Table II   National Income in Billions of Dollars

Year	GNP in Current Prices (1)	Capital Consumption (2)	Net National Product (3) = (1) − (2)	Indirect Business Taxes, etc.* (4)	National Income (5) = (3) − (4)	Minus Transfer Payments (6)	Personal Income (7) = (5) − (6)
1929	103.4	9.7	93.7	8.9	84.8	−0.2	85.0
1933	55.8	7.4	48.4	8.5	39.9	−38.0	47.0
1939	90.9	8.7	82.2	10.8	71.4	−1.0	72.4
1940	100.0	9.1	91.0	11.3	79.7	1.8	77.9
1941	125.0	10.0	115.0	12.3	102.7	7.3	95.4
1942	158.5	11.2	147.3	11.4	135.9	13.3	122.6
1943	192.1	11.5	180.7	11.4	169.3	18.5	150.8
1944	210.6	11.7	198.9	16.8	182.1	17.6	164.5
1945	212.4	12.2	200.2	19.5	180.7	10.7	170.0
1946	209.8	14.0	195.8	17.2	178.6	1.0	177.6
1947	233.1	17.3	215.7	20.8	194.9	4.8	190.1
1948	259.5	20.2	239.3	19.4	219.9	10.9	209.0
1949	258.3	21.8	236.5	22.9	213.6	7.2	206.4
1950	286.5	23.5	263.0	25.4	237.6	10.4	227.2
1951	330.8	27.2	303.6	29.5	274.1	19.2	254.9
1952	348.0	29.3	318.7	30.8	287.9	16.1	271.8
1953	366.8	31.0	335.8	33.7	302.1	14.4	287.7
1954	366.8	32.7	334.1	33.0	301.1	11.5	289.6
1955	400.0	34.8	365.3	34.8	330.5	20.2	310.3
1956	421.7	38.7	383.0	52.5	349.4	16.8	332.6
1957	444.0	41.7	402.3	37.1	365.2	14.2	351.0
1958	449.7	43.5	406.2	39.3	366.9	5.8	361.1
1959	487.9	44.9	443.0	42.2	400.8	16.4	384.4
1960	506.5	46.3	460.2	44.5	415.7	13.4	402.3
1961	524.6	47.5	477.0	48.2	428.8	11.0	417.8
1962	565.0	49.0	516.1	54.1	462.0	18.4	443.6
1963	596.7	50.6	546.1	57.6	488.5	22.3	466.2
1964	637.7	52.9	584.8	59.9	524.9	25.7	499.2
1965	691.1	56.0	635.0	62.6	572.4	31.7	540.7
1966	756.0	60.7	695.3	67.2	628.1	39.9	588.2
1967	799.6	65.9	733.7	71.5	662.2	32.2	630.0
1968	873.4	72.1	801.3	78.8	722.5	31.9	690.6
1969	944.0	80.0	864.0	84.7	779.3	24.6	754.7
1970	992.7	88.1	904.7	94.0	810.7	−0.4	811.1
1971	1,077.6	96.5	981.1	109.6	871.5	3.1	868.4
1972	1,185.9	106.4	1,079.5	115.9	963.6	12.2	951.4
1973	1,326.4	116.5	1,209.9	123.7	1,086.2	21.0	1,065.2
1974	1,434.2	136.0	1,298.2	137.5	1,160.7	−7.9	1,168.6
1975	1,594.2	159.3	1,389.9	150.5	1,239.4	−25.6	1,265.0
1976	1,718.0	175.0	1,543.0	163.8	1,379.2	−12.0	1,391.2
1977	1,918.3	195.2	1,723.2	175.5	1,550.5	10.1	1,540.4
1978	2,163.9	222.5	1,941.4	181.1	1,760.3	27.6	1,732.7
1979	2,417.8	256.0	2,161.7	195.0	1,966.7	15.5	1,951.2
1980	2,631.7	293.2	2,338.5	221.9	2,116.6	−48.7	2,165.3
1981	2,957.8	330.3	2,627.5	263.7	2,363.8	−65.7	2,429.5
1982	3,069.3	358.8	2,710.4	263.6	2,446.8	−137.8	2,584.6
1983	3,304.8	377.1	2,927.7	281.0	2,646.7	−97.5	2,744.2
1984	3,661.3	402.9	3,258.4	299.0	2,959.4	−53.8	3,013.2

*This category equals indirect business taxes plus business transfers plus government surplus plus statistical discrepancy minus subsidies.

Source: *Economic Report of the President*, 1982, pp. 254–55.

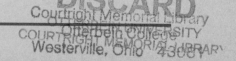

Principles of Economics

Second Edition

Principles of Economics

Second Edition

Roy J. Ruffin
University of Houston

Paul R. Gregory
University of Houston

Scott, Foresman and Company

Glenview, Illinois
London, England

To Patti Ruffin and AnneMarie Gregory

Library of Congress Cataloging-in-Publication Data

Ruffin, Roy
    Principles of economics.

    Also issued in two separate volumes under titles:
Principles of macroeconomics and Principles of
microeconomics.
    Bibliography
    Includes index.
    1. Economics.   I. Gregory, Paul R.   II. Title.
HB171.5.R82   1985   330   85–18307
ISBN 0-673-18225-8

Credits

Table 2 on page 144 from *Macroeconomics* by Robert J. Barro. Copyright © 1984, by John
    Wiley & Sons, Inc. Reprinted with permission.
Table 1, "Indicators of Economic Development, 1981," on page 422 from *World Tables,* Vol. I
    & II, 3rd ed., 1983. Reprinted with permission.
Table 2, "A Comparison of Developed Countries and Less Developed Countries (LDCs)," on
    page 425 from *World Tables,* Vol. I and II, 3rd. ed., 1983. Reprinted with permission.
Figure 1 on page 423, boxed figure on page 426, and Table 3 on page 435 from *World
    Development Report,* 1984. Reprinted with permission.
Figure on page 428 reprinted with permission of the Population Council from John Durand,
    "Historical Estimates of World Population: An Evaluation," *Population and Development
    Review* 3, no. 3 (September 1977): 253–96.
Figure on page 436, "Export Shares in Developing Countries," from "Trade as the Engine of
    Growth in Developing Countries Revisited" by James Riedel, *Economic Journal* 94, 1984,
    p. 373. Reprinted with permission of Cambridge University Press.
Table 4 on page 544, "The 50 Largest Industrial Corporations," reprinted by permission from
    the *Fortune* Directory; © 1985 Time Inc. All rights reserved.
Figure on page 571 from *Case Studies of American Industry*, 2nd edition by Leonard Weiss.
    Copyright © 1967, 1971 by John Wiley & Sons, Inc. Reprinted with permission.
Table on page 643 based on material from *Market Power and Economic Welfare: An Introduction*
    by William G. Shepard, © 1970 by Random House, Inc. Reprinted with permission.
Table on page 693, "Five Generations of Mainframes at IBM," reprinted with permission from
    International Data Corporation.
Table 3 on page 756 from *Econometric Contributions to Public Policy*, edited by Richard Stone
    and William Peterson. © International Economic Association 1978 and reprinted by permission
    of St. Martin's Press Inc. and Macmillan, London and Basingstoke.
Figure 5(a) on page 824 constructed from table from p. 48 of *Who Paid the Taxes, 1966–1985*
    by Joseph A. Pechman. Copyright © 1985. Reprinted with permission from Brookings
    Institution.
Figure 5(b) on page 824 constructed from table, "The Distribution of the Tax Burden," by Edgar
    Browning and William Johnson. © 1979 American Enterprise Institute. Reprinted by
    permission.

To the Instructor

In its second edition, PRINCIPLES OF ECONOMICS can restate its claim to be the most comprehensive introductory textbook in its coverage of modern micro- and macroeconomic theory. To maintain this reputation, this edition has been revised and updated to contain:

- a new chapter on interest rates and their interaction with government deficits, inflation, taxes, exchange rates, and the stock market.
- a full chapter on monetary policy with discussion of Fed policy since 1979 and the contribution of Chairman Volcker.
- a simplified discussion of the rational-expectations model with updated evidence for and against it and with the technical explanation of Lucas supply and demand curves moved to a separate appendix.
- a reworked chapter on Keynesian theory.
- a new appendix on the *IS/LM* model (following the chapter on output fluctuations).
- an expanded chapter on fiscal policy with coverage of the problems of deficit reduction and the relationships between deficits and inflation and between deficits and interest rates.
- further integration of the aggregate supply/aggregate demand model in all macro chapters.
- expanded discussions of the natural-rate hypothesis and the role of the self-correcting mechanism.
- the latest evidence on the relationship between money growth and inflation.
- extended clarification of the difference between long-run and short-run aggregate supply.
- the latest developments in the theory of labor-market search, search and layoff unemployment, and the nature of wage bargains.
- new sections on disinflation, the rise of the dollar in the 1980s, and many other macroeconomic topics.

- an updated chapter on public finance that covers the latest tax-reform proposals, including the flat tax and the Reagan Plan, and the problems of deficit financing.
- an explanation of substitution and income effects in the appendix on indifference curves.
- the introduction of the principal/agent theme to discussions of firms, monopolies, labor markets, and the Soviet economy.
- an explanation of the concept of Nash equilibrium and its application to advertising games, credible threats, and the prisoners' dilemma game in the chapter on oligopoly, along with an introduction to the concept of contestable markets.
- expanded discussions of the adverse-selection and moral-hazard problems in the chapter on information costs.
- new coverage of waste-disposal costs and the options available to the EPA in the chapter on market failure and the environment.
- references to the latest research in concentration trends, union effects on wages, causes of income inequality, environmental economics, and many other microeconomic issues.

- more than 100 new boxed examples.
- an expanded appendix on graphing, with explanations of growth distortion, scale distortion, and inflation distortion.
- more than 250 new end-of-chapter questions and problems.
- more than 100 new diagrams with explanatory captions.

The many strengths of the first edition are also preserved in this revision. The development of macroeconomic theory is logical and easy to follow. Money and banking is covered as a prelude to the presentation of modern aggregate demand/aggregate supply analysis. Logically, aggregate-demand analysis requires knowledge of the monetary sector because aggregate demand is influenced by real-balance and interest-rate effects; a complete examination of crowding out requires an understanding of liquidity-preference theory. The role of expectations is stressed throughout the presentation of macroeconomic theory. Although a full chapter is devoted to rational expectations, this chapter can be considered optional because the student is given the fundamentals of rational-expectations theory in the chapters on inflation and stabilization policy. The development of stagflation theory clearly distinguishes between the short-run and long-run Phillips curves. Microeconomic theory is brought closer to the real world by including a chapter on information costs that describes the workings of futures markets, speculators, and intermediaries. Price-theory discussions are enriched by the research of industrial-organization economists. An entire chapter is devoted to a comparison of monopoly and competition.

ORGANIZATION

This book is organized into six parts. Part I (Chapters 1–4) introduces the basic concepts of economics that must be learned before proceeding to the study of either macroeconomics or microeconomics. These four chapters contain the standard topics of economic methodology, scarcity, opportunity costs, the production-possibilities frontier, the law of diminishing returns, the law of comparative advantage, the workings of the price system, and the laws of supply and demand. A special appendix explains how to read graphs and avoid distortion pitfalls. In addition, the student is introduced to the concepts of relative prices and marginal decision making, which are crucial topics in both microeconomics and macroeconomics. From Part I, the instructor can move either to macroeconomics (Chapters 5–24) or to microeconomics (Chapters 25–43).

The development of macroeconomic theory begins in Part II by outlining the basic concepts of inflation, unemployment, and the business cycle(Chapter 5) and the basic principles of national income accounting(Chapter 6). Monetary economics, in Chapters 7(money and prices) and 8(banking and the Fed), precedes the chapters on Keynesian economics(9–11) and the determinants of aggregate demand and aggregate supply. This organization allows the instructor to present a full discussion of aggregate demand and a unified discussion of monetary and fiscal policy. Separate chapters on monetary policy (Chapter 12) and fiscal policy(Chapter 13) give up-to-date coverage of Fed policy since 1979 and the problems of deficit reduction. Chapters 14–16 on inflation (14), unemployment(15), and stagflation(16) use the natural-rate hypothesis and modern views of the Phillips curve to explain the causes of inflation and stagflation and the role of the self-correcting mechanism. Chapter 17 analyzes both sides of the debate about stabilization policy. The core macroeconomics section closes with a new chapter on interest rates and a revised version of the ground-breaking chapter on rational expectations.

Part III examines the world economy by first examining the determinants of economic growth (Chapter 20) and the problems of economic development (Chapter 21) and then moves to the discussion of international economics in Chapters 22–24. Chapter 22 shows how the law of comparative advantage applies on an international scale; Chapter 23 looks at the pros and cons of protection; Chapter 24 examines international monetary mechanisms and the balance of payments.

Part IV begins the microeconomics core with a ten-chapter unit on the product market (Chapters 25–

34). Chapter 25 teaches price elasticities of demand and supply as well as income and cross-price elasticities of demand. Chapter 26 deals with demand and utility (with an appendix on indifference curves). Business organization and corporate finance are discussed in Chapter 27, and short-run and long-run costs are explained in Chapter 28 (with an appendix on equal-output curves, or isoquants). The standard market models—perfect competition, monopoly and monopolistic competition, and oligopoly—are covered in Chapters 29–32, with a special chapter (31) devoted to comparing monopoly and competition. Chapter 33 introduces the role of information costs, and Chapter 34 discusses government/business relations, particularly government regulation and antitrust law.

Factor markets are taught as a five-chapter unit in Part V (Chapters 35–39). Chapter 35 gives a theoretical overview of the workings of factor markets, and Chapters 36 and 38 focus on specific factor markets. Chapter 37 considers the role of labor unions, and Chapter 39 considers the determinants of income distribution and proverty.

Microeconomic issues are the focus of Part VI (Chapters 40–43). Chapter 40 examines the issues of public finance and taxation; Chapter 41 explains the economics of exhaustible resources and of market failure (public goods and externalities); Chapter 42 discusses modern theories of public choice; Chapter 43 explores the Soviet economic system.

SUGGESTIONS FOR COURSE PLANNING

This book is intended for the two-semester sequence in microeconomics and macroeconomics that is traditionally taught as a first- or second-year college course. The book is available in both a combined hardbound volume and micro/macro split softbound volumes. The combined volume can also be used for an intensive one-semester course that covers both microeconomics and macroeconomics by selecting only core chapters (as suggested below). Since the book was written with the micro/macro splits in mind, even the instructor who is using the combined volume can teach either macro or micro first.

Suggested Outline for an Intensive One-Semester Course (30 chapters)

Introduction:
1   The Nature of Economics
2   The Economic Problem
3   The Price System
4   The Mechanics of Supply and Demand

Macroeconomics:
5   Macroeconomic Concepts
6   Measuring National Income and National Product
7   Money and Prices
8   Commercial Banking and the Federal Reserve
9   Keynesian Economics
10   Output Fluctuations: Aggregate Demand
11   Aggregate Supply
12   Monetary Policy
13   Fiscal Policy
14   Inflation
15   Unemployment
16   The Phillips Curve: The Interaction Between Inflation and Unemployment
17   Stabilization Policy

Microeconomics:

Suggested Outline for an Intensive One-Quarter Course (24 chapters)

Introduction:

Macroeconomics:

Microeconomics:

Instructors who want a course with a focus on growth and development should incorporate Chapters 20 on Economic Growth and 21 on Problems of Population and Economic Development. Instructors who want a course with a focus on international economics should incorporate Chapters 22–24 on International Trade and Comparative Advantage, Protection and Free Trade, and the International Monetary System and Chapter 43 on The Soviet Economy.

Instructors who want a one-semester course that is more heavily micro can choose the core macro chapters in the Quarter Course list above and the micro chapters from the Semester Course list above. Those who desire a course with a heavier macroeconomic emphasis can choose the micro chapters from the Quarter Course list above and the macro chapters from the Semester Course list.

SUPPLEMENTS

This book has a complete package of supplements, which includes an *Instructor's Manual, Study Guide, floppy disks, Test Bank,* and *Transparency Masters.*

The *Instructor's Manual* was written by the authors. Each of the 43 chapters contains sections on: points to learn in the chapter, chapter organization, special approaches, optional material, teaching hints and special projects, bad habits to unlearn, additional essay questions, answers to end-of-chapter "Questions and Problems," and answers to the "Review Quiz" for that chapter in the *Study Guide.*

The *Instructor's Manual* is a valuable teaching aid because it supplies the instructor with additional numerical examples not contained in the text and additional real-world illustrations not discussed in the text. A chapter outline gives a brief overview of the material in the chapter that assists the instructor in preparing lecture outlines and in seeing the logical development of the chapter. The special-approaches section tells the instructor how this chapter is different from other textbooks and explains why a topic was treated differently in this text or why an entirely new topic not covered by other texts was introduced in the chapter. The optional-material section gives the instructor a ranking of priorities for the topics in the chapter and enables the instructor to trim the size of each chapter (if necessary).

The *Study Guide* was written by Jeffrey Parker of the University of Houston and John Vahaly of the University of Louisville. Because the *Study Guide* is quite analytical, it will challenge the student and help him or her to better prepare for exams. The *Study Guide* supplements the text by providing summaries of the crucial concepts, but also takes the student step by step through a review of each new graph and equation presented in the text. It contains multiple-choice and true/false questions, but unlike other study guides, it contains not only the answers to the multiple-choice and true/false questions but also *explanations for the answers.* Instead of just giving lists of the correct *a, b, c* responses or a list of *T*s, and *F*s, the *Study Guide's* answer sections explain *why* a particular objective answer is the correct one. In addition to objective questions, each chapter of the *Study Guide* also contains analytical problems and essay questions. Again, the *Study Guide* provides not only the answers to the questions, but the step-by-step process for arriving at the answer.

At the back of the *Study Guide* is a "Review Quiz" for each chapter that contains multiple-choice questions the answers for which do *not* appear in the *Study Guide* but do appear in the *Instructor's Manual.* These quizzes can be used by the instructor as homework or as chapter quizzes.

Also available are two floppy discs for IBM PC and Apple computers: one containing seven interactive tutorial modules on basic microeconomic building blocks and the other containing seven tutorial modules on basic macroeconomic concepts.

The authors have also prepared a *Test Bank* that contains nearly 2000 multiple-choice questions—most of which have already been class tested. The answers have been checked and double-checked to minimize the chances that any of the questions have more than one answer. For each chapter in the text, the *Test Bank* contains 4 different tests (coded A, B, C, or D). Whether the instructor is trying to compose a one-chapter quiz or a 23-chapter final exam, that instructor can choose from among the questions in the *Test Bank,* the questions in the "Review Quizzes" at the back of the *Study Guide,* or the additional essay questions in the *Instructor's Manual*—more than 2500 questions in all. The *Test Bank* is available on perforated paper in book form, on computer tape, and on the EXAM system.

Transparency Masters suitable for overhead projectors are available for all key figures and tables (about 150 items).

To the Student

Many students find economics a difficult subject because, unlike many other courses a college student takes, economics cannot be mastered through memorization. Economics relies on economic theories to explain real-world occurrences—like why people tend to buy less when prices rise or why increased government spending may reduce unemployment. An economic theory is simply a logical explanation of why the facts fit together in a particular way. If the theory were not logical, or if the theory failed to be confirmed by real-world facts, it would be readily discarded by economists.

The successful student will be the one who learns that economics is built upon a number of fairly simple and easy-to-understand propositions. These propositions and assumptions—that businesses seek to maximize profits or that consumers base their expenditure decisions on disposable income, for example—form the building blocks upon which economics is based. These propositions are typically little more than common sense and should not intimidate a student. If a major building block is missing, however, the whole structure can fall apart. To prevent the student from overlooking or forgetting a crucial building block, we frequently engage in pedagogical review. In other words, when a new proposition is added to a theoretical structure, the underlying propositions are reviewed.

Another factor that can make economics difficult for a student is that economics—like other academic disciplines—has its own specific vocabulary. Unlike the physical sciences, however, where the student may be encountering a certain term for the first time, much of the vocabulary of economics—terms like *efficiency, capital, stock, unemployment*—has a common usage that is already familiar to the student. Economists, however, use the vocabulary of economics in a very exact way, and often the common usage of a term is not the same as the economic usage. In this book, each key term appears in boldface type where it is first discussed in text. Immediately following the paragraph where the term first appears in boldface type, the formal, economic definition of the term is set off in color. At the end of each chapter is a list of all the key terms that have been boldfaced and given formal definitions in that chapter; a glossary at the end of the book contains all the definitions of key terms and gives the chapter number in which the term was defined.

The modern developments in economics are simply new attempts to explain in a logical manner how the facts bind together. Modern developments have occurred because of the realization that established theories were not doing a good job of explaining the world around us. Fortunately, the major building blocks of modern theory—that people attempt to anticipate the future, that rising prices motivate wealth holders to spend less, that people and businesses gather information and make decisions in a rational manner—rely on common-sense logic.

Economics is valuable only if it explains the real world. Economics should be able to answer very specific questions like: Why are there three major domestic producers of automobiles and hundreds or even thousands of producers of textiles? Why is there a positive association between the growth of the money supply and inflation? Why does the United States export computers and farm products to the rest of the world? Why do restaurants rope off space during less busy hours? If Iowa corn land is the best land for growing corn, why is corn also grown in Texas while some land stands idle in Iowa? Why do interest rates rise when people expect the inflation rate to increase? What is the impact of the well-publicized government deficit? The successful student will be able to apply the knowledge he or she gains of real-world economic behavior to explain any number of events that have already occurred or are yet to occur.

In writing this book, we have made a conscious effort to present arguments and evidence on both sides of very economic controversy. We attempt to make a case for each distinct viewpoint, even if it would be more interesting and less complicated to come out strongly in one camp. Although we are aware of our own free-market bias, we believe it is best to allow the student to keep an open mind at this very early stage in the study of economics.

This book contains a number of important learning aids.

1. The *Chapter Preview* that precedes each chapter provides a brief overview of the important points to be learned in that chapter.
2. *Definitions of Key Terms* are set off in color following the paragraphs in which the terms are introduced in context.
3. *Key Ideas,* important economic principles or conclusions, are set off with color bars above and below.
4. *Boxed Examples* allow the student to appreciate how economic concepts apply in real-world settings without disrupting the flow of the text and supplement the numerous examples already found in the text discussions.
5. A *Chapter Summary* of the main points of each chapter is found at the end of each chapter.
6. *Key Terms* that were defined in color in the chapter are listed at the end of each chapter.
7. *Questions and Problems* that test the reader's understanding of the chapter follow each chapter.
8. *Suggested Readings* are listed for each chapter for the student who wishes to pursue an interesting topic even further.
9. A *Glossary,* containing all key terms defined in color in chapters and listed in chapter ''Key Terms'' sections, appears at the end of the book. Each entry contains the complete economic definition as well as the number of the chapter where the term was first defined.
10. A thorough *Index* catalogs the names, concepts, terms, and topics covered in the book.
11. Statistical data on the major economic variables are found on the front and back inside covers for easy reference.

Acknowledgments

We are deeply indebted to our colleagues at the University of Houston who had to bear with us in the writing of this book. John Antel, Richard Bean, Joel Sailors, Thomas DeGregori, Gerald Dwyer, Paul Evans, Louis Stern, and Thomas Mayor gave their time freely on an incredible number of pedagogical points in the teaching of elementary economics. Thanks are also extended to Colonel Kenneth Fleming and his colleagues at the Air Force Academy and to Manuel Reyes and his colleagues at Houston Community College for their many valuable comments on the first edition.

We are also grateful for the suggestions and contributions of numerous colleagues across the country who reviewed the manuscript for this revision:

Jack Adams	University of Arkansas (Little Rock)
Larry De Brock	University of Illinois, Urbana
James Dunlevy	University of Miami (of Ohio)
Anne Eicke	Illinois State University (Normal)
Randy Ellis	Boston University
Eugene Gendel	Lafayette College
Kathie Gilbert	Mississippi State University
Ann Hendricks	Tufts University
Jay Marchand	University of Mississippi
Ben Matta	New Mexico State University
Jerome L. McElroy	St. Mary's College
Mark Rush	University of Florida

It was a pleasure to work closely with John Vahaly and Jeffrey Parker, who, in addition to preparing the *Study Guide,* provided valuable and insightful comments on every chapter of this book.

We wish to thank George Lobell, economics editor at Scott, Foresman, who gave us encouragement and advice throughout the writing of this book. The skillful editing of the work was in the able hands of Mary LaMont, developmental editor at Scott, Foresman, whose contributions to style and content grace every page.

Roy J. Ruffin
Paul R. Gregory

Contents in Brief

Contents

Chapter 3   The Price System   46

Chapter 4   The Mechanics of Supply and Demand   66

Chapter 8   Commercial Banking and the Federal Reserve   151

Chapter 9   Keynesian Economics   174

Chapter 13   Fiscal Policy   261

Chapter 14   Inflation   282

Chapter 30   Monopoly and Monopolistic Competition   603

Chapter 31   Monopoly and Competition Compared   625

Chapter 32   Oligopoly   640

Chapter 33   The Economics of Information   666

Chapter 34   Antitrust Law and Regulation   687

Part VI   Microeconomic Issues   805

Chapter 40   Public Finance   806

Chapter 41   Market Failure, the Environment, and Energy   832

Basic Economic Concepts

1

The Nature of Economics

Chapter Preview

Understanding economics is important to each person as an individual, as a producer, and as a voter in a democratic society. Economists study many questions, but the central issue of economics is: How does the economy work? An understanding of how the economy works helps society as well as each individual. In a nutshell, the goal of economics is to sort out the sense from the nonsense in everyday economic affairs. Better information aids decision making at all levels.

Economics is an evolving and changing social-science field. Some parts of our economic knowledge are fairly certain; other parts are uncertain. Many areas of economics are in the process of development; many are controversial. That eco-

nomics is changing shows that economics is a challenging field in search of real answers. This book will explain the rudiments of how the economy works according to our present understanding of economics.

This chapter introduces the basic concepts and tools that economists use to understand how the economy works. The chapter explains the basic principles of scarcity, choice, specialization, and exchange and shows how economists use the scientific method to study the economy. The chapter warns about the pitfalls to avoid in studying economics and explains why (and about what) economists sometimes disagree. ■

WHAT IS ECONOMICS: BASIC THEMES

People are concerned with improving their standard of living; they are worried about inflation and unemployment; they may be disturbed by the poverty of the less fortunate. Newspapers tell people of the rising value of the dollar abroad, of the dangers of rising imports and trade deficits. Politicians and pundits warn of federal deficits. Families and businesses are alarmed by high interest rates. People must go about the ordinary business of making a living and balancing personal budgets. People are confronted with difficult personal choices: when to buy a home, whether or not to change jobs, whether or not to attend college, whether to buy stocks or bonds. People are often confused by the economic claims and counterclaims of opposing political parties. People can find help in dealing with these questions and concerns in the study of **economics.**

> **Economics** is the study of how people choose to use their limited resources (land, labor, and capital goods) to produce, exchange, and consume goods and services.

The above definition touches on several different themes of economic science. Economists agree that each theme is an essential feature of economics.

Scarcity

Scarcity is the most important fact of economics. If there were no scarcity, there would be no need to study economics. Scarcity is defined in a more formal manner in Chapter 2. For now, it is sufficient to say that scarcity occurs when a society's virtually unlimited wants exceed the ability of the economy to meet these wants. The existence of scarcity does not imply that people are necessarily poor or that their basic needs are not being met. Scarcity exists simply because it is human nature for people to want more than they can have, which forces people to make choices.

Choice

The second theme of economics is *choice*. Choice and scarcity go together. Individuals, businesses, and societies must choose among alternatives. An individual must choose between a job and a college education, between savings and consumption, between a movie and eating out. Businesses must decide where to purchase supplies, which products to offer on the market, how much labor to hire, whether to build new plants. Nations must choose between more defense or more spending for social-welfare programs; they must decide whether to grant tax reductions to business or to individuals.

Specialization

The third theme of economics is *specialization*. Economics studies how participants in the economy (people, businesses, countries) specialize in tasks to which they are particularly suited. The physician specializes in medicine, the lawyer in law, the computer scientist in data processing, Saudi Arabia in oil production, Cuba in sugar production, General Motors in automobile production, Lockheed in military hardware, the economics professor in teaching economics, the vacuum-cleaner salesperson in selling vacuum cleaners. Participants in the economy specialize in those things that they do better than others. (Chapter 3 will give more exact definitions of specialization.)

The principal message of Adam Smith, the founder of modern economics, in his 1776 masterwork, *The Wealth of Nations,* was that specialization creates wealth. To use Smith's words: "The greatest improvement in the productive powers of labor . . . seems to have been the effects of the division of labor."[1] *Division of labor* was Adam Smith's term for specialization.

Exchange

The fourth theme of economics is *exchange*. Exchange complements specialization. Specialized producers cannot meet their own consumption needs from their own production. Without exchange, the shoe manufacturer would not have sore feet but would have little else. The auto mechanic would have a smooth-running car but no shoes. Japan would have cars and electronic products but little food and raw materials. Without ex-

---

1. Adam Smith, *The Wealth of Nations,* ed. Edwin Cannan (New York: Modern Library, 1937), p. 3.

change, specialization would be of no benefit because individuals could not trade the goods in which they specialize for those that other individuals produce. Again, using Smith's words: "[Specialization] is the necessary . . . consequence of a certain propensity in human nature: the propensity to truck, barter and exchange one thing for another."[2] How exchange is organized is a major element in the study of economics.

Exchange is all around us. We exchange our specialized labor services for money and then exchange money for a huge variety of goods. A country like America exchanges its wheat for TV sets made in Japan. Within a business concern, different departments exchange skills in engineering, purchasing, and marketing to produce and sell the firm's output. A travel agency exchanges its ability to market group tours for discounted airline tickets. A foreign-car manufacturer may agree to supply fuel-efficient engines to an American auto manufacturer in return for marketing and repair outlets.

MARGINAL ANALYSIS

Scarcity forces people to make choices, and economics studies how these choices are made. Economics is people making decisions about the ordinary business of making a living and spending their money. If one can remember that individuals are the main actors, much of the mystery surrounding economics evaporates. The student of economics has an enormous advantage over the physics student who cannot ask, "what would I do if I were a molecule?" because the student of economics *is* one of the "molecules" economists study. Crucial to individual behavior are the incentives (that is, the carrots and sticks) that face people in any given situation. In economics, the "carrots" are the benefits that people receive from engaging in an economic activity; the "sticks" are the costs of the activity.

Individuals are guided in their economic decisions by costs and benefits. The most important tool used by economists to study economic decision making is the comparison of costs and benefits, or **marginal analysis.**

2. Smith, *Wealth of Nations*, p. 13.

Marginal analysis aids decision making by examining the consequences of making relatively small changes from the current state of affairs.

An example of marginal analysis is the way you might go about deciding how much studying is "enough." First, you would examine the benefits of a slight increase in your present amount of studying. If you study, say, 2 hours more per day, you will likely earn higher grades, the respect of your fellow students, and perhaps a better job upon graduation. All these benefits of studying 2 additional hours per day cannot be measured exactly, but you have an idea of the benefits that additional study will yield. Next, you would examine the costs of 2 more hours of studying per day. You might have to sacrifice earnings from a part-time job; you might have to give up leisure activities that you value highly (dating, your favorite soap opera, an extra two hours of sleep).

Finally, the answer to the question of whether you are studying enough would depend upon whether you feel that the benefits of the extra study outweigh the costs. If they do, then you would conclude that you are not studying enough, and you would study more. If the extra costs are greater than the extra benefits, you would conclude that you should not study the extra time.

How do businesses make choices? Consider the case of the selection of airline routes. How would an airline (United, Eastern, American, and so on) determine whether it is offering "enough" flights? It would do so by making decisions *at the margin*. That is, the airline would add flights so long as the expected revenues from any added flight exceed the expected costs. Let us say that United is considering adding a daily flight between Chicago and Seattle. The management of United would make an estimate of the benefits that the added flight would bring in (the additional ticket sales) and would compare these benefits with the extra costs that the new flight would create (added fuel, additional flight attendants, advertising for the new route). If the benefits of the new route are greater than the costs, then the new route would be added to United's schedule. If the costs exceed the benefits, the new route would probably be rejected. (See Example 1.)

Example 1   The "Waggle Dance" of Bees and Marginal Analysis

Microeconomics is based upon the principle that economic decisions are made by weighing costs and benefits at the margin. Economists believe that human beings behave in this way, and there is growing evidence that bees and other animals also implicitly use marginal analysis in their decision making.

A University of Miami biologist reports an experiment with two artificial flowers and a measured mixture of sugar and water. Bees—in their search for food—"waggle dance" when they find food to tell other bees of their find. The more vigorously they waggle dance, the stronger is the message to the other bees. The biologist found that bees

waggle dance more vigorously when the concentration of sugar rises and dance less vigorously as the distance the bee has to fly between the two flowers increases. In the language of marginal analysis, the higher the concentration of sugar, the greater the marginal benefit of the find; the further apart the two flowers, the greater the marginal cost of gathering the sugar. Thus, bees act in a rational manner in urging other bees on when the marginal costs are low and in discouraging the other bees when the marginal costs are high.   ■

Source: *Science,* October 1984, p. 12.

Decisions are made at the margin when a decision maker considers what the extra (or marginal) costs and benefits of an increase or decrease in a particular activity will be. If the marginal benefits outweigh the marginal costs, the extra activity is undertaken.

MICRO AND MACRO

Microeconomics

Economics is typically divided into two main branches called *microeconomics* and *macroeconomics*. Both **microeconomics** and macroeconomics deal with economic decision making but from different vantage points.

> **Microeconomics** studies the economic decision making of firms and individuals in a market setting; it is the study of the economy in the small.

Microeconomics focuses on the individual participants in the economy: the producers, workers, employers, and consumers. In everyday economic life, things are bought and sold, people decide where and how many hours to work. Business managers decide what to produce and how this production is to be organized. These activities re-

sult in *transactions* (business deals) that take place in markets where buyers and sellers come together. People involved in microeconomic transactions are motivated to do the best they can for themselves with the limited resources at their disposal. They use marginal analysis to determine their best course of action.

Because microeconomics deals with people weighing costs and benefits of actions at the margin, its range of application is broad. Microeconomics studies how business firms operate under different competitive conditions and how the combined actions of buyers and sellers determine prices in specific markets. Microeconomics studies households as earners of wages, interest, rent, and profit and, accordingly, studies the distribution of income. Microeconomics examines the causes and possible cures of pollution and even how voters and public officials make public-choice decisions. Microeconomics even looks inside the family to study marital behavior and fertility.

Macroeconomics

Instead of analyzing prices, outputs, and sales in individual markets, **macroeconomics** studies the production of the entire economy. Topics of investigation include the *general* price level (rather than individual prices), the national employment rate, government spending, the federal deficit, interest rates, and the nation's money supply.

> **Macroeconomics** is the study of the economy in the large. Rather than dealing with individual markets and individual consumers and producers, macroeconomics *examines* the economy as a whole.

Because macroeconomics studies the economy as a whole, measures of total economic activity are required. Important to macroeconomics is the definition and measurement of macroeconomic *aggregates,* such as gross national product (GNP), the consumer price index (CPI), the unemployment rate, and the government surplus and deficit. These measures are called *aggregates* because they add together (or aggregate) individual microeconomic components.

Just as microeconomics studies the relationships between individual participants in the economy, macroeconomics studies relationships between aggregate measures. What are the determinants of inflation? What is the relationship between inflation and interest rates? Is it necessary to trade off higher employment for lower inflation? What are the effects of government deficits on prices and interest rates? What is the relationship between the money supply and inflation?

In modern economics, there is a close relationship between microeconomics and macroeconomics. Macroeconomists have come to apply more and more microeconomic analysis to traditional macroeconomic questions such as the relationship between inflation and unemployment. The rationale behind using microeconomic tools to study macroeconomics is that the economy is made up of individuals; how these individuals behave *on the average* can explain how the economy in the large behaves.

> The modern convergence of microeconomics and macroeconomics follows from the realization that macroeconomic relationships cannot be analyzed without understanding the behavior of the individuals who make up the economy.

Five areas of investigation that exemplify the modern convergence of microeconomics and macroeconomics are:

1. How do generally rising prices affect the employment (and job search) behavior of individuals?
2. How do business output decisions respond to inflation or deflation?
3. Can unemployment be reduced by changing government policies that affect the costs of unemployment?
4. How do people's expectations of inflation affect interest rates in credit markets?
5. How are individual consumption and saving decisions affected by the presence of government debt?

To answer these questions the tools of microeconomic decision making (such as marginal analysis) can be applied to what are basically macroeconomic problems. In applying micro decision-making tools to macroeconomics, care must be taken not to assume automatically that what is true for the micro unit is true for the economy as a whole. This type of mistake (called the *fallacy of composition*) is discussed later in this chapter.

METHODOLOGY IN ECONOMICS

Economists rely heavily on economic theories to explain how the economy works. Why don't economists just go out and collect the facts and let the facts speak for themselves? The American economy includes millions of households and firms and thousands of separate federal, state, and local governments. All of these make decisions about producing millions of goods and services using millions of resources. Gathering information about economic choices from all these various sources is an incredibly complex and unmanageable task. Making sense of these millions of facts is even more difficult. Logical theories explain how the economy works by showing how the facts fit together in a coherent manner.

Theories and Hypotheses

A **theory** is simply a plausible and coherent explanation of how certain facts are related. A theory typically consists of at least one **hypothesis** about how a particular set of facts is related. Normally, but not always, theories contain some hypotheses of the form, "if A, then B." Two examples of hypotheses are: "if a good's price falls, people will want to buy more of it"; "if income rises, people will consume or save more."

A **theory** isolates those factors that may be crucial determinants of the phenomenon being explained.

A **hypothesis** is a tentative assumption made in order to test its logical or empirical consequences.

For example, economists' theories of demand hold that such things as consumer eye color, height, and IQ are relatively unimportant in explaining consumer purchases compared to such things as price and income. The process of zeroing in on a limited number of factors to explain a phenomenon is called *abstraction*.

Testing Theories: The Scientific Method

Since theories are abstractions from the real world (whatever that is!) it is necessary to test them. For example: Suppose one hypothesized that higher prices for gasoline induce people to buy less gasoline. This theory seems to make sense. But is it true? Some relevant data are shown in Table 1.

Clearly, as the price of gasoline in *constant dollars* (dollars that have been adjusted to eliminate the effect of inflation) rose by more than 50 percent between 1970 and 1981, gas consumption per *vehicle* fell dramatically—from an annual rate of 728 gallons to 568 gallons per year. Thus, the data on gasoline prices and gasoline consumption are consistent with our theory that higher prices for an item cause people to consume less of the item. The data *fail to refute* the theory but have not really *proved* the theory beyond any doubt. Data from another time or place may contradict the theory. When data are obtained that are *not* consistent with the theory, the theory must be reformulated or revised.

For example, Table 2 shows that egg prices fell substantially between 1974 and 1979, yet egg consumption per capita remained about the same. These data appear to contradict the theory that higher prices for an item induce people to consume less of the item. In this situation we could either say that the theory does not hold for eggs,

Table 1	Gasoline Prices and Gasoline Consumption	
Years	Price per gallon (constant 1981 dollars)	Average Fuel Consumption per Car (gallons per year)
1970–73	.83	728
1975–77	.94	683
1980–81	1.31	568

Source: *Statistical Abstract of the United States* (1984), pp. 619–20.

or we could revise the theory so that it would explain why eggs were an exception to the rule. The case of eggs suggests that things other than price influence consumption. The 1970s was a period in which the egg had lost some of its popularity because of allegations that egg consumption lowers human longevity. The unfavorable publicity might have had a substantial impact on consumption. The theory can be reformulated to reflect the fact that factors other than price influence consumption. Chapter 4 will do this more precisely, but for the moment the theory could be reformulated as follows: the higher the price of an item, the less of it people will want to buy, holding other factors (like unfavorable publicity, in this

Table 2	Egg Prices and Egg Consumption	
Year	Price per Dozen (1982 dollars)	Yearly per Capita Consumption (number of eggs)
1974	1.24	288
1975	1.12	279
1976	1.18	274
1977	1.00	272
1978	.92	273
1979	.92	278
1980	.79	272
1981	.78	266
1982	.74	263

Source: *Statistical Abstract of the United States* (1984), Tables 201, 805.

case) constant. The above examples illustrate how the scientific method can be applied to a simple economic theory:

1. a theory was formulated,
2. relevant facts were gathered (Tables 1 and 2) while irrelevant facts were discarded,
3. the theory was evaluated in light of the facts, and
4. when the facts failed to confirm the theory (Table 2), the theory was revised.

The **scientific method** is one of the truly great creations of the human mind. Hard as it is to believe, at one time people did not evaluate their beliefs in light of the facts or even formulate their beliefs in a way that could be tested by others. What makes the scientific method such a valuable tool is that it raises human thought above the level of the individual, separating the idea from the person as much as possible. Claude Bernard, a 19th-century writer, once perceptively summarized the orientation of all scientific subjects in comparison to artistic ones: "Art is I; science is we."

The process of formulating theories, collecting data, testing theories, and revising theories is called the **scientific method.**

The Uses of Economic Theories

Economic theories that use the scientific method allow us to make sense of an extremely complicated world. They enable us to understand economic relationships, to make sense of past events, and even to predict the consequences of actions that have yet to be taken. Economists have at their disposal well-tested theories of the relationship between product prices and the quantities purchased. For example, economists have established (largely on the basis of the experiences of other countries) that people cut back their gasoline consumption when gasoline prices rise substantially. Many government officials, consumer advocates, and politicians felt that this cutback would not happen in the United States, because Americans are so dependent on automobile transportation. The United States entered into uncharted territory when it left the age of cheap energy behind in the mid-1970s, and it was comforting at the time to have a scientifically

tested theory as a guide, despite its skeptics. True enough, after the higher prices went into effect, people did indeed cut back on their gasoline purchases just as economic theory predicted. This cutback became so strong that oil-producing countries had trouble finding buyers at the higher prices of the early 1980s.

Theory can say something about facts that have yet to be collected and about events that have yet to occur; that is, theory can be used to make *predictions.*

This discussion should lay to rest the erroneous notion that a theory can be a good one even if it does not work in practice. By the criterion of the scientific method, if a theory does not work in practice it cannot be a good theory.

COMMON FALLACIES IN ECONOMICS

False economic propositions can have substantial appeal when they appear on the surface to be eminently reasonable. Students of economics must be on guard against three logical fallacies that confound economic thinking. Examples of these logical fallacies can be found routinely in newspapers, statements of public figures, and even in the writings of professional economists. The three most common logical fallacies that plague economic thinking are the *false-cause fallacy,* the *fallacy of composition,* and the *ceteris paribus fallacy.*

The False-Cause Fallacy

The fact that Event A occurs with or precedes Event B does not mean that A has caused B. One well-known example of the **false-cause fallacy** is the so-called Superbowl phenomenon. In 15 of the last 16 years the stock market rose when the National Football conference team won the Superbowl and fell when it lost. To conclude that the one event (the NFC team winning the Superbowl) caused the other event (higher stock market prices) would be a false-cause fallacy. Believe it or not, there are people who buy or sell in the

Example 2   The Stock Market and the Hemline Index: The False-Cause Fallacy

Over the past 50 years, there has been an almost perfect correlation between stock-market prices and hemlines. The higher the hemline goes, the higher stock prices go. During the soaring stock market of the late 1920s, hemlines were above the knees (the "flapper" look). During the depression of the 1930s, hemlines fell lower and lower. During the rising market of the 1960s, miniskirts were in fashion. Some stock-market speculators even base their stock purchase and sales decisions on whether fashion designers intend to raise or lower hemlines. The hemline indicator is an example of the false-cause fallacy. Just because two indicators move together does not mean that one has caused the other, even if this correlation occurs over a 50-year period. In this case, it just happens to be a remarkable coincidence. In order to establish a cause-and-effect relationship, there must be some logical explanation as to why lower hemlines should cause stock markets to rise. ∎

---

stock market on the basis of which team wins the Superbowl!

> The **false-cause fallacy** is the assumption that because two events occur together one event has caused the other.

How does one determine whether or not two variables that are statistically correlated are involved in a cause-and-effect relationship? Economic theory attempts to determine in a coherent manner whether a logical case of cause and effect exists. Take the case of whiskey consumption: Between 1970 and 1980, U.S. whiskey consumption rose by 25 percent. During the same period, the number of public-school teachers rose by 30 percent and family take-home pay increased by 33 percent (after adjustment for inflation). Whiskey consumption is statistically correlated with both school teachers and income, yet there is no logical reason to think that an increase in the number of public-school teachers would cause increased whiskey consumption. On the other hand, a logical theory could be constructed that claims that increases in family income will be channeled into purchases of whiskey. Thus, one could argue that the rise in income is a possible cause of the rise in whiskey consumption. Economic theory supports a cause/effect relationship.

One of the most difficult problems of science is the determination of cause-and-effect relationships. Many of the unresolved controversies in economics center on cause-and-effect relationships. (See Example 2.)

A statistical correlation between two variables does not prove that one has caused the other or that the variables have anything whatsoever to do with one another. To establish causation, a logical theory explaining why a change in one variable causes a change in another variable must be supported with factual evidence.

The Fallacy of Composition

A classic example of the **fallacy of composition** would be to say that the best way to escape a fire in a crowded movie theater is to run to the exit. If *one* person runs from his or her seat to the exit, that person will escape unharmed. If *all* people run from their seats to the nearest exit, few will escape unharmed.

> The **fallacy of composition** is the assumption that what is true for each part taken separately is also true for the whole or that what is true for the whole is true for each part considered separately.

To illustrate the fallacy of composition with an economic example, consider what would happen if the government were to print money and give one person $10,000. Clearly, this action would make that individual better off. With the $10,000 windfall, the person could buy a new car, invest in the stock market, or finance a college education. But if the government were to give everyone a windfall of $10,000, consumer spending would

---

Example 3   Airline Pricing and Revenues: The Fallacy of Composition

---

The fallacy of composition is to conclude falsely that what is true for any part taken separately is also true for the whole. An economic example of the fallacy of composition is airline-ticket pricing in recent years. One airline, typically an airline experiencing financial difficulties, will lower air fares on its routes for the purpose of increasing the number of passengers. More business can mean substantially more traffic and, hence, higher revenues even at lower ticket prices. It is true that if one airline were to lower its fares, its traffic would

increase. What is true for the part is not true for the whole. Typically, when one airline lowers its fares, other airlines match the lower fares. While airline traffic may pick up generally due to lower air fares, no single airline gains a substantial increase in passengers. When all airlines lower their fares, the revenues of individual airlines tend to fall. What is true for the part (the lowering of fares by one airline will increase revenues) is not true for the whole (the lowering of fares by all airlines may lower revenues).   ■

---

increase, prices would generally rise, and it is likely society as a whole would not end up any better off. This example shows that what is true for each part taken separately—namely, that receiving money makes people better off—would not necessarily be true for the whole. (See Example 3.)

The *Ceteris Paribus* Fallacy

Ceteris paribus is a Latin term meaning "other things being equal." If the relationship between two variables is to be established, the effects of other factors that are changing as well must not be allowed to confuse the relationship, or the *ceteris paribus* **fallacy** will occur.

> The *ceteris paribus* **fallacy** occurs when the effects of changes in one set of variables are incorrectly attributed to another set of variables.

To show the dangers of the *ceteris paribus* fallacy consider the fact that the U. S. crime rate rose from 3,985 serious crimes per 100,000 inhabitants in 1970 to 5,553 crimes per 100,000 inhabitants in 1982. At the same time, the number of police per 1,000 residents rose from 2.2 to 2.8. If law-enforcement officers are doing their job, would one not logically expect the crime rate to drop as police protection increases? Should we conclude that increasing police protection "causes" more crime? Serious crime has a number of causes, and it so happens that nearly 75 percent of all serious crimes are perpetrated by

persons in the 20–44 age group. Population statistics show that while the overall U. S. population increased by 14 percent between 1970 and 1982, persons aged 20–44 increased by 39 percent. The composition of the U. S. population (as a consequence of the maturing of the "baby boom" generation) had become more concentrated in those age groups most prone to commit serious crime. The point of this example is that a factor other than the number of police officers changed in a direction that should lead to a higher crime rate. In addition, the police factor changed in a direction that should lead to a lower crime rate. To capture the true impact of police protection on crime, we must be able to ask: If all other factors that affect crime had remained the same and police protection had been increased, what would have been the effect of expanded police protection on crime?

To conclude in this case that increased police protection has caused a higher crime rate would be a *ceteris paribus* fallacy. To understand the relationship between two factors (like police protection and crime), the effects of all other relevant factors must be sorted out. Figuring out these other effects is not a simple matter. In fact, an entire branch of economics that combines economic theory and statistics, called *econometrics,* has been developed to deal with the *ceteris paribus* problem.

Economic events are complex. Prices are changing, incomes are changing, people's expectations are changing. To look at any two factors in isolation without understanding how they fit in

---

Example 4   Cigarette Prices and Consumption: The *Ceteris Paribus* Fallacy

---

The simple theory presented in this chapter stated that higher prices of a particular good would reduce the consumption of that good. The data on cigarette prices and per-capita cigarette consumption given in the accompanying table do not appear to support this theory. Although cigarette prices remained roughly constant (after adjustment for inflation) between 1965 and 1981, per-capita consumption of cigarettes fell by almost 50 percent. Looking at the price alone, we would expect stable consumption.

This example illustrates the dangers of the *ceteris paribus* fallacy. As is well known, factors other than the price of cigarettes have affected cigarette consumption. The Surgeon General of the United States has issued periodic warnings about the health hazards of cigarette smoking, and cigarette

smoking has become less popular. A factor other than the price (namely, the change in consumer

Year	Price per 1,000 Cigarettes (1981 dollars)	Per Capita Consumption (1,000 cigarettes per year)
1965	14.85	11.5
1981	14.88	7.5

Source: *Statistical Abstract of the United States* (1984), p. 783; *Handbook of Labor Statistics,* December 1983, pp. 342–43.

preferences) has apparently caused the decline in cigarette consumption. ■

---

with other factors that are also changing can lead to *ceteris paribus* fallacies. (See Example 4.)

WHY ECONOMISTS DISAGREE

Economists have received the unfair reputation of being unable to agree on anything. The image of economists in disagreement is part of our folklore. An English commentator wrote: "If parliament were to ask six economists for an opinion, seven answers could come back—two no doubt from the volatile Mr. Keynes." The *London Times* laments the "rise in skepticism about what economists can tell us," and *Business Week* complains about "the intellectual bankruptcy of the [economics] profession."[3]

The image of widespread disagreement among economists is overrated. The results of a survey of 100 professional American economists, reported in Table 3, confirm that there is considerable agreement among economists about *what can be done,* especially in a microeconomic context. However, there is more disagreement over *what ought to be done.* Questions of what ought to be done (Should we equalize the distribution of in-

come? Should we increase defense spending?) require moral and political value judgments on which individuals naturally differ. An international survey of economists finds that economists throughout the Western world tend to agree on positive economic issues and disagree on normative economic issues.[4] Disagreement among professional economists receives more publicity than other scientific professions, which contributes to the false image of economists in disaccord. In Table 3, more than 60 percent of the economists agree with each other on 21 of the 27 propositions.

Positive Economics

Economists generally agree that rising prices reduce consumption *(ceteris paribus),* that rising income will have differential but predictable effects on different products, that wage and price controls cause shortages, that tariffs and quotas raise prices to consumers, that rent controls reduce the quantity and quality of housing, that minimum-wage laws increase unemployment among youth and unskilled workers, and so on. The easiest

---

3. J. R. Kearl et al., "A Confusion of Economists," *American Economic Review* 69, 2 (May 1979): 28.

4. Bruno S. Frey, Werner Pommerehne, Friedrich Schneider, and Guy Gilbert, "Consensus and Dissension Among Economists: An Empirical Inquiry," *American Economic Review,* December 1984, pp. 986–94.

matters on which to achieve agreement involve the microeconomic relationships that actually prevail in an economy.

Positive economics is the study of *what is* in the economy.

The areas of disagreement in **positive economics** tend to be concentrated in the field of macroeconomics, which is, after all, a relatively young field. The points of controversy and disagreement in macroeconomics include such questions as: What are the causes of inflation and unemployment? What is the relationship between deficits and interest rates? Can we combine low unemployment and low inflation? Should activist government policy be used to achieve employment and inflation goals?

Why has economics still to resolve these vital issues? The basic answer is that the economy is an unbelievably complex organism, comprised of millions of individuals, hundreds of thousands of business firms, a myriad of local, state, and federal government offices. The economy is us, and our collective economic actions are difficult to analyze. Emotions are volatile; expectations can change overnight; relationships that held last year no longer hold today; it is costly and difficult to collect up-to-date economic facts. Unlike the physical sciences, economics is usually denied a laboratory setting; economists do not have the physicist's vacuum, the agronomist's experimental farm, the chemist's laboratory. In addition, many economic events are random and unpredictable. Bad weather can cause poor harvests; armed conflicts can occur without warning in different parts of the globe; oil-producing countries can form an oil-price-fixing alliance; consumer spending can shift in response to changing expectations.

Normative Economics

Economists do disagree—often strongly—about **normative economics.**

Normative economics is the study of *what ought to be* in the economy.

Economists disagree on whether we should have more unemployment or more inflation (a tra-

ditional Democratic/Republican difference over the years), over whether income taxes should be lowered for the middle class, the rich, or the poor, over job programs, over government-subsidized health programs. These disagreements are not over "what is"; opponents in a debate may agree on what will happen if Program A is chosen over Program B, but they may disagree sharply over their personal evaluation of the desirability of those consequences. As Table 3 shows, disputes over "what ought to be" are often the foundation for why economists disagree.

The Visibility of Economic Disputes

While disagreements in other sciences are as strong as or even stronger than those in economics, these other disagreements are less visible to the public eye. Theoretical physicists have disagreed about the physical nature of the universe since the foundation of physics, but this scientific controversy is understood by only a few theoretical physicists.

It does not require much disagreement to bring economic disputes to the public's attention. Everyone is interested in economic questions: Will inflation accelerate? Will I lose my job? When will interest rates fall? Why is the price of gasoline rising so fast? Why are home mortgages so hard to come by? Economists do disagree, particularly on some big macroeconomic issues. But often what the public perceives as disagreements over positive economics are really disagreements over what ought to be. In general, there is more agreement than disagreement among economists.

Economics studies how people use their limited resources to produce, exchange, and consume goods and services. The next chapter will begin to use the tools of the scientific method to explain how economic choices are made in a world of scarce resources. What are the costs of making choices? What arrangements are used to resolve the problem of choice? Answering these questions requires graphical analysis. The appendix to this chapter provides a review of guidelines for reading graphs.

Table 3   Do Economists Disagree?

Propositions	Agree
1. Tariffs and import quotas reduce general economic welfare.	97
2. The government should be an employer of last resort and initiate a guaranteed job program.	53
3. The money supply is a more important target than interest rates for monetary policy.	71
4. Cash payments are superior to transfers-in-kind.	92
5. Flexible exchange rates offer an effective international monetary arrangement.	95
6. A minimum wage increases unemployment among young and unskilled workers.	90
7. The government should index the income-tax rate structure for inflation.	68
8. Fiscal policy has a significant stimulative impact on a less than fully employed economy.	92
9. The distribution of income in the United States should be more equal.	71
10. National defense expenditures should be reduced from the present level.	66
11. Antitrust laws should be used vigorously to reduce monopoly power from its current level.	85
12. Inflation is primarily a monetary phenomenon.	57
13. The government should restructure the welfare system along lines of a "negative income tax."	92
14. Wage-price controls should be used to control inflation.	28
15. A ceiling on rents reduces the quantity and quality of housing available.	98
16. The Fed should be instructed to increase the money supply at a fixed rate.	39
17. Effluent taxes represent a better approach to pollution control than imposition of pollution ceilings.	81
18. The level of government spending should be reduced (disregarding expenditures for stabilization).	57
19. The Fed has the capacity to achieve a constant rate of growth of the money supply if it so desired.	66
20. Reducing the regulatory power of federal commissions would improve the efficiency of the U.S. economy.	78
21. The federal budget should be balanced over the business cycle rather than yearly.	83
22. The fundamental cause of the rise in oil prices in the mid-1970s is the monopoly power of the large oil companies.	25
23. The redistribution of income is a legitimate role for government in the context of the U.S. economy.	81
24. In the short run, unemployment can be reduced by increasing the rate of inflation.	64
25. The ceiling on interest paid on savings deposits should be removed.	94
26. "Consumer protection" laws generally reduce economic efficiency.	52
27. The economic power of labor unions should be significantly curtailed.	70

Source: Adapted from J. R. Kearl et al., "A Confusion of Economists?" *American Economic Review* 69, 2 (May 1979): 30.

Summary

1. Economics is important to each person as an individual, as a voter, and as a member of society. Increased knowledge improves the quality of decision making of individuals, voters, and members of society. The four themes of economics are scarcity, choice, specialization, and exchange.

2. Marginal analysis is an important tool of the economist. It aids economic decision making by examining the extra costs and benefits of economic decisions.

3. Microeconomics studies the economic decision making of firms and individuals in a

market setting; it is the study of the economy in the small. Macroeconomics studies the economy as a whole and deals with issues of inflation, unemployment, money supply, the government budget; it is the study of the economy in the large. Modern macroeconomics employs tools of microeconomics.

4.   Theory allows us to make sense of the real world and to learn how the facts fit together. There is no conflict between good theory and good practice. Economic theories are based upon the scientific method of hypothesis formulation, collection of relevant data, and testing of theories. Economic theory makes it possible to predict the consequences of actions that have yet to be taken and about facts that are yet to be collected.

5.   Three logical fallacies plague economic analysis: the false-cause fallacy (assuming that Event A has caused Event B because A is associated with B); the fallacy of composition (assuming that what is true for each part taken separately is true for the whole or, conversely, assuming that what is true for the whole is also true for each part); the *ceteris paribus* fallacy (incorrectly attributing to one variable effects that are caused by another).

6.   Economists tend to agree on positive economic issues (what is) while disagreeing on normative issues (what ought to be). The major unresolved issues of positive economics tend to be concentrated in macroeconomics, an evolving field in economics. Disagreements among economists are more visible to the public eye than disagreements in other scientific professions.

Key Terms

economics
marginal analysis
microeconomics
macroeconomics
theory
hypothesis
scientific method
false-cause fallacy
fallacy of composition
ceteris paribus **fallacy**
positive economics
normative economics

Questions and Problems

1.   Explain why specialization makes exchange essential. Why would people be unable to specialize if there were no exchange?

2.   Using the example of how to study enough on page 4, consider how to determine the optimal amount of study time.

3.   Again using the example of study time, assume that two days before an exam, your professor announces that this exam will account for 100 percent of your grade. How would this announcement affect your study time? Explain your answer using the logic of marginal analysis. From this answer, try to construct a general rule about changing costs and benefits and economic decision making.

4.   Which of the following topics would fall under macroeconomics? Which under microeconomics? Explain why in each case.
   a.   The price of cotton.
   b.   The interest rate.
   c.   Employment in the steel industry.
   d.   The general price level.
   e.   The national unemployment rate.

5. It was concluded that the data in Table 1 "failed to refute" the theory that higher prices reduce gasoline consumption. Why was it not said that the data in Table 1 "prove" the theory?

6. Explain how you would use the scientific method to determine what factors cause the grade-point averages of students in your class to differ. Explain why you must use abstraction.

7. "If I try to drive faster on the freeway, I will get home quicker." Explain under what conditions this statement is true and under what condition it is a logical fallacy. Also explain which logical fallacy is involved.

8. "The importation of cheap foreign cars has led to the decline of the American automobile industry." This statement is a potential example of which logical fallacy (or fallacies)?

9. Economists would be more likely to agree on the answers to which of the following questions? Why?
   a. Should tax rates be lowered for the rich?
   b. What would be the effects on economic output of a lowering of tax rates for the rich?
   c. What would be the effects of an increase in the price of home computers on purchases of home computers?
   d. Should government expenditures on welfare be reduced?
   e. What would be the effects of an increase in military spending on employment?

10. "The spring freeze in Florida has destroyed 25 percent of the citrus crop. The incomes of citrus farmers are, therefore, bound to fall." Which logical fallacy is possibly involved in this statement and why?

11. Try to construct from your own experience examples of the false-cause fallacy and the fallacy of composition.

Suggested Readings

Boulding, Kenneth. *Economics as a Science.* New York: McGraw-Hill, 1970.

Friedman, Milton. *Essays in Positive Economics.* Chicago: University of Chicago Press, 1953.

Kohler, Heinz. *Scarcity and Freedom.* Lexington, Mass.: D. C. Heath, 1977, part 1.

McCloskey, Donald. *The Applied Theory of Price.* New York: Macmillan, 1982, pp. 1–6.

Mundell, Robert A. *Man and Economics.* New York: McGraw-Hill, 1968, chap. 1.

Reading Graphs

Appendix Preview

Graphs are an important tool in learning economics. This appendix teaches the rudiments of working with graphs. It teaches graph construction, positive and negative relationships, dependent and independent variables, and the concept of slope for both linear and curvilinear relationships. It shows how slopes can be used to find the maximum and minimum values of a relationship, and it explains how to calculate the areas of rectangles and triangles. Finally, three common pitfalls of using graphs are discussed: the ambiguity of slope, the improper measurement of data, and the use of unrepresentative data.

Economics makes extensive use of graphs. A graph is simply a visual scheme for picturing the quantitative relationship between two different variables. This book contains graphs dealing with many different economic relationships, including the relationships between:
1. consumption and income.
2. the rate of inflation and time.
3. average costs of production and the volume of production.
4. profits and business decisions.
5. oil consumption and oil prices.
6. unemployment and inflation. ■

THE USE OF GRAPHS IN ECONOMICS

Relationships such as these can be pictured and analyzed by using graphs. Not only can a graph display a great deal of data; a graph can efficiently describe the quantitative relationship that exists between the variables. As the Chinese proverb says, ''a picture is worth a thousand words.'' It is easier both to understand and remember a graph than the several hundred or, perhaps, thousands of numbers that the graph represents. Graphs are important tools in learning economics. The reader must understand how to use graphs in order to master the basic economic concepts in this book.

Positive and Negative Relationships

The first important characteristic of a graph is whether there is a **positive (or direct) relationship** or a **negative (or inverse) relationship** between the two variables.

> A **positive (or direct) relationship** exists between two variables if an increase in the value of one variable is associated with an *increase* in the value of the other variable.

For example, an increase in the *horsepower* of a given car's engine will increase the *maximum speed* of the automobile. Panel (a) of Figure 1 depicts this relationship in a graph. The *vertical axis* measures the maximum speed of the car from the 0 point (called the *origin*); the *horizontal axis* measures the horsepower of the engine. When horsepower is zero (the engine is broken down), the maximum speed the car can attain is obviously 0; when horsepower is 300, the maximum speed is 100 miles per hour. Intermediate values of horsepower (between 0 and 300) are graphed. When a line is drawn through all these points, the resulting curved line describes the effect of horsepower on maximum speed. Since the picture is a line that goes from low to high speeds as horsepower increases, it is an example of an *upward-sloping curve*.

> When two variables are positively related the graph of the relationship is an upward-sloping curve.

> A **negative (or inverse) relationship** exists between two variables if an increase in the value of one variable is associated with a *reduction* in the value of the other variable.

For example, as the *horsepower* of the automobile increases, the *gas mileage* (for given driving conditions) will fall. In panel (b) of Figure 1, horsepower is still measured on the horizontal axis, but now gas mileage is measured on the vertical axis. Since the picture is a curve going from high to low values of gas mileage as horsepower increases, it is an example of a *downward-sloping curve*.

> When two variables are negatively related the graph of the relationship is a downward-sloping curve.

Dependent and Independent Variables

In some relationships involving two variables, one variable can be the **independent variable;** the other is the **dependent variable.**

> The **dependent variable** is the variable that changes as a result of a change in the value of another variable.

> The **independent variable** is the variable that causes the change in the value of the dependent variable.

An increase in engine horsepower *causes* an increase in the maximum speed of the automobile in the first graph. A horsepower increase *causes* a reduction in gas mileage in the second graph. In both examples, horsepower is the independent variable. The other two variables are said to ''depend upon'' horsepower because the changes in horsepower bring about changes in speed and gas

Figure 1   Graphing Positive and Negative Relationships

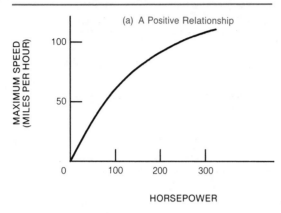

(a) A Positive Relationship

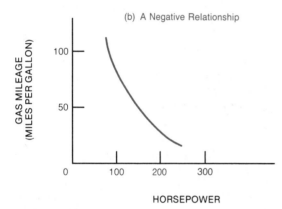

(b) A Negative Relationship

Panel (a) shows a positive relationship. As the horizontal variable (horsepower) increases, the value of the vertical variable (maximum speed) increases. The curve rises from left to right. Panel (b) shows a negative relationship. As the horizontal variable (horsepower) increases, the vertical variable (mileage) decreases. The curve falls from left to right.

mileage. Maximum speed and gas mileage are dependent variables.

One goal of economic analysis is to find the independent variable(s) that explain certain dependent variables. What independent variables explain changes in inflation rates, unemployment, consumer spending, housing construction, and so on? In many cases, it is not possible to determine which variable is dependent and which is independent. Some variables are interdependent (they both affect each other). In some instances, there is no cause-and-effect relationship between the variables.

RULES FOR CONSTRUCTING GRAPHS

A glance is sufficient to tell whether a curve is positively or negatively sloped. More work is required to read all the information that a graph contains. To read a graph properly, one must know how a graph is constructed.

The data for our sample graph are given in Table 1. The numbers in this table describe the quantitative relationship between *minutes of typing* and *number of pages typed*. Let us assume that the quantitative relationship between minutes and pages is known: every 5 minutes of typing will produce 1 page of manuscript. Thus, 5 minutes produces 1 page, 15 minutes produces 3 pages, and so on. Zero minutes will, of course, produce 0 pages.

Four steps are required to graph these data or any data. These steps have been carried out in Figure 2.

1. A vertical *axis* and a horizontal *axis* are drawn perpendicularly on graph paper, meeting at a point called the *origin*. The origin is labeled 0; the vertical axis is labeled Y; the horizontal axis is labeled X.
2. *Minutes of typing* are marked off along the horizontal X axis in equally spaced increments of 5 minutes, and the horizontal axis is labeled "Minutes of Typing."
3. The *number of pages typed* is marked off in equally spaced increments of 1 page along the vertical Y axis, and the vertical axis is labeled "Number of Pages Typed."
4. Each pair of numbers in Table 1 is plotted at the intersection of the vertical line that corresponds to that value of X and the horizontal line that corresponds to that value of Y. Point *a* shows that 5 minutes of typing produces 1 page. Point *c* shows that 15 minutes of typing produces 3 pages, and so on.

Table 1   **The Relationship Between Minutes of Typing and Number of Pages Typed**

	Minutes of Typing (X axis)	Number of Pages Typed (Y axis)
	0	0
a	5	1
b	10	2
c	15	3
d	20	4
e	25	5

Figure 2   **Constructing a Graph**

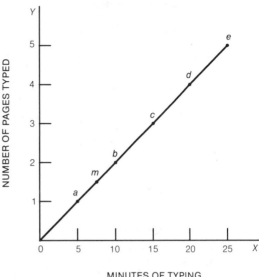

MINUTES OF TYPING

This graph reproduces the data in Table 1. Point *a* shows that 5 minutes of typing produces 1 page of typing; *b* shows that 10 minutes produces 2 pages, and so on. The upward-sloping line drawn through *a, b, c, d,* and *e* shows that the relationship between minutes of typing and number of pages typed is positive. The points between *a, b, c, d,* and *e* (such as *m*) show the number of pages typed for amounts of typing time between the 5-minute intervals.

Points *a, b, c, d,* and *e* completely describe the data in Table 1. Indeed, a graph of the data acts as a substitute for the table from which it was constructed. This is the first advantage of graphs over tables: they provide an immediate visual understanding of the quantitative relationship between the two variables just by observing the plot of points. Since the points in this case move upward from left to right, we know that there is a *positive relationship* between the variables.

This may not seem to be a great advantage for this simple and obvious case. However, suppose the data had been arranged as in Table 2.

If one spends some time inspecting the data, it becomes clear that there is a positive relationship between *X* and *Y;* however, it is not immediately obvious. In a graph, it is easier to see the relationship between the two variables.

The first advantage of graphs over tables is that it is easier to see the relationship that exists between two variables in a graph than in a table.

Suppose that in addition to the data in Table 1, we had data for the number of pages that could by typed at all kinds of intermediate values of typing time: 6 minutes, 13 minutes, 24 minutes and 25 seconds, etc. A large table would be required to report all these numbers. In a graph, however, all these intermediate values can be represented simply by connecting points *a, b, c, d,*

and *e* with a line. Thus, a second advantage of graphs is that large quantities of data can be represented in a graph more efficiently than in a table.

The second advantage of graphs over tables is that large quantities of data can be represented efficiently in a graph.

The data in Tables 1 and 2 reveal the relationship between minutes of typing and number of pages typed. This relationship was graphed in Figure 2. The relationship can change, however, if other factors that affect typing speed change. Assume that Table 1 shows minutes and pages typed on a manual typewriter. If the typist works with an IBM Selectric, a different relationship will emerge. With the IBM Selectric, perhaps the

Table 2   The Relationship Between Minutes of Typing and Number of Pages Typed (data rearranged)

	Minutes of Typing (X axis)	Number of Pages Typed (Y axis)
b	10	2
a	5	1
	0	0
e	25	5
c	15	3
d	20	4

typist can type 2 pages every 5 minutes instead of one. Both relationships are graphed in Figure 3. Thus, if factors that affect speed of typing change (for example, the quality of the typewriter), the relationship between minutes and pages can shift. Economists work frequently with relationships that shift, so it is important to understand shifts in graphs.

UNDERSTANDING SLOPE

The relationship between two variables is represented by a curve's **slope.** One cannot understand many central concepts of economics without understanding slope.

The slope reflects the response of one variable to changes in another. Consider the typing example. Every 5 minutes of typing on a manual typewriter produces 1 page; equivalently, every minute of typing produces ⅕ of a page. As we shall demonstrate below, the slope of the line *abcde* is ⅕ of a page of typing per minute.

The **slope** of a straight line is the ratio of the rise (or fall) in *Y* over the run in *X*.

To understand slope more precisely, consider in panel (a) of Figure 4 the straight-line relationship between the two variables *X* and *Y*. When *X* = 5, *Y* = 3; when *X* = 7, *Y* = 6. Suppose now that variable *X* is allowed to *run* (to change horizontally) from 5 units to 7 units. When this happens variable *Y* *rises* (increases vertically) from 3 units to 6 units.

Figure 3   Shifts in Relationships

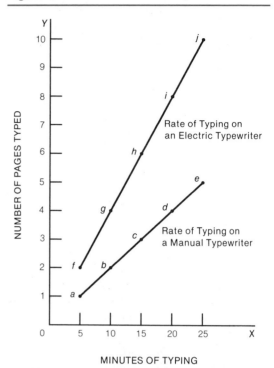

MINUTES OF TYPING

The curve *abcde* graphs the data in Table 1 that show the relationship between minutes and pages using a manual typewriter. The new (higher) curve *fghij* shows the relationship between minutes and pages with an electric typewriter. As a consequence of the change from the manual to the electric typewriter, the relationship has shifted upward.

The slope of the line in panel (a) is:

$$\frac{\text{Rise in } Y}{\text{Run in } X} = \frac{3}{2} = 1.5.$$

A *positive value of the slope signifies a positive relationship* between the two variables.

This formula works for negative relationships as well. In panel (b) of Figure 4, when *X* runs from 5 to 7, *Y falls* from 4 units to 1 unit, or rises by − 3 units. Thus, the slope is:

$$\frac{\text{Rise in } Y}{\text{Run in } X} = \frac{-3}{2} = -1.5.$$

A *negative* value of the slope signifies a *negative relationship* between the two variables.

Figure 4   Positive and Negative Slope

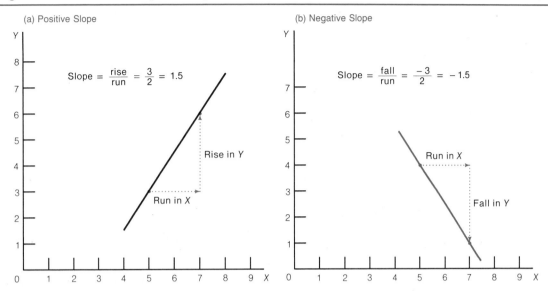

Positive slope is measured by the ratio of the rise in Y over the run in X. In panel (a), Y rises by 3 and X runs by 2, and the slope is 1.5. Negative slope is measured by the ratio of the fall in Y over the run in X. In panel (b), the fall in Y is -3, the run in X is 2, and the slope is -1.5.

If ΔY (delta Y) stands for the change in the value of Y and ΔX (delta X) stands for the change in the value of X,

$$\text{Slope} = \frac{\Delta Y}{\Delta X}.$$

This formula holds for positive or negative relationships.

Let us return to the typing example. What slope expresses the relationship between minutes of typing and number of pages? When minutes increase by 5 units ($\Delta X = 5$), pages increase by one unit ($\Delta Y = 1$). The slope is therefore $\Delta Y/\Delta X = \frac{1}{5}$.

In Figures 2, 3, and 4, the points are connected by straight lines. Such relationships are called *linear relationships*. The inquisitive reader will wonder how slope is measured when the relationship between X and Y is *curvilinear*.

A curvilinear example is given in Figure 5. When X runs from 2 units to 4 units ($\Delta X = 2$), Y rises by 2 units ($\Delta Y = 2$); thus, between a and b the slope is $\frac{2}{2} = 1$. Between a and c, however, X runs from 2 to 6 ($\Delta X = 4$), Y rises by 3 units

($\Delta Y = 3$), and the slope is $\frac{3}{4}$. In the curvilinear case, the value of the slope depends on how far X is allowed to run. Between b and c, the slope is $\frac{1}{2}$. Thus, the slope changes as one moves along a curvilinear relationship. In the linear case, the value of the slope will *not* depend on how far X runs because the slope is constant and does not change as one moves from point to point.

There is no single slope of a curvilinear relationship and no single method of measuring slopes. The slope can be measured between two points (say, between a and b or between b and c) or at a particular point (say, at point a). Insofar as the measurement of the slope between points depends upon the length of the run, a uniform standard must be adopted to avoid confusion. This standard is the use of *tangents* to determine the slope at a point on a curvilinear relationship.

To calculate the slope at a, let the run of X be "infinitesimally small," rather than a discrete number of units such as $\frac{1}{2}$, 2, 4, or whatever. An infinitesimally small change is difficult to conceive, but the graphical result of such a change can be captured simply by drawing a **tangent** to point a.

Figure 5   Calculating Slopes of Curvilinear Relationships

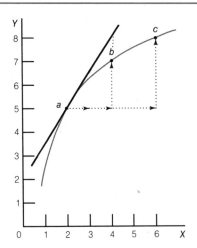

The ratio of the rise over the run yields a slope of 1 from *a* to *b* but a slope of ¾ from *a* to *c*. From *b* to *c*, the slope is ½. To compute the slope at point *a*, the slope of the tangent to *a* is calculated. The value of the slope of the tangent is ³⁄₂.

A **tangent** is a straight line that touches the curve at only one point.

If the curve is really curved at *a*, there is only one straight line that just barely touches *a* and only *a*. Any other line (a magnifying glass may be required to verify this) will cut the curve at two points or none. The tangent to *a* is drawn as a straight black line in Figure 5.

The slope of a curvilinear relationship at a particular point is measured using the tangent to that point:

> The **slope** of a curvilinear relationship at a particular point is the slope of the straight line tangent to the curve at that point.

The slope of the tangent at *a* is measured by dividing the rise by the run. Because the tangent is a straight line, the length of the run does not matter. For a run from 2 to 4 ($\Delta X = 2$), the rise (ΔY) equals 3 (from 5 to 8). Thus, the slope of the tangent is $\frac{3}{2}$ or 1.5.

Figure 6 shows two curvilinear relationships that have distinct high points or low points. In panel (a), the relationship between *X* and *Y* is pos-

Figure 6   Maximum and Minimum Points

(a) *Y* Is Maximized When Slope Is Zero

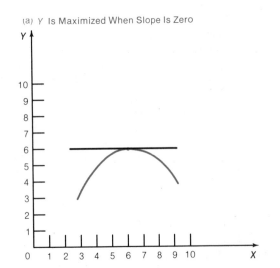

(b) *Y* Is Minimized When Slope Is Zero

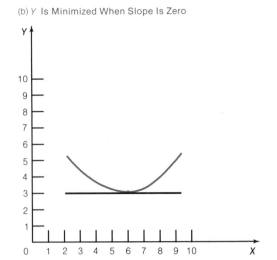

Some curvilinear relationships change directions. Notice that in panel (a), when the curve changes direction at *X* = 6, the corresponding value of *Y* is *maximized*. In panel (b), when *X* = 6, *Y* is *minimized*. In either case, the slope equals zero at the maximum or minimum value.

Figure 7   A Scatter Diagram Showing Mortgage Rates and Housing Starts, 1970–1983

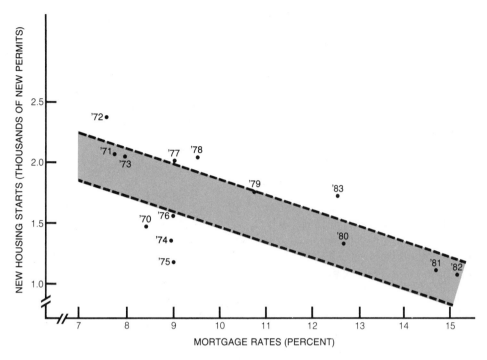

The generally falling pattern of dots suggests that there is a negative relationship between these two variables. The fact that not all dots lie on a single line suggests that other factors besides the independent variable (mortgage rates) affect the dependent variable (housing starts).

Source: *Economic Report of the President.*

itive for values of X less than 6 units and negative for values of X more than 6 units. The exact opposite holds for panel (b). The relationship is negative for values of X less than 6 and positive for X greater than 6. Notice that at the point where the slope changes from positive to negative (or vice versa), the slope of the curve will be exactly 0; the tangent at point $X = 6$ for both curves is a horizontal straight line that neither rises nor falls as X changes.

> **When a curvilinear relationship has a zero slope, the value of Y reaches either a high point—as in panel (a)—or a low point—as in panel (b)—at the X value where slope is zero.**

Economists pay considerable attention to the maximum and minimum values of relationships—

as when they examine how a firm maximizes profits or minimizes costs. Suppose, for example, that X in panel (a) represents the 1982 *production* of automobiles by General Motors (in units of 1 million) and that the variable Y represents GM's *profits from automobile production* (in billions of dollars). According to this diagram, GM should settle on $X = 6$ million units of automobile production because GM's profits would be higher at $X = 6$ than at any other production level.

Suppose that in panel (b), Y measures GM's costs of producing an automobile while X still measures automobile production. Production costs per automobile are at a minimum at $X = 6$. In other words, GM will produce cars at the lowest cost per car if GM produces 6 million cars.

The **scatter diagram** (see Figure 7) is a statistical tool frequently used to examine whether a positive or negative relationship exists between two variables. Statisticians have more powerful and exact tools to measure relationships, but the scatter diagram is a convenient analytical instrument.

> A **scatter diagram** consists of a number of separate points, each of which plots the value of the independent variable (measured along the horizontal axis) against a value of the dependent variable (measured along the vertical axis) for a specific time interval.

In Figure 7, mortgage interest rates are measured along the horizontal axis, and new housing starts (the number of new homes on which construction has started) are measured along the vertical axis. Each dot on the scatter diagram shows the combination of mortgage rate and number of housing starts for a particular year. Because mortgage rates are plotted against housing starts for the years 1970 to 1983, there are 14 dots on this particular scatter diagram (each labeled by year). The pattern of dots on a scatter diagram provides convenient visual information about the relationship between the two variables. If the dots tend to concentrate in a pattern where low mortgage rates accompany high housing starts and high mortgage rates accompany low housing starts, then the scatter diagram suggests a *negative relationship* between mortgage rates and housing starts. A negative relationship is indicated by a generally declining pattern of dots from left to right. If the relationship were positive, there would be a generally rising pattern of dots from left to right. If there were no relationship, the dots would be distributed randomly on the scatter diagram.

Figure 7 shows what appears to be a negative relationship between mortgage rates and housing starts. We have inserted a broad, negatively sloped band that traces out the general pattern of declining dots. This negative pattern indicated by the scatter diagram is not surprising. Most people would expect the number of houses being built to drop when the cost of borrowing to buy a home rises. The fact that all the dots do not lie neatly on a single negatively sloped line suggests that factors other than mortgage rates also affect housing starts. There are different levels of building activity in 1970 and from 1974–76 even though mortgage rates were about the same.

Figure 8   Calculating Areas of Rectangles and Triangles

(a) The Area of a Rectangle

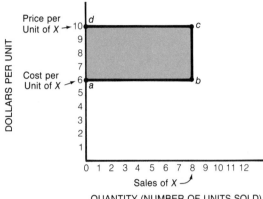

(b) The Area of a Triangle

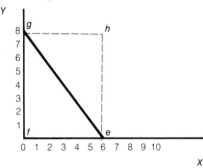

The area of the rectangle *abcd* is calculated by multiplying its height (*ad*, or equivalently, *bc*) by its width (*ab*, or equivalently, *dc*). The height equals $4 and the width equals 8 units; therefore, the area of the rectangle equals $32. As the text explains, $32 is the amount of this firm's profits. The area of the triangle *efg* is one-half of the area of the corresponding rectangle *efgh*. The area of the rectangle is $8 \times 6 = 48$. The area of the triangle *efg* is, therefore, $0.5 \times 48 = 24$.

AREAS OF RECTANGLES AND OF TRIANGLES

In economics, it is important to understand how areas of rectangles and areas of triangles are calculated. Panel (a) of Figure 8 shows how to calculate the area of a rectangle and panel (b) shows how to calculate the area of a triangle. Panel (a) uses a common economic example. It shows a firm selling 8 units of its product for a price of $10 while it costs $6 per unit to produce the product. The question is: How much profit is the firm earning? The answer is that the firm's profit is the area of the rectangle *abcd*. To calculate the area of a rectangle, the height of the rectangle (*ad* or *bc,* or $10 − $6 = $4 per unit) must be multiplied by the width of the rectangle (*ab* or *dc,* or 8 units). Multiplication shows that the area of the rectangle is $4 per unit times 8 units equals $32 of total profit.

Panel (b) of Figure 8 shows how to calculate the area of triangle *efg*. The triangle *efg* accounts for one half of the area of the rectangle *efgh*. The area of the triangle can, therefore, be calculated by first determining the area of the rectangle *efgh* (which equals $8 \times 6 = 48$) and then multiplying the rectangle area by ½ (because the triangle equals one half the area of the rectangle). In this example, the area of the triangle equals $0.5 \times 48 = 24$.

PITFALLS OF USING GRAPHS

When used properly, graphs illuminate the world in a convenient and efficient manner. Graphs may, however, be used to confuse or even misinform. Factions in political contests, advertisers of competing products, rivals in lawsuits can take the same set of data, apply the standard rules of graph construction, and yet offer graphs that support their own position and demonstrate the falsity of the opposition view. This misuse of graphs is especially apparent in national political campaigns, where the incumbent party or president seeks to demonstrate how well the country's economy has been managed, while the opposition attempts to show how badly the nation's economic affairs have been bungled.

It is important to be able to form an independent judgment of what graphs say about the real world. This section warns the graph consumer about three of the many pitfalls of using graphs: 1) the ambiguity of slope, 2) the improper measurement of data, and 3) the use of unrepresentative data.

The Ambiguity of Slope

The steepness of the rise or fall of a graphed curve can be an ambiguous guide to the strength of the relationship between the two variables because the graphed slope is affected by the scale used to mark the axes and because the slope's numerical value depends upon the unit of measure.

Panel (a) of Figure 9 provides an example of the ambiguity of slope. Both the right-hand and left-hand graphs plot exactly the same numbers: the sales of domestically produced cars for the years 1978 to 1982. In the left-hand graph (because each unit on the vertical axis represents 1 million cars), the decline in sales appears to be rather small. In the right-hand graph (because each unit now measures a half million cars), the decline appears to be quite steep. The impression one gets of the magnitude of the decline in auto sales is affected by the choice of units on the vertical axis even though both graphs provide identical information.

Improper Measurement

A second pitfall in reading and evaluating graphs is *improper measurement*. Improper measurement covers a multitude of sins but does not mean simply an incorrect count of a variable (counting 20 chickens instead of 15). A variable may give the appearance of measuring one thing while in reality measuring another. Improper measurement is often subtle and difficult to detect, and the user of graphs must constantly be on the alert for this misuse.

In economics, two types of improper measurement that are encountered most often with time-series graphs are 1) inflation-distorted measures and 2) growth-distorted measures. A *time-series graph* is one in which the horizontal *X* axis measures time (in months, quarters, years, decades, etc.), and the vertical *Y* axis measures a second variable whose behavior is plotted over time.

Panel (b) of Figure 9 gives an example of the importance of **inflation distortion** by graphing the per-capita national debt (the average person's share of the national debt) before and after adjustment for inflation. *Inflation* reduces the dollar's ' purchasing power and occurs when prices, on the average, rise. Per-capita national debt (without

Figure 9   Examples of Pitfalls in the Use of Graphs

(a) Ambiguity of Slope:
    Sales of U.S.-produced cars, 1978–1982

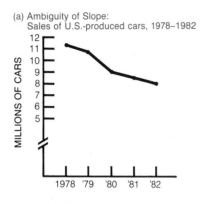

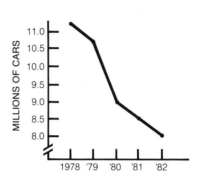

(b) Inflation-Distorted Measures:
    Per-Capita Government Debt, 1950–1980

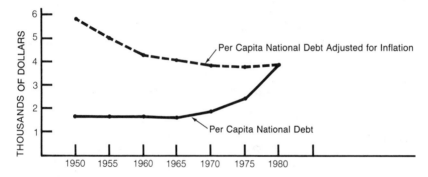

In panel (a), the choice of units on the vertical axis determines the steepness of slope. Although both figures plot the same data, the graph on the right appears to yield a steeper decline in domestic auto sales. In panel (b), the graph of per-capita government debt (not adjusted for inflation) shows a steady rise in per-capita debt. After the inflation distortion is removed (the dashed line), we find that per-capita debt has actually declined over a 30-year period. In panel (c), the left-hand graph shows that the output of the 100 largest manufacturing firms has been increasing since 1954 by substan-

adjustment for inflation) more than doubled between 1950 and 1980. We can make this rise appear as steep or as flat as we wish by changing the scale on the vertical axis, but that is not the point here. The dashed line shows the per-capita national debt adjusted for inflation. The rather surprising result is that, after the effects of inflation are removed, the per-capita national debt has decreased over the past 30 years. The graph of per-capita debt unadjusted for inflation is not a 'distortion in the strict sense of the word. It provides meaningful information: it is useful in many instances to know how much the federal government owes at prevailing prices. However, ma-

croeconomists tend to be more interested in series that have been adjusted for the effects of inflation.

Inflation distortion is the measurement of the dollar value of a variable over time without adjustment for the change in the inflation rate over that period.

Generally speaking, economic measures of output, employment, and the like tend to rise over time even after adjustment for inflation. They rise because population grows, the labor force expands, the number of plants increases, and the technology of production improves. To look at

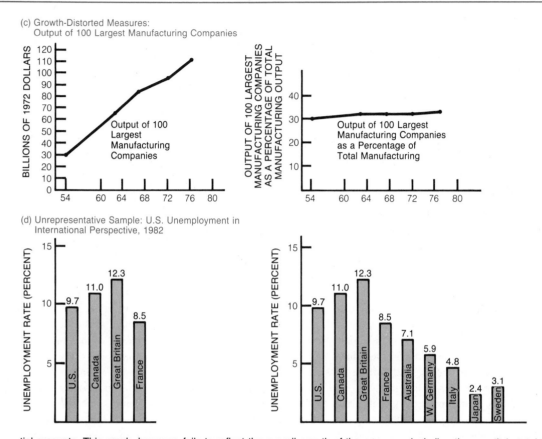

(c) Growth-Distorted Measures:
    Output of 100 Largest Manufacturing Companies

(d) Unrepresentative Sample: U.S. Unemployment in
    International Perspective, 1982

tial amounts. This graph, however, fails to reflect the overall growth of the economy, including the growth in total manufacturing. The right-hand graph adjusts for growth distortion and shows that the share of output of the 100 largest manufacturing firms has barely changed since 1954. In panel (d), when the sample is limited to four high-unemployment countries (the left-hand side), the U.S. unemployment rate does not appear to be high by international standards. When a broader and more representative sample is taken of nine countries (the right-hand graph), the U.S. unemployment rate does appear to be high by international standards.

the growth of a particular index without taking into account the fact that overall expansion is taking place elsewhere can lead to **growth distortion.** People who want to demonstrate alarming increases in alcohol consumption or in crime can point to increases in gallons of alcohol consumed or in crimes reported without noting that population may be increasing at a rate that is as fast or faster. Panel (c) of Figure 9 shows the problem of growth distortion. The left-hand graph shows the inflation-adjusted output of the 100 largest manufacturing concerns from 1954 to 1977. By looking at this graph, one might conclude that the dominance of American manufacturing by giant con-

cerns is on the rise because the output of these large concerns has risen by a considerable amount. However, by looking at the output share of the 100 largest manufacturing concerns in the context of rising total-manufacturing output (the right-hand chart), we find that the output of the 100 largest firms has just been keeping up with manufacturing output in general.

Growth distortion is the measurement of changes in a variable over time that does not reflect the concurrent change in other relevant variables with which the variable should be compared, such as population size.

Misinterpretations of time-series graphs can be avoided 1) by careful distinction between graphs that do and do not account for inflation and 2) by using per-capita figures where appropriate or expressing graphs as percentages or as shares of some total.

Unrepresentative Data

A final pitfall of using graphs is the problem of *unrepresentative or incomplete data*. The direction of a graphed relationship may depend upon the selection of the time period. For example, Soviet harvests have fluctuated dramatically in recent years with disastrous harvests following good harvests. If a good harvest year is chosen as the first year of a graph and a bad harvest year as the last, the assessment of Soviet agricultural performance will be unfavorable. It will be more favorable if the graph starts with a bad-harvest year and ends with a good one. Because the graphical relationship depends upon the choice of years covered by the graph, biased observers have the opportunity to present their version of the facts to the confusion of the user of the graph.

The problem of unrepresentative data also applies to comparisons across states, regions, or countries. The outcome can be manipulated by deliberate selection of which states or countries to include in the figure. Panel (d) of Figure 9 shows how unemployment-rate data can be manipulated. Suppose your goal is to demonstrate that the 1982 U.S. unemployment rate was not really that much above or below unemployment rates in other industrialized countries. The left-hand chart compares U.S. unemployment with three other countries, and from this chart one could conclude that U.S. unemployment is not different from that in other countries. However, when a larger sample is drawn in the right-hand chart of eight industrialized countries, then a different conclusion is reached. The U.S. unemployment rate in 1982 then appears high by the standards of other industrialized countries.

Summary

1. Graphs are useful for presenting positive and negative relationships between two variables. A positive relationship exists between two variables if an increase in one is associated with an *increase* in the other; a negative relationship exists between two variables if an increase in one is associated with a *decrease* in the other. In a graphical relationship, one variable may be an independent variable, and the other may be a dependent variable. In some relationships, it is not clear which variable is dependent and which variable is independent.

2. To construct a graph, four steps are necessary: 1) perpendicular vertical and horizontal axes are drawn on graph paper; 2) each variable is assigned to a particular axis; 3) units of measurement and scale are chosen for the X variable and for the Y variable; 4) each related set of variables is plotted at the intersection of the appropriate grid lines on the graph. The advantages of graphs over tables are that the relationship between the variables is easier to see and graphs can accommodate large amounts of data more efficiently.

3. For a straight-line curve, the slope of the curve is the ratio of the rise in Y over the run in X. The slope of a curvilinear relationship at a particular point is the slope of the straight line tangent to the curve at that point. When a curve changes slope from positive to negative as the X values increase, the value of Y reaches a *maximum* when the slope of the curve is zero; when a curve changes slope from negative to positive as the X values increase, the value of Y reaches a *minimum* when the slope of the curve is zero. Scatter diagrams are useful tools for examining data for positive or negative relationships between two variables.

4. The area of a rectangle is calculated by multiplying its height by its width. The area of a triangle is calculated by dividing the product of height times width by 2.

5. There are three pitfalls to be aware of when using graphs: 1) the choice of *units* and *scale* affects the apparent steepness or flatness of a curve; 2) the variables may be inflation-distorted or growth-distorted; 3) omitted data or incomplete data may result in an erroneous interpretation of the relationship between two variables.

Key Terms

positive (or direct) relationship
negative (or inverse) relationship
independent variable
dependent variable
slope
tangent
scatter diagram
inflation distortion
growth distortion

Questions and Problems

1. Graph the following data:

X:	0	1	2	3
Y:	10	20	30	40

What is the slope?

Figure A

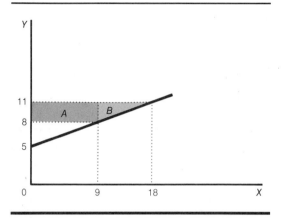

2. As income falls, people spend less on cars. Is the graph of this relationship positively or negatively sloped?

3. As the price of a good falls, people buy more of it. Is the graph of the relationship positively or negatively sloped?

4. Answer the following questions using Figure A.
   a. What is the slope?
   b. What is area A (shaded in grey)?
   c. What is area B (shaded in color)?

5. The Federal Government spent $96 billion in 1970 and $275 billion in 1983 on goods and services. What types of distortions affect this type of comparison?

2

The Economic Problem

Chapter Preview

The economic problem is how to use resources that are scarce. Society can't produce enough to meet society's virtually unlimited wants. Because all wants cannot be met, choices must be made among alternatives. Chapter 2 defines such crucial concepts as *resources, scarcity, scarce goods, free goods,* and *opportunity costs.* In solving its economic problem, every society must answer three questions: *What* should be produced? *How* should it be produced? *For whom* should it be produced? The production-possibilities frontier is used to illustrate the concepts of scarcity, opportunity cost, efficiency, and growth.

We live in what John Kenneth Galbraith has called "the affluent society."[1] Although many people in our society are poor, the standard of living of most American families is comparatively high. Is it appropriate to speak of scarcity in an affluent society?

This question underscores how important it is to understand the exact meaning of economic terms. In economics, *scarcity* has a specific meaning that differs from the one in the dictionary. Scarcity is not determined by one's standard of living, nor by whether one has life's basic necessities, but by comparison of wants with those resources available to satisfy wants. ■

---

1. John Kenneth Galbraith, *The Affluent Society* (Boston: Houghton Mifflin, 1957).

UNLIMITED WANTS VERSUS SCARCE RESOURCES

If we were to try to add up everyone's wants, it would soon become apparent that all wants could not be met. One person's list of wants might include a luxury car for each adult family member, a 10-bedroom and 7-bath home in the best part of town, a 15-room ski lodge in Colorado or in Switzerland, a full staff of 25 servants, 10 pounds of Maine lobster per month, a different 20-carat diamond ring for each day of the year. . . . the list could go on and on for pages. The only limits to wants are time, imagination, and appetite. If we added together the wish lists of everyone in the United States, the total number of luxury cars desired might equal 100 million per year; the total of Maine lobster might be 10 tons per week; the total number of domestic servants desired might be 50 million; Americans might want 1 million ski lodges in Vail, Colorado. People's wants are for all practical purposes unlimited.

It is immediately obvious that the economy could not conceivably produce enough goods and services to meet all these wants. There is not enough land in Vail, Colorado for 1 million ski lodges; virtually the entire adult population would have to become domestic servants to satisfy wants for domestic servants; there are not enough skilled engineers and craftspersons to build the millions of luxury autos; the waters off Maine would not yield the desired tonnage of Maine lobsters per week.

Suppose now that someone were given the task of allocating the goods and services that could be produced with society's resources among all the people who want these goods and services. The task would certainly not be easy because it is clear that only a small portion of society's wants could be met. The person in charge of allocation would have to make hard choices. Some wants could be met, but an even larger number would have to be denied. These decisions could be made randomly (perhaps through lotteries) or according to some rule. One rule might be to meet first the wants of those people who are prepared to offer something in return—such as hours of labor or goods and services they can supply. A committee might be appointed to determine which people have the best claim for the good in question. The committee might consider the social behavior of claimants or their contributions to society. The committee might decide to divide all goods equally among the members of society independently of their wants.

The imbalance between society's wants and society's ability to meet these wants illustrates the most basic facts of economic life: *scarcity* and *choice*. Scarcity is present because what people want far exceeds society's ability to meet these wants. Choice is necessary because someone or something must decide which wants are to be met. Scarcity exists whether claimants are rich or poor. It is likely that we would run out of luxury cars and ski lodges before we would run out of low-grade cuts of meat or seats on city buses.

> The most important fact of economics is the law of scarcity: there will never be enough resources to meet everyone's wants.

THE DEFINITION OF ECONOMICS

Chapter 1 noted that **economics** is the study of four themes: scarcity, choice, specialization, and exchange. Since economics deals with the process of choice, the definition of Chapter 1 can be shortened to:

> **Economics** is the study of how *scarce resources* are *allocated* among *competing ends*.

Four terms in this definition are emphasized because their meanings must be clear if the definition is to be properly understood. What are the exact economic meanings of *scarcity, resources, allocation,* and *competing ends?*

Scarcity

In September of 1980, Air Florida announced that any tickets that were not sold 10 minutes prior to departure on all its Houston-to-Dallas/Fort Worth flights would be given away free of charge. This offer was valid for only one week.

As you might have guessed, the Air Florida tickets were indeed a **scarce good.** Crowds of people gathered at the departure gate in the hope of getting one of the few available free tickets. Many disappointed travelers had to return home, after a long wait, without a ticket, because the "free" tickets were not a **free good.**

> An item is a **scarce good** if the amount available (offered to users) is less than the amount people would want if it were given away free of charge.

> A **free good** is one where the amount available is greater than the amount people want at a zero price.

The following examples will test your ability to distinguish between free goods and scarce goods.

Tumbleweeds.   Along an Idaho highway, one of the authors encountered the delightful sign: "Tumbleweeds are free, take one." Like the Air Florida ticket, tumbleweeds have a price of zero, but unlike the Air Florida ticket, tumbleweeds in Idaho are a free good. Why? Tumbleweeds may give satisfaction to the Eastern tourist, who may want to take one home as a souvenir, but the number of tumbleweeds available to takers far exceeds the number people want, even though they cost nothing. This example is limited by place and circumstances. In Alaska, tumbleweeds may be such a rarity that the number people want exceeds the number available. Exotic orchids can be freely picked in some remote Hawaiian islands, while commanding a high price in New York City. Mesquite used to be just a worthless bush to Texas ranchers. Fine restaurants started paying $1 or more per pound for mesquite chips when it was discovered that some kinds of mesquite bushes have excellent uses in food preparation.

La Guardia Airport.   Landing and take-off slots at major airports are not paid for by airlines. Instead, committees comprised of government officials and airline management determine which airlines will be allotted take-off and landing slots and on which days. At busy La Guardia Airport in New York City in 1984, 701 take-off slots were available on a daily basis.[2] The airlines that serve New York City collectively wanted more than these 701 slots and had to engage in intense

negotiation over which airlines got which slots. In fact, the La Guardia Airline Scheduling Committee received requests for 834 landing slots from airlines then landing at La Guardia. The negotiations were particularly intense for the popular 5 P.M. to 7 P.M. landing slots. Although the airlines do not pay for landing slots, they are nevertheless a scarce commodity at La Guardia Airport. Whether landing slots are scarce or free depends upon time and place. At 10 P.M., landing slots are virtually a free good at La Guardia. At uncongested airports (say, Champaign/Urbana, Illinois) landing slots are virtually a free good.

Los Angeles Air.   The early residents of Los Angeles did not have to worry about the scarcity of clean air, for prior to the automobile age and the mass migration to southern California, clean air was not scarce according to the economic definition. Now, although no one is explicitly charged for clean (or cleaner) air, it has become a scarce good. Residents are implicitly paying for clean air by purchasing homes in distant suburbs where smog is less severe, by making lengthy commutes to work, and by purchasing air-filtration systems for their homes.

Goods may be scarce even if they are free of charge, and goods may be free goods at one time and place and scarce goods in another time and place.

Unlike landing slots and clean air, scarce goods usually command a price. The next chapter will discuss how prices help allocate scarce resources.

Resources

Resources are the natural resources (land, mineral deposits, oxygen), the capital equipment (plants, machinery, inventories), and the human resources (workers with different skills, qualifications, ambitions, managerial talents) that are used as *inputs* to produce scarce goods and services. Productive resources are also called **factors of production.** These resources represent the economic wealth of

---

2. "Frustration Over Airline Slots," *New York Times,* November 9, 1984.

society because they determine how much output the society can produce from available resource inputs. Because the factors of production are limited, society's ability to produce output is limited. The limitation of resources is the fundamental source of scarcity.

> The **factors of production** are the resources used to produce goods and services; they can be divided into three categories—land, labor, and capital.

Sometimes, a fourth category—*entrepreneurship*—is considered a factor of production. The economic definitions of these factors differ somewhat from the dictionary usage.

Land represents those natural resources, unimproved or unaltered by inputs of the other two factors of production, that contribute to production. Desert land that had been transformed into arable land by irrigation would not be a free gift of nature. The application of the labor and capital used to build the irrigation system makes this desert land productive.

> **Land** is a catchall term that covers all of nature's bounty—minerals, forests, land, water resources, oxygen, and so on.

In 1984, the total value of all U.S. **capital** was approximately $13 trillion.[3] Unlike land, capital is not one of nature's gifts; capital is produced by combining the factors of production. *Plant-and-equipment capital* is long-lived: when it is used to produce output, it is not *consumed* (used up) immediately; it is consumed gradually in the process of time. An assembly plant may have a life of 40 years, a computer a life of 5 years, and a lathe a life of 10 years before it must be replaced.

> **Capital** is the equipment, plants, buildings, and inventories that are available to society.

When economists speak of capital, they mean physical capital goods—buildings, computers, trucks, plants. This concept of capital is distinct from *money capital*. Physical capital and money capital are related. Money capital is needed to purchase physical capital; money capital represents the ownership's claims to physical capital.

The owner of 1,000 shares of AT&T owns money capital, but these shares really represent ownership of a portion of AT&T's physical capital.

One final distinction should be made between the *stock* of capital and *additions* to the stock of capital. At one point in time, there exists a stock of capital. This stock consists of all the capital (plants, equipment, inventories, buildings) that exist *at that point in time*. Each year, this stock changes; it usually grows. New plants are built, new equipment is manufactured, new homes are constructed, additions are made to inventories. Through **investment,** society adds to its stock of capital.

> **Investment** is additions to the stock of capital.

The ditchdigger contributes muscles to the production process; the computer engineer contributes mental abilities; the airline pilot contributes physical coordination and mental talents. **Labor** resources can be measured in terms of the number of people in the work force, granted that people differ in skills, education, and natural ability. In the U.S. today, the labor force consists of more than 100 million individuals.

> **Labor** is the physical and mental talents that human beings contribute to the production process.

Just as a society can add to the stock of physical capital, so can it add to the stock of **human capital.**

> **Human capital** is the accumulation of past investments in schooling, training, and health that raise the productive capacity of people.

In 1984, the stock of human capital was valued at approximately $5.8 trillion.[4] By investing in the training and education of people, society adds to the productive capacity of labor and raises the wealth of society. Investments in physical capital and human capital accomplish the same goal: they increase the capacity of society to produce output. Certain persons, called **entrepreneurs,** possess a particular talent and perform a particular role that cannot be performed by land and capital.

---

3. OECD, Department of Economics and Statistics, *Flows and Stocks of Fixed Capital* (Paris: OECD, 1983), p. 9.

4. Calculated from John W. Kendrick, *The Formation and Stocks of Total Capital* (New York: Columbia University Press, 1976), Appendix B.

An **entrepreneur** organizes, manages, and assumes the risks for an enterprise.

Entrepreneurs are those people who organize the factors of production to produce output, who seek out and exploit new business opportunities, who introduce new technologies. The entrepreneur is the one who takes risk and bears the responsibility if the venture fails. The entrepreneur puts inventions into business practice.

Allocation

Scarcity requires that choices be made: if there is not enough of a commodity to meet unlimited wants, decisions must be made about who will receive the commodity and who will be denied it. A system of **allocation** of scarce resources must be employed. Societies cannot function unless the allocation problem is resolved in a satisfactory manner.

Allocation is the apportionment of scarce resources to specific productive uses or to particular persons or groups.

Consider what would happen if there were no organized allocation. People would have to fight or compete with one another for scarce resources. The timid would not compete effectively; the elderly or weak would have difficulty in obtaining goods, except through stronger, more aggressive benefactors. Such an allocation system was in effect for centuries in the dark and middle ages and explains much of the lack of economic progress of those eras. Such free-for-all allocation is rare in modern societies, but it reappears in cases of breakdowns of the social order. Floods, natural disasters, and wars bring out looting and violent competition for scarce goods. Martial law must be declared to prevent free-for-all allocation. If there were a drastic reduction in gasoline supplies (say, to one tenth of the current level), there would probably be considerable free-for-all allocation. Individuals armed with guns, wrenches, and nasty dispositions would seek to intimidate other customers at service stations to gain access to the scarce resource, gasoline.

It is important to have an allocation system that is not based upon strong-arm tactics. Society must develop a system for orderly allocation.

Market Allocation.   The allocation system that prevails in American society is the **market;** this book is devoted primarily to the study of market allocation.

The **market** is an arrangement by which buyers and sellers regularly exchange goods or services.

Market allocation works as follows: A commodity—let us say, a TV set—is scarce because the number desired at a zero price exceeds the number offered. Raising the price of TV sets encourages production and discourages consumption. Market allocation uses higher prices to restrict the number of buyers of the scarce commodity to the amount available. The market sets the price to encourage the *supply* of a resource (the amount offered for sale) to match actual *demand* for that resource (the amount buyers are prepared to purchase).

Market allocation and the price system are discussed in Chapter 3. Most goods and services are allocated by the market in our society—automobiles, hamburgers, computers, furniture, fresh fruits—the list is almost without end.

Government Allocation.   A second allocation system is *government allocation*. Governmental agencies, officials, and administrative authorities decide who, among all those who want the scarce commodity, will be accommodated. In Communist societies, most (but not all) allocation decisions are made by the government. In our economy, government allocation is typically used when it is felt that market allocation will not do a good job. Government allocates resources to national defense and to law enforcement, for example. Airport landing slots are assigned by government regulatory agencies. The regional distribution of gasoline supplies has at times been dictated by the federal government. Licenses for television and radio stations are granted by the federal government. In all these cases, access to the scarce resource is not determined by willingness to pay, but by some administrative authority.

Government allocation in no way eliminates the need to make hard choices. In Great Britain, the government National Health Service is responsible for allocating medical care. The number

Example 1   Lee Iacocca Is Not a Free Good

The new American institution, Chrysler chairman Lee Iacocca, is a popular person. His appearance at various functions is not a free good. How do we know this scientific fact? *Parade* magazine kindly supplied economists with a perfect economics experiment in the definition of a free good. A free good is one for which demand exceeds supply at a zero price. In late 1984, *Parade* erroneously reported that Iacocca makes free appearances at "birthday parties, benefits, and bar mitzvahs." At a zero price, the demand for Iacocca's services far exceeded the supply. The number of invitations he received rose to 1,000 letters a week. One woman invited him to her 25th birthday party; a small boy wanted Iacocca to serve as his confirmation sponsor (Chrysler had to hire one or two extra people to answer all the letters).

As this example illustrates, people have virtually unlimited wants. When goods and services are offered free, their desires are limited only by their imaginations. Just as Lee Iacocca cannot meet the demand for his services (at a zero price), the resources of society are no match for the people's wants. ∎

Source: "Lee Iacocca Wants You to Know: He Doesn't Do Free Bar Mitzvahs," *Wall Street Journal*, January 4, 1985.

---

of doctors, nurses, and hospital beds is not sufficient to meet wants for "free" medical care, and the National Health Service must decide who will receive medical care. Some procedures are denied to patients over 65—such as kidney dialysis or transplants. The desire for operations that are not required to save a life (elective surgery) is limited by requiring patients to wait weeks and months to see a specialist.[5] In effect, the National Health Service uses rules to allocate medical care. Of course, there is a private medical market as well that supplements the public market.

Scarce resources can be allocated by different allocation systems. There is endless controversy about which system (or combination of systems) is best. The allocation system has a substantial impact on how people live. Consider the differences between American society, which uses primarily market allocation, and Soviet society, which uses primarily government allocation. The allocation system affects personal lives, the political system, and freedom of choice. (See Example 1.)

Competing Ends

Economics is the study of competition for resources. Scarce resources must somehow be allocated among the **competing ends** of individuals, families, government agencies, and businesses according to an allocation system.

First, different individuals are in competition for resources. Which families will have a greater claim on scarce resources? Who will be rich? Who will be poor? How will income be distributed? There is also competition for resources between the private sector (individuals and businesses) and government. Third, there is competition for resources between current and future consumption. By investing scarce resources in physical and human capital, their current use is sacrificed to produce more goods and services in the future.

> The **competing ends** are the different purposes for which resources can be used.

Finally, the society must choose between competing national goals when allocating resources. Is price stability, full employment, elimination of poverty, or economic growth most important? Are we prepared to achieve one goal at the expense of another?

THE ECONOMIC PROBLEM

The economic problem is how to allocate scarce resources among competing ends. Three questions must be answered: *What* products will be produced? *How* will they be produced? *For whom* will they be produced?

---

5. Harry Schwartz, "What is a Life Worth?" *Wall Street Journal*, September 15, 1980, p. 22.

What?

Should society devote its limited resources to producing civilian or military goods, luxuries or necessities, goods for immediate consumption or goods that increase the wealth of society (capital goods)? Should small or large cars be produced, or should buses and subways be produced instead of cars? Should the military concentrate on strategic or conventional forces?

How?

Once the decision is made on what to produce, society must determine what combinations of the factors of production will be used. Will coal, petroleum, or nuclear power be used to produce electricity? Will bulldozers or workers with shovels dig dams? Should automobile tires be made from natural or synthetic rubber? Should Diet Coke be sweetened with saccharin or Nutra-Sweet? Should tried-and-true methods of production be replaced by new technology?

For Whom?

Will society's output be divided fairly equally, or will claims to society's output be unequal? Will differences in wealth be allowed to pass from one generation to the next? What role will government play in determining *for whom?* Should government intercede to change the way the economy is distributing its output?

Economic Systems

Societies must solve these economic problems of what, how, and for whom if they are to function. Different societies have different solutions. Some use private ownership and market allocation; others use public ownership and government allocation. Most use an **economic system** that is a combination of private and public ownership and a combination of market and government allocation.

> The set of organizational arrangements and institutions that are established to solve the economic problem is called an **economic system.**

Real-world economic systems exist in almost infinite variety; the list of labels for economic systems is also long. The two major alternatives are the capitalist (market) system and the planned socialist (communist) system. How the market system solves our economic problems is discussed in Chapter 3.

OPPORTUNITY COSTS

Scarcity requires that choices be made concerning what will be produced, how it will be produced, and for whom. Choice means that some alternatives must be forgone. A sacrificed opportunity is called an **opportunity cost** by economists because the economic cost of any choice is that which must be sacrificed in order to make that choice.

> The **opportunity cost** of a particular action is the loss of the next best alternative.

If a person buys a new car, its opportunity cost is the next best alternative that must be sacrificed. The next best alternative might have been a European trip, an investment in the stock market, or enrollment in a prestigious university. Because the person chose the car, he or she sacrificed these other things. The loss of the next best alternative is the true cost of the car. If the government increases defense spending, the opportunity cost is the best alternative government program that had to be sacrificed to make the funds available.

The notion of opportunity cost supplies a shortcut method of differentiating between free goods and scarce goods:

> **Free goods have an opportunity cost of zero.**
> **Scarce goods have a positive opportunity cost.**

Why does the Idaho tumbleweed have no opportunity cost? If one tumbleweed is taken, the amount available is still greater than the amount wanted. The taker has not had to give up anything as a consequence of taking the tumbleweed.

The opportunity cost of an action can involve the sacrifice of time as well as the sacrifice of goods. To gather the free tumbleweed, one would

Example 2   Medical Care and the Sinking Lifeboat: Opportunity Costs

The number of hospital beds, intensive-care personnel, kidney-dialysis machines, mechanical hearts, and so on required to care for the chronically ill are limited by the productive resources of society. On the other hand, the number of people requiring sophisticated, long-term medical care or major life-prolonging surgery is growing, especially with the aging of the American population. The number of people in need of chronic, long-term medical care, kidney dialysis, or cardiovascular surgery exceeds the resources available to meet these needs. In the language of economics, these forms of medical care are scarce resources. Growing scarcity has forced physicians and health officials to begin to think the unthinkable: exactly how should society decide who should get chronic medical care and who should not? The analogy is that of a slowly sinking lifeboat, where the boat can be kept afloat only by periodically pushing someone over the side. Insofar as medical resources are limited, they have an opportunity cost; one life may have to be traded for another. In fact, elaborate computer models have been developed which may eventually assist in the rationing of medical care to the chronically ill. These models are designed to predict the years of life to be saved by a medical procedure and even to assess according to some subjective standard the quality of life that a chronically ill patient would have. For example, an elderly person in need of constant kidney dialysis or someone who would have to live with chronic pain may be assigned a lower quality-of-life index number than a younger and otherwise healthier person with kidney problems.

The rationing of medical care to the chronically ill is one of the most explosive issues of our time, but the presence of scarcity requires that it be addressed. There has been a predictable outcry against computerized rationing, but whenever scarcity is present rationing must be done. The two polar choices are to let the marketplace decide who gets what or to let the decision be made according to administrative criteria. If the marketplace is used (supplemented by private and government health-insurance programs), those willing and able to pay for chronic care will receive it; those who do not want to pay or cannot pay will not receive the care. If administrative criteria are used, then panels of experts will indeed be required to establish rules to determine who gets chronic medical care. Neither choice appears attractive. This example dramatically illustrates why economics is a study of choice.   ■

---

need to sacrifice time. What is the opportunity cost of attending a football game? To pay the price of the ticket, the buyer has to sacrifice the purchase of other goods, and the next best purchase is the opportunity cost of buying the ticket. Even if the buyer had received the ticket free of charge, however, there would still be an opportunity cost. The two hours spent at the game could have been devoted to alternative uses. The buyer could have slept, studied, or listened to records, for example. If a major exam were scheduled for the next day, the opportunity cost of the game could be quite high. The notion of sacrificed time as an opportunity cost is an important ingredient of economics.

We shall show in the course of this book that virtually all economic decisions are affected by opportunity costs. In committing its resources to a particular action (producing cars, for example), the business firm must consider the opportunities forgone by not committing these resources to another activity (producing trucks, for example). Before signing a contract to work for Firm X, workers must consider the other employment opportunities that they are passing up. People with funds to invest must weigh the rates of return that will be sacrificed in alternative uses of the funds before they commit their funds to a particular stock-market investment. (See Example 2.)

Every choice involving the allocation of scarce resources involves opportunity costs.

PRODUCTION POSSIBILITIES

The **production-possibilities frontier (*PPF*)** is a useful analytical tool for illustrating the concepts of scarcity, choice, and opportunity costs.

Table 1   Production-Possibilities Schedule

Combination	Tanks (thousands)	Wheat (tons)	Opportunity Cost of Tanks (tons of wheat)
a	0	18	0
b	1	17	1
c	2	15	2
d	3	12	3
e	4	7	5
f	5	0	7

Suppose an economy produces only two types of goods: tanks and wheat. Of course, actual economies produce more than two goods, but a simple model aids our understanding. Table 1 gives the amounts of wheat and tanks that this hypothetical economy can produce with its limited factors of production and technical knowledge. These amounts are graphed in Figure 1. The table and the graph contain the same information.

What do these numbers mean? How are they to be interpreted? If our hypothetical economy chose to be at point *a,* it would be producing no tanks and the *maximum* of 18 tons of wheat from the factors of production available. At point *f* the economy would be producing no wheat and the *maximum* of 5,000 tanks. The points between *a* and *f* show the combinations of wheat and tanks that the economy is capable of producing from its available resources and technology. Point *c* shows that if 2,000 tanks are produced, the maximum number of tons of wheat that can be produced is 15. Each intermediate point on the *PPF* between *a* and *f* represents a different combination of wheat and tanks that could be produced using the same resources and technology.

The **production-possibilities frontier** (*PPF*) shows the combinations of goods that can be produced when the factors of production are utilized to their full potential. The production-possibilities curve reveals the economic choices open to society.

Our hypothetical economy is capable of producing output combinations *a* through *f.* The

Figure 1   The Production-Possibilities Frontier (*PPF*)

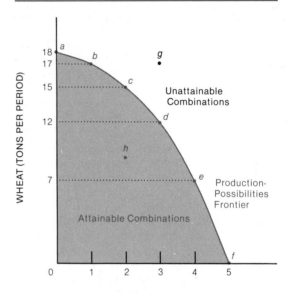

The *PPF* shows the combinations of outputs of two goods that can be produced from society's resources when these resources are utilized to their maximum potential. Point *a* shows that if 18 tons of wheat are produced, no tank production is possible. Point *f* shows that if no wheat is produced, a maximum of 5,000 tanks can be produced. Point *d* shows that if 3,000 tanks are produced, a maximum of 12 tons of wheat can be produced. Point *g* is above society's *PPF.* With its available resources, the economy cannot produce 17 tons of wheat and 3,000 tanks. Points like *h* inside the *PPF* and, therefore, attainable represent an inefficient use of the society's resources.

economy is unable to produce output combination *g* (17 tons of wheat and 3,000 tanks) because *g* uses more resources than the economy has available. Point *h* is an attainable combination because it lies inside the frontier. The economy can produce any combination of outputs on or inside the *PPF.*

The Law of Increasing Costs

The production-possibilities frontier is curved like a bow; it is not a straight line. Why does it have this shape? As noted earlier, the economic cost of any action is the loss of the next best opportunity. In our example, the economy produces only two goods. The opportunity cost of increasing the production of one of those goods is the amount of the other good that must be sacrificed. In this simple case, the measurement of opportunity cost is obvious: the opportunity cost of tanks is the wheat production that must be sacrificed.

At *a,* the economy is producing 18 tons of wheat and no tanks. The opportunity cost of increasing the production of tanks from zero to 1,000 is the 1 ton of wheat that must be sacrificed in the move from *a* to *b*. The opportunity cost of 1,000 more tanks (moving from *b* to *c*) is 2 tons of wheat. The opportunity cost of the fifth thousand of tanks (moving from *e* to *f*) is a much higher 7 tons of wheat. The amounts of wheat that must be given up to increase tank production are given in the last column of Table 1. The opportunity cost per thousand of tank production rises with the production of tanks, which is consistent with the **law of increasing costs.**

> The **law of increasing costs** states that as more of a particular commodity is produced, its opportunity cost per unit will increase.

The law of increasing costs is consistent with the bowed out shape of the *PPF*. Suppose our hypothetical economy were at peace, producing only wheat, no tanks (at *a* on the *PPF*). Its archenemy declares war, and the economy must suddenly increase its production of tanks. The amount of resources available to the economy is not altered by the declaration of war, so the increased tank production must be at the expense of wheat production. The economy *must move along* its *PPF* in the direction of more tank production.

As tank production increases, will the opportunity cost of a unit of tank production remain the same? At low levels of tank production, the opportunity cost of a unit of tank production will be relatively low. Some factors of production will be suited to producing both wheat and tanks; they can be shifted from wheat to tank production without raising opportunity cost. As tank production increases further, resources suited to wheat production but ill suited to tank production (experienced farmers make inexperienced factory workers, agricultural equipment is poorly adapted to tank factories) must be diverted into tank production. Ever-increasing amounts of these resources must be shifted from wheat to keep tank production expanding at a constant rate. The opportunity cost of a unit of tank production (the

amount of wheat sacrificed) will rise, as the law of increasing costs would predict.

The Law of Diminishing Returns

Underlying the law of increasing costs is the **law of diminishing returns.** Suppose that wheat is produced using land, labor, and tractors. The law of diminishing returns states that increasing the amount of labor in equal increments, holding land and tractors constant, eventually brings about smaller and smaller increases in wheat production.

> In general, the **law of diminishing returns** states that increasing the amount of one input in equal increments, holding all other inputs constant, eventually brings about ever-smaller increases in output.

The law of diminishing returns recognizes that output is produced by combinations of resources. Wheat is produced by combining labor, farm machinery, and chemical fertilizers. Tanks are produced by combining skilled mechanics, unskilled labor, assembly-line equipment, and managerial talent. For each output level, there will be an optimal combination of inputs. To produce 500 bushels of wheat requires little land, no heavy agricultural equipment, but some farm labor. To produce 10 tons of wheat requires a great deal more land and heavy machinery but not much more labor. Whenever some factors of production are fixed, output must be expanded by using more of the factors that can be varied. As more and more of the expandable factors are used, eventually there will be too much of the expandable factor relative to the fixed factors. Accordingly, the amount of extra output produced by additional inputs of the variable factor will decline.

Suppose a farm has a fixed amount of land (1,000 acres) and a fixed amount of capital (10 tractors). Suppose that initially 10 farm workers are employed, which means that each would have 100 acres to farm and that each would have one tractor. Increasing the number of farm workers to 20 would mean each worker would have 50 acres to farm and half of a tractor with which to work (2 workers would have to share one tractor). Increasing the number of farm workers to 1,000 would result in each worker farming one acre and

100 workers sharing each tractor. Obviously, each worker would be less productive if each had only an acre to farm and if each worker had to wait for 99 other workers to use the tractor.

Efficiency

The *PPF* shows the combination of goods an economy is capable of producing when its limited resources are utilized to their maximum potential. Whether an economy will indeed operate on its production-possibilities frontier depends upon whether or not the economy utilizes its resources with maximum **efficiency.**

In Figure 1, if the economy produces output combinations that lie on the *PPF* the economy is said to be *efficient*. Notice that when an economy is operating on its *PPF* it cannot increase the production of one good without reducing the production of another good. If the economy operates at points inside the *PPF,* such as *h,* it is said to be *inefficient* because more wheat could be produced without cutting back on the other good.

> **Efficiency** results when no resources are unemployed and when no resources are misallocated.

If workers are unemployed or if productive machines stand idle, the economy is not operating on its *PPF* because resources are not being employed. If these idle resources were used, more of one good could be produced without reducing the production of other goods. Misallocated resources are resources that are used but not to their best advantage. For example, if a surgeon works as a ditchdigger, if cotton is planted on Iowa corn land, or if jumbo jets are manufactured in India, resources are misallocated. Again, if resource misallocations are removed, more of one good could be produced without sacrificing the production of other goods.

Economic Growth

The production-possibilities frontier represents the economic choices open to society. It shows the maximum combinations of outputs the economy is capable of producing from its scarce resources. Economies that are efficient operate on their frontier; others that are inefficient operate inside their

Figure 2   The Effect of Increasing the Stock of Capital on the *PPF*

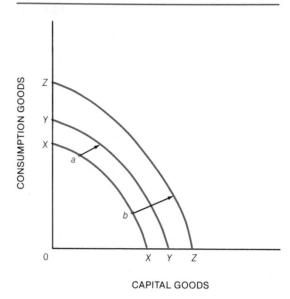

Suppose the current *PPF* is curve *XX*. If the economy chooses point *a*, allocating most resources to the production of consumption goods and few to the production of new capital goods, the *PPF* in the future will shift out to curve *YY*. But if the economy chooses point *b*, with comparatively little consumption and comparatively high production of new capital goods, the future *PPF* will shift out further—to *ZZ*.

frontier. Which combination of outputs lying on the frontier is best is a matter of economic choice.

Capital Accumulation.   Where to locate on the *PPF* may represent a choice between capital goods and consumer goods. Capital goods are the equipment, plants, and inventories that are added to society's stock of capital and can be used to satisfy wants in the future. Consumer goods are items like food, clothing, medicine, and transportation that satisfy consumer wants directly in the present. The capital goods/consumer goods choice is shown in Figure 2.

> **Economic growth occurs when the production-possibilities frontier expands outward and to the right. One source of economic growth is the expansion of capital.**

The economy on the *PPF* labeled *XX* must choose among those combinations of consumer

Example 3   Production Possibilities and the Military Buildup of the 1980s

The production-possibilities frontier can be used to assess the U.S. military buildup that occurred during the first four years of the Reagan administration (1980–1984). Between 1979 and 1984, the share of total resources devoted to the military rose from 4.5 percent to 6 percent of total output (still well below the 14–16 percent Soviet figure). In terms of the *PPF* in the accompanying figure, this shift in resources can be denoted as a shift along the *PPF* labeled *XX* from *a* to *b* (the movement is exaggerated to make the point of the diagram clearer). As a consequence of the movement from *a* to *b*, more military goods have been produced but at the opportunity cost of sacrificed civilian goods. A military buildup causes not only a shift in current production; it also causes a shift in research and development (R&D) priorities in favor of military technology. The additional resources flowing into military R&D will cause technological advances in military production and will shift the 1984 *PPF* to *YY*, say, by 1990. The improvement in military technology would allow the economy to produce at point *b'* in 1990. If the economy had not shifted priorities in favor of military technology, then civilian technology would have improved more rapidly, and the *PPF* would have shifted to *ZZ* in 1990. As long as society continues to favor the existing mix of civilian and military goods, the military buildup has allowed society to improve its position. At *b'* (with the buildup of military technology), it has more of both civilian and military goods than it has at *b''* (with the buildup of civilian technology). Suppose, however, that in 1990, relations with the Soviet Union improve, and society decides that it wants to return to its original mix of civilian and military goods. Be-

cause of the military buildup, society would have to move along *YY* from *b'* to *a'*. If there had been no buildup of military technology, a change in the

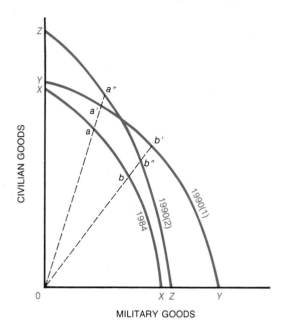

military civilian mix of output would have meant a movement along *ZZ* from *b''* to *a''*. With the return to the original mix of civilian and military output, the buildup in military technology has made society worse off because at *a'* it has less of both goods than at *a''*. ■

Source: Peter N. Hess, "An Introductory Economics Approach to the Current U.S. Military Buildup," *The Collegiate Forum,* Spring 1984, pp. 16–17.

goods and capital goods located on *XX*. What are the implications for the future of selecting *a* or *b?* If *a* is chosen, more consumer wants are satisfied today, but additions to the stock of capital are smaller. If *b* is selected, fewer wants are satisfied today, but additions to the stock of capital are greater. The creation of a larger stock of capital today means more production in the future. The society that selects *b* will, therefore, experience a greater outward shift of the *PPF* in the future and will be able to satisfy more wants in the future.

The society that selects *a* will satisfy more

wants today but will not be in as good a position to satisfy future wants.

These principles are illustrated in Figure 2. If society chooses *a,* then the *PPF* expands from *XX* now to *YY* in the furture. If it locates at *b,* the *PPF* expands more, from *XX* now to *ZZ* in the future. At *ZZ,* the economy will be able to satisfy more wants than at *YY*.

There are limits to the rule that less consumption today means more consumption tomorrow. If all resources are devoted to capital goods, the labor force would starve. If too large a share of

Figure 3   Technical Progress in Wheat Production

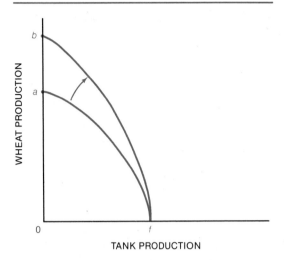

If a higher-yielding strain of wheat is discovered, a larger quantity of wheat could be produced with the same resources. Since this increase in wheat production would not influence tank production, the *PPF* would rotate from *af* to *bf*.

Figure 4   The Economic Problem: What? How? For Whom?

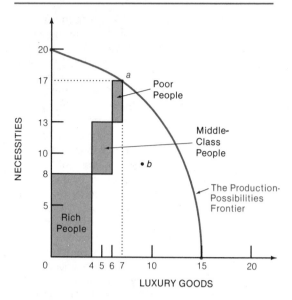

The *PPF* reveals the choices open to society. The *what* question is solved by the choice of where to locate on the *PPF.* Here society chooses *a,* or 7 units of luxuries and 17 units of necessities. The *how* question is solved when society decides how to combine resources to produce these outputs. Society can solve this problem efficiently and operate on the frontier (at *a*) or inefficiently and operate inside the frontier (at *b*). The *for whom* question is the division of society's output among the members of society. In this diagram, the rich get 4 units of luxuries and 8 units of necessitites; the middle class get 2 units of luxuries and 5 units of necessities; the poor get one unit of luxuries and 4 units of necessities.

resources is put into capital goods, worker incentives might be low and efficiency might be reduced. (See Example 3.)

> **Societies must choose between consumption today and consumption tomorrow. The society that devotes a greater share of its resources to producing capital sacrifices consumption now but enlarges its supply of capital and will, thus, have a higher rate of economic growth.**

Shifts in the Production-Possibilities Frontier.

The position of the production-possibilities frontier is based on the size and productivity of the resource base. Capital accumulation is only one reason for the *PPF* to shift. Increases in labor or land or discoveries of natural resources (coal, iron, oil) will also shift the *PPF* outward. Technical progress occurs when the society learns how to get more outputs from the same inputs. Thus, technical progress, or advances in productivity, will also shift the *PPF* outward.

Technical progress and accumulation of productive factors like land, labor, or capital have different effects on the *PPF*. Technical progress may affect only one industry or sector—whereas labor and capital and land can be used across all sectors. Figure 3 illustrates a technical advance in wheat production without a corresponding change in the productivity of the resources devoted to tank production. Accordingly, the *PPF* shifts from *af* to *bf*. Here the *PPF* shifts upward but not rightward. Figure 2 illustrates that a change in factor supply—illustrated in this case by capital accumulation—shifts the *PPF* both upward and rightward.

Production Possibilities and the Questions of *What, How,* and *For Whom.*

All societies must solve the economic problems of what, how, and for whom if they are to function. There are different methods of solving these problems. This book will concentrate on how market economies solve the economic problems but will also discuss how planned economies and mixed economies deal with them as well.

In market economies, the *what* problem is solved when consumers decide what they want to buy and how much they are willing to pay and when voters cast their ballots for or against public spending programs. The *how* problem is solved when producers determine how to combine resources to their best advantage. The *for whom* decision depends on who owns the economy's land, labor, and capital.

One solution to the *what, how,* and *for whom* problems for a hypothetical economy is shown in Figure 4. The *what* problem is nothing more than the choice of location on the *PPF*. In this diagram, society chooses point *a*. The *how* problem is solved behind the scenes by decisions on how the factors of production are to be combined. How well the *how* problem is solved can be read directly from the *PPF* diagram. If the economy is operating *on its PPF,* such as at *a,* it is solving the how problem with maximum efficiency. If it is operating inside the *PPF,* at *b* for example, it is not solving the how problem with maximum efficiency. The solution to the *for whom* problem also takes place behind the scenes. We can show the outcome of the *for whom* problem on the *PPF* diagram. How the consumer goods (necessities and luxury goods) are distributed among the members of society (the rich, the middle class, and the poor) is shown by the color-shaded rectangles. In the diagram, the rich receive most of the luxury goods; the middle class receive some luxury goods; the poor receive negligible luxury goods.

The next chapter explains how the price system solves the *what, how,* and *for whom* problems, how it facilitates specialization and exchange, and how it provides for the future.

Summary

1. Wants are unlimited; there will never be enough resources to meet unlimited wants.

2. Economics is the study of how scarce resources are allocated among competing ends.

3. A good is *scarce* if the amount available is less than the amount people would want if it were given away free. A good is *free* if the amount people want is less than the amount available. Goods may be scarce even though they are given away free of charge.

4. The ultimate source of scarcity is the limited supply of resources. The resources that are factors of production are land, labor, and capital. Society can add to its stock of resources by investment in physical capital and in human beings.

5. Because scarcity exists, some system of allocating goods among those who want the goods is necessary. The two major allocation systems are market allocation and allocation by government plan. These two types of allocation systems can be combined to create mixed allocation systems.

6. Allocation systems must determine what resources will be made available to which individuals, how resources are to be divided between the private and public sectors, and which resources will be devoted to current use and which to future consumption.

7. Economics is the study of how societies solve the economic problems of *what* to produce, *how* to produce, and *for whom* to produce.

8. The opportunity cost of any choice is the next best alternative that was sacrificed to make the choice. Scarce goods have a positive opportunity cost; free goods have an opportunity cost of zero.

9. The production-possibilities frontier *(PPF)* shows the maximum combinations of goods that an economy is able to produce from its limited resources when these resources are utilized to their maximum potential and for a given state of technical knowledge. If societies are efficient, they will operate on the production-possibilities frontier. If they are inefficient, they will operate inside the *PPF*.

10. The law of increasing costs says that as more of one commodity is produced at the expense of others, its opportunity cost will increase. This law applies to all economic systems.

11. According to the law of diminishing returns, increasing the amount of one input in equal increments, holding all other inputs constant, eventually brings about ever smaller increases in output.

12. The two sources of economic inefficiency are unemployed resources and misallocated resources.

13. Economic growth occurs because the factors of production expand in either quantity or quality, or because technological progress raises productivity. The choice of consumer goods versus capital goods affects economic growth. Generally, the greater the share of resources devoted to capital goods, the better is the economy able to meet wants in the future. The choice of consumer goods versus capital goods is really a choice between meeting wants now and meeting them in the future.

Key Terms

economics
scarce good
free good
factors of production
land
capital
investment
labor
human capital
entrepreneur
allocation
market
competing ends
economic system
opportunity cost
production-prossibilities frontier *(PPF)*
law of increasing costs
law of diminishing returns
efficiency

Questions and Problems

1. In the early 19th century, land in the western United States was given away free to settlers. Was this land a free good or a scarce good, according to the economic definition? Explain your answer. Explain why land in the United States today is no longer given away free.

2. "Desert sand will always be a free good. More is available than people could conceivably want." Evaluate this statement.

3. A local millionaire buys 1,000 tickets to the Super Bowl and declares that these tickets will be given away to 1,000 boy scouts. Are these tickets free goods? Why or why not?

4. In Israel, desert land has been turned into farm land by irrigation. Does this example demonstrate that nature's free gifts are not fixed in supply?

5. Do you consider your time spent in college as an investment in human capital? Is it investment or consumption? Make a brief list of the opportunity costs of attending college. Do these costs equal the dollar costs listed in the college catalog?

6. Consider an economy that has the choice of producing either guns or butter. All of its factors of production are equally well suited to producing either guns or butter. In this economy, what will be the shape of the production-possibilities frontier? Will the law of diminishing returns apply in such an economy?

7. Consider the data in Table A on a hypothetical economy's production-possibilities frontier.

Table A

Hundreds of Guns	Tons of Butter
8	0
7	4
5	10
3	14
1	16
0	16.25

a. Graph the *PPF*.
b. Does it have the expected shape?
c. Calculate the opportunity cost of guns in terms of butter. Calculate the opportunity cost of butter in terms of guns. Do your results illustrate the law of increasing costs?

d. If you observed this economy producing 700 guns and 3 tons of butter, what would you conclude about how this economy is solving the *how* problem?

e. If you observed this economy at some later date producing 700 guns and 12 tons of butter, what would you conclude?

8. By purchasing a new color TV set, I have passed up the opportunity to buy a personal computer, to take a vacation trip, to paint my home, and to earn interest on the money paid for the TV. What is the opportunity cost of the color TV? How would the opportunity cost be determined?

9. Goodwill and the Salavation Army are prepared to send trucks out to homes and apartments to pick up used household goods. In recent years, these agencies have begun to ask exactly what goods are to be donated before coming out for the pickup. Using the notion of scarcity and opportunity cost, explain why it is important for these agencies to gather this information.

10. Determine in which factor-of-production category—land, labor, or capital—each of the following items belongs.

a. A new office building.

b. A deposit of coal.

c. The inventory of auto supplies in an auto-supply store.

d. Land reclaimed from the sea in Holland.

e. A trained mechanic.

f. An automated computer system.

11. Draw two production-possibilities curves for tank production versus wheat production, like the one in Figure 1. In the first, show the effect of an improvement in the technology of tank production while the technology of wheat production remains the same. In the second, show simultaneous improvements in both the technologies of tank and wheat production.

12. Give the possible causes of an upward and outward movement in the production-possibilities frontier.

Suggested Readings

Franklin, Raymond S. *American Capitalism: Two Visions*. New York: Random House, 1977, chap. 1.

Gregory, Paul and Robert Stuart. *Comparative Economic Systems*. Boston: Houghton Mifflin, 1985, chaps. 1 and 2.

Heilbroner, Robert L. *The Making of Economic Society*. Englewood Cliffs, N. J.: Prentice-Hall, 1962, chap 1.

Heyne, Paul. *The Economic Way of Thinking,* 4th ed. Chicago: SRA, 1983, chap. 2.

Mundell, Robert A. *Man and Economics*. New York: McGraw-Hill, 1968, chap. 1 & 2.

North, Douglass C. and Roger LeRoy Miller. ''The Economics of Clamming and Other 'Free' Goods.'' In *The Economics of Public Issues,* 5th ed. New York: Harper and Row, 1980, pp. 152–56.

3

The Price System

Chapter Preview

This chapter will examine how resources are allocated and how the decisions of the millions of people in the typical economy are coordinated. Market allocation of resources is achieved through the price system. The prices people pay for things are like a number of cleverly placed thermostats that balance the decisions of thousands of producers and millions of consumers. The price system achieves this balance by operating according to the principle of substitution, the law of comparative advantage, and the principles of supply and demand. This chapter will explain the difference between relative prices and money prices and will examine the role of prop-

erty rights, specialization, and interest rates in the working of the price system. The chapter will conclude by discussing some of the limitations of the price system.

Economic activity is circular. Consumers buy goods with the incomes they earn by furnishing labor, land, and capital to the business firms that produce the goods they buy. The dollars that households spend come back to them in the form of income from selling productive factors. A starting point for understanding how the price system works is to examine this circularity in economic activity. ■

THE CIRCULAR FLOW OF ECONOMIC ACTIVITY

The **circular-flow diagram** illustrates how output and input decisions involving millions of consumers, hundreds of thousands of producers, and millions of owners of resources fit together.

The **circular-flow diagram** summarizes the flows of goods and services from producers to households and the flows of the factors of production from households to business firms.

The circular-flow diagram in Figure 1 illustrates the circular flow of economic activity. The flows from households to firms and from firms to households are regulated by two markets: the market for goods and services and the market for the factors of production. The circular-flow diagram consists of two circles. The outer circle shows the *physical flows* of goods and services and of productive factors. The inner circle shows the *flows of money expenditures* on goods and services and on productive factors. The physical flows and the money flows go in opposite directions. When households buy goods and services, physical goods flow to the households, but the sales receipts flow to the business sector. When workers supply labor to business firms, productive factors flow to the business sector, but the wage income flows to the household sector.

For almost every physical flow in the economy, there is a corresponding financial transaction. To obtain consumer goods, the consumer must pay for them. When firms deliver products, they receive sales revenues. When businesses hire labor or rent land, they must pay for them. When individuals supply labor, they receive wages.

There are two pairs of supply and demand transactions in the circular flow: 1) The supply and demand for consumer goods are mediated by the market for goods and services. 2) The supply and demand for factors of production are mediated by the market for the factors of production.

Two types of goods and services do not enter into the circular flow. *Intermediate goods* (discussed later in the chapter) are goods that businesses sell to other businesses. The steel industry supplies steel to the automobile industry, which produces the automobiles that enter the circular flow. The lumber industry provides lumber to home-construction firms, whose products enter the circular flow. Intermediate goods enter the circular flow only indirectly through the final goods they've helped to produce. The other goods and services that do not enter the circular flow are those produced within the household and used by the household. Homemakers provide cooking, cleaning, transportation, and other services to other family members. These services are both produced and consumed in the same household and, accordingly, do not enter into the circular flow. If the same services had been purchased from a business firm (eating in a cafeteria instead of at home), they would enter the circular flow.

RELATIVE PRICES AND MONEY PRICES

This chapter explains how a market economy, working through the price system, coordinates the millions of economic activities that enter the circular flow. We begin our tour of the price system with the concept of relative prices.

Prices in the Land of Orks

Suppose you find yourself in a strange land—strange in every respect except that you are able to communicate with the inhabitants. The hospitable natives welcome you with a gift of local currency, which you learn is called the *ork*. Being in a hurry to eat breakfast, you do not have time to count how many orks you have. You locate a diner and order coffe. A waitress brings you a cup of coffee and asks for 400 orks. Is coffee cheap or expensive? Is the price high or low? You have no idea. Given the information you have at this point, the price of 400 orks is meaningless.

How do you discover whether the price of coffee is high or low? You have to gather more information. You look at the menu and discover that a coke sells for 1,200 orks, and you learn in conversation with another customer that the typical worker earns something like 24,000 orks per hour. Now you decide that coffee is cheap by reasoning: ''Back home I pay $0.40 for a cup of coffee and $0.40 for a coke, and I earn $10.00 an hour. At home, an hour's work will purchase 25 cokes or 25 cups of coffee. Here an hour of work

Figure 1   The Circular Flow of Economic Activity

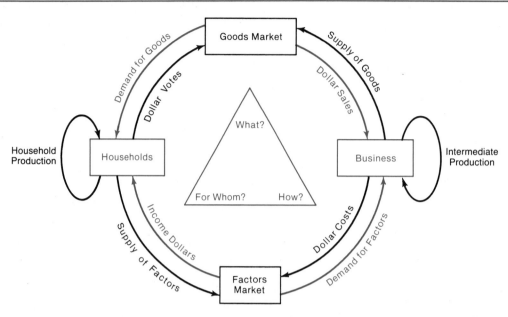

Economic activity is circular. The outside circle describes the flow of physical goods and services and productive factors through the system: business furnishes goods to households who furnish land, labor, and capital to business. The inside circle describes the flow of dollars: households provide dollar sales to business, whose costs become incomes to households. These two circles flow in opposite directions. The triangle gives a pictoral representation of the relationship of the circular flow to the solution to the *what, how,* and *for whom* questions. The circular-flow diagram shows that flows of intermediate goods remain entirely within the business sector and do not enter the circular flow. It also shows that because household-production services are produced and consumed within the family, they do not enter the circular flow.

will purchase 20 cokes and 60 cups of coffee.'' The moral of this parable is: A money price in isolation from other money prices is meaningless. What is important is how a particular money price stands relative to other money prices.

Calculating Relative Prices

A **relative price** indicates how one price stands in relation to other prices. A relative price is quite different from a **money price.** In the ork example, coffee sells for 400 orks and cokes for 1,200 orks. Three cups of coffee is the relative price of a coke, and one third of a coke is the relative price of coffee. If coffee and cokes had both sold for 400 orks, then the relative price of a coke would have been one cup of coffee.

A **relative price** is a price expressed in terms of other commodities.
A **money price** is a price expressed in monetary units (such as dollars, francs, etc.)

As these examples show, relative prices can be expressed in terms of anything. The relative price of coke can be expressed in terms of cups of coffee, cups of tea, hours of work, number of T-shirts, or anything else that has a money price.

Let P_A and P_B stand for the money prices of apples *(A)* and bananas *(B)*. The relative price of apples to bananas is the *ratio* of the two money prices, P_A/P_B. If the price of apples is \$0.50 per pound and the price of bananas is \$0.25 per pound, the relative price of one pound of apples is two pounds of bananas. Conversely, one pound of bananas costs 0.5 pound of apples. When coffee costs 400 orks and a coke costs 1,200 orks, the ratio of the price of coke to coffee equals 3, or the relative price of cokes equals 3 coffees.

Money prices are meaningful when they are related to prices of goods that are connected in some way with the good in question. For example, it might make sense to state the price of electricity in terms of natural gas because commercial

Table 1   Money Prices and Relative Prices, Residential Natural Gas and Electricity, 1970–1983

Year	Money Price of Natural Gas (dollars per million BTUs)	Money Price of Electricity (dollars per million BTUs)	Relative Price of Electricity (units of natural gas)
1970	0.79	5.83	7.37
1973	0.93	6.68	7.18
1975	1.32	9.23	6.99
1976	1.57	9.81	6.24
1977	1.92	10.65	5.54
1978	2.26	11.33	5.01
1979	2.75	12.20	4.44
1980	3.35	14.09	4.20
1981	3.90	16.32	4.18
1982	4.75	18.04	3.79
1983	5.70	19.49	3.41

Source: *Statistical Yearbook of the United States*, 1984, p. 500.

and residential users make choices between natural gas and electricity. Should we heat and air condition our homes with electricity or natural gas? Should manufacturers use electricity or natural gas as fuel? The money prices of natural gas and electricity are graphed in panel (a) of Figure 2 (from data in Table 1). They show that the money prices of both natural gas and electricity rose substantially over the last 13 years. However, panel (b) shows that the relative price of electricity (the price of electricity divided by the price of natural gas) fell during this same period. In 1970, a BTU of electricity cost 7.37 times as much as a BTU of natural gas. By 1983, a BTU of electricity had fallen to 3.41 times a BTU of natural gas.

The money price of a commodity can rise while its relative price falls. The money price can fall while its relative price rises. Money prices and relative prices need not move together.

Relative prices play a prominent role in answering the economic questions of *what, how,* and *for whom.* Money prices do not. Relative prices signal to buyers and sellers what goods are cheap or expensive. *Buying and selling decisions are made on the basis of relative prices.* If the relative price of one good rises, buyers substitute other goods whose relative prices are lower.

In Figure 2, we see that the relative price of electricity (expressed as a percent of natural gas) has been falling steadily since 1970. Conversely, it shows that the relative price of natural gas has been rising. This change in relative price signals to people and businesses making decisions on appliances and heating systems that electricity has become a better buy relative to natural gas. This signal should encourage the greater use of electricity and the decreased use of natural gas.

The emphasis on relative prices does not mean that money prices are unimportant. Money prices tend to be fairly important in the context of macroeconomics. For example, *inflation* is not a movement in relative prices but a general increase in money prices. Elections are won or lost on the basis of inflation; the living standards of older people on fixed incomes are damaged by inflation. Rampant inflation can destroy the fabric of society. Inflation is important. But notice that even in the case of inflation, money prices are not considered in isolation. Instead, the level of money prices today is compared to the level of money prices yesterday. Ultimately, this is also a form of relative price.

Generally speaking, in microeconomics there is greater interest in relative prices than in money prices. In macroeconomics, there is greater interest in the level of money prices than in relative prices. In modern macroeconomics, relative prices have come to play a greater role in explaining macroeconomic events.

Figure 2   Money Prices and Relative Prices of Natural Gas and Electricity

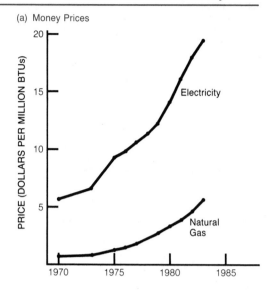

(a) Money Prices

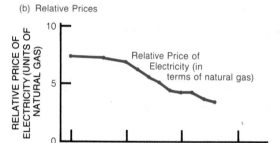

(b) Relative Prices

Panel (a) shows that the price of both electricity and natural gas rose from 1970 to 1983. Electricity prices tripled, but gas prices rose sevenfold. Panel (b) shows that the price of electricity *in terms of natural gas* actually fell.

THE PRINCIPLE OF SUBSTITUTION

Relative prices are important because of the fundamental **principle of substitution.**

> The **principle of substitution** states that practically no good is irreplaceable in meeting *demand* (the amount of a good people are prepared to buy). Users are able to substitute one product for another to satisfy demand.

Virtually no good is fully protected from the competition of substitutes. Aluminum competes with steel, coal with oil, electricity with natural gas, labor with machines, movies with TV, one brand of toothpaste with another, and so on. The only goods impervious to substitutes are such things as certain minimal quantities of water, salt, or food and certain life-saving medications, such as insulin.

To say that there is a substitute for every good does not mean that there is an *equally good* substitute for every good. One mouthwash is a close substitute for another mouthwash; a television show is a good substitute for a movie; apartments may be good substitutes for private homes. However, carrier pigeons are a poor substitute for telephone service;[1] costly insulation may be a poor substitute for fuel oil; public transportation may be a poor substitute for the private car in sprawling cities; steel is a poor substitute for aluminum in the production of jet aircraft.

Relative prices signal consumers when substitutions are necessary. If the price of one good rises relative to its substitutes, consumers will tend to switch to the relatively cheaper substitute.

Substitutions are being made all around us. As relative energy prices rise, people substitute insulation for fuel oil and natural gas, home-entertainment equipment for driving to movies, restaurants, and parties; carpools for driving one's own car. As the relative price of crude oil rises, utilities switch from oil to coal; retailers use fewer neon lights and hire more sales personnel. When the relative price of coffee increases, people consume more tea; when beef prices rise, the consumption of poultry and fish products increases. There is no single recipe for producing a cake, a bushel of wheat, a car, comfort, recreation, or happiness. Increases in relative prices motivate consumers to search out substitutes. (See Example 1.)

PROPERTY RIGHTS

Relative prices provide information to buyers and sellers on what goods are cheap and what goods are expensive. Substitutions depend on relative

---

1. In Buenos Aires telephone service at one time became so chaotic that businesses actually purchased carrier pigeons to substitute for telephone service.

Example 1   The Computer and the Middle Manager: Substitutions

The principle of substitution states that people will seek out substitutions for resources whose relative price has risen. One study of big firms in banking, insurance, manufacturing, and telecommunications suggests that the American middle manager is being replaced by the computer. The middle manager—whose main function is to collect and manage information—costs a company an average of $100,000 per year including salary, fringe benefits, office space, phone, and expense account. With the decline in computer prices that has accompanied the computer revolution, a company can purchase sophisticated computer equipment for $30,000 or less. In other words, the price of the middle manager has risen dramatically relative to the price of the computer. Opinions differ about the long-term fate of the middle manager. One management expert predicts a 30 percent decline in middle management employment within a few years. Other management experts believe that the rate of substitution for the relatively expensive middle manager by computers will be less rapid.   ■

Source: "Thanks to Computer, Middle Manager May be Businesses' Endangered Species," *Los Angeles Times,* June 1984.

prices. The manner in which buyers and sellers act on relative-price information depends on **property rights.**

> **Property rights** are the rights of an owner to use and exchange property.

Collective Ownership

There are different forms of ownership of property. In some societies, the bulk of property (capital, land, houses, etc.) is owned by the state. In the Soviet Union, virtually all plants, equipment, inventories, apartments, homes, and land are owned by the state. The state has rights to use and exchange the property that it owns. Individuals are limited in the property they are allowed to own; they may own a few head of livestock, a private home in some circumstances, a private car, a TV, and so on. In a **socialist society,** individuals have proscribed rights to use and exchange the property they own.

> A **socialist society** is characterized by collective ownership of property and government allocation of resources.

Private Ownership

Unlike in the Soviet Union with its extensive system of state ownership, in a **capitalist society,** the bulk of property is owned by private individuals.

> A **capitalist society** is characterized by private ownership of property and by market allocation of resources.

These two features of capitalism are intertwined. There is no such thing as a *pure* capitalist economy in which *all* property is owned privately and in which all allocation is done through the market. In the United States, local, state, and federal governments own trillions of dollars of property.

In a society where property rights are vested in private individuals, how will they exercise their property rights to solve the *what, how,* and *for whom* problems?

The individual owner of private property (whether it be land, a house, a horse, a truck, a wheat crop, or a can of peaches) has the legal freedom (the right) to sell that property at terms mutually agreed upon between the buyer and the seller. Normally, when property is sold, the buyer and seller agree on a dollar price. In some cases, there is an exchange of property on a barter basis; for example, a high-grade stereo may be *bartered* (traded) for a low-grade car. Instead of a dollar price, the price of the car is the stereo, and the price of the stereo is the car.

The legal system protects private-property rights. It protects private property from theft, damage, and unauthorized use and defines where property rights reside. The legal system generally places some restriction on property rights. Private

Example 2   Restrictions on Property Rights

The most basic property-right restriction in most societies is the restriction on the right to buy or sell people (slavery). Even if a person were willing to sell himself or herself to someone else (or to sell his or her lifetime earnings to someone else), the law would not permit such a transaction.

Complete freedom to exercise private-property rights does not exist in any society. Complete freedom could not work. Private property cannot be used in such a way as to injure a neighbor or harm the community. The injured party has the right to petition the legal system to prevent an owner from exercising property rights in this way and to seek compensation for the damage inflicted.

There are numerous examples of limitations on private-property rights. Most American cities have zoning laws that restrict the uses to which land can be put. The owner of land in a part of town zoned for residential use only cannot build a factory. Automobile manufacturers are subject to limitations on their property rights. They cannot use their plant and equipment to produce any type of car they (or the public) may want; instead, they must satisfy federal safety regulations, mileage standards, and pollution-emission standards.

There are limitations on the use of labor. In the United States, workers are prohibited from selling their labor at less than the minimum wage. A person cannot sell work as a plumber, electrician, pharmacist, barber, dentist, or attorney without first obtaining a license from the state. ■

---

owners of property may not be allowed to use their property in such a manner as to inflict damage on others or on themselves. For example, the owner of farmland should not be allowed to use dangerous pesticides that may poison the community's water supply; the owner of an oil tanker should not be allowed to dump excess fuel oil near beaches.

Unless such restrictions apply, an owner of private property has the right to use the property to the owner's best advantage and to sell the property at the best price possible. The actions of the owners of private property will be guided by relative prices. The private owner of an oil refinery will use the relative prices of gasoline, fuel oils, and kerosene to determine how much of each petroleum product to refine and will look at the relative prices of imported and domestic crude oil to determine whether to use domestic or imported crude.

The private owner of labor (that is, the individual worker) will look at the relative wage rates in different occupations to determine where to seek employment. The private owner of farmland will look at the relative prices of agricultural products to determine what mix of crops to plant.

Private owners of property are motivated to obtain the best deal possible for themselves; they are motivated by self-interest. Legal protection of private-property rights insures that owners will reap the benefits of decisions that benefit their self-interest and will suffer the consequences of decisions that don't benefit their self-interest. (See Example 2.)

THE PRICE SYSTEM AS A COORDINATING MECHANISM

An economy consists of millions of consumers and hundreds of thousands of enterprises, and virtually every member of society owns some labor, land, or capital resources. Each participant makes economic decisions to promote his or her self-interest. What coordinates the decisions of all these people and businesses? What prevents the economy from collapsing when all these decisions clash? If all participants are looking out for themselves, will not the end result be chaos? Is it not necessary to have someone or something in charge?

The Invisible Hand

Adam Smith describes how the price system solves economic problems efficiently without conscious direction:

> Every individual endeavors to employ his capital so that its produce may be of greatest value. He generally neither intends to promote the public interest, nor knows how much he is promoting it. He intends only his own security, only his own gain. And he is led by an *invisible hand* to promote an end which was no part of his intention. By pursuing his own interest he frequently promotes that of society more

Example 3   Specialization, Productivity Improvements, and the Pin Factory

Adam Smith, in his classic *Wealth of Nations,* used the pin factory as his example of the benefits of specialization and economies of scale. In Adam Smith's day (the late 18th century), pins were manufactured through a large number of separate operations. Then and now, pin making consists of seven basic operations: 1) drawing wire, 2) straightening, 3) pointing, 4) twisting, 5) cutting heads and heading the wire, 6) tinning and whitening, and 7) papering and packaging. According to Adam Smith's calculations, each worker could be considered as producing almost 5,000 pins a day (the number of pins produced per day divided by the number of workers in the pin factory). If each person worked alone, only a few pins would be produced per worker. In the late 18th century, the major advantages of specialization were achieved by separating pin production into many separate operations: One set of workers would do the straightening, another the pointing, another group the twisting, another group the cutting of heads, and so on.

Since the days of Adam Smith, there have been substantial changes in pin making. According to the 1832 study of English statistician Charles Babbage, by the 1830s, daily pin production per employee had risen to about 8,000 pins. By 1980, an astonishing 80,000 pins per day per employee were being produced in English pin factories! The change in worker productivity in pin factories since 1776 illustrates the importance of technolog-

ical change in expanding productivity. Basically, productivity has risen so much because of improvements in the speed of pin-making machines. In modern pin production, pin-making machines have integrated steps 2 through 5, replacing the many separate operations cited by Adam Smith. In 1830, pin-making machines turned out 45 pins per minute. In 1980, pin-making machines made in West Germany turned out 500 pins per minute. The number of machines controlled by each machine operator has risen. In an English factory, one operator runs as many as 24 pin-making machines. Because of automation, only 50 people were employed in pin making in Great Britain by 1980! The improvement in pin-making technology has been concentrated in the improvement in pin-making machinery. In 1832, 65 percent of the time required to make a pin was devoted to steps 2 through 5 (straightening through heading). In 1980, 18 percent of pin-making time was taken up by these operations. In 1832, 28 percent of pin-making time went for papering and packaging. In 1980, 73 percent of the time went for these activities. Labor productivity in packaging has been held back by the wide diversity of packaging required, which makes the packaging process difficult to automate. ∎

Source: Clifford Pratten, "The Manufacture of Pins," *Journal of Economic Literature,* March 1980, pp. 93–96.

---

effectively than when he really intends to promote it.[2]

The invisible hand works through the **price system.** A modern economy produces millions of commodities and services, each of which has a money price. These millions of money prices form millions of relative prices that inform buyers and sellers what goods are cheap and what goods are expensive.

> The **price system** coordinates economic decisions by allowing people with property rights to resources to trade freely, buying and selling at whatever relative prices emerge in the marketplace.

The principal function of the price system is to provide information in an efficient fashion to participants in the economy. Each participant will specialize in price information that is personally relevant. The worker will specialize in prices of those things that affect his or her well-being: wage rates in different occupations, relative prices of various consumer goods, interest rates on home mortgages. The steel-mill manager will specialize in relative prices of inputs used in the mill and in the prices of finished steel products. The money manager will specialize in the relative prices of stocks, bonds, and real estate.

No *single person need know all prices to function in daily economic life.* People and enterprises need to know only the prices of those things that are significant to them. (See Example 3.)

---

2. Adam Smith, *The Wealth of Nations,* ed. Edwin Cannon (New York: Modern Library, 1937), p. 423.

Equilibrium

Each participant makes buying and selling decisions on the basis of relative prices. The family decides how to spend its income; the worker decides where and how much to work; the factory manager decides what inputs to use and what outputs to produce. Insofar as all these decisions on what to buy and sell are being made individually in isolation, what is to guarantee that there will be enough steel, bananas, foreign cars, domestic help, steel workers, copper, lumber for homes? What is to ensure that there will not be too much of one good and too little of another? Is Adam Smith's invisible hand powerful enough to prevent shortage and surplus?

Consider what would happen if U.S. automobile producers, acting on the price information in which they specialize, produce more cars than buyers want to buy *at the price asked by the automobile producers*. The automobile manufacturers will be made aware of this fact, not by a directive from the government, but by the simple fact that excess inventories of unsold cars will pile up. Dealers must pay their bills and cannot live from unsold inventories; therefore, they must sell the cars at lower prices. As the money price of cars falls, its relative price tends to fall, and customers begin to substitute automobiles for European vacations, home computers, or a remodeled kitchen. The decline in the relative price of automobiles signals automobile manufacturers to produce fewer cars. Eventually, a balance between the number of cars people are prepared to buy (the demand) and the number offered for sale (the supply) will be struck, and the corresponding price is called an **equilibrium price.**

> The **equilibrium price** of a good or service is that price at which the amount of the good people are prepared to buy equals the amount offered for sale.

The economy's search for equilibria through changing relative prices is not limited to a single market. The search takes place in all competitive markets simultaneously. If too much is produced, the relative price will fall; if too little is produced, the relative price will rise. As relative prices change, so do buying and selling decisions, and these changes bring markets into equilibrium. The economy is in *general equilibrium* when all markets have achieved equilibrium prices. The mechanics of equilibrium of supply and demand are discussed in Chapter 4.

Checks and Balances

The functioning of the price system is analogous to the system of checks and balances at work in an *ecological system* (the pattern of relationships between plants, animals, and their environment). These checks and balances prevent one species of plant or animal from overrunning the entire area and, in the end, extinguishing itself. Relative prices provide the checks and balances in the economic system. If one product is in oversupply, its relative price will fall; more will be purchased and less will be offered for sale. If one product is in short supply, its relative price will rise; less will be purchased and more offered for sale.

Just as human beings can upset nature's delicate balance, the general equilibrium of prices can be upset by interference. For example, governments can regulate and freeze prices or producer organizations may manipulate prices. When are such interventions warranted? When do they do more harm than good? Examples will be studied later in this text. (See Example 4.)

How, What, and For Whom

The price system solves the *what, how,* and *for whom* problems without conscious direction. No single participant in the economy needs to see the big picture; each participant need only know the relative prices of the goods and services of immediate interest to that person. No single person or governmental organization is required to be concerned about the economy as a whole. The millions of individual economic decisions made daily are coordinated by the price system.

Consider an economy in which all property is privately owned; property rights are vested with the owners of the property; there are no imports or exports; there is no intervention in the setting of prices. Each individual owns certain quantities of resources—land, labor, capital—that are sold or rented to business firms that produce the goods and services people want. Private-property rights are exercised; everything is sold at a price agreeable to the buyer and seller.

What is produced in the economy is deter-

Example 4   Checks and Balances: The Whale-Oil Crisis and the Black Death

The checks and balances provided by the price system enabled the world economy to adapt to the oil crisis of the 1970s. As the relative price of crude oil skyrocketed in the mid and late 1970's, people and firms substituted relatively less expensive products for petroleum products; they drove less; they purchased fuel-efficient cars. In the 1980s, there is little talk of running out of oil; instead, there is fear of the adverse effects of an oil glut as oil producers scramble for customers. The oil crisis of the 1970s is not the only historical example of how the price system deals with the problem of growing scarcity. Another example is the great whale-oil crisis of the mid-19th century. Prior to the Civil War, whale oil was the prime lubricant and source of lighting fuel, but the relative price of whale oil rose as whales approached extinction. The rise in the relative price of oil encouraged the search for substitutes, and in 1859 underground oil was discovered in Titusville, Pennsylvania. The advent of commercial, under-ground-oil drilling lowered the relative price of oil below what was the relative price of whale oil some 20 years earlier.

The most dramatic example of how the price system deals with rising scarcity is the Black Death plague of the 14th century. Between 1348 and 1350, the Black Death killed from 35 percent to 65 percent of Europe's population. As population and work force declined, the relative price of labor (relative to draft animals and land) rose, and ways had to be found to conserve labor. Water power was frequently used to replace human power, and fields were converted from crop cultivation, which required large amounts of labor inputs, to sheep grazing which required few labor inputs. ∎

Source: Charles Maurice and Charles W. Smithson, *The Doomsday Myth: 10,000 Years of Economic Crises* (Stanford, Calif.: Hoover Institution Press, 1984).

---

mined by *dollar votes* cast by consumers for different goods and services and by the dollar costs of producing these goods and services. When consumers choose to buy a particular good or service, they are casting a dollar vote, which communicates their demand for that good or service. For example, assume two goods cost an equal amount to produce. If many dollar votes are cast for one good, this means that buyers are willing to pay a high relative price for the good. Producers will exercise their property rights to produce the good with a high relative price. If few dollar votes are cast for the other commodity, producers will have little incentive to produce that commodity. If consumers shift their dollar votes, producers will shift their production as well. Relative prices signal what actions to take. Relative prices signal to buyers what, where, and when to substitute and signal to producers what to produce.

The *what* problem is solved through the exercise of *consumer sovereignty* in a capitalist system. Consumers, in casting their dollar votes, determine what will be produced. If no dollar votes are cast for a particular product, it will not be produced. If enough dollar votes are cast for a product relative to its cost of production, it will be produced.

How goods are produced is determined by business firms who seek to utilize their land, labor, and capital resources as economically as possible. Business firms produce those outputs that receive high dollar votes by combining resources in the least costly way. Business firms follow the principle of substitution. If the relative price of land is increased, farmers will use less land and more tractors and labor to work the land more intensively. If the relative price of farm labor increases, farmers will use less labor and more tractors and land. If the relative price of business travel rises, businesses will travel less and use more long-distance telephoning. If the relative price of long-distance calls increases, businesses will telephone less and use more business travel. If business firms fail to reduce their costs through the use of the best available techniques and the best combination of the factors of production, the competition of other firms may drive them out of business.

Example 5   Pencils and New York City: The Price System at Work

This chapter has surveyed how the price system solves the *what, how,* and *for whom* problems in a capitalistic economy. Each of the following examples illustrates the principle that through voluntary exchange, the price system can coordinate the activities of many millions of people without centralized direction.

There are 12 million people living in the environs of New York City, each of whom is concerned with an infinitesimally small part of getting that city's work done. Each person is concerned—for the most part—with making a living. Imagine the numbers of trucks, airplanes, and trains moving people and goods to the right places at the right times. The logistics of these movements that keep the city going and prevent everyone from starving are enormously complicated (think of New York's well-publicized garbage-removal problems). Yet no single person or bureaucracy is in charge of the department-for-making-sure-the-city-does-not-starve. The city works by the millions of decentralized decisions of individuals responding to their own cost/benefit calculations. The price system and supply/demand coordination works so well that no one loses any sleep over the terrifying prospect of complete breakdown—no one even

gives it a thought. This classic example shows us how something that works smoothly often goes unnoticed. Adam Smith's term, the *invisible hand,* is an apt description.

Economist Milton Friedman relates the story called, "I, Pencil: My Family Tree as Told to Leonard E. Read," in which the pencil makes the startling announcement: *"not a single person . . . knows how to make me."* If one thinks about what it takes to make a pencil—the trees that produce the wood, the saws that fell the trees, the steel that makes the saws, the engines that run the saws, the hemp that makes the ropes that are necessary to tie down the logs, the training of loggers, the mining of graphite in Sri Lanka for the lead, the mining of zinc and copper for making the bit of metal holding the eraser, and the rape seed oil from the Dutch East Indies that is used in the eraser—it is clear that the pencil is correct. No one single person knows how to make a modern pencil. The decisions of the thousands upon thousands of people involved are coordinated through the price system; that all these activities have made it possible for you to go to the bookstore and buy a pencil for, say, a mere $0.25 boggles the mind. ■

For whom is determined by the dollar values the market assigns to resources owned by each separate household in the economy. The distribution of income between rich and poor reflects the prices paid for each resource and the distribution of ownership claims to scarce labor, land, and capital. People who own large quantities of land or capital will have a correspondingly large claim on the goods and services produced by the economy; those who are fortunate enough to provide high-priced labor services (doctors, lawyers, gifted athletes) will similarly receive a large share of the total output. At the other extreme, the poor are those who own few resources and furnish low-priced labor services to the market. (See Example 5.)

SPECIALIZATION

In a market economy, the price system accomplishes more than the simple balancing of the sup-

plies and demands for goods that enter the circular flow. It also automatically encourages the factors of production to specialize in those activities that they do better than others. Specialization raises efficiency and allows economies to produce ever larger output from their available inputs.

Productivity and Exchange

Suppose a sailor were stranded on a desert island with no other human beings around—a modern Robinson Crusoe. While the sailor would constantly have to make decisions about whether to make fish nets or fish hooks or whether to sleep or break coconuts, the economy of the desert island would lack many features of a modern economic system. The sailor would not be *specialized;* he would have to be a jack-of-all-trades. His consumption would have to be perfectly tailored to his production. Moreover, the sailor would not use *money.* He would still have to solve the problems of *what* and *how.* The *for whom* problem would be easy. Everything he produced would be for himself. He would have to solve *what* and *how* without explicit relative prices, property rights, or markets.

In the modern economy, it is somewhat unsettling to think about the degree to which people are specialized. The consumption of a typical household consists of thousands of articles; yet the principal breadwinner of the household may do nothing but align suspension components on an automobile production line. In short, everyone in our economy (except hermits) is dependent on the efforts of others. We produce one or two things; we consume many things.

Specialization obviously gives rise to exchange. Indeed, the exchange of one thing for another thing is the reverse side of the coin of specialization. If people consumed only those things that they produced, there would be no trade with anybody else and there would be no need for money. Money, trade, exchange, and specialization are all characteristics of a complicated economy.

Specialization means that people will produce more of particular goods than they consume and that these surpluses will be exchanged for the goods that they want.

Specialization raises productivity. Increased productivity was defined in Chapter 2 as the production of more output from the same amount of productive resources. We noted that Adam Smith began the *Wealth of Nations* with the observation that specialization is a basic source of productivity advances. Specialization raises the productivity of the economy and raises incomes in two ways. First, specialization allows resources, which have different characteristics, to be allocated to their best usage. Second, by concentrating certain resources in specific tasks, economies can produce outputs in large-scale production runs. In many industries, output can be produced more cheaply per unit if manufactured on a large scale.

Specialization allows people to work in jobs at which they are better suited than others. The individual with a good sense for numbers can work as an accountant, while the individual with an outgoing personality can work as a sales representative. On the loading dock, the muscular worker can do the heavy lifting, while the dextrous worker will drive the forklift. A specially designed precision machine tool will perform a specific task more quickly and accurately than an all-purpose machine tool. On a mass-production assembly line, workers can specialize in different tasks. Through repetition, each worker can perform his or her specialized task more quickly and accurately.

The Law of Comparative Advantage

Specialization makes possible higher productivity and higher incomes. The main reason for specialization is that people, land, and capital all come in different varieties. Some people are agile seven-footers; others are small and slow. Some are fast-talkers; others scarcely utter a word. Some people take easily to math and computers; others are frightened by numbers and technology. Some people have quick hands; others are clumsy. Some land is moist; other land is dry. Some land is hilly; other land is flat. Some land is covered with forests; other land is populated only with mesquite bushes. Capital is different too. Some machines can move large quantities of earth; others can lift heavy loads; others can perform precision metal work; others can heat metals to high temperatures.

Because the factors of production have different characteristics and qualities, specialization offers opportunities for productivity advances. Economists refer to the best employment of a resource as its *comparative advantage*. The agile seven-footer has a comparative advantage in basketball; the fast-talker can become a sales representative; the math whiz can become a computer specialist; the dextrous person might have a comparative advantage in operating a complicated machine tool. Land with high moisture content is best used in corn production; land with a relatively low moisture content is best used in wheat production. Earth-moving machinery can be used in road building: heavy-lifting equipment can be used in construction; precision tools can be used in aircraft manufacturing. Each resource has some comparative advantage.

The Kansas farmer will make more profits by

Example 6   The Comparative Advantage of Lawn Mowing Versus Typing

A simple numerical example of comparative advantage will illustrate the principle in a more concrete fashion. Imagine two people, Jack and Jill, both of whom can mow lawns and type. We assume that Jack and Jill do not really care whether they type or mow lawns. As the accompanying table shows, Jack can type 20 pages a day or mow 2 lawns a day. Jill, on the other hand, can type 50 pages a day or mow 8 lawns a day. Jill is clearly more efficient in absolute terms at both tasks than Jack; she can type 250 percent (50 ÷ 20) as fast and can mow lawns 400 percent (8 ÷ 2) as fast as Jack.

	Lawns per Day (1)	Pages per Day (2)	Opportunity Cost of Lawn Mowing (in pages) (3) = (2) ÷ (1)
Jack	2	20	10 pages
Jill	8	50	6.25 pages

Now what should Jack and Jill do? To answer this question, we must first determine the (relative) prices of mowing lawns and typing. Suppose typing earns $2 a page and mowing lawns pays $16 per lawn. If Jack mows lawns all day, his income would be $32 (= $16 × 2 lawns) per day; typing would earn Jack $40 (= $2 × 20 pages) per day. Thus, Jack would wish to type. Jill, on the other hand, could earn $128 mowing lawns (= $16 × 8 lawns) or $100 typing ($2 × 50 pages). Thus, Jill would prefer to mow lawns.

Jill has a comparative advantage in mowing lawns; Jack has a comparative advantage in typing. While Jill is better than Jack in all activities, her *greatest* advantage over Jack is in mowing lawns (she is 4 times as fast). In typing, Jill is only 2.5 times as fast. Jack's *least* disadvantage is in typing; thus, Jack prefers to be a typist.

Notice that Jill will earn $128 daily mowing lawns and Jack will earn $40 a day typing. Jill's superior productivity is reflected in higher earnings. Notice that Jack in effect competes with Jill in typing by charging a lower price per unit of his time. If there are 8 hours to the work day, Jill is earning a wage of $16 per hour ($16 = $128 ÷ 8 hours) and Jack is earning only $5 an hour ($5 = $40 ÷ 8 hours). Thus, Jill's hourly wage is slightly more than 3 times Jack's hourly wage. Jack's lower rate allows him to compete with Jill in typing: she is 2.5 times as efficient as a typist, but her wage is more than 3 times as high—which in the marketplace offsets her absolute advantage in typing.

To mow one lawn, Jack must sacrifice 10 pages of typing. Jack's opportunity cost of lawns equals 10 pages of typing. To mow one lawn, Jill must sacrifice 6.25 pages (50 ÷ 8). Jill mows lawns because her opportunity cost of lawn mowing is lower than Jack's. ■

growing wheat; the Iowa farmer will make more profits growing corn. The agile seven-footer will earn a larger income playing professional basketball than professional soccer. The extroverted fast-talker will earn more income as a sales representative than as a computer programmer. The person with quick hands will make more income as a surgeon than as a lawyer. The owner of the earth-moving equipment will make more income using it in roadbuilding; the owner of the heavy-lifting equipment will earn more by using it in construction. If all owners of labor, land, and capital resources use their resources in such a way as to make the most income possible, specialization will follow naturally.

Is this an oversimplification? What about the people who have both quick minds and quick hands, the math whiz with good verbal skills, the equipment that can move large amounts of earth and lift heavy weights, or the farm land that appears suited to growing both wheat and corn? Are not some people poor at just about everything in the sense that at every task they are less efficient than other people?

The price system ensures that the factors of production will be used to exploit their special characteristics and skills.

In 1817, the English economist, David Ricardo, formulated the **law of comparative advantage.**

The **law of comparative advantage** states that it is better for people to specialize in those activities in which their advantage over other people is greatest or in which their disadvantages compared to others are the smallest.

The easiest way to see this principle at work is to examine two extreme cases. Suppose that you can do any and every job better than anyone else. What would you as such a superior person do? You would not want to be a jack-of-all-trades because it is likely that your *margin* of superiority will be greater in one occupation than in another. The job in which your margin of superiority over others is *the greatest* is the job you will do because it will give you the highest income.

Now examine the other extreme. Suppose there is no person in the community to whom you are superior *in any job;* you are less productive than any other person in the society in every occupation. What would you do in such an unfortunate situation? The job in which your disadvantage compared to others is the smallest would be the job that maximizes your income.

A mediocre computer programmer could possibly be the best clerk in the local supermarket. The clerks in the local supermarket may not be able to stock shelves and work a cash register as well as the computer programmer, but they have a *comparative advantage* in that occupation. An attorney may be the fastest typist in town, yet the attorney is better off preparing deeds than typing deeds. An engineering major may have verbal skills that exceed those of an English major, but his or her comparative advantage is in engineering.

The law of comparative advantage is nothing more than the principle that people should engage in those activities where their opportunity costs are lower than others. The price system encourages the factors of production to work according to their comparative advantage.

Example 6 shows the relationship between the law of comparative advantage and opportunity costs. It shows that people specialize in those tasks in which their opportunity costs are lower.

In the time it takes Jill to mow one lawn, she must pass up the opportunity to type about 6 pages. In the time it takes Jack to mow one lawn, he could have typed 10 pages. Jill has a lower opportunity cost in lawn mowing than Jack. (See also Example 7.)

Economies of Large-Scale Production

If all people were the same, if all land were identical, and if all capital were the same, would there still be specialization? Even if all people in an automobile-manufacturing plant were identical, it would still be better to have one person install the engine, another bolt down the engine, and so on in an assembly line. Individuals who focus on one task can learn their jobs better and don't waste time switching from job to job. The per-unit costs of production are frequently higher at small volumes of output than at large volumes. Modern mass-production techniques require numerous specialized tasks to be carried out by the factors of production. Even if all agricultural land were identical, it would still be better to plant one farm with corn, another with wheat, and so on, than to plant smaller strips of corn and wheat on single farms because of the economies of large-scale production.

Specialization raises productivity not only through the lowering of opportunity costs through comparative advantage but also by allowing economies of large-scale production.

Money

Money is necessary because people are specialized and do not produce everything they need without any surpluses. Money is useful in an *exchange economy*—that is, an economy where people are specialized—because it reduces the cost of transacting with others. *Barter* is a system of exchange where products are exchanged for other products rather than for money. In barter, for example, it would be necessary for barefoot bakers to meet or exchange with hungry shoemakers. In other words, a successful barter deal requires that the two traders have matching wants. In barter, successful trades require a double coincidence of wants.

Example 7   Applications of the Law of Comparative Advantage

The law of comparative advantage explains patterns of specialization both within a country and among countries. It also explains why goods will not always be produced by the "best" producer. The fastest typist may be a lawyer; the best checkout clerk may be a skilled computer programmer.

The law of comparative advantage explains a wide variety of specialization patterns that would otherwise be difficult to explain. Here are three examples.

1. *GRE Exams:* The GRE (Graduate Record Exam) is an examination for students who wish to enter graduate school. It consists of two parts: a verbal exam to test verbal ability and a quantitative exam to test math ability. During the 1975–1980 period, physics majors recorded the higher scores on the verbal exam—higher than speech majors. Why would the student who appears to be better qualified for graduate study in speech choose a career in physics?

The law of comparative advantage explains this puzzling phenomenon: Although physics majors on average have an *absolute advantage* in both physics and English (they score higher on both the verbal and quantitative GREs), they have a strong *comparative advantage* in physics. On the GRE, they score 19 percent higher than speech majors on the verbal exam, but they score 55 percent higher than speech majors on the quantitative exam. The physics major is like Jill in Example 6; both the physics major and Jill are correct in their choice of specialization.

2. *Tobacco Growing in New England:* New England is a region poorly suited to agriculture. It is hilly, rocky, heavily wooded, and cold in the winter. New England seems an unlikely place for tobacco production, which requires a warm climate and rich, well-drained soil. Yet one of the agicultural crops of Massachusetts and Connecticut is tobacco. Why is tobacco grown in New England? Is the law of comparative advantage being violated?

Even California land would be better suited to tobacco production; an acre of land in California would yield much more tobacco than in New England. But New England produces tobacco, while California does not. The law of comparative advantage provides the explanation. Although California has an absolute advantage in tobacco production over New England, it has a much larger absolute advantage in alternative uses of the land (growing commercial vegetables and fruits). The alternative uses of rural New England land are limited (it is difficult to grow other crops; the land is not suited to commercial development); therefore, New England has a comparative advantage in tobacco. Stated in terms of opportunity costs: tobacco is grown in rural New England because the opportunity cost is relatively low.

3. *The Manufacture of Singer Sewing Machines in Asia:* The Singer Company, a U.S. company established by Isaac Singer in 1851, now manufactures many of its sewing machines in Asia—even though American Singer employees can produce more sewing machines per hour than their Asian counterparts. Why then did Singer shift sewing machine manufacturing to Asia? The answer is that the American worker has a much larger productivity advantage in high-technology manufacturing, such as mainframe computers and jet aircraft. The American Singer worker may be 10 percent more productive than an Asian counterpart, while the American IBM employee may be, say, 50 percent more productive than the Singer-employee. Because Asia, on the other hand, lacks the capital resources and know-how to produce mainframe computers, the productivity of an Asian worker in computer manufacturing would be less than in sewing-machine manufacturing. As in Example 6, the American worker's superior productivity would be reflected in higher earnings, and the Asian worker would compete by working at lower wages, reflecting lower productivity. The opportunity cost of an American worker producing sewing machines is high; the opportunity cost of an Asian worker producing sewing machines is low. ∎

Money is useful precisely because double coincidences of wants are rare. Money enables any person to trade with anyone else in a complicated economy. The form money takes differs from society to society. Money in a simple society will be quite different from money in a complicated society. In simple societies, things like fish hooks, sharks' teeth, beads, or cows have been used as money. In modern societies, money is issued and regulated by government, and money may (gold coins) or may not (paper money) have an intrinsic value of its own.

Money is anything that is widely accepted in exchange for goods and services.

HOW THE PRICE SYSTEM PROVIDES FOR THE FUTURE

We have shown how the price system provides checks and balances and how it promotes efficiency through specialization and exchange. The price system also provides for the future through the workings of interest rates.

Roundabout Production

Let us return to the shipwrecked sailor. Although he would not specialize, he would at least share a common problem with modern economies: how to provide for the future. In the sailor's case, he would be confronted with a clear choice of eating more today versus eating more tomorrow. If the water were clear, he could wade out and, with patient effort, catch fish with his bare hands. He may be successful in catching enough fish to survive. However, if the sailor were to devote a few days to making a fishing net from vines, he would be able to increase his catch and reduce his effort—but at the sacrifice of having less to eat for three days. Making a net to catch the fish is an example of **roundabout production** or the production of **intermediate goods.**

Roundabout production is the production of goods that do not immediately meet consumption needs.

Goods that are used to produce other goods are called **intermediate goods.**

There can be many stages of roundabout production. The good can be used directly to produce consumer goods. It can produce a good that produces another good that assists in the production of consumer goods, and so on.

When roundabout production is carried out, producers are dependent on things produced in the past for the things that are produced today. In modern economies, the degree of roundabout pro-

duction is striking. The wheat harvested today requires a harvesting machine produced in the past; the bread produced today is baked in ovens that were produced in the past; the shirt produced today is manufactured on a sewing machine produced in the past.

The responsibility for producing the capital goods that enable society to produce more in the future is left to the price system. Households set aside some of their income in the form of savings. Households save so that they can consume more tomorrow. They accumulate funds in savings accounts and retirement programs; they buy stocks, bonds, and life-insurance policies. How do their savings find their way into productive investments? Businesses borrow from financial institutions, sell bonds, and issue stock; they use the proceeds to build plants, to buy capital equipment, and to build up their inventories.

Interest Rates

Societies must refrain from consumption today to build capital goods. The stock of capital goods is one generation's legacy to the next. Long-lived capital goods can be used to produce goods in the future. The modern interstate highway system is being enjoyed not only by the generation that built it, but by future generations. The ultimate benefits of the investment in space exploration will not be enjoyed by this generation but by future generations. Households must sacrifice consumption today to save, but by saving the household will increase its consumption in the future. The sacrifice of current consumption is the cost of saving. The benefit of saving is that **interest** will be earned on savings. Thus, future consumption will increase by more than the sacrifice of current consumption. The higher the interest rate, the greater the inducement to save. The rate of interest acts not only as an inducement to save; it also signals to businesses whether they should borrow for investment.

Interest is the price of credit, usually a percentage of the amount borrowed.

Like any other price, the interest rate provides a *balance*—in this case balancing the amount people are willing to save with the amount of saving businesses want to borrow for investment. If the interest rate is low, businesses will clamor for the saving of individuals because they find it cheap to add to their capital stock. However, when the interest rate is low, few people will be willing to save. The reverse is true at high interest rates: few businesses will want to invest, but households will be quite willing to save.

> The interest rate balances the amount of saving offered by households with the amount of investment businesses wish to undertake. The price system, operating through the interest rate, solves the *what problem* of how to allocate resources between present and future consumption.

How interest rates are determined is much more complicated than this simplified story. Interest-rate determination will be examined in later chapters.

LIMITS OF THE INVISIBLE HAND

This chapter has emphasized the virtues of resource allocation through the price system. The price system solves the problems of *what, how,* and *for whom* without centralized direction. It balances the actions of millions of consumers and thousands of producers, and it even solves the difficult problem of providing for the future. The price system has great strength, but it has weaknesses as well. These weaknesses must be examined to determine the costs and benefits of interfering with the workings of the price system.

Income Distribution

There is no guarantee that resource allocation through the price system will solve the *for whom* problem in such a way as to satisfy the ethical beliefs of members of society. Some people believe that income should be distributed fairly evenly; others believe that the gap between rich and poor should be large. Many believe that it is unfair for people to be rich just because they were lucky enough to inherit wealth or intelligence.

Economics can shed little light on what is a "good" or "fair" solution to the *for whom* prob-

lem, because such decisions require personal value judgments. Economics is broad enough to accommodate virtually all views on the subject of income distribution. Judgments about income distribution are in the realm of normative economics.

Nevertheless, positive economics can make a contribution to the question of income distribution. Economists can indicate what may happen to efficiency or economic growth if the income distribution is changed, but they cannot make any scientific statements about the desirability of the change in the income distribution.

The Role of Government

Another weakness of the price system is that it cannot supply certain goods—called *public goods*—that are necessary to society. Public goods include defense, the legal system, highways, and public education. In the case of private goods, there is an intimate link between costs and benefits: The one who buys a car enjoys the benefits of the car; the one who buys a loaf of bread eats that loaf. Public goods, on the other hand, are financed not by the dollar votes of consumers but by the imposition of taxes. In most cases, the benefits each individual derives from public goods will not be known. Moreover, it is difficult to prevent nonpayers from enjoying the benefits of public goods. Even if someone does not pay taxes, the national defense establishment protects that person from enemy attack just as well as it protects the payers.

The price system, therefore, breaks down in failing to provide public goods. If private individuals were left with the choice of buying and selling public goods, few public goods would be produced. Yet society must have public goods to survive.

Monopoly

The invisible hand may not function well when a single person or single group gains control over the supply of a particular commodity. What makes Adam Smith's invisible hand work so well is that individual buyers and sellers compete with one another; no single buyer or seller has control over the price. The problem with *monopoly*—a single seller with considerable control over the price—is that the monopolist can hold back the amount of goods, drive up the price, and enjoy large profits. While the monopolist would benefit from such actions, the buyer would not. Monopoly threatens the smooth functioning of the invisible hand described in this chapter.

Macroeconomic Instability

The invisible hand may solve the economic problem of scarcity but may provide a level of overall economic activity that is unstable. It is a historical fact that capitalist economies have been subject to fluctuations in output, employment, and prices—called *business cycles*—and that these fluctuations have been costly to capitalist societies.

The study of the causes of the instability of capitalism was pioneered by John Maynard Keynes during the Great Depression of the 1930s, and this theme remains a principal concern of macroeconomics.

This chapter has described in general terms how scarce resources are allocated by the price system and has explained the organization of property rights. Equilibrium prices are an invisible hand that coordinates the decisions of many different persons. The next chapter examines the detailed workings of supply and demand in an individual market and answers the questions: How is the equilibrium price set? What causes equilibrium prices to increase or decrease?

Summary

1. The circular-flow diagram summarizes the flows of goods and services from producers to households and the flows of factors of production from households to producers.
2. Relative prices guide the economic decisions of individuals and businesses. They signal to buyers and sellers what substitutions to make.
3. The principle of substitution states that no single good is irreplaceable. Users substitute one good for another in response to changes in relative prices.
4. Property can be owned by private persons, by the state, or by combinations of the two. In capitalist societies, property is owned primarily by private individuals, who are permitted to exercise property rights over the use and sale of their property subject to the restriction that such exercise does not injure other people. Socialist societies are characterized by collective ownership of property.
5. The private decisions of the millions of consumers and producers are coordinated by the price system. The "invisible hand" analogy, originated by Adam Smith in 1776, describes how a capitalist system can allow individuals to pursue their self-interest and yet provide an orderly, efficient economic system that functions without centralized direction. The price system balances supplies and demands for individual products. If too much of a product is produced, its relative price will fall. If too little of a product is produced, its relative price will rise. The balance of supply and demand is called an equilibrium. The *what* problem is solved by dollar votes. Consumers determine what will be produced. The *how* problem is solved by individual producers. Competition among producers will encourage them to combine resource inputs efficiently. The solution of the *for whom* problem is determined by a) who owns productive resources and b) what the relative prices of resources are.
6. Specialization is responsible for productivity improvements. Specialization occurs because of the differences among people, land, and capital and because of the economies of large-scale production. The law of comparative advantage states that the factors of production will specialize in those activities in which their advantage is greatest or in which their disadvantages are smallest. Money enables a person to trade with anyone else in a complicated economy. The most basic characteristic of money is that it is widely accepted in exchange.
7. The price system provides for the future by allowing people to compare costs now with benefits that will accrue in the future. The interest rate balances the amount of savings offered with the amount of investment businesses wish to undertake.
8. The invisible hand can not solve the problems of income distribution, public goods, monopoly, or macroeconomic instability.

Key Terms

circular-flow diagram
relative price
money price
principle of substitution
property rights
socialist society
capitalist society
price system
equilibrium price
law of comparative advantage
money
roundabout production
intermediate goods
interest

Questions and Problems

1. Suppose 1 dollar will purchase approximately 9 French francs, 3 German marks, and 1.2 English pounds. From this information, can you determine which currency is cheap and which currency is expensive?

2. "The principle of substitution states that virtually all goods have substitutes, but we all know that there are no substitutes for telephone service." Comment on this statement.

3. If you own an automobile, what property rights do you have? What restrictions are placed upon these property rights?

4. Explain why you can usually find the items you want at a grocery store without having ordered the goods in advance.

5. From the data in Table A, calculate the relative price of coffee. Explain your answer. (As an exercise in graphing, you may want to plot the various prices).

Table A

	Price of Coffee (dollars per pound)	Price of Electricity (dollars per million BTUs)	Price of Tea (dollars per pound)
1970	.535	5.83	.390
1975	.683	9.23	.582
1980	1.70	14.09	.858
1982	1.40	18.04	.764

6. This chapter noted that not every product has a good substitute. Which of the following pairs of products are good substitutes? Which are poor substitutes? Explain the general principles you used in coming up with your answers.
  a. Coffee and tea.
  b. Compact Chevrolets and compact Fords.
  c. Cars and city buses.
  d. Electricity and natural gas.
  e. Telephones and express mail.

7. The rate of inflation in country X in year Y is 5 percent. Is this a high or a low rate of inflation?

8. You own a 3-carat diamond ring which you no longer like. In fact, you would like to have a new color television set. How would you go about getting the television set in a barter economy? From this generalize about the efficiency of exchange in a barter economy versus a monetary economy.

9. "Specialization takes place only when people are different. If all people were identical, there would be no specialization." Evaluate this statement.

10. Assume that while shopping, you see long lines of people waiting to buy bread while fresh meat is spoiling in butcher shops. From these observations, what can you say about prevailing prices? What is your prediction about what will happen to the relative price of bread?

11. Bill can prepare 50 hamburgers per hour and wait on 25 tables per hour. Mike can prepare 20 hamburgers per hour and wait on 15 tables per hour. If Bill and Mike were to open a hamburger stand, who would be the cook? Who the waiter? Would Bill do both?

12. Why would private industry find it difficult to organize national defense? How would they charge each citizen for national defense?

13. In an hour's time, Jill can lay 100 tiles and can mortar 50 bricks. Tom can lay 10 tiles and 20 bricks in an hour's time. What is Jill's opportunity cost of mortaring bricks compared to Tom's opportunity cost of mortaring bricks? In which activity should each specialize according to the law of comparative advantage? Explain why it is that Jill should not do both activities and let Tom rest simply because Jill is better at both activities?

14. Which of the following transactions would enter the circular flow and which would not?
a. U.S. Steel sells steel to General Motors.
b. General Motors sells a car to Jones.
c. Jones takes a job from General Motors and receives $100 pay.
d. Jones has his suit cleaned at the local dry cleaner and pays $5.
e. Jones washes his dress shirt.

15. Explain how an increase in the interest rate alters society's provision for the future.

Suggested Readings

Hayek, Frederick A. "The Price System as a Mechanism for Using Knowledge." American Economic Review (September 1945), pp. 519–28. Reprinted in *Comparative Economic Systems: Models and Cases,* 5th ed., ed. Morris Bornstein. Homewood, Ill.: Richard D. Irwin, 1985, pp. 49–60.

McKenzie, Richard B. and Gordon Tullock. *Modern Political Economy.* New York: McGraw-Hill, 1978.

Neuberger, Egon. "Comparative Economic System." In *Perspectives in Economics: Economists Look at Their Field of Study,* eds. Alan A. Brown *et al.* New York: McGraw-Hill, 1971, pp. 252–66.

Radford, R. A. "The Economic Organization of a P.O.W. Camp." In *Economica* 12 (November 1945): 189–201.

Smith, Adam. *The Wealth of Nations.* ed. Edwin Cannan. New York: The Modern Library, 1937, book 1.

4

The Mechanics of Supply and Demand

Chapter Preview

Chapter 3 described how capitalist economies solve the *what, how,* and *for whom* problems by market allocation that is guided by the price system. Property is owned predominantly by private individuals who exercise private-property rights. Each participant in the economy is motivated by self-interest. The actions of millions of buyers and sellers are coordinated by an invisible hand. No single buyer or seller is required to know more than the prices of those things of immediate interest to that person. Relative prices signal to buyers and sellers what they should do. If relative prices of some goods are rising, other goods will be substituted by buyers; sellers will tend to offer more for sale. If too much of a good is produced, its relative price will fall. If too little is produced, its relative price will rise. Through these changes in relative prices, the amounts of goods buyers are prepared to buy are brought into balance with the amounts of goods sellers are prepared to sell.

Chapter 3 provided a grand overview of how the price system works without getting into actual mechanics. This chapter will explain the workings of supply and demand and will define such terms as *demand, supply, shortage, surplus,* and *equilibrium* more exactly.

This chapter describes *how prices are determined by supply and demand.* There is a famous quip that if you teach a parrot the phrase "supply and demand," you will create a learned economist. This clever joke does not do justice to the complexity and the value of supply-and-demand analysis. An economist needs to know more than the parrot, just as the medical doctor must know more than the prescription: "Take two aspirin and call me in the morning." ■

WHAT IS A MARKET?

To develop the mechanics of supply and demand, we must narrow our vision to the study of how a *single market* works. In each **market,** buyers and sellers are guided by price in their buying and selling decisions.

> A **market** is an established arrangement by which buyers and sellers come together to exchange particular goods or services.

Types of Markets

A retail store, a gas station, a farmers' market, real-estate firms, the New York Stock Exchange (where stocks are bought and sold), Chicago commodity markets (where livestock, grains, and metals are traded), auctions of works of art, gold markets in London, Frankfurt, and Zurich, labor exchanges, university placement offices, and hundreds of other specialized arrangements are all markets. A market is an arrangement for bringing together buyers and sellers of a particular good or service. The New York Stock Exchange brings together by means of modern telecommunications the buyers and sellers of corporate stock. Sothebys auction in London brings together the sellers and buyers of rare works of art. The Rotterdam oil market brings together buyers and sellers of crude oil not under long-term contracts. The university placement office brings university graduates together with potential employers. The gas station brings together the buyers and sellers of gasoline. In some markets, the buyers and sellers confront each other face-to-face (roadside farm markets). In other markets, the buyer never sees the seller (the Chicago commodity markets).

Determinants of Market Form

The actual form a particular market takes depends on the type of good or service being sold and on the costs of transporting the good from the point of production to the point of sale. Some markets are local (bringing together local buyers and sellers); others are national (bringing together the buyers and sellers in all parts of the nation); others are international (bringing together the buyers and sellers in all parts of the world). Real estate is traded in local markets; houses and buildings cannot be shipped from one place to another (except at great expense). College textbooks are usually exchanged in a national market. The New York Stock Exchange, the various gold exchanges, and the Chicago commodity exchanges are markets in which buyers and sellers from around the world participate.

The study of marketing arrangements is a subject area in which economics and business administration overlap. Both disciplines presume that markets develop in an orderly fashion and teach that the market form that eventually evolves will be the one that keeps the cost of delivery (or marketing cost) to a minimum.

Perfectly Competitive Markets

The real world consists of an almost infinite variety of markets. This chapter deals with a very special type of market called a **perfectly competitive market.**

> A **perfectly competitive market** has the following characteristics: 1) The product's price is uniform throughout the market. 2) Buyers and sellers have perfect information about price and the product's quality. 3) There are a large number of buyers and sellers. 4) No single buyer or seller is large enough to change the price.

The principal characteristic of a perfectly competitive market is that buyers and sellers face so much competition that no person or group has any control over the price.

The markets where most people buy and sell goods are not perfect. Buyers and sellers may not be perfectly informed about prices and qualities. Two homemakers pay different prices in adjacent grocery stores for the same national brand of cookies. Houses that are virtually identical sell at different prices. Chemically equivalent brand-name and generic drugs sell at different prices. Italy and West Germany pay different prices for the same grade of imported crude oil. Two secretaries with the same qualifications, responsibilities, and disposition in the same company earn different wages. AT&T, General Motors, and Saudi Arabia exercise some control over the prices they charge. Large buyers exercise some control over the prices they pay. Coca Cola, the largest purchaser of sugar, exercises some control over sugar prices.

Many products, however, are exchanged in perfect markets. Stocks and bonds and commodities such as wheat, silver, copper, gold, foreign currencies, oats, pork bellies, soybeans, lumber, cotton, orange juice, cattle, cocoa, and platinum are bought and sold in perfectly competitive markets. Private investors, mutual funds, commercial banks, industrial buyers of commodities, and agricultural brokers participate in these markets. Although markets like the local grocery store, the dry cleaner, the gas station, the college placement office, or the roadside stand are not perfectly competitive, many of them function in a way that approximates perfect competition. In this respect, the behavior of perfectly competitive markets serves as a useful guide to the way many real-world markets function and is a valuable starting point for examining economic behavior.

DEMAND

Economics is based upon the principle of *unlimited wants*. Collectively, we all want more than the economy can provide, and scarcity is the consequence of the mismatch between wants and the ability of the economy to meet these wants.

The term *wants* refers to the goods and services that consumers would claim if they were given away free. *The list of goods consumers "want" is quite different from the list of goods they* **demand.** What consumers are actually prepared to buy depends on price and a variety of other factors, which will be studied in this chapter.

> The **demand** for a good or service is a schedule (which can be depicted by a curve) of the amounts of the good or service consumers are prepared to buy at different prices during a specified time period.

The Law of Demand

A fundamental law of economics is the **law of demand.**

The **law of demand** states that there is a negative (or inverse) relationship between the price of a good and quantity demanded, holding other factors constant.

Thus, if prices are lowered, **quantity demanded** increases, if other factors are held constant. The importance of the *ceteris paribus* ("holding all other factors constant") restriction on the law of demand will become apparent in the course of this discussion.

> The **quantity demanded** is the amount of a good or service consumers are prepared to buy at a given price (during a specified time period).

The basic reason for the law of demand is that as the price of any product goes up, people will tend to find substitutes for that product. If the price of gasoline rises, drivers will cut back on less essential driving, and more people will take the bus, or walk, or ride their bicycles to work. If the price of tea rises, more people will drink coffee, or heavy tea drinkers may cut back one or two cups a day and instead buy a soft drink. The universal and natural tendency is for people who consume or use the goods to *substitute other goods or services* when the price of a good goes up. Higher prices discourage consumption.

When a price rises by enough some people may even stop consuming the good altogether. Thus, as the price rises, the number of actual buyers may fall as some people *entirely* switch to other goods.

People also tend to buy less of a good as its price goes up because *they feel poorer*. If a person buys a new car every year for $5,000 (after trade-in), and the price rises to $9,000 (after trade-in), the person would need an extra $4,000 yearly income to maintain the old standard of living. The $4,000 increase in the price of the car is like a cut in income of $4,000.[1]

The law of demand shows that the everyday concept of *need* is not a very useful concept in

---

1. It is preferable to raise the price of the car by $4,000 than to reduce one's income by $4,000, because the change in income cannot be avoided; the change in the price of the car can be avoided by spending money elsewhere on the next best alternative.

Figure 1   The Demand Curve for Corn

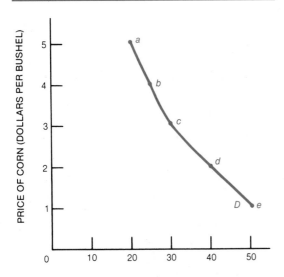

QUANTITY OF CORN
(MILLIONS OF BUSHELS PER MONTH)

Table 1 describes how the quantity of corn demanded responds to the prices of corn, holding all other factors constant. At *a,* when the price of corn is $5 per bushel, the quantity demanded is 20 million bushels per month. At *e,* when the price of corn is $1, the quantity demanded is 50 million bushels. The downward-sloping curve *(D)* drawn through these points is the demand curve for corn. Graphically, it shows the amounts of corn consumers would be willing to buy at different prices in the specified time period.

Table 1   Demand Schedule for Corn

	Price (dollars per bushel)	Quantity Demanded (millions of bushels per month)
a	5	20
b	4	25
c	3	30
d	2	40
e	1	50

mand 20 million bushels of corn per month at the price of $5 per bushel. Should the price of corn be lower—say, $4 per bushel—then the quantity demanded is higher. In this case, the quantity demanded at the lower price of $4 is 25 million bushels. By continuing to decrease the price, it is possible to induce or coax buyers to purchase more and more corn. Table 1 shows that at the price of $1, quantity demanded will be 50 million bushels. Notice that it is important to state the units of the measurement for both the price and the quantity. In this example, price is in dollars per bushel, and quantity is in millions of bushels per month. The time period, whether it be a minute, a day, a week, a month, or a year, must be specified before the demand schedule is meaningful.

economics. To "need" something implies that one cannot do without it. When the price of something changes, the law of demand says that quantity demanded will change. Since the word *need* implies an absolute necessity for something, this word is avoided whenever discussing demand.

The relationship between quantity demanded and price is called the *demand curve* or the *demand schedule.* The relationship is negative because of the law of demand. To avoid confusion, we shall henceforth talk about the *demand schedule* when the relationship is in tabular form and about the *demand curve* when the relationship is in graphical form. (See Example 1.)

The Demand Schedule

Table 1 shows a hypothetical demand schedule for corn. The buyers in the marketplace will de-

The Demand Curve

The demand schedule of Table 1 can be portrayed graphically (Figure 1) as the demand curve. For demand curves, price is on the vertical axis and quantity demanded is on the horizontal axis. In this demand curve, prices are in dollars per bushel and the quantities are in millions of bushels per month. When price is $5, quantity demanded is 20 million bushels per month (point *a* in Figure 1). Point *b* corresponds to a price of $4 and a quantity of 25 million bushels. When price falls from $5 to $4, quantity demanded rises by 5 million bushels from 20 million to 25 million bushels. The remaining Table 1 prices and quantities are graphed.

The curve drawn through the points *a* through *e,* labeled *D,* is the demand curve. The demand curve shows how quantity demanded responds to changes in price. Along the demand curve *D,* the

Example 1   M&Ms and the Law of Demand

The law of demand states that the quantity demanded will increase as the price is lowered as long as other factors that affect demand do not change. In the real world, factors that affect the demand for a particular product change frequently. Tastes change, income rises, and prices of substitutes and complements change. In 1984, the makers of M&M candy conducted an experiment that illustrates the law of demand, holding the necessary demand-affecting conditions constant. Over a 12-month test period, the price of M&Ms was held constant in 150 stores, while the content weight of the candy was increased. By

holding the price constant and then increasing the weight, the price (per ounce) is lowered. In the stores where the price was dropped, sales rose by 20 percent to 30 percent almost overnight, according to the director of sales development for M&Ms. As predicted by the law of demand, a reduction in price causes the quantity demanded to rise, *ceteris paribus*. ■

Source: "Why Do Hot Dogs Come in Packs of 10 and Buns in 8s and 12s?" *Wall Street Journal,* September 21, 1984.

---

price and the quantity are *negatively* related. This means the curve is downward-sloping.

Since the relationship between price and quantity demanded is downward-sloping, the law of demand is sometimes called the *law of downward-sloping demand*.

The demand curve shows that as larger quantities of corn are put on the market, lower prices are required in order to sell that quantity. The price needed to sell 25 million bushels of corn is $4 per bushel. To sell a larger quantity of corn (say, 30 million bushels) a lower price (of $3) is required.

Figure 1 is titled "The Demand Curve for Corn." But whose demand for corn does it represent? The units of measure are in millions of bushels, so it is definitely not the demand curve of an individual family. It could be the demand curve of all American buyers of corn, or it could be the demand curve of Ralston Purina, a major American buyer of corn. It could even be the world demand curve for corn. The national demand curve for corn is simply the demand curve of all American buyers combined. The world demand curve for corn is the demand curves of all nations added together. Just as one must state the units of measure of prices and quantities, so one must state whose demand curve it is.

The **market demand curve** is the demand curve of all persons participating in the market for that particular product.

Normally, this book will use a **market demand curve.**

The *demand curve for corn* therefore refers to all buyers in the corn market. The corn market is essentially a national market or even an international market that brings together all American (or even world) buyers of corn. For example, the demand curve for Hawaiian real estate brings together all buyers of Hawaiian real estate; the demand curve for U.S. automobiles brings together the demand schedules of all private, corporate, and governmental buyers of U.S.-produced automobiles.

Factors That Cause the Demand Curve to Shift

Factors other than the price of the good can change the relationship between price and quantity demanded, causing the demand curve to shift left or right. A demand curve assumes that all these other factors are held constant and shows what would happen to the quantity demanded if *only the price* were to change. In the real world, these other conditions are constantly changing; therefore, it is crucial to understand how changes in factors other than the good's own price affect the demand for a good. The nonprice factors that can affect the demand for a good include: 1) the prices of related goods, 2) consumer income, 3) consumer preferences, 4) the number of potential buyers, and 5) expectations.

The Prices of Related Goods. Goods can be related to each other in two ways: Two goods are **substitutes** if the demand for one rises when the price of the other rises (or when the demand falls when the price of the other falls). Examples of substitutes are: coffee and tea, two brands of soft drinks, stocks and bonds, bacon and sausage, pork and beef, oats and corn, foreign and domestic cars, natural gas and electricity. Some goods are very close substitutes (two different brands of fluoride toothpaste), and others are very distant substitutes (Toyota cars and DC-10 aircraft).

> Two goods are **substitutes** if the demand for one rises when the price of the other rises (or if the demand for one falls when the price of the other falls).

Two goods are **complements** if increasing the price of one good lowers the demand for the other. Examples of complements are: automobiles and gasoline, food and drink, white dress shirts and neckties, skirts and blouses. When goods are complements there is a tendency for the two goods to be used jointly in order to achieve something more general (for example, automobiles plus gasoline equals transportation). Thus, an increase in the price of one of the goods effectively increases the price of the joint product of the two goods together. Thus, an increase in the price of one of the goods will reduce the demand for the other. Examples of substitutes and complements are given in Example 2.

> Two goods are **complements** if the demand for one rises when the price of the other falls (or if the demand for one falls when the price of the other rises).

Income. It is easy to understand how income influences demand. A fact of economic life is that as incomes rise, people spend more on **normal goods** and services. But as income increases, people also spend less on other **inferior goods** and services.

> A **normal good** is one for which demand increases when income increases, holding all prices constant.
> An **inferior good** is one for which demand falls as income increases, holding all prices constant.

Lard, day-old bread, and second-hand clothing are examples of inferior goods for the market as a whole. For some people, inferior goods might be hamburgers, margarine, bus rides, or black-and-white TV sets. But most goods—from automobiles to water—are normal goods.

Preferences. To the economist, the word *preferences* means what people like and dislike without regard to budgetary considerations. One may *prefer* a 10-bedroom mansion with servants but may only be able to afford a 3-bedroom bungalow. One may prefer a Mercedes-Benz but may drive a Volkswagen. One may prefer T-bone steaks but may eat hamburgers! Preferences plus budgetary considerations (price and income) determine demand. As preferences change, demand will change. If people learn that walking will increase their lifespan, the demand for walking shoes will increase. Business firms spend enormous sums trying to influence preferences by advertising on television, in newspapers, and in magazines. The goal of advertising is to shift the demand curve for the advertised product to the right.

The Number of Potential Buyers. If more buyers enter a market, the demand will rise. The number of buyers in a market can increase for a number of reasons. Relaxed immigration barriers or a baby boom may lead to a larger population. The migration of people from one region to another changes the number of buyers in each region. The relaxation of trade barriers between two countries may increase the number of buyers. If Japanese restrictions on imports of U.S. meat products were removed, the number of buyers of U.S. meat products would effectively increase. Lowering the legal age for alcoholic-beverage purchases will increase the number of buyers of beer.

Expectations. If people believe that the price of coffee over the next year will rise substantially (for whatever reason), they may decide to stock up on coffee today. During inflationary times, when people find prices of goods going up rapidly, they often start buying up durable goods, such as cars and refrigerators. Thus, the mere expectation of a good's price going up can induce

Example 2   Substitutes and Complements in Transportation

Good X is a substitute for good Y if the demand for X increases as the price of Y increases. As panel (a) of the accompanying figure illustrates, airline travel is a substitute for intercity bus travel. Traditionally, intercity bus travel has been the cheapest way of traveling between two points. For many people, the cheaper fare compensates for the longer journey. The emergence of discount airlines has altered relative prices in favor of the discount airlines in certain markets. In late 1984, people could fly between Syracuse, New York and Newark, New Jersey or between Norfolk, Virginia and Newark for less than the price of a bus ticket. In the south and western United States, the bus lines were underpriced in specific markets by Southwest Airlines and Pacific Southwest Airlines.

Because airlines and intercity bus travel are substitutes, the demand for bus tickets has fallen as air fares have fallen.

Good X is a complement to good Y if the demand for X rises as the price of Y falls. As panel (b) of the accompanying figure illustrates, automobile rentals and air travel are complements. The bulk of automobile rentals are made at airports by business travelers who require the use of a rental car to conduct their business. A fall in the price of airline travel increases the amount of air travel. As the number of airline passengers increases, so does the demand for rental cars. ■

Source: "Bus Concerns Lose Business to Airlines," *The Wall Street Journal,* September 6, 1984.

(a) Substitutes: Intercity Bus Travel and Airline Travel

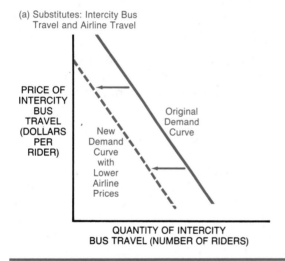

QUANTITY OF INTERCITY BUS TRAVEL (NUMBER OF RIDERS)

(b) Complements: Rental Cars and Airline Travel

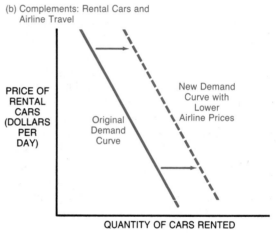

QUANTITY OF CARS RENTED

people to buy more of it. Similarly, people can postpone the purchase of things that are expected to get cheaper. For example: during the 1980s home computers grew cheaper and cheaper. Some buyers may well have postponed their purchase of home computers on the expectation that in the future the good could be purchased for an even lower price. Finally, expectations of future increases in income may have dramatic effects on consumer purchases in general.

Changes in any of the above nonprice factors will *shift the entire demand curve* for the good. Figure 2 shows the demand curve for white dress

shirts. This curve, *D,* is based on a $5 price for neckties (a complement), a $10 price of sport shirts (a substitute), and fixed income, preferences, and number of buyers.

An increase in the price of neckties (a complement for white shirts) from $5 to $7.50 shifts the entire demand curve for white shirts to the left from *D* to *D'* in panel (a). White dress shirts are usually worn with neckties. If neckties increase in price, consumers will buy less of them and will substitute less formal shirts for shirts that require neckties. As a result, the demand for white dress shirts will decrease, shifting left.

Figure 2   Shifts in the Demand Curve: Changes in Demand

(a) Decrease in Demand

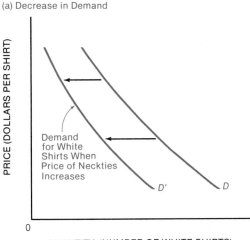

QUANTITY (NUMBER OF WHITE SHIRTS)

(b) Increase in Demand

QUANTITY (NUMBER OF WHITE SHIRTS)

The demand curve for white dress shirts depends on the price of neckties and on the price of sport shirts. When the price of neckties is $5 and the price of sport shirts is $10, the demand curve for white shirts is D. If the price of neckties rises to $7.50, holding the price of sport shirts at $10, then at each price for white dress shirts the demand falls. In panel (a), with a higher price of neckties the demand curve shifts to the left and depicts a decrease in demand from D to D'. In panel (b), keeping the price of neckties at $5 and raising the price of sport shirts to $15 will raise the demand for white shirts. The demand curve will shift rightward to D''. A rightward shift depicts an increase in demand, and a leftward shift illustrates a decrease in demand.

An increase in the price of sports shirts (a substitute for white dress shirts) from $10 to $15 shifts the demand curve for white shirts to the right from D to D'' in panel (b). When the price of sports shirts increases, consumers substitute white dress shirts for sports shirts. As a result of this substitution, the demand for white dress shirts will increase, shifting right.

> When the demand curve shifts to the left, *people wish to buy smaller quantities of the good at each price.* A leftward shift of the demand curve indicates a *decrease in demand.* When the demand curve shifts to the right, *people wish to buy larger quantities of the good at each price.* A rightward shift of the demand curve indicates an *increase in demand.*

Demand curves shift to the right or left when factors other than the good's own price change. If consumer income increases, and if white dress shirts are a normal good, demand will increase (D will shift to the right). If preferences change and white dress shirts fall out of fashion, demand will decrease (D will shift to the left). If buyers expect prices of white dress shirts to rise substantially in the future, demand will increase. (See Example 3.)

> A change in *product price only* will cause a movement along a demand curve. A change in a *demand-affecting factor other than the price of the good* (such as a related good's price, income, preferences, expectations, or the number of buyers) will cause the entire demand curve to shift.

SUPPLY

The quantities of goods and services firms are prepared to supply to the market depend on price and a variety of other factors. The term **supply** has a definite meaning for the economist.

> The **supply** of a good or service is a schedule (which can be depicted by a curve) showing the amounts of the good or service firms offer to sell at different prices during a specified time period.

Example 3   Factors That Cause a Demand Curve to Shift

Factor	Example
Change in price of substitutes	Increase in price of coffee shifts demand curve for tea to right.
Change in price of complements	Increase in price of coffee shifts demand curve for sugar to left.
Change in income	Increase in income shifts demand curve for automobiles to right.
Change in preference	Judgment that cigarettes are hazardous to health shifts demand curve for cigarettes to left.
Change in number of buyers	Increase in population of City X shifts demand curve for houses in City X to right.
Change in expectations of future prices	Expectation that prices of canned goods will increase substantially over the next year shifts demand curve for canned goods to right. ■

How much corn the farmer offers for sale depends on the price of corn. Generally speaking, the higher the price, the higher the **quantity supplied.**

> The **quantity supplied** of a good or service is the amount of the good or service offered for sale at a given price.

A higher price for corn will induce farmers to cultivate fewer soybeans and plant more corn. A higher price for corn will make farmers more willing to put out a little extra effort to make sure that corn is not wasted during harvesting or to prevent the crop from being harmed by the weather or pests. The fundamental reason for the normally positive relationship between quantity supplied and price is the *law of diminishing returns* (see Chapter 2). The law of diminishing returns states that with other factors of production fixed, the extra output obtained by adding equal increments of a variable factor to the process of production will eventually decline. To produce more of a good under the law of diminishing returns means that as more and more obstacles are encountered, a higher price is required to overcome these obstacles. For example, farmers may find that they have to plant additional corn in areas that are rockier or that the extra harvesting requires more maintenance or more reliance on undependable labor. Whenever fixed factors are present, the productivity of the extra variable factors used to produce more output falls, and the costs of producing each additional unit of output rise.

The Supply Curve

Consider now the normal case of a positive relationship between price and quantity supplied. Table 2 shows a hypothetical supply schedule for corn that is graphed in Figure 3. When the price of corn is $5 per bushel, farmers are prepared to supply 40 million bushels per month (point *a*). As the price falls to $4, the quantity supplied falls to 35 million bushels (point *b*). Finally, when the price is $1 farmers are prepared to sell only 10 million bushels (point *e*).

The smooth curve drawn through points *a* through *e*, labeled *S*, is the supply curve. It shows how quantity supplied responds to all price variations: *it shows how much farmers are prepared to offer for sale at each price.* Along the supply curve, the price of corn and the supply of corn are positively related: in order to induce farmers to offer a larger quantity of corn on the market, a higher price is required.

Factors That Cause the Supply Curve to Shift

Just as factors other than the good's own price can change the relationship between price and

Table 2	Supply Schedule for Corn	
	Price (dollars per bushel)	Quantity Supplied (millions of bushels per month)
a	5	40
b	4	35
c	3	30
d	2	20
e	1	10

Figure 3   The Supply Curve for Corn

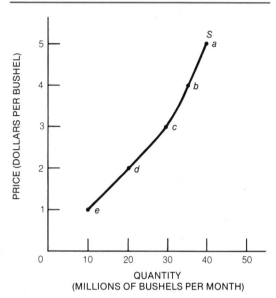

This graph depicts how the quantity of corn supplied responds to the price of corn. In situation *a*, when the price of corn is $5 per bushel, the quantity supplied by farmers is 40 million bushels per month. In the last situation, *e*, when the price is $1 per bushel, the quantity supplied is only 10 million bushels per month. The upward-sloping curve *(S)* drawn through these points is the supply curve of corn.

quantity demanded, nonprice factors can change the relationship between price and quantity supplied, causing the supply curve to shift. The nonprice factors that can cause the supply curve to shift include: 1) the prices of other goods, 2) the prices of relevant resources, 3) technology, 4) the number of sellers, and 5) expectations.

The Prices of Other Goods.   The resources that are used to produce any particular good can almost always be used elsewhere in the economy. Farmland can be used for corn or soybeans; engineers can work on cars or trucks; unskilled workers can pick strawberries or cotton; trains can be used to move coal or cars. As the price of a good rises, resources are naturally attracted away from other goods that use those resources. Hence, the supply of corn will fall if the price of soybeans rises; if the price of cotton rises the supply of strawberries may fall. If the price of trucks rises, the supply of cars may fall. If the price of fuel oil rises, less kerosene may be produced. (See Example 4.)

The Prices of Relevant Resources.   The production and provision of goods and services requires certain resources that must be purchased in resource markets. As these resource prices change, the supply conditions for the goods being produced change. An increase in the price of coffee beans will increase the costs of producing coffee and decrease the amount of coffee that coffee companies are prepared to sell at each price; an increase in the price of corn land, tractors, harvesters, or irrigation will tend to reduce the supply of corn; an increase in the price of cotton will tend to decrease the supply of cotton dresses; an increase in the price of jet fuel will decrease the supply of commercial aviation at each price.

Technology.   *Technology* is the knowledge that people have about how different things can be produced. If technology improves, more goods can be produced from the same resources. For example, if lobster farmers in Maine learn how to feed lobsters more cheaply due to a new and cheaper combination of nutritious food, the quantity of lobsters supplied at each price will tend to increase. If a firm finds that the assembly line can be speeded up by merely rearranging the order of assembly, the supply of the good will tend to increase. If new oil-recovery procedures are discovered, the supply of oil will increase.

The Number of Sellers.   If more sellers enter into the production of a particular good (perhaps because of high profits or in anticipation of high profits), the supply of the good will increase. The lowering of trade barriers (such as dropping cumbersome licensing requirements for foreign firms) may allow foreign sellers to enter the market, increasing the number of sellers.

Example 4   The Supply Curve and Broccoli Farming in Tobacco Country

The supply curve tends to be positively sloped. An increase in the price of a good should call forth a greater quantity supplied, *ceteris paribus*. An example of this phenomenon can be found in the tobacco-growing fields of Virginia. Virginia farm land is well suited for both tobacco and broccoli production. Both require irrigation systems, both are labor-intensive products that must be hand-picked over a period of weeks as they ripen. In recent years, broccoli prices have been rising while tobacco prices have been stable or falling. As the positive slope of the supply curve suggests, Virginia tobacco farmers have been switching their production from tobacco to broccoli in

response to current price movements. The increased production of broccoli in Virginia may also be the consequence of anticipated further reductions in relative tobacco prices (which cause the supply curve to shift to the right). In the face of increased competition from Brazil and Zimbabwe and the trend among Americans to smoke less, tobacco farmers are concluding that future price trends will move against tobacco and in favor of broccoli. ∎

Source: "Tobacco Farmers Would Rather Switch to Broccoli than Fight (Falling Profits)," special supplement to *Christian Science Monitor*, 1984.

Expectations.   It takes a long time to produce many goods and services. When a farmer plants corn or wheat or soybeans, the prices that are expected to prevail at harvest time are actually more important than the current price. A college student who reads that there are likely to be too few engineers in four years may decide to major in engineering in expectation of a high wage rate. When a business firm decides to establish a plant that may take five years to build, expectations of future business conditions in that industry are crucial to that investment decision.

Expectations can affect supply in different directions. If oil prices are expected to rise in the future, oil producers may produce less oil today to have more available for the future. In other cases, more investment will be undertaken if high prices are expected in the future. This greater investment will cause supply to increase.

Changes in each of the above nonprice factors *will shift the entire supply curve*. Figure 4 shows the supply curve, S, for corn. The supply curve is based on a $10-per-bushel price of soybeans and a $2,000 yearly rental on an acre of corn land. If the price of soybeans rises to, say, $15 a bushel, then the supply curve for corn will shift leftward to S' in panel (a) because some land used for corn will be shifted to soybeans. If the rental price of an acre of corn land goes down from $2,000 a year per acre to $1,000 a year, the supply curve will shift to the right—to, say, S'' in panel (b). The reduction in the land rental price lowers the

costs of producing a bushel of corn and makes the corn producer willing to supply more corn at the same price as before. (See Example 5.)

When the supply curve shifts to the left (for whatever reason), *producers are prepared to sell smaller quantities of the good at each price*. A leftward shift (as from S to S' in Figure 4) indicates a *decrease in supply*. When the supply curve shifts to the right, *producers are prepared to sell larger quantities at each price*. This rightward shift (as from S to S'' in Figure 4) indicates an *increase in supply*.

EQUILIBRIUM OF SUPPLY AND DEMAND

Along a given demand curve, such as the one in Figure 1, there are lots of price/quantity combinations from which to choose. Along a given supply curve, there are similarly lots of different price/quantity combinations. Neither the demand curve nor the supply curve is sufficient by itself to determine the *market* price/quantity combination.

Figure 5 puts the demand curve of Figure 1 and the supply curve of Figure 3 together on the same diagram. Remember that the demand curve indicates what consumers are prepared to buy at different prices; the supply curve indicates what

Figure 4   Shifts in the Supply Curve: Changes in Supply

(a) Decrease in Supply

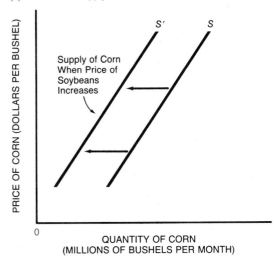

QUANTITY OF CORN
(MILLIONS OF BUSHELS PER MONTH)

(b) Increase in Supply

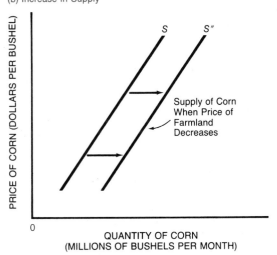

QUANTITY OF CORN
(MILLIONS OF BUSHELS PER MONTH)

The supply curve of corn depends on the price of soybeans and on the price of farmland. When farmland is $2,000 an acre per year and soybeans are $10 per bushel, S might be the supply curve for corn. Panel (a) shows that if farmland stays at $2,000 per acre per year but soybeans fetch $15 instead of $10, profit-seeking farmers will switch farmland from corn to soybeans and cause the supply curve for corn to shift to the left from S to S′ (a decrease in supply). On the other hand, panel (b) shows that if soybeans remain at $10 per bushel and farmland falls from $2,000 to $1,000 per acre, the supply curve for corn will shift to the right from S to S″ (an increase in supply).

producers are prepared to sell at different prices. These groups of economic decision makers are (for the most part) entirely different. How much will be produced? How much will be consumed? How are the decisions of consumers and producers coordinated?

Suppose that the price of corn happened to be $2 per bushel. Figure 5 tells us the same thing that Figures 1 and 3 tell us separately: at a $2 price consumers will want to buy 40 million bushels and producers will want to sell only 20 million bushels. This discrepancy means that at $2 there is a **shortage** of 20 million bushels.

> A **shortage** results if at the current price the quantity demanded exceeds the quantity supplied; the price is too low to equate the quantity demanded with the quantity supplied.

At a $2 per bushel price, some people who are willing to buy corn find themselves empty-handed. The demand curve shows that a number of consumers are willing to pay more than $2 per bushel. Such buyers will try to outbid each other for the available supply. With free competition, the price of corn will be bid up if there is a shortage of corn.

The increase in the price of corn in response to the shortage will have two main effects. On the one hand, the higher price will discourage consumption. On the other hand, the higher price will encourage production. Thus, the increase in the price of corn, through the action of independent buyers and sellers, will lead both buyers and sellers in the marketplace to make decisions that will reduce the shortage of corn.

According to the demand and supply curves portrayed in Figure 5, when the price of corn reaches $3 per bushel, the shortage of corn disappears completely. At this **equilibrium (or market-clearing) price,** consumers want to buy 30 million bushels and producers want to sell 30 million bushels.

> The **equilibrium (market-clearing) price** is the price at which the quantity demanded by consumers equals the quantity supplied by producers.

What would happen if price rose above the equilibrium price of $3 per bushel? At the price of $4 per bushel, consumers want to buy 25 mil-

Example 5   Factors That Cause a Supply Curve to Shift

Factor	Example
Change in price of another good	Increase in price of corn shifts supply curve of wheat to left.
Change in price of resource	Decrease in wage rate of autoworkers shifts supply curve of autos to right.
Change in technology	Higher corn yields due to genetic engineering shift supply curve of corn to right.
Change in number of sellers	New sellers entering profitable field shift supply curve of product to right.
Change in expectations	Expectation of a much higher price of oil next year shifts supply curve of oil today to left; expectation of higher ball-bearing prices in the future causes more investment, shifting supply curve to right. ■

lion bushels and producers want to sell 35 million bushels. Thus, at $4 there is a **surplus** of 10 million bushels on the market.

> A **surplus** results if at the current price the quantity supplied exceeds the quantity demanded; the price is too high to equate the quantity demanded with quantity supplied.

Some sellers will be disappointed as corn inventories pile up. Willing sellers of corn will not be able to find buyers. The competition among sellers will lead them to cut the price if there is a surplus of corn.

This fall in the price of corn will simultaneously encourage consumption and discourage production. Through the automatic fall in the price of corn, *the surplus of corn will therefore disappear*.

Again we find that the price will tend toward $3 and the quantity will tend toward 30 million bushels. This equilibrium point is where the demand and supply curves intersect. In Figure 5, there is no other price/quantity combination at which quantity demanded equals quantity supplied—any other price brings about a shortage of corn or a surplus of corn. The arrows in Figure 5 indicate the pressures on prices above or below $3 and how the amount of shortage or surplus—the size of the brackets—gets smaller as the price adjusts.

The equilibrium of supply and demand is stationary in the sense that price will tend to remain at that price once the equilibrium price is reached.

Movements away from the equilibrium price will be restored by the bidding of excess buyers or excess sellers in the marketplace. The equilibrium price is like a rocking chair in the rest position; give it a gentle push and the original position will be restored.

What the Market Accomplishes

The equilibrium price is discovered in the marketplace. The market coordinates the actions of a large number of independent suppliers and demanders. Their actions are brought together by the pricing of the good in a free market. The market can accomplish its actions without any one participant knowing all the details. Recall the pencil example (Example 5) of Chapter 3: pencils get produced even though no single individual knows *all* the details for producing a pencil (from making the saw to fell the trees to making the rubber eraser).

An equilibrium price accomplishes two basic goals. First, it *rations* the scarce supply of the commodity or service among all the people who would like to have it if it were given away free. Somebody must be left out if the good is scarce. The price, by discouraging or restraining consumption, rations the good out to the various claimants of the good.

Second, the system of equilibrium prices *economizes on the information required to match supplies and demands*. Buyers do not have to know how to *produce* the good, and sellers do not need

Figure 5   Market Equilibrium

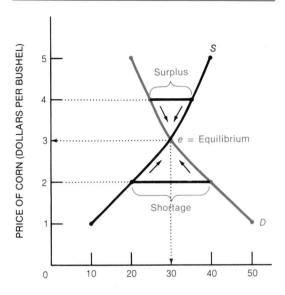

QUANTITY OF CORN
(MILLIONS OF BUSHELS PER MONTH)

This figure shows how market equilibrium is reached. On the same diagram are drawn both the demand curve for corn (from Figure 1) and the supply curve for corn (from Figure 3). When the price of corn is $2, the quantity demanded is 40 million bushels, but the quantity supplied is only 20 million bushels. The result is a shortage of 20 million bushels of corn. Unsatisfied buyers will bid the price up.

Raising the price will reduce the shortage. When the price of corn is raised to $4 per bushel, the quantity demanded is 25 million bushels while the quantity supplied is 35 million bushels. The result is a surplus of 10 million bushels of corn. This surplus will cause the price of corn to fall as unsatisfied sellers bid the price down to get rid of excess inventories of corn. As the price falls the surplus will diminish. The equilibrium price is $3 because the quantity demanded equals the quantity supplied at that price. The equilibrium quantity is 30 million bushels.

Figure 6   The Effect of Rent Ceilings on the Market for Rental Housing

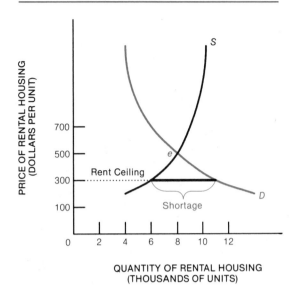

QUANTITY OF RENTAL HOUSING
(THOUSANDS OF UNITS)

If the equilibrium price/quantity combination for the rental market is $500 per unit and 8,000 units (point e), a rent ceiling of $300 per month on a standard housing unit would lower the quantity supplied to 6,000 units and raise the quantity demanded to 11,000 units, creating a shortage of 5,000 units of rental housing.

to know why people use the good. Buyers and sellers need only be concerned with small bits of information such as price or small portions of the technological methods of production. No one person has to know everything. (See Example 6.)

Disequilibrium Prices

To understand the rationing function of equilibrium prices, let us consider what happens when prices are not allowed to reach equilibrium. For many years, the price of natural gas shipped in-

terstate was held below equilibrium by the Federal Power Commission. During the Arab oil embargo during the summer of 1974, gasoline prices were held below market-clearing levels by government regulations. Prices of consumer goods in Poland and other East-bloc countries have been held below equilibrium by government pricing policies. In such cases, shortages and long lines resulted.

Rent control is an example of disequilibrium pricing. Laws are passed by some municipal governments *freezing* rents (that is, preventing rents from rising). The growing number of consumer groups demanding controls on rents is explained by a very simple fact: in the United States, the number of tenants is increasing relative to the number of homeowners.

Figure 6 shows the market for rental housing in a particular city. The supply curve is upward-sloping; the demand curve is downward-sloping. In a free market, the price of housing would settle at $500 per month for a standard rental unit. But

---

Example 6   Equilibrium Pricing and Information in the Case of Delta Airlines

Delta Airlines's pricing department currently employs 150 people who are responsible for setting fares for Delta's more than 5,000 routes. The goals of the pricing department are 1) to fly Delta planes with as few empty seats as possible and 2) to charge the highest price consistent with full planes. Delta, like most other airlines, has a two-tier price system for each flight: full-fare tickets and discount tickets. The effective price for each flight is determined by the proportion of full-fare tickets sold. Delta varies the number of discount seats per flight according to market conditions. If on a particular flight, the number of bookings rises above the historical pattern (which is calculated by computers), Delta will reduce the number of discount seats on that flight. If the number of bookings falls below the historical pattern, Delta will increase the number of discount seats. By increasing the number of discount seats, Delta is, in effect, lowering the price; by reducing the number of discount seats, Delta is, in effect, raising the price. Delta need not have specialized marketing information on why bookings are high or low; all

Delta has to do is to respond to ticket orders by raising or lowering the price.

Delta's pricing procedures are a classic example of how firms and markets *search* for equilibrium prices. Even though Delta is not operating in perfectly competitive markets, there is still a strong tendency to set prices at equilibrium. If they perceive an excess demand, the price is raised (fewer discount seats). If they see an excess supply, the price is lowered (more discount seats). These adjustments are made until equilibrium is reached (the plane is full or full enough). Delta's pricing department need not understand why bookings are up or down for a particular flight (whether there is a holiday, a strike on another airline, or whatever). All the information they need is that lowering the price tends to eliminate the empty seats and raising the price can reduce an excess number of buyers. ■

Source: "Fare Game: In Airline's Rate Wars Small Battles Can Decide Winner," *Wall Street Journal,* August 24, 1984.

---

suppose a price ceiling of $300 is established by municipal ordinance. If landlords are free to supply the number of apartments they wish, fewer units would be offered for rent the lower is the price: 6,000 units are supplied at a price of $300 and 8,000 units at a price of $500. The quantity demanded rises to 11,000 units as price falls. Accordingly, there will be a shortage of 5,000 units due to the rent-control price ceiling of $300. If the price could rise from $300 to $500, there would be no shortage.

Understanding Shortage and Surplus

The terms *shortage* and *surplus* (glut) are often misused. For example, the following statement (with certain details changed) was taken from a respected newspaper:

> Projections of supplies and demands reveal that there will be a large surplus of medical doctors by the end of the 1980s. The supply of M.D.s will exceed demand generally, but surpluses will be greatest in particular specialties.

One often hears reports about "shortages" of sugar or other commodities. In economics, a shortage occurs when the price is not allowed to *rise* to its equilibrium level. A surplus occurs when the price is not allowed to *fall* to its equilibrium level. If there are no impediments to these price adjustments, shortages and surpluses will disappear as prices adjust. A sugar shortage is not a shortage in the same sense as a shortage of rent-controlled apartments. By *a sugar shortage,* writers really mean that supply and demand conditions are pushing *up* the price of sugar. By *a surplus of doctors,* writers actually mean that supply and demand conditions push *down* the relative price of physicians' services, not that there will be doctors with no patients.

CHANGES IN THE EQUILIBRIUM PRICE

One important fact about market economics is that prices change. Sometimes prices go up, and

Figure 7   Change in Demand Versus Change in Quantity Demanded

(a) Change in Quantity Demanded

(b) Change in Demand

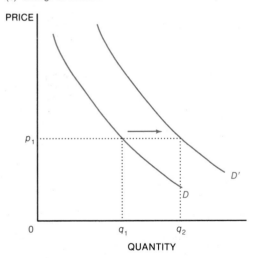

In panel (a), the increase in quantity demanded (from q_1 to q_2) is due to the change in price (from p_2 to p_1). The change in price causes the *movement along* the demand curve *(D)*. In panel (b), the increase in quantity (from q_1 to q_2) is due to a *shift* in the demand curve (an increase in demand) to D'. When demand increases, the whole demand curve shifts due to some change that leads consumers to buy more of the product *at each price.*

sometimes they go down—and in relative-price terms, price goes down as often as it goes up. This section will investigate the reasons for price changes. Thus far we have seen that the equilib-rium price is determined by the intersection of the demand and supply curves. The only way for the price to change is for the demand or supply curves themselves to shift. The supply and demand curves can shift only if one or more of the factors *besides the good's own price* changes.

Change in Demand (or Supply) Versus Change in Quantity Demanded (or Supplied)

A fall in the price of a good—as from p_2 to p_1 in panel (a) of Figure 7—induces a change in the quantity demanded but does not change the location of the demand curve. A change in demand occurs when a change in a factor other than the good's own price shifts the entire demand curve to the left or to the right.

> A *change* (increase or decrease) *in demand* is a shift in the entire demand curve because of a change in a factor other than the good's own price.

> A *change* (increase or decrease) *in quantity demanded* is a movement along the demand curve because of a change in the good's price (see Figure 7).

Similarly, panel (a) of Figure 8 shows that a rise in the price of a good (from p_1 to p_2) changes the quantity supplied but does not change the location of the supply curve. A change in supply occurs when a factor other than the good's own price changes, shifting the entire supply curve to the left or to the right.

> A *change* (increase or decrease) *in supply* is a shift in the entire supply curve because of a change in a factor other than the good's price.

> A *change* (increase or decrease) *in quantity supplied* is a movement along the supply curve because of a change in the good's price (see Figure 8).

Figure 8   Change in Supply Versus Change in Quantity Supplied

(a) Change in Quantity Supplied

(b) Change in Supply

In panel (a), the increase in quantity supplied (from q_1 to q_2) is due to a change in price (from p_1 to p_2). The change in price causes a *movement along* the supply curve *(S)*. In panel (b), the decrease in supply (from q_2 to q_1) is due to the *shift* in the supply curve (decrease in supply) from *S* to *S'*. Quantity drops without any change in price.

Figure 9   The Effects of a Natural Disaster on the Price of Wheat

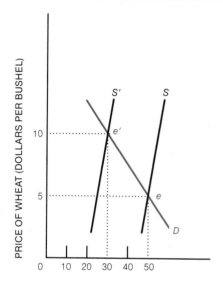

QUANTITY OF WHEAT
(MILLIONS OF BUSHELS PER YEAR)

In this graph, a natural disaster shifts the supply curve of wheat from *S* to *S'*. Where formerly $5 brought forth 50 million bushels of wheat (on *S*) now $5 brings forth only 25 million bushels of wheat (on *S'*). This decrease in supply raises the equilibrium price from $5 to $10. The *movement from e to e'* is a *movement along* the demand curve. Although the demand curve does not change, there is a decrease in quantity demanded from 50 million to 30 million bushels as the price rises from $5 to $10 per bushel.

The Effects of a Change in Supply

Changes in supply or demand factors can influence the equilibrium price and quantity in any given market.

Consider a natural disaster, such as severe flooding, a horde of locusts, or a drought, that affects the supply of an agricultural product, such as wheat. Figure 9 illustrates the effect of a natural disaster on the wheat market. The demand curve, *D,* and the supply curve, *S,* are based on given conditions *before* the natural disaster. Suddenly, and without warning, torrential rains hit the wheat fields prior to harvest, ruining about one half of the potential wheat crop. Now at a price of $5 per bushel, instead of 50 million bush-

---

Example 7   Supply and TV Advertising Prices for College Football

In June of 1984, the Supreme Court ruled that the National Collegiate Athletic Association (NCAA) no longer has the right to regulate the number of appearances on television by college football teams. Prior to 1984, the NCAA strictly limited the number of college games broadcast. Typically, only one or two college football games would be televised per week during football season. With the Supreme Court ruling, the television networks, independent stations, and cable broadcasters are allowed to compete for broadcast rights to college games, and, as a result of this competition, there may be as many as five college games on television on a Saturday afternoon. In the language of supply and demand, the supply of televised college football was increased dramatically by the breaking of the NCAA monopoly. When supply increases, the price should drop, *ceteris paribus*. As predicted, the price a network paid a college to televise a game did indeed drop, resulting in lower rates for TV advertisers buying commercial time during these games. The price of a 30-second commercial spot on an NCAA game on ABC fell from $57,300 in 1983 to $30,000 in 1984. On CBS, the price of a 30-second commercial fell from $59,000 in 1983 to $38,000 in 1984. The laws of supply and demand apply generally, even to the prices of advertising on television. ■

Source: "Madison Ave.'s Football Woe," *New York Times,* September 22, 1984.

---

els being offered, only 25 million bushels are offered by farmers. Similarly, at all other prices smaller quantities of wheat are offered on the market. The supply curve for wheat has shifted to the left to S' (the supply of wheat has decreased). How will this supply reduction affect the demand curve?

When the supply curve for a single good—like wheat—changes, the demand curve normally does not change. The factors influencing the supply of wheat *other than the price of wheat* have little or no influence on the demand for wheat. In our example, the severe rains will not shift the demand curve. Thus, in the analysis of a single market we can usually assume that the demand and supply curves are independent.

The supply curve has shifted to the left (supply has decreased); the demand curve remains unchanged. What will happen to the equilibrium price? Before the flood, the price that equated quantity supplied with quantity demanded was $5. After the flood, the quantity supplied at a $5 price is 25 million bushels and the quantity demanded is 50 million bushels. At the old price, there would be a shortage of wheat. Therefore, the price of wheat will be bid up until a new equilibrium price is attained (at $10), at which quantity demanded and quantity supplied are equal at 30 million bushels. As the price rises from the old equilibrium price ($5) to the new equilibrium price ($10), there is a movement up the new supply curve (S'). Even with a flood, a higher price will coax out more wheat. (See Example 7.)

A decrease in supply causes the price to rise and the quantity demanded to fall. An increase in supply causes the price to fall and the quantity demanded to rise.

The following newspaper report (with certain details changed) illustrates the danger of confusing changes in quantity demanded (or supplied) with changes in demand (or supply).

> The state agriculture office reports that warm weather and sufficient moisture have produced a plentiful supply of lettuce this year. However, lettuce prices are not expected to drop because consumers usually increase their demand for lettuce when prices fall. The demand increase will offset the supply increase.

The good weather reported by the agriculture office shifts the supply curve to the right and causes a movement along the demand curve. The increase in supply does not cause an increase in demand but *an increase in quantity demanded.*

The conclusion of the newspaper report (that prices will not drop) is incorrect given the stated

Figure 10   The Effects of an Increased Preference for Bread on the Price of Wheat

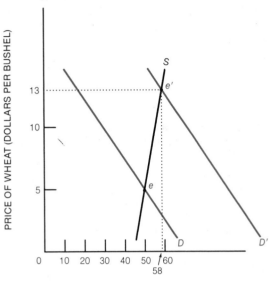

If for some reason people want to eat more bread due to a change in preferences, the demand curve for wheat will shift to the right. The shift in the demand curve from D to D' depicts an increase in demand. This increase in demand drives up the equilibrium price from $5 per bushel to $13 per bushel. As price rises from $5 to $13, there is an increase in quantity supplied from 50 million to 58 million bushels that results from the movement along the supply curve, S.

Figure 11   The Effects of an Increase in Demand and a Decrease in Supply on the Price of Wheat

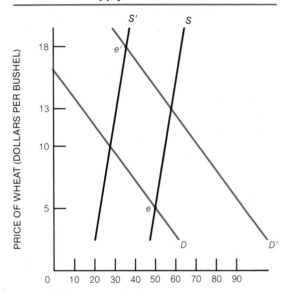

This graph combines the supply change of Figure 9 and the demand change of Figure 10. The original equilibrium was at a price of $5 and a quantity of 50 million bushels. After the shift in supply (from S to S') and the shift in demand (from D to D'), there is a shortage at the old price (quantity supplied equals 25 million bushels and quantity demanded equals 90 million bushels). The equilibrium price rises to $18 and the equilibrium quantity falls to 37.5 million bushels.

facts. As supply increases (as the supply curve shifts to the right), the price falls. As the price falls, there is a movement down the demand curve as consumers increase their quantity demanded in response to lower prices. When supply increases, the price will fall if the demand curve remains unchanged.

The Effects of a Change in Demand

A change in demand is illustrated in Figure 10. The initial situation is depicted by the demand curve, D, and the supply curve, S. The equilibrium price is $5 and the equilibrium quantity is 50 million bushels. Hence, D and S are the same curves as in Figure 9. Now imagine a change on

the demand side. Medical evidence is uncovered showing that eating bread will double one's life-span (purely hypothetical). This event would shift the demand curve for wheat sharply to the right (from D to D'). This massive increase in demand for wheat would drive the price of wheat up to $13 per bushel (from e to e'). When the price rises, the quantity supplied rises from 50 million to 58 million bushels. *There has been no increase in supply, only an increase in quantity supplied* in response to the higher price.

Notice again that when the demand curve shifts due to some change in demand factors other than the good's price, there is no shift in the supply curve—the supply curve remains the same. The supply curve and the demand curve should be considered to be independent of one another at this level of analysis. If a market is small enough relative to the entire economy, the link between the factors that shift demand curves (summarized in Example 3) and those that shift supply curves (summarized in Example 5) is weak. In our example, the change in preferences should not affect the willingness of farmers to supply wheat at different prices during any given time period.

An increase in demand causes the price to rise and the quantity supplied to rise. A decrease in demand causes the price to fall and the quantity supplied to fall.

Simultaneous Changes in Supply and Demand

Figure 11 combines the two previous cases and illustrates what happens to price and quantity if the two events (the flood and the change in preferences) occur together. The supply curve shifts to the left from S to S' (supply falls) and the demand curve shifts to the right from D to D' (demand increases).

Prior to these changes, equilibrium price was $5, and equilibrium quantity was 50 million bushels. The shifts in supply and demand disrupt this equilibrium. Now at a price of $5, the quantity supplied equals 25 million bushels, and the quantity demanded equals 90 million bushels—an enormous shortage. The new equilibrium occurs at a price of $18 and a quantity of 37.5 million bushels. The two shifts magnify each other's effects. As we have shown, if there had been only the supply change, price would have risen to $10. If there had been only the demand change, price would have risen to $13. The combined effects cause the price to rise to $18. In this case, the causes of the changes in supply and demand are independent.

Figure 12 shows the effects of all possible combinations of shifts in supply curves and demand curves. As panels (e), (f), (h), and (i) demonstrate, the effects of simultaneous changes in supply and demand are sometimes indeterminate. If supply increases (shifts right) and demand decreases (shifts left), the price will fall. If supply

decreases and demand increases, the price will rise. If, however, both the demand and supply curves move in the same direction (if both increase or if both decrease), the price effect depends upon which movement dominates.

These first four chapters focused on how market economies allocate resources through the price system. The tools of supply-and-demand analysis show how equilibrium prices are established and how and why prices change. Relative prices signal to buyers what to purchase and signal to firms what and how to produce. The economic problems of *what, how,* and *for whom* are solved by the invisible hand of the market-allocation system, which directs the circular flow of resources between households and businesses. The invisible hand of the market appears to work best under conditions of competition where no buyer or seller (or group thereof) can exercise control over prices.

Summary

1.   A perfectly competitive market consists of many buyers and sellers in which each buyer or seller accepts the market price as given.

2.   The law of demand states that as price goes up the quantity demanded falls, and vice versa; the demand curve is a graphical representation of the relationship between price and quantity demanded—other things equal. The demand curve is downward-sloping.

3.   As price goes up the quantity supplied usually rises; the supply curve is a graphical representation of the relationship between price and quantity supplied. The supply curve tends to be upward-sloping because of the law of diminishing returns.

4.   The equilibrium price/quantity combination occurs where the demand curve intersects the supply curve, or where quantity demanded equals quantity supplied at the market-clearing price. Competitive pricing rations scarce economic goods and economizes on the information necessary to coordinate supply/demand decisions. A shortage results if the price is too low for equilibrium; a surplus results if the price is too high for equilibrium.

Figure 12   Summary of Effects of Supply-Curve and Demand-Curve Shifts

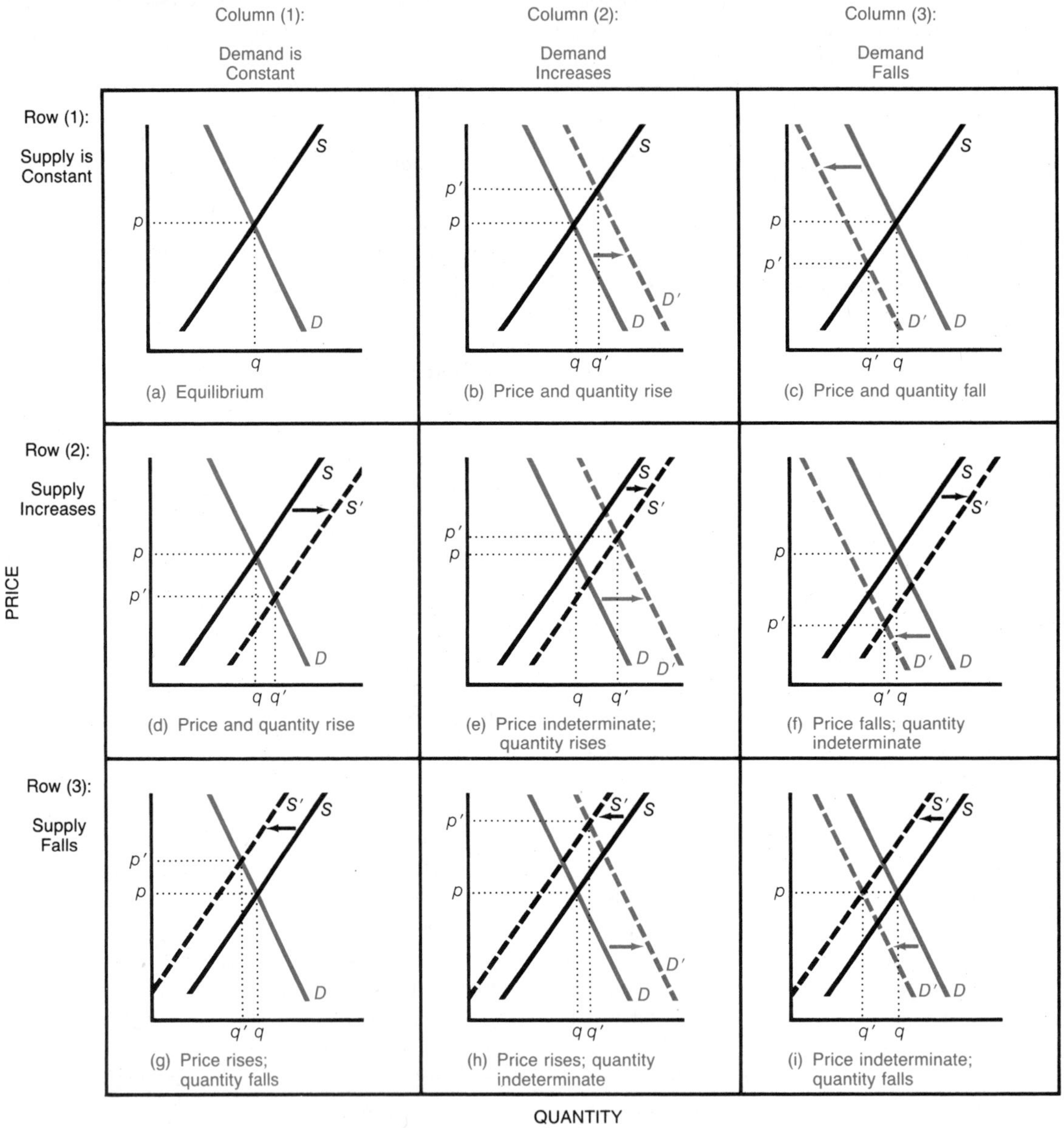

This figure gives the results of all possible combinations of supply-curve and demand-curve shifts. This figure can be read by matching rows and columns. For example, the figure in panel (e), at the intersection of row (2) and column (2), shows what happens when supply and demand increase simultaneously. The figure in panel (i), at the intersection of row (3) and column (3), shows what happens when both supply and demand fall.

5.   A change in quantity demanded means a *movement along* a given demand curve; a change in demand means the entire demand curve shifts. A change in quantity supplied means a *movement* *along* a given supply curve; a change in supply means the entire supply curve shifts. The demand curve will shift if a change occurs in the price of a related good (substitute or

complement), in income, in preferences, in the number of buyers, or in the expectation of future prices or income. The supply curve will shift if a change occurs in the price of another good, in the price of a resource, in technology, in the number of sellers, or in the expectation of future prices. A change in the equilibrium price/quantity combination requires a change in one of the factors held constant along the demand or supply curves. Supply-and-demand analysis allows one to predict what will happen to prices and quantities when supply or demand schedules shift.

Key Terms

market
perfectly competitive market
demand
law of demand
quantity demanded
market demand curve
substitutes
complements
normal goods
inferior goods
supply
quantity supplied
shortage
equilibrium (market-clearing) price
surplus

Questions and Problems

1. List the four characteristics of a perfectly competitive market. Explain why if any of the four conditions are not met, the principal characteristic of a perfectly competitive market (no person or group can control price) may not be met.

2. Suppose you live in a very cold climate and you pay on the average 25 percent of your income for fuel. If the price of fuel rises by 15 percent, and there are no good substitutes for fuel, why would you cut back on fuel consumption?

3. Plot the supply and demand schedules for the hypothetical product in Table A as supply and demand curves.

Table A

Price (dollars)	Quantity Demanded (units)	Quantity Supplied (units)
10	5	25
8	10	20
6	15	15
2	20	10
0	25	5

a. What price would this market establish?
b. If the state were to pass a law that the price could not be more than $2, what would happen to the equilibrium price? If the state were to pass a law that the price could not be more than $8, what effect would the law have on the equilibrium price?
c. If preferences changed and people wanted to buy twice as much as before at each price, what will the equilibrium price be?
d. If, in addition to the above change in preferences, there is an improvement in technology that allows firms to produce this product at lower cost than before, what will happen to the equilibrium price?

4. American baseball bats do not sell well in Japan because they do not meet the specifications of Japanese baseball officials. If the Japanese change their specifications to accommodate American-made bats, what will happen to the price of American bats?

5. "The poor are the ones who suffer from high gas and electricity bills. We should pass a law that gas and electricity rates cannot increase by more than 1 percent annually." Evaluate this statement in terms of supply-and-demand analysis.

6. Much of the automobile-rental business in the United States is done at airports. What would be the predicted effect of a reduction in air fares on automobile-rental rates?

7. If both the supply and demand for coffee increase, what would happen to coffee prices? If the supply increased and the demand fell, what would happen to coffee prices?

8. Which of the following statements uses incorrect terminology? Explain.

   a. ''The recent fare war among the major airlines has increased the demand for air travel.''

   b. ''The recession of 1981–82 has caused the demand for air travel to fall.''

9. What are the factors held constant along the demand curve? Explain how each can shift the demand curve to the right. Explain how each can shift the demand curve to the left.

10. What are the factors held constant along the supply curve? Explain how each factor can shift the supply curve to the right. Explain how each factor can shift the supply curve to the left.

11. Why is the demand curve downward-sloping?

12. Why is the supply curve normally upward-sloping? Can you think of any exceptions?

13. What is the effect of each of the following events on the equilibrium price and quantity of hamburgers?

   a. An increase in the price of steak (a substitute for hamburgers).

   b. An increase in the price of french fries (a complement.

   c. A given population becomes older.

   d. The government requires that all the ingredients of hamburgers be absolutely fresh (that is, nothing can be frozen).

   e. Beef becomes more expensive.

   f. More firms enter the hamburger business.

Suggested Readings

Kohler, Heinz. *Intermediate Microeconomics: Theory and Applications,* 2nd ed. Glenview, Ill.: Scott, Foresman, 1986.

Leftwich, Richard H. and Ansel M. Sharp. *Economics of Social Issues,* 3rd ed. Dallas: Business Publications, Inc., 1978, chap. 2.

Manne, Henry G. ''The Parable of the Parking Lots.'' In *The Public Interest* 23 (Spring 1971): 10–15.

North, Douglass C. and Roger LeRoy Miller. *The Economics of Public Issues,* 5th ed. New York: Harper and Row, 1980, chap. 1.

Stigler, George. *The Theory of Price,* rev. ed. New York: Macmillan, 1952, chaps. 1 & 3.

II

Macroeconomics

5

Macroeconomic Concepts

Chapter Preview

Microeconomics is the study of the economy "in the small." It explains the behavior of firms and households in the marketplace. The basic analytical tool of microeconomics is supply-and-demand analysis. The most important concept of microeconomics is the notion that market equilibrium occurs when the market price equates the quantity demanded with the quantity supplied.

In contrast, *macroeconomics* is the study of the economy "in the large." The basic analytical tools of macroeconomics are the aggregate demand and aggregate supply curves previewed in this chapter. Macroeconomics explains how the economy as a whole behaves: why the unemployment rate sometimes rises and sometimes falls, why inflation is high or low, why the total output of goods and services increases or decreases, why interest rates rise or fall, and what policies could be pursued to reduce inflation or to limit unemployment. Macroeconomics looks at the economy at the highest possible level of *aggregation* (or "grouping together"). Rather than studying consumers and producers in all possible single markets, all consumers in the entire economy are lumped together in an examination of total consumption spending; all business investment is lumped together to study total investment spend-

ing; all firms are lumped together to learn about the total production of the economy. Because macroeconomics examines the entire economy, aggregate measures of prices, employment, and production are necessary. Macroeconomists must be able to measure total economic output, the price level, and the national unemployment rate. Chapter 6 will be devoted to the measurement of total output, or *national income accounting*. This chapter will introduce the major problems of macroeconomics: inflation, unemployment, stagflation, and the business cycle.

Macroeconomics is in a state of flux. Economists disagree on the causes and cures of inflation and unemployment. They disagree on the effects of budget deficits on inflation and interest rates. They offer different explanations of the causes of high interest rates. Most of all, they disagree on the appropriate policy responses to macroeconomic problems. Societies must make macroeconomic policy even though these issues are far from resolved. As our understanding of macroeconomics improves, macroeconomic policy should improve as well. The following chapters will report the solutions to the major macroeconomic problems that have been offered by different economists. ■

THE SCOPE OF MACROECONOMICS

The Ideal Macroeconomic World

If we had our choice, we would like a world in which all able-bodied persons wishing to work had satisfactory jobs. Prices would be stable, and living standards would rise steadily. In such a world, the economy would avoid both *busts* (significant downward movements in economic activity) and *booms* (sharp upward movements in economic activity). Progress would be steady and secure. This ideal world would not be subject to sudden external shocks, such as worldwide crop failures or unexpected and dramatic movements in energy or raw-material prices. Businesses and consumers could be confident of a bright and predictable future.

This ideal macroeconomic world is far removed from economic reality. The pace of economic expansion is not steady. During one period, economic activity is expanding; in the following period, economic activity contracts. During the boom period, jobs are easy to find, but prices may be driven up. During the bust period, jobs are scarce, but prices are stable or even falling. Some people who wish to be employed are without jobs. They and their families suffer from the loss of income and society loses the output they would have produced if they had jobs. Prices are not stable. During some periods, prices rise at a rapid pace. At other times, they rise at a moderate rate. On rare occasions, prices even fall throughout the economy. In some countries (such as Germany from 1920 to 1923), there have even been episodes of price increases so rapid that the economy as a whole has been paralyzed.

Society would welcome an ideal world of ample jobs, stable prices, and steadily rising living standards. Although this ideal world has not been achieved, policymakers should at least strive to approximate it as closely as possible. The task of macroeconomics is to explain rising or falling prices, rising or falling unemployment, and movements in the level of business activity.

What Macroeconomics Must Explain

In microeconomics, supply and demand determine equilibrium prices and quantities in specific markets. In individual markets, it is useful to know the market price and the equilibrium quantity of the good traded in the marketplace. In macroeconomics, there is a similar interest in price—not in individual prices but in the *general price level* (or the movement of prices generally in the economy). The general price level is (roughly speaking) an average price of all goods and services in the economy. This chapter explains how to measure this average price and its movement over time. In macroeconomics, there is also an interest in output—not in the output of one good or service but in the output of all goods and services. Once we are able to explain movements in the general price level or movements in the total output of all goods and services produced by the economy, we are in a position to understand the two most important macroeconomic problems: inflation and unemployment. Inflation is nothing more than an upward movement in the general price level. By explaining how and why the general price level moves, we have explained inflation. The change in the total output of goods and services explains unemployment. In the short run, the amount of employment (and unemployment) in the economy is related to the total volume of goods and services produced. If the economy produces large amounts of goods and services, employment will be high and unemployment will be low. If the total output of goods and services is expanding, employment should be expanding and unemployment should be contracting. Moreover, material standards of living are determined by the total output of the economy. Living standards improve, on average, when the output of goods and services expands more rapidly than population expands.

UNEMPLOYMENT

The problems of unemployment and inflation are central issues of macroeconomics. The federal government is committed by the Employment Act of 1946 to create and maintain "useful employment opportunities . . . for those able, willing, and seeking to work." In devising macroeconomic policy, unemployment, therefore, has played and continues to play an important role.

Example 1   Unemployment Statistics and the Discouraged Worker

According to the official definition of unemployment, people who are without a job, looking for work, and available for work are classified as being unemployed. But what about the person who has looked for a job without success and decides that jobs are simply not available? If that person ceases to look for a job as a consequence of a disappointing job search, then that person would be counted officially as not being in the labor force. Because the person is not currently looking for work, he or she is not classified as being unemployed.

Workers who have dropped out of the search for jobs because they conclude they cannot find jobs are called *discouraged workers*. Some critics of established unemployment statistics claim that the number of discouraged workers should be added to the number of unemployed to obtain a more accurate picture of unemployment.

In its surveys, the Bureau of Labor Statistics does ask those persons not in the labor force their reasons for not seeking work. Of those not in the labor force, 90 percent answered (in 1982) that they "do not want a job now." The discouraged workers are those respondents who declared they were not looking for a job because they think they "cannot get a job for job-related factors." The number of such discouraged workers was 1.2 million. In 1982, the number of unemployed workers was 10.7 million for an unemployment rate of 9.7 percent. If discouraged workers were to be counted as unemployed, the 1982 unemployment rate would be raised from 9.7 to almost 11 percent. ■

Source: U.S. Department of Labor, Bureau of Labor Statistics, *Handbook of Labor Statistics,* December 1983, Bulletin 2175.

The Measurement of Unemployment

Every month, the Bureau of the Census surveys 60,000 households to gather information on their labor-market activities during the preceding week. The Bureau of Labor Statistics (BLS) then processes this information to estimate the number of Americans employed and unemployed in that month. An estimate of the total **unemployment rate** based on a scientifically selected sample of this magnitude should be reasonably accurate. The Bureau of Labor Statistics classifies each person 16 years or older into one of three categories: 1) employed[1] 2) unemployed, or 3) not in the **labor force**.

> The **unemployment rate** is defined as the number unemployed divided by the number in the labor force.

> The **labor force** equals the number of employed plus the number unemployed.

A person is classified as *unemployed* if he or she 1) did not work at all during the reference week, 2) actively looked for work during the previous four weeks, and 3) is currently available for work. "Actively looking for work" means registering at an employment office, being on a union or professional job register, answering help-wanted ads, or asking friends and relatives about job openings. Persons laid off from jobs or waiting to report to a new job within 30 days are also classified as unemployed.

Persons without jobs who do not meet these three conditions are classified as *not in the labor force*. A person is not in the labor force for one of two reasons: the person either chooses not to work or is a **discouraged worker**.

> A **discouraged worker** is a worker who does not actively seek work in the belief that no job is available in his or her line of work.

People may choose to remain outside the labor force for a variety of reasons. Examples of such people are women with young children, students, persons disabled or suffering prolonged ill health, or retired persons.

Unlike the first group, discouraged workers in an important sense do not choose to be out of the

---

1. One is employed if one worked at least one hour as a paid employee or in one's own business or at least 15 hours as an unpaid worker in a family business during the reference week. If a person had a job but was on vacation, ill, or absent due to poor weather or a labor dispute, that person is also counted as employed.

Figure 1   The Unemployment Rate, 1900–1985

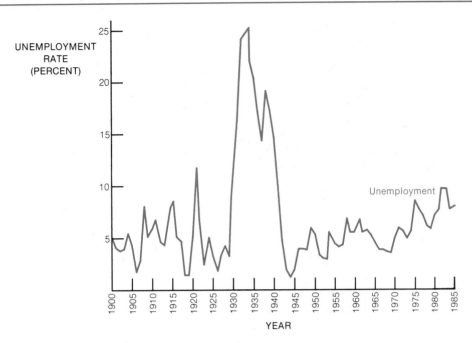

The unemployment rate has been rising in recent years, but it is far from reaching the level experienced during the Great Depression of the 1930s.

Source: *Historical Statistics of the United States,* 1970, p. 126; *Economic Report of the President.*

labor force. They remain out of the labor force because they have concluded that jobs are not available for them.

Government statisticians and economists have debated whether discouraged workers should be counted as unemployed or not in the labor force. The current practice is to publish separate statistics on discouraged workers but not to count them as unemployed. (See Example 1.)

Historical Trends in Unemployment

Figure 1 shows long-term trends in unemployment since 1900. The unemployment rate has been subject to significant year-to-year fluctuations. It has varied from lows of near 1 percent to a high of 25 percent during the Great Depression of the 1930s. The massive unemployment of the 1930s is the principal reason we refer to this period as the Great Depression. A 25 percent unemployment rate means that one out of every four

persons seeking work was out of a job. It is no wonder that the Great Depression had a great effect on macroeconomic theory and that many Americans who experienced the Great Depression firsthand harbor a deep fear of mass unemployment.

Between 1900 and 1947, distinct trends in the unemployment rate are not apparent, but since the 1960s, the unemployment rate has moved generally upward. During the period after World War II, the unemployment rate was generally in the range of 2.5 percent to 5.5 percent up to 1960. After 1960, unemployment rates of 5 to 9 percent became commonplace. In the 1960s, the unemployment rate ranged from 3.4 percent to 6.5 percent. In the 1970s, the annual average ranged from 4.8 percent to 8.3 percent. In the first half of the 1980s, the range was from 7 percent to 9.5 percent. As these figures show, there has been a distinct upward trend in the unemployment rate in the post–World War II period.

Types of Unemployment

Unemployment is a complex and varied phenomenon. It is clear that those people without jobs who do not want to hold jobs (such as full-time homemakers, retired people, or full-time college students) are not categorized as unemployed. They are simply not in the labor force. Of those who meet the three criteria of unemployment (being without a job, seeking work, and being available for employment), there are different degrees of *voluntariness* to their unemployment. At one extreme is the unemployed family head—the sole income-earner in the family—who cannot find work even though he or she is prepared to accept virtually any job offered. There is no question that this unemployment is entirely involuntary. At the other extreme is the unemployed person who narrows his or her job search to a difficult-to-find job (such as professional acting on Broadway). Until that specific job comes along, the person remains unemployed. Many would agree that there is a strong voluntary element to this unemployment. The majority of the unemployed fall in between these two extremes. People have job preferences; they have regional preferences; they have been trained through formal schooling or on-the-job training for jobs in specific fields. If they find themselves unemployed, they will not be prepared to accept any job that is available. The trained engineer would prefer to wait for a suitable job in engineering rather than to accept work as a janitor or fast-food manager. The textile worker whose mill has closed down in New England may be reluctant to relocate in the South where mill jobs are available. The fired corporation president, not wishing to return to the ranks of middle management, is prepared to wait for a corporation presidency to become available. For the unemployed person who passes up what appear to be suitable jobs given that person's skill, training, and regional preferences, there is a stronger voluntary element than for the unemployed person who is willing to accept virtually any reasonable job offer. There are no accepted ground rules for differentiating unemployment that is less voluntary from unemployment that is more voluntary. The issue of voluntariness in unemployment is highly controversial in macroeconomics.

Economists identify three types of unemployment—*frictional unemployment, cyclical unemployment,* and *structural unemployment*—that differ in degree of voluntariness. In the real world, it is often difficult to separate out the different types of unemployment, but economists find these distinctions useful in organizing their thinking about unemployment.

Frictional Unemployment.

Business conditions are constantly changing. Employment opportunities are being created in one business, region, or industry at the same time that they are being lost in others. Employed workers are usually on the lookout for better jobs; employers are usually on the lookout for better workers. The amount of information about job opportunities that one worker possesses is incomplete. The amount of information potential employers have about prospective employees is incomplete as well.

People are constantly entering and leaving the labor force. In this sense, the labor market is like a revolving door that is in constant motion. People and firms are constantly gathering information about jobs and worker qualifications. At any point in time, some workers will be changing from one job to another. Some will be reentering the labor force; others will be leaving the labor force. The labor force is in a constant state of flux, and the result is **frictional unemployment**.

> **Frictional unemployment** is the unemployment associated with the changing of jobs in a dynamic economy.

Frictional unemployment will always be with us. Its magnitude depends upon the age, sex, occupational, and racial composition of the labor force and upon how rapidly the economy itself is changing. At the individual level, frictional unemployment depends upon the costs and benefits of job searching and job changing. (Job search will be discussed in a later chapter.) Typically, frictional unemployment is of less concern to economists and policymakers than other types of unemployment. In fact, frictional unemployment may improve economic well-being. If the frictionally unemployed are moving into better jobs, then they (and society) are benefiting.

Frictional unemployment would disappear only if people were frozen into their current jobs by a static economy in which opportunities for job advancement had disappeared or if no one left a job until they had already found a new one. Although frictional unemployment is always present in a dynamic economy, society may wish to implement measures to keep it to a minimum. Any measure that increases the flow of information concerning job opportunities or that speeds up the job-search process tends to reduce frictional unemployment.

Cyclical Unemployment. Unlike frictional unemployment, **cyclical unemployment** carries with it no benefits for the unemployed (or society).

> **Cyclical unemployment** is unemployment associated with general downturns in the economy.

During cyclical downturns, fewer goods and services are purchased in the aggregate, employers cut back on jobs, and people find themselves without jobs. Many workers in basic industrial employment (steel, autos, farm equipment) will be unemployed for some period of time and return to their jobs only when the economy improves. Unlike the job changes associated with frictional unemployment, the job changes associated with cyclical unemployment are largely involuntary. People become unemployed because their jobs evaporate in a generally declining economy.

Structural Unemployment.   In a dynamic (changing) economy, some industries, companies, and regions experience a general increase in their economic fortunes at the same time that others experience a long-term decline. In declining industries—particularly those concentrated in specific regions of the country—employees suffer **structural unemployment**.

> **Structural unemployment** is the unemployment that results from the long-run decline of certain industries. Industries may decline because of rising costs, changes in consumer preferences, or technological advances that make the industry's product obsolete.

Long-term structural unemployment is especially prominent when it is concentrated in a specific region of the country. An example of such structural unemployment would be the high unemployment in the Appalachian coal-mining re-

gions associated with the long-term decline in underground coal mining prior to the energy crisis of the 1970s. More recent examples are the declining number of jobs in "smoke-stack America"—predominantly the steel industry. A primary concern about structural unemployment is that the people hit hardest by it are those who find it most difficult to relocate. Workers over fifty who have devoted a lifetime of work to underground coal mining would find it difficult (and perhaps not economically worthwhile) to leave family and friends behind to move to areas where jobs may be available.

Structural unemployment raises serious policy questions. On the one hand, economists and policymakers recognize the human hardship caused by structural unemployment. People are faced with the difficult choice of remaining unemployed, pulling up roots, or undergoing extensive retraining. But structural unemployment is, after all, caused by the declining fortunes of contracting industries. Most economists would agree that it would be unwise to counteract structural unemployment by propping up declining industries that cannot be operated profitably in the long run. It is within the power of government—through protection, subsidies, and other preferential treatment—to keep failing industries in business. If the industry cannot compete on its own, however, then government supports are simply delaying structural unemployment to some future date.

Involuntary unemployment, either cyclically induced or structurally induced, has both social and private costs. If an otherwise productive person remains involuntarily idle, society has lost the output that that person could have produced. The involuntarily unemployed person loses the income he or she would have earned. A later chapter will discuss in more detail the human costs of unemployment.

Full Employment

Must every able-bodied person currently have a job for full employment to exist? The answer is no because many people of working age do not wish to be employed—such as the full-time homemaker, the student, or the early retiree. Does full employment exist when everyone actively looking for work and available for work currently has a job? The answer is again no. If there were absolutely no unemployment, the economy would lack the frictional unemployment that any changing economy must have. People must have the opportunity to search out better jobs, to move from dead-end positions into more promising positions. Firms must have the opportunity to test the skills of new employees. People will naturally weigh the costs and benefits of changing jobs and of entering into the search for jobs.

Over the years, macroeconomists have come to accept the notion that full employment occurs when the ever-shifting labor market is in balance. In a dynamic economy, jobs are created while other jobs disappear. Some people enter or reenter the labor force while others withdraw or retire. In some professions, there may be more job applicants than jobs. In other professions, there may be more jobs than applicants. The complex labor market is in approximate balance when the number of jobs being created roughly equals the number of applicants available to fill those jobs. As new jobs are created or as people vacate established jobs, people with the appropriate skills and qualifications are entering the labor force or moving from other jobs to fill these vacancies. There may be imbalances in particular occupations or industries, but on average there can be a balance between the number of unfilled jobs and the number of qualified job seekers. The unemployment rate at which this balance is attained is called the **natural rate of unemployment**.

> The **natural rate of unemployment** is that unemployment rate at which there is an approximate balance between the number of unfilled jobs and the number of qualified job seekers. Modern macroeconomists consider the natural rate of unemployment to be full employment.

Economists' perception of what constitutes full employment has been changing over the years. In the early 1960s, the President's Council of Economic Advisers felt that full employment was reached at an unemployment rate of around 4 percent. In the late 1970s, the President's Council of Economic Advisers raised its estimate of full employment to an unemployment rate of 5 to 5.5 percent. In the 1980s, there is a continuing controversy about what to designate as the natural rate of unemployment. The full-employment rate depends upon a number of conditions that will be discussed in subsequent chapters. As subsequent chapters will explain, when labor markets are in balance, inflationary pressures remain the same. When an economy operates at its natural rate of unemployment, the prevailing rate of inflation should continue.

INFLATION

For much of our recent history (especially during the 1970s), **inflation** has been one of our economy's most persistent and intractable problems.

> **Inflation** is a general increase in prices.

A general increase in prices occurs when prices in the entire economy are rising on average. During an inflation, some prices rise faster than the average increase, and some rise slower. Some prices can even fall during inflations. For example, the prices of pocket calculators, home computers, and silicon chips fell throughout the inflationary 1970s and early 1980s. On the other hand, crude-oil prices rose between 1972 and 1981 five times faster than the average price increase. How the average rate of change of prices (the rate of inflation) is calculated in a world of changing relative prices is discussed below.

Whether inflation is perceived as moderate or rapid is a relative matter. In the mid-1950s, when prices were rising about 2 percent per year or less, an inflation rate of 5 percent would have been viewed with alarm. In fact, the "alarming" 1966 inflation rate of 3.3 percent motivated government authorities to impose strict anti-inflationary measures. By the mid-1980s, after several years of near double-digit inflation, an inflation rate of 5 percent was welcomed as a remarkable achievement. In countries like Israel and Brazil with prices that have more than doubled annually in recent years, the American inflation rates of the late 1970s and early 1980s would be the object of envy. The rate of inflation—just like any other measure of prices—must be evaluated in relative terms.

The Measurement of Inflation

If all prices rose at the same rate—say, 7 percent per year—there would be no problem measuring the general increase in prices. The inflation rate under these circumstances would obviously be 7 percent per annum. But prices do not change at the same rate; some prices rise more rapidly than others. For example, prices of food products rose 295 percent between 1967 and 1984, while housing prices rose 362 percent, apparel prices rose 200 percent, transportation prices rose 311 percent, and entertainment prices rose 255 percent. In other words, relative prices were changing while prices in general were rising.

A **price index** compares the cost of a given combination of goods in two or more different years. If a certain *market basket* (a combination of goods and services consumed by a typical family) costs $200 in 1985 and $220 in 1986, the price index is 110 ($220/$200 times 100) for 1986 in 1985 dollars. In other words, prices were 10 percent higher in 1986 than in 1985.

A **price index** shows the current year's cost of a particular market basket as a percentage of the cost of the same market basket in some base year.

Price index =

Cost of standard market basket in current year
————————————————————————————
  Cost of standard market basket in base year
  × 100.

Obviously, the value of this price index is 100.0 in the base year:

$$\frac{\$200}{\$200} \times 100 = 100.0.$$

To calculate the percentage change in prices between year 2 and year 1, the following formula can be used:

Percentage Change in Prices =

Year 2 Price Index − Year 1 Price Index
————————————————————————
          Year 1 Price Index

For example, if the year 2 price index is 150 and the year 1 price index is 125, then the percentage change in prices would be calculated as:

$$\frac{150 - 125}{125} = 20 \text{ percent.}$$

The Consumer Price Index (CPI).   The most prominent price index is the Consumer Price Index, or CPI.[2] The CPI is one of the most important statistics in the American economy. The CPI is calculated by the Bureau of Labor Statistics based on prices collected in 85 urban areas from about 24,000 establishments. Newspapers, radio, and television report monthly changes in the CPI. The public may form expectations concerning the future rate of inflation from past and current movements in the CPI. Presidents may be voted out of office because of public concern over soaring inflation. Moreover, the wages of some 8.5 million union workers and government employees are tied to the CPI: if the CPI goes up, wages are adjusted to reflect the higher cost of living. The rates of increase of many government pensions, including 38 million Social Security pensions and more than 3 million military pensions, are tied to the CPI. Starting in 1985, federal-income-tax rates are adjusted to prevent inflation-induced tax-rate increases. Government policies toward inflation tend to be based on the CPI. For these reasons, it is important that the CPI be an accurate gauge of the rate of increase in consumer prices.

There are several conceptual difficulties in measuring general trends in consumer prices. Because the CPI is calculated by determining how much a specified market basket of goods cost in different years, critics of the CPI maintain that it exaggerates the rate of inflation. The CPI assumes, in effect, that consumers do not make substitutions for products whose relative prices are increasing. In reality, if the relative price of beef rises, consumers substitute poultry, fish, or pork, often without a great loss of consumer satisfaction. Consumers respond to rising movie prices

---

2. The CPI is prepared by the Bureau of Labor Statistics (BLS). To compile the CPI, the BLS collects on a monthly basis prices from 85 areas across the country in about 24,000 trade and service establishments. The prices of thousands of goods and services are recorded. They are converted into a consumer price index by weighting each commodity group by its share of the average expenditures in 1972–73 of a typical urban family of four having an intermediate budget. In other words, the weights used to average the prices that enter into the CPI are taken to be the market basket of a hypothetical average American family. What does this typical market basket look like? In 1972–73, an average urban four-person family spent 24.8 percent of its budget on food, 22.5 percent on housing, 8.4 percent on transportation, and 44.5 percent on other items such as medical care, clothing, and services.

Figure 2   Inflation Measures: The Consumer Price Index and the GNP Deflator, 1951–1984

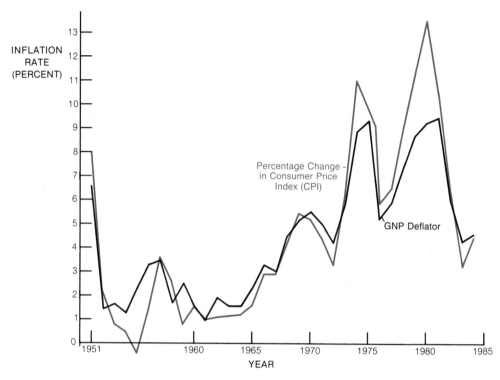

This chart shows that the rate of inflation as measured by the CPI and GNP deflator accelerated sharply from the early 1960s to 1980. After 1980, the inflation rate slowed down.

Source: *Statistical Abstract of the United States,* 1980, p. 486; *Economic Report of the President.*

by substituting other forms of entertainment, according to the law of demand. But the CPI assumes that consumers continue to consume the same mix of goods year after year even though relative prices are changing. By making substitutions, however, families can actually reduce the rate of increase in their cost of living below the measured CPI inflation rate.

The CPI measures the rate of inflation experienced by urban consumers (and by urban wage and clerical workers). Only those families that happen to consume the same market basket of goods as the hypothetical 1972–73 average urban family will have the same personal rate of inflation. A family's personal rate of inflation can be quite different from that indicated by the CPI. For example, housing costs have been one of the most rapidly rising components of the CPI. However, if a family happens to already own their own home financed at a fixed low mortgage rate, their

personal housing costs are not rising as rapidly as the CPI indicates. In this case, the CPI exaggerates the rate of inflation.[3] For other families (such as the elderly or ill who spend a large portion of their income on medical care that has a relatively high inflation rate), the CPI understates the family's rate of inflation.

The GNP Deflator.   The CPI measures changes in the prices of only those goods and services that families purchase for their own consumption. It does not measure the other goods and services that the economy produces for uses

3. In response to growing criticisms, the Bureau of Labor Statistics prepared a new variant of the CPI, which was officially issued in 1983. The revised CPI changes the way housing costs are treated by the CPI. Instead of measuring changes in housing prices and the costs of financing housing purchases, the revised CPI measures what it hypothetically costs homeowners to rent their own homes. The revised CPI is used to index Social Security benefits and to index individual income-tax rates as of 1985.

Figure 3   The U.S. Price Level, 1800–1984

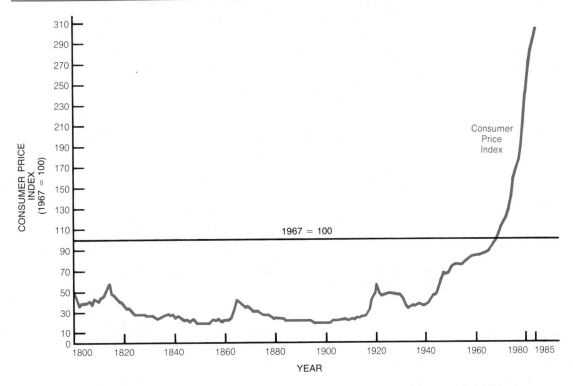

The price level has continuously risen since World War II, deviating from the pattern of the preceding 140 years.

Source: *Historical Statistics of the United States*, 1970, p. 291; *Economic Report of the President*.

other than personal consumption. In 1984, 65 percent of the *gross national product* (GNP), or the total output of the American economy, was devoted to personal consumption. The remaining 35 percent was expanded on business investment, government services, and exports and imports. The CPI, therefore, is not the most general measure of the rate of inflation. A more general measure is the *GNP deflator*. The GNP deflator measures the change in the prices of all final goods and services produced by the economy. Over the past 34 years, the GNP deflator has not behaved much differently from the CPI. Both the CPI and the GNP deflator show that prices have increased by a factor of 4.5 between 1950 and 1984, but in individual years the two indexes sometimes diverge. Because the GNP deflator is a more general measure of inflation, many of the inflation figures subsequently cited in this book are based on the GNP deflator.

Historical Trends.   Figure 2 shows the pattern of inflation since 1950 as measured by the annual rate of change in the Consumer Price Index and by the GNP deflator. This chart shows why most of the readers of this book have come to think of rising prices as one of the constants of life along with death and taxes: the CPI has shown a price decrease in only one of the last 34 years (1955). Figure 2 shows that the annual inflation rate trended upward from 1960 to the early 1980s. The average annual inflation rate in the 1960s was 2.5 percent (GNP deflator), in the first half of the 1970s was 5.8 percent, and in the second half of the 1970s was 7.6 percent. The mid-1980s, however, have witnessed a retreat from the high inflation rates of the late 1970s and early 1980s.

Trends in inflation over the past two centuries are plotted in Figure 3. This figure reveals that the sustained increases in consumer prices characteristic of the past 34 years are a fairly new phenomenon. If one stops at around 1930, U.S. experience shows that prices were as likely to fall as to rise. Prior to the Second World War, there were significant movements of the price level in both directions. *Deflations* (downward movements in prices) were just as common as *inflations* (upward movements in prices). The unusual features of the years since World War II has been the notable absence of periods of deflation. Unlike earlier periods when periods of inflation tended to be balanced by subsequent periods of deflation, the postwar era has been one of continuing increases in prices, albeit at different rates. The deflation of the early 1930s was clearly associated with the severe economic downturn of the Great Depression.

The facts show that inflation is not inevitable, even though it may appear so to the current generation. Later chapters will explore what is different about the postwar era.

Types of Inflation

A general rise in prices can occur for different reasons. Economists differentiate between two general types of inflation: demand-side inflation and supply-side inflation.

Demand-Side Inflation.   Inflation has been described as "too many dollars chasing too few goods." **Demand-side inflation** is the "too many dollars" side of the inflation equation.

> **Demand-side inflation** occurs when the amount of money purchasers of goods and services want to spend increases more rapidly than the supply of such goods and services, resulting in the bidding up of prices.

The increase in demand pulls up the general level of prices. Demand-side inflation is caused by any event that motivates consumers or firms to desire to purchase more goods and services than they previously desired to purchase. Subsequent chapters will discuss a number of factors that raise the number of desired purchases.

Supply-Side Inflation.   **Supply-side inflation** is the "too few goods" side of the inflation equation.

> **Supply-side inflation** occurs when increases in prices of inputs caused by autonomous reductions in their supply generally cause firms to reduce their offerings of goods and services to the market at prevailing prices, resulting in the bidding up of their prices.

The increase in costs pushes up the general price level. An example of supply-side inflation is the increase in energy prices that occurred in the 1970s due to the formation of OPEC and to the Iran-Iraq war, which raised costs of production generally throughout the world economy. In later chapters, we shall discuss both sides of the inflation equation. What causes the demand for goods and services to increase more rapidly than the supply of such goods and services? What causes business firms to reduce the quantities of goods and services they are prepared to supply at prevailing prices?

According to its definition, inflation is a general increase in prices. As such, inflation can be anything from a slow upward creep in prices to a runaway increase in prices, known as a **hyperinflation.**

> A **hyperinflation** is a very rapid and often accelerating rate of inflation.

At a minimum, prices would double every year in a hyperinflation. At worst, inflation could double daily or even hourly. Different countries have experienced hyperinflations in the course of their histories. A number of South American countries and Israel are among the many countries that are currently experiencing hyperinflation. In 1984, for example, the annual inflation rate in Israel was 800 percent, and the annual inflation rate in Argentina was 688 percent. The best known historical case of hyperinflation was the German hyperinflation of the 1920s which helped bring Hitler to power. In November of 1923, the German mark had fallen to the point where one American cent equaled 42 trillion marks! The American South experienced hyperinflation during the Civil War. People who have witnessed the destructive power of hyperinflation have a deep-rooted fear of inflation because they understand that hyperinflation can cause the destruction of the established social order.

Inflation and Interest Rates

High nominal interest rates tend to accompany high rates of inflation. The triple-digit inflation rates of Bolivia, Argentina, or Israel are accompanied by triple-digit interest rates. When U.S. inflation was running at its highest level in modern times in 1979–80 (see Figure 2), banks were charging credit-worthy customers more than 20 percent per year in interest charges. During the low inflation rates of the 1950s and early 1960s, banks charged credit-worthy customers 3.5 percent interest on bank loans. High inflation leads to a high **nominal interest rate.**

The **nominal interest rate** is the price of credit unadjusted for inflation. It is expressed as the ratio of annual dollar interest cost to the dollar amount loaned.

A 5 percent nominal interest rate means that the annual interest charge on a $1,000 loan is $50. A 10 percent nominal interest rate means that the annual interest charge on a $1,000 loan would be $100.

At a nominal interest rate of 10 percent, $100 not spent today will yield $110 that can be spent one year from today. A nominal interest rate of 5 percent means that $100 not spent today will yield only $105 that can be spent one year from today. Because lenders and borrowers are interested in how many goods and services can be purchased with money to be received in the future, they will consider both nominal interest rates and the rate of inflation.

Suppose that the nominal rate of interest is 10 percent and that prices are rising at 5 percent per year. In this case, a person lending $100 now will have $110 in one year. But $110 in one year buys only $105 worth of tomorrow's goods (approximately) because of generally rising prices (inflation). Because the $100 loaned today in reality buys only $105 worth of tomorrow's goods, the **real interest rate** is 5 percent.

The **real interest rate** is the price of credit adjusted for inflation. It is approximately equal to the nominal interest rate *minus* the annual rate of inflation.

It is important to distinguish between the *actual* real interest rate that is earned over a particular year and the real interest rate that is *antici-*

pated. No one knows for sure in advance what the rate of inflation will be. Therefore, no one will know in advance what the real rate of interest will be. When people borrow or lend money, they must make their best estimate of what the real rate of interest will be.

Logic tells us the general relationship between nominal interest rates and the rate of inflation. As the rate of inflation increases, people will be less willing to save at prevailing interest rates because rising prices reduce the purchasing power of tomorrow's income. Borrowers, on the other hand, will be more anxious to borrow as inflation increases. Rising inflation means that borrowers can repay loans in dollars that will purchase fewer goods than they could when the loan was made. These two forces tend to drive up nominal interest rates as the rate of inflation increases.

Decisions about providing for the future are guided by what people expect the *real* rate of interest to be in the immediate future. If the real interest rate is expected to be high, people will be more willing to refrain from consumption now; they will save for the future. If the real interest rate is expected to be low, businesses will be anxious to borrow for investment purposes. Because the future is uncertain (it is difficult to know what the inflation rate will be), lenders and borrowers may guess wrong about the real rate of interest, but it nevertheless serves as a guide to saving and investment decisions.

Effects of Inflation

People often worry about inflation out of a fear that rising prices will lower their standard of living. Alarming increases in housing prices, food prices, and so on are cited as proof that standards of economic well-being are falling. This fear is a classic example of the *ceteris paribus* fallacy discussed in Chapter 1. During inflations, prices of outputs and inputs, wages, rents, and interest rates tend to rise together. While the prices of the things we buy tend to rise, so do the prices of the things we sell (such as labor). Living standards are determined by the relationship between the income people have to spend and the prices they have to pay. If income (or the wage rate) is rising faster than prices, living standards are rising; if income is rising slower than prices, living standards are falling. The relationship between changes in income and changes in prices determines the direction of change in economic well-being.

To illustrate the logical fallacy of equating rising prices with falling living standards and of equating falling prices with rising living standards, we can compare the Great Depression of the 1930s with the inflationary 1970s. Between 1929 and 1933, there was a 25 percent drop in prices while people's incomes fell by 45 percent. Falling prices did not result in a rise in living standards. Because incomes fell more than prices between 1929 and 1933, living standards dropped even though prices were falling. Between 1970 and 1983, prices more than doubled (they went up by a factor of 2.4). However, people's incomes went up by more than three times (by a factor of 3.4). Even though the economy was experiencing high inflation, incomes rose more rapidly than prices; thus, living standards rose.

Although inflation does not automatically lower standards of living, inflation can be a serious problem for three reasons.
1. Inflation can redistribute income among members of society.
2. Inflation can cause a reduction in economic efficiency.
3. Inflation can cause changes in output and employment.

Income Redistribution.   Inflation tends to affect the economic well-being of members of society because it can redistribute income among families by causing the real incomes of some to rise and the real incomes of others to fall. Some people are poorly protected from inflation. In some professions, wages and earnings rise less rapidly than the rate of inflation. Examples of people who have a difficult time keeping up with inflation are persons on fixed pensions, domestic servants, some public employees (such as school teachers), and some recipients of public-welfare payments. Some workers and employees are protected or even benefit from inflation. Many union members have cost-of-living clauses in their contracts (called *COLAs* for "cost-of-living adjustments") that adjust wages based on the rate of inflation. In a typical COLA contract, wages are adjusted upward by an agreed-upon percentage of

the inflation rate. Borrowers who obtained loans when interest rates were low benefit from inflation by being able to pay off their loans in cheaper dollars. People who have purchased property—such as real estate, investment diamonds, or rare works of art—whose values have increased faster than inflation benefit from inflation.

Inflation is like a tax on fixed money receipts, or *assets,* and like a subsidy on fixed money payments, or *liabilities.* If one holds $10,000 or expects to receive $10,000 at some designated date in the future, inflation erodes its value. In this sense, inflation is like a tax on the $10,000. On the other hand, if one owes $10,000 to be repaid at some designated future date, inflation reduces the person's burden; in this sense, it is like a subsidy. During the period of time when payment obligations (rent payments, wage contracts, interest payments) are fixed, inflation redistributes real wealth from those who receive money to those who pay the money.

For example, suppose someone borrowed $40,000 in 1972 to buy a home at an annual interest rate of 7 percent to be paid over a 25-year period. In 1982, the borrower still owed the lender about $31,500 after 10 years. But over this 10-year period, the value of money that is still owed has been eroded by inflation. In 1982, $1.00 purchased what $.050 purchased in 1972 (the purchasing power of money in 1982 was about half of what it was in 1972). Hence, the borrower purchased a home by borrowing expensive dollars but repays in dollars that are growing cheaper as inflation continues. Wealth has been redistributed just as if the lender had paid a tax to the borrower.

The distributional effect of inflation depends upon the extent to which inflation is anticipated. Creditors and debtors are, of course, aware of the effects that inflation can have on their economic well-being. Is it not reasonable to assume that they will attempt to anticipate inflation in order to protect their economic interests? In our above example, the lender did not correctly anticipate the actual inflation that occurred between 1972 and 1982. (See Example 2.)

If in one year the rate of inflation is 8 percent, the next year it is 10 percent, and the next year it is 9 percent, people will begin to *anticipate,* say, a 9 percent rate of inflation per year, since the

Example 2   How Inflation Redistributes Income: Mortgages

Inflation redistributes income from lenders to borrowers when inflation is higher than generally expected, but the chances of incorrectly anticipating inflation are higher when inflation must be anticipated over a long time period. A classic case of incorrectly anticipating the inflation rate is the failure of savings-and-loan associations to anticipate the accelerating inflation of the 1970s. Savings & loans are the major suppliers of home-mortgage loans to home buyers. In the 1960s, such mortgage lenders made mortgage loans to home buyers for 15- to 30-year periods at fixed rates of interest. In making a 20-year mortgage in 1965, the mortgage lender had to estimate the average inflation rate through 1985 because the lender would receive fixed interest payments through 1985. The mortgage rate should be high enough to yield a reasonable return after adjustment for inflation.

In the second half of the 1960s, savings & loan mortgage rates averaged 6.5 percent per annum. These mortgage rates suggest that mortgage lenders in the second half of the 1960s were anticipating fairly low rates of inflation through the early 1980s. However, as Figure 2 shows, inflation ac-

celerated sharply in the 1970s, leaving savings & loans with a large volume of outstanding mortgage loans at low interest rates. The plight of the savings & loans is illustrated in the table below.

As a consequence of underestimating the long-run inflation rate, savings & loans were caught with outstanding loans with interest rates that were roughly equal to the annual inflation rate. After adjustment for inflation, the real interest rate was near 0 percent in 1980 and 1981. Even worse, savings & loans had to pay their depositors higher and higher interest rates as inflation soared. In 1981, they were paying their depositors 10.92 percent interest while their outstanding mortgage loans were yielding only 9.87 percent.

As a consequence of underestimating inflation, there was a transfer of income from the owners of the savings & loans to mortgage borrowers. Profits fell and stockholder dividends were reduced or eliminated. The stock prices of savings & loans fell, thereby reducing the wealth of the owners of savings & loans. ■

Sources: *Statistical Abstract of the U.S.* and *Economic Report of the President.*

	1970	1975	1978	1980	1981
Average interest return on home mortgages (%)	6.56	7.66	8.47	9.31	9.87
Average cost of borrowing funds (%)	5.3	6.32	6.67	8.94	10.92
Inflation rate (GNP deflator) %	5.4	9.3	7.4	9.2	9.4

actual rate will likely not diverge much from the average. Once an inflation becomes anticipated, individuals and firms will act to protect their interests. Fixed money contracts will be modified to take into account the erosion of money values. Creditors will realize that they are being paid in cheaper dollars and will ask for a higher interest rate to compensate them; debtors will realize that they are repaying in cheaper dollars and will be more willing to pay a higher interest rate. Landlords will ask for higher rents over the year or a shorter lease that they can renegotiate if inflation accelerates; workers will ask for a higher wage rate or a shorter contract period.

If inflation is correctly anticipated, it will not redistribute wealth from those scheduled to receive money to those scheduled to pay money. Money contracts will incorporate inflation premiums to protect recipients of payments from the effects of inflation.

Steady predictable inflation gives people the opportunity to avoid the inflation tax. If inflation is erratic and intermittent, it will be difficult for people to anticipate the actual rate of inflation. If the rate of inflation is 6 percent in one year, 18 percent the next, and 3 percent in the following

Figure 4   The Stagflation of the 1970s and Early 1980s

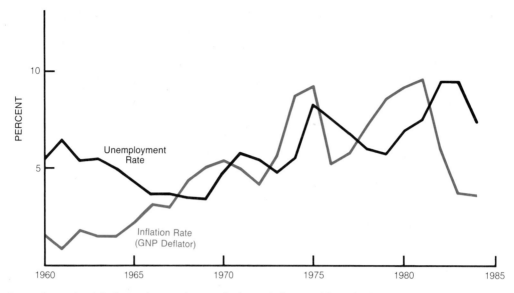

This figure shows that inflation and unemployment both trended upward from the late 1960s to the early 1980s. The combination of high inflation and high unemployment is *stagflation*.

Source: *Economic Report of the President*, 1984, pp. 225, 257.

year, the actual rate of inflation will be to a large extent unanticipated.

> **Inflation redistributes wealth from lenders to borrowers only when inflation is greater than anticipated.**

Inefficiency.   When inflation is intermittent, predicting the rate of inflation becomes a difficult business. The 1976 Nobel laureate in economics, Milton Friedman, points out that:

> Under such circumstances, the most valuable quality on the part of a businessman becomes his ability to forecast the changes in prices and to adjust rapidly to them. This becomes more important that his ability as organizer or as a manager or as a person who can see where there are profitable opportunities. The result is that some of the most valuable and scarcest resources in the economy are diverted into activities that are socially unproductive.[4]

4. Milton Friedman, *Dollars and Deficits* (Englewood Cliffs, N. J.: Prentice-Hall, 1968), pp. 49–50. Some examples of this can be found in the classic study of German hyperinflation by Costanino Bresciani-Turroni, *The Economics of Inflation* (London: Allen & Unwin, 1937).

Inflation leads to speculative practices that would otherwise be considered somewhat frivolous. By trying to outwit everyone else, those who expect more inflation than the marketplace expects will speculate in real estate, foreign currencies, gold (in January of 1981 the price of gold reached $850 per ounce), and art objects. Such speculative investments are made *in place of* investments in plants, equipment, and inventories that would raise the productive potential of the economy. Inflation causes people to rush to art auctions and to invest in questionable real-estate schemes to avoid the inflation tax. While the poor might be just trying to make ends meet, the rich are preoccupied in a rather useless game of musical chairs.

> **Anticipated inflation can divert resources from productive to unproductive investments and, thus, reduce the economy's productive capacity.**

The negative effects of inflation on economic efficiency are most pronounced during hyperinflations, when prices may double daily or even twice daily. Workers become reluctant to accept their wages in money (preferring to be paid in terms of products), and the money that is received is spent immediately. Businesses refuse to enter into fixed contracts, and most transactions involve barter exchanges of goods and services. In other words, hyperinflations result in the loss of the efficiency of money transactions. Most efforts in such an economy are directed at avoiding the inflation tax rather than at productive economic activities.

Changes in Real Output and Employment.

As just described, anticipated inflation can divert resources from productive to basically unproductive uses as people maneuver to avoid the inflation tax. But inflation can affect economic output and employment in a more direct manner by motivating firms to produce more or less than they would have otherwise and by motivating people to work or buy more or less than they would have otherwise.

Some economists believe that inflation (whether anticipated or unanticipated) has a negligible effect on output and employment. Other economists say that inflation, especially when it catches people by surprise, can have a significant and positive effect on output and employment. How inflation affects the amount of output produced will be explained in detail in later chapters. In fact, much of modern macroeconomic theory is devoted to this very question. For now, we can say that inflation (especially if it is not properly anticipated) can cause prices to rise more rapidly than costs. Wage rates may be subject to fixed contracts that do not allow wages to keep up with inflation. Input suppliers may have agreed to supply their products at fixed prices over a specified contract period. As prices rise more rapidly than costs, business firms consider themselves to be better off and increase their output and employment. In the course of an inflation, businesses and workers may even be fooled into thinking that inflation has made them better off in real terms when it has not.

STAGFLATION

Figure 1 shows that the unemployment rate trended upward from the 1960s to the 1980s. Figure 2 reveals that inflation also trended upward from the 1960s to the beginning of the 1980s. Figure 4 puts the information in these two figures together to show the problem of **stagflation.**

> **Stagflation** is the combination of high unemployment rates and high inflation over a period of time.

As Figure 4 shows, starting in the mid-1960s, both inflation and unemployment began to rise together. In fact, between 1966 and 1975, the two rose in almost perfect tandem. After 1975, inflation and unemployment continued to move together, following clear upward trends until the mid-1980s. The stagflation of the late 1960s and 1970s has spawned new macroeconomic theories of inflation and unemployment. Modern macroeconomic theory must be able to explain why inflation does not fall when unemployment is high.

BUSINESS CYCLES

Like prices and unemployment, trends in business activity are not smooth, neat, or completely predictable. Countries experience episodes of sharp reduction in the volume of total output and employment, which are followed by episodes of rapid growth of output and employment. Unemployment rates rise and then fall.

Over the very long run, economies tend to increase their total output of goods and services. The labor force grows with population; capital accumulation increases the nation's capital stock; technological improvements raise productive capacity. The American economy of 1985 produces a volume of output more than 20 times that of 1890. This increase translates into an annual rate of growth of 3.3 percent.

Many distinguished economists—such as Nobel laureate Simon Kuznets, Wesley Clair Mitchell, Joseph Schumpeter, Gottfried Haberler, N. D. Kondratieff, and Arthur Burns—have studied trends and movements in the level of business activity around the generally rising long-run trend in output, or the **business cycle.**

> A **business cycle** is the pattern of upward and downward movements in the general level of real business activity.

Economic research has discovered different types of business cycles: cycles of very short du-

Figure 5   The Phases of the Business Cycle

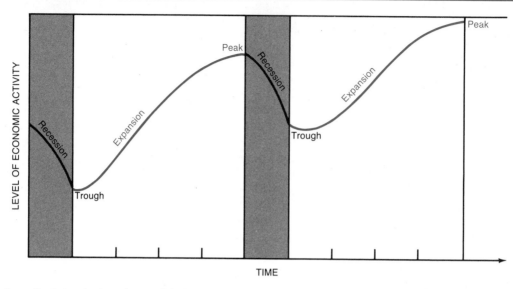

This figure illustrates the four phases of the business cycle. Since 1924, the average recession has lasted one year and the average recovery has lasted four years. Each peak in the figure is higher than the previous one because of the long-term growth of real GNP.

ration lasting one to two years, intermediate-term cycles lasting five years or so, and long-term cycles lasting a decade or more. There may even be *secular swings*—cycles lasting several decades or more. Some types of business cycles affect only one type of industry or business activity (such as home building or business inventory accumulation); other types of business cycles affect virtually all facets of business activity in all industries.

Recessions and Depressions

The terms *recession* and *depression* are commonly used in discussing business cycles, but few understand their exact meanings. The National Bureau of Economic Research (NBER) is a nonprofit private research organization that is accepted as an authority for deciding when a **recession** begins and ends.

> As a general rule, a **recession** occurs when real output declines for a period of six months or more.

The six-month-declining-output rule is not ironclad. If an economic downturn is especially severe, the NBER may classify it as a recession even if it lasts less than six months. A **depression** is more difficult to define precisely.

> A **depression** is a very severe downturn in economic activity that lasts for several years. Real output declines during this period by a significant amount, and the unemployment rate rises to very high levels.

A depression is a very severe and extended recession.

The Four Phases of the Business Cycle

Business cycles are divided into four phases, irrespective of their severity and duration. As Figure 5 shows, the four classic phases of the business cycle are:
1. downturn or recession (or depression if the decline in activity is prolonged and severe),
2. trough,

3. expansion (or recovery), and

4. peak.

During the *recession* phase, the level of business activity is in general decline. The various indexes of business activity (building permits, total output, employment, business formation, new orders) indicate that the economy is producing a declining rate of output. The unemployment rate rises, and the number employed declines (or the rate of increase in employment will slow down). The *trough* (or lowest point) occurs when the various indicators of business activity stop falling. The economy has reached a low point from which recovery begins.

During the *recovery* stage of the business cycle, the various output indicators point to expanding output. The final stage of the business cycle is reached at the *peak* when the various indicators of production and employment fail to yield further increases. When the next stage—recession—begins, the economy begins another business cycle.

Length of Cycles

The duration of a business cycle is the length of time it takes to move through one complete business cycle. The length of the business cycle can be measured either as the amount of time (number of months) between the peak of the cycle and the next peak or as the time it takes to move from trough to trough. The duration of the cycle varies by economy and time period and by the business-activity indicators being studied. No two business cycles are identical. Government studies of the American business cycle from 1924 to the present (see Table 1) show that the average duration of cycles is almost 5 years. The recession phase lasts, on the average, slightly less than one year. The expansion phase lasts, on the average, about four years.

Magnitude of Cycles

There is a big difference between small cyclical swings where the economy stays near full employment and large swings from boom to depression. During the Great Depression, real GNP fell in 1933 to 70 percent of its 1929 level. The unemployment rate rose from 3.2 percent in 1929 to

Table 1   American Business Cycles, 1924–1985

Trough	Peak	Length of Cycle, Peak to Peak (months)
July 1924	October 1926	41
November 1927	August 1929	34
March 1933	May 1937	93
June 1938	February 1945	93
October 1945	November 1948	45
October 1949	July 1953	56
May 1954	August 1957	49
April 1958	April 1960	32
February 1961	December 1969	116
November 1970	November 1973	47
March 1975	January 1980	62
July 1980	July 1981	12
November 1982	—	—

Source: U.S. Department of Commerce, *Handbook of Cyclical Indicators*, a Supplement to *Business Conditions Digest*, 1984, p. 178.

24.9 percent in 1933. During the recession of 1958, real GNP fell less than 1 percent, while the unemployment rate rose from 4.2 percent to 6.6 percent. The severe recession of 1982 saw a 2 percent fall in real GNP and a rise in the unemployment rate from 7.5 percent to 9.5 percent.

Business cycles affect different industries, occupations, and regions differently. Some industries, such as the auto, steel, and machine-building industries, are hit harder by economic downturns than others.

Leading Indicators

Literally hundreds of indicators may be used to measure the rhythm of the business cycle: the length of the average work week, the layoff rate, unemployment, total output, personal income, industrial production, stock prices, the number of new private housing units started, the volume of commercial and industrial loans, and so on. Such indicators tend to move together, but they do not move in the same phase with the basic rhythm of the business cycle. Some indicators lead the basic cycle; some are coincident with the cycle; others lag behind the basic cycle. From this point of view of economists and business forecasters, the

leading indicators are the most important because they may give information about the future.

> **Leading indicators** of business activity tend to rise or fall prior to the general rise or fall in business activity.

Figure 6 shows the composite (combined) index of 12 leading indicators from 1948 to 1984. The combined index is a weighted average of the 12 component indexes. The shaded areas show recession phases of the business cycle; the unshaded areas show expansion phases of the business cycle. Also shown are 4 of the 12 components of the composite index of leading indicators: new building permits, net inventory changes, stock prices, and the supply of money.

How good a job do the leading indicators do in warning of forthcoming recessions? Prior to each of the eight recessions shown in Figure 6, the index of leading indicators indeed dropped—but the amount of time between the drop and the recession varied. Sometimes the composite index begins to drop a year or more before the recession (two years before the 1957–58 recession, for example); other times it begins to drop just before the recession (4 months before the 1953–54 recession). Often drops in the index of leading indicators are not followed by recessions. For example, the 1960s was a decade of uninterrupted expansion, yet the index of leading indicators predicted three recessions during these years. Another problem is that the components of the composite index of leading indicators do not move together in exactly the same rhythm.

The role of leading indicators in predicting the future will be analyzed in more detail in later chapters. To devise sound countercyclical economic policy requires information about the timing, depth, and severity of recessions. Although the index of leading indicators is not a perfect guide to the future, it is one of the most important and widely used indicators in the economy.

A PREVIEW OF AGGREGATE SUPPLY-AND-DEMAND ANALYSIS

The behavior of aggregate supply and aggregate demand is as important to macroeconomics as the laws of supply and demand are to microeconom-

Figure 6   The Index of Leading Indicators and Four of Its Major Components (1967 = 100)

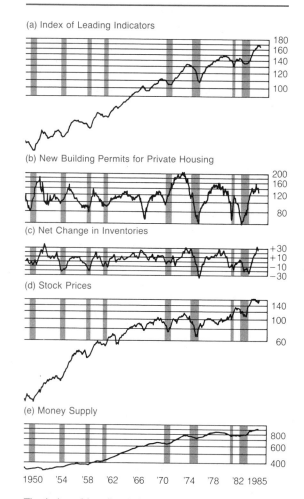

(a) Index of Leading Indicators

(b) New Building Permits for Private Housing

(c) Net Change in Inventories

(d) Stock Prices

(e) Money Supply

The Index of Leading Indicators is computed from 12 individual indexes, four of which are shown in this figure.

Source: Department of Commerce, *Business Conditions Digest.*

ics. Subsequent chapters will use aggregate supply-and-demand analysis to explain movements in general prices, total output, and employment. This section will briefly sketch the principles of aggregate supply-and-demand analysis and will allow later chapters to fill in the details.

Aggregate Demand

Aggregate demand *(AD)* is the relationship between the total demand for goods and services and the price level.

Figure 7   The Aggregate Demand and the Aggregate Supply Curves

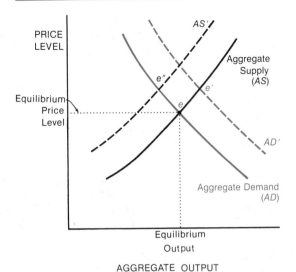

AGGREGATE OUTPUT

The aggregate demand curve, which shows the quantities of goods and services demanded at different price levels by all agents in the economy, will be negatively sloped. The aggregate supply curve, which shows the different quantities of goods and services supplied by all agents, will be positively sloped, at least in the short run. The intersection of the two curves determines the equilibrium level of aggregate output as well as the price level. An increase in aggregate demand (to the dashed color line) causes both prices and output to rise (to e'). A reduction in aggregate supply (to the dashed black line) causes prices to rise but output to fall (to e'').

Aggregate demand *(AD)* is a schedule of the amounts of goods and services agents in the economy (households, business firms, and government) are prepared to buy at different price levels.

The aggregate-demand curve in Figure 7 is negatively sloped. One cannot conclude that the aggregate demand curve is negatively sloping just because the demand curves of each product are negatively sloped. The law of demand is based upon relative prices and makes sense only when one price is changing relative to other prices. People substitute cheaper goods for more expensive goods when *relative* prices change. But if all prices rise (that is, if the *general* price level rises), there are no (or not enough) cheaper goods with which to substitute. Why does aggregate quantity demanded responds to changes in the general price level?

As will be explained in later chapters, a higher price level reduces the real value of financial wealth (the amount of goods and services that the accumulated money, stocks, bonds, and so on will purchase). Households, therefore, cut back on their purchases of cars, houses, clothing, and other items. A rising price level will also tend to raise interest rates, which tends to discourage purchases of investment goods and consumer goods. Higher prices mean that accumulated savings, for example, can buy fewer goods and services. Households with accumulated savings feel that they are less well off than before the price rise. As credit tightens, business firms cut back on investment spending. Households purchase fewer cars, washing machines, and houses. Tight credit motivates individuals and businesses throughout the economy to cut back on desired purchases.

Aggregate Supply

The black curve in Figure 7 is a curve of **aggregate supply** *(AS)*.

Aggregate supply *(AS)* is a schedule of various quantities of goods and services businesses are prepared to supply at different price levels.

Later chapters will demonstrate that the aggregate-supply curve is upward-sloping under certain conditions. Much of the discussion in modern macroeconomics today is over the shape and behavior of the aggregate-supply curve.

In the short run, the aggregate-supply curve can be positively sloped because a general rise in the price level will cause prices to rise more rapidly than costs, and this rate of increase will motivate profit-minded businesses to increase production and employment. Even if prices are not actually rising more rapidly than costs, businesses may perceive their prices to be rising when prices rise generally. Later chapters will show that a positive slope characterizes the aggregate-supply curve more in the short run than in the long run. In the long run, the aggregate-supply curve can be vertical: during inflations, prices, costs, and wages tend to rise at the same rate on average, leaving people and businesses no better or worse off than before the inflation. In such cases, inflation is little incentive to produce more.

Shifts in Aggregate Supply or Aggregate Demand

Aggregate supply-and-demand analysis is like microeconomic supply-and-demand analysis in the following way: the interaction of aggregate supply and aggregate demand determines the equilibrium price level and the equilibrium amount of goods and services produced. At point *e* in Figure 7, aggregate quantity demanded equals aggregate quantity supplied. As in microeconomics, changes in equilibrium will occur if the *AD* or *AS* curves shift.

Figure 7 illustrates the explanatory power of aggregate supply-and-demand analysis. The equilibrium point, *e,* represents the equilibrium level of prices and total output. Insofar as employment and unemployment are determined by the amount of output, the aggregate supply/demand equilibrium also explains employment and unemployment. Changes in aggregate supply and aggregate demand account for changes in the price level (inflation is an increase in the general price level), the unemployment rate, and the business cycle. An increase in aggregate demand (to the dashed color line) would tend to raise prices (demand-side inflation) and output and (hence) would reduce unemployment. On the other hand, a reduction in aggregate supply (to the dashed black line) would cause prices to rise (supply-side inflation) output to fall, and (hence) unemployment to rise. Considerable work is required to understand when, why, and how aggregate demand and aggregate supply curves shift.

The following chapters will explain how to work with aggregate-supply and aggregate-demand curves. Aggregate supply and aggregate demand have been previewed in this chapter to show their analytical power. By understanding aggregate supply and aggregate demand, one can deal with the major issues of modern macroeconomics. In order to understand macroeconomic effects on output, employment, and the price level, however, it is important to know how these economic variables are measured. The next chapter will examine how to define and measure aggregate economic output (Gross National Product) and its various components.

Summary

1. Macroeconomics is the study of the economy in the whole. Macroeconomists study inflation, unemployment, and the business cycle.

2. A person is unemployed if he or she is not working, is currently available for work, and is actively seeking a job. There are three main types of unemployment: frictional unemployment (normal changing of jobs in a changing economy), cyclical unemployment (associated with general downturns in the economy), and structural unemployment (resulting from long-term economic declines concentrated in specific industries or regions). Economists believe that full employment is reached at the natural rate of unemployment.

3. Inflation is a general increase in prices measured by price indexes that determine the changing cost of buying a standard market basket of goods. The most important price indexes are the consumer price index (the CPI) and the GNP deflator. The two types of inflation are demand-side inflation and supply-side inflation. Inflation can affect income distribution, efficiency, employment, and output.

4. In the United States, both the inflation rate and the unemployment rate trended up from the mid-1960s to the early 1980s. Modern macroeconomics must be able to explain the combination of high unemployment and high inflation, which is called *stagflation*.

5. A business cycle is the pattern of upward and downward movements in the level of business activity. A recession is a decline in real output that lasts six months or more. A depression is a very severe recession, lasting several years or more. The four phases of the business cycle are: recession, trough, recovery, and peak. Indicators of business activity that precede movements in the business cycle are leading indicators.

6. The aggregate-demand curve shows the quantity of goods and services demanded by all agents in the economy at different price levels. The aggregate-supply curve shows the quantity of goods and services supplied at different price levels. Aggregate supply-and-demand analysis is the principal tool of modern macroeconomics.

Key Terms

unemployment rate
labor force
discouraged worker
frictional unemployment
cyclical unemployment
structural unemployment
natural rate of unemployment
inflation
price index
demand-side inflation
supply-side inflation
hyperinflation
nominal interest rate
real interest rate
stagflation
business cycle
recession
depression
leading indicators
aggregate demand *(AD)*
aggregate supply *(AS)*

Questions and Problems

1. Explain why there tend to be both voluntary elements and involuntary elements to unemployment.

2. How would each of the following people be classified according to the official definition of unemployment?
a. The high-school student casually looking for an after-school job.
b. The person who quits his or her job to become a full-time homemaker.
c. The laid-off auto worker waiting to be recalled to his or her previous job.
d. The person who has quit a job to search for a better job.

3. Describe the relevant criteria by which government statisticians determine whether a person is ''unemployed'' or ''not in the labor force.''

4. Suppose economic conditions are generally good but that a further increase in gasoline prices has caused a slump in the automobile industry.

How would you classify unemployment in the automobile industry?

5. ''The rate of inflation has meaning only in relative terms.'' Evaluate this statement.

6. By analogy to microeconomics, explain why ''too many dollars chasing too few goods'' can cause inflation.

7. Explain how inflation can redistribute wealth from lenders to borrowers.

8. Explain why, in a society where prices are doubling every week, this hyperinflation would reduce economic efficiency.

9. In Figure 7, what would happen to prices, output, and unemployment if the aggregate-demand curve shifts to the left? What would happen to these variables if the aggregate-supply curve shifts to the right?

10. Explain the importance of leading indicators in predicting movements of the business cycle.

11. Use aggregate-supply and aggregate-demand curves to show how business cycles may arise.

12. Would an economy that is in a recession be at the natural rate of unemployment?

13. If normal frictional unemployment is 5 percent of the labor force, and the economy is currently operating at a 3 percent unemployment rate, speculate on what might happen to the inflation rate.

Suggested Readings

Bresciani-Turroni, Costanino. *The Economics of Inflation*. London: Allen & Unwin, 1937.

Friedman, Milton. *Dollars and Deficits*. Englewood Cliffs, N. J.: Prentice-Hall, 1968.

Gordon, Robert J. ''The Consumer Price Index: Measuring Inflation and Causing It.'' *Public Interest* 59 (Spring 1981): 112–34.

Samuelson, Paul A. *Economics,* 11th ed. New York: McGraw-Hill, 1980, chap. 14.

Triplett, Jack E. ''The Measurement of Inflation: A Survey of Research on the Accuracy of Price Indexes.'' In Paul H. Earl, ed. *Analysis of Inflation*. Lexington, Mass.: Lexington Books, 1975, chap. 2.

6

Measuring National Income and National Product

Chapter Preview

Because macroeconomics is the study of the economy in the large, economists must have ways of measuring the total output of the economy. **National-income accounting** is a relatively old branch of economics, which dates back to Gregory King's effort to measure the total output of England in the late 17th century. Not until the postwar era, however, did economists and international organizations like the United Nations agree upon uniform methods of national-income accounting. The most prominent pioneer in this field is Nobel Prize laureate, Simon Kuznets. His work in the 1930s was instrumental in developing many of the national accounting measures discussed in this chapter. The 1984 Nobel laureate, Richard Stone, played a prominent role in developing uniform national-income-accounting procedures for international organizations. This chapter will explain the relationship between an economy's total output and total income.

> **National-income accounting** is the study of methods of measuring the aggregate output and aggregate income of an economy.

National-income accounting is based upon the principles of the circular flow of output and income introduced in Chapter 2. The circular-flow diagram illustrates the basic principle of national income accounting: the value of total output equals the value of total income. If the economy produces a total output of, say, $500 billion, then a total income of $500 billion will automatically be created in the process. In producing output, costs are incurred. Workers must be paid, land must be rented, and capital costs must be paid. The act of producing goods and services, therefore, creates incomes for those supplying the factors of production. But what is to prevent the value of output from exceeding or falling short of the sum of factor payments? If, in our example, $500 billion worth of output is produced and sold but only $450 billion is paid to (earned by) the factors of production, the $50 billion that is left over accrues to entrepreneurs as profits—and profits are income just like wages, rents, and interest. If, in our example, $500 billion worth of output is produced and sold but $550 billion is paid to the factors of production, the $50 billion difference falls on entrepreneurs as losses—reducing their income. ■

THE CIRCULAR FLOW AND NATIONAL INCOME

To understand the basic principles of national-income accounting, consider a very simple hypothetical economy that consists of only five industries: 1) ore and coal production, 2) steel production, 3) automobile manufacturing, 4) cotton farming, and 5) clothing manufacturing. In this simple economy, steel is made from ore and coal (in addition to land, labor, and capital), autos are made from steel, and clothing is made from cotton. This simple economy does not use any capital goods to produce output. The annual sales of each industry are given in Table 1.

The upper half of the circular-flow diagram in Figure 1 shows the flows of goods and services from businesses to households. In our example, only the **final goods**—cars and clothing—flow from businesses to households. Ore and coal, steel, and cotton flow from one firm to another but do not flow to households. As the cars and clothing flow to households, money payments for the clothing and automobiles flow from households to businesses. As a first approximation, final goods can be defined as follows:

Final goods are goods that are not used up in the production of other goods in the current period.

To produce final goods and services, businesses must buy **intermediate goods** from other firms (automobile manufacturers must purchase steel; the clothing industry must purchase cotton). Intermediate goods do not enter the circular flow because they remain within the business sector.

Intermediate goods are goods that are completely used up in the production of another good. The value of the intermediate products is reflected in the price of the final goods.

In addition to buying intermediate goods, firms must also hire factors of production—land, labor, and capital—owned by households. The bottom portion of the circular-flow diagram represents the flows of the factors of production from households to businesses and the reciprocal factor payments made by businesses to households. The dollar flow of payments for goods and services in

Table 1   The Output of a Hypothetical Economy

Value of Intermediate Goods (billions of dollars of annual sales)	Value of Final Goods (billions of dollars of annual sales)
Ore, coal 20 → steel 100 → Cotton 50 →	Autos 200 Clothing 90 **Total** 290

In this example, ore and coal are used to produce steel, and steel is used to produce automobiles. Cotton is used to produce clothes. Goods used to produce other goods are called *intermediate goods*. Goods consumed by final consumers are *final goods*. The value of final goods in this example is the sum of the value of automobile sales and of clothing sales.

the upper half of the diagram exactly equals the dollar flow of factor payments in the bottom half.

GROSS NATIONAL PRODUCT

The circular-flow diagram provides a starting point for understanding the meaning of the total output of an economy. The circular-flow diagram includes only final goods in the flow of output from firms to households. Intermediate goods are not considered part of the total output of the industrial sector because they remain entirely within the business sector.

In our example, cotton is an intermediate good because it is used up in the production of another good—clothing. Automobiles are a final good because they are consumed by households and do not reenter the production process to produce other goods. Table 1 is divided into two parts. The left-hand side lists intermediate goods used within the business sector; the right-hand side shows the final goods that are produced.

The circular-flow diagram demonstrates that intermediate goods are not important in their own right; they are simply a means to an end. Economic well-being is determined by the final goods and services that the economy produces. Because an economy may produce large quantities of intermediate goods like ores, coal, steel, and raw cotton and yet use them inefficiently to produce final goods and services, the total output of the

Figure 1   The Circular Flow Revisited

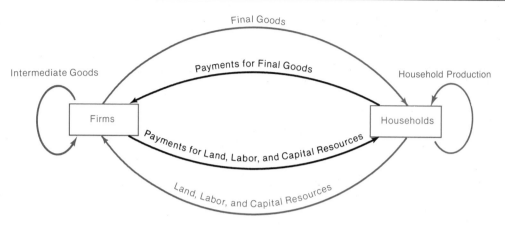

The top half of the circular-flow diagram highlights the flows of goods and services from businesses to households and the corresponding flow of money payments for these goods and services from households to businesses. The bottom half shows the flows of the factors of production from households to businesses and the reciprocal flow of factor payments (income) from the businesses to households. Intermediate goods traded within the business sector do not enter the circular flow.

The circular-flow diagram reveals the basic identity of national income accounting: the value of purchases of final goods and services equals the value of factor payments. It also shows that because we are interested in the flow of final goods, intermediate goods are important only because they are used to produce final goods.

economy is best defined in terms of the final goods and services it produces.

In our simple example, it is easy to distinguish between intermediate and final goods. In the real world, the distinctions are more difficult to make. As explained later, households are not the only ones that consume final goods.

The most comprehensive measure of the total output of the economy is **gross national product (GNP).**

> **Gross national product (GNP)** is the market value of all final goods and services produced by an economy in one year's time.

In our simple economy that produces only cars and clothing for final use, GNP equals the value of automobiles and of clothing produced by the economy in one year's time. In Table 1, the value of one year's automobile production is $200 billion, and the value of one year's clothing manufacture is $90 billion. GNP is, therefore, $290 billion.

GNP is not the sum of the production of both final and intermediate goods. In our example, this sum would be $460 bllion ($20 + $100 + $50 + $200 + $90). If the value of the production

of intermediate goods were included, some products would be counted two times or more. The value of ore and coal is already counted in the value of steel, and the value of steel is already counted in the value of autos. The value of cotton is already counted in the value of clothing. The measure of total output should not count products more than once.

CALCULATING GNP

The basic principle of national-income accounting illustrated in the simple example in Table 1 can be applied to real-world economies. Because the total output of the economy must equal the total income of the economy, GNP can be calculated either by summing the monetary value of all final goods and services produced in one year or by summing all factor incomes earned in one year. Both approaches yield the same answer.

The Flow of Products

In Table 1, GNP is the sum of the sales of the two final products—clothing and automobiles—

Table 2   1984 GNP by Final Expenditure (billions of 1984 $)

Expenditure Category	Amount (billions of 1984 dollars)	Percentage of Total
Personal-consumption expenditures	**2,342**	**64.0**
Durable goods	318	
Nondurable goods	858	
Services	1,166	
Gross private domestic investment	**637**	**17.4**
Nonresidential structures	150	
Equipment	276	
Residential structures	154	
Inventory investment	57	
Government purchases of goods and services	**748**	**20.4**
Federal government	296	
State and local government	452	
Net exports	**−66**	**−1.8**
GNP	**3,661**	**100.0**

Source: *Survey of Current Business.*

that were produced by the hypothetical economy. In this simplified example, only one type of final product was produced: goods for final consumption by households. In the real world, there are other types of final goods in addition to consumer goods. Table 2 shows U.S. GNP broken down into final products:

1. personal-consumption expenditures,
2. federal-, state-, and local-government purchases of goods and services,
3. investment, and
4. net exports.

Personal-Consumption Expenditures *(C).*

The goods and services that people buy and consume—the food, the entertainment services, the clothing, the airline tickets, the haircuts, the books, the television sets—are all final goods and services.

Personal-consumption expenditures are not used to produce other goods. They are consumed by households either immediately (such as food and entertainment) or gradually over time (TV sets, automobiles, and dishwashers). Long-lived consumer goods that are consumed over a period of time are called *consumer durables.*

Government Expenditures for Goods and Services *(G).*   Local, state, and federal governments purchase final goods and services. Governments spend money to run the legal system, to

provide for the national defense, and to run the schools. Although some government expenditures strongly resemble intermediate expenditures—such as government regulation of business or agricultural-extension services—by convention, almost all government expenditures for goods and services are counted as final goods and services in national-income accounting.

Government produces goods and services for society by hiring civil servants and school teachers, by constructing public buildings and building submarines, and by employing law-enforcement officers and judges. Because these government services are typically not sold to the final consumer, there is no market valuation for government services. Unlike other items that enter into GNP, government services are usually valued at the cost of *supplying* them rather than at the cost of purchasing them. For example, the value of public education is taken to be the sum of public expenditures on education; the value of national defense is assumed to equal expenditures on national defense.

Only government *purchases* of goods and services enter into GNP. **Transfer payments** are not included in GNP.

Transfer payments are payments to recipients who have not supplied current goods or services in exchange for these payments.

Example 1   The Internal Revenue Service and Final Goods

Whether an expenditure is intermediate or final is important for tax purposes. The dividing line between final and intermediate expenditures is often hard to draw. A sales representative may buy a car for business purposes (such as driving to sales meetings) or take his or her spouse along on a trip to Hawaii to attend a business convention. If these expenditures are intermediate (are business expenditures), the sales representative can de-duct them from taxable income and thereby reduce tax payments. On the other hand, a person who uses a car for shopping, commuting, and so on or who takes a trip to Hawaii cannot deduct these expenses from taxable income.

As one might imagine, the tax courts are crowded with disputes between taxpayers and the Internal Revenue Service over whether certain expenditures are final or intermediate. ■

Transfer payments, as the name implies, are simply transfers of income from one person or organization to another. Transfer payments are made by both private and governmental organizations. An industrial corporation may contribute to a worthy charity; government may transfer income from taxpayers to poor people through welfare programs. The largest transfer payments are handled by the Social Security Administration, which transfers incomes from those currently working to retired or disabled workers and their dependents.

Government purchases of goods and services are quite different from government transfer payments. As explained above, transfer payments are not made in exchange for current goods or services. Unlike payments for labor and capital, transfer payments are not factor income. Instead, transfer payments transfer income from individuals or organizations which have earned factor income to others. Because total output must equal total factor income, transfer payments do not belong in GNP: they produce neither income nor output.

Investment (I).   Investment has already been defined as expenditures that add to (or replace) the economy's stock of *capital* (plants, equipment, structures, and inventories). Why is investment then a final good? Is not capital used to produce other goods, just like intermediate goods in our opening example?

There is a big difference between capital goods and intermediate goods. Unlike intermediate goods that are used up entirely in the process of making other goods (steel is used up to make autos, cotton is used up to make clothing), capital is only *partially* used up in the process of making other goods. A steel mill may have a useful life of 40 years. In producing steel in any one year, only a small portion (say, 1/40th) of the mill is consumed. The ore and coking coal, on the other hand, is entirely consumed in producing steel. A computer may have a useful working life of seven years (before it becomes obsolete). The bank that uses the computer to manage its accounts also uses up only a portion (say, 1/7th) of the computer in producing one year's banking services. The using up of capital is called **depreciation.** Depreciation is a business cost, just like labor costs or material costs.

Depreciation is the value of the existing capital stock that has been consumed or used up in the process of producing output. Depreciation includes not only the physical wear and tear on capital goods but also the loss of value due to the obsolescence of old capital.

Investment is divided into two major categories called **inventory investment** and **fixed investment.** Both types of investment increase the productive capacity of the economy.

Inventory investment is the increase (or decrease) in the value of the stocks of inventories that businesses have on hand.

If business inventories are $200 billion at the beginning of the year and $250 billion at the end, inventory investment is $50 billion. Inventory investment can be either positive or negative. Year-end inventories can be larger or smaller than inventories at the beginning of the year.

> **Fixed investment** is the addition of new plants, equipment, commercial buildings, and residential structures.

Fixed investment is of two types: *nonresidential* and *residential* fixed investment. Nonresidential fixed investment is additions to the stocks of equipment, plants, and commercial buildings by business firms. Residential investment is additions to the stock of residential structures—apartment houses, condominiums, and private homes. The construction of private homes, cooperative housing, and private condominiums is classified as investment rather than as private consumption for two reasons: First, a home, like other types of capital, is long-lived and is consumed very slowly over the years. Second, the decision to buy a home is very much like a business-investment decision. The family contrasts the housing services it expects to obtain from the home over the years with the cost of the home just as business firms compare the expected returns from investment projects with their costs. Whether or not to buy private housing is as much a business-investment decision as is the decison to build a new plant or to buy new equipment.

Net Exports of Goods and Services *(X-M).*
All the final expenditures by American households, businesses, and government added together would not equal the total output of the American economy for one simple reason: some of the items purchased are produced by other countries (imported from abroad); these goods and services would have to be subtracted from total purchases. On the other hand, some of the domestic economy's output is exported to other countries; these goods and services would have to be added to total purchases.

GNP, therefore, cannot be accurately measured without adding in the nation's exports *(X)* of goods and services and subtracting out the na-

tion's imports *(M)* of goods and services. The value of exports minus the value of imports is called *net exports* of goods and services *(X − M).*

> The GNP formula for calculating the flow of final goods is simply the sum of 1) personal consumption expenditures *(C)*, 2) government purchases of goods and services *(G)*, 3) investment *(I)*, and 4) net exports of goods and services *(X − M)*. Thus, Method 1 for calculating GNP is:

$$GNP = C + G + I + (X - M).$$

The Flow of Income

As the circular-flow diagram shows, the value of final goods and services produced by an economy (GNP) exactly equals **gross national income (GNI).**

> **Gross national income (GNI)** is the sum of all factor incomes. Because GNP equals GNI, GNP can also be calculated by adding together all income earned from labor, land, capital, and entrepreneurship in the course of one year's time.

$$GNP \equiv GNI$$

GNI can be calculated either by adding up the incomes earned by the factors of production or by summing the incomes paid out by producing enterprises. Both methods yield the same total.

Factor Payments. GNP (or GNI) can be calculated by adding together all payments to labor, land, capital, and entrepreneurship. In national-income accounting, payments to labor are called *compensation of employees;* the payments to capital and entrepreneurship are *proprietors' income, corporate profits, net interest payments,* and *depreciation;* payments to land are *rental income of persons.*[1] The 1984 distribution of GNP

---

1. Indirect business taxes are also included in gross national income, although they are not really a payment to a factor of production.

Table 3   1984 Gross National Product by Type of Income

Type of Income	Amount (billions of 1984 dollars)	Percentage
Compensation of employees	2,159	59.2
Proprietors' income	150	4.1
Rental income of persons	62	1.7
Corporate profits	291	8.0
Net interest	283	7.8
Depreciation, indirect business taxes, and other adjustments	700	19.2
GNP = GNI	**3,645**	**100.0**

Source: *Survey of Current Business.*

among these categories is shown in Table 3. Payments to labor dominate, with almost 60 percent of GNP going to labor. Rental payments represent 1.7 percent of GNP, with the remaining 38 percent going to capital, entrepreneurship, and depreciation.[2]

With the exception of depreciation and indirect business taxes, all these payments are actual factor payments made to owners of the factors of production. Depreciation is a payment that businesses must charge themselves to make up for the capital they have used up in the process of producing output.

Method 2 for calculating GNP is:

GNP = Compensation of Employees + Proprietors' Income + Rental Income of Persons + Corporate Profits + Net Interest + Depreciation + Indirect Business Taxes

Value Added.   GNP (GNI) can also be calculated by adding together the income paid out by producing enterprises to the factors of production. In the example of a hypothetical economy in Table 1, the portion of GNP produced by any one in-

---

2. It is difficult to separate out payments to capital, labor, and entrepreneurship. Some payments to labor are really returns to human capital. Some corporate profits are returns to capital; others are returns to entrepreneurship. Proprietors' income includes returns to labor, capital, and entrepreneurship. Rental income also includes royalties on patents and copyrights.

Table 4   GNP Calculated as the Sum of Value Added of Each Hypothetical Industry

Industry	Industry Sales (billions of dollars) (1)	Purchases from Other Industries (billions of dollars) (2)	Value Added, or Net Output (billions of dollars) (3) = (1) − (2)
Ore and coal	20	0	20
Steel	100	20	80
Automobiles	200	100	100
Cotton	50	0	50
Clothing	90	50	40
GNP			**290**

Source: Table 1.

dustry—by ore and coal, by steel, by automobiles, by cotton, or by clothing—cannot be determined simply by dividing each industry's sales by total sales because of double counting. The automobile industry's share would be grossly overstated by this method because the dollar value of its sales includes the dollar value of the steel that it uses to produce cars. Instead, each industry's contribution to GNP can only be determined by calculating each industry's **net output,** or **value added.**

> The **net output,** or **value added,** of a firm is the value of its output minus the value of its purchases from other firms. Accordingly, the **net output,** or **value added,** of an industry is the output of that industry minus its purchases from other industries.

To return to the example in Table 1, the value added of the automobile industry is the output of automobiles ($200 billion) minus purchases from the steel industry ($100 billion). Its value added, therefore, is $100 billion ($200 billion − $100 billion). The value added of steel is the output of steel ($100 billion) minus its purchases from the ore and coal industries ($20 billion), or $80 billion ($100 billion − $20 billion). The value added of ore and coal equals its production ($20 billion), because in this example, ore and coal make no purchases from other industries.

Table 5   1984 Gross National Product by Industry

Industry	Value Added (billions of 1984 dollars)	Percentage
Agriculture, forestry, fisheries	80.5	2.2
Mining	124.5	3.4
Construction	146.4	4.0
Manufacturing	757.8	20.7
Transportation and utilities	340.5	9.3
Wholesale and retail trade	593.1	16.2
Finance, insurance, real estate	600.4	16.4
Services	530.9	14.5
Government and government enterprises	435.7	11.9
Rest of the world	51.5	1.4
GNP	**3,661.3**	**100.0**

Source: *Survey of Current Business.* (Figures are preliminary.)

The value of industry output minus the purchases from other industries equals the payments to labor, capital, land, and entrepreneurship.

An industry's value added is the sum of its factor payments.

Value added will equal the sum of factor payments; profits serve to insure the equality. Anything that is left over after purchasing materials from other firms and paying for labor, capital, and land will go into profits, which is also a form of factor income.

Method 3 for calculating GNP is:

GNP = the sum of the value added for all industries in the economy.

Table 4 calculates GNP for our hypothetical economy by adding up each industry's value added or by adding together the value of final products. The total GNP figure of $290 billion is the same figure yielded by Method 1 in Table 1.

Actual U.S. gross national product by industry value added is shown in Table 5. Each entry shows the net output or value added of each industry (sales minus purchases from other industries), which is the sum of factor payments made by that industry.

FROM GNP TO DISPOSABLE INCOME

Table 6 shows the step-by-step process for determining how much of gross national income households are actually free to spend.

Net National Product

Although gross national product is the broadest measure of the total output of an economy (and, therefore, of the economy's total income), it includes the value of the capital used up—depreciation—in producing output. If GNP is $2,500 billion and depreciation is $250 billion, then 10 percent of output simply replaces the capital that has been consumed. Only $2,250 billion (GNP minus depreciation) represents new goods and services available to society.

For this reason, economists often use a second, less comprehensive measure of total output, called **net national product (NNP)** to measure the total value of new goods and services available to the economy in a given year.

Net national product (NNP) equals GNP minus depreciation.

National Income

Both GNP and NNP are measured in the prices that buyers of final products pay. Included in these prices are a variety of sales and excise

Table 6   1984 GNP, NNP, National Income, Personal Income, Disposable Income

Item	Amount (billions of dollars)
Gross national product (GNP) = GNI	**3,661**
minus	
Depreciation (capital consumption)	−403
equals	
1. Net national product (NNP)	**3,258**
minus	
Indirect business taxes*	−299
equals	
2. National income	**2,959**
minus	
Corporate taxes, undistributed corporate profits, Social Security contributions	−346
plus	
Transfer payments	−400
equals	
3. Personal income	**3,013**
minus	
Personal taxes	−435
equals	
4. Personal disposable income	**2,578**

*plus minor items, such as business transfer payments and government subsidies.

Source: *Department of Commerce, Bureau of Economic Analysis.*

taxes—called *indirect business taxes.* These indirect business taxes do not actually represent a payment to the factors of production. While adding to the revenues of government, indirect business taxes do not generate income for individuals. When indirect business taxes are subtracted from NNP, only **national income,** or the total payments to the factors of production in the economy, remain.

> **National income** equals net national product minus indirect business taxes. National income equals the sum of all factor payments made to the factors of production in the economy.

Personal Income

Not all of earned national income is actually received by persons as income. Included in national income are three major accounts that do not enter into personal income: 1) undistributed corporate profits, 2) corporate income taxes, and 3) social-insurance contributions.

1. Corporations retain a portion of corporate profits for reinvestment. These earnings are not distributed to stockholders as dividend payments.
2. Corporations must pay corporate income taxes that do not enter personal income.
3. Contributions for social insurance (primarily for the Social Security system) are not received by households as income.

Transfer payments that individuals receive from government and business (which, remember, are not included in GNP) are a part of personal income. Transfer payments are not payments for the factors of production, but they are personal income. Interest payments of consumers and government are also not payments for factors of production, but they are eventually received by households as personal income. Transfer payments and the interest adjustments must, therefore, be added back in to determine **personal income.**

> **Personal income** equals national income 1) *minus* retained corporate profits, corporate income taxes, and social-insurance contributions 2) *plus* transfer payments and consumer interest payments and net government interest payments.

Personal Disposable Income

Finally, individuals must pay federal, state, and local income taxes. In order to determine potential spending power, income taxes must be subtracted from personal income to yield **personal disposable income.**

> **Personal disposable income** equals personal income minus income-tax payments.

The levels of national-income accounting categories, which are summarized in Table 6, may seem a bit bewildering. Each account gives economists a different perspective on the economy. Economists can see by comparing the different categories how income and Social Security taxes can change the relationship between the amount of income earned and the amount of income available for spending; they can see that only investment in excess of depreciation adds to the economy's capital stock.

THE EQUALITY OF SAVING AND INVESTMENT

As already noted, investment is the addition to (or the replacement of) the economy's stock of capital goods. Investment expenditures are made principally by the business sector. **Saving** makes resources available for investment and is done primarily by households. Savers and investors are typically different. An important theme of macroeconomics is the relationship between saving and investment.

> For the economy as a whole, **saving** is the amount of national income (total factor income) that is not spent on consumption or direct taxes.

Individuals save by *not spending* all their disposable income. Total saving for an economy is what remains of national income after personal consumption and government expenditures for goods and services.

Saving Equals Investment

Consider a hypothetical economy in which there is no government and, thus, no government spending for goods and services ($G = 0$) and in which there are no taxes ($T = 0$). Assume there is no depreciation and that imports equal exports ($X - M = 0$). Under these simplified conditions:

$$GNP = C + I \qquad (1)$$

because $G = 0$. In this economy, income can only be consumed or saved. There are no taxes; hence, saving is what remains of *GNI* after consumption:

$$S = GNI - C \qquad (2)$$

because $T = 0$. Because GNP and GNI are equal, $C + I$ must equal $C + S$. Hence, investment must equal saving:

$$I = S. \qquad (3)$$

The equality of actual saving and investment is an important cornerstone of macroeconomics. This equality does not mean that what people desire to save will always equal what businesses desire to invest. Instead, the amount *actually* invested will necessarily equal the amount *actually* saved. Some mechanism is required to bring desired saving and desired investment into equality, and there has been much controversy in the economic literature over how the disparate wishes of savers and investors are coordinated. The saving/investment equality means that the amount of saving the economy actually undertakes in one year will always equal the amount of actual investment in that year.

Investment Equals Personal Saving Plus Government Saving

The equality between saving and investment still holds in an economy with government spending and taxes, only now government saving (or dissaving) is included along with personal saving. Under such conditions, personal saving *(S)* equals the amount of income not spent on consumption *(C)* or used for taxes *(T)*, or:

$$S = GNI - C - T. \qquad (4)$$

GNP equals the sum of final expenditures, or:

$$GNP \equiv C + I + G. \qquad (5)$$

Since GNP = GNI ($C + I + G$) can be substituted for GNI in equation **(4).**

$$S = (C + I + G) - C - T. \qquad (6)$$

Simplifying equation **(6)** and solving for *I,* one can see that investment equals the sum of private saving *(S)* and public saving *(T − G)*:

$$I = S + (T - G), \qquad (7)$$

where $(T - G)$ is the government surplus (or deficit, if it is a negative number), which is simply government saving. In this respect, government is like a household (although government does not

Table 7   Personal Disposable Income and Personal Saving, 1950–1984

Year	Personal Disposable Income (billions of dollars)	Personal Saving (billions of dollars)	Saving Rate (percent)
1950	206.6	11.9	5.8
1955	275.0	16.4	6.0
1960	352.0	19.7	5.6
1965	478.5	33.7	7.1
1970	695.3	55.8	8.0
1975	1,096.1	94.3	8.6
1980	1,829	110	6.0
1984	2,578	157	6.1

Source: *Survey of Current Business.*

have to pay taxes). The government saves if its income *(T)* exceeds its expenditures *(G)*. It increases its debt if its expenditures exceed its income.

Saving still equals investment in an economy with government spending and taxes because saving includes both private and public saving.

The previous section showed the relationships between the income categories from GNP to personal disposable income. One final relationship is that between **personal saving** and disposable income.

> **Personal saving** equals personal disposable income minus personal-consumption expenditures.

Personal saving is what remains of personal disposable income after personal-consumption expenditures are made (remember, taxes are already subtracted from personal income to get disposable income). In other words, individuals save by refraining from consumption. Personal saving is only one component of total saving. Total saving is the sum of personal saving, business saving, and government saving (or dissaving).

Table 7 shows personal disposable income and personal saving during the period 1950 to 1984. It shows that private saving tends to rise with disposable income and that the saving rate (the ratio of personal saving to disposable income) has varied from lows of near 5 percent to highs of near 8.5 percent.

REAL GNP VERSUS NOMINAL GNP

Since GNP is measured in dollar values, the GNP of an economy can rise for two reasons: First, the *quantities* of goods and services produced can increase. Second, the *prices* of these goods and services can rise. Often both increases occur. GNP that is measured in current market prices is **nominal GNP,** or ''GNP in current dollars.''

> **Nominal GNP** (or ''GNP in current dollars'') is the value of final goods and services for a given year in that year's prevailing market prices.

When nominal GNP rises, it is not immediately apparent whether the increase is due to rising prices or to increasing outputs of real goods and services. Presumably, the material well-being of society is improved only by increasing the output of goods and services. Society as a whole is not made better off when prices rise and the quantities of real goods and services remain constant or decline. For this reason, when GNP is compared over a period of time, it is typically measured in a way that eliminates the effects or rising prices. This measure of GNP is called **real GNP,** or ''GNP in constant dollars.''

> **Real GNP** (or ''GNP in constant dollars'') measures the volume of *real* goods and services by removing the effects of rising prices on nominal GNP.

The GNP deflator was introduced in the previous chapter as the most general measure of the price level. The GNP deflator measures changes in the prices of consumption goods, investment goods, government goods and services, and net exports. The GNP deflator relates real GNP to nominal GNP. For example, nominal GNP in 1972 was $1,186 billion, and nominal GNP in 1984 was $3,661 billion. The ratio of the GNP deflator in 1983 to the GNP deflator in 1972 was 2.23 (that is, prices increased 2.23 times). The 1984 GNP in constant (1972) dollars can be calculated as

$$\frac{\text{Nominal GNP in 1984}}{\text{GNP deflator ratio}} = \frac{\$3,661 \text{ billion}}{2.23}$$

$$= \$1,640 \text{ billion in 1972 dollars.}$$

The real GNP ratio (the percent increase in real GNP) can then be determined as:

$$\frac{1984 \text{ GNP in 1972 dollars}}{1972 \text{ GNP in 1972 dollars}}$$

$$= \frac{\$1,640 \text{ billion}}{\$1,186 \text{ billion}} = 1.38.$$

In other words, real GNP increased by 38 percent between 1972 and 1984. Trends in real GNP and nominal GNP can be quite different, especially during periods of rapid inflation, as Figure 2 illustrates. This book concentrates primarily on real GNP in its discussions of aggregate output. Real GNP measures the output of goods and services. It shows movements in the level of real economic activity. The amount of employment (and unemployment) in the economy is related to real GNP.

OMISSIONS FROM GNP

The definition of GNP as the value of all final goods and services is not as simple as it appears. What should be done with goods that are not bought and sold in markets? Should the value of leisure be counted in GNP? How should illegal economic activities be handled? What about economic activities that may lower rather than raise economic well-being? Official measures of GNP ignore most of these questions. Illegal economic activities and household production are left out of GNP. Increases in leisure do not raise measured GNP. Well-accepted procedures to correct GNP for economic "bads" have not been developed. Although these items are not included in GNP, it is useful to consider whether they should be and, if so, what effect they would have on measured GNP.

Nonmarketed Goods

Many final goods and services are not acquired through regular market transactions. Instead of buying food at the grocery store, someone may consume the produce from a vegetable garden in the backyard. Instead of calling a plumber to repair a leaky faucet, some people may repair it themselves. A dentist may trade dental work for two weeks in a patient's vacation home.

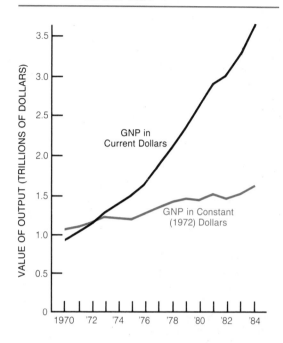

Figure 2   Gross National Product (GNP): 1970 to 1984

GNP in Current Dollars

GNP in Constant (1972) Dollars

VALUE OF OUTPUT (TRILLIONS OF DOLLARS)

Source: U.S. Bureau of the Census.

The common feature of these transactions of **nonmarketed goods** is that they have taken place without the use of organized markets.

The treatment of nonmarketed goods affects comparisons of countries at different stages of development. International statistics show, for example, that the per capita GNP of the United States is 52 times that of Zaire. How could anyone survive on so little? While the differences in living standards between countries like Zaire and the United States are indeed enormous, the statistics overstate the differential in material well-being. In a country like Zaire, more goods and services are acquired outside market transactions and, thus, do not enter measured GNP.[3]

Nonmarketed goods are goods and services exchanged through *barter arrangements* or acquired through *do-it-yourself activities* that

---

3. The nonmarketed goods that are allowed to enter into GNP are the value of agricultural products consumed on the farm and the imputed rental value of owner-occupied housing.

Example 2   How Much Is Being Saved?

Estimating aggregate economic measures like GNP, personal income, or personal saving is a difficult business. National-income accounting is not an exact science. Many figures must be approximated. Numbers reported to tax authorities play a prominent role in such calculations. Different calculation methods yield different outcomes. For example, the personal-saving statistics prepared by the Department of Commerce have differed in recent years from those prepared by the Federal Reserve Board.

By definition, personal saving is what is left over from personal income after personal-consumption spending and payment of direct taxes. But those engaging in saving add to their stock of financial and real assets. Therefore, personal saving also equals the net increase in personal holdings of financial assets (savings accounts, bonds, etc.) and real assets (such as homes and other fixed assets). Conceptually, personal saving could be calculated either as personal disposable income minus personal taxes and consumption or as the net increase in financial and real assets. The Department of Commerce saving figures are calculated by the first method; the Federal Reserve Board uses the increase in net assets for its saving measure. As the accompanying figure shows, the Department of Commerce saving figures have (since 1975) been well below those of the Federal Reserve. In fact, for 1983, the two figures are $117 billion apart. Because of this discrepancy, we do not know the true saving rate of the U.S. economy.

Which set of estimates is correct? Some argue that the Department of Commerce estimate is too low because earnings in the underground economy are left out. By subtracting personal consumption from personal disposable income (which does not include underground-economy earnings), the amount of saving is understated. Others

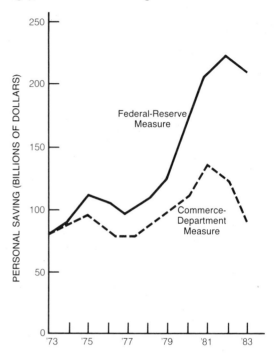

argue that the Federal Reserve figure is too high because it is difficult to determine the value of financial assets purchased by foreigners. What appears to be an increase in U.S. personal saving may actually be an increase in foreign purchases of U.S. assets. ■

Source: "Widely Disparate Savings Statistics Given by Fed, Commerce Officials," *The Wall Street Journal*, November 22, 1983.

take the place of goods and services that would otherwise have been purchased in organized markets.

Illegal Activities

GNP typically does not include illegal goods and services. Such goods and services otherwise meet all the requirements for inclusion in GNP: they are final products; they are purchased in market transactions. Yet they are goods and services—like illegal gambling, murder for hire, prostitution, illegal drugs—whose use and sale are proscribed by law. Semilegal activities—such as moonlighting, when the income is not reported to tax authorities—also belong to this category. Illegal income is not reported because of the desire to avoid paying taxes and because of restrictions on economic activities that are deemed criminal or illegal.

Example 3   Housework and GNP

How nonmarketed goods are treated can have a substantial effect on the size of GNP. For example, life-insurance companies advise families to carry life insurance on homemakers because it would cost the family tens of thousands of dollars per year to replace the homemaker in the household. If services performed by homemakers were purchased—if dirty clothes were taken to the laundry or if babysitters were hired—they would definitely enter GNP. The inclusion of homemakers's services would raise GNP dramatically. There are currently more than 29 million homemakers in the United States. If each produces household services worth, say, $20,000 per year, then the total value of their services would equal $580 billion or 15 percent of 1985 GNP. ■

No one knows for sure the dollar volume of illegal market activities. The available estimates of the size of the American underground economy vary considerably. An official Internal Revenue Service study places the volume at between 6 percent and 8 percent of legal GNP. Estimates of the value of illegal activities made by private economists range from 4 percent to 33.5 percent of legal GNP. Although the American underground economy is large in absolute size, it is still much smaller than in other countries, such as France and Italy, where it may reach 25 percent of legal GNP.[4]

Should illegal activities be included in GNP? If GNP is to be a measure of the level of economic activity, illegal economic activities would need to be included. Official GNP could show a slackening pace of production and employment when in reality, activity has simply shifted from the legal to the underground economy. Government economic policies are based upon measured GNP and measured poverty. If illegal activities are omitted, a false impression of economic activity and poverty may be obtained.

There are two basic arguments for not including illegal activities in GNP. The first is the impossibility of obtaining reliable statistics on the underground economy. The second is that since most underground activities are illegal, legislators, at least, do not believe they raise the material well-being of society. In fact, according to prevailing legislation, such activities lower material well-being. For example, the sale of drugs by a drug dealer to a 13-year-old lowers rather than raises material well-being.

The Value of Leisure

The number of hours the average American works per year has declined dramatically over the past 50 years. In effect, our society has chosen to produce a smaller flow of goods and services in return for more leisure. Should this voluntary choice of leisure be reflected in GNP? After all, voluntary increases in leisure raise material well-being just like increases in goods and services.

If the value of leisure were included in GNP, GNP would be dramatically increased. In 1900, workers in manufacturing worked, on average, a 60-hour week. By early 1985, this figure had fallen to 40 hours per week. If American workers worked the same number of hours now as they did in 1900, personal income would be much larger than it actually is. The fact that people have chosen leisure over higher money incomes means that they place a value on that leisure greater than the extra earnings sacrificed.

Leisure is not included in GNP because GNP is narrowly defined to encompass only tangible goods and services. It does not include intangibles such as the value individuals place on leisure.

Economic "Bads"

GNP measures the final goods and services that an economy produces. It is not a measure of well-being; it is only a measure of the total output of final goods and services. What if these goods and services are not economic goods but **economic "bads"**?

---

4. Vito Tanzi, "Underground Economy Built on Illicit Pursuits is Growing Concern of Economic Policymakers," *IMF Survey,* February 4, 1980.

Economic "bads" are goods or services that do not contribute to society's economic well-being.

Many "bads" are already excluded because they are illegal, but what about legal "bads" such as air, water, and noise pollution? What about the prison camps that are all too common in totalitarian countries or the cures offered for sale by medical quacks? Economic "bads" like pollution are particularly troublesome because economists have long recognized that polluters do not bear the full costs of their polluting activities. Insofar as firms are not charged fully for the pollution they create, society must pay some of these costs.

The existence of economic "bads" has caused some economists—most prominently James Tobin and William Nordhaus—to argue for a different measure of total output, called the *measure of economic welfare,* or MEW. MEW subtracts the value of economic "bads" from the value of economic goods.

The art of computing MEW is in its infancy. It remains to be seen whether MEW can be effectively measured. The basic problem is how to determine what is a "bad." How does one know whether something enters MEW as a plus or a minus and what its numerical value should be?

INCOME AND WEALTH

The different factors of production earn income. Table 3 showed the distribution of income among labor, land, capital, and entrepreneurship. As a percent of national income (GNP minus depreciation and indirect business taxes), labor accounts for 75 percent, land for 5 percent, and capital and entrepreneurship for the remaining 20 percent of income generated.

Net Worth

Nonlabor income (such as rental income from land or dividend and interest income from capital) is earned by individuals who own wealth. Personal wealth can be measured as either **gross wealth** or **net wealth.**

The **gross wealth** of an individual is the value of the assets owned by that individual.

Table 8	Net Wealth in the United States, 1980 (billions of dollars)	
Total assets		**19,282**
Reproducible assets (buildings, plants, equipment, inventories)	8,931	
Land	2,571	
Financial assets (bank deposits, currency, bonds, etc.)	7,765	
Total liabilities		**7,765**
Net worth		**11,516**

Source: *Survey of Current Business,* May 1982, pp. 36, 37.

Examples of assets owned by wealth-holding individuals are real estate, stocks, bonds, saving accounts, gold and other precious metals, and valuable art works. Gross wealth, however, can be a misleading indicator of financial health because people have *liabilities* (debts) as well as assets. As a first approximation, one can think of liabilities as the claims (such as loans) that other individuals have on that person's assets.

The **net wealth** of an individual is the value of assets minus the value of liabilities. Individual net wealth is typically called *net worth*.

If assets exceed liabilities, net worth is positive. If liabilities exceed assets, net worth is negative.

Stocks Versus Flows

Net assets, or net worth, can be measured at a single moment in time. On January 1, 1985, an individual can total the current value of all assets, subtract the value of all current liabilities, and obtain a measure of net worth on that date. On the other hand, income such as interest income, dividend income, and rental income, earned from assets is a *flow* because interest income, rental income, and dividend income are earned over time. Interest earned on a savings account may be compounded daily. Stock dividends are typically paid four times a year. Rental income is received on a monthly basis. It only makes sense to talk about income earned over a specified period of time (such as a year or a month). Unlike net worth,

Example 4   The Underground Economy

The underground economy of the United States is estimated to rival the annual output of the Canadian economy. As many as 20 million Americans may engage in illegal underground activities. More than $100 billion in taxes may be lost every year, forcing honest taxpayers to ante up more.

The underground economy includes both innocuous activities—unreported income from child care and housecleaning, occasional moonlighting by professionals and craft workers, the padding of expense accounts and the charging of personal expenses to corporate accounts—and organized crime activities, like casino skimming and drug and prostitution rings. Millions of workers, many of them illegal aliens, are paid in cash; there is no record of their employment on company books. No Social Security deductions are withheld.

Truckers, taxi drivers, and waitresses work to at least some extent for cash and pocket a percentage of their earnings (which are hard to document) and report only a portion of their earnings to tax authorities. Bars and jewelers fail to report a portion of cash sales.

Organized crime likely accounts for the bulk of underground economy receipts. Arson for profit, smuggling of goods, pirated tapes, records, and films, pornography, professional assassinations, and prostitution are the lifeline of organized-crime earnings. Experts estimate that almost half of the cigarette sales in New York City are of bootlegged cigarettes because of the New York cigarette tax.

How large is the underground economy in the United States and other countries? As might be expected, it is difficult to obtain firm answers. Studies based upon voluntary surveys and samples, tax audits, studies of cash circulation, and national-income accounting discrepancies yield different answers. Estimates for the United States, for example, range from 5 percent to 33 percent of GNP. One study that attempts to rank countries according to the relative size of their hidden economies shows that the United States ranks somewhere in the middle with a hidden economy equal to 8 percent of GNP. Countries with relatively small underground economies are Switzerland and Japan (with underground economies equal to 4 percent of GNP or less). Those with relatively large underground economies are the Scandinavian countries and Italy (with underground economies of more than 10 percent of GNP). The three factors that appear to account for the size of the underground economy are: the burden of taxation, the burden of regulation, and the amount of tax immorality. ■

Source: Bruno Frey and Werner Pommerehne, "The Hidden Economy: State and Prospects for Measurement," *Review of Income and Wealth,* Series 30, March 1984.

which is measured at a particular *point in time,* income can only be measured over a *period of time.* Net wealth is a **stock variable.** Income is a **flow variable.**

A **stock variable** is one that can be meaningfully measured at one point in time.

A **flow variable** is one that can be meaningfully measured only over a period of time.

What is the relationship between total net worth and income earned from net wealth for the U.S. economy as a whole? In 1980, the combined net worth of all persons was $11.5 trillion (see Table 8). Net worth consists primarily of the value of land and capital. In the case of financial assets, such as bonds or savings accounts, what is an asset for one person is a liability for another. For the economy as a whole, financial assets and liabilities cancel each other. Total income earned by the nonlabor factors of production was $517 billion in 1980. Total income earned by labor was $1,599 billion. The ratio of net wealth to income generated from wealth was, therefore, 22 to one. Viewed from the opposite angle, each dollar of net wealth earned slightly less than $0.05 per year in 1980.

This chapter explained how the economy's total output is measured and described its components. The next chapter will define money and examine money's impact on prices and output.

Summary

1. National-income accounting is the branch of economics that measures the total output of the economy. The value of total output equals the value of total income because the act of producing output automatically creates an equivalent amount of income.

2. Gross national product, or GNP, is the broadest measure of the total output of the economy. GNP is the value of all final goods and services produced by an economy in one year's time. Only final goods and services are included to avoid the double counting of products.

3. GNP can be calculated by measuring the total value of final products or by measuring the total value of income. The total value of income can be calculated as the sum of factor payments or as the sum of the value added by all industries. Therefore, the three methods for computing GNP are:

a. GNP = personal consumption expenditures + government expenditures for goods and services + investment + net exports.
b. GNP = compensation of employees + proprietors' income + rental income + corporate profits + interest + depreciation + indirect business taxes.
c. GNP = the sum of the value added of all industries in an economy. The value added of an economic sector equals the value of output minus purchases from other sectors. Value added also equals the sum of factor payments made by the sector.

4. Net national product equals GNP minus depreciation. National income equals NNP minus indirect business taxes. Personal income equals national income *minus* factor payments not received by individuals and Social Security deductions *plus* transfer payments. Personal disposable income equals personal income minus personal taxes.

5. National-income accounting shows that saving and investment are equal by definition. Investment is the addition to the economy's stock of capital. Saving is that portion of income that is not spent on consumption and taxes.

6. Nominal GNP is the value of final goods and services in current market prices. Nominal GNP can rise either because of increasing output or because of rising prices. Real GNP measures the volume of real goods and services by removing the effects of changing prices.

7. Nonmarketed goods, illegal goods, and the value of leisure are not included in GNP, although many economists argue that they should be included. Other economists argue that the appropriate measure of total output is the *measure of economic welfare,* which equals GNP minus the cost of economic ''bads.''

8. Net wealth (or net worth) equals assets minus liabilities. Nonlabor income is earned from net wealth. Net wealth is a stock variable that can be measured at a single point in time. The income earned from net assets (like any other form of income) is a flow variable that can be measured only over a period of time.

Key Terms

national-income accounting
final goods
intermediate goods
gross national product (GNP)
transfer payments
depreciation
inventory investment
fixed investment
gross national income (GNI)
net output
value added
net national product (NNP)
national income
personal income
personal disposable income
saving
personal saving
nominal GNP
real GNP
nonmarketed goods
economic ''bads''
gross wealth
net wealth
stock variable
flow variable

Questions and Problems

1. The economy produces final goods and services valued at $500 billion in one year's time but sells only $450 billion worth. Does this mean that the value of final output no longer equals the value of income?

2. Discuss the implications (in Table 1) of $5 billion worth of coal being purchased directly by households to heat their homes. Assume nothing else in Table 1 changes. How and why will this change GNP? Will it affect value added?

3. An industry spends $6 million on the factors of production that it uses (including entrepreneurship). It sells $10 million worth of output. How much value added has this industry created and how much has this industry purchased from other industries?

4. Explain why investment is regarded as a final product even though it is used as a factor of production to produce other goods.

5. A large corporation gives a grant to a classical musician to allow her to train her skills in Europe. How will this payment enter into GNP? Into personal income? Will this payment differ from one to an engineer employed by the company?

6. Which of the following investment categories can be negative: inventory investment, fixed investment, net fixed investment (gross investment minus depreciation)? Explain your answer.

7. Explain why GNP measures may tend to overstate the GNP of rich countries relative to poor countries.

8. In Economy X, personal disposable income is $100 billion, personal-consumption expenditures are $80 billion, taxes are $40 billion, and government expenditures for goods and services are $50 billion. How much total saving is there in the economy? How much is private saving?

9. Which of the following are stock variables? Which of the following are flow variables? Explain your answers.

a. Money in a savings account.
b. Interest on a savings account.
c. The market value of 10 shares of IBM stock.
d. Dividends on 10 shares of IBM stock.
e. The market value of an office building.
f. The monthly rental payment on an apartment.

10. In an economy, $300 billion of final goods and services are purchased. Explain under what conditions GNP will be more or less than $300 billion.

11. Calculate GNP, net national product, and national income from the following data: consumption equals $100; investment plus government spending equals $50; net exports equal $0; depreciation equals $10; indirect business taxes equal $5.

12. In year 1, nominal GNP was $200. In year 2, nominal GNP was $300. In year 1, the GNP deflator was 100. In year 2, the GNP deflator was 125.
a. Express year 2 GNP in the prices of year 1.
b. Calculate the growth of real GNP.

13. What happens to measured GNP when a person marries his or her housekeeper?

14. Explain why illegal goods are not counted in GNP.

Suggested Readings

Adams, F. G. *National Accounts and the Structure of the U.S. Economy.* New York: General Learning Press, 1973.

Dornbusch, Rudiger and Stanley Fischer. *Macroeconomics,* 2nd ed. New York: McGraw-Hill, 1981, chap. 2.

Kuznets, Simon. *Modern Economic Growth.* New Haven, Conn.: Yale University Press, 1966, chap. 1.

Ruggles, Richard and Nancy D. Ruggles. "Integrated Economic Accounts for the United States, 1947–1980." *Survey of Current Business* 62 (May 1982): 1–12.

Tanzi, Vito. "Underground Economy Built on Illicit Pursuits Is Growing Concern of Economic Policymakers." *IMF Survey,* February 4, 1980.

7

Money and Prices

Chapter Preview

To economists, the term **money** means the generally accepted commodity (or commodities) that can be exchanged for goods and services.

> **Money** is the medium of exchange used by an economy; it is the commodity ordinarily used in transactions that transfer ownership of goods and services from one person to another.

This chapter examines the functions of money, the types of money, the reasons why people desire to hold money, the relationship between money and prices. This chapter will also show how money is related—both theoretically and empirically—to inflation and the business cycle.

Money facilitates trade and commerce in economies that are characterized by specialization and exchange. In such economies, money performs four functions. Money serves as:

1. a medium of exchange,
2. a unit of value,
3. a standard of deferred payment, and
4. a store of value.

By performing these monetary functions, money allows people to specialize according to their comparative advantage and exchange goods and services with others. Thus, money allows people to earn higher incomes and, hence, to consume more goods and services than would otherwise be possible. In the language of Chapter 2, the use of money shifts the production-possibilities curve outward. By performing its four functions, money increases the efficiency of the economy. ■

THE FUNCTIONS OF MONEY

Money as a Medium of Exchange

The most important function of money is that of a medium of exchange. In a modern economic system, money enters almost all market transactions. The existence of a common object acceptable to all sellers eliminates the need for a *double coincidence of wants*. In a barter economy, in which goods are traded directly for other goods, a seller of wheat who wants to buy some sugar must find a seller of sugar wanting to buy wheat. Since double coincidences of wants are rare, in a pure barter economy a series of transactions would be required to obtain what one wants. The seller of wheat might first have to settle for potatoes, trade the potatoes for an axe, and then finally trade the axe for some sugar. The efficiency of the economy suffers as the efforts of the wheat grower (who wants sugar) are diverted from wheat cultivation into a long string of barter transactions.

> Money's most important function is to serve as the commodity that is generally acceptable as a means of payment (for buying things and paying debts).

Money eliminates the need for such costly intermediate exchanges. Because intermediate exchanges are so difficult, customs and laws designate some commodity to serve as the medium of exchange. Money allows the wheat farmer to sell wheat for money and to use the money to buy sugar. Converting wheat into sugar is easy, and the wheat farmer is free to concentrate on wheat growing. The sugar grower is left free to concentrate on sugar cultivation.

The object that society uses as money or the medium of exchange could be almost anything. Money is a social contrivance. The list of things that have been used as money staggers the imagination. American Indians used *wampum* (a string of shells); early American colonists used tobacco, rice, corn, cattle, and whiskey. Gopher tails were used as money in North Dakota in the 1880s. Cigarettes have served as money in prisoner-of-war camps. Farther from home more exotic things have been used as money: whale teeth in Fiji, sandalwood in Hawaii, fish hooks on the Gilbert Islands, reindeer in parts of Russia, red parrot feathers on the Santa Cruz Islands (as late as 1961), silk in China, slaves in Africa, rum in Australia. Thus, we see that money can grow on trees! Money can even walk, talk, fly, be eaten, or be drunk. Our modern paper money is boring by comparison.

Money as a Unit of Value

The value of a good or service is what it can be exchanged for in the market. In a barter economy, a cow might sell for two pigs, for an acre of land, for 50 bushels of corn, for a motorcycle, or for dozens of other things. It is, of course, inconvenient to keep track of the value of a cow or anything else in terms of every other thing it would trade for. Barter is also inconvenient when the units cannot be divided, as in a case where a pig is worth half a cow. Choosing a common unit of value—money—saves much time and energy in keeping track of the relative prices or values of different things and solves the problem of converting units. When the money prices of a number of common objects are known, it is easy to appraise the *relative* price of any item just from its money price. If an apple costs $0.50, an orange costs $0.25, and a banana costs $0.10, we know immediately that an apple is twice as expensive as an orange and five times as expensive as a banana and that an orange is 2.5 times as expensive as a banana. Money prices can also be used to add together apples and oranges. By reducing different economic entities to their dollar values, homemakers can add apples and oranges, firms can subtract expenses from revenue to obtain profit, and accountants can subtract liabilities from assets.

> Money serves as the common denominator in which the values of all goods and services are expressed.

Money as a Standard of Deferred Payment

When one good is used as the medium of exchange, it is almost inevitable that the good will be used as the standard of deferred payment on contracts extending over a period of time. There are numerous contracts that extend into the future: home mortgages, car loans, all sorts of bonds and promissory notes, credit charges at the department store and on credit cards, salaries, home rents, and so forth. That which serves as money will also be that in which payments deferred into the future will be made. If in the Santa Cruz Islands red parrot feathers are money, an agreement to pay for a cart one year in the future would call for payment one year hence in red parrot feathers. If dollars are money, contracts to pay for some good in the future would call for payment in dollars. When a home is purchased on credit, the mortgage loan calls for interest and principal payments over the loan period in dollars.

Money is a standard of deferred payment on exchange agreements extending into the future.

As pointed out in Chapter 5, inflation complicates money's role as the standard of deferred payment. Inflation means that deferred payments will be made in "cheaper" dollars because a unit of money buys fewer goods and services than it did before. If the inflation is foreseen, parties entering into deferred-payment contracts can build in safeguards. The parties may agree that the deferred payment will be adjusted upward at the same rate as inflation (a cost-of-living adjustment). Interest rates, rental payments, or even salary payments may include a premium to compensate the recipient of deferred payments for the anticipated rate of inflation. When inflation is foreseen, there are ways to protect money's role as a standard of deferred payment.

Chapter 5 showed that unanticipated inflation can redistribute wealth. Unanticipated inflation will benefit debtors and harm creditors who have not had the foresight to demand a higher interest rate to compensate them for the effects of inflation. Unforeseen inflation tends to redistribute wealth from those who receive deferred payments to those who make them.

Money as a Store of Value

People, on average, do not consume all their income, although some households do. When a family consumes less than its income, it saves, or (to say the same thing) it accumulates wealth. People can accumulate wealth in virtually any form that is not perishable—paintings, gold, silver, stocks, bonds, land, buildings, apartments—and money. A desirable characteristic of any *asset* (anything owned that has value) is that it should maintain or increase its value over time. During periods of rising prices, the value of money is eroded because the amount of goods and services one unit of money will purchase falls. Paper currency or coins that have a face value greater than the value of the substance of which they are made are particularly vulnerable to this erosion. Nevertheless, money, like other assets, serves as a store of value. If people accumulate wealth in the form of money, they can use this money at some future date to purchase goods and services. How good a store of value money is depends upon the rate of inflation. The higher is the rate of inflation, the less well money serves as a store of value.

Since money is the medium of exchange, it can also be used as a means of storing wealth.

THE SUPPLY OF MONEY

Money is anything that performs the four functions of money. (See Example 1.) Different objects and substances have served as money at different times and in different parts of the world. Money ranges from things that have no intrinsic value (such as a dollar bill) or little intrinsic value (such as a dime) to things that have considerable intrinsic value, such as gold coins.

Types of Money

Money comes in three basic varieties: *commodity money, fiat money,* and *bank money.*

Commodity Money.   Historically, the most important **commodity money** has been gold and silver. Gold and silver have nonmonetary uses in jewelry and industry; they can be easily coined, weighed, and used for large and small transactions. In early history, governments started minting gold and silver coins to avoid costly weighings each time a transaction occurred.

Example 1   When Money Stops Being Money: Israel's Shekel

Money is anything that is accepted as a medium of exchange, that serves as a unit of account and a store of value, and that is a standard for deferred payments. The minute money ceases to perform any of these functions, it ceases, for all practical purposes, to be money. A case in point is the Israeli shekel. After decades of rapid inflation, which had accelerated to a 1,000 percent inflation rate by 1984, the Israeli shekel (the official currency of Israel) showed signs of ceasing to be money. It became illegal in Israel to quote prices in dollars or to accept payments in dollars, but in hotels and restaurants, especially those catering to international tourists, discrete signs were mounted telling customers that they were ex-

pected to settle their accounts in dollars (not shekels). By 1984, many stores and businesses handled their accounting in dollars. The hyperinflation rendered the shekel virtually worthless as a store of value: if it were held for any length of time, its purchasing power fell dramatically. The shekel had virtually ceased to be the standard for deferred payment: merchants found that customers could pay their bills in cheaper shekels by delaying payment, so businesses and merchants linked deferred payments to the dollar. The standard for deferred payment, in effect, became the dollar. In the Israeli economy of late 1984, the dollar had become the unofficial money of Israel. ■

When gold or silver serve as commodity money, private citizens can produce money simply by taking mined gold to the government mint! In a commodity-money system there can also be paper currency, but the paper can be exchanged for gold at a fixed rate.

> **Commodity money** is money whose value as a commodity is as great as its value as money.

A commodity-money system is established when the commodity content of a unit of money is set at a fixed rate—say, $100 equals one ounce of gold. If the amount of gold mined jumps up (due to new discoveries), there is more money in circulation, prices are bid up, and one unit of money buys fewer goods and services. The relationship between money and prices will be discussed later in this chapter.) Gold's value as money has fallen. If the nonmonetary demand for the commodity increases (the demand for gold fillings increases), there is less money in circulation, prices fall, and a unit of money buys more. Gold's value as money has risen. In this way, the value of gold as a commodity and as money is kept equal. People cannot place a value on commodity money that is higher than its monetary value (dentists would never be willing to pay $110 for an ounce of gold when its monetary value is $100 per ounce) because gold would be shifted to commodity use whenever the commod-

ity price threatened to exceed the commodity's value as money.

Historically (and in some primitive societies today), agricultural products, such as rice, cattle, wheat, or sugar, have served as money. Whatever the commodity—gold, silver, rice, sugar, or cattle—the commodity value of money will be the same as its money value.

Commodity money suffers from an inherent problem, known as **Gresham's Law:**

> **Gresham's Law** states that *bad money drives out good*. When depreciated, mutilated, or debased currency is circulated along with money of high value, the good money will disappear from circulation; only the bad money will remain in circulation.[1]

When people shave or mutilate gold and silver coins, the bad currency will begin to circulate along with the good currency. The lesser-valued coins will be the ones spent while the more valuable coins will be hoarded. Tobacco money in colonial Virginia illustrates Gresham's Law. Initially, tobacco of both good and poor quality

---

1. Gresham's Law is named after Sir Thomas Gresham, who lived from 1519–1579. He was a successful banker and merchant, accumulated a great fortune, and endowed Gresham's College in London. Gresham's methods of making money were described as more effective than ethical. It may be that Gresham formulated his law on the basis of first-hand observation.

Example 2   The Stone Money of the Island of Yap

Anything acceptable as a medium of exchange by the population can serve as money. The island of Yap is a tiny U.S. trust territory in the South Pacific some 500 miles from Guam. For money, the Yapese—10,000 strong—use stone wheels, from 1 foot to 12 feet in diameter, made from stones found only on distant islands. Most of the stones are 2 to 5 feet in diameter. Each stone has a hole in the middle so it can be carried on a tree trunk. A private citizen could produce money only by making what was often a treacherous sea journey. Thus, Yap money could be called a commodity money. Interestingly enough, the value of the stones is related to their size as well as to their scarcity and the difficulty of acquiring them.

Each stone has its own history. A stone brought over during the days of the Yap empire is the most valuable. Next in line are stones fashioned in the 1870s by David Dean O'Keffe, a shipwrecked American sailor. Last in value are those few mechanically chiseled by German traders around 1900.

Physical possession is not necessary for ownership. A particular large stone may be owned by many residents, each of whom have received some part of the stone in exchange for some product or service. Larger stones, thus, stay put, with legal ownership being transferred from person to person. How the Yapese keep their book-keeping straight is not known. On at least one occasion, a family was considered wealthy because an ancestor was known to have discovered an extremely large and valuable stone that a storm sent to the bottom of the sea!

The Yapese have several media of exchange in addition to stone money: U.S. dollars, necklaces of stone beads, and large sea shells. The sea shells and stone beads are used as small change in traditional transactions, but U.S. dollars must be used to make deposits in banks or to buy goods in one of the few retail stores. Will the stone money last? Probably not. The informational requirements of stone money are too large (each stone has a history) for a complicated world. As retailing and banking displace traditional person-to-person exchange, stone money will doubtless become extinct.

As this example illustrates, money does not have to have intrinsic value; money must be scarce. What works as money in one society need not work as money in another society. As societies become more complex and impersonal, money must become more standardized. ■

Sources: William Furness III, *The Island of Stone Money* (New York: J. B. Lippincott Company, 1910), pp. 92–100; "Fixed Assets, Or: Why a Loan in Yap is Hard to Roll Over," *Wall Street Journal,* March 29, 1984.

---

circulated as money. As predicted by Gresham's Law, people came to hoard the good tobacco and only use the worst tobacco as money. Eventually, the tobacco used as money in colonial Virginia was only the scruffiest and foulest tobacco in the entire state. This opportunism tends to raise the cost of using the commodity money as a medium of exchange as sellers of goods become suspicious of the money being used.

The basic cost to society of using commodity money is that society must devote real resources to producing the commodity money. Gold and silver mines must be discovered and operated to produce gold or silver commodity money. This gold and silver must then be set aside to circulate as money and will not find its way into use as jewelry or dental fillings. (See Example 2.)

Fiat Money.   If society could use something as money that costs little or nothing of society's resources (such as pieces of engraved paper), resources could be devoted to other activities. For this reason, societies began to use **fiat money.**

> **Fiat money** is money whose value or cost as a commodity is less than its value as money.

Because governments have a monopoly over the issue of fiat money, governments may be tempted to issue too much fiat money. If everyone were allowed to produce fiat money, so much fiat money would be issued that its value as money would fall to its production cost. If anyone could go to private engravers and order paper currency that could be exchanged for goods and services,

Example 3   The Dollar and "In God We Trust"

The Federal Reserve System is a public agency charged with regulating the money supply and serving as the bankers' bank (the central bank). The Federal Reserve issues the paper currency of the United States, called *Federal Reserve Notes.* Nothing backs Federal Reserve Notes. If you examine one of these notes you will find that it states: "This note is legal tender for all debts public and private." You will also notice along the top of the note the phrase, "In God We Trust." Not too long ago, the legal declaration contained a promise. The old declaration read: "This note is legal tender for debts public and private and is redeemable in lawful money at any Federal Reserve Bank." This, of course, was an empty promise because the Federal Reserve Notes themselves were the lawful money of the United States! In the 1950s, a Cleveland businessman tested this promise by requesting that a $20 bill be converted into lawful money. The Federal Reserve Bank sent him two $10 bills! The businessman persisted, sending in one of the $10 bills, and ended up with two $5 bills and a letter explaining that "lawful money" was not defined. Soon after his incident, the promise for redemption was dropped and the phrase "In God We Trust" was added!   ■

everyone would place large orders with engravers. A flood of paper money would overwhelm the economy and push up prices. This rush to print money would only cease when the purchasing power of one unit of money equaled the bill's commodity value, or the cost of producing the unit of paper money (which is very low). When the amount of fiat money in circulation is determined by government, however, fiat money exchanges for more than its cost of production. People require money for transactions, but the supply of money is limited by the government monopoly. Because money is useful, people are willing to exchange goods and services for money in excess of the commodity value of money.

The two basic forms of fiat money are coins and paper currency. U.S. coins are issued by the U.S. Treasury, and the value of the metal plus the cost of minting is less than the value of the coins used as money. Sometimes such coins are called *token money.* The most important example of fiat money in the United States is paper currency, called *Federal Reserve Notes,* because they are issued by the Federal Reserve System rather than by the U.S. Treasury. (See Example 3.)

Fiat money has the advantage that it uses up little of society's resources. Critics of fiat money argue that it has one major flaw—there will be a constant temptation to produce too much fiat money because it is so cheap and easy to produce. Governments, which have a monopoly over printing fiat money, may be tempted to produce more fiat money to pay their bills. As more fiat money floods the market, prices are bid up throughout the economy, and the value of a unit of fiat money falls. The existence of a fiat money system increases the chances of inflation.

Bank Money.   In a modern economy, most transactions are conducted using **bank money.**

> **Bank money** is money that is on deposit in checking accounts.

About 90 percent of the dollar value of all transactions in the United States are carried out by the writing of a **check.**

> A **check** is a directive to the check writer's bank to pay lawful money to the bearer of the check.

Payments can be made more safely by check. Checks are a better record of transactions, and money is more secure from theft if it is in a checking account than in someone's wallet. A checkable deposit at a local bank is money, simply because it is a generally acceptable medium of exchange in the nation's marketplaces. The details on how bank money is created are described in the next chapter.

A customer's deposit at a bank can be either a **demand deposit** (a checking account) or a **time deposit** (a savings account).

Example 4   Financial Innovations of the 1970s and 1980s

The late 1970s and early 1980s saw rapid changes in the characteristics of bank monies as the amount of government regulation of the banking system decreased. These changes tended to blur the distinction between demand deposits and time deposits.

The long-standing technical distinction between *demand deposits* and *time deposits* is that banks can legally require at least 30 days' notice before withdrawal of a time deposit. For savings deposits of households, however, banks do not usually enforce their right to 30 days' notice.

Prior to the mid-1970s, it was against banking laws to write checks on interest-paying accounts. When checks were written they had to be drawn on a commercial bank on an account that paid no explicit interest. Thrift institutions such as credit unions, mutual-savings banks, or savings-and-loan associations were prohibited from handling checking accounts; commercial banks were prohibited from paying interest on demand deposits. The only checkable deposits from 1933 to the early 1970s were commercial-bank demand deposits. Time, or savings, deposits were not checkable deposits.

In the late 1970s, the banking system began to experiment with ways around the legal ban on banks' paying interest on demand deposits—a ban that remains in effect today. Clever lawyers and bankers figured a way around this prohibition: they called the checkable deposit by another name—a NOW (negotiable order of withdrawal) account—or they allowed automatic transfers out of savings into special checking accounts—called ATS (automatic transfer services) accounts—whenever a check is written.

In addition to NOW and ATS accounts, innovative brokerage firms created money-market funds on which checks could be written. These are basically *investment clubs* in various high-interest-paying assets that are not accessible to small savers. These *money-market mutual funds* allow their investors to write checks over a prescribed amount. Money-market mutual funds have grown rapidly, since they have tended to pay higher interest rates than those offered by conventional savings accounts or NOW accounts.

NOW and ATS accounts have experienced phenomenal growth since 1975. In 1975, they amounted to $1.6 billion. In August of 1984, they amounted to $140 billion. In 1975, money-market mutual funds amounted to $3.6 billion. By August 1984, they had risen to $193 billion. ■

A **demand deposit** is a deposit of funds that can be withdrawn (''demanded'') from a depository institution at any time without restrictions. The funds are usually withdrawn by writing a check.

A **time deposit** is a deposit of funds upon which a depository institution (such as a bank) can legally require 30 days' notice of withdrawal and on which the financial institution pays the depositor interest.

In recent years, the distinction between demand deposits and other types of bank deposits has become less pronounced, which complicates the definition of bank money. (See Example 4.)

Definitions of Money Supply

The definition of **money supply** incorporates all three types of money just described. A country's money supply is also known as its *stock of money*.

The **money supply** of a country is the sum of all commodity money, fiat money, and bank money that are held by the nonbanking public as of a given date.

In the United States, there is no commodity money; so the U.S. money supply is the sum of fiat money and bank money. Note that the fiat money *held by banks* is not a part of the money supply. When someone cashes a check, the bank money the person holds in a checking account is converted to fiat money. Thus, the supply of fiat money in circulation has increased by the same amount as the supply of bank money has decreased. The fiat money the bank holds as cash is not counted in the money supply until it is held by someone outside the bank.

The money supply is a stock variable that can be defined as of a given moment in time—say,

Table 1 The U.S. Money Supply, M1 and M2, February 1985

Component	Amount (billions of dollars)
Currency and coin	160.6
plus	
Demand deposits[a]	251.7
plus	
Travelers' checks	5.3
plus	
Other checkable deposits[b]	151.7
equals	
M1	**569.3**
plus	
Savings deposits at all depository institutions	289.5
plus	
Small time deposits at all depository institutions[c]	876.0
plus	
Money-market mutual-fund shares	237.6
plus	
Other	446.9
equals	
M2	**2,419.3**

[a]Demand deposits at all commercial banks other than those due to other banks, the U.S. government, and foreign official institutions.
[b]Other checkable deposits include NOW and ATS accounts, credit-union share-draft balances, and demand deposits at mutual savings banks. NOW (negotiated order of withdrawal) accounts pay interest and are otherwise like demand deposits. ATS (automatic transfer services) accounts transfer funds from savings accounts to checking accounts automatically when a check is written.
[c]A small time deposit is one issued in a denomination of less than $100,000.

Source: *The Federal Reserve Bulletin.*

midnight on April 15. One's personal money supply on a given date would be the total amount of one's holdings of commodity money (which is zero in the United States), of fiat money (paper money plus coins), and the balance in one's checking account on that date. The combined money supply of all individuals and nonbanking firms on that date is the total money supply of the country.

The process of determining how much money there is in the United States at any point in time has been complicated by innovations in banking that have created new types of accounts that are actually (or very nearly) demand deposits. These innovations have led to a number of changes in what bank monies are included in the nation's money supply (see Example 4).

People hold their assets in different forms: as currency, as a deposit in a checking account or a savings account, as stocks or bonds, as real estate, and so on. These assets vary according to their **liquidity.**

Liquidity is the ease with which an asset can be converted into a medium of exchange without risk of loss.

The most basic characteristic of money is that it is perfectly liquid—it is already a medium of exchange. People are prepared to accept money as a means of payment. Thus, currency and demand deposits are perfectly liquid. They are a medium of exchange, a store of value, and a unit of account. There is no question that they should be included in the money supply. But other types of assets can be converted to cash with varying degrees of ease. *Money-market funds* and savings deposits on which checks may be written can be converted into cash quickly, but not on weekends or if one is out of town. Time deposits with a fixed maturity date can be converted to cash but with some penalty. Government and corporate bonds can also be converted into cash quickly but only when the banks are open or the bond market is open. Also, when these bonds fall in value, they have to be sold at a loss. Even assets such as land or old paintings can be converted into cash, though a substantial penalty may be incurred if one cannot wait for the right buyer to come along. Where does one draw the line between *money* and *nonmoney?*

Because it is difficult to draw the fine dividing line between money and nonmoney, U.S. financial authorities use different definitions of the U.S. money supply for different purposes.

Table 1 shows the two definitions of the U.S. money supply that are most frequently used by financial authorities: **M1** and **M2.**

M1 is the sum of currency (paper money and coins), demand deposits at commercial banks held by the nonbanking public, travelers' checks, and other checkable deposits like NOW (negotiable order of withdrawal) accounts and ATS (automatic transfer services) accounts.

M2 equals M1 *plus* savings and small time deposits plus money-market mutual-fund shares plus other highly liquid assets.

M1 amounted to $569 billion in February of 1985. M1 is the most frequently cited measure of the money supply; it includes the most liquid assets available in the economy. About one half of M1 is held by nonbanking business enterprises, one third by households, and the rest by an assortment of financial institutions, foreigners, and others.

M2 amounted to $2,419 billion in February of 1985. In addition to M1, it includes assets such as savings and other time deposits that are less liquid than the items in M1. For example, many of these accounts have penalties for withdrawal before a specified maturity date. The largest component of M2 is small time deposits ($876 billion).

The $1,850 billion dollar difference between M1 and M2 is made up savings deposits, money-market mutual funds, and other highly liquid assets.

Savings accounts can be converted into currency or checking-account money simply by going to the bank and withdrawing cash or depositing the cash in a checking account. Banks typically allow depositors to withdraw small time deposits with little or no penalty. Money-market funds may, likewise, be converted quickly into cash. Because such funds are close substitutes for M1, people have a tendency to shift assets back and forth between M1 and M2. As banking institutions discover ways to make M2 a closer substitute for M1, the distinction between M1 and M2 becomes more blurred. (See Example 5.) Because new types of money are being created, the definitions of M1 and M2 change over time. The creation of NOW and ATS accounts required that the definition of M1 be amended to include NOW and ATS accounts.

Why is the distinction between the different money-supply definitions important? Because the supply of money has an important effect on the economy, the supply of money is controlled by government monetary authorities. Whether monetary authorities control M1 or M2 will affect the extent to which individuals and firms substitute one form of money for another. The development of checkable money-market funds and NOW and ATS accounts has diverted funds from conventional commercial bank demand deposits. Financial innovations have tended to offer people more substitutes for conventional demand deposits.

THE DEMAND FOR MONEY

Although money has a variety of benefits, as just described, there is also an opportunity cost to holding money. The basic opportunity cost of holding (''demanding'') money is that one is passing up the opportunity to accumulate other forms of wealth that promise higher returns. If one holds $10,000 in cash or in one's non-interest-bearing checking account, one is sacrificing the opportunity to buy goods now or to put that money into stocks, bonds, or real estate.

Economists differentiate among three motives for demanding money: 1) the **transactions motive,** 2) the **precautionary motive,** and 3) the **speculative motive.**

People motivated by the **transactions motive** hold money in order to carry out normal transactions.

People motivated by the **precautionary motive** hold money in order to protect themselves against unforeseen emergencies.

People motivated by the **speculative motive** hold money in order to take advantage of opportunities to profit from market fluctuations.

The Transactions Motive

Money is required for transactions purposes because money is perfectly liquid. As already mentioned, liquidity is the ease and speed with which an asset can be converted into a medium of exchange without risk of loss. One can measure the liquidity of an asset by the speed of its conversion to money or the ease of its acceptance as money. The holder of money does not have to go through the time and expense of selling a less liquid asset (like a stock certificate or a bond) in order to get money. Assets such as land, apartment buildings, and paintings may serve as good stores of value especially during inflationary periods, but they are

Example 5   Why Credit Cards Are Not Money

Today a large proportion of retail transactions are made not by cash or check but by credit card. With the major exception of most grocery stores, most retailers are prepared to part with goods for cash, check, or credit card. Credit cards appear to fulfill (somewhat imperfectly) the medium-of-exchange function of money, although some businesses (such as grocery stores, gas stations, dry cleaners, and some restaurants) do not accept credit cards. Credit cards do *not* fulfill the other three functions of money, however. Most notably, they do not serve as a store of value. When a person buys something with a credit card, the credit-card company is making that person a temporary loan. The person must repay the balance, often with interest. In the case of American Express cards, the balance must be paid in full within 30 days. Master Card and Visa require that a minimum balance be paid each month and charge interest on the unpaid balance. The credit card saves the cardholder the inconvenience of going to a bank or credit union for a loan every time he or she wants to make a large purchase. The card also allows a cardholder to buy something before saving up the necessary amount in cash or in a checking account. Money accumulated in cash balances or in checking accounts is an asset. This asset can either be used to buy goods and services now or can be held as a store of value for future purchases. On the other hand, to use a credit card is to incur a liability; the cardholder then owes the credit-card company the outstanding balance. This liability can be removed only by accumulating sufficient cash or checking-account money to pay off the balance. Credit-card money,

rather than being a store of value, represents a future claim on one's money assets.

Credit-card companies are currently experimenting with a new type of credit card, called a *debit card*. The holder of a debit card deposits money in the credit-card account to create a positive balance. When a purchase is made, the amount of the purchase is subtracted from the balance. No loan is being made because money has already been placed in the account. A debit-card account does serve as a store of value because the positive balance is an asset that can be left in the account as a store of value. It also serves as a medium of exchange to the same extent that regular credit cards do. There is really little difference between a checking account and a debit card. Although they look different (writing a check versus presenting a debit card), they are really the same. Debit cards are more like money than credit cards.

The most important issue raised by the move to plastic money is whether credit cards have changed the demand for money. Credit cards do allow their holders to reduce temporarily the amount of money held in cash or in checking accounts because credit cards can be substituted for cash transactions. However, credit-card customers must accumulate sufficient money balances to pay at least a percentage of their credit-card balances. One can only pay one's credit-card bills by accumulating money. It is not clear whether the existence of plastic money has substantially changed the quantity of money demanded by the economy as a whole. ∎

not liquid because some time or expense is involved in converting them to cash. Because people have to carry out regular transactions, they must hold part of their wealth in the form of money. The inconvenience of converting other assets into cash would be too great to allow individuals to conduct transactions without holding some money.

The Precautionary Motive

People demand money to carry out their normal transactions. They also hold money in their checking accounts as a precaution to handle un-

foreseen emergencies. If a family member becomes ill, medicine may have to be purchased at the pharmacy. If one's car breaks down, one may have to pay for emergency towing or repairs. Many people keep extra money in their wallets or hidden in their homes just for such emergencies.

The Speculative Motive

People demand money for speculative reasons as well. If a stock-market speculator gets the hunch that stock prices will fall through the floor within two months' time, he or she would likely sell current stock holdings, put the proceeds into an interest-bearing checking account, and wait for the stock market to fall. The speculator would then be in a position to buy stocks cheap with the money accumulated for speculative reasons. Today, the speculative motive is not important in the demand for M1 but would be important in the demand for M2 because M2 includes money-market mutual funds. Clearly, a speculator would not wish to hold large balances in low-interest-bearing checking accounts.

Factors Affecting the Demand for Money

The factors that cause the demand for money to change include the economy's level of real income, interest rates, inflation, and the price level.

First, as real incomes rise, people participate in more transactions; therefore, *the transactions demand for money should tend to rise with income.*

Second, the income that can be earned by holding assets other than money is the opportunity cost of holding money. Interest rates are one measure of the yields on other assets; therefore, *higher interest rates should reduce the quantity of money demanded.* The interest rate is really the *price* of holding assets in the form of money. According to demand theory, quantity demanded falls when price rises. This rule holds for the demand for money just as it holds for the demand for other commodities.

Third, when prices are rising, money ceases to be a good store of value. Although rising prices may require more money for transactions, a higher anticipated rate of inflation causes people to switch their wealth out of money into assets such as real estate, stock, or rare art works that promise to retain their value. Thus, *a higher inflation rate will lower the demand for money.*

Fourth, *a higher price level* with a given level of real GNP *increases the transactions demand for money.* As prices rise, even though people are making the same purchases as before, they require more money to make their transactions. A typical bag of groceries will have a higher dollar price as the price level rises. People, therefore, require higher cash balances to make their normal purchases.

The economy's demand for money depends upon the economy's real income, interest rates, inflation, and the price level.

THE RELATIONSHIP BETWEEN MONEY AND PRICES

Economists have long been interested in the relationship between money and prices. The previous section discussed the demand for money; the next chapter examines how monetary authorities control the supply of money. This section shows how prices are driven up when the quantity of money supplied exceeds the quantity of money demanded. Basic supply-and-demand analysis can provide the first insights into the relationship between money and prices. The chapter will close with a more sophisticated analysis of this relationship—the quantity theory of money.

A Money Supply/Money Demand Theory of Inflation

The supply-and-demand analysis presented in Chapter 4 sheds light on the relationship between the stock of money and prices. Remember from Chapter 4 that if the supply of a good rises relative to its demand, its price will fall to equate quantity demanded and quantity supplied. This elementary principle of supply and demand applies to money as well. As noted earlier, money is demanded, just as shoes, clothing, and beer are demanded. People hold money for transactions, precautionary, and speculative motives. If the supply of money rises more rapidly than its demand, the value of money should fall to again equate quantity demanded and quantity supplied. If the demand for money rises relative to its supply, the value of money should rise—again, to equate quantity demanded and quantity supplied.

The *value* of money is determined by what one can buy with it. The value of money is declining when each unit of money (say, each dollar) buys fewer goods. If the price of a candy bar is $0.25, $1 is worth 4 candy bars. If the price of a candy bar rises to $0.50, $1 is worth only 2 candy bars. In terms of a candy bar, the value of $1 is 1 divided by the price of a candy bar. Thus, the value of money falls when prices rise, and the value of money rises when prices fall. In other words, *there is an inverse relationship between the price level and the value of money.*

If *P* represents the general price level (as measured, say, by the GNP deflator), then the value of money is measured as the *inverse* of *P*, or as $1/P$. If prices rise by 10 percent, the value of money will fall by 10 percent.

The value of money falls in exact inverse proportion to the increase in the overall level of prices.

Supply-and-demand analysis predicts that when the money supply rises more rapidly than money demand, the economy will respond by raising the price level (lowering the value of money). When the money supply rises more slowly than money demand, the economy responds by lowering the price level (raising the value of money).

Since inflation is defined as an increase in the overall level of prices, inflation is associated with increases in money supply. If the money supply increases more rapidly than the demand for money, the price level will rise.

When the demand for money is constant and the supply of money is increased, people have excess cash balances that they do not want to hold. People try to get rid of their excess cash balances by spending them.

However, *it is impossible for the community as a whole to get rid of money.* When one person purchases a good with money, the seller's cash balance rises as the buyer's balance falls. Money is being passed from one person to another without changing the economy's supply of money. Individuals can spend excess cash balances, but the whole community cannot. As each person tries to get rid of an excess supply of money, prices are driven up because there are more dollars in the economy chasing the same number of goods. As prices rise, the community as a whole requires more money for its transactions. Thus, rising prices increase the quantity of money demanded until the excess supply of money disappears.

Figure 1   Increasing Money Supply Drives Up Prices When Money Demand Is Constant

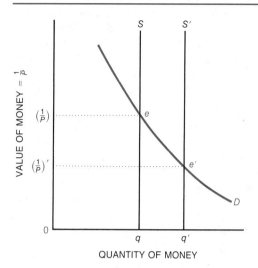

The equilibrium value of money ($1/P$) occurs at that price level at which the quantity of money supplied equals the quantity of money demanded. Initially, this equilibrium is at *e*. If the supply of money increases while money demand remains constant, at the old equilibrium value of money, there is a greater quantity of money supplied than people want to hold. People, therefore, speed up purchases in their effort to get rid of money balances. Increased spending drives up prices and lowers the value of money until a new equilibrium (at *e'*) is reached where the quantity of money demanded equals the quantity supplied. The increase in the supply of money has caused inflation.

Equilibrium is restored when the quantity of money demanded equals the quantity supplied, and prices stop rising. This process is shown in Figure 1.

Evidence: Money Growth and Inflation

The simple supply/demand theory of inflation says that inflation will occur when the increase in the supply of money is greater than the increase in the demand for money. If the quantity of money supplied exceeds the quantity demanded, the value of money falls. As we have seen, the value of money falls when the price level rises. Through price-level adjustments, the supply of and demand for money will reach an equilibrium.

To find evidence in the real world of the relationship between money and prices, we must contrast the *growth* of money supply with the *growth* in the demand for money. In modern economies, real GNP grows over time; the demand for money grows over time; the supply of money grows over time. In the real world it is hard to find one-shot changes in money supply, money demand, or real GNP. Instead, these variables tend to grow, with growth sometimes accelerating, sometimes decelerating, and even sometimes negative. This section examines the relationship between the growth rate of prices (the inflation rate), the growth rate of the money supply, and the growth rate of the demand for money.

The growth rate of any variable, x between year t and year $t + 1$ is

$$\frac{x_{t+1}}{x_t} - 1.$$

Thus, if real GNP is \$4.0 trillion in 1986 and \$4.4 trillion in 1987, the growth rate of real GNP between 1986 and 1987 is \$4.4 billion $\div$ \$4.0 billion $- 1 = 0.10$, or 10 percent.

The rate of growth of the supply of money is determined by monetary authorities (as the next chapter shows). What determines the rate of growth of the demand for money? The demand for money should rise with real GNP, *ceteris paribus,* because it takes more money to buy a larger volume of goods and services at the same prices. As a first approximation, one can say that the demand for money grows at about the same rate as the growth of real GNP. Inflationary pressures will appear, therefore, when the growth of the money supply exceeds the growth of real GNP. If the money supply grows more rapidly than the growth of money demand (as measured by the growth of real GNP), prices should rise because of this **excess monetary growth.**

Excess monetary growth occurs when the money supply grows more rapidly than money demand.

The adjective *excess* in the term *excess monetary growth* has a technical rather than a judgmental meaning; it is simply a reference to the situation that exists when the growth in the supply of money *exceeds* the growth in the demand for money and, hence, drives prices up.

The concept of excess monetary growth is explored in depth in Chapter 14 on inflation. As a rough measure, we can say that excess monetary growth occurs when the growth of the money supply exceeds the growth of real GNP.

Figure 2 plots excess monetary growth (measured as the growth rate of M1 minus the growth rate of real GNP) and the inflation rate (as measured by the annual growth rate of the GNP deflator) for the 13 five-year periods between 1915 to 1984. The supply/demand theory of inflation predicts that the inflation rate will be positively related to excess monetary growth. Figure 2 shows a strong correspondence between excess monetary growth and inflation. In periods when monetary growth exceeded real GNP growth (1915–20, 1945–50, the 1970s and 1980s), the inflation rate tended to be high. In periods when monetary growth was equal to or below real GNP growth (the 1920s, the 1950s, and the early 1960s) the inflation rate tended to be low (or even negative). The empirical relationship is not perfect, but it does provide strong support for the supply/demand theory of inflation.

For the 1915–1984 period covered by Figure 2, prices rose by more than 10 times, real GNP rose by 8 times, while money supply grew by almost 33 times. Prices rose because *when money supply grows at a more rapid rate than real GNP, there is an excess supply of money.* People increase their spending in an attempt to get rid of excess cash balances, the price level is bid up, and the value of money falls.

The evidence that money supply and price level are related is not limited to the United States. Table 2 compares the annual rates of growth of money and prices in a number of countries and the United States during various periods. The table shows a remarkable correspondence between the rate of growth in the money supply and the rate of inflation. Those countries that experienced the most rapid growth of money supply tend to have the highest rates of inflation.

Some countries have experienced dramatic historical episodes of runaway inflations, or hyperinflations. Hyperinflations essentially make the money of the country worthless. The economy must resort to barter and must seek out other

Figure 2   Excess Monetary Growth and U.S. Inflation, 1915 to 1984

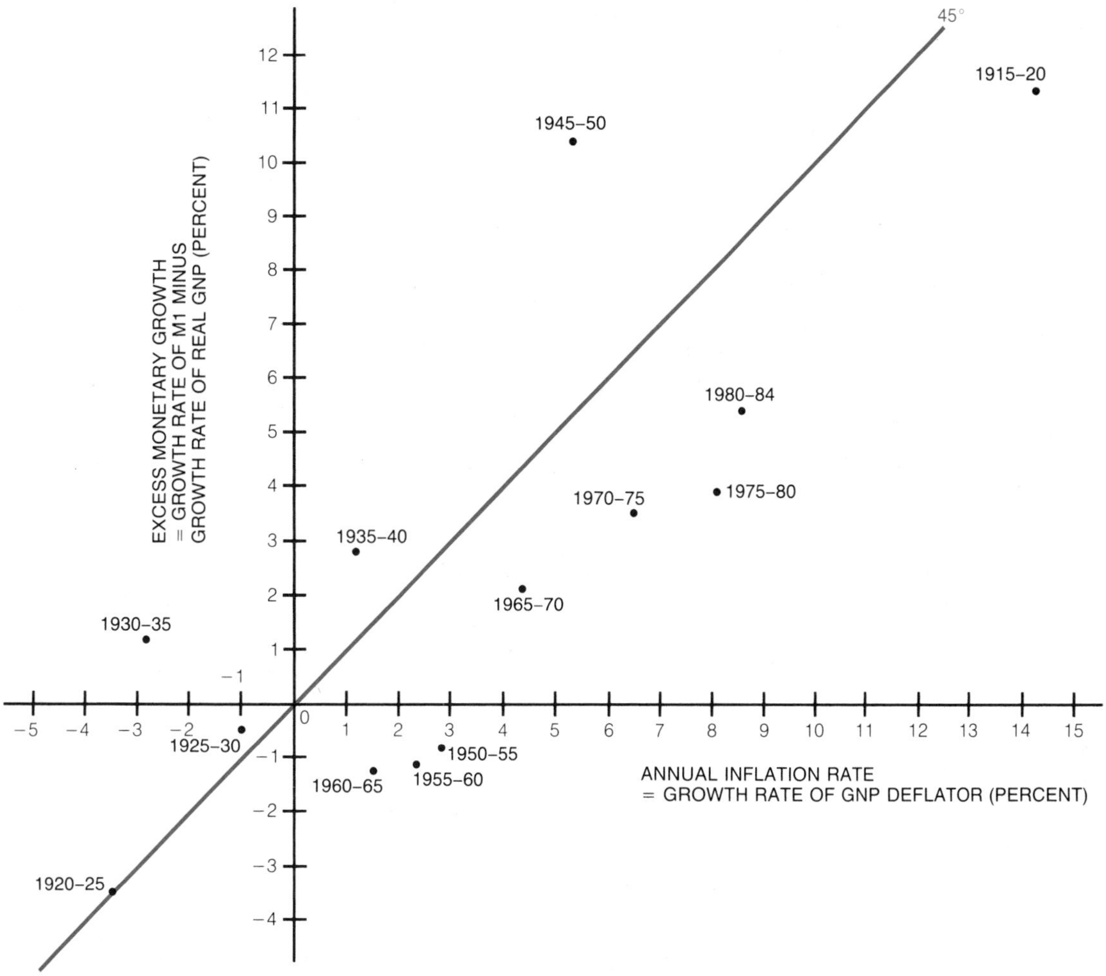

In this figure, *excess monetary growth* is measured as the growth rate of M1 minus the growth rate of real GNP, and the inflation rate is measured by the GNP deflator (the CPI is used for 1915 to 1930). Each dot shows the combination of excess monetary growth and inflation for a given period. If the dot for a particular period falls on the 45-degree line, inflation equals excess monetary growth during that period. As predicted by the supply/demand theory of inflation, there appears to be a positive correlation between excess monetary growth and inflation. The correlation, however, is not perfect (the dots do not all fall on the 45-degree line). Factors other than excess monetary growth also affect inflation.

types of money, often foreign currencies or commodity money.

How well do the historical episodes of hyperinflation support the money supply/money demand interpretation of inflation? The cause of each hyperinflation is well documented: the government printed too much money, often to finance wars or to pay the bills of past wars. Hyperinflations have been caused by excessive monetary growth. (See Example 6.) In each hyperinflation,

the cure was achieved only when the government slowed down the printing of money.

THE CLASSICAL QUANTITY THEORY OF MONEY

Chapter 1 warned against the false-cause fallacy. The fact that money and prices have tended to move together does not prove that increases in

Table 2 Annual Growth Rates of Price and Money for Selected Countries in the Post-World War II Period (arranged by decreasing order of the inflation rate)

Country	$\Delta P/P$	$\Delta M/M$ (Currency)	Time Span	Country	$\Delta P/P$	$\Delta M/M$ (Currency)	Time Span
Chile	89.1	97.1	1970–79	Nepal	6.6	11.8	1965–79
Argentina	72.8	70.2	1969–79	Greece	6.5	13.8	1950–79
Uruguay	42.2	41.5	1960–79	Libya	6.2	25.5	1964–78
Brazil	29.9	33.2	1963–79	New Zealand	6.2	5.7	1954–79
Zaire	27.7	18.8	1963–79	Thailand	6.2	11.4	1965–79
Bolivia	22.7	26.8	1950–79	United Kingdom	6.2	7.0	1951–79
Turkey	21.0	24.3	1968–78	Egypt	6.1	12.6	1965–79
Peru	16.1	20.7	1960–79	Italy	6.1	10.2	1950–79
Ghana	15.4	15.2	1959–77	Togo	6.0	13.9	1963–79
Israel	15.1	18.3	1950–79	France	6.0	7.5	1950–79
Korea (S.)	15.0	25.4	1953–79	Congo	6.0	9.5	1960–79
Iceland	14.1	15.8	1951–79	Australia	5.9	7.6	1950–79
Nigeria	14.0	26.4	1968–77	Denmark	5.9	6.7	1950–79
Yugoslavia	13.7	20.3	1960–79	Iran	5.9	16.0	1959–77
Colombia	11.7	17.1	1950–79	Philippines	5.9	9.0	1950–79
Sierra Leone	11.0	15.8	1971–78	Chad	5.8	7.2	1960–77
Paraguay	10.6	15.8	1952–79	Costa Rica	5.7	12.1	1960–79
Saudia Arabia	9.7	24.9	1967–69	Japan	5.7	12.9	1953–79
Central African Republic	9.3	11.6	1970–77	Ecuador	5.6	11.8	1951–79
Spain	9.1	12.9	1954–79	Netherlands	5.5	7.2	1960–79
Senegal	7.8	6.7	1964–79	Norway	5.5	7.0	1950–79
Mexico	7.8	14.0	1950–78	Sweden	5.5	7.5	1950–79
Pakistan	7.8	10.5	1961–79	Iraq	5.4	14.7	1965–76
Ivory Coast	7.6	14.0	1962–79	Madagascar	5.3	7.8	1964–78
Jamaica	7.6	13.5	1953–79	South Africa	5.2	8.0	1950–79
Portugal	7.5	10.4	1953–78	Upper Volta	5.1	10.2	1962–79
Niger	7.5	13.5	1963–79	Austria	4.8	8.2	1950–79
Mauritius	7.4	12.9	1963–79	Morocco	4.8	11.6	1960–78
Gabon	7.4	11.7	1962–79	Syria	4.8	14.0	1957–79
Somalia	7.1	16.8	1960–79	Guyana	4.2	9.7	1960–76
Cameroon	6.9	11.3	1962–79	Singapore	4.2	12.4	1963–79
Sudan	6.9	9.7	1951–79	Haiti	4.1	7.1	1953–78
Trinidad & Tobago	6.8	12.1	1960–78	Belgium	4.0	4.9	1953–79
Gambia	6.8	10.8	1964–79	Canada	4.0	7.1	1950–79
Ireland	6.7	9.0	1950–79	Tunisia	3.9	10.6	1960–78
Finland	6.6	8.7	1950–79	Dominican Republic	3.8	9.1	1950–79
India	6.6	8.7	1960–78	El Salvador	3.8	8.0	1951–79

Source: Robert J. Barro, *Macroeconomics* (New York: John Wiley & Sons, 1984), p. 153–54.

money supply have caused increases in the price level. A consistent and logical theory that explains why an increase in money supply will cause an increase in price level must be tested before this conclusion can be drawn. This section will elaborate further on a theory of why inflation is caused by excess monetary growth.

That inflation is caused by excess growth of the money supply is a fairly old notion. The classical economists of the 18th century, such as David Hume and Adam Smith, proposed a theory

to explain the relationship between money supply and price level. This theory was taken up by the great American economist Irving Fisher of Yale University (1867–1947) and by the great English economist Alfred Marshall (1842–1924) and has come to be called the **classical quantity theory of money,** or simply the *quantity theory*. The quantity theory is the antecedent of important modern macroeconomic theories. It is especially useful because it provides a powerful though simplified view of how the macroeconomy works.

Example 6   Bolivia: Living With the World's Highest Inflation Rate

---

In 1984, consumer prices rose by 2,700 percent in Bolivia with experts predicting a 1985 inflation rate of as high as 40,000 percent! What is it like to live in a country where prices go up by the hour? Banks no longer bother to count banknotes. Instead, they simply rely on the word of the depositor as to how much money is in the bundle of banknotes being deposited. It takes too much employee time to count "small" deposits like 32 million pesos. Tons of paper money must be printed each month. Planeloads of money arrive twice a week from printers in West Germany. Purchases of printed money cost the Bolivian government $20 million of scarce foreign exchange—making printed money Bolivia's third largest import. The 1,000 peso bill buys one bag of tea and costs more to print than it purchases. In November of 1984, the Bolivian government came out with a 100,000 peso bill (then worth about $1), but there aren't enough to go around. Business people carry large suitcases of cash with them, and people have to go shopping in twos to carry all the banknotes needed for that day's purchases. Prices go up by the hour. Merchants refuse to accept checks or credit cards because prices will rise before checks clear or credit-card balances are paid. Changes in the value of the Bolivian peso spread by word of mouth, and merchants adjust upward their prices constantly. Merchants demand payment in dollars for major purchases, and people get their dollars from streetside money vendors.

This example illustrates the destructive nature of hyperinflation. Bolivia's scarce dollar holdings must be devoted to paying for printed money. People are diverted from productive work activities. The disruptive effects of hyperinflation have manifested themselves in crippling strikes and a 25 percent decline in real wages. ∎

Source: "When Inflation Rate is 116,000%, Prices Rise by the Hour," *Wall Street Journal,* February 7, 1985.

The basic message of the **classical quantity theory of money** is that the price level is strictly proportional to the money supply.

In other words, the classical quantity theory taught that an *x* percent increase in money supply will lead to an *x* percent increase in the price level in the short run. In other words, if M1 increases 10 percent, the classical quantity theory would predict a 10 percent increase in the price level. The proponents of the quantity theory did not believe that this relationship would hold exactly in all instances, but they felt it was a reasonably close approximation of the reality of the economy in the late 19th and early 20th centuries.

Velocity of Circulation

The concept of **velocity of circulation** is essential to an understanding of the quantity theory.

The **velocity of circulation** is the number of times the average dollar is spent on final goods and services in one year's time.

In 1984, American GNP was $3,661 billion, which means that in 1984, households, government, and businesses spent this sum on final goods and services. The average 1984 supply of money (M1) was $543 billion. In order for the economy to make $3,661 billion worth of purchases in the course of one year with a stock of money of $543 billion, each dollar was spent on average 6.7 times (6.7 = $3,661 billion ÷ $543 billion). In other words, each dollar financed the purchase of $6.70 worth of final goods and services in the course of that year; the velocity of circulation was equal to 6.4.

The velocity of circulation *(V)* is the ratio of GNP to the money supply:

$$V \equiv GNP/M$$

The higher is the velocity of circulation, the faster people are turning over the available stock of money. In 1984, each dollar was turned over an average of 6.7 times. Velocity can rise or fall with changing economic conditions. In hyperinflations, for example, velocity tends to rise as people try to spend their money as fast as possible before its value declines even further. When prices are stable or falling, people are more inclined to hold on to their money longer.

Since nominal GNP equals real GNP (denoted here by Q) multiplied by the price level, P, the velocity of circulation can also be expressed as:

$$V \equiv \frac{PQ}{M},$$

where M represents money supply.

The Equation of Exchange

By multiplying both sides of the velocity-of-circulation equation by M, the equation becomes

$$MV \equiv PQ.$$

This equation is known as the *equation of exchange*.

The $\equiv$ symbol is used instead of the $=$ symbol because the equation of exchange is a tautology (identity), or an equation that is true by definition. Velocity is defined in such a way that the equation always works.

In effect, the equation of exchange says that the amount of final purchases in the economy (GNP) must equal the amount of money in circulation times the average number of times each dollar changes hands. Were this not true, then the observed amount of final spending would not have been possible.

The equation of exchange can be used to explain the quantity theory. Irving Fisher and Alfred Marshall both believed that the equation of exchange summarized the relevant factors determining the link between the money supply and the price level.

Changes in Money Supply and Prices

The equation of exchange does not guarantee that money supply and the price level will rise at the same rate. If V rises while M is constant, total spending *(PQ)* must rise. Unless Q rises to take up the slack, P must rise. Thus, P could rise

without there being any increase in M. The quantity theory assumes that:

1. the velocity of circulation, V, is fixed.
2. real GNP, Q, is fixed in the short run.

These assumptions turn the equation of exchange into a theory. The equation of exchange shows that if both Q and V are fixed, then P will be proportional to M. The equation of exchange, rewritten to solve for P, is $P = M\ (V/Q)$. If Q and V are both fixed, V/Q will be a constant. Therefore, an x percent increase in M will cause an x percent increase in P. With V and Q constant (no matter what their values), a 5 percent increase in M will cause a 5 percent increase in P; a 10 percent increase in M will cause a 10 percent increase in P. With Q and V both fixed, the quantity theory concludes that P is strictly proportional to M, or, in other words, that inflation is strictly a monetary phenomenon.

Why did the quantity theorists assume that velocity of circulation and real GNP were both fixed in the short run? They felt that velocity is fixed by the monetary habits and institutions of the community. A country with a large number of money substitutes may have a high velocity of circulation; a country with few money substitutes may have a low velocity. A country with frequent pay periods may have a high velocity; a country with few pay periods may have a low velocity. Whatever the case, because habits and institutions change very slowly, for all practical purposes, quantity theorists regarded velocity as constant.

The quantity theorists believed the size of real GNP is fixed in the short run by the size and productivity of the resources (land, labor, and capital) of the country. Land, labor, and capital grow slowly over time, but at any point in time they are essentially fixed in supply. The real output of the economy is fixed because resources will tend to be fully employed, particularly the most important resource, labor. In this view, changing resource prices ensure the full employment of resources. If workers are involuntarily unemployed, the wage rate will automatically adjust downwards until all those willing to work at the going wage will be employed. Over time as the labor force expands and technology improves, real output will rise. But in the short run, real output is fixed by the resource base and by technology.

The Money Sector and the Real Sector

The classical quantity theorists divided the economy into two sectors: a *real sector* and a *monetary sector*. In the real sector, resources are combined to produce full-employment output. The same amount of output will be supplied no matter what the price level. What counts is not the height of the general price level but the adjustment of relative resource prices to bring the economy to full employment. In the monetary sector, the price level is established by the amount of money in the economy. According to the quantity theorists, the two sectors do not overlap. Changes in money supply are not associated with changes in employment or real output, and vice versa.

The *quantity theory, therefore, denies a link between the money supply and unemployment.* According to the quantity theory, employment and output are determined in the real sector, and changes in money supply will affect only the price level, not real output or employment.

Aggregate Supply and Aggregate Demand in the Quantity Theory

Chapter 5 introduced the concepts of aggregate demand and aggregate supply. Aggregate supply-and-demand analysis can be used to illustrate the major propositions of the classical quantity theory. Aggregate demand *(AD)* is a schedule of the amount of real GNP demanded by all agents in the economy at different price levels. Aggregate supply *(AS)* is a schedule of the amounts of real GNP supplied at different price levels. Chapter 5 gave the *AD* curve a negative slope and the *AS* curve a positive slope.

What types of aggregate-demand and aggregate-supply curves are suggested by the quantity theory? To obtain the quantity-theory aggregate-demand curve, the quantity equation $MV = PQ$ can be rearranged as $Q = MV/P$. With this arrangement, the aggregate quantity demanded *(Q)* is a function of the price level *(P)*. The relationship between Q and P is inverse. A higher P causes a smaller Q to be demanded, *ceteris paribus*. Like microeconomic demand curves, the aggregate demand curve gives the relationship between output and price level when all other

Figure 3 The Classical Quantity Theory

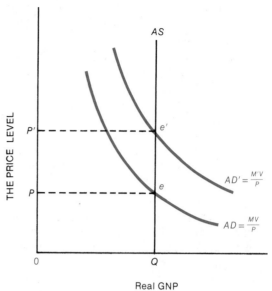

The aggregate quantity demanded of goods and services at each price level, according to the classical quantity theory, is simply *MV/P*, where *V* is a constant and *M* is held constant. Since real GNP is fixed, the aggregate-supply curve *(AS)* is vertical. If the money supply increases from *M* to *M'*, *AD* shifts to the right, and the equilibrium price level increases proportionately from *P* to *P'*.

factors that affect demand are held constant. According to the quantity theorists, velocity is already constant, so the aggregate demand curve can shift only if the money supply changes.

With money supply and velocity fixed, the quantity equation says that the aggregate demand for real GNP will vary inversely with the price level. The higher is the price level, the lower will be the quantity of real goods and services demanded. When money supply increases, aggregate demand increases (*AD* shifts to the right). The demand equation, $Q = MV/P$, shows that when M increases, more will be demanded *at each price level*. An increase in M causes aggregate demand to increase.

Figure 3 shows the aggregate-demand and aggregate-supply curves according to the classical quantity theory. The aggregate-demand curve is negatively sloped, and the aggregate-supply curve is a vertical line. *AS* is vertical because, according to the classical quantity theory, real GNP is fixed at full employment. Real GNP, therefore, cannot increase as the price level increases; all resources are already fully employed. With real GNP already determined, the intersection of *AD* and *AS* determines only the price level.

When the money supply increases, the aggregate-demand curve shifts right proportionately, and the equilibrium price level *P* rises to *P'*. If *M'* is twice *M*, then *P'* will be twice *P*.

According to the quantity theory, *the value of money depends on its nominal quantity not on the stuff from which it is made.* Money is valuable because of what it can buy. According to the quantity theory, it makes no difference whether the money is made out of gold, platinum, or just plain old paper on which some engravings of old men have been made. If the quantity of money is limited, the money will have value because it is the generally accepted medium of exchange.

This conclusion has policy implications. Why waste resources using a commodity money like gold or silver? Why not just print the money in a way that is difficult to counterfeit and limit its quantity? Sceptics doubt the ability of governments to resist the lure of printing too much money. For these critics, the cost of resources involved in commodity money is less than the inflationary costs of the excesses of government printing presses.

A PREVIEW OF MODERN QUANTITY THEORY

The classical quantity theory is a direct ancestor of modern monetary economics. Modern monetary economists have relaxed some of the more restrictive assumptions of the classical quantity theory and have turned it into a more sophisticated and realistic theory of the relationship between money, output, and prices. The development of the modern quantity theory is associated with the works of Irving Fisher, Milton Friedman, Allan Meltzer, and Karl Brunner.

Modern quantity theorists have had to adapt the classical quantity theory to two real-world phenomena not accounted for by the classical theory. First, the sharp and sustained drop of output and employment during the Great Depression demonstrated that economies can operate below full employment for lengthy periods of time. Moreover, in the post–World War II era, modern capitalist economies have continued to experience episodes of sharply rising output followed by episodes of falling output (the business cycle). The classical quantity theory argued that the supply of money affects only the price level, not output or employment. To say that money has no impact on output and employment—in the face of its perceived effects on interest rates, desired spending, and inflation—appeared unrealistic to the modern observer. Therefore, modern quantity theorists have had to explain how and under what conditions the quantity of money affects not only the price level but also output and employment. Second, the empirical record now clearly shows that velocity is not constant as the classical quantity theory assumed. The velocity of circulation has been subject to significant ups and downs, often within a brief period of time. If velocity behaves erratically without any apparent pattern, then the link between monetary growth and inflation can disappear. For example, a fall in *V* can neutralize the effects of monetary growth on the price level. Unless modern monetary economists could explain systematically the reasons for changes in velocity, they would not be able to account for the observed relationship between money and prices.

Later chapters will discuss how the modern monetary economists have dealt with changing velocity and with money's effects on output and employment. For now, we can only briefly summarize their major propositions. First, modern monetary theory emphasizes that there are systematic determinants of velocity, the most important being the anticipated rate of inflation. During an accelerating inflation, for example, people start to anticipate rising prices. People who anticipate inflation will not be content to sit with their pockets full of currency or with large sums in their checking accounts. Rather, they try to spend their money balances more quickly. As they speed up their purchases and find ways to hold down their cash balances, the velocity of circulation rises.

Modern monetary theory argues that velocity changes if people generally anticipate a change in the rate of inflation. If people expect inflation to rise, velocity rises. If people expect inflation to fall, velocity falls. If there is no change in inflationary expectations, velocity remains the same.

In effect, modern monetary theory tends to argue that *M* and *V* can move together. Excessive monetary growth sets off inflation, and inflation causes inflationary expectations to rise. As inflationary expectations rise, velocity rises. With rising velocity, the inflationary effects of excess monetary growth are worsened, and inflation intensifies.

Modern monetary theory maintains that the money supply can indeed affect output and employment, but more so in the short run than in the long run. The major effects of money on employment and output occur when people have not correctly anticipated inflation. When inflation is not correctly anticipated, workers are stuck with wage contracts that do not protect them from inflation. Firms find themselves with obligations to supply materials at contracted prices that do not protect them from inflation. On the other hand, producers find their selling prices rising more rapidly than anticipated. Producers believe that their selling prices are rising more rapidly than their costs, and they increase their employment and output. When inflation is unanticipated, a rising price level causes more output to be supplied to the economy. The aggregate supply curve is not vertical; rather, it is positively sloped—at least in the short run.

When inflation is steady, the conditions of the classical quantity theory are most likely to be met. Households and businesses will be able to anticipate correctly the rate of inflation when the inflation rate remains the same from year to year. As long as inflation is correctly anticipated, monetary effects on real output will be avoided as well—a second means of disrupting the proportionality of money supply to price level.

Although increases in anticipated inflation raise velocity, massive changes in the institutions of money and banking can also cause substantive changes in velocity and undermine the classical quantity theory. During periods when many new money substitutes are being created, the velocity of old money will increase as people switch from old money to new forms of money.

As the data cited in Figure 2 and Table 2 show, the classical quantity theory holds up fairly well. Money and prices do tend to move together. The determinants of velocity and the role of unanticipated inflation can be more fully explained in later chapters after an understanding of the analytical tools of macroeconomics is achieved.

This chapter has explained what money is and how to measure the money supply and has introduced the simplest theory of macroeconomics: the quantity theory of money. Before embarking on the task of explaining modern macroeconomics in Chapters 9 through 17, the next chapter will explain how the money supply is actually determined in a modern economy and will describe the role of the banking system.

Summary

1. Money is the medium of exchange ordinarily used in transactions. In addition, money serves as a unit of value, a standard of deferred payment, and a store of value. Inflation complicates the use of money as a standard of deferred payment and as a store of value. When inflation is foreseen, people may be able to protect money's role in these two functions.

2. The money supply consists of commodity money, fiat money, and bank money. Commodity money's value as a commodity is as great as its value as money. Fiat money's value as a commodity is less than its value as money. Bank money consists of checking deposits.

3. People demand money for transactions purposes, for precautionary motives, and for speculative motives. Interest rates measure the opportunity costs of holding money.

4. Supply-and-demand analysis suggests that when money supply increases more rapidly than money demand, the value of money should fall. When money-supply growth exceeds the growth of money demand, *excess monetary growth* occurs. The value of money falls when prices rise. A rise in the overall price level is inflation.

5. The classical quantity theory of money suggests that changes in money supply and price level will be strictly proportional. This conclusion follows from the equation of exchange *(MV = PQ)* and from the assumptions that velocity and output are fixed.

6. Modern theorists argue that unanticipated inflation can affect real output and employment. Thus, changes in the money supply can affect

real output. Anticipated inflation raises velocity as people adjust their spending habits to reduce their money balances. The classical quantity theory holds reasonably well when inflation is relatively stable over long periods.

Key Terms

money
commodity money
Gresham's Law
fiat money
bank money
check
demand deposit
time deposit
money supply
liquidity
M1
M2
transactions motive
precautionary motive
speculative motive
excess monetary growth
classical quantity theory of money
velocity of circulation

Questions and Problems

1. "Anything is money that is legally declared by the government to be money." Evaluate this statement.

2. During hyperinflations money loses its value as a medium of exchange, as a store of value, and as a standard of deferred payment. What would you expect to happen to the overall efficiency of the economy when this happens?

3. "It is foolish to talk about the demand for money. People want all the money they can get their hands on." Evaluate this statement.

4. Explain why the value of fiat money is determined by its relative abundance. What is the lower limit to which the value of fiat money can fall?

5. Discuss the social costs of having a commodity-money system. What are its benefits?

How does Gresham's Law enter into this issue?

6. If prices are rising 5 percent per year, what is happening to the value of money?

7. Assume that the demand for money is increasing at a rate of 20 percent per year and that the supply of money is increasing at a rate of 10 percent per year. What would you expect to happen to the value of money? to prices?

8. Why is the distinction between M1 and M2 important?

9. When answering the following questions, assume $M = \$100$, $Q = 400$ units, and $P = \$2$ per unit.
   a. What is the value of V?
   b. Determine the aggregate-demand schedule for a price level of $1, for a price level of $2, and for a price level of $3.
   c. If the money supply rose to $150, what would the aggregate-demand schedule be for the three price levels listed in part **b**?
   d. Use this example to illustrate the basic proposition of the classical quantity theory.
   e. In this example, show that if V is unstable and unpredictable, the basic proposition of the classical quantity theory does not hold.

10. Assume that in Economy X rice is the sole form of money. A rice blight wipes out half this year's crop and also spoils much of the rice in storage. Predict what effects these events will have on prices and output.

11. Explain why time deposits are not money.

12. Assume that in Economy Y cigarettes are used as money. What will happen to the price level if a health scare causes people to reduce their commodity demand for cigarettes?

Suggested Readings

Friedman, Milton. *Dollars and Deficits*. Englewood Cliffs, N.J.: Prentice-Hall, 1968.

Galbraith, John K. *Money*. Boston, Mass.: Houghton Mifflin, 1975.

Solow, Robert. "The Intelligent Citizen's Guide to Inflation." *The Public Interest* (Winter 1975), pp. 30–66.

8

Commercial Banking and the Federal Reserve

Chapter Preview

The last chapter discussed how the supply of money can affect prices, output, and employment. This chapter will explain how and by whom the money supply is determined. Why does money supply increase or decrease? Or, in other words, where does money come from? Where does money go?

The money supply can increase or decrease very rapidly. From 1929 to 1933, money supply fell by a gigantic 25 percent from $26.6 billion to $19.9 billion, yet the amount of currency held by the public actually increased. What happened to the missing $6.7 billion? Those who lived through the Great Depression will argue either that people had it under their mattresses or that Rockefeller had it all.

In order to see how the money supply expands or contracts, one must understand the business of banking and the relationship between banks and the Federal Reserve System. One must also understand the relationship between the money supply and credit conditions to see how the money supply affects interest rates. ■

THE BUSINESS OF BANKING: FINANCIAL INTERMEDIATION

Most of us have had some experience with banks: a commercial bank cashes our checks; a savings-and-loan association handles our savings account; the credit union at our place of work will give us a loan for new furniture. What services do these banks perform for us? How do they earn profits?

A savings-and-loan association, an insurance company, a commercial bank, a mutual-savings bank, a credit union, a retirement fund, and a mutual fund are all examples of **financial intermediaries,** of financial institutions that mediate between borrowers and lenders.

> **Financial intermediaries** borrow funds from one group of economic agents (people or firms with savings) and lend to other agents.

Financial intermediaries serve a useful purpose in our economy. With financial intermediation, borrowers and lenders do not have to seek each other out. The lender does not have to accept the borrower's IOU, investigate the borrower's credit worthiness, or pass on the wisdom of the borrower's spending plans. The commercial bank, for example, accepts a depositor's deposit with the promise to pay the depositor a specified interest rate and then lends these funds to a borrower at a higher interest rate. Borrowers and lenders, thus, pay a price for using the services of a financial intermediary. If they had sought each other out, the lender would have received more and the borrower would have paid less.

The Benefits of Financial Intermediation

Is the cost of financial intermediation worth its benefits? Financial intermediation offers at least three benefits: cost minimization, risk pooling, and high liquidity.

Cost Minimization.   If a large company wishes to borrow $5 million, it would be very costly to the firm to borrow $5,000 from 1,000 different lenders. An organized market is necessary to bring such a large number of lenders together. The public may not know the corporation, but the bank does. So the bank offers appropriate terms to ultimate lenders, and the bank alone investigates the credit worthiness of the company wanting to borrow $5 million. It would also be costly for 1,000 separate lenders to make their own credit investigations.

Risk Pooling.   For a lender, it is better not to put all eggs in one basket. If Jack lends $1,000 to Jill, and Jill cannot pay, Jack loses all his money. But if Jack lends $1 each to 1,000 different Jills, Jack can reduce his risks substantially by *risk pooling*. The financial intermediary pools the savings of smaller individuals and loans these savings to a diversified group of borrowers. When a financial intermediary loans to different borrowers, risks can be reduced because the odds of all borrowers not repaying are much greater than the odds of any one of the borrowers not repaying. If one borrower out of 100 defaults, the loss is still relatively small. Financial intermediaries can spread the pooled funds of their depositors over a variety of borrowers, while individual depositors with small sums of money to lend cannot.

High Liquidity.   A final benefit of deposit intermediaries, such as commercial banks, savings-and-loan associations, and mutual-savings banks, is that they *borrow short* and *lend long*. Borrowers usually prefer to borrow for a long term (to *borrow long*), because the services of the house, car, or business plant that the borrowed funds pay for last a long time. But lenders prefer to lend funds for a short period of time (to *lend short*) since unexpected needs could always arise. Thus, people in general prefer to lend short and to borrow long. Financial intermediaries fill the gap between borrowers and lenders by being willing to borrow short and lend long. Financial intermediaries offer deposits that are highly liquid. Commercial banks and savings-and-loan associations borrow money from depositors, who can withdraw their funds at any time. The bank may then turn around and lend to a home buyer on a 30-year mortgage.[1]

---

1. During periods of unanticipated inflation, financial intermediaries may become less willing to borrow short and lend long. In the late 1970s and early 1980s, savings and loans were stuck with large volumes of outstanding mortgage loans at 7 to 10 percent when they were borrowing short at 10 to 15 percent. For this reason, financial intermediaries have become cautious about making long-term loan commitments at a fixed rate of interest.

Table 1   Consolidated Balance Sheet of All Commercial Banks, December 1984

Assets (billions of dollars)		Liabilities (billions of dollars)	
Vault cash	23.3	Net demand deposits*	380.0
Reserves at Fed	20.5	Savings deposits	386.0
Securities	377.7	Time deposits	753.5
Loans and investments	1,487.4	Other borrowings	497.9
Other assets	254.3	Net worth	145.8
Total	**2,163.2**	**Total**	**2,163.2**

*Net demand deposits = demand deposits − items in the process of collection − balances with banks.

Source: *Federal Reserve Bulletin,* March 1985, p. A17.

The different types of financial intermediaries compete with each other for borrowers and lenders. Savings and loans, mutual-savings banks, and credit unions offer checkable accounts that compete with commercial banks. Financial intermediaries compete among themselves to make loans to qualified borrowers. On the average, profit rates in banking have not been above profit rates elsewhere in the economy.

The Magnitude of Financial Intermediation

In 1984, $649 billion in private domestic funds were advanced for private investment, short-term credits, and the purchase of government securities. This figure is the amount of funds supplied by ultimate lenders to ultimate borrowers. About $159 billion of the $649 billion (25 percent) was loaned directly from lenders to borrowers. The remaining $490 billion was channeled through commercial banks, insurance and pension funds, savings and loans, and other assorted financial intermediaries. These figures show that financial intermediaries handle most (about 75 percent) of the flows of private funds from lenders to borrowers.

COMMERCIAL BANKS

In 1984, there were about 15,000 **commercial banks** in the United States.

Commercial banks are banks that have been chartered either by a state agency or by the

U.S. Treasury's Comptroller of the Currency to make loans and receive deposits.

Prior to the mid-1970s, the differences between commercial banks and other financial intermediaries were more clear-cut than they are now. Historically, a commercial bank could be defined as a financial institution that offered its customers checking accounts (as well as savings accounts) and made short-term loans to the general public and to businesses. The feature of commercial banks that distinguished them from *thrift institutions* was that commercial banks offered checking-account deposits.

Thrift institutions, such as savings and loans, mutual-savings banks, and credit unions cater to noncommercial customers and traditionally could not offer checking-account services; instead, thrift institutions could offer only different types of savings accounts (hence, the name *thrift* institution). Thrift institutions now are able to offer checking accounts like NOW and ATS accounts to families.[2] Historically, commercial banks have been more important as financial intermediaries. However, recent innovations have led to a substantial rise in the importance of thrift institutions.

In December 1984, America's 15,000 commercial banks held assets of about $2.2 trillion (see Table 1). The largest 150 banks accounted for more than half of commercial-bank assets. Savings-and-loan associations, mutual-savings

2. Legislation proposed in 1981, but not enacted, would have expanded the powers of thrift institutions to include commercial checking accounts and commercial loans.

banks, and credit unions held assets of about $1.2 trillion.

Commercial banks also held virtually all the checkable deposits at the beginning of 1985, though most thrift institutions had been authorized to offer such accounts. Despite radical changes in the banking industry, it is fair to say that commercial banks remain the most important financial intermediaries in today's economy.

The financial system is in a state of flux. Commercial banks continue to dominate other financial intermediaries, but changing laws have modified the margin of competition between commercial banks and thrift institutions. In the 1980s, a bitter competitive struggle has been underway among the different financial intermediaries. (See Example 1 on nonbank banks.)

How Commercial Banks Make Profits

Mr. Dooley, the Will Rogers of his day, remarked that a banker is a "man who takes care of your money by lending it out to his friends." Humor and friends aside, this statement captures the essence of modern banking. Bankers ordinarily cannot earn substantial profits by lending only to their friends; to be profitable, a bank must lend funds only to businesses and households that offer the best return on their investment funds. Commercial banks make profits by borrowing from customers in the form of demand deposits and time deposits and then relending these funds in the form of automobile loans, real-estate loans, business loans, and student loans. Commercial banks earn profits by borrowing money at low interest rates and lending money at higher interest rates. The difference between the rate at which banks borrow and the rate at which they lend is called the *interest-rate spread*.

Balance Sheets

The concept of a **balance sheet** is essential to an understanding of how banks operate.

A **balance sheet** summarizes the current financial position of a firm by comparing the firm's *assets* and *liabilities*.

The **assets** of a firm can be buildings, equipment, inventories of goods, money, or even IOUs. A balance sheet lists the claims to these assets.

Assets are anything of any value that is owned.

The **liabilities** of a company include unpaid bills, tax obligations, and long-term debt.

Liabilities are anything owed to other economic agents.

The value (or net worth) of a company is measured as the excess of assets over liabilities. If a company owns assets worth $1 million and has liabilities of $900,000, the net worth of the company is $100,000.

Net worth = assets − liabilities

A bank's assets consist primarily of IOUs of one kind or another—the loans it has made to persons and to firms, the government bonds it has purchased, the deposits it has with other banks. Its liabilities consist principally of the various deposits that its customers have made—demand deposits, savings deposits, and time deposits.

The combined balance sheet of America's commercial banks as of December 1984 is shown in Table 1. As of that date demand-deposit liabilities accounted for 19 percent of liabilities, while savings and time deposits accounted for 56 percent.

The fact that commercial-bank demand-deposit liabilities are less than their savings and time-deposit liabilities is a recent development attributable to the increased use of credit cards, the rise of money-market mutual funds, and new bank overdraft facilities. Historically, demand-deposit liabilities exceeded time deposits. In other words, commercial banks have become more like thrift institutions. The asset side shows how commercial banks serve as financial intermediaries. Commercial-bank deposits are loaned to individuals and businesses and are used to purchase securities.[3] The asset statement shows that commercial

---

3. Further discussion of the bank balance sheet and recent changes can be found in Lloyd B. Thomas, *Money, Banking, and Economic Activity,* 2nd ed. (Englewood Cliffs, N.J.: Prentice-Hall, 1982), pp. 113–21.

Example 1   Sears Bank: The Problem of Nonbank Banks

A growing number of commercial and industrial companies are entering the business of banking through a back door in order to remain free of traditional bank regulation. Companies like Sears, J.C. Penney, American Express, the Commercial Credit Corporation, and the Dreyfuss Corporation have acquired banks and savings-and-loan associations through holding companies. With these acquisitions, Sears, Penneys, and American Express are attempting to establish themselves as one-stop financial centers where their customers can obtain loans, buy stocks and insurance, deposit money, and buy real estate. In order to engage in all these activities, these one-stop banking organizations prefer to be outside the control of the Federal Reserve. The loophole that allows them to avoid traditional banking regulation is the official definition of what constitutes a bank. According to existing legislation, a bank is a busi-

ness that offers checking accounts and makes commercial loans. If the business does not do either of these two things, it is not a bank. The nonbank banks, therefore, have abolished either checking accounts or commercial loans and thereby claim exemption from Federal Reserve regulation. The Fed has responded to nonbank banks by attempting to tighten up the definition of checking accounts and commercial loans. For example, the Fed wishes NOW accounts to be considered checking accounts. To this point, the Fed has failed in its attempts to get nonbank banks to register as banks. Eventually, the issue of nonbank banks will be resolved by the U.S. Supreme Court. ■

Sources: Thomas Buynak, "Banking and Commerce: To Mix or Not to Mix?" Federal Reserve Bank of Cleveland, December 5, 1983; *Economic Review*, Federal Reserve Bank of Atlanta, May 1983.

---

banks are primarily in the business of making loans.

The combined balance sheet in Table 1 reveals a remarkable feature of commercial banking: the demand-deposit liabilities of commercial banks far exceed the sum of commercial-bank reserves.

A large fraction of a bank's liabilities are *demand liabilities,* or obligations that can be called in by depositors. Any customer who withdraws a deposit is paid out of the bank's **reserves.**

Reserves are the funds that the bank uses to satisfy the cash demands of its customers.

Bank reserves consist of two components: *vault cash,* which is simply currency and coin in the vaults of the bank, and the *bank's balances with the Federal Reserve System* (explained below).

The combined balance sheet shows that bank reserves are much less than the liabilities of the banking system. In December 1984, bank reserves equaled $43.8 billion, or 11.5 percent of the net-demand-deposit liabilities to the nonbanking public. When savings deposits are included (because in practice banks also pay out their funds on demand), the reserve ratio falls to 6 percent.

Why are depositors and the banks not alarmed

by the imbalance between bank reserves and demand- or savings-deposit liabilities? On an ordinary business day, some customers deposit money in their checking accounts. Others withdraw money by writing checks on their accounts. If deposits come in at the same pace as withdrawals, bank reserves do not change. Reserves rise when deposits exceed withdrawals; they fall when withdrawals exceed deposits. The normal course of banking is for withdrawals and deposits to proceed at roughly the same rate.

Is it not precarious for bank reserves to be such a small fraction of deposits? What would happen if suddenly there were no deposits—only withdrawals? The reason why people have demand deposits is that checking-account money is safer and more convenient than currency and coin for many transactions. As long as depositors knew that they could get their money from the bank, they would want to leave it on deposit. The moment they felt that they could not get their money, they would want to withdraw it. Thus, people want their money if they can't get it and don't want their money if they can!

This paradox of banking has made commercial banks subject to *bank scares* at times. The history of banking is filled with episodes where large

---

Example 2   The FDIC and the Continental Illinois Bank Bailout

---

The best way to prevent a bank scare is to assure people that they can always withdraw their money. The Federal Deposit Insurance Corporation (FDIC) is an independent agency of the U.S. Government that was established by Congress in 1933 to insure bank deposits. An FDIC-insured bank pays FDIC insurance based on the volume of deposits. The deposit-insurance fund insures each depositor's funds up to $100,000. If an FDIC-insured bank should fail, each depositor would be fully reimbursed as long as the deposit did not exceed $100,000.

The creation of the FDIC was prompted by the massive bank failures from 1930–1933. Previously, some states had attempted without success to institute their own deposit-insurance schemes. Has the FDIC worked? Since 1934 the FDIC has paid out more than 99 percent of all deposits in banks that have failed. Today, all but a handful of commercial banks are insured by the FDIC. National banks and members of the Federal Reserve System must belong to the FDIC. Other banks find it advantageous to publicize to their customers that their accounts are insured. Every FDIC-insured bank proudly displays the FDIC emblem.

The FDIC's 1984 bailout of the failing Continental Illinois Bank is an example of how the FDIC (working in this case with the Federal Reserve) prevents depositor losses. Continental Illinois, one of the nation's largest banks, was threatened by bankruptcy as a consequence of making a number of bad loans abroad and in the energy industry. As these loans failed to be collected, the assets of Continental Illinois fell to dangerously low levels, and worried depositors began wholesale withdrawal of deposits. When Continental Illinois reserves proved insufficient to meet withdrawals, Continental Illinois was on the verge of failure. The FDIC and the Fed decided that a bank as large as Continental Illinois should not be allowed to fail because this collapse might trigger the failure of other banks both at home and abroad with similar problem loans. Accordingly, the FDIC rescued Continental Illinois by injecting some $4.5 billion dollars into Continental Illinois reserves. The management of Continental Illinois was dismissed, and the FDIC assumed control of 80 percent of Continental Illinois stock. The FDIC hopes eventually to return Continental Illinois to solvency, at which time Continental Illinois could be merged with another banking operation. Critics of the bailout point out that it cost one quarter of FDIC reserves and has weakened the ability of the FDIC to prevent other bank failures. Critics argue that it is not the FDIC's business to cover for the management mistakes of commercial banks. Supporters of the bailout argue that if Continental Illinois had been allowed to fail, other banks would have failed and the eventual bailout would have been even more costly. ∎

Source: Michael Boskin, "Going Overboard on Bank Bailouts," *Wall Street Journal,* August 23, 1984.

---

numbers of depositors lose confidence in the banks and demand their cash; when the banks cannot pay, a rash of bank failures occurs. The federal government's Federal Deposit Insurance Corporation (FDIC) was established to deal with this problem (see Example 2).

THE FEDERAL RESERVE SYSTEM

Bankers use the FDIC as their insurance agent and the Federal Reserve System as their banker. The *Federal Reserve System*—or *the Fed*—is the central bank of the United States. The first central bank was the Bank of Sweden. All modern countries have a central bank; the Bank of England, the Banque de France, the Deutsche Bundesbank, and the Bank of Japan are prominent in world financial circles. Even the Soviet Union has its central bank, Gosbank.

The United States did not have a central bank throughout most of the 19th century and into the second decade of the 20th century. During this period the United States became the most important industrial nation in the world without even having a central bank. A number of financial panics, culminating in the financial panic of 1907, convinced Congress that a central bank was needed to supervise and control private banks.

(The financial panic of 1907 was sparked by a severe business downturn; banks were forced to refuse to convert deposits into currency.) The Federal Reserve System became a reality in 1913 when President Woodrow Wilson signed the Federal Reserve Act.

Functions of the Fed

The Fed—like other central banks throughout the world—performs two primary functions:

1. The Fed controls the nation's money supply.
2. The Fed is responsible for the orderly working of the nation's banking system. It supervises private banks; it serves as the bankers' bank; it clears checks; it fills the currency needs of private banks; it acts as a lender of last resort to banks needing to borrow reserves.

The control of the money supply is the Fed's most important function. The supply of money is believed to have an important effect on prices, output, employment, and interest rates. The Fed's control of the money supply, therefore, places it in a position to influence inflation, output, unemployment, and interest rates.

The Structure of the Federal Reserve System

The 1913 Federal Reserve Act divided the country into 12 districts, each with its own Federal Reserve Bank. These banks are located in Boston, New York, Philadelphia, Cleveland, Richmond, Atlanta, Chicago, St. Louis, Minneapolis, Kansas City, Dallas, and San Francisco. Each Federal Reserve Bank issues currency for its district, administers bank examinations, clears checks, and is the nominal lender of last resort to depository institutions in the district.

The Federal Reserve System is controlled and coordinated by a seven-member *Board of Governors* (formerly known as the Federal Reserve Board) located in Washington, D.C. This powerful group is appointed by the President of the United States. Each member of the Board serves a 14-year term. Terms are staggered so that the appointees of a single U.S. President cannot dominate the Board. The President appoints the chair of the Board, who is the most powerful member

and serves for four years. Five of the seven current Board members are economists who have previously worked for the Fed. The Board is an inbred group.

The Federal Reserve System has much more independence than other governmental agencies. Independence is insured in part by the long terms of the Board members and because the Fed is self-financing. In a legal sense, the Fed is responsible to Congress. Although Fed actions can be taken without congressional approval, the Fed is not free of political pressures. There have been conflicts between the President and the Fed and between Congress and the Fed. There is always the threat that the independence of the Fed could be reduced by congressional action.

Reserve Requirements

Private profit-maximizing banks would choose voluntarily to hold a portion of their assets in reserves. A prudent banker knows that sufficient reserves must be on hand to meet the cash demands of customers. In the United Kingdom, the Bank of England does not impose legal reserve requirements on private banks, yet British banks hold prudent levels of reserves, and England has developed an excellent reputation for its banking services. In the United States, however, the Fed imposes uniform **reserve requirements** on all commercial banks, savings-and-loan associations, mutual-savings banks, and credit unions. U.S. banks are required by law to hold reserve levels that meet a standard **required-reserve ratio.**

> **Reserve requirements** are rules that state the amount of reserves a bank must keep on hand to back bank deposits.

> A **required-reserve ratio** is the amount of reserves required for each dollar of deposits.

A required-reserve ratio of 0.1 (10 percent) means that the bank must hold $0.10 in reserves for each dollar of deposits. The current prevailing reserve requirements are as follows: Transaction accounts, such as checking accounts, have reserve ratios ranging from 3 to 12 percent, depending on the size of the bank. The reserve requirements on time and savings accounts range from 0 to 3 percent depending on the size of the account and its maturity. The Fed has the power to raise or lower these required-reserve ratios and to impose supplemental requirements. (See Example 3.)

Borrowing from the Fed

Any depository institution holding reserves with the Fed is entitled to borrow funds from the Fed. Prior to the Monetary Control Act of 1980, only member banks had such borrowing privileges. A bank that is allowed to borrow from the Fed, in the technical banking language, has access to the *discount window*.

Banks do not have unlimited access to the discount window. They must have exhausted all reasonable alternative sources of funds before coming to the Fed. The discount window is available for temporary and immediate cash needs of the banks.

The rate of interest the Fed charges banks at the discount window is called the *discount rate*. The Fed sets the discount rate and can encourage or discourage bank borrowing by raising or lowering the discount rate. If the spread between the rate at which the banks themselves borrow (the discount rate) and the rates at which they lend is small, the bank's incentive to use the discount window is reduced.

The Federal Open Market Committee

The control of the money supply is the responsibility of the Federal Open Market Committee (FOMC). The FOMC meets once a month and holds telephone conferences between meetings. The FOMC consists of the seven members of the Board of Governors and presidents of five of the regional Federal Reserve Banks. The president of the New York Federal Reserve Bank is always one of these five; the presidents of the other regional Federal Reserve banks rotate in the four remaining slots.

The official function of the Federal Open Market Committee is to direct the buying and selling of government securities on the Federal Reserve's account. Since *government securities* are simply the IOUs of the federal government that are continuously traded on the open market, FOMC purchases or sales of government securities are called **open-market operations.**

Open-market operations are purchases and sales of federal government securities by the Fed (as directed by the Federal Open Market Committee).

The Monetary Base

The Fed can do something that other institutions cannot do: it can put money into the economy. Because the Fed can print money, whenever the Feds buys something, it puts money into the economy; whenever the Fed sells something it takes money out of the economy. Imagine, for the moment, that you could print money: whenever you bought something with the money you printed, everyone else (taken together) would have more money; whenever you sold something, you would get some of your money back and everyone else (taken together) would have less money. Similarly, Fed purchases inject money into the economy; Fed sales withdraw money.

As this chapter will later show, the Fed normally buys and sells government securities. It is simpler, however, to consider a more elementary case. For example, suppose the Fed hires a computer programmer, Jane, and pays her with a check for $5,000. Jane deposits the check in her commercial bank—the First National Bank of Clear Lake. The Fed's check is different from other checks. When the First National Bank of Clear Lake sends the check in for collection to the Fed, its balance sheet changes in two ways. On the asset side, the Bank of Clear Lake's "reserves with the Fed" have increased by $5,000; on the liability side, the Bank of Clear Lake's "demand deposits due Jane" have increased by $5,000, as shown in part (a) of Table 2. The charts in Table 2 are called **T-accounts.**

T-accounts show bank assets and liabilities.

The T-accounts in this table show only the *change* in bank assets and liabilities that result from the transaction under discussion.

At this point the money supply has increased by $5,000. Jane's bank account has increased by $5,000. Everyone else's bank account has remained the same, and the currency in circulation (outside banks) is still the same. (Remember the *money supply* is the quantity of checkable deposits plus the currency in circulation held by the nonbanking public.)

Table 2   Sample T-Accounts for the First National Bank of Clear Lake: Results of $5,000 Purchase by Fed

	Changes in Assets	Changes in Liabilities
Step 1: Jane deposits the Fed's $5,000 check.	Reserves at the Fed + $5,000	Demand deposits due Jane + $5,000
Step 2: The bank converts $5,000 of Fed reserves into $5,000 vault cash.	Vault cash + $5,000 Reserves at the Fed − $5,000	No change
Step 3: Jane withdraws $5,000 cash.	Vault cash − $5,000	Demand deposits due Jane − $5,000

These T-accounts show that when the Fed buys something (in this case, something for which it pays $5,000) three things happen: First, the receiving bank's reserves at the Fed increase (Step 1); second, the bank's vault cash can increase (Step 2); third, cash in circulation can increase (Step 3).

Had anyone but the Fed hired Jane, the money supply would have remained the same. Jane's bank account would have increased by $5,000, and the purchaser's account would have fallen by $5,000. The two transactions would cancel each other.

Suppose the Bank of Clear Lake does not wish to hold its new reserves as deposits at the Fed. Instead, the bank feels that it needs $5,000 more in vault cash. So the bank wires the Fed to send the $5,000 in cash. The Fed prints $5,000 in Federal Reserve Notes and issues this $5,000 to the Bank of Clear Lake. At this point, the Fed lowers the Bank of Clear Lake's deposit balance by $5,000. This conversion of reserve balances with the Fed into vault cash, shown in part (b) of Table 2, has no impact on the money supply because neither total demand deposits nor the currency outside of banks has changed.

Finally, suppose that Jane goes to the bank and cashes the $5,000 check. Again, nothing happens to the money supply. Her demand deposit account with the Bank of Clear Lake has fallen by $5,000, and the Bank of Clear Lake's vault cash has fallen by $5,000. Because there is $5,000 more in currency in circulation and $5,000 less in checkable deposits, the money supply is unchanged, as shown in part (c) of Table 2.

Of these three transactions, the only one that changes the money supply is the one where Jane deposited the check for $5,000 that she received from the Fed. The Fed could have simply printed $5,000 and issued the $5,000 to Jane in cash.

Purchases by the Fed 1) raise reserves at the Fed, 2) increase vault cash, or 3) increase currency in circulation. Sales by the Fed 1) reduce reserves at the Fed, 2) reduce vault cash, or 3) reduce currency in circulation.

Our simple example shows that the Fed can inject money into the economy by purchasing something; it can withdraw money from the economy by selling something. Fed purchases and sales alter the **monetary base.**

The **monetary base** is the sum of reserves on deposit at the Fed, all vault cash, and the currency in circulation.

When the Fed injects money into the economy, this money shows up either as an increase in reserves, as an increase in vault cash, or as an increase in currency in circulation. Only by looking at the sum of the three (the monetary base) can one gauge Fed injections or withdrawals of funds from the economy.

We have shown that Fed purchases raise the monetary base; Fed sales lower the monetary base. The Fed can control the monetary base by varying the amounts of things it buys or sells (whether those things are goods and services or government bonds).

Figure 1 compares the monetary base with the money supply (M1). The money supply is greater than the monetary base. In December 1984, for example, the money supply M1 was $555 billion,

Figure 1   The Monetary Base and the Money Supply, December 1984

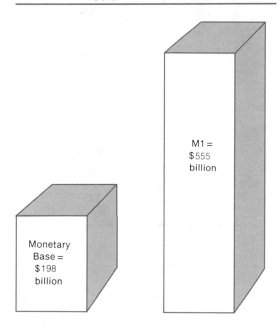

M1 = $555 billion

Monetary Base = $198 billion

This diagram illustrates the relative size of the monetary base in relation to the money supply as of December 1984.

Source: *The Federal Reserve Bulletin.*

and the monetary base was $198 billion ($158 billion in circulating currency, and the rest in reserves at the Fed and vault cash). Where did the $357 billion difference between M1 and the monetary base come from? To answer this question, one must consider how banks create money.

HOW BANKS CREATE MONEY

Banks can create bank demand deposits (money) by lending out the money that people and firms have deposited. Each bank is simply trying to make a profit from financial intermediation. By examining how banks create money, one can understand why the money supply exceeds the monetary base and how the Fed controls the money supply.

Monetization of Debt

Borrowers (business borrowers, home builders, car purchasers) come to the bank to borrow money. If the bank agrees to loan them money, an exchange takes place: the bank sets up a checking account equal to the sum of the loan, and the borrower gives an IOU to the bank spelling out the terms of repayment. In the process of this exchange, money has been created. Demand-deposit liabilities of the bank (remember, demand deposits are the main component of the money supply) have increased by the amount of the loan. Thus, banks create money through the **monetization of debt.**

> The **monetization of debt** is the creation of demand-deposit liabilities in the process of making bank loans.

The monetization of a debt can be illustrated by considering how banking first got started. Imagine an ancient goldsmith in the business of shaping gold into fine products used by kings, lords, princes, and wealthy merchants. The goldsmith must keep inventories of gold on hand and, therefore, must have safe storage facilities to prevent theft. Because the goldsmith has such facilities, people find it useful to store gold with the goldsmith. In return, the goldsmith might charge a fee to defray storage costs. When people deposit their gold with the goldsmith, they would want a receipt, and the goldsmith would return the gold only when a receipt is presented.

Assume that the gold is in the form of uniform bars. People would not care whether the goldsmith returns precisely the gold bars they deposited. By not having to keep track of who owns which bar, the goldsmith could hold down storage costs.

The goldsmith would soon discover that only a small amount of gold was needed to accommodate the gold withdrawals on any given day. Each day customers would bring in more gold to exchange for storage receipts; each day customers would bring in storage receipts to exchange for their gold. The goldsmith could keep most of the gold in the back room under strict lock and key, collecting dust, and maintain only a small inventory to service his customers. As long as they re-

Example 3   The Monetary Control Act of 1980

The Monetary Control Act of 1980 was designed to increase the Fed's control over all depository institutions. Prior to 1980, the Fed could impose reserve requirements only on its member banks (nationally chartered banks or state banks that elected to join the system). Nonmember state banks were allowed to hold reserves under the rules established by each state. Because state requirements were typically lower than those of the Fed, member state banks often opted to leave the system, and some national banks converted to state charters.

The 1980 Monetary Control Act expanded the power of the Fed to set required-reserve ratios for all depository institutions (not just national banks); all depository institutions were given the right to borrow from the Fed; it phased out interest-rate ceilings on deposits by 1986; it authorized banks and thrift institutions to offer interest on checking accounts (the NOW and ATS accounts).

The Monetary Control Act of 1980 has been described as the most significant banking legislation since the Federal Reserve Act of 1913. It changed the way in which various types of financial institutions compete with one another. Basically, all depository institutions received the right to issue checking accounts, and the differences between commercial banks and thrift institutions were blurred considerably. The Monetary Control Act sought to unleash competition in the banking industry and to reduce government controls on the banking industry Where this competition will eventually lead cannot be predicted at this point. ∎

---

ceive their gold upon presentation of a storage receipt, they are content.

As the custom of storing gold with the goldsmith becomes more and more widespread, people would find it convenient to use the storage receipts themselves, for transactions, rather than use the bulky gold. Although storage receipts are mere pieces of paper, because they are accepted as a medium of exchange, they are money just like circulating gold. As long as the goldsmith simply kept the gold in the back room, the money supply in such a world would be the gold in circulation (outside the goldsmith's back room) plus the storage receipts issued by the goldsmith. But the storage receipts would only add up to the amount of gold stored in the back room.

Now imagine one fine day the goldsmith discovers a method—presumably illegal—of making additional profit. A friend of the goldsmith might say, "Since all the gold is just sitting in the back room collecting dust, why not lend me some of it?" The goldsmith might at first object that this gold is somebody else's, but a high enough interest rate convinces the goldsmith to lend out some of the gold that is left to him for safekeeping. The friend gives the goldsmith an IOU; the goldsmith gives the friend some gold. The moment this transaction occurs, the money supply increases by the amount of the loan. The money supply now consists of the storage receipts, the gold previously in circulation, and the gold loaned out by the goldsmith. The goldsmith has *monetized* the debt by giving out gold in exchange for an IOU.

To make a long story short, the friend would even take a storage receipt instead of gold. Why? The storage receipt circulates as money. Indeed, what is to prevent the goldsmith from issuing many times his gold reserve in storage receipts as long as he knows very few storage receipts are going to be presented for gold? The goldsmith bank can create money provided that 1) the storage receipts circulate as money and 2) the goldsmith makes loans. If either condition is not satisfied, it is impossible for the goldsmith to create money.

Modern banks do not issue storage receipts for gold; they accept demand deposits and allow customers to write checks on those deposits. Checking-account money does not circulate like the storage receipts of the goldsmith. Indeed, the only time checking-account money has any real existence is when a check is being written. Most checking-account money is simply an entry on the books of some bank.

Table 3   The Effects of $100 Cash Deposit and $90 Loan

	Change in Assets		Change in Liabilities
Bank A			
(a) After $100 cash deposit:	Cash in vault	+$100	Demand deposits +$100
(b) After $90 loan but before loan funds are spent:	Reserves Loans	+$100 +$ 90	Demand deposits +$190
(c) After $90 loan proceeds are deposited in Bank B:	Reserves Loans	+$ 10 +$ 90	Demand deposits +$100
Bank B			
(d) After the $90 deposit but before new loans are made:	Reserves	+$ 90	Demand deposits +$ 90

The cash deposit in row(a) does not create money, since cash in the vault is not part of the money supply. The $90 loan and corresponding $90 demand deposit in (b) creates $90 worth of new money, since demand deposits have increased and currency in circulation has remained the same. When the $90 loan is deposited in Bank B in rows (c) and (d), no new money is created until Bank B makes a loan.

Loaning Out Reserves

Modern banks are prohibited from printing their own money like the goldsmith's storage receipts.[4] They can only make loans and accept deposits. How do modern commercial banks create money?

Consider what happens when someone makes a deposit of currency in a bank. Assume that $100 in currency is deposited in Bank A. Suppose the depositor has been keeping the cash in an old shoe. Prior to the deposit, the bank was in equilibrium—it was neither making new loans or calling in old loans. The moment the $100 cash deposit is made, Bank A's balance sheet changes as shown in part (a) of Table 3.

Nothing happens to the money supply as long as Bank A remains in this position. Currency in circulation has fallen by the amount that demand deposits have increased; the total money supply outside banks remains the same.

It is likely that Bank A will not be content to stay in this position. Banks have learned through experience that only a small fraction of deposits

must be kept as reserves—the rest can be loaned out. The bank is not making any profit from the $100 cash in its vault. Since the bank is interested in making profits, the $100 deposit will allow Bank A to expand its loans. What fraction of the new deposit will Bank A keep? In the United States, banks must maintain the required-reserve ratio of reserves to demand deposits imposed by the Fed. If the Fed requires a reserve ratio of 10 percent, banks must keep $10 as reserves for each $100 of demand deposits.

The Fed's reserve requirements have typically been more conservative than the reserve ratio a profit-minded banker would consider safe and prudent. Hence, reserves above required reserves would likely be considered **excess reserves.** Excess reserves will usually be loaned out.

> **Excess reserves** are reserves in excess of required reserves. Excess reserves equal total reserves minus required reserves.

Banks that have no excess reserves are said to be "loaned up."

Suppose that prior to the $100 cash deposit, the required reserves of Bank A equaled actual reserves (Bank A was loaned up), and suppose the Fed's required-reserve ratio is 10 percent. Because the new $100 deposit would require a $10 increase in required reserves, the bank would have $90 in excess reserves after the deposit. The bank, therefore, makes $90 worth of new loans to

---

4. At one time, state and national banks in the United States operated something like the goldsmith—they issued paper currency. Private bank notes circulated for more than a century. Eventually so many banks tried to get into the profitable business of money creation that it became impossible to determine the legitimacy of the bank notes issued by some of these wildcat banks. Eventually, the United States banned private note issue by banks.

eliminate the $90 of excess reserves. The moment the $90 loan is made, the borrower's demand deposit account is credited with $90. Before the borrower spends this $90, Bank A's balance sheet changes as shown in part (b) of Table 3.

Notice that in part (b) the money supply has increased by exactly $90. Bank A has created money! The bank exchanged the borrower's IOU for a demand deposit. The borrower's IOU *is not* money. The bank's IOU—the $90 demand deposit—*is* money. The bank has created money by monetizing debt. If demand deposits were not used as money or if the banks made no loans, banks could not create money.

Banks can create money when: 1) demand deposits are used as money, and 2) banks make loans out of excess reserves.

Part (c) of Table 3 takes this process a step further. When the loan recipient spends the $90, Bank A loses $90 of its reserves. The department store, grocery store, or plumber who is paid the borrowed $90 will either cash the $90 check or deposit the $90 check in some other bank.

Whether the $90 ends up in cash that remains in circulation or in a checking account in another bank, the money supply has still increased by $90 as a result of the loan. If the check is cashed, the amount of cash in circulation goes up by $90 and Bank A's deposit liabilities go down by $90. If the check is deposited in another bank, the increase in the depositor's account equals the decrease in the check writer's account. Most transactions (in terms of dollar value) are in checks, and the $90 will likely end up as a checking-account deposit in another bank.

Multiple Deposit Creation

The expansion of the money supply does not end with the $90 increase in the money supply as long as transactions continue to be in the form of checks (as long as people do not cash their checks). In our example, we assume that when Bank A loses the $90 in reserves, some other bank—Bank B—gains the entire amount in new deposits. Our example assumes that there is no **cash leakage** from the banking system to the public.

A **cash leakage** occurs when a recipient of a check converts it into cash rather than depositing it in a checking account. This cash remains in circulation outside of the banking system.

In this example, people are paid in checks, and they deposit these checks in their checking accounts.

Since Bank B receives $90 in new deposits, its balance sheet changes as shown in part (d) of Table 3. The transfer of $90 from Bank A to Bank B has no immediate impact on the money supply. The amount of demand-deposit liabilities remains the same, and no additional money is created.

If Bank B were originally in equilibrium with no excess reserves, it would now have excess reserves of $81. Since deposits increased by $90, required reserves increased by $9 with a 10 percent reserve requirement. Like Bank A before it, Bank B will loan out its excess reserves of $81. When the recipient of Bank B's loan spends this $81 (with zero leakages of cash), Bank C will receive a new deposit of $81.

The moment Bank B made the loan of $81, the money supply increased by that amount. Bank C will keep 10 percent of the $81 deposit as reserves and lend out the rest—$72.90—which again increases the money supply. When the borrower of $72.90 spends the funds, Bank D receives a new deposit of that amount (again assuming zero leakages of cash).

The $100 increase in reserves has set into motion a pattern of multiple expansion of the money supply. If there are no leakages of cash out of the banking system, the original $100 cash deposit in Bank A leads to demand deposits of $90, $81, and $72.90, with each succeeding figure being 90 percent of the previous deposit. If one sums $100 + $90 + $81 + $72.90 and so on down to the smallest amount, one obtains the total of $1,000.

Table 4 shows what happens to each bank as a consequence of a $100 cash deposit in Bank A. The original $100 cash deposit has led to the creation of $900 in additional deposits or money, or a **multiple-deposit expansion.**

A **multiple-deposit expansion** of the money supply occurs when an increase in reserves causes an expansion of the money supply that is greater than the reserve increase.

Notice that one bank out of many cannot create a multiple expansion of bank deposits. (See Example 4.) Each single bank can lend out only a fraction of its new deposits. In the above example, each bank can only create new money at a rate equal to 90 percent of any fresh deposit; that is, each bank can only loan out its excess reserves. But when there is no leakage of cash out of the system, an original cash deposit of $100 will lead to a multiple expansion of deposits: as long as the extra cash reserves are in the banking system, they provide the required reserves against deposits. If the reserve requirement is 10 percent, a $100 reserve will support $1,000 worth of deposits. When each bank lends out its excess reserves, it loses those reserves to other banks; these reserves then become the basis for further expansion of the money supply by other banks. The $100 initial cash deposit continues to be passed through the banking system until $900 in new money is created for a total of $1,000 in deposits.

One bank can lend out only its excess reserves. However, the banking system as a whole can lend out a *multiple* of any excess reserves.

Thus, what is true of all banks taken together is not true of any single bank (believing otherwise is an example of the fallacy of composition).

The Deposit Multiplier

Table 4 showed how the banking system was able to turn a $100 increase in reserves into $900 of new money for a total increase in demand deposits of $1,000. The factor by which demand deposits expand is the **deposit multiplier.**

The **deposit multiplier** is the ratio of the change in total deposits to the change in reserves.

A deposit multiplier of 10 indicates that for every $1 increase in reserves, demand deposits will increase by $10. We have already calculated the deposit multiplier when the required-reserve ratio is 10 percent (and when there are no cash leakages). With a 10 percent required-reserve ratio, banks will always lend out 90 percent of their excess reserves. Each dollar of new reserves adds

Table 4   The Multiple Expansion of Bank Deposits

Bank	New Deposits	New Loans or Investments	Additional Reserves
Bank A	$ 100.00	$ 90.00	$ 10.00
Bank B	$ 90.00	$ 81.00	$ 9.00
Bank C	$ 81.00	$ 72.90	$ 8.10
Bank D	$ 72.90	$ 65.61	$ 7.29
Bank E	$ 65.61	$ 59.05	$ 6.56
Sum A-E	$ 409.51	$368.56	$ 40.95
Sum of remaining banks	$ 590.49	$531.44	$ 59.05
Total for whole banking system	$1,000.00	$900.00	$100.00

The banking system as a whole can create a multiple expansion of bank deposits; a single bank can create only as much money as it has excess reserves. If the reserve requirement is 0.10 (10 percent), a fresh deposit of $100 will lead to $1,000 in total deposits and $900 in new money provided there are no cash leakages and no bank keeps excess reserves. The original deposit of $100 in Bank A leads to a $90 deposit in Bank B (due to Bank A's new loans), and so on. Thus, $10 is created out of $1, or $9 is manufactured by the multiple expansion of bank deposits.

$1 to deposits in Bank A, $0.90 to deposits in Bank B, $0.81 to deposits in Bank C, and so on. When all these deposits are added together, the result is a $10 increase in deposits for each $1 increase in reserves.

If the required-reserve ratio had been 20 percent in our example, the $1 increase in reserves would still add $1 to deposits in Bank A, but would now add $0.80 in Bank B, $0.64 in Bank C, and so on for a total increase of $5 in deposits. With a required-reserve ratio of 20 percent, the deposit multiplier is 5. These two examples suggest a formula for the deposit multiplier.

The deposit multiplier is the reciprocal of the reserve ratio (r) maintained by the banking system:

$$\text{Deposit multiplier} = \frac{1}{r}.$$

Example 4   Monopoly Banking and Multiple Expansion

The banking system of the United States is made up of many banks. The largest bank accounts for only a small fraction of bank assets. If, however, the entire banking system consisted of one bank— a giant monopoly bank—then that bank could create a multiple expansion of bank deposits all by itself. A monopoly bank that has excess reserves can lend out a multiple of those excess reserves because it knows that when those funds are spent they will be redeposited in the monopoly bank. A single bank out of many cannot be so bold. If a single bank loaned out more than its excess reserves, it would in all probability have to pay out those funds to other banks and would find itself with insufficient reserves.

If the banking system consisted of a few large banks, as in Canada or Great Britain, then each bank would be able to count on receiving some portion of its loans back as deposits. In such a case, a sufficiently large bank can itself create a multiple expansion of deposits. The Bank of America, the largest bank in the United States, consti-

tutes only 6 percent of the banking system. It would be imprudent even for the Bank of America to lend out much more than its excess reserves. But in England there is a "Big Five" that dominates the banking business, so that one of these banks could well create a small multiple expansion of bank deposits.

Does the number of banks affect the speed of multiple expansion of bank deposits? Although one could argue that the multiple expansion of bank deposits occurs much more quickly in England as compared to the United States, the multiple expansion of deposits takes place very quickly in the United States. One study found that most of the multiple expansion of deposits in the United States probably takes place within one month. ■

Source: Roy J. Ruffin, "An Econometric Model of Impact of Open Market Operations on Various Bank Classes," *Journal of Finance* (September, 1968), pp. 625–637.

When the reserve ratio is 10 percent, $r = 0.10$, and the deposit multiplier is 10. If the reserve ratio is 20 percent, $r = 0.20$, and the deposit multiplier is 5.

Money-Supply Expansion in the Real World

Our discussion of the multiple expansion of bank deposits assumed that no cash ever leaked out of the banking system and that banks keep excess reserves at zero. Both assumptions are not strictly true.

Cash Leakages.   The public does not hold all of its money balances in demand deposits. When banks begin to create new demand deposits, it is likely that the public will also want to hold more currency. Thus, there will be leakages of cash into hand-to-hand circulation as the multiple creation of bank deposits takes place.

Cash leakages reduce the deposit multiplier. Returning to our numerical example, when $100 was initially deposited in Bank A and $90 was lent out, the next generation of banks—Bank B—

might receive only $80 in new deposits rather than $90. Thus, Bank B could create only $72 in new deposits rather than $81. This erosion would occur all along the line in Table 4 and would reduce the deposit multiplier accordingly.

If one knows the total cash leakage that will take place, one can apply the deposit multiplier $(1/r)$ to the amount of the new reserves that are left with the banking system. Suppose that out of the $100 originally deposited with Bank A, $20 would eventually leak into hand-to-hand circulation. Since $80 of new reserves would remain in the banking system, then $800 of deposits must result from the $100 deposit. Thus, the 10-to-1 multiplier applies to the quantity of reserves permanently left with the banking system.

The effect of cash leakages on the total money supply explains the mysterious disappearance of $6.7 billion during the Great Depression noted at the beginning of this chapter. As already noted, the Fed controls the monetary base through its purchases and sales. From 1929 to 1933 the Fed did not attempt to pump reserves into the banking system, but the public did draw cash out of the banking system—partially in response to a loss of confidence in banks. These cash withdrawals lowered bank reserves and led to a multiple *contraction* of bank deposits. The $6.7 billion disappeared into thin air. Thus, the deposit multiplier works both in forward and reverse. If reserves contract, demand deposits will fall by a multiple of the fall in reserves.

Excess Reserves.

If *r* in the deposit-multiplier formula is interpreted as the required-reserve ratio, the formula applies only when there are no excess reserves. However, the *r* in the formula can also be interpreted as the *desired-reserve ratio* of banks. The desired-reserve ratio will depend on the required-reserve ratio and on the profitability of making loans.

In recent years, most banks have kept very small excess reserves. Thus, the desired reserve ratio has been only slightly larger than the required-reserve ratio. Before the Monetary Control Act of 1980, excess reserves remained at around 1 percent of total reserves. The 1980 Act substantially lowered required reserves. The consequence is that excess reserves have increased slightly. In 1984, excess reserves averaged from a low of 1.3 percent to a high of 2.5 percent of total reserves.

Excess reserves are small for two reasons. First, banks can usually borrow from the Federal Reserve System at the official discount rate to meet any reserve deficiency. Second, banks can always borrow reserves from other banks. The Federal Funds Market is a market in which any bank with excess reserves can lend its reserves to banks with deficient reserves at the Federal Funds rate. This rate varies substantially throughout the day, as banks are borrowing for very short periods of time (often just overnight).

The Money Multiplier

The process of multiple expansion of reserves explains why the money supply can exceed the monetary base (currency in circulation plus bank reserves). We have shown that the banking system as a whole—by lending out excess reserves—can create deposits that are a multiple of banking-system reserves. The size of this multiple depends upon required-reserve ratios, cash leakages, and banks' willingness to hold excess reserves.

The deposit multiplier measures by how much deposits increase for every $1 increase in bank reserves if there are no cash leakages. In reality, the deposit multiplier (1/*r*) exaggerates the actual increase in the money supply from a $1 increase in reserves because there are substantial cash leakages. The **money multiplier** is the measure of this *actual* increase.

The **money multiplier** measures the increase in the money supply for every dollar increase in the monetary base.

Because of cash leakages, the money multiplier is less than the deposit multiplier.[5]

Figure 1 illustrated the relationship between the money supply and the monetary base: the money supply (currency in circulation plus checkable deposits) was 2.8 times the monetary base in February 1985. This *money multiplier* is smaller than the deposit multiplier.

FEDERAL RESERVE POLICY

The most important function of the Fed is to control the quantity of money. The quantity of money can affect prices, output, and employment; therefore, the Fed controls—to some degree—the pulse rate of the economy. By expanding the money supply, the Fed can speed up the pulse rate; by contracting the money supply (or by slowing down its rate of growth), the Fed can slow down the pulse rate.

---

5. The money multiplier formula, for interested students, is derived as follows. Assume banks wish to hold the ratio *r* of Fed and vault reserves *(R)* to deposits *(D)*. Thus, $R = rD$. Assume the public wishes to hold the ratio *k* of currency *(C)* to deposits *(D)*. Thus, $k = C/D$ and $r = R/D$. The monetary base $(H) = R + C$. The money supply *(M)* $= C + D$. Thus,

$$\frac{M}{H} = \frac{D + C}{R + C}. \qquad (1)$$

Nothing is changed by dividing *D* into the numerator and denominator:

$$\frac{M}{H} = \frac{(1 + k)}{(r + k)}. \qquad (2)$$

This equation shows how the monetary base *H* is related to the money supply *M*. If $r = 0.2$ and $k = 0.3$, $M = (1.3)H/0.5 = 2.6H$. In this case, the money multiplier is 2.6, while the deposit multiplier is $D = 1/0.2 = 5$.

The Fed controls money and credit by:

1. controlling the monetary base through open-market operations,
2. controlling reserve requirements,
3. setting the discount rate,
4. applying moral suasion,
5. imposing selective credit controls, and
6. setting margin requirements.

Open-Market Operations

As already mentioned, the Fed can inject or withdraw money from the economy by buying or selling. An injection of money leads to a multiple expansion of deposits; a withdrawal of money leads to a multiple contraction of bank deposits.

The Fed controls bank reserves by buying and selling federal-government securities on the open market as directed by the Federal Open Market Committee. The Fed already owns a large sum of government securities. In 1983, the Fed acquired $11 billion in government securities to bring its total holdings to about $150 billion at the beginning of 1984.

A substantial portion of the Fed's open-market operations are purely defensive. The Fed responds to changes in the currency-holding habits of the public. For example, a large seasonal influx of cash from the public into the banking system tends to automatically increase bank reserves. When depositors deposit cash in their checking accounts, bank reserves rise and excess reserves are created. Without countering Fed action, banks would begin to loan out excess reserves. Likewise, spontaneous cash drains from the banking system cause a contraction of the supply of money in the absence of offsetting Fed actions. When depositors write checks to obtain cash, bank reserves fall, and banks can be left with insufficient reserves.

The mechanics of Fed open-market transactions are the same whether the Fed is simply offsetting actions in the private economy to hold money supply steady or embarking on a course of monetary expansion or contraction.

Open-Market Sales. Suppose the Fed sells $10,000 worth of government securities to an individual (by means of some intermediary). The individual sends a personal check written on a commercial bank to the Fed (although the exact same effect is achieved if the individual pays cash). Part (A) of Table 5 shows what happens to the balance sheets of the individual, the commercial bank, and the Fed. The individual's total assets stay the same. The individual's bonds increase by $10,000 and demand deposits decrease by $10,000. The commercial bank finds that its demand-deposit liabilities have fallen by $10,000, and its reserves with the Fed fall by $10,000. When the Fed receives the check drawn on the commercial bank, it reduces the bank's account by that amount. The Fed's stock of government securities falls by $10,000, and its reserve balance liability to the commercial bank falls by $10,000.

As a consequence of the Fed sale, the money supply falls by $10,000 because demand deposits fall by that amount. In addition, the monetary base also falls by $10,000. By selling $10,000 in securities, the Fed extinguishes $10,000 in reserves. Writing a check to the Fed, unlike writing one to someone else, destroys money instead of transferring it.

The extinction of $10,000 in reserves (monetary base) will cause a multiple contraction of deposits. With a deposit multiplier of 10, the deposits will fall by $100,000.

Open-Market Purchases. Now suppose the Fed purchases $10,000 worth of securities from a person (by means of some intermediary). That person receives a check from the Fed and deposits it in his or her bank. Part (B) of Table 5 shows what happens to the balance sheets of the person, the commercial bank, and the Fed. The individual's total assets remain the same: demand deposits increase by $10,000, and government bonds decrease by $10,000. The commercial bank finds that its demand deposits have risen by $10,000, and its reserves with the Fed rise by $10,000. Finally, the Fed's government securities and reserve balances of commercial banks both rise by $10,000. The monetary base has risen by the amount of the purchase. This expansion of bank reserves will set into motion a multiple expansion of deposits.

As a comparison of Parts (A) and (B) of Table

Table 5   Two Open-Market Transactions

(A) Effects of an Open-Market Sale of $10,000 in Government Securities

	Changes in Assets		Changes in Liabilities	
(1) Individual or household	Securities Demand deposits	+$10,000 −$10,000	No change	
(2) Commercial bank	Reserves at Fed	−$10,000	Demand deposits	−$10,000
(3) The Fed	Government securities	−$10,000	Reserve balances of banks	−$10,000

(B) Effects of an Open-Market Purchase of $10,000 in Government Securities

	Changes in Assets		Changes in Liabilities	
(1) Individual or household	Securities Demand deposits	−$10,000 +$10,000	No change	
(2) Commercial bank	Reserves at Fed	+$10,000	Demand deposits	+$10,000
(3) The Fed	Government securities	+$10,000	Reserve balances of banks	+$10,000

Part (A) of this table shows the effect of an open-market sale by the Fed. Rows (2) and (3) of Part (A) show that commercial-bank reserves fall by the amount of the sale. Thus, Fed *sales* of government securities *lower* commercial-bank reserves. Part (B) shows the effect of an open-market purchase by the Fed. Rows (2) and (3) show that commercial-bank reserves rise by the amount of the Fed purchase. Thus, Fed *purchases* of government securities *raise* commercial-bank reserves.

5 shows, open-market purchases have the exact opposite effects as open-market sales.

Open-market sales destroy reserves, and open-market purchases create reserve balances. *The Fed uses these operations to control the size of the money supply by controlling the size of the monetary base.* Open-market operations are the most potent weapon of Fed policy because the Fed can buy or sell small or large quantities of government securities and can do so quickly.

> **Open-market purchases increase the monetary base; open-market sales lower the monetary base. Open-market operations are flexible because they can be transacted quickly and in almost any desired amount. Open-market operations are powerful because they have a magnified impact on the money supply as new reserves are added or subtracted from the banking system.**

Changes in Reserve Requirements

The Fed has the power to change reserve requirements within broad limits. This power is potentially a very effective tool of monetary policy. For example, increasing reserve requirements from 10 percent to 12.5 percent would force banks to contract demand deposits by 20 percent. Recall that the deposit multiplier is $1/r$. When $r = 0.10$, $40,000 in reserves would support $400,000 in demand deposits. If reserve requirements were raised to $r = 0.125$, $40,000 in reserves would support only $320,000 in demand deposits; demand deposits would have to contract by $80,000. Conversely, lowering reserve requirements can have a massive impact on increasing the money supply.

Traditionally, the Fed has been reluctant to use this tool of monetary policy. From December 1976 until the Monetary Control Act of 1980 became effective in November 1980, the Fed never used this tool of monetary policy. One argument against reserve-requirement changes is that they are too blunt an instrument. An open-market operation, for example, can be carried out to offset a seasonal currency drain without any fanfare or comment from the press. But a reduction in reserve requirements that is used to simply offset a seasonal currency drain might be interpreted by the financial press as a fundamental change in monetary policy.

Increases in reserve requirements reduce the money supply; reductions in reserve requirements increase the money supply. Changes in reserve requirements, however, are a seldom-used instrument of monetary policy.

Changes in the Discount Rate

The discount rate is the interest rate the Fed charges depository institutions who wish to borrow reserves to meet reserve requirements. As indicated earlier, before 1980 only member banks had access to the discount window. Now all depository institutions with balances at the Fed can borrow from the Fed.

The basic function of the discount window is to perform the lender-of-last-resort function of the central bank. Unanticipated withdrawals from a bank can lead to a deficiency in reserves. The bank can make up this deficiency by borrowing from the Fed. The higher the discount rate relative to other interest rates that the bank can earn on its loans and investments, the more costly it is for the bank to keep a small margin of excess reserves. Thus, a lowering of the discount rate may encourage banks to follow a more lenient credit policy and may expand the money supply—but the effects are small.

Generally speaking, the Fed raises or lowers the discount rate in line with market interest rates on government securities. If market interest rates are rising on Treasury bills (government securities with a maturity of less than one year), banks will be tempted to invest all excess funds in such securities up to the loan limits imposed by reserve requirements. Raising the discount rate will reduce the temptation of banks to follow a more lenient loan-and-investment policy when interest rates are rising. Thus, raising the discount rate does not necessarily mean the Fed is trying to lower the money supply; the Fed may only be trying to control money supply by restricting Fed borrowing.

Other Instruments of Control

In addition to the three major instruments just mentioned, the Fed has three minor tools for controlling money supply: moral suasion, selective credit controls, and margin credit.

Moral Suasion.   The Chairperson of the Fed has been known at times to urge banks to expand their loans or to adopt more restrictive credit policies. *Moral suasion* is the process by which the Fed tries to persuade banks to voluntarily follow a particular policy.

Selective Credit Controls.   The Fed can use *selective credit controls* to affect the *distribution* of loans rather than the *overall volume* of loans. The Fed can control terms and conditions of installment credit and requirements for consumer credit cards. Until 1986, the Fed could set interest-rate ceilings on deposits at commercial banks, which can affect bank deposits.

Margin Credit.   When investors buy stocks, they are permitted to buy a portion on credit (this practice is called *buying on margin*). This credit, supplied by stock brokers, is called *margin credit*. The Fed sets margin requirements. Current margin requirements allow purchasers of stock to finance 50 percent of the purchase with margin credit. In the speculative stock-market boom of the 1920s, speculators could purchase stocks with as little as 10 percent down; the rest was financed with margin loans. Studies show margin requirements to be relatively ineffective. Thus, the Fed in January 1985 asked Congress to abolish margin requirements.

Problems of Monetary Control

The Fed controls the U.S. money supply by controlling the monetary base. By buying government securities, it injects reserves into the banking system, and the banks convert this addition to the monetary base into a multiple expansion of the money supply. The Fed can also control the money supply through reserve requirements and other instruments.

Fed control over the money supply is not perfect for a number of reasons. First, the Fed can never know for sure the size of the money multiplier when it injects reserves into the economy. The eventual expansion depends upon cash leakages and upon banks' willingness to loan out excess reserves. Although cash leakages and bank behavior are not normally subject to large swings, this does introduce a range of uncertainty into the Fed's control of the money supply. Second, the Fed cannot control banks or banklike organizations that lie outside the Fed's jurisdiction. For many years, American banks have been able to obtain reserves abroad by borrowing dollars held by foreign banks. In recent years, a number of corporations have entered the business of banking in such a way as to remain free of controls by the Fed (See again Example 1.)

Even if the Fed controlled M1 perfectly, however, as demonstrated in Chapter 7, there is still the problem of competing concepts of money supply. When the Fed controls M1, individuals and banks can switch to the money substitutes in M2. In early 1984, money-market mutual funds, on which people can write checks, were about 35 percent of the size of M1. If the Fed controls M2, people may find other forms of money substitutes that are not subject to Fed control.

MONEY AND INTEREST

This chapter has shown how the Fed controls the U.S. money supply through the commercial banking system. By injecting or withdrawing reserves from the economy, the Fed affects the amount of credit. When the Fed injects fresh reserves, banks receive excess reserves that they loan out in credit markets. When the Fed withdraws reserves, banks make fewer loans (and maybe even call in loans), and the credit market tightens. Generally, as credit eases, market interest rates fall. As credit tightens, interest rates rise.

Through its control of bank reserves, the Fed is able to make credit either easier or tighter. In this way, the Fed is able to affect market interest rates.

One of the most complicated relationships in economics is the relationship between money and interest rates. In this section, we begin to build the theory of money and interest. Subsequent chapters will discuss this issue in much more detail. Chapter 7 showed that the demand for money is negatively related to the interest rate. The interest rate is the opportunity cost of holding assets in money form. As the opportunity cost of money rises (as the interest rate rises), the quantity demanded of money should fall. An economywide demand curve for money is shown in Figure 2. A larger quantity of money is demanded at a low interest rate than at a high interest rate. The negatively sloped demand curve for money is also called the *liquidity-preference curve* because people are really demanding liquidity when they demand money. The supply of money is determined by the Fed. In Figure 2 the supply of money set by the Fed is not affected by interest rates (it is drawn as a vertical line at the money supply determined by the monetary authorities).

The rate of interest is the *price of credit*. How does the quantity of *money* demanded and supplied determine the interest rate? Panel (a) of Figure 2 shows that when the supply of money is S and the demand for money is D, the money market is in equilibrium when the interest rate is 10 percent. If the supply of money increases from S to S' either the Fed is purchasing government securities (supplying additional credit) or commercial banks are making additional loans and investments. In either case, additional credit is being supplied and downward pressure is put on interest rates. The new equilibrium interest rate is 6 percent when the supply of money increases to S'. In effect, the lower interest rate is required to induce the public to hold the larger stock of money.

Panel (b) of Figure 2 shows what happens if the demand for money increases. The demand for money will increase if GNP increases. Thus, an increase in GNP, holding the supply of money

Figure 2   Money Supply, Money Demand, and the Interest Rate

(a) An Increase in
    Money Supply

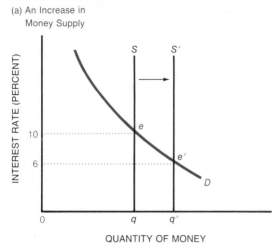

(b) An Increase in
    Money Demand

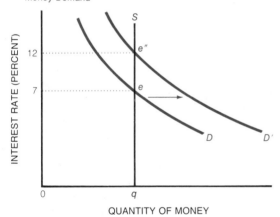

The money demand curve *(D)* is negatively sloped because the interest rate is the opportunity cost of holding money. The supply of money *(S)* is determined by monetary authorities and is not affected by the interest rate (therefore, it is drawn as a vertical line). The interest rate will settle at that rate at which the quantity of money demanded equals the quantity of money supplied (at *e*). As the money supply is increased from *S* to *S'* in panel (a), a new equilibrium is established at *e'* at a lower rate of interest. Panel (b) shows the effect of an increase in real GNP on the interest rate. An increase in real GNP raises the demand for money (From *D* to *D'*), and the equilibrium shifts from *e* to *e"* at a higher rate of interest.

constant, raises the rate of interest from 7 percent to 12 percent.

As later chapters will show, interest-rate movements are caused by a complex mixture of factors. Figure 2 shows what happens to interest rates when there is a change in only one factor at a time. In the real world, changes in money supply and money demand tend to be interrelated. Increases in the money supply can set into motion higher inflation (or the expectation of higher inflation). Increases in the money supply may also cause increases in real incomes (or the expectation of higher real incomes).

This chapter explained the relationship between the Federal Reserve System and the money supply. The money supply is important because it affects total expenditures for goods and services. The next chapter will examine a simple income/expenditure model of GNP that will provide the basis for our understanding of aggregate demand in later chapters.

Summary

1. Banks are financial intermediaries. Financial intermediaries borrow money from ultimate lenders and lend this money to ultimate borrowers. Most lending in the United States is done by financial intermediaries. Financial intermediaries offer three advantages: they minimize costs of lending and borrowing, they pool risks, and they offer liquidity to lenders by borrowing short and lending long.
2. Commercial banks are chartered by state banking authorities or by the U.S. Treasury. Commercial banks offer their customers checking-account services and savings accounts. They earn money by loaning out funds they have borrowed or by investing these funds in government securities. Banks make profits by borrowing at a lower rate of interest than that at which they lend or invest. Bank balance sheets summarize the claims on the assets of a bank. Banks must maintain reserves to meet the cash needs of their depositors. Reserves are held in two forms: cash in the vault and reserve balances at the Fed. Reserves are typically much less than the demand-deposit liabilities of the bank. The FDIC insures deposits and gives depositors the necessary sense of security.

3. The Federal Reserve System is the central bank of the United States and was established in 1913. The Fed consists of 12 district banks, a Board of Governors, and a Federal Open Market Committee in charge of buying and selling government securities for the Fed. Not all commercial banks are members of the Fed system, but the largest banks are. Since 1980, the Fed has the authority to exercise control over nonmember banks. The Fed imposes reserve requirements on banks and thrift institutions. A reserve requirement is a rule that the bank must hold a prescribed portion of their outstanding deposits as reserves. Depository institutions can borrow from the Fed to meet their temporary cash needs, and the interest rate at which they borrow is called the *discount rate*. By buying and selling things, the Fed injects money into the banking system and takes money out of the banking system. When the Fed buys anything, the sum of reserves on deposit with the Fed, vault cash in banks, and currency in circulation increases by the amount of the purchase. The monetary base equals reserve balances with the Fed, vault cash, and currency in circulation. The monetary base is smaller than the money supply.

4. Banks create money by monetizing debt. Banks can use reserves to make loans, and in the process of making loans, they create money. Private banks can create money because demand deposits are money and because banks make loans out of deposits. An increase in reserves leads to a multiple expansion of deposits. Although any one bank can lend out only its excess reserves, the banking system as a whole can lend out a multiple of an increase in reserves. The deposit multiplier is the ratio of the change in deposits to the change in reserves. If there are no cash leakages and banks lend out all excess reserves, the deposit multiplier is in the inverse of the required-reserve ratio.

5. The Fed has an arsenal of weapons to control the money supply: open-market operations, control of the discount rate, control of the required-reserve ratio, and selective credit controls. By buying government securities, the Fed injects reserves into the system and expands the money supply. By selling government securities, the Fed withdraws reserves, and the money supply contracts. Changing reserve requirements can have a large impact on the money supply because it creates excess reserves (when the rate is lowered) and it creates reserve deficiencies when the rate is raised. It is a seldom used policy. Changes in the discount rate have a modest effect on bank reserves. Cash leakages, nonuniform reserve requirements, and the existence of substitutes for M1 present problems for effective monetary control.

6. The interest rate is the opportunity cost of money. The demand for money is negatively related to the interest rate. The market rate of interest equates the quantity of money demanded with the quantity of money supplied by monetary authorities. If the supply of money is increased, the interest rate should fall, *ceteris paribus*. If the demand for money rises, the interest rate should rise, *ceteris paribus*. Interest-rate determination is one of the most complicated issues of macroeconomics.

Key Terms

financial intermediaries
commercial banks
balance sheet
assets
liabilities
reserves
reserve requirements
required-reserve ratio
open-market operations
T-accounts
monetary base
monetization of debt
excess reserves
cash leakage
multiple-deposit expansion
deposit multiplier
money multiplier

Questions and Problems

1. ''Banks get away with murder. They pay you no interest on your checking accounts and then they turn around and lend your money to some poor fellow at 18 percent.'' Evaluate this statement.

2. Table 1 shows that commercial banks in December 1984 had only $23 billion vault cash but had outstanding net-demand-deposit liabilities of $380 billion. Explain how banks can get by with so little cash.

3. Explain why even without required-reserve ratios bankers would maintain reserves.

4. Assume the Fed sells all its old office furniture to XYZ corporation for $10 million. What effect will this have on the money supply? What will happen if the Fed sells XYZ corporation $10 million worth of its holdings of government securities?

5. Explain why banks can create money only if bank deposits are accepted as money and only if banks are willing to make loans. Explain what is meant by the *monetization of debt*.

6. Assume the required-reserve ratio is 0.4 (40 percent) and there are no cash leakages. The Fed buys a government security from Jones for $1,000. Explain, using T-accounts, what will happen to the money supply. Answer the same question assuming only that Jones (and only Jones) takes payment from the Fed as follows: $500 cash (which he puts under his mattress) and a $500 check.

7. Rework Table 4 on the assumption that $r = 0.2$. In this case, the deposit multiplier is 5, so that the $100 fresh deposit in Bank A will ultimately lead to $500 in total deposits, or $400 in new money.

8. Consider what would happen to market interest rates if there were a simultaneous increase in the supply of and demand for money. Use supply and demand curves to support your answer.

9. What would you predict would happen to commercial-bank borrowing from the Fed if the Fed were to raise the required-reserve ratio?

10. Between year 1 and year 2, the amount of currency in circulation increased while the amount of vault cash and reserves at the Fed remained the same. Was the Fed purchasing or selling securities?

11. During the Christmas season, the public tends to withdraw large sums of cash from checking accounts. What effect would these withdrawals have upon the nation's money supply?

12. The previous chapter showed that the demand for money depends upon real income, the price level, and interest rates. If the economy is in a recession with falling real income and falling prices, what would happen to the market interest rate?

Suggested Readings

Burns, Arthur F. "The Independence of the Federal Reserve System." *Challenge* (July/August 1976), pp. 21–24.

Mayer, Martin. *The Bankers*. New York: Ballantine Books, 1974.

Mayer, Thomas *et al. Money, Banking, and the Economy*. New York: W. W. Norton, 1981.

Ritter, Lawrence S. and William L. Silber. *Money*, 3rd ed. New York: Basic Books, 1977.

Thompson, Lloyd B. *Money, Banking, and Economic Activity*, 2nd ed. Englewood Cliffs, N.J.: Prentice-Hall, 1982.

9

Keynesian Economics

Chapter Preview

Chapter 6 explained how GNP is measured. This chapter focuses on the determinants of aggregate supply and aggregate demand in an economy with substantial unemployed resources.

Classical economists tended to believe that unemployment was not a serious problem. This chapter will explain the basis for the classical theory. The Great Depression of the 1930s caused a watershed in macroeconomic thought because it showed that capitalist economies could operate for extended periods of time well below their potential output level, contrary to the prediction of the classical school. The British economist, John Maynard Keynes, offered an explanation of why economies could operate below their production potential for long periods of time. This chapter explains Keynesian economics and the shortcomings of the classical model.

Keynes shifted the focus of economics from the supply side to the demand side. On the supply side are those factors that determine the location of an economy's production-possibilities frontier. Keynes agreed with the classical economists that in the long run, the supply side would dominate the determination of real GNP, but in a famous quote declared that "in the long run, we are all dead." To Keynes, the interesting action is in the short run where the demand side dominates. Keynes felt, contrary to the teaching of his day, that an increase in demand for goods and services would increase real GNP because idle or unemployed resources would be available for producing the new, higher level of real GNP. Since any level of real GNP can be produced up to the full employment level, the Keynesian question is: what determines the level of real GNP at any given time? ∎

THE CLASSICAL MODEL

The classical model (discussed in an earlier chapter) can be credited to David Hume (1711–1766), David Ricardo (1772–1823), and Jean Baptiste Say (1767–1832). These classical quantity theorists taught that real GNP was determined by the supply side of the economy, while the price level was determined by the interaction of the supply and demand for money. Up until the work of Keynes, most economists believed that excessive unemployment was a short-lived affair that would quickly disappear if wages and prices are flexible.

According to the classical economists, whatever GNP can be produced will be demanded (Say's Law), and unemployment can only be the short-term consequence of money wages being temporarily too high. The determination of GNP was no mystery because the economy was assumed to operate at the full-employment level. The classical economists believed full employment to be the norm.

Say's Law

Chapter 6 explained that national income is the other side of the coin from national product. When an economy produces $3 trillion worth of final goods and services $(C + I + G + X - M)$, it also produces the income with which these goods can be purchased. It is always and everywhere true that *actual* aggregate income equals *actual* aggregate expenditures, but classical economists went one step further. They argued that *aggregate supply creates its own demand*. This assertion is called **Say's Law.**

> According to **Say's Law,** *desired* aggregate expenditures can never depart from *actual* aggregate expenditures. Whatever output is produced will be demanded.

How could the classical economists believe that consumers and firms will want to buy however much aggregate output is produced? Consider a hypothetical economy with no government that produces $600 billion worth of final goods and services, creating a total of $600 billion worth of income paid to land, labor, capital, and entrepreneurship. If households want to spend $500 billion on consumer goods and save $100 billion, the $100 billion saved is a withdrawal

Figure 1   The Interest Rate Equates Desired Saving and Desired Investment in the Classical Model

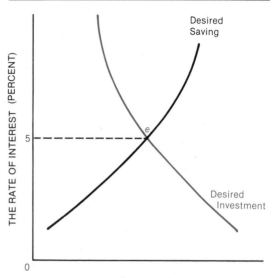

This figure measures the interest rate on the vertical axis and the amount of desired saving and desired investment on the horizontal axis. The saving curve shows the amount of desired saving at different interest rates. The higher is the interest rate, the greater is the amount of desired saving. The investment curve shows the amount of desired investment at different interest rates. The higher is the interest rate, the lower is the amount of desired investment. The interest rate equates the amount of desired investment and the amount of desired saving. In this example, the interest rate that equates desired saving and desired investment is 5 percent. At any interest rate above 5 percent, desired saving would exceed desired investment, and the interest rate would fall. At any rate below 5 percent, desired investment would exceed desired saving, and the interest rate would be driven up.

from the spending stream. According to Say, the desired saving of $100 billion will be exactly matched by desired investment of $100 billion. In this way, out of the $600 billion of income, households desire to spend $500 billion, and business firms desire to spend $100 billion. The investment injects the saving of households back into the spending stream.

How does the $100 billion of desired saving become $100 billion of desired investment? In Figure 1, the rate of interest is measured on the vertical axis, and desired saving and investment are measured on the horizontal axis. The saving curve shows how saving responds to the interest

Example 1   Unemployment, Wages, and Prices During the Great Depression

The classical theory taught that high unemployment would be self-liquidating. If a large number of people were involuntarily unemployed, they would be willing to work for less; wages would fall; thus, unemployment would fall. The Great Depression began in the late 1920s in Europe and spread to the United States in 1929. In Germany, France, the United States, and the Scandinavian countries unemployment rates rose to 25 percent or even higher in the early 1930s. In Europe and the United States, unemployment rates remained stubbornly high. The accompanying figures show unemployment rates and wage and price indexes in Great Britain, the United States, and Germany during the Great Depression.

The English figures clearly show why Keynes felt the classical model was not working: The English unemployment rate was above 10 percent from 1925 to 1937, rising to more than 20 percent in the early 1930s. During this same period, money wages in industry scarcely fell despite massive unemployment. Prices did decline somewhat, meaning that English real wages (money wages after adjustment for inflation) actually were rising during the Great Depression! It is no wonder that Keynes worried about the automatic self-correcting forces of falling wages and prices. The picture in the United States was slightly different. Money wages did fall substantially during the early 1930s, and prices fell slightly more rapidly. The surprising feature of the U.S. experience was the fact that both wages and prices were rising in the mid-1930s despite massive unemployment. The German case appears to conform most closely to the classical model. As the German unemployment rate rose to 30 percent of the labor force, the wage rate plummeted, falling more sharply than prices. Falling real wages accompanied rising unemployment in the German case. Of the three cases, the German unemployment rate returned most quickly to pre-Depression levels. There are a number of reasons for this (many cite Hitler's rearmament of Germany), but flexible wages and prices may have played a role. ∎

Sources: *Historical Statistics of the United States,* Series D1–10; D802–810; B. R. Mitchell, *European Historical Statistics, 1750–1970,* Tables C–2, C–4.

rate: generally speaking, the higher is the interest rate, the higher is desired saving. The higher is the interest rate, the greater is the incentive to save more and spend less on personal consumption. The investment curve shows how desired investment responds to the interest rate: generally speaking, the higher is the interest rate the less business managers and others want to invest in buildings, trucks, inventories, and equipment.

As Figure 1 shows, the market interest rate will be set at that rate at which *desired* saving equals *desired* investment. In the classical model, the interest rate coordinates saving and investment decisions. In Figure 1, the interest rate that equates desired saving and desired investment is 5 percent. At any interest rate above 5 percent, desired saving would exceed desired investment, and the interest rate would fall. At any rate below 5 percent, desired investment would exceed desired saving, and the interest rate would be driven up.

The interest rate equates desired saving and desired investment. If, for example, at any given level of income saving increases, consumption will fall. Interest rates will adjust downward sufficiently to insure that desired investment will increase by enough to offset the fall in consumption. Hence, desired aggregate expenditures would always equal aggregate income. Supply creates its own demand.

Unemployment

How did classical economists account for the cases where people are unemployed and the economy is operating below its production-possibilities frontier? To the classical quantity theorists, all unemployment was voluntary. Unemployment, in their opinion, could be looked upon as an excess supply of labor, and an excess supply of labor, wheat, or any other product results when the price is too high. In the case of labor, the price is

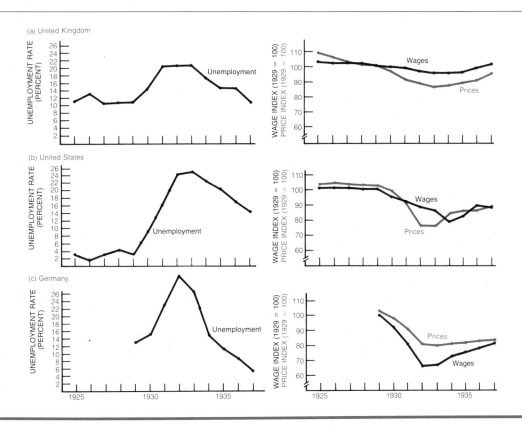

(a) United Kingdom

(b) United States

(c) Germany

the wage rate. If people complained that there was too much unemployment, the classical economist had a ready answer: if unemployed workers would accept a lower wage they would quickly be put back to work by eager employers. Unemployment was considered a problem that the unemployed themselves could correct by accepting lower wages.

Laissez-Faire Policy

The classical model supported a *laissez-faire* approach to macroeconomic policy, or a hands-off role for government. Classical economists believed the economy was capable of healing itself by allowing wages and prices to adjust to eliminate unemployment. No one needed to worry about an insufficiency of aggregate demand because Say's Law insured that supply creates its own demand. Government actions to regulate employment and real GNP could not be effective.

The classical model taught that the economy's real output would grow over time as its resources (labor and capital) expanded. This growth might not be steady insofar as resources might not grow at a uniform rate, but extended departures from long-term growth in the form of large downturns in output and employment would not be expected.

The Great Depression Sets the Stage for the Keynesian Revolution

The Great Depression of the 1930s shook economists' belief in the classical model. Between 1929 and 1933, real GNP in the United States declined by 30 percent. The 1929 output level was not regained until 1939. Unemployment rose from 3.2 percent of the labor force in 1929 to 24.9 percent in 1933 and was still 17.2 percent in 1939. Investment spending suffered much more than consumption spending. Between 1929 and 1933, real investment dropped by 75 percent, while real consumption fell by a more modest 20 percent. The change in net investment (after deducting depreciation) was even more dramatic: it fell from 18.6 billion dollars to −6.0 billion dollars.

Such a substantial downturn in real output and employment did not appear to contemporary observers as the temporary departure from equilibrium described by the classical model. There had been economic recessions and depressions before but none this severe or sustained. The Great Depression's impact on economic thinking and on public attitudes cannot be overestimated. A generation of Americans grew up during the Depression; for many it remains a frightening experience. The political influence of the Great Depression was enormous. A *laissez-faire* economic philosophy that instructed the government to do nothing while one out of four was unemployed became a political liability. The question of the times became: "Why can't the government do something to help us?"

The Great Depression set the stage for what has come to be called the *Keynesian revolution*. The Keynesian revolution was sparked by the publication in 1936 of *The General Theory of Employment, Interest, and Money*. In this landmark book, Keynes argued that economies can reach a fairly stable equilibrium—from which they will budge only slowly—at much less than full employment. Keynes believed that the cyclical instability of investment spending, while not a dominant portion of total spending, tended to have a magnified effect on the rest of the economy.

Keynes's empirical evidence for these propositions was the Great Depression itself, which demonstrated that substantial sustained declines in economic activity were possible. The Keynesian revolution opened up a new approach to macroeconomic policy: it argued that it is the responsibility of government to insure that the economy operates at an acceptable rate of output and employment. Keynes felt that the classical mechanism of letting wage and price adjustments raise output and employment was too slow, unreliable, and unnecessary. Government economic action could be used to restore the economy to full employment more quickly and at much lower social costs. (See Example 1, which describes economic conditions during the Great Depression.)

Figure 2   The Keynesian Aggregate-Supply Curve

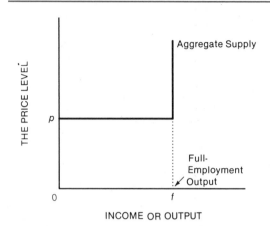

The Keynesian aggregate supply curve is horizontal at less than full-employment output—*f*—because money wages are "sticky" in a downward direction. Money wages do not fall in response to rising unemployment; therefore, different rates of aggregate supply (at less than full employment) are consistent with the same price level. Once the economy is at full-employment output (*f*), money wages rise, but prices are driven up at the same rate, and employment does not increase. At full-employment output, the supply curve becomes vertical. Thus, the Keynesian supply curve is a right-angled curve.

AGGREGATE SUPPLY

The Labor Market

The Keynesian approach to macroeconomics draws a picture of labor markets that is much different from the flexible labor market of the classical economist. According to Keynes, in a modern capitalist economy, the labor market can be inflexible because a variety of factors reduce the downward pressure on money wages when unemployment exists. These factors include union contracts that last two or more years, minimum-wage laws, and unemployment insurance that gives workers a financial backstop when laid off. Money wages, thus, tend to be sticky in the downward direction. In other words, if the demand for labor falls, money wages do not fall. Instead, they remain stuck at the prevailing rate.

This picture is not unreasonable for England at the time Keynes was writing. From 1921 to 1936,

Figure 3   A Keynesian Equilibrium

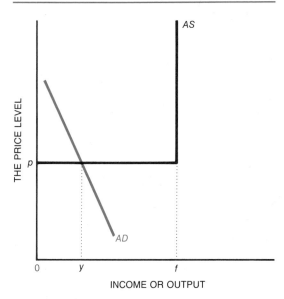

The equilibrium level of output in the Keynesian model occurs when the aggregate-demand curve intersects the horizontal portion of the aggregate-supply curve, where significant unemployment exists.

the unemployment rate in Great Britain varied between 9.7 and 22.1 percent. In the period 1921 to 1929, the British unemployment rate averaged 12 percent; from 1930 to 1936, it averaged 17.8 percent. Throughout this entire period, prices declined very slowly, and money wages remained more or less at the same level.

The Aggregate-Supply Curve

Remember from Chapter 5 that the aggregate-supply curve shows the levels of real output (real GNP) that are supplied by businesses at different price levels. Keynes tried to determine what this aggregate-supply curve would look like in a severe depression. In an economy in a depression it is possible to coax more production out of existing resources without raising wages and prices. A large number of people are out of work and are willing and anxious to work at going wage rates. People are, as it were, sitting around on the courthouse steps waiting for some business firm to give them a job. In addition, there is much idle plant-

and-equipment capital because many factories are not running at capacity. The firm need not raise wages to get more workers; it simply puts the unemployed worker back on the job. The worker is—according to Keynes—involuntarily unemployed. Because unemployed workers are willing to work at the going money wage, it is possible to expand aggregate expenditures without raising the price level. *At less than full employment, real GNP can increase without an increase in the price level.*

Figure 2 shows the Keynesian aggregate-supply curve. At levels of output less than full-employment output, wages and prices are sticky; workers willing to work at prevailing wages are unemployed. Therefore, aggregate real output can be increased without an increase in prices. For this reason, the Keynesian aggregate supply curve is horizontal below full-employment output, indicated by point *f* in Figure 2.

The picture changes when the economy reaches full employment. At full employment, an increase in aggregate expenditures will raise money wages. There is no involuntary unemployment, and it is not possible for the economy to increase its real output any further because resources are already fully employed. Instead, employers bid among themselves for labor and drive up wages; prices rise at the same rate as wages. Because wages and prices rise at the same rate, *real wages* remain the same. Despite the rising price level, the economy is producing the maximum possible output because all labor is employed.

The Keynesian supply curve is vertical at full-employment output. All those willing to work at the prevailing wage are employed; the economy cannot produce more real output. Instead, any effort to increase employment and output will drive up money wages and the price level without any increase in real output.

The *L*-shaped aggregate-supply curve plays a vital role in the Keynesian model. If the economy produces below the full-employment level of output, labor will be unemployed, and the economy has passed up the opportunity to produce a larger volume of output.

Figure 3 shows Keynes's explanation of why an economy can fall into a depression. When the aggregate-demand curve, *AD,* intersects the *L*-shaped aggregate-supply curve on its horizontal portion, the economy is operating below full employment. The farther to the left of full-employment output is the *AD/AS* intersection, the greater is the amount of unemployment. As Keynes saw it, the basic problem of an economy caught in a depression is too little aggregate demand. Keynes, therefore, devoted himself to explaining the determinants of aggregate demand. This chapter and the next will examine Keynes's analysis of the shape of the aggregate-demand curve and his explanation of how it shifts.

The aggregate-supply curve of Figures 2 and 3 is a gross oversimplification of the way real-world economies behave. Obviously, there are limits to the downward stickiness of wages. At very high rates of unemployment, money wages (and prices) would eventually fall, and the aggregate-supply curve would slope upward. Also, the full-employment threshold is not one single level of output. Economies do not reach a unique full-employment real output beyond which they cannot produce one more dollar of real output. Money wages may begin to rise at less than full employment as bottlenecks in particular labor markets develop. The dividing line between voluntary and involuntary employment is often poorly defined; there will be some frictional unemployment at full employment.

Like the rigid assumptions of the classical quantity theory, the simple Keynesian model offers the *L*-shaped aggregate-supply curve as an approximation of reality. Modern economists have substituted a more flexible version of full employment that will be examined in Chapter 11.

Figure 4 shows a Keynesian aggregate-supply curve modified by the existence of bottlenecks. Bottlenecks occur when some sectors of the economy reach full employment before others. As long as output is below point *b,* increases in aggregate demand bring important benefits but no inflationary costs. For example, the shift in the aggregate-demand curve from *AD* to *AD'* simply increases real GNP without raising prices. But an increase in aggregate demand from *AD'* to *AD"* moves the economy closer to full employment, but bottlenecks are created, and some upward pressure is put on wages and prices. Thus, real GNP increases but prices increase as well.

Figure 4   Keynesian Aggregate Supply with Bottlenecks

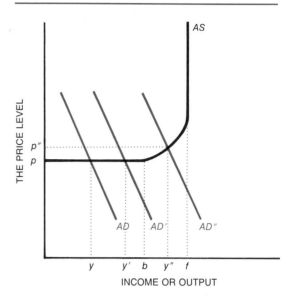

As the economy approaches full-employment output, the aggregate-supply curve begins to slope upward (at the output associated with point b) as resource bottlenecks are experienced. Thus, shifts in the aggregate-demand curve from AD to AD' do not affect the price level. But a shift from AD' to AD" raises prices because of bottlenecks.

Throughout the rest of this chapter it is assumed that the economy is operating in the horizontal portion of the Keynesian aggregate-supply curve.

The focus of Keynesian economics is on the demand side of the economy. What determines the shape and position of the aggregate-demand curve?

THE INCOME/EXPENDITURE APPROACH

Keynes's explanation of how an economy determines how much real output to produce relies on the relationship between income and expenditures. Thus, his approach is called the *income/expenditure approach.* The income/expenditure model of Keynes lays the foundations for an explanation of aggregate demand.

If real GNP is less than the full-employment level, what determines the level of real GNP at any given time? Why can it settle at less than full

Figure 5   U.S. Family Income and Expenditures, 1985

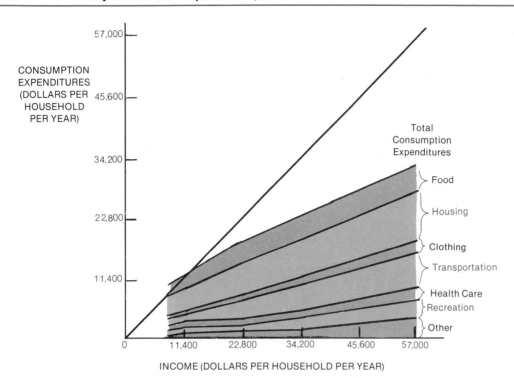

Total consumption expenditures vary positively with family income. The *pattern* of consumption also changes with income. Family saving is read as the difference between the 45-degree reference line and total consumption expenditures.

Source: U.S. Department of Labor, *Handbook of Labor Statistics*, December 1980. These are 1972–1973 data updated to 1985 by the authors.

employment? In Keynes's view there were two major flaws in the classical model. The first is that money wages did not have the necessary downward flexibility to eliminate unemployment. The second flaw Keynes saw in the classical model was Say's Law, which he rejected. Keynes believed that desired saving depended in only a minor way on interest rates. Instead, Keynes believed that desired saving depended primarily on disposable income. Thus, the interest rate could not be counted upon to equate desired saving and desired investment. Keynes did not believe that supply creates its own demand in the classical sense.

Chapter 16 on national-income accounting identified the major components of GNP as personal-consumption expenditures *(C),* private investment *(I),* government expenditures for goods

and services *(G),* and net exports *(X − M).* Since net exports make up only a small percentage of GNP, they will be ignored in this chapter. (Exports and imports will be discussed in Chapters 22 through 24.) Keynes's income/expenditure approach examined how the desired level of these expenditures (and, thus, the desired level of GNP) is determined.

The Consumption/Income Schedule

Of every dollar spent in our economy, about $0.64 is spent on private consumption—on purchases of food, clothing, shelter, services, and durable goods such as cars, TV sets, and refrigerators. If one examines how poor, middle-income, and rich families spend their income, three prominent patterns emerge (as shown in Figure 5).

Families with higher incomes tend to have higher consumption expenditures. Of course, there are exceptions to this rule; consumption spending does not depend on family income alone but will depend as well on the age and size of the family, expectations, the price level, taxation, and thriftiness—all of which will be examined shortly.

As a general rule, the higher is the family's disposable income, the higher is the dollar amount of its consumption spending.

The second pattern is that higher-income families spend a smaller percentage of their disposable income than do lower-income families. Figure 5 shows that the average family earning an income of $50,000 spent about $30,000, or about 60 percent, of its disposable income on consumer goods and services. The average family earning about $10,000, on the other hand, spent all of its income on consumption. When a family spends more than its disposable income, the family is either increasing its indebtedness (borrowing money for consumption) or financing consumption by drawing down its savings. The ones who spend less than their disposable income are saving and adding to their wealth, or reducing their indebtedness.

Higher-income families tend to save a larger portion of their disposable income than do lower-income families.

A third regularity that emerges from Figure 5 is that higher-income families have a different pattern of consumption spending: higher-income families tend to spend a smaller portion of their disposable income on food than do lower-income families. Figure 5 shows that the $50,000 family spends about 15 percent of its income on food, while the $10,000 family spends 25 percent of its disposable income on food.[1]

---

1. This pattern holds over time and across countries. The Prussian statistician, Ernst Engel, writing for the mid-19th century noted the universal tendency for the percentage of family income devoted to food to decline as income rises. Thus, the falling share of food expenditures with rising income has come to be called "Engel's Law."

Figure 6   U.S. Consumption Spending and Disposable Income, 1950–1984

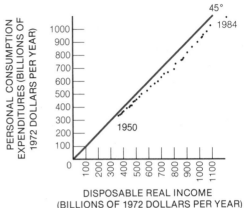

The spending habits of the U.S. economy as a whole are similar to those of average American families shown in Figure 5. U.S. total consumer spending tends to rise as disposable income rises.

Source: *Economic Report of the President.*

Higher-income families spend a smaller portion of disposable income on food than do lower-income families.

The most important fact about consumer-spending patterns is the positive relationship between consumption and income. The more income one earns, the more one is likely to spend on personal consumption. What is true for the individual and family should be true for the economy as a whole in this case, and the facts appear to support a positive consumption/income relationship.

In Figure 6 real personal-consumption expenditures of the United States are plotted against U.S. real personal disposable income for the period 1950 to 1984. As with the household data, the economy's total consumption spending tends to rise as disposable income rises. A line connecting the economy's consumption/income points would obviously be positively sloped.

Notably, the national pattern of saving does not follow the household pattern with equal clarity: the percentage of disposable income saved

Table 1 **The Aggregate-Expenditure Schedule with No Government Spending and No Government Taxes (billions of dollars)**

Output = Income, Y (1)	Consumption, C (2)	Saving, S (3)	Investment, I (4)	Desired Aggregate Expenditures (5) = (2) + (4)	Unintended Investment, S–I (6) = (3) – (4)
100	125	−25	50	175	−75
200	200	0	50	250	−50
300	275	25	50	325	−25
400	350	50	50	400	0
500	425	75	50	475	25
600	500	100	50	550	50

Columns (1) and (2) show the consumption/income schedule for our hypothetical economy. There are no taxes, so income and disposable income are the same. The marginal propensity to consume (MPC) in this example is 0.75 because for every $100 billion increase in income, consumption increases by $75 billion. The marginal propensity to save (MPS) is 0.25 because for every $100 billion increase in income, saving increases by $25 billion. The data in the first three columns are graphed in Figure 7. Panel (a) of Figure 7 graphs the consumption/income schedule of columns (1) and (2); panel (b) graphs the saving/income schedule of columns (1) and (3).

Aggregate expenditures equal the sum of desired consumption and desired investment at each income level. Desired investment is assumed to be constant at $50 billion. Unintended investment is the difference between desired saving and desired investment at each income level. Only at an income of $400 billion does desired saving equal desired investment or does the desired aggregate-expenditure level equal aggregate output. The equilibrium income is, therefore, $400 billion.

does not exhibit a distinctive upward trend with rising income. In 1950, the economy saved 7.2 percent (spent 92.8 percent of its disposable income on consumption). In 1983, it saved 7.6 percent (spent 92.4 percent)—a slight and scarcely noticeable change.

Why do saving rates of families increase as income increases while the same does not appear to be true for the economy as a whole? The reason has been explained by Milton Friedman and Franco Modigliani. The household data in Figure 5 are for a particular year. The national data in Figure 6 cover a very long period of time (1950–1984). Figure 5 is a short-run view; Figure 6 is a long-run view. The relationship between consumption and income in the short run is different than it is in the long run. For example, if your income *temporarily* increases, you will not increase your consumption as much as if your income *permanently* increases. In other words, people spend less out of a short-run increase in income than they do out of a long-run increase in their income. Thus, if we were to examine national consumption and saving at alternative levels of income over the short run (that is, at a given time), a pattern similar to the household pattern would emerge.

Table 1 provides hypothetical data on real consumption spending (C), real saving (S), and real GNP (Y) for an economy with no taxes. Because there are no taxes, every dollar earned is available as disposable income for either consumption or saving. In this special case, GNP equals disposable income. When income is $100 billion, then consumption is $125 billion, and saving is −$25 billion. At this level of income, households are borrowing or drawing down their financial assets (savings accounts, stocks, bonds). As Table 1 shows, when income rises from $100 billion to $200 billion, consumption rises by $75 billion to $200 billion. At this income level, households are now just breaking even. A further increase in income from $200 billion to $300 billion raises consumption spending to $275 billion. Households are now more than breaking even; they have unspent income left over for saving. At $300 billion, saving is a positive $25 billion. The schedules in the first three columns of Table 1 are the **consumption/income schedule** and the **saving/income schedule.**

The **consumption/income schedule** shows the amount of desired consumption at different levels of national income or output.

The **saving/income schedule** shows the desired amount of saving at different levels of national income or output.

The Marginal Propensity to Consume.

In the consumption/income schedule in columns (1) and (2) of Table 1, whenever income increases by $100 billion, consumption increases by $75 billion. Hence, in our hypothetical economy, every additional $1 of income increases desired consumption by $0.75. This relationship is very important to the income/expenditure model. Keynes called the fraction of additional income that is spent on consumption the **marginal propensity to consume (MPC)** because it refers to extra consumption induced by another dollar of disposable income.

The **marginal propensity to consume (MPC)** is the change in desired consumption (C) brought about by a change in income (Y) of $1.

$$MPC = \frac{\Delta C}{\Delta Y}$$

The symbol Δ placed before a variable is simply shorthand for "the change in" that variable.

The Marginal Propensity to Save.

In our hypothetical economy, every time income increases, saving increases as well. In Table 1, the saving/income schedule in columns (1) and (3) shows that saving increases by $25 billion for every $100 billion increase in income. Every extra $1 of income increases desired saving by $0.25. Keynes called the fraction of the increase in income that is saved the **marginal propensity to save (MPS)**.

The **marginal propensity to save (MPS)** is the change in desired saving (S) that is brought about by a change in income (Y) of $1.

$$MPS = \frac{\Delta S}{\Delta Y}$$

When there are no taxes in the economy (as in

this hypothetical example), an additional dollar of income is either consumed or saved. Hence,

$$MPC + MPS = 1.$$

When some income is spent in taxes, income and disposable income are no longer one and the same. It is, therefore, useful to refer to the marginal propensity to consume and the marginal propensity to save *out of disposable income*. If *MPC* and *MPS* are defined in relation to disposable income, then it is true that $MPC + MPS = 1$.[2]

Figure 6 graphs data on real consumption expenditures against real disposable income for the period 1950 to 1984. Although other factors that affect consumption were likely changing during this period along with income, the data in Figure 6 provide a preliminary idea of the values of *MPS* and *MPC* for this period. The *MPC* estimated from the 1950 to 1984 data is 0.91; the *MPS* equals 0.09. On average, out of every extra dollar of disposable income, $0.91 is spent on extra consumption and $0.09 is spent on extra saving in the long run. In the short run, for year-to-year changes, the *MPC* is significantly smaller than 0.91 (probably around 0.6).

The consumption/income and saving/income schedules of Table 1 are shown graphically in Figure 7. Consider first the consumption/income schedule in panel (a) of Figure 7. The 45-degree line from the origin has the property that any point on it is the same distance from the two axes. For example, the vertical line drawn from an income of $600 billion on the horizontal axis to the 45-degree line will be the same length as a horizontal line drawn from a consumption-spending level of $600 billion on the vertical axis to the 45-degree line. Each point on the 45-degree line is an equal distance from both axes. If the consumption/income curve were identical to the 45-

---

2. Keynes was also interested in the average relationships between desired consumption and income and between desired saving and income, which he called the average propensity to consume, *APC,* and the average propensity to save, *APS,* respectively. The average propensity to consume is defined as the ratio of desired consumption to income (*APC = C/Y*). The average propensity to save is defined as the ratio of desired saving to income (*APS = S/Y*).

degree line, all income would be spent on consumption. The vertical distance between the C curve and the 45-degree line is a visual measure of the difference between income and consumption, or a visual measure of saving. By comparing the 45-degree reference line with the consumption/income curve, the amount of saving at each level of income can be read directly from the diagram. For example, at an income level of $600 billion, saving equals $600 billion minus $500 billion, or $100 billion.

The intersection of the 45-degree reference line and the consumption/income curve (point *a*) is a very useful reference point: to the right of *a*, saving is positive since consumption is below income. For example, when income is $400 billion, consumption is $350 billion, and saving is $50 billion. To the left of *a* the economy is **dissaving** (saving is negative) because the economy's income is less than the amount of consumption spending. For example, when income is $100 billion, consumption is $125 billion and saving is − $25 billion.

> The economy is **dissaving**—total saving is negative—when consumption spending exceeds disposable income. The economy is either increasing its indebtedness or financing consumption by drawing down its savings.

At point *a*, the economy is neither saving nor dissaving. Total saving equals zero. In our example, the intersection occurs at an income level of $200 billion. At this income, the vertical distance to the 45-degree line is the same height as the vertical line to the consumption/income curve. At this point, income and consumption are the same; no income is left over for saving.

The corresponding relationship between saving and income is graphed in panel (b), which is directly below panel (a) in Figure 7. The saving/income curve shows the amount of saving at different levels of income. Whether saving is read from the 45-degree reference line of the consumption/income curve or directly from the saving/income curve, zero saving occurs on the saving/income curve at the same income ($200 billion). For income greater than $200 billion, saving is positive; for income below $200 billion,

Figure 7   The Consumption/Income Curve

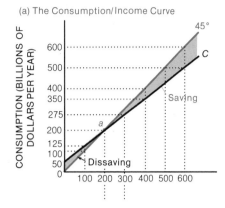

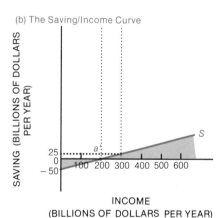

The C curve is the consumption/income curve graphed from the data in Table 1 and shows the amount of desired consumption at different levels of income. It is positively sloped because increases in income cause increases in consumption. The slope of C is the marginal propensity to consume, MPC, which in our example equals 0.75.

At any income measured on the horizontal axis, the vertical distance to the 45-degree line equals that income. The vertical distance to the C line equals consumption; the vertical distance between the 45-degree line and the C line equals saving. At the intersection of the 45-degree line and the C line (at point a), saving is zero. To the right of a, saving is positive; to the left of a, saving is negative (the economy is dissaving).

The saving/income curve (labeled S) shows the amount of real saving at each level of income. Saving is positive to the right of a', where income is $200 billion, and it is negative to the left of a'. By comparing panels (a) and (b), one can see that saving can be read from the consumption/income curve or from the saving/income curve.

Figure 8   Shifts in the Consumption/Income Curve

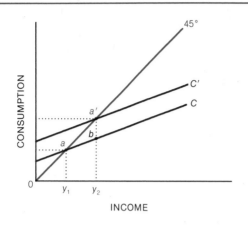

The original consumption/income curve, *C*, is drawn holding certain consumption-affecting factors other than income constant. Upward shifts in *C* are caused by increases in financial assets, reductions in the price level, reductions in taxes, a lowering of the average age of the population, a change in the distribution of income in favor of the poor, or the development of a more negative attitude toward thrift.

saving is negative (there is dissaving). Like the consumption/income curve, the saving/income curve is positively sloped.

Nonincome Factors That Affect Consumption

Income is not the only determinant of consumption. A number of other nonincome factors can also affect consumption. If any of these other consumption-affecting factors changes, the entire consumption/income curve will shift. It is important to distinguish between *movements along* the consumption/income curve and *shifts in* the consumption/income curve:

> A *movement along* the consumption/income curve occurs when income changes—with all other factors that affect consumption held constant. A *shift in* the consumption/income function occurs when a consumption-affecting factor other than income changes.

In Figure 8 a change in income from y_1 to y_2 will cause a movement along the consumption income curve from *a* to *b*. A change in a nonincome consumption-affecting factor could shift the entire curve from *C* to *C'*. A few of the many nonincome factors that affect consumption are: expectations, stocks of assets, the price level, taxation, age, income distribution, and attitudes toward thrift.

Expectations.   Consumption expenditures are often responsive to changes in consumer expectations about the future. People form expectations about how rapidly prices will rise, about the likelihood of becoming unemployed, or about whether a war will cause shortages of goods. Those who believe their jobs will remain secure may consume more than others earning the same income who believe they may lose their jobs sometime in the future. People who believe that inflation will be rapid may spend more than those who believe that inflation will be moderate. If people suddenly become convinced that inflation will speed up, they may accelerate their consumption spending—to buy before the price is too high.

Accordingly, the entire consumption/income curve can shift upward or downward when expectations change. As a general rule, it shifts upward when inflationary expectations increase or when there is a growing sense of job security and shifts downward when the reverse conditions hold.

Stocks of Assets.   Changes in the wealth of consumers can also cause shifts in the consumption/income curve. The money wealth of individuals is the net money value of the assets they own (stocks, cash balances, real estate). As the money value of these assets rises, people feel that they are better off and, if prices are not increasing, they are likely to increase their consumption expenditures. The stock market may rise and individuals who have seen the value of their assets rise respond by increasing their consumption—even though their annual income has not changed. For example, if wealth rises, one need not save as much out of current income to meet future retirement or vacation needs.

The Price Level.   Many financial assets in the economy are fixed in *nominal* value. The supply of money, the value of savings deposits, and money-market mutual funds are fixed in nominal value. When the price level changes, the purchasing power of these assets changes in inverse proportion. As prices rise, the purchasing power of a given volume of nominal financial assets falls. As prices fall, the purchasing power of a given volume of financial assets rises. For example, if a consumer held $100 in money, a doubling of the price level would reduce the purchasing power of the $100 in cash by exactly half. Thus, the higher is the price level, the lower is the purchasing power of any given stock of financial assets.

When the purchasing power of, say, the money supply increases, people feel better off and will increase their spending on goods and services even if their real income remains the same. For example, imagine your nominal income fell by 10 percent, prices fell by 10 percent, but your nominal holdings of money remained the same. Then the purchasing power of your income remains constant, but the purchasing power of your given money supply will increase by 10 percent. With larger real assets, you are likely to increase your consumption spending.

Taxation.   As income taxes rise, disposable income falls, *ceteris paribus*. As taxes increase, one would expect less consumption spending for the same amount of earned income. As income taxes are cut, disposable income rises; thus, one would expect more consumption spending from the same level of earned income.

Age, Income Distribution, and Attitudes toward Thrift.   A number of other nonincome factors can cause the consumption/income curve to shift. For example, the younger is the population, typically the higher is the percentage of income consumed. Younger families must acquire the durable goods to set up households. They must buy washing machines, cars, and other consumer durables. They must devote their incomes to raising and educating their children. On the other hand, families that have reached middle age have already accumulated a stock of durable goods; their children may have set out on their

own. Therefore middle-age families tend to spend a smaller portion of their income on consumption. To prepare for their retirement years they build up a nest egg by saving.

The *distribution of income* is also expected to affect the consumption/income curve: the rich tend to have a higher propensity to save than poor and middle-income families (as was shown by Figure 5). If the distribution of income is changed (say, by means of a tax reform) to raise the disposable income of the rich proportionally more than that of the poor, this change in distribution could shift down the consumption/income curve. If the distribution of income is changed in favor of the poor, the consumption/income curve should shift up.

Attitudes towards thrift also affect the consumption/income curve. If public attitudes toward saving and thrift change, the consumption/income curve will shift.

THE DETERMINATION OF EQUILIBRIUM EXPENDITURES

The Keynesian income/expenditure approach can be used to explain how real output, Y, is determined in the simple model described in this chapter. The basic ingredient of this explanation is the consumption/income schedule in the first three columns of Table 1, which assumed no government spending or taxes. We now add the assumption that the amount of desired investment is fixed. These assumptions simplify the explanation of income determination. In subsequent chapters, such unrealistic assumptions will be dropped. But this very simple hypothetical model sheds a great deal of light on the process by which income is determined.

The Aggregate-Expenditure Schedule

The consumption/income schedule in Table 1 relates the amount of consumption spending at each income (or output) level. The consumption/income schedule shows how much consumption would be *desired* at each income level. This desired amount of consumption will only be *realized* if the economy produces that amount of in-

Figure 9   Equilibrium Output

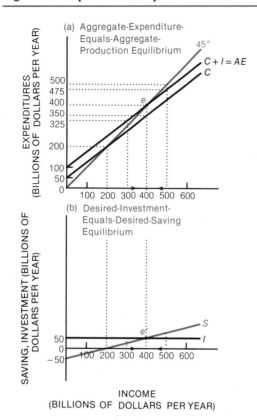

(a) Aggregate-Expenditure-
Equals-Aggregate-
Production Equilibrium

(b) Desired-Investment-
Equals-Desired-Saving
Equilibrium

INCOME
(BILLIONS OF DOLLARS PER YEAR)

This figure is drawn from the data in Table 1. In panel (a), the intersection of the *AE* curve with the 45-degree line occurs at an income of $400 billion (point e). If the economy were to attempt to produce an income greater than $400 billion (to the right of e), aggregate output would exceed desired aggregate expenditures, and income would fall. If the economy were to attempt to produce an income less than $400 billion (to the left of e), desired aggregate expenditures would exceed aggregate production, and income would rise. Panel (b) shows how the economy reaches equilibrium by contrasting desired investment and desired saving. At levels of income above $400 billion (e′), desired saving exceeds desired investment. Unintended inventory investment (the difference between desired saving and desired investment) signals firms to slow down their rate of output. At levels of income below $400 billion, desired investment exceeds desired saving. Unintended inventory disinvestment signals firms to increase their rate of production. Equilibrium income is reached at $400 billion where aggregate production equals aggregate expenditures, or where desired saving equals desired investment.

come. But consumption *(C)* is only one component of total spending; two other major components of total spending—investment *(I)* and government spending *(G)*—must be incorporated

into a schedule of **aggregate expenditures** *(AE)*. In our example, the business sector desires to spend a fixed amount on real investment—$50 billion dollars—at each level of income (and output) produced by the economy. In our simple economy, the government collects no taxes and purchases no goods or services.

A schedule of **aggregate expenditures** *(AE)* summarizes the relationship between the desired amount of total spending *(C + I + G)* and income.

Our example has eliminated government spending. Because investment is the same for each income level, desired aggregate expenditures at each income level are simply desired consumption plus desired investment, or the sum of columns (2) and (4) in Table 1.

In panel (a) of Figure 9, the consumption/income *(C)* curve is plotted from columns (1) and (2) of Table 1. The aggregate-expenditure *(AE)* curve is plotted from columns (1) and (5) but is simply the *C* curve shifted up by the amount of investment.

To understand income/expenditure analysis, it is important to understand that *desired* decisions are not necessarily *realized*. Whether they are indeed realized depends upon the relationship between desired aggregate expenditures and aggregate output.

Let us consider what would happen if our economy moved to an output of $500 billion. This decision is made by the hundreds of thousands of producers in the economy acting independently of one another. As Chapter 6 on national-income accounting mentioned, the act of producing $500 billion worth of output will create an income of $500 billion. If the economy were to continue to produce output at this rate, at the end of a year's time, it will have created $500 billion worth of income. At an annual income level of $500 billion, the economy would desire to spend $475 billion on consumption and investment, as shown in column (5) of Table 1. Desired aggregate expenditures would fall short of aggregate output by $25 billion, as shown in column (6) of Table 1.

The output rate of $500 billion worth of goods and services per year is, therefore, not an equilibrium output because the economy is producing output at a rate faster than purchasers in the economy are buying. Producers will know that too much output is being produced because unsold goods will accumulate in inventories higher than producers want to hold; excessive inventories of unsold cars, TV sets, sewing machines, and the like will build up. The accumulation of unwanted or excessive inventories will signal to business firms that their current production rates are excessive compared to what the market is prepared to purchase. Producers will have to slow down the rate of output production. (There might also be a tendency for prices to fall, but we are holding the price level constant in this chapter and the next.)

If business firms reduce their rate of production from $500 billion to $300 billion worth of output, desired aggregate expenditures will now exceed the rate of output by $25 billion. Producers will know that there is too little output because purchasers will be buying at too fast a rate. Inventories of goods—such as cars or TV sets— will fall below normal levels. Normal inventories can be replenished only by speeding up the rate of production.

Whenever aggregate production exceeds desired aggregate expenditures, the rate of production (and the rate of income creation) slows down. Whenever production falls short of desired aggregate expenditures, the rate of production (and income creation) speeds up. By adjusting the rate of output in response to total spending, the economy moves towards **Keynesian equilibrium.**

Keynesian equilibrium occurs when the economy produces an output that equals desired aggregate expenditures.

Panel (a) of Figure 9 shows how the equilibrium output is determined. The *AE* curve and the 45-degree reference line show the relationship between aggregate output (or income) and *desired* aggregate expenditures at each output level. Aggregate income (or output) can be measured along the horizontal axis or by the corresponding vertical distance to the 45-degree reference line at that level of income (or output). Point *e*, which is the intersection of the aggregate-expenditure curve with the 45-degree line, is the point where desired aggregate expenditures equal aggregate output. To the right of *e,* more output is being produced than the economy wishes to purchase: desired

spending falls short of output at every income level. To the left of *e,* less output is being produced than the economy wishes to purchase. The economy adjusts to such disproportions by changing output until it equals $400 billion (at *e*).

Saving and Investment

Investors and savers are typically different individuals. The most important savers in the economy are individual households who consume less than their disposable income. The typical investor is the business firm that invests in plant, equipment, and inventory expansion. Without a coordinating mechanism, there is no reason why desired saving *(S)* should equal desired investment *(I)* in the economy at any time. The classical economists had supposed that desired saving would be quickly translated into desired investment by changing the rate of interest (Say's Law). To Keynes, on the other hand, the main mechanism that coordinated desired investment and desired saving was change in the level of output.

Returning to our numerical example, the movement toward equilibrium output can be seen in the contrast of intended saving and investment decisions. In our example, the business community desires to invest $50 billion at all levels of income (or output). The amount of desired saving depends upon the amount of income.

If firms in the economy are producing an output of $500 billion. Table 1 shows that desired saving equals $75 billion because consumption equals $425 billion. Desired saving exceeds desired investment by $25 billion at this output. At an output of $500 billion, there is too much saving; $25 billion of output is unsold and accumulates as unintended inventory investment. *(Inventory investment* is the addition to the inventories of goods and materials held by business firms.) When goods are unsold (because aggregate expenditures are insufficient), actual investment exceeds planned investment by the sum of unplanned inventory investment. This unintended accumulation of inventories raises actual investment to $75 billion (the sum of desired and unintended investment) to equal desired saving. **Unintended investment** is shown in column (6) of Table 1.

Unintended investment is the difference between desired saving and desired investment at each level of income.[3]

Whenever there is unintended investment in unwanted inventories (caused by too little aggregate expenditures) or unintended reductions in inventories (caused by too much aggregate expenditure), producers change their rate of production and income changes. As income changes, so does desired saving (which depends upon income).

When unintended investment is taking place, output begins to fall. With prices fixed (as Keynes assumed), businesses have only one way to cut back on the amount of unsold goods piling up in unwanted inventories: they cut back on the rate of production. Since desired saving depends upon the amount of income, as output falls so does saving. As this adjustment continues, the disparity between desired investment and desired saving diminishes until income (or output) is $400 billion.

When desired saving is less than desired investment, there is too little saving. The withdrawal from the spending stream is smaller than the injection back into the spending stream by investment. Businesses will see their inventories being drawn down to low levels, and there will be unintended *disinvestment* in inventories. Again with prices fixed, firms have only one way to build their inventories back up to normal levels: they increase the rate of production. As the amount of income increases, the amount of desired saving increases along with income. As desired saving increases, the gap between desired saving and desired investment disappears. This analysis suggests a second definition of **Keynesian equilibrium:**

> **Keynesian equilibrium** is attained at that output at which desired investment equals desired saving.

In panel (b) of Figure 9, the movement to equilibrium output is shown in terms of the relationship between desired saving and desired investment. Point e' is the intersection of the horizontal investment curve with the saving/income curve (at an output of $400 billion). At levels of

3. The terms *ex ante* (before) and *ex post* (after) are sometimes used to describe desired *(ex ante)* and actual *(ex post)*.

income to the right of e', the withdrawal of saving from the spending stream exceeds the injection of investment back into the spending stream. Aggregate production exceeds desired aggregate expenditures; unsold goods accumulate in unintended inventories, and this unwanted inventory accumulation signals to producers that they are producing too much. At levels of income to the left of e', the injection of investment exceeds the withdrawal of saving. Desired aggregate expenditures exceed aggregate production; unwanted inventory disinvestment takes place, and firms are signaled to increase output. The level of income (or output) adjusts until desired investment equals desired saving. (See Example 2.)

Two Definitions of Equilibrium Are One

In the simple Keynesian model, the economy will adjust its rate of output until:

1. aggregate output equals desired aggregate expenditures $(Y = AE)$.
2. desired investment equals desired saving $(I = S)$.

As this chapter demonstrated, these two conditions are really different ways of looking at the same thing. When desired investment equals desired saving, output equals desired aggregate expenditures. Saving is the withdrawal households make from the spending stream, and investment is the injection firms put back. Whenever desired saving exceeds desired investment, more is withdrawn from spending than is put back in (desired aggregate expenditure is less than output). When desired saving is less than desired investment, less is withdrawn by savers than is put back in by business investment, or desired aggregate expenditure exceeds output. Because saving must equal investment, an increase in the desire to save may not increase actual saving. (See Example 3.)

Equilibrium with Government Spending and Taxes

To keep matters simple, the preceding model left government spending, G, and taxes, T, out of the picture by setting them equal to zero in our hypothetical economy. This section will bring gov-

Figure 10   Keynesian Equilibrium with Government Spending and Taxes

(a) Consumption/Income Curve

(b) Aggregate Expenditure Curve

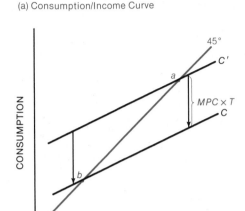
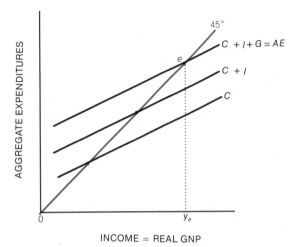

In panel (a) the introduction of taxes lowers disposable income by the amount of the tax. At each income level, consumption is lowered by *MPC* times the level of taxes. The introduction of taxes causes the consumption/income curve to shift down from *C'* to *C*. Panel (b) shows how desired aggregate expenditures *(AE)* are obtained at each income level. Government expenditures *(G)* and investment *(I)* are added to the *C* curve, shifting it up by those amounts. Panel (b) shows that the equilibrium level of output *(y$_e$)* is determined where the *AE* curve (which includes taxes, government spending, and investment) intersects the 45-degree reference line at point *e*.

ernment spending and direct (income) taxes back into the picture.

The introduction of government spending and taxes affects desired aggregate expenditures, *AE*, in two ways, as shown in Figure 10. First, the collection of direct taxes decreases aggregate expenditures at each level of income because the higher are the taxes, the lower is disposable income. Disposable income *(DY)* is the difference between income and tax payments: $DY = Y - T$. Because consumption is a function of disposable income, taxes have an indirect effect on aggregate expenditures: as taxes increase, disposable income falls by the amount of the tax increase; as disposable income falls, consumption falls. The amount of this decrease in consumption depends on the marginal propensity to consume *(MPC)*. When disposable income falls, consumption will fall by *MPC* times the decline in disposable income. Thus, the consumption/income curve in panel (a) will shift down by $MPC \times T$ from *C'* to *C*.

Second, government expenditures are a component of aggregate expenditures, along with consumption and investment spending. With positive government spending, the desired aggregate-expenditure schedule is the sum of the three types of spending desired at each income level: $AE = C + I + G$. To obtain the *AE* curve, investment and government spending are added to the consumption/income curve (that has been adjusted for taxes) at each income level. This section will simplify the discussion considerably by letting both investment and government spending be fixed sums that do not vary with income. The *AE* curve with government spending added is shown in panel (b) of Figure 10.

As panel (b) shows, the Keynesian equilibrium with government spending and taxes is similar to that with no government. Equilibrium income occurs where desired aggregate expenditures (which now include government spending) equal aggregate production (at the intersection of *AE* with the 45-degree reference line).

Example 2   Saving and Interest

A central proposition of the clasical model is that the amount of saving in the economy depends upon the interest rate. People would be prepared to save greater amounts from their disposable income at high interest rates than at low interest rates, *ceteris paribus*. Keynes argued that savings depended primarily on income and that saving would respond weakly, if at all, to the interest rate. The role of the interest rate in equating desired saving with desired investment was a key assumption of Say's law. Keynes felt that the equation of desired saving and desired investment would have to be accomplished by other means. The actual relationship between saving and the interest rate remains a topic of dispute among economists to the present day. In an influential study published in 1978, economist Michael Boskin calculated that a 10 percent increase in the interest rate (the real interest rate after taxes and inflation) tends to cause an increase in U.S. private saving from 2 percent to 6 percent. In other words, Boskin found a strong positive relationship between interest rates and saving. A later study published in 1983 by economists Irwin Freund and Joel Hasbrouck, however, found that private saving in the

United States is not affected by changes in the real interest rate. A 1984 study by economists Vito Tanzi and Eytan Sheshinski finds that the U.S. saving rate actually fell (after 1981) despite a considerable rise in real after-tax interest rates. Why have economists been unable to determine the real relationship between saving and interest rates? First, the relationship may be different during different periods of time. Second, it is difficult to measure the real after-tax interest rate that savers believed would prevail when they made their saving decisions. Third, higher interest rates mean more income for wealth-holding individuals. Individuals may react to higher interest rates by saving less. Were it not for this effect, higher interest rates would lead to more saving. Presumably, future research will shed a more definitive light on the relationship between interest rates and saving. ■

Sources: Michael J. Boskin, "Taxation, Saving, and the Rate of Interest", *Journal of Political Economy* 86, 2 (April 1978). Irwin Freund and Joel Hasbrouck, "Saving and After-Tax Rates of Return," *Review of Economics and Statistics,* November 1983; *IMF Survey,* November 26, 1984.

With government spending and taxes in the picture, the equality of saving and investment is still an equilibrium condition, but now saving includes both private saving *(S)* and government saving *(T − G)*. Chapter 6 showed that government saving is the difference between government income—taxes—and government spending. Thus, equilibrium occurs when $I = S + (T − G)$.

With government spending included, desired aggregate expenditures *(C + I + G)* equal aggregate production *(Y)*. With taxes included, aggregate income *(Y)* is used either for consumption, taxes, or saving and, therefore, equals $C + S + T$. Because aggregate production *(Y)* and aggregate income *(Y)* are the same,

$$C + I + G = C + S + T,$$

or, to simplify,

$$I + G = S + T.$$

Therefore,

$$I = S + (T − G).$$

AGGREGATE DEMAND

When prices are constant, of course, it is more convenient to work with aggregate-expenditure curves than with aggregate-demand and aggregate-supply curves. But when prices change, it is far more convenient to work with the aggregate-demand curve. In Figures 9 and 10, it is assumed that the level of prices is fixed. In the aggregate supply/aggregate demand approach, different price levels are associated with different levels of output.

Chapter 10 will give two reasons why the aggregate-demand curve is downward-sloping; this chapter provides one of these reasons. Earlier it

Figure 11   Derivation of Aggregate Demand

(a) Aggregate Expenditures Versus Income

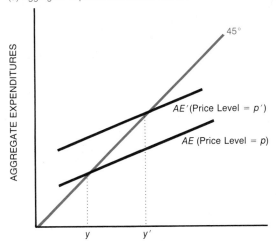

(b) Aggregate Demand

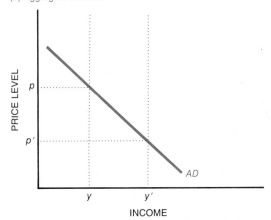

INCOME

Panel (a) shows that if the price level falls from p to p' the aggregate-expenditure curve shifts up because the purchasing power of the money supply increases. The lower price level is associated with a higher equilibrium income or output. Panel (b) shows the relationship between the price level and the equilibrium income—or the aggregate-demand curve.

was explained that an increase in the value of real financial assets will stimulate consumption. The link between the income/expenditure approach and the aggregate-demand approach is shown in Figure 11. As the price level falls, holding the money supply constant, real money balances increase. Thus, the consumption/income curve will

shift up at each level of income. In panel (a) of Figure 11, when the price level falls from p to p', the aggregate-expenditure curve shifts upward from AE to AE'. The equilibrium level of output, thus, increases from y to y' as the price level falls from p to p'. The aggregate-demand curve, AD, in panel (b) of Figure 11 links each price level with the corresponding equilibrium level of output. Thus, p is associated with y, and the lower price level p' is associated with the higher level of output y'.

This chapter showed how the equilibrium level of output is determined when the price level is fixed, as explained by the income/expenditure model, or the simple Keynesian model. The next chapter will study the workings of the simple Keynesian model. It will consider the impact of changing investment, government spending, and taxation on equilibrium output under differing aggregate-supply conditions.

Summary

1.   Keynes studied economies operating with unemployed resources. Increases in aggregate expenditures could cause increases in real output and employment. Because of the emphasis on aggregate demand, Keynesian economics has been called *demand-side economics*. Keynes rejected the classical full-employment model. He rejected Say's Law that supply creates its own demand and believed that money wages were not sufficiently flexible to eliminate involuntary unemployment. According to Keynes, desired saving and desired investment would be equated not through the interest rate but through changes in income. The Great Depression of the 1930s created the appropriate climate for the Keynesian notion that the government should ensure full employment.
2.   Keynes assumed money wages were sticky in the downward direction. When there is substantial unemployment, additional workers are available at the going set of wage rates. Thus, the aggregate-supply curve is L-shaped in the Keynesian model.

Example 3   The Paradox of Thrift

Saving is a virtue—or is it? The simple Keynesian model implies saving may not be such a good thing.

What will happen to output if thrift increases? An increase in *thrift* is a decrease in the amount of desired consumption at each level of income and an increase in the amount of desired saving at each level of income. An increase in thrift shifts the *AE* curve down and shifts the saving/income curve up.

The accompanying figure shows the effect of an increase in thrift on equilibrium income. As the saving/income curve shifts up, desired saving at the equilibrium income level, y_1, exceeds desired investment. Withdrawals from the spending stream exceed injections back in through investment. The economy's aggregate production exceeds desired aggregate expenditures, and unintended inventory investment takes place. This unintended inventory investment signals to firms that they are producing too much. The level of output, therefore, adjusts downward until a new equilibrium income is established (at e') where desired saving equals desired investment.

Notice that at the new equilibrium, actual saving is still the same as before, even though people have tried to save more.

The increase in thrift has caused a reduction in aggregate income; as aggregate income falls, so does desired aggregate saving. Since desired investment is assumed fixed, the economy ends up with the same saving.

Although individuals can save more if they increase their thrift, economies as a whole cannot increase their saving if there is a general increase in thrift. This paradox is a classic example of the fallacy of composition: what is true for each one considered separately need not be true for all to-

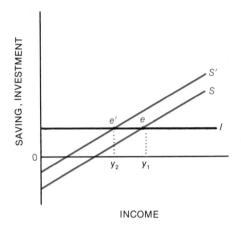

gether. A general increase in thrift means that less is being spent on consumption at each level of income. More saving is being withdrawn from the economy for each level of income. But investment decisions govern what is being injected back into the economy. Greater thriftiness means that more is being withdrawn than is being injected, and the economy must respond by a reduction in aggregate production and income. When aggregate income falls sufficiently to equate the withdrawals of saving with the injections of investment, the savers in the economy can end up with as much or less saving as before, but with lower incomes (y_2 is less than y_1 in the accompanying figure).   ∎

---

3. The Keynesian income/expenditure model explains how economies determine their real output. The consumption/income schedule shows the amount of desired consumption at each income level. The saving/income schedule shows the amount of desired saving at each income level. The marginal propensity to consume *(MPC)* is the fraction of an extra dollar of income that is consumed. The *MPS* is the fraction of an extra dollar of income that is saved. In a world without taxes, *MPC* + *MPS* = 1. Factors that cause the consumption/income (and saving/income) curves to shift are expectations, the real value of assets, taxation,

income distribution, age, and attitudes toward thrift.

4. The aggregate-expenditure *(AE)* curve shows the amount of desired aggregate expenditures, *C + I + G*, at each income level. The economy will produce that income at which a) aggregate production equals desired aggregate expenditures and b) desired investment equals desired saving. These two equilibrium conditions are two ways of looking at the same thing. When government spending is introduced into the income-expenditure model, the same two equilibrium conditions still determine output: aggregate production equals desired aggregate expenditures, and desired investment equals desired saving. Saving, however, now includes both public $(T - G)$ and private (S) saving.

5. The aggregate-demand curve shows the equilibrium levels of income as the price level changes, holding the nominal money supply (and other factors) constant. Because a lower price level shifts up the aggregate-expenditure curve and increases the equilibrium level of income, the aggregate-demand curve is downward-sloping.

Key Terms

Say's Law
consumption/income schedule
saving/income schedule
marginal propensity to consume *(MPC)*
marginal propensity to save *(MPS)*
dissaving
aggregate expenditures *(AE)*
Keynesian equilibrium
unintended investment

Questions and Problems

1. "Savers and investors are different people. There is no way desired saving will equal desired investment." Describe how quantity theorists and Keynesian economists might respond to this statement.

2. Explain why the classical economists felt that there would be no long-term involuntary unemployment.

3. Why is the Keynesian aggregate-supply curve horizontal when there is substantial unemployment?

4. How does the Keynesian aggregate-supply curve differ from the aggregate-supply curve of the classical quantity theorists?

5. How could the classical economists believe that aggregate supply created its own demand?

6. To the classical economists, what mechanism coordinated business investment with consumer saving?

7. What is the marginal propensity to consume? How is it related to the marginal propensity to save?

8. Using the consumption/income schedule in Table A,
   a. calculate the saving/income schedule.
   b. determine the *MPC* and the *MPS*.
   c. determine at what level of income the break-even point of zero saving is reached.
   d. determine the aggregate-expenditure *(AE)* schedule if investment is a constant $50.
   e. find equilibrium output and demonstrate that at this equilibrium, desired investment and desired saving are equal.
   f. determine what happens to equilibrium output if investment falls to zero. What happens to the savings/investment equality?
   g. answer **d** if an increase in thrift occurs and people now desire to consume $50 less at each income (save $50 more at each income); determine equilibrium income and compare income and saving both before and after the increase in thrift.

Table A

Income, (billions of dollars), Y	Consumption, (billions of dollars), C
0	50
100	100
200	150
300	200
400	250

9. Explain what is meant by unintended investment. How will businesses respond to unintended investment in the simple Keynesian model? If prices were flexible, would the response of businesses to unintended inventory investment perhaps be different?

10. In Keynesian economics, what mechanism coordinates business investment with consumer saving?

11. What would happen to the aggregate-expenditure curve in each of the following cases?
   a. Investment demand increases.
   b. The money supply increases.
   c. The price level increases.
   d. Consumers anticipate a sharp increase in prices in the next year.

12. Optional question: Suppose the consumption schedule is $C = \$100$ billion $+ .75y$.

    a. Draw the consumption/income schedule for income levels of $200 billion, $400 billion, $600 billion, and $800 billion. What is the *MPC?*

    b. What is the equation for saving?

    c. If $I = \$50$ billion, what is the equilibrium level of $Y?$

13. If there were no government spending, even though the government collected taxes, what would the saving/investment equality look like?

14. Assume that in economy Z, $I = \$25$ billion, and the relationship between consumption and income *without taxes* is given in Table B.

Table B

Income (billions of dollars), Y	Consumption (billions of dollars), C
0	75
100	150
200	225
300	300
400	375
500	450
600	525

    a. What is the *MPC?* the *MPS?*

    b. What is the equilibrium $Y?$

    c. Now assume $T = \$100$ billion and $G = \$125$ billion. What is the new consumption/income schedule?

    d. When $T = \$100$ billion, $G = \$125$ billion, and $I = \$25$ billion, what is the equilibrium $Y?$

Suggested Readings

Gordon, Robert J. *Macroeconomics,* 3rd ed. Boston, Mass.: Little, Brown, 1984, chap. 3.

Keynes, John Maynard. *The General Theory of Employment, Interest, and Money.* New York: Macmillan, 1936, preface, chaps. 1–3.

Samuelson, Paul A. *Economics,* 11th ed. New York: McGraw-Hill, 1980, chaps. 11–12.

10

Output Fluctuations: Aggregate Demand

Chapter Preview

Chapter 9 showed that the equilibrium level of national income is achieved when desired aggregate expenditures equal national income or, equivalently, when desired investment equals desired saving.

This chapter first explains the simple multiplier effect of a change in autonomous spending on equilibrium national income when both the price level and interest rates are assumed constant. The theory of investment will then be developed to show why investment is an unstable component of GNP. The simple multiplier must be modified when the interest rate is allowed to change (but when the price level is still assumed to be constant). Finally, the theory of aggregate demand itself is developed to show how real-world multipliers must be modified when both the interest rate and the price level are allowed to change. An appendix provides a discussion of the demand

side of the complete Keynesian model (called the *IS/LM* model), where both interest rates and national income are mutually determined.

The previous chapter showed that the income/expenditure equilibrium is achieved at that output level at which desired aggregate expenditures $(C + I + G)$ equal actual output. This chapter considers what happens to the income/expenditure equilibrium when desired aggregate expenditures change. In the first part of this chapter, we examine the effects of changes in government and investment spending on output in a world in which such changes do not change interest rates or the price level—which is only possible if the economy has considerable unemployed resources and, thus, can expand output without raising prices and if the Fed holds interest rates constant. ■

Figure 1   A Shift in Aggregate Expenditures Changes Equilibrium Output

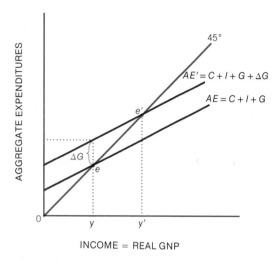

An increase in government spending *(ΔG)* causes the aggregate-expenditure curve to shift from *AE* to *AE'*. At the old equilibrium income, *y,* desired aggregate expenditure exceeds output, and producers are signaled to increase production. The new equilibrium income is reached at *y',* where output and desired aggregate expenditures are again equal.

FACTORS THAT CHANGE EQUILIBRIUM INCOME

As long as desired aggregate expenditures do not change, the equilibrium level of output will remain the same. Figure 1 shows that any change that shifts the aggregate-expenditure curve *(AE)* will cause equilibrium income to change. If the *AE* curve shifts upward, desired aggregate expenditures $(C + I + G)$ will exceed the initial equilibrium output, *y*. In Figure 1, an increase in government spending shifts the *AE* curve to *AE'*. The economy is now purchasing output at a rate faster than output is being produced; inventories are drawn down to subnormal levels; firms respond by increasing their production. Upward shifts in *AE*, therefore, shift equilibrium from *e* to *e'* and cause output to increase from *y* to *y'* (if there are unemployed resources).

Had *AE* shifted down instead of up, desired aggregate expenditures would have been below the original equilibrium output, *y;* unwanted inventories would have built up; the economy's pro-

Figure 2   The Impact of a $50 Billion Autonomous Increase in Investment on Equilibrium Output

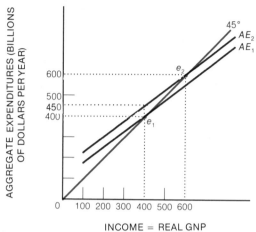

The $50 billion increase in investment causes the aggregate-expenditure curve to shift up vertically by $50 billion from AE_1 to AE_2. At the original equilibrium, output is $400 billion; desired aggregate expenditures now exceed aggregate production, and desired saving exceeds desired investment. The previous chapter demonstrated that the economy's producers will, therefore, increase their output. Equilibrium is restored at an output of $600 billion. The $50 billion increase in investment has caused a $200 billion increase in output.

ducers would be forced to move to a lower output.

A change in investment or government spending will directly change desired aggregate expenditures. If one or both of these factors increase, there will be more desired aggregate expenditures at each level of income. Graphically, a change in investment or government spending will cause a vertical shift in the *AE* curve by the amount of the change in *I* or *G*. Expenditures that shift the level of desired aggregate expenditures are called **autonomous expenditures** if they are independent of the level of national income.

Autonomous expenditures are determined independently of income changes.

Increases or decreases in government spending result when federal, state, and local governments change their level of expenditures for goods and

Table 1   Keynesian Equilibrium with Government Spending but No Taxes (billions of dollars)

Output = Income, Y	Consumption Spending, C	Investment Spending, I	Government Spending, G	Aggregate Expenditures, AE = C + I + G
(A) With I at $20 billion; equilibrium Y = $400 billion				
100	125	20	30	175
200	200	20	30	250
300	275	20	30	325
400	**350**	**20**	**30**	**400**
500	425	20	30	475
600	500	20	30	550
(B) With I at $70 billion; equilibrium Y = $600 billion				
100	125	70	30	225
200	200	70	30	300
300	275	70	30	375
400	350	70	30	450
500	425	70	30	525
600	**500**	**70**	**30**	**600**

services. Changes in investment occur when the business community decides to either increase or decrease its investment spending.

Autonomous changes in consumption are caused by changes in attitudes toward thrift, expectations, age structure, or the distribution of income. Changes in consumption that result from changes in income are *induced* rather than autonomous.

Shifts in the aggregate-expenditure curve can also result from changes in taxes. Consumers base their consumption decisions on disposable income, not on total income. As taxes are raised, disposable income *(DY)* is reduced by the amount of tax increase. As disposable income declines, so does consumption spending at each level of national income.

SIMPLE MULTIPLIERS

Autonomous-Expenditure Multipliers

Table 1 explores the effects of a permanent change in autonomous investment on equilibrium output. (Remember, we are first considering cases where the change in autonomous spending does not affect interest rates or the price level.) In part (A), the first two columns show the consumption/income schedule of Table 1 of the previous

chapter. The marginal propensity to consume *(MPC)* is 0.75 (every $1 increase in income results in a $0.75 increase in consumption), investment is constant at $20 billion, and government spending is constant at $30 billion. There are no taxes; they will be added to the picture shortly. As part (a) shows, equilibrium output is $400 billion, because desired aggregate expenditures equal total output at $400 billion. The original aggregate-expenditure curve is labeled AE_1 in Figure 2.

Part (B) of Table 1 shows what happens when there is a permanent autonomous increase in investment spending of $50 billion (from $20 billion to $70 billion). A $50 billion increase in government spending or in a combination of investment and government spending would have the same effect on desired aggregate expenditures, shifting AE_1 to AE_2 in Figure 2, as the $50 billion increase in investment spending. Because autonomous investment is a final demand for goods and services, the AE curve shifts up by the vertical distance of the change in investment.

The position of the AE_2 curve shows that the economy's desired aggregate expenditures are now greater at each income level than at AE_1. Point e_1 represents the original equilibrium for curve AE_1. When increased investment shifts AE_1 to AE_2, the old equilibrium output of $400 billion is less than the desired expenditure level of $450 billion for that level of income. Now the economy wishes to purchase $450 billion worth of goods and services, but the economy is only producing $400 billion worth. Inventories throughout the economy are being drawn down below desired levels, signaling to producers that they should increase their rate of output. The economy raises output until it arrives at its new equilibrium at e_2, where it produces $600 billion worth of output. The output of $600 billion is the new equilibrium output because at that output, desired aggregate expenditures are also $600 billion.

Notice that the $50 billion increase in investment spending causes a $200 billion increase in output (from $400 billion to $600 billion). The increase in output is 4 times the increase in investment. The tendency for an increase in investment or government spending to cause magnified increases in output is called the *expenditure multiplier effect*. An **expenditure multiplier** can be either an **investment multiplier** or a **government-expenditure multiplier.**

The **expenditure multiplier** is the ratio of the change in output to the change in autonomous expenditures. The two expenditure multipliers are the *investment multiplier* ($\Delta Y/\Delta I$) and the *government-expenditure multiplier* ($\Delta Y/\Delta G$).

The **investment multiplier** ($\Delta Y/\Delta I$) is the ratio of the change in output to the change in investment.

The **government-expenditure multiplier** ($\Delta Y/\Delta G$) is the ratio of the change in output to the change in government spending.

Why should an autonomous change in investment cause a much larger change in output? When investment expenditures are increased by $100 billion, the immediate effect is for incomes in the economy to increase by $100 billion. These expenditures, after all, end up in the pockets and purses of the suppliers of the factors of production that produced the $100 billion worth of investment goods. If this immediate effect were the only effect, then the increase in investment would cause an equivalent increase in output. But the process does not stop here. *Those households whose incomes have gone up by a total of $100 billion will increase their consumption spending.*

Table 2   The Multiplier Principle Illustrated (billions of dollars)

Round	Amount of Increase in Income (Δy)	Amount of Increase in Consumption (ΔC)	Leakages (increase in saving) (Δs)
1	**100.00**	75.00	25.00
2	75.00	56.25	18.75
3	56.25	42.19	14.06
4	42.19	31.64	10.55
5	31.64	23.73	7.91
6	23.73	17.80	5.93
All other	71.19	53.39	17.80
Totals	400.00	300.00	**100.00**

A $100 billion increase in investment sets the multiplier process off (marginal propensity to consume = 0.75). The $100 billion increase in investment creates $100 billion in additional income, 75 percent of which is spent in round 1. In round 2, the $75 billion extra consumption enters as a $75 billion increase in income, and 75 percent of this increase is spent on additional consumption ($56.25 billion). This $56.25 billion enters as additional income in round 3, and 75 percent of this income is spent on additional consumption. This process continues through a large number of rounds until income has increased by $400 billion and consumption has increased by $300 billion. The process continues until the sum of leakages into saving equals the initial increase in investment. The investment multiplier equals 4 because a $100 billion increase in investment has caused a $400 billion increase in income.

When income increases, consumption increases according to the economy's marginal propensity to consume, or by *MPC* times the increase in income. Aggregate incomes again increase by the amount of the injection of more consumption, and the recipients of this extra income again increase their consumption by *MPC* times the amount of the income increase. This process continues until the successive increases in spending dwindle to zero.

Table 2 shows how an increase in investment leads to a magnified increase in output. A $100 billion increase in investment immediately creates $100 billion worth of additional income. With a marginal propensity to consume of 0.75, this increase in income causes an increase in consumption of $75 billion. In round 2, this $75 billion increase in consumption creates another $75 billion in income. Of this $75 billion, 75 percent ($56.25 billion) is spent on additional consump-

Example 1   The Algebra of the Expenditure Multiplier

The relationship between the marginal propensity to consume and the expenditure multiplier can be demonstrated with some simple algebra.

The investment-expenditure multiplier is the ratio of the increase in income (Y) to the increase in investment (I). The increase in Y equals the increase in I plus the change in C, or

$$\Delta Y = \Delta C + \Delta I. \qquad (1)$$

But ΔC will equal MPC times ΔY:

$$\Delta C = MPC \times \Delta Y. \qquad (2)$$

Substituting equation **(2)** into equation **(1)** yields:

$$\Delta Y = MPC \times \Delta Y + \Delta I, \qquad (3)$$

or

$$\Delta Y (1 - MPC) = \Delta I. \qquad (4)$$

Dividing both sides by $(1 - MPC)$ yields:

$$\Delta Y = \frac{\Delta I}{1 - MPC} \qquad (5)$$

Equation **(5)** is the expenditure-multiplier formula when both sides are divided by ΔI:

$$\frac{\Delta Y}{\Delta I} = \frac{1}{(1 - MPC)} = \frac{1}{MPS}. \qquad (6)$$

A simpler derivation is to note that $\Delta S = \Delta I$. Since $\Delta S = MPS \times \Delta Y$, it follows that $\Delta I = MPS \times \Delta Y$ or $\Delta Y/\Delta I = 1/MPS$. ∎

tion, creating $56.25 billion of additional income. In round 3, this $56.25 billion worth of new income stimulates a consumption increase of another $42.19 billion, and so the multiplier process continues until the full effect of the multiplier is felt. In our example, the investment multiplier is 4 because the $100 billion increase in investment eventually causes a $400 billion increase in income.

At each stage, income is leaking out of the circular flow of expenditure in the form of saving. As Table 2 shows, of the initial $100 billion increase in income, when $75 billion is consumed, $25 billion is saved. At the next stage, when $56.25 billion is consumed $18.75 billion of the newly generated $75 billion in income is saved, and so on. These leakages in the form of saving limit the ultimate increase in income in response to an increase in investment (or government spending). The increase in income stops when the total leakages equal the initial $100 billion increase. The same result would have been obtained if the original increase in spending had been in government spending rather than in investment. The government-spending multiplier would also have equaled 4. The investment and government-expenditure multipliers have the same numerical value because government spending is assumed

not to be a substitute for private spending. (This chapter will discuss this assumption later in more detail.)

One can see in our numerical example that the MPC has a great deal to do with the value of the multiplier. If the MPC had been 0.9 rather than 0.75, the initial increase in consumption would have been larger in the first and in subsequent rounds. The smaller the leakages (or the larger MPC) the greater is the amount of additional income created at each stage, and the larger is the multiplier. The larger the leakages (or the smaller MPC) the smaller is the amount of income generated at each stage, and the smaller is the multiplier.

The formula for determining the investment-expenditure multiplier $(\Delta Y/\Delta I)$ is:

$$\Delta Y/\Delta I = \frac{1}{1 - MPC} = \frac{1}{MPS},$$

where there are no taxes ($MPC + MPS = 1$ in the absence of taxes). If investment increases by $1, in the new equilibrium, saving must also increase by $1 since $S = I$. If MPC equals 0.75, however, $MPS = 0.25$, and $4 of extra income is necessary to increase saving by the necessary $1. Thus, income must increase by $4 to generate the extra saving to match the $1 increase in investment. (See Example 1.)

The higher is the *MPC*, the higher is the multiplier. An *MPC* of 0.75 yields a multiplier of 4; an *MPC* of 0.9 yields a multiplier of 10. The economy's response to autonomous expenditures, therefore, depends on the *MPC* (or *MPS*). The higher is the *MPC*, the higher is the induced expenditures from any given rise in income. In other words, the higher is the *MPC*, and the lower is the *MPS*, the more income must change in order to get the saving leakages to match the injection of new investment.

> **The higher is the *MPC*, the higher is the expenditure multiplier. The lower is the *MPC*, the lower is the expenditure multiplier.**

The Tax Multiplier

The effect of changes in taxes can be different from the effect of changes in investment or government spending. Because taxes affect aggregate expenditures only indirectly through their effect on consumption expenditures, taxes do not lower consumption expenditures dollar for dollar. Therefore, the tax multiplier will be smaller than the expenditure multiplier.

Figure 2 retained the assumption of zero taxes in demonstrating the effect of a $50 billion increase in investment. Figure 3 illustrates the effect of a permanent $40 billion increase in taxes (from $0 to $40 billion).

The $40 billion increase in taxes (with an *MPC* of 0.75) will cause consumption to drop by $30 billion at each income level. At each level of income, the tax increase causes disposable income to fall by $40 billion. Consumption will, therefore, fall by 0.75 (the *MPC*) times the $40 fall in disposable income ($40 billion), or by $30 billion. A $30 billion decrease in consumption is less than the increase in taxes. In panel (a) of Figure 3, the increase in taxes lowers the consumption/income curve from C_1 to C_2. When consumption decreases from C_1 to C_2, aggregate expenditures also decrease from AE_1 to AE_2 in panel (b). The amount of the downward shift from C_1 to C_2 in panel (a) is the same as the

Figure 3   The Effect of Increasing Taxes on Equilibrium Output

(a) The Consumption/Income Curve

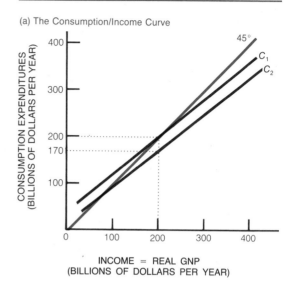

(b) The Aggregate-Expenditure Curve

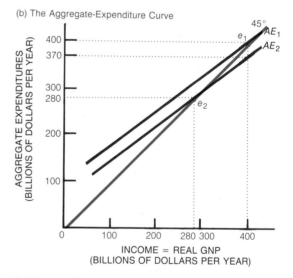

In this example, taxes rise from $0 to $40 billion. In panel (a), the original consumption/income curve, C_1, shifts down to C_2, but the vertical downward shift in the consumption/income curve is less than the $40 billion increase in taxes. The tax increase causes disposable income to fall by the amount of the tax increase, but with an *MPC* of 0.75, *C* falls by only $30 billion. In panel (b), aggregate expenditures shift downward (from AE_1 to AE_2) by $30 billion, not by the amount of the full tax increase. Equilibrium output will be restored at $280 billion. Output has fallen by $120 billion as a consequence of the $40 billion increase in taxes; the equilibrium point has shifted from e_1 to e_2.

amount of the downward shift from AE_1 to AE_2 in panel (b)—$30 billion.

Point e_1 represents the original equilibrium where output equals desired expenditures at $400 billion. When aggregate expenditures decline by $30 billion to $370 billion, while output is still $400 billion, the economy is buying at a rate slower than the economy is producing; excessive inventories build up; firms cut back on production. The new equilibrium is established at point e_2, where output equals desired expenditures at $280 billion.

The impact of a change in taxes will be different from that of changes in investment or government spending. If investment or government spending were to decline by $40 billion (with an MPC of 0.75), output would decline by 4 times this amount, or by $160 billion. A $40 billion increase in taxes, however, causes output to drop by only $120 billion. The **tax multiplier** is smaller than the government expenditure or investment multiplier for the same size change.

> The **tax multiplier** ($\Delta Y/\Delta T$) is the change in output divided by the change in the tax.

In the above example, the tax multiplier equals -3. The $40 billion increase in taxes caused output to drop by $120 billion. The tax multiplier is a negative number because *increases* in taxes cause *reductions* in output. The investment and government-spending multipliers are positive because *increases* in investment or government spending cause *increases* in output.

The tax multiplier is the expenditure multiplier applied to the shift in the AE curve due to the increase in taxes. A $1 tax shifts the AE curve by $-MPC$. In other words, expenditures *fall* by MPC. Thus, the tax multiplier is:

$$\frac{\Delta Y}{\Delta T} = \frac{-MPC}{1 - MPC}$$

Because the economy's *MPC* is less than unity, tax changes will cause shifts in the consumption/income curve that are less than the change in taxes. Accordingly, changes in taxes will cause shifts in desired aggregate expenditures that are less than the change in taxes.

The Balanced-Budget Multiplier

The absolute value of the tax multiplier subtracted from the expenditure multiplier is 1.

$$\frac{1}{1 - MPC} - \frac{MPC}{1 - MPC} = \frac{1 - MPC}{1 - MPC} = 1$$

If the expenditure multiplier is one greater than the tax multiplier in absolute value, then, surprisingly, *equal changes in government spending and taxes will change income by the amount of the change in government spending.* For example, if the government-spending multiplier is 4, the tax multiplier is -3. If government spending and taxes both rise by $10 billion, the effect of the rise in government spending would be to *raise* output by $40 billion; the rise in taxes would *lower* output by $30 billion. The net effect of the simultaneous equal increases in government spending and taxes is, therefore, to raise output by $10 billion—the amount of the increase in government spending.

The multiplier effect of equal changes in government spending and taxes is called the **balanced-budget multiplier.**

> The **balanced-budget multiplier** is the ratio of changes in income to equal changes in government spending and taxes and always equals 1 because equal increases (or decreases) in government spending and taxes will cause income to increase (or decrease) by the amount of the change in government spending.

All the multipliers discussed thus far are simple multipliers because they are based on two simplifying assumptions: First, they assume that increases in autonomous spending do not affect interest rates; that is, there can be more autonomous spending on government, investment, or consumption without driving up interest rates. Second, the simple multipliers assume that there can be more autonomous spending without driving up prices. (See Example 2.) This chapter will close with a discussion of multipliers in a world of rising interest rates and changing prices. The next section examines the theory of investment spending, the most unstable form of autonomous spending.

Example 2　Using Econometric Models to Estimate Multipliers

Much of this chapter is devoted to discussing multipliers. Real-world multipliers are likely to be smaller than the simple expenditure and tax multipliers because of crowding out and price-level increases. The branch of economics that estimates actual expenditure and tax multipliers is called *econometric modeling*. Econometric modeling of the U.S. economy was pioneered by Nobel laureate Lawrence Klein of the University of Pennsylvania. Currently, econometric modeling of the U.S. and other world economies has become a major activity of academic, business, and government economists. There are a number of competing econometric models of the U.S. economy from which to choose. Perhaps the best known are the Wharton Econometric Model, the Data Resources Inc. (DRI) model, and the econometric models of major private banks and regional Federal Reserve banks that are used by many corporations, investment firms, and government agencies.

These econometric models are estimated from historical U.S. data on consumption, investment, and government spending. Unlike the simple hypothetical multiplier models discussed in this chapter, econometric models often consist of hundreds of equations that are designed to describe the behavior of the U.S. economy.

The various econometric models do not agree among themselves on the values of real-world expenditure and tax multipliers. The accompanying table records the estimates of various econometric models of the government—expenditure and tax multipliers after a government spending increase (or tax decrease) has had two years to work its way through the economy. As the table shows, estimates of the government-expenditure multiplier range from 0 (no effect on real output) to 2.7 (a $1 billion dollar increase in G causes a $2.7 billion increase in real output). The various models illustrate the theory that the tax multiplier is less (in

absolute value) than the expenditure multiplier. The tax multipliers range from a low of 1.1 to a high of 2.1.

Despite their shortcomings, econometric models perform a valuable function: they allow participants in the economy to look into the future, albeit imperfectly, and attach probabilities to different economic outcomes. The fact that American business spends large sums on econometric forecasting suggests that econometrics is performing a positive function. The main reason for forecasting errors is that econometrics must predict the future on the basis of what has happened in the past. Although past behavior is often a good guide, it is far from foolproof.　■

Econometric Model	Government-Expenditure Multiplier, $\Delta Y/\Delta G$	Tax Multiplier, $\Delta Y/-\Delta T$
Bureau of Economic Analysis	2.2	1.4
Brookings	2.7	1.6
University of Michigan	1.4	1.1
Data Resources, Inc.	0.9	1.1
Federal Reserve Bank St. Louis	zero	n.a.
MPS Model, University of Pennsylvania	2.2	2.1
Wharton Model	2.4	1.7
H-C Stanford University	1.4	n.a.

Sources: Gary Fromm and Lawrence Klein, "A Comparison of Eleven Econometric Models of the United States," *American Economic Review,* May 1973; Robert Gordon, *Macroeconomics,* 3rd ed. (Boston: Little, Brown and Company, 1984), pp. 410–412.

THE THEORY OF INVESTMENT

Multiplier analysis attempts to explain why changes in income occur. Fluctuations in autonomous expenditures, such as investment spending and government spending, exert a magnified effect on income through the multiplier. Real GNP

fluctuates because expectations change, because spending habits change, or because government changes taxes or government spending. The effect of each of these changes may be magnified through the multiplier.

Keynes felt that the fundamental source of output instability was the instability of investment

Figure 4   The Instability of Investment Compared to GNP

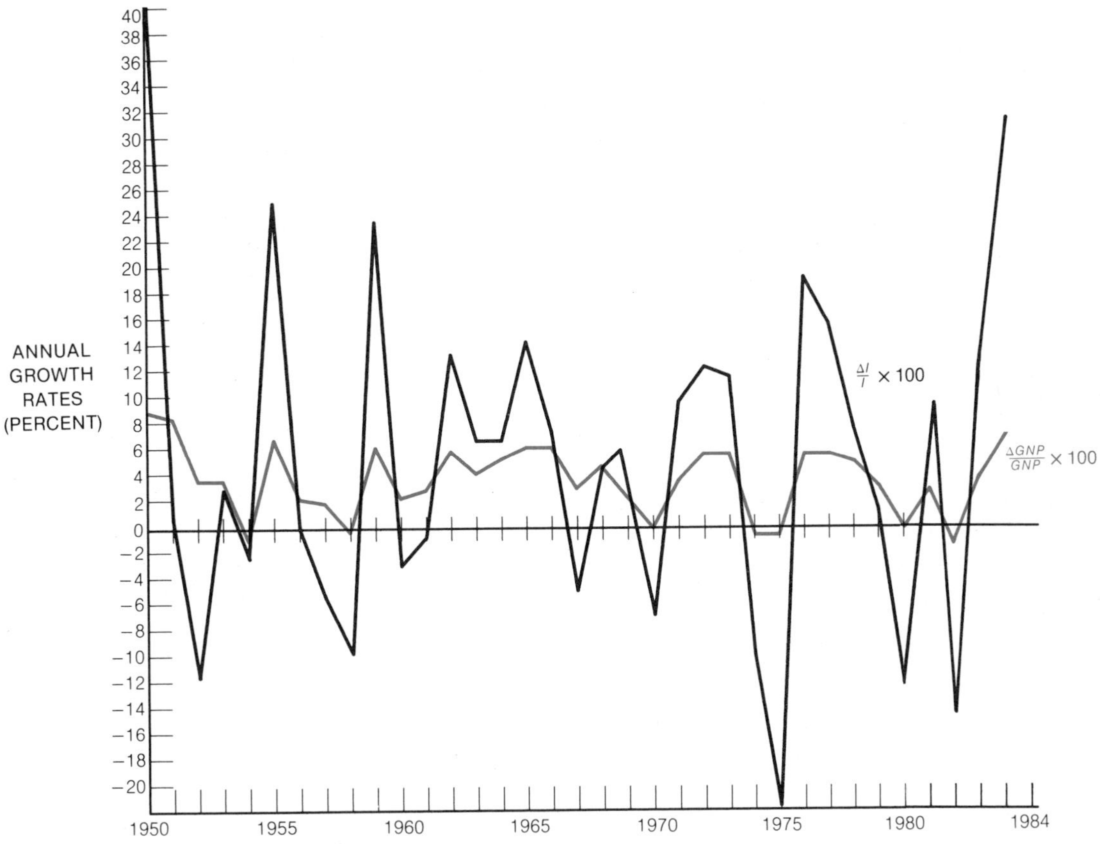

The growth rate of investment fluctuates much more than the growth rate of GNP.

Source: *Economic Report of the President.*

spending. If investment is highly unstable—increasing rapidly in one year and falling sharply in the next—the multiplier would magnify this instability, causing substantial fluctuations in output.

Figure 4 shows that over the years, real investment spending has fluctuated much more erratically than real GNP, as Keynes had observed. Why is investment so unstable? This question can be answered by realizing that investment is determined by profit-seeking businesses and by looking at the determinants of investment. Businesses decide whether or not and how much to invest based on 1) the change in the level of sales a business firm anticipates, 2) the rate of interest the

firm must pay on borrowed capital, and 3) their general expectation about the future. The first and third of these factors help explain why investment is unstable.

The Accelerator Principle

In producing output (whether shoes or cars or whatever), firms seek to use that stock of capital (machines, inventories, plants) that allows the most profitable operation of the firm. A grocery store that sells $1 million per year of goods may need an average inventory of $100,000; a manufacturer of steel plates may need $2 million worth of capital to manufacture $1 million worth of output per year.

Net investment is the addition to the stock of capital, but the stock of capital needs to grow only if the level of output or sales increases. For example, if the steel manufacturer can sell another $2 million of output per year, it may need additional investments in plant and equipment. At the economywide level, final business sales approximate national income. Since the stock of capital needs to grow only if income (and output) grows, net investment requires growth in income or business sales. If business sales are not growing, investment can fall off rapidly.

The relationship between capital and output illustrates this point. For example, if for every $1 of output, the economy requires $1.50 worth of capital, the **capital/output ratio** would be 1.5.

> The **capital/output ratio** (K/Y) is the value of capital (K) needed to produce a given level of output divided by the value of that output (Y).

If the capital/output ratio remains steady (and capital is fully utilized), capital must increase for the economy to produce more output. With a capital/output ratio of 1.5, for example, a $10 billion increase in output would require a $15 billion increase in capital. Because investment is the increase in capital $(I = \Delta K)$ investment must also depend upon the rate of increase in output. With a fixed capital/output ratio of 1.5, the relationship between investment and output is:

$$I = 1.5\Delta Y,$$

or

$$I = \frac{K}{Y} \times \Delta Y$$

This equation illustrates the **accelerator principle** of investment. It shows that investment will increase only if the growth of output increases. If output fails to increase, gross investment will fall to zero. If output declines, there will be net disinvestment as business firms allow their capital stock to depreciate without replacement. Thus, investment in an economy depends not on the level of income but on how fast output—or the level of business sales—is rising or falling. To get invest-

Table 3   The Accelerator Principle Illustrated (billions of dollars)

Year (1)	Output (2)	Growth of Output over Previous Year (3)	Investment (4)
Increasing growth			
0	600	—	—
1	1,000	400	600
2	1,600	600	900
Declining growth			
3	1,900	300	450
4	2,000	100	150
Zero growth			
5	2,000	0	0
Constant growth			
6	2,200	200	300
7	2,400	200	300

The capital/output ratio in this example is 1.5. Investment will, therefore, equal 1.5 times the increase (or decrease) in income. This example shows that investment will grow only if the output growth increases. If the output growth remains constant, there will be no net investment.

ment to rise, output not only has to grow; it has to grow *by increasing increments.*

> The **accelerator principle** of investment is that investment depends upon the growth of output and implies that investment will be unstable. Investment will fall simply because output grows *at a slower rate.* For investment just to remain stable, output growth must be constant.

The investment accelerator can explain why investment spending is so unstable. Table 3 shows the behavior of investment when output is experiencing rising, stable, and declining growth. The real GNP and investment figures of Table 3 are plotted in Figure 5. Investment fluctuates much more than output when investment depends on the *growth* of output. (See Example 3.)

Multiplier/Accelerator Interaction.   The investment accelerator is only part of the picture because, as demonstrated earlier, increases in investment cause a magnified increase in output through the mutliplier effect. The multiplier and accelerator interact. The outcome of this interac-

Figure 5   The Accelerator Principle

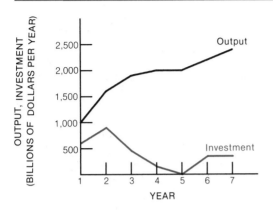

These two curves are plotted from data in Table 3. Output in the first year equals $1,000. Output in each year is, therefore, the previous year's output plus the growth of output. This figure illustrates that the accelerator principle causes investment to fluctuate more than output.

tion can cause sharp upward and downward movements in output *(business cycles).*

Consider what happens when investment starts to grow. The increase in investment will have a magnified impact on output through the multiplier. The growth of output will increase, and investment will accelerate as a result. This *multiplier/accelerator interaction* causes a boom with output and investment growing at ever-faster rates. The increasing rate of growth of output causes increasing growth of investment, which pushes up output growth even more. When the boom ends, however, the growth of output slows down, and investment starts to fall. As investment falls, the multiplier will cause output to decline. The accelerator causes investment to become negative, and output falls even further. The boom is, therefore, followed by a bust with falling output and negative net investment.

Limitations of the Accelerator.   The accelerator and accelerator/multiplier interaction suggest serious cyclical problems. Investment will fluctuate wildly, and interactions with the multiplier will cause boom-and-bust business cycles. In the real world, cyclical fluctuations are nowhere as large as suggested in our hypothetical examples. The accelerator is based upon the notion that

more capital is required to produce more output—which is true when all resources are fully utilized—but an economy operating well below full employment can increase output by other means. As a result, the link between the growth of output and investment is not strong when the economy is operating well below full employment. Moreover, for reasons to be discussed below, real-world multipliers are likely to be smaller than the simple multipliers discussed so far.

The Cost of Capital

The profit-seeking firm will add to its capital stock (invest) using the same rules it uses to buy materials, to rent land, or to hire labor. It compares the marginal costs and benefits of acquiring more or less of the resource in question—in this case, capital.

The accelerator principle attributes increases in investment to its benefits: the greater is the increase in expected sales, the more profitable is new investment. But the firm must also incur costs when it borrows or uses financial capital for financing its investment plans. The firm's cost of acquiring additional capital is, basically, the prevailing cost of borrowing loanable funds: *the interest rate.*

How much investment a typical firm will want to carry out at different interest rates will depend upon the *rates of return* that the firm believes it can earn on the various investment projects that its engineers and managers suggest.

For example, an investment project that promises to add each year an additional $1 million to the profits of the firm for a very long (almost infinite) period costs $10 million. The *rate of return* on this $10 million investment, in this special case, is 10 percent—the annual addition to profit divided by the cost of the project.[1] Investment projects are typically more complicated than this one, but the principle remains: investment decisions are based upon the relationship between the rate of return and cost.

---

1. The rate of return is the rate that equates the present discounted value of the additions to profits to the cost of the project. In this case, a 10 percent rate equates the present value of the perpetual $1 million profit stream to the cost.

Example 3   The Accelerator Principle: GNP Growth and Inventory Investment

According to the accelerator principle, investment can depend upon the growth of output. If output ceases to grow, or even grows at a slower rate, investment will drop. Investment will remain stable, according to the accelerator principle, only if output growth is steady. The chapter shows that overall investment is not as unstable as the accelerator principle predicts. A major reason for this is that, with the capital stock not fully utilized, output can increase without an accompanying increase in capital.

The most unstable form of investment is inventory investment. Inventory investment is positive when the inventories held by businesses at the end of the year exceed those inventories held at the beginning of the year. Inventory investment is negative if end-of-year inventories are smaller than beginning-of-year inventories. Businesses tend to hold inventories as a fixed percentage of sales. If

sales are increasing (GNP is growing), firms must increase their inventories. If sales are falling, businesses can allow their inventories to fall. If sales are flat (GNP is not growing), there is no need for businesses to increase their inventories.

The accompanying figure plots the relationship between business inventory investment (in billions of 1972 dollars) and the annual growth rage of real GNP. The relationship is remarkably close to that predicted by the accelerator principle. When output is growing rapidly, firms build up inventories rapidly. When output contracts, inventory investment drops sharply. When the rate of growth of output falls, inventory investment falls. The accelerator appears to provide a good explanation for the behavior of inventory investment. ■

Source *Economic Report of the President.*

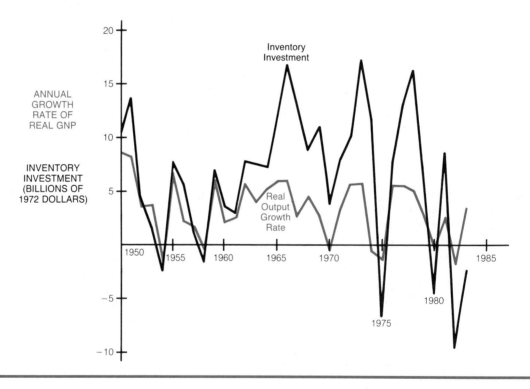

In any year, a firm would choose among a number of potential investment projects. Some would offer higher rates of return; others would offer lower rates of return. In making its investment decisions, the firm would rank its invest-

ment projects by rate of return. As long as a project promised a rate of return higher than the rate at which capital funds had to be borrowed (the interest rate), the firm would want to carry out the project. The profit-maximizing firm would, therefore, carry out all those projects that promised returns greater than the interest rate. The last project financed would have a rate of return just equal to the market interest rate.

> Firms carry out additional investments as long as their rate of return *(R)* exceeds the market rate of interest, *r*. Therefore, the last (marginal) investment project should yield a rate of return equal to the market interest rate *(R = r)*.

The investment-demand curve of an individual firm should be negatively sloped just like other demand curves (see Figure 6). At high rates of interest, there are fewer projects that offer rates of return equal to or greater than the interest rate. The lower is the interest rate, the greater is the number of investments that will be undertaken. In this case, what holds for individual firms also holds for the economy as a whole: at low interest rates, there is a greater quantity demanded of investments than at higher interest rates.

The negative slope of the investment-demand curve illustrates that *the amount of investment increases as the interest rate is lowered*. In Figure 6, an interest rate of 10 percent yields an investment of $100 billion. An interest rate of 8 percent yields an investment of $120 billion.

> The investment-demand curve reveals that desired investment spending increases as the interest rate falls.

Business taxes and investment tax incentives can shift investment demand. When tax laws are changed in such a manner as to lower the after-tax costs of investment projects, more investment will tend to be undertaken at each interest rate. For example, by allowing businesses to depreciate business investments over a period of time much shorter than their useful lives, the investment-demand curves will shift to the right. Such accelerated depreciation schedules make investments more profitable by increasing after-tax profits.

Expectations and Business Psychology

If the investment-demand curve shifts to the right as in panel (b) of Figure 6, the demand for in-

Figure 6   The Investment Demand Curve for an Entire Economy

(a) Derivation of Investment Demand

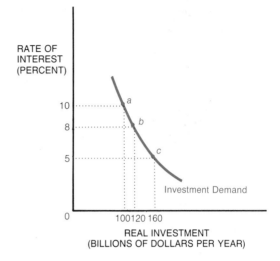

(b) A Shift in Investment Demand

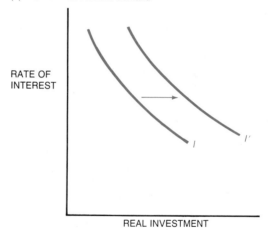

Firms in the economy will be prepared to carry out investment projects as long as the rate of return promised by the project equals or exceeds the interest rate. As panel (a) shows, insofar as there are fewer investment projects that offer rates of return of 10 percent and above than those that offer 5 percent and above, the quantity of investment demanded at an interest rate of 5 percent is greater than the quantity of investment demanded at a 10 percent rate. Panel (b) shows an increase in investment demand from *I* to *I'*.

vestment is rising; if it shifts to the left, investment demand is falling. The accelerator model showed that a slowdown in the growth of output can cause a decrease in investment demand. But the accelerator is the only one potential explanation for instability in the investment-demand curve.

Changing expectations concerning the future on the part of businesses can also alter desired investment. Insofar as rate-of-return calculations depend upon perceptions of prices, costs, and profits in the often-distant future, a shift in expectations towards a more pessimistic outlook can cause desired investment at each interest rate to fall.

Animal Spirits.   Keynes himself thought that business psychology played a key role in determining desired investment. Keynes, however, attributed most fluctuations in business investment to disturbances in the "animal spirits" of business entrepreneurs. Shifts in investment could occur even if, on objective grounds, nothing changed in the business environment. As time passes, the captains of industry accumulate much elusive information about future products, future technology, and the future attitude of government toward business. Much of this information is qualitative and subjective. Investment demand increases or decreases when the collective intuition of business entrepreneurs turns "optimistic" or "pessimistic".

According to Keynes, spontaneous changes in "animal spirits" mean "not only that slumps and depressions are exaggerated in degree, but that economic prosperity is excessively dependent on the political and social atmosphere which is congenial to the average business man. . . . In estimating the prospects of investment, we must have regard, therefore, to the nerves and hysteria and even the digestions and reactions to the weather of those upon whose spontaneous activity it largely depends."[2]

Stock-Market Speculation.   Keynes also felt that stock-market speculation increased the instability of business investment. On the organized stock markets, existing or past investments in companies are constantly being revalued. For ex-

ample, in the summer of 1984, IBM stock could have been purchased for about $100 a share. In the fall of 1984, IBM stock could be purchased for $120 a share. Such revaluations of past investments have a decisive influence on current, new investments. As Keynes said, "there is no sense in building up a new enterprise at a cost greater than that at which a similar existing enterprise can be purchased" on the stock market. (See Example 4.)

If the prices of stocks are determined by irrational processes, as Keynes himself believed, business investment would be too unstable. To Keynes the stock market devoted far too much attention "to anticipating what average opinion expects the average opinion to be."

Keynes's view of the irrationality of stock prices has been amended by modern students of finance. Perhaps in the 1920s and 1930s, the stock market was irrational. But modern experts on the stock market claim that the prices of stocks roughly reflect what the company is worth at any given time. There is a constant stream of news about profits, technology, and opportunities. In a world of uncertainty, the financial community will, thus, revalue old investments differently from day to day as the news unfolds. To the extent that unfolding news is misleading, it still may be the case that stock-market speculation leads to excessive fluctuations in investment. According to Keynes, "Speculators may do no harm as bubbles on a steady stream of enterprise. But the position is serious when enterprise becomes the bubble on a whirlpool of speculation. When the capital development of a country becomes a by-product of the activities of a casino, the job is likely to be ill-done." (See Example 5.)

THE CROWDING OUT OF EXPENDITURES

According to Keynes the instability of the economy could be traced to the instability of the investment-demand curve and the magnified effects on aggregate spending of fluctuating investment spending. To this point, we have assumed that any expenditure multiplier was a **simple multi-**

2. See John Maynard Keynes, *The General Theory of Employment, Interest, and Money* (New York: Harcourt, Brace and Company, 1936), Ch. 12, from which all the quotes in this section were taken.

Example 4   Tobin's *q* and Finding Oil in Wall Street

Nobel laureate economist James Tobin has analyzed how the stock market affects investment demand. "Tobin's *q*" is the ratio of the current stock-market value to the book value of a corporation. *Book value* represents the current value of the corporation's net assets (its plants, equipment, oil reserves, and so on); whereas stock-market value is the share price times the number of shares. Whenever, Tobin's *q* falls below unity, the stock market is placing a lower value on the corporation than that for which the company's assets could be sold. By buying all the shares of such a corporation, the buyer can acquire the assets of the corporation for less than the book value.

Corporations can build up their physical assets either by investing in plant, equipment, and inventories or by buying the assets of existing companies. When they decide to buy existing companies (through corporate takeovers), no new capital is created. Capital is merely being transferred from one owner to another. When a corporation decides

to build new plants and equipment, new capital is created and investment takes place.

What is the relationship between Tobin's *q*, the stock market, and investment? When the stock market falls, the market value of some companies falls below book value. Corporations with investment funds, therefore, decide to apply these funds to corporate takeovers rather than to new investment projects. Declining stock prices can, therefore, lead to less investment throughout the economy as investment funds are diverted to buying established companies. An example of this phenomenon was the takeover activity in the oil industry in the early 1980s. The share prices of some oil companies had sunk so low that it became cheaper in some instances to acquire oil reserves by buying existing oil companies with established reserves than to invest in seismic exploration and drilling rigs to find oil. The low stock prices discouraged investment in the oil industry. ∎

---

plier—that increases in autonomous spending did not push up interest rates or prices.

A **simple multiplier** shows the impact on income of a change in autonomous spending or taxes when the price level and interest rates are not affected by such changes.

In the real world, increases in autonomous spending are indeed likely to affect interest rates and prices, and multiplier analysis needs to take these effects into consideration. Moreover, increases in government spending may affect private spending decisions—another factor multiplier analysis must consider. The final sections of this chapter are devoted to a more complete analysis of multipliers.

Indirect Crowding Out

It is now time to drop the assumption that interest rates are constant, but we will assume the price level is still constant. When autonomous spending

increases, real GNP rises. Chapter 8 showed that an increase in real GNP will increase the demand for money. Hence, there will be a tendency for interest rates to rise. As interest rates rise, the quantity of investment demanded will be reduced.[3] Higher interest rates crowd some private investors out of the market. Even if the price level is fixed, an increase in government spending, a reduction in tax rates, or a rightward shift in the investment-demand curve will all cause the rate of interest to rise. Thus, any increase in autonomous spending will cause **indirect crowding out** of private spending. The upward shift in the aggregate-expenditure curve that would have resulted from a spending increase will be reduced by the impact of the rising interest rate.

---

3. Thus, we cannot know how much real GNP increases until we know the increase in interest rates. Moreover, we cannot know the increase in interest rates until we know how much real GNP increases. The precise effects of an increase in autonomous spending are shown in the appendix, where it is shown that the changes in GNP and the interest rate are simultaneously determined.

Example 5   Why Investment Collapsed During the Great Depression

Keynes believed that the Great Depression was caused by the collapse of business investment. In the United States, real investment (measured in constant 1972 dollars) dropped from $51.2 billion in 1929 to $13.2 billion in 1933. The theories of investment developed in this chapter allow us to speculate on the causes of this investment collapse. First, there was a general collapse of business expectations concerning the future. This collapse is reflected in the collapse of stock prices. Standard and Poor's index of common stocks fell from 26.02 in 1929 (1941–43 = 100) to 13.66 in 1931 to 6.93 in 1932. In addition to measuring business optimism, declining stock prices can adversely affect investment. Second, as the accelerator principle suggests, declining real output can

choke off investment as business firms find themselves with idle capacity. From 1929 to 1933, real GNP declined each year. Third, although interest rates on business loans did fall from 5.8 percent in 1929 to 4.3 percent in 1933, this decline in interest rates was not strong enough to offset the sharp decline in investment demand that resulted from waning business optimism and the accelerator effect. Fourth, the world depression began to hit Europe in the late 1920s. As Europe went into depression, European purchases of U.S. products declined, thereby reducing autonomous spending. ■

Source: *Historical Statistics of the United States.*

Indirect crowding out occurs when an increase in autonomous spending pushes up interest rates and crowds out some of the private investment spending that would otherwise have taken place.

Figure 7 shows the effect of an autonomous increase in government spending, ΔG, when there is indirect crowding out. Without crowding out, the aggregate-expenditure curve shifts up from AE_1 to $AE_1 + \Delta G$. But the fall of investment spending due to the higher interest rate partially offsets the increase in government spending. Thus, the actual shift in the aggregate-expenditure curve is from AE_1 to AE_2. The difference between AE_2 and $AE_1 + \Delta G$ represents indirect crowding out. Instead of a change in government spending, ΔG, we also could have considered an autonomous change in private consumption or private investment—the effect of indirect crowding out would be the same.

Direct Crowding Out

Indirect crowding out applies to all increases in autonomous spending—government or private. But increases in government spending can have additional crowding-out effects. So far our analysis has supposed that when government expendi-

ture increases by one dollar, holding interest rates constant, private spending remains the same. However, this assumption may hold only for certain types of government expenditure (for example, national defense). It is quite possible that government expenditures on health care, education, police protection, roads, and parks will directly reduce some private expenditure. Thus, when the government purchases and provides at a low cost goods that are substitutes for private goods, it is likely that increasing government expenditures on those substitutes will cause the **direct crowding out** of some private expenditures.

Direct crowding out occurs when an increase in government spending substitutes for private spending by providing similar goods.

If direct crowding out is complete, there would be no shift in the *AE* curve and the multiplier would be zero. Complete crowding out means that the increase in government spending causes an equal decrease in private spending. If direct crowding out is partial, Figure 7 could also be used to describe the direct-crowding-out impact of a change in government spending. The crowding out shown in Figure 7 now results from the substitution of public spending for private spending rather than from the higher interest rates.

Figure 7   Crowding Out

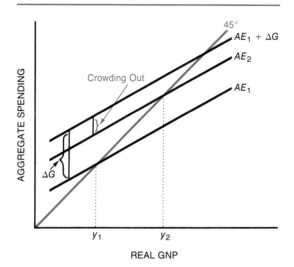

An increase in government spending or autonomous investment spending of ΔG will shift the aggregate-expenditure curve from AE_1 to only AE_2 because of the indirect crowding out of some private expenditures (through higher interest rates). Along AE_2, the interest rate is higher than along AE_1. The equilibrium level of GNP rises by the simple multiplier of the vertical shift from AE_1 to AE_2.

THE AGGREGATE-DEMAND CURVE

This chapter first considered the effects of changes in autonomous spending in a world in which autonomous spending does not affect interest rates or prices. The preceding section analyzed how changes in autonomous spending affect output, taking into consideration indirect (interest-rate) and direct crowding-out effects. This section presents the final building block for the analysis of autonomous spending and output: the aggregate-demand curve. The analysis of the aggregate-demand curve formally considers the relationship between the price level and the aggregate quantities of goods and services demanded by agents in the economy.

The concept of **aggregate demand** was introduced briefly in Chapter 5. The shape of the aggregate-demand curve was derived using the classical quantity theory in Chapter 7. The relationship between aggregate expenditures and aggregate demand was described briefly at the end of Chapter 9. Knowledge of the theory of aggregate expenditures, of muliplier analysis, and of the theory of investment can be used to define aggregate demand in a more exact fashion.

> **Aggregate demand** is a schedule that shows the equilibrium aggregate expenditures at different price levels, holding the nominal money supply, tax rates, and real government expenditures constant. In other words, for any given price level, the aggregate-demand schedule shows the level of income where desired expenditures and actual income are equal.

The income/expenditure model of Keynes can be used to determine what the economy's aggregate-demand curve looks like.

Although the aggregate-demand curve follows from the Keynesian model of equilibrium output determination, there is a clear distinction between the aggregate-demand curve and the aggregate-expenditure curve.

> The aggregate-expenditure *(AE)* curve shows *desired* aggregate expenditures *at each level of income.* The aggregate-demand *(AD)* curve shows *equilibrium* aggregate expenditures *at each price level.*

As noted in Chapter 5, one cannot argue by analogy to single markets that aggregate demand will fall as the price level rises due to the law of demand because the law of demand depends upon relative prices, not price-level changes. The income/expenditure model identifies two major factors that cause equilibrium output to decline as the actual (not expected) price level changes: the real-balance effect and the interest-rate effect.

The Real-Balance Effect

Individuals accumulate assets, such as money, bonds, or stocks. The money value of these assets minus the money value of their debts represents the net wealth (or net worth) of the individual. These assets can be converted into a medium of

Figure 8   The Derivation of Aggregate Demand

(a) A Change in Price Level Shifts the Aggregate-Expenditure Curve

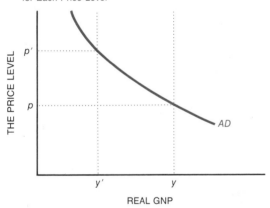

(b) Aggregate Demand as Equilibrium Output for Each Price Level

Panel (a) shows that an increase in the price level from p to p' will shift down the AE curve as a result of interest-rate and real-balance effects. The aggregate-demand curve (AD) in panel (b) associates each price level with the corresponding equilibrium GNP; thus, p corresponds to y and p' to y'.

therefore, cause asset-holding individuals to conclude that they are better off, and they tend to increase their purchases of goods and services. Rising prices cause the purchasing power of assets to fall; people conclude they are worse off and reduce their purchases of goods and services. The effect of the change in the price level on real consumption spending is called the **real-balance effect.**

> The **real-balance effect** occurs when desired consumption at each income level changes as price-level changes alter the purchasing power of assets, including money balances. Price increases reduce purchasing power and reduce desired consumption at each income level; price declines raise purchasing power and raise desired consumption at each income level.

The real-balance effect shifts the aggregate-expenditure curve. As the price level rises, consumers desire to spend less on real consumption at each level of income. As the price level falls, the aggregate-expenditure curve shifts up.

The Interest-Rate Effect

As the price level rises, the demand for credit increases. When the cost of goods and services financed by credit—cars, plants, equipment, inventories—rises, businesses and households must borrow more. The increased demand for credit causes interest rates to rise, and the higher interest rates discourage business investment. The **interest-rate effect** shifts the aggregate-expenditure curve. As prices rise, interest rates rise, and real investment declines. The aggregate-expenditure curve shifts down as investment declines. As the price-level falls, interest rates fall, investment increases, and the aggregate-expenditure curve shifts up.

> The **interest-rate effect** occurs when rising interest rates discourage investment expenditures and, thus, reduce aggregate spending as rising prices increase the demand for credit, given the money supply or when falling interest rates encourage investment spending and raise aggregate spending.

exchange (money assets are already a medium of exchange) for use in purchasing goods and services. The purchasing power of assets rises and falls with the price level. If prices are generally falling, people realize that their assets, including money balances, can buy more. Falling prices,

Why the *AD* Curve is Downward-Sloping

Because of the real-balance effect and the interest-rate effect, the aggregate demand for real goods and services will decline as the price level rises. When monetary and fiscal policy are constant, a once-and-for-all increase in the price level reduces aggregate expenditures because of reductions in desired consumption and desired investment. As the aggregate-expenditure curve shifts down, equilibrium output falls. Because *higher* prices mean a *smaller* aggregate demand for goods and services, the aggregate-demand curve has a negative slope.

The link between the income/expenditure approach and the aggregate demand/aggregate supply approach is shown in Figure 8. As the price level rises, holding the money supply constant, real-money balances decrease. In panel (a) of Figure 8, when the price level rises from *p* to *p′*, the aggregate-expenditure curve shifts down from *AE* to *AE′*. The equilibrium level of output, thus, decreases from *y* to *y′* as the price level rises from *p* to *p′*. The combinations of points *(p, y)* and *(p′, y′)* lie on the aggregate-demand curve *(AD)* in panel (b) of Figure 8. In other words, each price level is associated with a unique aggregate-expenditure curve and a unique equilibrium output. The association between the given price level and the equilibrium value of aggregate expenditure is the aggregate-demand curve.

Shifts in Aggregate Demand

Revealing the determinants of the aggregate-demand curve is Keynes's fundamental contribution to macroeconomics. Even if one disagrees with the policies associated with Keynesian economics, the analysis of aggregate demand forms one of the twin foundations of modern macroeconomics (the other being the analysis of aggregate supply that begins in the next chapter).

The aggregate-demand curve shows how the Keynesian equilibrium varies when only the price level changes. If government spending, tax rates, the money supply, the consumption/income curve, or the investment-demand curve changes, the aggregate-demand curve will shift. As noted above, in the absence of indirect-crowding-out ef-

Figure 9   Shifts in Aggregate Demand

(a) A Shift in the Aggregate-Expenditure Curve

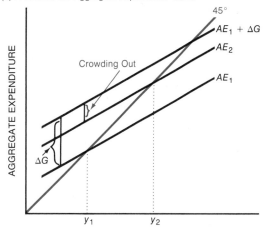

(b) The Resulting Shift in the Aggregate-Demand Curve

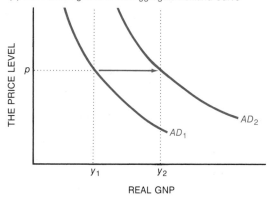

When government spending (or autonomous investment spending) increases by ΔG, the aggregate-expenditure curve shifts up from AE_1 to AE_2 (less than ΔG) because of the crowding out of other expenditures by high interest rates. For the given price level (p) the equilibrium level of GNP increases from y_1 to y_2. The AD curve shifts to the right by a distance equal to the simple multiplier times the vertical shift in the AE curve.

fects, the change in real output should equal any change in autonomous spending times the appropriate multiplier. Indirect crowding out occurs when interest rates rise in response to the increase in real GNP, which partly counters the initial output shift.

Figure 9 illustrates a situation that results in an increase in aggregate demand. In Figure 9, the money supply and the price level are assumed to be fixed, and an increase in government spending

Figure 10   The Role of Aggregate Supply

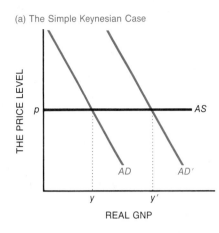
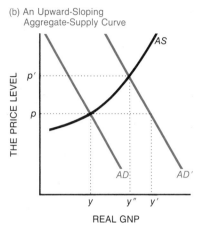

Panel (a) shows that when the price level is constant, an increase in aggregate demand from *AD* to *AD'* has the maximum impact on equilibrium real GNP. Panel (b) shows that when the aggregate-supply curve is upward-sloping, an increase in aggregate demand raises real GNP from *y* to only *y"* and raises the price level from *p* to *p'*. Had the price level remained at level *p*, real GNP would have increased to *y'*.

occurs that does not directly crowd out any private expenditure. Panel (a) of Figure 9 copies Figure 7. Government spending increases by ΔG, but indirect crowding out (resulting from higher interest rates) causes the aggregate-expenditure curve to shift up from AE_1 to only AE_2 rather than to $AE_1 + \Delta G$. In panel (b), the fixed price level is *p*. The aggregate-demand curve shifts from AD_1 to AD_2, since at the price level *p* the Keynesian equilibrium increases from y_1 to y_2. The shift in the aggregate-demand curve at the price level *p* is exactly the full multiplier effect of the *net* change in autonomous spending (the change in government spending minus the indirectly crowded out private spending). The same would be true of *any* change in autonomous spending.

> **The horizontal shift in the aggregate-demand curve at any price level is the full multiplier effect of the change in autonomous spending minus any crowded out spending.**

Figure 10 shows how the *effect* of a shift in the aggregate-demand curve depends on the shape of the aggregate-supply curve. In the Keynesian case, in panel (a), where the aggregate-supply curve is horizontal, a rightward shift in the aggregate-demand curve causes real GNP to rise by the maximum amount because the equilibrium price level remains the same.

Panel (b) of Figure 10 shows that if the aggregate-supply curve is upward-sloping—the normal case—then a rightward shift in the aggregate-demand curve causes real GNP to rise by less than when the *AS* curve is horizontal because the equilibrium price level rises, which discourages some consumption and investment spending. When the aggregate-demand curve shifts to the right from *AD* to *AD'*, real GNP increases from *y* to *y"* and the price level rises to *p'*. Had the price level remained constant at *p*, real GNP would have increased to *y'*, as in panel (a). The difference between y' and y" is due to the increase in the price level from *p* to *p'*. Thus, when the aggregate-supply curve is upward-sloping an increase in aggregate demand is not as effective in increasing aggregate output as in the Keynesian case because part of the increase is absorbed in higher prices.

Multipliers in the real world are smaller than the simple Keynesian multiplier, which assumes that interest rates and the price level are constant.

Even if the price level is constant, the real-world multiplier is smaller than the simple multiplier because of the indirect-crowding-out effect. If the price level increases, the real-world multiplier is smaller yet because interest rates rise even more, leading to more indirect crowding out. Price-level increases also discourage private spending through the real-balance effect. Clearly, price increases reduce the multiplier. In the case of a perfectly vertical aggregate-supply curve, for example, the price level would rise so much that the multiplier would have to be zero.

Government-spending multipliers in the real world may be smaller than the simple multiplier because of both indirect and direct crowding out.

The shape of the aggregate-supply curve is also important. The next chapter examines the short-run and long-run properties of aggregate supply.

Summary

1.   Changes in income (and output) can be caused by either direct factors, such as a change in investment spending or government spending, or by indirect factors, such as a change in taxes.
2.   Changes in autonomous expenditures—those that are determined independently of income changes—change desired expenditures dollar for dollar. The expenditure multiplier indicates by how much output will change for each change in government spending or investment. The value of the multiplier depends upon the marginal propensity to consume; the higher is the *MPC*, the higher is the multiplier. The expenditure-multiplier formula is $1/(1 - MPC)$ or $1/MPS$. The tax multiplier indicates by how much output will fall for each \$1 increase in taxes. The tax multiplier is $-MPC/(1 - MPC)$. The tax multiplier equals (in absolute value) the expenditure multiplier minus 1. For this reason, the balanced-budget multiplier equals unity.
3.   The accelerator principle explains why investment expenditures tend to be unstable. It postulates that investment depends upon the rate of increase of output. Investment remains constant only if output grows at a constant rate.

If the rate of output growth falls, investment will suffer a decline. When the accelerator interacts with the multiplier, booms and busts may result. Increases in investment cause output to grow, and as output growth increases, investment increases further. Desired investment depends upon the interest rate, government tax policy, and expectations concerning the future. Keynes felt investment was also unstable because of spontaneous changes in business psychology and excessive stock-market speculation.
4.   Indirect crowding out occurs when an increase in autonomous spending crowds out some private spending due to the increase in interest rates. Direct crowding out occurs when an increase in government spending directly substitutes for private consumption or investment spending.
5.   The aggregate-demand curve is downward-sloping because as the price level rises, holding the nominal quantity of money constant, there is an increase in interest rates and a reduction in real money balances. The increase in interest rates cuts investment and the reduction in real money balances (the real-balance effect) reduces consumption. Shifts in the aggregate-demand curve are less than the simple multiplier because the interest rate will not be constant (indirect crowding out will occur). If the aggregate-supply curve is upward-sloping, the effect of an increase in aggregate demand will be even less.

Key Terms

autonomous expenditures
expenditure multiplier
investment multiplier $(\Delta Y/\Delta I)$
government-expenditure multiplier $(\Delta Y/\Delta G)$
tax multiplier $(\Delta Y/\Delta T)$
balanced-budget multiplier
capital/output ratio (K/Y)
accelerator principle
simple multiplier
indirect crowding out
direct crowding out
aggregate demand
real-balance effect
interest-rate effect

Questions and Problems

1. In Economy V, there is no government spending and no taxes. Evaluate the impact of an increase in investment from $30 billion to $50 billion, assuming the price level is constant. The consumption schedule is given in Table A
  a. What is the *MPC?* What is the *MPS?*
  b. What is the equilibrium income when investment spending is $30 billion? When *I* = $50 billion?
  c. What is the expenditure multiplier?

Table A

Income (billions of dollars), Y	Consumption (billions of dollars), C
0	10
50	50
100	90
150	130
200	170
250	210
300	250

2. Assume that in Economy V in problem (1) investment spending is $30 billion.
  a. What is the effect on income of introducing government spending in the amount of $20 billion (but with no taxes!)?
  b. What is the effect on income of introducing government spending of $20 billion and taxes of $25 billion?

3. Will a cut in personal income taxes of $100 billion raise or lower equilibrium real output? Does the answer depend upon whether there are unemployed resources in the economy? Will the effect on equilibrium output be larger if the *MPS* is 0.2 or 0.1? Explain.

4. "Changes in attitudes towards thrift and personal income taxes both affect the consumption/income curve. Therefore, a $100 billion increase in taxes will have the same effect as a $100 billion decrease in desired consumption expenditures caused by an increase in thrift." Evaluate this statement.

5. Economy W has substantial unemployed resources. The *MPS* out of disposable income is 0.25. Government spending increases by $100 billion and taxes are lowered by $100 billion. Using the Keynesian multiplier analysis, by how much would one expect equilibrium output to change?

6. Explain why changes in expectations concerning the future can shift the investment-demand curve.

7. What assumptions are made in simple-multiplier analysis?

8. Compare and contrast direct and indirect crowding out.

9. Is the following statement true or false? "There will be no indirect crowding out of government spending if direct crowding out is complete."

10. Explain the difference between the aggregate-expenditure curve and the aggregate-demand curve. What is being held constant along these curves?

11. Give two reasons why the aggregate-demand curve is downward-sloping?

12. Why is the shift in the aggregate-demand curve smaller than the simple-multiplier effect?

13. How does the shape of the aggregate-supply curve alter effect of, say, a change in autonomous spending on equilibrium real GNP?

14. How does the shape of the aggregate-supply curve affect the shift in the aggregate-demand curve when autonomous spending changes?

Suggested Readings

Fusfeld, Daniel. *The Age of the Economist.* Glenview, Ill.: Scott, Foresman, 1982.

Keynes, John Maynard. *The General Theory of Employment, Interest, and Money.* New York: Harcourt, Brace and Co., 1936, chap. 12.

Mathews, R.C.O. *The Business Cycle.* Chicago, Ill.: University of Chicago Press, 1958.

Stein, Herbert. *The Fiscal Revoluton in America.* Chicago, Ill.: University of Chicago Press, 1969.

The IS/LM Model

Appendix Preview

The aggregate-demand curve shows how the Keynesian equilibrium varies with different price levels. The description of the Keynesian equilibrium in Chapter 10 is incomplete because interest rates are determined simultaneously with income. This appendix describes the *IS/LM* model, which shows how both the interest rate and the level of real GNP are the outcome of two equilibrium conditions: goods-market equilibrium and money-market equilibrium. The *IS/LM* approach explicitly incorporates crowding-out effects and clearly separates monetary factors from fiscal factors in the determination of output. It also can be used to rigorously derive the aggregate-demand curve.

The following analysis is conducted under the assumption that the price level is fixed. This assumption will be relaxed when the aggregate-demand curve is discussed. ■

THE *IS* CURVE: INTEREST RATE AND GOODS MARKET IN EQUILIBRIUM

When aggregate production equals desired aggregate expenditure, the market for goods is in equilibrium. The condition for equilibrium is that desired investment *(I)* equals desired saving *(S)*. The *IS* curve answers a simple question: how is the equilibrium level of income related to the interest rate, holding the price level constant? Thus, the *IS* curve shows, for each interest rate, the level of real GNP that is consistent with equilibrium in the market for goods and services.

Panel (a) of Figure 1 shows how higher interest rates lower the aggregate-expenditure curve (because of the induced reduction in desired investment). Consider three interest rates, r_1, r_2, and r_3, and assume that $r_3 > r_2 > r_1$. Clearly, the higher is the interest rate, given the price level, the lower will be the aggregate-expenditure curve. Thus, as the interest rate rises, the aggregate expenditure curve shifts down from AE_1 to AE_2 to AE_3. Thus, the three interest rates are associated with three equilibrium levels of income, y_1, y_2, and y_3.

Panel (b)'s *IS* curve relates each interest rate to the corresponding equilibrium level of real output. The **IS curve** is negatively sloped because higher interest rates lower the equilibrium level of real GNP.

> The **IS curve** shows all the combinations of interest rates and real income that are consistent with goods-market equilibrium (in which desired investment equals desired saving).

THE *LM* CURVE: MONEY MARKET IN EQUILIBRIUM

The *LM* curve takes its name from the fact that when the money market is in equilibrium, the demand for money—often denoted by *L* in economics—equals the supply of money—often denoted by *M* in economics. The demand for real money balances, depends on two factors: the nominal interest rates and real income or GNP. Since the price level is assumed to be fixed, the expected

Figure 1   The *IS* Curve

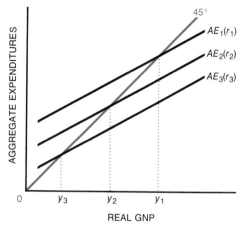

(a) The Aggregate-Expenditure Curve Shifts Down as the Interest Rate Rises

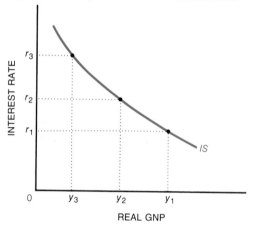

(b) Equilibrium Output Falls as the Interest Rate Rises

Panel (a) shows that as interest rates rise from r_1 to r_2 to r_3, the aggregate-expenditure curve shifts downward from AE_1 to AE_2 to AE_3. The *IS* curve in panel (b) associates the corresponding equilibrium levels of income to each interest rate.

inflation rate is 0, making the nominal rate of interest equal to the real rate of interest. The *LM* curve answers the question: For a given supply of real balances, how does the equilibrium interest rate respond to changes in real income?

Panel (a) of Figure 2 measures the interest rate on the vertical axis and real money balances on

Figure 2   The *LM* Curve

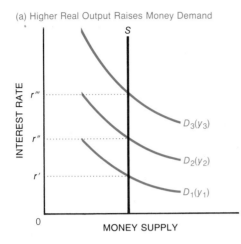

(a) Higher Real Output Raises Money Demand

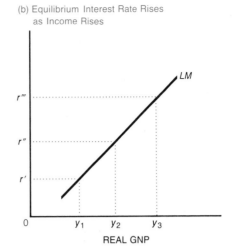

(b) Equilibrium Interest Rate Rises as Income Rises

Panel (a) shows that as real income rises from y_1 to y_2 to y_3, the demand for money shifts to the right from D_1 to D_2 to D_3. Thus, as income rises the interest rate equating the fixed supply of money balances, S, to the quantity of money demanded increases from r' to r'' to r'''. The *LM* curve in panel (b) associates each equilibrium interest rate to each level of real income.

the horizontal axis. Consider three levels of real income: y_1, y_2, and y_3. The demand curves D_1, D_2, and D_3 illustrate how the demand for real balances decreases as the level of real income falls. Since $y_1 < y_2 < y_3$, the demand curve D_3 is to the right of D_2 and the demand curve D_2 is to the right of D_1. The supply of real money balances is shown by the vertical line, S. When the real income level is y_1, the interest rate that brings about money-market equilibrium is r'. When real incomes are y_2 and y_3, the equilibrium interest rates are r'' and r''', respectively. Clearly, the interest rate that equates quantity of money demanded to quantity of money supplied rises as the level of real income rises.

Panel (b)'s **LM curve** shows the combinations of interest rates and real income that are consistent with money-market equilibrium. The curve is upward-sloping because higher real income increases the demand for real money balances and higher interest rates are required to maintain the same demand for real balances. In other words, higher interest rates are required to choke off the extra demand for money created by a higher level of real income.

The **LM curve** shows all the combinations of interest rates and real income that bring about equality between the demand for money and supply of money.

THE *IS/LM* EQUILIBRIUM

Figure 3 combines the *IS* and *LM* curves on the same graph. Point e_0 represents the equilibrium level of interest rate and real income. The interest rate r_0 and income level y_0 are the only levels compatible with equilibrium in both the goods market and the money market simultaneously.

Fiscal Policy: Shifts in the *IS* Curve

Shifts in the *IS* curve can be explained by shifts in the aggregate-expenditure curve that are not caused by changes in the rate of interest. As explained in Chapter 10, an increase in the aggregate-expenditure curve by the amount ΔA will cause the equilibrium level of output to increase by $\Delta Y = \Delta A/(1 - \text{MPC})$. Thus, the *IS* curve

Figure 3   The *IS*/*LM* Equilibrium

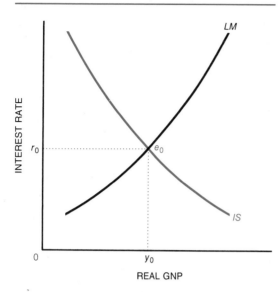

The combination of the interest rate r_0 and the income level y_0 brings about equilibrium in both the goods market and the money market, because e_0 falls on both the *IS* and *LM* curves.

Figure 4   Fiscal Policy

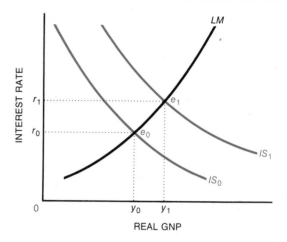

If the *IS* curve shifts to the right from IS_0 to IS_1—due to, say, an increase in government spending or a reduction in tax rates—the equilibrium level of real income will rise from y_0 to y_1. The equilibrium interest rate will rise from r_0 to r_1 along a given *LM* curve.

shifts by the simple multiplier of the change in autonomous spending.

Figure 4 shows a rightward shift in the *IS* curve from IS_0 to IS_1. This rightward shift can be the result of any of the following events:

1. An increase in the real level of government spending.
2. A decrease in tax rates that shifts the consumption/income curve up.
3. An upward shift in the consumption/income curve due to an increased propensity to consume.
4. A rightward shift in the investment-demand curve due to the expectation of an acceleration in sales or simple business psychology.
5. An autonomous increase in exports or an autonomous decrease in imports.

Obviously, the *IS* curve will shift to the left if the reverse of any of the above five events occurs. Events 1 and 2 are examples of an expansionary fiscal policy, through which the government deliberately shifts the *IS* curve to the right in order to increase real GNP.

In Figure 4, the *IS* curve shifts from IS_0 to IS_1, indicating an expansionary fiscal policy or an au-

tonomous expansionary change in consumption, in investment, or in net exports. The equilibrium interest rate rises from r_0 to r_1 and the equilibrium level of real GNP rises from y_0 to y_1. Notice that the change in real GNP is *smaller* than the horizontal shift in the *IS* curve (the full multiplier effect of the change in autonomous spending). The explanation, of course, is that interest rates rise and crowd out some private investment (or even consumption) spending.

> An expansionary fiscal policy that raises real GNP (or anything that shifts the *IS* curve to the right) will also raise interest rates. A contractionary fiscal policy that lowers real GNP (or anything that shifts the *IS* curve to the left) will also lower interest rates.

Monetary Policy: Shifts in the *LM* Curve

What about the effects of monetary policy? To simplify the disussion, assume an increase in the supply of real money balances has a negligible effect on private consumption. Thus, changes in the real money supply can exert only indirect effects on the goods market.

Shifts in the *LM* curve are caused by fluctua-

Figure 5   Monetary Policy

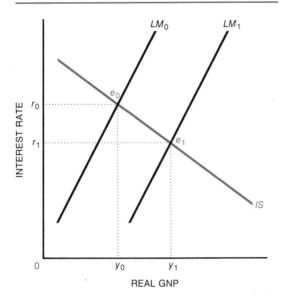

If the *LM* curve shifts to the right from LM_0 to LM_1—due to an increase in the nominal money supply (holding the price level constant)—the equilibrium level of real income will rise from y_0 to y_1. The equilibrium interest rate will fall from r_0 to r_1 along a given *IS* curve.

tions in the demand for money that are not due to changes in interest rates or real income and by changes in the real supply of money. An increase in real money will require a larger real GNP to maintain money-market equilibrium at a constant interest rate. Alternatively, an increase in real money will lower the interest rate needed to maintain money-market equilibrium for a constant real GNP. Thus, a larger real money supply will shift the *LM* curve to the right; a smaller real money supply will shift the *LM* curve to the left.

An expansionary monetary policy that raises real GNP will lower interest rates. A contractionary monetary policy that lowers real GNP will raise interest rates.

Suppose the Federal Reserve System increases the nominal supply of money by one of its instruments of monetary control (for example, by making open-market purchases or lowering reserve requirements). If the price level is assumed fixed, the real money supply will rise. Figure 5 shows a rightward shift in the *LM* curve from LM_0 to LM_1

due to an increase in the real supply of money. The equilibrium interest rate falls from r_0 to r_1 and the equilibrium level of real GNP rises from y_0 to y_1. The mechanism underlying the increase in real GNP, of course, is that the higher supply of real money balances lowers interest rates, causing the quantity of investment demanded to increase.

DERIVING THE AGGREGATE-DEMAND CURVE

The above analysis assumes that the price level is fixed. What happens when the price level changes? The effect is similar to a change in the money supply. If the money supply is fixed and the price level is *reduced* from p_0 to p_1 to p_2, the real money supply will *rise* because the purchasing power of the given nominal money supply increases. Thus, just as in the above analysis of monetary policy, the *LM* curve shifts to the right each time the price level falls. In panel (a) of Figure 6, LM_0, LM_1, and LM_2 are the *LM* curves for the price levels p_0, p_1, and p_2, respectively. As the price level falls, real income rises and the interest rate falls.

Panel (b) of Figure 6 associates each price level with the resulting equilibrium level of real GNP. Thus, p_0, p_1, and p_2 are associated with the real GNPs y_0, y_1, and y_2, respectively. The underlying mechanism is that a lower price level increases the real money supply, which in turn lowers interest rates and encourages private investment spending. The output level associated with the *LM*/*IS* equilibrium point for each price leve is plotted against that price level to generate the aggregate-demand curve relating different price levels to the Keynesian level of equilibrium GNP.

The aggregate-demand curve is derived by plotting the association between each price level and the equilibrium level of real GNP corresponding to the *IS*/*LM* equilibrium for each price level.

Shifts in the aggregate-demand curve are caused by changes in the nominal money supply (which changes the *LM* curve) or any of the factors that cause shifts in the *IS* curve. Unlike a shift in the IS curve, the aggregate-demand curve

Figure 6   The Derivation of Aggregate Demand

(a) The Effect of a Change in the Price Level on the IS/LM Equilibrium

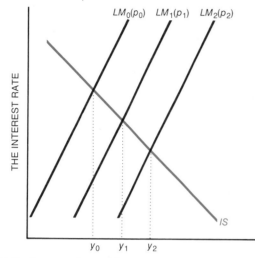

(b) The Aggregate-Demand Curve

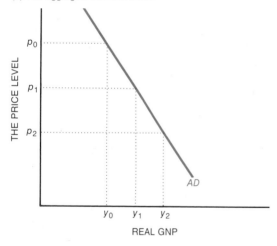

REAL GNP

Panel (a) shows that the *LM* curve shifts to the right each time the price level falls from p_0 to p_1 to p_2 (holding the nominal money supply constant). Thus, LM_0, LM_1, and LM_2 are associated with p_0, p_1, and p_2, respectively. Panel (b) plots the corresponding levels of real income against each price level, forming the aggregate-demand *(AD)* curve.

(AD) will shift by *less* than the full multiplier effect of a change in autonomous spending because for any price level, a rightward shift in the *IS* curve will drive up interest rates and choke off some investment demand, which partly offsets the initial change in autonomous expenditure.

Summary

1. The *IS* curve shows all the combinations of interest rates and real income that are consistent with goods-market equilibrium (in which desired investment equals desired saving).
2. The *LM* curve shows all the combinations of interest rates and real income that bring about equality between the demand for money and supply of money.
3. The *IS/LM* interesection point simultaneously shows the interest rate and income level compatible with equilibrium in both the goods market and the money market. An expansionary fiscal policy that raises real GNP will also raise interest rates. An expansionary monetary policy that raises real GNP will lower interest rates.
4. The aggregate-demand curve is derived by plotting the association between each price level and the equilibrium level of real GNP corresponding to the *IS/LM* equilibrium for that price level.

Key Terms

IS **curve**
LM **curve**

Questions and Problms

1. Why is the *IS* curve downward-sloping?

2. What factors are held constant along the *IS* curve?

3. Why is the *LM* curve upward-sloping?

4. What factors are held constant along the *LM* curve?

5. Describe the impact of increasing tax rates on the *IS/LM* equilibrium.

6. Describe the impact of reducing the money supply on the *IS/LM* equilibrium.

7. How is the simple multiplier modified by the *IS/LM* model?

11

Aggregate Supply

Chapter Preview

This chapter formally brings together the demand side and the supply side of macroeconomics to study the relationships between real output, the price level, and unemployment in the short run and in the long run.

Keynes studied a depression economy—an economy operating with a stable price level and large quantities of underutilized resources. In such an economy, Keynes concluded that policymakers should focus on the demand side of the economy: if aggregate expenditures could be increased, idle resources could be brought into use, and real GNP and employment could be increased without prices being driven up. Aggregate supply was of little concern to the depresson economy; the existence of idle resources meant that increases in aggregate expenditures would bring about increases in real output. For this reason,

Keynesian economics has come to be called *demand-side economics*.

This chapter analyzes aggregate supply under more general conditions than those assumed by Keynes. This chapter assumes that prices could rise before the economy reaches full employment, that in general prices are more flexible than they would be in a depression economy. This chapter examines the relationship between real output, unemployment, and the price level in a world of flexible prices—a key issue of modern macroeconomics. It shows the circumstances under which the supply side of the economy can drive unemployment down to the *natural* (or *full-employment*) unemployment rate. The economy may have a self-correcting mechanism in the long run. ■

MODERN INSIGHTS ABOUT AGGREGATE SUPPLY

Keynes viewed the money wage rate as fixed in the short run. Chapter 9 pointed out that wages were more or less constant in Great Britain during the Great Depression. In the United States, wages fell significantly in the first few years of the Great Depression. In 1929, the average production worker in the United States earned $0.56 an hour. By 1933, in the face of a 25 percent unemployment rate, the hourly wage had fallen by 21 percent to $0.44 an hour. The price level itself fell about 25 percent over the same period. But after 1933, wages and prices actually rose despite high unemployment rates. The Great Depression appears to have been a time when wages and prices were usually flexible.

Since the time of Keynes, economists have put a great deal of thought into the question of the flexibility of money wages and prices and the effect of wages and prices on employment and output. The modern view of aggregate supply is that *in the short run,* prices and wages are somewhat flexible in both the upward and downward direction. The degree of flexibility can vary from economy to economy and from time to time. *In the long run,* however, prices and wages may be regarded as perfectly flexible in the upward or downward direction.

The Nature of Wage Bargains

At any given time in the economy, some employers and employees are striking new wage bargains. At the same time, a number of existing wage bargains have contract expiration dates weeks, months, or years in the future, depending on the length of the contract and the amount of time already expired. Some wage contracts are struck daily; others set wage rates over a number of years. Clearly, when enough time passes, every wage contract is going to have to be renegotiated. Thus, in the long run, all wages are flexible.

The wage bargain depends on demand and supply factors. On the demand side, determining factors are the worker's productivity and the expected monetary value of the goods being produced. Because money is the standard of deferred value, wage bargains will be struck in nominal

terms. The prices that the business firm anticipates over the period of the wage contract will clearly influence the firm's demand for labor. If prices are expected to rise, the business firm's demand for labor will increase.

On the supply side, workers will be concerned with the purchasing power of their wages (the real wage) and the value they place on their leisure time. The nominal wage to which the worker will agree will depend in part on the prices the worker expects to pay for food, rent, clothing, utilities, and so on. If prices for these goods are falling, then the worker can accept lower nominal wages and at least maintain current real wages. The value of leisure is the forgone earnings a worker gives up by not working. The higher is unemployment, the lower is the value of leisure for many workers. Thus, lower nominal wages would be accepted by workers during periods of high unemployment. Using similar reasoning, workers would be expected to ask for higher nominal wage rates when prices are rising or unemployment rates are low.

Thus, supply and demand will condition all new wage bargains. When unemployment is high or prices are falling, newly negotiated wages will fall. When unemployment is low or prices are rising, newly negotiated wages will rise.

Figure 1 shows the impact of rising prices on nominal wage rates (in the long run). When prices are rising, firms will expect the market value of their output to rise. Thus, the increase in prices shifts the labor-demand curve to the right from D_L to D_L' as firms are willing to pay more per unit of labor. Similarly, the increase in prices causes workers to reduce the amount of labor they are prepared to supply at each nominal wage rate. Thus, the supply curve of labor will shift from S_L to S_L'. In this case, the new equilibrium nominal wage rate rises from w to w' and employment remains the same.

Money Illusion

A key issue in the determination of aggregate supply is how workers and firms view changes in money, wages, and prices. Will changes in the price level affect output and employment? Economists have tended to believe that rational consumers and firms are not subject to **money illusion.**

Figure 1   The Long-Run Effect of Rising Prices on the Demand and Supply of Labor

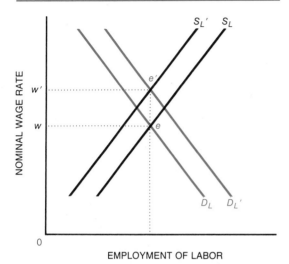

When the price level rises, the demand for labor increases from D_L to D_L' because business firms find that the value of their output rises. Similarly, as prices rise the supply of labor decreases from S_L to S_L' because workers wish to maintain their real wages. Thus, the nominal wage rate will rise from w to w' under the pressure of rising prices, but in this case, the amount of employment remains the same.

Economic decision makers are subject to **money illusion** when a proportionate change in all money prices and money wages causes them to think that real wages or relative prices have changed.

If economic actors are not subject to money illusion, changes in the price level that leave relative prices unchanged should not affect output or employment decisions. For example, suppose a worker's *money* wage is rising by 10 percent while consumer prices are also rising by 10 percent. The worker's *real* wage has not been altered by the 10 percent increase in the money wage. If this worker is not subject to money illusion, this worker's real behavior—purchases of goods and services, offerings of labor services to employers—will not change as a consequence of the money-wage increase. The worker will not increase total purchases or work longer hours. The worker will know that real purchasing power has not changed and that real wages have not risen.

Business firms that are not subject to money illusion will not change their behavior if money prices rise, either. Suppose shoe prices are rising 10 percent per year, while the shoe-manufacturing firm's input prices—leather, electricity, money wages—are also rising 10 percent per year. If the manufacturer is not subject to money illusion, its real behavior—number of shoes produced, number of workers hired—should not change.

When Chapter 5 first introduced the aggregate-supply curve, it was drawn with an upward slope on the assumption that business firms supply more goods and services at higher price levels. In the discussion of the classical quantity theory in Chapter 7, the aggregate-supply curve was drawn as a vertical line on the assumption that money prices should not affect real economic activity because economic actors are not subject to money illusion. As long as money prices, input prices, and money wages all rise at the same rate with a rising price level, higher money prices should not call forth more real output.

The vertical supply curve of the classical economists, in effect, assumes that inflation (a rising price level) has no real effects on the economy. Modern economists, however, have come to recognize that inflation can change the output decisions of business firms and the employment decisions of individuals. This chapter will be exploring modern views of the effects of the price level on the aggregate supply of real goods and services in an attempt to answer the question: How can a higher price level bring about more real output if people are generally not subject to money illusion?

The Natural Rate of Unemployment

Macroeconomics groups together many sectors of the economy, but the composition of the economy is in a constant state of flux. Some industries are expanding; others are contracting. The labor force is being shuffled from industry to industry and from job to job. In a fully static economy, the full-employment level of output would be that level of employment at which each and every worker would be allocated to his or her best job; unemployment would be essentially zero. Zero unemployment, however, is a fiction in a complicated dynamic economy. Within the aggregates of consumption, investment, government spending, exports and imports, there is constant change. As a result, there will always be some frictional unemployment (job changing) and some structurally unemployed workers (moving from contracting to expanding industries). There is a constant search for new workers and new jobs.

"Natural" unemployment arises from the inevitable frictions that characterize complicated labor markets in which people are constantly looking for jobs and firms are constantly looking for workers.

The **natural rate of unemployment** was defined in Chapter 5 as that unemployment rate at which there is an approximate balance between the number of unfilled jobs or vacancies and the number of qualified unemployed workers. Since the number of unfilled jobs in an economy cannot be measured accurately by government statisticians, economists prefer another definition.

The **natural rate of unemployment** is that rate of unemployment that can be sustained without accelerating or decelerating inflation.

This definition can be understood by considering how the labor market works under different conditions. As explained earlier, the wage bargain partly reflects the value workers place on their leisure (or nonworking) time. Thus, in the labor market, wages will behave differently at different rates of unemployment. When the unemployment rate exceeds the natural rate of unemployment—when the number of people looking for work exceeds the number of unfilled jobs—the current rate of wage increase or inflation (on average) will tend to fall. When the unemployment rate falls short of the natural rate—when the number of unfilled jobs exceeds the number of people looking for work—the current rate of wage increase or inflation (on the average) will tend to rise.

The behavior of wages depends on the momentum of wages and prices. For example, suppose there is zero wage or price inflation and that the economy is at the natural unemployment rate. Wages and prices have been steady for some time, and everyone expects them to remain stable in the future. For purposes of illustration, assume the unemployment rate of 5 percent is the natural rate. If the unemployment rate were to rise above 5 percent, wages would begin to fall; if the rate of unemployment were to fall below 5 percent, wages would begin to rise. Only at 5 percent

would wages remain stable. Next, suppose wages have been rising steadily at 10 percent per annum for a number of years. The natural rate of 5 percent would be that rate at which this rate of wage inflation would continue. If unemployment rose above 5 percent, the rate of wage inflation would decelerate below 10 percent. If unemployment fell below 5 percent, inflation would accelerate above 10 percent.

The natural rate of unemployment does not depend on the rate of inflation. The natural rate of unemployment is consistent with different rates of inflation.

The natural rate of unemployment depends not on the price level, but on long-run demographic and cost factors that will be discussed in a later chapter. (See Example 1 for different estimates of the natural rate of unemployment.)

Natural Real GNP

Corresponding to the natural rate of unemployment is a **natural level of real GNP (y_n).**

The **natural level of real GNP** (y_n) is the output produced when the economy is operating at the natural rate of unemployment.

At output levels above the natural output level, y_n, the unemployment rate will be below the natural rate of unemployment; wage inflation will accelerate and price increases will accelerate. If output is below natural output, the unemployment rate will be above the natural rate; wage and price inflation will decelerate.

Consider an economy where prices have been holding steady for a number of years, where the economy is at the natural rate of unemployment, and where the real output corresponding to the natural rate is $3 trillion. If output rose above $3 trillion, prices would rise. If output fell below $3 trillion, prices would fall. Only at the natural output level would prices remain stable.[1]

---

1. There is no assurance of symmetrical behavior of prices for outputs above or below y_n. If output rises above natural output, prices may rise rapidly. If output falls below natural output by the same amount, the fall in prices may be small.

Example 1   Overlapping Union Contracts and Inflation

Unanticipated inflation or deflation changes the relationship between selling prices and costs. Union wage bargains set pay and work conditions typically for periods of two to three years. A three-year union contract, for example, would specify wage increases to be granted during the first, second, and third years of the contract along with other provisions such as cost-of-living adjustments. The wage increases negotiated over the life of the contract would depend upon the employer's anticipation of the rate of increase in selling prices and upon the union's anticipation of the cost-of-living rise over the life of the contract (as well as unemployment conditions). A number of union settlements include *cost-of-living-adjustments* (COLAs) that tie wage increases in subsequent years of the contract to the rate of inflation. A COLA clause in a contract might, for example, call for the wage rate in each year of a contract to be raised automatically by 50 percent of the previous year's inflation rate.

The accompanying figure shows how unanticipated inflation can change the relationship between selling prices and labor costs. The color line shows the actual inflation rate in each year for the period 1973–1984. The solid black line shows the percentage wage increase in the first year of new union contracts negotiated in each year. The dashed black line shows the percentage wage increase in each year mandated under the terms of existing union contracts. The two union-wage series are for union contacts with no cost-of-living adjustments because they give better information on the rate of inflation anticipated over the life of the union contract. If the contract contains no automatic cost-of-living adjustments, the union must make every effort to incorporate anticipated inflation into the terms of the contract.

What does this figure show? First, it gives a rough picture of the relationship between actual inflation and the rate of inflation anticipated by existing union contracts. In 1974 and 1975, actual inflation was higher than that anticipated by unions. The sharp drop in inflation in 1976 was not anticipated by unions, and anticipated inflation was higher than actual inflation. From 1978 to 1981, actual inflation was higher than anticipated inflation. The sharp drop in inflation after 1981 was not anticipated by existing contracts, and actual inflation was below anticipated inflation. Second, the figure shows that first-year wage increases, negotiated as they are with good knowledge of existing labor-market conditions and inflation, closely mirror the actual inflation rate, although actual first-year wage increases are more sticky in a downward direction than inflation (at least as far as 1976 and 1977 are concerned).

If inflation were fully anticipated by unions, the three lines would closely coincide. The figure shows that accelerations and decelerations of inflation are not fully anticipated. This fact changes the relationship between selling prices and wage costs. During periods of accelerating inflation (1973–75, 1976–81), selling prices were generally rising more rapidly than wages governed by existing union contracts. Only new contracts generally kept up with inflation. With wage increases lagging behind price increases, firms were made better off. During periods of decelerating inflation (1976, 1981–84), prices rose more slowly than wage increases mandated under existing contracts. ■

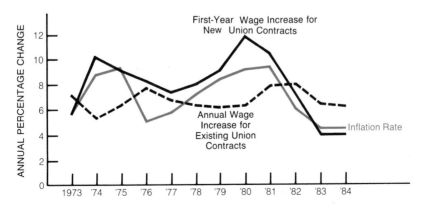

Source: *Statistical Abstract of the U.S.,* 1984, p. 439; *Federal Reserve Bulletin,* December 1984, p. 845.

Aggregate Supply in the Long Run

A vertical line drawn at the natural level of output, y_n, represents **long-run aggregate supply** *(LRAS)*. The *LRAS* curve is vertical because in the long run consumers and firms do not have money illusion and all expectations regarding prices will be fulfilled. Doubling all prices does not affect the incentive of anyone to produce more because both prices and costs are perceived to rise by the same amount.

> **Long-run aggregate supply** *(LRAS)* is a schedule of output supplied by business at different price levels, assuming that all wages and prices are flexible, that all expectations are fulfilled, and that the quantity and productivity of resources are constant. It is represented by a vertical line at the natural level of output.

The notable fact demonstrated by the long-run aggregate-supply curve is that the amount of output supplied is the same, in the long run, no matter what the price level. As long as money illusion is not present and price expectations are fulfilled, the economy will produce the natural level of output. The natural level of output is the modern economist's notion of full employment.

Aggregate Supply in the Short Run

Short-run aggregate supply *(SRAS)* is a schedule of the real GNP that business firms supply at different price levels, holding constant the expected price level, the resources available to the economy, and the efficiency with which the resources are used.

> **Short-run aggregate supply** *(SRAS)* is a schedule of the quantities of real output the economy is prepared to supply at different price levels, holding other factors (especially the expected price level) constant.

In the short run, the most important condition that the aggregate-supply holds constant is the expected price level. If inflation is expected to be 10 percent, a worker may be satisfied with a one-year wage of $31,500. If the worker expected no inflation, he or she might agree to a $30,000 wage over the next year. As noted at the begin-

Figure 2   Short-Run and Long-Run Aggregate Supply

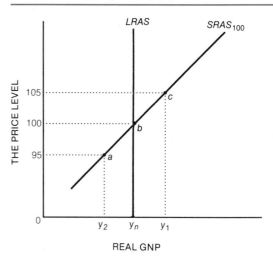

The long-run aggregate-supply *(LRAS)* curve is vertical at the natural output level, y_n. The short-run aggregate-supply curve $SRAS_{100}$ is based on the expected price level of 100. The natural-rate hypothesis requires that when the actual price level is the same as the one expected, output equals the natural level, y_n. Hence, $SRAS_{100}$ intersects *LRAS* at the price level of 100. If inflation rises to a level higher than anticipated—say, to a price level of 105—output rises to y_1. Unanticipated inflation stimulates output because prices of products rise faster than producing firms' costs. When prices fall more than anticipated—say, from 100 to 95—output falls to y_2. Unanticipated deflation discourages output because prices of products fall slower than producing firms' costs.

ning of this chapter, price expectations condition the wage bargains between employers and employees. The higher are expected prices, the higher are expected business costs. In the **natural-rate hypothesis,** modern macroeconomists make the assumption that the relationship between expected and actual prices determines whether output exceeds or equals the natural level of real GNP.

> The **natural-rate hypothesis** is that prices must be higher than expected for output to exceed the natural output level and that prices must be lower than expected for output to fall below the natural output level.

Figure 2 shows the short-run aggregate-supply curve, $SRAS_{100}$, drawn holding the expected price level constant at 100. According to the natural-

Example 2   Estimating the Natural Rate of Unemployment

The natural rate of unemployment was defined operationally in this chapter as that unemployment rate at which inflationary pressures are constant. If the actual unemployment rate falls below the natural rate, inflationary pressures will intensify (the rate of inflation will increase). If the actual unemployment rate rises above the natural rate, inflationary pressures will lessen (the inflation rate should drop).

The natural rate of unemployment at a particular point in time depends upon demographic factors (such as the proportions of women and young people in the labor force), productivity factors, supply shocks, and the tax system. Different estimates of the 1984 natural rate of unemployment offered by different economists are shown in the accompanying table.

As these figures show, the various estimates of the natural rate of unemployment range from a low of 4 percent to a high of 6.5 percent. A later chapter will outline the inflationary dangers of aiming for an unemployment rate below the natural rate that

make an accurate estimate of the natural rate of unemployment so important. ■

Source of Estimate	Estimate of the Natural Rate of Unemployment (percent)
Council of Economic Advisors	6.5
Congressional Budget Office	6.0
Robert Gordon (Northwestern University)	6.0
Michael Wachter (University of Pennsylvania)	5.7
LaSalle Econometrics, Inc.	4.0–4.5

Sources: "Some Economists Call for Lowering Natural Jobless Rate to Cut Deficit," *The Wall Street Journal,* Tuesday, September 11, 1984; Robert Gordon, *Macroeconomics,* 3rd ed. (Boston: Little, Brown, and Company, 1984), Table B–2. The Gordon figure is for the second quarter of 1983.

---

rate hypothesis, the $SRAS_{100}$ curve must intersect the *LRAS* curve at the price level 100 because at this point the actual price level equals the expected price level.

Whether or not firms increase their output as the price level rises unexpectedly from 100 to 105 depends upon their *perception* of the relationship between their selling prices and their costs. If selling prices rise more rapidly than costs (or even if firms only think this is happening), firms will increase production. If selling prices and costs rise at the same rate (and if firms correctly recognize this fact), firms will have no incentive to produce more.

Actual output can rise above y_n (by definition) only if the actual unemployment rate falls below the natural unemployment rate. When unanticipated inflation occurs, some workers are on contracts that stipulate fixed money wages. Other contracts may have been written with a lower inflation rate in mind. Firms may have negotiated to purchase material inputs at prices that do not escalate as fast as their selling prices. As long as some fixity in input costs is present, selling prices rise faster than costs during an unanticipated infla-

tion, and production is raised as business profitability improves. (See Example 1.)

Individuals and businesses may be fooled by the unanticipated inflation. People who are out of work and looking for jobs will find that wages are rising beyond their expectations and will be tempted to accept the next job offer. Firms may begin to overestimate the tightness of the labor market and become more hesitant to fire or lay off workers. Firms may lower their requirements on worker quality and step up their hiring. The rise in employment is the other side of the coin of increasing output. Unemployment falls below the natural rate when output rises above the natural level. Thus, the short-run aggregate-supply curve to the right of the natural level of output is upward-sloping.

If the price level unexpectedly falls—say, from 100 to 95 in Figure 2—the firms perceive that their profitability is falling. Their workers may be on contracts calling for fixed or rising wages; they have negotiated the purchase of materials at fixed prices. Their selling prices are falling more rapidly than their costs, and they respond by producing less. When unemployed workers see wages starting to fall, they are less inclined to accept job offers. Firms become more willing to fire unsatisfactory workers and to lay off workers not currently needed. In sum, unanticipated deflation should cause less real output to be produced. To the left of the natural level of output, the short-run aggregate supply curve is also positively sloped.

SHORT-RUN EQUILIBRIUM

Short-run macroeconomic equilibrium occurs where the *SRAS* and *AD* curves intersect.

> **Short-run macroeconomic equilibrium** occurs at that price level at which aggregate quantity demanded and short-run aggregate quantity supplied are equal.

If the economy were to attempt to settle at a price level at which the aggregate quantity demanded exceeded the aggregate quantity supplied, the price level would rise and output would increase. If the economy tried to settle at a price level at which the aggregate quantity demanded fell short of the aggregate quantity supplied, the price level would drop and output would fall. Such adjustments would take place until the economy settled at a macroeconomic equilibrium where aggregate quantity demanded equaled aggregate quantity supplied (see Figure 3).

Shifts in Short-Run Aggregate Supply

The short-run aggregate-supply curve shows what happens to output as the price level rises and falls in an unanticipated manner. It suggests that the quantity of output supplied tends to rise and fall with the price level in the short run. Like the aggregate-demand curve, factors other than the price level can affect short-run aggregate supply. When these factors change, the short-run aggregate-supply curve will shift. Any event that changes the price level at which the business sector will be willing to supply a given volume of real output will change short-run aggregate supply (cause a leftward or rightward shift in *SRAS*). Events that change aggregate supply include supply shocks, the expectation of inflation, changes in productivity, and changes in labor-market conditions.

Figure 3   Short-Run Macroeconomic Equilibrium

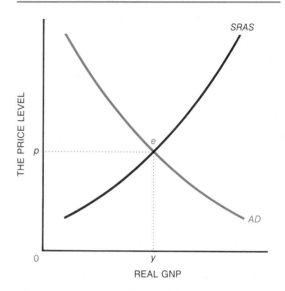

Short-run macroeconomic equilibrium occurs where the *SRAS* and *AD* curves intersect. If the price level is below *p*, aggregate quantity demanded exceeds aggregate quantity supplied; if the price level is above *p*, aggregate quantity demanded falls short of aggregate quantity supplied.

Supply shocks, such as the creation of a monopoly over a natural resource (like OPEC's acquisition of control over crude-oil exports in the early 1970s), poor worldwide harvests, or natural disasters, reduce aggregate supply. When supply shocks raise the input costs of businesses, they raise the price level at which businesses are willing to supply a given volume of real output. At higher energy prices or higher raw-material prices, business firms as a whole are willing to supply less output at the same price level as before.

If households and businesses raise their *inflationary expectations,* businesses will be less willing to supply output at the prevailing price level, and aggregate supply will decline.

When *increases in productivity* due to technological innovations or improved management techniques lower the unit costs of producing output, firms are prepared to supply more output at the same price as before.

Changing labor-market conditions—such as a change in the willingness of workers to supply la-

Figure 4   Supply Shocks

(a) An Adverse Supply Shock

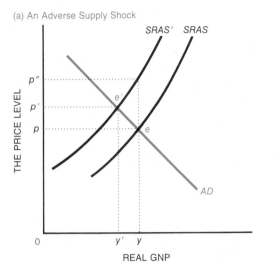

(b) A Beneficial Supply Shock

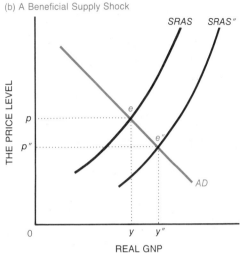

The economy is initially operating at point *e* in panel (a). Aggregate supply is reduced (from *SRAS* to *SRAS'*) by disasterous harvests. At the original price level, *p,* aggregate demand exceeds aggregate supply, and prices begin to rise. As prices rise, the economy moves along *AD* (from *e* to *e'*) until a new equilibrium is established at *e'*. Supply shocks reduce real output and raise prices in the short run.

Panel (b) shows a beneficial supply shock. The economy is initially operating at point *e,* where the *AD* and *SRAS* curves intersect. Due to a good harvest or a reduction in the price of imported oil, the *SRAS* curve shifts right to *SRAS''*. The short-run equilibrium price level falls from *p* to *p''* and real output rises from *y* to *y''*.

bor at different wage rates or an influx of foreign labor—can cause aggregate-supply shifts as well.

Later chapters focus on supply shocks and inflationary expectations in shifting short-run aggregate-supply curves. Changes in productivity and labor-market conditions tend to occur slowly over time and in a more regular pattern. In a short-run setting, supply shocks and inflationary expectations have more significant effects on prices and output.

Supply Shocks

Figure 4 shows the effect of an adverse supply shock on prices and real output in the short run. The economy is initially operating at point (the intersection of *SRAS* and *AD*), where the level of output is *y* and price level is *p*. People expect this situation to continue into the future, but bad harvests occur on a worldwide basis or the price of imports (such as oil) rise sharply. The prices of foods, fibers, feed, and fuel rise. Because these price increases represent cost increases to producers, the short-run aggregate-supply curve in panel

(a) shifts left from *SRAS* to *SRAS'*. Firms will cut back on employment unless prices rise to *p''*. But at the price level *p''* aggregate quantity supplied exceeds aggregate quantity demanded. A higher price level reduces the aggregate quantity demanded as the real-balance and interest-rate effects take hold. The new equilibrium price level is *p'* and the new equilibrum GNP is *y'*. Thus, the end result of an **adverse supply shock** is one-time inflation (a shift from *p* to *p'*) and smaller real output.

A similar supply-side inflation occurred when OPEC raised the price of oil in 1973–74 and 1980–81. The fall in real output was accompanied by a reduction in employment (an increase in unemployment rates).

Panel (b) of Figure 4 illustrates the effects of a **beneficial supply shock.** The economy is initially operating at point *e,* where the output level is *y* and the price level is *p*. Good harvests occur on a worldwide basis, or the prices of imports fall. Because these price decreases represent cost decreases to producers, the short-run aggregate-supply curve will shift right from *SRAS* to *SRAS''*.

The price level will now fall from p to p'' and real GNP will increase from y to y''. A beneficial supply shock will cause supply-side deflation and raise employment (or lower the unemployment rate).

> An **adverse supply shock** occurs when the short-run aggregate supply curve shifts to the left, causing the price level to rise and output to fall.

> A **beneficial supply shock** occurs when the short-run aggregate-supply curve shifts to the right, causing the price level to fall and output to rise.

Shifts in Aggregate Demand

Figure 5 illustrates the effects of an increase in aggregate demand on real output and prices. The economy is initially producing below the natural level of output, at point e. Thus, the SRAS curve intersects the AD curve to the left of LRAS. An increase in government spending shifts the aggregate demand curve from AD to AD'. At the initial price level, p, aggregate quantity demanded exceeds short-run aggregate quantity supplied, so the price level begins to rise. As the price level rises, there is a movement up the short-run supply curve, SRAS, from e to e'. The new equilibrium is established at e', where the economy is producing output y_n at price level p'.

The effect of the increase in aggregate demand in the short run is that real output has risen to the natural level, unemployment has fallen to the natural rate, and prices have risen. For an economy operating below the natural level of output, an increase in aggregate demand can raise output to the natural level but at a higher price level.

Inflationary and Deflationary Gaps

Macroeconomic equilibrium occurs where the SRAS and AD curves intersect. In the short-run, because these curves are independent, the equilibrium level of output may be larger or smaller than the natural level of output. The equilibrium output, y, in panel (a) of Figure 6 falls short of the natural level of output, y_n. In panel (b), the equilibrium level of output, y', exceeds y_n. Differences between current output and y_n indicate a **deflationary gap** or an **inflationary gap**.

Figure 5   The Effect of an Increase in Aggregate Demand on Short-Run Equilibrium

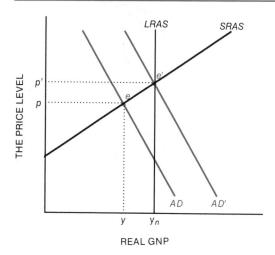

The economy is initially producing y at the price level p. Government expenditures increase and aggregate demand shifts from AD to AD'. As prices begin to rise, the economy moves along its short-run aggregate-supply curve until a new equilibrium is established at e'. The increase in aggregate demand raises output and prices and lowers the unemployment rate—in this case, to the natural rate.

> A **deflationary gap** exists if the equilibrium level of output falls short of the natural level of output.

> An **inflationary gap** exists if the equilibrium level of output exceeds the natural level of output.

If a deflationary gap exists, as in panel (a), the unemployment rate exceeds the natural rate of unemployment. Because the SRAS curve interesects the LRAS at the expected price level, it is clear that the equilibrium price level falls short of the expected price level. For example, in panel (a) the anticipated price level is 100 and the actual price level is 90.

On the other hand, if an inflationary gap exists, as in panel (b), the unemployment rate falls short of the natural rate of unemployment. The short-run equilibrium price level must now exceed the expected price level. For example, in panel (b) the actual price level is 110 and the expected price level is 100. (See Example 3.)

Figure 6   Inflationary and Deflationary Gaps

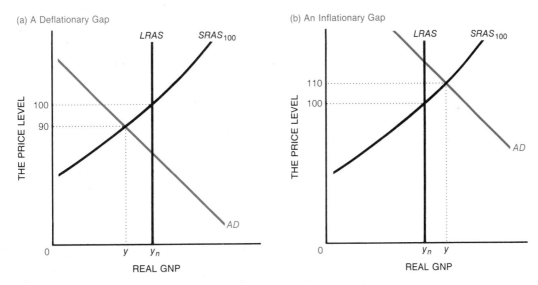

(a) A Deflationary Gap

(b) An Inflationary Gap

Panel (a) shows a deflationary gap. The *expected* price level is 100. The $SRAS_{100}$ curve interesects the AD curve to the *left* of $LRAS$ and y is less than y_n, the natural output level. The equilibrium price level is 90.

Panel (b) shows an inflationary gap. The *expected* price level is 100. The $SRAS_{100}$ curve intersects the AD curve to the *right* of $LRAS$ and y exceeds y_n. The equilibrium price level is 110.

The next two chapters will show how fiscal or monetary policy can be used to remove an inflationary or deflationary gap. Fiscal policy (Chapter 13) regulates aggregate demand by changing government spending and taxes. Monetary policy (Chapter 12) regulates aggregate demand by controlling the money supply.

A rightward shift in the AD curve could remove a deflationary gap (see Figure 5). Similarly, a leftward shift in the AD curve could remove an inflationary gap. Such activist policies will be studied in detail in Chapters 12 and 13. The question we now seek to answer is: What happens to output, prices, and employment in the long run if the government does *nothing?*

LONG-RUN EQUILIBRIUM: THE SELF-CORRECTING MECHANISM

Up to this point, we have discussed shifts in short-run aggregate-supply or aggregate-demand curves and their short-run effects on prices, real output, and unemployment. Shifts in short-run aggregate supply and aggregate demand can cause an inflationary or deflationary gap.

The *short run* is a period of time so short that households and businesses cannot adjust their expectations to the change in the inflation rate. The short-run aggregate-supply curve is upward-sloping simply because economic agents have not fully anticipated the change in prices. In our examples, economic agents initially expected the prevailing price level to continue into the future. Unanticipated inflation caught workers off guard with wage contracts that failed to protect them from the unanticipated inflation. Business firms had contracts for the purchase of inputs at prices that were rising less rapidly than selling prices. Moreover, some people were simply fooled by the unanticipated inflation. Firms were fooled into thinking that prices were rising more rapidly than costs. Unemployed workers were fooled into thinking that their real wage offers were improving. Other workers were fooled into working longer hours. Thus, *in the short run, people are subject to a certain amount of money illusion.*

Abraham Lincoln once noted that you can fool all the people some of the time and some of the people all of the time but that you can't fool all of the people all the time. Once people are able to anticipate inflation, the short-run supply effects

Example 3   Inflationary and Deflationary Gaps: 1929 to 1984

As Example 2 demonstrated, there is disagreement about what unemployment rate represents the natural rate of unemployment for any particular year. But the range of disagreement typically falls within a couple of percentage points. Moreover, the natural rate tends to change slowly, while the actual unemployment rate can vary sharply from one period to the next. To determine trends in inflationary and deflationary gaps, one must be able to compare the actual unemployment rate with the natural rate of unemployment. A *deflationary gap* is present if the actual unemployment rate is above the natural rate. An *inflationary gap* is present when the actual unemployment rate is below the natural rate. The accompanying figure shows Robert Gordon's estimates of inflationary and deflationary gaps from 1929 to 1984. Economists may disagree with some of Gordon's estimates of the natural rate, but most would agree with the

general trends shown in the figure. The color shaded areas are periods of deflationary gaps. The grey shaded areas are periods of inflationary gaps. The figure shows the enormous deflationary gaps of the Great Depression, which persisted from 1930 to 1942. The World War II era was a period of inflationary gaps as most able-bodied males were drawn into military service, creating exceptionally low unemployment. The 1950s and late 1960s were periods of inflationary gaps, while the early 1960s and the period after 1975 were characterized by deflationary gaps. ■

Source: Robert Gordon, "Inflation, Flexible Exchange Rates, and the Natural Rate of Unemployment," in Martin N. Bailey, ed., *Workers, Jobs, and Inflation* (Washington, D.C.: Brookings, 1982) and Gordon, *Macroeconomics,* 3rd ed. (Boston: Little, Brown, and Company, 1984), Table B–1.

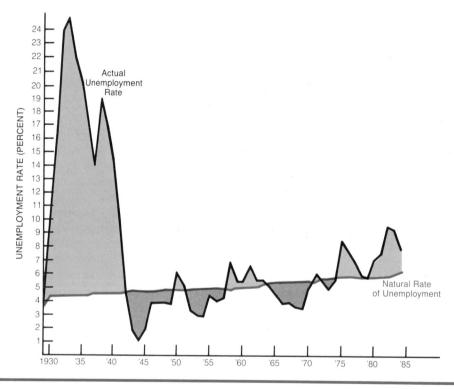

studied above tend to disappear. In the long run, there is no money illusion.

Chapter 5 showed that there is a big difference between reactions to anticipated and unanticipated inflation. Once the inflation comes to be antici-

pated, people are able to protect themselves from the inflation "tax": workers are no longer willing to accept money-wage contracts that do not protect them from anticipated inflation; business firms refuse to supply goods on fixed long-term contracts in an inflationary environment. Long-term building leases have become a thing of the past; instead, they are renegotiated at short intervals.

The following sections demonstrate how the economy moves automatically to the natural level of output when people have time to adjust inflationary expectations because a *self-correcting mechanism* removes deflationary and inflationary gaps.

The Automatic Removal of a Deflationary Gap

The adjustment to long-run equilibrium for a deflationary gap is illustrated in Figure 7. The economy is initially at point *e,* where the output level, *y,* is less than the natural level, y_n. In other words, the unemployment rate exceeds the natural rate of unemployment. Monetary and fiscal policies are not changing, so aggregate demand does not change.

When there is a deflationary gap, actual prices fall short of expected prices. As old wage bargains expire, firms will be able to pay workers lower wages because unemployment is high and real wages look high to workers covered by old contracts. Thus, wages and costs will drift downward. When costs fall, business firms will begin to cut prices. The short-run aggregate-supply curve will eventually shift to the right from *SRAS* to *SRAS'* as the expected price level falls. Falling prices will cause the economy to move down along the established negatively sloped aggregate-demand curve, *AD.* Falling prices raise the real value of financial assets (stimulating consumption) and falling interest rates stimulate investment. The economy moves from point *e* toward point *e'.* As long as the economy's output is less than y_n, prices will continue to fall and move the economy closer and closer to y_n. This process stops when the economy is producing y_n at price level *p',* where the actual price level equals the expected price level.

This self-correcting long-run adjustment to the natural level of output takes place with constant monetary and fiscal policies. The economy adjusts by moving down a fixed aggregate-demand curve, not by altering monetary or fiscal policy to shift the aggregate-demand curve.

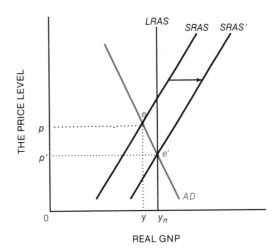

Figure 7   A Self-Correcting Deflationary Gap

Initially, the economy's short-run aggregate-supply *(SRAS)* curve intersects the aggregate-demand *(AD)* curve at e. At this point, y is less than y_n, and the unemployment rate exceeds the natural rate. Wages fall and prices fall. As prices fall, the economy moves down AD toward e' even though there have been no changes in monetary or fiscal policy. The short-run aggregate-supply curve's move to the right causes this movement along the AD curve. As the inflation rate drops, individuals and businesses adjust downward their inflationary expectations and become willing to supply more at the same price level as before. The long-run equilibrium occurs at the intersection of the AD and SRAS' curves where the natural level of output, y_n, is produced. At this point (e'), there is no longer any tendency for prices to fall further. It is the fall in the price level from p to p' that brings about this automatic adjustment.

> As long as the unemployment rate remains below the natural rate, falling wages and prices will in the long run move the economy to the natural rate of unemployment. This adjustment is self-correcting; it takes place without the need for changes in monetary or fiscal policy.

The self-correcting mechanism works because the aggregate-demand curve is negatively sloped and eventually intersects the *LRAS* curve. For the economy to move down the aggregate-demand curve, the short-run aggregate-supply cuve must be shifting to the right (see Figure 7). As people and firms experience declining prices and wages, they adjust their inflationary expectations downward. Firms are willing to supply more output at the same price level as before when they expect less inflation. In **long-run equilibrium,** the short-run aggregate-supply curve is *SRAS,* which intersects *AD* at the natural level of output.[2] Shifts in aggregate supply and aggregate demand may cause the economy to produce more or less than y_n in the short run, but in the long run, the economy should gravitate toward producing y_n.

> **Long-run macroeconomic equilibrium** is the equilibrium of price level and aggregate output that occurs when aggregate demand equals long-run aggregate supply.

The Automatic Removal of an Inflationary Gap

The self-correcting mechanism can also eliminate an inflationary gap without benefit of changes in monetary and fiscal policy. Consider the inflationary gap in Figure 8. The initial level of output is y and the price level is p. When there is an inflationary gap, actual prices exceed expected prices. As old wage bargains expire, workers bargain for higher wages because unemployment is low and real wages look small to workers covered by past contracts. Thus, wages and costs will drift upward. When costs rises, business firms will begin to raise prices. The short-run aggregate-supply curve will begin to shift left. In long-run equilibrium, the *SRAS* curve shifts to *SRAS'* as the expected price level rises. Increasing prices will cause the economy to move up the negatively sloped aggregate-demand curve, *AD*. The economy is in long-run equilibrium when the level of output is y_n and the actual price level equals the expected price level.

There is a symmetry between the automatic removal of an inflationary gap and the automatic removal of a deflationary gap. The elimination of deflationary gaps requires falling wages and prices, while inflationary gaps require rising wages and prices. Generally speaking, wages and prices are far more flexible in the upward direction than in the downward direction. Workers and business firms do not like accepting lower wages

and prices even if those cuts do not represent real wage or price cuts. On the other hand, workers and firms are eager to raise money wages and prices to prevent real wages or prices from falling or even to increase real wages or prices. A wage cut may cause a strike or extended negotiation. A wage increase will be praised.

Does the Self-Correcting Mechanism Really Work?

The self-correcting mechanism carries a soothing message: in the long run, economies will automatically return to the natural rate of unemployment (full employment). The theory of the self-correcting mechanism does not tell us how quickly this return will occur (in a few months, in five years?), but it does appear to rule out long-run economic disasters such as an ever-worsening unemployment rate.[3] It recognizes that economies will be buffeted from all sides—by supply shocks, by fluctuations in investment spending, by accelerating government spending—but that movements in wages and prices will eventually restore the economy to the natural rate of unemployment without any assistance from government policymakers.

What evidence is there that the self-correcting-mechanism actually works? Chapter 9 explained that the self-correcting mechanism did not appear to be working with acceptable speed during the Great Depression. This does not mean that the self-correcting mechanism would not have eventually worked—just that it was working too slowly. The most convincing evidence that a self-correcting mechanism exists comes from the long sweep of recorded economic history. Although reliable statistics on unemployment rates from the late 19th through the early 20th centuries are hard to produce, the available evidence suggests that there was no long-term trend in unemployment rates from the 1880s to the Great Depression. Unemployment rates fluctuated from year to year, but they seemed to return to a fairly "normal" unemployment rate. In France, for example, the unemployment rate ranged from a low of 4.7 percent to a high of 10.2 percent from 1895 to 1913,

---

2. Our examples are of a noninflationary economy that begins to experience inflation. The self-correcting mechanism then restores this economy back to its noninflationary equilibrium. We could just as well have dealt with an economy experiencing a constant rate of inflation. Demand or supply shifts then cause the rate of inflation to accelerate, and the self-correcting mechanism restores the economy back to its original constant rate of inflation.

---

3. The socialist philosopher Karl Marx predicted that capitalism would experience a long-run rise in unemployment that would contribute to its overthrow.

Figure 8   A Self-Correcting Inflationary Gap

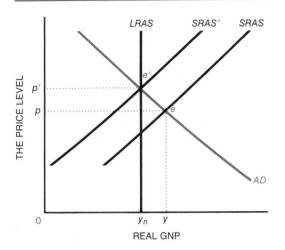

Initially, the economy's short-run aggregate-supply *(SRAS)* curve intersects the aggregate-demand *(AD)* curve at *e*. At this point, there is an inflationary gap because *y* exceeds y_n and unemployment is less than the natural rate. Wages rise and prices rise. In the long run, the *SRAS* curve shifts left to reflect the higher level of expected prices. The long-run equilibrium occurs at the intersection of the *AD* and *SRAS'* curves where the natural level of output, y_n, is produced and where the *AD* curve intersects the *LRAS* curve.

yet it appeared to return after such fluctuations to a 6.5 percent unemployment rate. The German unemployment rate ranged from 0.2 percent to 7.2 percent between 1887 and 1922, yet always seemed to return to an unemployment rate of around 2 percent. From 1887 to 1920, the English unemployment rate ranged from 0.4 percent to 7.8 percent, but seemed to return to an unemployment rate of around 3 percent. From 1890 to 1929, there was no discernible trend in the U.S. unemployment rate, which ranged from a low of 1.4 percent to a high of 18.4 percent and tended to return to an unemployment rate in the 4 to 5 percent range.[4]

The late 19th and early 20th centuries were periods of all kinds of supply and demand shocks—wars, investment booms and busts, shifts of employment from agriculture to industry and services, stock-market binges, major technological changes, new resource discoveries. It was also

---

4. These figures are from B. Mitchell, *European Historical Statistics, 1750–1970* (New York: Columbia University Press, 1975), Table C–2.

a period of *laissez-faire* macroeconomic policy. Governments did not attempt consciously to use monetary and fiscal policy to eliminate inflationary or deflationary gaps. The data from the 19th and early 20th centuries is consistent with the theory of the long-run self-correcting mechanism.

According to the natural-rate hypothesis, in the long run, the level of real output or the rate of unemployment cannot be controlled by monetary or fiscal policy. There is surprising degree of consensus among modern economists about the natural-rate hypothesis. What divides economists is how quickly and with what social costs the self-correcting mechanism operates. If inflationary expectations adjust slowly, if wages and prices tend to be sticky, if the real-balance and interest-rate effects are weak, progress from a rate of unemployment above the natural rate may be slow and painful.

Some economists think that reliance should be placed on the self-correcting mechanism; others feel that the government should take an active role. The following two chapters examine the benefits and costs of using monetary and fiscal policies.

Summary

1. Money wages and prices are more flexible in the long run than in the short run. Money-wage bargains are affected by unemployment rates and expected inflation. In the long run, all wages and prices are perfectly flexible upward or downward because in the long run all contracts will be renegotiated and there is no money illusion. The natural rate of unemployment can be sustained indefinitely without accelerating inflation or deflation. The natural level of real GNP is the real GNP that is produced when the economy is operating at the natural rate of unemployment. The long-run aggregate-supply *(LRAS)* curve is vertical at the natural rate of real GNP. The short-run aggregate-supply *(SRAS)* curve is upward-sloping and intersects the *LRAS* curve at the expected price level. The *SRAS* curve is upward-sloping because unanticipated increases in the price level relative to business costs encourage firms to produce more.

2.   Short-run macroeconomic equilibrium occurs where the aggregate-demand curve intersects the *SRAS* curve. Adverse supply shocks shift the *SRAS* curve leftward, raising prices and lowering real output. Beneficial supply shocks shift the *SRAS* curve rightward, lowering prices and raising real output. Monetary and fiscal policy can shift the aggregate-demand curve to the right or left to increase or decrease real output in the short run. A deflationary gap prevails if the short-run equilibrium real GNP falls short of the natural level. An inflationary gap prevails if short-run equilibrium real GNP exceeds the natural level. Long-run equilibrium occurs when the aggregate-demand curve interesects the *LRAS* curve.

3.   In the long run, there is a self-correcting mechanism that automatically removes an inflationary or deflationary gap. Deflation in the long run shifts the *SRAS* curve down until it intersects the *LRAS* curve at the long-run equilibrium price level. Inflation in the long run shifts the *SRAS* curve up until the long-run equilibrium is reached.

Key Terms

money illusion
natural rate of unemployment
natural level of real GNP (y_n)
long-run aggregate supply*(LRAS)*
short-run aggregate supply*(SRAS)*
natural-rate hypothesis
short-run macroeconomic equilibrium
adverse supply shock
beneficial supply shock
deflationary gap
inflationary gap
long-run macroeconomic equilibrium

Questions and Problems

1.   Why are wages and prices more inflexible in the short run than in the long run?

2.   Explain why in the long run wages and prices may be regarded as flexible in either the upward or the downward direction.

3.   Explain why the long-run aggregate-supply curve is vertical.

4.   Can actual unemployment be less than the natural rate of unemployment? How?

5.   How is the increase in the expected price level reflected in short-run aggregate supply?

6.   Explain why the *SRAS* curve is upward-sloping.

7.   What would happen to the slope of the *SRAS* curve if the workers in the economy were covered by fewer long-term wage contracts?

8.   How is the *SRAS* curve affected by each of the following events?
   a.   An increase in the expected price level.
   b.   An increase in the price level in the short run.
   c.   A reduction in the price of imported steel.
   d.   An increase in labor productivity.

9.   How is the *LRAS* curve affected by a change in the expected price level?

10.   Compare and contrast a short-run macroeconomic equilibrium to a long-run macroeconomic equilibrium?

11.   What does an inflationary gap imply about:
   a.   the unemployment rate?
   b.   the actual versus the expected price level?

12.   Explain how the self-correcting mechanism drives unemployment to the natural level. Can you think of any conditions under which the mechanism would not work?

13.   Is there any empirical evidence in support of the self-correcting mechanism?

Suggested Readings

Dornbusch, Rudiger and Stanley Fischer. *Macroeconomics,* 2nd ed. New York: McGraw-Hill, 1981, chap. 11.

Gordon, Robert J. *Macroeconomics,* 3rd ed. Boston, Mass.: Little, Brown and Co., 1984, chap. 6.

Maisel, Sherman. *Macroeconomics.* New York: W. W. Norton, 1982.

12

Monetary Policy

Chapter Preview

This chapter looks at how monetary policy can be used to reduce the inflationary and deflationary gaps discussed in the preceding chapter. It first describes the tools available to the Federal Reserve System for controlling the supply of money and then traces the Keynesian theory of the link between changes in the money supply and shifts in the aggregate-demand curve. The chapter later examines how the Fed's targets and goals of monetary policy have been and are now being set and evaluates the effectiveness of the Fed's monetary policy in achieving its goals. The theory of monetarism is introduced as a response to the limitations of monetary policy. The chapter closes with a discussion of the issue of Fed independence from the federal government.

As we learned in Chapter 7, one measure of the money supply is the sum of currency in circulation plus the checkable deposits and travelers checks the public holds in depository institutions, such as commercial banks and savings-and-loan associations. The above definition of money, known as M1, is quite narrow. A broader concept of money, M2, consists of M1 plus money-market deposit accounts, savings accounts, and small-denomination time deposits at all depository institutions. In 1985, M1 averaged around $570 billion while M2 averaged about $2,400 billion. ■

THE FEDERAL RESERVE SYSTEM'S CONTROL OVER THE MONEY SUPPLY

Chapter 8 explained how the money supply is determined by the actions of the Fed, the public, and the banking system. How closely can the Fed control the supply of money? To answer this question it is necessary to take another look at the Fed's main instruments of **monetary policy**. These main instruments are 1) open-market operations, 2) discount-rate changes, and 3) changes in reserve requirements.

> **Monetary policy** is the deliberate control of the money supply and, in some cases, credit conditions for the purpose of achieving macroeconomic goals, such as a certain level of unemployment or inflation.

Open-Market Operations

The Fed conducts open-market operations by buying or selling government securities. As explained later, when the government finances its deficits, it borrows by selling various kinds of IOUs. What is important here is that such IOUs (government securities) are held by both the Fed and by the public. If the Fed purchases government securities from the public, bank reserves are increased by a corresponding amount because the Fed pays for the government securities by issuing a check drawn on itself. The seller of the government security then deposits the check in his or her bank, thereby increasing bank reserves (or increasing currency in circulation if the seller of the government security withdraws some of the deposit in the form of currency). When the Fed sells some of its own government securities to the public, bank reserves are decreased by a corresponding amount because the buyer of the government security writes a check to the Fed, which receives payment from the buyer's bank by deducting the amount of the check from the bank's deposit with the Fed.

Recall that the *monetary base* is defined as the sum of currency in circulation and bank reserves. Thus, open-market operations directly affect the monetary base. Fed purchases of government securities increase the monetary base; Fed sales of government securities decrease the monetary base.

The chief advantage of open-market operations as a tool of monetary policy are:

1. Open-market operations give the Fed more precise control over the monetary base. By purchasing or selling $X of government securities, the Fed adds or subtracts exactly $X to or from the monetary base.
2. *Flexible* monetary control is possible through open-market operations because the Fed can buy or sell securities each day. The Fed can reverse itself if new information becomes available.

Thus, it is hardly surprising that the Fed relies more heavily on open-market operations than on any other tool of monetary control (See Example 1.)

The Setting of the Discount Rate

Recall from Chapter 8 that depository institutions, such as commercial banks and savings-and-loan associations, can borrow from the Fed at the *discount rate*. The amount that banks borrow from the Fed directly affects the monetary base. When banks borrow from the Fed, they are said to be using the "discount window." As depository institutions borrow more or less from the Fed, the monetary base increases or decreases. A key feature of the discount rate is that it is lower than bank lending rates. For example, in 1984 banks on the average charged their best customers 12 percent per year while they could borrow from the Fed at an average discount rate of 8.8 percent. Thus, banks normally have an economic incentive to borrow from the Fed and then lend those funds at a higher rate.

The Fed, of course, does not want depository institutions to make opportunistic use of their borrowing privileges. By administrative action, the amount banks can borrow at the discount window is limited to their seasonal borrowing needs or to help banks in financial trouble. The Fed takes a close look at depository institutions that use the discount window too frequently and can refuse to make loans. Nevertheless, the higher are market interest rates relative to the discount rate the greater is the incentive of depository institutions to borrow from the Fed.

In order to limit the incentive of depository institutions to use the discount window, the Fed attempts to keep the discount rate in line with market interest rates. As market interest rates rise or fall, the discount rate is raised or lowered.

Some have suggested that the discount rate can be used to indicate the Fed's future monetary policy. Increases in the discount rate are said to be indicative of tight monetary policy and decreases are said to suggest an easy monetary policy. Thus, discount-rate changes can have an *announcement effect* by letting people know what the Fed is doing. Economists are usually suspicious of this argument, however, because no one has yet shown that changes in the discount rate can be used to predict the future monetary base or money supply.

The Fed's use of the discount rate as a tool of monetary policy has been criticized by many economists. First, the availability of borrowing from the Fed reduces the Fed's control over the monetary base. If banks borrow when the Fed is interested in lowering the monetary base, the Fed must sell government bonds to offset such borrowing. Second, allowing banks to borrow at an interest rate less than the market interest rate amounts to a subsidy to those depository institutions. Generally speaking, the banks that avail themselves of the discount window are usually in financial trouble. Critics cannot understand why imprudently run banks should be subsidized.

Reserve-Requirement Policy

A *reserve requirement* is a rule that sets the minimum percentage of deposits a bank must keep on hand to back those liabilities. If reserve requirements are reduced, banks will increase loans and thereby increase the supply of money. As shown in Chapter 8, a change in reserves has a multiplied impact on the money supply. The lower is the required-reserve ratio of deposits to reserves that banks maintain, the higher is the multiplier. Thus, changes in reserve requiremnts are a potent tool of monetary policy.

The current policy of the Fed is to not use reserve-requirement changes as a tool of day-to-day monetary policy. Whatever can be achieved by changes in reserve requirements can also be achieved with more precision and flexibility by open-market operations, although the tool is availiable for wartime or other emergencies. Monetary experts do not dispute the Fed's rare use of reserve-requirement changes.

THE MONEY MULTIPLIER

When the monetary base increases, banks have a larger base on which to make loans. As loans increase, the money supply increases. If there were no drain of reserves into currency in circulation, and if the ratio of reserves to deposits was about 10 percent, a $1 increase in the monetary base would increase the money supply by approximately $10. As explained in chapter 8, the deposit multiplier equals $1/r$, where r is the reserve/deposit ratio.

In reality, an increase in the monetary base by $1 will not raise the money supply by $10. People hold their money balances in both checking accounts *and* currency. As the quantity of checking accounts expands, currency in circulation will also increase. Thus, as banks make loans out of additional reserves, some of those reserves will leak out into currency in circulation. If bank A received $1 in extra reserves as a result of a Fed open-market purchase, the money supply would rise by $1. When bank A then increases its loans by about $0.90, the money supply increases again by another $0.90 (as explained in Chapter 8). If the proceeds of this loan ended up entirely as currency in circulation, the process of money expansion would stop there. Thus, the money supply would increase by $1.90 as the result of a $1 open-market purchase. Consequently, the ratio of the money supply, M, to the monetary base, H, could under these extreme circumstances be either 10 or 1.9. What is the actual **money multiplier?** In February, 1985 the money supply was approximately $560 billion and the monetary base was about $200 billion, a ratio of 2.8. Thus, the money multiplier equalled 2.8 in 1985. As the above discussion shows, the money multiplier depends negatively on the reserve ratio and upon the ratio of currency in circulation to deposits.

The **money multiplier** is the ratio of the money supply, *M,* to the monetary base. *H*. If *k* is the ratio of currency in circulation to deposits, and *r* is the reserve/deposit ratio, the money multiplier is

$$M/H = \frac{1 + k}{r + k}.$$

The money-multiplier formula[1] informs us about the determinants of the money supply. Since

$$M = \frac{H(1 + k)}{r + k},$$

the money supply *increases:*

1. whenever the monetary base (*H*) increases,
2. whenever the currency/deposit ratio, *k,* falls,[2] and
3. whenever the reserve/deposit ratio, *r,* falls.

The money supply *decreases* for exactly the opposite reasons.

Clearly, the money supply is determined by a combination of forces. The size of the monetary base can be changed by the Fed without much difficulty by varying the size of open-market operations. But the currency/deposit ratio depends upon the public's willingness to hold currency relative to checking deposits. The reserve/deposit ratio is primarily a function of the required-reserve ratio, but because banks can hold excess reserves it partly depends on the desire of banks to hold excess reserves. This factor is relatively unimportant, however, compared to changes in the cur-

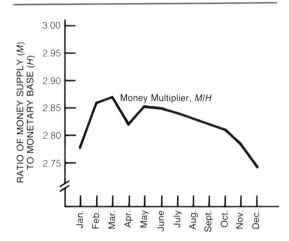

Figure 1   The Money Multiplier, 1983

The money multiplier (*M/H*) is the ratio of the money supply (*M*) to the monetary base (*H*) and varies considerably from month to month. For example, in 1983 the money multiplier ranged from a low of 2.74 in December to a high of 2.87 in March.

Source: *Economic Report of the President,* 1984.

rency/deposit ratio. The money multiplier (and the money supply) responds much more strongly to a given percentage change in the currency/deposit ratio than to the same percentage change in the reserve/deposit ratio.[3] (See Example 2.)

Figure 1 shows the money multiplier on a month-to-month basis for the year 1983. It varied between a low of 2.74 (in December) to a high of 2.87 (in March). From January to February, the money multiplier increased from 2.78 to 2.86. While this appears to be a small change, it is in fact a large change. Had the monetary base remained the same, such an increase in the money multiplier would have resulted in a nearly 3 percent increase in the money supply within one month. Many economists think a 3 percent increase in the money supply is sufficient for an entire *year.* At the rate of 3 percent per month, the money supply would increase by more than 36

---

1. The money multiplier is derived in Chapter 8, footnote 5. An alternative derivation is given here. Remembering that the money supply (*M*) equals currency in circulation (*C*) plus checking deposits (*D*) and that the money base (*H*) equals reserves (*R*) plus *C:*

$$M/H = \frac{(C + D)}{(R + C)}$$

Dividing both numerator and denominator by *D* and noting $k = C/D$ and $r = R/D$,

$$M/H = \frac{(C/D + D/D)}{(R/D + C/D)} = \frac{(1 + k)}{r + k}.$$

2. In the equation $M = H(1 + k)/(r + k)$, *k* is in both the numerator and denominator. In the numerator, *k* is added to unity. In the denominator, *k* is added to a fraction (*r*). Therefore, a given reduction in *k* will affect the denominator proportionally more than the numerator. Therefore, when *k* falls, *M* rises; when *k* rises, *M* falls.

3. For example, in 1984 the currency/deposit ratio (*k*) was about 0.4, and the reserve/deposit ratio was about 0.1 resulting in a money multiplier of $M/H = (1 + 0.4)/(0.1 + 0.4) = 2.8$. If the currency/deposit ratio fell by exactly one half, the money multiplier would increase from 2.8 to 4 [= (1 + 0.2)/(0.1 + 0.2)] But if *k* remained at 0.4 while the reserve/deposit ratio (*r*) fell by one half to $r = 0.05$, the money multiplier would increase from 2.8 to only 3.11 [= (1 + .4)/(.05 + .4)].

Figure 2   Growth Rates of the Money Supply and the Monetary Base, August 1982 to October 1984

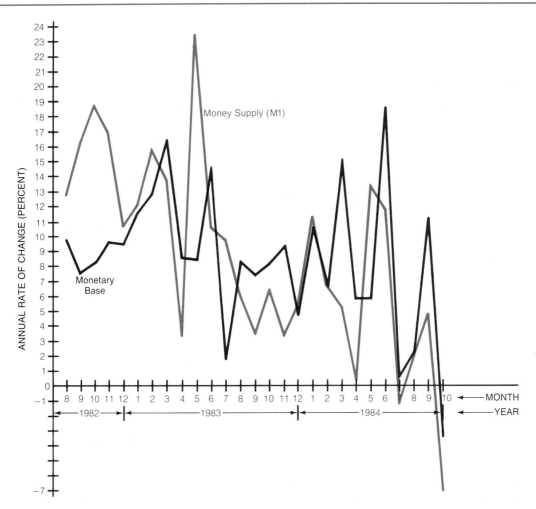

This graph shows the monthly variations in the annual rates of change in the money supply and in the monetary base. While the two move together in general, the month-to-month deviations reflect the short-run instability of the money multiplier.

Source: Federal Reserve Bank of St. Louis.

percent per year! The conclusion seems inescapable: short-run, unpredictable changes in the money multiplier prevent the Fed from exercising precise short-run control over the money supply.

Unpredictable changes in the money multiplier from month to month reduce the ability of the Fed to control the money supply from month to month.

Figure 2 shows the percentage rate (on an annual basis) of change in the monetary base and the money supply (defined as M1) on a month-to-month basis from late 1982 to late 1984. The black line shows the change in the monetary base. The color line shows the change in the money supply. Notice that over the entire period the two move together rather closely. But in any given month the two measures can diverge considerably. For example, in October 1982 the Fed be-

Example 1   The Open-Market Room of the New York Fed

Open-market operations are conducted at the New York Federal Reserve Bank. The nerve center of the New York Fed is the open-market room. Instead of the usual Fed opulence, the open-market room has formica-top tables and vinyl furniture. The room has a blackboard, covering an entire wall, that is about one fourth the size of a basketball court. TV monitors display the latest Federal funds rate, and that rate is duly recorded into one of the hundreds of squares filling the blackboard.

The open-market room routinely carries out purchases or sales of $1 billion or more in government securities. To raise interest rates, the Fed's traders begin to phone various government securities brokers for bids. If the Federal funds rate is falling, and the Fed does nothing to stop it, the Fed's inaction will announce to people intimately associated with the government-securities market that the Fed may be following an easier monetary policy. Thus, by not doing anything, the Fed may well indicate future policy stances. If the Fed wants to stop a decline in the Federal funds rate, the trading room becomes a beehive of activity: telephones directly connected to more than three dozen dealers in government securities begin ringing off the wall as brokers bid on the Fed's sale of government securities. What the Fed is doing is, therefore, known throughout the market for government securities. ■

Source: Winston Williams, "The Inaction That Makes Things Happen," *New York Times,* December 30, 1984.

gan to increase the rate of growth in the monetary base. From October 1982 to March 1983, the growth rate of the monetary base increased from 8 percent per year to 16 percent per year. But from October 1982 to December 1982 the rate of growth in the money supply fell from an annual rate of about 19 percent to an annual rate of about 11 percent. The rate of growth in the money supply did not begin to increase until January 1983. In other words, there was a three-month *lag* between the Fed's action on the monetary base and the resulting change in the money supply!

The relationship between the growth of the monetary base and the growth of the money supply is flexible, at least in the short run.[4] There can be lags or very rapid responses. In late 1982 and early 1983, the money supply responded to a change in the monetary base with a lag, but Figure 2 shows that in late 1984 the monetary base and the money supply moved together in nearly perfect harmony without any lag. Our discussion of the money multiplier and the data in Figure 2 suggest the following conclusions:

---

4. In early 1984 the Fed instituted a measure that may have substantially increased its short-run control over the money supply, but it is too early to appraise the new policy. Prior to January 1984, reserve requirements in any given two-week period were based on the deposits of banks in the previous two-week period. Now reserve requirements are imposed contemporaneously: depository institutions in any two-week period must maintain reserves corresponding to deposits in that period.

The Fed does not have direct control over the money supply. It can control only the monetary base. The money supply itself will depend on 1) the reserve deposit ratio that banks hold, which depends in part on the reserve requirements imposed by the Fed as well as on the excess reserves desired by depository institutions, and 2) the public's desired currency/deposit ratio. The Fed's short-run (month-to-month) control is less effective than its long-run (year-to-year) control.

KEYNESIAN MONETARY POLICY

The income/expenditure model pioneered by Keynes viewed the role of money much differently from the classical quantity theorists, whose views were summarized in Chapter 7. The classical economists believed that the supply of money affected the level of money expenditures directly. With velocity (V) constant and the economy tending to operate automatically at full employment, the equation of exchange ($MV = PQ$) showed that aggregate expenditures rise at the same rate as the money supply (M). However, classical theorists did not believe that the quantity of money had any effect on real GNP or employment because of the natural tendency for economies to operate at full employment. Increases in money supply would translate into proportionate increases in the price level.

Keynes viewed the link between the money supply and desired aggregate expenditures in a different light. He rejected the two classical notions of fixed velocity and full employment. Keynes felt that velocity could fluctuate unpredictably, as could real GNP; therefore, he believed the direct link between the money supply (M) and aggregate expenditures (PQ) was weak and unstable.

Instead, Keynes proposed an indirect link between the money supply (M) and real GNP (Y). This indirect relationship would operate through the effect of money supply on interest rates. By affecting real investment and perhaps even real consumption expenditures, changes in the interest rate would have an indirect effect on real output.

In the Keynesian model, monetary policy affects output *indirectly* through interest rates.

The following sections will trace these indirect linkages between money and output, starting with the relationship between money and interest rates.

Bond Prices and Interest Rates

The financial pages of the daily newspaper often contain the descriptions of interest rates and bond prices that sound something like the following: "Bond prices drifted lower yesterday as interest rates moved up for the second day in a row. Last week bond prices were higher and interest rates lower." As such statements suggest, there is an inverse relationship between bond prices and interest rates.

A *bond* is a promise to pay future dollars. The issuer of the bond promises to deliver a certain number of dollars at certain dates in the future. Thus, bonds promise a stream of future returns. For example, the simplest bond is the famous 3-month Treasury bill (called a *T-bill*). The U.S. Treasury promises to pay the face amount—$1,000—of the bill in 3 months. The price of the T-bill will be some discount from $1,000; otherwise, the buyer would earn no interest. If the price of the bill were $985, the buyer would earn $15 ÷ $1,000 = 1.5 percent interest over 3

months, or 6 percent per year (there are four 3-month periods in a year, so the annual rate of 6 percent is four times the 3-month rate of 1.5 percent). If the interest rate increased to 12 percent, the buyer would pay only $970 for the T-bill ($30 ÷ $1,000 = 3 percent; 4 × 3 percent = 12 percent). Clearly, the interest rate on a T-bill rises if the price of the T-bill falls (and vice versa).

The same relationship between bond price and interest rate holds for any bond, only the calculations are harder if bonds pay interest periodically over several years. Whatever the case, the lower is the price of the bond today, the greater is the return the investor is making because the bond specifies fixed dollar payments in the future.

Since bonds promise fixed dollar payments in the future, the lower is the current price of the bonds, the higher is the interest rate yielded. Similarly, the higher is the current price of bonds, the lower is the interest rate.

When the financial section of the newspaper talks about a bond-market *rally* (bond prices rising rapidly), one knows that interest rates are falling. When the newspaper talks about the bond market being *bearish* (bond prices falling), one knows that interest rates are rising.

Given the relationship between bond prices and interest rates, Fed open-market operations can have a direct impact on interest rates. When the Fed purchases government securities, the increase in demand for those bonds will drive up their prices and, thus, lower interest rates. When the Fed sells government securities, the increase in the supply of those bonds will drive down their prices and, thus, raise interest rates. A similar phenomenon occurs if banks purchase or sell government securities. If banks expand the money supply by buying government securities, bond prices will rise and interest rates will fall. If banks contract the money supply by selling government securities that they own, bond prices will fall and interest rates will rise.

Interest Rates and Money Demand

The exact impact of changes in the money supply on interest rates depends on the responsiveness of the quantity of money demanded to the rate of interest. The Keynesian view of interest-rate de-

Figure 3   The Demand and Supply of Money and the Interest Rate

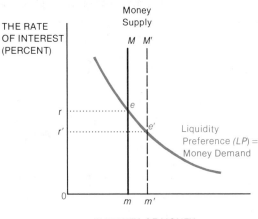

The money-demand curve, or *liquidity-preference curve,* has a negative slope. The amount of money demanded by the economy is greater at low rates of interest than at high rates of interest because the interest rate is the opportunity cost of holding money. The supply of money is determined by monetary authorities. The market interest rate (*r*) will be the equilibrium rate at which the quantity of money demanded (*m*) equals the quantity of money supplied. There will be an excess supply of money as the interest rate exceeds the equilibrium rate or an excess demand for money as the interest rate falls short of the equilibrium rate. As monetary authorities increase the supply of money from *m* to *m'*, the interest rate falls from *r* to *r'*, *ceteris paribus.*

Figure 4   The Effect of Interest-Rate Changes on Investment

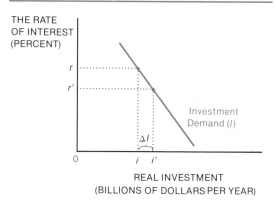

More loanable funds are demanded for capital investment at lower rates of interest than at higher rates of interest, *ceteris paribus.* Any monetary policy that lowers the interest rate will stimulate investment, *ceteris paribus.*

termination is called the **liquidity-preference theory.**

> According to the **liquidity-preference theory,** the opportunity cost of holding money—a completely liquid asset—is the interest sacrificed, and the interest rate is determined by the supply of and demand for money.

Cash in one's pocket earns no interest. Money in a checking account earns little or no interest. The higher is the opportunity cost of holding money, the lower is the quantity demanded. Therefore, as argued in Chapter 8, the money-demand curve (the demand curve for liquidity) will have a negative slope relative to the interest rate. At high interest rates, the opportunity cost of holding money is high, and the quantity of money demanded will be low. At low interest rates, the opportunity cost is low, so the quantity of money demanded will be greater.

The Demand for Money.   Figure 3 shows a representative money-demand curve. The money-demand curve is also called a *liquidity-preference curve* because people are demanding liquidity when they demand money. The liquidity-preference curve is like any other demand curve in that the quantity demanded (money) is inversely related to the commodity's price (the interest rate). Like other demand curves, there are a number of demand factors that are held constant, which will be discussed later. The other factors, as we will later see, play an important role in interest-rate determination.

The Supply of Money.   The market rate of interest is established as that rate at which the quantity of money demanded equals the quantity of money supplied. In Figure 3, the initial money supply is represented by the vertical line, *M.*

At interest rates above the equilibrium rate (*r*), the quantity of money supplied will exceed the quantity of money demanded. When there is an excess supply of money, people and firms will find credit easier to obtain; as the supply of credit is increased interest rates will be driven down. If the interest rate is less than the equilibrium rate (*r*), there will be an excess demand for money, and the interest rate will rise. In other words, if there is an excess supply of money, people will buy bonds and drive interest rates *down* as bond prices *rise*. If there is an excess demand for money, people will sell bonds and drive interest rates *up* as bond prices *fall*.

Controlling the Interest Rate.
According to the simple liquidity-preference theory, monetary authorities can control interest rates by means of their control of the supply of money. By increasing the money supply, monetary authorities can drive down the rate of interest. By reducing the supply of money, monetary authorities can raise the rate of interest.

In Figure 3, the interest rate falls from r to r' when the money supply increases from M to M', *ceteris paribus*. A greater supply of money induces lending institutions (banks, savings and loans, insurance companies) to make more loans, which drives down the market rate of interest.

> **An increase in the supply of money drives down interest rates as long as the money-demand—or liquidity-preference—curve is constant.**

From Interest Rates to Aggregate Demand

Figure 4 shows that at higher interest rates, less investment is demanded and that at lower interest rates, more investment is demanded. Figure 5 shows how the interaction between money and investment markets depicted in Figures 3 and 4 can affect the economy's level of output.

If the Fed increases the money supply, the rate of interest falls and the quantity of investment demanded increases. This increased investment shifts up the AE curve and (as in the analysis of Chapter 11), hence, shifts the AD curve to the right. Figure 5 shows what happens when the money supply *doubles* if the initial price level is p_0. As the AD curve shifts *horizontally* (from AD to AD'), the economy moves from point e_0 to e_1 where it has increased its output level from y_0 to y_1 *at the initial price level p_0*. The AD curve will shift to the right for any increase in the money supply as long as interest rates fall and investment increases in response to lower interest rates.

The case of doubling the money supply allows us to examine the *vertical* distance between the

Figure 5   The Effect on Aggregate Demand of Doubling the Money Supply

(a) An Increase in Aggregate Expenditures

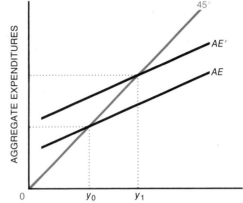

(b) The Resulting Increase in Aggregate Demand

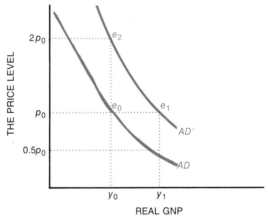

As panel (a) shows, when the money supply increases, the interest rate falls, increasing investment and shifting up the AE curve. The increase in aggregate expenditures results in a rightward shift in the AD curve, as shown in panel (b). The vertical shift in the AD curve is in the same proportion as the increase in the money supply. If the money supply doubles, AD' will be exactly twice as high as AD.

AD curve and the AD' curve. To determine what the vertical distance is between the two curves we must find out at which price level the new aggregate-demand curve (AD') intersects the original output level y_0. In order to return to an output of y_0, investment must return to its original level, so the interest rate must return to its initial rate. It

Example 2   The Currency/Deposit Ratio and the Underground Economy

One interesting puzzle is that the currency/deposit ratio has tended to increase from 1960 to 1984. In 1960, the ratio was about 30 percent. In 1984, the ratio was about 40 percent. This increase is puzzling in view of the introduction of interest-earning checking accounts in recent years. One would think that the currency/deposit ratio would fall as the public shifted from currency (paying zero interest) to deposits (paying some interest).

An explanation for this puzzle is the rise of the underground economy (see Chapter 6). In the underground economy, people may find it easier to avoid detection if they use cash rather than check-

ing deposits. If this hypothesis is correct, the currency/deposit ratio could fall substantially if the underground economy stopped growing. If the government lowered tax rates, the underground economy could contract, and the currency/deposit ratio might fall. In early 1985 and late 1984, the United States was seriously considering the adoption of a simpler tax system (with lower tax rates and fewer loopholes). A side effect of such legislation might be a higher money multiplier!   ■

Source: Vito Tanzi, "The Underground Economy in the United States: Annual Estimates," *International Monetary Fund Staff Papers,* 30 (June 1983): 283–305.

was the lowering of the interest rate, after all, that raised investment and, hence, raised aggregate demand. Figure 5 shows that the price level must rise to $2p_0$ (twice the initial price level) in order for the economy to move up the AD' curve to where the AD' curve intersects y_0 at e_2. If there is no money illusion in the economy, a doubling of the money supply combined with a doubling of prices would leave everyone the same as before. Even though money balances have doubled, the doubling of prices leaves *real money balances* (the supply of money adjusted for inflation) the same as before. People who now hold twice as much money as before (in the absence of money illusion) recognize there has been no real change. Accordingly, the interest rate and the quantity of investment demanded return to their original levels. Thus, when M doubles and p_0 doubles to $2p_0$, equilibrium output stays the same at y_0. The new aggregate-demand curve, AD', must, therefore, pass through the price level $2p_0$ at the income level y_0.

> When the money supply increases, the *horizontal* shift in the AD curve depends on the sensitivity of interest rates and investment to the money supply (as well as the multiplier). The *vertical* shift, however, will be in exact proportion to the increase in the money supply as long as there is no money illusion.

Removing Deflationary and Inflationary Gaps

Chapter 11 explained that if there were a deflationary gap, monetary and fiscal authorities could follow a policy of nonaction and the self-correcting forces of deflation would return the economy to the natural level of output. In Figure 6, the economy finds itself in such a deflationary gap where the aggregate-demand (AD) curve intersects the short-run aggregate-supply ($SRAS$) curve to the left of the long-run aggregate-supply ($LRAS$) curve. The self-correcting mechanism would eventually move the economy from point e_0 at price level p_0 to point e_1 at lower price level p_1, restoring the economy to full-employment output, y_n.

Keynes felt that waiting for deflation to solve the problem wasted far too many economic resources. Instead of letting the self-correcting mechanism use deflation to return the economy to the natural level of output (which could be slow and painful), Keynes thought the money supply should be increased immediately. An appropriate increase in the money supply could shift AD to AD', where the deflationary gap would be removed when the economy moved along the $SRAS$ curve to e_2. Output would increase from y_0 to y_n and the price level would rise from p_0 to p_2. Since the vertical shift in the demand curve (from p_0 to p_3 at y_0) corresponds to the proportional shift in

Figure 6   Removing a Deflationary Gap

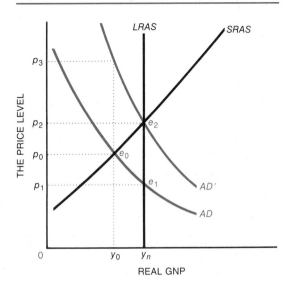

The economy is originally in short-run equilibrium at e_0, where the *AD* curve intersects the *SRAS* curve. A deflationary gap exists because y_0 is less than the natural level of output, y_n. The self-correcting mechanism would require deflation until the economy reaches e_1 on the *AD* curve. Increasing the money supply sufficiently, however, could shift the *AD* curve to *AD'*, thereby eliminating the deflationary gap.

Figure 7   Removing an Inflationary Gap

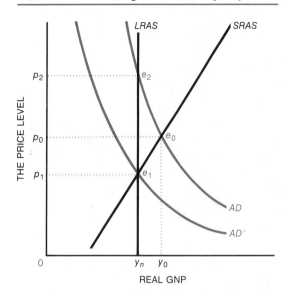

The economy is originally in short-run equilibrium at e_0, where the *AD* curve intersects the *SRAS* curve. An inflationary gap exists because y_0 exceeds the natural level of output, y_n. The self-correcting mechanism would require inflation until the economy reaches e_2 on the original *AD* curve. A sufficient decrease in the money supply, however, can shift the *AD* curve to *AD'*, thereby eliminating the inflationary gap.

the money supply (as shown in the last section), the price level would not increase proportionately as much as the money supply. On this point, Keynes differed with the classical economists described in Chapter 7. The classical economists thought increasing the money supply by, say, 10 percent would merely raise prices by 10 percent (since V and Q were assumed to be constant in the equation $MV = PQ$). Keynes showed that with unemployed resources (a deflationary gap), an increase in the money supply would cause a less-than-porportionate change in the price level. Instead of prices rising by the full amount indicated by the quantity theory, real output would increase to keep the percentage price increase below the percentage increase in the money supply.

Figure 7 shows how an *inflationary gap* could be removed by deliberately changing the money supply. The economy finds itself in an inflationary-gap equilibrium at point e_0. Without a monetary-policy action, the economy would experience inflation; the self-correcting mechanism would move the economy along the *AD* curve to point

e_2 at price level p_2. However, by simply lowering the money supply sufficiently, aggregate demand will fall (the aggregate-demand curve will shift to the left from *AD* to *AD'*). Modern Keynesians (like Keynes himself) believe that inflationary gaps will be removed more quickly than deflationary gaps by the self-correcting mechanism. Prices and wages rise more readily than they fall. Hence, Keynesians tend to be more activist with respect to expansionary monetary policy than contractionary monetary policy.

An important characteristic of Keynesian monetary policy is its potential *inflationary bias*. If money-supply increases are used to eliminate deflationary gaps and the self-correcting mechanism is used to eliminate inflationary gaps, a Keynesian would be reluctant to recommend reducing the money supply. Thus, even in a world of no long-term economic growth, such a policy position leads to long-term increases in the money supply. In this sense, Keynesian monetary policy is said to have an inflationary bias. This bias is not necessarily bad; it may be the optimal monetary policy if prices and wages are less flexible downward than they are upward.

Credit Rationing

In the Keynesian model, monetary policy works primarily through interest rates. When the Fed reduces the money supply, interest rates rise to choke off some investment. **Credit rationing** can, however, be used as a subsidiary instrument of monetary policy.

> **Credit rationing** occurs when interest rates are not allowed to rise to the rate at which the demand for loans equals the supply of loans. In this situation, the demand for investment funds at the prevailing interest rate exceeds the supply.

Credit rationing limits investment by making investment funds unavailable to some firms that are prepared to invest at prevailing interest rates. Although credit rationing and a decrease in the money supply work generally in the same direction, there is an important difference. A decrease in the money supply raises the interest rate, and as the interest rate rises, less investment is demanded. Credit rationing works differently: when the supply of money is reduced, controls on interest rates prevent interest rates from rising to a new equilibrium. Firms are discouraged from investing not because of a reduced demand for investment but because of the reduced availability of loans. Moreover, credit rationing typically tends to be less even-handed. Often rules are set by the Fed or by the lending institutions themselves as to which customers will be granted credit.

Credit rationing requires the existence of government controls over interest rates. Left uncontrolled, interest rates would adjust to equate the supply and demand for loans. The Fed does have the tools for credit rationing: the Fed can set interest-rate ceilings; it can enact rules for making loans; it can penalize lending institutions that fail to follow its rules. Through credit rationing, the monetary authorities can affect investment in a more direct fashion by regulating the availability of investment funds.

THE FED'S TARGETS AND GOALS OF MONETARY POLICY

Countercyclical Versus Procyclical Monetary Policy

According to Keynesians, **countercyclical monetary policy** is preferable to **procyclical monetary policy.**

> A **countercyclical monetary policy** is one that increases aggregate demand when output is falling too much (or when its rate of growth is declining) and reduces aggregate demand when output is rising too rapidly.

> A **procyclical monetary policy** is one that decreases aggregate demand when output is falling and increases aggregate demand when output is rising.

The countercyclical prescription is clear: if there is a deflationary gap (a recession), increase the money supply; if there is an inflationary gap (a boom), possibly reduce the money supply. In an economy where, over time, the resource base and the natural level of real GNP grow, these policy rules translate into changes in the *rates of monetary growth*. In recessions, the Fed should raise the rate of monetary growth; in booms, the Fed should not raise (or should possibly lower) the rate of monetary growth.

Has Fed policy been countercyclical? What have been the Fed's monetary targets? A useful distinction can be drawn between *intermediate targets* and *ultimate targets,* or *goals.* The ultimate targets of policy would be to achieve certain levels of unemployment or output, a certain rate of inflation, a certain interest rate, or perhaps even a certain exchange rate for the U.S. dollar (how many French Francs or British Pounds it takes to buy a U.S. dollar). This chapter will concentrate on the output goals of monetary policy. Other chapters will examine how monetary policy can affect inflation, the interaction of inflation and unemployment, interest rates, and the value of the dollar. The intermediate targets of the Fed would be the monetary and credit conditions the Fed manipulates in order to achieve these goals. We shall use the term *targets* to refer to intermediate monetary targets and the term *goals* to refer to such objectives as reducing unemployment or reducing inflation.

Figure 8 shows the yearly rates of growth in the money supply (measured from December of the previous year to December of the indicated year) from 1960 to 1984. The graph shows that the Fed has not succeeded in pursuing countercyclical monetary policy.[5] Notice that over the period the rate of monetary growth passed through various peaks and troughs. If monetary policy were *countercyclical,* the *peaks* of monetary growth should correspond to recessions and the *troughs* of monetary growth should correspond to inflationary gaps. *In general, the opposite holds:* monetary policy has been procyclical (troughs of monetary growth correspond to recessions and peaks of monetary growth correspond to booms.)

Each recession (growth rates in real GNP either negative or significantly less than average) is marked on the curve by an *R*. With only one exception (1982), the recessions occur at the troughs of monetary expansion. Rather than having rapid monetary growth to pull the economy out of recession, the historical record shows that monetary growth has been slow during the recession stage of the business cycle. The year 1982 was an exception; monetary growth was actually increased during the 1982 recession. The "trough" of monetary growth in 1984 was also an exception because 1984 was a boom period, which should have called for slow monetary growth. Thus, in 1982 and 1984 the Fed did follow countercyclical policies. Figure 8 tells us that, historically, Fed policy has been procyclical; in 1982 and 1984, Fed policy was countercyclical (but not in 1983 when real GNP grew at a rapid rate of about 6 percent and money growth peaked).

Historically, the Fed has followed policies that are procyclical (that is, money-growth rates have decreased in recessions or increased in booms). Recently, the Fed has tended to follow countercyclical monetary policies.

---

5. *See* Robert J. Gordon, *Macroeconomics,* 3rd ed. (Boston: Little, Brown and Company, 1984), pp. 507–517. For a more detailed study, *see* Alan S. Blinder, *Economic Policy and the Great Stagflation* (New York: Academic Press, 1979).

Figure 8   Yearly Growth Rates in M1: 1960–1984

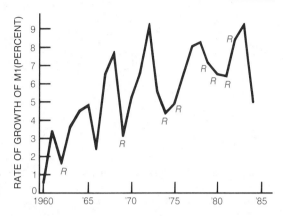

Yearly growth rates in the money supply (from December of the preceding year to December of the given year) from 1960 to 1984 fluctuated between highs (peaks) and lows (troughs). With the exception of 1982, years of recession (marked with an *R*) were accompanied by troughs in the rate of monetary growth. In the later years, policy apparently changed. In 1984, monetary growth was relatively low yet the economy was booming.

Sources: *Economic Report of the President,* 1984 and the *Federal Reserve Bulletin.*

Control Interest Rates or Control the Money Supply?

Why has the Fed been unable historically to follow a countercyclical monetary policy? One answer is that the Fed up until recently has preferred to set an **interest-rate target** rather than a **monetary-aggregate target.**

An **interest-rate target** is a rate of interest that the Fed seeks to achieve through monetary policy.

A **monetary-aggregate target** is a particular money supply or growth rate of the money supply that the Fed seeks to achieve through monetary policy.

According to the Keynesian model, monetary policy works through interest rates. Should monetary policy try to set interest rates and not worry about how much money supply must rise or fall to achieve the desired interest rate? Or should monetary authorities set a target money supply

Table 1   M1 Growth Versus Fed Targets

Time Period[a]	Targeted Range of M1 Growth (annual percentage)	Actual M1 Growth (percentage)
1976–1977	4½–6½	7.4
1977–1978	4–6½	7.3
1978–1979	1½–4½	5.5
1980–1981	3–5½	5.1
1981–1982	2½–5½	8.5
1983 (2nd quarter)– 1983 (4th quarter)	5–9	6.1
1983–1984	4–8	5.3[p]
1984–1985	4–7	

[a]Time periods are from the fourth quarter of the start year to the fourth quarter of the end year, unless otherwise indicated.
[p]Preliminary.

Source: *Federal Reserve Bulletin.*

and not worry about the effect of this money supply on interest rates?

Monetary economists generally favor controlling the money supply without excessive worry about interest rates. They argue that the pursuit of interest-rate targets destabilizes the economy.

Assume that the economy is in a boom period and that monetary authorities (following an interest-rate policy) decide to hold interest rates constant. But economic expansion increases the demand for credit, and this increased demand starts to drive up interest rates. To hold interest rates down, therefore, the Fed must create even more money. The increase in money supply will further feed the boom. Likewise, when the economy is depressed, the demand for credit will contract and threaten to push down interest rates. For monetary authorities to hold the interest rate constant, they must reduce the supply of money, thereby depressing economic conditions even further.

Monetary economists warn that the pursuit of rigid interest-rate targets exaggerates the business cycle by leading to a procyclical monetary policy.

Setting interest rate targets would work if the Fed knew the interest rate compatible with achieving full employment. The Fed could then change the money supply until that interest-rate target was achieved. Unfortunately, it is very difficult to know the right interest rate. Recall from Chapter 5 the distinction between nominal and real interest rates: *nominal interest rates* are the explicit rates charged by banks or earned (in nominal dollars) on various bonds; *real interest rates* adjust the nominal interest rates for inflation. The rate of interest the Fed should target to obtain full employment is the expected real interest rate (the nominal interest rate minus the expected inflation rate) which generates the level of investment demand corresponding to the natural level of real GNP. *But nobody knows the expected inflation rate that is in the mind of people at every point in time.* The Fed can only affect the nominal rate of interest. The Fed does not control inflationary expectations. Economists can only guess at the expected inflation rate. Thus, any interest-rate target is likely to be wrong at any given time.

Prior to October 1979, the Fed's monetary policy was directed toward setting interest-rate targets—although these targets were flexible. This policy meant that the growth of the money supply was dictated by the interest-rate targets and the demand for money. If very rapid growth of the money supply was required to achieve a target rate of interest, so be it.

Thus, before October 1979, the Fed paid primary attention to interest-rate targets rather than to money-supply targets. The procyclical behavior of the money supply observed in Figure 8 is clearly consistent with the hypothesis of interest-rate targeting by the Fed. As we pointed out, the pursuit of interest-rate targets is likely to speed monetary expansion during booms (since the demand for money is high) and to slow monetary expansion during recessions (since the demand for money is low).

Fed Policy Since 1979

In October 1979, in a historic decision, the Fed decided to base monetary policy on monetary-aggregate targets and let interest rates settle at the level dictated by the targeted money supply. The Fed now sets a target range of growth rates for the money supply and uses its control of the money supply to keep monetary growth within these target ranges. The Fed's move was inspired by Fed Chairman Paul T. Volcker, who argued that control of the money supply was necessary to control the rate of inflation (in 1979, inflation was running at an annual rate of 11 percent). According to the operating procedure adopted in October 1979, the Fed would set specific target growth rates for the money supply. While the Fed had set money growth targets prior to 1979 (see Table 1), the new procedure called for the Fed to stop manipulating interest rates and to take the money-supply targets seriously. The Fed would still be monitoring interest rates, but only to prevent wild swings in interest rates arising from short-run changes in the demand for money. (See Example 3.)

The dramatic difference between Fed performance before and after October 1979 is evident in Table 1, which compares the Fed's money-supply targets to actual money-supply growth for several years before and after 1979. The Fed's money-supply targets were not achieved in 1977, 1978, or 1979. In each of those years, the money supply grew more rapidly than the Fed's targeted growth rate. But in the post-1979 period, the Fed failed to achieve its money-growth target only once—in 1982. The Fed suspended its 1982 target of 2½ to 5½ percent money growth (and allowed 8½ percent monetary growth) because the unemployment rate in September 1982 was 10 percent of the labor force and Fed Chairman Volcker was worried about the foreign debt crisis (Mexico and Argentina had notified their American bank cred-

Figure 9   **Interest Rates, 1979–1984**

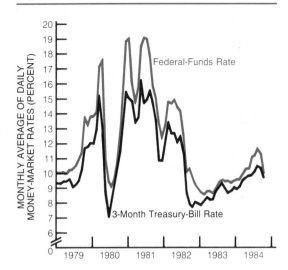

Interest rates were far more volatile in 1980 and 1981 than in the preceding or following years.

Source: St. Louis Federal Reserve Bank.

itors that they could not make their loan payments). Table 1 shows that the Fed in late 1983 and 1984 appeared to return to its October 1979 policy decision to stay within the target ranges of money growth.

What happened to interest rates after October 1979? Figure 9 shows the course of interest rates from 1979 to 1984. The color line is the *federal-funds rate,* which is the interest rate banks charge each other for overnight loans of bank reserves. The federal-funds rate is the actual target rate of interest pursued by the Fed. The solid line is the 3-Month Treasury-bill rate discussed above. Notice in 1980 how the T-bill rate varied from a low of 7 percent in mid-year to highs around 15 percent earlier and later in the year. The federal-funds rate also varied dramatically: from a low of 9 percent to a high of 19 percent in 1980. But in 1983 and 1984 the wild swings of 1980 and the roller-coaster swings of 1981 were avoided.

Short-run changes in the demand for money can cause wild swings in the federal-funds rate. The Fed establishes a target range for the federal-funds rate along with its monetary-growth targets. For example, in late 1984 the Fed established a target range of 7 percent to 11 percent for the federal-funds rate. The federal-funds rate may be usefully considered the price of bank reserves. If that rate rises above 11 percent, the Fed is likely to carry out open-market purchases that inject reserves into the system and lower the federal-funds rate; if that rate falls below 7 percent, the Fed is likely to absorb reserves with open-market sales and raise the federal-funds rate. This approach smacks of interest-rate targeting in the short run, but not necessarily in the long run. When the Fed sets *both* a monetary-growth target and an interest-rate target, the important issue becomes which target has priority if both cannot be achieved at once. Prior to October 1979, the Fed tended to meet its interest-rate targets and to sacrifice monetary-growth targets where necessary. After 1979, the reverse has tended to be true. If the money-supply targets override the interest-rate targets, the Fed presumably would change the interest-rate targets in such a way as to maintain money-growth targets on a year-to-year basis. For example, as interest rates fell in late 1984, the Fed lowered its interest-rate targets while maintaining its money-supply targets.

Current Fed policy is to follow flexible money-growth targets. The Fed is likely to depart from its long-run targets in the case of serious recession (as it did in 1982). The Fed will vary from its long-run targets for a short-period of time if interest rates fluctuate much beyond its short-run interest-rate targets.

THE EFFECTIVENESS OF MONETARY POLICY

The Limitations of Monetary Policy

The old saying: "You can take a horse to water but you can't make him drink" has been applied to monetary policy. Basically, all the Fed can do is to make additional monetary reserves available to the banking system if it wishes to expand the money supply. It cannot force banks to lend out these reserves and expand the money supply. Nor can it force businesses to increase their investment borrowing when interest rates drop. The use

of monetary policy to induce the economy to increase investment can be like pushing on a string. If banks do not loan out additional reserves or if business firms do not invest more when interest rates drop, the monetary authorities are pushing on a string. Many economists dispute the pushing-on-a-string analogy. They argue that lower interest rates provide adequate incentives for businesses and consumers to increase their spending.

Most economists agree that monetary authorities are more effctive when they *pull* on the string. When they wish to contract the money supply, authorities can withdraw reserves and force a contraction of the money supply. If firms do not respond to higher interest rates by investing less, the monetary authorities can always use credit rationing to restrict investment.

The link between the money supply and desired aggregate expenditures in the Keynesian model could be very fragile. The link could be broken at any point in the chain. If increases in money supply fail to lower interest rates, or if changes in interest rates fail to elicit changes in investment, money supply would exert no effect on desired aggregate expenditures. Moreover, even if the chain is not broken, the effects may be very weak or take some time to occur. Interest rates may respond only weakly to changes in money supply; investment demand may be very insensitive to changes in interest rates.

For these reasons, Keynes felt that monetary policy would be less effective than fiscal policy in combating severe unemployment. (Fiscal policy is the subject of the next chapter.)

The Problem of Lags

If the monetary authorities can recognize an inflationary or a deflationary gap, and if the effects of the change in the money supply take place *before* the self-correcting mechanism solves the problem, discretionary monetary policy can stabilize the economy. Another possible problem with discretionary monetary policy is that there is a **recognition lag** and an **effectiveness lag** between a monetary-policy action and its desired effect.

A **recognition lag** is the time it takes the Fed to actually change the supply of money in response to a change in economic conditions.

Example 3   Behind the Scenes of the Fed's 1979 Decision

Prior to October 1979, the Fed conducted monetary policy by controlling interest rates, not the growth rate of the money supply. On August 6, Paul Volcker, a banker with many years of experience at central banking, was appointed to chair the Fed by President Jimmy Carter. On September 17, 1979, slightly more than one month after Volcker's appointment, the Fed announced that it had raised the discount rate after a 4–3 vote. The close vote sent financial markets into panic because it appeared that Volcker would be a weak chairperson, unable to control the Fed and rigorously fight inflation. After the September 17th meeting, Volcker determined that a dramatic step was required to convince the world that the Fed was serious in its fight against inflation. Although not a monetarist, Volcker decided that the dramatic move would be to change Fed operating policy from interest-rate controls to slowing the growth of the money supply. In late September, in an unusual move, Volcker met with top administration officials to inform them of his intentions. The Secretary of the Treasury, the Chair of the Council of Economic Advisors, and eventually the President of the United States all opposed the change in Fed operating procedures, preferring to continue the battle against inflation with interest-rate targeting. At a meeting of the world's central bankers on October 2, 1979 in Yugoslavia, Volcker was urged by fellow central bankers to take prompt action against U.S. inflation. Although Volcker, like other board members, officially has only one vote on policy matters, he does control the agenda of the Federal Open Market Committee (FOMC) and does direct the Fed's professional Washington staff. Moreover, there is a long tradition of loyalty of the staff to their leader. In an unprecedented move, Volcker began lobbying the members of the FOMC to support the change in operating procedures. As a consequence of these lobbying efforts and the support of the Fed's professional staff, the change in operating procedures was approved by the FOMC at an emergency meeting on October 6, 1979. The Carter administration, even though it disapproved of the action, was forced to publicly support it because criticism would further undermine confidence in the Fed's inflation-fighting ability.

The inflation consequences of the change in Fed operating procedures will be discussed in a later chapter on inflation. ■

Source: Paul Blustein, "How Federal Reserve Under Volcker Finally Slowed Down Inflation," *The Wall Street Journal,* December 7, 1984.

An **effectiveness lag** is the time it takes the change in the money supply to affect the economy.

Modern economics, even with extensive data-gathering facilities, can never be sure of *current* economic conditions. We do not have an accurate estimate of GNP until 6 months after the fact. Unemployment and inflation data come in more quickly but are still a couple of months old. To know whether an expansionary or contractionary policy is required, one must be able to compare actual unemployment to the natural rate of unemployment. As we pointed out in an earlier chapter, economists are not even certain about what unemployment rate is the natural unemployment rate or whether deviations from the natural rate are temporary aberrations or a part of a serious trend. Thus, nobody knows for sure what is happening right now. The recognition lag may be about 4 months (as estimated by Robert Gordon). In other words, the Fed may need 4 months or so to identify an inflationary or deflationary gap and to initiate the appropriate technical procedures to expand or contract the money supply. For example, in May 1985 Fed officials were sharply divided over whether the U.S. economy was headed toward recession or growing at a healthy pace.

Estimates of the effectiveness lag vary widely. Robert Gordon estimates the effectiveness lag as short—from 5 to 10 months. Milton Friedman estimates the effectiveness lag as long and variable—from 6 months to 2 years.

The total lag (the sum of the recognition and effectiveness lags), according to Gordon, varies from 9 to 14 months; the total lag according to Friedman varies from 10 months to more than two years. Who are we to believe? It could be that both are right. Gordon's estimates are based on recent business-cycle experience; Friedman's estimates are based on averages over nearly a century's time. It is possible that, as a result of improvements in communication and information, the lags have become shorter in recent years. Time will tell whether the lags are short but variable or long but variable.

If lags are short, the argument for activist monetary policy is stronger. With short lags the monetary authorities stand a better chance of adopting the correct countercyclical policy. If a deflationary gap develops (threatening a recession), a 5-month total lag means that an expansionary monetary policy will be felt 5 months after recognition of the problem. A 2-year lag means that the effects of the policy will be felt 2 years after recognition of the problem. By that time, the economy may be in a boom that requires a contraction in the money supply. Keynesian economists tend to believe that lags are short and that activist policy can be used to iron out many fluctuations in real GNP.

Even if lags are short but variable, monetary policy should not try to iron out every small inflationary or deflationary gap. If a deflationary gap is relatively small, the self-correcting mechanism may do its work before the effects of the monetary policy can take place. Thus, most Keynesians now believe that policymakers should not try to fine-tune the economy but should rather aim only at correcting significant inflationary or deflationary gaps.

The Monetarist Response to Monetary-Policy Limitations

If lags are long but variable, then what monetary policy should be followed? Milton Friedman has argued that the Fed should follow a **constant-money-growth rule:** the money supply should grow at a fixed percentage (Friedman usually says 3 percent) per year. The justification for the constant-growth rule is that if the monetary lag varies between 10 months and 28 months, by the time the effects of any monetary policy are felt the original reasons for the policy may have disappeared through the self-correcting mechanism. More likely than not, by the time the policy is felt, it may be the exact opposite of the policy

required at that time. The choice of the constant-growth rate (whether it be 2, 3, or 4 percent) depends on the long-term growth of real GNP (which, historically, has averaged about 3 percent per year). Friedman argues that if we knew more about the economy (for example, if we knew the size of the effectiveness lag), we could possibly control the business cycle better. But given present knowledge and the lags involved, monetary policy (or fiscal policy) may be destabilizing. The nonactivist policy of Milton Friedman and economists such as Karl Brunner and Allan Meltzer is known as **monetarism.**

> The **constant-money-growth rule** holds that the money supply should increase at a fixed percentage each year.

> **Monetarism** is the doctrine that monetary policy should follow a constant-money-growth rule.

Many journalists and politicians have identified the Fed's October 1979 decision to hold to monetary-growth targets as an experiment in monetarism. This interpretation is not strictly correct. Monetarism requires pursuing a constant-monetary-growth target, where the monetary-growth target is set near the growth of real GNP. Under the October 1979 operating rules, the Fed did not pledge itself to follow a constant-growth rule. In fact, Table 1 shows that there have been changes in the Fed's monetary-growth targets after October 1979. Our discussion already noted that the Fed exceeded its monetary-growth target in 1982 to combat the high unemployment rate. Monetarists have always maintained that their constant-money-growth rule should be followed indefinitely into the distant future (or until more is learned about the economy) and should not be affected by current economic conditions.

The debate between the monetarists and the Keynesians over whether or not to pursue an activist monetary policy is an important one and will be discussed extensively in the next few chapters.

THE INDEPENDENCE OF THE FED

The Fed's power to set money-supply and interest-rate targets is independent of Congress and the executive branch of the government. Recall from

Chapter 8 that the Fed does not require financing from Congress; it is self-supporting. Moreover, members of the Board of Governors have 14-year, nonrenewable terms. The Fed can make decisions that the Secretary of the Treasury, the President of the United States, and congressional leaders all oppose. The authors of the 1913 Federal Reserve Act believed the Fed should be independent of political pressures. Opponents of an independent Fed disagree.

The Case For Fed Independence

The basic case for independence rests on three observations. First, if the Fed were under the direct control of politicians, the Fed would exhibit a stronger inflationary bias because, it is argued, politicians like to spend money but do not like to tax. With a cooperating Fed, government deficits could be easily financed by money expansion and inflation would be encouraged. Many countries with high rates of inflation have a central bank that is not independent. It is easier for nonelected, relatively anonymous central bankers than for elected officials to adopt anti-inflationary policies.

Second, proponents of independence argue that the Fed can carry out long-term plans while politicians can see no farther than the next election. There are fears of a so-called ''political business cycle'' (discussed in the next chapter): politicans may try to engineer Fed policy to help them get reelected.

Third, proponents of Fed independence argue that the Fed will never go too strongly against the wishes of the electorate because the real independence of the Fed is somewhat constrained by political reality. If the Fed got out of hand, Congress could pass legislation reducing the Fed's independence.

The Case Against Fed Independence

Critics of Fed independence cite two important arguments. First, independence means that what may be the most important flexible policy tool available to the government is out of the hands of the electorate. If the public does not like Paul Volcker or the other members of the Board of Governors, there is nothing that can be done. The Fed cannot be thrown out of office like an unpopular and, perhaps, incompetent politician. Many

feel that in a democracy policy should be sensitive to the wishes of the public.

Second, critics of Fed independence point out that monetary policy and fiscal policy should be coordinated. Under the current system, monetary and fiscal policy could work at cross-purposes. President Reagan's then Treasury Secretary, Donald Regan, argued in late 1984 that the Fed's 1985 money targets were too low. Secretary Regan predicted that the Fed's tight money policy would hurt the economy, lower Treasury tax revenues, and, thus, raise the government deficit to more than the $205 billion deficit projected for fiscal 1985. In other words, the Fed's tight money policy of 1984 was considered to make President Reagan's 1984 election-year promise to reduce the deficit more difficult to achieve.

The next chapter examines how fiscal policy is conducted and evaluates its effectiveness as a countercyclical tool. Is the government deficit something we should worry about?

Summary

1. The Fed can change the money supply through its open-market operations, reserve-requirement changes, and discount-rate changes. Open-market operations are the principal tool of Federal Reserve monetary policy.
2. The money multiplier is the ratio of the money supply to the monetary base. On a month-to-month basis, it fluctuates enough to reduce the Fed's short-run control over the money supply. In the long run (year to year), the Fed can take changes in the money multiplier into account.
3. Keynesian monetary policy is based on the indirect link between money supply and real GNP. Because bond prices and interest rates move inversely, increases in the money supply (in the short run) lower interest rates. The quantity of investment demanded rises when interest rates fall. In principle, inflationary and deflationary gaps can be removed by changes in the money supply.
4. The Fed's use of interest-rate targets rather than monetary-growth targets tends to cause changes in the money supply to be procyclical. Prior to October 1979, the Fed's interest-rate

targets had priority over money-growth targets, and Fed policy tended to destabilize the economy. After October 1979, the Fed's policy has been to rely more heavily on money-growth targets. Current policy appears to be more countercyclical.

5. Keynesians believe that monetary policy should be used actively to remove major deflationary and inflationary gaps. Monetarists believe that lags in the effectiveness of monetary policy imply that a constant-money-growth-rate rule should be used and that activist monetary policy can destabilize the economy.

6. Defenders of Fed independence stress that being independent reduces the inflationary bias of government policy and allows the Fed to have a longer time horizon than politicians have. An independent Fed can follow politically tough policies. Critics of Fed independence worry about the Fed being irresponsible to the electorate and working at cross-purposes with fiscal policy.

Key Terms

monetary policy
money multiplier
liquidity-preference theory
credit rationing
countercyclical monetary policy
procyclical monetary policy
interest-rate target
monetary-aggregate target
recognition lag
effectiveness lag
constant-money-growth rule
monetarism

Questions and Problems

1. Describe briefly how Fed uses its three major instruments of monetary control.

2. What is the most important instrument of monetary policy and why?

3. Define the money multiplier. How does it vary from month to month?

4. Explain the relationship between interest rates and bond prices.

5. If the newspaper reports that: "The bond market is in the doldrums; it has been depressed all week," what is happening to interest rates?

6. Compare the impact on interest rates of a change in the money supply when:
   a. the quantity of money demanded is highly responsive to interest rates.
   b. the quantity of money demanded is relatively insensitive to interest rates.

7. How does a change in the money supply increase real GNP?

8. What problems could arise to reduce the impact of a change in the money supply on real GNP?

9. Explain why the vertical shift in the *AD* curve due to monetary policy equals the percentage increase in the money supply.

10. What decision did the Fed make in October 1979?

11. Why might interest-rate targeting destabilize the economy?

12. Historically, has the Fed been Keynesian or monetarist?

13. Describe recent Fed policy.

14. How do lags in the effectiveness of monetary policy affect the design of a good monetary policy?

15. How can Fed independence reduce inflation?

16. How can Fed independence result in poor monetary policies?

Suggested Readings

Bryant, Ralph C. "Money and Monetary Policy." *The Brookings Review,* Spring 1983.

Gordon, Robert J. *Macroeconomics,* 3rd ed. Little, Brown and Company, 1984, chaps. 15 and 16.

"How Fed Reserve Under Volcker Finally Slowed Down Inflation." *The Wall Street Journal,* December 7, 1984.

"Monetary Policy, Money Supply, and the Federal Reserve's Operating Procedures." *Federal Reserve Bulletin,* January 1982.

"U.S. Monetary Policy in Recent Years: An Overview." *Federal Reserve Bulletin,* January 1985.

13

Fiscal Policy

Chapter Preview

Chapter 12 explained how monetary policy—altering the money supply and credit conditions—could be used to pursue macroeconomic goals. This chapter will explain how fiscal policy—changing government-spending and taxation programs—can affect aggregate demand (and even aggregate supply) and how some government-spending and tax programs respond automatically to changes in economic conditions. The chapter will also explore the effect of budget deficits on prices, interest rates, and output before closing with a discussion of the effectiveness of fiscal policy.

Currently, there are more than 82,000 governmental units in the United States. We have one federal government, 50 state governments, and more than 82,000 townships and county and municipal governments. Each government unit carries out a spending program and collects revenues through a variety of means. Most government units collect taxes from their residents; some government units earn revenues by selling goods and services to residents—although the revenues from this source tend to be relatively minor compared to taxes. ■

Table 1   The Projected 1985 Federal Budget

Category	Amount (billions of dollars)	Percent
Total receipts	**799**	**100**
Personal tax and nontax receipts	340	43.6
Corporate income taxes	93	11.9
Indirect business taxes	55	7.1
Social-insurance contributions	289	37.1
Total expenditures	**948**	**100**
Purchase of goods and services	340	35.9
Transfer payments to persons	377	39.8
Grants in aid to state and local governments	96	10.1
Net interest payments	117	12.3
Other	18	1.8
Deficit (total revenues minus total expenditures)	**169**	

Source: *Economic Report of the President.*

GOVERNMENT FINANCE

The Federal Budget

A projected 1985 budget of the U.S. government is shown in Table 1. Projected federal government receipts are made up primarily of personal tax receipts and contributions to social-insurance programs. Corporation income taxes make up only a small portion of the federal government's receipts. On the expenditure side, only about 36 percent of federal government expenditures are for purchases of goods and services. About 40 percent of spending goes for transfer payments to individuals, and the remaining 24 percent goes for grants to state and local governments and for interest payments on the national debt.

The federal budget shows that almost two thirds of federal government spending pays for activities that transfer income from one person or organization to another. *Transfer payments to persons* are income that is transferred from taxpayers to recipients of welfare payments, unemployment insurance, and Social Security benefits. *Grants in aid to states and local governments* transfer income from the federal government to state and local governments. *Interest payments* on the national debt transfer income from taxpayers to the owners of government bonds.

Surpluses and Deficits

There is a strong resemblance between the finances of a governmental unit and the finances of a household. Both governments and households take in income. Households receive income through factor payments and the receipt of transfer payments; government units take in income by collecting taxes, receiving transfer payments from other government units, and selling services (such as municipal water or sewerage connections, tuition at state universities). Both governments and households spend their income. Households spend income on consumer goods and services; governments spend income on purchases of goods and services and on transfer payments. When a household spends more than its income, it is *dissaving*. Dissaving means that it must borrow money (or draw down accumulated savings). Similarly, when a government unit spends more than it takes in, it is dissaving. Government dissaving also means that it must borrow money (or draw down accumulated savings).

Any difference between the total revenues and total outlays of a government unit is either a **government surplus** or a **government deficit**.

A **government deficit** is an excess of total government spending over total revenues from taxes and fees.

Table 2   Private and Public Saving, 1983 (billions of dollars)

Saving Category		Amount of Saving (+) or Dissaving (−) (billions of dollars)
Personal saving		156.9
Business saving		518.4
Government dissaving		−124.4
Federal deficit	−176.4	
State- and local-government surplus	52.1	
Total Saving		551.0

Source: *Economic Report of the President*, February 1985, p. 262.

A **government surplus** is an excess of total government revenues from taxes and fees over total spending.

If total government revenues from taxes and fees equal total government expenditures, the government unit has a *balanced budget*.

Private and Public Saving

As noted in earlier chapters, there are three sources of saving (or dissaving) in the economy: household saving, business saving, and government saving. If all government units combined are running a surplus, government as a whole is saving. If all government units combined are running a deficit, government is dissaving.

Table 2 shows the total public and private saving of the U.S. economy in the year 1984. Total saving (personal saving plus business saving minus government dissaving) equalled $551 billion. Households and businesses as a whole were saving a total of $675 billion, while government was dissaving, or saving −$124 billion. The federal deficit was $176 billion, while state and local governments ran a combined surplus of $52 billion. The actual division of government dissaving between federal government and state and local governments is not clearcut because in 1984, the federal government transferred $93 billion in federal grants in aid to state and local governments. If the federal government had kept these funds (and in the unlikely event that the states had continued to spend the same amount), then the fed-

eral deficit would have been $83 billion and the state-and-local-government surplus would have become a $41 billion deficit.

FISCAL-POLICY GOALS

Chapter 12 showed how the money supply could be used to pursue macroeconomic goals. If the economy were in a deflationary gap (output below natural real GNP), the money supply could be expanded (and credit loosened) to move the economy toward full-employment output. If the economy were in an inflationary gap, the money supply could be contracted (and credit tightened) to reduce aggregate demand to move the economy back to the natural rate of output. **Fiscal policy** can also be used to attack inflationary and deflationary gaps.

Fiscal policy is the deliberate control of government spending and taxation to pursue macroeconomic goals.

Most government spending and taxation is determined by factors that are totally unrelated to fiscal policy. Government spends money to provide for the national defense, to care for the poor and hungry, to provide for public education, and so on. Government tax policy may aim to equalize the distribution of income. It may be designed to promote certain activities and to discourage others. Such spending and taxation decisions are made independently of their impact on output and employment. Fiscal policy, by contrast, is the *de-*

liberate control of government spending and tax policy for the purpose of affecting output, employment, or inflation.

Fiscal Multipliers Revisited

Chapter 10 showed that an autonomous increase in government spending tends to increase aggregate demand. The amount of the increase in aggregate demand depends upon the amount of crowding out in the economy. Crowding out occurs in two ways: First, an increase in autonomous government spending tends to increase the demand for credit, thereby driving up interest rates. Higher interest rates choke off some investment. In the extreme case, crowding out is complete; that is, the resulting reduction in investment fully offsets the initial increase in government spending. In other cases, crowding out is incomplete; the initial increase in government spending is greater than the resulting reduction in investment spending. Second, a rise in government spending may directly crowd out private spending. As the government spends more for public education, for example, people reduce their spending on private education. The increase in government spending is partially offset by a reduction in personal spending.

Chapter 10 showed that the increase in aggregate demand resulting from a $1 billion increase in autonomous government spending equals $1 billion times the simple-expenditure multiplier minus all crowding-out effects. The ultimate effect of the increase in aggregate demand on output and prices is determined by the shape of the short-run aggregate-supply (*SRAS*) curve. If the *SRAS* curve is horizontal (output can be increased without driving up prices), output will increase by the full amount of the aggregate-demand increase. If the *SRAS* curve is upward-sloping, output will increase by less than aggregate demand as prices are pushed up.

Chapter 10 also showed that changes in taxes could raise or lower aggregate demand. If taxes are lowered autonomously, personal disposable income rises, the consumption/income curve rises, and aggregate demand increases. Although it was not mentioned in Chapter 10, an autonomous tax cut should also set into motion some interest-rate crowding out. The increase in desired spending should raise the demand for credit, push up interest rates, and choke off some investment. The increase in aggregate demand resulting from a tax cut will, therefore, be less than the simple tax multiplier discussed in Chapter 10.

Inflationary and Deflationary Gaps

Chapter 12 discussed how monetary policy could be used to eliminate deflationary and inflationary gaps. The removal of deflationary and inflationary gaps is also a goal of fiscal policy. Chapter 12 showed that inflationary or deflationary gaps are self-liquidating in the long run through the automatic adjustment of wages and prices. When an economy is in a deflationary gap, prices and wages tend to fall, and falling wages and prices will eventually cause short-run aggregate supply to increase to eliminate the deflationary gap. Similarly, when an economy is in an inflationary gap, wages and prices are rising. Rising wages and prices will eventually cause short-run aggregate supply to fall to eliminate the inflationary gap. Once the inflationary or deflationary gap is eliminated, the economy is again operating at the natural level of output, and the prevailing price level (or prevailing rate of inflation) will continue.

Fiscal policy, like monetary policy, can be a tool policymakers use to speed up the adjustment to the natural level of output. Panel (a) of Figure 1 shows an economy in a deflationary gap; the intersection of the aggregate-demand (*AD*) and short-run aggregate-supply (*SRAS*) curves occurs below the natural level of output at *e*. An autonomous increase in government spending or an autonomous reduction in taxes increases aggregate demand. If fiscal policymakers could manipulate government spending and taxes to increase aggregate demand so that the aggregate supply/demand equilibrium occurs at the natural level of output, the deflationary gap would be eliminated. Moreover, the deflationary gap could then be removed without having to wait for the self-correcting mechanism to work. Because the short-run aggregate-supply curve is upward-sloping, fiscal policy could raise both output and prices by moving the economy along *SRAS* to point *e'*. The self-correcting mechanism would have eventually yielded the same output (at point *a*) but with a lower price level.

Figure 1   Fiscal Policy with Deflationary and Inflationary Gaps

(a) Expansionary Fiscal Policy for a Deflationary Gap

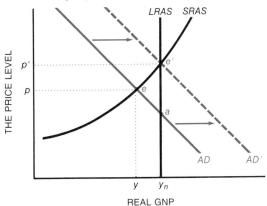

(b) Contractionary Fiscal Policy for an Inflationary Gap

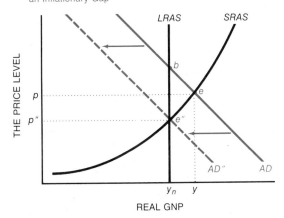

Panel (a) shows how expansionary fiscal policy could be used to eliminate a deflationary gap. By increasing autonomous government spending or by autonomously reducing taxes, the aggregate-demand curve could be shifted to the right (from AD to AD'), restoring the economy to the natural rate of output, y_n. Panel (b) shows how contractionary fiscal policy could be used to eliminate a deflationary gap. By reducing autonomous government spending or by autonomously lowering taxes, the aggregate-demand curve could be shifted to the left (from AD to AD'') to restore the economy to the natural rate of output.

Panel (a) of Figure 1 shows how an **expansionary fiscal policy** could remove a deflationary gap. Panel (b) shows how a **contractionary fiscal policy** could remove an inflationary gap.

An **expansionary fiscal policy** increases aggregate demand by raising autonomous government spending and or by autonomously lowering taxes.

A **contractionary fiscal policy** lowers aggregate demand by lowering autonomous government spending or by autonomously raising taxes.

AUTOMATIC STABILIZERS VERSUS DISCRETIONARY POLICY

Governments spend money and collect taxes on a continuous basis. Whether intended or not, their spending and taxing actions affect aggregate demand.

Many fiscal-policy actions take place automatically and require no policy decisions on the part of government—as in the case of an **entitlement program**, such as Social Security or unemployment-compensation payments.

An **entitlement program** requires the federal government to pay benefits to any person or unit of government that meets the eligibility requirements stated in the entitlement legislation.

To receive entitlement payments, recipients need only demonstrate that they qualify under established rules. Once the rules are set, the government does not determine the magnitude of such entitlement-program payments. Instead, the payment totals tend to depend on general economic conditions. At the Federal level, 75 percent of all federal outlays in 1984 were for relatively uncontrollable items like entitlements, permanent appropriations, and interest on the national debt.[1] Federal tax revenues come in on much the same basis. Once income-tax rates are set and rules concerning depreciation, personal exemptions, and the like are set, government tax revenues depend upon general economic conditions.

Other government revenues and expenditures

---

1. Stanley E. Collender, *The Guide to the Federal Budget, 1984 edition* (Washington, D.C.: The Urban Institute Press, 1983), pp. 5–6.

Table 3   Tax Rates and Multipliers: The Effect of a $100 Billion Increase in Income with an *MPC* out of Disposable Income of 0.8

Tax Rate	Change in Income, ΔY	Change in Disposable Income, ΔPDY	Change in Consumption, ΔC	Marginal Propensity to Consume (ΔC/ΔY)	Simple Multiplier, $\left(\dfrac{1}{1-MPC}\right)$
0.	$100 billion	$100 billion	$80 billion	0.80	4.0
0.10	$100 billion	$ 90 billion	$72 billion	0.72	3.57
0.20	$100 billion	$ 80 billion	$64 billion	0.64	2.78

As the tax rate rises, the marginal propensity to consume (*MPC*) falls and the multiplier falls. As explained in Chapter 10, the multiplier equals $1/(1 - MPC)$.

are determined by deliberate, discretionary decision making on the part of government. For example, rules concerning eligibility for entitlement programs can be changed; income-tax rates can be raised or lowered; major new defense-expenditure or public-works programs can be started.

Economists distinguish between two types of fiscal policy: **automatic stabilizers** and **discretionary fiscal policies.**

Automatic stabilizers are government spending or taxation actions that take place without any deliberate government control and that tend automatically to dampen the business cycle.

Discretionary fiscal policies are government spending and taxation actions that have been deliberately taken to achieve specified macroeconomic goals.

Automatic Stabilizers

Consider an economy that is subjected to disruptive cyclical disturbances caused by fluctuating investment. If investment declines, output falls. If investment rises, output rises. The multiplier analysis of Chapter 10 showed how fluctuations in investment spending could result in magnified fluctuations in output. This section explains how automatic stabilizers moderate the effects on output of such changes.

Two automatic stabilizers are built into most modern economies: 1) the income-tax system and

2) unemployment-compensation and welfare payments.

The Tax System.   The amount of income tax a government can collect is determined by applying the tax rate to the amount of the economy's taxable income. If an economy has an average tax rate of 20 percent of income, and if total income is $100 billion, the government will collect $20 billion in income taxes (20 percent times $100 billion). If total income rises to $150 billion, the government will collect $30 billion (20 percent times $150 billion). Thus, it is easy to see that the amount of income tax collected tends to rise and fall with income.

Chapter 10 showed that the simple multiplier depends upon the marginal propensity to consume (*MPC*), where the *MPC* is the change in consumption (ΔC) divided by the change in income (ΔY). To this point, our analysis has not taken into account the fact that taxes tend to rise and fall with income. The *MPC* out of *disposable income* reflects the fundamental propensities of households to consume and save as their income changes. The *MPC* out of GNP and, hence, the multiplier depend upon the tax rate.

Table 3 shows that *MPC* out of GNP depends upon the tax rate. The higher is the tax rate, the lower is the *MPC* and, hence, the lower is the multiplier. In Table 3, the *MPC out of disposable income* (income after taxes) is 0.8. If disposable income goes up by $100 billion, consumption goes up by $80 billion. If the tax rate is 0 percent (there are no income taxes), the *MPC* is also 0.8

Example 1   Unemployment Compensation and Welfare Payments

One of the most important automatic stabilizers is the system of unemployment compensation and welfare payments. The accompanying table relates the magnitude of unemployment to the amounts of transfer payments (in 1984 dollars) made by federal, state, and local governments. The table shows that these payments tend to rise with the unemployment rate. Unemployment compensation appears to be most sensitive to unemployment; state and local transfer payments are least sensitive to unemployment.

These numbers suggest the importance of unemployment compensation and general transfer payments as automatic stabilizers in our economy. Between 1970 and 1975, for example, the unemployment rate rose from 4.9 percent to 8.5 percent while federal transfer payments rose by 77 percent in constant dollars. Between 1970 and 1975, unemployment compensation tripled. Between 1978 and 1983, the unemployment rate rose from 6.1 percent to 9.6 percent while unemployment compensation rose more than 50 percent and federal transfers went up by 31 percent (in constant dollars). ∎

Source: *Economic Report of the President.*

Year	Unemployment Rate (percent)	Transfer Payments (billions of 1984 dollars)		
		Federal Transfer Payments	State and Local Transfer Payments	Unemployment Compensation
1960	5.5	66	18	10.3
1965	4.5	87	23	7.4
1968	3.6	116	29	5.7
1970	4.9	133	35	10.1
1973	4.9	185	44	9.5
1975	8.5	235	44	30.0
1978	6.1	269	50	13.5
1980	7.1	296	49	20.5
1983	9.6	351	51	21.0
1984	7.5	341	55	12.0

because total income and disposable income are the same. If the tax rate in our example rises from 0 percent to 10 percent, and if income rises by $100 billion, taxes rise by $10 billion, leaving an increase in disposable income of $90 billion. With an *MPC out of disposable income* of 0.8, consumption increases by $72 billion. With a 10 percent tax rate, the $100 billion increase in income has resulted in a $72 billion increase in consumption. Therefore, the *MPC* is 0.72 ($72 billion/$100 billion.) Table 3 shows that if the tax rate is raised to 20 percent, a $100 billion increase in income leads to a $64 billion increase in consumption, for an *MPC* of 0.64.

The last column of Table 3 shows the simple multipliers associated with each tax rate. The simple multiplier ranges from 4 at a 0 tax rate to 2.78 at a 20 percent tax rate. The higher is the tax rate, the lower is the multiplier.

The above analysis explains how the tax system acts as an automatic stabilizer, moderating the effects of cyclical disturbances. If there is a sudden drop in autonomous investment spending, the multiplier effect on output will be smaller the higher is the tax rate because when investment increases, income goes up but so do taxes. Thus, consumption rises by less than it would if taxes were constant. With smaller multipliers, the effect of cyclical disturbances on output and employment will be lessened.

Unemployment Compensation and Welfare Payments.   If investment declined substantially, and the economy dropped below full employment, more people would be unemployed and would be eligible for unemployment entitlement benefits. Moreover, families whose incomes have declined due to fewer hours of work or unemployment would become eligible for welfare assistance. Unemployment compensation and increased welfare payments soften the fluctuation of the cycle by preventing consumption expenditures from falling as much as they would have if these programs had not been in effect. Unemployment-compensation and welfare programs also soften the business cycle on the upswing. Welfare recipients are taken off the welfare and unemployment-compensation rolls as they find jobs, and increased deductions from payrolls (to state and local programs and union unemployment funds) reduce the amount of disposable income going to employed workers. (See Example 1.)

> Government spending tends to rise automatically during recessions as more people become eligible for entitlement programs. Government spending, therefore, acts as an automatic stabilizer.

There are two problems with relying exclusively on automatic stabilizers to iron out business cycles: 1) they don't eliminate fluctuations but only moderate them, and 2) they are counteracted by *automatic destabilizers.*

First, automatic stabilizers cannot fully neutralize the business cycle. If the economy is operating at full employment and investment falls, the automatic stabilizers will neutralize only a part of the decline in output. The effect of taxes will be to reduce the multiplier effect of the reduced investment. Unemployment compensation and other welfare payments will restore only a portion of lost disposable income.

Second, not all automatic aspects of federal spending and taxation are stabilizing (cause the economy to soften the fluctuations of the business cycle). An important case in point is the **fiscal drag** of the pre-1985 U.S. progressive tax system. A *progressive income tax* is one where higher-income taxpayers have higher tax rates. During periods of rapid inflation, the tax system has tended to push individuals into higher tax brackets. When prices are rising at the same rate as money income, real income is constant; yet the share of income being paid in federal income taxes is increasing because inflation pushes people into higher tax brackets. If real income is constant, yet the proportion of disposable income left over after taxes is falling, real disposable income is falling. Thus, inflation acts to increase tax rates when taxes are progressive and tax schedules aren't adjusted downward (indexed) for inflation. Starting in 1985, however, the United States began indexing its tax schedule so that real tax rates do not increase with the level of prices.

> **Fiscal drag** is the tendency for nonindexed progressive taxes to act as an automatic destabilizer. If inflation accompanies excessive unemployment, progressive taxes lead to automatic destabilizing increases in taxes.[2]

Discretionary Fiscal Policy

Because automatic stabilizers can only ameliorate cyclical instability—not eliminate it—the proponents of activist (discretionary) macroeconomic policies believe discretionary fiscal policy can play an important stabilizing role. Like discretionary monetary policy, the aim of discretionary fiscal policy is to eliminate inflationary and deflationary gaps. The direction of activist discretionary fiscal policy was pointed out in Figure 1: *discretionary fiscal policy should change government spending and government taxes to close in-*

---

2. An earlier notion of fiscal drag formulated in the late 1950s originated from the concern that a proportional tax system would act as a *drag* on the economy—keeping it at less than full employment. Taxes would rise automatically with income, but there would be no similar automatic force causing government spending to rise at the same rate. With taxes rising faster than government spending, drag would be placed upon aggregate expenditures. Today there is less concern that government spending will fail to keep up with government tax collection.

flationary or deflationary gaps. If an inflationary gap is present, government should cut government spending or raise taxes. If a deflationary gap is present, the government should raise spending or cut taxes to raise output.

Discretionary fiscal policy operates through **autonomous changes** in tax rates and 2) government expenditures.

> **Autonomous changes** are changes in tax rates or government spending that are independent of changes in income.

Policies for a Deflationary Gap.

Panel (a) of Figure 1 showed an economy in a deflationary gap, operating below the natural level of output. The long-run self-correcting mechanism would eventually restore the economy to full employment through deflation, but discretionary fiscal policy offers an opportunity to restore the economy to full employment without waiting for the self-correcting mechanism. In this situation, government tax and spending authorities could lower tax rates and raise discretionary government spending (adopt an expansionary fiscal policy). If they lowered tax rates or raised discretionary spending by the right amounts, the aggregate-demand curve could be shifted to the right to intersect the *SRAS* curve at *e'* at the natural level of output.

As output falls in response to cyclical pressures, the government could raise its expenditures above and beyond the increases called for by the automatic stabilizers (such as unemployment-compensation and welfare programs). The government could spend additional money on relatively controllable programs like dams, public parks, increased police protection, and the like. The government could liberalize unemployment-compensation rules and change eligibility requirements for welfare, thereby raising the incomes of the unemployed and the poor. Discretionary increases in government spending shift the aggregate-demand curve to the right.

Policies for an Inflationary Gap.

Panel (b) of Figure 1 shows an economy in an inflationary gap. If left alone, the economy would return to the natural level of unemployment through the process of inflation. In this situation, government tax and spending authorities could raise tax rates and reduce discretionary government spending (adopt a contractionary fiscal policy). If tax rates were raised or discretionary government spending reduced by the right amounts, the aggregate-demand curve could be shifted to the left to intersect the *SRAS* curve at point *e″* at the natural level of output.

There are different political costs and benefits to expansionary and contractionary fiscal policies. Expansionary fiscal policies tend to be politically more popular. Tax rates are lowered; it becomes easier to qualify for entitlement benefits; members of Congress find it easier to get their favorite spending programs funded. Expansionary fiscal policies tend to win many friends and make few enemies. Contractionary fiscal policies, on the other hand, tend to make many enemies and win few friends. The voters do not like tax increases, or more restrictions on eligibility for entitlement benefits. Special-interest groups would oppose the nonpassage of pork-barrel spending legislation. For these reasons, the government is more willing to use expansionary fiscal policy than contractionary fiscal policy.

The Full-Employment Surplus

Because many government taxes and expenditures respond automatically to changes in GNP, the direction of discretionary fiscal policy cannot be gauged simply by looking at government spending, taxes, and the government surplus or deficit (see Figure 2). During periods of declining GNP, the government deficit tends to become more negative. As income falls, so do tax collections. But government obligations, in the form of unemployment-compensation payments and welfare transfers, rise as income falls. Therefore, the automatic stabilizers automatically push the government budget in the direction of deficits. Figure 2 illustrates this trend. Rising government deficits (color shaded areas) have been associated primarily with recessions. During recessions, government revenues fall steeply while government expenditures continue to rise. The

Figure 2   Government Expenditures, Revenues, and Deficits as a Percentage of GNP, 1960–1984

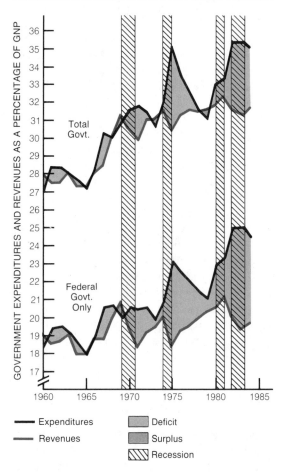

- —— Expenditures
- —— Revenues
- ▨ Deficit
- ▨ Surplus
- ▨ Recession

This figure shows that since 1960 deficits tend to be associated with recessions. During recessions, government revenues fall while expenditures rise. The late 1960s (the Vietnam years) were an exception to this rule.

Source: *Economic Report of the President.*

deficits of the Vietnam War (in the late 1960s) were characterized by government spending that rose more rapidly than rising government revenues and are an exception to this rule. To measure discretionary fiscal policy, the effects of automatic stabilizers must be removed from government revenues and expenditures. The yardstick against which economists measure the direction of discretionary fiscal policy is the **full-employment surplus (deficit)**.

The **full-employment surplus (deficit)** is what the government budget surplus or deficit would have been had the economy been operating at the natural rate (full employment).

To illustrate, assume that the natural rate of unemployment is 6 percent and that the economy is operating at 8 percent unemployment. Because the economy is 2 percentage points below full employment, the government must make substantial payments for welfare and unemployment compensation, and it will collect fewer taxes. The actual budget deficit (actual revenues minus actual expenditures) will be $40 billion, but at full employment revenues would have been $15 billion more and expenditures would have been $10 billion less. The full-employment deficit, therefore, is $15 billion (= $40 − $15 − $10)—a deficit much smaller than the actual deficit.

Full-employment budget figures do not have an exact meaning for a single year, but when compared with the full-employment budget for other years, they should indicate the direction of government discretionary fiscal policy. Figure 3 supplies data on the actual government budget and the full-employment budget from 1950 to 1984. Since there are difficulties associated with defining full-employment output, these figures must be regarded as approximate. Many economists and government officials regard them as quite useful despite their arbitrary element, however.

An examination of Figure 3 shows that, although the actual and full-employment surpluses tend to move generally together, they are far from the same. In the 1980s, for example, the full-employment deficit has been much smaller than the actual deficit. The most useful function of the full-employment budget is to show changes in discretionary fiscal policy. A decrease in the full-employment surplus (or an increase in the full-employment deficit) signals a move to a more expansionary fiscal policy. According to Figure 3, the 1960s was a period of fiscal expansion up to the late 1960s. The first half of the 1970s was a period of fiscal expansion, while the second half of the 1970s was a period of fiscal contraction. So far, the 1980s has been a period of fiscal expansion because the full-employment deficit has been increasing.

Figure 3   The Actual Budget Versus the Full-Employment Budget of the United States, 1950–1984

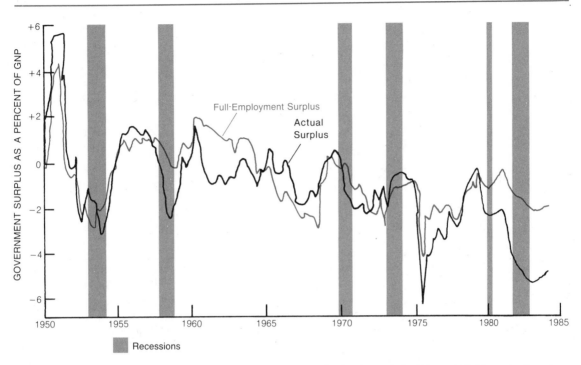

Recessions

The black line shows the actual federal-government surplus or deficit for the period 1950 to 1985. The color line gives the full-employment surplus or deficit for the same years. The full-employment budget should reveal changes in discretionary fiscal policy over this period. Crosshatched areas are periods of recession.

Source: Robert J. Gordon, *Macroeconomics*, 3rd ed. (Boston: Little, Brown & Co., 1981), Appendix B.

Fiscal Policy and Aggregate Supply

Figure 1 showed the effects of fiscal policy on aggregate demand. Discretionary reductions in tax rates or discretionary increases in government spending affect output and prices by increasing aggregate demand. Discretionary increases in taxes or discretionary reductions in government spending affect output and employment by reducing aggregate demand.

Changes in tax policy may affect both aggregate demand *and* aggregate supply, as in the case where tax authorities generally lower income-tax rates paid by individuals and corporations. These lower tax rates can affect an individual taxpayer's **average tax rate** and **marginal tax rate**.

The **average tax rate** is the individual's tax payment divided by taxable income.

The **marginal tax rate** is the increase in the individual's tax payment caused by a $1 increase in taxable income.

A taxpayer who pays $10,000 in taxes on a $50,000 income has a 20 percent average tax rate. If that person's tax payment rises to $15,000 when income rises to $60,000, the marginal tax rate is 50 percent. The $10,000 increase in income has caused a $5,000 increase in taxes—for a marginal tax rate of 50 percent.

In the case of corporations, the reduction in tax rates could take the form of tax reductions for additional investment. Corporations may be granted *investment tax credits*, whereby for every dollar the corporation invests in equipment it can reduce its tax payments by a certain fraction of a dollar—say, $0.10. Corporations may also be given increased tax incentives to acquire capital equip-

Figure 4   Demand-Side Versus Supply-Side Views of the Effects of a Tax Cut

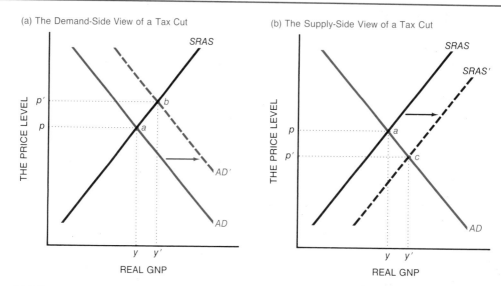

(a) The Demand-Side View of a Tax Cut

(b) The Supply-Side View of a Tax Cut

As panel (a) illustrates, the demand-side view of a tax cut is that a tax cut will affect output and prices through an increase in aggregate demand (from *AD* to *AD'*). The increase in aggregate demand raises both output and prices. The supply-side view, in panel (b), is that the tax cut affects output and prices through an increase in short-run aggregate supply (from *SRAS* to *SRAS'*). The increase in short-run aggregate supply raises output and lowers prices.

ment by permitting them to depreciate capital more rapidly.

Some economists (called *supply-side economists*) argue that tax cuts of the sort described above will increase short-run and long-run aggregate supply. Individuals will respond to lower marginal tax rates by working more, taking more risks, and perhaps saving more. Businesses will respond to investment incentives by investing in new technology. As people increase their work effort and as businesses modernize their plant and equipment, aggregate supply increases.

Figure 4 contrasts the two potential effects of discretionary tax cuts. In panel (a), the tax cuts cause an increase in aggregate demand only. In panel (b), the tax cuts cause an increase in short-run aggregate supply only. In general, when tax rates fall, both aggregate demand and a short-run aggregate supply increase. If the aggregate-demand increase dominates, output increases and *prices increase*. If the aggregate-supply increase dominates, output increases but *prices fall*. If authorities could cut taxes and count on substantial increases in short-run aggregate supply, the result would be the best of both worlds: more output and lower prices. Whether tax cuts cause signifi-

cant aggregate-supply increases is an empirical issue to which we shall return in a later chapter.

Fiscal Policy and Deficits

Keynesian Policy.   Discretionary fiscal policy was highly touted by the Keynesian model as a weapon for dealing with inflationary and especially deflationary gaps. Keynes feared that monetary policy would not be effective with vast unemployed resources. Automatic built-in stabilizers would ameliorate business cycles but would not eliminate them. In Keynes's view, discretionary fiscal policy would have to carry the heaviest load in the conduct of activist policies.

The proponents of activist fiscal policy maintain that government expenditures and taxes should be set in order to induce the economy to produce at full employment. If budget deficits (or surpluses) are required to raise output to full employment, then these budget deficits (or surpluses) are a small price to pay for full employment. The actual size of the government surplus or deficit is not critical at any one point in time. The budget surplus or deficit should not be allowed to stand in the way of important macroeconomic goals.

Example 2   Measuring the Deficit

In a world of changing interest rates and prices, the true deficit is the change in the *real value* of the federal government's net debt (the difference between total liabilities and total financial assets). Economists Robert Eisner and Paul J. Pieper argue that if we correctly measure the deficit, taking into account the fact that the federal government owns certain financial assets (such as gold) and that inflation and interest rates change the value of these assets, then the federal budget is more frequently in surplus than in deficit. First, inflation reduces the purchasing power of the nominal value of the debt owed by the federal government. Second, an increase in prices may be associated with an increase in the price of gold, which will reduce the net federal debt because the government holds stocks of gold. Third, when interest rates change, the market value of the federal government's outstanding debt changes. The Eisner-Pieper adjustment factors can either increase or decrease the nominal deficit: if prices fall, if the gold price falls, or if interest rates fall, nominal deficits may be smaller than the corrected deficit. When Eisner and Pieper recalculated the deficit or surplus for the years 1976 to 1980, they found that the federal government had a real *surplus* in the years 1978–1980 instead of a deficit. ∎

Source: Robert Eisner and Paul J. Pieper, "A New View of the Federal Debt and Budget Deficits," *American Economic Review,* 74 (March 1984): 11–29.

According to this budgetary philosophy, it would be very unwise to adopt the goal of a balanced federal budget. If the economy is experiencing a cyclical disturbance (say, a reduction in private investment) that causes output to fall below full employment, as output declines, so do tax revenues. Therefore, to balance the budget, government expenditures must be reduced by the amount of the reduction in tax collections. To pursue a balanced budget during a cyclical downturn would only make the downturn worse. A balanced-budget policy would also intensify inflationary cyclical upturns. A balanced budget requires that government expenditures rise with the increase in taxes; therefore, income will increase by the amount of the increase in government spending (the balanced-budget multiplier again).

In the early 1960s, economists and public officials almost unanimously embraced the Keynesian budgetary philosophy. Balanced budgets were no longer regarded as desirable *per se;* instead, budgets were to be constructed to meet macroeconomic goals. The decline in popularity of the balanced-budget philosophy signaled an important triumph for the Keynesian revolution. In 1964, taxes were cut, and the deficit was deliberately increased to reduce unemployment. Taxes were *cut* in 1981 because of the supply-side arguments raised above; this tax cut could be a test of Keynesian budget philosophy (see Example 2).

A Cyclically Balanced Budget. The Keynesian budgetary approach does not advocate *sustained* deficits or surpluses. During periods of excessive unemployment, budget deficits would be called for, but budget surpluses would be required during inflationary upswings. Therefore, although there was no rule that the budget should be balanced each year, it was expected that budget surpluses and deficits would even out in the long run—especially if cyclical downturns would be equal in duration and magnitude to cyclical upturns.

As Figure 2 showed, the early expectation of a long-run balanced budget has not materialized. Since 1960, the federal budget has had only 2 years of surpluses and more than 24 years of deficits. In recent years public alarm over the growing size of the federal deficit has grown, setting off bitter political struggles. Annual deficits of more than $200 billion are being forecast for the near future. Deficits are still with us and are growing despite the campaign promises of several presidents to balance the budget.

The Classical Case for Balanced Budgets.

The Keynesian argument against a strict balanced-budget rule was a substantial departure from the philosophy of the classical school. If, as the classical economists maintained, economies tend to operate at full employment, increases in government expenditures could not raise real GNP.

Rather, increased government spending would push up interest rates and would be perfectly offset by an equivalent reduction in investment. This result is the extreme case of complete crowding out in which every extra dollar of government spending is matched by a dollar reduction in private investment.

In the classical view, government deficits, therefore, tend to increase government spending at the expense of investment. But economic growth in the long run will suffer if government spending crowds out investment. Lower rates of capital accumulation translate into lower rates of growth of real GNP in the long run. In the long run, growing government deficits can mean lower standards of living.

The crowding-out problem remains in the case of incomplete crowding out, in which government deficits choke off some private investment and reduce the capital stock available to the economy for long-run growth.

Modern-day advocates of balanced budgets echo the fears of the classical economists that growing government deficits can crowd out private investment. They also maintain that one of the major advantages of requiring a cyclically balanced budget is the prevention of excessive growth of government. If it were clear that government programs would have to be paid for over the business cycle out of tax revenues, voters and politicians would limit government spending to socially necessary programs. As long as governments can borrow to pay for their programs, the temptation may be too great to have too large a government.

The Effectiveness of Fiscal Policy

The aim of discretionary fiscal policy is to eliminate inflationary or deflationary gaps more quickly than the self-correcting mechanism can eliminate them. Critics of the use of discretionary fiscal policy cite the difficulties of conducting effective fiscal policy in a real-world setting. These critics believe that: 1) fiscal policy is too slow-moving and cumbersome and often inappropriate or counterproductive; (2) the effects of fiscal policies (especially tax policies) on aggregate demand are uncertain and, in certain cases, even negligible; 3) increased government spending may

crowd out private investment and reduce the long-run growth prospects of the economy.

Lags in Fiscal Policy.   Changes in taxation and government spending must be approved by Congress and supported by the President. Changes in tax policies and revisions in tax codes often take several years or more between their inception and enactment. Public-works programs must be approved by Congress, and they are often handled on a case-by-case basis. The President must either accept or veto budgets forwarded by Congress. The President cannot selectively veto specific spending proposals within a budget because the President is not authorized to use a *line-item veto*. Often logrolling overrides considerations of macroeconomic stabilization policy. There are actually three fiscal-policy lags: a *recognition lag,* an *implementation lag,* and an *effectiveness lag.* First, Congress and the President may be slow in recognizing that a change in fiscal policy is necessary. Reliable statistics on real output become available only six months after the fact. No one knows for sure whether a downturn is temporary or the start of a serious downtrend. It is difficult to recognize when a change in fiscal policy is required.

Second, unlike monetary policy, fiscal policy is subject to a substantial implementation lag—by the time the program goes through Congress and becomes implemented, the policy may no longer be the correct one. Third, the effectiveness lag is the amount of time it takes between implementation of a fiscal-policy action and an actual change in economic conditions. Statistical evidence on the length of the effectiveness lag is mixed, but it does appear that the effectiveness lag is longer for fiscal policy than for monetary policy.[3]

Critics of activist fiscal policy ask whether a country can carry out effective discretionary fiscal policy when such enormous time lags and political delays are involved.

Permanent Income.   The effects of discretionary tax policy are reduced by *permanent-income effects*. Tax cuts affect aggregate demand only if lower tax payments cause the consumption

3. Robert Gordon, *Macroeconomics,* 3rd ed. (Boston, Mass.: Little, Brown and Co., 1984), p. 549.

income curve to shift up. As long as the marginal propensity to consume (*MPC*) remains stable, tax-induced changes in disposable income should elicit predictable changes in consumption. But how stable is the consumption/income relationship? Keynes felt it would be one of the most stable relationships in the whole economy, but economists after Keynes have come to question this proposition.

Many modern economists argue that people tend to base their consumption decisions on life-cycle income, or **permanent income**, not on transitory changes in current income.

> **Permanent income** is an average of the income that an individual anticipates earning over the long run.

If there is a transitory change in this year's income—say, due to a tax increase that is generally regarded as a one-shot affair—the effect on current consumption will be minimal. The impact of the tax on long-run income is so small that few people will change their current consumption.

If people do indeed base their spending decisions on permanent income, the relationship between this year's income and this year's consumption can be quite unstable. This instability means the *MPC* and, hence, the tax multiplier cannot be known in advance. Discretionary tax policy is difficult to pursue if its effects on private spending are unknown.

Crowding Out.   We have already pointed out that expansionary fiscal policies may crowd out private investment by pushing up interest rates. When this happens, the growth of the nation's capital stock has been retarded, and the long-run growth of the economy has been reduced. Moreover, because the amount of crowding out (either direct or indirect) is difficult to predict, the exact effects of fiscal stimulus are difficult to predict.

THE ECONOMICS OF THE PUBLIC DEBT

Figure 3 showed that the federal government has run a deficit in at least 23 of the last 25 years. Although many people had hoped that the budget would be balanced over the business cycle, this balancing has not occurred. The federal budget has been in deficit during periods of rising prosperity as well as during periods of recession.

When the federal budget is in deficit, the federal government is *dissaving*. Like individuals who dissave, the federal government must borrow to finance the difference between expenditures and revenues. The federal government borrows by selling IOUs in the form of U.S. government bonds or bills to private individuals (both at home and abroad), to banks, corporations, and to the Federal Reserve banks. The cumulated outstanding debt of the federal government is the **national debt.**

> The **national debt** is (approximately) the sum of outstanding federal government IOUs upon which interest and principal payments must be made.

The *federal deficit* is the *annual addition* to the national debt. If the federal deficit is $180 billion in 1990, then the national debt will grow by that amount in that year.

People tend to be concerned about the national debt for three reasons.

1. People fear that the deficits that cause the national debt to grow create inflation.
2. People fear that large deficits cause interest rates to rise.
3. People fear that the national debt will either bankrupt the nation or place an unbearable tax burden on future generations.

Deficits and Inflation

When the federal government runs a deficit, it must sell IOUs to someone. If the IOUs are sold to the public, either at home or abroad, the money supply is not affected. Bank reserves are not altered, and the amount of checking-account money in the economy is not changed. If, however, the federal government's IOUs are purchased by the Fed, then new reserves are pumped into the banking system. As these new reserves enter the banking system, the money supply expands. If the Fed's purchase of U.S. Treasury securities leads to excess monetary growth, inflation can result. Deficits can increase the money supply and, hence, cause inflation. Second, if deficits are caused by a rapid expansion of government spending (rather than by shrinking revenues), such deficits can cause aggregate demand to rise and, hence, cause inflation to rise.

The next chapter discusses in detail the relationship between deficits and inflation. This section gives a brief summary of this deficit/inflation relationship. In the short run, the relationship between deficits and inflation is weak. Over the course of the business cycle, the relationship can change. During the recession phase the deficit tends to grow, but product and labor markets are weak, and prices remain stable. During the recovery stage, the deficit falls, but product and labor markets are tight and inflation heats up. Increases in the deficit can have a number of causes: income and tax revenues can be falling, the government may be following an aggressive expansion of government spending, taxes may have been cut. Each of these factors should have different effects on inflation.

When cyclical effects are averaged out over the long run, there is a positive relationship between deficits and inflation. The reason for this long-run pattern will be discussed in the next chapter.

Deficits and Interest Rates

A second concern about deficits stems from the belief that large deficits push up interest rates. The logical argument is that when the U.S. government runs a deficit, it must borrow funds in credit markets just like any other borrower. When the U.S. government runs a large deficit, it increases the demand for credit, and an increase in the demand for credit should raise interest rates. As interest rates rise, private businesses reduce their borrowing for investment purposes, and the federal deficit crowds out private investment.

Although this proposition has gained wide acceptance, the empirical relationship between federal deficits and interest rates is surprisingly weak. Figure 5 plots interest rates and the federal deficit (as a percent of GNP) for the period 1960 to 1984 but 5 fails to reveal the expected positive relationship between interest rates and the deficit. When interest rates rose in the late 1960s, the federal deficit was falling. Interest rates fell in the early 1970s as the deficit was rising. In the 1980s,

Figure 5   The Federal Deficit and Interest Rates, 1960–1984

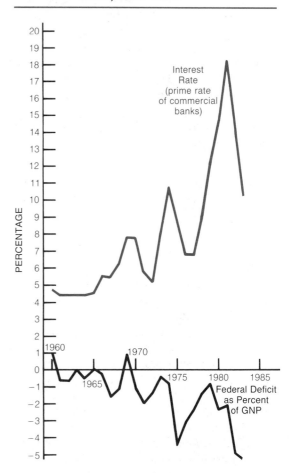

This figure fails to demonstrate a positive relationship between the federal deficit as a percent of GNP and interest rates.

Source: *Economic Report of the President.*

the deficit was soaring while interest rates were falling. However, the high interest rates in the mid 1970s did correspond to rising federal deficits.

The relationship between deficits and interest rates will be explored in more depth in Chapter 18 on interest rates. For now, it is interesting to ask why the relationship between federal deficits and interest rates appears weak. First, deficits appear to be highest during recessions when credit demand is low. Therefore, government borrowing may not necessarily push up interest rates. Second, as Figure 2 revealed, the deficits of total government (including state and local government) tend to be smaller than the federal deficit. In recent years, some of the federal deficit has been offset by budget surpluses at the state and local level. Third, the credit market has indeed become a world credit market over the last decades. People with funds to loan can now place these funds in London, New York, Tokyo, Hong Kong, or Latin America on a moment's notice. Cast in this global perspective, the large U.S. deficits of the early 1980s make up only a small percentage of the credit demand in world credit markets. It may be that U.S. deficits (even though they appear large in absolute size) are too small to affect interest rates in world credit markets.

Fourth, increases in government debt may motivate taxpayers to increase their saving. If taxpayers recognize that higher deficits now mean higher taxes in the future, they may increase private saving to be in a position to handle the future tax burden. In this case, if the increase in private saving offsets the increase in public dissaving, the interest should rate be unaffected.[4] (See Example 3.)

The Burden of Debt

Debt Relative to GNP.   Figure 6 provides some facts on the public debt that shed light on the burden of the debt. Whether the debt of the federal government is unreasonably large should be determined just like private debt. The person who goes to a bank to borrow money will be asked what he or she earns and about existing liabilities. The borrower who reports an annual income of $100,000 and no outstanding debts will be able to borrow much more than the borrower reporting a $15,000 annual income with annual debt payments of $5,000. Debt must be judged relative to the ability of the debtor to pay the interest and principal on the debt.

What determines the U.S. government's ability to carry debt? Insofar as tax collections (the government's income) are closely tied to GNP, ultimately the federal government's income depends upon the amount of GNP produced. Government tax receipts since 1960 have averaged around 20 percent of GNP; a GNP of $4 trillion would give

4. See Robert J. Barro, *Macroeconomics* (New York: John Wiley and Sons, 1984), chap. 15.

Figure 6   Public Debt as a Percent of GNP, 1945–1984

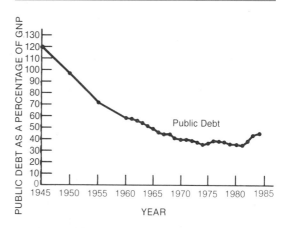

Despite growing concern about the size of the public debt, public debt as a percent of GNP has been steadily falling throughout the postwar period, although it did rise between 1981 and 1984.

Source: *Statistical Abstract of the United States,* 1981, p. 245; *Economic Report of the President.*

the federal government income of $800 billion. A GNP of $3 trillion would give the government a smaller annual income of $600 billion. The amount of GNP produced now and in the future is a critical determinant of the reasonableness of the national debt.

As Figure 6 indicates, public debt as a percentage of GNP has been declining since the end of World War II. In 1945, public debt was 1.2 times GNP. By 1981, the ratio of debt to GNP had fallen to 34 percent. Between 1981 and 1984, the national debt rose from 34 percent to 44 percent of GNP. If one compares these figures with the indebtedness of individuals, one can see that in 1980 the private debt of families (consumer installment credit plus mortgages) equaled about 80 percent of personal disposable income. On average, the American family has an accumulated personal debt equal to 80 percent of one year's income after taxes.

The burden of the public debt can also be measured by the proportion of current income that is devoted to paying interest and principal on the debt. In 1984, 13 percent of federal government expenditures were devoted to interest payments

Example 3   Another View of Deficits and Interest Rates

One reason people fear the deficit is that they believe high deficits raise interest rates. Just as one can look at the effect of the deficit on interest rates, so can one look at the effect of interest rates on the deficit. The accompanying figure supplies data on the federal deficit since 1959. The color line shows the actual deficit as a percent of GNP. The black line shows the *primary deficit;* that is, the deficit with interest payments excluded. With interest payments excluded, the primary deficit would have been a surplus throughout most of the 1960s and would have showed surpluses in some years during the mid 1970s and late 1970s. According to the more conservative Congressional Budget Office projections, the primary deficit will be in balance in 1989 while the actual deficit will be around 5 percent of GNP. These figures again underscore the important role that recessions play

in causing deficits. The primary budget deficits occur primarily in recession years. ■

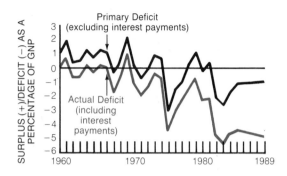

Source: Peter L. Bernstein, "When Public Borrowing Isn't a Burden," *The Wall Street Journal,* January 8, 1985. Figure data from the Congressional Budget Office.

on the national debt. For the average American family, approximately 6 percent of personal disposable income was devoted to interest payments on mortgages and consumer debt in the same year. In general, the burden of private debt appears to be less than that of national debt, but there are important reasons (discussed below) why the federal government can safely carry more debt relative to income than can private individuals.

In accumulating public debt, will the United States ever run the risk of bankruptcy? As long as GNP continues to grow at a rate as rapid or more rapid than the public debt, the burden of the debt will remain the same or decline. Therefore, a growing economy is the best protection against an increasing burden of the national debt.

Unlike private individuals, the federal government has a guarantee in addition to earning sufficient income that it will be able to handle the public debt. If the Fed is willing to cooperate, the federal government can finance the national debt by creating money! If the federal government runs a $50 billion deficit in a particular year, the U.S. Treasury can either sell $50 billion of bonds to the public or can ask the Fed to buy $50 billion worth of bonds. The Fed does not have to finance the federal deficit by buying federal government securities, but if it does, the Fed will have

pumped $50 billion worth of additional reserves into the economy. In other words, the federal government has financed its deficit by printing money. Individuals and corporations do not have this option for financing their debt; they are not able to create money; only the federal government can do so.

Internal Versus External Debt.   In the early 1950s, only 5 percent of the national debt was owned by foreigners. By 1984, the proportion had risen to 12 percent. Whether debt is held internally or externally makes a difference. If the debt is *internal,* then the United States basically owes it to itself. When interest payments are made on the national debt or when a government bond matures, income is transferred from one U.S. citizen to another. The taxpayers' dollars are used to pay interest and principal to the owner of the government bond. Insofar as the recipient of interest and principal payments is typically a taxpayer as well, the net transfer of income may be small. In the case of an internal debt, servicing the debt does not alter the amount of income in the country; it affects only the distribution of that income between public-debt owners and nonowners.

An *external* debt works differently: interest and principal payments represent transfers of income from U.S. taxpayers to residents of other countries. In 1983, $17.9 billion in interest and principal was paid to foreign owners of the national debt. The amount of income left in the country is affected by this type of transaction. Foreign ownership of the national debt has increased over the years for many reasons. The main reason is that the United States has come to be regarded as a safe haven by foreign investors. One need not conclude that external debt is bad. Had the United States not borrowed abroad, U.S. interest rates might have been much higher and private investment might have been much lower in the early 1980s.

Public Debt and Capital Accumulation

The fact that the U.S. government is not about to be bankrupted by rising public debt does not mean that there are no negative consequences of public debt.

Economists generally worry that a large public debt could lead a myopic population to save less and, hence, in the long run, would lead to less capital accumulation. Chapter 9 showed that an increase in assets held by the public could increase consumption and reduce saving. People who have already accumulated wealth do not have to save as much. The public debt is an asset to those who hold the IOUs, but it is a liability that must be met by future taxpayers. If present taxpayers do not fully recognize the taxes that they must ultimately pay to carry this debt, the public could spend more and save less than otherwise. In other words, the public debt might be treated as net wealth—even though it is not. In a long-run full-employment setting, a smaller capital stock is available for future generations. Empirical evidence on this effect is not decisive.

Problems of Deficit Reduction

The impact of deficits on the economy has been a hotly debated issue over the last decade. Economists are still uncertain about the effects of deficits on inflation, on interest rates, and on capital formation, but it is quite possible for rising deficits to crowd out private investment. Even if the historical association between deficits and interest rates is weak, there is still the widespread fear

that deficits cause high interest rates. These fears by themselves can raise inflationary expectations. Moreover, there is concern about the share of government in total economic activity; many people would like to see a lower share of government (or at least a stable share of government) in total economic activity.

For these reasons, most politicians and economists favor deficit reductions. Although several American presidents have made strong deficit-reduction pledges in their campaign platforms, over the past 15 years, no president has been able to produce a balanced federal budget. Why is it so difficult to achieve a balanced budget despite the best of intentions?

First, approximately 75 percent of all federal-government spending is for **relatively uncontrollable outlays.**

> **Relatively uncontrollable outlays** are government expenditures whose outlay level is determined by existing statutes, by contracts, or by other obligations. The President must by law include such items in the annual budget as submitted.

Examples of relatively uncontrollable outlays are Social Security benefits, military retirement pensions, unemployment assistance, public-assistance and related programs, farm-price supports, and outlays from prior-year contracts and obligations.

The predominance of relatively uncontrollable outlays means that in any given budget year, only about one quarter of federal-government outlays are subject to the discretionary control of budgetary authorities. The major expenditure category that is not dominated by uncontrollable outlays is national defense; only one quarter of national-defense outlays are relatively uncontrollable.

To cut the size of the federal deficit, federal revenues must be increased, federal outlays must be reduced, or a combination of the two must take place. In any particular year, budgetary authorities do not have much leeway in reducing outlays because of relatively uncontrollable outlays. Insofar as tax revenues depend upon the state of the economy (with given tax rates), they are largely out of the control of budgetary authorities as well. Therefore, to reduce the federal deficit, basic changes in entitlement programs are required to reduce *future* outlays on relatively uncontrollable items. In addition, changes in tax rates must be put into effect, and new sources of revenue must be found. Moreover, society may wish to reduce the amount of resources being devoted to defense spending. Examples of proposals currently under consideration to increase revenues in future years are: the taxation of certain entitlement benefits, the taxation of fringe benefits, the elimination of investment tax credits, and the raising of excise taxes. Proposals currently under consideration to reduce federal expenditures in future years are: slowing down the growth of defense spending, cutting back on the growth of Social Security pensions, scaling back military pensions, and eliminating farm-support programs.

The above lists of spending cuts and tax changes show the types of changes necessary to reduce the federal deficit. The problem is that any spending cut will be vigorously opposed by those who benefit from the spending program, and tax changes that raise government revenues will be just as vigorously opposed by those who would end up paying higher taxes. Affected parties are able to lobby their elected officials, making it difficult for elected officials to vote in favor of unpopular spending cuts or tax increases. Tax-increase proposals are further complicated by the need to raise only those tax items that will not result in a reduction of work effort or capital formation. If work effort and capital formation drop, income drops and there is less income to tax.

Although everyone favors deficit reductions, few are willing to pay the personal price of a lower deficit, particularly when it comes to giving up spending and tax programs that are of benefit to that individual. This fact, more than any other, explains why it is difficult to substantially reduce the deficit.

The next chapter will investigate the causes and cures of inflation and will examine in more detail the relationship between the deficit and inflation.

Summary

1.   Government budgets show the relationship between government revenues and outlays. A budget deficit means that the government unit is dissaving; a surplus means the government unit is saving. Currently, the federal government is running deficits while state and local governments combined run a surplus.

2.   The objective of discretionary fiscal policy is to eliminate inflationary and deflationary gaps. Fiscal policy is the deliberate control of government spending and taxation to achieve macroeconomic goals. Real-world government expenditure and tax multipliers determine how much fiscal stimulus or restraint is required to return the economy to the natural rate of output.

3.   A portion of government spending and tax collections depends upon income. Tax collections fall as income falls; welfare payments and unemployment compensation rise as income falls. Such automatic stabilizers soften the business cycle, but they cannot eliminate the business cycle. Discretionary policies are required to fully counteract cyclical disturbances.

4.   Because of automatic stabilizers, economists use the full-employment budget as a yardstick against which to measure changes in discretionary fiscal policy. The full-employment budget is the surplus or deficit that would have prevailed had the economy been producing full-employment output. Supply-side economists maintain that tax cuts that lower marginal tax rates and raise business investment incentives affect output and prices by increasing aggregate supply. Keynesian policy argues that deficits should be accepted if necessary to achieve full employment. Keynes, however, hoped that the budget would be balanced over the business cycle, but the federal budget has been in deficit during periods of both prosperity and recession.

5.   Critics question the effectiveness of fiscal policy because of lags, permanent-income effects, and the crowding out of private investment.

6.   The national debt is the sum of outstanding federal government IOUs. People fear the national debt because they believe it may cause inflation, high interest rates, and national bankruptcy, but sober analysis suggests that these fears may be exaggerated. Deficit reduction is difficult because most federal spending is relatively uncontrollable in the short run. In the long run, deficit reduction requires unpopular spending cuts and unpopular tax increases.

Key Terms

government deficit
government surplus
fiscal policy
expansionary fiscal policy
contractionary fiscal policy
entitlement program
automatic stabilizers
discretionary fiscal policies
fiscal drag
autonomous changes
full-employment surplus (deficit)
average tax rate
marginal tax rate
permanent income
national debt
relatively uncontrollable outlays

Questions and Problems

1. In Economy Z, private saving is $500 billion. Expenditures of the federal government are $700 billion, and its revenues are $650 billion. The combined expenditures of state and local government are $300 billion, and their combined revenues are $350 billion. What is the total amount of saving in the economy?

2. Economy Y is operating below the natural rate of output and autonomous government spending is increased by $50 billion. As a consequence of this action, private spending is reduced by $50 billion. What will be the impact of the increase in government spending on output and employment?

3. An economy goes into a recession and tax collections fall. Would it be correct to call this fall in tax collections an *autonomous change?*

4. Use the permanent-income hypothesis to predict which type of tax cut is more likely to affect aggregate output: a one-year tax surcharge or a permanent lowering of tax rates.

5. "If wages and prices are flexible in both inflationary and deflationary gaps, there is no need for activist macroeconomic policy." Evaluate this statement.

6. What is the difference between automatic stabilizers and discretionary fiscal policy? Are they not the same because they both work through government spending and taxes?

7. If actual government expenditures are $200 billion and actual government revenues are $100 billion, and if the economy is at less than full employment, would the full-employment budget show a larger or smaller deficit than the actual budget? Explain.

8. Why is crowding out important to the debate over activist policy?

9. Contrast the Keynesian position on balanced budgets with that of the classical school.

10. Explain why the U.S. government can afford to carry a heavier debt burden than private individuals.

11. In 1992, the actual deficit is $100 billion and the full-employment deficit is $80 billion. In 1993, the actual deficit is $200 billion and the full-employment deficit is $80 billion. From these figures, speculate about what has happened to the economy in this year.

12. If deficits are highest during recessions, explain why the link between large deficits and inflation may be weak.

Suggested Readings

Barro, Robert J. *Macroeconomics*. New York: John Wiley & Sons, 1984, chap. 15.

Collander, Stanley E. *The Guide to the Federal Budget, 1984 ed*. Washington, D.C.: The Urban Institute Press, 1983.

Mills, Gregory B. and John L. Palmer. *The Deficit Dilemma: Budget Policy in the Reagan Era*. Washington, D.C.: The Urban Institute Press, 1983.

Pechman, Joseph A. *Federal Tax Policy*. Washington, D.C.: The Brookings Institution, 1966, chaps. 1–3.

Samuelson, Paul A. *Economics,* 11th ed. New York: McGraw-Hill, 1980, chaps. 13 & 18.

Schultz, George P. and Kenneth W. Dam. *Economic Policy Beyond the Headlines*. New York: W. W. Norton, 1977, chaps. 2 & 3.

Thomas, Lloyd B., Jr. *Money, Banking, and Economic Activity,* 2nd ed. Englewood Cliffs, N.J.: Prentice-Hall, 1982, chap. 18.

14

Inflation

Chapter Preview

One way to appreciate the seriousness of inflation during the postwar period is to look at how many years it takes the price level to double during different periods of U.S. history. Between 1947 to 1972 it took a quarter of a century for the price level to double. Between 1974 to 1984 a span of only a decade—the price level doubled again. Why did it take 25 years to double prices in one period and only 10 years in another period?

This chapter focuses on the causes of inflation. It considers the relationships between the money supply and inflation, between government deficits and inflation, and between supply shocks and inflation. The chapter describes the possible causes of the wage/price spiral and spells out various approaches to curbing inflation, along with the costs of each approach. Inflation's impact on income distribution was discussed in Chapter 5, and *stag-*

flation—the combination of high unemployment and rapid inflation—is the focus of Chapter 15.

Five fundamental facts about inflation that require explanation are:

1. Inflation is not inevitable (in the sense that the sun must rise or set).
2. High inflation rates are associated with high rates of growth of money supply, especially in the long run.
3. Inflation was more rapid in the 1970s than can be explained by the long-run historical association between money and prices.
4. In the long run, high inflation rates and high interest rates go hand in hand.
5. There has been a clear-cut inflationary trend since the 1930s. ■

Figure 1   The U.S. Price Level, 1800–1984

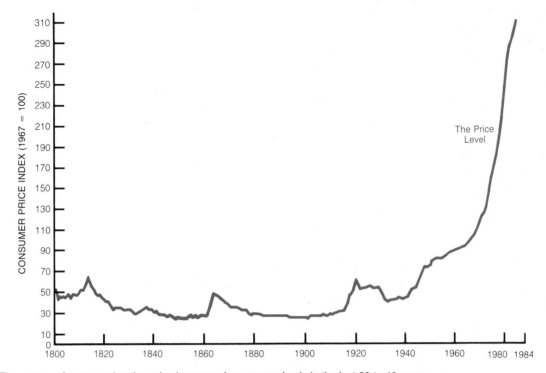

The pattern of ever-accelerating price increases has emerged only in the last 30 to 40 years.

Sources: *Historical Statistics of the United States,* 1970, p. 211; *Economic Report of the President.*

THE FACTS OF INFLATION

Inflation Is Not Inevitable

Figure 1, which shows the U.S. price level from 1800 to 1984, demonstrates that, over the very long run, inflation is not inevitable. Prices in 1943 were about the same as prices in 1800! Until the Second World War, there was no definitive upward trend in prices. Instead, periods of inflation were followed by periods of deflation; the two tended to cancel each other. Over the entire 19th century, the general price level went up and down again and again. The clear-cut inflationary trend did not begin until the mid-1930s, when the U.S. economy began its recovery from the Great Depression.

Politically, it may be difficult to reduce the inflation rate to zero. Some may argue that under present circumstances inflation is a fact of life. However, objective economic science cannot regard inflation in the same way as the laws of scarcity or diminishing returns. Scarcity will always be present, as will diminishing returns. This chapter points out that society can eliminate inflation if it is prepared to pay the ensuing costs.

Money and Prices Are Positively Associated

In the long run, Figure 2 shows a positive empirical association between the growth of money and the growth of prices. Money and prices have not grown at the same rate in the long run, however. The money supply (M1) rose about 43 times

Figure 2   The Growth of the U.S. Money Supply and the Price Level, 1915–1984

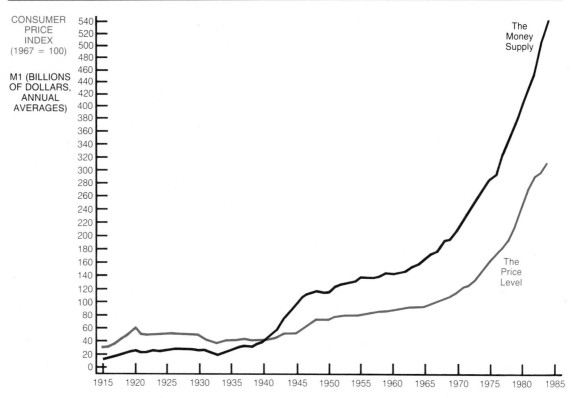

Changes in money supply and changes in the price level have tended to move together, although without exact agreement. M1 has grown faster than the price level because the increase in real GNP over time absorbs some of the increase in M1.

Sources: *Historical Statistics of the United States*, 1970, pp. 210–11, 992; *Economic Report of the President*.

while the price level rose by more than 10 times over the 1915–1984 period. One reason the money supply has grown more rapidly than the price level is that real GNP has been growing along with prices, and more money is required to accommodate the larger quantity of real GNP. Between 1915 and 1984, real GNP increased nearly 9 times.[1] In the long run, money tends to grow more rapidly than prices because rising real output holds down price increases.

The relationship between monetary growth and inflation from 1966–1984 is shown in Figure 3. Figure 3 is a *scatter diagram* that compares the

annual percentage change in the money supply with the annual inflation rate in the next year. The vertical height of each dot shows the rate of inflation in a particular year; the horizontal distance of each dot from the vertical axis shows the rate of growth of money in the *previous* year. (Presumably, the effect of monetary growth on inflation would not be immediate. The change in the money stock affects economic activity with a lag, as Chapter 12 explained.)

The 45-degree reference line (not to be confused with the 45-degree line in the income/expenditure model) shows where points would appear if there were equal percentage changes in money supply and the price level. If the price level grows faster than the money supply, the dots will lie above the line. If the dots lie

---

1. The equation is $MV = PQ$. In the long run, Q rises with advancing technology and labor force growth. So M must rise to accommodate more Q, with V and P constant.

Figure 3   The Yearly Change in the U.S. Money Supply Versus the Yearly Change in the Price Level, 1966–1984

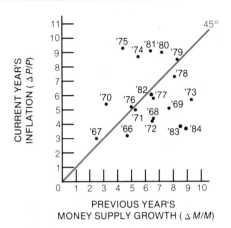

This scatter diagram compares the annual inflation rate for each year with the rate of change in the previous year's money supply. The 1966–1984 period saw more inflation than the growth in money supply alone can explain, because money usually grows faster than prices.

Source: *Economic Report of the President.*

Figure 4   Inflation Rates and Interest Rates, 1966–1984

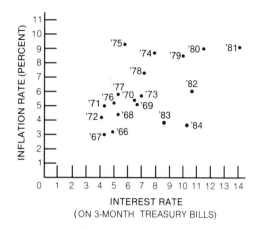

This scatter diagram reveals a strong positive relationship between rapid inflation and high interest rates.

Source: *Economic Report of the President.*

below the line, the price level grows slower than the money supply. Of the 19 dots, 5 are clearly above the line, 7 are on the line (or very close), and 7 are below the line. Our expectation would be that the majority of the dots would fall below the line because of the long-run tendency for prices to rise slower than the money supply rises. Indeed, Figure 3 confirms this expectation with most of the dots either close to the line or below the line. It appears that the high inflation rates of 1974–75 and 1980–81 represent a departure from the general trend with prices rising much more rapidly than the money supply. In general, the period from the mid-1970s to 1981 saw more inflation than the growth in the money supply alone can explain.

Inflation and Interest Rates Are Positively Associated

Figure 4 shows the relationship between recent inflation rates and the interest rate for the period 1966 to 1984. If the relationship between inflation

and interest rates is positive, the graph should show that interest rates tend to be high when inflation is high and low when inflation is low. The scatter diagram reveals a strong positive relationship: periods of rapid inflation tend to be periods of high interest rates, and vice versa. For example, in 1980 and 1981, when the inflation rate was near 9 percent, the interest rate was between 12 and 14 percent. In 1971 and 1972, when the inflation rate was between 4 and 5 percent, the interest rate was less than 5 percent. Figure 4 shows that the relationship between inflation and interest rates is not simple. The fact that the dots do not lie on a straight line indicates that factors other than the current rate of inflation also affect real interest rates.

THE CAUSES OF INFLATION

Any good theory of inflation should account for the five facts of inflation discussed above. The previous chapter used the tools of aggregate supply and aggregate demand to explain how real output, employment, and the price level are determined. Chapter 11 showed how the short-run aggregate-supply curve can be positively sloped and

Figure 5   Demand-Side Versus Supply-Side Inflation

(a) Demand-Side Inflation

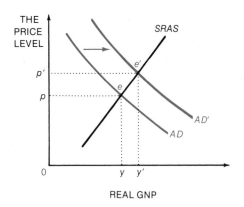

(b) Supply-Side Inflation

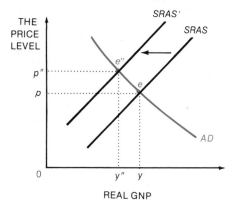

Panel (a) illustrates demand-side inflation. The economy is initially in equilibrium at e. Aggregate demand increases from AD to AD' and causes the price level to rise from p to p' as the economy moves up along the short-run aggregate-supply curve, $SRAS$, to e'. In the short run, output increases from y to y'. The increase in aggregate demand has pulled prices up.

Panel (b) illustrates supply-side inflation. The economy is initially in equilibrium at e. A reduction in short run aggregate supply from $SRAS$ to $SRAS'$ causes a movement back along the aggregate-demand curve from e to e''. Prices frise from p to p''; output declines from y to y''; unemployment increases. The reduction in short run aggregate supply has pushed prices up.

why the aggregate-demand curve is negatively sloped. It also discussed the tendency of economies to produce the natural level of output in the long run.

Aggregate supply-and-demand analysis suggests two general types of inflation: **demand-side inflation** and **supply-side** (or *cost-push*) **inflation.** Figure 5 illustrates both types of inflation using the tools of aggregate supply-and-demand analysis. These diagrams show short-run effects only; they do not show what happens to prices, output, and employment as the automatic-adjustment mechanism does its work.

Demand-Side Inflation

In panel (a) of Figure 5, the economy is initially operating at point e, where output is y and the price level is p. The short-run aggregate-supply curve, $SRAS$, is positively sloped—which means that the economy will produce more output only at a higher price level. If aggregate demand increases—for example, through an increase in the money supply, a lowering of taxes, an increase in

government spending, or an autonomous upward shift in consumption—the aggregate-demand curve, AD, will shift to the right. At the new equilibrium, e', more output (y') is produced (and unemployment falls). The increase in demand has caused the equilibrium price level to rise (to p').

> **Demand-side inflation** (or *demand-pull inflation*) occurs when aggregate demand increases and pulls prices up.

Supply-Side Inflation

In panel (b) of Figure 5, the economy is initially operating at point e again, producing output y at price level p. A reduction in aggregate supply—due to a decline in productivity, poor harvests, or autonomous increases in energy prices—shifts the aggregate-supply curve to the left from $SRAS$ to $SRAS'$. The drop in aggregate supply disrupts the initial equilibrium of output and prices and shifts the equilibrium to e''. At price level p, aggregate demand exceeds aggregate supply, and prices rise (from p to p''). As prices rise, the economy moves back along the aggregate-demand curve; output falls to y'', and the unemployment rate rises. The reduction in aggregate supply has raised both the price level and unemployment.

Supply-side inflation (or *cost-push inflation*) occurs when aggregate supply declines and pushes prices up.

Confusing Demand-Side and Supply-Side Inflation

Demand-side and supply-side inflation are often confused when inflation is moderate. For example, suppose the quantity of money increases, so that the aggregate demand for goods and services is raised throughout the economy. As each sector seeks to meet the increase in demand, its prices and wages rise. Individual business managers will not see the increase in the money supply; they will see only that their wage costs, material costs, and interest charges are rising, and they will raise prices in response to higher costs. Thus, pure demand-side inflation may look like supply-side inflation on an individual level.

To the microeconomic unit—the individual and the firm—moderate demand-side inflations look similar to supply-side inflations. To determine whether inflation is demand-side or supply-side, one must know the source of rising wages and prices.

When inflation is excessive and there is widespread knowledge that the government is printing money at a rapid rate, there is less chance observers will think the demand-side inflation is really supply-side inflation. In order to decide on the best cure, it is important to know whether inflation is caused by demand-side or supply-side forces.

THE DEMAND SIDE: MONEY AND INTEREST

Many economists believe that protracted inflation is a monetary phenomenon caused by *excess monetary growth* (introduced in Chapter 7). According to the equation of exchange, $MV = PQ$,

where M is money supply, V is velocity, P is price level, and Q is output.

With constant velocity, excess monetary growth occurs when money supply grows more rapidly than output.

The effects of monetary growth on inflation, output, unemployment, and interest rates can be determined using the tools of aggregate supply-and-demand analysis. Money's effects on prices would be simple to predict if velocity and real output were constant, as the classical quantity theory assumed, but changes in real output and velocity complicate the relationship between money supply and prices.

Inflationary expectations affect the relationship between money and prices. Changes in the anticipated rate of inflation can change velocity. It is, therefore, important to consider how people form inflationary expectations and how the expected rate of inflation affects velocity through interest rates. The following sections explore the different effects of anticipated and unanticipated inflation on interest rates and the effect of changes in velocity on the inflationary aspects of monetary growth.

Unanticipated Inflation with a One-Shot Monetary Injection

Inflation is not likely to be anticipated if it is caused by a one-shot or once-and-for-all increase in aggregate demand. If prices have been increasing steadily (or even erratically), people will do their best to anticipate inflation to prevent being caught off guard. In the example that follows, the economy has had stable prices for a number of years and is not likely to anticipate inflation. Although we have experienced inflation (sometimes low, sometimes high) for more than 30 years, consideration of a permanent one-shot increase in demand that moves the economy from one stable price level to a higher demand-side stable price level simplifies the understanding of demand-side inflation. After this section, we will turn to the more common case of continuing inflation.

In Figure 6, a once-and-for-all increase in the money supply causes a one-shot permanent in-

Figure 6   The Effects of Increases in Money Supply on Interest Rates, Output, and Prices

(a) Aggregate Supply and Aggregate Demand

(b) The Money Market

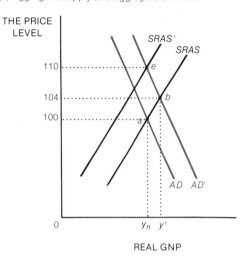
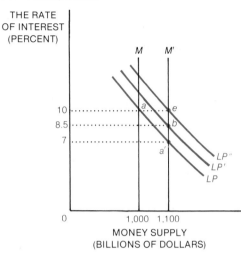

The economy is initially operating at point *a* in both panels, producing an output of y_n with an interest rate of 10 percent. As a result of an unanticipated move by the Fed, money supply increases, and the interest rate drops to 7 percent. At the lower interest rate, aggregate demand increases (due to higher investment spending) from *AD* to *AD'*. As aggregate demand shifts up along *SRAS*, both prices and output rise. As prices start to rise, the demand for money increases (the liquidity-preference curve starts to shift to the right). As the price level rises initially from 100 to 104, the money-demand curve shifts from *LP* to *LP'* to establish a higher interest rate (8.5 percent) in the money market. The interest rate has risen from 7 to 8.5 percent, but it is still below its original rate of 10 percent. However, the economy is now operating above the natural level of output at point *b*; therefore, the price level continues to rise. As the price level continues to rise, people adjust to the higher price level. Businesses are no longer willing to supply the same real output at the same price level as before, and there is a reduction in short-run aggregate supply (the short-run aggregate-supply curve shifts to the left). The rise in the price level will stop only when the economy returns to producing y_n, which occurs at the price level 110. The economy is restored to producing y_n when the short-run aggregate-supply curve shifts all the way to *SRAS'*. The movement of the price level to 110 affects the credit market by continuing to increase the demand for money. Eventually, the liquidity-prefernce curve shifts all the way to *LP'*. At this intersection of *L'* and *M'* (at point *e*), the interest rate is restored to the original 10 percent rate. The long-run equilibrium occurs at point *e* in both diagrams. (The diagram ignores the effect on the *LP* curve of the temporary increase in output from y_n to y'.)

crease in aggregate demand. We assume that people do not expect any future changes in the money supply. The increase in money supply comes as a surprise to everyone because the money supply had been held constant by monetary authorities up to that point.

The Short Run.   In panel (a) of Figure 6, the economy is initially operating at point *a*, producing the natural level of output, y_n, at a price level of 100. In panel (b), the increase in money supply (from *M* to *M'*) adds reserves to the commercial banking system. Banks can use these excess reserves to make loans and other investments. The increase in the supply of credit causes the interest rate to fall along the money-demand

or liquidity-preference *(LP)* curve (from 10 percent to 7 percent in our example).

In order to keep the interest rate this low (at 7 percent), the price level and real output must remain unchanged. If the price level rose, the demand for money would rise, pushing up interest rates. An increase in real output would also push up interest rates by increasing the demand for money. But in this situation, both the price level and output should rise. The short-run aggregate-supply curve is upward-sloping, and aggregate demand increases from *AD* to *AD'* (due to the increase in investment spending stimulated by the lower interest rate). Therefore, output rises to y' and the price level rises to 104 as the economy moves from *a* to *b*. As the price level rises to

104, the demand for money increases, and the interest rate rises from 7 percent to 8.5 percent—from a' to b in panel (b).

The Long Run.   As explained in Chapter 11, an increase in aggregate demand can raise output and employment in the short run above the natural rate, but in the long run, both output and employment should return to the natural rate. Is there an equivalent rule for interest rates?

At b in panel (a), output is above the natural level, and the price level begins its long-run ascent towards e (where the price level is 110 and output is y_n). But what happens to the liquidity-preference curve as prices rise? At higher prices, people need more money balances to carry out their transactions; the demand for money increases (LP' shifts towards LP'' in panel (b). The interest rate rises as the demand for money increases; it will continue to rise as long as prices are rising. Prices rise until e is reached (at a price level of 110), and the interest rate rises as long as prices are rising. When the price level is 110 (at point e), prices no longer rise (the inflation rate goes back to being zero, and output is restored to its original level, y_n). The interest rate should be restored to its original rate of 10 percent when the economy reaches e in panel (a). At e, the economy is operating with the same real income and the same rate of inflation (zero) as before the increase in money supply. The only thing that has changed is that the price level has risen.[2] The economy has moved from one stable price level to another stable but higher price level.

There is no money illusion in the long run. If inflation is zero, both the nominal and real interest rate must be equal (at 10 percent in this example). In the long run, a once-and-for-all permanent change in the nominal money supply has no impact on real GNP, the real interest rate, or the real money supply. Thus, in the long run, the interest rate tends to be restored to its original rate after a one-shot change in the money supply. Increases in money supply can drive down interest

rates only in the short run. In the long run, rising prices return the interest rate to its original position.

Chapter 18 will examine the case where unanticipated increases in the money supply are considered to be temporary.

If the economy starts from a long-run equilibrium, an unanticipated *one-shot* increase in the money supply (that people expect to be permanent) lowers the rate of interest and raises output above the natural rate in the short run. But in the long run, the economy returns to the natural level of output, and the interest rate will be restored to its original level. Unanticipated increases in money supply will lower interest rates only in the short run.

Anticipated Inflation with Steady Monetary Injections

It is difficult to anticipate inflation in a world where there are one-shot injections of money following long periods of a constant money supply. Instances of one-shot unanticipated inflation like the one just described are rare. Both the money supply and real GNP typically grow. People come to expect a certain rate of inflation or deflation. The economy does not usually bounce back and forth between inflation and deflation or between skyrocketing and moderate inflation. In the real world, people presumably form inflationary expectations using their experiences from immediate and past history.

Adaptive Expectations.   How do people form expectations of the future? There is no way to know for sure the mental process by which expectations are formed, but economists have offered two competing hypotheses, viewing expectations either as **adaptive expectations** or as **rational expectations.**

> **Adaptive expectations** are expectations of the future that people form from past experience and only gradually modify as experience unfolds.

For example, if the annual inflation rate has been 10 percent year in and year out for the past 10 years, people would probably expect the infla-

---

2. To simplify the above explanation, we have ignored the shifts in the liquidity-preference curves due to the temporary changes in real GNP. In the long run, real GNP is y_n—the natural level. Thus, LP, LP' and LP'' are drawn on the assumption that real GNP equals y_n. LP assumes the price level is 100; LP' assumes the price level is 104; LP'' assumes the price level is 110.

tion rate to remain at 10 percent. If the inflation rate jumps to a steady 15 percent, the adaptive-expectations hypothesis argues that people would not immediately adjust their expected inflation up to 15 percent. In the first year, they might raise their expected rate of inflation to 11 or 12 percent. As the rate of inflation continues at 15 percent, people would continue to adjust upward their expected rate of inflation each period until they finally reach a 15 percent expected inflation rate.

The main implication of the adaptive-expectations hypothesis is that *it takes time for people to adjust to a new rate of inflation. In the meantime, there will be a difference between the actual and the anticipated rate of inflation*. If the rate of inflation rises, the anticipated rate of inflation will rise by less than the actual rise. If the rate of inflation falls, the anticipated rate of inflation will fall by less than the actual fall. Only gradually will people raise or lower their anticipated rate of inflation to bring it in line with the actual rate of inflation.

Rational Expectations.

The adaptive-expectations hypothesis maintains that people change their expectations of inflation slowly in response to changing circumstances. The rational-expectations hypothesis assumes that people change their expectations more quickly and use more information in forming their expectations.

> **Rational expectations** are expectations that people form by using all available information and by relying not only on past experience but also on their predictions about the effects of present and future policy actions.

A major difference between adaptive and rational expectations is the speed of adjustment of expectations. It is conceivable that people could change their rational expectation of the anticipated rate of inflation simply on the basis of a policy pronouncement from monetary or fiscal authorities. If they believe a change in policy will raise a current 10 percent inflation rate to a permanent 15 percent rate, they will immediately raise their inflation projection to 15 percent.

Many people and businesses do indeed study the latest economic projections, money-supply growth statistics, and fiscal-policy changes. Banks, investment firms, labor unions, and small

investors gather information that they hope will allow them to anticipate the future. It is, therefore, possible that expectations are indeed formed according to the rational-expectations hypothesis. Which hypothesis is correct is an empirical issue that has been the subject of much research and controversy. Do people actually use all the available information on economic policy to form their expectations, or do they simply respond slowly to past experience? Chapter 19 will return to the rational-expectations hypothesis in more detail.

Anticipated Inflation, Velocity, and Interest Rates

Consider an economy in which inflation has been present for some time, and people are attempting to anticipate the future rate of inflation. For the time being, we shall assume that they form their expectations adaptively.

Chapter 5 explained that when people begin to anticipate more inflation, the nominal interest rate rises. When more inflation is anticipated, lenders will be less willing to lend at prevailing interest rates because they know they will be paid back with cheaper dollars. Borrowers will be more anxious to borrow at prevailing interest rates because they can pay back their loans with cheaper dollars.

As noted earlier, the interest rate is the opportunity cost of holding money. The higher is the opportunity cost of money, the lower is the quantity of money demanded and the more work each dollar must accomplish for each dollar of GNP. Higher interest rates should, therefore, cause people to turn over their money more often—to raise velocity.

What do the data tell us? Do interest rates rise with the anticipated rate of inflation? Does velocity rise with the interest rate? To answer these two questions requires information on the anticipated rate of inflation. One simple approach (among many) is to say that the anticipated inflation rate is simply the average of the inflation rates of the past few years.[3] This measure of anticipated infla-

---

3. For example, if the inflation rate in the current year is 10 percent and if it was 9 percent last year and 8 percent the year before, people would expect 9 percent (the average of 10, 9, and 8) for the next year. If the inflation rate jumps to 14 percent, the new expected inflation rate is 11 percent, the average of 14, 10, and 9.

Figure 7   Velocity and Inflation

(a) The Relationship Between Anticipated
Inflation and Interest Rate, 1966–1984

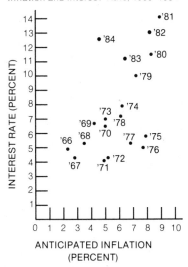

ANTICIPATED INFLATION
(PERCENT)

(b) The Relationship Between the Interest
Rate and Velocity, 1966–1984

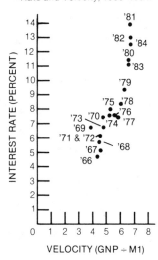

VELOCITY (GNP ÷ M1)

In panel (a), the anticipated inflation rate is measured as the average inflation rate over the last three years. The interest rate in both panels is the interest rate on 10-year U.S. government bonds. The positive slope of the scatter diagram in panel (a) reveals a positive relationship between anticipated inflation and the interest rate. In panel (b), velocity is the ratio of GNP to M1. This scatter diagrams clearly shows a positive relationship between interest rates and velocity. The results of panels (a) and (b) together show that velocity tends to increase as anticipated inflation rises.

tion can then be compared with interest rates, and interest rates can be compared with velocity.

Panel (a) of Figure 7 shows the relationship between our measure of the anticipated rate of inflation and the rate of interest for the period 1966 to 1984. This scatter diagram shows a strong positive relationship between the interest rate and the anticipated rate of inflation. The higher is the anticipated rate of inflation, the higher is the rate of interest.

Panel (b) of Figure 7 shows the effect of interest rates on velocity. As predicted by theory, there is a strong positive correlation between velocity and interest rates. At high interest rates, velocity is high because the opportunity cost of holding cash balances is high.

Figure 7 partly explains why prices rose more rapidly than the money supply rose during the period 1975 to 1981. As the inflation rate rose during the 1970s, inflationary expectations pushed up interest rates, and this increase in interest rates raised velocity. With rising velocity, a given increase in the money supply will yield a larger increase in prices. The normal relationship between

monetary growth and inflation (prices rising slower than money rises) was disrupted by rising inflationary expectations, which raised velocity.

Monetary Growth and Interest Rates

Figure 6 showed that when inflation is not anticipated, a one-shot increase in money supply lowers the interest in the short run. However, in the long run, the economy is restored through the rise in the price level to the natural level of output (at a stable but higher price level) at the original interest rate.

A similar distinction holds for an economy that is experiencing continuous excess monetary growth (as opposed to a one-shot permanent increase in the money supply). If there is an unanticipated (permanent) acceleration in monetary growth that unexpectedly raises the inflation *rate*, interest rates should drop in the short run. Because the acceleration of inflation is unanticipated, lenders expect the prevailing rate of inflation to continue and do not cut back on their willingness to lend. Borrowers also expect the

Example 1   The Fed's Five-Year War on Inflation

The following is a list of Fed-related actions undertaken between 1979 and 1984 that had a key effect on inflation. Table 1 shows the behavior of interest rates, the unemployment rate, and the inflation rate during this period.

1. On August 6, 1979, Volcker became the Fed chairman.
2. On October 6, 1979, the Fed changed its operating procedure to target money-supply growth instead of interest rates.
3. On March 14, 1980, the Fed imposed credit controls.
4. In the summer of 1980, the credit controls were lifted.

5. On September 25, 1980, the Fed raised its discount rate one full point five weeks before the election.
6. On August 31, 1981, the Reagan tax-cut and spending-restraint legislation was passed.
7. On October 5, 1982, the Fed modified its money-supply targets and adopted a more flexible approach.
8. On June 18, 1983, Reagan nominated Volcker for a second term.
9. In May 1984, the Reagan administration attacked the Fed's policy as too tight and as a threat to the economy's expansion. ■

Source: *The New York Times,* December 7, 1984, p. 16.

prevailing rate of inflation to continue and do not increase their willingness to borrow. Yet the increase in the growth rate of money has speeded up the injection of credit into credit markets. Accordingly, interest rates drop. If the higher inflation brought about by the faster growth in money supply is anticipated perfectly, however, the interest rate will not fall at all. Lenders and borrowers will correctly anticipate that prices will increase; lenders will be more reluctant to lend money at prevailing interest rates, and borrowers will be more anxious to borrow at prevailing interest rates. The nominal interest rate will rise with anticipated inflation as lenders protect themselves from the declining value of the dollar.

The real interest rate (the nominal interest rate minus anticipated inflation) need not change. For example, assume an economy has had an annual growth of money supply of 5 percent for the last five years. Real GNP has been rising at 2 percent per year, and the annual inflation rate has been 3 percent. The nominal interest rate has been steady at 7 percent and the real interest rate is 4 percent. Monetary growth accelerates unexpectedly to a permanent 8 percent, which eventually raises the inflation rate to 6 percent. The anticipated rate of inflation is still 3 percent, and the increased growth of money and credit temporarily drives down the interest rate below the original 7 percent. The drop in the interest rate will be only temporary. As people come to expect a higher in-

flation rate, the interest rate rises to protect lenders from higher inflation. Eventually (in the long run), people will come to anticipate (correctly) the higher 6 percent rate of inflation. The nominal interest rate will rise to 10 percent (the sum of the 6 percent anticipated rate of inflation and the 4 percent real interest rate). In real terms, the economy is back at the original real rate of interest and the original level of output but at a higher inflation rate.

The Dilemma Faced by Monetary Authorities

Monetary authorities face a dilemma during periods of rapid and anticipated inflation. When inflation is high, nominal interest rates will have to be high enough to incorporate a premium for anticipated inflation. But the response to such high rates will be a public outcry against high interest rates, and pressure will build on the Fed to lower interest rates. In order to lower nominal interest rates when inflationary expectations are high, monetary authorities must lower inflationary expectations.

In the case of adaptive expectations, people will lower their inflationary expectations only slowly as they see inflation actually dropping. In this situation, the Fed must lower actual inflation to reduce inflationary expectations. In an inflation, both the money supply and the price level

Table 1   Money Growth, Inflation, Unemployment, and Interest Rates During the Reagan-Volcker Years, 1978–1984

	Year-to-Year Growth Rate in M1 (percent)	Inflation Rate: GNP Deflator (percent)	Yearly Average Unemployment (percent)	Year-End Rate for 3-Month T-Bill (percent)
1978	8.2	7.4	6.1	9.1
1979	7.7	8.6	5.8	12.1
1980	6.4	9.2	7.1	15.7
1981	7.0	9.4	7.6	10.9
1982	6.6	6.0	9.7	8.0
1983	11.1	3.8	9.6	9.0
1984	6.6	3.8	7.4	8.2

Sources: *Economic Report of the President; Federal Reserve Bulletin.*

are rising; to lower inflation the Fed must reduce the growth of money supply. The demand for money remains strong because people require more money to carry out their transactions with rising prices. When the supply of money is growing less rapidly than the demand, interest rates rise!

To *lower* nominal interest rates in an environment of rapid anticipated inflation requires that nominal interest rates be *raised* in the short run. When monetary authorities reduce the growth of money supply, nominal interest rates rise further. When the rate of inflation slows, inflationary expectations begin to fall, and only then will nominal interest rates come down.

The U.S. experience with rising interest rates in 1979 and 1980 illustrates the dilemma faced by monetary authorities. Interest rates were driven up in the short run when monetary authorities cut the growth of the money supply during a period of high inflation and high inflationary expectations. The Fed decided in October 1979 to reduce money-growth rates in order to combat inflation (see Example 1). Table 1 shows that from 1978 to 1980 the rate of monetary growth was gradually reduced from 8.2 percent per year to 6.4 percent per year. During this same time period, the rate of interest on 3-month treasury bills rose from 9.1 percent in December 1978 to 15.7 percent in December 1980. As one would expect, in-

terest rates rose when monetary growth was reduced in the presence of high inflationary expectations. But as the anti-inflation policy began to take hold in 1982 and 1983 (at the cost of driving unemployment up from 6.1 percent in 1978 to 9.7 percent in 1982), interest rates started to fall. The inflation rate fell to less than 4 percent per year in both 1983 and 1984 from a peak inflation rate of 9.4 percent in 1981. As inflation rates fell, people lowered their expected inflation rates. When buyers of bonds have lower inflation expectations, they bid more for bonds. Higher bond prices lower interest rates. The drop in interest rates from late 1980 to late 1984 reflects lower inflationary expectations. The T-bill rate in late 1983 and late 1984 (9 percent and 8.2 percent, respectively) was at about the same level as when the Fed experiment began.

Government Deficits

Although it has become increasingly popular to blame inflation on the deficit, the government deficit *per se* may not add to inflation. As already noted, U.S. inflation was falling after 1982 despite record U.S. deficits. What is the relationship between inflation and deficits? The connection between deficits and inflation appears to depend on whether short-run or long-run periods are examined.

The Short Run.   The short-run relationship between government deficits and inflation is am-

Figure 8   **The Yearly Change in the Price Level Versus the Yearly Change in National Debt, 1975–1984**

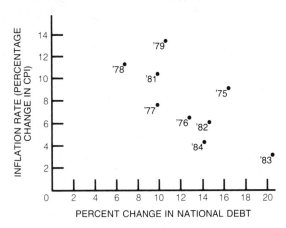

This diagram reveals a negative relationship between yearly inflation rates and yearly increases in the national debt (the deficit). The evidence from the last 10 years suggests that in the short run, there may be a negative relationship between inflation rates and the deficit, but a positive relationship is also possible.

Source: *Economic Report of the President.*

Figure 9   **The Five-Year Change in Prices Versus the Change in National Debt, 1955–1984**

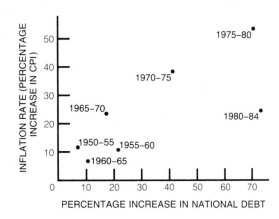

This scatter diagram reveals a positive relationship between percentage changes in the price level and percentage changes in the national debt over five-year intervals (except for 1980–1984, which is a four-year interval). If a five-year period can represent the long run, there is a long run positive association between deficits and inflation.

Sources: *Economic Report of the President* and *Statistical Abstract of the United States.*

biguous because deliberate fiscal policy, automatic stabilizers, and monetary policy often work in opposite directions. On the one hand, deficits produced by deliberate increases in government spending or reductions in tax rates will raise the rate of inflation as the aggregate-demand curve shifts to the right. On the other hand, deficits produced by falling tax revenues induced by a weak economy (aggregate demand shifting to the left due to reductions in private spending) will be associated with a falling rate of inflation. A tight money policy will also reduce the rate of inflation and increase the deficit by driving up unemployment and decreasing government tax revenues. It would be surprising, therefore, to find a strong short-run empirical association between deficits and inflation. The scatter diagram in Figure 8 shows a distinct negative correlation between inflation rates and deficits over the 1975–1984 period. Deficits (measured by the yearly percentage increases in the national debt) are plotted against inflation rates (measured by the yearly change in the consumer price index). The years of lowest

inflation (1983 and 1984) were also years of larger than average increases in the national debt! The government's anti-inflation policy lowered the rate of inflation in 1983 and 1984 but at the expense of driving up unemployment and increasing the deficit. It appears that over the 1975–1984 period the impact of the Fed's anti-inflation policy and the workings of the automatic stabilizers dominated the relationship between inflation and the deficit.

The Long Run.   Is there a long-run relationship between inflation and the deficit? Economists have advanced three theories that claim a definite long-run relationship between deficits and inflation.

1. The federal deficit can contribute to inflation indirectly through its effect on the money supply. If the newly issued government bonds are sold only to the public, the money supply is not affected, but interest rates may be driven up as government and private borrowers compete for

available investment funds. If there is an unwillingness to raise interest rates in the short run, the Fed—although it is not obligated to do so—will purchase the federal debt. When the Fed purchases government bonds, it injects new reserves into the banking system, and the money supply expands. In effect, the government deficit is financed by printing money. The Fed has shown no short-run tendency to finance the Federal deficit. For example, from September 1983 to September 1984 the government had a deficit of $172 billion, as measured by the increase in the net national debt. But the Fed's holdings of government securities slightly declined from September 1983 to September 1984. Over the long run, however, the Fed has increased its holdings of government securities. Thus, in the long run at least, the Fed's financing of the government deficit has been inflationary. Whether this financing has been intentional or unintentional is not known.

2. The federal deficit can also contribute to inflation indirectly through the impact of the national debt on spending plans. If people treat the government IOUs that they own as net wealth, a larger national debt means that people will spend more. In other words, if people look only at their increased holdings of federal-government IOUs and ignore the future taxes that must be collected to finance the debt, an increase in the national debt may motivate them to spend more and, thus, to drive up prices. This issue was addressed in Chapter 13. The extent to which the national debt is treated as net wealth is not known.

3. Inflation can also increase the deficit. In other words, inflation can cause the deficit, rather than vice versa! This argument is simple: higher inflation rates—in the long run—raise interest rates. Higher interest rates increase the federal deficit by increasing the interest cost of the national debt. (See Example 3 in Chapter 13.)

A long-run empirical relationship between inflation and federal deficits does exist. The last quarter century has been characterized by both inflation and deficits. Figure 9 shows that over five-year time periods inflation and deficits appear related. When changes in the national debt over 5 years (the accumulated deficit over 5 years) are compared to changes in the price level over the same period, the two rates of change are positively related between 1955 and 1984. A combination of the above three theories likely explains the long-run empirical relationship between inflation and deficits.

THE SUPPLY SIDE: SUPPLY SHOCKS

Supply-side inflation occurs when there is a reduction in aggregate supply—when the *SRAS* curve shifts to the left, as in panel (b) of Figure 5. The drop in aggregate supply causes the economy to move up the aggregate-demand curve to a lower level of output and to a higher price level. Unlike demand-side inflation—which tends to raise output and employment in the short run—supply-side inflation brings the worst of both worlds: rising prices *and* lower output and employment.

Shifts in aggregate supply can be expected or unexpected. For example, the generally rising trend in technological advances would be expected to increase aggregate supply over time in a fairly predictable manner. Of greater interest to the study of inflation is an unexpected shift in aggregate supply, called a **supply shock.**

A **supply shock** is an event that unexpectedly causes the short-run aggregate-supply curve to shift.

An adverse supply shock is one that causes a reduction in aggregate supply (the short-run aggregate-supply curve shifts to the left). A favorable supply shock causes an increase in aggregate supply.

Causes of Supply-Side Inflation

There is no single cause of supply-side inflation. Any factor that causes aggregate supply to decrease can initiate supply-side inflation. Changes in labor productivity, autonomous increases in raw-material prices, crop failures, and changes in the way labor and product markets work can all cause reductions in aggregate supply.

If the costs of production rise spontaneously without being pulled up by increases in demand, the economy will experience a supply shock. Firms, on average, will supply fewer goods and services than before the shock at prevailing

Table 2   OPEC Crude-Oil Prices and Average Inflation Rates in the Big Seven Countries (U.S., Germany, Japan, France, Canada, Italy, and the U.K.), 1971–1984

Year	Oil Price (dollars per barrel)	Average Inflation Rate (percent)
1971–73	2.13	6.4
1974	10.77	14.5
1975	10.72	13.0
1976	11.51	10.0
1977	13.12	10.1
1978	12.93	7.6
1979	18.67	9.7
1980	30.87	9.1
1981	34.50	10.1
1982	33.63	8.4
1983	29.31	6.0
1984	28.00*	5.0*

*preliminary

Sources: *Handbook of Economic Statistics, 1984; pp. 53;* James Griffin and Henry Steele, *Energy Economics and Policy* (New York: Academic, 1980), p. 18; *Economic Report of the President,* 1981, p. 189.

prices, and aggregate supply will fall. As the aggregate-supply curve shifts to the left, the general price level is pushed up.

The most dramatic case of supply-side inflation in recent years is the 1475 percent rise in the price of imported oil between 1973 and 1980. When the Organization of Petroleum Exporting Countries (OPEC) discovered the magic of cartel pricing in 1973, the oil-importing countries of the world were hit with an enormous adverse supply shock. OPEC inflicted leftward shifts in the aggregate-supply curves of every oil-importing country. The oil-induced reductions of supply pushed up the general price level. Table 2 supplies data on the price of OPEC oil and the average inflation rate in seven major countries.

The upsurge of world inflation rates coincided with the increase in energy prices. Although OPEC was not the only cause of the inflation, the oil shock likely did contribute to the inflation of the 1970s.

Price shocks can also emanate from agriculture. Poor weather and bad harvests throughout the world can raise agricultural prices, and because agricultural goods are a major input for the world economy, this price rise can shift the aggregate-supple curve. The year 1973 brought with it not only the beginning of the oil shock, but an increase in the price of wheat from $70 per ton to $140 per ton—due largely to a poor harvest in the United States in 1973 and a crop disaster in the Soviet Union the year before.

Supply shocks can also lower the rate of inflation if the *SRAS* curve shifts to the right. Table 2 shows that as the OPEC cartel weakened in the early 1980s, price inflation also dropped.

Ratification of Supply-Side Inflation

As Figure 5 demonstrated, supply-side inflation causes a reduction in output and, hence, more unemployment. Demand-side inflation, on the other hand, may cause increases in output and employment. The combination of rising prices and rising unemployment characteristic of supply-side inflation puts pressure on government to do something about rising unemployment.

The decline in output and employment that accompanies supply-side inflation can be prevented by raising aggregate demand to offset the reduction in aggregate supply. Since it is difficult (due to recognition, implementation, and effectiveness lags) to use fiscal policy to raise aggregate demand, the most common instrument for shifting aggregate demand is monetary policy. The use of monetary policy to increase aggregate demand, however, can result in the **ratification of supply-side inflation.**

> **Ratification of supply-side inflation** results if the government increases the money supply to prevent supply-side shocks from raising unemployment.

Figure 10 illustrates the ratification of supply-side inflation. The economy is initially producing output of y_1 at a price level of p_1 (at point e_1). The economy now suffers a supply shock—aggregate supply shifts to the left (from *SRAS* to *SRAS'*). If aggregate demand is unchanged, the economy moves to e_2, producing less output but at higher prices (prices rise from p_1 to p_2). As output declines, the unemployment rate rises.

When the government feels pressure to combat the rising unemployment, it raises the money supply and increases aggregate demand (from *AD* to *AD'*). The price level rises even further—from p_2

Figure 10   The Ratification of Supply Shocks

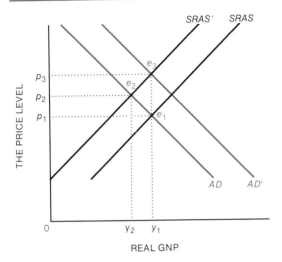

The economy is initially operating at e_1—producing y_1 at price level p_1. When aggregate supply falls from SRAS to SRAS', the price level rises to p_2, and output falls to y_2 (unemployment rises). The government ratifies the cost-push inflation by increasing aggregate demand from AD to AD'. The price level rises to p_3, and output (and unemployment) returns to its original level.

to p_3, and the economy returns to its original level of output and unemployment. As a consequence of the ratification, the supply-shock-induced unemployment has been eliminated, but the price level has been driven up even further.[4] If nothing else happens, the price increase stops at p_3.

THE WAGE/PRICE SPIRAL

When inflation has continued for some time, workers and firms will not longer be caught off guard by inflation. They will attempt to anticipate inflation. Contracts between workers and their employers will reflect the anticipated rate of inflation. Workers who anticipate a 10 percent annual inflation rate over the life of a wage contract will negotiate a contract that will protect them from this amount of inflation. Anticipated inflation causes higher wages to be demanded, and firms will be willing to pay. In an inflationary setting, firms can pass these wage increases along in the

form of higher prices. Sellers entering into sales contracts will also factor the anticipated rate of inflation into their sales contracts.

In such a situation, the economy gets caught in a **wage/price spiral.** Workers anticipate inflation and demand higher wages. Higher wages raise production costs and shift the aggregate supply curve in Figure 10 to the left. To prevent unemployment from increasing, the monetary authorities ratify the supply-side inflation and drive prices even higher. Workers now anticipate a higher price level; they demand higher wages; aggregate supply falls again; the whole process repeats itself.

> The **wage/price spiral** is the phenomenon of higher prices pushing wages higher and then higher wages pushing prices higher, or vice versa. This spiral occurs when workers anticipate inflation and demand and get higher wages and when the monetary authorities ratify the supply-side inflation. This process repeats itself.

As long as monetary authorities continue to ratify the increase in wages, the wage/price spiral can continue indefinitely. A necessary component of the wage/price spiral is the accompanying rise in the money supply.

Is this type of inflation an example of supply-side or demand-pull inflation? The argument is circular: If workers did not demand higher wages, it would not be necessary to ratify this supply-side inflation by increasing the money supply. Or if the money supply had never increased and the economy were not on an inflationary path, workers would not demand wage increases in excess of productivity advances.[5] In a wage/price spiral,

---

4. Our example illustrates a perfectly matched demand response of monetary policy to the supply shock. In practice, this match may be difficult to achieve.

---

5. Is the wage/price spiral caused by anticipated inflation that is ratified by monetary authorities or by people asking for a greater share of the economic pie? Abba Lerner has advanced the notion that inflation is caused by sellers of goods and services trying to get more and more rather than trying to protect themselves by correctly anticipating inflation. Remember, the wage/price spiral is initiated by a supply shock that is ratified, after which workers come to anticipate inflation. Seller's inflation could be self-generating. All that is necessary is a little greed.

If inflation is caused by seller's inflation, why has it not always been with us? We can presume that people who lived in the 19th century were as greedy as those of the 20th century; yet we have shown that there was no secular inflation in the 19th century. This discrepancy would suggest that the root cause of the wage/price spiral must be the expectation of more inflation. These expectations would not be self-generating.

the growth of the money supply is always present but so also is the supply-side element of anticipated inflation forcing up wage contracts. The debate over who has caused the wage/price spiral is also like the argument over which comes first, the chicken or the egg.

One explanation for the existence of wage/price spirals only in recent decades may be the postwar Keynesian policy of attempting to maintain full employment. When aggregate demand falls and threatens unemployment, full-employment policy calls for a stimulation of aggregate demand. If the economy suffers a supply shock, supply-side inflation will be ratified to prevent unemployment, and prices will rise more than they would have. In an economy that experiences demand changes and supply shocks, government policy is more likely to prevent price declines than price increases, building an inflationary bias into the economy.

The wage/price spiral cannot be halted painlessly. If the government ceases to ratify supply-side inflation (by refusing to let the money supply grow), the wage/price spiral will be broken, but the economy will have to live with the unemployment generated by the supply shock until the long-run self-adjustment mechanism works its course.

In the 1970s, inflation rates reveal a shift in the historical relationship between the money supply and the price level. As noted earlier, the percentage increase in money supply usually exceeds the percentage increase in price level. As output rises, it absorbs some of the increase in money supply and holds down the increase in prices.

From 1970 to 1981, however, the money supply grew at approximately 6 percent per year and real GNP grew at an annual rate of 2.5 percent, but prices rose on the average by almost 8 percent per year. With these growth rates of the money supply and of real GNP, one would expect lower rates of inflation. The increase in output did not hold the rate of inflation below the growth of money supply for three reasons:

1. Supply shocks—in the form of OPEC-induced oil-price increases and weather-induced agricultural-price increases—combined to create extraordinary and unexpected price increases in the early 1970s. These supply shocks may also have raised inflationary expectations.

2. Between 1970 and 1981, there were sustained increases in the rate of growth of both the money supply and the price level. The inflation rate was 5.4 percent in 1970 and 9.4 percent in 1981. As the inflation rate rose from 5.4 percent to 9.4 percent, there was an increase in inflationary expectations. Increases in the anticipated rate of inflation fuel inflation by increasing velocity, as noted earlier. As the equation of exchange shows, rising velocity causes a given percentage growth of the money supply to yield more inflation, *ceteris paribus*.

3. The increase in velocity was fed not only by rising inflationary expectations but also by changes and innovations in the financial system (described in Chapter 8). People began to use credit cards; brokerage firms began to offer money-market funds with check-writing privileges. NOW accounts were introduced that allowed customers to write checks on savings accounts. Money management by firms was made easier by computerization. With computers, firms could more easily manage their cash balances and thereby lower the demand for money and increase velocity. These innovations increased the number of close substitutes for money (M1). Velocity was 4.7 in 1970 and 6.6 in 1981; hence, velocity increased by 40 percent. In terms of the exchange equation, while the increase in M averaged 6 percent per year, the rise in MV was almost 10 percent per annum due to the increase in V.

SUGGESTED CURES FOR INFLATION

How can inflation be brought under control? In particular, how can a rapid or accelerating inflation accompanied by high inflationary expectations be controlled by government authorities?

The Keynesian Solution

There is no unique Keynesian solution to the problem of rapid inflation because Keynesians do not believe in a single cause of inflation.[6] Most

---

6. This section is based largely on Arthur Okun, *Prices and Quantities* (Washington, D.C.: Brookings Institution, 1981), chap. 8.

Keynesians believe that the best approach is active aggregate-demand management combined with some sort of **incomes policy.**

An **incomes policy** is a set of rules, guidelines, or laws devised by government to influence wage and price increases.

The basic fear of such well-known Keynesians as Paul Samuelson, Franco Modigliani, James Tobin, and the late Arthur Okun would be that a pure anti-inflation strategy (such as monetarism) would result in excessive unemployment. For example, Keynesians note that when the Fed tightened monetary policy after 1979, unemployment rose from an average 5.8 percent in 1979 to 9.7 percent in 1982 until the rate of inflation dropped. Critics of Fed policy ask: was the drop in inflation worth the resulting rise in unemployment?

Nobel prize laureate James Tobin argues, along with many other Keynesians, that moderate inflation is not nearly as bad as unemployment. The basic cost of inflation is that people move away from money. Anticipated inflation causes people to hold smaller money balances per dollar of expenditure. Hence, people will make extra shopping trips and extra trips to the bank.

. . . the ultimate social cost of anticipated inflation is the wasteful use of resources to economize holdings of (money). . . . I suspect the intelligent layman would be utterly astounded if they realized that this is the great evil economists are talking about. They have imagined a much more devastating cataclysm, with Vesuvius vengefully punishing the sinners below. Extra trips between savings banks and commercial banks? What an anti-climax.[7]

When inflation becomes immoderate—near the double-digit rate from the late 1970s to 1981—the crawl from money becomes more serious. Runaway inflations can be very dangerous as the economy resorts more and more to barter. Keynesians then suggest restraint in the growth of nominal aggregate demand using a combination of monetary and fiscal policy. This restraint has to be tempered, though, with an eye to the unemployment rate. Countercyclical policy cannot be given up in an inflationary world. If recession threatens, the Keynesian would likely use expansionary policies. Keynesians hope that in recessions an incomes policy would help keep the inflation rate down when expansionary policies are applied.

Wage/Price Controls

One approach to controlling the inflationary wage/price spiral is to use *wage and price controls,* or government-imposed rules and laws to govern prices and wages. In their mild form, such controls could be an incomes policy of voluntary rules and guidelines concerning wage and price increases. For example, the government may decree that prices can be raised only at the same rate as costs; it may say that wages and prices cannot increase by more than x percent in a given year; it may set rules on profit margins. These rules can be anywhere from mandatory to voluntary. The wage/price controls system often requires a substantial bureaucracy to monitor compliance.

In their more extreme form, wage and price controls use rigid wage and price freezes that prohibit raising wages and prices above the level at which they were on a certain date prior to the freeze. Such freezes are usually not all-inclusive; agricultural commodities and imports, whose prices are set in world markets, are typically exempted. (See Example 2.)

Arguments For.   The principal argument for wage and price controls is that they might break inflationary expectations. If people form expectations adaptively, these expectations will fall only slowly as inflation rates fall. As long as inflationary expectations remain high, interest rates will remain high, workers will continue to demand wage increases in excess of productivity, and so on. The problem, therefore, is to get people to adjust their inflationary expectations downward in a hurry. A temporary wage/price control system would put an immediate damper on inflationary expectations.

Arguments Against.   The basic argument against rigid wage/price controls is that the productive efficiency of the economy will decline. If relative wages and prices are not allowed to move freely, the economy will be deprived of valuable signals. Higher relative wages can no longer signal to workers which sectors of the economy are

7. James Tobin, "Inflation and Unemployment," *American Economic Review* 62, 1 (March 1972): 15.

Example 2   The U.S. Wage-and-Price-Controls Program of 1971–1974

On August 15, 1971, President Richard Nixon announced a 90-day freeze on almost all wages and prices. The control program ran through four phases and was dismantled in late 1973 and early 1974. The first phase was the 90-day freeze from which only taxes, mortgage interest rates, and raw agricultural commodities were exempted. Phase II began in November 1971. A Pay Board was established to enforce Phase II, which set a standard for wage increases of 5.5 percent per year with certain exceptions. A parallel Price Board operated on the rule that firms would be allowed to pass cost increases on in the form of higher prices only on a strict percentage basis. Phase III began in January 1973. The Pay and Price Boards were abolished; the 5.5 percent wage-increase standard was retained, but a more flexible approach was followed in its enforcement; standards for passing on cost increases were loosened. Inflation accelerated alarmingly during Phase III, and a second freeze was announced in June of 1973. Freeze II froze prices but not wages! Phase IV went into effect in August of 1973, and the standards and regulations of this phase were very much like those of Phases II and III. On April 30, 1974, the President's authority to control wages and prices lapsed, and the experiment with wage/price controls ended.

Why were wage and price controls introduced in 1971? Although the inflation rates of this period appear to us as relatively mild (they averaged 5.1 percent between 1969 and 1971), they were alarming to a country accustomed to much lower inflation rates. The unemployment rate had risen from 3.3 percent in 1969 to 6 percent in January of 1971. Moreover, the value of the dollar abroad was being attacked. How was unemployment to be brought down without a further acceleration of inflation? Wages and price controls were seen as the answer.

The goal was to freeze wages and prices to shock inflationary expectations out of the economy. As inflationary expectations subsided, aggregate demand could be increased without pulling up the inflation rate. What happened to the inflation rate during the controls program? During Phase I prices were basically unchanged. During Phase II the inflation rate averaged 3.6 percent. There was an alarming resurgence of inflation during Phase III—inflation rose to a 9.1 percent annual rate.

More important than what happened to prices during the controls program is what happened to inflation after the program: the annual inflation rate was 4.3 percent in 1970 on the eve of the controls. At the end of the controls program (1974), the inflation rate was averaging 9.4 percent. In the two years after controls were lifted (1975 and 1976), inflation averaged 5.9 percent. What happened to unemployment? During the controls program unemployment remained between 5 and 6 percent. After the controls were lifted, the unemployment rate rose to 8.5 percent.

It, thus, appears that the controls program failed to meet its objective to bring down inflation and unemployment at the same time. There are many possible explanations for this failure, but one of the most important is that nothing was done to prevent a price "catch-up" as the controls were being lifted. The rate of growth of the money supply accelerated from 6.6 percent in 1970, to 7.1 percent in 1971, to 7.5 percent in 1972, and then down to 5.0 percent in 1973. If inflation is everywhere a monetary phenomenon, why should prices not catch up to what they would have been without the controls after the controls are lifted? Economists who have studied the controls program conclude that the controls likely held down the inflation rate somewhat when they were in effect, but they raised the inflation rate in 1974 when the controls were removed. ∎

Source: Alan Blinder, *Economic Policy and the Great Stagflation* (New York: Academic Press, 1979), chapters 3 and 6.

rising. Branches experiencing rising demand can not raise their prices sufficiently to equate supply and demand, and shortages will develop. Economic activity will tend to spill over into industries that are not frozen—such as agriculture and imports and even the underground economy. Supply and demand pressures will encourage evasion of rules.

All economists agree that rigid wage/price controls cannot be used over an extended period because of their effect on efficiency; they can only be used in the short run. If people are aware that these controls are of limited duration, they will attempt to anticipate what will happen to inflation when the controls are lifted. If people generally expect a price explosion when the program runs out, they will not wind down their inflationary expectations. If the controls program fails to wind down inflationary expectations, it will not have accomplished its goal.

Tax-Based Incomes Policy (TIP)

Experience teaches that wage and price controls inflict all sorts of inefficiencies and shortages on the economy. Economists have suggested ways of using incomes policies to control wage and price increases while still using the market to allocate resources. Henry Wallich, now a member of the Broad of Governors of the Fed, and Sydney Weintraub have suggested that a *tax-based incomes policy (TIP)* can meet the inefficiency objection to controls. The purpose of a TIP is to use the tax mechanism to accomplish the goals of an incomes policy within the framework of a market economy.

A TIP works as follows. Business corporations are sensitive to the income taxes they pay and will go through considerable effort to reduce their taxes. The TIP imposes a penalty on firms whenever they grant average pay boosts in excess of some norm—say 5 percent per annum. The tax would then vary proportionately to the extent that actual pay increases exceed the percentage norm. Because such a plan would meet substantial opposition from business and labor, Arthur Okun suggested another version: giving tax *credits* to firms that meet the norm, with the credits being paid to the employees of the firm.

The major difficulty with TIP plans is that a TIP would be an administrative nightmare. The average pay of a firm would reflect the skills and education of the firm's employees, and a TIP would give the firm the incentive to hire lesser skilled employees or to engage in other tax-avoidance schemes. To stay within the norm, firms could simply raise the fringe benefits of employees.

The proponents of TIPs recognize these problems but maintain that the administrative costs are less than the benefits TIP would bring. The other alternative—reducing inflation by raising the unemployment rate—is more costly.

Monetarism: Monetary Rules

The major proponent of monetarism, Milton Friedman, argues that "inflation is always and everywhere a monetary phenomenon," that inflation cannot persist unless it is supported by monetary growth. According to Friedman, supply-side inflation is just a temporary phenomenon that is important only in the short run. The major cause of inflation is demand pull, and demand pull is caused by excess monetary growth. For example, from 1915 to 1984 the average annual growth in the money supply has been 5.5 percent per year. During that same period, inflation has averaged 3.4 percent per year and real GNP has grown at about 3.1 percent per year.

If inflation is "always and everywhere" caused by excessive monetary growth, it is easy to predict Friedman's solution: strict limitation of the growth of the money supply. Insofar as real GNP over the long run has grown at about 3 percent per year, Freidman would limit the rate of growth of money supply to about 3 percent per year.

Friedman's "3 percent rule" is that the Fed should increase the money supply by 3 percent every year, give or take some small margin of error. Of course, the fixed rate of monetary growth could be any other small number—anywhere from 3 to 5 percent—depending on the output growth rate. Friedman's constant-money-growth rule is sometimes called the "k percent rule." Under these circumstances, the Fed's decision-making power would be reduced to mere technical matters.

Although detailed discussion of monetarism will be postponed until Chapter 17, the general rationale for the constant-money-growth rule follows.

1. Studies of the business cycle reveal that recessions and depressions are always associated with prior sharp reductions in monetary growth. Hence, monetarists argue that it is monetary instability that is largely responsible for the apparent instability of capitalism. Under a constant-money-growth rule, cyclical ups and downs would still exist, but their magnitude would be smaller.

2. The empirical relationship between changes in the rate of monetary growth and nominal GNP growth is lagged. Milton Friedman argues that the

lag between money supply and GNP is long and variable (sometimes 6 months; sometimes 2 years). Since the business cycle cannot be forecasted accurately, attempts to use countercyclical policy can destabilize the economy. A fixed growth of money supply would bring more stability than countercyclical policy.

3. The historical relationship between excessive monetary growth and inflation is impressive and cannot be denied.

The Supply-Side Program

The equation of exchange shows that the rate of inflation will be lower, *ceteris paribus,* the higher is the rate of growth of output. Some believe that inflation could be controlled by increasing the growth of real output. The appeal of this proposition is enormous because it obviates the need for pain and suffering (in the form of high unemployment or high interest rates) while curing inflation. If inflation can be cured by the rapid expansion of real goods and services, as real output expands, unemployment will fall along with the inflation rate.

Tax Incentives.   Supply-side economists have argued that it is possible to bring about substantial increases in the growth of output. The supply-siders maintain that the progressive tax system discourages people from working and business firms from investing in plants and equipment.

Arthur Laffer uses his "Laffer Curve" to show the relationship between tax rates and tax collections. If tax rates were to rise to 100 percent of income, there would be little or not output since all incentives to produce and work would have been removed. At a 100 percent tax rate, tax revenues would be essentially zero. At the other extreme, if the tax rate were 0 percent of income, incentives to work and produce output would be strong since no taxes are being paid. Although incomes would be high, zero taxes would be collected because of the 0 percent tax rate. Thus, tax collections would be zero at both a 100 percent and a 0 percent tax rate; there must exist some tax rate between these two extremes at which tax revenues are maximized. For example, one might argue that if the tax rate rises above 45 percent, tax revenues would actually fall because people's

work effort and earnings would fall off more rapidly than the tax rate would be increasing.

If an economy has a tax rate above the rate that yields maximum tax revenues, it can attack inflation by reducing the tax rate. If tax rates are reduced, the economy will produce more real output because of improved economic incentives; the government will actually gain tax revenues from the lower tax rate. Both of these effects will reduce inflation. The increase in real output increases the supply of goods and services, and the increase in tax collections reduces the budget deficit. A smaller deficit could mean a slower rate of growth of money supply if the deficit is financed by Fed purchases.

The supply-siders propose that cuts in personal and business taxes combined with limited monetary growth would result in smaller increases in aggregate demand. Increases in aggregate output would, therefore, insure that inflation drops in an environment of rising employment.

President Ronald Reagan was much influenced by the ideas of the supply-side school. Indeed, the tax cut passed in 1981 was designed to stimulate work effort by lowering marginal tax rates and offering investment incentives to business firms. The tax-simplification proposal advocated by President Reagan in 1985 would also lower marginal tax rates.

Return to the Gold Standard.   Another plank of the supply-side cure of inflation is that the United States should return to the gold standard. As noted in Chapter 8, our money supply is no longer backed by gold. The price of gold is set like that of other raw materials by market forces. It rises and falls relative to the value of the dollar as the market dictates.

The ideal gold standard as proposed by supply-siders would work as follows. The value of the dollar would be fixed in terms of gold—say, one ounce of gold would equal $400. The U.S. Treasury would guarantee the value of the dollar in terms of gold. Anyone with $400 could always buy one ounce of gold from the U.S. Treasury. Likewise, the U.S. Treasury would always stand ready to sell one ounce of gold for $400. By buying and selling gold at a fixed price, the relative price of dollars for gold would be fixed.

Under the gold standard, the money supply would be tied to the underlying stock of gold.

Example 3   A Free Market in Money?

A most ingenious and radical solution to the inflation problem has been advanced by Nobel laureate Friedrich A. von Hayek. Hayek proposes that each country of Europe and North America bind themselves to an agreement "not to place any obstacles in the way of the free dealing throughout their territories in one another's currencies or of a similar exercise of the banking business by any institution established in any of their territories." In short, Hayek proposes the denationalization of money and free competition among different types of money. Why should governments have a monopoly on the issue of money?

What Hayek supposes would eventually happen is that large banks would get into the profitable business of issuing currencies. The Bank of America might issue the BAM, the Bank of France the BAF, the First City Bank the FCB, and so on. These banks would then compete with one another for customers for their currency. Banks that succeeded in keeping the value of their currency stable would do well in this competitive struggle.

How would people manage with all these currencies? Within any one city there would be a number of currencies with different rates of exchange. Would money's value as a medium of exchange be hampered by the existence of different currencies? With computers, the checkout clerk at the grocery store need only pass each item over the eye of the computer, which will then announce each price and figure the total amount including change. Computers could easily handle 50 separate currencies simultaneously.

The idea of different currencies competing with one another is not as strange as it sounds. Long before the German hyperinflation had destroyed the value of the mark in the 1920s, foreign currencies had begun to circulate in Germany. Those familiar with American banking history will know of the history of wildcat banking during which American banks issued their own currencies. The system did not work well then, but that was before the age of the computer.

Denationalization of money means the end of monetary policy because the government no longer controls the money supply. Hayek would feel more comfortable if money were taken out of the hands of government where he believes it has been abused for centuries. The same distrust of government lurks in the minds of modern proponents of the gold standard. ∎

Source: Friedrich A. von Hayek, *Denationalization of Money* (Great Britain: Institute of Economic Affairs, 1976).

Monetary authorities would no longer be able to freely expand or contract the money supply as they have done over the years. The control of the money supply would effectively be taken out of their hands under a gold standard.

Under a gold standard, when inflation threatens, gold production would slack off because the value of gold would fall (a dollar would purchase fewer goods). The supply of gold and, hence, the money supply would no longer grow rapidly, and the rate of inflation would fall. When prices fell, the production of gold would become more profitable because of the increasing value of the dollar. The gold supply would increase more rapidly, and price deflation would disappear. While inflation or deflation would remain under the gold standard, private producers of gold would engage in the appropriate anti-inflationary or anti-deflationary monetary policy. Inflation discourages gold production; deflation encourages gold production (as long as the price of gold remains fixed in terms of the dollar).

Criticisms.   Critics of the supply-side approach point out two problems. The first is that most economists are sceptical about the possibility of obtaining sustained increases in real output from tax incentives. Tax reductions are likely to bring about relatively small, one-shot increases in real output, not sustained increases in the rate of growth of real output. Historically, it is very difficult to raise the growth of output; very substantial increases in resources or efficiency are required to raise the annual real growth rate by even 0.5 percent per annum. Note that increasing the output growth rate by a full percentage point will lower the inflation rate by about 1 percentage point. Thus, even under the most favorable of circumstances, supply-side increases will not have much of an effect on inflation.

Critics of the gold-standard plank of the supply-side school argue that a return to the gold standard would make the money supply a hostage of the two leading gold-producing countries (South Africa and the U.S.S.R.). It also seems unwise to dig up gold and then turn around and bury it again in Fort Knox, all for the purpose of restraining the growth rate of the money supply. There must be cheaper ways of limiting monetary growth.

The basic problem with the gold standard is that the economy is still subject to the random shocks of wars, changes in gold production, crop failures, and so on. Economies on the gold standard went through painful periods of deflation and inflation and depression. As noted earlier, prices were anything but stable during the 19th century. The United States was on the gold standard from 1879 to 1914. During this period, prices fell 47 percent from 1882 to 1896 and then rose 41 percent from 1896 to 1913.

Both monetarists and Keynesians alike would tend to be suspicious of returning to the gold standard. Monetarists would be opposed because the gold standard could not guarantee a steady and moderate rate of money growth. Keynesians would be opposed because the gold standard disallows the use of monetary policy as a discretionary instrument of economic policy.

This chapter discussed the facts, causes, and possible cures of inflation. The next chapter will turn to the combination of high unemployment and high inflation called stagflation.

Summary

1. The five facts of inflation are the noninevitability of inflation, the positive historical relationship between the money supply and the price level, the correlation between high inflation and high interest rates, the inflationary trend in recent years, and the fact that recent inflation has sometimes been higher than can be accounted for by the historical relationship between money supply and prices.

2. Demand-side inflation is caused by increases in aggregate demand. Supply-side inflation is caused by decreases in aggregate supply.

3. If inflation is unanticipated, increases in the money supply will increase aggregate demand, causing output and prices to rise. The increase in output beyond the natural level will be only temporary and will be eliminated in the long run by the self-adjustment mechanism. In the short run, an increase in the money supply will drive down interest rates, but in the long run, interest rates will tend to return to their original level. Excess monetary growth occurs when the growth of money supply exceeds the growth of output. The growth of the price level will equal the growth of money supply minus the growth of output with constant velocity. When inflation is persistent, people come to anticipate inflation. Inflationary expectations can be formed either through adaptive expectations or through rational expectations. When inflation is anticipated, monetary authorities can lower interest rates in the long run only by raising interest rates in the short run. The short-run relationship between the government deficit and inflation rates is ambiguous. In the long run, deficits and inflation appear to be related because deficits may be financed by the Fed, because a larger national debt encourages spending, and because inflation increases the deficit directly through higher interest payments.

4. Supply-side inflation can be caused by supply shocks. Ratification of supply shocks is the process of raising aggregate demand to prevent unemployment from rising as a consequence of the supply shock.

5. The wage/price spiral is caused by anticipated inflation and the ratification of supply-side inflation by monetary authorities. Recent inflation experience is explained by the supply shocks of the early 1970s, the increase in velocity, the increase in anticipated inflation, and recent financial innovations.

6. The proposals to cure inflation include: the monetarist constant-money-growth rule; the complex Keynesian package of demand management, incomes policy, and antirecession policies, wage/price controls, tax-based incentive programs; supply-side economics.

Key Terms

demand-side inflation
supply-side inflation
adaptive expectations
rational expectations
supply shock
ratification of supply-side inflation
wage/price spiral
incomes policy

Questions and Problems

1. The owner of the apartment you are renting complains: "Wages, utilities, and other costs are rising too rapidly. I have no choice but to raise your rent." Is this a case of supply-side inflation?

2. Economists classify inflation as either supply-side inflation or demand-side inflation. Using aggregate supply-and-demand analysis, explain the differences between these two types of inflation. Is it possible to distinguish between the two types of inflation from observed information on output, employment, and prices?

3. In a particular economy, the money supply has been growing at 8 percent per annum, and output has been growing at 3 percent per annum. If velocity is constant, what would the rate of inflation be? If velocity is declining at a rate of 2 percent per year, what would the rate of inflation be?

4. Explain why increases in money supply that are unanticipated are likely to cause the interest rate to drop. Why may the drop in the interest rate be short-lived? If the increase in money supply is fully anticipated, what would happen to interest rates?

5. Using the adaptive-expectations hypothesis, what do you think the expected rate of inflation would be in 1992 if past inflation rates were 10 percent in 1991, 8 percent in 1990, and 6 percent in 1989?

6. How does the rational-expectations hypothesis differ from the adaptive-expectations hypothesis?

7. What would you expect to happen to velocity as inflationary expectations increase? What is the actual relationship between velocity and anticipated inflation?

8. Why is the short-run relationship between inflation and government deficits ambiguous?

9. What are some reasons that there might be a long-run relationship between inflation and the government deficit?

10. Using aggregate supply-and-demand analysis, explain why adverse supply shocks combine the worst of two worlds: more inflation and higher unemployment. Also explain why governments tend to ratify supply-side inflation.

11. The wage/price spiral is blamed on unions and management and on expansionary economic policy. Explain why it is difficult to assign the blame for the wage/price spiral.

12. Evaluate the following statement: "Both the Keynesians and monetarists believe that inflation is primarily caused by demand-side factors. Therefore, there really is not any difference between the two schools' approaches to the inflation problem."

13. What are some arguments for wage and price controls?

14. What are some arguments against wage and price controls?

15. How would monetary policy work under a gold standard?

Suggested Readings

Blinder, Alan. *Economic Policy and the Great Stagflation*. New York: Academic Press, 1979.

Lerner, Abba P. "Stagflation—Its Cause and Cure." *Challenge* 20 (September/October 1977): 14–19.

Perry, George L. "Slowing the Wage/Price Spiral: The Macroeconomic View." *Brookings Papers on Economic Activity* 2 (1978): 259–91.

Seidman, Laurence S. "A New Approach to the Control of Inflation." *Challenge* 19 (July/August 1976): 39–43.

15

Unemployment

Chapter Preview

The Employment Act of 1946 commits the federal government to "maintain useful employment opportunities . . . for those able, willing, and seeking work." The full-employment goal was reaffirmed by the Full Employment and Balanced Growth Act of 1978 (also called the Humphrey-Hawkins Bill) wherein Congress declared the achievement of full employment a central economic goal. Full employment, unlike other macroeconomic goals, such as price stability or economic growth, has been clearly established as a national economic goal by federal legislation.

This chapter examines the determinants of employment and unemployment in the short run and in long run, reviews the different types of unemployment (frictional, structural, and cyclical), and

considers the problems of defining unemployment. Trends in employment and unemployment reveal that the relationships between employment, unemployment, and the unemployment rate are complex. With the possible exceptions of layoff unemployment and chronic unemployment, the phenomenon of unemployment can be studied as a process whereby workers and firms are involved in search activities. This chapter shows how job seekers and employee seekers rationally conduct search activities and discusses how job-search behavior is affected by inflation and other factors in both the short run and the long run. The chapter analyzes the causes of long-run changes in the natural rate of unemployment and the cost of unemployment. ■

DEFINING UNEMPLOYMENT

Types of Unemployment

Chapter 5 explained that economists distinguish among three types of unemployment: **frictional unemployment, structural unemployment,** and **cyclical unemployment.**

Frictional unemployment is the unemployment associated with the normal changing of jobs in a dynamic economy.

Structural unemployment is the unemployment associated with long-run structural changes in a dynamic economy and is created by long-run declining employment in specific industries.

Cyclical unemployment is the unemployment associated with reductions in aggregate demand or with supply shocks that cause the economy to operate below full employment.

The precise dividing lines between the three types of unemployment are difficult to draw. We cannot say with any certainty whether a particular person is frictionally, structurally, or cyclically unemployed. Although we cannot identify what proportions of the unemployed fall into which category, dividing unemployment into three types helps us to separate the causes, conseqeunces, and cures for unemployment.

The problem of unemployment is the task of matching unemployed people to unfilled jobs. In the case of frictional unemployment, there is no great imbalance between the number of job seekers and the number of unfilled jobs. In the normal course of business, people move from one job to another. In the case of structural unemployment, the matching task is more difficult as people must move from one industry or region to another industry or region to avoid unemployment. In the case of cyclical unemployment, declines in aggregate demand or adverse supply shocks reduce the number of unfilled positions, making it more difficult for job seekers to locate jobs.

From the point of view of the economy as a whole, unemployment can have both a positive and a negative side. Cyclical unemployment has little to recommend it. Cyclical unemployment is the result of an imbalance between the number of unemployed people and the number of vacant jobs for which the unemployed are suited. During business-cycle downturns, it becomes more difficult for people to find jobs. The unemployed are unemployed for longer and longer periods as a business downturn worsens. Family incomes fall, marriages break apart; even the suicide rate turns up during periods of cyclical unemployment. Chronic long-term unemployment also has no redeeming features. A smoothly functioning labor market matches people to jobs for which they are suited within a reasonable amount of time. In the case of certain individuals, this process breaks down. Even after searching for jobs for 6 months, a year, or longer, the chronically unemployed person still cannot find a job. (See Example 1.) Cyclical unemployment has social as well as private costs. Having otherwise productive workers sitting on the sidelines without jobs reduces the efficiency of resource utilization and causes the economy to produce less output than it is capable of producing from its existing resources.

The effects of unemployment are not uniformly negative, however. Frictional unemployment plays a generally positive role in the economy; it is one of the costs of achieving economic efficiency. Through frictional unemployment people move to better jobs. Frictional unemployment is the oil that lubricates structural change in the economy. As tastes change and as costs change, economies must change their mix of output. When employment opportunities decline in agriculture and smokestack industries and rise in service and high-tech industries, labor-markets are adapting to changes in the economy. If unemployed workers were to accept the first job that came along (thereby removing themselves from the unemployment ranks)—even if it were below the salary and skill level to which they were accustomed—their long-run incomes would suffer. Even structural unemployment—a type of unemployment that imposes substantial burdens on the unemployed—can play a productive (albeit painful) role. Industries that are in inevitable decline will be unable to provide attractive employment opportunities in the long run. Both the affected worker and society as a whole benefit if the worker makes the (often painful) move from employment in a declining industry to employment in a rising industry. Workers must move out of

Example 1   The Human Costs of Unemployment

Economists typically concentrate on the easily measurable dollar costs of unemployment. Unemployed workers lose income and, when the unemployment rate exceeds the natural rate, society loses output that could have been produced without heating up inflation. Researchers find that unemployment has human costs effects as well that rise during periods of high cyclical unemployment. Scientific statistical studies and newspaper accounts report that family conflict and child-abuse rates, alcoholism, and divorce rates rise as the unemployment rate rises. Unemployed workers often lose their health insurance. Rising unemployment is found to be statistically related to the suicide rate, the homicide rate, admissions to prisons and mental hospitals, and deaths from heart attacks. ∎

Source: Barry Bluestone and Bennett Harrison, *The Deindustrialization of America* (New York: Basic Books, 1982), chap. 3.

employment in declining industries if they are to earn decent lifetime incomes and if the economy is to progress.

> While some types of unemployment, such as cyclical and chronic unemployment, impose personal and social costs that we would like to avoid, some types of unemployment are essential and beneficial to society and even to the unemployed.

In order to be able to analyze movements in the rate of unemployment over time, it is necessary to understand how unemployment is measured. The measurement of unemployment is not as straightforward as it might seem.

The Official Definition

The official definition of unemployment was introduced in Chapter 5. Chapter 5 explained that in order to be counted as unemployed by the Bureau of Labor Statistics, a person must meet three conditions:

> A person 16 years or older is unemployed if he or she: 1) is not currently working, 2) has actively looked for work during the previous four weeks, and 3) is currently available for work.

Persons aged 16 or older who are not unemployed fall into two other categories. They can either be *employed,* or they can be *not in the labor force.* Employed persons are either currently working at jobs or have jobs but are currently not working due to bad weather, labor disputes, illness, or other temporary factors. Persons not in the **labor force** remain *voluntarily* outside of the labor force for a variety of reasons. Such reasons include raising children, attending school, retirement, or long-term mental or physical illness. Some workers may even remain outside the labor force involuntarily, as will be explained in a later discussion of *discouraged workers.*

> The **labor force** consists of those employed and unemployed persons 16 years of age or older who either have jobs or who are looking for jobs and available for jobs.

The possible flows of persons into and out of the labor force and into and out of employment are shown in Figure 1.

The Treatment of Layoffs

The official definition of unemployment requires that persons without jobs and currently available for work be "actively searching" for a job in order to be classified as unemployed. The official definition allows an important exception to this rule: workers unemployed as a result of a **layoff.** Workers who have been laid off from a job and who are waiting to be recalled to their previous job are counted as unemployed even though they are not actively looking for another job.

> A **layoff** is a suspension of employment without pay and without prejudice that lasts 7 days or more. The laid-off workers may be recalled to his or her old job if economic conditions improve.

Figure 1   Flows Into and Out of the Labor Force, 1983

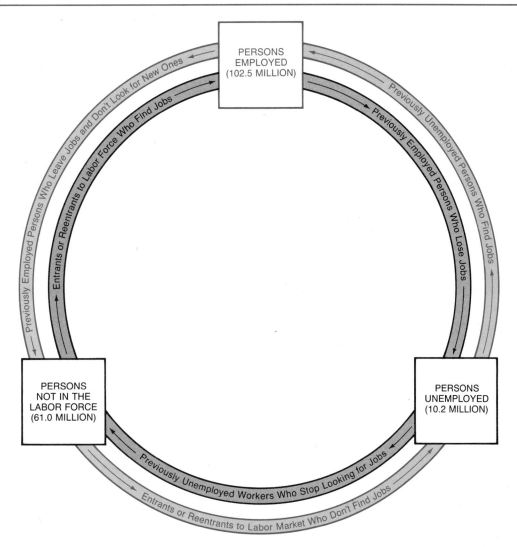

Persons can enter the ranks of the unemployed either by moving from the ranks of the employed or by not finding a job upon entering the labor force. People can drop out of the labor force either by departing from jobs or by giving up the job search once unemployed.

The laid-off worker who chooses not to search for a new job makes this decision on the grounds that he or she expects to be recalled within a reasonable period of time and feels that another job would not provide the same pay or benefits.

Definitional Problems

The definition of unemployment, while appearing straightforward, raises a number of questions that underscore the difficulty of measuring unemploy-

ment. Whether someone should be counted as unemployed or not in the labor force is not always clear-cut. In a number of cases, it is a close judgment call as to whether a particular person is unemployed, employed, or not in the labor force. In principle, the unemployment rate should be a measure of those persons who are *involuntarily* without jobs. Yet, as we shall show below, unemployment has both voluntary and involuntary elements. In some cases, such as an unemployed parent who is willing to accept virtually any pay-

Table 1   Job-Search Methods of Unemployed Workers (percent using method), 1982

Method	By Sex		By Age				
	Men	Women	16–19	20–24	25–34	35–44	45–54
Public employment agency	26.9	20.9	17.9	31.6	30.1	29.4	28.7
Private employment agency	5.8	5.8	3.1	5.9	7.4	8.5	8.3
Direct contact with employer	78.8	76.5	80.3	75.2	71.9	70.9	68.8
Friends or relatives	18.3	13.8	12.9	14.3	14.7	15.7	14.4
Want ads	32.6	37.3	25.8	33.2	36.3	33.8	34.2
Other	5.8	3.4	3.9	3.9	5.6	6.9	7.7
Average number of methods used	1.68	1.58	1.44	1.64	1.66	1.65	1.62

Source: *Handbook of Labor Statistics*, December 1983, p. 88.

ing job but is still unable to find work, the involuntary element clearly dominates. In other cases, such as the spouse of a well-paid executive making a casual job search to find a job compatible with his or her social position, there is a stronger voluntary element to being without a job. In principle, economists would like to be able to draw a clear line between voluntary and involuntary unemployment, but this is not possible. In most cases, there is a mixture of voluntary and involuntary elements that could not be separated without being able to look inside the minds of people. Persons differ in the intensity of their job search, in the extent to which they will accept positions that don't exactly match their experience and qualifications, in the extent to which they are willing to accept underground employment, and in the extent to which they are willing to continue their search.

Intensity of Job Search.   A person without a job and available for work is unemployed as long as that person is engaged in a job search. There is no operational way to gauge the intensity of the job search. Some people may be looking rather casually for a job (such as the full-time high-school student who is casually looking for an after-school job). Other persons may be conducting a very intensive job search, spending 15 hours a day on the telephone, reading want ads, visiting employment agencies, and attending interviews. Government statistics cannot distinguish among the unemployed according to intensity of job search. The Bureau of Labor Statistics does gather data on job-search methods (see Table 1), but these data fail to shed much light on the inten-

sity of job search. What they do show is that the most common method of searching for a job is to contact potential employers directly. They also show the importance of placing or answering want ads and the use of public employment agencies. They also show that young people use different search methods than more mature workers.

Matching Jobs and Qualifications   The unemployed seek jobs that are consistent with skills, qualifications, and previous work experience. The unemployed ditchdigger does not seek work as a certified public accountant. The unemployed aeronautical engineer would like to find employment in aeronautical engineering. The Ph.D. in English literature would like to find a college or university job teaching English literature. Insofar as people are not all the same, because they have different educational and work-experience backgrounds, they tend to restrict their search for jobs to employment options that they regard as suitable. Although a job may be available managing a fast-food restaurant, the unemployed automotive design engineer will likely not take such a job. The unemployed English Ph.D. may choose to remain unemployed until a college teaching job comes along rather than accept employment as a public-school teacher. If people's job expectations are not met, they typically choose to remain unemployed. These decisions depend upon the magnitude of the mismatch (the automotive design engineer taking a job as a janitor is more of a mismatch than the automotive design engineer taking a job as an automotive assembly engineer) and upon personal preferences. The problem of matching available jobs with

Example 2   Job Openings and Help-Wanted Ads

The U.S. Employment Service reports statistics on job openings as reported by state employment agencies. The Conference Board compiles totals of help-wanted ads placed in various newspapers. These figures are reported in the accompanying table along with the national unemployment rate for the period 1974 to 1982. Reported job openings and the number of help-wanted ads fall when the unemployment rate rises. When the labor market turns around and the unemployment rate is falling, job openings and help-wanted ads increase. As these statistics demonstrate, there are unfilled jobs even during periods of very high unemployment. Job openings continue to be reported to state employment agencies, and help-wanted ads continue to be placed in newspapers. In 1982, when the unemployment rate was 9.5 percent, there were more than 6 million job openings reported from the beginning to the end of 1982. An examination of the types of job openings listed by state employment agencies and in help-wanted ads shows why unfilled jobs continue to

exist even with large numbers of people unemployed. The job openings tend to be for people with special skills and training (such as for certain engineering or accounting specialties) or for positions that require extensive and careful job search on the part of the employee-seeking firm (such as executive positions in corporations). The existence of unfilled jobs during periods of high unemployment does not prove that people are voluntarily unemployed. It underscores the fact that unemployment is a task of matching people to jobs. These figures show that this task is more difficult during downturns in the business cycle. ■

Sources: *Statistical Abstract of the United States 1984*, p. 424. The help-wanted ad index is compiled by the Conference Board and is based upon the number of advertisements in classified sections of newspapers. The help-wanted index is quoted by permission of the Conference Board, New York, New York.

Year	Unemployment Rate (percent)	Job Openings (thousands)	Help-Wanted Index (1967 = 100)
1974	5.5	9,439	110
1975	8.3	7,889	80
1976	7.6	7,668	95
1977	6.9	8,396	118
1978	6.0	9,534	150
1979	5.8	9,477	158
1980	7.0	8,122	129
1981	7.5	7,548	119
1982	9.5	6,150	86

worker qualifications again underscores the difficult distinction between voluntary and involuntary unemployment. The matching problem also explains why unemployment continues to exist even in an economy with an apparently large number of unfilled positions. High unemployment combined with a large number of unfilled positions means a mismatching of available jobs with available skills (see Example 2).

Underground Workers. Official unemployment figures fail to capture the hundreds of

thousands, or perhaps millions, of people who work in the underground economy. As Chapter 6 demonstrated, the underground economy is a multibillion dollar business that employs a large number of people. It is likely that many people working in the underground economy also have regular jobs and are, thus, counted as employed. The electrician or plumber who also does cash business under the table is classified as employed. The drug smuggler may have a regular job to cover his or her illegal activities. The **underground worker** most likely to be missed by official employment statistics are those who are officially counted as "not in the labor force." The retired carpenter who continues a thriving under-the-table home-repair business, the homemaker who runs an unreported typing pool in the home, the full-time college student who moonlights as a waiter (and whose boss does not report his or her earnings) are all officially counted as not in the labor force even though they have underground employment. Some of the people who are counted as unemployed may also have underground employment. The "unemployed" construction worker may work part-time on a construction project on an off-the-books basis. An "unemployed" domestic worker may work full time for an employer on a cash-only basis.

> An **underground worker** is a worker whose income is unreported or not fully reported to the government.

Because workers in the underground economy have a strong incentive to conceal their activities, government statisticians cannot estimate the effect of underground-economy activity on measured unemployment. We do not know by how much the inclusion of underground workers would lower the amount of unemployment or affect its changes over time.

Discouraged Workers.   How does the Labor Department classify the unemployed worker who concludes that his or her job search is hopeless and who, thus, stops looking for a job? According to the official definition, that person is out of the labor force because he or she is not actively looking for a job. Such persons are called **discouraged workers.**

> A **discouraged worker** is a person who has stopped looking for a job after becoming convinced (after an unsuccessful job search) that it is not possible to find a suitable job.

Discouraged workers are not counted as unemployed because they do not meet the second unemployment condition: they are not actively looking for work. Some economists have argued that discouraged workers should be included in the ranks of the unemployed. They argue that there is a big difference between the voluntarily retired person or the full-time homemaker and the

Table 2   Reasons Job-Wanting Persons Are Not Job Hunting, 1982

Reason	Total (thousands)	Percent
School attendance	1,732	26.4
Ill health, disability	769	11.7
Home responsibilities	1,391	21.2
Belief that job can't be found	1,568	23.9
Other reasons	1,099	16.8
Total	**6,559**	**100.0**

Source: *Handbook of Labor Statistics*, December 1983, p. 34.

discouraged worker, all of whom are classified uniformly as not in the labor force. Again, it is difficult to judge the seriousness of the discouraged worker's job search or whether the discouraged worker was looking for a job that was unattainable with given skills, training, and work experience. Although discouraged workers are not counted among the nation's jobless (they are officially not in the labor force), government statisticians do provide some data on the number of discouraged workers (see Table 2). In 1982, of the 62 million people not in the labor force, 6.6 million declared that they wanted a job. Of this number, 5 million cited school attendance, ill health, and home responsibilities as the factors that kept them from looking for a job. The remaining 1.6 million—the discouraged workers—declared that they weren't job hunting because they thought they could not get a job. As the 1.6 million figure suggests, the decision not to include discouraged workers in the ranks of the unemployed has a significant effect on the unemployment rate. In 1982, 10.7 million persons were unemployed, according to the official definition. Adding to these the number of discouraged workers would have raised the number of unemployed to 12.3 million (the unemployment rate would have increased from 9.5 percent to 10.9 percent.

Involuntary Part-Time Work.   A final ambiguity in the official unemployment definition is the treatment of involuntary part-time work. According to the official definition, a person is counted as employed even if that person wishes to work full time but can only get a part-time job.

Employment is an either/or proposition as far as the labor statisticians are concerned; one is either employed or one is not. There is no such thing as being half employed even though that may be the most accurate description of a person's employment situation. The Bureau of Labor Statistics does report statistics on part-time employment broken down by those on voluntary and involuntary part-time work schedules. In 1982, for example, 12.5 million workers worked on a voluntary part-time basis (71 percent of them were women). In the same year, 6.2 million workers were on part-time schedules for "economic reasons" (such as slack work, inability to find full-time work, job changing during the reference week, and material shortages).[1]

The Unemployment Rate

Figure 2 graphs the trends in employment and unemployment from 1950 to 1984. Panel (a) shows the total labor force broken down into those employed and those unemployed and also shows the number of persons not in the labor force. Panel (b) shows the **unemployment rate.**

> The **unemployment rate** is the number of unemployed divided by the total labor force.

Figure 2 reveals some important facts about the U.S. labor market. First, it shows that employment and unemployment move in a complex pattern. In the long run, both employment *and* unemployment have risen, but the relationship is far from exact. The 1960s was a decade of low and slightly falling unemployment. The 1970s was a decade of high and generally rising unemployment. The rates of increase in *employment,* however, were virtually identical in the 1960s and 1970s!

A generally rising economy allows both employment and unemployment to rise together. In 1950, employment was 60 million and unemployment was 3.3 million. In 1984, employment was 105 million and unemployment was 8.5 million. During certain periods between 1950 and 1984, employment and unemployment moved in opposite directions (such as during most of the 1960s

1. *Handbook of Labor Statistics,* December 1983, Tables 19–20.

Figure 2   Employment and Unemployment, 1950–1984

(a) The Employment Status of Workers

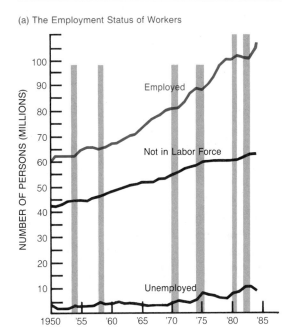

(b) The Unemployment Rate

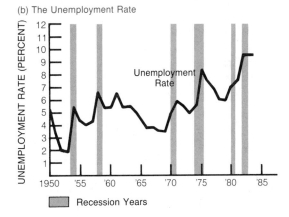

Recession Years

Employment often just increases at a slower rate during periods of rising unemployment except in the case of major recessions, as in 1975 or 1983.

Sources: *Handbook of Labor Statistics,* December 1983; *Federal Reserve Bulletin,* December 1984.

or during the mid-1970s). In other periods, employment and unemployment moved together (such as during the early 1970s and during the early 1980s). The relationship between employment and unemployment is not a simple one.

Table 3   Proportion of Unemployment by Duration During Contractions and Expansions

Year	Cycle	Percent of Unemployed Out of Work for:		Average Duration of Unemployment (weeks)
		Less than 5 Weeks	27 Weeks or More	
1959	Expansion	44.4	15.3	14.4
1961	Contraction	38.3	17.1	15.6
1965	Expansion	48.4	10.4	11.8
1975	Contraction	37.0	15.2	14.2
1978	Expansion	46.2	10.4	11.9
1981	Contraction	41.7	14.0	13.7
1984	Expansion	39.2	19.1	18.2

Source: *Economic Report of the President.*

Second, there is a cyclical pattern to the relationship between the number employed, the number unemployed and the number of people not in the labor force. During economic downturns, there is a general tendency for unemployment to rise and for employment to fall or to slow its pace of increase. There is a tendency for people to drop out of the labor force during recessions; the number of persons not in the labor force rises during recessions. Third, the unemployment *rate* (as the ratio of unemployed to the number in the labor force) does not necessarily move with unemployment. From 1971 to 1973, there was a sharp drop in the *unemployment rate* even though the *number of unemployed* remained fairly stable because there was an enormous expansion of employment. The denominator in the unemployment rate equation rose to drive down the unemployment rate. The same pattern occurred during the substantial expansion of employment from 1975 to 1979. Fourth, since the early 1950s, the unemployment rate has been generally rising. The exception was the period of declining unemployment rates in the 1960s.

> Employment statistics show that employment and unemployment can move either in opposite directions or together. During recessions, employment tends to fall as unemployment rises, and the number of people not in the labor force rises. Unemployment and the unemployment *rate* can move inversely during periods of rapidly expanding employment.

THE THEORY OF CYCLICAL UNEMPLOYMENT

Cyclical unemployment occurs when there is a decline in the number of vacant jobs relative to the number of qualified job seekers. Figure 2 showed that there is a distinct pattern of employment and unemployment during recessions and recoveries. During the downturn, the unemployment rate rises, employment falls (or its rate of increase drops), and people drop out of the labor force. During recoveries and booms, unemployment falls, the growth of employment accelerates, and people return to the labor force either as job holders or job seekers. Table 3 shows what happens to the duration of unemployment during the business cycle. During cyclical downturns, the duration of unemployment spells rises. During periods of prosperity, the duration of unemployment spells shortens. The proportion of long-term unemployment also rises during cyclical downturns. The phenomenon of cyclical unemployment can be studied using the tools of aggregate supply-and-demand analysis developed in previous chapters.

Previous chapters explained the role of the natural rate of unemployment in modern macroeconomic thinking. Economists now use the natural rate of unemployment as the standard for full employment. Cyclical unemployment results when forces cause the economy to operate below the natural rate (see Figure 3). For example, if an economy is initially operating at the natural rate

Figure 3   How a Reduction in Aggregate Demand Raises Unemployment: Cyclical Unemployment

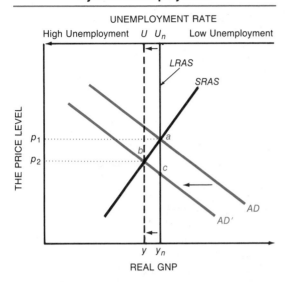

A reduction in aggregate demand (the movement of *AD* to *AD'*) causes output to drop from the natural level of output (y_n) to a level (y) below the natural rate. The horizontal axis that appears in color at the top of the diagram shows the movements in unemployment that accompany movements in output level. As output falls below y_n, the unemployment rate rises above the natural rate of unemployment (u_n).

natural rate as the aggregate-demand curve shifts to the left starting from an initial equilibrium at the natural rate of unemployment. This increase in unemployment is considered cyclical unemployment.

Previous chapters have also described the tendency for economies to return to the natural level of output (and to the natural rate of unemployment) in the long run. The self-correcting mechanism is set in motion whenever the economy departs from the natural rate of unemployment. If unemployment is above the natural rate (as it is in Figure 3), there is a tendency for the price level to fall (or for the rate of inflation to slow down); short-run aggregate supply increases; eventually unemployment falls to the natural rate. If unemployment falls below the natural rate, there is a tendency for the price level to rise (or for the inflation rate to accelerate); short-run aggregate supply falls, and unemployment rises to the natural rate.

The Search Behavior of Employers and Employees in Labor Markets

The unemployment rate is difficult to analyze because it depends upon millions of individuals making decisions about whether they should go to school, stay home to raise children, retire at age 60, or enter or remain in the labor force. Once an individual decides to be in the labor force, that person must decide whether to remain at his or her current job (if employed) or to seek another (presumably better) job. The person without a job must decide what kind of job to seek, what job-search method to use, and how intensively to search for a job. The unemployment rate also depends upon the actions of the hundreds of thousands of employing firms. These firms must decide how many employees to have on the payroll, and whether to retain or fire existing workers. If firms decide to hire new workers, they must determine the job requirements, their employee-search procedures, and how intensively to search the labor market for potential employees. To understand the phenomenon of unemployment, one must understand how these microeconomic decisions are made by workers and by firms.

of unemployment (and, accordingly, producing the natural level of output), an unexpected reduction in aggregate demand shifts the *AD* curve to *AD'*, and the economy moves down the short-run aggregate-supply curve from *a* to *b*. The price level is lower at the new short-run equilibrium, and the economy is producing an output below the natural level of output. The upper horizontal axis (in color) in Figure 3 measures *the unemployment rate associated with each level of output* being measured along the lower horizontal axis (in black). The natural rate of unemployment (u_n) coincides with the natural level of output (y_n) by definition. Note that because output and the corresponding rate of unemployment tend to move in opposite directions, the unemployment rate starts out high to the left of u_n and gets progressively lower as it moves to the right of u_n. Figure 3 shows that the unemployment rate rises above the

Sources of Unemployment

The labor market is a vast information-processing network that must match an incredible variety of jobs—from brain surgeon to store clerk—to an equally staggering variety of workers. How are workers to be matched with jobs efficiently? In a world in which everyone possesses complete information, matching jobs to people would be a relatively simple task. Everyone would be aware of all jobs in the economy, and employers would know the skills and qualifications of all potential employees. Presumably, in such an economy there would be little or no unemployment.

In our complex economy, frictional and structural unemployment are an inevitable result of the interplay of supply and demand in constantly changing labor markets. Every day, new people enter the labor force; older people retire; new products compete in the market; unprofitable businesses fold; new methods of production are found; people change their attitudes toward working. In a dynamic economy, workers do not stay put. If they did, the economy would be unable to change for the better. The opportunity for people to change jobs is good for society.

When one thinks of the source of unemployment, one tends to think of job losses (firings and layoffs). While firings and layoffs are indeed important sources of unemployment, there are other ways of becoming unemployed. Table 4 shows the sources of unempoyment for those unemployed in December 1983. Of those unemployed, 37 percent had just entered or reentered the labor force after a period of schooling, work in the household, or whatever people do when they are outside the labor force. These people were unemployed not because they had been fired or laid off but because they had not succeeded in finding jobs upon entry (or reentry) into the labor force. The entry and reentry of people into the labor market goes on all the time and accounts for a significant percentage of total unemployment. Table 4 shows that about 54 percent of those employed were fired (33 percent) or were *laid off* (21 percent) and that 9 percent quite their jobs.

The sources of unemployment change over the course of the business cycle. During periods of business expansion, the proportion of those that become unemployed through firings or layoffs falls and the proportion of those who quit jobs

Reason for Unemployment		Percent
Job losers		54.1
Fired	33.1	
Laid off	21.0	
Job leavers		9.2
Reentrants		24.2
New entrants		12.4
		100.0

Table 4   Reasons for Unemployment, December 1983

Source: *Economic Report of the President.*

rises. During the prosperous late 1960s, job losses accounted for only 40 percent of the unemployed while 14.5 percent were quits. During the recession of 1981, 59 percent were job losses and 8 percent were quits. Figure 4 illustrates the distinctive pattern of quits and layoffs over the business cycle, showing how quits move with the business cycle (rising in importance during prosperity and falling during recessions), whereas layoffs move *counter to* the business cycle (rising with recession and falling with prosperity).

Search Unemployment

The above data on the reasons for unemployment demonstrate that with the possible exceptions of some who have quit their jobs and those on layoff waiting to be recalled to their old jobs, the unemployed are involved in searching for jobs. By definition, those who are unemployed are actively looking for employment. Firms are also searching for workers. How the unemployed go about searching for jobs or how firms search for workers affects both the amount of unemployment at one point in time and trends in unemployment over time.

The economic theory of job search maintains that both individuals searching for jobs and firms searching for workers will search in a rational manner. Both job search and employee search incur costs.

The Rational Search for Jobs.   When the economy is operating at the natural rate of unemployment, there is a rough balance between the number of people seeking jobs and the number of

Figure 4   Quit Rates and Layoff Rates, 1950–1984

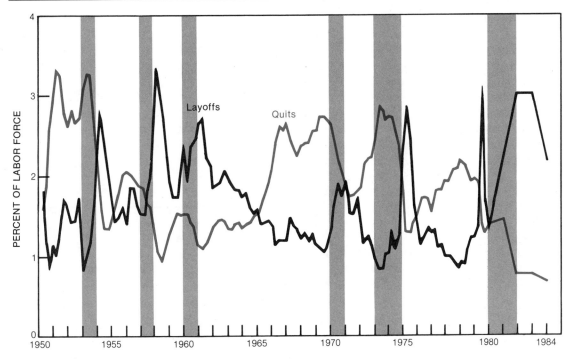

Quite rates tend to drop and layoff rates tend to rise during periods of recession.

Sources: *Economic Report of the President; Survey of Current Business.*

unfilled jobs for which job seekers are qualified. When unemployment is above the natural rate of unemployment, this balance is broken; the result is cyclical unemployment. In the absence of significant cyclical unemployment, however, appropriate jobs are available, but it is up to the job seekers to find them. People cannot know about all the jobs that are currently available to them or may become available in the near future. Taking a job now means passing up the opportunity to find a better job. If a person knew all the unfilled jobs that were available to that person, there would be no need to search. The person with a job could immediately transfer to a new and better job without first undertaking a job search. The entrant to the job market could instantly accept the best of all jobs open to him or her. In such a world of perfect information about jobs, there would be little if any frictional unemployment.

In the real world, people do not have perfect information about jobs. They do not know all the

unfilled jobs for which they are qualified. They do not know if the number of unfilled jobs will expand or contract over time. Job seekers must make decisions based upon uncertain information. To gain job information, job seekers must spend their time reading newspaper ads, making telephone calls, setting up interviews, traveling to distant cities, hiring private placement firms. The gathering of such information is costly, both in time and money. Perhaps the most significant cost of continued job search is the opportunity cost of not accepting a job sooner. When a job searcher turns down a job offer in order to search further for a better job, that person is forgoing earnings from the job he or she rejected.

Job searching costs time, money, and forgone earnings. These costs will be different for different people. One individual may spend two 5-hour days per week searching for a job and a few dollars for bus fare. A terminated executive may spend 8 hours every day of the week searching for a job and spend thousands of dollars on travel and professional placement fees to locate a new executive position. One person may turn down a high-paying job on the conviction that a better-paying job is just around the corner; another person may be unwilling to pass up a reasonable job offer even though by waiting longer that person might locate a better job. The longer one searches, the greater is the cost. Presumably, the longer one searches, the greater also are the benefits in the form of finding a higher-paying and more satisfactory job. The theory of job search maintains that rational people will weigh these costs and benefits in deciding on the amount of search time.

The rational worker should search in the labor market as long as the expected benefits from more searching (the marginal benefits) exceed the expected costs of more searching (the marginal costs).

The economic behavior of the rational job searcher is shown in panel (a) of Figure 5. The job search ends when the unemployed worker accepts a job. The longer the worker searches, the greater are the search costs. In panel (a), *marginal* search costs are assumed to *rise* with the length of the search. At the initial phase of the search, the costs of an extra unit of search (say, another week) are expected to be low. The worker can do the easy things first (such as telephoning, reading want ads). The costs incurred during each succeeding week are higher than the costs incurred the week before. As the search lengthens, the worker must pass up jobs to continue the search or must hire an expensive private placement service. The marginal benefits (obtaining a higher wage or better working conditions) from extra search are assumed to *fall* as the search lengthens. The value of job information brought in by successive units of search time should be generally falling because there are diminishing returns to finding a higher wage rate or better working conditions. For these reasons, the marginal-benefits curve in panel (a) is negatively sloped, and the marginal-cost curve is positively sloped.

The rational job searcher should search to the point at which the expected marginal benefits from search equal the expected marginal costs of

Figure 5   Rational Search by a Job Seeker

(a) Equilibrium Search

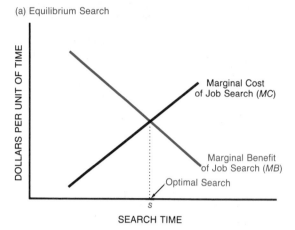

(b) An Increase in Marginal Search Costs Reduces Search Time

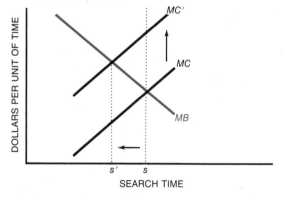

Panel (a) shows that the amount of search time chosen by a rational job-seeking individual will be that amount (s) at which the marginal costs of job search equal the marginal benefits. Panel (b) shows that an increase in the marginal costs of job search (depicted as an upward movement of the marginal-cost curve from MC to MC') will reduce the length of the job search (from S to S').

search. If the job seeker were to search less than this amount of time, the marginal benefits from extra search would exceed the marginal costs, and the worker could improve his or her welfare by searching more. The job-search equilibrium occurs at the intersection of the marginal-cost and marginal-benefit curves.

The Rational Search for Employees.

The economic theory of search analyzes the search behavior of employee-seeking firms using the same principles that apply to job search.

Figure 6   Rational Search by an Employee-Seeking Firm

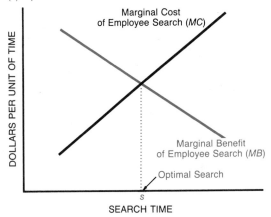

(a) Equilibrium Search

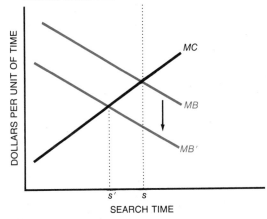

(b) A Reduction in Marginal Search Benefits Reduces Search Time

Panel (a) shows that the amount of employee-search time that a rational firm will select. The amount of time a firm spends searching for an employee is that amount (s) at which the marginal costs of employee search equal the marginal benefits of employee search. Panel (b) shows that a reduction in the marginal benefits of employee search will motivate the firm to reduce its search time (from S to S').

Firms have a variety of jobs that are made available by quits, layoffs, firings, and general business expansion. The objective of the firm is to staff available jobs with the best possible people. Just as job searchers do not know everything about available jobs for which they are suited, firms do not know everything about the character-

istics of potential employees. They gather such information by searching for new employees, but searching incurs search costs. Firms must place ads in newspapers, assign management personnel to recruiting committees, pay the training costs of new employees. Moreover, the firm incurrs an opportunity cost by leaving positions vacant and continuing to search for more qualified employees.

The firm derives benefits from searching. The firm benefits from careful selection procedures because it is able to find new employees whose benefits to the firm exceed their wage plus their hiring costs. The longer is the search, the more likely it is that the firm will be staffed by the most qualified employees. As in the case of job search, economists assume that the marginal costs of employee search rise as the length of search increases and that the marginal benefits of employee search fall as the length of the search increases. These assumptions are built into panel (a) of Figure 6, which shows that the employee-searching firm searches to the point where marginal costs equal marginal benefits.

Firms will search for new employees in the labor market as long as the cost of more searching (the marginal cost) is less than the expected benefits of more searching (marginal benefit).

Factors that Affect the Duration of Unemployment

The theory of search suggests that the amount of search time selected by job-seeking persons and by employee-seeking firms depends upon the marginal costs and marginal benefits of search. If the marginal benefits of search fall, there will be less search activity. If the marginal costs of search rise, there will also be less search activity. Less search means that job seekers accept jobs more quickly and that employee-seeking firms hire more quickly.

As a general rule, the duration of unemployment falls (and the amount of unemployment normally falls) when job seekers and employee seekers reduce their search time.

Table 5   Duration of Job Search by Different Demographic Characteristics, 1982

	Average Duration (weeks)	Percent Unemployed Less Than 5 Weeks	Percent Unemployed 15 Weeks or More
Men	15.4	31.1	31.2
Women	12.7	39.5	25.9
Males married with spouse present	75.8	27.7	32.2
Single males, never married	14.2	35.1	28.2
Age			
16–21	14.3	34.5	29.1
20–24	10.5	44.4	21.3
25–34	15.5	33.6	32.6
35–44	15.7	30.3	31.3
45–54	16.1	29.6	31.7
55–64	16.4	31.2	33.3
Occupation			
White collar	14.1	35.2	28.9
Blue collar	15.2	30.7	30.9

Source: Bureau of Labor Statistics, *Employment & Earnings*, March 1982, p. 28.

A number of factors can change the marginal costs and marginal benefits of search for individuals and firms.

Unanticipated Inflation.   The next chapter explains more completely how unemployment responds to unanticipated inflation. In brief, unanticipated inflation causes wage-rate offers to job seekers to rise unexpectedly, especially for job seekers in labor markets where wages are negotiated at frequent intervals. As wage offers rise more rapidly than anticipated, workers' real wages *appear* to rise. This apparent wage increase raises the perceived marginal costs of search by raising the opportunity cost of not accepting job offers on hand. Unanticipated inflation, therefore, motivates the job seeker to shorten the search by accepting employment. This process is shown in panel (b) of Figure 5. Less job search translates into a greater willingness to accept jobs that have been offered and a lesser willingness to continue the search in the hopes of finding a superior job.

Employee-seeking firms also respond to changing marginal search costs and benefits by altering the amount of search time. As inflation rises unexpectedly, the perceived benefits to further job search decline. In labor markets governed by fixed union-wage contracts, the selling prices of the goods or services the firm produces are rising faster than costs, and the marginal benefits to continuing the employee search fall. Rather than leaving positions unfilled, the firm steps up its hiring of new workers whose wages are rising more slowly than product selling prices. The reduction in marginal benefits to search also motivates firms to hold on to existing employees, who are a known quantity. Unanticipated inflation also signals to employers that labor markets are growing tighter. Extending the search for employees means that the firm may find itself searching in the future in labor markets in which fewer and fewer qualified workers are available. Again, the marginal benefits to continued job search fall. In panel (b) of Figure 6, a reduction in a firm's marginal benefits of search motivates the firm to search less. When hiring firms decide to devote less time to search, they hire more quickly, the duration of unemployment falls, and the unemployment rate should fall.

The theory of search predicts that unanticipated inflation causes unemployment to fall by reducing the search time of job seekers and of employee seekers. Unanticipated inflation raises the marginal search costs of job seekers and lowers the marginal search benefits of employee seekers.

Unemployment Benefits.   The marginal costs of job search are affected by unemployment benefits. Workers must compare the opportunity cost of forgone earnings from jobs that have been

Table 6   Shares in the Labor Force by Sex and Age

	Percent	
Category	1950	1984
Men	70	56
Women	30	44
Persons 16–24	18	23
Persons 35–44	22	20

The shares in the labor force of women and younger workers have increased over the past 35 years; women and younger people also tend to have higher unemployment rates.

Source: U.S Department of Labor, *Handbook of Labor Statistics.*

declined with unemployment benefits to determine their net marginal search costs. If unemployment benefits fall, the opportunity cost of turning down jobs to continue the search rises: a decline in unemployment benefits raises the marginal cost of search. As in panel (b) of Figure 5, the increase in marginal cost reduces optimal search time, thereby causing workers to accept jobs more readily. (See Example 3.)

A reduction in unemployment benefits should reduce both the duration of unemployment and the amount of unemployment by raising the marginal costs of job search.

Other Factors that Affect Search.   Any factor that alters the marginal costs or marginal benefits of job search or employee search will affect the duration of unemployment and the amount of unemployment. If the amount of job information increases—say, through the creation of local or regional employment offices (where there had been none before)—the benefits of search will fall, and the duration of unemployment will fall. Changes in demographic composition and the occupational distribution of the population will also affect search time. Insofar as different groups of people (by age, sex, race, skills, training, occupation) have different costs and benefits of search, changes in the shares of such groups in the labor force affect search time

Table 5 presents some data on the duration of

unemployment according to different demographic characteristics. The table shows that the duration of unemployment for males tends to be higher than for females and that males experience proportionally less short-term unemployment and proportionally more long-term unemployment than females. The best explanation of these figures is that the marginal benefits of search are higher for males than for females. The table also shows that the duration of unemployment is higher for married males with spouse present than for never-married males. One possible explanation for this strange finding is that the marginal costs of search may be lower for married men because of the presence of a working wife. Table 5 also shows that there is a positive correlation between age and duration of unemployment: the older is the unemployed worker, the longer is the duration of unemployment. The theory of search provides some partial explanations. The search costs to firms of hiring older workers may be higher because the worker will not be with the firm for as many years before retirement as will a younger employee. A second explanation is that younger workers have less diverse employment opportunities. With employment opportunities limited to a relatively small number of entry-level jobs, the marginal benefits to searching for a better job are limited.

CAUSES OF RISING UNEMPLOYMENT

Figure 2 revealed that the unemployment rate in the United States has been generally rising over the last 25 years. This section explores some possible explanations for this rise in the unemployment rate.

The Changing Composition of the Labor Force

The fact that different workers have different rates of unemployment accounts for part of the long-term increase in the unemployment rate. The composition of the American labor force has changed dramatically since the end of World War II. In 1950, women accounted for 29.5 percent of the labor force; in 1984 they accounted for 44 percent (see Table 6). In 1950, only 1.4 million

Figure 7   Selected Unemployment Rates, 1948–1984

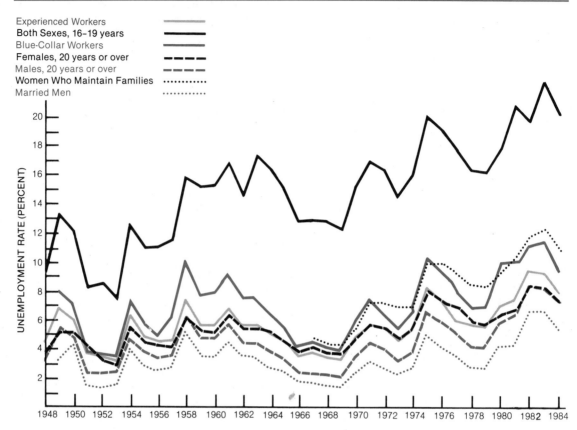

Experienced Workers
Both Sexes, 16–19 years
Blue-Collar Workers
Females, 20 years or over
Males, 20 years or over
Women Who Maintain Families
Married Men

Unemployment rates vary for different segments of the labor force. Teenagers and women who maintain families have experienced rising unemployment rates in recent decades.

Source: *Economic Report of the President.*

women with children under 6 years of age were in the labor force; by 1984, their number had increased to almost 5 million. Table 6 also shows that the labor-force share of persons aged 16–24 has also increased.

Figure 7 shows that different groups of workers have experienced different rates of unemployment since 1947 (see Figure 7). The unemployment rate of married men, while varying from year to year, has not increased over the long run. The unemployment rates of males and females 20 years and older have been rising only slightly in the long run. The unemployment rates of young people 16–19 years of age reveal a distinct upward trend, as do the unemployment rates of women who maintain families. The unemploy-

ment rates of experienced wage and salary workers have risen less than those of blue-collar workers.

To what extent can the rise in the American unemployment rate be explained by the rising labor-force shares of those groups (like women and young workers) that have higher-than-average unemployment rates? Although the labor-force shares of women with children and of teenagers have increased, so have the shares of professional workers and employees in low-unemployment sectors, like the service industries.

The effect of the changing composition of the labor force on the national unemployment rate can be determined by calculating what current unemployment rates would have been if today's labor-

Example 3   Unemployment Benefits

Detroit Michigan had one of the highest unemployment rates in the country in 1980. Yet even in Detroit many jobs went unfilled. Burger Chef restaurants reported 40 unfilled jobs for cooks and counter jobs paying $3.50 per hour. Why are jobs unfilled in cities like Detroit with soaring unemployment? Our answer is that the available jobs are mismatched with those who are unemployed. In 1980, out-of-work auto workers were accustomed to earning $10.75 per hour. They prefered to wait for economic conditions to improve. Moreover, unemployed auto workers are entitled to collect 90 percent of their former pay for one year from state unemployment insurance and employer-financed benefits. Some of these benefits are not taxed;

therefore, their after-tax income did not actually fall during their first year of unemployment. Such workers, as one might imagine, would not be attracted to jobs earning $3.50 per hour.

Unemployed auto workers are an exceptional case where the costs of the first year of unemployment (measured in strictly economic terms) are relatively low. But this example does show how unemployment benefits can affect the costs and benefits of being unemployed and, thus, the unemployment rate. ■

Source: "The Unemployed Shun Much Mundane Work, at Least for a While," *Wall Street Journal*, December 5, 1980.

---

force composition were the same as in the 1950s. One calculation shows that approximately one third of the increase in the unemployment rate between the late 1950s and the mid-1970s was explained by changes in the composition of the labor force.[2] In other words, factors other than the changing composition of the labor force must be considered in explaining the rise in the unemployment rate.

> The rising U.S. unemployment rate is not just the result of more women, minorities, and teenagers in the labor force. The changing composition of the U.S. labor force may account for only one third of the long-term increase in unemployment.

Changing Private Costs and Private Benefits

Modern economists maintain that much unemployment can be explained in cost/benefit terms: if the costs of being unemployed are reduced, the

unemployment rate should rise. The costs of unemployment are affected by a number of institutional arrangements, including unemployment insurance, taxes, and minimum-wage laws.

Multiple Earners.   In 1960, about 23 percent of the U.S. female population over the age of 16 was employed. By 1984, this figure was more than 50 percent. The trend toward two or more working members in a household has changed the costs of unemployment. Before 1960, the unemployment of a household head meant an almost total loss of family income in the majority of cases. In the 1980s, the earnings losses to a household of one unemployed member are cushioned by the earnings of other employed members. In the recession year of 1982, for example, only 28 percent of families with an unemployed member had no employed person in the family. Only in single-parent families with children was the percent of families with unemployment and no employed member high (47 percent for single-parent families headed by females and 37.5 percent for single-parent families headed by males).

Unemployment Insurance.   Martin Feldstein and other economists have argued that rising coverage and rising benefits offered by unemployment insurance have markedly altered the costs of

---

2. For example, N. J. Simler has calculated what the 1976 unemployment rate would have been had the labor-force composition not changed over the preceding 20 years. Simler finds that the 1976 unemployment rate would have been only one third lower. See Simler, "Employment and Unemployment," *Federal Reserve Bank of Minneapolis Review*, April 1978, p. 13.

unemployment. According to Feldstein, the substantial decline in the personal costs of unemployment over the past 20 years can explain much of the rise in the unemployment rate.[3]

Unemployment benefits affect the behavior of an unemployed worker in a predictable manner. If unemployment benefits are generous and can be drawn upon for a long period of time, it may not be worthwhile for the worker to continue to search for a better job, especially if that worker places a high value on leisure. The benefits of unemployment may exceed the costs in the case of the laid-off worker who has good prospects of being recalled to a former job where the worker has built up seniority rights and a pension. In fact, laid-off workers usually do not search for new jobs unless it becomes apparent that there is no chance of recall. Instead, they wait to be recalled to their old job. In addition, most unemployment benefits are not taxed. A worker who pays 30 percent of his or her income in income taxes and who receives 70 percent of former income in unemployment benefits receives the same after-tax income whether he or she is unemployed or employed.

Over the past 20 years, the proportion of *covered employment* (workers and employees covered by state and federal unemployment insurance) has risen dramatically. In 1950, 58 percent of the labor force was covered. By 1984, 95 percent of the labor force was covered. In 1950, the average weekly unemployment benefit represented 39 percent of average weekly earnings when working. In 1981, it accounted for 43 percent. State and federal unemployment benefits averaged about 50 percent as much as after-tax wage incomes.[4]

The average unemployed worker in the United States can, therefore, count on state and federal programs to cover roughly one half of after-tax wage income. This figure does not include employer-provided benefits and union unemployment funds that in certain instances (such as the case of the auto workers in Example 3) raise benefits well above 50 percent of former wage income. Moreover, the duration of unemployment is typically short enough so that unemployment benefits are not exhausted. At the end of 1983 (a recovery year), only 2.0 percent of unemployment-benefit recipients had exhausted their benefits.

Minimum-Wage Laws.   Statistics show that teenage unemployment is significantly higher than adult unemployment (see Figure 7).

Many economists argue that the minimum wage has contributed to high teenage unemployment. The minimum wage is too high to encourage employers to spend money on training teenage employees for skilled positions. As a consequence, teenagers occupy menial positions, receive little on-the-job training, see little opportunity for eventual advancement, and leave unappealing jobs at high rates.

Government statistics show that the minimum wage as a percentage of average wages has actually declined (from 54 percent in 1950 to 43 percent in 1983). This fact suggests that minimum-wage laws should not necessarily have priced more teenagers out of the market. However, as the relative minimum wage declined, the percentage of those covered by minimum-wage legislation increased. It is, therefore, difficult to determine the overall effect of minimum-wage legislation on the relative wage of teenagers.

Progressive Taxation.   Some economists argue that the combination of a progressive tax system with rapid inflation has pushed up the unemployment rate. First, highly progressive tax rates pushed middle- and upper-income households into higher and higher tax brackets in the period under consideration. It was not until 1985 that the tax schedules were indexed to remove the impact of inflation. Thus, as the aftertax rewards to employment are reduced by progressive taxes during inflations, the costs of being unemployed are reduced. The benefits of nontaxed unemployment benefits increase as the costs of unemployment decline. Moreover, the combination of inflation and progressive taxes pushes people into the underground economy where, although they are actually working, they will not be counted as employed.

It is easy to document changing institutions

3. Martin Feldstein, "The Economics of the New Unemployment," *Public Interest* 33 (Fall 1973).
4. These figures are from *The Economic Report of the President*, January 1982, p. 272 and from Rudiger Dornbusch and Stanley Fischer, *Macroeconomics,* 2nd ed. (New York: McGraw-Hill, 1981), p. 523.

like unemployment benefits and minimum-wage laws that potentially could account for rising unemployment. It remains difficult to document their exact impact on unemployment over the years.

Other factors that may have raised the unemployment rate over the years are more difficult to quantify. The organization of the labor market can affect the unemployment rate. How rapidly and effectively information on job availabilities and job specifications is disseminated and how big a role labor unions play in the market can also affect unemployment. If jobs are expanding more rapidly in industries that have higher than average rates of unemployment, the unemployment rate should rise.

THE SOCIAL COSTS AND SOCIAL BENEFITS OF UNEMPLOYMENT

During the contraction phase of the business cycle, the unemployment rate rises above the natural rate. If cyclically unemployed resources had been productively employed, more output could have been produced, and society could have had a higher standard of living, *ceteris paribus*. The aggregate loss of income and output due to cyclical unemployment is the social cost of cyclically unemployed resources.

Social Costs

Economist Arthur Okun measured the social cost of unemployment in terms of the loss of output for each percentage-point increase in the unemployment rate. The relationship that Okun found between changes in the unemployment rate and changes in output is called **Okun's law.**

> **Okun's law** is that for every 1 percentage point increase in the unemployment rate there is a 2.5 percent drop in real GNP.[5]

Thus, if the unemployment rate rises from 6 to 7 percent, Okun's Law predicts a 2.5 percent drop in real GNP. In 1984, according to Okun's law, a 1-percentage-point increase in the unemployment rate cost American society approximately $93 billion, or $435 for every person in the United States.

Okun's Law measures the short-run losses of output due to a cyclical increase in the unemployment rate above the natural rate. Okun's Law assumes that cyclical increases in employment are accompanied by rising employment, rising hours worked per person, and increased productivity. Thus, in the short run, there are substantial output gains when people return to productive employment. Idle capital will be utilized more efficiently, and people doing part-time work will return to full-time jobs.[6]

The private costs of unemployment are not evenly distributed across society. The long-term unemployed with minimal unemployment-insurance protection bear a substantial burden of the private unemployment cost, especially if they place a low value on their leisure. The unemployed with generous unemployment benefits suffer less. Employees of declining industries who must pull up stakes to find employment in rising industries must also pay a personal cost. The worker in a cyclically depressed industry must bear the anxiety of waiting to be recalled and the belt tightening associated with layoffs. It is obviously not pleasant to be unemployed, except when it is a short interruption to move up the job ladder.

Social Benefits

As already noted, the effects of unemployment are not all negative, especially when the economy is operating at the natural rate of unemployment. Job turnover allows workers to seek out better jobs. As workers move into jobs in which they are more productive, real GNP increases. If un-

5. Arthur Okun, "Upward Mobility in a High Pressure Economy," Brookings Papers in Economic Activity (1973:2) estimates the ratio to be 3 rather than 2.5. More recent estimates place the ratio at 2.5. On this, see Jeffrey Perloff and Michael Wachter, "A Production Function Non-Accelerating Inflation Approach to Potential Output," eds. Karl Brunner and Allan Meltzer, *Carnegie-Rochester Conference Series,* North Holland.

6. Okun's law applies only to cyclical fluctuations in the unemployment rate. It overstates the effects of a permanent increase in the natural rate of unemployment. In the long run, the sole effect of the increase in the unemployment rate is the decrease in numbers employed; long-run effects on productivity and hours worked are not expected. In the long run, a 1 percentage point increase in the natural rate of unemployment is calculated to yield about a 1 percent reduction in real GNP.

employed workers were to accept the first job that came along—even if it were below the salary and skill level to which they were accustomed—short-run incomes would increase, but long-run incomes would suffer. From the standpoint of society. it is sometimes better for individuals to opt for unemployment to wait for better jobs. In the long run, society and the individuals involved benefit more from the efficient allocation of people into jobs than from the automatic acceptance of the first job that comes along.

Although there is a rational case to be made that some unemployment is essential and beneficial—even to the unemployed—our society's attitude is that all unemployment is bad and that social policy should be geared to minimizing all types of unemployment, even the socially beneficial kind.

REDUCING UNEMPLOYMENT

Can the government do anything to control long-term unemployment? If the government can enact programs that improve the efficiency of labor markets and provide job skills to those with limited training and experience, the long-term unemployment rate should decline.

The Employment Act of 1946 gave the federal government responsibility for fighting excessive unemployment. Cyclical unemployment was to be attacked using monetary and fiscal policy, but monetary and fiscal policy cannot affect the structural unemployment that results from a declining industry or a severe lack of employable skills. For this reason, the federal government—in conjunction with state governments—instituted a series of job programs designed to combat structural unemployment.

The most ambitious programs of the federal government in the area of labor-force training were enacted during the Johnson administration's drive for the "Great Society." Programs such as the Job Corps, Manpower Training and Development, and Neighborhood Youth Programs were enacted in the 1960s. The first full-scale government training program was established in 1962 under the Manpower Development and Training Act. The programs provided under this act were designed to provide vocational and remedial train-

ing for those with low skills and high unemployment rates (particularly disadvantaged youths). The intent of such programs was to train workers to do jobs that are in high demand. In 1971, the Public Employment Program was passed, and in 1973 the Comprehensive Employment and Training Act (CETA) was enacted.

In 1978, almost 1 million workers—mainly under age 20—were enrolled in federally funded classroom or on-the-job training programs at a cost of around $2,000 per person. In 1982, the CETA program was abolished. How successful were these programs? As noted above, the unemployment rates of those whom the training programs were designed to help—particularly teenagers—*increased* over a period of time when massive government outlays were being devoted to training. These statistics do not demonstrate the failure of such programs—the rise in unemployment could have been much worse without them—but they do not indicate outstanding successes either.

The next chapter analyzes the stagflation—the combination of rising inflation and rising unemployment—for the 1970s and early 1980s.

Summary

1. The three types of unemployment are frictional unemployment, structural unemployment, and cyclical unemployment. Unemployment is the problem of matching people with jobs. When the economy is at the natural rate of unemployment, there is a rough balance between the number of unfilled jobs and the number of job seekers. When the economy is operating above the natural rate of unemployment, the result is cyclical unemployment. A person is unemployed if not currently working, if actively looking for work, and if available for work. Persons on layoff waiting to be recalled are counted as unemployed. The amount of unemployment is difficult to measure because of differing intensities of job search, problems matching qualifications to jobs, underground employment, discouraged workers, and involuntary part-time work. The unemployment rate is the number

unemployed divided by the total labor force. Employment and unemployment statistics show that employment and unemployment can rise or fall together as well as move in opposite directions. There is a distinct cyclical pattern in which unemployment and the number of people not in the labor force rise during recessions.

2. Cyclical unemployment occurs when the economy rises operates above the natural rate of unemployment. In the long run, the economy should return to the natural rate. Unemployed people usually search for jobs. People become unemployed not only because of quits, firings, and layoffs but also because they do not find jobs upon entering or reentering the labor force. Both job seekers and employee-seeking firms will search in the labor market until the marginal costs of search equal the marginal benefits. If something happens to change the costs or benefits of search, the amount of search time changes. When people and firms choose to search less, the unemployment rate should generally fall. Unanticipated inflation tends to reduce search time and, thus, lower unemployment. Reductions in unemployment benefits raise search costs to individuals and lower search time.

3. Only about one third of the rise in the unemployment rate is explained by the changing composition of the labor force. The rise in the long-term unemployment rate has likely been affected by changing unemployment benefits, families with more than one income earner, minimum-wage laws, and progressive taxation. The unemployment rate is affected by both the costs and benefits to workers of being unemployed.

4. The principal social cost of unemployment is the loss of output that unemployed labor would have produced. Okun's Law states that in the short run, every 1 percentage point increase in the unemployment rate causes output to fall by 2.5 percent. Unemployment does yield benefits to society. Society benefits when workers move to better jobs and when the overall allocation of labor improves.

5. Government programs that improve the efficiency of labor markets and provide job skills to those with limited training and experience might reduce unemployment.

Key Terms

frictional unemployment
structural unemployment
cyclical unemployment
labor force
layoff
underground worker
discouraged worker
unemployment rate
Okun's law

Questions and Problems

1. To what extent can the different types of unemployment—cyclical, structural, and frictional—be considered voluntary or involuntary?

2. Brown is prepared to take a job that pays $25,000 per year with a two-week paid vacation in the first year, but Brown cannot find such a job. Would Brown be classified as unemployed?

3. Explain why it is unlikely for cyclical unemployment to account for the long-run rise in unemployment in the United States.

4. ''Economists are on the wrong track when they say that unemployment decisions are based upon cost/benefit analysis. Cost/benefit analysis applies to most economic decision making, but not to unemployment. Able-bodied people want to work.'' Evaluate this statement.

5. Using cost/benefit analysis, explain why rising coverage for unemployment benefits may affect the unemployment rate.

6. Assume that tax rates are substantially reduced. In what ways would you expect the natural unemployment rate to react?

7. Okun's law underlines the high costs of unemployment. Yet this chapter stated that unemployment has a positive side as well. Are these two views of unemployment inconsistent?

8. Explain, using job-search theory, why the duration of unemployment is lower for teenagers than for adult workers.

9. What happens to the number of people not in the labor force during recessions? Give some reasons for this pattern.

10. Draw a diagram showing the relationship between the marginal costs and marginal benefits of job search for a laid-off worker who decides not to search for a new job in order to be recalled to his or her old job.

11. Assuming that the Bureau of Labor Statistics could detect all underground employment and, thus, exclude underground workers from among the officially unemployed, in which of the following cases would measured unemployment fall?

    a. A full-time student is detected working on an unreported basis as a waiter.

    b. An electrician is caught working after hours installing wiring.

    c. A woman who gives her occupation as a homemaker is caught conducting a cosmetics business from her house.

12. Explain how the unemployment rate can fall when unemployment is rising.

13. What is the predicted effect of each of the following on search time?

    a. The amount of time an unemployed worker can draw unemployment benefits is lowered from 6 months to 3 months.

    b. The spouse of an unemployed worker loses his or her job.

    c. State employment offices increase the amount of information they make available on job vacancies.

    d. Wages fall generally in the economy and are perceived to be falling more rapidly than prices.

14. What shifts in the composition of the American labor force would have contributed to rising unemployment?

Suggested Readings

Benjamin, Daniel K. and Levis A. Kochin. "Searching for an Explanation of Unemployment in Interwar Britain." *Journal of Political Economy* 87 (June 1979): 441–74.

Feldstein, Martin. "The Economics of the New Unemployment." *Public Interest* 33 (Fall 1973).

Feldstein, Martin. "The Private and Social Costs of Unemployment." *American Economic Review* 68 (May 1978): 155–58.

16

The Phillips Curve: The Interaction Between Inflation and Unemployment

Chapter Preview

This chapter will explore one of the great questions of macroeconomics: What is the relationship between inflation and unemployment? The 1970s and the early 1980s showed that high unemployment and high inflation could occur simultaneously. A new term entered the economist's vocabulary: **stagflation.**

Stagflation is the combination of high unemployment and high inflation.

Stagflation presents a serious policy dilemma. As preceding chapters showed, contractionary monetary and fiscal policies are the traditional remedy for demand-side inflation, while high unemployment calls for expansionary policies. If an economy has both unemployment and inflation, what should policymakers do? To answer this question, one must understand the relationship between inflation and unemployment.

In 1958, A. W. Phillips of the London School of Economics published a paper that Nobel laureate James Tobin calls "the most influential macroeconomic paper of the last century."[1]

Phillips collected data on the relationship between wage inflation and unemployment in the United Kingdom for the years 1861 to 1913. When Phillips fit a curve to the 1861–1913 data, he found that it sketched out a relationship much like the experience of the United Kingdom through 1957. The famous **Phillips curve** suggested a stable and long-lasting trade-off between inflation and unemployment.

The **Phillips curve** shows the relationship between unemployment and inflation and seems to reveal that a reduction in the rate of unemployment requires an increase in the rate of wage (or price) inflation. ∎

---

1. A. W. Phillips, "The Relation Between Unemployment and the Rate of Change of Money Wages in the United Kingdom, 1861–1957," *Economica* (November 1958), pp. 283–99.

THE ORIGINAL PHILLIPS CURVE

Figure 1 reproduces the original Phillips curve. It shows a scatter diagram of the rate of change of wage rates and the unemployment rate in the United Kingdom for the years 1861 to 1913. Each dot represents a single year. The vertical height of each dot shows the average rate of change of money wages during the year; the horizontal distance between the vertical axis and the dot shows the average unemployment rate for the year. The line fitted through these points is the famous Phillips curve. The Phillips curve has a negative slope: low unemployment rates are accompanied by high inflation, and high unemployment is accompanied by low inflation rates.

Phillips's work in England motivated economists to examine the relationship between inflation and unemployment in other countries. American economists Paul Samuelson and Robert Solow fit a Phillips curve to the American experience from 1935 to 1959. Instead of looking at wage inflation, as Phillips did, they drew a Phillips curve relating the rate of price inflation and unemployment. Samuelson and Solow discovered that the U.S. data told the same story: to lower inflation, the unemployment rate must rise. In the American case, Samuelson and Solow estimated that an unemployment rate of between 5 and 6 percent was required in order to have an inflation-free economy. The socially acceptable unemployment norm in 1960 was perhaps 3.5 percent (which sounds low today but did not then). The American Phillips curve, therefore, implied a difficult social choice: low unemployment required living with inflation. The policy implication: Inflation could be eliminated only if society was prepared to tolerate an unemployment rate well above full employment. Inflation was the price of low unemployment![2]

Figure 2 shows a hypothetical Phillips curve—much like the one Samuelson and Solow found for the United States—that illustrates the hard choices that society must make. Point *a* combines low inflation with high unemployment; point *b* combines high inflation with low unemployment.

---

2. Paul A. Samuelson and Robert M. Solow, "Analytical Aspects of Anti-Inflation Policy," *American Economic Review* (May 1960), pp. 177–94.

Figure 1   The Original Phillips Curve: Wage Inflation and Unemployment in the United Kingdom, 1861–1913

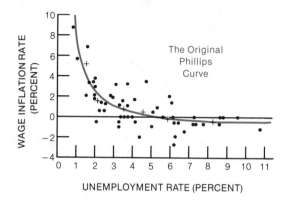

UNEMPLOYMENT RATE (PERCENT)

Phillips's research revealed a negative correlation between inflation and unemployment: as wage inflation fell, unemployment increased.

Source: A. W. Phillips, "The Relation Between Unemployment and the Rate of Change of Money Wages in the United Kingdom, 1861–1957," *Economica* 25 (November 1958); 285.

The Phillips curve made economists the bearers of bad news. The dismal science of the Phillips curve condemned society to either perpetual inflation or perpetual unemployment or to some combination of an unacceptable level of unemployment and too high inflation. Despite its gloomy message, however, the Phillips curve at least appeared to give society a choice.

The Phillips curve seemed to rule out the combination of high unemployment and high inflation. The stagflation of the 1970s and the early 1980s burst this bubble. The data on the relationship between U.S. inflation and unemployment from 1961 to 1984 are graphed in Figure 3. The annual inflation rate in each year is measured along the vertical axis, and the unemployment rate for that same year is measured along the horizontal axis.

The work of Phillips would lead one to expect a negative relationship between unemployment and inflation: the higher is the unemployment rate, the lower is the inflation rate. In Figure 3, the dots that represent each year's combination of inflation and unemployment are connected sequentially to show the history of inflation and unemployment as it unfolded after 1960.

Figure 2   A Hypothetical Phillips Curve: The Inflation/Unemployment Trade-Off

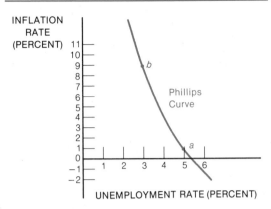

The hypothetical Phillips curve has a negative slope. Point *b* combines high inflation with low unemployment. Point *a* combines high unemployment with low inflation. The Phillips curve reflects the menu of inflation/unemployment choices open to society.

Figure 3   U.S. Inflation and Unemployment, 1961–1984

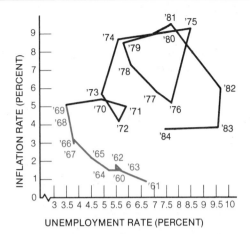

The annual growth rate of the GNP deflator is shown on the vertical axis. Each dot shows the inflation/unemployment combination for that year. The 1960s are connected with a color line, which shows the typical Phillips curve trade-off. The 1970s line in black fails to reveal the expected trade-off between inflation and unemployment.

Source: *Economic Report of the President; Federal Reserve Bulletin.*

The 1960s are connected with a color line. The 1960s dots show a classical Phillips curve relationship: unemployment fell from a 5–7 percent level in the early 1960s to a 3–4 percent level in the late 1960s while inflation rose from 1–2 percent in the early 1960s to 4–5 percent in the late 1960s.

The traditional Phillips curve relationship fell apart in the 1970s. The black line in Figure 3 connects the years 1969 to 1984. The headline story of the 1970s was stagflation. The 1970s failed to yield anything resembling the traditional Phillips curve. Instead of a neat negative relationship, the traditional Phillips curve dissolved into a swirling pattern. For the 1970s as a whole, both unemployment and inflation rose together. According to commentators of the 1970s, the "laws of economics" (namely, the Phillips curve) were no longer working. Economists had been so impressed with the Phillips curve that noneconomists should not be blamed for believing that stagflation violated some basic law of economics.

Indeed, during the 1960s it was difficult to dispute the Phillips curve. The Phillips curve was generally consistent with the teachings of Keynesian economics—which was riding a crest of popular and academic prestige. During the Kennedy-Johnson years, Keynesian economics and the

Phillips-curve analysis found an eloquent voice in Walter Heller, Gardner Ackley, and Arthur Okun.

In 1968 two economists, working independently, made a very simple point about the Phillips curve. Milton Friedman and Edmund S. Phelps noted that the Phillips curve makes a key assumption: it assumes that the *anticipated* rate of inflation remains constant. According to Friedman and Phelps, if the anticipated rate of inflation changes, the entire Phillips curve will shift. Friedman and Phelps claimed that the inflation/unemployment relationship discussed by Phillips and by Samuelson and Solow is stable *only when anticipated inflation is not changing.*

Much of this chapter is devoted to explaining the Friedman-Phelps view of the Phillips curve. We begin with a thumbnail sketch of their ideas that will be fleshed out in the following sections. According to Friedman and Phelps, anticipated inflation will not change during periods when there is no distinct trend in inflation. However, if the rate of inflation increases significantly over a number of years, the anticipated inflation rate will increase (recall from Chapter 14 that according to the adaptive-expectations hypothesis, expectations adapt slowly to current and past experience). As the anticipated rate of inflation increases, the entire Phillips curve will shift upward.

Figure 4 depicts the Friedman-Phelps view of the shifting Phillips curve. PC_0 is the Phillips curve for an anticipated inflation rate of 0 percent, and PC_{10} is the Phillips curve for an anticipated inflation rate of 10 percent. As the anticipated inflation rate rises, so does the entire Phillips curve.

The Friedman-Phelps Phillips curve suggests that stagflation does not violate the laws of economics. If the anticipated rate of inflation is rising, both inflation and unemployment could rise—say, from a on PC_0 to c on PC_{10}. The stable Phillips curve trade-off between inflation and unemployment holds only when anticipated inflation is not changing.

The Friedman-Phelps analysis has led to a new Phillips curve that is the focus of this chapter. It has altered the way economists view the inflation/unemployment relationship. To understand this new view, one must relate the workings of the labor market and unemployment to inflation.

LABOR MARKETS AND INFLATION

The previous chapter on unemployment explained that people become unemployed by being fired or laid off, by quitting, or by failing to find a job upon entering (or reentering) the labor force. With the exception of the laid-off worker who decides to wait to be recalled to his or her old job, the unemployed are searching for jobs. The unemployed (by definition) are actively looking for jobs, trying to find the best jobs possible given their skills and qualifications. As jobs open up, firms are also searching for workers. If there were perfect information in the hands of job seekers and employee seeking firms, the matching of people to jobs would be very easy. In accepting a job, the job-seeking worker would know exactly what potential jobs he or she was passing up. Job seekers would know all the jobs that are available now and that will be available in the immediate future. Employee-seeking firms, armed with per-

Figure 4 The Short-Run Friedman-Phelps Curve

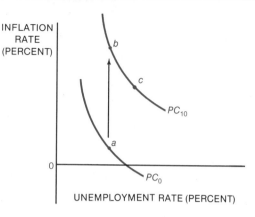

This figure illustrates the Friedman-Phelps analysis of the Phillips curve. PC_0 is the initial Phillips curve when the anticipated inflation rate is 0 percent. PC_{10} is the Phillips curve when the anticipated inflation rate is a higher 10 percent. A higher anticipated inflation rate shifts the entire Phillips curve up.

fect information, would know everything there is to know about the job-seeking individuals available for work now or in the future. In hiring an employee, the firm would know exactly whom they have passed up in order to hire someone now.

Labor-Market Search

If labor markets operated on the basis of perfect information, there would be little unemployment. People would move quickly from one job to another; new entrants to the job market would find employment quickly; employee-seeking firms would not have to engage in drawn-out searches for new employees.

Labor markets are characterized by imperfect information and considerable uncertainty. From the vantage point of job seekers, it is difficult to know exactly what jobs are available now or will be available in the immediate future, where these jobs are located, and what the chances are of successfully landing any particular job. From the vantage point of the firm, it is difficult to know exactly what types of people are available to fill job vacancies. If current employees are fired, can they be replaced by better people? If the firm delays filling positions, will better qualified people be in the labor market in the next period? If the firm lays off workers, will they wait to be recalled?

Because of imperfect information, both job seekers and employee-seeking firms must search in the labor market. The previous chapter emphasized that search incurs costs. Job seekers incur out-of-pocket costs (such as transportation expenses, hiring someone to write a resume, placing job-wanted ads, making long-distance calls to potential employers). The longer is the job search, the greater are these costs. If job seekers pass up the opportunity to accept an offered job in order to look for something better, continued job search also incurs the opportunity cost of forgone earnings. When rational individuals continue their job search in the face of job-search costs, they expect the benefits (in the form of a better eventual job) from more search to outweigh the costs of more search.

Employee-seeking firms also incur costs in searching for employees. They must place want ads, assign employees to search committees, or send recruiters on business trips. They may pass up a willing job seeker in the hope of finding a better prospect and sometimes find that no better prospect comes along. When employee-seeking firms continue their employee search, they expect the benefits from more searching to outweigh the costs of more searching. Both job seekers and employee-seeking firms search to the point where the marginal costs of more search equal the marginal benefits expected from more search.

How people and firms search in the labor market affects the unemployment rate. When job seekers decide to reduce the amount of search, they accept jobs more quickly; they are less willing to hold out for better jobs. They may even decide to withdraw from job seeking and leave the labor force entirely. When employee-seeking firms decide to reduce the amount of search, they hire more quickly; they are more reluctant to fire current employees; they may lower their skill requirements for jobs.

Unemployment tends to fall when job seekers and employee-seeking firms decide to reduce the amount of search in the labor market.

The previous chapter showed that people reduce their search in the labor market when the marginal costs of search rise and when the marginal benefits expected from search fall. Employee-seeking firms also reduce their search when the marginal costs of search rise and the marginal benefits expected from search fall.

Expectations of Inflation

The traditional Phillips curve shows a stable, inverse relationship between inflation and unemployment. Why would unemployment be expected to respond to inflation? The classical economists argued that there is no reason for inflation to affect output or employment decisions because people are not subject to money illusion. Inflation does not, on average, change real wages; so why should inflation (which raises nominal wages but not real wages) change the amount of unemployment in the economy? The economics of labor-market search shed light on this question.

Search and Contracting with Unanticipated Inflation.   Inflation (or deflation) that is *unanticipated* can affect unemployment. If the inflation rate rises above the anticipated rate, search activities can be affected in a number of ways:

1.   When prices and wages are rising above expectations, wage offers will start to look more attractive to people looking for jobs. If wages and prices both rise, on average, by 7 percent while people anticipate a 5 percent inflation rate, workers will think they are being offered higher real wages, and job seekers will be more inclined to take jobs sooner. In effect, unanticipated inflation misleads people into thinking that the marginal costs of job search have risen because the cost of forgoing the offered job has (apparently) risen. Accordingly, they reduce search time by accepting employment offers more readily. Those receiving unemployment insurance will find that market wages are rising relative to insurance benefits (which respond slowly to rising living costs) and will be more likely to accept jobs. Again, unanticipated inflation has raised the marginal costs of continued job search by making it more costly not to take available jobs.

2. Firms who were anticipating or contemplating firing marginal workers may now reconsider the costs and benefits of such an action. As wages rise in the marketplace, it may be better for the time being to keep the marginal worker (who is a known quantity) rather than try to replace him or her. If the labor market is tight, the expected benefits from search fall, and it pays to keep the marginal worker. Tight labor markets reduce the probability of finding willing prospective employees. When the firm's expected inflation is less than actual inflation, it overestimates the tightness of the labor market. As firings slow down, the actual tightness of the labor market increases.

3. Firms and employees set wage contracts on the basis of anticipated inflation rates as well as anticipated employee productivity. Employees seek to protect their real wage by factoring the anticipated inflation rate into their money-wage contracts. When the actual inflation rate exceeds the anticipated rate, employees are stuck with contracts that do not protect them fully from inflation. The firm finds that its product-selling prices (that are being pulled up by inflation) are rising faster than production costs since wages were set on a lower basis. The firm has an incentive to hire more and to fire less.[3] With selling prices rising more rapidly than contractual wages, firms find that the marginal costs of search rise—the costs of keeping positions vacant has risen.

> **When inflation is greater than anticipated, unemployment falls. When inflation is less than anticipated, unemployment rises.**

When inflation is less than anticipated, the three factors noted above now work in reverse to increase unemployment. Fixed-wage contracts factor in a higher rate of inflation than actually occurs and reduce business profitability. The firm

increases its firings of marginal workers and reduces its search for new employees. Unemployment insurance looks better to the unemployed, and so on.

Layoffs and Implicit Contracts.   In 1982 (a year of 9.7 percent unemployment), layoffs represented about 20 percent of total unemployment. Unlike firings, quits, and new entrants, layoffs cannot be classified as search activity (except in a broad sense). How will layoff unemployment be affected by inflation? Layoffs are used by firms that require a career labor force. Companies like General Motors or Boeing want a labor force that is attached more or less permanently to the firm because the firm requires a quality labor force with a good deal of on-the-job experience. On the other hand, the firm cannot guarantee employment to all its workers all the time. In some years, business may be bad, and fewer workers will be required.[4]

The firm strikes an explicit or implicit contract with its workers. It guarantees them a given wage plus generous fringe benefits and overtime pay but does not guarantee the hours of employment. In most cases, there is an explicit contractual agreement concerning hourly wages and fringe benefits. Such contracts are typically negotiated union contracts that cover a multiyear period. In addition to the negotiated wage-and-benefits package, the company promises (either explicitly or implicitly) to rehire laid-off workers rather than someone else when business is good. In this way, firms that experience cyclical fluctuations in demand attempt to keep an experienced cadre of quality workers who know that they may be laid off from time to time.

Such a firm has an implicit contract with the worker to vary employment (or unemployment) more than the worker's wage rate. When the demand for labor falls, the wage rates of workers on such contracts will not fall to prevent layoffs. Instead of wages adjusting, the amount of employment declines; some workers are laid off.

Layoff unemployment is an important compo-

---

3. These factors explain why firings and entrant and reentrant unemployment fall when the actual inflation rate exceeds the anticipated inflation rate. Quits do not follow the Phillips-curve pattern. When unemployment is falling, quit rates tend to increase as workers become more confident about securing a better job. Therefore a higher-than-anticipated inflation rate should cause quits to rise. But as noted above, quits are a small fraction of total unemployment, and most workers who quit already have another job arranged beforehand. Their unemployment—if any—will be of very short duration.

---

4. This discussion is based on Arthur Okun, *Prices and Quantities* (Washington, D.C.: Brookings Institution, 1981). Okun draws on the research of Martin N. Bailey, Donald F. Gordon, and Costas Azariadis on implicit contracts.

nent of total unemployment. Its relative importance appears to rise during periods of high unemployment. To understand the relationship between unemployment and inflation, it is necessary to understand how inflation affects layoff unemployment. The amount of layoff unemployment depends upon the actions of firms and of laid-off workers. The firm must do a balancing act between its desire to retain, in the long run, a career labor force and its need to reduce employment during cyclical downturns. The laid-off worker must decide whether to wait to be recalled or to actively seek another job. The outcome of the worker's decision depends upon the attractiveness of the wage-and-benefits package he or she would receive if recalled and the probable duration of the layoff. If the layoff threatens to be a lengthy one or if the pay and benefits are not that much better than alternative jobs, the laid-off worker is likely to search actively for another job. When a firm lays off workers, it runs the risk of losing part of its career labor force to other employers.

How would unanticipated inflation affect the amount of layoff unemployment? First, unanticipated inflation means that inflation has not been properly factored into multiyear wage contracts. With selling prices rising faster than wages, the firm will lay off fewer workers and will recall workers who are on layoff. By temporarily lowering real wages, unanticipated inflation causes employment to expand, the number of layoffs to contract, and the amount of unemployment to fall. Second, unanticipated inflation motivates firms to worry about the loss of their career labor force. Business firms take unanticipated inflation to be a sign that positions will be harder to fill. If workers are laid off when positions are hard to fill, their alternative employment opportunities are good, and they are more likely to take jobs with other firms. If laid-off workers are not recalled quickly, they may be lost to the firm forever. As a consequence of unanticipated inflation, there are fewer layoffs, and the labor market does indeed tighten. The anticipation of difficulty in filling positions tends to be a self-fulfilling prophecy as employers become increasingly wary of laying off workers and start recalling workers.

If the anticipated rate of inflation is less than the actual rate, firms will find their costs rising faster than their prices; they will step up the pace of layoffs. Workers who believe jobs are harder to find are prepared to accept less employment in return for a long-term employment contract that offers them the prospect of being recalled at an attractive wage.

Search and Contracting with Anticipated Inflation.

As just described, unanticipated inflation changes the costs and benefits of search and, thus, can alter the amount of unemployment. Generally speaking, unanticipated inflation reduces unemployment, while unanticipated deflation raises unemployment. Unanticipated inflation also reduces layoff unemployment because firms that rely on a career labor force must worry about laying off workers when positions are hard to fill.

What will be the effect of *anticipated* inflation on the amount of unemployment? As long as an economy operates at the natural rate of unemployment, where the number of job seekers and the number of vacant jobs for which the unemployed are qualified are in balance, the prevailing rate of inflation can continue. At the natural rate, people are properly anticipating inflation; they are not caught off guard by inflation. As long as inflation is properly anticipated, workers and firms are aware that real variables are not changing. Nominal wages are rising at an average rate of 7 percent per year, but workers are also aware that prices are rising at the same rate, so they know there has been no real change. Rising wages and prices do not change perceived costs and benefits of job search or of employee search. With inflation properly anticipated, inflation is fully factored into multiyear contracts so that nominal wages and selling prices rise at the same rate. With inflation properly anticipated, people and firms will not take rising nominal wages as a sign that jobs are easier for workers to find or harder for employers to fill.

When inflation is anticipated, unemployment will equal the natural rate—no matter what the anticipated rate of inflation. When inflation exceeds the anticipated rate, unemployment falls below the natural rate. When inflation is less than the anticipated rate, unemployment rises above the natural rate.

The natural-rate hypothesis of Milton Friedman and Edmund Phelps (discussed in Chapter 11) bears repeating at this point because it is analyzed here from the viewpoint of the labor market.

Analysis of labor-market behavior again shows why the natural rate of unemployment is independent of the rate of inflation when inflation is anticipated. If wages and prices rise at an anticipated rate of inflation of, say, 7 percent, no real variables are changing, so there will be no change in search or layoff behavior, and the unemployment rate will remain at the natural rate. At an anticipated inflation rate of 12 percent, the result will be the same. Insofar as the 12 percent inflation is anticipated, there will be no change in real behavior, and the economy will remain at the natural rate of unemployment. Only *unanticipated* inflation causes the amount of unemployment to depart from the natural rate.

> The natural rate of unemployment is independent of the rate of inflation because in the long run people and firms are not subject to money illusion. In the long run, people will anticipate any given rate of inflation. Anticipated inflation has no effect on the employment actions of people and firms.

THE NEW PHILLIPS CURVE

We are now ready to return to the puzzle of stagflation and the deteriorating Phillips curve of the 1970s and early 1980s. The analysis of search and contracting and the natural-rate hypothesis explain these phenomena.

The Friedman-Phelps analysis differentiates between two Phillips curves: the short-run Phillips curve and the long-run Phillips curve. The short-run curve can be recognized as the original Phillips curve. The long-run Phillips curve indicates *no* trade-off between inflation and unemployment in the long run.

The **short-run Phillips curve** shows the inflation/unemployment relationship when anticipated inflation remains constant. The **long-run Phillips curve** shows the inflation/unemployment relationship when the anticipated rate of inflation is changing and equals the actual rate of inflation.

Figure 5   The New Phillips Curve

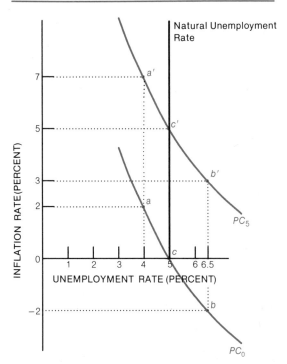

The economy is initially operating at the natural rate (assumed to be 5 percent) at point c on the Phillips curve PC_0. The actual and anticipated inflation rates are 0 percent. An expansionary policy raises the inflation rate, and the unanticipated inflation moves the economy to a, where the unemployment rate is 4 percent. If the economy had been instead at c' with an anticipated inflation rate of 5 percent, the Phillips curve would be PC_5. On PC_5, a 7 percent inflation rate is required to move the economy to a' where the unemployment rate is again 4 percent.

The Short-Run Phillips Curve

Suppose that the rate of inflation is 0 percent and people expect no inflation (the anticipated inflation rate is also 0 percent). According to the natural-rate hypothesis, under these conditions, the actual unemployment rate will be the natural rate. If the natural rate of unemployment is 5 percent, this economy is operating at point c in Figure 5. The Phillips curve that prevails when the anticipated inflation rate is 0 percent is PC_0. Now suppose a sudden increase in aggregate demand raises the rate of inflation to 2 percent. People have failed to anticipate the increase in inflation (they still anticipate 0 percent inflation). The economy will, therefore, move to point a on the same Phillips curve where the unemployment rate is 4 percent.

The economics of search and contracting explains why the economy moves to an unemployment rate below the natural rate. Contracts written with a 0 percent anticipated inflation cause wage increases to fall behind price increases. Firms increase their output and employment. Those unemployed perceive money wages to be rising faster than prices; they accept job offers more readily. Firms also can be misled into thinking their selling prices are rising more rapidly than their costs. They, therefore, expand output and employment.

If aggregate demand had fallen unexpectedly and brought about a 2 percent rate of deflation, the economy would move down to point b where the unemployment rate is 6.5 percent. At b, the unemployment rate exceeds the natural rate because the actual rate of inflation is less than the anticipated rate of inflation (-2 percent is less than 0 percent). Again, the search and contracting behavior of firms and individuals explains why unanticipated deflation causes more unemployment.

The **short-run Phillips curve,** like the original Phillips curve, shows a negative relationship between inflation and unemployment. In the short run, less inflation means more unemployment.

The Long-Run Phillips Curve

Suppose now that the rate of inflation has risen to 5 percent instead of the original 0 percent and that the anticipated rate of inflation has also risen to 5 percent. According to the natural-rate hypothesis, the Phillips curve has shifted up from PC_0 to PC_5 in Figure 5. The economy is now at c' on PC_5. When inflation is anticipated, no one will be fooled by money illusion. The employment decisions of individuals and firms will not be different at a 5 percent anticipated inflation rate than at a 0 percent anticipated inflation rate. Therefore, the shifted Phillips curve PC_5 maintains the same shape as curve PC_0.

The upward shift in the Phillips curve has now disrupted the negative statistical correlation between inflation and unemployment. To have a 4 percent unemployment rate (point a') now re-

quires a 7 percent inflation rate (one that exceeds the anticipated rate). To have a 6.5 percent unemployment rate (point b') requires a 3 percent inflation rate (one that is below the anticipated rate of inflation).

The Phillips curves shift up along the vertical natural-unemployment-rate line as anticipated inflation increases. Each PC curve passes through the vertical natural-rate line at exactly the point where the anticipated inflation rate equals the actual inflation rate. This result follows from the natural-rate hypothesis; there is an entire family of short-run Phillips curves—one for each anticipated rate of inflation. The long-run Phillips curve is the curve that connects each of the short-run curves at the point where actual inflation equals anticipated inflation.

The **long-run Phillips curve** is a vertical line that shows that in the long run, the unemployment rate is independent of the inflation rate. Unemployment will not decline with more inflation in the long run.

Inflation greater than the anticipated rate moves the economy up the short-run Phillips curve (from c to a in Figure 5). Inflation less than anticipated moves the economy down the short-run Phillips curve (from c to b). When actual inflation is different from a given rate of anticipated inflation, a trade-off exists between inflation and unemployment. In the long run, the economy comes to anticipate a higher rate of inflation, and the short-run Phillips curve shifts up as anticipated inflation increases to match actual inflation.

EXPLAINING STAGFLATION, DISINFLATION, AND ACCELERATING INFLATION

The new theory of the Phillips curve predicts that there will be a trade-off between inflation and unemployment *only if the anticipated rate of inflation does not change.* It predicts that the Phillips curve will shift up as the anticipated rate of inflation increases. Once the higher rate of inflation is anticipated, the economy will operate at the natural unemployment rate. How well does the available evidence support the Friedman-Phelps theory of the Phillips curve?

Figure 6   U.S. Unemployment and Unanticipated Inflation, 1966–1984

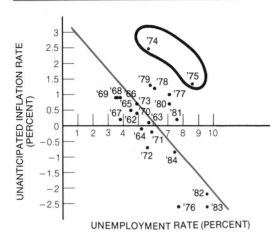

In this graph, the *anticipated inflation rate* is calculated as the average inflation rate over the past three years. The *unanticipated* rate is the GNP deflator minus this anticipated rate. The graph shows that the unemployment rate tends to drop when there is unanticipated inflation and tends to rise when actual inflation is below anticipated inflation.

Stagflation, 1966–1981

The period 1966 to 1981 was one of sharply accelerating inflation—a period in which there was likely unanticipated inflation. Figure 6 is a scatter diagram showing the unemployment rate on the horizontal axis and a simple measure of the unanticipated rate of inflation on the vertical axis. Each dot represents a single year. The *unanticipated inflation rate* is measured as the difference between the actual annual percentage change in the GNP price deflator and the anticipated inflation rate for that year. The anticipated rate of inflation is calculated using adaptive expectations as the average rate for the last three years. For example, in 1978, 1979, and 1980 the inflation rates were 7.3, 8.5, and 9.0 percent. The anticipated inflation rate in 1980 is, therefore, taken to be 8.3 percent, the average of the three years. No one knows for sure what the anticipated inflation rate is in any year, but this method gives a reasonable approximation.

If the new theory is correct, there should be a negative relationship between unemployment and the *unanticipated* inflation rate. Remember, un-

anticipated inflation causes unemployment to decline. If the inflation is *anticipated,* it should have *no effect* on unemployment. The data shows that except for 1974 and 1975, there is indeed a negative relationship between unemployment and unanticipated inflation. The years 1974 and 1975, it might be noted, were exceptional years when the extraordinary effects of the quadrupling of oil prices were most severe. Supply shocks of this type would be expected to disrupt the normal relationship between unanticipated inflation and unemployment.

Except for 1974 and 1975, the dots are generally consistent with the Friedman-Phelps theory. For instance, in 1976 people expected a 7.7 percent inflation rate but experienced only a 5.2 percent inflation rate. As the theory predicts, unemployment was quite high in that year. In 1979, the anticipated inflation rate was 7.2 percent, and the actual rate was 8.5 percent. As predicted by the theory, unemployment was a relatively low 5.8 percent. (See Example 1 for international evidence of stagflation.)

Disinflation, 1982–1984

The Friedman-Phelps hypothesis predicts that unanticipated inflation causes the unemployment rate to fall. Figure 6 appears to confirm this proposition for the period 1966–1981. During this time period, inflation was generally accelerating and people were surprised by unanticipated inflation. During the years when unanticipated inflation was highest, the unemployment rate tended to drop (except during the supply shocks of 1974 and 1975). In the years when unanticipated inflation was lowest, the unemployment rate tended to rise.

As Chapter 14 reported, the 1982–1984 period was a time of marked and generally unexpected decline in the rate of inflation. The annual inflation rate (as measured by the GND deflator) dropped from 9.2 percent per annum in 1982 to 3.7 percent in 1984. The period 1982 to 1984 was a period of unexpected **disinflation.**

Disinflation is a decline in the rate of inflation.

The Friedman-Phelps hypothesis predicts that an unexpected decline in the rate of inflation should cause the unemployment rate to rise. When inflation is less than anticipated, firms find themselves stuck with nominal wages rising faster than product selling prices. Firms see positions becoming generally easier to fill and lay off more workers and recall fewer workers. Search time in the labor market rises, and the unemployment rate rises.

Figure 6 shows that the Friedman-Phelps hypothesis accurately predicted the unemployment effects of unanticipated disinflation. In 1982 and 1983, the actual inflation rates were well below the anticipated inflation rates, and the unemployment rate rose to 9.5 percent in both years. By 1984, the actual inflation rate was closer to the anticipated inflation rate (but still slightly below it), and the unemployment rate dropped from 9.5 percent to 7.4 percent. Presumably, when actual and anticipated inflation are equal, the economy will return to the natural rate of unemployment—an unemployment rate somewhere between 5 and 6.5 percent. (See Example 2.)

Figure 3 presented actual U.S. inflation and unemployment rates for the period 1960–1984. The deterioration of the stable Phillips-curve relationship after 1969 has given credence to the Friedman-Phelps view of the inflation/unemployment relationship. The basic proposition of the new Phillips curve is that the short-run Phillips curve shifts upward when inflationary expectations rise and shifts back down when inflationary expectations fall.

We are now in a position to make more sense out of the confusing swirls of Figure 3. Figure 7 again plots the unemployment/inflation combinations for the period 1960–1984 (leaving out the supply-shock years 1974 and 1975). Four free-hand curves are then superimposed over the dots: one through the dots of the 1960s, one through the dots of the early 1970s, one through the dots of the late 1970s, and one through the dots of the early 1980s. The result is four short-run Phillips curves. Each short-run Phillips curve has a negative slope, and each successive one is higher than the previous one. These freehand representations show how the short-run Phillips curve has been shifting upward as inflationary expectations rose from the 1960s to the 1980s. As one would expect, the dot for 1984 falls below the 1980–83 short-run Phillips curve. As inflationary expecta-

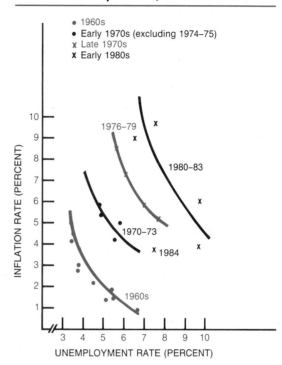

Figure 7 Upward Shifts in the Short-Run Phillips Curve, 1960–1984

This diagram plots the inflation/unemployment combinations for the period 1960–1984 (omitting the supply-shock years 1974 and 1975). When the dots for subperiods are connected, they trace out short-run Phillips curves, each higher than the preceding one. The short-run Phillips curve is expected to rise as inflationary expectations rise. The fact that the 1984 dot is below the 1980–83 short-run curve may suggest that the short-run Phillips curve is shifting down as inflationary expectations fall.

tions fall, there should be a drop in the short-run Phillips curve.

Accelerating Inflation

The new Phillips-curve doctrine is consistent with the accelerating inflation of the 1970s. Recall that from the mid-1960s to the late 1970s, inflation rates as measured by the GNP deflator rose from 1.5 percent per annum to near double-digit levels (9.4 percent in 1981). In 1979, the CPI rose by 11.3 percent, and the GNP deflator rose by 8.5 percent. The new Phillips curve offers an explanation for accelerating inflation.

Figure 8   Accelerating Inflation

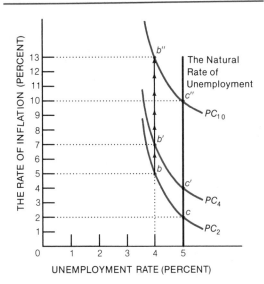

Maintaining a 4 percent unemployment rate causes accelerating inflation. For unemployment rates below the natural rate, actual inflation must exceed anticipated inflation, but this requirement increases the anticipated rate of inflation. Hence, the Phillips curve shifts ever upward.

Suppose the economy is operating at point c in Figure 8. The inflation rate is 2 percent, the anticipated inflation rate also equals 2 percent, and unemployment is at the natural rate of 5 percent. The government now decides to lower the unemployment rate to 4 percent and to hold it at that level. By increasing aggregate demand, the inflation rate rises unexpectedly to 5 percent (there is a 3 percent unanticipated inflation), and the unanticipated inflation lowers the unemployment rate to 4 percent. The economy has moved along the established short-run Phillips curve, PC_2, from c to b.

At a 5 percent inflation rate, however, people will raise their inflation expectations. People might raise the anticipated rate of inflation initially from 2 to 4 percent. When the anticipated rate of inflation rises, the entire short-run Phillips curve shifts up (from PC_2 to PC_4). With the new and higher short-run Phillips curve, PC_4, a 7 percent inflation rate is required to keep the economy at a 4 percent unemployment rate (point b' on PC_4). A 7 percent inflation rate causes the Phillips curve to shift up again, and an even higher

inflation rate is required to keep the economy at a 4 percent unemployment rate. Figure 8 warns of the inflationary implications of aiming for an unemployment rate below the natural rate.

If monetary and fiscal authorities try to hold the unemployment rate below the natural rate, they must continuously keep the inflation rate above the anticipated inflation rate. Inflation will continue to accelerate as long as the unemployment rate is held below the natural rate. The process of accelerating inflation is shown by the continuous upward shifting of the short-run Phillips curve.

Stop-and-Go Policies

The world does not proceed as smoothly as in Figure 8. As the government sees the inflation rate accelerating, political pressures will build up to stop inflation. Hence, it is likely that the government will respond to these pressures by cutting the growth of money supply. For example, the U.S. economy experienced accelerating inflation from 1964 to 1968. The growth of the money supply trended upward, and by 1968 money was growing at an 8 percent annual rate. In the next year, 1969, money supply growth was cut to 3 percent per year. When money-supply growth is cut, the effect on inflation is typically not immediate. Inflation does not immediately fall; instead, the inflation rate will first peak and then eventually slow down.

As the inflation rate falls, the actual inflation rate will fall below the anticipated rate. As already demonstrated, unemployment rises when the actual rate of inflation falls below the anticipated rate. Now the problem is rising unemployment, not inflation. Political pressure now builds to combat high unemployment. Monetary authorities may be persuaded to step up the growth of the money supply once again. For example, in the early 1970s, the unemployment rate was around 6 percent—which was considered high for the time. The monetary authorities began speeding up the rate of monetary growth. By 1972, the money supply was growing at an annual rate of 9.2 percent—the highest monetary growth rate since World War II.

Figure 9 shows the effects of such stop-and-go policies. First, the unemployment rate is pushed below the natural rate (at *a*) by expansionary policies that create unanticipated inflation. As the inflation rate accelerates (at *b*), the monetary authorities become concerned about inflation, and they cut back on monetary growth, pushing the economy to point *c*, where unemployment is high but the inflation rate is falling. Monetary authorities respond to high unemployment by stepping up the growth of the money supply and moving the economy to *d*. Accelerating inflation again becomes a problem at *e,* and authorities reduce monetary growth, moving the economy to *f*. The cycle may repeat itself.

The spiral movements in Figure 9 look uncannily like the U.S. data in Figure 3 with one important difference. The U.S. data in Figure 3 reveal stop-and-go movements with the unemployment rate trending up—unlike our hypothetical stop-and-go diagram with fluctuations around a stable natural rate of unemployment.

Political Business Cycles

Stop-and-go policies can generate *political business cycles*. The alternating concern of the monetary authorities may represent the Fed's response to political pressures. When inflation is singled out as public enemy number one, the executive branch and the Congress put pressure on monetary authorities to reduce the inflation rate. If the public regards inflation as getting out of hand, the party in power will worry about the next election. When unemployment is regarded as the main villain, political pressure is put on the Fed to lower the unemployment rate. Alternating the focus between fighting inflation and fighting unemployment leads to the spiral motions of Figure 9. Insofar as these cycles are caused by responses to political pressures, they have been dubbed political business cycles.

Is it in the interests of democratic governments to induce business cycles? Will not the voters recognize what is going on and "throw the rascals out"? Unfortunately, politics is a short-run business. In good times, the politicians in power are usually rewarded by reelection; in bad times, they are penalized by losing their offices. Voters do not have long memories and are impatient for

Figure 9   Stop-and-Go Economic Policies

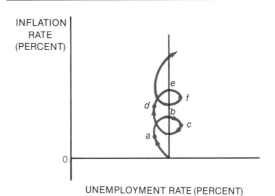

The economy is initially experiencing unanticipated inflation that drives the unemployment rate below the natural rate (point *a*). Accelerating inflation moves the economy to *b*. Political pressure builds to stop inflation, and the growth of money supply is reduced. Unanticipated deflation causes unemployment, and the economy moves to point *c*. Monetary authorities are now pressured to fight unemployment. The growth of money supply is speeded up, and the economy moves to *d*, where inflation becomes the major political problem once again. This process may repeat itself.

good times to reappear. A politician who enacts a policy of slowly reducing inflation and unemployment over a 10-year period would stand little chance of reelection—even though the problem of anticipated inflation may have been decades in the making. The politician who wants to get reelected must act now. The price of acting now to achieve a low unemployment rate at election time may be a high rate of anticipated inflation in the future. But the vote-maximizing politician cannot afford to worry about such long-range concerns. The politician's attitude often is to worry about tomorrow when tomorrow comes.

A number of economists and political scientists have studied the political business cycle. Edward Tufte, a political scientist from Yale University, looked at U.S. data on real disposable income from 1947 to 1976. He found that, excluding the Eisenhower years of 1953 to 1960, about 80 percent of the election years showed an increase in the growth of real disposable income and about 80 percent of the nonelection years showed a decrease in the rate of growth of real disposable income. Tufte found that this phenomenon is not

Example 1   Stagflation as an International Phenomenoñ

From 1960 to the early 1980s, the United States experienced stagflation—the combination of rising inflation and rising unemployment. Stagflation was not confined to the United States during this period. The accompanying figure gives average inflation rates and average unemployment rates in seven industrialized capitalist countries (Canada, France, West Germany, Italy, Japan, the United Kingdom, and the United States). As the figure shows, unemployment and inflation rose in these seven countries from the mid-1960s to 1980. The rise in unemployment was more gradual than the rise in inflation, which was accentuated by two energy shocks in the mid- and late 1970s. After 1980, the seven countries experienced substantial disinflation, while the unemployment rate continued to rise. ■

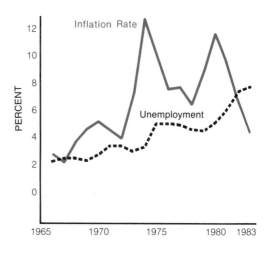

Source: OECD, 1983.

---

unique to the United States and that a similar pattern existed in 27 different democratic countries.[5]

The evidence on the political business cycle is still inconclusive, but if there is indeed a political business cycle, what can be done about it? One proposal is to increase the term of the President from 4 to 6 years and to limit the President to one term in office. The advocates of this proposal maintain that this system would allow the President to pursue more long-term economic goals with less concern about the reelection just a couple of years away.[6]

WHAT TO DO ABOUT STAGFLATION

Stagflation presents policy makers with the serious dilemma of how to fight inflation without worsening unemployment or how to fight unemployment without worsening inflation.

---

5. Edward Tufte, *Political Control of the Economy* (Princeton, N.J.: Princeton University Press, 1978).

6. Politicians are well aware of the power of the political business cycle. In his memoirs, Richard Nixon blames his loss of the close 1960 election on Eisenhower's failure to reduce unemployment prior to election time.

The Unemployment Costs of Reducing Inflation

The new Phillips-curve analysis suggests that there may be substantial unemployment costs to reducing inflation if expectations are slow to adjust. Anti-inflationary monetary policy will raise the unemployment rate if the anticipated rate of inflation does not drop at the same rate as the inflation rate. If the actual inflation rate is below the anticipated inflation rate, unemployment will rise, according to the new Phillips-curve analysis.

Figure 10 illustrates this problem. The economy is initially operating at the natural rate of unemployment (5 percent) with an inflation rate of 10 percent. Because the economy is operating at the natural rate, actual and anticipated inflation are equal. How can the economy move from a high rate of inflation to a 0 rate of inflation without causing unemployment (how can it move from c' to c)?

According to the new Phillips-curve analysis, getting from c' to c is very difficult because inflationary *expectations* must be beaten down to 0 percent! If expectations are adaptive, a number of years must be endured in which the actual rate of inflation is less than the anticipated rate. But unemployment increases when actual inflation is below anticipated inflation. During this period, a simplified picture of the path of the economy might look something like the loop $c'bc$. The economy starts at c' with inflation at 10 percent, unemployment at 5 percent, and the anticipated inflation rate at 10 percent. When contractionary policies are applied, the economy moves to b. At the intermediate point b, the unemployment rate has risen to 10 percent and the inflation rate has dropped to 4 percent, but the anticipated inflation rate is 8 percent. Unemployment above the natural rate has been caused by an anticipated rate of inflation higher than actual inflation. The hardships of unemployment at b may be considerable. As the inflation rate continues to drop towards 0 percent, inflationary expectations will continue to drop. Once the economy reaches point c, the natural rate of unemployment is restored, and the actual and anticipated rates of inflation are both 0 percent.

Suggested Remedies

The price paid for a sudden shift to an anti-inflationary policy is unemployment when inflationary expectations are adjusting downward. Two policies have been suggested for lightening this load: gradualism and indexation.

Gradualism. To move from c' to c requires reducing the rate of growth of the money supply drastically. Even if this is done all at once—say, the rate of growth of money supply is cut from 13 percent to a permanent 3 percent—the economy may require 3 to 5 years to move along $c'bc$ to c. During these years, the economy would have to endure considerable unemployment. A gradualist policy might lessen the impact on unemployment. Instead of reducing the growth of money supply from 13 percent to 3 percent all at once, monetary authorities might do it gradually over a period of, say, 5 years. Moreover, in order to persuade the public to lower its expectations about inflation, the monetary authorities would announce in advance the scheduled reductions in the rate of monetary growth. If expectations are rational, when people believe the government policy announcements they will immediately lower the anticipated rate of inflation. If the people do not believe the government's monetary-growth

Figure 10   The Unemployment Costs of Reducing Inflation

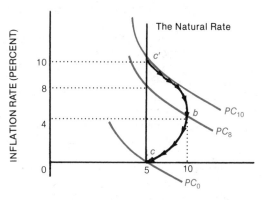

The economy is initially operating at c'—at the natural rate of 5 percent unemployment with an anticipated inflation rate of 10 percent (which equals the actual inflation rate). Monetary authorities reduce the growth of the money supply and the rate of inflation begins to slow down. The economy begins to move along $c'bc$. Point b is a representative intermediate point: at b, the inflation rate is 4 percent, but the anticipated inflation rate is 8 percent; unemployment is 10 percent. Until the expected rate of inflation falls to 0 percent, the economy will continue to experience unemployment above the natural rate.

plans (they may have long ago lost faith in such pronouncements), the anticipated inflation rate will drop only when people see the actual inflation rate dropping.

Indexing. Some economists suggest that **indexing** the income tax, private wage contracts, unemployment insurance, and Social Security benefits to the actual rate of inflation will reduce the unemployment costs of reducing inflation.

> **Indexing** is the tying of the rate of increase of the variable being indexed (wages, income taxes, Social Security benefits) to the actual inflation rate. Because Social Security payments are indexed to the inflation rate, for example, they will rise by the rate of actual inflation.

One reason an unanticipated decline in the rate of inflation increases unemployment is that wage contracts are fixed in money terms. A three-year wage contract builds in an anticipated rate of in-

Example 2   Disinflation and Distressed Bargaining in the 1980s

One reason that unanticipated deflation (or disinflation) increases unemployment is the existence of overlapping union contracts. During an unanticipated deflation, selling prices are free to fall, but union wages tend to remain rigid because of wage adjustments negotiated earlier. As selling prices fall while nominal wages remain rigid, real wages rise, and firms cut back on employment.

A typical union contract is negotiated on a multiyear basis. A first-year wage increase is specified in the contract along with specific nominal-wage increases over the remaining years of the contract. In many cases, the contract contains a *cost-of-living adjustment* (COLA), which automatically raises nominal wages in subsequent years by a certain percentage of the inflation rate. The nominal-wage increases dictated for later years of the contract reflect the union's inflationary anticipations at the time the contract was negotiated. Thus, 4-year contracts signed during a time of high inflationary expectations tend to call for substantial nominal-wage increases over the life of the contract.

When unanticipated deflation (or disinflation) strikes (as it did between 1982 and 1984), the extent of the rise in unemployment will depend upon the rigidity of union wages. One of the surprising features of the 1982–84 disinflation was the unexpected downward flexibility of union wages. In 1981, the average wage adjustment under major collective bargaining agreements was 9.5 percent. In the first 9 months of 1984, this figure had fallen to 4.0 percent. The rapid and substantial drop in

union-wage increases between 1982 and 1984 can be attributed to several factors. First, first-year wage adjustments under new settlements fell abruptly from an annual change of 9.8 percent in 1981 (slightly in excess of actual 1981 inflation) to 2.5 percent in 1984 (well below the actual rate of inflation in 1984) as outlined in the accompanying table. In 1981, only 8 percent of workers had first-year settlements that either reduced nominal wages or held them steady. In 1983, 37 percent of workers received either a wage cut or no wage increase under first-year settlements. The second factor accounting for the surprisingly rapid adjustment of union wages was the effect of COLAs. With declining inflation, automatic wage adjustments became smaller. A third factor was the growing incidence of *distressed bargaining.* In a growing number of distressed industries, unions agreed to renegotiate existing contracts. Unions in distressed industries agreed to forgo cost-of-living adjustments mandated in their union contracts in order to preserve jobs. Distressed bargaining also resulted in contract modifications that deferred wage adjustments.

Collective bargaining has showed considerably more flexibility in adjusting union wages to disinflation than most economists would have predicted. ∎

Source: Robert S. Gay, "Union Wage Settlements and Aggregate Wage Behavior in the 1980s," *Federal Reserve Bulletin,* December 1984, p. 848.

Major Collective-Bargaining Agreements	Percentage Increase					
	1979	1980	1981	1982	1983	1984
Total effective wage change	9.1	9.9	9.5	6.8	4.0	4.0
First-year adjustment, new settlements	7.4	9.5	9.8	3.8	2.6	2.5
Inflation rate (GNP deflator)	8.6	9.2	9.4	6.0	3.8	3.7

flation. If the actual inflation rate is below the anticipated rate, wage costs will rise more rapidly than product prices, and there will be less employment. If money wages are indexed to the actual inflation rate, the rate of increase of money

wages will automatically respond to reductions in the inflation rate. As Friedman has written:

> Here is an employer who has committed himself to paying higher and higher wages at a fixed rate without an escalator clause. When the process of slow-

ing inflation starts, he suddenly discovers that the prices at which he sells his product aren't going up as fast as they were before. What's he going to do? His costs stay up. He can't do anything about costs, so he has to cut down on his output. With indexation, his costs would, after a lag . . . also adjust. Therefore he would not be under anything like as much pressure to reduce his output and employment.[7]

The main objection to indexing is that it may formalize the wage/price spiral. On the way down, indexing might prove beneficial, but on the way up, wages would increase more than they otherwise would have. The fear is that indexation would feed inflation on the way up.

The main difficulty with Friedman's proposal is how to put it into operation. The indexing of income taxes has already been accomplished through legislative action, but what about private wage and price contracts? Friedman opposes passing a law that requires indexing of private contracts, and so would most other economists. The question, therefore, is: why should business firms start indexing on their own?

The last two chapters were concerned with inflation and unemployment and have suggested possible policies to deal with reducing the rate of inflation with minimum effects on unemployment. If the problem of inflation were solved, the economy would still be subject to ups and downs in unemployment—the business cycle. The next chapter explores how the business cycle can be stabilized.

Summary

1. Stagflation is the combination of high unemployment and high inflation in a stagnant economy. The original Phillips curve showed a stable negative relationship between unemployment and inflation. It predicted that to reduce inflation, a higher unemployment rate had to be accepted and that to reduce unemployment, a higher inflation rate had to be endured. Recent U.S. history shows that the typical Phillips-curve relationship held for the 1960s but not for the 1970s, when increasing inflation was accompanied by increasing unemployment.

2. Quits, firings, new entrants, and reentrants account for most of unemployment. Individuals unemployed for these reasons are engaged in searching in the labor market. An actual inflation rate that is greater than the anticipated rate will cause the unemployment rate to fall because of less searching. An actual inflation rate that is less than the anticipated rate will cause unemployment to rise because of more searching. Layoff unemployment also rises when actual inflation is less than anticipated (and falls when the reverse is true).

3. Milton Friedman and Edmund Phelps offered the natural-rate hypothesis to explain the phenomenon of stagflation. They argued that the Phillips curve will shift up with the anticipated rate of inflation. Because the economy tends to return to the natural rate in the long run, the different Phillips curves tend to pass through the natural rate.

4. The new Phillips-curve hypothesis is consistent with recent American experience. Unemployment does vary with unanticipated inflation, and the new Phillips curve does explain accelerating inflation. If the government attempts to hold the unemployment rate below the natural rate, inflation will accelerate. Unanticipated reductions in the rate of inflation cause increases in unemployment. Therefore, political pressures will cause the government to use stop-and-go economic policies. Stop-and-go economic policies may lead to the political business cycle.

5. Inflation can be reduced by permanently lowering the rate of growth of the money supply, but until inflationary expectations fall, the unemployment rate will rise. The unemployment costs of fighting inflation can extend over a period of years. Gradualism is one solution to the problem of fighting inflation without creating too much unemployment in the process. Instead of a once-and-for-all reduction in money-supply growth, the government could announce and carry through a policy of gradually reducing money-supply growth. Another solution is indexing private contracts, income taxes, and government benefit programs.

7. The American Enterprise Institute for Public Policy Research, *Indexing and Inflation* (Washington, D.C.: AEI Institute, 1974), p. 21.

Key Terms

stagflation
Phillips curve
short-run Phillips curve
long-run Phillips curve
disinflation
indexing

Questions and Problems

1. ''The Friedman-Phelps natural-rate hypothesis unites microeconomics and macroeconomics.'' Evaluate this statement.

2. Explain why inflation will likely not affect real behavior (the job choices of individuals, the production decisions of firms) when it is anticipated. Why would it then affect real behavior when it is unanticipated?

3. How are actual and anticipated inflation related when unemployment is above the natural rate? When unemployment is below the natural rate?

4. Explain why the short-run Phillips curve shows a negative relationship between inflation and unemployment. Explain why the long-run Phillips curve is vertical.

5. If the rate of inflation anticipated by workers is 5 percent, but the actual rate of inflation turns out to be 10 percent, how would this surprise affect employment decisions?

6. What will be the consequences when monetary authorities attempt to hold the unemployment rate permanently below the natural rate? Explain your answer with aggregate supply-and-demand diagrams.

7. Evaluate the ability of different proposals to combat inflation without creating serious unemployment in the process.

8. In the inflation/unemployment scatter diagram (Figure 3), the dots for 1974 and 1975 appear to be unusual. Explain why they are unusual.

9. Explain why firms would be more reluctant to lay off workers when a firm finds it harder to fill positions with qualified applicants.

10. What happens to the unemployment rate in the following situations?
   a. Initially, the anticipated rate of inflation is 5 percent and the actual rate of inflation is also 5 percent.
   b. In the next period, there is an unexpected decline in the inflation rate to 2 percent. Show what will happen to the unemployment rate.
   c. In the following period, inflationary expectations drop to 2 percent, and the actual inflation rate is also 2 percent.

11. Explain what happens to the costs of job search from the perspective of the unemployed job seeker when there is unanticipated inflation. What happens when inflation is anticipated?

12. Why would a worker on layoff behave differently from a worker who has been fired? What factors determine whether the worker on layoff actively searches for a different job?

13. This chapter considered the consequences of monetary and fiscal authorities aiming for an unemployment rate below the natural rate. What would happen if they aimed for an unemployment rate above the natural rate?

14. Explain why some reformers believe that lengthening the term of the Presidency would help eliminate the political business cycle.

Suggested Readings

Friedman, Milton. *Dollars and Deficits*. Englewood Cliffs, N.J.: Prentice-Hall, 1968.

Okun, Arthur. *Prices and Quantities*. Washington, D.C.: Brookings Institution, 1981.

Phelps, Edmund S. *Inflation Policy and Unemployment Theory*. New York: W. W. Norton, 1972.

Tobin, James. "Inflation and Unemployment." *American Economic Review* 62 (March 1972): 1–18.

17

Stabilization Policy

Chapter Preview

The most controversial question in macroeconomics today is how to stabilize business cycles. Economists are widely agreed about many things, but economists still disagree on how best to keep inflation under control, and how to keep unemployment from getting out of hand. These issues worry the average person on the street who looks to policymakers and economists for answers.

Activists argue that monetary and fiscal policies should be deliberately used to moderate the business cycle. *Nonactivists,* on the other hand, argue that deliberate countercyclical policies should not be followed. They believe that deliberate policy should be replaced by a stable monetary and fiscal framework and that rules should be established in place of activist policies. Activist economists usually follow the tradition of Keynes; nonactivists are usually monetarists or proponents of *rational-expectations theory* (described in Chapter 19). The monetarist/Keynesian controversy began with arguments over whether monetary or fiscal policy is more important but has spilled over into the broader debate of activism versus nonactivism.

This chapter focuses on the activist/nonactivist debate. It presents the cases for and against activism and nonactivism. It also describes actual macroeconomic policy over the past quarter century in terms of the activist/nonactivist debate.

Fiscal-policy actions are changes in government expenditures or tax schedules for the purpose of achieving macroeconomic goals. *Monetary-policy* actions are changes in the money supply or the rate of growth of the money supply for the purpose of achieving macroeconomic goals. As noted in earlier chapters, both monetary and fiscal policy work through their effect on aggregate demand (and sometimes aggregate supply). The discussion that follows refers to aggregate-demand policies if no distinction between monetary and fiscal policy is needed. ∎

THE POLICY OPTIONS

Activism

Activist policy deliberately manipulates fiscal and monetary policies to iron out fluctuations in the business cycle.

> An **activist policy** is one that selects monetary- and fiscal-policy actions on the basis of perceived economic conditions and that changes as economic conditions change.

An activist policy does not include the use of built-in fiscal stabilizers or changes in government spending or taxation carried out for reasons of public finance (for example, raising revenue to support public goods like police protection or national defense). The objective of activist policy is to soften the fluctuation of the business cycle. Activists argue that it is too costly to sit on the sidelines and wait for the economy to cure itself. They argue that the tools are available to moderate (if not eliminate) the ups and downs of economic activity. Activist policies can be carried out either through *feedback rules* or *discretionary policy*.

Feedback Rules.   Activist policy can be rigid in the sense that one can set policy dials to respond in a predetermined manner to changes in the state of the economy through the use of a **feedback rule.**

> A **feedback rule** establishes a feedback relationship between activist policy and the state of the economy.

For example, a simple monetary-policy feedback rule might be to raise monetary growth by 1 percent for every 1 percent increase in the unemployment rate above a specified unemployment-rate target. A fiscal-policy feedback rule might be to increase government expenditures by a certain percentage for every 1 percent increase in the unemployment rate above a target rate. Once the state of the economy changes in a specific manner, feedback rules prescribe the monetary and fiscal policies that respond to the change.

Discretionary Policy.   Feedback rules are fixed rules. Opponents of fixed rules argue that different economic situations may call for subtle policy differences. The optimal feedback rule may be difficult to determine. If policy making is an art rather than a science, it is better to let the President's Council of Economic Advisers, the Treasury, Congress, and the Fed decide what monetary and fiscal policies are appropriate in each circumstance. Economic policymakers can look at a number of indicators of the state of the economy—inflation, unemployment, interest rates, the balance of payments, and political factors—to determine monetary and fiscal policy. Rather than tying their hands with rigid feedback rules, it may be better to rely on the judgment of those responsible for the economic health of our nation.

How active should activist policies be? Should stabilization policies respond only to major disturbances or to small changes in the business cycle? In the heady days of the 1960s, economists spoke of **fine tuning.**

> **Fine tuning** is the frequent use of discretionary monetary and fiscal policy to counteract even small movements in business activity.

Today few economists argue for fine tuning but believe that the dials should be adjusted only in response to major movements in real GNP and inflation. Feedback rules could be written in a way that allows for a range of fluctuation in real GNP and unemployment to occur before any policies are activated.

Nonactivism

The major spokesperson for nonactivism, Milton Friedman, argues for a stable monetary and fiscal framework without activism. In the view of nonactivists, attempts to deliberately manage monetary and fiscal policy should be scrapped as ineffective and even harmful; **nonactivist policy** will yield macroeconomic results that are superior to activism.

> A **nonactivist policy** is one that is independent of prevailing economic conditions and that is held steady when economic conditions change.

Friedman's proposal for nonactivism consists of two parts:

Figure 1   The Policy Options

(a) How Activist Policy can Restore the Economy to the
    Natural Rate of Output

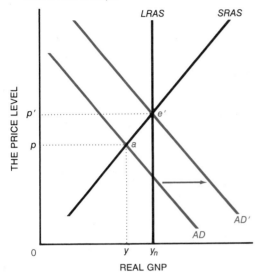

(b) How Nonactivist Policy (the self-correcting mechanism)
    can Restore the Economy to the Natural
    Rate of Output

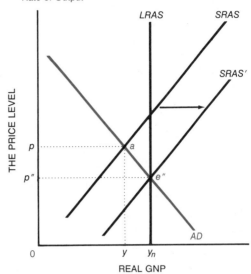

Panel (a) shows how activist policy can be used to return an economy that is in a deflationary gap (producing output below the natural level) to the natural level of output. Activist policy could be used to increase aggregate demand (shifting AD to AD'). At the higher aggregate demand, the economy produces y_n and the price level has risen from p to p'. Panel (b) shows how nonactivism (working through the self-correcting mechanism) restores the economy to the natural level of output. Because the economy is producing less than y_n, the price level will fall. As prices and wages fall, short-run aggregate supply increases from $SRAS$ to $SRAS'$. The economy is restored to producing y_n and the price level has fallen from p to p''.

1. There should be a fixed monetary rule that requires constant (or nearly constant) growth of the nominal money supply year after year at a rate equal to the long-run average growth rate of real GNP.

2. The federal budget should be balanced over the business cycle. Surpluses during the recovery phase should cancel out deficits during the recession stage. Government spending should be dictated by the need for public spending and not by the needs of discretionary fiscal policy.

Nonactivists argue that such a stable monetary and fiscal framework would provide the proper setting for long-run economic stability. The self-correcting mechanism would work at its maximum efficiency under a fixed monetary rule and a cyclically balanced budget.

The Self-Correcting Mechanism Versus Activist Policy

The choice between activism and nonactivism is illustrated using the now-familiar tools of aggregate demand and short-run and long-run aggregate supply. Figure 1 shows an economy (at point a) that is in a deflationary gap—producing output below the natural level of output. The goal is to return the economy to the natural level of output. Panel (a) shows the activist approach. In response to the prevailing deflationary gap ($y < y_n$), expansionary monetary and fiscal policies are applied. Aggregate demand increases from AD to AD'. The economy moves up the short-run aggregate-supply curve from a to e', and the economy returns to producing the natural level of output y_n. The increase in aggregate demand has raised the price level (from p to p').

Panel (b) shows the nonactivist approach to restoring equilibrium through the self-correcting mechanism. The economy is initially operating at point *a* once again, in a deflationary gap. As a consequence of operating below the natural level of output, the price level starts to fall (deflation). As the price level drops (and wages fall), the willingness of firms in the economy to supply output at each price level increases. The short-run aggregate-supply curve shifts to the right from *SRAS* to *SRAS'*. Insofar as the price level will continue to fall until the natural level of output is restored, the aggregate-supply curve will shift until the economy reaches point *e''*, where it is producing y_n at the new price level p''.

As these diagrams show, both approaches (if followed properly) yield the same output result: the economy ends up producing the natural level of output. In the activist case, there has been an increase in the price level (from p to p'). In the nonactivist (self-correcting) case, the price level has fallen (from p to p''). The discussion that follows focuses on the pros and cons of the activist and nonactivist approaches in a real-world setting. Which approach should policymakers follow?

POLICY INSTRUMENTS

Previous chapters have described the **policy instruments** that can affect output, employment, and prices.

> **Policy instruments** are variables that affect output, employment, and prices.

The two major types of policy instruments are monetary-policy instruments and fiscal-policy instruments. They can be supplemented by a third type of policy instrument: **human-resource policy** (also known as *manpower policy*). Monetary policy is the deliberate control of the money supply (and sometimes credit conditions) for the purpose of achieving macroeconomic goals. Fiscal policy is the deliberate control of government spending and taxation for the purpose of achieving macroeconomic goals.

Although human-resource policy can have shorter-run effects on the economy, its primary effect is on the natural rate of unemployment.

The fact that there is more than one policy instrument means that policymakers may be able to select what they consider to be the appropriate blend of monetary growth, credit restrictions, government-spending level, tax rates, and training programs to achieve their macroeconomic goals.

> **Human-resource policy** is the use of government training programs, unemployment services, and unemployment-insurance programs to lower the natural rate of unemployment over the long run.

Differences in Potency

In the 1960s, there was a lively debate among economists over the relative potency of monetary versus fiscal policy. The Keynesians argued that fiscal policy, which in the Keynesian model has a more direct effect on aggregate demand, would be the most potent policy instrument. Monetary policy, which works indirectly through interest rates and investment demand in the Keynesian model, would be a less reliable and less powerful policy instrument. Monetarists argued that fiscal policy is a weak policy instrument, first, because increases in government spending would tend to crowd out (either directly or indirectly) private investment or consumption spending and, second, because tax changes may not affect permanent income. People base their consumption decisions on permanent income, not on current income; therefore, changes in tax policy that are not perceived as permanent changes are unlikely to affect private consumption spending.

The debate over the relative potency of fiscal and monetary policy led to the accumulation of a great quantity of historical and econometric evidence in the 1960s supporting both sides of the issue. Large econometric models of the U.S. economy based on Keynesian principles found that both fiscal and monetary variables affect output and prices. Milton Friedman and Anna Schwartz, in their authoritative study of the monetary history of the United States,[1] found that changes in fiscal policy did not appear to affect the steady historical relationship between money, GNP, and prices. In a famous study conducted by

---

1. Milton Friedman and Anna Schwartz, *A Monetary History of the United States,* 1867–1960 (Princeton, N.J.: Princeton University Press, 1963).

the Federal Reserve Bank of St. Louis,[2] no significant correlation was found between fiscal-policy instruments and real GNP, while significant correlations were found between monetary instruments and real GNP.

In recent years, there has been a convergence of activist and nonactivist opinion that has shifted attention away from this debate. Activist Keynesians agree that monetary policy is a potent policy instrument, while Milton Friedman has admitted that fiscal policy can affect output and prices.[3] The contemporary policy debate has shifted to the issue of activism versus nonactivism and away from the potency of different policy instruments.

Differences in Flexibility

Monetary policy is conducted by the Fed. As noted in the chapter on monetary policy, the Fed was set up in such a way as to insulate it from current political pressures, but the independence of the Fed is not complete. The Fed must take certain major political factors into consideration, but it is generally agreed that the Fed is more independent of political pressures than the President, the Treasury, or the Congress. The Fed is also in a position to act quickly, quietly buying or selling government securities, to change the money supply. The Fed can buy or sell government securities daily or once a year, largely hidden from public view. On a more visible level, the Fed can raise or lower the discount rate, change reserve requirements, and even impose credit controls. As earlier chapters have shown, the Fed's control of the money supply is not perfect (especially in the short run), but the Fed does possess the flexibility to change monetary policy on short notice.

The two instruments of fiscal policy are discretionary government spending and tax policy. The President of the United States submits spending budgets to Congress, but actual spending authorization can be granted only by Congress. The President must either sign or veto the spending bills approved by Congress. The President does not have the authority to cut out only parts of approved spending packages; instead, the President must accept or reject the entire bill. On occasion, the President can simply not spend the money authorized by Congress (called *impounding*), but the constitutional legality of this practice has been questioned. Although Congress has sought to develop procedures for gearing the total amount of federal spending to specific macroeconomic goals, this approach has never worked out well in practice. Given the current appropriation system, it is very difficult to conduct macroeconomic policy by manipulating the amount of federal-government spending. Tax policy is also determined by Congress. Proposals for tax changes can be made by the Treasury or can originate within the Congress. The current tax system is very complex and has developed in response to special-interest pressures. Nevertheless, the Congress has succeeded in the past in passing a number of tax bills that were specifically designed to achieve macroeconomic goals. Taxes were lowered in 1964, 1975, and 1981 for the express purpose of stimulating economic activity. The tax changes under consideration by Congress in 1985 and 1986 aimed more at simplifying existing tax codes than at manipulating aggregate demand.

Because of its independence and the flexibility of open-market operations, the money supply is the most flexible policy instrument.

Monetary policy is the preferred instrument of modern activists because of its greater flexibility and the ability of the Fed to act quickly.

Because of the inflexibility and uncontrollability of federal spending, the major instrument of fiscal policy is tax policy.

Matching Policies to Macroeconomic Goals

There is no single goal of macroeconomic policy. Everyone agrees that it would be desirable to have full employment, stable prices, and real GNP growth. Everyone agrees that it would be desirable to avoid the ups and downs of the business

---

2. The St. Louis model was developed by Leonall C. Andersen and Jerry L. Jordan, then of the St. Louis Federal Reserve Bank in "Monetary and Fiscal Actions: A Test of their Relative Importance in Economic Stabilization," *Federal Reserve Bank of St. Louis Review* 50, 11 (November 1968): 11–23.

3. Robert Gordon, *Macroeconomics* 3rd ed. (Boston: Little, Brown and Company, 1984), p. 389.

cycle (especially the downs). Business managers and families would like to have moderate interest rates. In the international arena, most people would like to avoid extreme fluctuations in the international value of the dollar and to achieve stable and growing world trade.

The full-employment target has been established as a national economic goal by the Employment Act of 1946. Although politicians understand quite well that people generally do not like high rates of inflation (and the accompanying high interest rates), price stability has not been entrenched as a legislative goal toward which policy makers are legally bound to strive. In making decisions on macroeconomic policy, politicians must be conscious not only of the economic health of the nation but also of their election prospects.

Rather than pursuing one single goal, macroeconomic policy aims to achieve a combination of goals. We want full employment combined with reasonable price stability and steady economic growth.

Conditions for Ideal Activist Policy

All economists agree the world would be a better place if the economy operated continuously at the natural rate of unemployment with moderate inflation or deflation. If activist policy could indeed be used to tame the business cycle, economists of all persuasions would embrace the notion of activist policymaking. The question is how effectively activist monetary and fiscal policy can be used to combat the business cycle. Can the activist approach achieve a result that is superior to the do-nothing approach?

The chapters on monetary policy and fiscal policy explained how, in principle, activist monetary and fiscal policy could be employed to combat deflationary or inflationary gaps. These chapters also described briefly the difficulties of selecting the appropriate monetary or fiscal policy in a real-world situation. The list of things that policymakers must know to conduct perfect activist policy for a particular time and place is fairly long:

First, policymakers must be able to anticipate perfectly impending changes in the private economy; that is, they must be able to foresee turning

points in the business cycle. They must know in advance that the economy is about to enter a recession and its exact timing and magnitude. They must know in advance when the recovery stage is to begin. In other words, policymakers must be able to anticipate exactly impending inflationary or deflationary gaps. Not only must they anticipate the gaps, they must also know the exact magnitude and duration of the gap.

Second, they must know what the natural rate of unemployment is at every point in time. As the previous chapter showed, the economy can suffer if policymakers aim at an unemployment rate that is either too high or too low. Yet the natural rate depends upon a wide variety of factors. It depends upon the demographic composition of the labor force; it changes when there are fundamental changes in job-search behavior. The natural rate also depends upon the success or failure of human-resource policies. There is no easy way to measure the natural rate, but it is important that policymakers know the natural rate at every point in time.

Third, they must be able to use their policy instruments in a timely fashion without undue political or other delays. If policymakers have perfect information about impending inflationary or deflationary gaps, this information is of little use if they cannot make necessary changes in policy instruments.

Fourth, policymakers must know with some precision when the policy actions will affect economic activity. They must know when a change in tax laws will actually begin to affect private spending. They must know when a change in the money supply will affect interest rates and aggregate demand. If policymakers do not know when policy actions will affect output, employment, and prices, they will not know which policy to select. They may select a policy that is appropriate for a deflationary gap only to have its effects felt when the economy has moved to an inflationary gap.

Fifth, policymakers must know by how much selected policy actions affect the economy. If the effects of a given change in taxes, government spending, or the money supply are larger than policymakers calculate, it is possible that the economy will move from, say, too much unemployment to too much inflation.

Finally, the policy moves of fiscal and monetary authorities should not be generally anticipated by firms and households.

As the above list reveals, the opportunities for policy miscues are great. Activist policymakers may respond to a nonexistent impending recession. Even if policymakers correctly anticipate a turning point in the business cycle, they may not be able to get the policy instrument into position in time (it may take years to pass a tax cut, for example). Policymakers will find the timing of policy moves difficult if the effects of policy changes on the economy are felt with some delays (and the delays are not always the same).

Both activists and nonactivists agree that policy makers must have the above information in order to conduct perfect activist policy. They also agree that policy makers unfortunately operate with less than perfect information. Thus, there is no disputing the fact that activist policy will not be error-free. The disagreement concerns just how imperfect the information can be without impairing the effectiveness of activist policy. Is activist policy conducted with imperfect information better than doing nothing?

THE CASE FOR ACTIVISM

The key conflict between the activists and nonactivists is whether or not deliberate monetary and fiscal policy should be used to stabilize the economy. The modern Keynesians support an activist policy. The monetarists believe that activist policy is ineffective at best and destabilizes the economy at worst. Rational-expectations economists believe that activist policy cannot stabilize the economy in the long run and will, at best, have only a short-run effect when the activist policy is not anticipated.

The GNP Gap

Modern Keynesian economists believe that the self-correcting mechanism does indeed operate in a stable monetary and fiscal framework. The private economy can generate enough steam on its own power to reach the natural rate of unemployment in the long run. No change in monetary or fiscal policy is required for this correction to oc-

cur; the adjustment to the natural rate is automatic. Even Keynes felt that in the long run, the economy would tend toward full employment. Some early Keynesians doubted even that; according to their doctrine of *secular stagnation,* as the economy grew the gap between full-employment saving and investment would widen, and a growing government sector would be required to achieve full employment. Modern evidence on the consumption function has demonstrated that secular stagnation is not a threat.

In spite of the operation of the self-correcting mechanism, modern Keynesian economists assert that sharp fluctuations in real GNP and employment will naturally occur if monetary and fiscal policy are held constant. The economy is subject to all kinds of shocks. Investment is naturally unstable because of the accelerator and changing expectations; supply shocks can disrupt the economy; unpredictable shifts in consumer demand take place. Changes in autonomous spending induce magnified changes in real GNP and unemployment through the multiplier. If the economy is beset by adverse supply shocks, both unemployment and prices can be pushed up.

The modern Keynesian rationale for activist stabilization policy is that *waiting for the economy to cure itself by wage and price adjustments (the self-correcting mechanism) is too costly.*

When the economy is subjected to an adverse demand or supply shock, the economy will not be operating at full employment. In addition to the private anguish of unemployment, society must bear a social cost—the cost of lost output. If the economy had been operating at full employment, a larger real GNP would have been produced. The **GNP gap** measures this loss of output.

> The **GNP gap** is the difference between current GNP and *potential GNP* (the output the economy would conceivably have produced at full employment) and is a measure of the social costs of unemployed resources.

No one knows for sure the exact size of the GNP gap. First, full employment is difficult to define exactly. How much unemployment is voluntary? Are discouraged workers unemployed? How much unemployment is the result of hidden employment in the underground economy? Sec-

Example 1   How Well Can We Predict the Economic Future?

Effective activist policy requires being able to foresee turning points in the business cycle. To apply the policy tools of discretionary monetary and fiscal policy, we need to know in advance if the economy is about to enter a recession. We need to know if a recovery is about to turn into an inflationary boom.

The two most widely used sources of information concerning the future of the economy are the index of leading indicators, released on a monthly basis by the Department of Commerce, and economic forecasts prepared by private and government economists. How useful are the index of leading indicators and economic forecasts in predicting the future?

As discussed in Chapter 5, the *index of leading indicators* is based upon the principle that certain measures of economic activity (such as the stock market, the number of housing starts, the length of average work week) will turn down before the general downturn in business activity. The index of leading indicators did indeed turn down before each recession, but as Chapter 5 explained, there are two problems. The first is that the index of

leading indicators gives off false alarms. The 1960s was a decade of uninterrupted expansion, but the index of leading indicators signaled three recessions that never occurred. The second problem is that the lag between the leading-indicator signal of a downturn and the actual downturn varies. The index peaked 23 months before the 1957-58 recession, 5 months before the 1974-75 recession, and only 3 months before the 1982 recession. Even if we know that a recession is coming, the leading indicators still do not tell us when.

Both government and private forecasters failed to forecast the 1974–75 recession (missing the mark by about 35 percentage points) and in 1982, private forecasters were off by 2 percentage points while government forecasters missed by an astonishing 45 percentage points. Forecasters also failed to foresee the vigorous recovery after 1982.

The record of the index of leading indicators and of economic forecasters has not been good. At this point, we are not able to foresee the economic future with a reasonable amount of accuracy. ■

---

ond, it is difficult to estimate what unemployed resources would have produced had they been employed. Table 1 supplies estimates of the GNP gap for the period 1975 to 1984. These figures show that the economy lost an estimated $1.5 trillion worth of output between 1975 and 1984 by operating at less than full employment. As a percent of actual GNP, the GNP gap totals 4.8 percent. By operating below full employment, the economy lost about 5 percent of its potential output. The GNP gaps are greatest during recession years and in years immediately following a recession (1975–76, 1980–81, 1981–82).

According to the Keynesian position, the GNP gap is the price society must pay while waiting for the self-correcting mechanism to operate. In the Keynesian view, it is better to use activist policies to speed up the movement toward full employment.

If the figures in Table 1 are at all accurate, they suggest that the economy in the past decade has been subject to a number of shocks (the sup-

ply shocks of the mid- and late 1970s, the unanticipated disinflation after 1982). Each of these disturbances cost the economy lost output.

The objective of activist policy is to limit the private and social costs of unemployed resources by speeding up the economy's adjustment toward full employment.

Once the economy experiences such a disturbance, modern Keynesians question how rapidly it can respond through the natural self-correcting mechanism. They point back to the Great Depression when real wages actually rose after 1932 even though there was massive unemployment. They point to the experience of England during the Great Depression when money wages refused to fall despite massive unemployment. For the modern period, they cite the downward inflexibility of wages introduced by overlapping multiyear contracts. They warn that, as long as wages and

Table 1   The GNP Gap (billions of 1984 dollars)

Year	Potential GNP	Actual GNP	GNP Loss
1975	2891	2701	−190
1976	2987	2847	−140
1977	3089	3003	−86
1978	3194	3145	−49
1979	3293	3245	−48
1980	3389	3241	−148
1981	3491	3322	−169
1982	3592	3264	−328
1983	3699	3371	−328
1984	3811	3753	−58
Total	33,436	31,892	−1,544

GNP gap ÷ Actual GNP = 4.8%

Source: *Economic Report of the President,* 1980, p. 181. These figures are updated to 1984 using data from Robert Gordon, *Macroeconomics,* 3rd ed. (Boston: Little, Brown, and Company, 1984), Table B-1 and the authors' own calculations for 1983–84 from Department of Commerce news reports.

prices are rigid (or slow to adjust) in the downward direction, the self-correcting mechanism of deflation (or disinflation) will be very slow in restoring the economy to full employment.

Activism Versus Doing Nothing

Proponents of activism admit that the conduct of discretionary activist policy is difficult. They readily admit that mistakes have been made in the past and that mistakes will continue to be made in the future. Activists have never promised perfect activist policy. Rather their main argument is that imperfect activist policy is superior to a do-nothing policy. The best criterion for judging activism is whether it has produced results that are better than those that would have been produced by nonactivism.

Throughout most of the period (from the 1960s to 1985, activist policies of one kind or another were used to combat the business cycle. Discretionary monetary and fiscal policies were used in an attempt to soften the fluctuations of unemployment and inflation. Yet even activist economists agree that the last 25 years have seen considerable unemployment, recessions, inflation, and even stagflation.

The fact that the business cycle remains de-

spite the use of activist policy does suggest that discretionary policies have not worked perfectly. In defense of activism, it could be argued that activist policies prevented the business cycle from fluctuating even more. Perhaps activist policies avoided a Great Depression or a hyperinflation. At least two pieces of evidence support the claim that activism has reduced the GNP gap.

1. The history of fluctuations in real output is shown in Figure 2, which plots the annual rates of growth of real GNP from 1890 to 1984. The historical data show that, while the business cycle has not been eliminated, it has become less severe since activist policies first came into use after World War II. Episodes of negative real growth still occur, but severe depressions have been avoided. According to Keynesians, the experience of the last 30 years provides dramatic evidence that activist policy has reduced the amplitude of economic fluctuations.

2. The experience of high unemployment that accompanied the roughly constant monetary policy in the mid-1970s has been cited by Keynesians in support of activist policies. Franco Modigliani in his 1976 address to the American Economic Association pointed to this period as an example of how the absence of activism can lead to excess unemployment.[4]

In 1973, 1974, and 1975, the annual rates of growth of money supply were 5.5 percent, 4.3 percent, and 4.8 percent, respectively. These percentages indicate an almost constant rate of growth of the money supply over a three-year period. During this time, the economy went through a great recession. Unemployment was 5.6 percent in 1974, soared to 8.5 percent in 1975, and then declined slightly to 7.7 percent in 1976. According to Modigliani, the constant growth of the money supply cost the economy dearly in unemployment and lost output.

The recession of 1974 to 1976 was in large measure caused by the explosion of oil prices. When an adverse supply shock of this magnitude occurs, activist Keynesians find it wasteful to let the economy grind back to full employment under

---

4. Franco Modigliani, ''The Monetarist Controversy, or, Should We Forsake Stabilization Policy?'' *American Economic Review* (March 1977), pp. 1–19.

the self-correcting mechanism. Policymakers must choose between doing nothing and paying the price of higher unemployment and lost output and following an activist policy of monetary and fiscal expansion that brings a higher rate of inflation.

Third, advocates of activism point to the successful use of discretionary tax cuts to stimulate employment and economic growth. Keynesian economic policy was first used in the 1960s in the Kennedy and Johnson administrations. During the 1960s, Keynesian economics was given its first test, and the first major use of discretionary fiscal policy was the Revenue Act of 1964.

The 1950s saw two recessions in which the unemployment rate rose to 5.5 percent (1954) and to 6.8 percent (1958). In the early 1960s, the unemployment rate remained in the 5–7 percent range. According to the Keynesian activists, this period illustrated a classic case of underemployed resources. Keynesians called for activist fiscal policies to lower unemployment and raise the growth of real GNP. The 1964 Revenue Act cut personal taxes by $10 billion—the equivalent of a 20 percent cut—and reduced corporate taxes by $3 billion, for an 8 percent reduction in corporate taxes.

How did Keynesian economics score on its first test? According to the calculations of Arthur Okun—one of the architects of economic policy during the 1960s—the 1964 tax cut increased GNP by $36.2 billion (GNP in 1964 was $638 billion). In 1964, the unemployment rate was 5.2 percent; two years later it had dropped to 3.8 percent. In the four years prior to the tax cut, real GNP increased by a total of 11.3 percent. From 1964 to 1967, real GNP expanded by a total of 15.4 percent. For the decade of the 1950s, real GNP grew by 38 percent; for the decade of the 1960s, real GNP grew by 47 percent. Fiscal policy operating from a starting point of unemployed resources did indeed appear to raise real output and employment.

In 1968, in response to relatively high inflation and low unemployment, a tax surcharge was imposed. By the standards of the 1960s, the 1968 inflation rate of about 4.5 percent was considered excessive. In 1975, in response to a high unemployment rate (8.3 percent), taxes were cut.

Most economists agree that tax policy changes in 1968 and 1975 did not have the desired effects on the economy, but critics point out that the tax increase of 1968 and the tax cut of 1975 were both billed as one-time tax changes and were, thus, unlikely to change permanent disposable income. It is still too early to assess the tax cuts put into place by the 1981 tax bill. Although the 1981 tax cuts initiated in 1981 and 1982 were motivated by supply-side considerations, they nevertheless should provide a useful test of activist Keynesian principles. They were initiated during a period of high unemployment, and the tax cuts were billed as permanent changes in tax rates. There has been an impressive economic recovery in 1983 and 1984 with rapid rates of real GNP growth and capital formation being recorded. More sophisticated analysis will be required before we know the role played by the 1981 tax-code revision in this recovery.

Fourth, activists argue that the known is better than the unknown. The United States has had 30 years of activism without major economic catastrophes like a Great Depression or a hyperinflation. Without activist policies, the United States might not be able to respond to some major economic emergency in the future with a suitable policy.

Activists argue that there is no way to know how the economy will behave if policymakers commit themselves to fixed rules. With a cyclically-balanced-budget rule, what would happen if the government were to receive unexpected revenue windfalls? How would one know when to suspend a fixed budgetary rule, as in the case of national emergency? With fixed-monetary-growth rules, how should the Fed respond to unforeseen types of new monies that the banks and near banks are so good at creating? Would we be able to suspend the fixed-monetary-growth rule in a national emergency? If so, how big an emergency would be required to suspend the rule? In effect, activists argue that nonactivism represents uncharted waters for a complex, modern economy. The unknown risks of nonactivism may be great.

Fifth, activists argue that our ability to carry out effective activist policy is improving over time. As time passes, we learn more about how the economy functions. The data-gathering and data-processing ability of private and government agencies is improving. Policymakers have learned from past mistakes. In the past quarter century, a number of important social experiments have been tried. There have been four discretionary tax changes. The basic operating rules of the Fed have been changed, and the Fed's countercyclical performance has improved since 1979. We have lived with both high and low federal deficits. The experiences gained from each of these social experiments form the basis for better activist policy today and in the future.

Activism and Inflation

Activism calls for expansionary policies when unemployment rises. Yet the modern experience with stagflation is that expansionary policies induce accelerating inflation.

To justify activist policy in a world of high inflation, policymakers must find some means of expanding aggregate demand—when deemed necessary for activist policy—without increasing the inflation rate. Modern Keynesians such as James Tobin, Paul Samuelson, Franco Modigliani, and Arthur Okun suggest incomes policies as a solution to this dilemma. The greatest challenge currently facing activist stabilization policies is to design a workable incomes policy.

Activists maintain that efficient market-based incomes policies can allow the use of activist countercyclical policy. As Chapter 14 explained, a tax-based incentive program (TIP) seeks to accomplish the goal of fighting inflation without driving up unemployment. Arthur Okun supports the TIP program:

> . . . The U.S. inflation rate will be lowered over the next decade; the serious question is whether that is going to be accomplished by inefficient and inhumane recessions, by stifling wage-price controls, or by some innovative, sensible method like TIP.[5]

THE CASE FOR NONACTIVIST RULES

The case for activist policy is that it is too costly to do nothing. Modern Keynesians, therefore, maintain that activist monetary and fiscal policies must be used to fight the business cycle. Mone-

tarists and rational-expectations economists offer a radically different policy prescription.

> The monetarist and rational-expectations view is that it is better to do nothing in the face of demand and supply shocks and to let the self-correcting mechanism work without interference.

The nonactivists have a more difficult task ahead of them to prove their case. They must not only show that the costs of the business cycle cannot be reduced by activist policies but that activist policies actually make the business cycle worse.

The monetarists, led by Milton Friedman, Karl Brunner, and Allan Meltzer, maintain that activist policies either fail to improve the business cycle or actually make the cycle worse. The rational-expectations school, led by Robert Lucas, Thomas Sargent, and Robert Barro, maintains that activist policies affect only inflation, not cyclical unemployment. Activist policies can make inflation better or worse but have no lasting effect on reducing real GNP fluctuations.

The case for nonactivism rests upon four claims: 1) the economy is much more stable than the activists contend; 2) it is too difficult to select appropriate activist policies; 3) activist policies are likely to make matters worse rather than better; 4) rational expectations may defeat activist policies.

The Stability of the Economy

Nonactivists grant that the private sector is subject to all kinds of disturbances. Private investment can change with the whims of the business community. There can be radical autonomous changes in raw-material prices. Families can go on an unexpected buying spree in one year and become thrifty in the next. The economy is constantly buffeted by disturbances. The question raised by the nonactivists is: Just how adept is the economy at returning itself to equilibrium?

Activist thinking has been heavily influenced by the experiences of the 1930s when the self-correcting mechanism appeared to work slowly (if at all) at restoring the economy to full employment. Nonactivists maintain, first, that the Great Depression was largely the result of policy blun-

---

5. Arthur Okun, "Implications for Policy: A Symposium," Brookings Economic Papers, *Innovative Policies to Slow Inflation* (1978:2), p. 522.

ders that prevented the self-correcting mechanism from working (a point to be discussed below). Second, nonactivists maintain that the 1930s was a highly unusual period unlikely to be repeated. In the postwar era, economies have demonstrated greater flexibility. Nominal wages and prices do respond to the business cycle. The previous chapter, for example, demonstrated the abrupt drop in union wages after 1982 in response to high unemployment and disinflation. Even multiyear union contracts (supposedly the most downwardly rigid wage in the economy) can respond to changing economic conditions.

Nonactivists maintain that there is sufficient flexibility in wages and prices in modern economies to allow the self-correcting mechanism to work with reasonable speed.

The Difficulty of Devising Activist Policy

The monetarist attack against countercyclical policy rests upon the proposition that countercyclical policy historically has destabilized the economy. Monetarists conclude from the policy blunders of the 1930s that a constant growth rate of money supply is preferable to activist policy. Although the proponents of activism could defend activist policy by saying the biggest policy blunders were made when economists did not understand how the economy works, there are four reasons why countercyclical policy—even in this modern age—will still be destabilizing.

1. *There are long and variable lags in the effect of money on the economy.* If monetary authorities decide to combat a rising unemployment rate by increasing the growth of the money supply, this monetary expansion will not have an immediate effect on real output and unemployment. Friedman's own research suggests that there is a lag of from 6 months to 2 years before changes in money supply affect GNP. Thus, monetary authorities can never be sure when the change in money supply will begin to affect real output and employment. If the lag is short, the chances are less that the monetary policy will be inappropriate, but if the lag is long (say, 2 years), it may be that the policy will take effect when contraction rather than expansion is called for.

2. *The effects of fiscal policy are uncertain.* Because of permanent-income and crowding-out effects, it is virtually impossible to predict in advance the impact of fiscal policy. An accurate estimate would require knowledge in advance of the amount of crowding out and the effects of tax changes on consumption expenditures. Moreover, just like monetary policy, fiscal policy—if the fiscal multiplier is not zero—affects the economy only after a lag. Not only is fiscal policy difficult to implement because of recognition lags and implementation lags, fiscal planners must also be able to determine when the change in fiscal policy will affect economic activity.

3. *It is difficult for activist policymakers to know if the economy is approaching a recession.* Because of the lagged effects of monetary and fiscal policy, it is very important to be able to anticipate changes in the business cycle. If policymakers knew 6 months in advance, for example, that a recession was coming, it would be much easier to devise countercyclical policy. But recessions vary in length and in predictability. Through econometric models and indexes of leading indicators, policymakers attempt to anticipate recessions, but these models and indexes are far from accurate guides to the future.

Monetary and fiscal authorities who attempt to carry out activist countercyclical policies at the wrong time run the risk of actually destabilizing the economy. Monetarists believe policymakers do not possess sufficient information to diagnose and cure the disease before it spontaneously corrects itself. By acting without adequate information, they may actually use the wrong medicine and make the patient even worse.

4. *Activist policies can aim for the wrong target.* Most modern economists agree that the appropriate target of activist policy is the natural rate of unemployment. If the economy is operating with an unemployment rate above the natural rate, expansionary policies can lower unemployment without accelerating inflation. But policymakers may not always know what the natural rate is at any point in time. The natural rate itself changes from year to year. Changes in the composition of the labor force change the natural rate. Substantial raw-material price changes may permanently affect the natural rate. Since the natural rate itself fluctuates, it is difficult to chase it with deliberate policy actions. As Chapter 15 showed,

Figure 2   The Annual Rate of Growth of Real GNP, 1890–1984

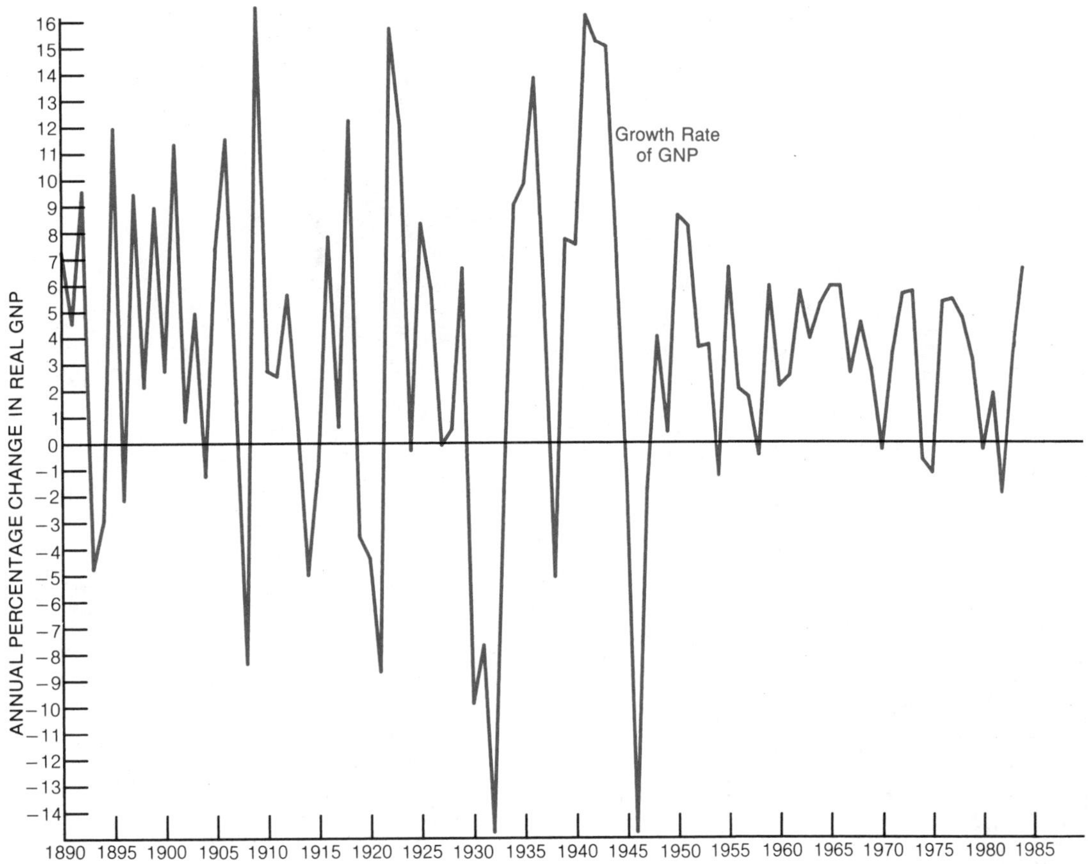

The business cycle has become less severe since the end of World War II.

Sources: *Historical Statistics of the United States; Economic Report of the President.*

aiming for a natural-rate target that is too low (a rate that is below the natural rate) leads to accelerating inflation.

The Counterproductive Effects of Activism

Figure 2 shows that the swings of the business cycle have narrowed in the postwar period—after activist policies came to be used to moderate the business cycle. According to the monetarists, the cycle was *not* moderated by countercyclical policy. Friedman and Schwartz, in their study of the U.S. business cycle over a century's time, conclude that discretionary policy was *destabilizing*

the economy, not stabilizing it. In their view, the Great Depression was a business downturn that was turned into a Great Depression because of a series of incredible government blunders and because the natural self-correcting mechanism was not allowed to work.

What were the policy blunders of the 1930s?

1. From 1929 to 1933, the nominal supply of money (M1) fell 25 percent. The price level also fell nearly 25 percent. Therefore, there was no change in the real money supply, but an increase in the real money supply was required to get the economy moving again. If monetary policy had been stable in the early 1930s, falling prices

Figure 3   The Annual Growth Rate of Money Supply, 1890–1984

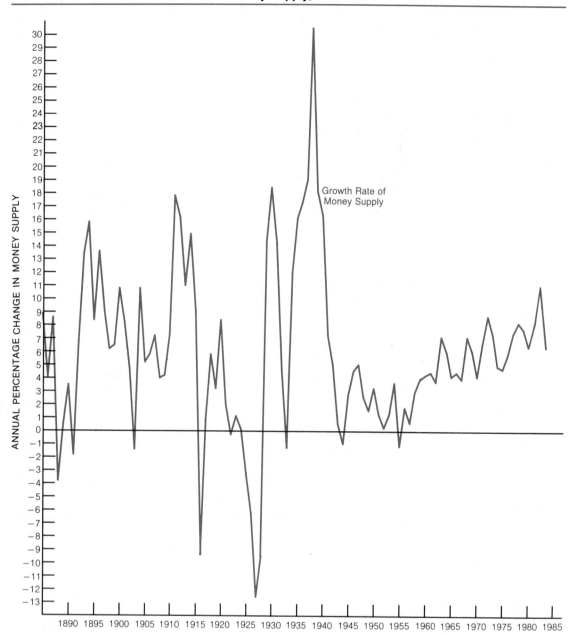

A comparison of this figure with Figure 2 shows that the reduction in the amplitude of GNP fluctuations coincides with the reduction in fluctuations in the growth rate of money supply in the past 30 years.

Source: *Historical Statistics of the United States; Economic Report of the President; Survey of Current Business; Federal Reserve Bulletin.* The percentage growth rate in money supply is based on M1 for the years 1915 to 1981 and includes time deposits (formerly M2) for the years 1890–1915.

Example 2   Monetary Rules: The Case of Switzerland

One objection to monetarist rules is that the known (activism) is better than the unknown (monetarist rules). The truth is that several countries (Switzerland, West Germany, and to a degree Japan) have been following monetarist rules in recent years without apparent damage. The most notable case is Switzerland—a country noted historically for its price stability. Over the past three years, the Swiss have set a target of 3 percent growth in the monetary base and each year the target has been met within half a percentage point. Stable monetary policy has been accompanied by steady noninflationary growth of real GNP. Being a part of the world economy, Switzerland was not spared the world recession of 1982, but the drop in output in Switzerland was modest compared to the drop in the rest of Europe, and its recovery was quicker. Because of its steady monetary policy, there is little interest in the release of monetary-growth data by the Swiss central bank (unlike the U.S. situation where the release of monetary data sets off fluctuations in interest rates). Monetary growth has been steady and predictable, and Swiss interest rates have remained around 5 percent even when interest rates in other countries were reaching new highs.   ■

Source: The Swiss—with a Grateful Yawn—have Steady Money Supply," *Christian Science Monitor,* December 20, 1984.

---

would have caused the real money supply to increase; the economy would not have fallen into the Great Depression.

2.   As Nobel prize winners James Tobin and Milton Friedman have pointed out, various government actions taken by Roosevelt's New Deal program caused wages and prices to rise after 1933 even though there was massive unemployment, while the self-correcting mechanism required falling wages and prices. The New Deal increased the power of labor unions, gave more monopoly power to business firms, and encouraged them to raise prices. In short, from 1933 to 1936 a supply-side inflation in the middle of a deep depression retarded the move towards full employment.[6] In terms of the aggregate supply/aggregate demand model, the *SRAS* curve shifted to the left while the *AD* curve may have remained constant.

3.   In 1937, in perhaps the most incredible act of self-destruction in American economic history, the Federal Reserve System doubled reserve requirements. The banking system did have large excess reserves at the time, but excess reserves were being held by banks because of the prevailing economic situation. Accordingly, the increase in the reserve requirement brought the needed money growth to a halt and sent the economy into another recession within the Great Depression.

4.   Large tax increases were passed in 1932 and 1937 during periods of massive unemployment.

Keynesians maintain that activist countercyclical policy is responsible for the reduced fluctuations in real GNP after the Second World War. Monetarists counter that the reduced amplitude of the business cycle is a consequence *not* of countercyclical policies but of a reduction in the amplitude of money-supply growth. The major episode of cyclical instability prior to the Second World War—the Great Depression—was itself caused by improper monetary policy, not by natural cyclical forces.

The monetarist evidence is presented in Figure 3 which shows the annual growth rate of the money supply since 1890. Comparison of money growth (in Figure 3) and output growth (in Figure 2) reveals that the reduction in the amplitude of GNP fluctuations coincides with the sharp reduction in the amplitude of money-supply growth. From this evidence, the monetarists conclude that

---

6. James Tobin, "Inflation and Unemployment," *American Economic Review* 62 (March 1972): 14; Milton Friedman, *Dollars and Deficits* (Englewood Cliffs, N.J.: Prentice-Hall, 1968).

the greater relative stability over the past 35 years is not the result of activist policy but of the increased stability of the rate of growth of the money supply.

In most cases, reductions in the rate of growth of money supply lead to recessions. Consider again the case of the Great Depression. Figure 3 shows that, beginning in 1926, the growth *rate* of money supply was reduced almost every year until 1933. This pattern holds up in the postwar period as well; postwar recessions were preceded by reductions in the *rate* of growth of money supply.

If the business cycle is caused by fluctuations in the rate of growth of money supply, monetarists believe that cyclical instability can be reduced or eliminated by eliminating the unstable growth pattern of the money supply. This belief is the rationale for Milton Friedman's 3 percent rule.

Monetarists argue that monetary authorities should be ordered to expand the money supply at a constant annual rate year in and year out. If the growth of money supply is held constant at a rate equal to the long-run growth of real GNP, cyclical instability and inflation could be reduced at the same time.

The Negating Effect of Rational Expectations on Activist Policy

Even if countercyclical policy is not destabilizing, as the monetarists claim, the logical case that activism should be used still has potential flaws. Some members of the rational-expectations school argue that countercyclical policies—*if predictable*—will have no impact on the business cycle. If both monetary and fiscal policies lead to predictable shifts in aggregate demand, as the Keynesians assume, shifts in aggregate demand that are correctly anticipated will be offset by rising prices and wages.

If monetary and fiscal authorities want to reduce unemployment, they might use monetary and fiscal expansion to stimulate aggregate demand. In order to persuade people to work more hours and firms to produce more real output, workers would have to perceive that their real wages were rising, and firms would have to perceive that their prices were rising more rapidly

than their costs. If people correctly anticipate the effects of expansionary policies on wages and prices, they will realize that real wages are not rising and that prices are not rising more rapidly than costs. Unless people are fooled by the expansionary policies, their real behavior will not change. Workers and firms will raise prices right along with the expansion of aggregate demand. At the economywide level, real GNP will not change and unemployment will not change. The expansionary policies will cause nominal GNP to rise as a consequence of rising prices, but real GNP will remain unchanged.

The full implications of the rational-expectations approach and the evidence for it are presented in Chapter 19.

IS THERE A MIDDLE GROUND?

The disagreement between activist Keynesians and nonactivist monetarists and rational expectationists appears profound. One side believes in activist policy; the other side says that countercyclical policies either do not matter or make matters worse.

If one examines the postwar development of macroeconomics, faint signs of agreement between activists and nonactivists are beginning to emerge. First, the two positions have come much closer in the last 25 years. The Keynesians began with the notion that money scarcely matters at all; now Keynesians and monetarists hold a more balanced view that both monetary and fiscal policy matter. Because of the greater flexibility of monetary policy, even Keynesians probably regard monetary policy as the major tool of countercyclical policy. Modern Keynesians have also largely abandoned the notion of fine tuning—the constant fiddling with the dials of discretionary policy. Instead, it is agreed that activist policy should respond only to major cyclical disturbances.

The fundamental monetarist critique of activist policy is that it is more likely to do harm than good. Activists also realize that policymakers have committed costly errors in the past. It is unlikely that policy blunders as large as those committed in the 1930s will ever be repeated. Presumably, the ability to forecast the business cycle improves over time; economists learn more from

Example 3   Lags and Monetary Policy

Economist Robert Gordon provides some informal estimates of the total lag involved in activist monetary policy. Gordon identifies five lags. First, the *data lag,* estimated to be 2 months long, occurs because the economic data must become available before a problem can be recognized. Second, the *recognition lag,* with an estimated length of 2 months, arises because once the data is available, the Fed must recognize that a problem exists. Third, a *legislative lag,* of approximately half a month, results when the Fed must decide on the appropriate policy. Fourth, the *transmission lag,* estimated at 1 month, occurs

because the Fed must use open-market operations and its other instruments to vary the money supply. Fifth, the longest lag (7.8 months) is the *effectiveness lag.* The effects of changes in the money supply on the economy are not felt immediately because it takes time for them to work their way through the economy. Can effective activist monetary policy be conducted with a total lag of 13.3 months? Activists would answer yes; nonactivists would say no. ∎

Source: Robert Gordon, *Macroeconomics,* 3rd ed. (Boston: Little, Brown and Co., 1984), p. 521.

experience about the effects of past policies. Yet economists are far from reaching the point where monetarists would be satisfied that policymakers know enough to devise error-free activist policy.

Monetarists have done the Keynesians a favor by pointing out how complex our economy actually is. They have shown that the multiplier analysis of Keynes paints too simple a picture. Crowding out, permanent-income effects, accelerating inflation, and expectations all markedly affect the way economic policy works.

The activists have pointed out the potential weaknesses of fixed rules. If money substitutes can be created, which money concept is to be used in applying fixed-monetary-growth rules? What type of default rules would be used to suspend the fixed monetary and fiscal rules in case of national emergency? These criticisms have prompted the nonactivists to reexamine and refine their proposals.

The activists and nonactivists do share an important common ground. They wish to achieve the same targets: full employment, moderate inflation, and real economic growth. Both schools dislike unnecessary unemployment; both schools recognize the private and social costs of recessions. They both agree that, in the long run, nonactivism would yield the desired end result. Both activists and nonactivists believe that the self-correcting mechanism works in the long run. The disagreement is basically over the amount of time required to allow the self-correcting mechanism to

do its work. Activists argue that it is important to use discretionary policy to speed up the return to full employment. The self-correcting mechanism works slowly, and activist policy (however imperfect) can return the economy to equilibrium more quickly than reliance on automatic forces. Nonactivists maintain that the self-correcting mechanism works with reasonable dispatch. Even if the self-correcting mechanism were slow-moving, the nonactivists would argue that the chances of activist policy blunders are too great to warrant interfering with automatic forces.

ACTIVISM AS THE CHOICE OF U.S. POLICYMAKERS

This chapter and previous chapters have shown that U.S. policymakers have chosen the activist-policy approach. Monetary growth rates have fluctuated considerably over the years, although the fluctuations have decreased in recent years (see Figure 3). Fluctuating growth rates of money do not by themselves prove that the Fed was intentionally pursuing activist monetary policies. As we pointed out in the chapter on money and banking, changes in economic activity and in currency-holding patterns can by themselves alter bank reserves and the money supply. Yet most economists agree that the Fed has used activist monetary policy (either directed toward interest-rate targets or monetary-growth targets) to attempt to moderate the business cycle. It is clear from the evidence that the Fed has not followed a fixed-monetary-growth rule—even after October 1979 when the Fed placed a higher priority on monetary-growth targets. There is an important distinction between following monetary-growth targets (which can be changed as economic conditions change) and a fixed-monetary-growth rule. The inflation chapter (14) pointed out that the Fed has altered its monetary-growth targets in response to changing economic conditions. Activist monetary policy is perfectly consistent with monetary-growth targets.

U.S. policymakers have made relatively frequent use of activist tax policy since the 1964 tax cut. In the postwar era, there have been four tax revisions that have been passed largely for activist policy reasons. These tax revisions have had different degrees of success, but it is clear that U.S. policymakers regard tax revision as a major instrument of activist fiscal policy. The data presented earlier in this book on federal deficits clearly demonstrate that U.S. policymakers have not followed the cyclically-balanced-budget rule advocated by the nonactivists. In fact, the inability of policymakers to balance the budget over the cycle despite the best intentions of several Presidents makes one sceptical about our ability to implement the balanced-budget rule.

The debate between activism and nonactivism continues. As new middle ground is discovered, new differences of opinion will emerge. The next chapter looks at how interest rates are determined, a key issue in macroeconomic policy.

Summary

1.   The two main macroeconomic policy options are activist policy and nonactivism. Activist policies aim to stabilize the business cycle; activist policies can be either discretionary or can use feedback rules. Nonactivist policy uses fixed rules. The two rules suggested by Friedman for nonactivism are: a) let the money supply grow at a constant rate and b) have a cyclically balanced budget.

2.   The policy instruments of macroeconomic policy are monetary policy, fiscal policy, and human-resource policy (which has long-run effects). Monetary policy is the most flexible policy instrument. In order to devise perfect activist policy, policymakers must: know about impending changes in the business cycle, know the level of the natural rate, be able to use policy instruments in a timely fashion, and know when policy changes will affect the economy.

3.   The chief argument for activism is that the self-correcting mechanism is too slow. The main evidence in favor of activism is the long-term reduction in GNP fluctuations since the Second World War. The negative experience with constant money growth between 1973 and 1976 is cited by some Keynesians in support of activism. Activists also point to successful countercyclical tax cuts and warn against the possible dangers of fixed rules. Activists must solve the problem of how to use discretionary policy without increasing inflation. Innovative incomes policies are seen by some Keynesians as the answer.

4.   The case for nonactivism rests on the following points: the economy is not as unstable as the activists believe; instability has been caused by policy blunders; the reduced GNP fluctuations since the Second World War are due to smaller fluctuations in monetary growth. Activist policy tends to be destabilizing because monetary lags make it difficult to devise discretionary policy, because the effects of fiscal policy are uncertain, because it is difficult to know when a recession is coming and how severe it will be, and because activist policy can aim for the wrong employment target (the natural rate is not known with certainty). Rational-expectations theory teaches that activist stabilization policy will not stabilize the economy if policy is anticipated.

5.   Modern Keynesians now take into account many of the monetarist points, such as crowding out, permanent income, accelerating inflation, and the role of expectations.

6.   U.S. policymakers have used activist policy to try to moderate the business cycle and have been unable to follow a cyclically-balanced-budget rule.

Key Terms

activist policy
feedback rule
fine tuning
nonactivist policy
policy instruments
human-resource policy
GNP gap

Questions and Problems

1. Distinguish between feedback rules and discretionary policy. What is meant by *fine tuning?*

2. Explain how crowding out affects the Keynesian analysis of fiscal multipliers.

3. If, as most economists believe, there is a self-correcting mechanism that automatically moves the economy toward full employment, how can anyone advocate discretionary policy? Will the economy not take care of itself?

4. This chapter pointed out that the advocates of nonactivism must demonstrate that activist policies tend to worsen the business cycle. What arguments are there that activism actually makes matters worse?

5. How could we have had the Great Depression of the 1930s if there is a self-correcting mechanism at work in the economy?

6. The rational-expectations argument is that expectations can defeat activist policy. Assume Congress decides to pass a tax cut to stimulate the economy. How could rational expectations defeat the purpose of the tax cut?

7. Explain the difference between monetary targets and monetarism. Is it correct to call the Fed's decision in October 1979 to follow monetary-growth targets a victory for monetarism?

8. This chapter showed that the conditions required for conducting ideal activist policy cannot be met in the real world. What is the activist defense of activist policy given the fact that conditions are imperfect?

9. Both activists and nonactivists use the greater stability of the economy after the Second World War in support of their positions. Explain how both sides can use the same data to support entirely different positions.

10. Some studies show that wages have responded more sensitively to unemployment in the 1980s than in the 1960s. For which period would the case for nonactivism be stronger if this is indeed the case?

Suggested Readings

Carlson, Keith and Roger Spencer. ''Crowding Out and Its Critics.'' Federal Reserve Bank of St. Louis, *Review* (December 1975), pp. 2–17.

Friedman, Milton and Walter W. Heller. *Monetary Versus Fiscal Policy.* New York: W. W. Norton, 1969.

Friedman, Milton. *A Program for Monetary Stability.* New York: Fordham University Press, 1960.

Meltzer, Allan H. ''Monetarism and the Crisis in Economics.'' *The Public Interest* (Special Issue, 1980), pp. 35–45.

Modigliani, Franco. ''The Monetarist Controversy, or Should We Forsake Stabilization Policies?'' *American Economic Review* 67 (March 1977): 1–19.

18

Interest Rates

Chapter Preview

This chapter examines different types of interest rates and analyzes why different interest rates are paid on different types of IOUs. It also distinguishes between the nominal interest rate and the real interest rate. This chapter will show how real interest rates depend upon the productivity of capital and upon the saving habits of the population and how a number of other factors, such as inflation, government deficits, international capital flows, taxes, monetary policy, and stock markets can also affect interest rates. Finally, this chapter considers how monetary policy can be used to control interest rates.

Why are so many people—from a business manager to a young married couple—so concerned about interest rates? Examples of businesses in which interest costs represent an important component of total costs are retailing (where inventories are financed by credit), residential and commercial construction (where new projects are financed by construction loans), farming (where spring planting is financed by bank loans), airlines (where new aircraft are purchased with borrowed funds), and electrical utilities (whose huge capital outlays must be financed through borrowing). Other businesses are affected by interest rates through the effect of rising interest rates on

the demand for their product. Residential home builders are hit twice by rising interest rates. Higher interest rates raise the cost of constructing new homes and reduce the demand for new homes. Rising interest rates raise the monthly mortgage payments and motivate prospective home buyers to remain in rented apartments or in their old homes. Rising interest rates tend to reduce the demand for *consumer durable goods*—new cars, washing machines, expensive television sets—which are typically purchased with credit.

Industries that are negatively affected by rising interest rates are called **interest-sensitive industries**. (See Example 1.)

> **Interest-sensitive industries** are industries, like automobile manufacturing, construction, farming, and retailing, whose sales and/or profits fall when interest rates rise.

Interest rates also affect the operation of state, local, and national government. State and local governments must borrow funds to build schools, highways, and public buildings. The federal government must borrow funds to finance the federal deficit. (See Example 2.) ■

THE VARIETY OF INTEREST RATES

The Prime Rate

The most highly publicized interest rate is the **prime interest rate.**

> The **prime interest rate** is the base, or reference, rate on which banks decide to price their loans. It may be regarded as the base cost of commercial bank credit.

The bulk of the value of business loans is made at the prime rate. The business firms that are able to borrow at the prime rate are those that have excellent credit ratings. It is a market interest rate that reflects the demand for and supply of bank credit. At one time, the prime rate was the rate of interest charged to the strongest, or "prime," business borrowers (GM, IBM, AT&T, Exxon). Now such firms have access to bank loans all over the world. In order for domestic banks to compete with banks elsewhere, those firms with the best credit ratings can borrow from domestic banks at less than the prime rate.

Figure 1 shows yearly averages of the prime rate from 1955 to 1984. Over this period the average prime rate was 7.5 percent. Over this nearly 30-year period the yearly average prime rate varied from a low of 3.2 percent in 1955 to a high of 18.9 percent in 1981. Figure 2 shows the prime rate on a monthly basis from January 1981 to the end of 1984. What is clear is that the prime rate—viewed either monthly or yearly—has been very volatile in the 1970s and 1980s.

Corporate Bonds (Aaa)

Triple-A (Aaa) corporate bonds are the long-term IOUs of virtually default-free corporations (General Motors, International Business Machines, and many others). There is virtually no risk that the company will not pay its interest and principal obligations. The holders of such bonds are exposed only to **price risk.** As we learned in Chapter 12, bond prices and interest rates vary inversely. When a bond offers fixed interest payments into the future, and the bond can be freely sold in secondhand bond markets, the higher is the interest rate, the lower is the market price of the bond.

Figure 1   The Prime Rate, Yearly, 1955 to 1984

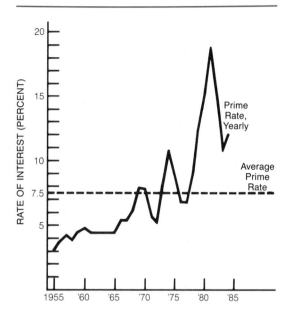

From 1955 to 1984 the average prime rate was 7.5 percent, but the prime rate has varied substantially over the years, reaching historic highs in 1981.

Source: *Federal Reserve Bulletin.*

> The **price risk** of a bond is the chance that the price of the bond will fall in secondhand markets. If the bond had to be sold before its maturity date (when the principal is due), it must be sold at a loss if interest rates rise.

The price risk long-term bondholders face is substantial. For example, suppose a bond promises a **coupon payment** of $100 a year in perpetuity.

> The **coupon payment** is the fixed interest-payment obligation due to the owner of a bond at stated regular intervals.

If the interest rate were 10 percent, a bond paying a $100 coupon every year would be worth $1,000. But if the interest rate rose to 15 percent, a bond paying the $100 a year would be worth only $667 (15 percent = $100/$667). As a consequence of the interest rate rising from 10 to 15 percent, the price of the bond falls from $1,000 to $667. The decline in the bond's price that ac-

Figure 2   The Prime Rate, Monthly

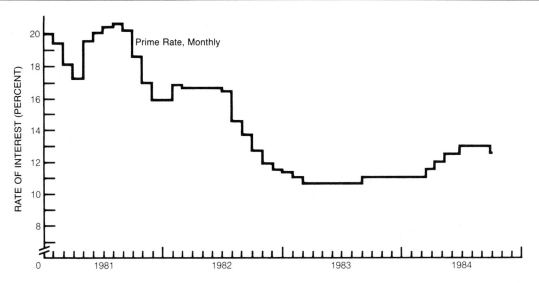

Prime Rate, Monthly

Month-to-month changes in the prime rate can be quite dramatic. From mid-1981 to late 1982, the prime rate dropped by almost half from more than 20 percent to about 11 percent.

Source: Board of Governors of the *Federal Reserve* System.

companies a rise in interest rates is the price risk.

Figure 3 shows the yearly averages of the Aaa corporate-bond rate from 1955 to 1984. The Aaa rate varied from a low of 3.1 percent to a high of 14.2 percent, with an average yield of 7.3 percent over the nearly 30-year period. Notice that the corporate-bond rate averages about the same as the prime rate, but the corporate-bond rate fluctuates less than the prime rate.

High-Grade Municipal Bonds

Municipal bonds are the IOUs of state governments, water districts, school districts, and other governmental units at the state or local level. High-grade municipal bonds bear very little default risk (many are backed by the state's power to tax), but, like corporate bonds, they are subject to considerable price risk.

Figure 3 also shows the history of interest rates on high-grade municipal bonds from 1955 to 1984 (on a yearly basis). Notice that the municipal-bond rate is always lower than the corporate-bond

rate. The municipal-bond rate has varied from a low of 2.5 percent in 1955 to a high of 11.6 percent in 1982, with an average rate of only 5.5 percent. Why is the interest rate on municipal bonds lower than the prime rate or the corporate-bond rate? The answer is that the federal government exempts the interest income from municipal bonds from the federal income tax. A corporate bond paying 8 percent nets only 6 percent after taxes if the holder is in a 25 percent tax bracket. Thus, investors will not be willing to buy corporate bonds unless they pay interest rates sufficiently higher than the tax-free municipal-bond rate on which they pay no taxes.

Federal Government Bills and Bonds

Chapter 12 described the 3-month Treasury bill, or "T-bill" (a promise by the U.S. Treasury to pay $1,000 in 90 days). T-bills sell at a discount from $1,000; the higher is the discount (or, in other words, the lower is the price), the higher is the interest rate. For example, a $1,000 3-month T-bill may sell for $985. Over a three-month pe-

Figure 3   Aaa Corporate and Municipal Bonds, 1955 to 1984

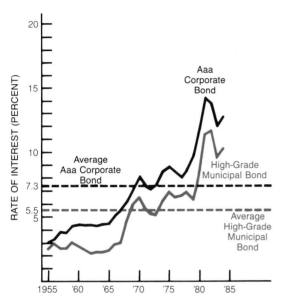

From 1955 to 1984 the Aaa corporate-bond yield averaged 7.3 percent while the high-grade municipal-bond rate averaged 5.5 percent because municipal bonds are tax-exempt.

Source: *Federal Reserve Bulletin.*

Figure 4   Short-Term Versus Long-Term Interest Rates

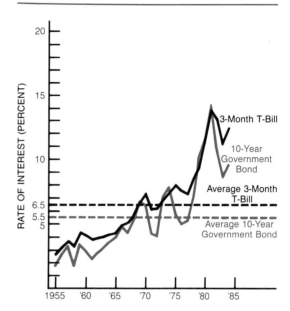

From 1955 to 1984 the interest rate on 3-month Treasury bills was generally less than the interest rate on 10-year government bonds (5.5 percent versus 6.5 percent, on the average). Long-term government bonds must pay a premium to compensate for their greater price risk. Generally speaking, however, the two interest rates moved up and down together. Short-term interest rates can exceed long-term rates when interest rates are expected to fall (notice the short-term interest rates exceeded long-term rates only on upswings).

Source: *Federal Reserve Bulletin.*

riod, $15 interest would be earned for a 3-month rate of 1.5 percent ($15/$1,000), or an annual rate of 6 percent (1.5 percent times 4). If the interest rate were 12 percent, the price of the T-bill would drop to $970: $30/$1,000 × 4 = 12 percent. Figure 4 shows the rate of T-bills from 1955 to 1984. It has varied from a low of 1.8 percent per year in 1955 to a high of 14 percent per year in 1981, with an average of 5.5 percent per year. T-bill rates have averaged about the same as tax-free municipal-bond rates. While investors must pay income tax on T-bill interest, T-bills pay a lower interest rate to compensate for their great liquidity. T-bills can be sold very quickly (the investor does not have to hold them for 3 months) and at very little price risk. For example, suppose you buy a new T-bill for $985 (an interest rate of $15/1,000 × 4 = 6 percent). A subsequent rise in interest rates to 12 percent in the next month would have a devastating effect on holders of

long-term bonds. But the T-bill would now be due in 2 months and could be sold for $980 ($20/1,000 × 6 = 12 percent). The loss is only $5 per $1,000.

Figure 4 also shows the interest rate on long-term U.S. government securities from 1955–1984. While the government issues many long-term bonds (longer than one year in maturity), Figure 4 shows the yield on only 10-year government bonds. This long-term rate has averaged 6.5 percent over the 1955–84 period, with a low of 2.8 percent and a high of 13.9 percent. The interest rates on long-term U.S. government securities has been slightly lower than those on Aaa corporate bonds.

Example 1   Interest-Sensitive Industries

The accompanying figure shows the empirical relationships between interest rates and residential construction (as measured by new housing starts), automobile production (as measured by the index of automobile production), and business failures for the period 1966 to 1984. Although the relationship is far from perfect, the figure shows the general tendency for housing starts and automobile production to be low when interest rates are high, and for housing starts and automobile production to be high when interest rates are low. The troughs for residential construction and automobile production (1970, 1975, 1981–82) correspond to peaks in interest rates. The relationship between the business-failure rate and interest rates is also apparent from the figure. Low rates of business failure tend to coincide with low interest rates and high rates of business failure tend to coincide with high interest rates, although the agreement between the two is not exact. ■

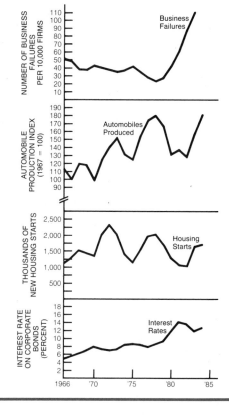

Source: Data from *Economic Report of the President*, February 1985.

Long-Term Versus Short-Term Rates

Two facts are important in comparing short-term and long-term rates. First, the long-term interest rate generally exceeds the short-term interest rate because the long-term rate must be higher to compensate the holder for the greater price risk. As already explained, the prices of long-term bonds fluctuate significantly when interest rates change. Exceptions occurred in the years 1973, 1974, and 1979–1981. What explains the exceptions? Generally speaking, when people have strong expectations that interest rates in the future will be lower than current interest rates, then long-term rates will reflect those expectations. For example, suppose the interest rate on a one-year security is 10 percent. If in one year people expect the interest rate on one-year securities to drop to 4 percent, today a two-year security need pay only

about 7 percent per year because $100 invested for two years at 7 percent yields about $114 in two years. The $100 invested for one year at 10 percent for one year and then reinvested as $110 at 4 percent also yields about $114 in two years. In other words, long-term interest rates are averages of current and expected future short-term interest rates. The data in Figure 4 are consistent with this explanation because short-term interest rates exceed long-term interest rates only when interest rates peak and might, thus, be expected to fall.

Second, short-term and long-term interest rates move together. While the short-term rates vary more than long-term rates, the cyclical behavior of the two interest rates is virtually identical. Since interest rates tend to move together, it is sometimes convenient to speak of "the" interest rate even though there are many different interest rates.

Figure 5   Anticipated Inflation and Interest Rates

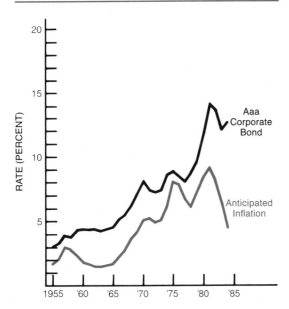

The anticipated inflation rate is here measured as the average of actual inflation over the preceding three years. Notice how the anticipated inflation rate and the nominal interest rate, measured by the Aaa corporate-bond yield, move together.

Source: Data on nominal interest rates and inflation from *Federal Reserve Bulletin.*

Figure 6   Real Interest Rates, 1955 to 1984

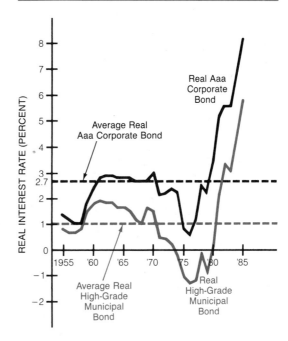

What is remarkable about real interest rates is how low they are. Real yields on Aaa corporate bonds averaged only 2.7 percent and real yields on high-grade municipal bonds averaged less than 1 percent. Real interest rates were at historic highs in the early 1980s.

Source: Data on nominal interest rates and inflation from *Federal Reserve Bulletin.*

Real Versus Nominal Interest Rates

Each of the rates just discussed is an example of a **nominal interest rate**.

The **nominal interest rate** is the interest rate expressed in current dollars (unadjusted for inflation).

But the dollar is an ever-changing standard. To compute the **real interest rate,** it is necessary to deduct the inflation rate from the nominal interest rate.

The **real interest rate** is the nominal rate minus the anticipated rate of inflation; it is the interest rate expressed in constant dollars (adjusted for inflation).

Figure 5 measures the anticipated rate of inflation as the average of the inflation rates (measured by the GNP price deflator) over the past three

years. Notice how the anticipated inflation rate and the nominal interest rate (using the corporate-bond rate) move together. Increases in the anticipated inflation rate push up nominal interest rates. When anticipated inflation falls, nominal interest rates fall.

Since 1955 the real interest rate on Aaa corporate bonds has (on the average) been about one third of the nominal interest rate on such bonds. In other words, anticipated inflation has explained about two thirds of the nominal rate.

Figure 6 shows the real interest rate on corporate bonds. The real interest rate varied from a low of 0.6 percent in 1976 to a high of 5.6 percent in 1982–83. On the average, the real interest rate on corporate bonds from 1955 to 1984 was

Figure 7   The Real Prime Rate, 1955 to 1984

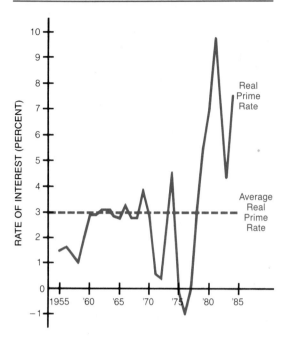

The real prime rate has varied more than real interest rates on Aaa corporate bonds. Notice that the real prime rate was even negative or zero from 1975 to 1977. In 1984, the real prime rate appeared to be heading toward the historical average of nearly 3 percent.

Source: Data on nominal interest rates and inflation from *Economic Report of the President.*

only 2.7 percent. The average expected inflation rate was 4.6 percent. Clearly, therefore, the largest component of the nominal interest rate is the expected rate of inflation.

Figure 6 also shows the real interest rate on high-grade municipal bonds. The real rate on these bonds varied from a low of −1.2 percent in 1976 to a high of 3.4 percent in 1982. The average real (tax-free) rate was only 0.9 percent over the 1955–84 period. A question that will be answered later is why muncipal bonds have earned so little compared to corporate bonds in real terms.

The real prime rate from 1955–1984 is shown in Figure 7. This rate varied from a low of −1 percent in 1976 to the astronomical high of 9.8 percent in 1981. Yet, on the average, the real prime rate was only 2.9 percent over the entire period.

In looking at the overall behavior of real interest rates over the past 30 years, two questions emerge. First, why were real interest rates so low in the mid-1970s? Second, why were real interest rates so high in the early 1980s? We shall try to answer these questions in the next section.

THE DETERMINANTS OF INTEREST RATES

Since interest rates tend to move together, we can discuss interest rates as if there were only a single interest rate. Except in the inflation chapter, our analysis has usually assumed that the price level is constant or has simply changed from one level to the next on a one-time basis. Thus, the aggregate-demand and aggregate-supply models in Chapters 11, 12, and 13 usually ignored the distinction between nominal and real interest rates, but this distinction is an important one.

Thrift and Productivity

When we studied the determinants of the level of real output, it was assumed that we knew the level of real interest rates in order to specify the quantity of investment demanded. The investment-demand curve showed that the quantity of investment demanded varied inversely with the (real) interest rate. To study the determination of real interest rates, we will now assume that we know the level of real output (or income).[1]

Real interest rates are the outcome of saving and investment decisions. The decision to save depends on two economic factors: the level of real income and the level of real interest rates. Income is the most important determinant of saving and was studied in detail in Chapter 9. The real interest rate measures the extra quantity of future goods that a dollar's worth of real saving this year will buy next year. If the real interest rate is zero, a dollar saved today will still be worth a dollar (in constant dollars) tomorrow. If the real interest rate is positive—say, 5 percent—then one dollar saved today will be able to purchase 5 percent more goods and services in one year than it can

---

1. Appendix 10A shows how real interest rates and real income are determined simultaneously.

today. Obviously, the higher is the real interest rate, the greater are the benefits of saving. Generally speaking, people save more when the real interest rate rises, but people save to reach certain objectives. As the real interest rate rises to high enough levels, less needs to be saved in order to pay for the children's college education, a vacation home, or that dream boat. Figure 8 shows how the quantity of saving supplied generally rises with the real rate of interest, but when real rates are high enough the curve bends back slightly. The saving supply curve, S, reflects the thriftiness of the population. Generally speaking, the thriftier or more patient is the population, the more will be saved for any given real interest rate or real income.

The quantity of investment demanded also depends on the real interest rate, as argued in Chapter 10. Businesses are prepared to carry out investment projects whose real rate of return exceeds or equals the real rate of interest. At higher real rates of interest, the number of investment projects that offer high enough rates of return is less than the number of such projects at low real interest rates. The higher is the real interest rate, the lower is the quantity of investment demanded. As this analysis shows, investment demand depends on the underlying productivity of capital: the higher is the productivity of capital, the higher is the real rate of return on capital.

Figure 8 shows that the real interest rate is determined by the interaction of saving supply and investment demand. The investment-demand curve, I, reflects the productivity of a country's capital investments. The saving-supply curve, S, reflects the thriftiness and patience of the population. The equilibrium real interest rate is the rate that corresponds to the intersection of the S curve and the I curve.

At the equilibrim real interest rate, the quantity of saving supplied equals the quantity of investment demanded.

In the Keynesian model, the condition that $S = I$ (in the absence of government spending and taxes) is the condition for equilibrium real output. But at any given level of output, the condition $S = I$ determines the real interest rate.

Figure 8   Equilibrium Real Interest with No Government Deficit

Without government spending or taxes, the equilibrium real interest rate equates desired saving with desired investment. The saving curve, S, is based on a given level of real income.

Government Deficits

Figure 8 illustrates the case in which government spending and taxes are zero. As shown in Chapter 10, a condition of equilibrium for real output (when there is government spending, G, and taxes, T) is that $S + T = G + I$. If D is the deficit ($D = G - T$), the equilibrium condition is $S = I + D$. Thus, Figure 9 shows how the real interest rate is determined when there is a government deficit. The demand for saving now includes private investment demand *plus* the government deficit. It may appear from Figure 9 that the existence of a government deficit must increase the real interest rate by increasing the demand for saving. This tempting conclusion has been the subject of much dispute among professional economists.

Some economists dispute the hypothesis that government deficits raise real interest rates for two reasons. First, Figure 9 does not show how private saving, S, responds to the deficit. Econo-

Figure 9   Equilibrium Real Interest With Government Deficit

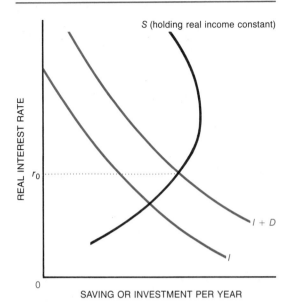

S (holding real income constant)

REAL INTEREST RATE

r_0

I + D

I

0

SAVING OR INVESTMENT PER YEAR

When there is a government deficit (measured by *D*), the equilibrium real interest rate equates desired saving with desired investment plus the deficit. While it appears from the diagram that deficits increase real interest rates, it is possible for the deficit to be financed by foreigners, or to shift the saving curve leftward by a compensating amount.

mists such as Robert Barro and Milton Friedman have argued that the government deficit may motivate people to increase private saving by an offsetting amount. If people realize that a government deficit today implies higher taxes in the future, they may save more today to be able to pay higher future taxes. The present value of the future interest payments on the debt issued to cover the deficit equals the deficit itself. According to Barro and Friedman, people pay attention to both current and future taxes. At an interest rate of 10 percent people might be indifferent between paying $100 in taxes today and $110 in taxes in one year. After all, if someone knows for certain that his or her taxes will increase by $110 next year, he or she must save $100 or so this year (depending on the interest rate) in order to pay $110 next year in taxes.[2]

2. David Ricardo made this argument more than 150 years ago. For a modern discussion, see Robert Barro, *Macroeconomics* (New York: Wiley, 1984), chap. 15.

Second, an increase in the government deficit may attract investment from foreign countries. Even if an increase in the deficit does not affect private saving in the offsetting manner noted above, it is still possible for an increase in the deficit to partly result in an increase in the saving supplied for American investment by foreign countries. If the deficit threatens to raise real interest rates above those prevailing in other countries, there may be an influx of foreign saving that tends to push rates back down—as there was in the United States in 1984 when it had an enormous $200 billion deficit. In the first half of 1984, between $64 billion and $100 billion (at an annual rate) of foreign capital was attracted into the United States at least in part by relatively high U.S. real interest rates. In other words, as much as one half of the government deficit was financed by foreigners! This trend partly explains why the government deficit was not associated with an enormous squeeze on private investment.

The relationship between government deficits and real interest rates is inconclusive. At the simplest level, real interest rates rose from 1955 to 1970 while the national-debt-to-GNP ratio was falling; real interest rates rose from 1975 to 1984 when the national-debt-to-GNP ratio was rising. Sophisticated statistical analyses of this relationship likewise yield inconclusive results.[3]

The Real Rates of the 1970s and 1980s

In 1976 the real rate of interest on Aaa corporate bonds fell to a miniscule 0.6 percent. What explains the low real rates of interest in the mid-1970s? The theory presented thus far suggests that any factor that reduces the productivity of capital investments will lower real interest rates, *ceteris paribus*. The falling productivity of capital investment is, therefore, a possible explanation. Why, then, would capital productivity have fallen in the mid-1970s? The most plausible explanation is the quadrupling of the price of oil in 1973–74. When the price of oil increased, the productivity of capital investments was reduced substantially—shifting the investment curve in

3. See Willem Buiter and James Tobin, ''Debt Neutrality: A Brief Review of Doctrine and Evidence,'' in George M. von Furstenburg, ed., *Social Security vs. Private Saving* (Cambridge, Mass.: Ballanger, 1979).

Example 2   Interest Rates and Farming

Interest-sensitive industries are hit harder than others by high interest rates. Farming is an example of an industry that tends to suffer disproportionately when interest rates rise. The business of farming is heavily dependent upon credit. Farmers must borrow to finance their spring planting. The farm may produce one cash crop that is sold at a particular time in the year. During the low interest rates of the 1960s, interest expenses equaled roughly 5 percent of farm operating costs. In 1983, interest expenses equaled 12 percent of farm operating costs.

As a consequence of being so dependent upon bank loans to operate their farms, farmers have accumulated massive debt, as shown in the accompanying figure. By the mid-1980s, farm debt was about 10 times annual farm income. In order to continue farm operations, farmers must continue to qualify for new loans. The disinflation after 1982, however, severely restricted farmers' ability to qualify for loans. The principal collateral for farm loans is agricultural land; yet market prices of farm land fell after 1982 as inflation subsided. Lower inflation meant lower values on farm land, yet interest rates remained stubbornly high with interest expenses equaling about one half of farm income in 1983. Farm banks found that the assets of farmers (consisting primarily of the value of their farm land) had fallen below their outstanding debt. As a consequence, a number of rural banks had to write off outstanding loans as uncol-

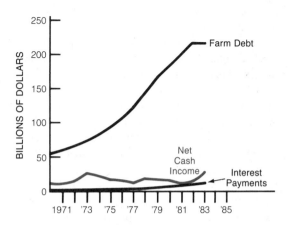

lectable, and rural bank failures increased in 1983 and 1984. Farm foreclosures also increased as farmers were unable to meet their interest and principal payments out of their farm income. The plight of the farmers received considerable publicity in late 1984 and early 1985. Congress passed legislation to provide loan guarantees for farmers, but this legislation was subsequently vetoed by President Reagan on the grounds that it contributed to the federal deficit. ■

Source: "As Many Farms Fail, More Rural Banks at Risk of Dying," *The Wall Street Journal,* January 24,1985. Data from *Statistical Abstract of the United States and Economic Report of the Presdent,* February 1985, p. 343.

Figure 9 to the left and, thus, reducing real interest rates. There may have been other factors that help explain the low real interest rates of the mid-1970s, but the energy shock likely played a contributing role.[4]

In 1983, the real rate of interest on Aaa corporate bonds was 5.6 percent. What explains the high real rate in the early 1980s? Three factors played a clear role. First, in the early 1980s the real price of oil dropped significantly. Just as the increase in the real price of oil in the 1970s lowered the productivity of capital investments, a re-

duction in the price of oil would raise the productivity of those investments. Second, the Economic Recovery Tax Act of 1981 changed the tax system by lowering taxes on capital income, which encouraged an investment boom in the early 1980s. Investment tax credits and accelerated depreciation raised the productivity of capital investments, measured on an after-tax basis. Third, personal-saving rates fell from nearly 8 percent of disposable income in the 1970s to 6 percent of disposable income in the 1980s. The decline in personal saving relative to income would be expected to drive up real interest rates.

Other factors may have raised real interest rates in the early 1980s. As we have shown, the growing federal deficit may have contributed to higher real interest rates. Yet another explanation

---

4. The argument that real interest rates rise or fall as the price of oil decreases or increases is in James A. Wilcox, "Why Real Interest Rates Were so Low in the 1970s, "*American Economic Review* 73 (March 1983): 44–53.

for the high rates of the 1980s has been offered by three economists in a report published by the National Bureau for Economic Research.[5] After the Fed dropped (or moderated) interest rate targeting in October of 1979, interest rates soared as the Fed applied the monetary brakes. Since 1979, interest rates have experienced wider fluctuations than had previously been the case when interest-rate targets were used. When interest rates fluctuate, bond prices fluctuate in the opposite direction, and bond owners run the risk of capital losses. Standard investment theory teaches that risky investments require a higher rate of return to compensate for extra risk taking. If the riskiness of an investment is gauged by the amount of variation in price, then bonds have become relatively more risky (relative to stocks and short-term bills). As a consequence of the growing riskiness of bonds, real interest rates have had to rise to induce people to buy long-term bonds.

Anticipated Inflation

Once the real interest rate is known, the nominal interest rate is determined simply by adding the anticipated inflation rate to the real interest rate.

The nominal interest rate = the real interest rate + the anticipated rate of inflation.

The real rate of interest is in equilibrium when the amount of saving people desire to accumulate equals the amount of investment businesses desire to undertake. The nominal interest rate is in equilibrium when the quantity of money demanded equals the quantity of money supplied.

The *liquidity-preference theory* of interest (explained in detail in Chapter 12) explains how the nominal interest rate reaches equilibrium. Figure 10 shows the liqudity-preference (*LP*) curve, or the demand-for-money curve. Holding the level of real income constant, the higher is the nominal interest rate the lower is the quantity of money, or liquidity, demanded. No matter what the inflation rate, the nominal interest rate measures the

5. Zvi Brodie, Alex Kane, and Robert McDonald, "Why Are Real Interest Rates So High?" *NBER Working Paper*, Number 1141, 1983.

Figure 10   Equilibrium Nominal Interest Rate

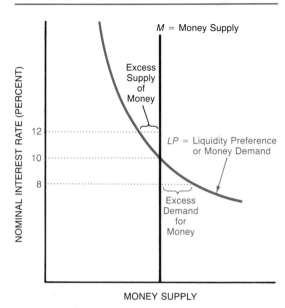

The nominal interest rate is the opportunity cost of holding money. Thus, the equilibrium nominal interest rate equates the quantity of money demanded and the quantity of money supply. The equilibrium nominal interest rate minus the anticipated inflation rate must also equal the equilibrium real interest rate in Figures 8 or 9.

---

opportunity cost of holding money balances versus interest-paying assets. Imagine holding $100 in cash versus putting that cash in a security paying 10 percent per year. An inflation rate of 15 percent per year, therefore, affects the real value of both cash and securities equally. An investor is still 10 percent better off putting his or her money in securities rather than in cash. The liquidity advantages of money must offset the opportunity costs of holding money. Thus, the equilibrium nominal interest rate is that rate at which people are just willing to hold the existing supply of money.

In Figure 10, the quantity of money supplied equals the quantity of money demanded at the equilibrium nominal interest rate of 10 percent. If the interest rate were less than the 10 percent equilibrium rate—say, 8 percent in Figure 10—there would be an excess demand for money. To satisfy their excess demand for money, people would sell bonds to gain money, thereby depressing bond prices and driving up interest rates. If

Example 3   The Treasury Proposal to Tax Real Interest Rates

In early 1985, the U.S. Treasury proposed a tax reform affecting the taxation of interest earnings. Under this plan, rather than pay income taxes on nominal interest earnings, taxpayers would pay taxes on only real interest earnings. The accompanying table explains why taxing real interest as opposed to nominal interest would tend to lower nominal interest rates and to make nominal interest rates less volatile during inflationary periods.

Table A shows the nominal interest rates necessary to yield a 2 percent real after-tax interest rate with different inflation rates (4 percent and 10 percent) and with different marginal tax rates (50 percent and 25 percent). With an inflation rate of 4 percent, a taxpayer in the 50 percent marginal-tax bracket must earn 12 percent nominal interest to have a 2 percent after-tax real interest rate. With an inflation rate of 10 percent, the same taxpayer would have to earn a nominal rate of 24 percent to earn a 2 percent after-tax real rate. The effect of higher inflation is smaller for a taxpayer in the 25 percent marginal tax bracket. For this hypothetical taxpayer, a rise in the inflation rate from 4

percent to 10 percent would require an increase in the nominal interest rate from 8 percent to 16 percent. Table A demonstrates that taxing nominal interest (especially for persons in high marginal-tax brackets) increases nomininal interest rates dramatically when inflation rises.

Table B (the U.S. Treasury tax proposal) shows the nominal before-tax interest rates necessary to yield a 2 percent after-tax real return when taxes are levied on real interest rather than nominal interest. The taxpayer in the 50 percent tax bracket must now earn a lower 8 percent nominal interest rate with a 4 percent inflation rate (versus 12 percent in Table A). The same taxpayer would have to earn a 14 percent nominal rate with a 10 percent inflation rate (versus 24 percent in Table A). The taxpayer in the 25 percent tax bracket would have to earn a 6⅔ percent nominal rate at 4 percent inflation and a 12⅔ nominal rate with a 10 percent inflation.

As these figures show, if the Treasury proposal were put into effect, nominal interest rates would drop. ∎

Table A   Taxing Nominal Interest

Nominal Before-Tax Interest (percent)	Tax Rate (percent)	Nominal After-Tax Interest (percent)	Inflation Rate (percent)	Real After-Tax Interest (percent)
12	50	6	4	2
24	50	12	10	2
8	25	6	4	2
16	25	12	10	2

Table B   Taxing Real Interest

Nominal Before-Tax Interest (percent)	Inflation Rate (percent)	Real Before-Tax Interest (percent)	Tax Rate (percent)	Real After-Tax Interest (percent)
8	4	4	50	2
14	10	2	50	2
6⅔	4	2⅔	25	2
12⅔	10	2⅚	25	2

the interest rate were greater than 10 percent—say, 12 percent—there would be an excess supply of money. The excess supply of money would move into bonds, driving up bond prices, and

lowering interest rates. As people shift into and out of money assets, the nominal interest rate adjusts until the equilibrium rate of interest is established—at 10 percent in Figure 10. As already noted, this equilibrium interest rate will be compatible with the real interest rate (shown in Figure 8) once the anticipated rate of inflation is taken into account.

The equilibrium nominal interest rate equals the equilibrium real interest rate plus the anticipated rate of inflation.

INFLATION AND TAXES

Figure 6 showed the low real interest rate on high-grade municipal bonds. From 1955 to 1984, the real rate on municipal bonds averaged only 0.9 percent. On the other hand, the real rate on Aaa corporate bonds averaged 2.7 percent over the same period. How can we account for this rather substantial difference? The difference is explained by inflation and by the fact that taxes are imposed on nominal rather than on real interest rates.

The average rate of expected inflation over the 1955–84 period was approximately 4.6 percent, and the average Aaa corporate bond rate was 7.3 percent. With a 25 percent marginal tax rate, 7.3 percent yields a 5.5 percent after-tax nominal return (0.75 × 7.3 percent) for Aaa corporate bonds. Deducting 4.6 percent inflation from the 5.5 percent after-tax nominal return, yields an actual 0.9 percent after-tax rate of return. Thus, investors with a 25 percent marginal tax rate earned exactly the same return from Aaa corporate bonds as they did from high-grade municipal bonds on an after-tax basis. If after-tax returns had not been so similar, funds would flow to the higher-return bond and drive down its after-tax return.

Example 3 shows how changes in expected inflation have a magnified impact on nominal interest rates when people pay taxes on nominal interest rather than on real interest. If taxpayers paid taxes on real interest rather than on nominal interest, nominal interest rates would drop and would be less sensitive to changes in inflation. For these reasons, the U.S. Treasury proposed in early 1985 to tax real interest rather than nominal interest, but the proposal was dropped from the Reagan tax-simplification package presented to Congress in the summer of 1985.

Figure 11   Interest Rates and the Stock Market

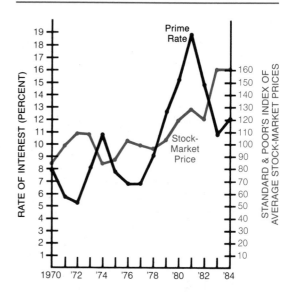

The stock market—as measured by the Standard & Poors Index of average stock-market prices—tends to rise when the prime rate goes down and to fall when the prime rate rises. There are significant exceptions (as in 1981), but the overall relationship is clear.

Source: Data on interest rates from *Federal Reserve Bulletin*.

THE STOCK MARKET

Stocks and bonds are substitutes. The stock market places values on the shares of existing companies. Unlike bonds, when savers "invest" in stocks they acquire an ownership interest in the company itself; they become part owners of the company. The income earned from holding stocks consists of dividends and whatever capital gains can be earned by increases in the value of the stock itself. Unlike the bondholder, who has a prior claim on the profits of the corporation, the stockholder has a residual claim on the profits of the corporation. The stockholder is the capitalist; he or she is the prime risk taker. When the profits of a company like General Motors go up, the stockholder benefits; the bondholder, on the other hand, scarcely benefits. Similarly, if the profits of General Motors falls, the stockholder suffers while the bondholder is basically unaffected (as long as the change in profits does not affect the credit worthiness of the company).

Thus, stocks and bonds are alternative instruments of saving or financial investment. When interest rates rise, bonds look more attractive; when interest rates fall, stocks look more attractive. (This simple theory assumes that everything else that affects the stock market is being held constant.)

Figure 11 shows that higher interest rates do appear to depress the stock market, while lower interest rates stimulate the stock market. The year 1981 is an interesting and important exception—the prime rate hit record levels and the stock market also peaked. In addition to a growing sense of optimism concerning the prospects of economic recovery, the Economic Recovery Tax Act of 1981 gave big tax breaks to corporations. These tax advantages benefited stockholders relative to bondholders and made stocks more attractive relative to bonds. Thus, the general relationship between interest rates and the stock market was affected until the one-time effects of the tax act were exhausted.

THE DOLLAR EXCHANGE RATE

Although world credit markets are not perfectly free, there is a powerful tendency for savings to seek out their highest rate of return. A typical saver in West Germany, who must choose between putting his or her funds into German corporate bonds yielding 8 percent or U.S. corporate bonds yielding 12 percent (with the same risk and maturity), will tend to puchase the IOUs of U.S. corporations. When the German saver purchases U.S. IOUs, he or she must purchase U.S. dollars with German marks in order to carry out the transaction. Thus, higher interest rates in the United States attract savings from other countries, and, in the process, foreign investors in U.S. bonds must buy U.S. dollars with their respective national currencies.

The external value of the dollar (as measured by its rate of exchange with other currencies) is, therefore, affected by the relationship between U.S. interest rates and interest rates in other countries. The exchange rate of the dollar (in relation to the German mark, the English pound, the Italian lira, or any other currency) is determined in international foreign-currency markets by the forces of supply and demand. When the U.S. interest rate rises above interest rates in other countries, foreign investors who want to buy U.S. IOUs increase their demand for U.S. dollars and drive up the dollar exchange rate, *ceteris paribus*. A number of complex factors in addition to interest rates determine exchange rates, as Chapter 24 will describe. For now, it is enough to say that one possible reason for the phenomenal rise in the U.S. dollar in the early 1980s in international currency exchanges was the relatively high U.S. interest rates. Foreign savers, attracted by U.S. political stability, relatively stable U.S. monetary policy, the strong economic recovery after 1982, and relatively high U.S. interest rates, have assisted in raising the external value of the dollar. For instance, in 1980, it took $0.55 to buy one German mark and $2.32 to buy one English pound. In early 1985, it took $0.29 to buy one German mark and $1.08 to buy one English pound. In both cases, the external value of the dollar roughly doubled over a four-year period!

A rising dollar may be good news for American tourists and for purchasers of German cars and English tweeds, but it is bad news for American companies seeking to sell high-priced American goods abroad. Those people hurt by the rising value of the dollar may lobby against high U.S. interest rates as a contributing factor to the rising dollar. Moreover, other countries, who see their domestic savings being invested in the United States, may be inclined to lobby for lower U.S. interest rates. As U.S. interest rates rise, other countries must raise their own interest rates to prevent a more serious outflow of savings.

IMPLICATIONS FOR MONETARY POLICY

The relationship between monetary policy and interest rates depends on whether we take a long-run or a short-run view. In the long run, the relationship is simple. In the short run, the relationship is complicated by short-run changes in the expectations of bond-market speculators.

The Long Run

As a result of the self-correcting mechanism studied in Chapters 11 and 12, a once-and-for-all change in the money supply will simply cause a

Example 4   Predicting Interest Rates

One of the most perilous forecasting feats is the proper forecasting of interest rates. Economic forecasters who were asked their interest-rate forecasts in June 1984 for interest rates at the end of 1984 (only 6 months later) missed the mark (on average) by 3 percentage points. The average prediction was 10.6 percent, and the actual rate was 7.8 percent. The interest-rate experts were off the target by about 25 percent.

Perhaps the most highly publicized guru of interest rates is Henry Kaufman, the chief economist of the investment firm Salomon Brothers, Inc. Kaufman predicted that interest rates would rise sharply in 1984 when in reality interest rates dropped sharply in 1984. As late as May 1984, Kaufman was still predicting an increase in interest rates. Despite such forecasting errors, interest-rate forecasters, like Henry Kaufman, continue to have a wide following. When Kaufman gave his predictions for 1985 interest rates (first higher and then lower interest rates in 1985), 1,250 clients were in attendance along with more than 75 reporters from countries as far away as Australia and Brazil. ■

Source: "So, Who's Perfect?" *The Wall Street Journal,* December 13, 1984.

---

proportionate change in the price level starting from a situation where output equals the natural, full-employment level. The interest rate—both real and nominal—will return to its initial rate after the self-correcting mechanism has worked its course in the long run. Nominal interest rates cannot rise above real rates unless continous inflation is expected.

Continuous growth of the money supply has a different effect on interest rates than a once-and-for-all change. If there is excessive growth in the money supply year after year, people will eventually catch on and begin to expect inflation. When inflation is expected, nominal interest rates will rise. If excessive monetary growth accelerates, nominal interest rates will rise even further. Thus, in the long run, there should be a powerful correlation between interest rates and rates of growth in the money supply. Long periods of easy money (high money-growth rates) should be associated with long periods of high nominal interest rates. Likewise, tight money and low interest rates should go together in the long run. Since inflation rates are intimately linked to money-growth rates, Figure 5 establishes this connection for the United States. Nominal interest rates and anticipated inflation definitely move together. (See Example 4.)

The Short Run

Chapter 12 argued that, in the short run, an increase in the money supply will work to increase real output by first depressing real interest rates. Moreover, since a short-run increase in the money supply will have little effect on inflation expectations, an increase in the rate of growth in the money supply in any given month or quarter should depress both real and nominal interest rates. Similarly, reducing rates of monetary growth should raise both nominal and real interest rates. For example, when the Fed reduced money-growth rates after October 1979, both nominal and real interest rates increased.

Recent evidence indicates that this simple story does not fully explain the current complex relationship between monetary policy and interest rates in the short run. Increases in monetary growth can either raise or lower nominal interest rates in the short run! Since the Fed adopted money-supply targeting in October 1979, unexpected increases in the money supply now increase interest rates when the Fed announces its money-supply figures (every Thursday)! This *money-supply announcements puzzle* occurs because of the usual negative association between the money supply and interest rates in the short run. The *money-supply announcements puzzle* is the observed increase in interest rates when the announced money supply is unexpectedly large. This puzzle did not exist prior to October 1979. What explains it? To make the argument simple, imagine the Fed announces a 12 percent annual money-growth rate (= 1 percent per month) as a target over the next year. Assume, though, that in a given month the money supply increases by 2 percent (or 24 percent per year). Speculators in the bond market will most likely think that the Fed will reduce its rate of growth in future months in order to get back on target. Hence, when people are told that the money supply is unexpectedly large, the same people will expect that the Fed will have to move to reduce money growth in the next few weeks. People, therefore, expect the Fed to engage in additional open-market sales of government securities, which will lower bond prices and raise interest rates. The mere expectation of higher interest rates, however, will then bring them about. People who expect lower bond prices will either sell bonds today or postpone purchases today, which causes bond prices to fall and interest rates to rise. Thus, an unexpected increase in the money supply—under money-growth targeting—should raise interest rates.

When there is announced money targeting, an unexpectedly large increase in the money supply is a temporary increase in the money supply. Only permanent increases in the money supply should lower interest rates in the short run, however. Thus, the money-supply announcements puzzle can be resolved once we make the distinction beween temporary and permanent increases in the money supply.[6]

The next chapter, will examine the new classical macroeconomics and will analyze how expectations are formed and the effects of expectations on policy.

Summary

1. The prime rate is the base rate on which banks decide to price their loans. Triple-A (Aaa) corporate bonds are the long-term obligations of default-free companies. High-grade municipal bonds are issued by state and local authorities and have been exempt from federal income tax. Long-term bonds are subject to considerable price risk. The rates for 3-month Treasury bills are generally lower than those for long-term Treasury bonds because of the latter's price risk. Nominal interest rates generally rise and fall together. The real interest rate is the nominal interest rate minus the anticipated inflation rate. The major component of nominal interest rates is the anticipated inflation rate. Only about one third of the nominal rate represents the real rate of return.

2. The equilibrium real interest rate equates desired saving with desired investment plus the government deficit (holding real income or output constant). The government deficit may or may not increase real interest rates, depending on the extent to which future taxes are anticipated and on international capital flows. Real interest rates were low in the 1970s because of adverse oil-price shocks; real interest rates were high in the early 1980s because of beneficial oil-price shocks, the Economic Recovery Tax Act of 1981, and the decline in personal saving relative to income.

3. When nominal interest rates are taxed, an increase in anticipated inflation increases nominal interest rates by even more. The relatively low real rates on municipal bonds compared to corporate bonds is due to the taxing of nominal interest and to inflation.

4. Generally speaking, the higher are interest rates, the lower are average stock-market prices because stocks and bonds are substitutes.

5. Relatively high U.S. interest rates tend to raise the external value of the dollar.

6. In the long run, increases in the rate of growth of the money supply will be related to increases in the nominal rate of interest (due to the impact on anticipated inflation). In the short run, a permanent increase in the money supply will lower nominal and real interest rates. Unexpectedly large increases in the money supply, however, will be associated with higher interest rates in the short run.

Key Terms

interest-sensitive industries
prime interest rate
price risk
coupon payment
nominal interest rate
real interest rate

---

6. For a review of different explanations of the money-supply announcements puzzle, see Bradford Cornell, ''The Money-Supply Announcements Puzzle: Review and Interpretation, '' *American Economic Review* 73 (September 1983): 644–57.

Questions and Problems

1. Interest rates on personal car loans are often tied to the prime rate, but why are they higher than the prime rate?

2. *True or false:* The prime rate shows a lot of rigidity. Explain your answer.

3. Is the prime rate of interest significantly higher than the Aaa corporate-bond interest rate, on the average?

4. If a bond pays—in perpetuity—$100 a year in coupon payments and if the interest rate is 20 percent, what would be the price of the bond?

5. Why do long-term bonds expose the bondholder to price risk?

6. Why do high-grade municipal bonds pay a lower interest rate than, say, Aaa corporate bonds?

7. Why are short-term interest rates usually lower than long-term interest rates?

8. Under what circumstances might short-term interest rates exceed long-term interest rates?

9. Suppose the nominal interest rate is 18 percent and a bondholder is in the 50 percent tax bracket. If the inflation rate is 8 percent, what is the after-tax real rate of return?

10. What appears to be the most important component of nominal interest rates, historically?

11. Why might not government deficits push up real interest rates?

12. If the government decided to end favorable tax treatment of the income from capital investments, what would you expect to happen to real interest rates *(ceteris paribus)?*

13. If the equilibrium real rate of interest is 5 percent and the equilibrium nominal interest rate is 7 percent, what is the anticipated inflation rate?

14. How are stock-market prices related to interest rates, generally speaking?

15. What is the long-run relationship between rates of monetary growth and interest rates? Why?

16. How is the short-run relationship between increases in the money supply and the interest rate affected by whether the change in the money supply is permanent or expected to be temporary?

17. If U.S. interest rates were to fall below interest rates in other countries, what would happen to the dollar exchange rate, *ceteris paribus?*

Suggested Readings

Feldstein, Martin. "Inflation, Income Taxes, and the Rate of Interest." *American Economic Review* 66(December 1976): 809–20.

Fisher, Irving. *The Theory of Interest.* New York: Macmillan, 1930.

Friedman, Milton. "Factors Affecting the Level of Interest." In eds. Donald Jacobs and Richard Pratt. *Saving and Residential Financing: 1968 Conference Proceedings.* Chicago: U.S. Savings and Loan League, 1968.

Miller, Norman C. *Macroeconomics.* Boston: Houghton-Mifflin, 1983, pp. 570–82.

19

Rational Expectations

Chapter Preview

This chapter will introduce a theory of macro-economics, called the *new classical macroeconomics,* or *rational-expectations theory*. This theory was formulated in the 1970s and provides an alternative to the Keynesian model. Its proponents believe that it accounts for the basic facts of the business cycle but still explains why countercyclical policy appears not to work.

Just as the Great Depression of the 1930s brought forth the Keynesian Revolution, so the apparent inability of the Keynesian model to resolve the stagflation problems of the 1970s and the early 1980s spawned a new alternative theory of macroeconomics.

The dissatisfaction with the Keynesian prescription is reflected in a remarkable speech by former Primer Minister of Great Britian, James Callaghan, in 1976:

> We used to think you could just spend your way out of a recession and increase employment by cutting taxes and boosting government spending. I can tell you, in all candour, that option no longer exists, and that, insofar as it ever did exist, it only worked by injecting bigger doses of inflation into the economy followed by higher levels of unemployment as the next step. This is the history of the past 20 years.

In the United States, government officials and economists, confronted with both rising unemployment and accelerating inflation, complained that "things don't work the way they used to" and that traditional economic remedies were no longer effective.

Economists Robert Lucas and Thomas Sargent, contributors to this new theory, summarize their dissatisfaction with Keynesian economics:

> . . . The inflationary bias *on average* of monetary and fiscal policy during this period (the 1970s) should, according to (Keynesian economics) . . ., have produced the lowest average unemployment rates for any decade since the 1940s. In fact, as we know, they produced the highest unemployment since the 1930s. This was . . . failure on a grand scale.

This chapter introduces the new classical macroeconomics using the analytical tools of aggregate demand and short-run and long-run aggregate supply. The appendix to this chapter provides more sophisticated analysis that relates aggregate quantity supplied and aggregate quantity demanded to price surprises. ■

THE NEW CLASSICAL MACROECONOMICS

Keynes rejected the old classical macroeconomics—the classical quantity theory—as unrealistic. The facts of the business cycle (studied in Chapter 5) clearly supported Keynes's criticism. The level of real GNP has fluctuated substantially over time, and some explanation of this fact was needed. The perceived need for a theory to explain large fluctuations in real GNP originally accounted for the extraordinary success of Keynesian economics.

The new classical macroeconomics was developed by Robert Lucas by combining the Friedman-Phelps analysis of the Phillips curve with the innovative rational-expectations hypothesis of John F. Muth.[1] Muth himself applied the rational-expectations hypothesis only to commodity markets at the microeconomic level. But Lucas went much further; he applied the rational-expectations idea to the entire macroeconomy. Thomas Sargent and Robert Barro also contributed important empirical work and have helped develop the theory.

The central idea of rational expectations is that consumers and business managers are more than just passive observers of the economic scenery. People are active observers; they *think*. A person will, in making economic decisions, not only take objective economic data into account but will also form **rational expectations** about the future course of economic activity and governmental policy. People use their best available information about what the government (or other people) are going to do in the future. People then combine the limited information they have about how the economy works to form expectations about the future. For example, if people expect the government to increase money-supply growth by a substantial amount, they will raise their inflationary expectations.

Rational expectations are expectations that people form about macroeconomic variables, such as the inflation rate and the unemployment rate, using their knowledge about current and future monetary and fiscal policy, business and consumer spending plans, and how the macroeconomy works.

The basic premise of rational-expectations theory is simply that people pursue their self-interest as far as possible. Households and business firms who maximize satisfaction try to anticipate what is going to happen using the best available information. Employers and employees negotiate wage contracts not only on the basis of current prices and costs but also on the basis of wages and prices rationally expected to prevail in the future. Individuals base decisions to purchase homes not only on current housing prices, on interest rates, and on personal income but also on their perceptions of *future* home prices, interest rates, and income that are rationally expected to prevail.

The difference between adaptive expectations and rational expectations was explained in Chapter 14 on inflation. Adaptive expectations are based on what is happening now and on what has happened in the past. Rational expectations are based on people's rational analysis of current economic theories, conditions, and policies.

Do People Anticipate Policy?

Do consumers and producers form expectations concerning government monetary and fiscal policy from which they rationally forecast expected wages and prices? The average person likely does not keep up with the latest moves of the Fed or analyze changes in the federal budget. Most people do not understand enough economics to use an economic model for forming rational expectations. Many individuals and businesses, however, do subscribe to newsletters and commercial reports or use the services of macroeconomic forecasting firms, such as Data Resources, Inc. or Wharton Econometrics, that in effect perform the needed claculations. The President's Economic Report, published yearly, also contains predictions for real GNP, the inflation rate, and the unemployment rate for the next five years. Business firms and labor unions hire their own economists

1. This discussion is based on Robert E. Lucas, Jr., "Some International Evidence on the Output-Inflation Trade-Off," *American Economic Review* 63 (June 1973); Robert Lucas and Thomas Sargent, "After Keynesian Macroeconomics," Thomas J. Sargent and Neil Wallace, "Rational Expectations, the Optimal Monetary Instrument, and the Optimal Money Supply Rule," *Journal of Political Economy* 83 (April 1975) and "Rational Expectaions and the Theory of Economic Policy," *Journal of Monetary Economics* 2 (April 1976).

Example 1   Rational Expectations and Fed Watching

Major banks, industrial concerns, and labor unions hire *Fed watchers* to keep an eye on the actions of the Fed in an attempt to anticipate Fed policy. In the vocabulary of rational expectations, the job of the Fed watcher is to prevent policy surprises. Professional Fed watchers are recruited from the ranks of former Fed employees out of a belief that someone who has seen the workings of the Fed from the inside will be able to anticipate changes in Fed policy. New York investment firms pay Fed watchers $200,000 and up per year—

more than three times what Fed Chairman Volcker earns. One professional Fed Watcher charges $1,800 per hour.

The existence of high-paid Fed watchers shows the lengths to which businesses are willing to go to try to anticipate policy. They are not sitting passively, waiting to be surprised by changes in policy. ■

Source: "More Concerns Hire Fed Watchers to Interpret Central Bank's Policies," *The Wall Street Journal,* October 21, 1983.

to make predictions about the variables that are of greatest concern to them. When prominent economists predict the future inflation rate, that prediction often makes the newspapers or evening television news. Thus, even though most people do not make elaborate economic predictions, they can use data provided by economists and by government officials to form rational expectations about future prices and wages.

Generating information and projections about the government monetary and fiscal policy has become a substantial industry in the United States. Business and organized labor do form expectations about monetary and fiscal policy. What about the average person on the street? It might be argued that the average person is scarcely aware of current monetary and fiscal policies, let alone surprised by them. Yet most people are reasonably well informed about the taxes they pay and form expectations of changes in tax policy. People do pay attention to the national debt and form expectations about the possibilities of deficit reductions. When individuals decide whether to place their funds in real estate (buy a home), in the stock market, or in money-market certificates, they must make some guesses about future monetary policy. Even average citizens, whether they are aware of it or not, form some expectations or guesses concerning government economic policies. They, like the large corporation or the labor union, can guess correctly, or they can be surprised. To say that people do not attempt to anticipate government economic policy is almost like

saying that they are not interested in maximizing their own personal well-being. (See Example 1.)

The World Is Uncertain

The next key hypothesis of the new classical macroeconomics is that even though people form rational expectations, no single person has perfect information. Individuals do not and, indeed, cannot be expected to know everything, especially when it comes to predicting the future.

This mundane observation has profound implications when combined with another observation: *people are more specialized in their selling activities than in their buying activities.* The line of products a business manager sells is much smaller than the myriad of products that manager needs to purchase in order to produce and market the product. The wheat farmer sells wheat but buys fertilizers, rents land, hires workers, and purchases tractors and equipment. Workers sell only the services of their labor, but they buy a vast array of consumer goods. Thus, virtually every economic agent—whether a firm or a worker—sells fewer things than it buys.

The typical producer (worker, business firm, farm) knows the prices of the things it sells better than the prices of the things it buys.

Because people have less information about the prices of the things they buy than about the prices of the things they sell, there is a distinct possibility that they will be confused by price and wage movements (even if their wages and prices are renegotiated frequently). They may mistake changes in nominal wages and prices for changes in real wages and relative prices.

ANTICIPATED VERSUS UNANTICIPATED POLICY

Can the economy be deliberately manipulated to produce more (or less) real GNP through the use of activist monetary and fiscal policy? If there is significant unemployment, can policymakers increase real output to create more jobs using expansionary monetary and (demand-side) fiscal policies? Activist policy is based on the notion that output and employment can be manipulated by changing aggregate demand. According to the new classical macroeconomics, the desired result will be achieved only if people are surprised or fooled. For the effect to be long lasting, people must be continuously fooled. If the countercyclical policy is anticipated, it will have no effect on output and employment. Fiscal policies that have supply-side affects (that raise the natural level of output) can affect output and employment.

Price-Level Surprises

Almost everyone has had the experience of discovering that prices are higher or lower than others. The national news media described in the 1970s how engineers attracted to California by high-paying jobs experienced unpleasant price surprises in the form of housing prices higher than anticipated. These engineers were specialized in the prices of the thing they sold (their engineering skills) and not in the prices of the things they bought (homes in southern California). There are numerous examples of businesses ruined by agreeing to supply their product at a price that leads to losses when production costs rise more rapidly than expected.

A *price surprise* occurs when the actual price is different from the price expected to prevail. Just as individuals experience price surprises, so the economy as a whole can experience a **price-level surprise**. The price level (P) is a weighted average of the prices of all the individual goods

and services the consumer or firm purchases and can be measured by a price index such as the CPI or the producer price index. When prices are higher than consumers expect (on the average), the actual price level is higher than the price level that people expect. The price level that people expect to prevail is called the *expected price level* (P_e).

> A **price-level surprise** occurs when the actual price level, P, is not equal to the expected price level, P_e.

A convenient way to measure the extent to which people are surprised is to take the ratio of P to P_e. If $P/P_e = 1$, people (on the average) are not surprised by the prices they encounter in the marketplace; if $P/P_e > 1$, prices are higher than expected; if $P/P_e < 1$, prices are lower than people expected. For example, if P/P_e is 1.05, prices are 5 percent higher than expected.

Demand and Supply Shocks

A price-level surprise is caused either by a **demand shock** or by a **supply shock**.

> A **demand shock** is an *unanticipated* shift in aggregate demand due to an *unanticipated* change in monetary or fiscal policy or a sudden change in private consumption or investment behavior.

According to rational-expectations theory, people attempt to anticipate all factors that affect inflation. Previous chapters have shown how changes in aggregate demand affect output and inflation. If people are interested in anticipating inflation, they must attempt to anticipate changes in aggregate demand. *The fact that people attempt to anticipate changes in aggregate demand does not necessarily mean that they will succeed.* Until the Fed began announcing (and generally observing) monetary-growth targets in 1979, it was very difficult to anticipate changes in the money supply. In some years, money-supply growth would accelerate; in other years, money growth would be unusually slow. Even after 1979, there was still no assurance that the Fed would actually meet its stated monetary-growth targets. As we have shown, the Fed has been willing to overshoot its announced targets during years of very high unemployment.

Figure 1   Rational-Expectations Theory in Terms of Aggregate Supply and Demand

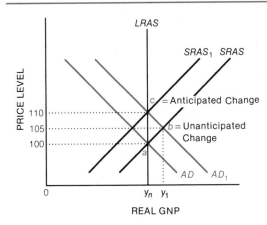

The initial equilibrium of aggregate supply and aggregate demand is at point *a*, where *AD* intersects *SRAS*. *AD* shifts upward to AD_1 as a result of monetary or demand-side fiscal policy. If the increase in aggregate demand is not anticipated, people and firms will be caught off guard by inflation, and the economy will move along the *SRAS* curve from *a* to *b*. If the policy is anticipated, the rational-expectations hypothesis implies that the short-run aggregate-supply curve will shift up at the same time to $SRAS_1$. The new equilibrium is then *c*, with the same GNP but a higher price level. When policy is anticipated, the economy adjusts directly from *a* to *c*. The movement from *b* to *c* (after an unanticipated demand increase) takes place as people gradually adjust to the higher price level. They realize that real money balances and real interest rates have not changed (if the demand increase was of a monetary origin), or they realize that higher government spending means a higher future tax burden (if the demand increase was of a fiscal origin).

Demand shocks can also be caused by unanticipated increases in government spending. It is possible, for example, that the public may have underestimated the acceleration of government spending associated with the Vietnam War in the late 1960s.

Demand shocks are not the only source of price-level surprises. A price surprise can also be caused by a *supply shock*.

A **supply shock** is an unanticipated shift in the aggregate-supply curve.

For example, the unanticipated 4-fold increase in OPEC oil prices in 1974 was a supply shock that caused an extensive price-level surprise. The decline in OPEC oil prices after 1982 may have

set into motion a price-level surprise in the opposite direction: prices rising less rapidly than anticipated.

Policy Surprises

Consumers, workers, unions, small producers, and giant corporations all form expectations concerning government monetary and fiscal policy. Participants in the economy will seek to anticipate changes in the money supply and in government spending and taxation. A price-level surprise can originate from a policy action that causes either a **money surprise** or a **fiscal surprise.**

A **money surprise** occurs if the actual money supply is different from that generally expected.

A **fiscal surprise** occurs if government spending or taxation turns out different than people anticipated.

As already mentioned, labor unions, corporations, and individuals expend a great deal of effort to predict (or anticipate) future government monetary and fiscal policies. Unions must anticipate government economic policy to avoid price surprises. If a major union were to incorrectly anticipate a slowing in the inflation rate and then settle for a smaller wage package, it would be in deep trouble with its members. If a major bank were to guess wrong on monetary policy, its profits could be damaged. Corporations must anticipate changes in corporate taxation if they are to make rational economic decisions.

The Self-Correcting Mechanism

Figure 1 shows an economy that is initially in long-run equilibrium at point *a*. It is producing the natural level of output (it is at the natural rate of unemployment), and there are no price-level surprises. People are correctly anticipating the price level (or equivalently, are correctly anticipating the inflation rate).

Adjustment with Price Surprises. As preceding chapters have shown, an *unanticipated* increase in aggregate demand (from *AD* to AD_1 in Figure 1) would set off an increase in prices that would catch people off guard. Workers on multiyear contracts would find that their wages were not keeping up with prices. Selling prices would rise more rapidly than costs. Some people would experience money illusion and think that real wages and relative prices had changed when they had not. As a consequence of these price-level surprises, the economy would move up the short-run aggregate-supply curve (from *a* to *b*). The economy would produce more output (output would increase from y_n to y_1), and the price level would rise (from 100 to 105). The increase in output would, to some extent, moderate the increase in prices.

An important feature of the new classical macroeconomics model is that there need not be any long-term contracts for unanticipated inflation to increase output—all wages and prices could be perfectly flexible upward or downward. How would the *SRAS* curve still be upward-sloping under these conditions? Recall that people know the prices of the things they sell better than the things they buy. If prices are higher than people have anticipated, the sellers of products (firms) or of labor (workers) will think that the prices of the goods they sell have risen *relative* to the things they buy. This mistaken belief will induce producers (in the aggregate) to supply more real GNP. Sellers will think they are being offered a good deal in the marketplace and will try to take advantage of it by increasing their output (for example, labor will work harder). With positive price surprises people will try to "make hay while the sun shines." If prices are lower than people have anticipated, real output will shrink because sellers will mistakenly assume that selling prices have fallen relative to buying prices.

For example, suppose increases in aggregate demand are pushing up wages and prices throughout the country. Machinists in Topeka, Kansas have just received a 9 percent wage increase—of which they are well aware. Collectively, they anticipate a 5 percent increase in the prices they pay. It is more difficult for them to judge what is happening to the prices of the things they buy, but they believe that their *real wage* has risen by 4 percent (their wage has increased more than the prices of the things they buy). They, therefore, increase the quantity of the labor they supply in order to increase their income before prices catch up with wages. Their labor-supply actions are based upon their *expectation* of prices. Even if

prices rise at the same rate as their wage (9 percent), they have been fooled (by incorrectly anticipating price increases) into working more even though their real wage may be unchanged.

The short-run aggregate-supply curve passes through the natural level of real GNP, y_n, when there are no price surprises because when inflation is perfectly anticipated, the economy will automatically operate at the natural level of unemployment, by definition as we learned in Chapter 11.

To the new classical macroeconomist, there is a different level of output and employment for each level of price surprise. Prices higher than expected lead to higher employment and more output; prices lower than expected lead to lower employment and less output. Here they part company with the old classical economists, who were unable to explain fluctuations in real GNP. When the level of prices is the same as expected ($P/P_e = 1$), or, in other words, when price inflation and deflation are perfectly anticipated, the resulting natural level of real GNP, y_n, can be maintained indefinitely (in principle). As in the old classical system, y_n will rise slowly over time with rising productivity and growth in the labor force. However, price surprises can cause fluctuations around the natural level of output.

In the long run, however, any multiyear contracts can be renegotiated, wage and cost increase will catch up with price increases, and people will no longer be fooled into thinking real wages have changed or that relative prices have changed. When these long-run adjustments are made, short-run aggregate supply falls (there is a leftward move of the *SRAS* curve to $SRAS_1$). As short-run aggregate supply falls, prices are pushed up further. The increases in prices stops only when the economy returns to the natural level of output (at *c*). At the natural level of output, the prevailing price level (or the prevailing rate of inflation) will remain constant.

The long-run self-correcting mechanism restores the ecomomy to the natural rate by gradually eliminating the effects of price surprises from the economy.

The economy moves from *a* to *b* in Figure 1 because of price surprises. It then moves from *b* to *c* because, in the long run, price surprises are eliminated automatically as people adjust price expectations.

Adjustment With No Price Surprises.

Let us now consider what will happen if the increase in aggregate demand is *fully anticipated*. As in the case of an unanticipated demand increase, the demand increase causes prices to rise, but if the increase in aggregate demand is fully anticipated, there will be no price surprise. Union contracts will have anticipated the rise in prices, and nominal wages will be set to rise at the same rate as prices. Firms will recognize that their selling prices are not rising more rapidly than costs. Consumers will recognize that income and prices are rising at the same rate. Workers will not mistake nominal wage increases for real wage increases. Because people in the economy realize that real wages and prices are not changing, there is no change in output or employment. *The economy continues to produce the natural level of output even though prices are rising.* In Figure 1, there is no movement up the short-run aggregate-supply curve (from *a* to *b*) to moderate price increases. Instead, the short-run aggregate-supply curve shifts immediately to the left (from *SRAS* to *SRAS₁*) to offset the increase in aggregate demand, and prices rise (from 100 to 110) immediately from the original price level corresponding to the equilibrium at *a* to the price level at the new long-run equilibrium at *c*. There is no short-run effect on output and employment (there is no short-run movement from *a* to *b*). The economy moves directly from the initial position, *a,* to the final position, *c.* An anticipated change in policy raises the price level without any stimulus to real GNP.

> When policy effects are correctly anticipated, there can be no price-level surprises without a demand or supply shock. Previously announced fiscal and monetary policies will be anticipated and will simply raise (or lower) the price level without any change in real GNP. Without price surprises, real GNP stays at the natural level of output.

When people correctly anticipate price-level changes, *the automatic adjustment mechanism works instantaneously.* Firms and workers anticipate the full magnitude of the price increase, and

the short-run aggregate-supply curve shifts immediately from *SRAS* to *SRAS₁*.

The rational-expectations economist knows as well as the Keynesian economist that an economy is unlikely to remain tranquil in the real world for any length of time. Numerous shifts occur in aggregate demand and short-run aggregate supply. Not all these shifts can be anticipated even assuming expectations are rational. The new classical macroeconomist assumes that demand and supply shocks are an inevitable feature of economic life. Had the policy change in Figure 1 been *unanticipated,* the new short-run equilibrium position would have been point *b* with prices higher than anticipated. When a *price surprise* occurs, the economy moves up its short-run aggregate supply curve to a *higher output* and a higher price level.

MONETARY AND FISCAL POLICY

Anticipated Policy

According to the new classical macroeconomics, if the government embarks on a fully anticipated monetary or fiscal policy, real GNP and, hence, unemployment will not change. Only the rate of inflation or price level will be affected by an anticipated policy change, as shown in Figure 1. The expansionary policy shifts up the original aggregate demand curve, *AD,* but since the policy is anticipated the short-run aggregate-supply curve shifts up to offset the impact on real GNP.

Only if the government fools the public will there be a change in output and unemployment. *A policy change can cause a demand shock only when people fail to anticipate the policy.* The aggregate-demand curve shifts whenever monetary or fiscal policy is changed; the short-run aggregate-supply curve fails to shift to offset this change only when there is an *unanticipated* demand shock or policy surprise.

Anticipated Monetary Policy.

A monetary policy is anticipated when the public correctly anticipates the rate of growth in the nominal money supply. As the money supply increases, consumers and producers anticipate that prices and wages will increase at the same rate as the money supply. Even though the supply of money in the hands of the public is increasing, it is generally recognized that prices will increase at the same rate as the money supply. Because the public realizes it is no better off in real terms than before the monetary expansion, there is no reason for aggregate quantity demanded to increase in real terms.

As shown in Chapter 18, the effect of a policy change on interest rates depends on whether the *rate* of monetary expansion is increased or not. If the *rate* of money growth has been increased, and the public anticipates it, the expected rate of inflation will increase. Hence, an increase in the rate of monetary growth will increase interest rates as lenders require a premium for higher anticipated inflation. Nominal interest rates will rise by precisely the increase in the anticipated rate of inflation. The *real interest rate,* defined as the nominal rate minus the anticipated inflation rate, does not change; real business investment stays the same. When people on average anticipate a higher rate of inflation, the corporations that borrow for real investment are willing to pay the higher nominal interest rate; lenders then demand a higher interest rate—an inflation premium—in order to insulate themselves from the inflation tax.

According to the new classical macroeconomic theory, an anticipated increase in the rate of growth in the money supply will leave real GNP unchanged (because participants will act to neutralize the monetary policy) but will *raise* the rate of inflation and the nominal rate of interest.

The aggregate-demand and short-run aggregate-supply curves of Figure 1 can again be used to show why anticipated monetary policy changes only prices, not output. Because there are no price surprises, the economy continues to produce y_n. When there is a fully anticipated increase in aggregate demand (from AD to AD_1), people are not caught off guard by inflation. The short-run aggregate-supply curve instantaneously adjusts (from $SRAS$ to $SRAS_1$) to offset the aggregate-demand increase. Thus, the economy automatically adjusts by moving from point a, where the original aggregate-demand and short-run aggregate-

supply curves intersect, to point c, where the new aggregate-demand and offsetting short-run aggregate-supply curves intersect. Fully anticipated inflation offsets the greater nominal supply of money in the hands of the public, and fully anticipated inflation raises nominal interest rates sufficiently to keep real interest rates constant. With a constant real money supply and constant real interest rates, there is no reason for the aggregate quantity demanded to increase when there is fully anticipated inflation.

Anticipated Fiscal Policy. Expectations can defeat the demand-side effects of fiscal policy as well as monetary policy. Consider, once again, the aggregate-demand and short-run aggregate-supply curves in Figure 1. The initial equilibrium is point a, where the equilibrium price level is 100. If real government expenditures increase, the aggregate-demand curve shifts to the right to AD_1. Because there is no change in monetary policy, the nominal money supply will not change as aggregate demand increases.

When aggregate demand increases to AD_1, short-run aggregate supply decreases to $SRAS_1$ because firms and workers know there is no change in real wages or in relative prices. At the new price level of 110, total GNP doesn't change, but desired consumption and desired investment decline just as much as government expenditures rise, and the real money supply falls. In other words, the price level of 110 *crowds out* a quantity of private expenditures equal to the increase in government expenditures. When policy is fully anticipated, the short-run aggregate-supply curve shifts to $SRAS_1$ as workers and firms perceive that prices and wages will rise due to the expansionary fiscal policy.

Does it make any difference whether government expenditures are financed out of taxes or by selling public debt (assuming that deficit financing does not lead to increases in the money supply)? According to rational-expectations theory, when fiscal policy is fully anticipated so-called deficit financing is an unimportant detail because rational taxpayers will consider the long-term implications of financing the increased government spending. If government spending increases by $20 billion and is financed by selling $20 billion worth of government bonds, the rational taxpayer will realize that the obligation to pay the interest income and the principal on this debt will call for higher taxes in the future. Although current tax obligations are not being increased, the taxpayer might cut back on current consumption to save for the increased tax burden in future years.

Unanticipated Monetary and Fiscal Policies

If the public is fooled by monetary and fiscal policy, rational-expectations theory predicts results similar in some respects to those predicted by the Keynesian model. Obviously, the public cannot always anticipate government policy. The future is uncertain, and the government may, without warning, change the monetary and fiscal rules under which it operates. For example, the Federal Reserve System in October 1979 without warning changed its goals from maintaining interest-rate objectives to maintaining specified monetary-growth targets.

If the Fed surprises the public with an *unanticipated increase* in the money supply, the public sees its money balances increasing but fails to recognize that price increases will soon wipe out any real gains. Real spending, therefore, increases. The increase in the money supply starts to drive down interest rates, and savers (who fail to anticipate the impending increase in inflation) do not require an added inflation premium on interest rates. The interest rates falls, and real business investment increases.

A similar effect would result from unanticipated fiscal policy. If the public had had no prior experience with deficit financing and the government added $20 billion worth of government spending to its budget without raising taxes, the unanticipated fiscal policy would raise the aggregate quantity demanded.

Figure 1 can again be used to illustrate why an *unanticipated* monetary or fiscal expansion causes output and employment to increase. The unexpected shift of the aggregate-demand curve to the right (from *AD* to *AD*₁) creates unanticipated inflation, and the economy moves along the short-run aggregate-supply curve *SRAS* from *a* to *b*. Because there is a price surprise, short-run aggregate supply does not fall immediately to offset the increase in aggregate demand. Accordingly, the movement from *b* to *c* along the new aggregate-demand curve does not take place immediately.

Learning from the Past

The public, however, learns from these experiences. As Abraham Lincoln said, "you can't fool all the people all the time." Policy surprises occur because the public cannot anticipate all policy changes of the government. As the public learns about the new policy (that the rate of monetary growth was higher than expected or that deficit financing raises future taxes), they will make adjustments, and the economy will return to the natural level of output. *Anticipated* shifts in aggregate demand *do not* change output and employment in the short run because such shifts will be offset by shifts in short-run aggregate supply. Over time, the economy will tend to return to the original natural level of real GNP.

How does the public adjust over time to policy surprises? Unions that have underestimated the degree of inflation will renegotiate contracts to catch up with inflation. Lenders, initially caught unawares by unanticipated inflation, will require inflation premiums from borrowers. Thus, it is unlikely that policy by surprise can be applied successfully in the long run. People learn through experience. They learn that when the unemployment rate is high, the Fed increases monetary growth. They learn that taxes tend to be raised when the deficit is large. They learn that a larger deficit today means more taxes tomorrow. If the public is no longer surprised by monetary and fiscal policy, countercyclical policies will have no systematic impact on real GNP and employment.

> Countercyclical policy cannot be used to stabilize fluctuations in real GNP unless the public fails to learn from past experience.

The Good News About Inflation

This new theory of classical macroeconomics gives a very optimistic report about inflation: like the new Phillips curve, it says that there is no long-run trade-off between inflation and unemployment; rational-expectations theory even claims that there need be no short-run trade-off either.

Chapter 14 on inflation emphasized that the cost of curing inflation is likely to be a substantial rise in unemployment in the short run. People will respond slowly to a decline in inflation brought about by tightening money. In the mean time, unemployment must be borne until inflationary expectations are slowly beaten down.

Rational-expectations theorists recommend that the government tell the public what fiscal and monetary policy will be—say, a stable growth policy of 4 percent monetary growth per year. There will be no price and policy surprises; as the inflation rate drops, inflationary expectations will adjust downward instantly, and the economy will settle down to the natural level of real GNP and employment with a low rate of inflation.

However, if government officials announced in an inflationary period that henceforth the rate of monetary growth would equal 5 percent a year, the public simply would not believe them. In terms of the rational-expectations model, the result would be an actual price level *below* the anticipated level ($P/P_e < 1$). The sharp recession in late 1981 and 1982 can be interpreted as the unbelieving response of the public to the Fed's restrictive monetary policies. When the actual price level fell below that expected, the public experienced a price surprise ($P/P_e < 1$) and moved down the short-run aggregate-supply curve to a lower real GNP. The high levels of unemployment in late 1981 and early 1982 suggest that preannounced policies will not work if people don't believe the government.

As long as policy is discretionary, the public's disbelief of government promises is entirely rational. Therefore, many rational-expectations theorists believe in fixed constitutional rules of the game that bind the government's actions.

EVALUATING THE NEW MACROECONOMICS

The new theory of classical macroeconomics portrays the world quite differently from the activist Keynesian model. Whereas, the activist Keynesian says that shifts in aggregate demand or aggregate supply have relatively predictable effects on output and employment, the new classical macroeconomist maintains that only unanticipated shifts affect output and employment. The Keynesian model pays little attention to whether people attempt to anticipate policy changes; the rational-expectations model assumes that people do their

best to anticipate policy. Their success or failure in anticipating policy determines that policy's effect on output and employment. The Keynesian model underscores the painful trade-off between inflation and unemployment. To stop an inflationary trend people must pay high high unemployment costs until expectations gradually adjust downward. In the new classical macroeconomics model, if there is a trade-off at all, it will be transitory and will be present only if people fail to anticipate policy. If people adjust inflationary expectations instantaneously, the trade-off disappears.

The policy differences between the new classical macroeconomists and the Keynesian activists have been discussed briefly in Chapter 17. Rational-expectations economists would agree with the monetarists that activism is just as likely to do harm as good. The rational-expectations school opposes activism for two basic reasons: First, activist policy can have, at best, transitory effects on output and unemployment. Effects on output are achieved only if the policy fools people, and people cannot be fooled permanently. For activist policy to have a lasting effect, activist policymakers must somehow figure out how to continuously fool people which is an impossible task. Second, the new theory of classical macroeconomics argues that the trade-off between inflation and unemployment is, at best, transitory. As people become more adept at anticipating policy shifts, the employment gains that result from expansionary monetary and fiscal policies will become even more transitory or even nonexistent. The sure price of expansionary policies is inflation. If the extra inflation does not bring about any lasting reduction in unemployment, there is no reason not to aim for a low rate of inflation.

Supporting Evidence

The rational-expectations model is very difficult to test against real-world data. In fact, a considerable amount of attention has been devoted to figuring out exactly how to test the rational-expectations model. The basic hypothesis of the new classical macroeconomics is that only unanticipated policy affects output and employment. In order to test this proposition, one must know 1) to what extent a policy has been anticipated and 2) if the policy is anticipated, whether people

Figure 2 The Relationship Between Unanticipated Money-Supply Growth and Unemployment

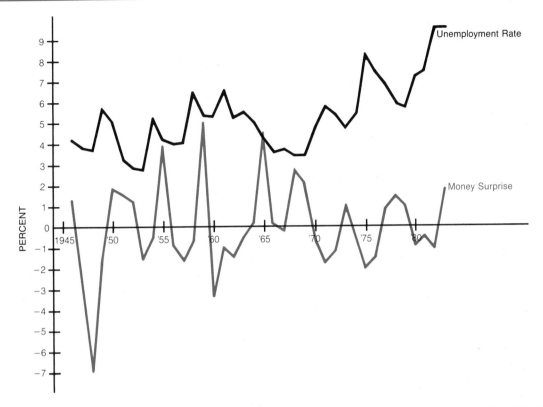

Robert Barro's estimates of the money surprise is the unanticipated rate of growth of the money supply (measured as the actual money-growth rate minus the anticipated money-growth rate). These estimates assume that people believe the rate of growth of the money supply depends on past rates of growth, the unemployment rate, and the federal fiscal deficit. The unemployment rate for different years tends to fall when there is unanticipated growth of the money supply.

Source: Based on Robert Barro, "Unanticipated Money, Output, and the Price Level in Its Natural State," *Journal of Political Economy* 86 (August 1978). Updated by Mark Rush, "On the Policy Ineffectiveness Proposition and a Keynesian Alternative", unpublished paper, University of Florida.

properly understand the manner and extent to which that policy will affect aggregate demand and aggregate supply.

The most direct evidence that it is possible for people to forecast the effects of future policies is the rather dramatic endings to the hyperinflations that have plagued the world. Following World War I, Austria, Germany, Hungary, and Poland experienced enormous inflation rates (in Germany they were more than 300 percent per month). Each hyperinflation stopped suddenly without plunging these economies into deep recessions, as would be predicted by the old Phillips-curve theory. In each case, the governments took concrete and widely announced steps to end government

deficits and runaway monetary growth. By changing the name of the monetary unit and by radically reconstructing the monetary and fiscal rules of the game, inflation was brought to an abrupt halt. In June 1985, Argentina changed the name of its currency from the *peso* to the *austral,* letting 1,000 old pesos equal 1 austral, to end a hyperinflation of 1,000 percent per year.

Evidence that only unanticipated monetary policy affects real GNP and employment has been compiled by Robert Barro, who compared unanticipated increases in the rate of growth of the money supply with the rate of unemployment. Figure 2 shows Mark Rush's updates of Barro's measure of the unanticipated growth in the money supply. (A negative number indicates that monetary growth was lower than anticipated, a positive number indicates that it was higher than expected.) As the Barro/Rush analysis shows, when money growth was higher than anticipated, the unemployment rate would fall. This evidence is consistent with the rational-expectations view that only unanticipated monetary policy will affect real GNP and employment.

Third, experience with postwar fiscal policy appears to be generally consistent with the rational-expectations hypothesis. The 1964 tax cut is commonly credited with having a larger effect on real output and unemployment than subsequent tax cuts. On the other hand, the 1981–82 tax cuts may have successfully stimulated output and employment. The 1964 tax cut was the first use of discretionary tax policy. People would have had great difficulty anticipating its effect on aggregate demand. The impact of subsequent tax changes would be easier to predict and, hence, offset. For example, the period of the 1970s is associated with tax cuts in 1972 and 1975 but rising levels of unemployment and inflation.

Fourth, the evidence concerning the new Phillips curve (presented in Chapter 16) is consistent with the new classical macroeconomics. Indeed, Chapter 16 showed that unanticipated inflation affected unemployment in a consistent manner. The widely accepted Friedman-Phelps analysis of the Phillips curve is part of the rational-expectations story. The additional ingredient added by the new classical macroeconomics is that expectations are formed rationally rather than adaptively. The rational-expectations model allows for more rapid (in some cases even instantaneous) shifts in the short-run Phillips curve.

How would one expect rational workers to behave during periods of rapid inflation? First, there would be a tendency for more workers to insist on cost-of-living escalator clauses during periods of high inflation, which has been the case. Second, one would expect shorter contracts to be negotiated during periods of high inflation because workers would want to avoid getting locked in to long-term contracts.[2] The move toward shorter

wage contracts during episodes of high inflation can also be documented.

Criticism

There is little disagreement among modern economists that people do indeed attempt to anticipate inflation. To do otherwise would be to behave irrationally, and economists believe that people behave rationally in the conduct of their economic business. In attempting to anticipate inflation, people would be interested in policy changes, such as impending tax revisions or changes in Fed operating rules. The heart of the dispute between activist Keynesians and the new classical macroeconomists, however, concerns whether or not people really are able to anticipate the inflationary implications of policy changes and how people react to policy changes.[3] Rational-expectations economists believe that people (if convinced that a policy change will lower the inflation rate) will react quickly and decisively in lowering their inflationary expectations. Activist Keyenesians maintain that reactions will be slow and indecisive and that this behavior is entirely rational.

The Keynesians argue that people understand quite well the prevailing institutional arrangements that govern wage and price contracts. They maintain that, in the real world, most wages and prices are not set in an **auction market**. Instead, most wages and many prices are set in long-term contracts.

> An **auction market** is a market in which the market price is renegotiated on a regular basis.

For example, the prices of stocks are determined in auction markets (the various stock exchanges) in which prices are renegotiated every minute in response to changing supply and demand conditions. The wage rate of day laborers who gather at hiring halls every morning is subject to renegotiation every morning. The price of oil on the Rotterdam spot market is renegotiated continuously as supply and demand conditions change. All the basic commodities (wheat, cot-

---

2. This section is based upon Gardner Ackley, "Commodities and Capital: Prices and Quantities," *American Economic Review* (March 1983); and Robert Gordon, *Macroeconomics*, 3rd ed. (Boston: Little, Brown and Co., 1984), pp. 271–73.

3. The literature on testing the rational-expections theory is surveyed in Steven M. Shefrin, *Rational Expections* (New York: Cambridge University Press, 1983) and in Frederick S. Mishkin, *Rational Expectations Approach to Macroeconomics* (Chicago, University of Chicago Press, 1984).

ton, coffee, sugar, corn, soybeans, cattle, oats, gold, silver, etc.) are bought and sold in auction markets.

If most wages and a number of important input prices are set in long-term contracts, people will recognize that policy changes cannot bring about quick changes in wage and price inflation. If important union wage contracts are predetermined over a three-year period and the Fed puts on the monetary brakes, union wages will not respond until the contract is renegotiated. People may simply be unable to realize their actual inflation expectations because prior contracts freeze historical, rather than current, price expectations.

As long as important wages and prices are set in long-term contracts, a great deal of inertia is built into the system. Even if there are substantial changes in policy that people correctly anticipate, many wages and prices cannot respond quickly because they are not set in auction markets.

Thus, many Keynesians still believe that discretionary monetary and fiscal policy can be used to stabilize the economy. The main problem, as the Keynesians see it, is that the government often follows the wrong monetary and fiscal policies (see Chapters 12 and 13). Keynesians cite the 1981–82 tax cut and the Fed's 1982 easing of monetary policy as examples of successful discretionary policy. It remains to be seen whether the improvement in the economy in 1983 and 1984 can be attributed to Keynesian policies or to other favorable economic events.

This chapter completes our analysis of the basic workings of the macroeconomy. The next five chapters will turn to broader aspects of the world economy: economic growth, development, and international trade.

Summary

1.   Rational-expectations theory offers an explanation for why countercyclical policy appears not to have worked well in recent years. The central idea of rational-expectations theory is that people use all the information available to them to attempt to anticipate the future. People combine their knowledge of the macroeconomy with forecasts of government policy to form their expectations about future prices. The typical producer knows the prices of the things it sells better than the prices of the things it buys. General inflation or deflation can, therefore, cause errors of judgment.

2.   A price surprise occurs when the actual price level is different from the expected price level. Price-level surprises are caused by supply and demand shocks. A supply shock is an unexpected shift in aggregate supply. A demand shock is an unexpected shift in aggregate demand. Unanticipated changes in policy (policy shocks) are an important source of demand shocks. When a shift in aggregate demand is anticipated, it will have no effect on output or employment. It will affect only the price level; the self-correcting mechanism works instantaneously. Because the resulting change in the price level is anticipated, the economy will move immediately to the higher price level but will remain at the same level of real GNP. Only when the demand change is not anticipated will there be a change in output. Demand shocks change real output only temporarily.

3.   Only if people fail to learn from past experience will they be continuously surprised by policy. Anticipated monetary and demand-side fiscal policy should have no effect on real output and employment. Rational-expectations theorists argue that there may be no short-run trade-off between unemployment and inflation.

4.   The evidence on the rational-expectations hypothesis is still being gathered. Evidence in favor of rational-expectations theory is found in the quick ends to historical episodes of hyperinflation and the fact that unanticipated monetary growth appears to affect real output and employment. Keynesians argue that institutional arrangements (overlapping contracts) prevent inflationary expectations from adjusting quickly.

Key Terms

rational expectations
price-level surprise
demand shock
supply shock
money surprise
fiscal surprise
auction market

Questions and Problems

1. "I do not know much about economics. In fact, before this course I did not even know that the Fed controls the money supply, and I am not much different from other people. How can the rational-expectations theory claim that people in general attempt to anticipate the effects of monetary and fiscal policy?" Evaluate this statement.

2. Consider a very simple economy that consists of four people. One anticipates that prices will rise 10 percent; another thinks prices will not rise at all; the other two expect prices to rise 5 percent. The actual price increase turns out to be 7 percent. What is the expected price increase? What is the price-level surprise?

3. "How can there be price-level surprises in the economy? After all, all we have to do is turn on the radio or television to learn how rapidly prices are rising." Evaluate this statement.

4. In a secret session of Congress, the President and Congress agree on a 20 percent tax cut. Would this tax cut affect real output and employment?

5. Explain why the long-run response to the tax cut described in question 4 may be different from the short-run response.

6. Under which of the following conditions would people be more likely to adjust their inflationary expectations rapidly?
    a. All prices are set in auction markets.
    b. Wage rates are set in 3-year contracts.

7. A weakness of the old classical economics was that it could not explain the business cycle. How does the new classical macroeconomics explain the business cycle?

8. If there were only three products in the economy, what would happen to the basic argument of rational-expectations theory? Would there still be price surprises?

9. Contrast the positions of the old classical macroeconomics, Keynesian economics, and rational-expectations theory concerning the self-correcting mechanism.

10. How can rational expectations negate the effects of activist of activist policy?

11. Let there be an expansion of aggregate demand as a consequence of increased government spending that is financed by raising the federal deficit. Why would the effect of this action on output depend upon the extent to which people change their view of their future tax liabilities?

Suggested Readings

Begg, David. *The Rational Expections Revolution in Macroeconomics*. (Baltimore: The Johns Hopkins University Press, 1982).

Fisher, Stanley, ed. *Rational Expectations and Economic Policy*. Chicago: University of Chicago Press, 1980.

Forman, Leonard. "Rational Expectations and the Real World." *Challenge* (November/December 1980).

McCallum, Bennett. "The Significance of Rational Expectations Theory." *Challenge* (January/February, 1980), pp. 37–43.

Willes, Mark H. " 'Rational Expectations' as a Counterrevolution." *The Public Interest* (Special Issue, 1980). pp. 81–96.

19A

Lucas Supply and Demand Curves

Appendix Preview

The discussion of the new classical macroeconomics in Chapter 19 uses aggregate-supply and aggregate-demand curves to explain the propositions of rational-expectations theory. This appendix develops a slightly more sophisticated set of analytical tools to explain the rational-expectations model and uses the tools to demonstrate the effects of both demand shocks and supply shocks on economic activity.

Since the distinction between anticipated and unanticipated demand or supply shifts is so critical in the new classical macroeconomics, it is useful to be able to represent the degree of surprise graphically. The Lucas demand and supply curves described in this appendix can illustrate better than aggregate-demand and aggregate-supply curves the effect of demand and supply shocks on output.

After first deriving the Lucas supply and Lucas demand curves, this appendix will illustrate the effect on output of shifts in the Lucas supply or Lucas demand curves. ■

THE LUCAS SUPPLY CURVE

The **Lucas supply curve,** named for Robert Lucas, the pioneer of rational-expectations theory, shows the relationship between output and the degree to which a change in aggregate demand was anticipated.

> The **Lucas supply curve** shows the quantity of real GNP supplied for every level of price surprise (P/P_e).

The derivation of the Lucas supply curve is shown in Figure 1. The economy is initially in equilibrium at point a, where AD equals $SRAS$ at the natural level of output. An unanticipated increase in aggregate demand (a demand shock) causes a price surprise. Actual prices are higher than expected prices, and firms supply more output in the short run. Thus, the price surprise has caused more real output to be produced. The curve in panel (b) shows the real output that is supplied at different levels of price surprise. At the initial equilibrium, a', there is no price surprise $(P/P_e = 1)$, and the economy supplies the natural level of output. When there is a positive price surprise $(P/P_e > 1)$, the economy supplies an output greater than the natural level. The curve associating each level of price surprise with the corresponding quantity supplied of real output is the Lucas supply (LS) curve.

If the increase in demand had been anticipated, the short-run aggregate-supply curve would have shifted immediately to the left, until it intersected y_n, so that the economy would have continued to supply the same real output as at a'. In this case, there would have been no price surprise $(P/P_e = 1)$, and the economy would continue to supply the same real output, as again shown by point a'.

If there had been an unanticipated *reduction* in aggregate demand (not shown in Figure 1), there would have been a *negative* price surprise $(P/P_e < 1)$, and the economy would have supplied less real output in the short run. When the price surprise is less than 1, a real output below the natural level will be supplied. Because the economy supplies more real output when prices are higher than expected, the Lucas supply curve is upward-sloping.

Figure 1   Derivation of the Lucas Supply Curve

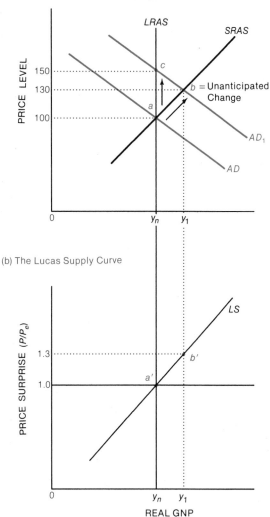

(a) Aggregate Supply and Aggregate Demand

(b) The Lucas Supply Curve

Panel (a) shows that the economy is initially at a, producing the natural level of output (y_n) with a price level of 100. A demand shock increases aggregate demand unexpectedly from AD to AD_1. Because economic agents have not anticipated the demand shock, the resulting inflation (prices rise from a level of 100 to a level of 130) catches people off guard. The economy is fooled into producing more real output and moves from a to b.

Panel (b) relates the increase in the supply of aggregate output to the price surprise itself rather than to the price level. The price level of 130 in panel (a) translates into a price-level surprise of 1.3 $(= 130 \div 100)$ in panel (b).

THE LUCAS DEMAND CURVE

A **Lucas demand curve** shows the relationship between the output level and the degree to which a change in aggregate supply is anticipated.

> The **Lucas demand curve** shows the quantity of real GNP demanded at each level of price surprise (P/P_e).

The Lucas demand curve shows demand at a given level of demand shock. In other words, it shows the reaction of the quantity demanded of real GNP to price-level surprises when there are no demand shocks (or when the level of demand shocks is not changing). Demand shocks cause the Lucas demand curve to shift, as explained below.

Figure 2 shows the relationship between aggregate supply-and-demand analysis and the Lucas demand curve. In panel (a), the economy is initially in equilibrium at point a, where the economy is producing the natural level of output with no price surprises. A temporary unexpected supply shock shifts the short-run aggregate-supply curve to the left. The supply shock sets off unanticipated inflation. When people who anticipate a lower price level believe the higher prices are reducing real money balances (they perceive prices to be rising faster than their nominal money balances), they cut back on their demand for real output. The adverse supply shock, thus, moves the economy along the aggregate-demand curve from a to b, where less real output is produced at a higher price level. If there were an even larger temporary adverse supply shock, the economy would move further up the AD curve to c, where real GNP is even lower.

In panel (b), the Lucas demand curve plots the level of real GNP demanded at each level of price surprise. It shows the equilibrium levels of output (y_n, y_1, y_2) at each level of supply shock (1.0, 1.1, 1.2).

Temporary and fairly permanent shifts in short-run aggregate supply have different effects on the level of price surprise. A temporary supply shift (such as an unexpectedly poor harvest) would have no effect on the natural level of output because the amount of resources and their

Figure 2 Derivation of the Lucas Demand Curve

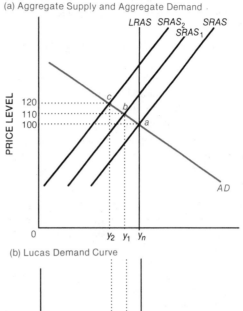

(a) Aggregate Supply and Aggregate Demand

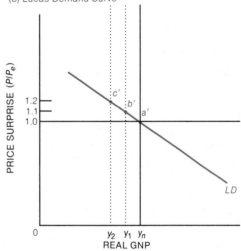

(b) Lucas Demand Curve

Panel (a) shows the effect of a temporary and unanticipated reduction in short-run aggregate supply (an adverse supply shock). When the normal short-run aggregate-supply curve, $SRAS$, shifts to $SRAS_1$, the economy moves along AD from a to b. At b, the economy produces less than the natural level of output. If there is a further unanticipated supply shock (to $SRAS_2$) the economy moves to c at a still higher price level and a still lower real output.

Panel (b) shows the same sequence of events on the Lucas demand curve—which plots the aggregate demand for real GNP at different levels of price surprise. The economy is initially at the natural level of output with no price surprise $(P/P_e = 1)$. At b', the price surprise is 1.1 and y_1 is demanded. At c', the price surprise is 1.2 and y_2 is demanded.

productivity would not have changed. The transitory supply reduction would, therefore, have no impact on the expected price level because the short-run aggregate-supply curve would be expected to return to its original position. The expected price level would remain at 100 in Figure 2.

A permanent supply shift, on the other hand, would change the natural level of output. For example, the reduction in world oil supply engineered by the OPEC cartel in the early 1970s raised world oil prices and reduced the effective resource base of oil-importing economies. Such a fundamental change lowers the natural rate of output. People would come to expect a permanently higher price level (once they realized OPEC was not a temporary phenomenon), and the natural rate would shift to the left (say, to output y_1 in Figure 2).

LUCAS EQUILIBRIUM

Equilibrium With No Shocks

Figure 3 shows a Lucas equilibrium in a tranquil economy in which there are no supply or demand shocks. Equilibrium occurs at that output and level of price surprise where LD and LS intersect. All fiscal and monetary policies are fully and completely anticipated. There are no supply shocks. Suppliers and demanders (on average) correctly anticipate the price level. Therefore, the natural level of real GNP is produced (y_n), and there is no price surprise at the macro level $(P/P_e = 1)$.

Equilibrium With a Demand Shock

Figure 4 shows an adverse demand shock, due either to an unanticipated reduction in the growth of the money supply or a contractionary fiscal policy that catches people by surprise. The adverse demand shock could also arise from unexpected changes in private behavior—sudden reductions in exports or sudden increases in imports, an unanticipated reduction in business investment, or a change in consumer preferences. In this case, the demand shock comes from an unanticipated increase in the money supply. The adverse demand shock shifts LD to the left to LD_1. At the equilibrium of LD_1 and LS at point e,

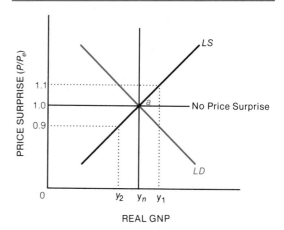

Figure 3   A Tranquil Economy

The Lucas supply *(LS)* curve and the Lucas demand *(LD)* curve both pass through point *a* when there are no supply or demand shocks. At point *a*, the economy is producing at the natural or full-employment level with no price surprises. Price surprises are measured by the ratio of actual prices *(P)* to the expected price level *(P_e)*. The *LS* curve shows that the supply of real output increases when P/P_e increases; the *LD* curve shows that the demand for real output decreases when P/P_e increases.

people experience lower prices than they anticipate. Output has decreased and unemployment has increased. The unanticipated decrease in the money supply shifts the Lucas demand curve to the left from LD to LD_1. Real GNP decreases from y_n to y_1, and there is a price surprise of 0.8 (prices are 20 percent below the expected level). As wage rates fall (in response to the decrease in aggregate demand), the supply of labor falls as workers fail to anticipate that deflation will ultimately cancel the losses from falling money wages. Thus, the economy moves down the Lucas supply schedule from point a to point e. If the demand reduction had been anticipated, there would have been no price surprise $(P/P_e = 1)$, and the economy would have continued to produce an output of y_n. Only unanticipated shifts in aggregate demand affect output.

Equilibrium With a Supply Shock

In Figure 5, the Lucas demand curve, LD, passes through point a, where there are no demand-shock-induced price surprises and where the demand for real GNP equals the natural level. An

Figure 4   An Adverse Demand Shock with No Supply Shocks

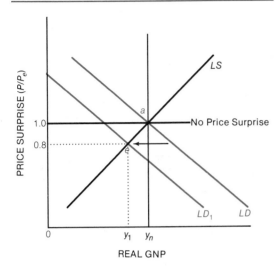

Since there are no supply shocks, the *LS* curve passes through point *a*. An adverse demand shock—such as an unexpected reduction in government spending or in the rate of monetary growth—shifts the *LD* curve to the left of point *a* and shifts the *LS/LD* intersection to point *e*. Real GNP falls below the natural level, and prices are lower than expected.

Figure 5   An Adverse Supply Shock: The Unanticipated Increase in OPEC Prices

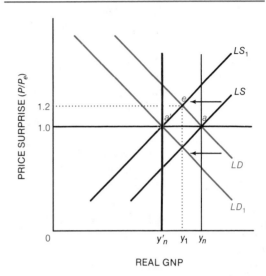

The economy is initially at equilibrium at *a* with no price surprises and with production at the natural level of real GNP, y_n. The unanticipated increase in OPEC prices shifts the *LS* curve to LS_1, and a new equilibrium is achieved at *e* at a lower real GNP and higher price level and price surprise. As the public adjusts to this price surprise, aggregate demand will shift from *LD* to LD_1, and a new and lower natural level of real GNP, y_n', will be established at *a'*.

adverse supply shock causes the original *LS* curve to shift to the left to LS_1. The economy reaches equilibrium where *LD* crosses LS_1 at point *e*. At this equilibrium, prices are higher than anticipated ($P/P_e > 1$), and output is less than the natural level. A supply shock in the next period might shift the Lucas supply curve to the right or even further to the left. If the supply shock is only temporary and there is no supply shock in the next period, the Lucas supply curve will shift back to the right and again pass through point *a*. A temporary supply shock is random and reversible—due to the weather or a strike, for example.

Figure 5 shows what can happen in the case of a fairly permanent supply shock, such as an unanticipated increase in the price of oil that persists over a number of years. An unanticipated increase in the price of crude oil would cause a shift in aggregate supply from *LS* to LS_1. This supply shock would create a price surprise; that is, prices would rise to well above the anticipated level, and the economy would move along the demand schedule, *LD*, to a new equilibrium at *e* (at a lower real GNP and a higher price level). This

equilibrium, however, would be only a temporary one because consumers and producers would have the opportunity to adjust to the oil price surprise as time passes.

Consumers and businesses would realize that the purchasing power of their money assets had declined more than anticipated and would reduce their real consumer and investment spending. The Lucas demand curve would decrease (shift down from *LD* to LD_1). Gradually, the economy would adjust to a *new* equilibrium (at *a'*), where the economy would produce a new natural level of real GNP (y_n') with a lower level of real output.

Countercyclical monetary and demand-side fiscal policies cannot return the economy to the original higher natural level of real GNP unless the public could be surprised, and it is unlikely that the public could be surprised permanently. According to the rational-expectations approach, real-GNP declines caused by supply shocks cannot be bought off with higher prices.

Summary

1.   The Lucas supply curve shows the aggregate supply of real GNP at each level of price surprise. The Lucas supply curve is positively sloped.

2.   The Lucas demand curve shows the aggregate demand for real GNP at each level of price surprise. The Lucas demand curve is downward-sloping.

3.   Macroeconomic equilibrium occurs at the intersection of the Lucas supply and Lucas demand curves. The long-run equilibrium occurs when the Lucas curves intersect at the natural level of output where there are (by definition) no price surprises. An unanticipated increase in aggregate demand shifts the Lucas demand curve to the right and will temporarily raise output. In the long run price surprises will be eliminated, and the Lucas demand curve will shift back to intersect the Lucas supply curve at the natural level of output but at a higher price level. The effect of a supply shock depends upon whether it is transitory or permanent. A permanent supply shift will change the natural level of output.

Key Terms

Lucas supply curve
Lucas demand curve

Questions and Problems

1.   Show the effects of random and fluctuating supply shocks on the Lucas supply/demand equilibrium.

2.   Figure 1 shows the effects of an increase in aggregate demand. Derive the Lucas supply curve for a reduction in aggregate demand.

3.   Explain why the economy moves instantaneously from *b* to *c* in Figure 1 when there is no policy surprise.

Part III

The World Economy

20

Economic Growth

Chapter Preview

The material well-being provided by an economy is measured by the material goods and services that it produces. *Growth economics* is the study of how the capacity of economies to produce goods and services changes over time. Why are some economies rich in material goods while others are poor? Why does the output of goods and services expand rapidly in some countries while it expands slowly or even contracts in others? This chapter will examine why economies grow and will try to determine the sources of growth.

This chapter marks a change of pace. We are no longer interested in the business cycle or the forces that cause the economy to operate above or below its natural level of output. Instead, we are examining those long-run forces that cause the natural level of output to expand over time. In this chapter, we leave Keynes's short run to consider the long run.

The definition of economic growth uses the measure of an economy's total output developed by national income accounting. Because the value of the total output of goods and services can rise with price increases, the measure of material well-being must be corrected for price changes to reflect only the value of the real goods and services produced. **Economic growth** is, therefore, defined in terms of changes in real GNP in two ways:

Economic growth is an increase from one period to the next in *real GNP*.

Economic growth is an increase from one period to the next in *real GNP per capita*, which is real GNP divided by the country's population.

Typically, economic growth is calculated in terms of annual percentage rates of growth. If real GNP in 1989 is $500 billion and was $450 billion in 1988, then the annual growth rate of GNP is 11.1 percent, or ($500 − $450)/$450. ■

WHY IS ECONOMIC GROWTH IMPORTANT?

Each of the two measures of economic growth provides different information about the change in the real output of an economy. The rate of increase in GNP is a measure of how much the total output of goods and services has increased and is a valuable indicator of the change in the economic power of an economy. Economies that produce large volumes of goods and services—such as the United States, Japan, the Soviet Union, West Germany, China, and India—tend to have more military power, greater influence on the world economy, and more political influence. The rate of increase of GNP per capita indicates the rate at which the amount of goods and services available, on average, to each person in the economy is increasing. Short-run changes in GNP indicate the course of the business cycle. If GNP is increasing rapidly, employment opportunities are likely expanding, and unemployment is likely contracting. If GNP growth is slowing down (or is even negative), employment opportunities contract, and the unemployment rate rises.

Per capita GNP is a measure of average living standards. Materially speaking, people who live in economies that produce large GNPs per capita are better off, on average, than those who live in economies that produce small GNPs per capita.

The two rates of economic growth can be quite different for any given country. Some countries with rapid GNP growth also have rapid population growth; such a country may have a smaller increase in living standards than a country in which GNP growth is more modest but in which there is little or no population growth. Table 1 shows the differences between the rate of growth of GNP and of GNP per capita for 13 countries.

The difference between the two measures of economic growth are most prominent in international comparisons of countries at the same point in time. The total output of The Peoples Republic of China in 1982 was $300 in 1982 U.S. dollars, that of India was $186 billion, and that of the Netherlands was $156 billion. China and India are large countries; the Netherlands has a fairly small population. On a per capita basis, the output of China was $310, that of India was $260, and that of the Netherlands was $10,930. Although the to-

Table 1 Average Annual Growth Rates of GNP and GNP per Capita, 1970–1982

Country	Annual Growth Rate of GNP (percent)	Annual Growth of Population (percent)	Annual Growth Rate of GNP per Capita (percent)
United States	3.2	1.0	2.2
Japan	7.1	1.1	6.1
West Germany	3.2	0.1	3.1
Italy	3.8	0.4	3.4
U.S.S.R.	3.1	0.9	2.2
China	7.3	2.3	5.0
Kuwait	6.2	6.3	−0.1
Venezuela	5.5	3.6	1.9
Greece	6.2	1.0	5.2
Kenya	6.8	4.0	2.8
Hong Kong	9.4	2.4	7.0
India	3.6	2.3	1.3
Chile	2.3	1.7	0.6

Sources: World Bank, *World Development Report 1984*, Tables 1 and 19. Data for the Soviet Union from Paul Gregory and Robert Stuart, *Comparative Economic Systems*, 2nd ed. (Boston: Houghton-Mifflin, 1985), p. 480.

tal output of the Netherlands was below that of China and India, Dutch living standards were 35 times China's and 42 times India's.

Economists typically pay more attention to the long-run growth of per capita GNP than to the long-run growth of GNP because standards of living are considered to be a better measure of economic well-being. Nevertheless, there is no universal agreement on which objective is more important: the growth of GNP or the growth of GNP per capita. In the Soviet Union and many less developed countries, the growth of the absolute size of the economy is considered of great importance. In other countries, absolute size is less important than the growth of living standards.

Economic growth is affected by changes in the output of material goods and services. Economic growth is not directly related to changes in happiness or contentment; philosophers and psychologists are better able to delve into the determinants of happiness than economists. Yet changes in material well-being or in total output are extremely important. The economic rise of the Soviet Union has definitely changed the social politics of the 20th century. Japan's phenomenal growth after the Second World War has materially altered Japan's position in the world economic order. Declining living standards in countries that are accustomed to improving living conditions can be a national trauma. One need only consider the dramatic decline in living standards in Poland or in Iran in the years 1980 and 1981 and its effect on everyday living to understand the importance of trends in material well-being. A less dramatic case is the gradual decline in England's living standard relative to England's European neighbors, which has had a profound impact on life and politics in the United Kingdom. The severe recessions of the 1970s and early 1980s caused people in the industrial world to question for the first time in a long time whether their material well-being would continue to increase.

THE CLASSICAL GROWTH MODEL

Economists first became interested in economic growth in the late 18th and early 19th centuries. The classical economists—particularly David Ricardo and Thomas Malthus—devoted much of their attention to explaining the factors that cause economies to grow.

Ricardo and Malthus were interested in explaining why predominantly agricultural economies reach an upper limit to economic growth, which they called a *stationary state*. Modern economists have addressed another issue: why economies continue to grow over long periods of time.

From the perspective of the classical economists, writing at the very beginning of the industrial revolution, the stationary state of zero growth seemed the normal state of affairs. The classical economists were interested in explaining the stationary state because there was very little growth of output or of population prior to 1750, the approximate starting point of modern economic growth in Great Britain.

Diminishing Returns

Ricardo and Malthus were interested in explaining the growth of a traditional agrarian economy. In such an economy, modern science and technology

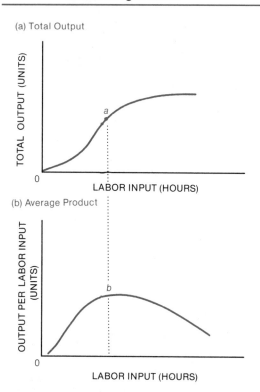

Figure 1   An Agricultural Economy with Diminishing Returns

(a) Total Output

TOTAL OUTPUT (UNITS)

LABOR INPUT (HOURS)

(b) Average Product

OUTPUT PER LABOR INPUT (UNITS)

LABOR INPUT (HOURS)

In this economy, the amount of agricultural land is fixed. As the variable factor, labor, is combined with the fixed factor, output initially rises at an increasing rate. Panel (a) shows that as more and more units of the variable factor are added beyond point a, output increases at a decreasing rate. Panel (b) shows that the average product of labor first increases and then decreases.

had yet to be applied to agriculture, and capital equipment (such as hoes or plows) was a relatively minor input. Output was produced primarily by combining land and labor, and agricultural land was essentially fixed in supply.

As earlier chapters explained, the *law of diminishing returns* applies to situations where more and more units of a variable factor (labor) are being added to a fixed factor of production (land). According to this law, at low levels of population and labor force, increases in labor initially yield fairly substantial increases in output, but eventually additional inputs of labor bring in smaller and smaller additions to output as more and more labor is combined with the fixed factor of production. The average product of labor, after first rising, will fall as diminishing returns set in.

Figure 2   The Classical Stationary State

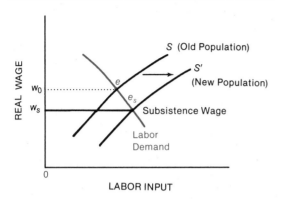

In the short run, the market wage rate will be w_0—the equilibrium wage rate. The horizontal line shows the subsistence wage rate, w_s. If the market wage is above subsistence, as it is in this case, population will expand, and the labor-supply curve will shift to the right (supply will increase). As long as the market wage remains above subsistence, population will continue to expand, thereby driving wages down even further. Population growth will cease when the market wage is driven down to subsistence. At this point, the economy is in a stationary state. The growth of output ceases, and wages are stuck at the subsistence level.

Panel (a) of Figure 1 shows the behavior of the aggregate output of such an economy as more and more units of the variable input (labor) are combined with the fixed input. Initially, output rises at an increasing rate, but the rise in output tapers off and eventually output could even decline as more units of labor are added. Panel (b) of Figure 1 shows how the average product of labor first rises but then declines.

The law of diminishing returns suggests that an agricultural economy with a fixed amount of land, primitive technology, and rudimentary capital resources should avoid excessively large inputs of labor insofar as these labor injections would drive down the average product of labor. Labor productivity determines real wages; therefore, an economy that had too large a population and labor force should expect to experience falling real wages and falling living standards for laborers.

Malthusian Population Laws

Because of the writings of Thomas R. Malthus, whose *Essay on the Principle of Population* was published in 1798, classical economics came to

be called the "dismal science." Malthus believed that there would be a long-term disproportion between the rate of growth of population and the rate of growth of food production. Population, Malthus argued, tends to increase at *geometric* rates (the *ratio* between each rate and its predecessor is constant) because the "passion between the sexes" and factors such as disease and war remain constant throughout human history. On the other hand, food production tends to increase at *arithmetic* rates (the *difference* between each rate and its predecessor is constant) due to the law of diminishing returns. Because a geometric series, such as 1, 2, 4, 8, 16, . . . , grows at a faster rate and will inevitably overtake an arithmetic series, such as 10, 11, 12, 13, . . . , Malthus felt that humanity would eventually find itself on the verge of starvation, living at subsistence wages.

Basically, the root of the Malthusian population problem is that because people tend to reproduce whenever their wages rise above subsistence, wages can never rise above subsistence for long periods of time. Once wages rise above subsistence level, the population and labor force will expand geometrically, and the increase in the supply of labor will drive wages back down to subsistence level. If wages fall below subsistence level, famine and higher mortality will reduce the population and allow wages to rise back to subsistence level.

The Classical Dynamics

The classical economists came to the pessimistic conclusion that there were distinct limits to growth. In the long run, economies would end up in a stationary state characterized by 1) a zero growth rate of output, population, and per capita output and 2) subsistence wages.

In Figure 2, the quantity of labor is given on the horizontal axis, and the real wage rate is shown on the vertical axis. The downward-sloping labor-demand curve shows the economy's demand for labor at different wage rates, and the upward-sloping labor-supply curve shows the amounts of labor supplied at different wage rates. The subsistence wage (w_s) is drawn as a horizontal line.

In the short run, the supply of labor is determined by the size of the population and by the proportion of the adult population that works—both of which change slowly over time. In the short run, wages can be above subsistence level; they are determined by the forces of supply and demand. If the wage rate is above subsistence level, as in Figure 2, the birth rate will rise, and death rates will fall due to better nutrition and health. The increase in population will cause the labor supply to increase (the curve will shift to the right), thereby driving down the equilibrium wage rate. Not until population growth shifts the labor-supply curve to S' will population growth cease. At this point, wages are driven down to subsistence level, population growth ceases, and wages stabilize at the subsistence level.

According to the classical model, in the long run, economies will find themselves in a stationary state where there is no expansion of population, no growth of output, and subsistence wages.

If a severe famine or war reduces the number of workers, wages will temporarily rise above subsistence level, the population will begin to reproduce, and wages will be driven back to subsistence level. During the Black Death plague of the Middle Ages, which destroyed one third of Europe's population, studies show that real wages rose substantially but declined thereafter as population growth accelerated.

MODERN ECONOMIC GROWTH

Modern economic growth since the 18th century has contradicted the pessimistic conclusions of the classical economists, at least as far as the industrialized countries are concerned. The classical model appears to have greater value for poor countries, as the next chapter will show. The historical record of economic growth of the industrialized countries indicates that these countries managed to escape the stationary state of diminishing returns and overpopulation.

The Historical Record

The dismal predictions of the classical growth model were far off the mark for the countries of Europe, North America, and Japan. Beginning in the mid-18th century—first in the United Kingdom and then spreading to the European continent

Figure 3   The Effects of Technological Progress and Capital Deepening

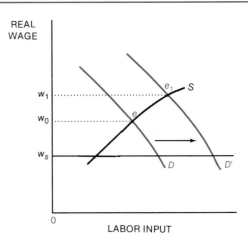

The market wage is initially above subsistence at w_0. Technological advances and capital deepening raise labor productivity and increase the demand for labor (from D to D'). Even if population were to grow, the increased demand for labor would prevent the wage rate from falling to subsistence. Furthermore, if population fails to respond to rising prosperity by expanding, productivity increases will raise wage rates even more (to w_1).

and to the areas of European settlement in North America and Australia—*industrial revolution* occurred. The result of these industrial revolutions in all these economies was the acceleration of the growth rates of real GNP and of population. The growth of output exceeded the growth of population, however, and per capita GNP began to grow at a sustained or increasing rate. In the past, there had been isolated episodes of economic growth at the rise of the Egyptian, Greek, and Roman empires. Each of these episodes of past growth was followed by a reversal, however, so that living standards always reverted more or less back to what they had been.

The principal feature of modern economic growth has been its sustained nature. There is no simple explanation for why the industrialized world was able to sustain economic growth for the first time in human history. The industrial revolution was accompanied by a technological revolution. Productivity-increasing inventions produced by 18th- and 19th-century science, including the steam engine, the mechanized cotton spindle, and the blast furnace, help explain modern economic growth. Modern economic growth was also accompanied by the expansion of trade and the growth of free-market institutions.

Modern economic growth brought about substantial changes in lifestyles. In all countries that experienced industrial revolutions, the share of economic activity devoted to industry and services rose; the share devoted to agriculture declined. The declining share of agriculture was accompanied by rising urbanization; the typical worker was no longer a farmer but an industrial worker. Rising per capita income translated into rising real wages, and items that had previously been available only to the rich—quality textiles, long-distance transportation, phonographs, automobiles—became items of mass consumption. With rising living standards, birth rates began to fall—contrary to the Malthusian proposition that prosperity would bring rising fertility. After the initial acceleration of population growth, the rate of population growth began to decline in industrialized countries. In the late 20th century, a number of affluent countries are even worried about declining population.

The Limitations of the Classical Model

The classical growth model failed to anticipate three forces that would indefinitely avoid diminishing returns and prevent a stationary state in the industrialized world: 1) sustained technological advances, 2) rising capital per worker, and 3) declining fertility.

Technological advances allowed the existing work force to become more productive with the same quantity of land and capital. As the amount of capital per worker increased, the productivity of the existing work force was raised as well. A slowly growing population (and labor force) meant that diminishing returns could be avoided.

Figure 3 illustrates why the classical model's dire predictions failed to materialize. In the industrialized countries, advances in technology caused the productivity of labor to increase. As workers became more productive, the demand for labor increased, thereby raising market wages. In the industrialized countries, capital was accumulated at a rate higher than the growth rate of labor. Capital per worker rose, and the amount of output pro-

duced by a given quantity of labor increased as the added equipment made existing workers more productive. Rising capital per worker—called **capital deepening**—also caused labor demand to increase.

> **Capital deepening** is an increase in the ratio of capital to workers in an economy.

The process of economic growth is a race between diminishing returns and those forces (such as technological advances and capital deepening) that cause labor productivity to increase. In Figure 3, without technological progress or capital deepening, labor productivity would remain constant, and the labor-demand curve would not shift. If, on the other hand, technological progress and capital deepening increase the demand for labor, wages can be kept above the subsistence level as long as labor productivity continues to rise.

The increase in real wages is reinforced if population fails to respond to rising prosperity by increasing in size. Real wages are not bid down by an increasing labor force, and the economy is not pushed in the direction of diminishing returns.

SOURCES OF ECONOMIC GROWTH

Since the beginning of modern economic growth, industrialized economies have experienced sustained growth of GNP and of GNP per capita. Although there have been cyclical episodes of zero or negative growth—the most serious such episode was the Great Depression of the 1930s—the industrialized economies have continued to grow with surprising strength over the long run (see Table 2).

Economies grow when

1. when the total amount of land, labor, and capital inputs expands and
2. when available inputs are used more effectively.

The more effective use of inputs shows up as increases in output per unit of input; that is, as increases in factor productivity. Economists therefore distinguish between **extensive growth** and **intensive growth.**

Table 2   Long-Term Average Annual Growth of Real GNP and Real GNP per Capita for Selected Countries, 1929–1984

Country	1929–1950 Growth Rate (percent)		1950–1960 Growth Rate (percent)		1960–1984 Growth Rate (percent)	
	GNP	GNP per Capita	GNP	GNP per Capita	GNP	GNP per Capita
United States	2.9	1.8	3.2	1.4	3.5	2.5
Canada	3.2	1.8	4.6	1.9	4.6	3.1
France	0.0	−0.1	4.6	3.6	4.2	3.3
West Germany	1.9	0.7	8.0	6.4	3.3	2.7
Italy	1.0	0.3	5.5	4.8	3.7	3.0
Japan	0.6	NA	8.0	6.9	7.2	6.1
United Kingdom	1.6	1.2	2.8	2.4	2.4	2.0
U.S.S.R.	5.4*	3.5*	6.0	4.2	3.2	2.3

*1928–1940

Sources: *Statistical Abstract of the United States,* 1980, p. 439; Paul Gregory and Robert Stuart, *Comparative Economic Systems,* 2nd ed. (Boston: Houghton-Mifflin, 1985), Table 12–2. The 1983–84 data are from the International Monetary Fund.

Extensive growth is economic growth that results from the expansion of factor inputs.

Intensive growth is growth that results from increases in output per unit of factor input.

To expand labor inputs, people must sacrifice leisure or household production to produce more market output. To expand capital inputs, people must sacrifice current consumption for future consumption. Compared to these costs of extensive growth, the costs of intensive growth are smaller. More output can be produced without the sacrifices just described.

The Growth of Inputs

Factor inputs can grow in two dimensions: they can grow quantitatively and qualitatively. Inputs grow quantitatively when more hours are worked in the economy, when more machines are placed in service, or when more factories are built. As workers acquire additional education or industrial skills and become physically healthier and stronger, the labor input grows qualitatively. As the quality of the labor force increases, one hour's work produces more output than it did previously.

Economists disagree about whether increases in output brought about by increases in input quality should be classified as intensive or extensive growth. This chapter treats quality improve-

ments—particularly improvements in labor quality—as intensive growth.

The Growth of Productivity

The second source of economic growth is advances in productivity. A productivity improvement has occurred when more output is produced from the same volume of factor inputs. A major source of productivity improvements is technological change. Scientists and engineers may discover new and improved technologies for combining industrial inputs. Agronomists may develop new drought-resistant grains or new types of chemical fertilizers or insecticides. New modes of transportation—the railroad, the jet aircraft, the space shuttle—may make it possible for manufacturers to deliver their products at lower costs. All such efficiency improvements can be attributed to technological advances.

Improvements in the way resources are combined can also lead to efficiency improvements. Managers may develop new business techniques that allow them to combine resources in a more effective manner. The assembly line may replace handicraft production. New management techniques may make possible the efficient management of huge enterprises. Government restrictions and rules that prevent the private sector from utilizing available resources in the most cost-effective manner may be withdrawn. (See Example 1.)

Table 3   **Annual Growth Rates of U.S. Inputs and GNP, 1800–1981**

Category	Annual Growth Rates (percent)				
	1800–1855	1855–1898	1899–1919	1919–1948	1948–1981
Real GNP	4.2	4.0	3.9	3.0	3.3
Labor inputs (hours)	3.7	2.8	1.8	0.6	0.7
Capital inputs	4.3	4.6	3.1	1.2	3.6
Combined inputs	3.9	3.6	2.2	0.8	1.7
Output per unit of labor	0.5	1.1	2.0	2.4	2.6
Output per unit of capital	−0.1	−0.6	0.7	1.6	−0.2
Output per unit of combined inputs	0.3	0.3	1.7	2.2	1.6
Proportion of growth explained by inputs	93%	90%	46%	20%	51%
Unexplained residual	7%	10%	54%	80%	49%

Source: John W. Kendrick, "Survey of the Factors Contributing to the Decline in U.S. Productivity Growth," Federal Reserve Bank of Boston, *The Decline in Productivity Growth*, Conference Series No. 22, June 1980, p. 2; U.S. Department of Labor, Bureau of Labor Statistics, *Trends in Multifactor Productivity, 1948–81*, September 1983, p. 24.

Past U.S. Economic Growth

Has economic growth resulted from the growth of inputs or by improvements in efficiency? American economists such as Edward Denison, John Kendrick, and Robert Solow have all studied the empirical record of American and European growth to find the answer to this question.

Table 3 supplies long-term data for American economic growth. The first row gives the growth rates of real GNP for different periods from 1800 to 1981. The next two rows give the corresponding growth rates of labor inputs (measured in hours) and of capital inputs. To obtain the growth rates of labor and capital inputs combined, the two input growth rates are averaged using labor's share and capital's share of national income as weights. During this period, labor earned from 60 to 75 percent of all income; therefore, the growth of labor inputs is the prime determinant of the growth of combined labor and capital inputs. (In 1981, labor's share was 65 percent.)

If labor earns 65 percent of income and capital the remaining 35 percent, then the growth rate of both factors combined is 0.65 times labor growth rate plus 0.35 times capital growth rate.

From 1948 to 1981 in the United States, the labor input grew by a 0.7 percent annual rate and capital grew at a 3.6 percent annual rate. Applying the above formula, we find that the combined growth rate of capital and labor was 0.65(0.7) + 0.35(3.6) = 1.7.

To determine what proportion of growth is accounted for by the growth of inputs and what proportion is explained by the growth of input productivity (output per unit of input), the growth of inputs is subtracted from growth of output. During the period 1948–1981, combined inputs grew at 1.7 percent per year. If there had been no improvements in productivity, GNP would have grown at the same rate as inputs (also at 1.7 percent per year). But GNP actually grew much faster than inputs, at 3.3 percent per year. The difference between the growth of output and the growth of inputs (3.3 − 1.7 = 1.6) is productivity growth, or the *residual*. The term *residual* is used because economists can only guess what factors are in the residual. For the 1948–1981 period, the residual explains 49 percent of GNP growth, while the growth of factor inputs explains the remaining 51 percent of growth. As Table 3 points out, the unexplained residual accounted for a much higher percentage of growth between 1919 and 1948 than between 1948 and 1981.

But, over the last 50 years, the major portion of American—or western European or Japanese—economic growth is explained by the growth of productivity. The exact causes of productivity growth will never be known. Some economists—such as Edward Denison and John Kendrick—

Table 4 Sources of Growth of Real GNP in the United States, 1948–1978

Sources	Annual Growth Rate (percent)	
	1948–1966	1966–1978
Real GNP	3.9	3.0
Labor (hours)	0.4	1.4
Capital	2.8	2.9
Combined inputs	1.1	1.8
Total factor productivity	2.8	1.2
Sources of Factor Productivity Growth		
Advances in knowledge	1.4	1.0
Changes in labor quality	0.6	0.5
Changes in land quality	0.0	−0.2
Resource reallocations	0.8	0.5
Other factors	0.4	−0.8
Sum	**2.8**	**1.2**

Source: John W. Kendrick, "Survey of the Factors Contributing to the Decline in U.S. Productivity Growth," Federal Reserve Bank of Boston, *The Decline in Productivity Growth*, Conference Series No. 22, June 1980, p. 2. The data to 1969 are based upon Edward Denison, *Accounting for U.S. Economic Growth, 1948–1969* (Washington, D.C.: Brookings, 1974).

have attempted to break down the residual into different sources: advances in knowledge, changes in the quality of labor and land inputs, resource reallocations, and other factors. The results of Denison's and Kendrick's research are given in Table 4. They find that the major source of productivity growth is advances in knowledge obtained through formal investment in research and development and through informal advances in knowledge. The second major factor in productivity advances is improvements in the quality of labor, primarily the consequence of improvements in education and training.

Future U.S. Growth

Just as it is difficult to project the business cycle, so it is difficult to project U.S. economic growth over the next decade. This chapter has pinpointed the factors that will determine whether the next decade will see low, average, or high growth. Economic growth depends upon the growth of factor inputs and the efficiency with which they are used. Efficiency depends upon technological progress. We cannot predict the course of technological progress, which depends upon scientific

discoveries and new organizational and managerial arrangements, among other factors. We do have a better perspective on the growth of factor inputs. Because all the people who will be at work over the next decade have already been born, the number of people available for work can be specified with some precision. The major uncertainty is the proportion of the working-age population that is prepared to work and the average number of hours they will work. Currently, the Department of Labor projects a 1.5 percent annual growth rate of the U.S. workforce over the next decade. The growth of the capital stock depends upon the investment decisions to be made over the next decade. As we have shown in previous chapters, investment spending is the most unstable (and unpredictable) component of GNP. The amount of investment will depend upon the general level of business optimism, tax incentives to invest, and real interest rates.

As we have shown, the long-term growth rate of labor productivity has ranged from 1.5 percent to as high as 3.3 percent per annum. At this point, there is no reason to believe that the future will be different from the past. Combining the projected growth of labor (1.5 percent per annum) with the extreme ranges of labor-productivity growth yields a growth rate of real GNP of 3 percent to 4.8 percent per annum over the next decade (see Example 2).

LABOR PRODUCTIVITY

Figure 4 shows the annual rate of growth of labor productivity in the U.S. business sector from 1958 to the present. Labor productivity growth—as measured by the rate of growth of real GNP per hour of labor—fluctuates a great deal from year to year. The annual fluctuations in labor productivity make it difficult to estimate long-run trends in productivity. The period from the late 1950s through the mid-1960s was one of high labor-productivity growth. From the late 1960s to the mid-1980s, labor-productivity growth was erratic, falling with recessions and rising with recoveries.

Figure 4 illustrates why fears of a long-term productivity decline were widespread in the late 1970s. From high and steady productivity growth in the 1960s, the economy experienced negative

Figure 4   Annual Growth Rates of U.S. Labor Productivity, 1958–1984

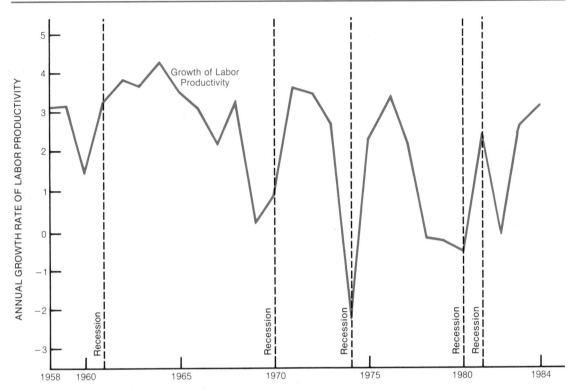

The growth rate of labor productivity tends to fluctuate from year to year. Productivity growth was high from the late 1950s through the late 1960s, fell during the recessions of the 1970s and early 1980s, and rose sharply during the recovery phase of the cycle.

Source: *Economic Report of the President.*

productivity growth in the late 1970s. The economic recovery after 1982 generated positive and reasonably rapid labor-productivity growth, again underscoring the fact that labor productivity is heavily dependent upon the state of the business cycle. At this point in time, we do not know whether the rest of the 1980s will see steady and rapid labor-productivity growth or slow and erratic labor-productivity growth. The outcome appears to depend upon the growth of real GNP. If GNP growth is steady and rapid, labor-productivity growth will likely be steady and rapid as well.

It is worthwhile to examine the causes of the productivity slowdown from the mid-1960s to the early 1980s. We have already described the close relationship between real wages and productivity. Rising productivity typically translates into rising real wages.

A slowdown in labor-productivity growth means that increases in money wage rates are not being offset by increased output per worker. Average costs of production should, therefore, rise. Because, as already demonstrated, productivity growth is the major source of economic growth, if the growth of productivity of a major factor like labor declines, the growth of output should decline, *ceteris paribus.*

Much attention has been devoted to explaining the decline in American labor productivity from the mid-1960s to 1980. Labor productivity, as measured by output per hour of labor, rises 1) because other factors that cooperate with labor in the production process grow (qualitatively or quantitatively) more rapidly than labor hours, 2) because the quality of the labor input rises, or 3) because technological advances or better ways of

Example 1   Affluence and Growth Rates

The accompanying table shows the change in rankings by national income per capita for 10 countries between 1960 and 1980. The figures cited (in 1984 dollars) come from a study of world income sponsored by the World Bank and directed by Irving Kravis. The study makes exact purchasing-power calculations to measure per capita income in dollars. As such, it should provide reasonable estimates of relative per capita income. The numbers illustrate what can happen when countries grow at different rates of per capita growth. The most notable example is the changing position of Japan. In 1960, Japan's per capita GNP was only 32 percent that of the United States. By 1980, per capita GNP in Japan had risen to 74 percent of that in the United States. If Japan's rapid growth of per capita GNP were to continue at this rate, the Japanese would eventually enjoy the highest standards of living in the world. As a consequence of relatively slow growth, the United Kingdom between 1960 and 1980 fell from a per capita income equal to 65 percent of the U.S. per capita income to one that is 60 percent of the U.S. per capita income. ■

Source: I. Kravis, A. Heston, and R. Summers, "Corrigendum to 'New Insights into the Structure of the World Economy,'" *Review of Income and Wealth* 28 (September 1982):362–63.

	1960 Per Capita Income		1980 Per Capita Income	
	Amount (1984 dollars)	Rank	Amount (1984 dollars)	Rank
United States	9,274	1	14,721	1
Luxembourg	7,020	2	12,071	4
Federal Republic of Germany	6,779	3	12,969	2
Denmark	6,510	4	11,865	5
United Kingdom	6,065	5	8,921	9
Netherlands	5,880	6	10,614	8
France	5,713	7	12,145	3
Belgium	5,453	8	11,335	6
Italy	4,062	9	8,229	10
Japan	2,931	10	10,835	7

combining resources (so that labor productivity rises without an increase in cooperating factors) are made available.

Cooperating Factors

The data show that the decline in labor productivity between 1965 and 1980 was partially caused by a deterioration in the relationship between the number of machines and the number of hours worked. From 1955 to 1965, capital grew 5 times faster than hours worked. From 1965 to 1973, capital grew 2.4 times faster than hours worked. From 1973 to 1981, capital grew 1.8 times faster than hours worked.[1] One reason why the growth

of labor productivity slowed during this period was the significant decline in the growth of capital per hour worked.

There has also been a decline in a particular type of investment spending—*research and development (R&D)*—relative to gross national product. In the early 1960s, more than 2 percent of GNP was devoted to R&D spending. Since the mid-1960s, this percentage has fallen to slightly less than 1.6 percent of GNP.

Composition of the Labor Force

A second potential cause of the labor-productivity slowdown is a decline in the quality of the labor force. The productivity decline began approximately at that time when those people born during the "baby boom" of the 1950s entered the labor force in large numbers. As young, relatively inexperienced workers replaced older experienced

1. John Kendrick, "Survey of the Factors Contributing to the Decline in U.S. Productivity Growth," Federal Reserve Bank of Boston, *The Decline in Productivity Growth*, Conference Series No. 22, June 1980, p. 3; OECD, *Flows and Stocks of Fixed Capital* (Paris: OECD, 1983), pp. 10–11; and *Economic Report of the President*.

workers, the overall quality of the labor force declined. In addition to the baby-boom effect, more women entered the labor force after having forgone experience and on-the-job training in order to carry out homemaking or child-rearing activities.

Did these labor-force-composition changes have a major effect on labor productivity? Studies show that the labor productivity of experienced adult workers continued to increase at about historical rates throughout the productivity slowdown of the mid-1960s to 1980. The declines in productivity growth were exhibited by young and inexperienced workers.[2] It is unlikely that changes in the composition of the labor force played a prominent role in the productivity decline.[3] The shifts in the composition of the labor force and the productivity differentials were not dramatic enough to account for substantial productivity changes.

The Residual

The changing relationship between capital and labor and the changing composition of the labor force explain only a portion of the decline in the growth of labor productivity between 1965 and 1980. Economist William Nordhaus, for example, estimated that only 20 percent of the decline results from these two factors.[4]

The major portion of the labor-productivity slowdown between 1965 and 1980 can be attributed to factors not associated with the qualitative or quantitative growth of the factors of production. From Figure 4, it is clear that the four recessions that occurred between 1970 and 1981 played a critical role. Productivity growth during recovery periods (the early 1970s, 1976–77, 1982–84) was quite respectable. If real GNP had grown steadily at average rates (by historical standards), the picture of productivity growth would have been quite different. The stagflation of the

Table 5   Long-Term Trends in U.S. Labor Productivity Growth

Period	Average Annual Growth Rate in Output per Hour (percent)
1900–16	1.5
1916–29	2.3
1929–48	1.6
1948–65	3.3
1965–73	2.3
1973–85	1.5

Source: Michael Darby, "The U.S. Productivity Slowdown: A Case of Statistical Myopia," *American Economic Review* (June 1984), p. 302. Darby's figures are updated to 1985 (using projected 1985 productivity growth) from *Economic Report of the President.*

1970s also hurt business confidence. As confidence in the future fell, stock prices declined, making it more difficult for corporations to raise capital for expansion. Stagflation pushed businesses and people into higher tax brackets while their real income was steady or falling. The 1970s was also a period of increasing governmental environmental and safety regulations that required businesses to invest in pollution-reduction and safety equipment rather than in regular plant and equipment. These regulations, while improving the environment and worker safety, likely had a negative effect on labor productivity. The 1970s were also the years of the energy crisis. As relative energy prices rose, firms substituted more workers for less energy and may have acquired less capital than they would otherwise have acquired. The effects of rising relative energy prices on the productivity slowdown have been disputed among economists. Dale Jorgenson finds that the energy crisis explains much of the productivity decline, while Michael Darby finds that the energy crisis played virtually no role.[5]

Historical Perspective

Table 5 gives a long-run perspective on labor productivity in the United States. It gives annual growth rates of labor productivity (per hour

2. Jeffrey Perloff and Michael Wachter, "The Decline in Labor Productivity: A Labor Problem?" in Federal Reserve Bank of Boston, *The Decline in U.S. Productivity Growth,* Conference Series No. 22, June 1980, p. 125.

3. Michael Darby, "The U.S. Productivity Slowdown: A Case of Statistical Myopia," *American Economic Review* (June 1984), pp. 318–20.

4. William Nordhaus, "Policy Responses to the Productivity Slowdown," Federal Reserve Bank of Boston, *The Decline in U.S. Productivity Growth,* Conference Series No. 22, June 1980, p. 153.

5. Dale Jorgenson, "The Great Transition: Energy and Economic Change," Harvard Institute for Economic Research, Discussion Paper No. 1103, November 1984; Darby, "The U.S. Productivity Slowdown," p. 301.

Example 2   Future U.S. Growth: The 3-Percenters Versus the 5-Percenters

Policymakers in Washington frequently debate the future-growth potential of the U.S. economy. Has the United States entered a new era of markedly higher long-term growth? The optimists (the 5-percenters) argue that the Reagan tax cuts in 1981 put the U.S. economy on a new growth trajectory. Because of lower personal marginal-tax rates, the reduction in corporate tax rates, and added tax breaks for capital investment, the U.S. labor-productivity growth rate from 1985 to 1995 will be much like that of the 1960s. With a 1.5 percent annual growth of labor and a 3.5 percent annual growth of labor productivity, real GNP should be able to expand at 5 percent per year without experiencing inflationary pressures. The pessimists argue that there has been no fundamental change in the U.S. economy and that the labor-productivity growth of the 1960s cannot be dupli-

cated. They, therefore, anticipate that productivity growth will average around 1.5 percent per year. This rate plus the 1.5 percent labor growth rate yields a 3 percent growth rate for the next decade.

The debate between the 3-percenters and the 5-percenters has important policy implications. With 5 percent real growth, the Fed can afford to pursue a more expansionary monetary policy. The Fed can aim for 5 percent monetary growth without heating up inflation. On the other hand, if the real growth rate turns out to be 3 percent, and the Fed pursues a more liberal monetary policy (anticipating 5 percent growth), the result will be inflationary. ■

Source: "Extent of Future U.S. Growth Is at Center of Debate Over Monetary and Fiscal Policy," *The Wall Street Journal,* December 13, 1984.

---

worked) from 1900 to 1985 and sheds a different light on recent productivity performance. First, Table 5 shows that the period from the end of the Second World War to the mid-1960s was one of unusually high productivity growth (3.3 percent per annum) by historical standards. Therefore, to use the 1960s as a standard for contemporary productivity performance may be too difficult a test. Second, it shows that productivity performance tends to be weakest during periods of cyclical instability. Productivity growth from 1973–1985 was virtually identical to productivity growth from 1929 to 1948 (a period that includes the Great Depression). Third, it shows that recent productivity performance was virtually identical to that of two earlier periods: 1900–1916 and 1929–1948.

In a major review of the long-run historical evidence, Michael Darby concludes that there has been no major change in U.S. productivity growth. If one adjusts for the changing quality of the U.S. labor force over time, productivity growth in recent years is not statistically distinguishable from long-run historical trends. Darby, therefore, labels the productivity slowdown scare of the 1970s a case of "statistical myopia."[6] (See Example 3.)

DOOMSDAY FORECASTS

The sustained growth of GNP per capita over a long period of time has provided Americans with a high standard of living. The average citizen of the United States has the ability to acquire enough goods and services to enjoy a comfortable standard of living. In recent years, some social critics have come to question the wisdom of further economic growth. They argue that economic growth increases environmental problems (more factories create more pollution) and that economic growth threatens to exhaust the globe's scarce natural resources. Insofar as there are only finite supplies of natural resources, clean air, and pure water, economic growth may some day in the future threaten our very existence.

Modern doomsday forecasts are reminiscent of the predictions of the classical stationary state; instead of seeing agricultural land as the limiting factor of production, doomsday forecasters see natural resources (arable land, minerals, air, and water) in this role. The most famous doomsday model is that published by the Club of Rome, using the computer models developed at MIT by Dennis L. Meadows and Jay Forrester.[7]

---

6. Darby, "The U.S. Productivity Slowdown."

7. Dennis Meadows et al., *The Limits to Growth* (Washington, D. C.: Potomac Associates, 1972).

Example 3   The Pros and Cons of Industrial Policy

The 1970s was a period of stagflation. Both inflation and unemployment were rising, and the rate of labor-productivity growth was falling. Unemployment was especially high in the heavy industries (steel, textiles, automobiles, machine tools, and rubber) that had been the engine of U.S. growth over the last 50 years. U.S. basic industries lost markets to Japan, Taiwan, Brazil, and other countries as a consequence of losing their competitiveness in world markets. The declining fortunes of U.S. basic industries ("smokestack America") caused many people to call for an *industrial policy* in the United States. Proponents of industrial policy argue that the government should do something to speed up the adjustment of the U.S. economy to changing economic conditions at home and in world markets. Some advocates of industrial policy favor emulating the Japanese model. In Japan, the powerful Ministry for Industry and Trade attempts to select industrial winners and losers and to speed up the shift of labor and capital from declining to rising industries by means of subsidies and low-interest loans. Other advocates of industrial policy favor more government involvement in speeding up the transition from declining to rising industries. For example, government could pay part or all of the retraining costs of workers in declining industries, give tax credits to companies for remaining in communities and retraining older workers for new jobs, establish regional-development banks to provide low-interest loans to promising industries within a region, or fund applied-research centers to develop new technologies.

Opponents of industrial policy argue that government is ill suited to deciding what industries and industrial activities are promising. Private entrepreneurs will be more likely to spot industries with potential for future profits and employment opportunities than government officials. Opponents of industrial policy also argue that political pressures will result in government funds being used to prop up declining industries (which have accumulated considerable political power over the years).

The strong recovery of the U.S. economy after 1982 has quieted proposals for a new U.S. industrial policy. In fact, U.S. economic performance since 1982 has been stronger than in countries like West Germany, France, and Sweden that have long-established industrial policies. ■

Source: Robert B. Reich, "Industrial Policy: Ten Ways to Create a Dynamic American Economy," *New Republic*, March 31, 1982, pp. 28–31.

The 1972 Club of Rome computer model—like the stationary state models of the 19th century—predicted that continued economic growth will put such a severe strain on our natural resources and on our environment that shortly after the turn of the 21st century, GNP per capita will begin to decline. The basic conclusion of this doomsday model is that our planet cannot sustain further economic growth and that humanity should adopt social policies to stop the growth of GNP and of population in order to avoid catastrophe.

Since the appearance of its doomsday model in 1972, the Club of Rome has decided that our planet can continue to grow without catastrophe if growth is well managed.

How much credence should one attach to the dire predictions of the doomsday philosophers? Economists can raise certain legitimate questions about the assumptions of their models. First, such doomsday models are based upon the assumption that the world economy will continue to use resources at the same rates as they have been used in the past. If, in the past, petroleum usage grew at the same rate as real GNP, the doomsday prophets assume that this relationship will continue in the future. Economists—using the elementary laws of supply and demand—argue that when a natural resource becomes short in supply, its relative price will rise, and the higher relative price will reduce its quantity demanded. For example, the rising relative price of oil has resulted in a major shift in the amount of oil used per dollar of GNP. The oil/GNP ratio has dropped substantially since the energy price explosion. Most economists, therefore, maintain that a freely functioning price system will retard the depletion of scarce natural resources. Second, the doomsday models—like the models of Malthus and Ricardo—assume static technology. (See Example 4.)

Example 4   An Economist's Critique of Doomsday Forecasts

Economist Julian Simon has conducted a careful investigation of charges that our globe is running out of resources and that there is a growing disproportion between our resources and the growing world population.

Simon finds that these charges are based upon very flimsy evidence:

1. Contrary to doomsday claims that economic growth is robbing the world of arable land, the quantity of arable land has actually increased markedly in recent years. In fact, the amount of land taken out of cultivation by the much publicized urban sprawl has been more than offset by the amount of arable land added by swamp drainage and land improvement.

2. Contrary to doomsday forecasts, Simon finds that the incidence of famine is actually decreasing rather than increasing. In reality, per capita food production has been increasing at nearly 1 per-

cent per annum—25 percent over the last 25 years—and even countries like India are becoming increasingly self-sufficient in grains.

3. Contrary to doomsday warnings against overpopulation, Simon finds no negative statistical correlation between population growth and per-capita-income growth.

4. Contrary to doomsday warnings that we are running out of natural resources and raw materials, Simon finds that the most direct measure of rising scarcity—rising relative prices—does not support the thesis of growing shortages of natural resources and raw materials. Relative to other prices paid by consumers, raw materials and natural resources are growing cheaper, not more expensive. ■

Source: Julian Simon, "Resources, Population, Environment: An Oversupply of False Bad News," *Science* 208 (June 27, 1980): 44–51.

The world economy in the 21st century may very well develop new energy-saving technologies or may discover good substitutes for natural resources that are rising in relative price. If the world supply of petroleum and natural gas threatens to run out, for example, scientists may discover new energy sources that will be economically feasible.

Only the future will show whether the gloomy predictions of the doomsday philosophers will prove true or whether technological progress will continue to save the day, as it did in the case of the classical stationary state. Economists tend to be sceptical of doomsday models because they believe that a correctly functioning price system will motivate people and firms to economize on the use of scarce resources and create incentives to develop new technologies to replace depleting resources. Our experience with rising energy prices suggests how market economies will deal with future shortages of natural resources. Rising relative prices have forced our economies to combine economic growth with declining usage of petroleum inputs. In this case, economic growth has proven to be compatible with declining usage of a scarce natural resource.

The industrialized countries of the world have enjoyed sustained economic growth for more than a century, thanks largely to technological advances. The next chapter will turn to an examination of less developed countries.

Summary

1. Economic growth can be defined either as an increase in real GNP or as an increase in real GNP per capita. The latter measure tells more about the growth of living standards. Economic growth is important because a country's position in the world economic order is determined by the size of the economy and by its relative affluence.

2. Classical economists David Ricardo and Thomas Malthus predicted that economies would reach a stationary state of zero growth and subsistence living standards. The stationary state would be caused by the law of diminishing returns and by the tendency of the population to expand whenever wages rose above subsistence. Because of its teachings on the stationary state, classical economics was called the ''dismal science.''

3. The industrialized countries have grown at a sustained rate since the mid-18th century. Modern economic growth is characterized by sustained growth of per capita GNP and by structural changes in the economy. The stationary state has been avoided by rapid technological progress, capital deepening, and by slow population growth.

4. Economies grow for two reasons: because the total amount of factor inputs increases and because output per unit of input (or productivity) increases. Research shows that the major factor causing economic growth is the growth of productivity.

5. Labor productivity declined from the mid-1960s to the beginning of the 1980s partially because of the change in the relationship between capital and labor and because of the change in the composition of the labor force. The major portion of the decline remains unexplained as a residual. This productivity decline likely does not signify a significant departure from long-term-trends.

6. Doomsday forecasts predict that economic growth cannot be sustained because the exhaustion of scarce natural resources and pollution will cause a new stationary state to be reached. Doomsday predictions, however, are based upon the assumption that scarce resources will continue to be used at the same rates as in the past.

Key Terms

economic growth
capital deepening
extensive growth
intensive growth

Questions and Problems

1. Explain why the two measures of economic growth can yield different results.

2. The amount of land in the world is fixed. The law of diminishing returns indicates that, with a fixed input, the marginal productivity of variable inputs will ultimately decline. Will we not ultimately reach Ricardo's stationary state?

3. Malthus maintained that whenever wages rise above the subsistence level, the population will grow. Has this prediction proven to be true in the industrialized countries? Why not?

4. Explain why intensive growth is less costly than extensive growth.

5. Over a 10-year period, real output grew at 5 percent per annum, combined inputs at 2 percent per annum, and population at 1 percent per annum. What is the annual growth rate of per capita GNP? What is the annual growth rate of factor productivity? What proportion of the 5 percent growth rate is explained by productivity growth (the residual)?

6. Economists criticize the doomsday models on the grounds that they don't take the effects of relative prices into account. Why should prices matter if the supply of natural resources is fixed?

7. From 1973 to 1981 capital grew twice as fast as labor hours (approximately). If capital grows at three times the rate of labor hours, what would you expect to happen to labor productivity?

Suggested Readings

Congressional Budget Office. *The Industrial Policy Debate*. Washington, D.C.: U.S. Government Printing Office, 1983.

Federal Reserve Bank of Boston. "The Decline in U.S. Productivity Growth." *Conference Series No. 22*, June 1980.

Meadows, Dennis *et al. The Limits to Growth*. Washington, D.C.: Potomac Associates, 1972.

Phelps, Edmund, ed. *The Goal of Economic Growth*. New York: W. W. Norton, 1969.

Simon, Julian. "Resources, Population, Environment: An Oversupply of False Bad News." *Science*, June 27, 1980.

21

Problems of Population and Economic Development

Chapter Preview

The industrialized countries first experienced modern economic growth in the 18th and 19th centuries. Since then, they have continued to grow steadily over the long run. For these fortunate countries, a century's growth of per capita GNP has brought higher living standards and, for the average citizen, has made problems of malnutrition and inadequate shelter and clothing less common.

Affluence is, however, still a relatively rare phenomenon, even in the 1980s. Affluence is the product of sustained growth of per capita GNP, but relatively few countries have experienced steady long-term growth of living standards. Affluence, as we know it, is still limited to a relatively small circle of countries—to the countries of Europe and to the areas of European settlement in North America and Australia. The list of newcomers to this circle is short. In Asia, only Japan has been able to make the transition from poverty

to relative affluence. Although living standards in the Soviet Union remain well below those of Europe and North America, the U.S.S.R. has also succeeded in making the transition from backwardness to industrialization. The most recent newcomers to affluence (Kuwait, Saudi Arabia, the Arab Emirates) have achieved this status not through a century of patient growth of living standards but through enormous windfalls brought about by the ownership of mineral resources.

This chapter will examine why the fruits of industrialization have been denied to so many and why affluence is still a relatively rare phenomenon in today's world.

Development economics is the study of why most countries are poor. It seeks to explain the causes of poverty and to determine how poor countries can make the transition from poverty to relative affluence. ■

THE CHARACTERISTICS OF NATIONAL POVERTY

Economists and international organizations (such as the United Nations or the World Bank) group the countries of the globe according to their level of economic development. At the very top are the industrialized or affluent capitalist countries. At the very bottom come those unfortunate countries that are still living on the margin of physical subsistence. Most of the world's population lives in countries that lie between these two extremes of poverty and wealth and that are generally closer to the bottom group than to the top group.

The Level of Economic Development

There is no single measure of economic development because economic development is a multidimensional phenomenon. The most frequently used measure is per capita income. Under most circumstances, the higher is per capita income, the higher is the country's level of development. Yet per capita income does not tell the whole story. A country's level of industrialization or modernization is another indicator of the level of economic development. Some countries—such as the oil-rich nations—may earn substantial per capita incomes but have yet to develop a domestic industry. Such countries may retain the features of a traditional premodern society. Although wealthy in terms of per capita income, they may lack certain characteristics of modern life—urbanization, jobs in offices or factories, social mobility, universal education—that are available in less wealthy countries. Income is highly concentrated in the hands of a very few who were born into this wealth. Other countries with more modest per capita GNPs may be highly urbanized, educated, and industrialized societies. Alternatively, the levels of economic development may be measured in terms of the health and education of its population. Some countries provide their residents with good educational and public-health facilities that raise life expectancy, lower infant mortality, allow families the choice of limiting family size, and provide a wide range of cultural facilities.

A country's level of economic development cannot be fully captured by any one statistical measure. In most cases, however, the various indicators of economic development move together, except in the case of high-income countries that are not industrialized, urbanized, or well educated. Table 1 ranks countries according to per capita income, life expectancy, urbanization, and agriculture's share of GNP. Although the correlation among these different measures of economic development is not perfect, especially for the oil-rich countries, it is nevertheless a close one.

Conditions in Less Developed Countries (LDCs)

In contrast to **less developed countries (LDCs),** countries that have attained a high level of economic development are called *developed countries* or *industrialized countries*.

> **Less developed countries (LDCs)** are countries that have yet to reach a reasonably high level of economic development.

Optimists like to refer to such countries as *developing countries*.

Where does one draw the line between an LDC and a developed country? Is a less developed country one that is unable to meet certain subsistence requirements, or should an LDC be defined in relation to a developed country? This issue of how to define an LDC is very much like the problem of defining who is poor in a given country. Poverty definitions can be either *absolute* or *relative*. An absolute definition of an LDC might be a country in which per capita income is less than that required to purchase the basic essentials of food, clothing, shelter, and education. However, national poverty exists just as strongly in a relative sense. If the citizens of one country know that their standard of living is only a small fraction of that of other countries, they will likely conclude that they are poor even if they can afford the basic necessities of life. According to this relative definition of poverty, an LDC can become developed only if it can narrow the gap between itself and the more affluent countries. Economists and international organizations typically use the relative standard of poverty to distinguish LDCs from developed countries. An exact dividing line between developed and less developed countries cannot be drawn. Instead, the in-

Table 1   Indicators of Economic Development, 1981

	GNP per Capita, (as a percent of U.S. GNP)	Agriculture's Share of GNP (percent)	Percent of Urban Population	Life Expectancy (years)
United States	100.0	2.9	77.4	75.0
Denmark	104.5	4.8	84.5	75.2
Germany	94.7	3.4	88.6	77.4
Luxembourg	90.2	2.7	79.1	73.5
France	89.6	3.9	78.4	75.7
Belgium	87.8	3.6	72.6	73.5
Netherlands	84.5	4.1	76.3	76.0
Austria	69.8	4.2	54.6	73.5
Japan	62.3	6.1	78.7	76.8
United Kingdom	57.6	1.9	91.0	73.7
Italy	47.9	5.9	69.8	73.8
Spain	41.0	6.3	74.9	73.9
Ireland	37.2	14.0	58.4	73.3
Poland	36.0	17.3	57.1	72.8
Hungary	29.6	19.0	54.4	70.7
Romania	24.3	—	50.3	71.4
Yugoslavia	23.2	12.1	43.1	70.8
Iran	22.1	19.4	50.7	58.0
Mexico	20.4	8.1	67.3	65.6
Jamaica	19.6	7.9	41.9	71.2
Brazil	16.0	10.1	68.2	63.6
Malaysia	10.9	23.8	29.8	64.7
Syria	10.0	18.7	48.5	65.3
Korea	8.1	17.2	55.9	66.1
Colombia	7.9	26.9	64.4	63.3
Philippines	5.2	22.8	36.7	63.2
Thailand	5.0	24.3	14.6	63.1
Kenya	3.4	32.4	14.7	56.0
Pakistan	2.6	30.0	28.7	50.2
Sri Lanka	2.6	27.7	27.2	69.4
India	2.0	36.1	23.7	52.2

Source: World Bank, *World Tables*, vols. I and II, 3rd ed., 1983. The per capita GNP figures are based upon a World Bank study under the direction of Irving Kravis that calculated relative per capita GNP using purchasing-power parities to convert the domestic currency of each country into dollars. The figures cited above are for 1981 except for the per capita income figures, which are for 1975.

ternational organizations charged with classifying countries as developed or less developed call all those countries that have yet to attain a high level of economic development *developing countries*. Within the developing-country group, a distinction is made between those LDCs that operate at the margin of subsistence (called *low-income LDCs*) and those that have per capita incomes well above subsistence (called *middle-income LDCs*). The low-income countries are sometimes called "fourth-world nations" because they show few signs of progress toward overcoming their development gap.

What proportion of the world's population, according to this classification, resides in LDCs? As Figure 1 shows, approximately 3 out of every 4 persons lives in an LDC if the U.S.S.R. and Eastern Europe are classified as belonging to the developed countries. Only 15 percent of the world's population lives in the developed capitalist countries of the United States, Canada, Australia, Japan, and Western Europe, and 10 percent of the world's population lives in the European communist countries of the U.S.S.R. and Eastern Europe. Of the 75 percent of the world's population that lives in LDCs, about 50 percent resides in countries outside the communist bloc, and about 25 percent lives in Asian communist countries. Figure 1 shows that the LDC share of world population has been rising since 1900. In 1900, approximately two thirds of the world's population lived in today's LDCs. By 1980, this percentage

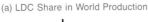

Figure 1   The Share of Less Developed Countries in Population and Production, 1800–1980

(a) LDC Share in World Production

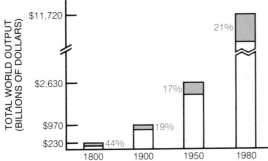

(b) LDC Share in World Population

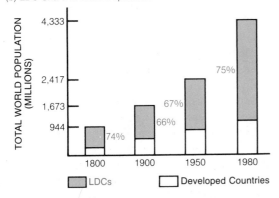

This figure shows that the less developed countries' share of population far exceeds their share of income. It also shows the decline in their share of world output since 1800.

Source: Adapted from World Bank, *World Development Report 1984*, p. 6.

had risen to three quarters. The LDCs' share of world population is projected to rise throughout the rest of the 20th century.

Comparing the Haves and the Have-Nots

A comparison of the distribution of world population with the distribution of world income dramatizes how unequally income is distributed among the different countries of the globe. As Figure 1 shows, the developed countries, which account for only 25 percent of the world's population, account for 79 percent of the world's GNP. The LDCs account for 75 percent of world population but only 21 percent of world GNP. Therefore, per capita GNP in the developed countries is, on average, about 11.4 times that in the LDCs. World output is concentrated in the United States, western Europe, and Japan. The unequal distribution of income among countries also leads to an unequal distribution of the consumption of natural resources between the rich and poor countries. The industrialized capitalist countries, for example, consume 70.5 percent of the world's oil production. After allowing for consumption by the U.S.S.R. and Eastern Europe, only 9 percent of the world's oil production is available for the LDCs. Figure 1 shows vividly how the LDCs missed the industrial revolution. In 1800, the LDCs accounted for 44 percent of total world production. The developed countries began to experience modern economic growth and by 1900 the LDC share of world production had fallen to 19 percent. The declining LDC share of world production was the result of rapid growth in the developed countries combined with slow or stagnant growth in the LDCs after 1800.

Life in a low-income LDC is very different from life in the United States. Only one of 5 people in a low-income LDC lives in an urban area (as opposed to 78 percent in the industrial market economies). One out of every 7 children dies before the age of four (as compared with one out of every 200 in the industrial market economies). In a community of 6,000 people, there is one physician (as opposed to 11 in the industrial market economies). Life expectancy is 58 years in a typical low-income LDC and 75 years in a typical industrial market economy. Only one out of every 2 adults can read or write, and only one out of 4 school-age children attend secondary school. There is a better than 50/50 chance that a girl will never attend school. Only 2 out of every 100 persons own their own radio receiver, and a private automobile is a virtually unheard-of luxury. LDC residents come from large families and plan on having a large number of children, many of whom will not survive their infancy.[1]

---

1. World Bank, *World Tables*, Vol. II, 3rd ed, 1983, pp. 142–45.

The Problem of World Poverty

The picture of life in a low-income LDC is not a very pretty one. Is material life in LDCs getting better? Have there been significant improvements in living conditions that might suggest that third-world proverty is a temporary inconvenience to be suffered only by the current generation?

Table 2 gives data on average rates of growth of population and per capita GNP and on changes in two social indicators from 1950 to 1980. On the whole, there is little evidence that the LDCs are catching up with per capita incomes in the developed countries. The evidence suggests that low-income LDCs have fallen even further behind since 1950, while the middle-income LDCs have just about held their own. LDCs have clearly experienced more rapid population growth than the developed countries. Both the low- and middle-income LDCs have experienced GNP growth as rapid or more rapid than that of the developed countries, but more rapid population growth has meant equivalent or slower per capita GNP growth.

In terms of life expectancy and literacy, the LDCs have indeed been catching up with the developed countries. The developed countries are approaching natural upper limits (one cannot raise the literacy rate above 100 percent, and human beings are mortal), and the LDCs have succeeded in improving the health and education of their populations.

On the basis of absolute poverty standards, LDCs have made significant progress. If the low-income LDC per capita GNP were to continue to grow at the annual rate of 1.5 percent experienced between 1960 and 1981, today's per capita income of $525 (in 1985 dollars) will be $710 20 years from now. Such a rate of growth, while not earthshaking, would slowly take the populations of the LDCs away from the edge of physical subsistence. The continuation of the 3 percent growth rate of the middle-income LDCs would mean a doubling of their per capita income within 25 years.

Significant improvements in agricultural output per capita have been achieved over the last decade even in some very poor LDCs. Countries like India are nearing self-sufficiency in food production

according to the statistical studies of international organizations. As a group, the LDCs have significantly lessened their dependence upon grain imports from the developed countries. These important improvements in agricultural production are called the "Green Revolution" and are the consequence of the application of new developments in seed technology in the LDCs. (See Example 1.)

If a relative poverty standard is used, then the progress of the LDCs has not been satisfactory. There is no significant trend toward reducing the income gap between the rich and the poor countries. Per capita incomes in the rich and poor countries appear to be growing at roughly the same rate.

As already demonstrated, most of the world's population lives in material conditions that would be intolerable to those accustomed to the affluence of the developed countries. Just as poverty at home amid conditions of general affluence can create moral pressure to redistribute income to the poor, so the existence of international poverty can motivate the more fortunate countries to assist the poor countries. The poor countries are an economic problem because international poverty may violate individual notions of justice and fair play. Many individuals have ethical objections to the poverty that exists in the very poor LDCs.

International poverty is also a political problem for the capitalist West. The noncommunist third- and fourth-world countries (with capitalist and communist countries making up the first two "worlds") represent more than 50 percent of the world's population, and, in most instances, they remain ideologically and politically uncommitted. Will they ultimately decide that Soviet or Chinese communism offers them the best opportunity to overcome their relative poverty, or will they decide that ideological and political commitment to capitalism and participatory democracy offers them the best prospects for progress? Or will they develop some other ideology?

Soviet ideologists have long argued that the ideological struggle between capitalism and socialism will be decided in the third and fourth worlds. Would the LDCs be willing to embrace capitalism and democracy if the Western world fails to assist the LDCs and if they continue to

Table 2   A Comparison of Developed Countries and Less Developed Countries (LDCs)

	1950–1960	1960–1970	1970–1980
1. Rate of population growth:			
in developed countries	1.2	1.0	0.7
in middle-income LDCs	2.4	2.5	2.4
in low-income LDCs	2.0	2.4	1.9
2. Rate of per capita GNP growth:			
in developed countries	2.5	4.0	2.3
in middle-income LDCs	2.8	3.7	3.0
in low-income LDCs	1.8	2.1	1.0
	1960	**1970**	**1980**
3. Life expectancy (years):			
in developed countries	68.9	71.8	74.9
in middle-income LDCs	50.6	54.9	59.9
in low-income LDCs	40.8	45.3	58.4
4. Adult literacy (per 100):			
in developed countries	96.9	98.3	98.9
in middle-income LDCS	44.0	56.2	65.2
in low-income LDCs	22.6	31.0	51.0

Source: World Bank, *World Tables* 1980, series III; World Bank, *World Development Report,* published for the World Bank by Oxford University Press, 1981, p. 5; World Bank, *World Tables,* Vols I & II, 3rd ed., 1983, p. 486 (Vol. I), pp. 143–144 (Vol. II).

fall farther and farther behind the affluent West? There is no way of knowing for sure. As individuals accumulate private wealth, they have more to lose under a communist regime; the chances of a country choosing communism are diminished by the existence of private wealth.

Resentment and envy can also play a role in the LDCs' choice of capitalism or communism. Modern telecommunications have made everyone, even in the poor countries, aware of their relative standard of living. Even in some remote villages in the LDCs, villagers watch American and European television programs, which make them painfully aware of their relative poverty. This information means that the residents of the LDCs are unlikely to be satisfied with absolute improvements in their standard of living but may judge their own economic progress and form their expectations of the future on the basis of living standards in the more affluent countries.

WHY ARE THE LDCs POOR?

Although economic development means more than a high per capita income, a rising per capita income is indeed a necessary condition for economic development. If per capita income is to grow, real GNP must grow more rapidly than population.

The classical stationary state of Ricardo and Malthus described in the preceding chapter provides one explanation of why the LDCs are poor. LDCs are typically economies that rely primarily on agricultural output for their income, where arable land is limited in supply, where population is growing at a rapid rate, and where technological improvements are practically nonexistent. Thus, LDCs contain all the basic ingredients of the stationary state. Population pressure forces such an economy to operate with diminishing returns as technological progress fails to offset declining labor productivity. Wages are kept near the subsistence level, and population growth is regulated by rising and falling mortality. Good harvests cause lower mortality but more population pressure. Poor harvests cause higher mortality and less population pressure.

The classical model supplies a first approximation of why the LDCs are poor. It is especially appropriate for the low-income LDCs, which appear to be caught in something approaching a sta-

Example 1   Population and Food: The Case of India

One of the overlooked features of economic growth since the end of the Second World War has been the growing agricultural self-sufficiency of even the poor LDCs. There are exceptions to this rule (such as the severe droughts in Ethiopia in 1984 and 1985). The accompanying figures show the relationship between population growth and the production of food in India. Even in a very poor country like India, the use of modern fertilizers, mechanization, and new drought-resistant seed (the "green revolution") has allowed agricul-

tural output to grow more rapidly than population. Between 1950 and the present, Indian population growth has been quite rapid at 2.1 percent per annum. Yet the annual growth rate of foodgrains has exceeded even the rapid Indian population growth (at an annual growth rate of 2.7 percent). The growing ability of the LDCs to feed themselves is one of the promising signs for the world's LDCs. ∎

Source: World Bank, *World Development Report 1984*, p. 93.

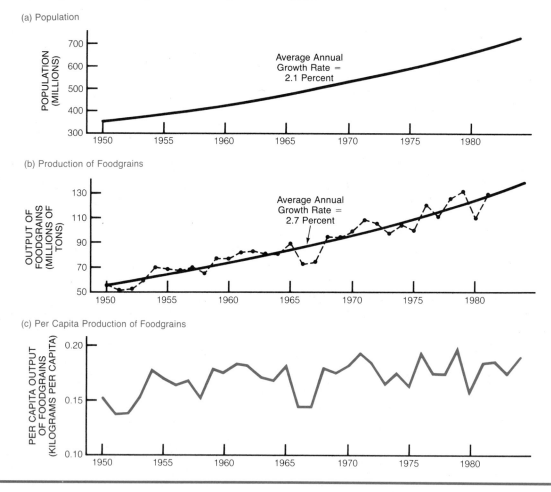

(a) Population

(b) Production of Foodgrains

(c) Per Capita Production of Foodgrains

tionary state. The classical model also suggests what could be done to release the LDCs from the confines of the stationary state:

1. If capital formation could be accelerated, labor productivity could be raised.

2. If technological progress could be achieved, diminishing returns could be avoided.

3. If the rate of population growth were to decline, the pressures of diminishing returns would be abated.

Why are most countries still underdeveloped if these solutions to national poverty are available? The answer is that serious obstacles make it difficult to slow population growth, to achieve technological progress, or to accelerate capital formation.

Population Pressures

The rate of growth of per capita GNP equals the rate of growth of GNP minus the rate of growth of population. Per capita growth can, therefore, be accelerated either by increasing the growth of GNP or by decreasing the growth of population. This simple exercise in arithmetic explains why many analysts of LDCs tend to regard rapid population growth as an enemy of economic development. As already noted, if population growth had been less rapid in the LDCs (and if GNP growth had remained the same), the per capita income of the LDCs would have done some catching up with that of the developed countries.

The Demographic Transition.   Why is population growth more rapid in the LDCs than in the developed countries? Demographers have long studied a "law" of population growth called the **demographic transition.**

The **demographic transition** is the process by which countries change from rapid population growth to slow population growth as they modernize.

To understand why the demographic transition tends to accompany the process of modernization, one must first understand the fundamental equation of population growth. The **rate of natural increase** is the net addition to the population and is determined by the relationship between the **crude birth rate** and the **crude death rate.**

The **rate of natural increase** equals the *crude birth rate* minus the *crude death rate*.

The **crude birth rate** is the number of births per 1,000 population.

The **crude death rate** is the number of deaths per 1,000 population.

In a country's premodern era, there is little or no population growth because the birth rate and death rate are roughly equal, and there are no net additions to the population. However, as the process of modernization begins, there is an acceleration of population growth. Modernization brings with it better health care and nutrition, and the death rate declines. In addition, rising incomes may cause birth rates to rise in the early phases of modernization. The first phases of modernization are, therefore, characterized by an acceleration in the rate of population growth. (See Example 2.)

As modernization proceeds, further reductions in the death rate become harder to achieve. Mortality due to infectious diseases has already become rare, and medical science is left with harder-to-combat chronic diseases, such as heart disease and cancer. On the other side of the population equation, modernization eventually causes the birth rate to decline. As married couples become more educated, they regulate more effectively the number of births through the practice of contraception. The desired number of children decreases. In modern societies, a large number of children is no longer the ticket to old-age security. Infant mortality has been reduced, so it is no longer necessary to have many children to insure that some will survive to adulthood. Employment opportunities for women improve, and the opportunity costs of having children increase. All of these factors combine to reduce the birth rate.

As the death rate stabilizes and the birth rate declines, a demographic transition from high rates of population growth to low rates takes place. The Malthusian spectre of overpopulation is removed, and some advanced societies must even start to worry about underpopulation—about negative population growth.

The gap between birth and death rate remains quite large in the developing countries. In the developed countries, the gap is narrow and stable. As a consequence, the LDC share of total world population is projected to expand throughout this century. The LDCs as a group have failed to participate in the demographic transition for a number of reasons.

1.   Unlike the industrialized countries, declines in death rates in the LDCs were not coordinated

Example 2   World Population Growth from 1 Million B.C. to the Present

Three views of world population growth are presented in the accompanying diagrams. Panel (a) shows world population from 9000 B.C. projected to the year 2000 A.D. This long-run view shows that the world population remained quite small until the industrial age began in the late 19th century. Prior to the industrial age, the world's economies were unable to support a large population. The era of a large world population represents only a brief interval in the history of humanity.

Panel (b) shows the annual growth rates of the world population from 1750 to the present (and projected to the year 2000). It shows that rapid population growth (annual growth rates of more than 1.5 percent) have occurred only in the post–World War II era. Moreover, world-population-growth rates appear to be tapering off, moving back toward the lower growth rates that were typical prior to the Second World War.

Panel (c) shows world population from 1 million B.C. to the year 2000 A.D. World population growth is divided into three eras. In each era, there was a burst of population growth until a new equilibrium (determined by the resource limits of society) was reached. The first expansion shows a gradual expansion of population up to the limits allowed by economies of hunters and gatherers. The second expansion was initiated by the move to farming and animal husbandry. The population limits of this expansion were reached more quickly. We are now in the third wave of population expansion. The limits are now dictated by the amount of population sustainable by modern manufacturing and science-based agriculture. We cannot predict when this third wave of growth will reach its equilibrium, but there are visible signs of movements toward lower birth rates and the reaching of lower limits on death rates. ■

Sources: John D. Durand. "Historical Estimates of World Population: An Evaluation," *Population and Development Review* 3 (1977): 253–96.

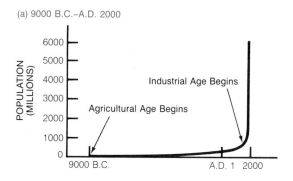

(a) 9000 B.C.–A.D. 2000

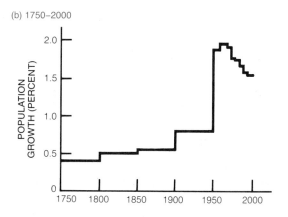

(b) 1750–2000

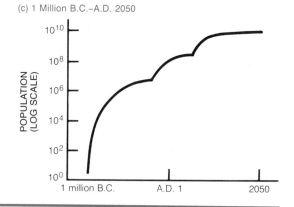

(c) 1 Million B.C.–A.D. 2050

with rising modernization and prosperity. Instead, public-health improvements (such as typhoid and cholera immunizations) were introduced by the colonial powers prior to significant economic development. Improved health care and sanitation in the LDCs caused significant declines in mortality *prior* to modernization.

2. In many LDCs—which remain rural societies without government old-age-security programs—children are still the only guarantee that one will

be looked after in one's old age. Parents that have many children stand a better chance of health and income security in their old age.

3. In many LDCs, there are century-old traditions that favor large families. The proof of manhood may be the number of children fathered. Immortality is considered assured by having many children, grandchildren, and great grandchildren.

4. As long as the country remains underdeveloped and employment opportunities are primarily in agriculture, the opportunity costs to women of having additional children are low. In many LDCs, having a baby means the loss of only a few days or weeks in the fields. At an early age, the child becomes productive in the fields and helps his or her parents.

5. As long as education—particularly the education of women—remains unavailable, the ability to practice birth control remains limited.

For these reasons, the LDCs are caught in a vicious circle: rapid population growth inhibits increases in per capita income; without substantial increases in per capita income (and the modernization that accompanies rising incomes) it is difficult to bring about substantial reductions in birth rates.

Optimal Population Growth.   Many development economists and public officials have concluded that the LDCs would be better off with zero population growth. The advantages of zero population growth are that there would be less pressure on land resources, larger per capita growth per percentage increase of GNP, and a lower ratio of dependent children to working adults. But there are also disadvantages to zero population growth. If there were no population growth, the population would begin to age. An aged population is less productive than a young population. Zero population growth means that the domestic economy would grow less rapidly, but growing markets encourage investment and risk taking. Growing populations also mean more minds, and more minds increase the opportunity for more scientific knowledge and technological progress.[2]

---

2. Julian Simon, *The Economics of Population Growth* (Princeton: Princeton University Press, 1977).

Public officials who follow simple rules like zero population growth could do more harm than good. But even if the optimal rate of population growth could be determined, the difficult task of achieving this rate through appropriate public policies—perhaps in the face of considerable public opposition—remains. Governments in LDCs such as India have been toppled by public opposition to government population policies.

Capital-Formation Problems

The LDCs encounter another vicious circle in the area of capital formation. The major portion of a nation's saving is carried out by the affluent; the poor save little or nothing. Therefore, if a whole country is poor—with most of its population living near a subsistence level of income—its saving rate should be low. Moreover, the wealthy in the LDCs tend to invest their savings into nonproductive areas, such as land, precious metals, and foreign bank accounts. The wealthy are simply reacting to the realities of LDC life: the political uncertainties and the apparently poor development prospects of their own countries.

The Saving Rate.   The English economist Sir Roy Harrod and Evsey Domar studied in the 1950s the relationship between a nation's rate of saving and its economic growth. Their work is summarized in the *Harrod-Domar growth model*.

The Harrod-Domar growth equation is based upon two definitions and an identity. The identity is the macroeconomic equality of investment and saving $(I = S)$. The first definition is that investment (I) is the addition to the stock of capital, or $I = \Delta K$, where ΔK denotes the change in the stock of capital. The second definition is the **marginal output/capital ratio (MOCR)**.

The **marginal output/capital ratio (MOCR)** is the change in output divided by the change in capital:

$$MOCR = \Delta Q/\Delta K,$$

where ΔQ is the change in output.

From the definition of the *MOCR*, one can see that the increase in output equals the *MOCR* times the increase in capital:

$$\Delta Q = MOCR \times \Delta K$$

Dividing both sides of the equation by Q yields an equation for the growth rate of output ($\Delta Q/Q$):

The growth rate of output ($\Delta Q/Q$) = MOCR $\times$ $\Delta K/Q$

Because investment *(I)* is simply the change in the capital stock (ΔK), and saving *(S)* identically equals investment *(I)*, the term $\Delta K/Q$ equals the percentage of output saved—the saving rate.

The growth rate of output equals the *MOCR* times the saving rate.

If, for example, the *MOCR* equals 0.5 and the saving rate equals 0.1 (10 percent), the growth rate of output is 0.05 (5 percent) per year (0.5 $\times$ 0.1). The growth rate can be increased by raising the saving rate: if the saving rate had been 0.2 (20 percent), the growth rate would be 0.1 (10 percent) per year if the *MOCR* does not change. By doubling the saving rate, the growth rate of output is doubled.

The Harrod-Domar growth model implies that the LDCs could solve many of their problems by raising national saving rates. As long as the *MOCR* remains stable, every 1 percentage point increase in the saving rate would mean a 1 percentage point increase in the growth rate.

Contemporary growth theory (described in the preceding chapter) teaches that economic growth depends as much or more on the growth of labor inputs (in both quantity and quality) and on technological progress as on capital accumulation. The Harrod-Domar growth equation does not contradict this more modern approach. Growth depends not only on the saving rate but also on the behavior of *MOCR*. Because technological improvements raise the productivity of existing factors, they raise the *MOCR*. If increases in the saving rate cause the *MOCR* to fall, the growth rate will rise more slowly than the percentage increase in the saving rate. Modern growth theory teaches that the relationship between the saving rate of a country and its growth rate is very complex. It does not deny that increases in capital formation have a beneficial effect on economic growth; however, it does demonstrate that limited capital formation is only part of the problem.

Social Overhead Capital.   Modern economic growth began in the developed countries after centuries of preparation. Canals, schools, roads, and cathedrals had been built in the centuries that preceded the industrial revolution. By the time of the industrial revolution, the developed countries had accumulated an impressive stock of **social overhead capital** goods.

> **Social overhead capital,** such as roads, canals, schools, and hospitals, is capital that benefits society more than it benefits specific individuals.

Some development economists argue that the LDCs have not had the luxury of centuries of steady accumulation of social overhead capital. In effect, an infrastructure of social overhead capital is required before real economic development can take place. Yet it may take years or decades to accumulate sufficient social overhead capital.

Technological Backwardness

On the surface, it would appear that the industrialized countries have already developed modern technology that need simply be borrowed by the LDCs. The technology of the industrialized countries represents a response to the factor endowments that are present in these countries. Relative to the LDCs, capital is abundant in the developed countries; the quantity of labor is scarce, but the quality of each worker (in training, health, and education) is quite high. Because of these factor endowments, the industrialized countries have developed over the years technologies that emphasize labor saving and require large inputs of highly skilled labor and capital.

The modern production techniques of the developed countries are, therefore, not well suited for application in the LDCs. The LDCs require technologies that take advantage of their abundant supplies of unskilled labor and do not place heavy burdens on their more limited resources—skilled labor and capital. Although a wealth of sophisticated technology is on hand in the industrialized countries, the LDCs remain in the ironic position of having to develop their own technologies. Although there is evidence that Japan was successful in adapting modern technology to its particular needs, most LDCs have been less successful.

Not only must production techniques suited to LDC factor endowments be developed, but these new techniques must be put into productive use. They must be accepted by farms and factories in the LDCs. In the developed countries, particularly the United States, Canada, and Australia, new agricultural technology—such as new seed types, chemical fertilizers, or automated farm equipment—were put into practice by farmers with few delays because profit-motivated farmers realized these new technologies were good for business.

In the LDCs, where peasant farming dominates and traditional forms of agriculture still prevail, there is a great reluctance to adopt new ways of doing things. There is also the unanswered question of the economic motivation of peasant families. Are they, like western farmers, profit maximizers or has diminishing returns and surplus labor forced them to use other criteria for allocating resources?[3]

SOLUTIONS TO WORLD POVERTY

The LDCs are poor because they have fewer economic resources—labor, entrepreneurs, capital, and technology—than the developed countries. Moreover, obstacles in the form of tradition, religious tabus, and bureaucratic restrictions have prevented them from utilizing their limited resources as effectively as the industrialized countries. The LDCs are caught in a vicious circle: low income prevents them from accumulating new resources, and the failure to accumulate new resources leaves them poor.

Preconditions Versus Substitutions

Economic historian W. W. Rostow, in *The Stages of Economic Growth,* formulated the notion that economies must pass through a series of stages or phases on their way to economic development. Rostow wrote that economies, in preparation for industrialization—or the "take-off" as he called it—must first establish the preconditions for economic development. As a precondition to take-off, a country must first develop a middle class to assume entrepreneurial responsibilities; it must accumulate social overhead capital; it must create a literate population; it must establish a legal system compatible with economic development. The length of time required to establish these preconditions may be substantial; countries that lack these preconditions must establish them before the take-off can occur.

Rostow's view of preconditions is basically a pessimistic one as far as the contemporary LDCs are concerned. Most of them lack the necessary social overhead capital or a strong middle class, for example. Must they patiently wait for all the preconditions to be met before they can hope for sustained economic development?

Prominent economic historian Alexander Gerschenkron offers a markedly different vision of the process of economic development. Gerschenkron maintained that countries can substitute for missing preconditions and in this way speed up economic development. Relying primarily on the historical experiences of Japan and czarist Russia, Gerschenkron described how these economies found suitable substitutes for missing preconditions. Foreign capital and foreign entrepreneurs were substituted for inadequate domestic savings and for missing entrepreneurial skills. Government bureaucracies took the place of the missing middle class. Capital-intensive techniques were substituted for scarce trained industrial workers.

The views of both Rostow and Gerschenkron have been disputed, and many exceptions to their general rules have been found. Must LDCs go through the laborious process of establishing preconditions or can they skip over the most hard-to-create preconditions by making innovative substitutions?

Bootstrap Solutions

The most optimistic analysts of economic development believe that the LDCs, by following the appropriate policies, can generate economic de-

---

3. Economists and social scientists have studied the rationality of peasant behavior. The most famous analysis is that by Nobel laureate, Sir W. Arthur Lewis, who concludes that peasants in traditional labor-surplus economies cannot employ profit-maximization rules because the opportunity cost of additional workers is zero in a labor-surplus economy. Paying workers their opportunity costs would suggest widescale starvation. Therefore, traditional methods of allocating resources are used instead.

velopment without outside assistance. In other words, the LDCs can "pull themselves up by their own bootstraps."

The Labor-Surplus Economy.

One bootstrap approach to economic development has been offered by Nobel laureate Sir W. Arthur Lewis. Lewis maintains that many LDCs suffer from a surplus of labor in agriculture. Agricultural overpopulation is so severe in many instances that labor could be shifted from agriculture to industry without a loss of output in agriculture. If a method could be found for shifting some of the redundant labor into alternative employment in industry, an *agricultural surplus* could be created to finance overall economic development.

When redundant workers are shifted from agriculture to industry, the economy is able to produce more output. Agricultural output has not declined, but industrial output has increased. To motivate workers to move voluntarily from agriculture to industry, it is only necessary for industry to pay a slight premium over agricultural wages. As long as there is redundant labor in agriculture, agricultural wages will not rise; shifting surplus workers to industry will not raise the total wage bill of the economy (wages in industry and agriculture) even though more output is being produced.

If income from this surplus output is channeled into industrial investment, more jobs are created in industry, more redundant workers are drawn from agriculture, and more surplus is earned to be plowed back into industry. This process of reinvestment continues until all surplus labor has been drawn out of agriculture and the agricultural surplus has been exhausted. By this time, the economy will be well on the way to economic development.

The utilization of a hidden agricultural surplus to pull an economy up by its own bootstraps is an appealing notion, especially to independent-minded LDCs. Development economists have pointed out two problems with the Lewis approach. The first is that there is little evidence to support the view that large numbers can indeed be drawn out of agriculture without a loss of agricultural output. Most studies of LDC agriculture show that the amount of rural overpopulation has

been overestimated and that most agricultural workers make a positive contribution to agricultural output. The second problem is the mechanism whereby redundant labor, if it indeed exists, is to be withdrawn from agriculture. One option would be a Soviet-type forced collectivization, but this approach would likely meet with fierce peasant opposition. Other approaches—the use of rapid inflation or government taxation—remain untested.

Unbalanced Growth.

Balanced growth is a broad-based simultaneous advance of all branches of the economy. Ragnar Nurkse and Paul Rosenstein-Rodan—early proponents of balanced growth—point out that without balanced growth, the national market in an LDC would be too small to support isolated modern industrial branches. Economic branches are interdependent; one sector cannot prosper in isolation from other branches upon which it depends for its inputs and sales. The basic problem with balanced growth is that it requires more resources than are available to the LDCs. If an LDC had the resources to support a broad simultaneous expansion of all branches, it would not be underdeveloped. The only way balanced growth appears feasible is with enormous sums of foreign assistance.

Albert Hirschman has argued that LDCs can pull themselves up by their own bootstraps by pursuing an *unbalanced-growth strategy*. The unbalanced-growth approach requires that the LDCs determine which of their economic branches require substantial inputs from other industries (the steel industry, for example, relies on inputs from the coal and ore industries) and which industries are significant suppliers of other industries (again, the steel industry is an important supplier for automobile-production, machinery, and bridge-building industries).

According to Hirschman, LDCs should one-sidedly push the development of industries that require inputs from other industries or supply inputs to other industries. Enterpreneurial talent is a very scarce resource in the poor countries; the domestic price system may be distorted. Consequently, there are risks that incorrect economic decisions will be made. Unbalanced growth will force correct resource-allocation decisions. The growth of the steel industry will create an excess demand for coal and ore that will signal that resources should be devoted to developing these industries. The greater availability of steel will also signal to steel-using industries that they should expand. By deliberately pursuing unbalanced growth, economic decision making is simplified. The economy will move spontaneously from one shortage to another, and, in the process, one branch of the economy will develop after another.

The Soviet Union in the 1930s, for example, pursued a deliberate policy of unbalanced growth in favor of heavy industry, while starving agriculture and light industry of resources. As a consequence of this unbalanced-growth policy, the Soviet economy was transformed in less than one decade from a fairly backward agricultural economy to a self-sufficient industry-oriented economy that was capable of producing its own machinery and weapons.

The unbalanced-growth model assumes that the pattern of sectoral expansion must be planned. A deliberate plan that specifies which industries are to be favored must be established, and the state must have the authority to enforce the plan. It is unlikely that spontaneous market forces would result in unbalanced growth. Therefore, unbalanced growth and economic planning are deeply intertwined.

Trade Policies.   The examples of Great Britain in the 19th century and Hong Kong, Taiwan, and Singapore today show how extensive international trade can bring many benefits to a country. Trade harnesses the power of specialization to raise national income beyond what is possible in isolation. Some LDCs have tried to grow by denying the benefits of specialization and have attempted to copy the industrialized countries. They want their own automobile and steel industries even though it is cheaper to buy cars and steel indirectly by producing goods for which the economy's resource base is suited (textiles, natural resources). Countries such as Argentina and India have attempted to follow the inward-looking policy of **import substitution.**

Import substitution occurs when a country substitutes domestic production for imports by subsidizing domestic production through tariffs, quotas, and other devices.

Cases of successful import substitution are rare, primarily because the products manufactured with the assistance of tariffs and other forms of protection are not competitive.

An alternative course followed by countries such as Hong Kong, South Korea, Taiwan, Brazil, and Singapore has been the outward-looking policy of **export promotion**—encouraging exports through various types of incentive schemes.

Export promotion occurs when a country encourages exports by subsidizing the production of goods for export.

In general, those LDCs that have followed export-promotion policies have done better as a group than those that followed import-substitution policies. The major success stories in the third world are those countries that have become fully integrated into the world economy, competing successfully with more affluent countries in the area of manufacturing.

External Assistance

Can the LDCs realistically expect to develop on their own, or must they have outside assistance? The issue of assistance from the industrialized countries is an explosive one in the third world because many LDCs blame their poverty on exploitation by the developed countries. Because many LDCs believe the developed countries are responsible for the low income of the LDCs, they believe the developed countries are obligated to help.[4]

For both humanitarian and political reasons, the industrialized capitalist countries have concluded that they should assist LDCs.

Foreign Aid.   If the industrialized countries give foreign aid to the LDCs, will this aid stimulate economic growth or make the LDCs more dependent on the developed countries?

Foreign economic assistance adds a new source of saving to an LDC economy. With foreign aid, total saving equals domestic saving plus

---

4. The belief that the developed countries are responsible for the plight of the LDCs is widely held in the LDCs. This conclusion has been supported by the Marxist-Leninist theories of colonialism that maintain that the wealth of the industrialized countries was created by exploiting the labor and natural resources of the poor countries.

foreign assistance. Using the Harrod-Domar growth equation, with foreign assistance, the rate of economic growth is:

$$\Delta Q/Q = MOCR \times (s + f),$$

where s is the domestic saving rate and f is foreign aid as a percentage of GNP. If the $MOCR$ is 0.5 and s equals 0.1 (10 percent), the growth rate is 0.05 (5 percent). If f equals 0.1 (10 percent), then the growth rate is raised to 0.1(10 percent). Foreign assistance increases a low domestic saving rate.

Hollis Chenery, a former vice-president of the World Bank, and Allen Strout conclude that if the LDCs use their foreign assistance wisely they will eventually be able to stand on their own feet without assistance.[5]

A New International Economic Order.
Direct foreign assistance is one means by which the industrialized countries assist the LDCs. In the view of the LDCs, the current level of foreign assistance (approximately $35 billion annually, not including foreign aid from communist countries), while welcome, is grossly inadequate. The LDCs call for a doubling of foreign assistance, suggesting that the industrialized countries should donate approximately 1 percent of their GNP to the LDCs. Few industrialized nations, including the United States, contribute anything close to the 1 percent figure. In 1983, foreign assistance as a percentage of GNP ranged from 1.1 percent (Norway) to 0.23 percent (Austria). The U.S. ratio of foreign assistance to GNP was 0.24 percent. (See Table 3.)

According to the LDCs, the industrialized countries could (and should) provide forms of assistance other than direct foreign aid. Most LDCs trade raw materials for the machinery and equipment required for economic development. The LDCs complain that their dependence upon raw-material exports places them at a disadvantage in the world economy. Their earnings from raw ma-

terials—coffee, rubber, flax, sugar, ores—fluctuate more dramatically than the prices of manufactured goods. The LDCs believe as well that there is a long-run tendency for the prices of raw materials to fall relative to manufactured goods. Such a decline would cause the incomes of the LDCs to continue to fall in the long run relative to the developed countries, but studies show no clear-cut trends. Even the low-income LDCs have experienced a significant movement away from dependence on one raw-material export (see Example 3). It appears that only the low-income African LDCs have not been able to loosen their dependence on a single raw-material export. Representatives of the LDCs allege that they are in a boom-or-bust environment and that they are unable to develop in a steady and predictable manner.

In the United Nations, a coalition of the poor countries has argued that the developed countries should set up commodity-stabilization funds to control the fluctuations of raw-material prices. This fund would operate under the auspices of the United Nations and would be funded by contributions from the rich countries. Dialogues between the LDCs and the industrialized countries—called "North-South dialogues" by the press—could yield long-term raw-materials pricing agreements that earn a fair and predictable return for the LDCs. If the world price threatens to fall below a specific price, then the commodity-stabilization fund would buy the commodity to prevent the price decline.

The commodity-price-stabilization program is the centerpiece of the New Order, but a number of economic studies indicate that export instability may promote economic development for two reasons. First, export instability will be correlated with international-trade policies that promote international specialization and, thus, enable the LDCs to capture the gains from specialization. Second, export instability will tend to decrease the average propensity to consume, since individuals faced with greater variation in income tend to consume less. Thus, export instability can raise saving rates and capital formation. A substantial amount of empirical research supports the conclusion that export instability actually promotes eco-

5. Hollis Chenery and Allen Strout, "Foreign Assistance and Economic Development," *American Economic Review* 56, 4 (September 1966): 679–733.

Table 3   Official Development Assistance to LDCs, 1983

	Amount (millions of U.S. dollars)	Percentage of Donor Country's GNP
Italy	827	0.24
New Zealand	61	0.28
United Kingdom	1,601	0.36
Austria	157	0.23
Japan	3,761	0.33
Belgium	477	0.59
Finland	153	0.33
Netherlands	1,195	0.91
Australia	754	0.49
Canada	1,424	0.47
France	3,915	0.76
Federal Republic of Germany	3,181	0.48
Denmark	394	0.73
United States	7,950	0.24
Sweden	779	0.88
Norway	584	1.10
Switzerland	318	0.31
Saudi Arabia	4,428	2.82
Kuwait	1,295	4.86
United Arab Emirates	563	2.06
Qatar	251	3.80
Total	34,068	

Source: World Bank, *World Development Report 1984*, pp. 252–53.

nomic development.[6] Paradoxically, commodity-price-stabilization funds might backfire and hurt the LDCs.

In addition to more foreign aid and commodity stabilization, the LDCs have called for improved access to the markets and technology of the industrialized countries and reforms of the international monetary system.[7]

Capitalism or Socialism?

The LDCs must decide which economic system offers them better prospects for economic development. Studies of comparative economic systems reveal that, as a group, the LDCs have a greater tendency to substitute administrative resource allocation for market resource allocation, but the rigid authoritarian control required to carry through a regimented economic plan is typically not present in the LDCs.

Some Western economists argue that one reason the LDCs remain poor is the very fact that they have allowed too little market resource allocation. The LDCs have numerous barriers to market decision making—commodity-price controls, tariffs, franchises and monopolies, and social barriers—that prevent the LDCs from efficiently utilizing their resources. Moreover, the lack of market resource allocation and the weak protection of private-property rights discourage investment by the wealthy and by foreign capitalists. Advocates of a greater role for capitalist market forces cite the success stories of Hong Kong, South Korea, Taiwan, and Singapore as proof of their position.[8]

6. See Odin Knudsen and Andrew Parnes, *Trade Instability and Economic Development* (Lexington, Mass.: D. C. Heath, 1975), chap. 6. This study confirms the pioneering study of Alastair MacBean, *Export Instability and Economic Development* (Cambridge, Mass.: Harvard University Press, 1966), chap. 4.

7. Mordecai E. Kreinin and J. M. Finger, "A Critical Survey of the New International Economic Order," *Journal of World Trade Law* (November/December 1976).

8. For a case study of the Hong Kong free-enterprise experiment, see Steven Chow and Gustav Papanek, "Laissez Faire, Growth, and Equity—Hong Kong," *Economic Journal* 91, 362 (June 1981): 466–85.

Example 3   The Declining Dependence of LDCs on Single Primary Exports

Many LDCs tend to export a single primary export. Reliance on one exportable primary product (whose price may fluctuate) makes sustained economic development difficult. Between 1960 and 1980, there has been increasing diversification in the exports of countries that have traditionally relied on a single primary export. A group of 11 LDCs, including India (but excluding the major exporters such as Korea, Hong Kong, Taiwan, and Singapore), which accounts for two thirds of the LDC population (excluding China), has managed to raise its share of manufactures to about 50 percent of nonfuel exports. Africa is the only region that has not succeeded in reducing its dependence upon a single primary export. ∎

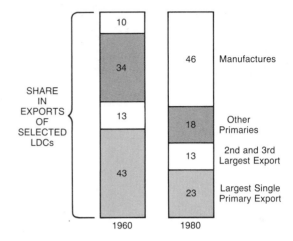

Source: James Riedel, "Trade as the Engine of Growth in Developing Countries Revisited," *Economic Journal* 94 (1984): 373.

Economic growth in the industrialized countries has been very different from that in the third world. The next three chapters will examine international economics, beginning with an exploration of the advantages of international trade.

Summary

1. Affluence is still a rare phenomenon in the world today. About 75 percent of the world's population lives in poor countries. Less developed countries, or LDCs, are those countries that have a low level of economic development relative to the developed countries. National poverty can be defined in absolute terms (countries that live close to subsistence) or in relative terms (low income relative to more affluent countries). LDCs are characterized by low per capita income, high mortality, low life expectancies, low rates of urbanization, and high illiteracy. The LDCs are poor because they have fewer economic resources than the rich countries and because they use their resources less efficiently than the developed countries. While poor countries have made considerable progress to reduce their *absolute* poverty, the LDCs have failed to overcome their backwardness *relative* to

the rich countries. International poverty is a political as well as an economic problem.

2. The classical-stationary-state model provides a first explanation of LDC poverty. The combination of rapid population growth and limited technological progress has caused diminishing returns to be a serious problem in LDCs. Possible solutions to the diminishing-returns problem are reduced population growth, increased capital formation, and more rapid technological progress. The demographic transition is the process by which countries change from rapid to slow population growth during the course of modernization. The LDCs have yet to experience as a group the demographic transition. The LDCs suffer from inadequate capital formation. Because the growth rate equals the marginal capital/output ratio times the saving rate, an increase in the saving rate will cause an increase in growth, *ceteris paribus*. LDCs also lack adequate social overhead capital to support economic growth. Although it appears that the LDCs could borrow the advanced technology of the developed countries, this technology is generally not well suited to the factor endowments of the LDCs.

3. One approach to the poverty problem of the LDCs is to help the economy become self-

sufficient. The labor-surplus model and the unbalanced-growth model have been suggested as possible bootstrap approaches to economic development. The LDCs must also choose between import-substitution and export-promotion policies of economic development. A second general approach to economic development is to use outside assistance. Foreign aid raises the saving rate and, thus, raises economic growth. The LDCs have asked for a New International Economic Order, the cornerstone of which is an international commodity-stabilization program funded by the developed countries. Its benefits have been questioned by some Western economists. The LDCs must decide whether planned or market allocation systems offer them a better chance for economic development.

Key Terms

less developed countries (LDCs)
demographic transition
rate of natural increase
crude birth rate
crude death rate
marginal output/capital ratio *(MOCR)*
social overhead capital
import substitution
export promotion

Questions and Problems

1. Explain why GNP or GNP per capita can be an imperfect guide to the level of economic development.

2. "The stationary state of Ricardo and Malthus is not an accurate description of the industrialized countries. On the other hand, it does appear to describe accurately the LDCs." Evaluate this position.

3. Describe the demographic transition. Why has the demographic transition not occurred in many of the LDCs?

4. Using the Harrod-Domar model, calculate the growth of output if the marginal output/capital ratio is 0.4 and the national saving rate is 0.2 (20 percent). What happens to the growth rate if the *MOCR* rises to 0.5? What happens if the saving rate rises to 0.3? According to this model, what role could foreign aid play in raising the growth rate?

5. Explain how the existence of an agricultural surplus could lead to bootstrap economic development.

6. Contrast the different trade policies that an LDC might pursue in trying to promote its economic development.

7. Describe the New International Order that the LDCs want from the industrialized countries.

8. Evaluate the following statement: "The LDCs should not have any problem with technology. All they have to do is to adopt the technologies that have been developed in the industrialized world."

9. Using the data presented in this chapter, indicate in which area—economic growth or social indicators—the LDCs have made the most progress relative to the industrialized world.

10. Describe the difference between an absolute measure of national poverty and a relative measure of national poverty.

Suggested Readings

Hagar, Everett C. *The Economics of Development,* 3rd ed. Homewood, Ill.: Richard D. Irwin, 1980.

Hughes, Jonathan. *American Economic History.* Glenview, Ill.: Scott, Foresman, 1983.

Kreinin, Mordecai E. and J. M. Finger. "A Critical Survey of the New International Economic Order." *Journal of World Trade Law* (November/December 1976).

Lewis, W. A. "The State of Development Theory." *American Economic Review* (March 1984), pp. 1–10.

Maddison, Angus. *Economic Progress and Policy in Developing Countries.* New York: W. W. Norton, 1970.

Simon, Julian. *The Economics of Population Growth.* Princeton, N.J.: Princeton University Press, 1977.

22

International Trade and Comparative Advantage

Chapter Preview

International economics is divided into two branches: 1) the study of international trade in physical goods and services and 2) the study of monetary consequences of international payments between countries. This chapter studies the reasons for and consequences of international trade; Chapter 23 will study the effects of tariffs and quotas on trade; Chapter 24 will study foreign-exchange rates, the balance of payments, and the evolution of the international monetary system. International economics is the oldest branch of economics: David Hume laid out the basic monetary mechanism of international trade in 1752; David Ricardo established the famous law of comparative advantage in 1817. This chapter will describe the workings of the law of comparative advantage and the comparative advantages of the U.S. economy.

This book has emphasized that people benefit from specialization. People find that their incomes are increased by specializing in those tasks for which they are particularly suited. Different jobs have different intellectual, physical, and personality requirements. Since people are all different and since each person has the capacity to learn, it pays to specialize. As Adam Smith stated:

> It is the maxim of every prudent master of a family never to attempt to make at home what it will cost him more to make than to buy.

Trade among persons takes place because each individual is endowed with a mix of traits that are different from most other people. Some of these traits are an inherent part of the individual that cannot be shared with other individuals. Trade between individuals has much in common with international trade between countries. ■

THE REASONS FOR INTERNATIONAL TRADE

Each country is endowed with certain traits: a particular climate, so much fertile farm land, so much desert, so many lakes and rivers, and the kinds of people that comprise its population. Over the years, some countries have accumulated a lot of physical and human capital while other countries are poor in capital. In short, each country is defined in part by the endowments of productive factors (land, labor, and capital) inside its borders. Just as a person cannot transfer intelligence, strength, personality, or health to another, a country's land and other natural-resource deposits cannot be transferred to another country. Similarly, the labor force that resides within a country is not easily moved; people have friends and family ties in their native land and share a common language and culture with their fellows. Even if they wish to leave, immigration laws may render the labor force internationally immobile. Thus, each country will have different (to some degree) proportions of the supplies of land, labor, and capital. A country like Australia has very little labor compared to land and, hence, will devote itself to land-intensive products like sheep farming or wheat production. A country like Great Britain will tend to produce goods that use comparatively little land but more of the other factors of labor and capital. Sweden's Nobel-prize-winning economist Bertil Ohlin pointed out that when each country specializes in those goods for which its factor proportions are most suited, international trade in goods and services acts as a substitute for movements of the various productive factors.

> The fundamental fact upon which international trade rests is that goods and services are much more mobile internationally than the resources used in their production. Each country will tend to export those goods and services for which its resource base is most suited.

It is easier to transfer the goods and services produced by land, labor, and capital to another country than to transfer the land, labor, and capital itself. As Adam Smith noted,

What is prudence in the conduct of every private family can scarce be folly in that of a great kingdom. If a foreign country can supply us with a commodity cheaper than we ourselves can make it, better buy it with some part of the produce of our industry employed in a way in which we have some advantage.

International trade allows a country to specialize in the goods and services that it can produce at a relatively low cost and export those goods in return for imports whose domestic production is relatively costly. As a consequence, international trade enables a country—and the world—to consume and produce more than would be possible without trade. We shall later show that a country can benefit from trade even when it is more efficient (uses fewer resources) in the production of *all* goods than any other country.

Aside from the tangible benefit of providing the potential for greater totals of all the goods and services the world consumes, trade has intangible benefits as well. The major intangible benefit is the diversity trade offers to the way people live and work. The advantages of particular climates and lands are shared by the rest of the world. The United States imports oil from the hot desert of Saudi Arabia to drive cars in cool comfort. Americans can enjoy coffee, bananas, and spices without living in the tropics. The economy and durability of Japanese cars can be enjoyed without driving in hectic Tokyo. Thus, international (and interregional) trade enables us to enjoy a more diverse menu of goods and services than would be possible without trade. World trade also encourages the diffusion of knowledge and culture because trade serves as a point of contact between people of different lands.

THE UNITED STATES IN WORLD TRADE

The Volume of U.S. Trade

The U.S. share of world exports was about 15 percent in 1965. Although the U.S. *share* of world trade dropped to 11 percent by 1984, the *volume* of U.S. trade increased astonishingly. In real terms, the volume of merchandise exports from the United States has almost tripled over the

Table 1   Size of Exports in Seven Major Countries, 1982

Country	Exports as Percent of GNP	Total Exports (billions of dollars)
United States	7	212
West Germany	28	176
Japan	13	139
United Kingdom	23	97
France	19	93
Italy	21	73
Canada	22	68
The Netherlands	52	66

Source: *Statistical Abstract of the United States*, 1984.

Table 2   Principal Commodities of U.S. Merchandise Trade, 1983

Commodities	Quantity (billions of dollars)	Percentage of Total[a]
Exports		
Agricultural	36.5	18
Chemical	16.4	8
Business machines, computers	12.5	6
Civilian aircraft	10.7	5
Construction machinery	6.5	3
Other exports	117.9	59
Total	**200.5**	**100**
Imports		
Petroleum	53.6	21
Consumer goods (nonauto)	44.9	17
Automotive vehicles	42.0	16
Iron and steel	6.8	3
Coffee, cocoa, sugar	4.0	2
Other imports	106.7	41
Total	**258.0**	**100**

[a]Totals may not sum to 100 due to rounding.

Source: U.S. Department of Commerce, *Survey of Current Business*, March 1984, pp. 52–53.

past two decades, while the rest of the world has been running even faster. For example, Japan's merchandise exports rose between 1965 and 1984 by about 7 times in real terms.

Currently, the United States is still the world's largest exporting country but may not be for long. The United States exported $212 billion in 1982, while the second-largest exporting nation, West Germany, trailed at $176 billion. Table 1 shows the merchandise exports of the United States, Japan, France, Italy, the United Kingdom, West Germany, and the Netherlands. These countries account for about half of world trade. Because of its size and diversity, the United States is less dependent on trade than any of these 6 countries, as the lower U.S. ratio of exports to GNP demonstrates.

U.S. Exports and Imports

Table 2 shows the principal commodity exports and imports of the United States in 1983. About 18 percent of American exports consist of agricultural goods, such as wheat, soybeans, corn, cotton, and tobacco. Chemicals, business machines and computers, and aircraft make up about 19 percent of total merchandise exports. Petroleum products dominate American imports. The American propensity to drive foreign cars, wear clothes made in Taiwan or shoes made in Italy or Brazil, and watch Japanese TV sets shows up in the heavy imports of consumer goods and automotive vehicles. These aggregate statistics hide the fact that the United States is almost entirely

dependent on foreign suppliers for bananas, cocoa, coffee, diamonds, manganese, cobalt, nickel, natural rubber, tea, tin, natural silk, and spices.

The major trade partner of the United States is Canada, which bought 22 percent of U.S. exports and supplied 21 percent of U.S. imports in 1983. Japan supplied 16 percent of U.S. imports and bought 16 percent of U.S. exports. Over one fourth of U.S. exports go to Western Europe; about one fifth of U.S. imports come from Western Europe.

Figure 1 shows how the U.S. involvement in foreign trade has increased from 1960 to 1984. In 1960, the United States exported about 4 percent of GNP, and imports were only 3 percent of GNP. In 1984, imports had grown to about 7.5 percent of GNP, and exports had risen to about 6 percent of GNP. Since 1980, however, there has been a sharp decline in the relative importance of foreign trade to the U.S. economy. For example, the ratio of exports to GNP has fallen from 8.5 percent in 1980 to 6 percent in 1984.

Figure 1   U.S. Merchandise Exports and Imports

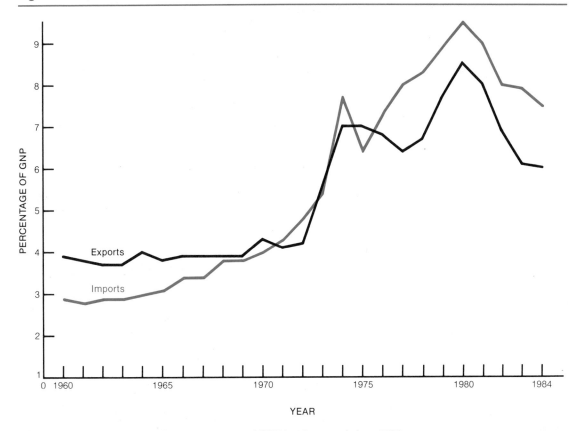

U.S. trade (exports and imports) as a percentage of GNP has increased since 1960.

Source: *Economic Report of the President.*

These increases are only partly due to America's growing dependence on foreign oil since the spectacular increases in oil prices beginning in the early 1970s. The acceleration of imports as a percentage of GNP had already begun to rise in the late 1960s and early 1970s before the oil cartel was established. In 1983, nonpetroleum imports constituted more than 6 percent of GNP, which is double the rate of total merchandise imports in 1960. The fall in the importance of foreign trade to the American economy since 1980 partly reflects the falling world price of oil. Thus, the benefits the U.S. enjoys from international trade have been increasing.

THE LAW OF COMPARATIVE ADVANTAGE

Chapter 3 showed how the **law of comparative advantage** could be used to explain the benefits people enjoy from specialization. Individuals are made better off by specializing and engaging in trade with other people. The law of comparative advantage can also help explain the gains from international specialization. Interpersonal trade and international trade are very similar because many of the individual traits of persons and nations cannot be transferred to other persons and nations. David Ricardo proved in 1817 that international specialization pays if each country devotes its resources to those activities in which it has a comparative advantage.

> The **law of comparative advantage** is that people or countries specialize in those activities in which they have the greatest advantage or the least disadvantage compared to other people or countries.

Profound truths are sometimes difficult to discover; the real world is so complex it can hide their working. Ricardo's genius was that he was able to provide a simplified model of trade without the thousands of irrelevant details that cloud our vision. He considered a hypothetical world with only two countries and only two goods. The two ''countries'' could be America and Europe; the two goods could be food and clothing. For the sake of simplicity, let us assume also that:

1. labor is the only productive factor, and there is only one type of labor (the assumption that labor is the only factor does not compromise the fact that resources are used to produce goods and services).
2. labor cannot move between the two countries (this assumption reflects the relative international immobility of productive factors compared to goods).
3. the output from a unit of labor is constant (in other words, productivity is constant no matter how many units of output are produced).
4. laborers are indifferent between working in the food or clothing industries, provided only that wages are the same.
5. there is no unemployment (each worker can produce food or clothing on his or her own without being attached to a firm that has capital).

An immediate objection to all of these simplifications is that the assumptions remove a reason for protecting domestic industry from foreign competition. In the real world, foreign competition can throw people out of work in a particular domestic industry and idle fixed plant and equipment. This objection is well taken and will be addressed in Chapter 23 on protection and free trade.

Table 3 shows the hypothetical output of food or clothing from one unit of labor in each of the two hypothetical countries. America can produce 6 units of food with 1 unit of labor and can pro-

Table 3   Hypothetical Food and Clothing Output from One Unit of Labor

Country	Units of Food Output from 1 Unit of Labor	Units of Clothing Output from 1 Unit of Labor
America	6	2
Europe	1	1

Trade patterns depend on comparative, and not on absolute, advantages. In our hypothetical example, America is 6 times more efficient than Europe in food production and twice as efficient in clothing production. America has an absolute advantage in both food and clothing but has only a comparative advantage in food production. Europe has an absolute disadvantage in both goods but has a comparative advantage in clothing production. Europe will export clothing to America in return for food, and both will gain by this pattern of trade. Each country exports the good in which it has the greatest efficiency advantage (in the case of America) or the smallest inefficiency disadvantage (in the case of Europe). America's opportunity cost of clothing production is 3 units of food; Europe's opportunity cost of clothing production is only 1 unit of food. Equivalently, each country exports the good for which it has the lowest opportunity cost of production compared to the rest of the world.

duce 2 units of clothing with 1 unit of labor. Europe can produce either a unit of food or a unit of clothing with 1 unit of labor. America is 6 times more efficient than Europe in food production (it produces 6 times as much with the same labor); America is only twice as efficient in clothing production (it produces twice as much with the same labor).

We have deliberately constructed a case where America has an **absolute advantage** over Europe in all lines of production.

> A country has an **absolute advantage** in the production of a good if it uses fewer resources to produce a unit of the good than any other country.

Even under these circumstances, however, both countries stand to benefit from specialization and trade according to comparative advantage, as demonstrated below.

The Case of Self-Sufficiency

Assume that each country in our hypothetical world is initially self-sufficient and must consume only what it produces at home.

Figure 2   Hypothetical American and European Production-Possibilities Frontiers

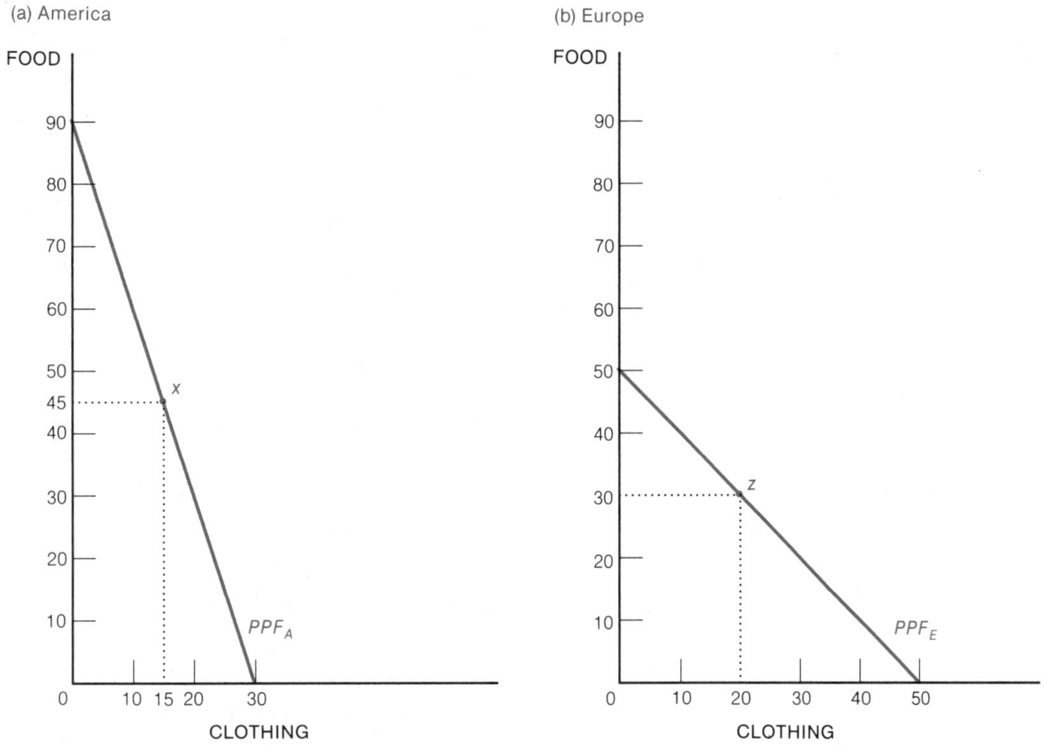

Panel (a) shows a hypothetical production-possibilities frontier for America. Based on the labor-productivity rates in Table 3, if 15 units of labor are available and labor is the only factor of production, America could either produce 30 units of clothing, 90 units of food, or some mixture of the two—such as point x where 45 units of food and 15 units of clothing are produced. Panel (b) shows a hypothetical PPF for Europe, where 50 units of labor are available. Europe could produce 50 units of clothing, 50 units of food, or a combination, such as z, where 30 units of food and 20 units of clothing are produced. (The productivity of European labor is also given in Table 3.)

America.   A self-sufficient America must produce both food and clothing. American workers can produce 6 units of food or 2 units of clothing from a unit of labor (see Table 3). Thus, in the marketplace, 6 units of food will have the same value as 2 units of clothing. In other words, 3 units of food (F) will have the same value as 1 unit of clothing (C), since these quantities use the same amount of labor. In opportunity-cost terms, to acquire 1 unit of clothing, a worker must sacrifice 3 units of food.

America's opportunity cost of 1 unit of clothing is 3 units of food:

$$3F = 1C.$$

Under conditions of self-sufficiency the Amer-

ican price of a unit of clothing will be 3 times the price of a unit of food.

These same facts are shown in panel (a) of Figure 2. Panel (a) shows America's production-possibilities frontier. Labor is the only factor of production, and a total of 15 units of labor are assumed to be available to the American economy. America's production-possibilities frontier is a straight line because opportunity costs are constant in our example. If everyone worked in clothing production, 30 ($= 15 \times 2$) units of clothing could be produced. If everyone worked in food production 90 ($= 15 \times 6$) units of food could be produced. The economy would likely produce a mix of food and clothing to meet domestic consumption. Such a combination could be point x where 45 units of food and 15 units of clothing are produced and consumed in America. Without trade, America consumes 45F and 15C, the combination of which reflects America's preferences.

Europe.   In a self-sufficient Europe, workers can produce 1 unit of food or 1 unit of clothing with a unit of labor. A unit of clothing and a unit of food have the same labor costs and, hence, the same price. In other words, Europeans must give up 1 unit of food to get 1 unit of clothing.

Europe's opportunity cost of a unit of clothing is a unit of food:

$$1F = 1C.$$

Panel (b) of Figure 2 shows Europe's production-possibilities frontier. In our example, Europe is more populous than the United States; it has 50 units of labor available. Europe has a straight-line production-possibilities frontier as well and can produce either 50 units of food, 50 units of clothing, or some combination of the two. A likely situation would be for Europe to produce and consume at a point such as z, where 30 units of food and 20 units of clothing are produced. Without trade, Europe consumes 30F and 20C, the combination that reflects Europe's preferences.

Without trade, each country must consume on its production-possibilities frontier. To produce (and consume) more requires either a larger labor force or an increase in the efficiency of labor.

The World.   If both Europe and America were self-sufficient, the total amount of food and clothing produced would be the amount produced by America (45F and 15C) plus the amount produced by Europe (30F and 20C). Thus, the total amount of food produced would be 75 units (45F + 30 F), and the total amount of clothing produced would be 35 units (15C + 20C).

The Case of International Trade

If trade opened up between Europe and America, an American trader would find that 1 unit of clothing sells for 1 unit of food in Europe but sells for 3 units of food in America. If the trader applies 1 unit of labor in American food production and ships the resulting 6 units of food to Europe, he or she can obtain 6 units of clothing instead of only 2 by producing it at home! It makes no difference that clothing production is half as efficient in Europe. What matters is that in Europe food and clothing use the same amount of labor and so food and clothing sell for the same price in Europe.

Americans would soon discover that clothing could be bought more cheaply in Europe than at home. Soon the law of supply and demand would do its work. Americans would stop producing clothing to concentrate on food production and would begin to demand European clothing. This increased demand would drive up the price of European clothing. Europe would presumably shift from food production to clothing; eventually the pressure of American demand would lead Europe to specialize completely in clothing production.

The end result would be that Americans would get clothing more cheaply (at less than 3F for 1C) than before trade; Europeans would receive a higher price for their clothing (at more than 1F for 1C).

In making decisions about trading, each country needs to know how much clothing is worth in terms of food, or the **terms of trade.**

The **terms of trade** is the rate at which two products can be exchanged for each other between countries.

The terms of trade between Europe and America will settle some place between America's and Europe's opportunity costs. If America's opportunity cost of 1 unit of cloth is 3 units of food, and Europe's opportunity cost of 1 unit of cloth is 1 unit of food, the terms of trade will settle between 1C = 3F and 1C = 1F. Europe is willing to sell 1 unit of cloth for at least 1 unit of food; America is willing to pay no more than 3 units of food for 1 unit of cloth.

The cheap imports of clothing from Europe will drive down the price of clothing in America. When Europe exports clothing to America, the European price of clothing will rise.

Although the final equilibrium terms of trade cannot be determined without knowing each country's preferences, one can determine the range in which the terms of trade will settle. If the world terms of trade at which both Europe and America can trade are set by the market at 2F = 1C, Americans would no longer get only 2 units

Example 1 The Multinational Corporation

The multinational corporation has been the focus of much debate. Some have considered its development to be a major event in economic history, on a par with the development of the steam engine or the automobile. Others consider it an engine of monopoly capital and a sinister agent of capitalistic imperialism. Thus, the analysis of the multinational corporation is clouded by the polarization in the positions taken by different experts.

The multinational corporation (MNC) is an enterprise that has subsidiaries or branches in more than one country. The crucial element is that the MNC controls the decision-making processes of a business enterprise in a foreign country. More simply, it is a corporation that controls income-generating assets in more than one country. Thus, the MNC engages in international production of goods and services, rather than simple exporting or importing.

Who are the MNCs? The largest 10 are Exxon, General Motors, Royal Dutch/Shell, Ford, Texaco, Mobil, Standard Oil, British Petroleum, Gulf Oil, and IBM. Of the 260 largest MNCs (in 1973), 126 were U.S. companies, 49 were British companies, 21 were West German companies, and 19 were French companies.

The Exxon Corporation—a multinational corporation for 80 years—has 400 corporate entities operating in 100 countries. It is the world's largest industrial company. The name *Exxon* (chosen in 1972) even had to be selected by a computer in order to guarantee that the new name would not have an adverse connotation in any one of the many languages of the world (to select the name itself cost $100 million!). That's big business.

The MNCs have been criticized on a broad front. Some think that a country (like Canada) whose economic structure is dominated by MNCs loses some of its national sovereignty. MNCs, for example, might be able to escape domestic taxation (for valuable social programs) by simply shifting taxable profits from high-tax countries to low-tax countries *(tax havens)* and by using creative accounting. Moreover, MNCs may even be able to neutralize domestic monetary policies by shifting funds abroad when home credit is easy and borrowing abroad when home credit is tight. Another basic criticism is that the MNCs exercise too much market power—exploiting consumers, workers, or the valuable natural resources of some small country.

Many also favor the rise in the MNC. The rise in the MNC in the last several decades has been accompanied by enormous increases in worldwide competition. But the most fundamental argument in favor of the MNC has been that it is an instrument of progress: it serves to diffuse technical and managerial know-how from rich countries to poor countries.

Do MNCs encourage trade along lines of comparative advantage and so promote world efficiency? No one really knows the answer to this question. On the one hand, it can be argued that since the MNCs operate on a worldwide basis they can—better than anyone else—produce output in the least-cost locations, clearly enhancing world efficiency. On the other hand, it has been charged that sometimes MNCs use the wrong technology in the less developed countries. Moreover, trade may be distorted away from true comparative advantage by the creative-accounting techniques employed by MNCs. These techniques involve pricing goods at less than cost in some locations and at more than cost in other locations; this practice may distort trade.

It is difficult to evaluate the MNCs. People tend to line up on one side if they are sympathetic to big business and on the other side if they instinctively dislike big business, but the hard evidence is not clear-cut. ■

Source: Neil Hood and Stephen Young, *The Economics of Multinational Enterprise* (New York: Longman, 1979).

of clothing for 1 unit of labor but could produce 6 units of food and trade that food for 3 units of clothing (because $2F = 1C$) in Europe. Europeans would no longer have to work so hard to get a unit of food. They could produce 1 unit of clothing and trade that clothing for 2 units of food instead of getting only 1 unit of food for the hour of work.

When the terms of trade in the world are $2F = 1C$, Americans will devote all their labor to food production, and Europeans will devote all their labor to clothing production. (If increasing,

Figure 3   The Effects of Trade

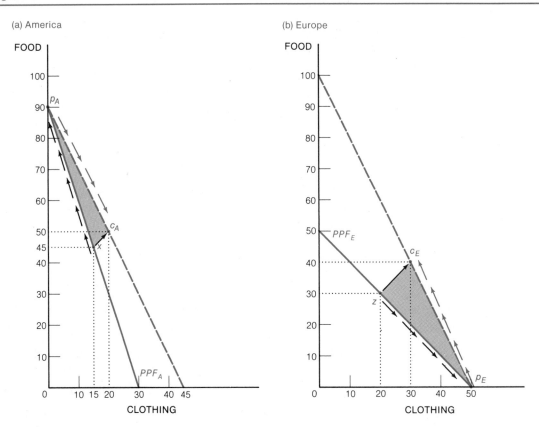

(a) America

(b) Europe

As shown in panel (a), before trade America produces and consumes at point x. When trade opens up at the terms of $2F = 1C$ (where F = units of food and C = units of clothing), America produces at p_A, specializing in food production, and trades 40 units of food for 20 units of clothing. America, therefore, consumes at point c_A, where it consumes 50 units of food and 20 units of clothing. Trade shifts American consumption from x to c_A. As shown in panel (b), before trade Europe produces and consumes at point z. When trade opens up, Europe shifts production to p_E, specializing in clothing production, and trades 20 units of clothing for 40 units of food. Europe, therefore, shifts consumption from z to point c_E, where 30 units of clothing and 40 units of food are consumed. In both panels, the black arrows show the effects of trade on domestic production, and the color arrows show the effects of trade on domestic consumption. Both countries consume somewhere on the dashed line above their original production-possibilities frontiers.

rather than constant, opportunity costs had been assumed, the two countries need not have been driven to such complete specialization.)

THE GAINS FROM TRADE

When American workers are specialized in food, and European workers are specialized in clothing, the gains to each may be measured by their sacrifices before and after trade. Americans before trade sacrificed 3 units of food for 1 unit of clothing. After trade, Americans need sacrifice only 2

units of food for a unit of clothing (with terms of trade $2F = 1C$). Europeans before trade sacrificed 1 unit of clothing for 1 unit of food. After trade, Europeans need sacrifice only half a unit of clothing (since clothing sells for twice as much as food after trade).

The gains from trade are shown more dramatically in Figure 3. Before trade, America is at point x in panel (a), and Europe is at point z in panel (b). When trade opens up at the terms of trade $2F = 1C$, America moves its production to point p_A (specialization in food production), as the arrows show. Thus, America increases its

Table 4   The Effects of International Trade (F = unit of food; C = unit of clothing)

Country	Consumption and Production Before Trade (1)	Production After Trade (2)	Exports (3)	Imports (4)	Consumption After Trade (5)	Gains (6)
(a) America	45F	90F	40F	0F	50F	5F
	15C	0C	0C	20C	20C	5C
(b) Europe	30F	0F	0F	40F	40F	10F
	20C	50C	20C	0C	30C	10C
(c) World	75F	90F	—	—	90F	15F
	35C	50C	—	—	50C	15C

food production from 45 units to 90 units. America can now trade each unit of food for half a unit of clothing. America trades 40 units of food for 20 units of clothing. Now America consumes at point c_A, with consumption at 50 units of food and 20 units of clothing. Trade enables America to consume above its production-possibilities frontier. In this example, trade shifts consumption from x to c_A.

As column (1) of Table 4 shows, America produces 45F and 15C before trade. The opening of trade causes America to shift labor entirely out of C production. As column (2) shows, America produces only F (90F) after trade opens. Columns (3) and (4) describe America's trade: America keeps 50F for domestic consumption and sells 40F for 20C. Column (5) shows consumption after trade and column (6) shows America's benefits from trade. As a result of trade, America can consume more of both products (5 more of each) than before trade.

Europe's story is told in panel (b) of Figure 3. Europe shifts production from z, where 30F and 20C are produced, to point p_E, where 50 units of clothing are produced. The terms of trade are 2F = 1C; when Europe trades 20 units of clothing for 40 units of food, Europe's consumption shifts from z to c_E—which is above the original production-possibilities frontier. Europe is also better off. Row (b) of Table 4 tells the same story in simple arithmetic. Columns (3) and (4) show that Europe's trade is consistent with America's. For example, America exports 40F and Europe imports 40F.

In this simple world, the benefits of trade are dramatic. America consumes 5 units more of both food and clothing; Europe consumes 10 units

more of both food and clothing. Row (c) of Table 4 shows that the world increases its production of food by 15 units, or by 20 percent (from 75 to 90 units), and increases its production of clothing by 15 units, or by 43 percent (from 35 to 50 units). Everybody is made better off; nobody is hurt by trade in this case. In effect, trade has the same effect on consumption as an increase in national resources or an improvement in efficiency of resource use. As a consequence of trade, countries are able to consume beyond their original production-possibilities frontiers.

In the real world, imports of goods from abroad displace the domestic production of competing goods, and in the process some people may find that their income falls. Since the Ricardian model assumes only one factor of production, the model simply cannot account for changes in the distribution of income. The model does demonstrate that in a world with many factors and shifts in distribution of income, trade increases average real income. Although trade makes the average person better off, some people are made even better off than the average while others are made worse off.

Small and Large Countries

If America began to grow due to some shift of population from Europe to America, America would want to buy more European clothing, and the supply of European clothing would tend to fall. To maintain equilibrium between the demand and supply for clothing in the world, the price of clothing would rise above the original 2F = 1C terms of trade. If America became so large that Europe could not satisfy its enormous demands for clothing, the terms of trade for Europe would have to rise all the way to $3F = 1C$—which is the exchange ratio America has under self-sufficiency. America gains from trade only when it can buy clothing at less than $3F = 1C$. When $3F = 1C$, a large enough America gains nothing from trade. The remaining Europeans, however, now find that exporting 1 unit of clothing brings them 3 units of food instead of only 2 units of food; Europeans are better off. When the small country trades at the large country's opportunity costs, it receives all the gains from trade. Thus, small countries tend to gain more from trade than large countries.

Some people argue that small countries cannot gain as much as the large countries from trade because they have less power. There is a germ of truth in this argument. Theoretically, it is possible for large countries to use trade restrictions, such as tariffs and quotas, to gobble up the trade gains of the small countries. But the facts speak otherwise. Small countries tend to restrict trade more than large countries. Both Mexico and Canada, America's smaller neighbors, restrict imports from the United States more than the United States restricts imports from them. The poor, uninformed resident of the small country loses. Ignorance of economics can be costly.

Low-Wage and High-Wage Countries

U.S. hourly wages are more than 3 times hourly Mexican wages. Hourly Japanese wages are about 4 times higher than hourly Korean wages. Yet the United States and Japan are two of the world's largest exporting countries; Korea and Mexico are comparatively small exporting countries. The law of comparative advantage explains how high-wage countries can compete with low-wage countries.

Table 3 assumed that America is 6 times as productive in food and 2 times as productive in clothing production as Europe. Therefore, American wages should be between 6 and 2 times as high as European wages. When the world terms of trade are $2F = 1C$, the price of clothing is twice that of food. In our example, the price of food could be $3 per unit and the price of clothing could be $6 per unit. If Americans are specialized

in food production, food is $3 per unit, and a unit of labor produces 6 units of food, wages must be $18 ($=$ 3×6 units) per unit of labor in America.

Europeans are specialized in clothing production. Since clothing is $6 per unit, and a unit of European labor produces 1 unit of clothing, wages must be $6 ($=$ 6×1 unit) per unit of labor in Europe. (Prices are measured in dollars to avoid currency differences.) Thus, with the given terms of trade, America's wages are 3 times Europe's wages.

Reports that high-wage countries like the United States cannot possibly compete with low-wage countries like Taiwan or Korea are nonsense. Wages are higher in the United States because productivity is higher. Reports that people who live in low-wage countries cannot compete with high-productivity countries like the United States are also nonsense. When comparative advantage directs the allocation of resources, both high-wage and low-wage countries will share in the benefits of trade. The high-productivity country's wage rate will not be high enough to wipe out all the productivity advantage or low enough to undercut the low-productivity country's comparative advantage. Likewise, the low-productivity country's wage will not be high enough to make it impossible to sell goods to the rich country nor low enough to undercut the rich country's comparative advantage. Given the productivity data in Table 3, both countries will be able to show their comparative advantage to the world if American wages are no more than 6 times higher than European wages nor lower than twice as high as European wages.

American wages will be somewhere between 6 and 2 times as high as European wages (depending on the terms of trade). If American money wages were 7 times higher than European money wages, American money prices would be higher than European money prices for both food and clothing, since America's labor-productivity advantage could not offset such a high wage disadvantage. This situation could not persist. The demand for American labor would dry up while the demand for European labor would rise. With American wages 7 times European wages, forces would be set into operation to reduce American wages and raise European wages until the ratio of

American to European wages returned to a level between 6 and 2.

Differences in opportunity costs are one reason for international trade. Two other reasons for trade are 1) decreasing costs, or economies of scale, and 2) differences in consumer preferences.

Economies of Scale

The discussion thus far assumed that food and clothing were produced under constant returns to scale. If America and Europe could produce food and clothing with the same labor costs but with **decreasing costs** as production increases (economies of scale), advantages of large-scale specialization would be gained if each product were produced by only one country.

> **Decreasing costs** are present when each unit costs less to produce the more units are produced.

Good illustrations are the Japanese shipbuilding industry and the American commercial-aircraft industry. Both of these industries are characterized by economies of large-scale production. America's early start in the aircraft industry and Japan's in shipbuilding explain in part the current competitive advantage of each country. America is the dominant world exporter of commercial aircraft. Japan is the dominant world exporter of large cargo ships. Without economies of scale, the competitive advantage of each country would be smaller.

Preference Differences

If our two countries had identical productivities but were subject to **increasing** (opportunity) **costs** of production, there would be no trade *unless consumer preferences in the two countries were different.*

> **Increasing costs** are present when each unit has a greater opportunity cost as more units are produced.

If America's preference for clothing increased relative to Europe's preference for clothing in the absence of international trade, the relative price of clothing would increase in America compared to Europe. If trade were opened up, America would import clothing and export food!

For example, some Asian countries can produce rice easily because they have the necessary rainfall, but some of these countries actually import rice because of the enormous importance of rice in their diets. For example, Indonesia is a traditional rice importer and yet devotes about one third of its resources to agricultural output. The United States, which devotes less than 3 percent of its resources to agriculture, is a rice exporter. This rice trade is explained in part by preference differences.

U.S. COMPARATIVE ADVANTAGE

According to Bertil Ohlin, countries tend to export those goods that intensively use the abundant productive factors they are blessed with. The Ohlin theory is based on the relative abundance of different productive factors. For instance, if a country has a lot of labor relative to land or capital, its wages will tend to be lower than wages in countries with abundant land or capital. Even if technical know-how were the same across countries, labor-cheap countries would have a comparative advantage in the production of labor-intensive goods. While the Ricardian theory assumes only one factor and takes cost differences as given, the Ohlin theory explains comparative advantage as the consequence of differences in the relative abundance of different factors.

The United States has an abundance of two factors: fertile farm land and highly skilled, technical labor. The United States tends to export farm goods and goods that use highly skilled labor. The United States also has a comparative advantage in manufactured goods that require intensive investment in research and development (R&D); industries with relatively high R&D expenditures contribute most to American export sales. Chemicals, nonelectrical or electrical machinery, aircraft, and professional and scientific instruments are the major R&D-intensive industries. In 1982, these industries generated a surplus of exports over imports of $49 billion. The manufacturing industries that were not in this category—like textiles or paper products or food manufactures—generated a trade deficit (a surplus of imports over exports) of about $53 billion.

The products of R&D industries tend to be new products, which are nonstandardized and not well suited to simple, repetitive mass-production techniques. The older these products become, such as hand-held calculators, the more standardized the production process can become. The longer a given product has been on the market the easier it is for the good to become standardized and the smaller is the need for highly trained workers. When new goods become old goods, other countries can gain a comparative advantage over the United States in these goods. The United States then moves on to the next new product generated with its giant research establishment and abundant supply of engineers, scientists, and skilled labor in order to fulfill its comparative advantage. It is the nature of U.S. comparative advantage in manufacturing to be in new products and processes.

This chapter studied the law of comparative advantage, the gains from trade, how high-wage countries compete with low-wage countries, and the pattern of U.S. trade. The next chapter will examine the arguments for and against protection of American industries and the arguments for and against free trade.

Summary

1.   Just as trade and specialization can increase the economic well-being of individuals, so specialization and trade between countries can increase the economic well-being of the residents of the trading countries. The basic reason for trade is that countries cannot readily transfer their endowments of productive factors to other countries. Trade in goods and services acts as a substitute for the transfer of productive resources among countries. The Swedish economist, Bertil Ohlin, has demonstrated that countries specialize in those goods for which its factor proportions are most suited. In 1817, David Ricardo formulated the law of comparative advantage, which demonstrates that countries export according to comparative, not absolute, advantage. Countries export those goods in which they are most efficient, or least inefficient, compared to the rest of the world.

2.   The United States is the world's largest exporting country, but trade as a percentage of GNP is less in the United States than in most other countries.

3.   In a simple two-country two-good world, even if one country has an absolute advantage in both goods, both countries can still gain by specialization and trade. If the two countries were denied the opportunity to trade, they would have to use domestic production to meet domestic consumption. With trade, specialization allows them to consume beyond their domestic production-possibilities frontiers by producing at home and then trading the product in which the country has comparative advantage. Countries will specialize in those products whose domestic opportunity costs are low relative to their opportunity costs in the other countries. Through trade, countries are able to exchange goods at more favorable terms than those dictated by domestic opportunity costs.

4.   Unless large countries use trade restrictions, small countries gain more from trade than do large countries. Money wages are set to reflect the average productivity of labor in each country. Higher average labor productivity will be reflected in higher wages. Money wages are not set in such a manner as to undercut each country's comparative advantage. Economies of scale and preference differences are also reasons for trade among countries.

5.   The United States has an abundance of two factors: fertile farm land and highly skilled, technical labor. America's exports of agricultural products and high-technology research-and-development products are determined by the relative abundance of these two factors.

Key Terms

law of comparative advantage
absolute advantage
terms of trade
decreasing costs
increasing costs

Questions and Problems

1. The text quoted Adam Smith's statement that "What is prudence in the conduct of every private family can scarce be folly in that of a great kingdom." Strictly speaking, a fallacy of composition is involved in Smith's famous remark. But when applied to international trade, what is true of the family is also true of the kingdom. Why does not the fallacy of composition apply?

2. Suppose that 1 unit of labor in Asia can be used to produce 10 units of food or 5 units of clothing. Also suppose that 1 unit of labor in South America can be used to produce 4 units of food or 1 unit of clothing.

a. Which country has an absolute advantage in food? In clothing?

b. What is the relative cost of producing food in Asia? In South America?

c. Which country will export food? Clothing?

d. Draw the production-possibilities frontier for each country if Asia has 10 units of labor and South America has 20 units of labor.

e. What is the range for the final terms of trade between the two countries?

f. If the final terms of trade is 3 units of clothing for 1 unit of food, compute the wage in Asia and the wage in South America on the assumption that a unit of food costs $40 and a unit of clothing $120.

3. What happens to the answers to parts *a, b,* and *c* of question 2 when the South American productivity figures are changed so that 1 unit of labor is used to produce 40 units of food or 10 units of clothing?

4. In Congressional hearings, American producers of such goods as gloves and motorcycles claim they are most efficient in the world but have been injured by domestic wages being too high compared to foreign wages. Without disputing the facts of their case, how would you evaluate their plight?

Suggested Readings

Hood, Neil and Stephen Young. *The Economics of Multinational Enterprise*. New York: Longman, 1979.

Kreinin, Mordecai E. *International Economics,* 3rd ed. New York: Harcourt Brace Jovanovich, 1979), chaps. 11–12.

Lindert, Peter H. and Charles P. Kindleberger. *International Economics,* 7th ed. Homewood, Ill.: Richard D. Irwin, 1982, chaps. 1–4.

23

Protection and Free Trade

Chapter Preview

This chapter examines the economics of trade barriers. The Greek apple industry contends that imported bananas hurt their business. Greeks love bananas, but the Greek government loves the apple industry even more. The absolute prohibition on imported bananas is an example of a trade barrier. When each country specializes and trades according to comparative advantage, each country can consume more than would be possible if it had to produce at home everything that it consumed. With **free trade**, a country can consume above its production-possibilities frontier.

Free trade is international trade unimpeded by artificial barriers, such as tariffs (import taxes) or import quotas.

Is it to a country's advantage to adopt complete free trade or is it to a country's advantage to interpose some trade barriers between it and the rest of the world? This chapter discusses the nature of trade barriers, the case against protection, the arguments for trade barriers, and American trade policies.

TRADE BARRIERS

Tariffs

An import **tariff** raises the price paid by domestic consumers as well as the price received by domestic producers of similar or identical products.

A **tariff** is a tax levied on imports.

A tariff on clothing from Taiwan will raise the prices paid by American consumers of clothing imports and the prices charged by American clothing producers.

Suppose a country levies a $1 tariff on imported shoes that cost $10 in the foreign market. If domestic and foreign shoes are the same, both imported and domestically produced shoes will sell for $11 in the home market. Because consumers will pay more for shoes than otherwise, the tariff discourages shoe consumption. Because the domestic producer of shoes will be able to charge more for shoes, the tariff encourages domestic production. The $1 tariff discourages shoe imports and foreign shoe production.

The same result (of discouraging shoe consumption and encouraging domestic production) could also be accomplished by taxing domestic consumption of shoes by $1 and giving every domestic firm a $1 subsidy per pair of shoes produced.

Import Quotas

An **import quota** sets the number of units of a particular product that can be imported into the country during a specified period of time. U.S. import quotas on imported steel, for example, might specifiy the number of tons of steel of a specified grade that can be imported into the United States in a particular year.

An **import quota** is a quantitative limitation on the amount of imports of a specific product during a given period.

Generally speaking, importers of products that fall under quota restrictions must obtain an import license to import the good. By limiting the number of licenses issued to the number specified by the quota, the quantity of imports cannot exceed the maximum quota limit.

Import licenses can be distributed in a variety of ways. One option is for import licenses to be auctioned off by the government in a free and fair market. If import licenses are scarce (more importers want licenses than are available), they will sell for a price that reflects their scarcity. In such a case, an import license is similar to tariff: it restricts imports and raises revenue for the government.

Import licenses may also be handed out on a first-come-first-served basis, on the basis of favoritism, or according to the amount of past imports by the importer. When import quotas are not auctioned off, the potential revenue that the government could collect goes to the lucky few importers who get the scarce import licenses. For this reason, some importers, especially those who are likely to obtain import licenses, prefer import quotas to tariffs. Instead of the government collecting the revenue, the importers can cash in on the scarcity value of the import licenses. The license permits them to buy a product cheaply in the world market and then to sell it at a handsome profit in the home market. For example, in May 1985, world sugar prices were about $0.03 a pound. The U.S. sugar quota keeps domestic sugar prices at about $0.20 a pound. The importers collect the difference! American consumers pay higher prices, and the government gains no revenues.

Voluntary Export Quotas

A **voluntary export quota** is a popular trade barrier in use by the United States.

A **voluntary export quota** is effected when the home government bargains with the foreign government to impose export quotas that will limit the foreign country's exports over a specified period of time.

Voluntary export quotas (or *orderly marketing arrangements*) are especially popular in the United States. The U.S. government has negotiated a number of voluntary export quotas with foreign governments that limit the foreign country's volume of commodity exports to the U.S. market. Unlike tariffs or import quotas, voluntary export quotas do not generate any revenue for the importing country or its government. Instead, foreign exporters or the foreign government collect the scarcity value of the right to export to the huge American market.

Voluntary export restrictions are particularly widespread in textiles. An agreement among 29 countries restricts trade in textiles. The importing country induces the exporting country to impose export quotas under the threat of imposing tariff or import quotas. Under these quota agreements, not all those who wish to export textiles to the United States can do so. First, they must acquire scarce export licenses. The privilege to export textiles to the United States is a property right that can be bought and sold in several Asian countries. The voluntary export quotas imposed by Japan on automobile exports to the United States is another example. Under the U.S. threat of imposing an import quota, the Japanese government ordered its auto companies to voluntarily limit exports to the United States to about 1.8 million units a year from 1981 to 1985. These restraints resulted in raising the average price of imported cars by $851 and of domestic cars by $324 in the early 1980s.[1] In 1985, the "voluntary" export limit was raised to 2.3 million units per year.

Over the last decade, animal feeds, brooms, color TV sets, cattle, cotton, crude petroleum, dairy products, fish, meat, peanuts, potatoes, sugar, candy, textiles, stainless-steel flatware, steel, wheat and wheat flour, and automobiles have been subjected to import quotas or voluntary export quotas. According to C. Fred Bergsten, a Washington-based trade expert, "The U.S. now has an array of quotas and 'voluntary' export restraints that have an even greater price effect than tariffs."[2]

Like import tariffs, import quotas and voluntary export quotas limit the quantity of foreign goods available in the domestic market. Such nontariff barriers raise the price paid by domestic consumers and the price that can be charged by domestic producers on their import-competing products. Domestic producers benefit from quotas by being able to charge higher prices. The importer who receives a license to buy cheap imports gains, or, if licenses are auctioned, the government gains some revenues. The loser from quotas is the consumer who pays higher prices.

Other Nontariff Barriers

The importance of nontariff barriers in world trade has grown in the last decade. It has been estimated that nearly 50 percent of world trade is conducted under some sort of nontariff barrier. Import and voluntary export quotas are not the only nontariff barriers. Two other major impediments to trade are government procurement practices and technical standards. Governments tend to give preferential treatment to domestic producers when they purchase goods and services. Further, the free flow of products can be impeded by technical standards that imported products must meet. For example, imported cars must pass American pollution-control and safety standards; imported foods and drugs must meet U.S. food and drug standards. American autoworker unions have proposed *domestic-content rules,* which would require domestic automakers to use American-made parts for a certain fraction of a car's cost. Recent agreements among the major trading nations indicate a desire to limit such nontariff barriers, but no agreements have been forthcoming on limiting import quotas or voluntary export quotas.

Tariffs and nontariff barriers raise costs to consumers and protect the domestic producers of import-competing products. The following discussion of the economics of protection applies to tariffs, but tariff and nontariff barriers have similar effects.

THE CASE AGAINST PROTECTION

According to a recent study, 97 percent of economists agree that tariffs and quotas lower real income. Probably no other issue in economics commands so much support among economists.[3] Economists' enthusiasm for free trade has remained steadfast for more than 210 years.

The Costs of Protection

According to the law of comparative advantage, specialization benefits the country as a whole,

1. Keith Maskus, "Rising Protectionism and U.S. International Trade Policy," Federal Reserve Bank of Kansas City, *Economic Review* (July/August 1984), p. 9.

2. C. Fred Bergsten, *The Cost of Import Restrictions to American Consumers* (New York: American Importers Association, 1972).

3. J. R. Kearl, et al., "A Confusion of Economists?" *American Economic Review* 69 (May 1979): 28-37.

Figure 1   Consumer Benefits from Lower Prices

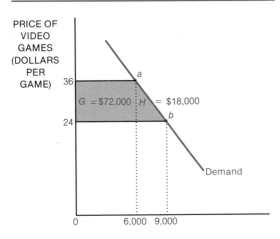

When the price falls from $36 to $24 per video game, consumers benefit by the area G + H. Those who would buy 6,000 units at $36 each (point a) benefit by area G because they save $12 per unit. Those new customers who buy the 3,000 additional units when the price is $24 (point b) benefit by area H.

Figure 2   Producer Benefits from Higher Prices

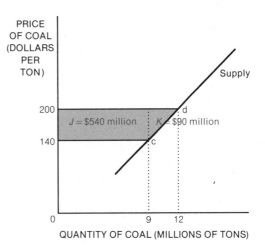

When the price rises from $140 to $200, producers benefit by the area J + K. Those who would sell 9 million tons at $140 per ton (point c) benefit by area J. Those new suppliers who sell 3 million additional tons when the price is $200 per ton (point d) benefit by area K.

while tariffs or quotas eliminate or reduce those gains from specialization. The argument for free trade presented thus far has rested on the rather simple Ricardian model of the last chapter, which, for simplicity, ruled out the existence of different types of land, labor, and capital. In the real world, when trade opens, some people are hurt. The import of Japanese cars keeps domestic car prices lower than otherwise, which keeps car buyers happy but certainly hurts domestic auto producers. The export of American wheat keeps domestic prices of bread higher than otherwise but makes wheat farmers happy. The law of comparative advantage, however, guarantees that the *net* advantages are on the side of trade rather than protection.

Figure 1 shows why consumers benefit from lower prices. If the price of a Pac Man video game is $36, the demand curve in Figure 1 shows that 6,000 games are demanded. If the price of the game were to fall to $24, 9,000 games would be demanded. The gain to consumers of the lower price is the area G + H. The people who would have bought 6,000 units at $36 only have to pay $24 and, therefore, save $12 per unit. Their gain

is $12 × 6,000 or $72,000 (area G). When the price is $24, new customers come into the market who buy 3,000 additional video games. The average new customer would have been willing to pay $30 (the average of $36 and $24). Since new customers are paying only $24 per game, their gain is $6 × 3,000 or $18,000 (area H). Thus, if the price falls from $36 to $24 per game, consumers gain G + H. Conversely, if the price rises from $24 to $36, consumers lose G + H.

The demand curve in Figure 1 showed how consumers benefit from lower prices. Similarly, the supply curve in Figure 2 can show how producers benefit from higher prices. If the price of a ton of coal is $140, Figure 2 shows that at that price 9 million tons of coal would be supplied. If the price of coal were $200, 12 million tons would be supplied. The gain to producers from raising the price from $140 to $200 is the area J + K. Coal producers who would have supplied 9 million tons at a price of $140 receive $200 per ton (a $60 gain on each of the 9 million tons). Their gain is $60 × 9 million or $540 million (area J). When the price rises to $200 per ton, 3 million additional tons are produced. The average producer of this new coal would have been will-

Figure 3   The Costs of a Prohibitive Tariff

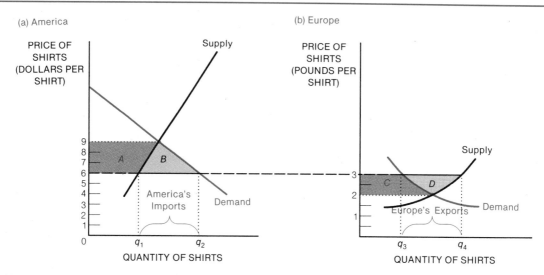

With a prohibitive tariff, the prices paid in each country are determined by the supply and demand curves in each country. To compare prices, we assume that $2 = £1. If there were no tariff, prices would be the same in the two countries. The prohibitive tariff in America raises the price in America from $6 to $9. Consumers lose area *A* + *B*, but producers gain area *A*. The net loss to America is area *B*. In Europe, prices fall from £3 to £2, and producers lose area *C* + *D*, while consumers gain *C*. The gain to consumers is less than the loss of producers. The net loss to Europe is area *D*.

ing to receive $170 (the average of $200 and $140) for a ton of coal. Since the new suppliers are in fact receiving $200, their gain is $30 × 3 million or $90 million (area *K*). Thus, if the price of a ton of coal rises from $140 to $200, producers gain *J* + *K*. Conversely, if the price falls from $200 to $140, producers lose *J* + *K*.

A Prohibitive Tariff.   The costs of protection are easiest to understand by examining the effects of a **prohibitive tariff** (as opposed to a **nonprohibitive tariff**).

A **prohibitive tariff** is a tariff that is high enough to cut off all imports of the product.

A **nonprohibitive tariff** does not wipe out all imports of the product.

Panel (a) of Figure 3 shows the hypothetical demand-and-supply situation in America for shirts; panel (b) shows the hypothetical demand-and-supply situation in Europe for shirts. For each "country," the supply curve shows the quantity of shirts supplied by domestic producers at each price, and the demand curve shows the quantity demanded by domestic consumers at each price.

For simplicity, we will assume that American and European shirts are the same and that the European currency is the pound, where $2 equals £1. For simplicity, we will also assume that Europe and America are the only countries in the world economy.

Using these simple assumptions, one can determine the gains from trade in shirts. With free trade, the price of shirts would be the same in America and Europe. If prices were different, importers would buy in the cheap market and sell in the dear market until prices were equalized. In our example, the price in America under free-trade conditions would be $6 (in Europe £3). America would be importing shirts from Europe. America's excess of consumption over production (imports) would just match Europe's excess of production over consumption (exports).

Suppose America imposed a prohibitive tariff on shirt imports high enough to cut off all shirt imports. Without any trade, the prices in the two countries would diverge; they would be determined exclusively by domestic supply and demand conditions. Europe's price of shirts would be £2 (or the equivalent of $4) and America's price would be $9 (or the equivalent of £4.5).

Without trade, the difference between American and European shirt prices is $5. Thus, if America imposed a tariff exceeding $5, the incentive to trade would be wiped out because imported shirts would cost more than the domestic price ($4 plus the tariff of more than $5).

As demonstrated earlier, the increase in price from $6 (with trade) to $9 (with a prohibitive tariff) would result in consumers losing the shaded areas $A + B$. America's shirt consumers lose, but American producers gain, as a consequence of higher prices. The producers of shirts in America would gain area A. In panel (a) of Figure 3, the cost of tariff protection to consumers $(A + B)$ exceeds the gains to producers (A). The net cost of tariff protection to the whole American economy is area B.

Europe also loses from a prohibitive tariff, as shown in panel (b). With free trade, Europe's price of shirts is £3 (or $6). A prohibitive tariff eliminates exports, and the European price must equate domestic supply with domestic demand. If Europe cannot export shirts, the price of its shirts must be £2. The prohibitive American tariff hurts European shirt producers by the area $C + D$ but benefits European shirt consumers by area C. The gain to consumers (C) is less than the loss to producers $(C + D)$. Thus, Europe suffers a net loss of area D.

A Nonprohibitive Tariff.

As just demonstrated, a prohibitive tariff causes losses in both the exporting and importing countries. Nonprohibitive tariffs, however, do not eliminate imports entirely. Figure 4 shows the supply and demand conditions in a country whose imports of a particular good are so small relative to the world supply that the world price (p_w) is taken as given. The amount imported by this country will not affect the world price.[4]

With a zero tariff, consumers can purchase all they want at the prevailing world price, p_w. According to Figure 4, the quantity represented by the distance between q_1 and q_4 would be imported because this quantity is the difference between the quantity demanded at p_w and the quantity supplied by domestic producers.

Figure 4   The Effects of a Nonprohibitive Tariff

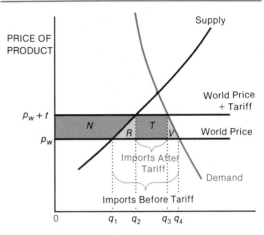

Before the nonprohibitive tariff, the price of the product is p_w. The tariff raises the price to $p_w + t$; that is, the world price plus the amount of the duty. Consumers lose area $N + R + T + V$. Producers gain N. The government gains the tariff revenue T, which equals the tariff per unit times the quantity of imports. The net loss is $R + V$. The tariff lowers imports from $(q_4 - q_1)$ to $(q_3 - q_2)$.

When a tariff (t) is imposed, the price rises to $p_w + t$; the new domestic price equals the world price plus the tariff rate. The country now imports only that quantity represented by the distance between q_2 and q_3.

The tariff benefits domestic producers by the area N. The government (or public) benefits by area T—which equals the revenue from the tariff (the tariff rate times the quantity of imports). The loss to consumers from the increase in price is the sum of areas $N + R + T + V$. If the gains (area $N + T$) are subtracted from the losses (area $N + R + T + V$), the nonprohibitive tariff imposes a net loss to the country of area $R + V$.

The bottom line is that protection imposes costs on society that are greater than the benefits received by the individual industries being protected. Trade barriers raise prices and lead to economic inefficiency (shifting resources from efficient to less efficient industries). In 1980, protection cost each U.S. family an estimated $1,020.[5] Another way of looking at the costs of

---

4. Note that this assumption is not satisfied in Figure 3: there are only two countries, and the number of shirts imported by America affects the world price of shirts.

5. M. Weidenbaum and M. Munger, ''Protection at Any Price?'' *Regulation* (July/August 1983), pp. 14-18.

protection is to examine the cost of maintaining a job through protection. A trade barrier increases the number of jobs available in the protected industry (but not necessarily in the economy). Example 1 estimates the annual costs to consumers per job protected by different trade barriers. In general, the cost per job is more than twice as much as the average earnings in that job. In other words, if trade barriers save a $20,000-a-year job, that job costs the rest of the community more than $40,000.

Such losses may be an underestimate, according to economists Gordon Tullock and Anne Krueger. Tullock and Krueger argue that because producers have an incentive to expend resources to get the tariff passed, the import-competing industry may form a committee, lobby Congress, or advertise the plight of its industry. When the color-TV industry was hurt by imports, the industry formed COMPACT (the Committee to Preserve American Color Television). Such expenditures reduce gains to protected producers and, thus, further increase the costs of protection.

Exports Pay for Imports

Exports subtract from domestic consumption; imports add to domestic consumption. The gains from trade consist of imported goods that can be gained cheaper by importing them than by producing them at home.

From 1970 to 1983, the United States exported goods and services worth $2,891 billion and imported $2,858 billion worth of goods and services. Over the last 13 years, the United States has exported about the same amount as it has imported in goods *and* services. The close correspondence is no accident. In the long run, exports must pay for imports. Chapter 22 described a simple world where America trades only with Europe and simply ships food in return for clothing. In this case, American exports of food are paying for clothing imports from Europe. The more America exports food the more clothing imports are brought in, and vice versa. The reason exports of goods and services must pay for imports of goods and services is that, in the long run, countries want each other's goods, not each other's money. The next chapter describes how a surplus of imports over exports must be financed by foreign investment in domestic industries.

If the United States, or any country, restricts imports it necessarily restricts exports. In other words, subsidizing import-competing industries by means of tariff or nontariff barriers penalizes a whole host of unseen export industries. Imports can be more visible than exports.[6]

If tariffs impose a cost on the community, why do they exist? Why would a representative democracy, which is supposed to represent consumer interests, establish trade barriers?

The explanation for tariffs is that the costs imposed by a tariff are highly diffused among millions of people, while the (smaller) benefits are concentrated among specific sectors of the economy associated with the protected industry. The costs imposed on the community are large in total but so small per person that it is not worth the trouble to any one person to join a committee to fight tariffs on each and every imported good, while the benefits to protected sectors are well worth the costs of lobbying. For example, assume people devote about 0.5 percent of all consumption to sugar (in all its various forms). A trade barrier that raises the price of sugar by 50 percent helps domestic sugar producers enormously, but it raises the cost of living to consumers by only 0.25 percent (50 percent of 0.5 percent). To the consumer, this cost is just too small to worry about. The costs of fighting against each request for protection are prohibitive.

The people who would have an incentive to lobby Congress heavily would be the foreign competitors of the domestic import-competing industry seeking protection. But these foreign competitors have comparatively little political clout in the United States.

PROTECTIONIST ARGUMENTS

Preventing Unfair Foreign Competition

The economy gains from foreign trade because it can obtain imports cheaper from abroad than by

---

6. One of the authors was once on a flight to Europe to sell his services to a foreign university for a short time (exporting). Sitting next to him was an engineer off to Europe to sell his engineering talents. Even the Boeing 747 was an export to the foreign airline. The engineer fretted that the United States ''can't export anything and imports too much.'' The author decided it was better to have a pleasant trip than win a debating point!

Example 1   The Costs of Protection

The costs of protection are vividly illustrated by the annual costs to consumers per protected job. The accompanying table draws on studies by M. Markre, D. Tarr, M. Weidenbaum, M. Munger, R. Crandall, and Wharton Econometrics. Trade barriers protect jobs in particular industries at the cost of higher prices for consumers. What is the ratio of annual costs to benefits? The table shows that the ratio of cost to benefits ranges from 10 for citizen's band transceivers to 3.6 for autos. In other words,

the trade barrier for citizen's band transceivers costs consumers $85,539 for each $8,500 job saved! The trade barrier for autos costs consumers $85,400 for each $23,566 job saved. Thus, the hidden costs of protection far exceed the visible benefits. ∎

Source: Keith E. Maskus, "Rising Protectionism and U.S. International Trade Policy," Federal Reserve Bank of Kansas City, *Economic Review* (July/August, 1984), pp. 3-17.

Product and Restriction	Number of Jobs Protected	Average Earnings	Cost Per Job	Ratio of Cost to Earnings
Citizens' band transceivers (tariffs, 1978–81)	587	$ 8,500	$85,539	10.1
Apparel (tariffs, 1977–81)	116,188	6,669	45,549	6.8
Footwear* (tariffs and quotas, 1977)	21,000	8,340	77,714	9.3
Carbon Steel* (tariffs and quotas, 1977)	20,000	24,329	85,272	3.5
Autos* (proposed local content law, 1986–91)	58,000	23,566	85,400	3.6

*In 1980 dollars.

making them at home. The domestic producers of goods that are close or perfect substitutes for these imports try to convince their governments, and others, that such competition is unfair. This argument takes many forms and is probably the most widely used protectionist argument.

Low Foreign Wages. According to the theory of comparative advantage, high-wage countries will be able to export to or compete effectively against low-wage countries in those industries in which their productivity advantage more than offsets their wage disadvantage. Likewise,low-wage countries will be able to export to or compete effectively against high-productivity countries in those industries in which their wage advantage more than offsets their productivity disadvantage (see Chapter 22). The industries in the high-wage country that can export are the industries in which the country has a comparative advantage. The industries in the high-wage country that cannot compete, due to their low productivity advantage, are the industries in which the high-wage country has a comparative disadvantage. Moreover, every country will have industries in

which it has a comparative advantage and industries in which it has a comparative disadvantage. If one country could undercut every other country in every good, its wages (relative to the rest of the world) would be bid up until the country would begin to import.

The industries in the advanced countries that cannot compete complain that they are subjected to unfair competition because of the low wages abroad. Some years ago during a House Committee hearing, Representative Noah Mason observed:

We have just listened to the American Knit Handwear Association and the America Seafood Association and the Harley-Davidson Motorcycle Co. representative, and all three state that they represent an industry that is most efficient in the world, as compared to the industries abroad. But they all three stated that they are being injured because of imports from abroad . . . because . . . of low wages there, high wages here.

If our people are to compete against the people of the other countries then we have got to cut our wages in half.

To some business managers and politicians, it

seems unfair to be more efficient on a productivity basis and yet be unable to compete because wages are too high. If the above view were sound, it would be necessary to erect trade barriers so that all of the industries in which the United States had a comparative disadvantage could supply the home market. The erection of such barriers, however, would destroy U.S. export trade and would severely lower the real income of the American people. One could argue that it is unfair to erect trade barriers that would raise the incomes of those hurt by import competition but would lower the incomes of the rest of the community even more. This trade-off is a key element of the theory of comparative advantage.

Dumping.   Another version of the complaint that foreign competition is unfair alleges that foreign goods are ''dumped'' on the home market at a cost less than the foreign cost.

The **dumping** complaint is even enshrined in law. The U.S. Tariff Act of 1930, as amended by the Trade Agreements Act of 1979, provides for special antidumping duties to be imposed when foreign goods are sold in the home market for less than the price they would fetch in the foreign market. The original Anti-Dumping Law was passed in 1921.

> **Dumping** occurs when a country sells a good in another country at a price less than the price charged in the home country.

Public attitudes towards dumping are peculiar. As Charles P. Kindleberger has pointed out, most people appear to have a subconscious producer's bias, which leads them to applaud antidumping actions. When dumping occurs, however, domestic consumers are buying goods more cheaply than foreign consumers. The beneficiaries are the domestic consumers, and the losers are the domestic firms competing with the dumped products. The theory of comparative advantage points out that the advantage of foreign trade is that a country (as a whole) is made better off if it can obtain goods more cheaply abroad than at home; the cheaper are the foreign goods, the greater is the consumer benefit.

International-trade economists are suspicious of antidumping laws. The case against them has been made by Charles Kindleberger:

Countervailing measures against alleged dumping are obnoxious because they reduce the flexibility and elasticity of international markets and reduce the potential gain from trade. From 1846 to 1913, when Britain followed a free-trade policy, distress goods in any part of the world could be disposed of in London . . . to the benefit of the British consumer and the overseas producer. With antidumping tariffs everywhere, adjustment after miscalculations which result in overproduction is much less readily effected.[7]

The only time antidumping duties might be appropriate is in the case of predatory dumping, where the foreign firm monopolizes the domestic market by temporarily lowering prices and then raising them to an even higher level after the domestic competitors have been driven out of business.

Foreign Export Subsidies.   One of the most important arguments for protection in today's world is similar to the dumping complaint, but the ''dumping'' is caused by the actions of a foreign government rather than the actions of a foreign firm. Business managers who must compete against foreign imports argue that if a foreign government provides export subsidies to their exporters, then domestic firms face unfair competition. This argument, like the dumping argument, is supported by the U.S. **countervailing duty.**

> A **countervailing duty** is a duty imposed on foreign imports which are subsidized by their home governments.

When a foreign government subsidizes exports to, say, the United States, the ultimate beneficiaries are the American people. The losers are the residents of the foreign country and the special interests in the United States that produce domestic import substitutes. Textiles from Argentina, radial tires from Canada, sugar from the European Economic Community, molasses from France, tomato products from Greece, refrigerators from Italy, and chains from Spain are all actual examples of goods exported to the United States that have received governmental subsidies. Even the United States, which has a solid comparative advantage

---

7. Charles P. Kindleberger, *International Economics,* 5th ed. (Homewood: Richard D. Irwin, 1973), p. 156.

in commercial aircraft, subsidizes the export of aircraft through below-market loans to the Boeing and McDonnell-Douglas corporations.

Those who desire protection from subsidized foreign exports have a powerful political argument, but there is no economic argument for countervailing duties. The benefit of foreign trade is imports; the opportunity cost of foreign trade is exports. Protectionists reason that exports are good and imports are bad. This reasoning is true for the businesses that must compete with foreign imports but not for the economy as a whole. Foreign export subsidies are a gift to the American people. To offset this gift by imposing countervailing duties is a perverse policy—like the dog biting the hand that feeds it. (See Example 2.)

Protecting Infant Industries

Alexander Hamilton, the first U.S. Secretary of the Treasury, argued that the "infant" or new industries of newly developing economies need protection in their initial stages. This Hamiltonian argument is repeated today by many economists and politicians interested in accelerating the economic development of nonindustrialized countries. There are two versions of the infant-industry argument. One version is difficult to defend in terms of economic theory; the other makes more sense.

The most frequently encountered infant-industry argument amounts to a disguised brand of simple protectionism. It is argued that in many industries economies of scale are present and that an initial stage of learning by doing is necessary to make the plant competitive on an international basis. A small, new plant must face higher costs than its foreign rivals because the rivals are larger and have been in the business a long time. Hence, some argue that it is necessary to protect new industries until they can stand on their own feet.

This argument ignores the fact that in virtually every business enterprise the first few years of activity are characterized by losses. Until businesses become known externally, until a competent staff is acquired, and until early production difficulties are overcome, it is difficult to make a profit. Most successful businesses are characterized by losses in the first few years and profits thereafter. To wait five or ten years or even more for a business venture to pay off is not unusual in business. Capital markets allow business firms to borrow the funds from lenders or venture capitalists to finance their investments. If these investments paid profits from the beginning, it would not be necessary to borrow.

To argue that the government must protect an industry from foreign competition implies that the private market has failed to see the profit opportunities in the infant industry. Given the way information is distributed in this world the argument is highly improbable. Information is costly to acquire. Those who are most likely to have information are those who would benefit the most from it. Thus, it is very unlikely that a government bureaucracy or a House committee would have more valuable information about the future course of profits in an industry than potential investors.

While there are isolated examples of the ability of government to pick out winners in the race for comparative advantage, the general record has not been impressive. The most famous result of government policy that fostered a particular industry is the Concorde supersonic jet. The Concorde cost French taxpayers $4.4 billion by 1979, and since that time revenues have fallen far short of its actual operating costs. Both Britain and France have attempted to encourage an internationally competitive computer industry, but none of the firms involved has been able to turn a profit.

Economists Leland Yeager and David Tuerck have found that historically new industries do not need protection:

> Manufacture of iron, hats, and other goods got a foothold in Colonial America despite British attempts at suppression. Manufacture of textiles, shoes, steel, machine tools, airplanes, and countless other goods has arisen and flourished in the American West and South despite competition under internal free trade with the established industries of the Northeast.[8]

Another version of the infant-industry argument is that a particular industry may yield external benefits to the rest of the community for a certain period of time. These external benefits cannot be captured by the initial investors and,

---

8. Leland B. Yeager and David G. Tuerck, *Trade Policy and the Price System* (Scranton, Pa.: International Textbook Company, 1966). This excellent book contains almost all the arguments pro and con for free trade but is strongly opposed to protection.

Example 2   The U.S. Countervailing-Duty Statute

The U.S. has had a *countervailing-duty* statute since the late 1890s. Such a statute requires a countervailing duty if a foreign government subsidizes its exports to the United States. The current countervailing-duty code passed in 1979 is an example of how an understanding of the law of comparative advantage helped to frame a better statute.

For many years the United States had a countervailing-duty code that caused two basic conflicts with the code approved by European countries and GATT (the General Agreement on Tariffs and Trade). The first conflict was that the United States did not have an "injury test" included in its code. Hence, even if a foreign-export subsidy did not do serious harm to a domestic industry, the United States was still bound to impose a countervailing duty. This provision, of course, conflicts seriously with the law of comparative advantage. When the foreign government subsidizes exports to the United States, the United States benefits. The next best thing to no countervailing duties is to have an injury test, which reduces the range of application of the countervailing-duty statute. The Trade Agreements Act of 1979 included an injury test in the new code. Now significant injury to domestic industry must be demonstrated before a countervailing duty can be imposed.

The second conflict in the old U.S. code was its failure to distinguish between pure export subsidies and rebates of sales or value-added taxes levied on foreign exporters. A typical European firm pays a *value-added tax (VAT)* on the value of the labor, land, and capital used in the business. If the firm exports goods to another country, the value-added tax is rebated. Many argued, incorrectly, that American firms were handicapped in world trade because the corporate income tax was not rebated to American exporters.

This argument conflicts with the theory of international trade because exports pay for imports. Import restrictions ultimately restrict exports. Export encouragements ultimately encourage imports. Restricting imports by a 10 percent tax can be offset by encouraging exports by a 10 percent subsidy. The European VAT tax applies to Europe's imports. Thus, a European country imposes extra duties on imports that correspond to the VAT on that category of goods. The extra import duties restrict trade away from the European comparative advantage. To offset the VAT on imports, the European countries use an export subsidy equal to the VAT on the category of goods being exported. This export subsidy encourages trade. As the outstanding economists who advised the European Common Market countries had perceived, a general export subsidy of *x* percent merely offsets a general import duty of *x* percent. Except for the short-term impact on exchange rates, the European export subsidies and added import duties (called *border-tax adjustments*) have little influence on Europe's trade with the rest of the world.

The new U.S. code distinguishes between price export subsidies and rebates of sales or VAT taxes—an important improvement over the old law. ■

---

thus, will not be included in private profitability calculations. A new firm might have to adapt from foreign to local conditions. The knowledge it acquires about new technology would not be patentable and later users could take full advantage of their experience. The knowledge acquired by the one firm could be used by all; hence, public action in the form of protection may be called for to promote this activity.

Robert Baldwin of the University of Wisconsin has pointed out that even this reason for supporting an infant industry does not justify import duties. Baldwin argues that even if external benefits are present, a tariff does not guarantee that the most desirable type of knowledge-acquisition ex-

penditures will be made. It may be better to subsidize firms who make the initial contacts or first acquire the knowledge to use new technology.

Another reason why tariffs are a poor device for subsidizing an industry is that tariffs raise costs to consumers. Hence, if it is desirable to stimulate some industries, a direct subsidy that can be easily measured and does not lead to higher costs to consumers would be the preferred option.

Economists, however, do not adamantly oppose protection of infant industries if it is temporary and carried out in selected circumstances where it is apparent that a country has a long-run comparative advantage (see Example 2 again).

Keeping Money in the Country

Some protectionist arguments are grossly false. The first is one attributed (perhaps falsely) to Abraham Lincoln: "I don't know much about the tariff. But I do know that when I buy a coat from England, I have the coat and England has the money. But when I buy a coat in America, I have the coat and America has the money."

While this argument is appealing at first glance, it contains an error in logic. It supposes that money is somehow more valuable than goods. This *mercantilist fallacy* was committed by the mercantilist writers of the 17th and 18th centuries who feared that unrestricted trade would lead to the loss of gold. Writers such as David Hume and Adam Smith pointed out that this argument confuses ends with means. The end of economic activity is consumption; money is only a means to that end. When England sells an American a coat, the money is eventually used to buy, say, American wheat. The cost is the wheat, not the money.[9]

Saving Domestic Jobs

Another false protectionist argument is that imports deprive Americans of jobs: "The American market is the greatest in the world, and necessarily it should be reserved for American producers . . .," we hear from a 1952 Senate speech. An American Senator once explained the mysterious mechanism by which foreign imports cause unemployment:

> The importation of . . . foreign beef is not a stimulant to our economy. For foreign producers do not employ American labor; they do not buy our feed grain and fertilizers; they do not use our slaughterhouses; they do not use our truckers; they do not invest in or borrow from our banks; they do not buy our insurance; they do very little to stimulate the national economy.[10]

9. Under the existing international monetary system, trade imbalances do not even lead to the loss of money (currency) to other countries. The "prices" of foreign currencies are set in foreign-exchange markets, where the supply and demand for each currency is equated. A foreign currency is demanded to pay for goods purchased from the foreign country. No actual money crosses foreign borders. Transactions in each country must be carried out in that country's currency, not in the currency of another country.

10. The quotes in this section come from Yeager and Tuerck, *Trade Policy and the Price System.*

As already demonstrated, if each country specializes according to its comparative advantage, every country has more real GNP. The presumption the above senator makes is that when a job is lost through import competition, a job is lost forever to the economy—which is simply untrue.

In the long run, a country must export in order to import. Jobs destroyed by competition from imports are eventually restored by increased exports. Foreign trade increases economic efficiency. In the long run, import barriers simply make it costlier to purchase the goods and services. The enormous efficiency changes over the last century did not result in permanent unemployment but rather in a higher standard of living for all. Trade according to comparative advantage raises economic efficiency. A country would not benefit by forgoing long-term efficiency gains for short-term reductions in unemployment. Even if there is a trade deficit (imports greater than exports), greater unemployment is not the result.

NONPROTECTIONIST ARGUMENTS FOR TARIFFS

Protectionists argue that tariffs should be used to benefit certain special interests (at the public expense). Four arguments for tariffs are not protectionist in nature.

The National-Defense Argument

An industry that is essential to the national defense presumably should be subsidized to encourage it to produce at a prudent level for the public safety. Although this argument does make some sense, it is not entirely applicable to the United States. A look at the comparative advantage of the United States reveals that the manufacturing industries in which the United States excells—chemicals, machinery, transportation equipment, aircraft—are the same ones that would be important in times of war. Significant exceptions to this, perhaps, are shipbuilding, which the United States does subsidize, and steel. The industries that for the most part would gain from protection—such as handbags, pottery, flatware, fish, nuts, cheese, cherries, hats, furs, pianos, toys, TV sets, and so forth—are not essential to a defense effort.

In some cases, protection even appears contrary to defense interests. Consider oil imports. The United States protected domestic oil by a tariff from the 1950s to the early 1970s. One could argue that it would be better to import foreign oil, save domestic oil reserves, and follow a policy of stockpiling imported oil in the case of war. The U.S. policy instead used up American oil.

Many industries that have little to do with national defense have used the national-defense argument as a rationale for protection. These industries are, to name but a few, gloves, pens, pottery, peanuts, paper, candles, thumbtacks, pencils, lacemaking, tuna fishing, and even clothespins.

If an industry is deemed essential for the national defense, a better way of obtaining more peacetime production by that industry is the domestic-production subsidy. Such subsidies could be handed out by the Department of Defense, where the experts on defense presumably reside. As noted, a tariff has the same effect as the combination of a production subsidy and a consumption tax. A direct subsidy is almost always better than a tariff since the tariff also raises the cost of living of consumers.

The Terms-of-Trade Argument

International economists have long recognized that it is logically possible for a country to raise tariffs and, so, shift the terms of trade to raise the country's real income. If a country imports widgets under free trade at a price of $10 a widget and this country is a major importer of widgets, the less the country imports, the lower is the world price. In the extreme case, a $1 tariff might drive down the world price of widgets from $10 to $9. The country's consumers would still pay a $10 price for widgets, but the country could then import them for $9 and fill the national treasury with the tariff revenues, benefiting the entire country.

A famous turn-of-the-century British economist, Francis Edgeworth, warned that the terms-of-trade argument is like a bottle of poison that is useful in small doses: one should always label it *DANGER*. The argument presupposes that the rest of the world cannot retaliate. Very special circumstances would have to be present for one country to be able to beat down everybody else's terms of trade by tariffs while the rest of the world could not respond. Once the possibility of retaliation is present, countries that try to use this policy might simply start a tariff war that would result in everybody being made worse off.

The Diversification Argument

An argument closely related to the infant-industry argument is that free trade may lead an economy to specialize too much and expose it to the risks of putting all its eggs in one basket. When an economy is highly dependent on only one export good—such as Ghana on cocoa, Bolivia on tin, or Colombia on coffee—the fortunes of the country wax and wane with the price of the main export good. Such cyclical fluctuations in raw-material prices allegedly impose hardships on the specialized economy.

Raul Prebisch, a well-known Latin American economist, has argued that if such countries impose tariffs to protect their domestic industry, this protection would permit them to diversify their industrial base. The greater is the range of goods produced, the smaller is the risk imposed on the economy by price changes.

One seldom hears this argument in fair weather, only in foul. No one questioned the wisdom of the oil-exporting countries' specialization in oil. Kuwait is heavily dependent on oil exports and is the richest country in the world (on a per capita basis) because of this specialization. When prices are going up, the diversification theorists remain strangely quiet. Private investors find it profitable to invest in the goods that promise to bring the highest return. In nondiversified economies, investors have concluded that only a few goods are worthy of their attention. To conclude that diversification should be forced by government policy is sound only if the policymaker has more information about the future of an economy than private investors. It is difficult to determine which industries will be profitable in the future. If one industry is risky and another is not so risky, private investors will demand a risk premium in the risky industry—such as copper in Chile, cocoa in Ghana. Only if governments can make better decisions than investors about future comparative advantage can a case be made for deliberate diversification.

Figure 5   Average U.S. Import Duties, 1980-83

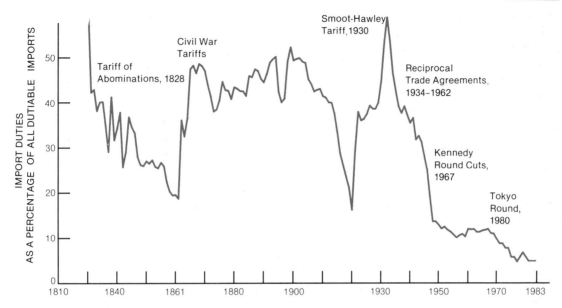

As attitudes toward free trade and protectionism have fluctuated in the United States, average tariff rates have also fluctuated but have shown a distinct downward trend.

Source: *Historical Statistics of the United States; Statistical Abstract of the United States.*

The Tariffs-for-Revenue Argument

Tariffs provide protection and raise government revenue. The two goals are partly in conflict. A perfect protectionist tariff would eliminate trade entirely and, so, would eliminate tariff revenue!

A nonprohibitive tariff does raise government revenue. Tariffs are not an important source of revenue in the United States (slightly more than 1 percent of the federal government's revenue), but in some countries tariff revenue is significant. Indeed, 19th-century America relied heavily on tariff revenues.

A revenue tariff has special justification if it is difficult for a country to raise revenues in other ways. In a poor country where tax avoidance and nonmarket transactions restrict the amount of revenue yielded by income taxes, the government may be forced to collect its revenues by imposing taxes on traded goods. Customs officers located in airports and ports may be able to collect tax revenue to pay for roads, education, and other public goods. Under these circumstances, a tariff

probably has greater justification than in any other case.

U.S. TRADE POLICIES

The tariff history of the United States is shown in Figure 5, which shows that tariffs have fluctuated up and down with the ebb and flow of protectionism in the U.S. Congress. In modern times, tariffs hit their peak with the infamous Smoot-Hawley Tariff of 1930. Economists were so appalled by the prospect of this tariff bill that in a rare show of agreement 1,028 of them signed a petition asking President Hoover to veto the bill. Since politics tends to override economics in tariff legislation, the bill was signed.

The Trade-Agreements Program and GATT

The Smoot-Hawley tariff, like most of the preceding 18 tariff acts stretching back to 1779, was the result of political *logrolling* in the U.S. Congress. Logrolling occurs when some politicians trade their own votes on issues of minor concern to their constituents in return for other politicians' votes on issues of greater concern to their constituents. Tariffs, historically, are the best example of the sacrifice of general interests for special interests.

Having established the highest tariff rates in U.S. history, the Smoot-Hawley Act triggered angry reactions overseas, as predicted by economists. As one nation after another erected trade barriers, the volume of world trade declined more than it would have due to the Great Depression. The export markets of the United States shrunk at a time of a very deep domestic depression.

In order to secure a larger market for U.S. exports, Congress amended the Tariff Act of 1930 with the Reciprocal Trade Agreements Act of 1934. The President was authorized to negotiate reciprocal agreements that promised to lower U.S. trade barriers or tariffs in return for similar concessions abroad. The fact that Congress did not have to approve the tariff cuts marked a significant change in the power of special interests to influence U.S. tariff policy.

The Trade Agreements Program has been broadened under successive extensions and modifications. The Trade Expansion Act of 1962 gave the President the power to reduce tariffs by up to 50 percent and to remove duties of less than 5 percent. Under the authority of this act, the United States engaged in multilateral negotiations, known as the Kennedy Round, which resulted in an average reduction of 35 percent on industrial tariff rates. The Trade Reform Act of 1974 allowed the President to reduce tariffs by up to 60 percent and to eliminate duties of less than 5 percent. This act resulted in the Tokyo Round (1980) of multilateral reductions, in which the United States agreed to cut tariffs on industrial goods by 31 percent, the European Community agreed to cut tariffs by 27 percent, and Japan agreed to cut tariffs by 28 percent.

Clearly, the Trade-Agreements Program has been an enormous success. In 1932, the average tariff rate was about 59 percent; today the average tariff rate is about 5 percent. The trade-agreement obligations of the United States and other countries are carried out under the General Agreement on Tariffs and Trade (GATT), established in 1948. GATT is an agreement that spells out rules on the conduct of trade and procedures to settle trade disputes. GATT is also the forum in which international tariff negotiations now take place. As of 1982, 87 countries belonged to GATT, and several other countries conform to its codes without being formal members.

Escape Clauses

The President's authority to reduce tariffs in reciprocal trade agreements can be used only if the anticipated increases in imports are considered unlikely to threaten or cause serious injury to a domestic industry. Protectionists can now use this "escape clause" to avoid competition from cheaper foreign imports. But an escape clause (Section 201 of the Trade Act of 1974) can be invoked only if three conditions are met: 1) imports must be increasing, 2) the domestic import-competing industry must be (or must potentially be) seriously injured, and 3) the increased imports must be a substantial cause of the serious injury or threat to the domestic import-competing industry. Escape-clause cases are initiated by petition from the industry to the U.S. International Trade Commission.

The escape clause cannot be invoked simply because the increased imports affect a domestic industry adversely or because the domestic industry is seriously depressed. For example, the Trade Commission did not grant the U.S. automobile industry escape-clause protection because the major difficulties in the auto industry have been caused by the reduced demand for automobiles. Even if imports had not increased their penetration, the U.S. auto industry would have been depressed in the early 1980s.

Economists tend to be critical of escape clauses because the greater are the net social gains that can be expected from tariff cuts, the larger will be the reallocation of resources away from the import-competing industries into export industries and other industries. Thus, escape clauses are invoked presumably in those industries where trade gains may be the greatest. In recent years, escape-clause protection has been granted sparingly. In 1985, escape-clause relief was in effect for motorcycles and several kinds of steel products. The International Trade Commission recommended relief for the domestic copper industry, but President Reagan overturned the commission's unanimous decision.

Trade-Adjustment Assistance

When tariffs are lowered and, say, textile or auto workers are thrown out of jobs, hardships are imposed on them. If escape-clause action is inefficient, an alternative is to assist workers and firms to adjust to the changed conditions by supplementing unemployment insurance, giving job counseling and training, or providing grants for moving expenses.

A case can be made that government trade-adjustment assistance is necessary because a government policy (tariff reductions) brought about the short-term unemployment of the workers. The question is how to provide this assistance without discouraging the transfer of resources out of declining protected sectors into the exporting sectors of the economy.[11]

From 1975 to 1981, the United States had a liberal trade-adjustment program in effect. The program basically extended unemployment insurance benefits and did little to encourage workers to move from declining to expanding industries. Another problem with the program (officially ended in 1983) was that the benefits were for the most part given to only one industry—the automobile industry.

A Drift Toward Protectionism?

The fall in average tariff levels for the United States recorded in Figure 5 indicates a move toward free trade. Similar changes have occurred abroad. But tariff rates do not adequately measure protection in today's world. When the Trade-Agreements Program took the power of tariff making away from Congress, the United States began to lower tariff rates but raise nontariff barriers, such as import quotas and voluntary export restrictions. Industries obtain protection today by lobbying Congress. When Congress threatens to impose import quotas, the Executive Branch, to keep the peace, arranges for a voluntary export quota with the foreign exporter.

11. For a further discussion of Trade Adjustment Assistance, see J. David Richardson, *Understanding International Economics: Theory and Practice* (Boston: Little, Brown, 1980), pp. 340-50.

Fears have been expressed that high unemployment rates in the United States, Britain, France, Italy, and elsewhere in the early 1980s would lead democratic governments to make compromises with the special interests seeking protection. The protectionist argument that imports cause unemployment becomes *politically* effective in periods of high unemployment. Whether protection will increase in the future remains to be seen. The forces tending toward greater protectionism have so far been neutralized by the realization that everybody loses if all countries adopt protectionist policies.

This chapter examined the nature and consequences of trade barriers. Imports are bought with money; exports are sold for money. The next chapter will examine how monetary relationships fit into the international exchange of goods and services.

Summary

1. The major trade barriers are tariffs, import quotas, voluntary export quotas, and other nontariff barriers. A *tariff* is a tax levied on imports. It raises both the price paid by the domestic consumer and the price received by the domestic producer of the import-competing product. *Import quotas* limit the amount of imports of specified products. They raise the prices paid by domestic consumers and the prices received by domestic producers of import-competing products. Quotas are normally regulated by import licenses. If import licenses are sold to importers, the government receives their scarcity value. If they are not sold, private importers benefit from their scarcity value. *Voluntary export quotas* direct governments to restrict their exports to another country.
2. The basic argument against protection is that the costs of protection outweigh the benefits of protection. The loss to consumers from a tariff is greater than the gain to the protected producers. Additional losses from tariffs are the costs of lobbying for tariff or quota protection.
3. The politics of tariffs explains why tariffs are passed. Although the costs of tariffs are large in total, these costs are small per person. Special-interest groups, therefore, lobby and

spend funds to obtain tariff protection. The major economic arguments for protection are that protection is necessary to avoid unfair foreign competition (low foreign wages, dumping, foreign export subsidies), to protect infant industries, to keep money in the country, and to save domestic jobs.

4.   The nonprotectionist arguments for tariffs are the national-defense argument, the terms-of-trade argument, the diversification argument, and the tariffs-for-revenue argument. The national-defense argument is potentially valid but tends to be misused and applied to industries of little importance to national defense. The terms-of-trade argument works only if the nation's trading partners fail to retaliate against protective tariffs. The diversification argument fails to take into account the fact that private investors prefer to specialize their investments in specific domestic industries. The tariff-revenue argument may have a special justification in poor countries that have difficulty raising revenues through other means.

5.   U.S. trade policies have changed over the years. The Smoot-Hawley Tariff of 1930 caused a further restriction of trade during the Great Depression by setting very high tariff rates. Since then, legislation has been passed that allows the U.S. President to negotiate tariff reductions. As a consequence of this legislation, the average tariff rate declined from 59 percent in 1932 to 5 percent in 1984. Existing legislation does contain escape clauses that can reverse the trend towards free trade. Prior to 1974, tariff reductions could be prevented if the tariff reduction threatened to harm domestic industry. The Trade Act of 1974 required proof that increasing imports would seriously injure the domestic industry and that increasing imports were a substantial cause of the serious injury.

Key Terms

free trade
tariff
import quota
voluntary export quota
prohibitive tariff
nonprohibitive tariff
dumping
countervailing duty

Questions and Problems

1.   What are the differences and similarities between an import duty and an import quota?

2.   What is the difference between an import quota and a voluntary export quota?

3.   Economists agree that tariffs hurt the countries that impose them. Yet nearly all countries impose tariffs. Is something wrong with the economists' argument?

4.   Assume a country can export all the wheat it wants at the world price of $5 per bushel. Using an analysis parallel to the discussion of Figure 4 in the text, show the impact of imposing a $1 per bushel export tariff on every bushel exported. Does the benefit to consumers and government exceed the cost to producers of wheat? (*Hint:* an export tariff means that if a foreigner purchases wheat he or she must pay the domestic price plus the $1 export duty).

5.   What are the best arguments that can be made for tariffs? What are the worst arguments that can be made for tariffs?

6.   Frederic Bastiat, a 19th-century French economist/journalist, called tariffs "negative railroads." In what respects are tariffs negative railroads? In what respects is the analogy faulty?

7.   "Ignoring political considerations, importing from the Soviet Union may not benefit the United States because under communism prices need not correspond to the true Soviet comparative advantage." Evaluate this statement.

Suggested Readings

Bergsten, C. Fred. *The Cost of Import Restrictions to American Consumers*. New York: American Importers Association, 1972.

George, Henry. *Protection or Free Trade?* New York: Doubleday and Page, 1905.

Richardson, J. David. *Understanding International Economics: Theory and Practice*. Boston: Little, Brown, 1980, chaps. 9-10.

Yeager, Leland B. and David G. Tuerck. *Trade Policy and the Price System*. Scranton, Pa.: International Textbook, 1966.

24

The International Monetary System

Chapter Preview

Money is the medium of exchange for domestic transactions because it is accepted by all sellers in exchange for their goods and services. Each seller generally wants the national currency of his or her own country. Thus, Americans want U.S. dollars, the English want pounds sterling, the Japanese want yen, Germans want marks, and the French want francs.

When an international transaction takes place, buyers and sellers reside in different countries. An American farmer sells wheat to a British miller or a British firm sells a bicycle to an American cyclist. To make the purchase, the buyer needs the currency of the seller's place of residence. The currency of another country that is needed for international transactions is called **foreign exchange.**

> **Foreign exchange** is the national currency of another country that is needed to carry out international transactions. Normally, foreign exchange consists of bank deposits denominated in the foreign currency but may sometimes consist of foreign paper money when foreign travel is involved.

This chapter will examine the monetary mechanism behind the international exchange of goods and services. How does the foreign-exchange market work? What happens when a currency depreciates? Why are exchange rates between the currencies of different countries allowed to fluctuate? What are the advantages and disadvantages of the present international monetary system?

These questions and others will be answered as this chapter discusses the U.S. balance of payments, international capital movements, fixed versus floating exchange rates, the gold standard, the European currency unit, special drawing rights, the International Monetary Fund (IMF), international monetary speculation, the high value of the dollar in the early 1980s, and the recycling of OPEC oil revenues. ■

INTERNATIONAL MONETARY MECHANISMS

The Foreign-Exchange Market

The buyer of international goods and services obtains his or her currency requirements from the foreign-exchange market. This market is highly dispersed around the world. Exchange between different currencies takes place between large banks and brokers. For example, an American importer of a British bicycle priced in pounds sterling pays in sterling that is deposited in a British bank. The money is transfered by a check or draft or cable that is purchased with dollars from the importer's American bank that holds a sterling deposit in a British bank. Where does the American bank get these sterling deposits? They come from British importers of American goods who want dollars and supply pounds.[1]

America's demand for foreign exchange comes from its demand for the things that residents of the United States want to buy abroad; America's supply of foreign exchange comes from the demand by foreign residents for the things that they want to buy in the United States.

The price of one currency in terms of another is the *foreign-exchange rate*. These exchange rates change from day to day and from hour to hour. In the first week of February 1985, the British pound cost about $1.12, the German mark about $0.31, the French franc about $0.10; $1 was worth about 259 Japanese yen and about 230 Mexican pesos.

Foreign-exchange rates are needed to convert foreign prices into American prices. When the exchange rate is expressed in terms of dollars per unit of foreign currency, the rate can be multiplied by the foreign price to obtain the American price. For example, if a British bicycle costs 80 pounds (£), the American importer pays $96 when the pound is worth $1.20 ($96 = $1.20 × 80). When the exchange rate is expressed in terms of foreign currency per dollar, the foreign price can be divided by the rate to obtain the American price. For example, a Japanese car costing 1,560,000 yen costs $6,000, when 260 yen equal $1.

Floating Exchange Rates

How the exchange rate is determined depends upon whether the rate is a **fixed exchange rate** or a **floating exchange rate**.

A **fixed exchange rate** is an exchange rate that is set by government decree or intervention within a small range of variation.

A **floating exchange rate** is an exchange rate that is freely determined by the interaction of supply and demand.

The real world is a blend of these two polar cases. The floating system is easier to understand and roughly corresponds to the present regime adopted by the United States, Great Britain, Canada, Japan, and other nations (about 23 countries in total). Many small countries maintain fixed exchange rates against the dollar, the English pound, the French franc, or some basket of currencies. Eight European countries (including France, Germany, and Italy) have formed a European Monetary System and maintain fixed exchange rates relative to each other but not relative to the United States. But even the floating systems of today's world have some of the characteristics of the fixed-exchange-rate system.

Americans demand foreign exchange to buy imported commodities, to use foreign transportation services and insurance, to travel abroad, to make payments to U.S. troops stationed abroad, to remit dividends, interest, and profits to the foreign owners of American stocks, bonds, and business firms, to grant foreign aid, and to make short-term and long-term investments in foreign assets.

America's supply of foreign exchange is generated by foreigners' demand for American dollars to buy American exports, to travel in America, to pay American owners of stocks, bonds, and businesses, and to invest in American assets.

To simplify the explanation of the foreign-exchange market, imagine again that the world consists of two countries: America and England. The

---

1. For a further discussion of the foreign-exchange market, see Peter H. Lindert and Charles P. Kindleberger, *International Economics,* 7th ed. (Homewood, Ill.: Richard D. Irwin, 1982), pp. 243–62.

American demand for foreign exchange is, thus, a demand for British pounds sterling. Also assume that exports and imports of goods and services are the only things traded internationally.

Figure 1 shows the demand curve for foreign exchange by Americans. On the vertical axis is measured the dollar price of pounds; on the horizontal axis is measured the flow of pounds coming into the foreign-exchange market during the relevant period of time. The demand curve is downward-sloping because the higher is the price of pounds in dollars, *ceteris paribus,* the higher is the cost of British goods to American importers. For example, if a British bicycle costs 80 pounds and the pound price rises from $1.20 to $1.60, the bike's price rises from $96 to $128 for the American importer. This price increase will induce Americans to buy fewer bikes or switch to an American-made brand. Thus, the higher is the price of pounds, the lower is the quantity of foreign exchange demanded by Americans.

The American supply curve of foreign exchange depends on British importers of American goods. When the English buy American wheat, they supply pounds to the foreign-exchange market (because pounds must be exchanged to buy U.S. goods). The supply curve is upward-sloping because when the dollar price of pounds rises— or when the dollar falls in value—American goods appear cheaper to foreigners. As a result, they will buy more American goods, thereby increasing the quantity of pounds supplied to Americans in the foreign-exchange market. For example, if a bushel of U.S. wheat costs $3.60, a fall in the value of the dollar from £1 = $1.20 to £1 = $1.60 will lower the cost of a bushel of wheat to foreigners from £3 to £2.25. The English will then shift their demand for wheat from British to American wheat and increase wheat consumption, stimulating American exports.

When the price of pounds is $1.60, Figure 1 shows that there is an excess supply of pounds on the foreign-exchange market. At the $1.60 exchange rate, desired U.S. exports exceed U.S. imports. With a floating exchange rate, the dollar price of a pound could not be high enough to cause an excess supply. An excess supply of pounds bids the price of pounds down, as in any competitive market. Similarly, at a price of $0.80, there would be an excess demand for

Figure 1   The Foreign-Exchange Market

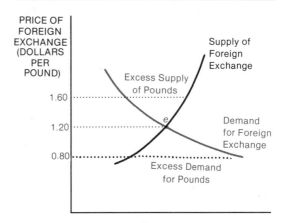

QUANTITY OF FOREIGN EXCHANGE
(BRITISH POUNDS)

The dollar price of pounds is measured on the vertical axis; the flow of pounds on the foreign-exchange market per unit of time is measured on the horizontal axis. The equilibrium exchange rate is $1.20 = £1. If the exchange rate were $1.60 = £1, the excess supply of pounds on the market would drive down the price. At a price of $0.80, there would be an excess demand for pounds on the market, bidding the price up.

pounds and the price of pounds would be bid up. The market-clearing price of $1.20 in Figure 1 not only equates the supply and demand for foreign exchange but also maintains an equilibrium between U.S. exports and imports. Equilibrium between imports and exports is achieved because they are the mirror image of the demand and supply for foreign exchange.

Exports and imports will be equal only if there are no other factors besides exports or imports (tourism, paying dividends, foreign investments) entering the foreign-exchange market. Suppose in addition to exporting and importing, some Americans wish to invest in foreign securities. The demand curve *(D)* in Figure 2 reflects America's foreign-exchange requirements for imports of goods. The desire for making new foreign investments shifts the demand curve for foreign exchange outward to *D'*. The dollar price of pounds rises, or the dollar gets cheaper. This depreciation in the dollar, or appreciation in the pound, makes American goods cheaper and brings about the required excess of exports over imports needed to

Figure 2   The Effect of an Increase in American Investment in England

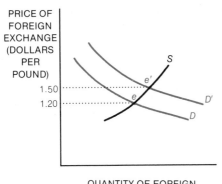

QUANTITY OF FOREIGN
EXCHANGE (BRITISH POUNDS)

If Americans decided to invest more in England, the demand curve for foreign exchange would shift from *D* to *D'*. The equilibrium price of pounds would rise to $1.50 and would allow a surplus of exports over imports to pay for the increased foreign investment abroad.

accommodate the outflow of American capital to a foreign country.[2]

> A currency is said to *depreciate* if it falls in value on the foreign-exchange market (if it buys less foreign exchange) and to *appreciate* if it rises in value on the foreign-exchange market (if it buys more foreign exchange).

In our example, the depreciation of the dollar is the same thing as the appreciation of the pound because the dollar/pound exchange rate reflects the relative values of the two currencies: when one goes up the other must go down. In the actual world, of course, the dollar can rise in terms of the pound while falling in terms of the franc or the mark. For this reason, the value of the dollar on the foreign-exchange market as a whole is best expressed in terms of a **currency basket:**

2. The foreign-exchange market is explained here in terms of the flows of exports, imports, investment, and so forth entering the channels of international exchange. An alternate approach to explaining the foreign-exchange market is the *monetary approach to the balance of payments*. This approach focuses on the demand and supply for different national monies. At any given time, the array of exchange rates that prevails must induce people around the world to be willing to hold the various money supplies (as stocks) that each country has chosen to produce. An excellent introduction to the monetary approach can be found in Lindert and Kindleberger, *International Economics*, pp. 319–35.

A **currency basket** is simply a bundle of currencies such as 2 French francs, 1 German mark, 400 Japanese yen, and so on. The dollar, on the average, depreciates if this currency basket becomes more expensive and appreciates if this currency basket becomes less expensive.

Purchasing-Power Parity

Inflation rates in different countries play an important role in determining floating exchange rates. Countries that have enormous rates of inflation can still trade with the rest of the world because the exchange rate reflects the relative purchasing power of the two currencies in their respective countries.

This theory, popularized by Sweden's Gustav Cassel around 1917, works well when the inflation rates between two countries are quite different. When inflation rate differentials are small, exchange-rate movements will be dominated by other developments, such as fluctuations in the business cycle, capital movements, and changes in comparative advantage.

Suppose England and America were in equilibrium with an exchange rate of $1.20 = £1. If England doubles its supply of money while America maintains a constant money supply, there will be a tendency for the price of all English goods to double. If the price of the pound falls to a mere $0.60 (it falls to one half its previous exchange value), English prices appear exactly the same to Americans. The British bike that used to cost £60 rises to £120; but since the pound falls from $1.20 to $0.60, the bike still costs Americans $72. The exchange rate has maintained its **purchasing-power parity (PPP)**. A dollar still buys the same goods in England as before the inflation.

> **Purchasing-power parity (PPP)** exists between two currencies when changes in the exchange rate reflect only relative changes in the price levels of the two countries.

The Rise of the Dollar in the 1980s

The theory of flexible exchange rates helps explain the sharp increase in the value of the dollar from 1981 to 1984. From 1981 to the end of 1984, the dollar rose by about 65 percent in terms

Figure 3   Price-Adjusted Dollar and Long-Term U.S./Europe Real Interest Differential

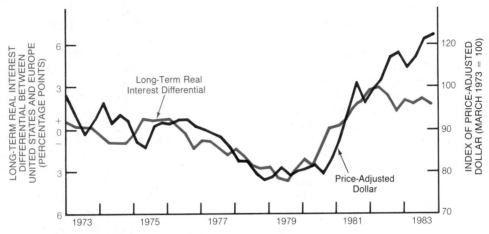

The black line shows that the price-adjusted value of the dollar kept pace with the long-term real interest rate differential of the United States over Europe until 1981, when the dollar began to appreciate even faster.

Source: *Federal Reserve Bulletin.*

of the British pound, by 10 percent in terms of the Japanese Yen, and by about 40 percent in terms of an average of the currencies of 11 industrial countries.

There are three reasons for the rise of the dollar. First, the U.S. inflation rate in the early 1980s fell more rapidly than the average inflation rate of America's main foreign competitors. Thus, on purchasing-power-parity grounds alone the dollar should have increased in value. Second, in the early 1980s U.S. real interest rates were relatively high compared to the rest of the world and attracted foreign investment to the United States. These two factors alone still cannot explain the entire change.

Figure 3 shows the long-term real-interest-rate differential between the U.S. and the rest of the world compared to the price-adjusted value of the dollar. (The price-adjusted dollar would remain constant if purchasing-power parity held at all points in time.) From 1973 to 1980, the price-adjusted value of the dollar kept pace with the interest-rate differential. But from 1980 onward the price-adjusted value of the dollar increased by more than the real-interest-rate differential could explain. Thus, a third factor appeared to be at work. Most economists attribute the unexplained

appreciation of the dollar to America being a safe haven for foreign funds. As measured by the amount of foreign investment entering the United States, foreign confidence in America soared during the early 1980s. The safe-haven hypothesis is, however, very difficult to quantify.

The dollar's real appreciation (beyond purchasing-power parity) had both costs and benefits. On the benefit side, a higher dollar means that imports are cheaper to Americans. This price decrease raises American living standards by lowering the U.S. inflation rate relative to the increase in U.S. incomes. Moreover, the fact that the United States was attracting so much capital from abroad meant that Americans could consume and invest more than they otherwise could. Despite a massive government deficit and an unusually low rate of private saving, foreign investment in the United States enabled Americans to continue to build plant and equipment for the future.

While economic theory suggests that an improvement in a country's terms of trade due to incoming foreign investment has more benefits than costs, there are important costs of a dollar appreciation. First, a higher dollar makes America's exports of wheat and other goods much more expensive in foreign markets. Cutting exports

Example 1   Bumblebees Cannot Fly

Economists are currently divided over whether governments should try to manage exchange rates. The argument for managing exchange rates rests on three observations. First, the government can determine the fundamental equilibrium exchange rate. Second, floating exchange rates have been too volatile. Third, under floating exchange rates currencies can become significantly overvalued or undervalued.

The first and third points are related. If the information exists for determining whether an exchange rate is in "fundamental equilibrium," it is possible also to determine whether a currency is overvalued or undervalued (misaligned). A currency is overvalued if the exchange rate is higher than can be explained by changes in purchasing-power parity or improvements in the country's productivity relative to other countries. For example, the U.S. dollar was said to be "overvalued" in 1984 and 1985. The dollar appreciated by more than 40 percent from 1981 to the end of 1984, which could not be explained by fundamentals (differential inflation rates and productivity improvements). Critics of the current floating-exchange-rate system hold that currency misalignments impose many costs on the economy, such as unemployment and the adjustment costs caused by rapidly changing exchange rates (when exchange rates appreciate, export industries and import-competing industries are hurt).

Critics of floating rates also argue that excessive exchange-rate volatility reduces the volume of international trade by making international transactions more uncertain.

Supporters of the current system argue that the very concept of currency misalignment supposes that economists have the correct model of exchange-rate determination. Economists' exchange-rate models have not worked very well (such models focus on fundamentals), but is the exchange rate misaligned or are the models simply wrong? According to the laws of aerodynamics, a bumblebee cannot fly. According to economic models of exchange rates, the U.S. dollar is too high. Until better models of exchange rates are developed, economists should be slow in pronouncing whether an exchange rate is "overvalued" or "undervalued" (loaded terms).

Supporters of floating exchange rates point out that volatile exchange rates may or may not have reduced the volume of international trade. The evidence is mixed. Moreover, it is not clear that exchange rates have shown excessive volatility. For example, in the United States, Canada, Germany, Great Britain, and Japan, both interest rates and their domestic stock markets have been more volatile than their exchange rates. ∎

Sources: John Williamson, *The Exchange Rate System* (Cambridge: MIT Press, 1983); Jeffrey H. Bergstrand, "Is Exchange Rate Volatility 'Excessive'?", *New England Economic Review,* Federal Reserve Bank of Boston (Sept/Oct 1983); and Douglas K. Pearce, "Alternative Views of Exchange Rate Determination," Federal Reserve Bank of St. Louis, *Economic Review* (February 1983).

causes hardships in those export industries. Second, when America repays its foreign debts it will have to consume and invest less sometime in the future. Any country that borrows today is trading future goods against more present goods: more today, less tomorrow.

Some economists have argued that the rise of the dollar was excessive up to early 1985 and that the dollar would eventually have to drop again (see Example 1). The dollar will certainly drop again. Every flexible exchange rate goes up and down. The question is: *when* will the dollar fall? If the value of the dollar is excessive, speculators could make a lot of money betting against the dollar. It is too early to decide whether the dollar appreciation of the early 1980s was excessive.

Fixed Exchange Rates and the Gold Standard

The gold standard is the prototype of the fixed-exchange-rate system. The classical gold standard was in its heyday before World War I, from about the 1870s to 1914. The United Kingdom was on the gold standard as far back as the 1820s and used both gold and silver during the 18th century—the century in which David Hume and Adam Smith lived.

A fixed-exchange-rate system does not have to use gold, silver, or any commodity, but *each country must adopt monetary rules that correspond to those of the classical gold standard.*

When Spain conquered the New World, it brought back enormous quantities of gold. As the quantity theory predicts, a major consequence of the inflow of gold into Spain was inflation of wages and production costs. This inflation made it more difficult for Spain to compete with other European countries in world markets. Thus, Spain developed an excess of imports over exports and shipped gold to pay for the difference. Eventually, this gold caused inflation elsewhere, and Spain's exports and imports were brought into approximate balance.

The blueprint for an international gold standard, brilliantly outlined by David Hume in 1752, showed how a fixed-exchange-rate system can work to maintain equilibrium in the balance of payments with the rest of the world.

The gold-flow mechanism can be explained using our hypothetical two-country world. If America defined the dollar as equal to $\frac{1}{20}$ of an ounce of gold and England defined the pound as equal to $\frac{1}{4}$ of an ounce of gold, an English pound would contain 5 times as much gold as a U.S. dollar. England would convert gold into pounds (and vice versa) at the established rate of £1 = $\frac{1}{4}$th of an ounce of gold; America would convert gold into dollars at the rate of $1 = $\frac{1}{20}$th of an ounce of gold. Under these circumstances, the exchange rate would be $5 = £1. No rational person would pay more than $5 for an English pound, because $5 would buy $\frac{1}{4}$ of an ounce of gold from the U.S. Treasury and that amount of gold would buy one £1 note from the British Treasury.[3] The next key ingredient of the gold standard is that England and America let their money supplies depend on how much gold is in their national treasuries.

If America had a surplus of exports over imports in our hypothetical world, gold would be shipped from England to America to pay for the surplus of exports over imports. This gold shipment would raise the money supply in America and reduce the money supply in England. As a result, inflation of costs and prices would occur in America, and a deflation of costs and prices would occur in England. Thus, America's exports would become less competitive and England's exports would become more competitive. As America's exports decreased and England's exports increased, America's surplus of exports over imports would disappear—as long as the rules of the gold-standard game were followed.

The equilibrating mechanism of the international gold standard is the *relationship between the domestic money supplies and the state of the balance of payments.* It is not actually necessary for gold or silver to be involved. If the country with a payments deficit allows its money supply to fall, while the country with a payments surplus allows its money supply to rise, automatic adjustment mechanisms will tend to restore equilibrium. In the country with a payments surplus, the expansion of the money supply will 1) lower exports because of higher prices and costs, 2) raise imports because prices and costs are now cheaper abroad, and 3) raise imports because real GNP may be increased due to expansion in the money supply. In the deficit country, the contraction of the money supply will 1) raise exports because prices and costs are lower, 2) lower imports because prices and costs are now higher abroad, and 3) lower imports because real GNP may be lower due to the contraction of the money supply.

The central objection to the equilibrating mechanism of a fixed-exchange-rate system is that balance-of-payments surpluses and deficits may produce unwanted inflationary or deflationary pressures. During the Great Depression, with its enormous unemployment, countries could no longer afford to allow a deficit to produce further deflation and unemployment. Hence, country after country left the gold standard during the 1930s.

Gold is not necessary to establish a fixed-exchange-rate system that works like the gold standard. Fixed exchange rates can be established by official decree reinforced by central-bank inter-

---

3. Since shipping gold back and forth between American and England is costly (transportation and insurance), the dollar price of pounds might range between $5.02 and $4.98, if it costs 2 cents to ship $\frac{1}{4}$ ounce of gold between the countries. These upper and lower limits of exchange rate are called the *gold points.*

vention in the foreign-exchange market. For example, in Figure 4, America is assumed to maintain its currency at a $2 exchange rate against the English pound, but the equilibrium exchange rate is $1.75. Thus, at the official rate there is an excess supply of foreign exchange, because the pound is overvalued (or the dollar is undervalued). To maintain the $2 price of pounds, America's central bank must purchase the excess supply of pounds coming onto the foreign-exchange market. While America is experiencing this balance-of-payments surplus, the American central bank is adding to its inventory of pounds. This inventory of pounds can later be used as international reserves to defend the value of the dollar when a deficit appears—when the supply and demand curves intersect above the $2 official price.

The surplus of exports over imports in the above example will not persist if America and England follow the rules of the gold-standard game. If America lets its money supply rise and England allows its money supply to fall, mechanisms will be set in motion that will shift the demand curve to the right and the supply curve to the left. When America suffers inflation relative to England, America exports less (decreasing supply) and imports more (increasing demand).

In a floating-exchange-rate system, if the dollar/pound exchange rate changes from $1.80 to $1.90, the dollar *depreciates* and the pound *appreciates*.

The term *devaluation* refers to official changes in the exchange rate in a fixed-exchange-rate system. Under the old gold standard, a devaluation of the dollar occurred when the price of gold rose. Today, a country with a fixed exchange rate devalues its currency simply by lowering the official price of its currency. The country announces that it will no longer defend the old price and sets a new price to maintain by official intervention.

In Figure 4, America has a surplus and England has a deficit at the official price of $2 per pound. This price can be maintained if the American central bank buys pounds or if the English central bank sells dollars (or if both actions take place). To avoid this inflation in America and deflation in England, England might, with America's agreement, decide to simply devalue its currency! In Figure 4, lowering the price of pounds to $1.75 will (temporarily at least) solve En-

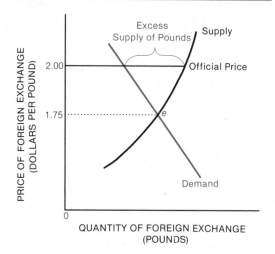

Figure 4   American Balance of Payments

If the exchange rate were $1.75 = £1, America's balance of payments would be in equilibrium. If the dollar price of pounds is fixed at $2.00 = £1, however, the dollar will be undervalued (the pound will be overvalued), and America's balance of payments will be in surplus by the excess supply of pounds on the foreign-exchange market. These pounds will have to be purchased by the central banks of either America or England.

gland's deficit and America's surplus. When the official value of a currency is raised, a *revaluation* is said to occur. Thus, in this case, England *devalues* its currency, and America *revalues* its currency.

THE BALANCE OF PAYMENTS AND INTERNATIONAL CAPITAL MOVEMENTS

The Balance of Payments

A country's **balance of payments** is a source of much information about the country's exports, imports, earnings by domestic residents on assets located abroad, earnings on domestic assets owned by foreign residents, international capital movements between countries, and official transactions by central banks and governments.

A country's **balance of payments** is a summary record of its economic transactions with foreign residents over a year or any other period.

The balance of payments is a two-sided summary of international transactions. Each transaction is recorded by standard double-entry bookkeeping. In other words, every transaction has two sides, each of which is entered on one of the two sides of the balance-of-payments account. For example, when America exports wheat, the foreign importer might simply give an IOU in exchange for the wheat. The wheat sale is recorded on the minus (debit) side and the IOU is recorded on the plus (credit) side. Because each amount recorded on the minus side is recorded on the plus side, the balance of payments record will always be *in balance.*

Although the balance of payments always balances if all transactions are considered, specific *accounts* of the balance of payments need not balance. U.S. merchandise exports need not equal U.S. merchandise imports, for example. Thus, a specific account of the balance of payments may have a surplus or deficit, but all the surpluses in the balance of payments as a whole will cancel out the deficits. Since the balance of payments as a whole must balance, a deficit on one account implies a surplus on some other account.

These observations should serve as a warning that a deficit in a particular account should not be treated as unfavorable and a surplus should not be treated as favorable to a country. Mercantilists, those 17th and 18th century writers whom Adam Smith and David Hume criticized, treated a surplus of exports over imports as a good thing and even called it a "favorable trade balance." That such a surplus benefits a country more than an "unfavorable" trade balance is a fallacy. A trade deficit may be a good thing. If a country is importing more than it is exporting, more goods are being brought in than are being sent out. Mercantilists committed the fallacy of treating exports as business sales and imports as business expenses. The **mercantilist fallacy** still lingers on in many press reports and in the minds of many people.

The **mercantilist fallacy** is that exporting is better than importing.

International-trade economists view exports as the cost of imports.

As noted above, the balance of payments records each transaction on two sides: the credit side and the debit side. In the plus or credit column is

Table 1   The U.S. Balance of Payments, 1983

Item		Amount (billions of dollars)
1. **Exports of goods and services**		**+334.2**
	a. Exports of merchandise	200.2
	b. Military sales	12.7
	c. Services	43.3
	d. Income from U.S. investments abroad	78.0
2. **Imports of goods and services**		**−366.4**
	a. Imports of merchandise	−260.8
	b. Military purchases	−12.2
	c. Services	−38.9
	d. Income on foreign investments in U.S.	−54.5
3. **Net unilateral transfers abroad**		**−8.6**
	a. U.S. government grants and pensions	−7.5
	b. Private remittances	−1.1
4. **Balance on current account**		**−40.8**
5. **Net capital movements**		**+33.7**
	a. U.S. capital outflow	−49.3
	b. Foreign capital inflow	+83.0
6. **Allocations of new SDRs to U.S. by IMF**		**0**
7. **Statistical discrepancy**		**+7.1**
8. **Increase (−) in U.S. official reserve assets**		**−1.2**
9. **Increase (+) in foreign official assets in the U.S.**		**+5.8**
10. **Total**		**0**

Source: *Survey of Current Business*, March 1984. (Categories may not add to totals because of rounding errors.)

placed the part of the transaction that increases the *supply* of foreign exchange: the payments for exports of merchandise or the income earned by providing services like transportation, insurance, and even capital to foreigners. In the minus or debit column is placed the part of a transaction that increases the demand for foreign exchange: payments for imports of merchandise and the income earned by foreigners when they provide domestic residents with transportation, insurance, or capital.

Exports and Imports.   Table 1 shows the U.S. balance of payments for 1983. The most important categories are found under items 1 and 2. U.S. merchandise imports (item 2a) exceeded U.S. merchandise exports (item 1a) by $60.6 billion. The **merchandise-trade balance** is sometimes called the *visible trade balance,* because it is easy to see physical movements of goods, such as wheat, cars, airplanes, computers, and steel. Yet the visible trade balance does not give an accurate picture of what the U.S. exports and imports from abroad. There are also many invisible items in the balance of payments. The United States furnishes transportation, insurance, and capital to foreigners. Payments are received in exchange for these services. When these less visible items are taken into account, the United States imports more goods and services than it exports by $32.2 billion (item 4).

> The **merchandise-trade balance** equals exports of merchandise minus imports of merchandise. If positive, it is the (merchandise) *trade surplus.* If negative, it is the (merchandise) *trade deficit.*

Net Unilateral Transfers Abroad.

If an American sends money to a relative in a foreign country, if the government gives money to a foreign country as a gift or grant, or if an American decides to retire in a foreign country and receives a pension check there, such transactions enter the balance of payments as *unilateral transfers.* Nothing concrete is exchanged for these payments, but these transactions do give rise to a demand for foreign exchange. In 1983, the United States made $8.6 billion worth of such transfers, most of which consisted of government grants in one form or another. The net difference between exports of goods and services and imports of goods and services minus net unilateral transfers is the **current-account balance.**

> The **current-account balance** equals exports of goods (merchandise) and services minus imports of goods (merchandise) and services minus net unilateral transfers abroad.

The United States had a deficit on the current account because the income from U.S. investments abroad (item 1d) exceeded the income on foreign investments in the United States by only $23.5 billion, which did not offset the deficit on the merchandise-trade balance and gave the U.S. an overall current-account deficit. The current-account deficit in 1984 swelled to more than $100 billion. From 1960 to 1984, the United States had only 7 current-account deficits and 18 current account surpluses. The United States can typically import more merchandise from foreign countries than it sells in return because income is earned on capital located abroad. The United States exchanges the goods and services its capital could produce at home for the goods and services that its capital could produce abroad. Such a situation usually results in a merchandise trade deficit.

Net Capital Movements.

When Americans buy foreign bonds, stocks, and invest in foreign factories, capital that would otherwise be available for investment at home becomes invested abroad. This capital outflow was $49.3 billion in 1983 (item 5a). When foreigners invest in U.S. stocks, bonds, and factories, there is a capital inflow. In 1983, the capital inflow into the United States was estimated to be $83.0 billion. Capital outflows—sometimes called *capital exports*—are a debit item, since they give rise to a demand for foreign exchange and, like imports, represent an increase in a domestically held asset (the foreigner's IOU), Capital inflows—sometimes called *capital imports*—are a credit item, since they give rise to an increase in the supply of foreign exchange and represent an increase in U.S. liabilities to foreigners.

The excess of capital imports over capital exports of $33.7 billion (item 5) is atypical for the United States. From 1917 to the early 1980s, the United States was a net capital exporter. Americans invested more in the rest of the world than foreigners invested in America. The United States was a net capital exporter for about 65 years (1917 to 1982). Beginning in 1983, the huge inflow of capital from the rest of the world swamped America's net creditor position (accumulated over 60 years) and turned America into a net debtor. It has been estimated that by 1987 the United States will owe the world a net $300 billion to $400 billion. The U.S. will no longer earn more from foreign investments than it pays out. In 1983, the United States still earned more from investments it made abroad than the investments foreigners made in the United States. U.S. net income from foreign investment—about $24 billion in 1983—is a reflection of exporting more capital than was imported over many decades. In 1984, U.S. net income from foreign investment fell to $17 billion.

Item 7 in Table 1 is "statistical discrepancy." In 1983, the statistical discrepancy was a $7.1 billion credit item. From 1975 to 1983, the statistical discrepancy was an average $19 billion credit item. This statistical discrepancy arose from the fact that when all the observable credits and debits were recorded, the debits outweighed the credit items by this amount. Thus, unobserved credits, such as spending by foreign tourists here, hidden exports, or unnoticed capital inflows, must have occurred. It is generally believed by international-finance experts that these substantial credits represent unrecorded capital inflows.

Official Reserve Assets.   A country's *official reserve assets* are that country's gold, special drawing rights (SDRs), its reserve position in the International Monetary Fund (discussed later), foreign exchange, or any financial assets held in official agencies, such as the central bank or treasury.

Item 9, *the increase in foreign official assets in the U.S.*, records the investments of official agencies of foreign countries in the United States. In 1983, official foreign agencies invested a net $5.8 billion in the United States.

Government agencies engage in buying and selling assets and foreign exchange. When official agencies like the central bank or the treasury take such an action, there is a presumption that the agency is demanding or supplying foreign exchange for the purpose of stabilizing the exchange rate. The $5.8 billion increase in foreign official assets in the United States (item 9) does supply foreign exchange and helps increase the value of the dollar. Item 8, the increase in U.S. offical reserve assets, consists for the most part of foreign currencies. It is a debit item, since it is a demand for foreign exchange and represents an increase in an asset, as when a good is imported on private account. Since these actions increased the supply of dollars on the foreign-exchange market, the exchange value of the dollar was kept lower.

The allocations of new special drawing rights by the International Monetary Fund (IMF) are included in item 6 and item 8. These new allocations can be used as an official reserve asset of the United States—namely, to buy foreign exchange. SDRs are allocated to every member of the IMF on a regular basis, but not in 1983.

When the deficits and surpluses on all the individual accounts are summed, the total deficit or surplus must be zero, as indicated earlier. For example, in 1983, the $41 billion deficit on the current account was offset by a $34 billion net capital inflow and the statistical discrepancy of more than $7 billion. (Many analysts treat the statistical discrepancy as an unrecorded capital inflow.) Similarly, in 1984, the current-account deficit of more than $100 billion was offset by a net capital inflow of more than $70 billion and a statistical discrepancy of about $30 billion.

International Capital Movements

International capital movements considerably complicate what is happening to a country's balance of payments. Without such capital movements, exports would more closely approximate imports, and there would be fewer measures of deficit or surplus in the balance of payments.

Capital movements enable capital-importing nations to raise their physical capital stocks—dams, buildings, roads—above what such stocks would be in the absence of international capital flows. When a country exports capital, it is furnishing residents of another country with funds for financing investments in plant and equipment. Thus, capital exports divert one country's saving into investments in another country. Saving still equals investments in the world as a whole, but when international trade is involved, this equality need not hold for any individual country.

Recall from Chapter 6 that GNP = consumption (C) + government spending (G) + investment (I) + exports (X) − imports (M). Because GNP equals income, GNP = consumption (C) + saving (S). If government spending and taxes are assumed to be zero (for simplicity),

$$C + S = C + I + X - M,$$

or

$$S = I + X - M,$$

or

$$S - I = X - M.$$

This equation shows that the excess of saving over investment in a country is reflected in the excess of exports over imports. The excess of

---

Example 2   The World Debt Problem

In August 1982 the finance minister of Mexico served notice to Citibank: Mexico cannot pay its foreign loans on time. Since then countries such as Argentina, Brazil, the Philippines, Chile, and Nigeria have joined Mexico as having a potential debt-repayment problem.

The world debt problem does not mean that the sky is falling. Financial collapse is not around the proverbial corner. It simply means that a group of countries borrowed more than they can easily repay. Why did it happen? To see why, imagine someone told you that your future income would rise. If your banker agreed with you, then it would be easy for you to borrow now against your future income. Clearly, if your future income did not rise as much as you and your banker anticipated (or, worse yet, fell), then you would have trouble meeting your payments. Happily, individuals can get out of some of their debts by selling the assets backing up the loan. But in the case of the world debt problem, this is not so easy. Mexico was able to borrow money on the basis of high oil prices. When oil prices softened, the value of Mexico's oil reserves dropped along with its income. Thus, in order for Mexico to meet her international debts, she must reschedule her payments due Western banks, which is exactly what happened.

Journalists and politicians expressed the fear of imminent financial collapse during most of 1984. Visions of Western banks falling like a row of dominoes have been drawn: country A fails to pay bank X; bank X calls on country B to pay its debt; country B fails to pay bank Y; bank Y calls on country C to pay its debt; and so on. These fears were probably not grounded. For example, Chile, which has the largest debt-to-income ratio of any of the problem countries, had a 1983 foreign debt of about $19 billion, but Chile's GNP (in 1980) was $23 billion. Many individuals are quite solvent with a debt-to-income ratio of far greater than unity. If a couple with a $30,000 income buys a $60,000 house and a $10,000 car, the couple may well have a debt-to-income ratio of 2. Argentina's foreign debt was $45 billion in 1983, but her GNP (in 1980) was $118 billion. To an individual, a debt of $20,000 with an annual income of $52,000 (the same ratio of debt to income as Argentina) would be regarded as highly prudent.

A reasoned look at the world debt problem suggests that while the problem was uncomfortable for the banks and countries involved, the world's monetary system was not likely to collapse. As events unfolded, the world debt problem became a simple irritation rather than a crisis. ■

---

saving over investment is the net export of capital to other countries. Thus, the export of capital is transferred into physical goods through the current-account surplus.

Capital movements take place for two reasons: investors wish to take advantage of earning a higher interest rate on their capital, or investors wish to gain some measure of security. Capital seeks higher returns and lower risks.

The capital account of any country's balance of payments contains both capital inflows and outflows because investors are seeking to diversify their portfolios of investments and securities. A fundamental principle of sound investment strategy is not to put all of one's eggs in one basket. By holding a portfolio of international securities—for example, investments in German companies, Japanese companies, and American companies—an investor can reduce the risk of achieving a given expected rate of return.

Net capital movement is governed by the desire for higher interest rates. For example, in a simple world with no risks, investors would place their capital in the country that paid the highest interest rate (the highest rate of return on investments). This process of capital exportation would raise interest rates in low-interest-rate regions and lower interest rates in high-interest-rate regions. This allocation of capital gives rise to greater production everywhere in the world and, thus, a more efficient utilization of the world's scarce stock of capital.

Stages of the Balance of Payments. When a country first begins to export capital, the country's earnings on previous foreign investments are small or zero. To finance this export of capital, it is essential to generate a surplus of merchandise exports over merchandise imports. The merchandise-trade surplus of such an immature creditor country enables the world to use the scarce capital stock efficiently. As time goes on the country begins to collect on its investments. As it becomes a mature creditor country, it is able to import more than it was exporting. The United States was an immature creditor country in the 1920s; partly because it was a mature creditor country until 1984 it had a merchandise-trade deficit year in and year out.

When a country first begins to import capital, the country's payments on past indebtedness are small or zero. Thus, an immature debtor country will be able to finance an excess of imports over exports (a trade deficit). As the debtor country matures, its interest obligations will grow relative to its net borrowing until it must generate an export surplus to pay for its past borrowings. As indicated earlier, the United States has recently become an immature debtor country. It has a trade deficit for two powerful reasons. First, it borrows more from foreigners than it lends out; second, up until at least 1984, America's income from foreign investments still exceeded is interest obligations to foreigners.

Why has the United States become a net capital importer? Will its net debtor position become a permanent feature of the U.S. balance of payments? Several factors have played a role. First, as indicated earlier, high real interest rates in the United States relative to the rest of the world led to inflows of capital. Second, the world debt crisis (see Example 2) led many foreign investors to believe in the United States as a safe haven for their investments. This caused American banks to lend much less to underdeveloped countries. Third, it has become easier for foreign residents to invest in the United States because of changes in the laws abroad. For example, the guidelines for foreign investment by Japanese and British institutions were loosened in the 1980s. Whether or not America remains a capital importer depends on whether the fundamental factors determining U.S. real interest rates (see Chapter 18) remain favorable to the United States.

Foreign Investment and Nationalism.
When capital is exported from the United States, labor complains that the United States is giving employment to foreigners and depressing home wages. When capital is imported, capitalists com-

plain that their rate of return is depressed. When a foreign country takes over a particular business firm, many people will regard this takeover as a bad thing. In recent years, for example, the Japanese have bought up some American banks, trading companies, and hotels and office buildings. Is it somehow to the disadvantage of the United States to allow foreigners to take over American businesses?

When foreign investment takes the form of actual control of a domestic firm, another issue is at stake: trade in entrepreneurial services.[4] Like trade in all goods and services, if the Japanese can operate American business more efficiently than the former management, the American people will benefit—just as they benefit from buying cheaper foreign imports of TV sets or cars.

THE EVOLUTION OF THE INTERNATIONAL MONETARY SYSTEM

In 1870, the world was not on an international gold standard; in 1900 the world was on an international gold standard. The gold standard was dead in 1945 and was replaced by a system of fixed but adjustable exchange rates. The postwar system was dead by 1973, and today the world is on a system of floating exchange rates with active exchange-rate-stabilization policies by the major central banks. To understand the current system, it is useful to take a backward look at this evolution.

The Breakdown of the Gold Standard

An international gold standard requires that 1) each country set a price of its currency in terms of gold, 2) each country allow anyone to convert gold into its currency and vice versa at the set price, and 3) the domestic money supply be tied to the domestic stock of monetary gold so that deficits reduce the money supply and surpluses in-

---

4. Indeed, there is no reason why the taking over of a domestic firm by a foreign firm should be associated with foreign investment because a Japanese firm can take over an American firm by borrowing in the American capital market.

crease the money supply. Under a gold standard, balance-of-payments deficits are defined as the reduction in the supply of monetary gold used for financing an excess of debits over credits by ordinary market participants; a surplus means the supply of monetary gold rises.

If these rules are followed, each country is giving up its own monetary autonomy because the money supply takes a course dictated by the state of the balance of payments. Indeed, the gold standard may be considered a rather cumbersome way of setting up a world currency. A more straightforward method would be to set up a world currency directly with a single central bank or monetary authority.

The pre-1914 gold standard, centered in the United Kingdom, appeared to work well from 1870 to 1914. The balance-of-payments adjustment mechanism worked smoothly to eliminate surpluses and deficits. After World War I, the gold standard broke down. While a "new" gold standard was established in the 1920s, the turbulent 1930s brought it to an end. The gold standard broke down for three main reasons:

1. After World War I, many countries, especially the United States, began to depart significantly from the rules of the gold-standard game. To abide by the gold standard, a country must let its money supply rise and fall with inflows and outflows of gold. The United States, an important country after the war, abandoned this principle.

2. When Britain and France tried to restore the old gold standard in the 1920s, they set inappropriate exchange rates. The United Kingdom overvalued the pound sterling; France undervalued the French franc. Since Winston Churchill was the Chancellor of the Exchequer in Britain, John Maynard Keynes wrote an essay entitled, "The Economic Consequences of Mr. Churchill," in which he spelled out the consequences of an overvalued exchange rate. With Britain on an overvalued rate and France with an undervalued rate, large deficits in Britain and surpluses in France were inevitable. To make the system work along the lines of Hume's gold-flow mechanism, Britain would have had to deflate substantially and France would have had to inflate substantially. It is safe to say that in the 1920s countries were not that interested in sacrificing themselves to the discipline of the gold standard.

3. The Great Depression of the 1930s put the final nail in the coffin of the gold standard. With widespread unemployment, deficit countries would never accept the discipline of further unanticipated deflation and more unemployment. Indeed, countries tried to do precisely the opposite; that is, they tried to export their unemployment to other countries. The opposite of the gold standard is to engage in so-called competitive devaluations. If Country A can unexpectedly devalue its currency, its exports will become more competitive, and it will find importing more expensive. With widespread unemployment, an unanticipated competitive devaluation (without retaliation from other countries) might increase employment at home at the expense of employment abroad. While such policies were not as widespread as sometimes alleged, the 1930s were characterized by exchange-rate gyrations and numerous currency devaluations.

In retrospect, it is easy to see that the 1930s were not a laboratory for studying a flexible-exchange-rate system. Throughout the 1930s governments were controlling changes in exchange rates or, after letting exchange rates find their own level, setting new exchange rates. With the world economy grinding through one of the worst depressions in history, it would be foolish to associate the gyrating exchange rates with a floating-exchange-rate system.[5]

The Bretton Woods System

The International Monetary Fund (IMF) was established in 1947 after a 1944 conference in Bretton Woods, New Hampshire. The international monetary arrangements set up at this conference are now called either the "old IMF" system or the "Bretton Woods" system.

Each member of the IMF was assigned a quota that was determined by its trade and national income. A country contributed 25 percent of its quota in gold or U.S. dollars and 75 percent in its own currency. Thus, the IMF consisted of a pool of gold, dollars, and all other major currencies

---

5. A good review of the 1930s will be found in Leland B. Yeager, *International Monetary Relations: Theory, History, and Policy,* 2nd ed. (New York: Harper & Row, 1976), chap. 18.

that could be used to lend assistance to any member country having balance-of-payments difficulties.

A country's international reserves under the old IMF consisted of gold, dollars, its drawing or borrowing rights from the IMF, and foreign exchange.

The Bretton Woods system was set up on the theory that balance-of-payments *deficits* and *surpluses*—reductions or increases in international reserves—were usually temporary in a fixed-exchange-rate system. Thus, the discipline of the Hume reserve-flow mechanism—deflation for deficit countries and inflation for surplus countries—could in many cases be avoided. Thus, each country pledged to maintain a par value for its currency in gold or in dollars that were worth ⅟₃₅ of an ounce of gold and to maintain the exchange rate of its currency within 1 percent of this par value. Should a deficit develop, the country could rely on its international reserves to help it weather the storm until a surplus on the balance of payments developed. In the meantime, the country would not have to go through the adjustment of a domestic deflation.

If the deficit did not reverse itself, the country was considered to be facing a "fundamental disequilibrium" and was then allowed to adjust its exchange rate. A country in fundamental deficit could devalue its currency; a country in fundamental surplus could revalue its currency.

The Fall of Bretton Woods

The United States was the center of the Bretton Woods system. Under the old IMF system, countries tied their currencies to the U.S. dollar. The United States, in turn, tied the dollar to gold. Until 1971, the United States allowed foreign monetary authorities to convert dollars into gold at the rate of $35 an ounce. The dollar became a crucial source of international reserves. Countries obtained dollars by accepting dollar payments in exchange for their goods and services. With other countries needing international reserves, the United States could run an import surplus, or a surplus of capital exports over capital imports, without too much difficulty. In other words, be-

cause the United States could buy the goods and factories of the rest of the world with its own dollars, it was in a very enviable position during this period.

The expectation was that when the U.S. import surplus came to an end, the Bretton Woods system would begin to work smoothly. In the 1950s and 1960s the United States had a deficit in its official accounts virtually every year. The expectation of the deficit turning into a surplus or at least equilibrium never materialized.

The fact that the U.S. dollar was the international money of the world also made it very difficult for the United States to adjust the value of its own currency. If the United States devalued the dollar, every country holding dollars as reserves would find itself losing a substantial fraction of its wealth. Thus, the most important member of the IMF could not use its safety valve when its deficit was permanent.

Special Drawing Rights (SDRs).   In the late 1960s, it was believed that part of the U.S. deficit problem was caused by inadequate international reserves. Thus, at the IMF's annual meeting in 1967, a new kind of international money was created—the **special drawing right (SDR).**

The **special drawing right (SDR) is** essentially an international money that can be used between monetary authorities.

Basically, the IMF simply creates SDRs out of thin air and allocates them to the various member countries in accordance with their quotas. If a deficit country needs international reserves, it can transfer its SDR balance to other countries. The rate of exchange that a country gets for SDRs depends upon the prevailing value. At first, 1SDR = $1. Later the SDR's value was determined by making 1SDR equal to a bundle of currencies. In the early 1980s, for example, an SDR was worth more than $1.

But SDRs were essentially a stopgap measure. While they may eventually become the basis for an international currency, the SDR solution did nothing to solve the fundamental problem of the Bretton Woods system: speculation.

Speculation.   In addition to the U.S. official deficit, another problem was that the currency adjustment system itself suffered from incompatibility with relatively free international capital movements. If a country had a fundamental deficit and needed to devalue its currency, speculators would know this fact better than anyone else. The chances of the country revaluing or raising the value of its currency would be virtually zero. The speculators would be in a no-lose situation if they sold weak currencies with a vengeance and bought strong currencies. For example, the British pound was often weak and the German Deutschmark (DM) was often strong. Accordingly, speculators would sell pounds and buy DMs. This exacerbated the deficit in the United Kingdom and the surplus in Germany.

In 1971, speculators began to speculate against the U.S. dollar. President Nixon, in August 1971, changed the fundamental character of the IMF system when he severed the dollar's link with gold. No longer could countries convert dollars into gold at $35 an ounce; the dollar was essentially set free to fluctuate. After a few attempts to fix up the system, by March 1973 all major currencies of the world were on a managed floating system, and the Bretton Woods system was shattered.

The Current International Monetary System

The Jamaica Agreements.

At a conference in Kingston, Jamaica in early 1976, the original IMF charter was amended to legalize the widespread managed floating that replaced the Bretton Woods par-value system.

According to the new agreements, each country can adopt whatever exchange-rate system it prefered (fixed or floating). Countries are asked to "avoid manipulating exchange rates . . . in order to prevent effective balance-of-payments adjustment or to gain an unfair competitive advantage over other members." The IMF is directed to "oversee the compliance of each member with its obligations" in order to "exercise firm surveillance of the exchange-rate policies of its members." Monetary authorities of a country can buy and sell foreign exchange in order to "prevent or moderate sharp and disruptive fluctuations from day to day and from week to week," but it

is considered unacceptable to suppress or reverse a long-run exchange-rate movement.

The policy of the Reagan administration is to limit intervention in the foreign-exchange markets. Under a policy announced in 1981, intervention will occur only if there is unusual disorder in foreign-exchange markets. The United States did not intervene in foreign-exchange markets until early 1985. The rising dollar and farm problems (associated with falling exports) led to the belief that the dollar appreciation was excessive (see again Example 1). But intervention by the United States and by other countries had little impact as of the summer of 1985, since private foreign-exchange trading is on the order of $45 billion a day in New York alone.

Advantages.

All the major countries are floating against the dollar. A number of small countries are tied to the dollar, and some others are tied to the French franc and the pound sterling. Thus, the entire system is one of individual floating, joint floating, and intervention in the foreign-exchange markets to keep the exchange rate from appreciating or depreciating too sharply. The advantages of this system are 1) monetary autonomy, 2) ease of balance-of-payments adjustment, 3) recycling of oil revenues, and 4) market efficiency.

When exchange rates are flexible, one country's monetary policy does not have to be dictated by the monetary policies of other countries. If everybody else wants to inflate, a country can maintain stable prices simply by following a long-run monetary policy of tight money (low monetary growth) and allowing its exchange rate to appreciate relative to the countries that choose to follow inflationary policies. Likewise, flexible exchange rates enable a country to follow highly inflationary policies by simply allowing its rate of exchange to depreciate.

Under a fixed-exchange-rate regime, a deficit can be solved by internal deflation or unemployment. If this solution is not in the best interests of the country, a flexible exchange rate allows a country to depreciate its currency rather than undergo the discipline of Hume's reserve-flow mechanism. It is much easier to lower the value of a country's currency than to lower every internal commodity price and wage rate!

The most dramatic achievement of the current system is that when the OPEC countries quadrupled the price of oil in 1973-74, the resulting shock to the world economy was absorbed by floating exchange rates. The enormous deficits that developed in the oil-importing countries and the necessity of the oil-exporting countries to invest their oil revenues meant that the foreign-exchange markets had a lot of recycling of oil revenues to process. The previous Bretton Woods system could not have accomplished this recycling. Indeed, the Bretton Woods system could not take much smaller pressures. While exchange rates fluctuated dramatically after the oil shock, the system worked. It did not break down or cause crises like those that the world witnessed in the late 1960s and early 1970s.

Proponents of floating exchange rates argue that the foreign-exchange market, while volatile, is efficient. If a market is efficient, the price of the commodity being traded should reflect all currently available information. For example, on February 6, 1985, the British pound was worth $1.1122. The same day a person could arrange a futures contract to buy a British pound in 90 days for $1.10. Thus, on February 6, people expected the pound to be $1.10 in 3 months. If the market works efficiently such predictions (that are made daily) should not be biased one way or the other. Sometimes the futures price will overestimate the exchange rate and sometimes it will underestimate the exchange rate, but on the average it will turn out to be right. This view appears to be supported by some studies of the foreign-exchange market, but other economists argue the exact opposite.[6]

Disadvantages.   Critics of the present system of floating exchange rates claim that the system 1) is a nonsystem, 2) is characterized by exchange-rate volatility, 3) has increased world inflation, and 4) requires monetary unification for efficiency. According to critics of floating rates, the world would be better off going back to the Bretton Woods System or to some system of managed exchange rates.[7] Establishing such a system,

however, would require that the monetary authorities of each country set up and defend an exchange rate.

Others argue that it is impossible for the monetary authorities to know what the equilibrium exchange rate should be. Hence, any attempt by the monetary authorities to intervene in the foreign-exchange markets will inevitably reflect other goals. When an exchange rate appreciates, for example, exporters may complain that it is harder to sell in foreign markets. By moderating the appreciation of an exchange rate by purchasing foreign currencies, of which the Federal Reserve System did quite a bit in 1980-81, exporters are not hit quite as hard. With each country having all sorts of such domestic objectives, manipulation of exchange rates is inevitable and does not foster the achievement of long-run equilibrium. Because the economics of managing exchange rates is not well understood, it is difficult to evaluate this criticism.

The fact that world inflation rates increased (until recently) after the adoption of generalized floating has led some to believe that there is a link between floating rates and inflation. Under a fixed exchange rate, a country is constrained from following an inflationary policy because balance-of-payments deficits are produced. A floating exchange rate removes this constraint on domestic monetary policy. Hence, as a practical political matter, one should expect greater inflation with floating rates than with fixed rates. Some economists, such as Arthur Laffer and Robert Mundell, are now suggesting that the United States should return to the gold standard in order to prevent inflation.

Figure 5 shows the volatility of the exchange rate by calculating the actual versus the predicted change in the U.S. dollar/German mark exchange rate from 1973 to 1984. Some suggest that volatile exchange rates indicate that the system is not working. The world economy is subject to many real shocks (like the oil shock) and monetary shocks. Changes in the exchange rate reflect these shocks and changing expectations. One criterion for determining whether exchange rates are too volatile is whether or not exchange-rate uncertainty contributes to a lower volume of real international trade and, hence, fewer benefits to the world from international specialization, but the

---

6. See John Williamson, *The Exchange Rate System* (Washington: Institute for International Economies, 1983).

7. It was confirmed in Jacob A. Frenkel, "Flexible Exchange Rates, Prices, and the Role of 'News': Lessons from the 1970s," *Journal of Political Economy* (August 1981): 665–705.

Figure 5   Percentage Changes in the U.S. Dollar/German Mark Exchange Rate from June 1973 to April 1984

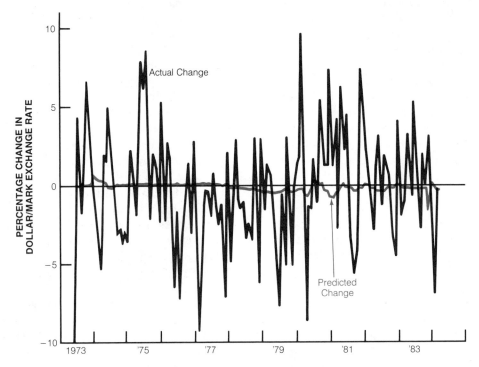

This diagram shows why some economists think that floating exchange rates fluctuate excessively. The actual dollar/mark exchange rate varies much more than the predicted exchange rate, based on existing models.

Source: Federal Reserve Bank of Kansas City, *Economic Review.*

evidence is mixed.[8] Another criterion is to compare exchange rates to other prices—such as the stock market or interest rates. On this scale, exchange rates may not be that volatile.

A final criticism of the present system is that the only way to enjoy the full benefits of a monetary economy is for every country to adopt the same currency. In other words, the current system is just a long detour away from the most efficient monetary arrangement. Presumably, in a world without nationalism and with free trade, the adoption of a truly international currency unit would come almost automatically. An international cur-

rency, however, requires the sacrifice of national monetary autonomy and other nationalistic goals. One unified world is a long way off.

Summary

1.   Foreign exchange is the national currency of another country that is needed to carry out international transactions. America's demand for foreign exchange increases when U.S. residents demand more foreign goods and services. America's supply of foreign exchange increases when residents of foreign countries demand more U.S. goods and services. The demand curve for foreign exchange is downward-sloping because the higher is the dollar price of foreign currency, the higher is the cost of foreign goods to American importers. The supply curve of foreign

8. Leland Yeager, in *International Monetary Relations,* chap. 13, argues that exchange-rate fluctuations do not reduce trade. For the opposing view see "International Trade Flows under Flexible Exchange Rates," *Economic Review* 65 (March 1980): 3–10 (Federal Reserve Bank of Kansas City).

exchange tends to be upward-sloping because as the dollar price of foreign currency rises, American goods appear cheaper to foreigners. Under a floating-exchange-rate system, the exchange rate is allowed to float to the point where the demand for foreign exchange equals the supply. When the exchange rate reflects the relative purchasing power of the currencies of two different countries, purchasing-power parity prevails between the two currencies. Under a fixed-exchange-rate system, equilibrium in the demand for and supply of foreign exchange is brought about by Hume's gold-flow mechanism. The key to this mechanism is that surplus countries (experiencing an inflow of gold) allow their money supplies to rise while the deficit countries (experiencing an outflow of gold) allow their money supplies to fall. The ensuing inflation in the surplus countries and deflations in the deficit countries correct the imbalance in the demand for and supply of foreign exchange.

2. A country's balance of payments provides a summary record of its economic transactions with foreign residents over a period of one year. It is a two-sided (credit/debit) summary that must always be in accounting balance. International capital movements raise the physical capital stocks in the capital-importing countries and lower them in the capital-exporting countries.

3. Today the world is on a system of floating exchange rates with active exchange-rate stabilization by the major central banks. The Bretton Woods system set up after World War II broke down because a currency-adjustment system is fundamentally in conflict with free international capital movements. Speculation destroyed the old Bretton Woods System. The new international monetary system involves a mixture of floating and fixed exchange rates. Since 1973 the U.S. dollar has floated with respect to all the major currencies of the world.

Key Terms

foreign exchange
fixed exchange rate
floating exchange rate
currency basket
purchasing-power parity *(PPP)*

balance of payments
mercantilist fallacy
merchandise-trade balance
current-account balance
special drawing right (SDR)

Questions and Problems

1. In February 1985, the West German mark was worth $0.31 (in U.S. dollars) and $1 was worth about 260 Japanese yen. How much would a Mercedes-Benz cost in U.S. dollars if the German price were 30,000 Deutsch-Marks (DM)? How much would a Toyota cost in U.S. dollars if the Japanese price were 1,165,000 yen?

Table A

	Foreign Currency in Dollars		Dollar in Foreign Currency	
	Wed.	Tue.	Wed.	Tues.
British pound	1.1122	1.1150	0.8990	0.8970
Japanese yen	0.003843	0.003855	260.15	259.4

2. Table A shows part of an actual newspaper report on the foreign-exchange market. Did the British pound rise or fall from Tuesday to Wednesday? Did the Japanese yen rise or fall from Tuesday to Wednesday? What happened to the dollar in terms of the pound? What happened to the dollar in terms of the yen?

3. If there were a floating exchange rate between Japan and the United States, which of the following events would cause the Japanese yen to appreciate? Which would cause the yen to depreciate? Explain your answers.

a. The government of Japan orders its automobile companies to limit exports to the United States.
b. The United States places a quota on Japanese automobiles.
c. The United States increases its money supply relative to Japan's money supply.
d. Interest rates in the United States rise relative to Japanese interest rates.

e. More Japanese decide to visit America.

f. Japanese productivity growth rises relative to the United States.

4. Indicate whether each of the following transactions represents a debit (a supply of U.S. dollars) or a credit (a demand for U.S. dollars) in the U.S. balance of payments:

a. An American commercial airline buys the European-made Airbus (an airplane competing with the Boeing 747).

b. A European airline buys an American Boeing 747.

c. An American makes a trip around the world.

d. A French company pays dividends to an American owning its stock.

e. An American buys stock in a French company.

f. An American company borrows from a European investor.

g. A Canadian oil company exports oil to Japan on an American tanker.

h. An American banker makes a loan to a European manufacturer.

5. Explain the mechanism under which U.S. restrictions on its imports will lead to fewer U.S. exports under a floating-exchange-rate system.

6. What would happen if Mexico and the United States had a fixed exchange rate but for 20 years Mexico had more inflation than the United States?

7. What are some arguments for floating exchange rates?

8. What are some arguments against floating exchange rates?

Suggested Readings

Adams, John, ed. *The Contemporary International Economy: A Reader*. New York: St. Martins Press, 1979.

Lindert, Peter H. and Charles P. Kindleberger. *International Economics,* 7th ed. Homewood, Ill.: Richard D. Irwin, 1982, pp. 243–62.

Rolfe, Sidney E. and James L. Burtle. *The Great Wheel: The World Monetary System*. New York: McGraw-Hill, 1973.

Yeager, Leland B. *International Monetary Relations,* 2nd ed. New York: Harper & Row, 1976, chaps. 13, 18.

Yeager, Leland B. *The International Monetary Mechanism*. New York: Holt, Rinehart and Winston, 1968.

Part IV

Product Markets

25

Elasticity of Demand and Supply

Chapter Preview

One of the most important tools of applied economics is *elasticity*. Economists use the concept of elasticity to measure responsiveness to price changes. An understanding of elasticity helps economists answer an enormous range of questions, such as: Will the price of oranges rise very much if there is a freeze in Florida? How much will oil imports fall if the government raises the excise tax on gasoline? If a company raises the prices it charges for the goods or services it produces, will dollar sales rise or fall?

This chapter shows how to measure the responsiveness of quantity demanded to price changes, or the *price elasticity of demand,* and describes the determinants of price elasticity of demand. The chapter also explains the concepts of *price elasticity of supply, income elasticity,* and *cross-price elasticity.* ■

THE PRICE ELASTICITY OF DEMAND

Remember that the demand curve shows how quantity demanded responds to different prices, *ceteris paribus;* the supply curve shows how quantity supplied responds to different prices, *ceteris paribus.* In both panels (a) and (b) of Figure 1, the equilibrium intersection of *S* and the demand curve (whether *D* or *D'*) is at point *e,* where price is $10 and quantity is 100 units. The only difference between the two diagrams is in the demand curve. *D* in panel (a) is much flatter than *D'* in panel (b). The supply curves *(S)* are identical.

Suppose that the supply curve shifts leftward. The supply curve shifts if any of the factors held constant along a supply curve change. Chapter 4 explained what factors cause shifts in supply curves. Let us assume that input prices rise, and there is a reduction in supply. The supply curve shifts to the left—as illustrated in panels (a) and (b). The supply shift from *S* to *S'* is the same in both panels (a) and (b).

When there is a decrease in supply, equilibrium price rises and equilibrium quantity falls. As the supply curve shifts, price rises and quantity falls; the equilibrium point *e* moves in panel (a) to *e'* on *D* and in panel (b) to *e"* on *D'*. In panel (a), the price increase (from $10 to $14) is relatively small compared to the substantial reduction in quantity demanded (from 100 units to only 20 units). In panel (b), on the other hand, the price increase (from $10 to $20) that clears the market is relatively large compared to the small reduction in quantity demanded from 100 to 80 units. The difference between the two demand curves in panels (a) and (b) is in the *responsiveness of quantity demanded to a price increase*. In panel (a), quantity demanded is very responsive to the price change; in panel (b), it is less responsive to a price change. **Price elasticity of demand (E$_d$)** is a measure of this responsiveness. (See Example 1.)

Absolute changes in price or quantity demanded are poor measures of responsiveness. If a $1 increase in the price of coal lowers quantity demanded by 1 ton, one cannot determine whether these changes are large or small unless

Figure 1   Response to a Reduction in Supply

(a) Quantity Demanded Is More Responsive to Price Change

(b) Quantity Demanded Is Less Responsive to Price Change

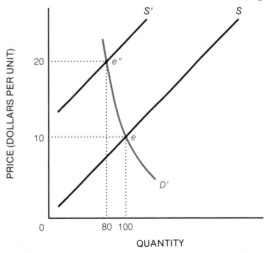

In both panels (a) and (b), *S* intersects the demand curve at the equilibrium price/quantity combination of $10/100 units. The supply conditions are exactly the same in each diagram, but the quantity demanded is less responsive to price changes in panel (b) than in panel (a). A decrease in supply from *S* to *S'* causes a sharper increase in the equilibrium price when quantity demanded is less responsive to price. Although the price increase in (b) from $10 to $20 is greater than the price increase in (a) from $10 to $14, quantity demanded falls more in (a) than it does in (b).

Example 1   Consumer Resistance and Competitive Pressure

In the financial press and in corporate reports, one frequently comes across the term *consumer resistance* or *competitive pressure*. To quote from an annual report to stockholders: "We regret that we are unable to raise prices commensurate with the increase in costs because our product would meet with increased resistance at higher prices." Another quote from an annual report of an airline: "Competitive pressure prevents us from recovering additional fuel costs by raising fares." Why is it that some industries appear to be more prone to consumer resistance or competitive pressure than others?

High consumer resistance is another way of saying *high price elasticity of demand*. A percentage increase in price causes a substantial percentage reduction in the number of units sold. If the price elasticity of demand is high, consumers will resist price increases by substituting other products. Firms whose products face a high price elasticity of demand find it difficult to pass on cost increases in the form of higher prices because they lose too many sales. The term *competitive pressures* is also used in this situation as a recognition of the number of substitutes to which consumers will turn if the price is raised.   ■

---

one knows the initial price and quantity. If the initial price is $2 per ton, a $1 change in price represents a 50 percent increase in price. If the initial price is $1,000, a $1 change in price represents a miniscule change in price. The same principle applies to quantity changes. The measure of responsiveness of quantity demanded to price changes must therefore be the relative (or percentage) change in price or quantity demanded.

> The **price elasticity of demand** (E_d) is the percentage change in the quantity demanded divided by the percentage change in price.

Calculating the Price Elasticity of Demand

Because of the law of demand, if the price rises the quantity demanded falls, and if the price falls the quantity demanded rises. Thus, since a negative number will always appear in the numerator or denominator, the sign of the price elasticity of demand will always be negative. It is a convention in economics when calculating the *coefficient* of the price elasticity of demand to drop the negative sign and to use the *absolute value* of the elasticity.

> **The coefficient of the price elasticity of demand(E_d) is the absolute value of the** percentage change in quantity demanded divided by the percentage change in price. The coefficient measures the percentage change in quantity demanded per 1 percent change in price.

$$E_d = \left| \frac{\%\Delta Q}{\%\Delta P} \right|,$$

> where %Δ stands for "percentage change."

For example, if P rises by 10 percent and Q falls by 20 percent, E_d equals 20 percent divided by 10 percent, or 2. An elasticity coefficient of 2 means that if prices were raised from the prevailing rate, the percentage change in quantity demanded would be 2 times the percentage change in price.

The price-elasticity-of-demand coefficient can range from a value of zero to a value that is infinitely large, but economists typically divide elasticity coefficients into three broad categories:

> 1.   When $E_d > 1$, demand is *elastic* (Q is strongly responsive to changes in P).
> 2.   When $E_d < 1$, demand is *inelastic* (Q responds weakly to changes in P).
> 3.   When $E_d = 1$, demand is *unitary elastic* (a borderline case).

Price-elasticity-of-demand coefficients are divided into these three categories because total rev-

Example 2   Titanium and Cuban Tobacco

Titanium and Cuban tobacco have one thing in common: in 1980 both shrank in supply. The supply curves for both products shifted to the left. In the titanium case, the supply reduction was the direct result of a decision by the Soviet Union (the major producer of titanium) to restrict its sales of titanium to the world market, which reduced the number of sellers (a factor that shifts a supply curve). In the Cuban case, the reduction in supply was the aftermath of a blue mold fungus that destroyed almost 90 percent of Cuba's tobacco crop.

The supply curves of titanium and Cuban tobacco both shifted to the left. In fact, the shift in the Cuban tobacco supply curve was, relatively, much greater than the shift in the titanium curve. The reduction in supply increased the market price, but the price of titanium rose from approximately $4 per pound to a high of $20 per pound, while the price of Cuban tobacco rose only slightly. The Cuban economy lost almost $100 million dollars in tobacco earnings. Although the Soviets reduced their supplies of titanium to the world market, their titanium earnings actually increased.

Why did titanium prices rise so dramatically while Cuban tobacco prices scarcely rose at all?

Why did Cuban earnings from tobacco sales fall while Soviet earnings rose?

The demand for titanium is very inelastic because it is used in aircraft production, and there is no known substitute that combines its lightness with its high resistance to heat and stress. If demand is highly inelastic and supply shifts to the left, the price will skyrocket. Cuban tobacco, on the other hand, has many good substitutes. Cuban refugees now grow cigar tobacco in Florida, Jamaica, and the Canary Islands the quality of which is comparable to or better than the quality of Cuban tobacco. As a consequence, the demand for Cuban tobacco is highly elastic. When the supply curve shifts to the left along an elastic demand curve, the price rises little. The total-revenue test explains the behavior of revenues. Titanium is inelastic in demand; therefore, total revenue will rise as price increases. Cuban tobacco is elastic in demand; therefore, total revenue falls as price rises. ∎

Sources: "Titanium Pinch Felt by Aircraft Builders as Soviets Cut Shipments to World Market," *Wall Street Journal,* November 14, 1979; and "Funguses Attack Cuba's Tobacco Fields, Sending the Cigar Industry Up in Smoke," *Wall Street Journal,* March 26, 1980.

---

enue responds differently to price changes in each category.

Elasticity and Total Revenue

The coefficient of the elasticity of demand can be used to show what will happen to the **total revenue *(TR)*** of sellers or—what is the same thing—what will happen to the total expenditures of consumers when price changes.

> The **total revenue *(TR)*** of sellers in a market is equal to the product of the price of the commodity times the quantity sold:
>
> $$TR = P \times Q.$$

Along a demand curve, price and quantity demanded will always move in opposite directions.

Although a fall in price tends to lower total revenue, a rise in quantity demanded tends to raise total revenue. What actually happens to total revenue depends upon the responsiveness of quantity demanded to changes in price. For example, a relatively small rise in quantity demanded will not offset the decline in revenue caused by a fall in price. A substantial rise in quantity demanded could offset the loss in revenue due to a lower price. The response of total revenue to price changes depends on the price elasticity of demand. (See Example 2.)

Elastic Demand.   If $E_d > 1$, the percentage rise in quantity demanded is greater than the percentage fall in price. Revenue increases because the increase in quantity demanded more than offsets the decrease in price.

Table 1   Total Revenue and Elasticity

Price (dollars per unit), P (1)	Quantity (units), Q (2)	Total Revenue, TR = P × Q (3) = (1) × (2)	Direction of Change in Revenue (4)	Percentage Change in Quantity Demanded, $\dfrac{\Delta Q}{(q_1 + q_2)/2}$ (5)	Percentage Change in Price, $\dfrac{\Delta P}{(p_1 + p_2)/2}$ (6)	Coefficient of Price Elasticity, E_d (7) = (5) ÷ (6)	Conclusion (8)
9	15	135					
(a)			Increase	$\dfrac{10}{20} = 50\%$	$\dfrac{2}{8} = 25\%$	$\dfrac{50}{25} = 2$	Elastic
7	25	175					
(b)			No change	$\dfrac{10}{30} = 33.3\%$	$\dfrac{2}{6} = 33.3\%$	$\dfrac{33.3}{33.3} = 1$	Unitary elastic
5	35	175					
(c)			Decrease	$\dfrac{10}{40} = 25\%$	$\dfrac{2}{4} = 50\%$	$\dfrac{25}{50} = 0.5$	Inelastic
3	45	135					

Columns (1) and (2) show a demand schedule. Column (3) is the total revenue of sellers—or the total expenditure of buyers. Column (4) shows what happens to revenue as *P falls*. Column (6) shows the percentage change in price using the midpoint between p_1 and p_2 as the base. Column (5) shows the percentage change in quantity using the midpoint between q_1 and q_2 as the base. Finally, column (7) shows the ratio of column (5) to column (6)—the elasticity of demand, E_d. Notice that when demand is elastic ($E_d > 1$), revenue rises when price falls; when demand is inelastic ($E_d < 1$), revenue falls when price falls.

When $E_d > 1$, $| \%\Delta Q | > | \%\Delta P |$.
If $|\%\Delta Q | > | \%\Delta P |$, *TR* will move in the opposite direction of price.

Inelastic Demand.   If $E_d < 1$, the percentage rise in quantity demanded is less than the percentage fall in price. Revenue falls because the decline in price is not offset by the relatively small rise in quantity.

When $E_d < 1$, $| \%\Delta Q | < | \%\Delta P |$.
If $| \%\Delta Q | < | \%\Delta P |$, *TR* will move in the same direction as price.

Unitary Elastic Demand.   If $E_d = 1$, the percentage rise in quantity demanded equals the percentage fall in price. Revenue is unchanged because the decline in price is just offset by the rise in quantity.

When $E_d = 1$, $| \%\Delta Q | = | \%\Delta P |$.
If $| \%\Delta Q | = | \%\Delta P |$, *TR* will not change.

The Total-Revenue Test.   One can determine whether demand for a particular product is elastic, inelastic, or unitary elastic by applying the **total-revenue test,** which combines the above observations.

The **total-revenue test** is:
1.   If price and total revenue move in different directions, $E_d > 1$ (demand is elastic).
2.   If price and total revenue move in the same direction, $E_d < 1$ (demand is inelastic).
3.   If total revenue does not change when price changes, $E_d = 1$ (demand is unitary elastic).

There are, then, two ways to determine whether demand is elastic, inelastic, or unitary elastic. The first method is to calculate the coefficient of the price elasticity of demand from price and quantity information.

The second method is to observe what happens to total revenue when price changes and apply the total-revenue test. Although this second method also indicates whether demand is elastic, inelas-

Figure 2   The Midpoints Elasticity Formula

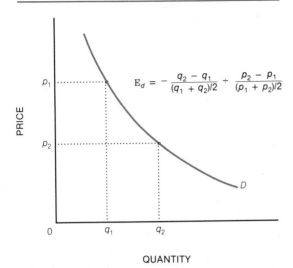

$$E_d = -\frac{q_2 - q_1}{(q_1 + q_2)/2} \div \frac{p_2 - p_1}{(p_1 + p_2)/2}$$

To calculate the elasticity of demand between any two prices, p_1 and p_2, along a given demand curve, D, requires three steps: 1) calculating the percent change in quantity demanded by dividing the change in quantity by the average of the quantities, 2) calculating the percent change in price by dividing the change in price by the average of the two prices, and 3) calculating the ratio of the percent change in quantity demanded to the percent change in price.

tic, or unitary elastic, it does *not* give a value for the coefficient.

The Midpoints Formula

To calculate the price elasticity for a given segment of a demand curve, the percentage change in quantity demanded and the percentage change in price must be computed for that segment of the curve. Consider columns (1) and (2) of Table 1.

The percentage *decrease* in price from $9 to $7 could be calculated by dividing the change in price ($2) by the *initial* price ($9). In this case, the percentage decrease would be 2/9 = 22 percent (approximately).

If we had started with $7 and raised the price to $9, the percentage *increase* in price would be the increase in price ($2) divided by the *initial* price of $7, or $2/7 = 28 percent (approximately). The problem with dividing by the initial price is that the price elasticity is different depending on the direction of the price change.

There should not be one elasticity for price de-

creases and another one for price increases. This problem can be avoided by using an *average* of the initial and new prices instead of using the initial price alone as the base in calculating the percentage change. (The initial price is added to the new price and the total is divided by 2 to obtain the arithmetic average of the two prices.) In the present case, where $7 and $9 are the two prices, the average price is ($7 + $9)/2 = $8; thus, the percent change in price is the change in price ($2) *divided* by the average price ($8), which yields a price change of 25 percent (2/8 = 25 percent). The same technique can be applied to quantity demanded. Table 1 shows that in the segment of the demand curve where price falls from $9 to $7, quantity demanded rises from 15 to 25 units. The appropriate percent increase in quantity demanded is the change in quantity demanded (10) divided by the average of the two quantities [(15 + 25)/2 = 20]. Hence, the percent change in quantity demanded is 10/20 = 50 percent. The percent change in quantity demanded is given in column (5) and the percent change in price appears in column (6).

Once the percentage change in quantity demanded (50 percent) and the percentage change in price (25 percent) for a given segment of a demand curve are known, the price elasticity of demand can be computed using the **midpoints formula.**[1]

The **midpoints formula** is:

$$E_d = \frac{\text{Percent Change in Quantity Demanded}}{\text{Percent Change in Price}}$$
$$= \frac{\dfrac{\text{Change in Quantity Demanded}}{\text{Average of Two Quantities}}}{\dfrac{\text{Change in Price}}{\text{Average of Two Prices}}}$$

Dividing the percent change in quantity demanded (50 percent) by the percent change in price (25 percent) in our example yields a price-elasticity-of-demand coefficient (E_d) of 2, as given in column (7) of Table 1. Figure 2 provides a graphical

---

1. In symbols, if p_1 and p_2 are the two prices and q_1 and q_2 are the two quantities, the midpoints formula can be simplified as follows:

$$E_d = -\frac{q_2 - q_1}{(q_1 + q_2)/2} \div \frac{p_2 - p_1}{(p_1 + p_2)/2} = \frac{q_2 - q_1}{p_1 - p_2} \times \frac{p_1 + p_2}{q_1 + q_2}.$$

Figure 3   Elasticity Rises as Price Increases

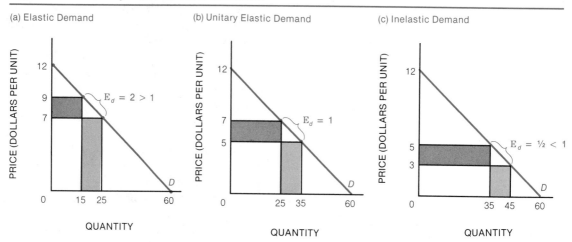

The linear demand curve, *D*, is the same in panels (a), (b), and (c). Between the prices of $9 and $7, the elasticity of demand (E_d) is 2; demand is elastic. Panel (a) shows that a reduction in price raises revenue. The black shaded rectangle shows the revenue lost due to the lower price, and the color shaded rectangle shows the revenue gained due to the greater number of units sold. Because the color rectangle is greater in area than the black rectangle, more revenue is gained than lost.

Between prices of $7 and $5, E_d equals 1; panel (b) shows that the reduction in price has no impact on revenue. Finally, between the prices of $5 and $3, E_d is ½; demand is inelastic. Panel (c) shows that the reduction in price lowers revenue because more revenue is lost (black shading) than gained (color shading). Thus, the elasticity of demand varies along a linear demand curve with constant slope. *Elasticity and slope are different.*

illustration of how price elasticity of demand can be determined.

Elasticity Along a Demand Curve

Total revenue (price times quantity) along the demand curve is given in column (3) of Table 1. Column (4) indicates whether total revenue rises or falls as prices decline from $9 to $7 to $5 to $3. The demand schedule from columns (1) and (2) is depicted by curve *D* in Figure 3. Column (4) in the table summarizes the visual information contained in the shaded areas of the graphs in Figure 3. In panel (a), the price is reduced from $9 to $7; 15 units were sold at $9, and now 25 units are sold at $7. The area shaded in black indicates the loss in revenue from having to sell the first 15 units at the lower price of $7. But more units are sold at $7 than at $9. The color shaded area indicates the revenue gained from selling more units. Total revenue rises since the color shaded area is larger than the black shaded area when demand is *elastic*. The revenue that is lost through

the lower price is more than offset by the revenue that is gained selling substantially more units.

If price now falls from $7 to $5 as in panel (b), demand is now unit elastic; in this case, revenue remains constant since the revenue lost (the black area) equals the revenue gained (the color area). As price falls further from $5 to $3, demand is inelastic. In panel (c), the revenue lost (the black area) exceeds the revenue gained (the color area) from selling a few more units, so total revenue falls.[2]

Notice that E_d *falls* in value along the demand curve as price falls. A characteristic feature of demand curves that are linear or approximately linear is that *the elasticity coefficient tends to increase as a good increases in price.*[3] In other

---

2. The total-revenue test can be applied to the data listed in Table 1 and graphed in Figure 3. Where price decreases and total revenue increases—in panel (a)—E_d ($= 2$) > 1. Where total revenue does not change when price changes—in panel (b)—$E_d = 1$. Where price and total revenue both decrease—in panel (c)—E_d ($= 0.5$) < 1.

3. It is possible to have demand curves that are curved in such a manner that the elasticity coefficient does not change as prices rise.

Figure 4   Perfectly Elastic and Perfectly Inelastic Demand Curves

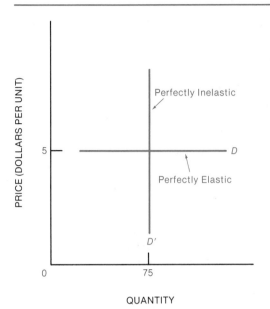

The demand curve *D* is perfectly elastic; it is perfectly horizontal or parallel to the quantity axis. The demand curve *D'* is perfectly inelastic; it is perfectly vertical or parallel to the price axis. The elasticity-of-demand coefficient of *D* is infinitely large along the entire demand schedule. The elasticity-of-demand coefficient of *D'* is zero along the entire demand curve.

words, consumers tend to be more responsive to price changes at high prices than at low prices for the same product. If the initial price of gasoline is $0.25 per gallon and rises by 10 percent, the elasticity coefficient would likely be lower than if the initial price were $2 per gallon and then rises by 10 percent. People are more likely to accept substitutes at high prices than at low prices.

Perfectly Elastic or Perfectly Inelastic Demand Curves

The highest degree of elasticity possible—the greatest responsiveness of quantity demanded to price—is a perfectly horizontal demand curve. In Figure 4, any amount on demand curve *D* can be sold at the indicated price ($5). Such a horizontal demand curve demonstrates **perfectly elastic demand.**

The midpoints elasticity formula shows that E_d is infinitely large ($E_d = \infty$) when the demand curve is horizontal. The quantity demanded can be increased indefinitely without a decrease in price. Because there can be a percentage increase in quantity demanded with no change in price, the midpoints formula yields an infinitely large coefficient of price elasticity of demand.

Although perfectly elastic demand curves represent an extreme, they are common in the real world. In perfectly competitive markets—defined in Chapter 4 as markets in which no single producer (or group of producers) is large enough to influence the market price—each seller can sell all he or she wants at the market price. Single sellers do not have to lower their prices to sell more. The price of wheat is determined in the world commodity exchanges. American corn or wheat farmers can sell all they want at that price and can't sell anything at a higher price.

A horizontal demand curve demonstrates **perfectly elastic demand** ($E_d = \infty$); quantity demanded is most responsive to price.

The lowest degree of inelasticity possible—the least responsiveness of quantity demanded to price—occurs when the demand curve is perfectly vertical. In Figure 4, the vertical demand curve *D'* demonstrates **perfectly inelastic demand.** With demand curve *D'*, 75 units of the good will be sold regardless of the price. The coefficient of the elasticity of demand is zero because if the price were to rise above $5, the percentage change in the quantity demanded would be zero. When zero is divided by the percentage change in price, E_d is zero.

A perfectly inelastic demand curve suggests that no matter how high the price rises, consumers will not cut back on the quantity demanded. The closest example would be insulin for the diabetic, but even in this case if the price rose higher and higher, eventually diabetics might reduce their dosages and accept some health loss rather than pay the higher price.

Demand curves can be perfectly inelastic *within a range of prices.* If insulin prices were to rise by 10 percent, the quantity demanded of insulin would probably not change. If the price of salt were to rise from $0.20 to $0.21 per pound, the quantity demanded would probably stay the same.

> A vertical demand curve demonstrates **perfectly inelastic demand** ($E_d = 0$); quantity demanded is least responsive to price.

Determinants of Price Elasticity of Demand

The price elasticity of demand measures the degree to which consumers respond to changes in prices. Price elasticity can tell producers what will happen to their sales revenue if they change their pricing strategy or if they offer more or fewer units for sale.

The four determinants of the price elasticity of demand for a good are: 1) the availability of substitutes, 2) the relative importance of the good in the budget, 3) the amount of time available to adjust to the price change, and 4) whether the good is a necessity or luxury.

Availability of Substitutes.

Telephones are the principal means of communicating with friends, neighbors, and businesses within a city or town, but they are not the only means. There are commercial messenger services, citizen-band radios, and the postal service. One could even drive or walk and talk in person. Because most of these alternatives are poor substitutes for the telephone, one would not expect a substantial percentage change in quantity demanded in response to a 1 percent change in price.

Next, consider movie tickets. Movies are only one form of entertainment; there are quite a few substitutes, including subscribing to a cable TV service, watching commercial television, or going to a stage play. Because of the availability of close substitutes, the elasticity of demand for movie tickets would likely be high.

The availability of substitutes depends in part upon how broadly a good is defined. The elasticity of demand for automobiles is lower than that for Chevrolets. The demand for energy will be less elastic than the demand for coal. The demand for entertainment will be less elastic than the demand for movie tickets. The more narrowly defined the product (Chevrolets vs. automobiles, coal vs. energy, movie tickets vs. entertainment), the greater the number of close substitutes (Plymouths for Chevrolets, natural gas for coal, cable TV for movies), and the higher the elasticity of demand. For example, the price elasticity of demand for lettuce has been estimated to be in the vicinity of 0.3; the demand is highly inelastic.[4] But the demand for Farmer Smith's lettuce would be very elastic (nearly perfectly elastic) because there are many perfect substitutes for the lettuce produced on Smith's farm: the lettuce of equal quality and freshness produced on any other farm.

> The greater the number of substitutes for a good, the *more elastic* is its demand. The fewer the number of substitutes for the good, the *more inelastic* is its demand.

The Relative Importance of the Good in the Budget.

Both gasoline and salt have few close substitutes. Which one would be expected to be more elastic?

Would an increase in the price of salt from $0.20 to $0.25 a package (a 22 percent increase by the midpoints method) have a substantial percentage effect on purchases of salt? The average consumer might buy two boxes of salt per year, and a 22 percent price increase would raise the family's cost of living by only $0.10 per year. A 22 percent increase in the price of gasoline, however, translates into a price increase from $1.50 per gallon to $1.83 per gallon. The average family consumes about 1,000 gallons of gas per year, so the cost of living of the average family would be increased by $330 per year. Because consumers would scarcely notice the salt price increase, their purchases would be little affected. The gasoline price increase, however, would lower real income by a noticeable margin and would, therefore, depress gasoline purchases.

---

4. George E. Brandow, "Interrelation Among Demands for Farm Products and Implications for Control of Market Supply," *Pennsylvania Agricultural Experimental Station Bulletin* 680, 1961, Table 1.

As this comparison shows, the price elasticity of demand will depend upon the relative importance of the good in the budget.

Goods that are a small fraction of the consumer's budget (salt, pepper, drinking water, matches) are more inelastic in demand than products that constitute a large fraction of the consumer's budget (automobiles, fuel oil, mortgage payments, television sets), other things equal.

Time to Adjust to Price Changes. Demand is more elastic the longer consumers have to adjust to price changes. This pattern is explained by a number of factors. Consider the response of consumers to higher electricity prices. Immediately after electric utility rates are increased, consumers can do little more than lower their heating thermostats in the winter and raise their air-conditioning thermostats in the summer. How much they adjust their thermostats depends upon their income and their tolerance for uncomfortable temperatures. As time passes, additional substitutes for electricity become available. Extra insulation and more energy-efficient heating and air-conditioning equipment can be installed. If natural gas prices have not risen as much, the family can convert to natural-gas appliances when their old system needs to be replaced.

Some expenditures require a long period of advance planning. If transatlantic air tickets fall dramatically in price in the winter, consumers whose employers allow only summer vacations must wait until summer to take advantage of the lower prices. Other expenditures are conditioned by habit formation. Consumers are accustomed to buying certain products, and habits are often hard to break. The family may be used to setting the thermostat at 78 degrees. If families are accustomed to having fresh vegetables and the price of fresh vegetables rises substantially, it may take a while before the habit is broken.

Generally speaking, the longer is the time period in which consumers can adjust to changes in prices, the more elastic is the demand.

Necessities Versus Luxuries. As this chapter will discuss later in more detail, economists distinguish necessities from luxuries by defining *necessities* as products whose demand increases less rapidly than income. For example, according to *Engel's Law,* there is a tendency for families to spend a smaller portion of their income on food as their income rises.[5] *Luxuries,* on the other hand, are goods whose demand increases at a more rapid rate than income. Foreign travel is a luxury because the demand for foreign travel increases at a more rapid rate than that of income.

What is the expected relationship between necessities and luxuries (defined in this manner) and the elasticity of demand? Chapter 4 noted that a reduction in price is very much like an increase in real income. Price reductions have an income effect on quantity demanded because real income increases when prices fall. Hence, a reduction in price will stimulate the demand for luxuries more than it will stimulate the demand for necessities, if everything else (the availability of substitutes, the importance of the good in the budget, the time allowed for adjustment) is equal. The income effect is larger for luxury goods than for necessities.

There is a tendency for luxury goods to have more elastic demands than necessities.

Actual Prices Elasticities of Demand. Table 2 gives estimates of actual price elasticities. Most were compiled by Hendrick Houthakker and Lester Taylor in their noted study of consumer demand in the United States. These elasticities of demand are calculated in two variants: one is the *short-run* E_d (where the consumer has not had much time to adjust to price changes). The other is the *long-run* E_d (where the consumer has had more time to adjust to price changes).

This evidence generally supports the claim that the long-run elasticities are larger than the short-run elasticities. In the case of electricity, E_d equals 0.13 in the short run (highly inelastic) but

---
5. Ernst Engel, a German statistician, in the mid-19th century conducted pioneering studies of European spending patterns.

Table 2   Price Elasticities of Demand for U.S. Consumers

	E_d in Short Run	E_d in Long Run
Tobacco products	0.46	1.89
Jewelry	0.41	0.67
Toilet articles	0.20	3.04
Owner-occupied housing	0.04	1.22
China and glassware	1.55	2.55
Electricity	0.13	1.89
Water	0.20	0.14
Medical care and hospitalization	0.31	0.92
Tires	0.86	1.19
Auto repairs	0.40	0.38
Durable recreation equipment	0.88	2.39
Motion pictures	0.88	3.69
Foreign travel	0.14	1.77
Gasoline	0.15	0.78

Source: Hendrick S. Houthakker and Lester D. Taylor, *Consumer Demand in the United States: Analyses and Projections* (Cambridge, Mass.: Harvard University Press, 1970), pp. 166–67; James L. Sweeney, "The Demand for Gasoline: A Vintage Capital Model," Department of Engineering Economics, Stanford University.

equals 1.89 in the long run (elastic). In the case of foreign travel, E_d rises from 0.14 in the short run to 1.77 in the long run. The elasticities of Table 2 illustrate the important role of substitutes. Medical care has fewer good substitutes than most of the other products listed, and it has lower short-run and long-run elasticities than products, such as motion pictures, recreation equipment, gasoline, and foreign travel. In the short run, electricity has no good substitutes, and the short-run electricity E_d is low.

OTHER ELASTICITIES OF DEMAND

Chapter 4 showed that consumer demand depends not only on the product's own price, but also upon consumer preferences, the prices of substitutes and complements, and consumer income. Although economists devote most of their attention to *price* elasticity of demand, the elasticity concept can also be applied to the other factors affecting demand. For example, economists try to measure the responsiveness of demand to the prices of related goods (cross-price elasticity) and the responsiveness of demand to consumer income (income elasticity).

Cross-Price Elasticity

A change in the price of one product can cause a shift in the demand schedules of other products that are related to the first product. This responsiveness of demand to other prices is **cross-price elasticity of demand (E_{xy}).**

> The **cross-price elasticity of demand (E_{xy})** is the percentage change in demand of the first product (x) divided by the percentage change in the price of the related product (y).[6]

Unlike the price elasticity of demand, which will always be negative (due to the law of demand), the cross-price elasticity can be either positive or negative because the demand for x can increase or decrease when the price of y increases.

A positive cross-price elasticity of demand means that an increase in the price of one product will cause an increase in the demand for the other product. Consider beef and chicken. As the price of beef rises, the quantity demanded of beef falls because substitutes have been purchased in place of beef. Chicken is a substitute for beef; therefore, the beef price increase causes an increase in the demand for chicken.

A negative cross-price elasticity means that an increase in the price of one product will cause a decrease in the demand for the other product. Compare airline travel and auto rentals. The two are complements because a large proportion of auto rentals are made by airline travelers. If the price of airline tickets rises, the number of airline passengers declines. As the number of air passengers declines, so does the demand for automobile rentals.

---

6. The cross-price elasticity of demand is calculated by the same midpoints formula. The only difference is that instead of having the "own price" (p^x) in the denominator, the price of the related product (p^y) is in the denominator:

$$E_{xy} = \frac{q_2^x - q_1^x}{(q_1^x + q_2^x)} \div \frac{p_2^y - p_1^y}{(p_1^y + p_2^y)}.$$

If the cross-price elasticity of demand is positive, the two products are *substitutes*. If the cross-price elasticity is negative, the two products are *complements*. If the cross-price elasticity is zero, products *x* and *y* are unrelated.

Income Elasticity

A rise or fall in consumer income will affect the demands for different products. As consumer income rises, the demand for most products increases—but not always. The responsiveness of demand to consumer income is measured by the **income elasticity of demand (E_i).**

> The **income elasticity of demand (E_i)** is the percentage change in the demand for a product divided by the percentage change in income *holding all prices fixed.*[7]

The income elasticity of demand will be positive for most goods because the higher their income, the more consumers demand of most goods. If the income elasticity equals unity, a 1 percent increase in income will lead to a 1 percent increase in the demand for the good. Hence, consumers would continue to spend the same fraction of their income on the good as before income increased. If the income elasticity exceeds 1, people will spend a larger fraction of their income on the good as income rises. If the income elasticity for some good is less than 1, people will spend a smaller fraction of their income on a good as income rises. The definitions of **necessities** and **luxuries** given earlier in this chapter can be refined using the income-elasticity-of-demand concept.

> **Necessities** are those products that have an income elasticity of demand less than 1.

> **Luxuries** are those products that have an income elasticity of demand greater than 1.

---

7. The midpoints formula for the income elasticity of demand is:

$$E_i = \frac{q_2 - q_1}{(q_1 + q_2)} \div \frac{i_2 - i_1}{(i_1 + i_2)},$$

where *i* denotes consumer income.

Using this criterion, goods such as food items would be necessities, while recreational vehicles would be luxury items. Notice, though, that the economist allows the terms *luxury* and *necessity* to be defined by the market choices people make rather than by individual perceptions about what is more "necessary" than something else. (See Example 3.)

THE PRICE ELASTICITY OF SUPPLY

The price elasticity of demand measures the responsiveness of *consumers* to price change. The **price elasticity of supply (E_s)** measures the responsiveness of *producers* to price changes. The elasticity of supply is calculated in the same way as the elasticity of demand, only now the *qs* refer to quantities *supplied*, not quantities demanded.

> The **price elasticity of supply (E_s)** is defined as the percentage change in the quantity supplied divided by the percentage change in price.

According to the midpoints formula, E_s is calculated:

$$E_s = \frac{q_2 - q_1}{(q_1 + q_2)/2} \div \frac{p_2 - p_1}{(p_1 + p_2)/2}$$

Like the elasticity of demand, the E_s coefficients are divided into three categories: elastic ($E_s > 1$), unitary elastic ($E_s = 1$), and inelastic ($E_s < 1$). The direction of movement of total revenue along a supply curve, however, will not depend upon the value of E_s. The E_s coefficient is positive except in rare cases; increases in price usually raise the quantity supplied. Because both price and quantity supplied are rising, total revenues rise as well.

Perfectly Elastic and Perfectly Inelastic Supply Curves

The highest degree of elasticity possible for a supply curve is a perfectly horizontal supply curve. In Figure 5, the supply curve, *S*, illustrates the case of **perfectly elastic supply.** At the price of $10, producers of the good (in the aggregate) are

Example 3   Cyclical Stocks and the Income Elasticity of Demand

Stock-market analysts consider automobile stocks (such as shares in Ford, GM, and Chrysler) and airline stocks (such as shares in United, Pan Am, and Eastern) to be *cyclical stocks* because they are shares in companies whose profits and stock prices move up at a rapid rate during prosperous times and fall at a rapid rate during hard economic times. The high income elasticity of demand for the goods or services these companies sell is the reason these stocks are so cyclical. During periods of rising prosperity, incomes are generally rising (after adjustment for inflation). If the income elasticity of demand for automobiles, for example, is 2, a 10 percent increase in income will lead to a 20 percent increase in automobile sales. It is, therefore, easy to see why automobile manufacturers will share disproportionately in rising prosperity. There is a reverse side to this coin: during hard times when incomes are falling (after adjustment for inflation), automobile manufacturers will also suffer disproportionately. A 10 percent reduction in income could lead to a 20 percent reduction in automobile sales. A cyclical industry, like automobile manufacturing, tends to feel exaggerated effects of the ups and downs of the economy. Stock-market analysts, therefore, recommend buying cyclical stocks shortly before prosperity breaks out and selling them before hard times set in. Unfortunately, it is very difficult to know when each event is about to occur.

The accompanying table illustrates the volatility of sales in an industry with a high income elasticity for the period 1970–1982. As a general tendency,

	Annual Growth Rate of Auto Sales (millions of cars per year)	Annual Percentage Growth Rate of Income (adjusted for inflation)
1973	0.9	5.8
1974	−22.0	−0.6
1975	−3.0	−1.2
1976	17.4	5.4
1977	11.0	5.5
1978	0.9	5.0
1979	−5.0	2.8
1980	−16.0	−0.3
1981	−6.0	2.6
1982	−6.0	−1.9

Source: *Statistical Abstract of the United States,* 1984, 1980 editions.

the percentage increase (or decrease) in automobile sales tends to be much greater than the percentage increase in income (after adjustment for inflation). ∎

willing to supply any amount of the good to the market at that price.

Most of the supply curves that the average consumer deals with are perfectly elastic. The grocery store is willing to sell any person all the milk, canned goods, and dairy products that person wants to buy at the prices set. Under normal circumstances, however, all buyers together (the market) must offer higher prices to induce producers to increase the quantity supplied.

The lowest degree of elasticity occurs when the supply curve is perfectly vertical, as shown in Figure 5 by the supply curve S'. Such a supply curve demonstrates **perfectly inelastic supply.** The coefficient of E_s in this case equals zero. An increase in price has no effect on quantity supplied; therefore, the percentage change in quantity supplied is zero.

Like perfectly inelastic demand curves, supply curves can be perfectly inelastic over one range of prices but not perfectly inelastic for all prices. The supply curves of perishable agricultural products tend to be perfectly inelastic. The supply of lakefront or oceanfront locations is fixed and perfectly inelastic as is the supply of agile seven-foot tall athletes. Such supply curves will be discussed in the chapter on rent, interest, and profit.

Most market supply curves fall between the two extremes of perfect elasticity ($E_s = \infty$) and perfect inelasticity ($E_s = 0$).

Figure 5   Perfectly Elastic and Perfectly Inelastic Supply Curves

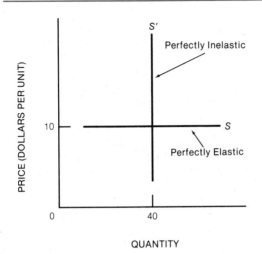

The supply curve S is perfectly elastic because at a price of $10 any quantity of output can be offered on the market by sellers. The supply curve S' is perfectly inelastic because no matter how much the price rises, the quantity supplied remains the same.

A horizontal supply curve demonstrates **perfectly elastic supply** ($E_s = \infty$); quantity supplied is most responsive to price.

A vertical supply curve demonstrates **perfectly inelastic supply** ($E_s = 0$); quantity supplied is least responsive to price.

Elasticity of Supply in Three Time Periods

Just as the elasticity of demand depends upon the amount of time the consumer has to respond to price changes, the elasticity of supply also depends upon time.

In general, the longer the period of time the producer has to adjust to changes in prices, the greater the elasticity of supply.

When prices change, economists distinguish between three time periods during which producers adjust their supply to the new prices: the **immediate run,** the **short run,** and the **long run.**

The **immediate run** is a period of time so short that the quantity supplied cannot be changed at all. In the immediate run—sometimes called the *momentary period* or *market period*—supply curves are perfectly inelastic.

The **short run** is a period of time long enough for existing firms to produce more goods but not long enough for existing firms to expand their capacity or for new firms to enter the market. Thus, output can be varied but only within the limits of existing plant capacity.

The **long run** is a period of time long enough for new firms to enter the market, for old firms to disappear, and for existing plants to be expanded. In the long run, firms have more flexibility in adjusting to price changes.

These three time periods cannot be closely associated with calendar time. The amount of calendar time required to move from the short run to the long run varies with the type of industry. The electric-power industry may require a decade to expand existing power-generating facilities and to bring new plants on line. On the other hand, the fast-food industry can construct and open a new outlet in a few months. Example 4 shows how the time period affects the elasticity of supply of eggs.

ELASTICITY AND THE TAX BURDEN

Local, state, and federal governments tax a variety of goods and services, including tobacco, alcohol, gasoline, and various foreign imports. Elasticity analysis can be used to determine how a tax on a particular good will affect consumers and producers. Who will pay the tax?

How the Burden Is Shared

Suppose that a tax is imposed on a luxury good like perfume. Figure 6 shows the supply curve and the demand curve for perfume before the tax is imposed. The equilibrium price is $2 per gram and the equilibrium quantity is 8 million grams per month at point *e* before the tax is imposed.

Let a tax of $1 per gram be imposed by the government. In order for sellers to earn $2, they must now charge $3; or to earn $1.25 they must charge $2.25. The tax will cause the supply curve to shift *up* by exactly $1—the amount of the tax. Before the tax, suppliers were prepared to supply 8 million grams per month at a price of $2 per gram, but after the tax, suppliers will be prepared to supply the same 8 million grams per month only if the price is $3 (because they will receive $2 per gram after the tax). Since the conditions affecting the demand curve for perfume (consumer income, other prices, consumer preferences, number of buyers) are not changed by the tax, the demand curve for perfume will remain the same. As long as buyers are charged the same price (including the tax), their quantity demanded will remain the same. The new equilibrium price must be less than $3 (the original price plus the $1 tax) because at $3, the quantity supplied is the same as without the tax but the quantity demanded is lower.

The new equilibrium point is *e'*. The buyers will pay $2.25 for perfume and sellers will receive $1.25, with the tax collector picking up the $1.00 difference. The equilibrium price *paid* by consumers goes up only $0.25, but the net price (price minus tax) received by producers goes down by $0.75. In this particular case, the greater burden of the tax is on the sellers who pay three quarters of the tax. Buyers pay only one quarter of the tax.

The Elasticity Determines Who Bears the Burden

Why is it that the producer bears a greater part of the burden than the consumer in our perfume example? The answer is found in the elasticities of demand and supply.

The demand curve in Figure 6 is more elastic than the supply curve in the vicinity of the equilibrium point *e,* as evidenced by the fact that curve *S* is steeper than curve *D*. Consumers, therefore, respond more to the price than do producers. Hence, consumers have a greater oppor-

Figure 6   The Burden of a Tax

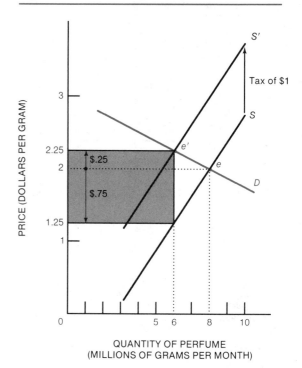

D and S are the demand and supply curves for perfume before the tax; the equilibrium price is $2. A tax of $1 per unit on sellers shifts the supply curve upward by exactly $1 as sellers recoup their tax payments to the state. The new equilibrium price to buyers is where the new supply curve, S', intersects the old demand curve, D, at point e'; thus, the new price is $2.25 to buyers. Sellers must send $1 (per gram sold) to the tax collector; hence, sellers keep only $1.25 after paying tax. Notice that one fourth of the burden of the $1 tax ($0.25) falls on buyers and three fourths of the burden ($0.75) falls on sellers. This incidence reflects the fact that the elasticity of demand is approximately 4 times greater ($E_d = 2.4$) than the elasticity of supply ($E_s = 0.6$).

tunity to avoid the tax than producers. In fact, the elasticity of demand along *D* between $2 and $2.25 is 2.4; the elasticity of supply along *S* between $1.25 and $2 is approximately 0.6.

Had we assumed instead that the supply curve was more elastic than the demand curve, then the consumer would bear the greater burden of the tax. If consumers have a more inelastic demand, it is easier to shift the price forward to them and harder to reduce the price paid to producers. For the consumer to bear the greater burden of the tax requires that demand elasticities be *smaller* than

Example 4   The Market for Eggs and the Elasticity of Supply

Since 1960, per-capita egg consumption in the United States has fallen more than 15 percent. In 1960, people consumed on the average about 28 dozen eggs per year, but in 1982 they each consumed only about 22 dozen eggs on average. The reasons for this decline are complicated, but two important factors were the trend toward smaller breakfasts and the fear that cholesterol is a contributing factor in heart disease. The U.S. demand curve for eggs, thus, shifted to the left during this period.

Panel (a) of the accompanying figure shows what happens in the immediate run in the egg market. When the demand schedule shifts to the left from D to D', egg producers are unable to cut back on the current supply of eggs. The hens to lay these eggs have already been raised or purchased; the chicken coops have already been built; they have or are about to produce eggs for sale. When the demand reduction hits, the supply curve of eggs is perfectly inelastic. With the per-capita supply fixed at 28 dozen eggs per year, the price must drop in order to induce consumers to buy all the eggs on the market. In our example, the price of eggs drops sharply, from $1 per dozen to $0.50 per dozen.

As the price of eggs falls, egg producers will find it worthwhile to start selling their laying hens. Egg prices will have fallen substantially, and egg farmers will find that they can reduce losses by selling their hens to slaughtering houses, where hens will be converted into canned meat, chicken soup, and pot pies. The amount of calendar time required to make this adjustment is short. All the egg growers have to do is sell their hens.

As time passes from the immediate-run period to the short run, the quantity of eggs supplied falls to 26 dozen eggs per year per capita. The supply schedule is no longer perfectly inelastic. Producers respond to lower prices by offering less output for sale. At the immediate-run price of $0.50, the quantity demanded exceeds the quantity supplied, and the price rises to $0.75 in the short run. The short-run price is lower than the original equilibrium price (of $1), but it is higher than the price in the immediate run (of $0.50).

If demand remains at D', there will be further supply adjustments as egg producers enter the long-run period. Some producers will go out of business; they will convert their chicken coops to raising minks or some other venture. Others will remain in business but will decide not to replace buildings and equipment that have worn out. These actions mean a further reduction in the quantity supplied (the supply curve pivots around the old equilibrium price), and the long-run supply curve is even more elastic than the short-run supply curve. In panel (c) of the figure, as the supply curve becomes more elastic, the price rises further to $0.90—still below the original price of $1 but above the immediate-run price of $0.50 and the short-run price of $0.75.   ■

Source: "Egg Prices Are Likely to Climb Further as Producers Trim Output to End Losses," *Wall Street Journal*, October 7, 1980, p. 36.

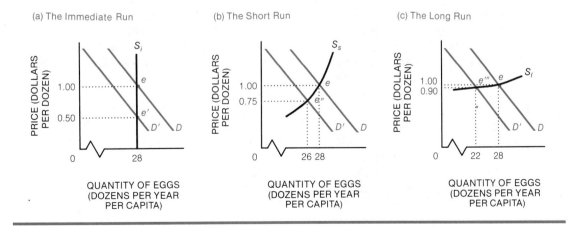

(a) The Immediate Run   (b) The Short Run   (c) The Long Run

supply elasticities—which in the long run, in many industries, is likely to be true.

The concept of elasticity allows us to understand the extent to which changing prices and income affect supply and demand. The next chapter will look behind the demand curve to explain the law of demand and consumer surplus.

Summary

1. The *price elasticity of demand* (E_d) is a measure of the responsiveness of consumers and producers to changes in price and is the absolute value of the percentage change in quantity demanded divided by the percentage change in price. The price elasticity of demand can be either elastic ($E_d > 1$), unitary elastic ($E_d = 1$), or inelastic ($E_d < 1$). If demand is elastic, price and total revenue move in opposite directions. If demand is inelastic, price and total revenue move in the same direction. If demand is unitary elastic, total revenue is not affected by price changes. E_d can be calculated using the midpoints formula; the change in quantity is divided by the average quantity, and the change in price is divided by the average price. The price elasticity of demand changes as one moves along the demand schedule. At higher prices, demand tends to become more elastic. Demand is perfectly elastic when the demand curve is horizontal; demand is perfectly inelastic when the demand curve is vertical. The price elasticity of demand is determined by the availability of substitutes (more substitutes mean higher elasticity), the amount of adjustment time (more time means higher elasticity), the importance in the budget (the more important the higher the elasticity), and whether the good is a necessity or a luxury (necessities tend to have lower elasticities).

2. Elasticities can also be used to measure the responsiveness of consumer demand to changes in income and the prices of other goods. Cross-price elasticity is the percentage change in the demand of one good divided by the percentage change in the price of the other good. If this number is positive, the two goods are substitutes. If it is negative, the two goods are complements. Income elasticity of demand is the percentage change in the demand divided by the percentage change in income. If this number is greater than one, the good is a luxury; if it is less than one, the good is a necessity.

3. The price elasticity of supply is the percentage change in quantity supplied divided by the percentage change in price. Supply is perfectly elastic when the supply curve is horizontal; supply is perfectly inelastic when the supply curve is vertical. The price elasticity of supply depends upon the time period of adjustment. In the immediate run, supply is fixed, and the supply schedule is perfectly inelastic. In the short run, firms can produce more or fewer goods but do not have sufficient time to alter their capital stock or enter or leave the industry. In the long run, supply can be altered through changes in capital stock and through the entry and exit of firms. Elasticity of supply is greater in the long run than in the short run.

4. Elasticity analysis can be used to determine whether producers or consumers will bear the greater burden of a tax on a particular good.

Key Terms

price elasticity of demand (E_d)
total revenue (*TR*)
total-revenue test
midpoints formula
perfectly elastic demand
perfectly inelastic demand
cross-price elasticity of demand (E_{xy})
income elasticity of demand (E_i)
necessities
luxuries
price elasticity of supply (E_s)
perfectly elastic supply
perfectly inelastic supply
immediate run
short run
long run

Questions and Problems

1. Using the demand schedule in Table A, calculate the price elasticities of demand for each successive pair of rows.

Table A

Price (dollars)	Quantity (units)
5	1
4	2
3	3
2	4
1	5

2. Suppose the price elasticity of demand for rental housing is 0.6 and the average rent increases from $275 per month to $325 per month. At $275 per month, 100,000 rental units are rented. What percentage decrease in quantity demanded would you predict from this information? How many units would be rented at $325 per month?

3. The price of gasoline rises from $1.50 per gallon to $4.00 per gallon. Why would one's short-run adjustment to this price change be different from the long-run adjustment?

4. Assume the basic monthly charge for a private telephone is $10.50 per month. If the rate were to rise to $11.00, would you expect a substantial reduction in the quantity demanded? Explain your answer. If, on the other hand, the basic monthly charge were $250.00 per month and the rate were to rise by the same percent as in the first case, what is your prediction about the change in quantity demanded?

5. When a professional football team raises its ticket prices by 10 percent, its sales revenues decline. From this information, what can you say about the price elasticity of demand for its tickets?

6. If the price of tennis balls were to go up, what impact would this price increase have on the quantity demanded of tennis rackets? What sign (+ or −) would the cross-price elasticity have? What sign would the cross-price elasticity of tennis balls and golf balls have?

7. The income elasticity of demand for all services taken together is greater than one. As the economy grows, what would you expect to happen to the share of service industries in total output?

8. Used-car sales typically rise during economic recessions, while new-car sales decline during recessions. Explain why.

9. Assume that you have a product called *args*. The elasticity of demand is 2 and the elasticity of supply is 0.2. If government imposes a tax of $1 per unit on args, who would end up paying more of the tax (bearing the larger burden of the tax): the consumer or the producer? Why? Draw a diagram illustrating your argument.

10. Evaluate the following statement: "The elasticity of demand for oranges is 0.2; therefore, California orange growers could raise their income by restricting their output."

11. Suppose the supply curve for product X shifts to the right (supply increases). What happens to the total expenditure of consumers under the following conditions?
   a. The demand for X is price elastic.
   b. The demand for X is price inelastic.
   c. The demand for X is perfectly elastic.
   d. The demand for X is perfectly inelastic.

12. Suppose the supply curve for product X shifts to the left (supply decreases). What happens to the total expenditure of consumers under the following conditions?
   a. The demand for X is price elastic.
   b. The demand for X is price inelastic.
   c. The demand for X is perfectly elastic.
   d. The demand for X is perfectly inelastic.

13.   Suppose the demand for product X increases. What happens to the total revenue of sellers under the following conditions?
   a.   The supply of X is elastic.
   b.   The supply of X is inelastic.

14.   What determines the size of the price elasticity of demand for a product? Using these determinants, indicate for each of the following pairs of goods which one has the highest elasticity.
   a.   Wheat and grains.
   b.   Soft drinks and beverages.
   c.   Cars and clothing.
   d.   Toothpicks and beef.

15.   Double the quantities demanded at each price in Table A above (for example, when the price is $5 assume 2 units are demanded, when the price is $4 assume 4 units are demanded, and so on). What happens to the slope of the demand curve? What happens to the elasticity of demand between each successive pair of prices?

16.   Who bears the burden of a tax on a good in each of the following circumstances?
   a.   The supply curve is upward-sloping; demand is perfectly inelastic.
   b.   The supply curve is upward-sloping; demand is perfectly elastic.
   c.   The demand curve is downward-sloping; supply is perfectly inelastic.
   d.   The demand curve is downward-sloping; supply is perfectly elastic.

Suggested Readings

Kohler, Heinz. *Intermediate Microeconomics: Theory and Applications,* 2nd ed. Glenview, Ill.: Scott, Foresman, 1986.

Mansfield, Edwin. *Microeconomics: Theory and Applications,* 5th ed. New York: W. W. Norton, 1985, chap. 4.

26

Demand and Utility

Chapter Preview

Adam Smith, in his *The Wealth of Nations,* writes in 1776 that "Nothing is more useful than water; but it will purchase scarce anything; scarce anything can be had in exchange for it. A diamond, on the contrary, has scarce any value in use; but a very great quantity of other goods may frequently be had in exchange for it."

This chapter will explain the paradox that Smith writes about by building a model of consumer behavior that is based on the principle that the consumer will allocate (spend) income in such a manner as to gain maximum satisfaction. The model can be used to deduce the law of demand. This chapter will also show how to combine individual demand curves to determine market demand curves and how to measure the consumer gains and losses that result from price changes.

Wants and *demand* are two different things in economics. *Wants* are those goods and services that households would consume if there were no budgetary limitations. *Demand* denotes those goods and services that households are prepared to buy given relative prices and the consumers' income level. The amounts of goods and services that households purchase depend not only on relative prices and income, but also on preferences or tastes. Some families might not want pork even if it were given away free. The individual with a fear of flying will not want free airline tickets. The opera lover would welcome a free concert ticket but might throw away a free ticket to the World Series that a baseball fan would treasure. To understand why consumers are prepared to buy a given quantity of a given good, it is necessary to first understand the nature of consumer preferences. ■

THE NATURE OF CONSUMER PREFERENCES

People are different; they have different **preferences.**

> **Preferences** are people's evaluations of goods and services independent of budget and price considerations.

Consumer preferences—when broadly defined—are remarkably stable. In a sense, the consumer wants the *services* that goods provide, not the goods themselves. Rather than wanting an automobile, the consumer wants the transportation *services* that an automobile will provide. Rather than wanting theater tickets, admission to bowling alleys, or tickets to sports events, the consumer desires the entertainment *services* that these goods provide. Rather than wanting a house or condominium, the consumer wants the shelter that these goods provide.

Stated in these terms, consumer preferences for the service different goods provide will be more stable than preferences for the specific products that provide the consumption service. The taste for transportation services may be stable, but, because transportation services can be provided by a variety of goods (the private automobile, taxis, buses, trains, airplanes, one's feet), how these services are purchased will be less stable. The preference for entertainment may be quite stable, but the exact manner in which the consumer satisfies that taste can vary dramatically. One consumer watches television; another goes to a movie; another learns how to pilot an airplane; yet another buys a book.

Technology and innovations alter preferences for specific goods. For example, transportation innovations over the years have been dramatic: the consumer who used to be content to move about by horse 200 years ago may now prefer jet-powered transportation. To the casual observer, this transformation might seem like a radical change in preferences, but economists would argue that the preference for the transportation service itself has remained relatively stable. Example 1 shows that preferences are basically uniform from one country to another. (See Example 1.)

THE CONCEPT OF UTILITY

A consumer's preferences determine how he or she would rank different *market baskets* (combinations of goods and services) in all conceivable situations. Nineteenth-century economists introduced a simple way of representing preferences. They assumed people's preferences for goods or services are based on their perception of how the goods or services add to their **utility.**

> **Utility** is the satisfaction that a person enjoys from consuming goods and services.

The Law of Diminishing Marginal Utility

It is not possible to attach a util-o-meter to a person's arm to measure the satisfaction that is being experienced from consuming goods and services. (The appendix to this chapter explains why it is not even necessary to be able to measure utility in specific units.) Suppose, however, that one could measure utility in terms of imaginary *utils,* or units of utility. From consuming 50 gallons of water per week, for example, a consumer might enjoy 3,000 utils of satisfaction. The **marginal utility (*MU*)** of water is the extra utility enjoyed by increasing water consumption by one gallon. If 51 gallons yields 3,010 utils, the marginal utility of the last gallon of water is 10 utils.

> The **marginal utility (*MU*)** of any good or service is the increase in utility that a consumer experiences when consumption of that good or service (and that good or service alone) is increased by one unit. In general,
>
> $$MU = \frac{\Delta TU}{\Delta Q},$$
>
> where *TU* is total utility and *Q* is the quantity of the good.

The **law of diminishing marginal utility** states that, as a general rule, as more of a good or service is consumed, its marginal utility declines. Thus, the first gallon of water (in a given week) has an enormous marginal utility because a

Example 1 The Universality of Wants

That wants are uniform is supported by a major study of spending patterns in 34 countries commissioned by the World Bank. The World Bank examined the spending patterns of 34 countries and found great diversity among the individual product categories. The Japanese eat more fish; the French dine out more; the Americans spend little on public transportation (they use their private cars instead); the Indians spend a great deal on spices; the Kenyans spend little on clothing and footwear. These differences are explained in large part by difference in climate, religion, and custom. Yet if one examines broad consumption catego-ries that satisfy basic preferences for services that goods provide, one finds much more uniformity. The differences that remain, moreover, are primarily the consequence of differences in income levels and differences in relative prices. The World Bank study shows that as countries become more similar in income levels and relative prices, their patterns of consumption become more similar.   ∎

Source: Irving B. Kravis et al., *A System of Interventional Comparisons of Purchasing Power* (Baltimore, Md.: The Johns Hopkins Press, 1975); Kravis et al., *World Product and Income* (Baltimore: Johns Hopkins Press, 1982).

---

consumer who has no water would consider 1 gallon to be very valuable. The 20th gallon of water has a relatively small marginal utility because a person who already has 19 gallons would not value a 20th as highly. The *total utility* from all 20 gallons of water would be the total of the marginal utility of all units. Why does the utility of water decline so rapidly as more water is consumed? Because the first gallon of water is essential to sustaining life, its marginal utility is astronomical. As more water becomes available, water can be applied to less urgent uses: to washing oneself, to washing one's clothes, to feeding pets, and eventually even to watering one's lawn. By the time sufficient water is available for watering the lawn, the marginal utility of the last gallon is much smaller than the marginal utility of the first gallon.

> The **law of diminishing marginal utility** states that as more of a good or service is consumed during any given time period, its marginal utility declines, holding the consumption of everything else constant.

There are some rare exceptions (the marginal utility of the stamps of the stamp collector may rise for quite some time as additional stamps are acquired), but these exceptions need not concern us here because they do not change the general pattern of consumer behavior. The law does not say how rapidly marginal utility will decline as consumption increases; this rate will vary. For some goods (food products, for example), marginal utility declines rapidly. The marginal utility of the second hamburger is much less than that of the first. The marginal utility of the third hamburger will be very small. For other goods, such as women's shoes, marginal utility may decline slowly as consumption increases.

The Diamond/Water Paradox

In the quotation that opens this chapter, Adam Smith poses the famous *water/diamond paradox*. Smith is asking why prices often fail to reflect the usefulness of goods. Goods like water and salt, without which human beings would perish, have low relative prices, while goods that have little practical value, such as diamonds, gold, and high fashion, have high relative prices.

The law of diminishing marginal utility provides the answer to the diamond/water paradox. Why do diamonds, whose total utility is much less than the total utility of water, have a higher relative price than water? The answer is that the consumption of water takes place at a low marginal utility because the supply of water is large, while the supply of diamonds is usually so limited that consumption takes place at relatively high marginal utility. Although water's total utility is high, its marginal utility will be small. Since the marginal utility of water is low no one will sacrifice very much for an additional gallon.

Example 2   Marginal Utility and Being Snowed in at JFK

At John F. Kennedy International Airport in New York, a sandwich can be purchased for from $2 to $3, a hot meal in an airport restaurant for $15, a ride by bus or subway into Manhatten for $6, and a trip by taxi for $15 to $25 depending upon time of day and traffic. When a blizzard hits and thousands of passengers are stranded, these prices change radically. People gratefully pay vendors $10 for a sandwich, $50 for the same hot meal that cost $15 the day before, $100 for a blanket, and $200 for a ride on a snowplow truck into town. Marginal-utility theory explains this unusual behavior. When the airport is cut off from its normal supplies and transportation, stranded passengers are forced back up their marginal-utility curves. Some stranded passengers who have skipped a meal or two place a very high marginal utility on one sandwich. Even at $10 per sandwich, their marginal utility per dollar is high. In such a situation, people compare the marginal utility per dollar of purchasing a sandwich, a hot meal, a blanket, or a ride into town with marginal utilities per dollar of things that they will be able to buy after things return to normal. Insofar as the marginal utility of a sandwich, a hot meal, a blanket, or a ride home is so high at the time, some of the people who pay these extraordinary prices are acting completely rationally. ■

The diamond/water paradox holds under normal supply conditions, but what happens when normal conditions are disrupted? In the confusion at the end of the Second World War, food supplies were interrupted, and people gladly exchanged diamonds and precious metals for bread and potatoes in parts of Europe. Supplies of food products were so limited that food products yielded a higher marginal utility (by preventing malnutrition) than did diamonds and precious metals. When the American West was being settled in the 19th century, range wars were fought (and people were killed) over the control of water holes. In arid parts of the world (Africa, Middle East), armed conflicts still break out over water. (See Example 2.)

MARGINAL UTILITY AND THE LAW OF DEMAND

The law of diminishing marginal utility explains the diamond/water paradox. Relative prices reflect marginal utility rather than total utility. The exact linkage between the law of diminishing utility and the law of demand remains to be established.

Consider an individual consumer, Mr. Ruffgreg, who purchases only two goods—ale (A) and bread (B).

Ruffgreg's preferences for both ale and bread are summarized in Table 1. They are stable and do not change as time passes and as other things change. Columns (2) and (6) show the total utility of ale (TU_A) and bread (TU_B), respectively; columns (3) and (7) show the marginal utility of ale (MU_A) and bread (MU_B), respectively. These utility schedules apply to Ruffgreg's consumption over a particular time period—say, a week.

Ruffgreg's marginal utility schedule for ale is shown in Figure 1 and is graphed from the data in column (3) of Table 1. The first pint of ale (per week) yields Ruffgreg a marginal utility of 40 utils; the second yields 30 utils; the third yields 20 utils; the fourth pint of ale yields a marginal utility of 10 utils. The total utility from consuming different quantities of ale is the sum of the bars up to the quantity of ale consumed. The total utility from consuming three pints of ale during a week, for example, is 90 (= 40 + 30 + 20).

We cannot determine Ruffgreg's demands for ale and bread from his preferences alone. As noted in Chapter 4, demand depends not only on consumer preferences, but also on consumer income and prices. To keep our example simple, let us assume Ruffgreg has $8 to spend on ale and bread per week. The price of ale (P_A) is $2 per pint, and the price of bread (P_B) is $0.50 per loaf. Ruffgreg could spend the entire $8 allowance on ale, buying 4 pints of ale, or he could spend all $8 on bread, obtaining 16 loaves of bread. The most likely case, however, is that Ruffgreg will spend part of the money on ale and part on bread.

Table 1   The Utility of Ale and Bread

Quantity of Ale (pints), Q_A (1)	Total Utility of Ale (utils), TU_A (2)	Marginal Utility of Ale (utils), MU_A (3)	Marginal Utility of Ale per Dollar (utils), MU_A/P_A (4)	Quantity of Bread (loaves), Q_B (5)	Total Utility of Bread (utils), TU_B (6)	Marginal Utility of Bread (utils), MU_B (7)	Marginal Utility of Bread per dollar (utils), MU_B/P_B (8)
1	40	40	20	1	15	15	30
2	70	30	15	2	23	8	16
3	90	20	10	3	30	7	14
4	100	10	5	4	35	5	10
5	105	5	2.5	5	38	3	6
6	107	2	1	6	40.5	2.5	5

This table lists the quantities of ale and bread consumed per week by Ruffgreg along with the utility Ruffgreg attaches to each quantity. The price of ale equals $2 per pint and the price of bread equals $0.50 per loaf. The marginal-utility columns illustrate the *law of diminishing marginal utility:* the marginal utility of each product falls as the amount consumed increases.

For instance, he could purchase 3 pints of ale per week costing a total of $6 and 4 loaves of bread per week costing a total of $2 for a total weekly expenditure of $8.

Maximizing Satisfaction

How will Ruffgreg allocate his $8 between ale and bread? All consumers (if they behave rationally) will seek to obtain as much satisfaction as possible from the amount of income they have to spend.

> To achieve maximum utility the consumer allocates the budget on goods in such a way that it is impossible to find a better buy by spending a bit more on one good or a bit less on the other.

We will now try to demonstrate that Ruffgreg maximizes his satisfaction when his budget is spent so that *the last dollar spent on each product (ale and bread)* yields the same marginal utility. The intuitive sense of this rule is that if the marginal utility per dollar is not the same for two products, a consumer can get more utility by switching an extra dollar to the good with the greater marginal utility per dollar.

Figure 1   Marginal Utility

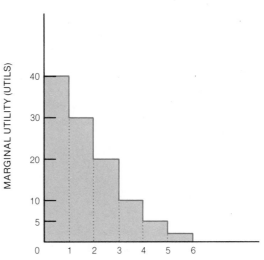

QUANTITY OF ALE (PINTS PER WEEK)

This figure graphs the data in columns (1) and (3) of Table 1. The width of each bar represents one pint of ale. The vertical height or area of each bar represents marginal utility for that extra unit of ale. Total utilty up to some quantity of ale is the sum of the areas of the bars to the left of that quantity of ale. For example, the total utility of 2 pints equals 70 (= 40 + 30); the total utility of 5 pints equals 105 (= 40 + 30 + 20 + 10 + 5).

Table 2   The Steps to Consumer Equilibrium

	Available Choices	Decision	Income Remaining
1st Purchase ↓	1st pint of ale: $MU_A/P_A = 20$ 1st loaf of bread: $Mu_B/P_B = 30$	Buy 1st loaf of bread for $0.50	$8.00 − $0.50 = $7.50
2nd Purchase ↓	1st pint of ale: $MU_A/P_A = 20$ 2nd loaf of bread: $MU_B/P_B = 16$	Buy 1st pint of ale for $2.00	$7.50 − $2.00 = $5.50
3rd Purchase ↓	2nd pint of ale: $MU_A/P_A = 15$ 2nd loaf of bread: $MU_B/P_B = 16$	Buy 2nd loaf of bread for $0.50	$5.50 − $0.50 = $5.00
4th Purchase ↓	2nd pint of ale: $MU_A/P_A = 15$ 3rd loaf of bread: $MU_B/P_B = 14$	Buy 2nd pint of ale for $2.00	$5.00 − $2.00 = $3.00
5th Purchase ↓	3rd pint of ale: $MU_A/P_A = 10$ 3rd loaf of bread: $MU_B/P_B = 14$	Buy 3rd loaf of bread for $0.50	$3.00 − $0.50 = $2.50
6th Purchase and 7th Purchase	3rd pint of ale: $MU_A/P_A = 10$ 4th loaf of bread: $MU_B/P_B = 10$	Buy 3rd pint of ale for $2.00 and 4th loaf of bread for $0.50	$2.50 − $2.00 = $0.50 $0.50 − $0.50 = $0 }Equilibrium

This table shows the step-by-step process by which a consumer makes purchasing decisions that will maximize satisfaction. In choosing at each step between a unit of ale and a unit of bread, the consumer determines which commodity has the highest marginal utility per dollar and buys that commodity. The data are taken from Table 1. The consumer has $8 to spend. The consumer ends up buying 3 pints of ale and 4 loaves of bread, which is the equilibrium combination because marginal utility per dollar is equal for the two goods and all income is spent.

Maximum satisfaction requires that marginal utility per extra dollar spent on A be the same as the marginal utility per extra dollar spent on B.

In columns (4) and (8) of Table 1, *marginal utility per dollar* is calculated by dividing marginal utility by the price. Since the price of ale is $2 per pint, column (4) is half of column (3); since the price of bread is $0.50 per loaf, column (8) is twice column (7). Ruffgreg is now ready to spend the $8 on ale and bread.

Note that the concept of marginal utility per dollar is a rate measure like miles per hour. Just as one can drive 50 miles per hour without driv-

ing for a full hour, marginal utility per dollar does not require the spending of a full dollar.

Table 2 shows the step-by-step process by which Ruffgreg allocates his income between bread and ale. The first loaf of bread costs $0.50 and yields a marginal utility of 15; the marginal utility *per extra dollar* spent on bread is 30 (= 15/$0.50) for the first loaf. The first pint of ale costs $2 and yields a marginal utility of 40, but the marginal utility *per dollar* is only 20 (= 40/$2) for the first pint. Because the first loaf of bread has a higher marginal utility per dollar, Ruffgreg would first buy one loaf of bread at a cost of $0.50, leaving $7.50 to spend. Ruffgreg now finds that the marginal utility per dollar is higher for the first pint of ale (20) than for the

Figure 2   The Individual Demand Curve Derived from Ruffgreg's Marginal-Utility Schedule

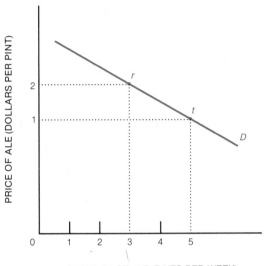

This curve shows Ruffgreg's demand curve for ale calculated from Table 1. If the price of bread is $0.50 per loaf and weekly income is $8, consumer equilibrium can be calculated at the price of ale equal to $2 per pint. The equilibrium quantity of 3 pints of ale is the quantity of ale demanded when the price of ale equals $2 (point r). The equilibrium quantity can also be calculated for a price of ale equal to $1 per pint. The resulting equilibrium quantity of ale (5 pints) is the quantity of ale demanded when the price of ale equals $1 (point t).

second loaf of bread (16), so he purchases a first pint of ale for $2, leaving $5.50 to spend. Marginal utility per dollar is higher for the second loaf of bread (16) than for the second pint of ale (15), so Ruffgreg's third purchase is the second loaf of bread. Ruffgreg continues to select the product with the higher marginal utility per dollar until his budget is exhausted. Ruffgreg is in **consumer equilibrium** when he buys 3 pints of ale and 4 loaves of bread—where he has spent his entire income of $8 (3 loaves at $2 each and 4 pints at $0.50 each) and where the marginal utility per dollar is 10 utils for both ale and bread.

Consumer equilibrium occurs when the consumer has spent all income and marginal utilities per dollar spent are equal on each

good purchased ($MU_A/P_A = MU_B/P_B$). At this point, the consumer is not inclined to change purchases unless some other factor (such as prices, income, or preferences) changes.

The law of demand can be deduced from this theory of consumer behavior. When the price of ale is $2, Ruffgreg purchases (demands) 3 pints of ale, given that his income is $8 and the price of bread is $0.50. The price/quantity combination of $2/3 pints of ale is one point (r in Figure 2) on Ruffgreg's demand curve.

Other points on the demand curve can be calculated by repeating the whole process at a different price of ale, keeping income at $8 per week and the bread price at $0.50 per loaf.

If the price of ale falls from $2 to $1 per pint, the marginal utility of ale and the marginal utility per extra dollar spent on ale are the same thing ($MU_A \div 1 = MU_A$). Because of the lower price of ale, the marginal utility per dollar spent on ale is now higher than the marginal utility per dollar spent on bread at the old equilibrium of 3 pints of ale and 4 loaves of bread. Ale purchases will be increased; expenditures will be reallocated between the two goods until the $8 is spent and marginal utilities per dollar are again equal—this time at 5 pints of ale and 6 loaves of bread purchased. Thus, when the price of ale is $1, the quantity demanded of ale is 5 pints. This price/quantity combination of $1/5 pints is a second point (t) on the demand curve. As the law of demand predicts, holding all other factors constant, a decrease in the price causes an increase in the quantity demanded.[1]

> **Every point on a given consumer's demand curve satisfies the conditions that MU/P is the same for all goods the consumer is buying and that all income is spent—that is, the consumer is maximizing utility at that price/quantity combination.**

1. The mathematics is simple. Start with the consumer in equilibrium with $MU_A/P_A = MU_B/P_B$. If P_A falls, $MU_A/P_A > MU_B/P_B$. To restore equilibrium, MU_A must fall. The law of diminishing marginal utility states that MU_A will fall if consumption of A *increases*. From this, the negative relationship between P_A and Q_A is established.

Income and Substitution Effects

When the price of a good falls, two things happen. First, consumers can buy the goods and services they used to buy *plus* more goods and services. A decrease in price is like an increase in income in the sense that it enables consumers to purchase more goods of any type, including more of the good whose price has fallen. The part of the increase in quantity demanded caused by such an increase in income is called the **income effect.** Second, the cheaper good now yields a higher marginal utility per dollar. Consumers bent on maximizing satisfaction will substitute this now cheaper good for other products. This part of the increase in the quantity demanded of the cheaper good is called the **substitution effect.**

> When the price of a good falls people buy more of it because 1) the price reduction is like an increase in income that in itself normally leads to larger demands for all goods and services, including the one whose price has fallen (the **income effect**) and 2) consumers tend to substitute that good for other relatively more expensive goods (the **substitution effect**).

In Table 2, before the drop in the price of ale from $2 to $1, the consumer purchased 3 pints of ale and 4 loaves of bread for a total of $8 worth of ale and bread. At the lower price of $1 per pint of ale, the consumer can purchase the same 3 pints of ale and 4 loaves of bread for $5. The consumer now has $3 left over that can be spent on either ale or bread. This $3 is like an increase in income. The effect of this increase in real income on purchases of ale is the income effect.

In addition to having the extra $3, the relative price of ale has dropped (the ratio of ale price to bread price has fallen from 4 to 2). Because of the lower relative price of ale, the consumer is now getting more marginal utility *per dollar* out of ale than bread and, therefore, switches to buying more ale. This switch from bread to ale is the substitution effect.

Consider the following real-world example: In 1979, the average American family spent almost $1,500 per annum on energy consumption (utili-

ties, gasoline, and oil).[2] In 1980, energy prices rose by 15 percent, which means the real income of the average American family declined substantially *(ceteris paribus)* as a consequence of the energy-price increase. The average family would have to spend $225 more in 1980 to buy the same amount of energy purchased in 1979. The decrease in energy consumption noted in 1980 would be the consequence of both the income effect and the substitution effect. The income effect would be the impact of the $225 reduction in real income on energy purchases. The substitution effect would be the impact of the rising price of energy that would make energy substitutes more attractive to the consumer.

Is the Model Realistic?

Do people really behave in the mechanical fashion depicted by the model of rational consumer behavior? Few people keep marginal-utility schedules in their heads or calculate marginal utility per dollar to determine the best buys at every given moment.

But people—on the average—behave as if the above theory were more or less true. Have you ever stood at the meat counter in a supermarket and observed sharp-eyed customers sifting through the packages of meat? The customer is in effect calculating *best buys*. A *best buy* at any moment is the good that yields the highest marginal utility *per extra dollar* spent. A consumer may get the most marginal utility from a delicious T-bone steak, but that consumer gets the most marginal utility *per dollar* from simple hamburger meat. The consumer may decide that: "instead of buying the T-bone steak, I'll buy the hamburger *and* take in a movie." The steak does not yield enough marginal utility per dollar compared to the hamburger and the movie.

The actual decision process of the individual is far more complicated than that described by marginal-utility theory; human beings are complicated and must choose from among more than just two goods. Yet when one cuts through all the apparent inconsistencies and irrationalities (like keeping up with one's neighbors), the average consumer is

---

2. *Statistical Abstract of the United States* (101st edition, 1980).

Figure 3   From Individual to Market Demand

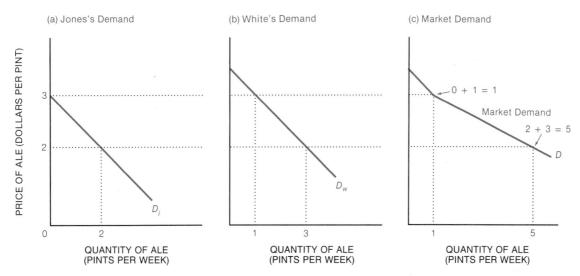

The market demand curve is the *horizontal* summation of all individual demand curves; it is calculated by summing all individual quantities demanded at each price. Here, the market has only 2 consumers, but the principle applies to markets with any number of consumers.

surprisingly rational. Individual examples cannot prove the rationality of the average consumer, but observed consumer behavior taken as a whole is consistent with the predictions of the theory. The theory of rational consumer behavior predicts that the law of demand holds and explains why people consume a variety of goods and services.

MARKET DEMAND

The theory of consumer behavior explains how individual consumers make buying decisions. The law of diminishing marginal utility implies that rational consumers will purchase less of a product, *ceteris paribus,* if its price rises. According to the law of demand, the demand schedules of individual consumers will have negative slopes.

But prices are established in markets, and the individual consumer is only a small part of the total market. Recall from Chapter 4 that if the market is competitive, each individual participant will represent such a small share of the total that the individual will have no impact on the price.

Individual demand curves must be combined to determine the **market demand curve** for a particular good.

> The **market demand curve** shows the total quantities demanded by all consumers in the market at each price. It is the horizontal summation of all individual demand curves in that market.

Figure 2 showed the demand curve for ale for one consumer—Ruffgreg. Figure 3 shows the demand curves for ale for two consumers, Jones and White, who, we now assume, constitute all the buyers in the market for ale. At a price of $3 per pint, Jones demands 0 pints and White demands 1 pint. The market quantity demanded at the $3 price can be obtained by adding the two quantities demanded together (0 + 1 = 1 pint). At a price of $2 per pint, Jones demands 2 pints and White demands 3 pints. The market quantity demanded at the $2 price is 2 + 3 = 5 pints.

The market demand curve in Figure 3 is downward-sloping for the same reasons that the individual demand curves are downward-sloping. In addition, as price decreases more consumers might be enticed to buy a product. In Figure 3, for example, when the price of ale is above $3 Jones is not in the market; at a price of $0.50, even more buyers may enter the market. Along the market demand curve, just as along an individual demand curve, the consumers who are purchasing the good are achieving (individually) maximum satisfaction at that price.

CONSUMER SURPLUS

We have shown that a high-priced good (diamonds) has a proportionately higher marginal utility than a low-priced good (water). When consumers maximize their satisfaction, consumption of each good is pushed to the point where marginal utility *(MU/P)* is the same for all goods consumers are buying. *The theory of consumer demand shows that price reflects marginal utility.*

> **When consumers are in equilibrium, the price of a good is a *dollar measure* of what the *last unit* of the good is worth (its marginal utility).**

Figure 4 shows the market demand curve for a product. At the current market price of $5, the quantity demanded is 6 units (point *m*). The demand curve shows that if only one unit of the product were available, some consumer would have been willing to pay a price of $10 for it. If only two units of the product were available, someone would have been willing to pay $9 for the second unit. If 6 units were available, someone would have been willing to pay a price of $5 for the sixth unit. The current market price therefore reveals what consumers are willing to pay for the *last unit* of the product sold.

When the market price is $5 and the quantity demanded is 6 units (point *m*), the price reflects what the sixth unit is worth to the last consumer. Even though the first of those 6 units is still worth $10 to someone, the second of the 6 units is still worth $9 to someone else, and so on to the sixth unit, which is worth $5 to someone, each consumer actually pays only $5 for each of the 6 units. The total of what the 6 units combined are worth ($10 + $9 + $8 + $7 + $6 + $5 =

Figure 4   Consumer Surplus

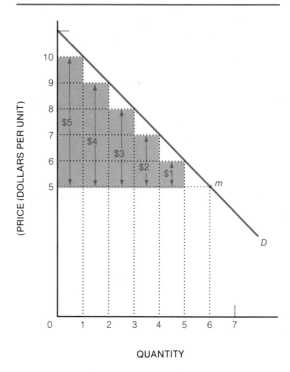

The demand curve shows that consumers are prepared to buy a sixth unit of this good for $5 but were prepared to spend $10 for the first unit, $9 for the second unit, $8 for the third unit, $7 for the fourth unit, and $6 for the fifth unit. When they buy six units, however, the need pay only $5 each for all six units. Thus, they pay for each of the six units only what the sixth unit is worth to them. The difference between what each unit is worth to consumers and what the consumers actually pay is shown by the height of the shaded area for each unit. Adding these surpluses for all units yields a total consumer surplus of $5 + $4 + $3 + $2 + $1 = $15.

$45) is greater than the total of what consumers pay for all 6 units (6 × $5 = $30) because each consumer pays for each of the 6 units only what the *last* unit is worth.

Consumers pay the same market price for each unit, but the market price reflects only what the *last unit sold* is worth. Because earlier units have a higher marginal value than later units, consumers enjoy a surplus on all the earlier units. The surplus on each unit is the excess of what that unit is worth over what the consumer must pay.

For example, at a price of $5 the first unit is worth $10 to someone but costs $5 so that person enjoys a surplus of $5 on the first unit. Someone enjoys a surplus of $4 on the second unit, because the second unit is worth $9 to that person but costs $5. Only the last unit sold (the sixth) will yield no surplus, for its price will reflect exactly what that unit is worth to the consumer. Adding these surpluses together, one obtains the total **consumer surplus** of $15.

> **Consumer surplus** is the excess of the total consumer benefit that a good provides over what the consumers actually have to pay.

The great British economist, Alfred Marshall (1842–1924), introduced the concept of consumer surplus. The consumer-surplus concept provides another perspective for viewing the water/diamond paradox. Consumer surplus is a measure, to use Adam Smith's words, of the difference between the "use value" of a good and its market value. Consumer surplus on low-priced but essential goods like water will be substantial. On high-priced but nonessential goods like diamonds, consumer surplus will be low.

Consumer surplus measures how much the total benefits consumers obtain from a good or service exceed what consumers pay for the product. The lower the price of water, the higher the consumer surplus, *ceteris paribus*. As consumers move along a demand curve, consumer surplus changes. If the price increases, the excess of consumer benefits over consumer costs falls; if the price falls, the excess of consumer benefits over consumer costs rises.

Consumer surpus can be used to measure consumer gains and losses from price changes along a given demand curve. If electric utility rates are raised, what have consumers lost? If airline fares are lowered, what have consumers gained? These losses and gains are the changes in consumer surplus.

Figure 5 shows how to calculate consumer surplus when the demand curve is a straight line. At *f*, the price is $15, and the quantity demanded is 1,000 units. Consumers, therefore, pay a total of $15,000 ($15 × 1,000 units) for the product. Consumer surplus is equal to the area of the color triangle labeled *A*. At quantities below 1,000 units, consumers are willing to pay more than the $15 they have to pay. The vertical distance between the demand curve and the horizontal line at

Figure 5   The Gain in Consumer Surplus Resulting from a Reduction in Price

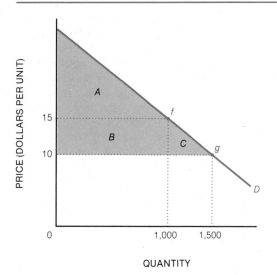

When price is $15 and quantity demanded is 1,000 units, the consumer surplus is the area *A*, the excess of what people would be willing to pay over what they actually pay. If the price falls to $10, quantity demanded increases to 1,500 units and consumer surplus is the area *A* + *B* + *C*. Consumer surplus, therefore, increases by *B* + *C*, or by $6,250.

$15 is the surplus for each unit.[3] Adding all these surpluses together yields the consumer surplus, or the area of the triangle *A*.[4]

What happens to consumer surplus if the market price drops to $10? Logically, it should be clear that consumer surplus will increase because now there is a surplus at all quantities less than 1,500, whereas the surplus stopped at a quantity of 1,000 before the price drop. Consumer surplus at point *g*, where price is $10, is the area of the triangle formed by the demand curve and the hor-

---

3. By changing quantity demanded in very small increments, the demand schedule approximates a smooth line. Thus, instead of a series of rectangles added together as in Figure 4, consumer surplus is measured by the smooth area of a triangle.

4. As explained in Appendix 1A, areas of *rectangles* are computed by multiplying the horizontal width of the rectangle times the vertical height of the rectangle. The width of rectangle *B* is 1,000; the height is $5. Areas of triangles are calculated by multiplying the width of the triangle by its height and dividing by 2 (or multiplying by ½). The area of the triangle will be ½ that of the rectangle formed by the height and width of the triangle.

Example 3   Consumer Surplus and Directory Assistance: Why Free Calls Are Not Free

In some states in the United States, telephone customers pay for calls to directory assistance. These charges average around $0.20 per call—which is the averge cost per call to the phone company of supplying directory assistance. In other states, telephone customers can call directory assistance free of charge. Because the telephone company must hire operators to handle these calls, however, every phone customer has an extra charge incorporated in the basic monthly rate. This charge does not vary with the number of directory-assistance calls but is the total cost of providing operator assistance divided by the number of customers—that is, the average cost per call to the phone company—which is around $0.20 per call.

In states where the phone company has tried to introduce a specific charge for directory-assistance calls, telephone customers have resisted. They reason that being charged for something that was previously free would make them worse off. The concept of consumer surplus can help us see why this reasoning is not correct.

To keep the example very simple, take the case of a phone company with 5 customers, each making no more than one call to directory assistance per week. The hypothetical demand schedule for directory assistance is given in the accompanying table.

Let us now compare the case where people are charged directly $0.20 per call to the case where they can make all the calls they wish but the cost of the service per customer ($0.20) is automatically added to their phone bills. According to the demand schedule, when the price per call is $0.20 (as it is when people are charged for each call), 3 calls would be made per week. The first customer has a surplus of $0.20, the second a surplus of $0.10, and the third pays exactly what the service is worth to that person: the total consumer surplus is $0.30 per week. When the price per call is $0

(as it is when the service is "free"), 5 calls will be made per week. The total consumer surplus equals $1.00 (the first customer has the full $0.40 because the price is zero, the second has $0.30, the third has $0.20, the fourth has $0.10, and the fifth has no surplus), but each customer must pay a fixed charge of $0.20 when the phone bill is due to cover the cost of the service. Together, the five customers pay 5 × $0.20, or $1.00. Their total consumer surplus of $1.00 is eaten up entirely by the fixed charge.

Price of Directory Assistance (dollars per call)	Quantity Demanded (calls per week)
$0.40	1
$0.30	2
$0.20	3
$0.10	4
$0.00	5

The conclusion: people are better off being charged directly for each directory-assistance call. If the service is free, people who place a low (or even zero) marginal value on the service use directory assistance and then end up paying the average cost of providing the service. This makes them worse off than they would be under a direct-charge system in which they would place directory-assistance calls only if the marginal value of the call is greater than or equal to its price. Take the case of the fifth person who places a zero marginal value on directory-assistance calls. That person receives no benefits (a zero marginal value is placed on the call) but is still charged $0.20 at the end of the month. ∎

Source: George Daly and Thomas H. Mayor, "Estimating the Value of a Missing Market," *Journal of Law and Economics,* April 1980.

izontal line at $10. The new triangle is the sum of the three areas $A + B + C$. Consumer surplus at a price of $15 was area $A;$ at a price of $10, consumer surplus is $A + B + C$. Therefore, the *increase* in consumer surplus as a consequence of the drop in price is $B + C$. The area $B + C =$

$5,000 (area of B) + $1,250 (area of C) = $6,250.

The segment of the demand curve between f and g in this example was deliberately constructed to have an elasticity of demand of unity, so that the amount of consumer spending at the two points on the demand schedule are equal. At both prices, consumers spend $15,000, but at the lower price, consumer surplus is $6,250 greater than at the higher price. (See Example 3.)

This chapter has examined the relationship between consumer behavior and the demand curve for goods and services. The next chapter will shift to the supply side of the market for products and will examine how businesses are organized and the different types of markets in which firms operate.

Summary

1. *Preferences* are people's evaluations of goods and services independent of budget and price considerations. Consumer preferences are fairly stable when the services that the consumer goods provide are broadly defined. For example, the preference for transportation services is more stable than the demand for a particular type of transportation service.

2. The satisfaction that is obtained from consuming goods and services is called *utility*. *Marginal utility* is the increase in total utility obtained when consumption of a good is increased by one unit. The law of diminishing marginal utility states that the marginal utility declines as more of a good or service is consumed. The fact that market prices reflect marginal utility rather than total utility explains the diamond/water paradox (why diamonds are more expensive than water).

3. The law of diminishing marginal utility is consistent with the law of demand. When the rational consumer equates marginal utility per dollar on the last purchases of each commodity, the consumer is in equilibrium. If the price of one good falls, its marginal utility per dollar initially rises, and more of the commodity will be consumed. Rational consumers will spend their money in a way that maximizes their satisfaction (utility). When the price of a commodity drops, two effects will be set in motion: The income effect occurs when the price decrease raises the real income of the consumer and when this increase in income is used to purchase additional goods and services. The

substitution effect occurs because the fall in the relative price of the good motivates the consumer to substitute the good for other goods.

4. The market demand schedule is the horizontal summation of the demand schedules of all individuals participating in the market. The market demand schedule will have a negative slope because its individual components have negative slopes.

5. *Consumer surplus* is the excess of consumer benefits over consumer costs for a particular product. Consumer surplus follows from the law of diminishing marginal utility. Consumers pay the same market price for each unit they buy, but the market price reflects only what the last unit sold is worth. The marginal utility of earlier units exceeds the market price. Adding these surpluses together yields total consumer surplus. The consumer-surplus concept permits the measurement of consumer losses and gains from price changes.

Key Terms

preferences
utility
marginal utility *(MU)*
law of diminishing marginal utility
consumer equilibrium
income effect
substitution effect
market demand curve
consumer surplus

Questions and Problems

1. In some parts of Africa today, sick people go to witch doctors. In the United States, most people seek out medical doctors when they are ill; a few seek out faith healers. Are consumer preferences for medical care, then, basically unstable?

2. One of the most basic changes in consumer buying patterns in the late 1970s and early 1980s was the switch from "gas guzzlers" to fuel-efficient cars. Does this switch indicate that consumer preferences are unstable? Why is the *ceteris paribus* qualification important in this example?

3. If the marginal utility of a good *(A)* were to increase as consumption of the good increased (in opposition to the law of diminishing marginal utility), would $MU_A/P_A = MU_B/P_B$ still be the equilibrium condition?

4. Use the marginal-utility information in Table 1 to calculate the quantity demanded of ale at a price of $4 per pint. What do you do when marginal utility per dollar cannot be exactly equated on the last units sold?

5. Again using Table 1, calculate the quantity demanded of ale at the price of $2 but at a weekly income of $11. Compare this result with the answer at $8. Which is larger? Why?

6. Assume that there are 1,000 identical consumers in the market with the same income and the same preferences. When the price of *X* is $50 per unit, the typical consumer is prepared to purchase 20 units of *X*. When the price is $40 per unit, the typical consumer is prepared to purchase 25 units of *X*. Construct from this information the market demand curve for *X* (assume the demand curve is a straight line). Then calculate the loss of consumer surplus when the price rises from $40 to $50 per unit.

7. A consumer is spending an entire weekly income on goods *A* and *B*. The last penny spent on *A* yields a marginal utility of 10; the last penny spent on *B* yields a marginal utility of 20. Is it possible for the consumer to be in equilibrium? If so, what are the exact conditions?

8. Ms. White consumes only goods *X* and *Y*. Column (1) of Table A shows the marginal utility she derives from various units of *X;* column (2) shows the marginal utility she derives from various units of *Y*. Her income is $20, the price of *X* is $2 per unit, and the price of *Y* is $4 per unit.

Table A

(1)		(2)	
Units of *X*	MU_X	Units of *Y*	MU_Y
1	20	1	2,000
2	16	2	200
3	12	3	20
4	10	4	10
5	6	5	4

a. How much of *X* and *Y* will Ms. White demand?

b. Check your answer by using the consumer-equilibrium conditions. (Is all income spent? Does $MU_X/P_X = MU_Y/P_Y$?)

9. Can the equilibrium conditions be applied to more than two goods? How?

10. The price of ale is $10, the price of bread is $5, and the marginal utility of bread is 50 utils when the consumer is in equilibrium. Can you deduce how much is spent on ale? Can you deduce the marginal utility of ale?

11. *Optional Question:* Income and substitution effects can be measured. Suppose that the income elasticity of demand for housing is 1 and that the price elasticity of demand is 0.3 (these numbers are close to actual estimates). Furthermore, suppose that housing accounts for 20 percent of the average household's budget. A decrease in income of 2 percent would decrease the demand for housing by 2 percent because the income elasticity is 1. Now suppose that income is held constant and that the price of housing rises by 10 percent. Since the price elasticity is 0.3, a 10 percent increase in price will lower quantity demanded by 3 percent. What portion of this 3 percent decrease in quantity demanded is due to the income effect? What portion is due to the substitution effect? (*Hint:* a 10 percent increase in the price of housing raises the cost of living by 2 percent since there is a 10 percent increase in 20 percent of the budget. Observe also that an increase in the cost of living of 2 percent has the same effects as a 2 percent reduction in income. Therefore, a 10 percent increase in the price of housing, holding income and other prices constant, is like a 2 percent reduction in real income.)

Suggested Readings

Mansfield, Edwin. *Microeconomics: Theory and Applications,* 5th ed. New York: W. W. Norton, 1985, chap. 3.

Stigler, George. *The Theory of Prices,* 3rd ed. New York: Macmillan, 1966, chap. 4.

Walsh, Vivian Charles. *Introduction to Contemporary Microeconomics.* New York: McGraw-Hill, 1970, chaps. 4–5.

Indifference Curves

Appreciation Preview

The preceding chapter on demand and utility showed how the law of diminishing marginal utility can be used to explain the law of demand. In equilibrium, consumers will equate marginal utilities per dollar on the last unit of items consumed. If the price of good *A* rises, the marginal utility per dollar of *A* will be *less* than that of other goods. The law of diminishing marginal utility states that the marginal utility of *A* will increase if less of *A* is consumed. Therefore consumer equilibrium is reattained by consuming less of *A*. Because of diminishing marginal utility, there will be a negative relationship between price and quantity demanded.

The law of diminishing marginal utility does explain the law of demand, but its claim to realism is limited. It requires that people be able to

measure the *utility* they obtain by consuming various quantities of goods and services.

Because of skepticism about the measurement of utility, economists were forced to find an alternative approach to understanding consumer behavior. The culmination of this search is *indifference-curve theory*. This theory does not require that consumers be able to measure utility in any specific units of measurement but does assume that consumers are able to rank their preferences for combinations of goods. The consumer should be able to choose between 4 pints of ale and 5 loaves of bread on the one hand and 8 pints of ale and 1 loaf of bread on the other. If the consumer does not prefer one combination to the other, the consumer is said to be *indifferent*. ∎

CONSUMER PREFERENCES

As noted above, the indifference-curve approach does not require consumers to know util values of goods in order to decide how much of each good is desired. Rather, the consumer must be able to decide only how much of one good he or she is willing to give up in trade for one unit of another good without experiencing a loss in total satisfaction. When one combination of goods yields the same satisfaction as another combination, the consumer is indifferent between the two combinations.

In Figure 1, the horizontal axis measures the quantity of ale consumed by the individual per week. The vertical axis measures the quantity of bread consumed by the individual per week. At point *a*, 6 loaves of bread and 1 pint of ale are consumed. At *a*, the consumer is willing to give up 3 loaves of bread for 1 more pint of ale. This trade-off would move the consumer to point *b* where 3 loaves of bread and 2 pints of ale are consumed. At point *b*, the consumer is no longer willing to give up 3 loaves of bread to acquire 1 more pint of ale. The consumer is now willing to give up only 1 loaf of bread to acquire 1 more pint of ale. This trade-off would put the consumer at point *c*, consuming 2 loaves of bread and 3 pints of ale per week. Finally, to acquire 1 more pint of ale, the consumer is willing now to give up only half a loaf of bread, moving the consumer to point *d*. The consumer is indifferent between points *a, b, c,* and *d* and feels equally well off at any of these points.

A curve can be drawn, through points *a, b, c,* and *d*, which represents all possible trade-offs that keep the consumer at the same level of satisfaction. This curve is called an **indifference curve** because every point on the curve yields the same satisfaction even though the consumption pattern is different at each point.

> An **indifference curve** shows all the alternative combinations of two goods that yield the same total satisfaction and among which the consumer is indifferent.

An indifference curve is downward-sloping because as long as both goods yield satisfaction,

Figure 1   An Indifference Curve

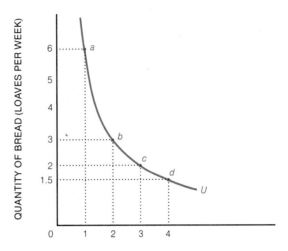

QUANTITY OF ALE (PINTS PER WEEK)

When given the choice among the commodity bundles along an indifference curve the consumer is indifferent. Consumption pattern *a* yields the same satisfaction to the consumer as *b, c,* or *d*. The absolute slope of an indifference curve is the marginal rate of substitution and shows—in this case—how much bread the consumer is just willing to sacrifice for one more pint of ale.

more is better than less. The only way for the consumer's satisfaction to stay the same when more of one good is consumed is to consume less of the other good.

The Law of the Diminishing Marginal Rate of Substitution

The shape of an indifference curve provides useful information about preferences. Indifference-curve analysis substitutes the concept of the **marginal rate of substitution *(MRS)*** for the concept of marginal utility.

> The **marginal rate of substitution *(MRS)*** is how much of one good a person is just willing to give up to acquire one unit of another.

Thus, the marginal rate of substitution is just a fancy name for an acceptable trade-off between two goods or for the person's *valuation* of an additional unit of one good in terms of the other.

An indifference curve is always convex when viewed from below (bulges toward the origin.) The convex curvature of the indifference curve follows from the **law of diminishing marginal rate of substitution:** as more ale is consumed relative to bread, the consumer is willing to give up less and less bread to acquire additional units of ale. When one moves from point *a* down to point *d* and beyond, the indifference curve gets flatter and flatter since the relative valuation placed on ale is decreasing compared to bread.

> The **law of diminishing marginal rate of substitution** is that as more of one good *(A)* is consumed, the amount of the other good *(B)* that the consumer is willing to sacrifice for one more unit of *(A)* declines.

The flatter the slope of the indifference curve, the lower the relative valuation the consumer places on *A* (compared to *B*). The slope of the tangent at any point on the indifference curve measures the marginal rate of substitution of bread *(B)* for ale *(A)*.

Indifference curves can be drawn to represent any level of satisfaction. Figure 2 shows the same consumer at three different levels of satisfaction. Higher indifference curves for any one consumer represent higher levels of satisfaction. Each consumer has an entire map of indifference curves, one for every level of satisfaction. Figure 2 shows only three indifference curves. Whether a person is poor or well off is determined by the person's income and the relative prices of goods.

Indifference curves have five properties:

1. They are bowed toward the *origin* (the point where the axes meet), which reflects the law of diminishing marginal rate of substitution.
2. The consumer is better off when he or she moves to a higher indifference curve.
3. Indifference curves that show preferences between two goods from which consumers derive benefits are downward-sloping.
4. Indifference curves cannot intersect each other, because an intersection would indicate that the consumer is simultaneously worse off and better off. (Even though indifference curves do not intersect, they need not be parallel.)

Figure 2   The Map of Indifference Curves

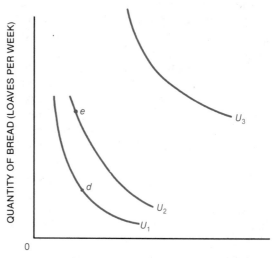

QUANTITY OF ALE (PINTS PER WEEK)

There is an infinite number of indifference curves for each consumer; three indifference curves for a particular consumer are shown here. The higher the indifference curve, the greater the well-being of the consumer. The indifference map shows that commodity bundle *e* is preferred to bundle *d* because the former is on a higher indifference curve. Indifference curve U_3 represents a higher level of satisfaction than U_2, and U_2 represents a higher level than U_1. The level of satisfaction along each indifference curve is constant.

5. Indifference curves do not move as a result of market circumstances (changes in income or prices).

A consumer's position on an indifference curve is determined by the consumer's budget.

The Budget Line

Suppose the price of ale is $2 a pint and the price of bread is $0.50 a loaf, as in the chapter. Assume the consumer has $8 to spend per week on ale and bread. If the entire $8 is spent on ale, the consumer can buy 4 pints of ale. This combination corresponds to point *m* in Figure 3. If the entire $8 is spent on bread, 16 loaves of bread can be purchased. This combination corresponds to point *n*. The **budget line** connecting points *m* and *n* represents all the other combinations of ale and bread the consumer is able to buy by spending the entire $8 income on the two goods.

Figure 3   The Budget Line

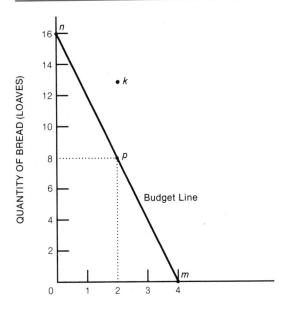

QUANTITY OF ALE (PINTS)

With a budget of $8, the consumer can buy 16 loaves of bread at a price of $0.50 a loaf or 4 pints of ale at a price of $2 a pint. Spending $4 on each good would buy 8 loaves of bread and 2 pints of ale (point p). The budget line shows the choices open to the consumer. The consumer can afford to buy any combination of goods on the budget line. Points above the budget line, such as k, cannot be purchased with the consumer's income. The slope of the budget line is the ratio of the price of ale to the price of bread—here 4.

The **budget line** is all the combinations of goods the consumer is able to buy given a certain income and set prices. The budget line shows the choices of consumer goods available to the consumer.

The budget line in Figure 3 has the slope $^{16}/_4$ = 4. This slope is the price of ale in terms of bread: P_A/P_B = \$2/\$0.50 = 4. The slope indicates that if the consumer wants to buy one more pint of ale, the consumer must give up 4 loaves of bread.

Algebraically, point m in Figure 3 is income divided by the price of ale because point m shows the maximum possible consumption of ale. Point n is income divided by the price of bread. The absolute slope of the line nm is then determined as follows:

$$\text{Slope} = \frac{\text{Income}}{P_B} \div \frac{\text{Income}}{P_A} = \frac{P_A}{P_B}.$$

Indifference curves show how the consumer ranks *different* market baskets; the budget line shows what the consumer *is able* to buy. Combining the information represented by the indifference curve and the budget line shows what combination the consumer *will* buy.

CONSUMER EQUILIBRIUM

The consumer achieves equilibrium by choosing a consumption pattern that maximizes the consumer's satisfaction on the budget line. Figure 4 shows the optimal consumption pattern. The consumer is *able* to locate anywhere on the budget line, but *the rational consumer will select that consumption combination that falls on the highest attainable indifference curve*. This combination is point *e:* by consuming 4 loaves of bread and 3 pints of ale the consumer can reach indifference curve U_1. Any other point on the budget line will fall on a *lower* indifference curve. At the optimal consumption pattern *e*, the budget line is tangent to (touches the curve only at one point end and has the same slope as) the indifference curve.

Equivalently, consumer equilibrium occurs at that point on the highest attainable indifference curve where the marginal rate of substitution equals the price ratio. At *e*, the consumer's marginal rate of substitution is 4 since the consumer is willing to trade off 4 units of bread for one unit of ale. The price ratio, as we have shown, is also 4.

The consumer is in equilibrium when the budget line is just tangent to the highest attainable indifference curve. Two conditions are then satisfied: 1) The consumer is on the budget line. 2) The consumer's marginal rate of substitution of bread for ale equals the price ratio of ale to bread (P_A/P_B).

There is a link between indifference-curve analysis and marginal-utility theory. The marginal rate of substitution of bread for ale can also be indicated by the marginal utilities of ale and bread. For example, if the marginal utility of ale

Figure 4   Consumer Equilibrium

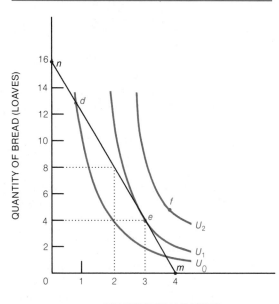

QUANTITY OF BREAD (LOAVES)

QUANTITY OF ALE (PINTS)

The consumer's optimal consumption pattern is at e. A point like d is attainable (on the budget line) but is not as good as e because it places the consumer at a lower indifference curve (U_0). Point f is better than e (the consumer is on a higher indifference curve, U_2) but is not attainable with the given set of income and prices. At e, the indifference curve U_1 is tangent to the budget line. Thus, the slope of the indifference curve equals the slope of the budget line. This tangency is equivalent to the marginal-utility rule for maximizing utility ($MU_A/P_A = MU_B/P_B$) discussed in the chapter.

(MU_A) is 20 and the marginal utility of bread (MU_B) is 5, it takes 4 extra loaves of bread to compensate the consumer for the loss of only 1 pint of ale. But if $MU_A = 10$ and $MU_B = 5$, the marginal rate of substitution of bread for ale is only 2.

The marginal rate of substitution of bread for ale ($MRS_{B/A}$) equals the ratio of the ale's marginal utility (MU_A) to the bread's marginal utility (MU_B):

$$MRS_{B/A} = \frac{MU_A}{MU_B}.$$

The condition for equilibrium can now be translated into the equal-marginal-utility-per-dol-

lar rule for consumer equilibrium described in the preceding chapter. At e, the slope of the indifference curve is MU_A/MU_B. The slope of the budget line is P_A/P_B. The indifference-curve equilibrium rule is equivalent to $MU_A/MU_B = P_A/P_B$. A little algebraic manipulation shows that this is equivalent to the marginal-utility-per-dollar rule for equilibrium: $MU_A/P_A = MU_B/P_B$.

THE EFFECT OF AN INCOME CHANGE

The consumer's equilibrium position will be affected if income changes, if the price of ale changes, or if the price of bread changes. Figure 5 shows how a reduction in the consumer's income from $8 to $4 leads to a reduction in the demand for both ale and bread. We assume the price of ale stays at $2 per pint and the price of bread remains at $0.50 per loaf. The budget line shifts down from mn to hj, because now the consumer can purchase only a maximum of 2 pints of ale or 8 loaves of bread. Instead of 4 loaves of bread and 3 pints of ale being consumed, now only 2 loaves of bread and 1.5 pints of ale are consumed at the new equilibrium (point e_0).

Notice that when income changes, holding prices constant, the budget line shifts in a parallel fashion. This shift occurs because the slope of the budget line is P_A/P_B, which has been assumed constant. The budget line shifts down when income falls and up when income rises. Clearly, utility falls as income falls and rises as income rises.

THE EFFECT OF A PRICE CHANGE

Now consider the effects of a change in one of the prices, holding income and the other price constant. Figure 6 shows how a fall in the price of ale from $2 to $1 a pint leads to an increase in the quantity of ale demanded. The initial equilibrium situation is represented by the combination e_1, where the price of ale is $2 and the price of bread is $0.50. Reducing the price of ale to $1 will allow the consumer the option of purchasing as many as 8 pints of ale, since the income re-

Figure 5   The Effect of an Income Change

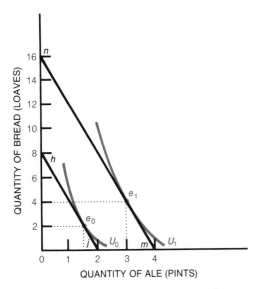

When the price of ale is $2 per pint and the price of bread is $0.50 per loaf, a fall in income from $8 to $4 causes a parallel shift in the budget line from nm to hj. The equilibrium changes from e_1 to e_0, which is on a lower indifference curve.

Figure 6   The Effect of a Price Change on Consumer Equilibrium: The Law of Demand

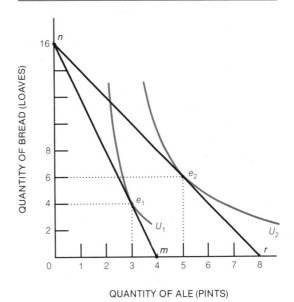

QUANTITY OF ALE (PINTS)

Assuming that income is $8 and the price of bread is $0.50, when the price of ale falls from $2 to $1 per pint, the budget line swings outward from nm to nr because the consumer is able to buy as many as 8 pints of ale. The consumer seeks out a new equilibrium combination, e_2, where indifference curve U_2 is tangent to the new budget line nr. A fall in the price of ale from $2 to $1, thus, increases the quantity of ale demanded from 3 pints at point e_1 to 5 pints at point e_2.

mains $8. The budget line will now swing outward from *nm* to *nr*.

> **When the price of one good falls, an increase in real income occurs, as shown by an outward swing of the budget line.**

The new equilibrium position occurs at e_2. At this point, the consumer buys 5 pints of ale and 6 loaves of bread. Before the price change, the consumer bought 3 pints of ale and 4 loaves of bread. The law of demand is confirmed: lowering the price of ale increases the quantity of ale demanded.

The consumer is clearly made better off (moves to a higher indifference curve) by the fall in the price of ale. Clearly, the consumer gets a bonus from low prices; the lower the price of a good bought by a consumer, holding income and other prices constant, the greater the consumer's welfare.

Why are demand curves downward-sloping? The chapter pointed out that there are two reasons

for the law of demand: the substitution effect and the income effect. When the price of a good falls, people will tend to substitute the good for other goods because its relative price has fallen. Thus, the substitution effect tends to increase the quantity of a good demanded when the price falls. In addition, when the price of a good falls people have more money to spend on all goods. If you are accustomed to buying one $10,000 car per year, a price reduction to $8,000 is like a $2,000 increase in income! If a good is normal, increases in income increase demand for the good. Thus, the income effect of a price reduction will also increase the quantity demanded of the good. Indifference-curve analysis can be used to illustrate the income effect and the substitution effect.

Figure 7 shows a consumer with the initial budget line *vw* and the initial equilibrium at point *e*. The consumer is purchasing *q* units of ale.

When the price of ale falls, the budget line shifts to *vz*. The quantity of ale demanded is now *q″* at the new equilibrium point, *e″*. The consumer is better off after the drop in the ale price because curve *U″* is higher than curve *U*.

The change in equilibrium from *e* to *e″* can be broken down into a two-step process to isolate the roles of the *income effect* and the *substitution effect* on the change in the equilibrium position.

When the price of ale falls, the ratio of the price of ale to the price of bread changes. *If the consumer were interested only in maintaining the current level of welfare achieved on curve U*, the consumer would increase the quantity demanded of ale until he or she reached the point on curve *U* where line *st* is tangent to *U*(*st* is a budget line with a slope that reflects the *new* ratio of ale price to bread price that results when the price of ale falls). The point on curve *U* where *st* is tangent to *U* is point *e′*. At *e′*, the consumer buys more ale and less bread without changing the level of satisfaction. This change in the quantity demanded of ale from *q* to *q′* is the **substitution effect** of the change in the price of ale.

At point *e′*, however, the consumer is not spending all the income available to him or her. Because of the drop in the price of ale, the consumer has more income available to spend on *both* bread and ale. The consumer's new budget line resulting from the lower ale price is *vz*, which has the same ale-price-to-bread-price ratio as *st* but which makes possible for the consumer a position on a higher indifference curve. The consumer who wished to maximize satisfaction would not stay at *e′* but would shift to *e″*, a point on the highest indifference curve attainable given budget line *vz*. The consumer making this shift would increase the quantity demanded of ale still further from *q′* at *e′* to *q″* at *e″*. This new equilibrium, unlike *e′*, *does* satisfy all the conditions of consumer equilibrium. The increase in quantity demanded from *q′* to *q″* as a result of the additional income made available is the **income effect** of the change in the ale price.

> The **substitution effect** is the change in quantity of *X* demanded that occurs when the price of *X* changes and the consumer is compensated to keep utility or welfare constant.

Figure 7   Substitution and Income Effects

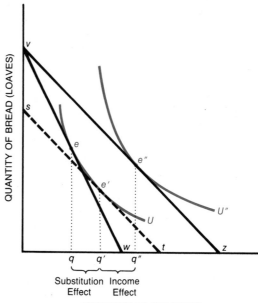

When income is $8 per week, bread costs $0.50 per loaf, and ale costs $2 per pint, the initial equilibrium is point *e*. When the price of ale falls from $2 to $1 per pint, the budget line swings outward from *vw* to *vz*. The new equilibrium is point *e″*. The substitution effect is obtained by drawing the budget line *st* parallel to *vz* but tangent to the original indifference curve, *U*. Thus, the substitution effect is the distance *qq′* and the income effect is the distance *q′q″*. In the case of a normal good, the income effect reinforces the substitution effect.

> The **income effect** is the change in the quantity of *X* demanded that is attributable to the welfare change that accompanies the price change.

The importance of the distinction between the substitution and income effects is that we can see that if a good is normal the income effect reinforces the substitution effect. In Figure 7, the price of ale falls and the substitution effect increases quantity demanded from *q* to *q′* along the convex indifference curve *U*. The move from *e′* to *e″* is like any income increase. If ale is a normal good, more ale will be consumed. In effect, a reduced price of ale gives the consumer more income to spend on both ale and bread. Thus, for a normal good, the income effect also indicates more ale will be consumed. It follows from the above analysis that if a good is normal, the demand curve for the good must be downward-sloping.

Summary

1. Indifference-curve analysis requires only that consumers be able to state whether they prefer one combination of goods to another combination or whether they are indifferent. An indifference curve plots those combinations of goods that yield the same level of satisfaction to the consumer. Indifference curves are negatively sloped (because more is better than less), and they are bowed toward the origin. Indifference maps show the preferences of individual consumers. If preferences differ, this will be reflected in different shapes of the indifference maps. The higher the indifference curve in the indifference map, the higher the level of satisfaction that the consumer receives. In indifference-curve analysis, the law of the diminishing marginal rate of substitution replaces the law of diminishing marginal utility. It states that the greater the quantity of good X that the individual consumes relative to good Y, the smaller the quantity of good Y that the consumer will be willing to sacrifice to obtain one more unit of good X. The budget line shows the choices of goods open to the consumer.

2. Maximizing satisfaction requires that the consumer seek out the highest indifference curve while remaining on the budget line. This point occurs at the tangency of the indifference curve and the budget line. The indifference-curve rule for maximizing satisfaction can be translated into the marginal-utility-per-dollar rule.

3. A change in income causes a parallel shift in the budget line. The budget line shifts down if income decreases and up if income increases. The new equilibrium is simply the new tangency of the new budget line with an indifference curve.

4. A reduction in the price of one commodity causes the budget line to swing outward. The new equilibrium takes place at the point of tangency between a higher indifference curve and the new budget line. The consumer is made better off by the price reduction because the consumer is able to locate on a higher indifference curve. The effects of a price change on quantity demanded can be broken down into a substitution effect, which maintains the existing utility level, and an income effect, which results from the change in the consumer's level of utility.

Key Terms

indifference curve
marginal rate of substitution *(MRS)*
law of diminishing marginal rate of
  substitution
budget line
substitution effect
income effect

Questions and Problems

1. a. Draw the consumer's budget line if income is $100, the price of ale is $5 per pint, and the price of bread is $4 per loaf.
   b. How does the budget line shift if the price of bread rises to $10, holding the price of ale at $5?
   c. How does the budget line shift if the price of ale rises to $10 holding the price of bread at $10?
   d. How does the budget line shift if income doubles to $200, holding the prices of ale and bread at $5 and $10, respectively?

2. a. Why are indifference curves downward-sloping?
   b. Why are they bowed toward the origin?

3. Why must the equilibrium position be a point of tangency between the budget line and an indifference curve?

4. Illustrate a situation in which income increases and the demand for one of the goods falls.

5. Deduce the law of demand for a normal good using the distinction between substitution and income effects when the price of the good rises.

27

Business Organization

Chapter Preview

In studying consumer behavior, the previous chapter examined the demand side of the market for products. This chapter will examine the suppliers of products: firms. Firms can be owned by a single individual or by several individuals, or they can be controlled by a board of directors on behalf of stockholders. This chapter will discuss the role of business firms in the economy, the principal/agent relationship within a firm, the advantages and disadvantages of various forms of business organization, the elements of corporation finance (stocks and bonds), and the four market models used by economists to study the different degrees of competition in an industry.

The circular-flow diagram on page 48 in Chapter 3 showed that firms can be involved in transactions with final consumers and in transactions among firms. For example, IBM might sell personal computers to households, while RCA sells parts and supplies to IBM. In the first case, the transaction enters the circular flow between businesses and households; in the second case, the transaction is an intermediate transaction that re-

mains entirely within the business sector. Transactions between firms and final consumers and transactions among firms are conducted through markets. As shown in Chapter 4, market prices coordinate the quantities of goods to be sold by buyers to sellers. Resources are allocated between firms and consumers and among firms by the impersonal forces of supply and demand. The equilibrium price coordinates the allocation of scarce resources.

Resources are allocated within the firm by *managerial coordination*. All business firms need a person or group of persons to make managerial decisions. The firm's manager may be the owner or owners, or it may be someone hired by the owners to make managerial decisions. The firm's managerial coordinators allocate the resources of the firm. These resources consist of the capital and land either owned or leased by the firm. The firm also has labor resources at its disposal—employees working according to written or unwritten contracts and prepared to follow the directives and orders of the firm's management. ■

BASIC CONCEPTS

Unlike market resource allocation in which resources are directed to various uses by the forces of supply and demand, within the firm resources are directed to various uses by **managerial coordination.**

> **Managerial coordination** is the disposition of the firm's resources according to the directives of the firm's manager.

Principals and Agents

Business firms must enter into a wide variety of contractual relationships in which they can act either as a **principal** or as an **agent.**[1]

> An **agent** is a party that acts for, on behalf of, or as a representative of a principal.

> A **principal** is a party that has controlling authority and that engages an agent to act subject to the principal's control and instruction.

Firm A is a principal when it enters into a contract with Firm B that requires Firm B (the agent) to supply it with specified amounts of a product at specified prices over a specified period of time. Firm A is a principal when it signs a contract with an employee (the agent) that calls for the employee to perform specific services at a specified wage for a specified period of time for Firm A. The Lockheed Corporation acts as a principal when it contracts with Rolls Royce (the agent) to supply jet engines for its aircraft. Chrysler Corporation acts as a principal when it hires Lee Iacocca (the agent) to serve as its chief executive officer. Mr. Jones acts as a principal when he signs a contract with a national moving firm (the agent) to move his household belongings from one city to another. Once an agency relationship is established, the principal is responsible for monitoring the performance of the agent to ensure that the agent is providing the services specified in the contractual agency agreement. When both the principal and the agent are motivated toward the same goal, or when it is not difficult for the principal to monitor the performance of the agent, conflicts between the principal and the agent are unlikely to arise. When the principal and the agent have different goals, however, or when it is difficult for the principal to monitor the performance of the agent, then conflicts between principal and agent are expected. This chapter discusses some examples of principal/agent conflicts.

The Role of Business in the Economy

Why do we even need business firms? Earlier chapters discussed the role of *entrepreneurs*—individuals who combine the factors of production to produce output. It is theoretically possible for entrepreneurs to work entirely through the market without business firms. A single entrepreneur may build a home by contracting through the market with the numerous carpenters, plumbers, electricians, and lumber and glass suppliers needed to build the home. Or an entrepreneur may supply individual artisans with materials to produce goods. Such instances are, however, rare in modern economies. Most products are produced by firms that integrate operations and combine the factors of production according to the directives of an employed manager.

The construction firm builds homes by having its agent, the manager, direct employees—carpenters, electricians, and unskilled laborers—to perform particular tasks. The furniture manufacturer employs skilled workers for carpentry work and unskilled workers for packing and delivery and maintains a fleet of delivery trucks.

The most basic reason for the existence of business firms is that in a number of cases managerial allocation is more effective than market allocation. Economists have pointed out four roles firms are able to play in the economy: they can take advantage of *economies of scale;* they can bear risk individuals are unwilling to bear; they can limit the costs of market transactions; they can monitor team production.

Economies of Scale.   As Adam Smith pointed out, one strong reason for business firms is the presence of **economies of scale.**

---

1. This distinction is made in Stephen A. Ross, "The Economic Theory of Agency: The Principal's Problem," *American Economic Review Papers and Proceedings,* May 1973, p. 134. The agency literature was developed by Robert Wilson, A. Michael Spence, Richard Zeckhauser, and Stephen Ross.

Economies of scale are present in the production process when large output volumes can be produced at a lower cost per unit than small output volumes.

Such economies are present in many production processes (Smith's example was a pin factory) in which costs per unit are reduced by the specialization of labor and equipment that is possible at a sufficiently large scale of output. The business firm brings together workers, land, and capital; the manager directs them to specialize in different tasks; output is produced in larger production runs and at lower cost per unit than if each worker had worked alone.

Risk Bearing.

Economist Frank Knight cites a second reason for business firms.[2] Some individuals are more willing to bear risk than others. Business ventures typically involve risk (markets can change, factor prices can fluctuate, and so on). The owner of the enterprise (the principal) will be the one who is willing to bear the risks. The employees (the agents) will be those individuals who dislike risk. The employer will hire workers and rent land and equipment at negotiated prices. The employer provides the suppliers of the factors of production with security, in return for which they agree to follow the owner's business directives. If the business is successful, the owner will reap the rewards; if it fails, the owner will suffer the consequences.

In the language of agency, the firm acts as the principal who contracts with agents to perform services for and represent the firm. The agents receive for their services a fee (in the form of a wage, salary, or bonus) for serving as agents. This contractual fee partly insulates them from risk and uncertainty. As long as the firm is solvent and the agency agreement is in effect, the agents will receive their fees even when the firm encounters ups and downs. The principal bears the risks by absorbing business losses when they occur. (The chapter on interest, rent, and profits will show that profits fluctuate much more than wages.)

The Costs of Using Markets.

Ronald Coase outlines a third reason for business firms.[3] Market coordination has its costs. The participants in market-coordinated activities must negotiate contracts, must do all sorts of paper work, must search out the best prices, and must bear the legal expenses if contracts are not fulfilled. Business firms can limit the costs of market transactions. Imagine, for example, the enormous transactions costs of using market coordination instead of managerial coordination to produce a modern commercial jet aircraft. If market coordination were used, thousands of subcontracts would have to be negotiated to produce the instruments, the hydraulic control systems, the airframe, and the interior furnishings. The expense of using market coordination would be enormous in this instance. Managerial coordination can reduce these transactions costs. Instead of negotiating thousands of market contracts, the manager simply directs employees to perform designated tasks, allocates the plant and equipment of the business enterprise, and works with fewer subcontractors.

In the Coase system, the dividing line between activities undertaken within the firm and those undertaken by the market would be determined by comparing the cost of market coordination with the cost of managerial coordination. As long as the marginal cost of organizing an activity inside the firm remains below the marginal cost of organizing that activity on a market basis, the task is carried out within the firm. When the marginal cost of organizing the activity within the firm exceeds the marginal cost of using the market, then the task is carried out by the market.

Monitoring Team Production.

Armen Alchian and Harold Demsetz emphasize that business enterprises are formed when there are substantial gains from team production.[4] Alchian and Demsetz believe there are situations where more output can be produced by employees working as a group than if each employee had worked alone.

---

2. Frank H. Knight, *Risk, Uncertainty, and Profit* (New York: Harper Torchbooks, 1957).

3. Ronald H. Coase, "The Nature of the Firm, "*Economica* 4 (1937): 386–405. Reprinted in George Stigler and Kenneth Boulding, eds. *Readings in Price Theory* (Homewood, Ill.: Richard D. Irwin, 1952).

Where there is team production there is the problem of monitoring the performance of individual employees, because it is not easy to determine the contribution of each team member.

The role of the owner/manager, therefore, is to monitor the performance of team members and to prevent shirking of work. Because the owner of a firm is paid out of the gains to team production, the owner will be motivated to do a good job of monitoring. Moreover, the owner has the authority to change the composition of the production team by changing contractual arrangements between the business enterprise and its inputs.

One reason why team monitoring is essential is that agents may have goals that are different from those of the principal. The principal wants, for example, the firm to earn a maximum profit from its resources. Employees (agents) may want a lighter work load, or they may be unwilling to acquire skills that only the principal would need. Hired managers (agents) may value job security more than profits. As long as the goals of agents are different from those of the principal, the principal must monitor the actions of agents.

Limits to Managerial Allocation

If managerial coordination is such a good idea in all the above situations, then what reasons are there *not* to have managerial coordination of all resource-allocation decisions? First, there are limits to the gains from economies of scale. If enterprises become too large, their costs of production per product may be higher than those of a smaller firm. Second, as the number and scope of managerial decisions increase, so do the costs of managerial coordination. The manager in this case is called upon to do too many things and to have to know too much information about prices, equipment, and so on. As the business enterprise grows, an optimal size will be reached beyond which the gains to managerial coordination (in the form of reduced transactions costs) will be overwhelmed by the rising costs of managerial coordination.

The real world consists of a mixture of managerial coordination and market coordination. Some activities are carried out within firms; other activities are the result of market coordination among firms. One automobile manufacturer will produce and market automobiles entirely within the business enterprise's own plant and sales offices. Another automobile manufacturer will purchase engines and other parts from foreign and domestic manufacturers, will assemble the automobile, and will leave the marketing of the product to independent distributors. Whether the first or second mode of coordination is used depends upon economies of scale, risk, costs of arranging market transactions, and the benefits of team production.

PROFIT MAXIMIZATION

Before one can understand the behavior of business firms, one must examine what motivates a business firm. What is the goal of a business firm? Most economists have a simple answer: the objective of all business firms (other than nonprofit organizations) is **profit maximization.**

> **Profit maximization** is the search by firms for the product quality, output, and price that give the firm the highest possible profits.

Opposing Theories

Some prominent economists disagree with the assumption that all firms seek to maximize profits. William J. Baumol argues that firms seek to maximize their sales. Robin Marris maintains that firms seek to maximize the growth of the firm after they have insured the security of the management in its position. A. A. Berle and Gardner Means argue that the separation of ownership and management has allowed managers to neglect the profit-maximization goal desired by shareholders and to concentrate on other objectives (such as the size of the firm, the number of employees reporting to them, and so on). John K. Galbraith argues in a similar vein that the separation of ownership and management has spawned a managerial elite—called the *technostructure*—whose goals are to limit risks and reduce uncertainty and surprises. Oliver Williamson maintains that managers will not pursue their own self-interests until they have kept profits and dividends at a level acceptable to shareholders. Finally, there are those like Richard Cyert, James March, and Herbert Simon who argue that managers set a goal for satisfactory profits and then pursue other goals, including perhaps what they regard as their social responsibilities.

Natural Selection

The major defense of profit maximization is the **natural-selection theory.**

> According to the **natural-selection theory,** if business firms do not maximize profits, they will be unable to compete with other firms and will be driven out of the market.

Obviously survival is important to all managers and owners; any firm or management that does not seek to maximize profits may not pass the ''survival of the fittest'' test. The natural-selection argument is compelling in the case of firms that face competition. It is less compelling for monopolists who (at least in theory) do not have to deal with competition.

The ultimate test of any behavioral assumption is whether the predictions that emerge from the assumption appear to describe reality. As subsequent chapters shall demonstrate, the real power of the profit-maximization assumption is that it appears to describe the reality of business behavior quite well.

FORMS OF BUSINESS ORGANIZATION

Business enterprises are customarily classified into three categories: *sole proprietorships, partnerships,* and *corporations.* Which form a business enterprise takes determines who makes business decisions, how capital is raised, who bears the risk of business failures, how principal/agent problems are resolved, and how profits are taxed.

Sole Proprietorships

The **sole proprietorship** is the least complex form of business enterprise.

The **sole proprietorship** is a form of business that is owned by one individual who makes all the business decisions, receives the profits that the business earns, and bears the financial responsibility for losses.

From this description, the simplicity of the individual proprietorship is apparent. Barring legal restrictions any individual can simply decide to go into business. The individual proprietor need not seek permission to enter into business except in areas of enterprise where business licenses are required, where health permits must be obtained, or where permission must be granted by zoning boards. Such restrictions aside, the individual who has accumulated or borrowed sufficient funds to set up a business can do so. No legal work is required to set up a sole proprietorship, although the individual proprietor will often seek legal and accounting advice.

Once in business, the proprietor is responsible for all business decisions. The owner determines how many employees to hire, when they should be rewarded or penalized, what products to produce, how they are to be marketed. The owner need not seek anyone's permission to make such decisions. The basic limitation upon decision making is that the owner must observe the law and honor contracts. Otherwise, the owner is free to make wise or foolish decisions.

Advantages.   The first advantage of the sole proprietorship is that decision-making authority is clear-cut: it resides with the owner. In making business decisions, the owner need not consult anyone. *The owner is the sole decision maker.* The owner (the principal) does not typically share decision-making authority with a hired managerial agent.

The second advantage of the sole proprietorship is that the profits of the business enterprise are *taxed only once.* The individual proprietor will receive any profits that the business earns after meeting its expenses. The proprietor pays personal income taxes on these profits.

Disadvantages.   There are three basic disadvantages of the sole proprietorship. The first is that the owner must assume *unlimited liability* (responsibility) for the debts of the company. The owner enjoys the profit of the business if it is successful, but if the business suffers a loss, the owner is personally liable. If the company borrows money, purchases materials, and incurs other bills that it cannot cover out of its revenues, the owner must personally cover the losses. The owner stands to lose personal wealth accumulated over the years in paying off the debts of the company.

The second disadvantage of the sole proprietorship is its *limited ability to raise financial capital*. This limitation makes it difficult for sole proprietorships to grow to a large size and explains why most proprietorships are small businesses. Financial capital for the expansion of the company can be raised in several ways in the case of the sole proprietorship. The owner can choose to plow profits back into the business. The owner can dip into personal wealth to invest in the company, or the owner can borrow money from relatives, friends, and lending institutions. The ability of the owner to borrow is determined by the owner's earning capacity (which will depend upon the success of the business) and personal wealth. Lending money to an individual proprietorship can be risky because the success of the business depends very much on one person, and if that person dies or becomes incapacitated, the lender will have to stand in line with other creditors.

The third disadvantage is that the business will typically die with the owner. Since the firm does not have a permanent existence, it may be difficult to find reliable employees; many employees prefer to work in firms that will be around long enough to offer employees career advancement.

Partnerships

A **partnership** is much like an individual proprietorship but with more than one owner.

> A **partnership** is a business enterprise that is owned by two or more people (called partners), who make all the business decisions, who share the profits of the business, and who bear the financial responsibility for any losses.

Like the individual proprietorship, partnerships are easy to establish. Most partnerships are based upon an agreement that spells out the ownership shares and duties of each partner. The partners may contribute different amounts of financial capital to the partnership; there may be an agreement on the division of responsibility for running the business; partners may own different shares of the business. One partner may make all the business decisions, while the other partner (a "silent partner") may simply provide financial capital. A partnership can be a corner gas station owned by three brothers or a nationally known law firm or brokerage house.

Advantages. The advantages of partnerships are much like those of the sole proprietorship. Partnerships are easy to set up. The profits of the company accrue to the partners and are taxed only once as personal income.

Unlike the sole proprietorship, however, there is a greater opportunity to specialize and divide managerial responsibility because the partnership consists of two or more individuals. The partner who is the better salesperson will be in charge of the sales department. The partner who is a talented mechanical engineer will be in charge of production. "Two heads are better than one" when each has different talents that are useful to the business enterprise. Second, a partnership can raise more financial capital than a sole proprietorship because the wealth and borrowing ability of more than one person can be mobilized. In fact, if a large number of wealthy partners can be assembled, such partnerships can indeed · e large sums of capital.

Disadvantages. The ability ، the partnership to raise financial capital is limited by the amount of money the partners can raise out of their personal wealth or from borrowing. The partners have unlimited liability for the debts of the partnership. A business debt incurred by any of the partners is the responsibility of the partnership. Each partner stands to lose personal wealth if the company is a commercial failure. Clearly, a conflict in goals can arise because the richer partner may be more risk-averse than the poorer partner.

"Two heads are better than one" *if* the two heads agree. But if partners fail to agree, decision making can become quite complicated. In a partnership where all partners are responsible for management decisions, there is no longer one single person who is in charge. Partnerships can be immobilized when partners disagree on fundamental policy. It may be difficult to reach decisions if one partner is out of town. Partnerships involve a more complicated decision-making process that can become more complicated as the number of partners grows.

Partnerships can also be unstable. If disagreements over policy cause one partner to withdraw from the partnership, the partnership must be reorganized. When one partner dies, again the partnership agreement must be renegotiated.

Finally, partnerships can involve a considerable risk for the individual partners. The sole proprietor does bear unlimited liability for the debts of the company, but at least the owner is the one who makes the business decision that may turn out to be bad. In the case of the partnership, each partner is responsible for business debts incurred by another partner even if that partner acted without consent of the other partners.[5] For this reason, partnerships are often made up of family members, close relatives, and close personal friends who have come to trust one another over the years. Partnerships with more partners would have a greater ability to raise capital. However, because additional partners complicate decision making and increase the likelihood of an irresponsible act being committed by a partner, many partnerships have a limited number of partners.

Corporations

The **corporation** came into existence to overcome some of the disadvantages of the proprietorship and partnership noted above.

> A **corporation** is a form of business enterprise that is owned by a number of stockholders. The corporation has the legal status of a fictional individual and is authorized by law to act as a single person. The stockholders elect a board of directors that appoints the management of the

corporation, usually headed by a president. Management is charged with the actual operation of the corporation.

Unlike sole proprietorships and partnerships that can be established with minimal paperwork, a *corporate charter* is required to set up a corporation. The laws of each state are different, but, typically, for a fee, corporations can be established (incorporated) and can become legal "persons" subject to the laws of that state. According to state and federal laws, the corporation has the legal status of a fictional individual. Officers of the corporation can act in the name of the corporation without being personally liable for its debts. If corporate officers commit criminal acts, however, they can be prosecuted as individuals.

The corporation is owned by individuals (stockholders) who have purchased shares of *stock* in the corporation. A stockholder's share of ownership of the corporation will equal the number of shares owned by that individual divided by the total number of shares *outstanding* (owned by stockholders). If a person owns 100,000 shares of AT&T stock and there are 630 million AT&T shares outstanding, then the person would own only 0.016 percent of AT&T. Owners of shares of stock have the right to vote for the board of directors and to vote on special referenda at the annual meeting of the corporation. The management of the corporation is required by law to issue periodic reports to its shareholders describing the financial and business activities of the corporation during the reporting period. The stockholders may cast their votes in person at the annual meeting (the greater the number of shares owned, the greater the weight of the individual's vote) or can vote *by proxy* (that is, turn over voting privileges to the current management or to some other group).

The stockholder who owns 1 percent of the stock of AT&T will receive 1 percent of the dividends the AT&T management chooses to pay to its shareholders out of profits and is entitled to vote on matters affecting the corporation and to vote for its board of directors. Unlike the sole proprietor who has title to 100 percent of the profits of the company or the partner who may have title to 50 percent of the profits of the company, the typical stockholder owns a miniscule portion

---

5. There are partnerships in which some partners have limited liability—as in real estate and sports, for example. In these partnerships, however, there must be one or more general partners with unlimited liability.

Table 1 Types of Business Organization

Type of Firm	Advantages	Disadvantages
Individual proprietorships	1. Business is simple to set up. 2. Decision making is clear-cut; the owner makes the decisions. 3. Earnings are taxed only once as personal income.	1. The owner has unlimited liability; the owner's personal wealth is at risk. 2. The company has a limited ability to raise financial capital. 3. Business dies with owner.
Partnership	1. Business is relatively easy to set up. 2. More management skills are available; two heads are better than one. 3. Earnings are taxed only once as the personal income of the partners.	1. There is unlimited liability for the partners. 2. Decision making can be complicated. 3. The company has a limited ability to raise capital. 4. Partnerships can be unstable.
Corporation	1. There is limited liability for owners. 2. Company is able to raise large sums of capital through issuing bonds and stock. 3. Company has an eternal life. 4. Company is able to recruit professional management and to change bad management.	1. Corporate income is taxed twice: once as corporate profits, then as personal income (dividends). 2. There are greater possibilities for management disagreements. 3. There is the possibility of conflicting goals between the owners of the corporation (the *principals*) and management (the *agents*).

of the total number of shares outstanding. In the case of the sole proprietorship and partnership, the owners decide what to do with the profits. In the case of the corporate stockholder, the management determines what to do with the profits of the corporation. The shareholder who does not approve of the way these profits are handled can vote to change the current board of directors or sell the stock and buy some other asset. **Common stock, preferred stock,** and **convertible stock** are three types of corporate stock.

Common stock confers voting privileges but no prior claim on dividends. Common stock dividends are paid only if they are declared by the board of directors in any given year.

Preferred stock confers a prior claim on dividends but no voting privileges. Dividends on preferred stock must be paid before paying common stock dividends but after meeting interest obligations.

Convertible stock is a hybrid between a stock and a bond. The owner of convertible stock receives fixed interest payments but has the privilege of converting the convertible stock into common stock at a fixed rate of exchange.

Corporations often have thousands or millions of shares outstanding, and these shares are typically owned by a large number of stockholders. In the case of closely held corporations, the number of stockholders is limited, and each stockholder owns a substantial share of the corporation's stock. Unlike the sole proprietor or the partner, stockholders do not participate directly in the running of the corporation unless they happen to own a substantial share of the outstanding stock. Moreover, even if an effort were made to involve shareholders in corporate decision making, there would be too many of them, they would be geographically dispersed, and they would be too involved in their own business affairs to devote sufficient attention to corporate affairs.

For these reasons, there is usually a *separation of ownership and management* in the modern corporation. The board of directors appoints a professional management team that makes decisions for the corporation. The professional management team serves as agents for the corporation. As long as the corporation is run successfully, the management team is allowed to continue. If the corporation falls on hard times, then the stockholders may vote out the current board of directors or the board of directors itself may decide to bring in a new management team.

Statistical studies of modern corporations have demonstrated the magnitude of the separation of ownership and management.[6] In most instances, the people who actually run the corporation own only a small portion of the shares. In the case of giant corporations, the officers of the corporation may own only 2 to 3 percent of the stock.

Stockholders, however, can exercise substantial indirect control over management by simply selling their stock. The sale of stock by enough unhappy stockholders will depress the price of each share and invite possible takeovers by other corporate teams.

Advantages.   The first advantage of the corporation is limited liability. The owners of the corporation (the stockholders) are not personally liable for the debts of the corporation. If a corporation incurs debts that it cannot meet, its creditors can lay claim to the assets of the corporation (its bank accounts, equipment, supplies, buildings, and real-estate holdings), but they cannot file claims against the stockholders. The worst thing that can happen to stockholders is that the value of their stock will decline (in extreme circumstances, it can become worthless).

Limited liability contributes to a second advantage of the corporation: corporations can raise large sums of financial capital by selling corporate bonds, by issuing stock, and by borrowing from lending institutions. (How corporations raise capital will be described in more detail later in the chapter.)

The third advantage of the corporation follows from its status as a legal individual distinct from the officers of the corporation. A change in the board of directors, the death or resignation of the current president, or a transfer of ownership could destroy a partnership or sole proprietorship, but these events do not alter the legal status of the corporation. The continuity of the corporation is a distinct advantage. Many major U.S. corporations are more than a century old. Few corporations have the same owners and officers that they had when the corporation was founded. Continu-

ity is an advantage in raising financial capital. Lending institutions are willing to make long-term loans to corporations because they know the corporation will outlive its current owners and officers. In fact, U.S. corporations have loans outstanding that are not due until the 21st century. New stockholders can also be brought into the corporation because they know that the existence of the corporation is not dependent upon the individuals that currently run the corporation. Continuity also makes it easier for the firm to hire a career-minded labor force.

The fourth advantage of the corporation follows from the separation of ownership and management. Because the two functions are separated, professional managers who specialize in running different parts of the corporation's operations can be hired. Experience shows that the owners of businesses (those individuals with money to invest) do not always make the best managers. In the modern corporation, talented officers can be brought into the business who own little (or no) company stock. For example, Lee Iaccoca was an ''outsider'' when he was appointed President of the Chrysler Corporation. Iaccoca helped save the car manufacturer from bankruptcy through his considerable skills in manufacturing and marketing cars (and in securing necessary government loan guarantees).

Disadvantages.   The major disadvantage of the corporation is the double taxation of corporate income. The profits (earnings) of the corporation can either be distributed to shareholders as *dividends* or kept as *retained earnings* to be reinvested (plowed back) in the corporation. The profits of the corporation are subject to a federal income tax. Corporations pay a tax rate of from 15 percent (on profits of $25,000 or less) to the full rate of 46 percent (on annual profits in excess of $100,000) of company earnings. In many states, corporations must also pay a state income tax. If the corporation chooses to plow back all profits into the company, corporate profits will be taxed only once, but if it distributes some of its profits to shareholders in the form of dividends, shareholders must pay personal income tax on these dividends.

The double taxation of corporate earnings is indeed a disadvantage, but the fact that the cor-

---

6. The pioneering study of the separation of ownership and management was published in 1932 by A. A. Berle and Gardner Means, *The Modern Corporation and Private Property* (New York: Commerce Clearing House, 1932).

Figure 1 Proprietorships, Partnerships, and Corporations, 1984

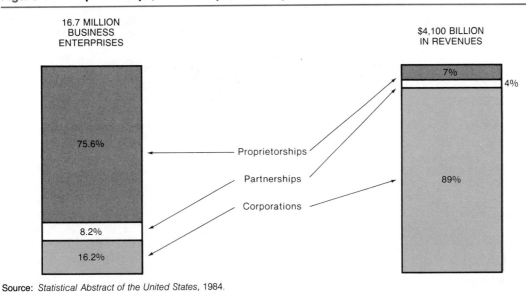

Source: *Statistical Abstract of the United States*, 1984.

porate form of business enterprise is so prevalent suggests that the advantages of corporations (most specifically limited liability) can compensate for double taxation.

A second disadvantage of the corporation is its complexity. A modern corporation can have thousands or even millions of different owners (stockholders). Often ownership is so dispersed that it is difficult to get the owners to agree (or even assemble) even when important issues are at stake. Power struggles among shareholder factions can break out and paralyze decision making. It is difficult to mobilize widely dispersed stockholders to get rid of incompetent management. The costs of gathering information about the complex dealings of the corporation are high to individual shareholders, who are often poorly informed about the corporation.

A third disadvantage of the corporation is the possibility of conflicting objectives between the principals (the shareholders) and the agents (the corporation's professional management team). Shareholders are interested in maximizing the long-run profits of the corporation (thereby getting the best return from their shares of stock). The professional management team may be more interested in preserving their jobs or in maximiz-

ing their personal income or perquisites than in profit maximization (see Example 1).

The Role of Big Business in the Economy

In the United States, there are roughly 17 million business enterprises (see Figure 1). The overwhelming majority of these are proprietorships (75.6 percent); the rest are corporations (16.2 percent) and partnerships (8.2 percent). Although proprietorships dominate in number, their share of business revenues is relatively small, accounting for only 7 percent of total revenues. Corporations, on the other hand, account for 89 percent of business revenues.

The average corporation is 12 times larger than the average partnership and 70 times larger than the average proprietorship. In 1980, the average corporation had dollar receipts of about $2.1 million.

Proprietorships are concentrated in agriculture, trade, and services, where the family farm and small family business are common (see Table 2). Corporations are especially active in manufacturing and trade. Partnerships are important in trade, finance, and services.

Table 2   Proprietorships, Partnerships, and Corporations, by Industry, 1980

Industry	Number (thousands)			Business Revenues (billions of dollars)		
	Proprietor-ships	Active Partner-ships	Active Corpo-rations	Proprietor-ships	Active Partner-ships	Active Corpo-rations
Total	12,702	1,380	2,711	505.9	286.0	5,731.6
Agriculture, forestry, and fishing	3,279	126	81	101.1	21.6	48.9
Mining	120	35	26	8.6	13.2	167.4
Construction	1,073	67	272	47.8	18.4	260.4
Manufacturing	296	30	243	14.8	15.3	2,301.1
Transportation, public utilities	439	20	111	20.0	5.9	507.4
Wholesale and retail trade	2,527	200	800	202.3	65.8	1,919.3
Wholesale	330	32	281	42.7	28.4	1,104.4
Retail	2,066	168	515	153.8	37.3	813.0
Finance, insurance, real estate	1,049	637	493	21.5	87.1	697.5
Services	3,843	263	671	88.0	58.6	266.1

Source: *Statistical Abstract of the United States* 1984, p. 533.

Large corporations (with revenues of more than $1 million) account for 92.5 percent of corporate business revenues (see Table 3), while large proprietorships (sales of over $100,000) account for only 42.1 percent of proprietor revenues. The large corporation accounts for 82 percent of all *business* revenue.

Figure 2 shows the number of industrial and commercial failures resulting in some loss to creditors for the years 1970 to 1983. Retail failures are largest in number. The post-1978 in-crease resulted from the 1980–1981 business recession and the easing of bankruptcy laws. As the economy recovers from the 1980–1981 recession, the number of business failures would be expected to drop.

As noted above, the large corporation accounts for a substantial share of business sales and profits. The *absolute* size of giant corporations is awesome (see Table 4). The annual sales of certain large U.S. industrial corporations—like General Motors and Exxon—exceed the annual output

Table 3   Size of Business Revenues of U.S. Proprietorships, Partnerships, and Corporations, 1980

	Proprietorships			Partnerships			Corporations		
	Under $50,000	$50,000-$99,999	$100,000 or More	Under $100,000	$100,000-$499,999	$500,000 or More	Under $500,000	$500,000-$999,999	$1,000,000 or More
Number of enterprises (in thousands)	10,516	1,082	1,104	1,003	291	85	2,013	280	418
Average revenues of these enterprises (dollars)	10,289	70,610	290,761	24,322	221,079	232,045	121,945	685,985	12,665,224
Percent of total business revenues for category	42.8	15.1	42.1	8.5	22.4	69.1	4.2	3.3	92.5

Source: *Statistical Abstract of the United States*, 1984, p. 533.

Figure 2   Business Failures in the United States, 1970–1983

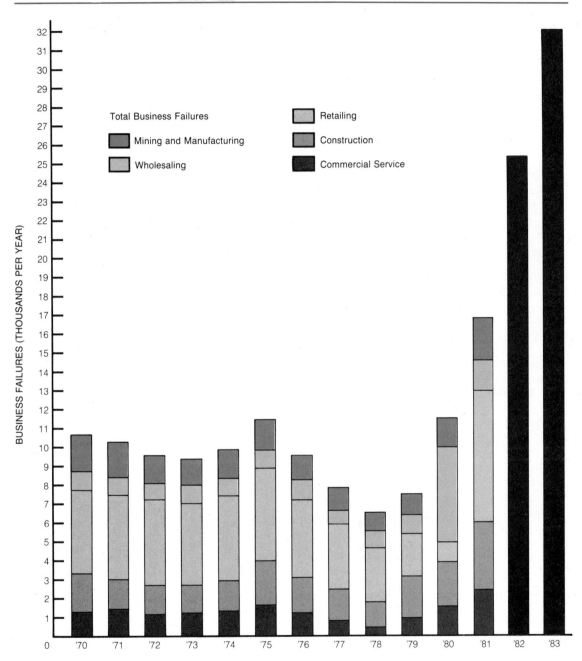

Source: *Survey of Current Business.*

of many industrial economies. The annual sales of General Motors, for example, equals the annual production of Belgium. The annual sales of the six largest U.S. industrial corporations (Ford, GM, Exxon, Mobil, Texaco, and Standard Oil of California) exceed the annual production of the United Kingdom—a fact that underscores the importance of big business in the U.S. economy.

Table 4   The 50 Largest U.S. Industrial Corporations, Ranked by Sales

Rank 1983	1982	Company	Sales (thousands of dollars)
1	1	**Exxon** (New York)	88,561,134
2	2	**General Motors** (Detroit)	74,581,600
3	3	**Mobil** (New York)	54,607,000
4	5	**Ford Motor** (Dearborn, Mich.)	44,454,600
5	6	**International Business Machines** (Armonk, N.Y.)	40,180,000
6	4	**Texaco** (Harrison, N.Y.)	40,068,000
7	8	**E.I. du Pont de Nemours** (Wilmington, Del.)	35,378,000
8	10	**Standard Oil (Indiana)** (Chicago)	27,635,000
9	7	**Standard Oil of California** (San Francisco)	27,342,000
10	11	**General Electric** (Fairfield, Conn.)	26,797,000
11	9	**Gulf Oil** (Pittsburgh)	26,581,000
12	12	**Atlantic Richfield** (Los Angeles)	25,147,036
13	13	**Shell Oil** (Houston)	19,678,000
14	15	**Occidental Petroleum** (Los Angeles)	19,115,700
15	14	**U.S. Steel** (Pittsburgh)	16,869,000
16	17	**Phillips Petroleum** (Bartlesville, Okla.)	15,249,000
17	18	**Sun** (Radnor, Pa.)	14,730,000
18	20	**United Technologies** (Hartford)	14,669,265
19	19	**Tenneco** (Houston)	14,353,000
20	16	**ITT** (New York)	14,155,408
21	29	**Chrysler** (Highland Park, Mich.)	13,240,399
22	23	**Procter & Gamble** (Cincinnati)	12,452,000
23	25	**R. J. Reynolds Industries** (Winston-Salem, N.C.)	11,957,000
24	24	**Getty Oil** (Los Angeles)	11,600,024
25	21	**Standard Oil (Ohio)** (Cleveland)	11,599,000
26	22	**AT & T Technologies** (New York)	11,154,700
27	34	**Boeing** (Seattle)	11,129,000
28	27	**Dow Chemical** (Midland, Mich.)	10,951,000
29	49	**Allied** (Morris Township, N.J.)	10,351,000
30	26	**Eastman Kodak** (Rochester, N.Y.)	10,170,000
31	28	**Unocal** (Los Angeles)	10,065,600
32	37	**Goodyear Tire & Rubber** (Akron, Ohio)	9,735,800
33	30	**Dart & Kraft** (Northbrook, Ill.)	9,714,000
34	31	**Westinghouse Electric** (Pittsburgh)	9,532,600
35	32	**Philip Morris** (New York)	9,465,600
36	35	**Beatrice Foods** (Chicago)	9,188,200
37	33	**Union Carbide** (Danbury, Conn.)	9,001,100
38	38	**Xerox** (Stamford, Conn.)	8,463,500
39	40	**Amerada Hess** (New York)	8,368,946
40	53	**Union Pacific** (New York)	8,352,585
41	39	**General Foods** (White Plains, N.Y.)	8,256,433
42	43	**McDonnell Douglas** (St. Louis)	8,111,000
43	42	**Rockwell International** (Pittsburgh)	8,097,900
44	41	**PepsiCo** (Purchase, N.Y.)	7,895,936
45	36	**Ashland Oil** (Russell, Ky.)	7,852,299
46	46	**General Dynamics** (St. Louis)	7,146,300
47	44	**Minnesota Mining & Manufacturing** (St. Paul)	7,039,000
48	48	**Coca-Cola** (Atlanta)	6,990,992
49	51	**Consolidated Foods** (Chicago)	6,572,298
50	56	**Lockheed** (Burbank, Calif.)	6,490,300

Source: *Fortune*, April 30, 1984.

Example 1   Greenmail, Hostile Takeovers, and the Agency Problem

An *agency problem* exists when principals and agents have conflicting objectives and the principal is unable to monitor and control the performance of the agent. In the case of corporations, an agency problem exists when the corporation's management has goals that differ from those of the average shareholder. The behavior of corporate management during hostile takeover attempts can be used to illustrate the agency problem.

A *hostile corporate takeover* occurs when an outside group (or another company) buys sufficient shares of a corporation to be in a position to name a new management, which will run the corporation more in line with the wishes of the new group. From the viewpoint of existing stockholders, a hostile takeover attempt should be welcome news (as long as the stockholders are currently not members of the management or employees who may be fired by a new management). In order to gain control of the company, the hostile group must buy a large number of shares. The demand for shares increases, and the stock price rises—sometimes quite substantially. Existing shareholders can, therefore, sell their shares, if they so desire, at a high price, and the takeover has increased their wealth. The corporation's management, however, views hostile takeovers differently. A takeover may mean the loss of one's job, a reduction in salary, or the loss of prestige. Accordingly, management typically attempts to resist the takeover. One means is to go further into debt to acquire other companies or to invest in risky ventures to make the corporation a less attractive takeover target. Another means is to pay *greenmail;* that is, to pay the person or persons attempting the hostile takeover a substantial amount—usually by buying back stock at a premium stock price—to refrain from the takeover attempt. The widely dispersed shareholders, who stand to lose from these anti-takeover measures, are often unable to monitor and control the actions of their agents. ∎

CORPORATE FINANCE

Limited liability and continuity give corporations an edge in raising large sums of financial capital. Corporations have options for raising capital that are not available to sole proprietorships or to partnerships. Corporations, like proprietorships and partnerships, can borrow money from banks and from other lending institutions, and they can plow profits back into the business. In addition to these traditional forms of raising capital, corporations can 1) *sell* **bonds** (also called *issuing debt*), or they can 2) *issue (sell) additional shares of stock*.

Corporate **bonds** are IOUs of the corporation that bind the corporation to pay a fixed sum of money (the principal) at maturity and also to pay a fixed sum of money annually until the maturity date. This fixed annual payment is called *interest* or the *coupon payment*.

Present Value and Discounting

Bonds are obligations to make specified payments at specific dates over a specified period of time.

Bonds cannot be understood without an understanding of present and future values of money. To understand the difference between present and future payments, one must keep in mind a fundamental principle:

A dollar today is worth more than a dollar tomorrow because it can earn interest.

For the sake of simplicity, assume that an annual interest rate of 10 percent is the prevailing rate of interest paid throughout the economy. In other words, if $100 is deposited in a savings account, $10 interest will be earned at the end of one year. At 10 percent interest, $100 today will be equal to $110 a year from now. If the interest rate had been 20 percent, $100 today would equal to $120 a year from now.

Looking at the process in reverse, if the bank were to offer to pay someone $110 one year from now, what would that person be willing to pay today in order to receive $110 in one year? At 10 percent interest, the most this person would be willing to pay now in order to receive $110 in one year is $100. Thus, the **present value (PV)** of a future payment of $110 is $100 at 10 percent interest.

> The **present value (PV)** of money to be received in the future is the most anyone would pay today in order to receive the money in the future. The present value is sometimes called the *discounted value* because it is smaller than the amount to be received in the future.

The price (market value) of an IOU (such as a bond) that promises to make specified payments at specified future dates will be the present value of those payments. The present-value calculation can be summarized in a formula. The present value (PV) of each dollar to be paid in one year at the interest rate i (i stands for the rate of interest in decimals) is:

$$PV = \frac{\$1}{1 + i}.$$

If the interest rate is 10 percent, then $i = 0.10$ and $1 + i = 1.10$. The PV of each dollar equals $0.9091. If $10,000 is the sum to be paid in one year, the PV equals $9091 ($10,000 times 0.9091).

The present-value formula becomes more complicated when the time span is greater than one year. At an annual interest rate of 10 percent, how much would someone be willing to pay now to have $121 two years from now? The answer follows the same reasoning as before. At an interest rate of 10 percent, how much money would a person have to deposit today to have an account worth $121 in two years? If the sum PV were deposited at interest rate i, it would be worth $PV \times (1 + i)$ one year from now. That sum would then earn a second year's interest and by the end of the second year would be worth $PV \times (1 + i) \times (1 + i)$, or $PV(1 + i)^2$. Setting the sum, $PV(1 + i)^2$, equal to $121 and dividing by $[(1 + i)^2]$ yields:

$$PV = \frac{\$121}{(1 + i)^2}$$

At a rate of interest of 10 percent, the PV of $121 to be received two years from now is $100 ($= $121/1.1^2$).

This result can be generalized to show that the present value of a sum to be received in three years is that sum divided by $(1 + i)^3$; the present value of a sum to be received in four years is that sum divided by $(1 + i)^4$; and so on.

The present value (PV) of a dollar to be received in n years is

$$PV = \frac{1}{(1 + i)^n}.$$

At a 10 percent interest rate, $100 received one year from now has a present value of $90.91; $100 to be received five years from now has a present value of only $62.27.

The further out in the future the money is to be paid, the lower is its present value.

These present-value formulas bring home an important point: the present value of money to be received in the future falls as the interest rate rises. In the above example, the PV of $121 to be received two years from now is $100 at an interest rate of 10 percent; that is, $121 \div 1.1^2 = $100. At an interest rate of 20 percent, the PV of $121 to be received two years from now falls to $84; that is, $121 \div 1.2^2 = $84.

The present value of a dollar to be received in the future falls as the interest rate rises and rises as the interest rate falls.

Now suppose someone has an *asset* (an income-producing property) that yields $100 per year *in perpetuity* (forever). What is such an asset worth today? What would its price be if it were to exchange hands?

If the interest rate were 10 percent, a $1,000 interest-yielding asset would generate $100 per year in interest income. This $1,000 is the present value of the $100 perpetual income stream. If the interest rate doubled to 20 percent, a $500 investment would earn $100 a year in perpetuity. Hence, $500 would be the present value of an asset that yielded $100 per year at a 20 percent rate of interest.

The general formula for calculating the present value *(PV)* of an asset that yields a perpetual income stream is:

$$PV = \frac{R}{i}$$

where R = the annual income stream, and i = the rate of interest expressed in decimal form. At an interest rate of 10 percent, the present value of $100 a year in perpetuity is $100 ÷ 0.10, or $1,000.

The Selling of Bonds

The financial section of the newspaper usually contains a comprehensive listing of corporate bonds. By selling bonds, corporations can acquire funds to finance business expansion. Once the bond is sold, the buyer can resell it, but such trades in second-hand bonds no longer directly affect the corporation.

The interest or principal payments on corporate bonds represent a legal obligation for the corporation, just like any other debt of the corporation. The purchaser of the bond has loaned the corporation money, and in return the corporation has promised the lender fixed interest payments until maturity and payment of the principal at the date of maturity. Interest and principal payments on corporate bonds have a claim on company earnings prior to dividends. The company has no choice but to make interest payments unless it is to be declared in a state of **bankruptcy.**

A corporation can be declared in a state of **bankruptcy** if the corporation cannot pay its bills or its interest obligations.

Because purchasers of corporate bonds have prior claim on company earnings, bonds offer a relatively secure return on corporate investments. As long as the corporation does not become bankrupt, the bondholder will receive the promised annual coupon payment (as well as the principal payment at the date of maturity).

Nevertheless, corporate bonds are not a riskless investment. In fact, purchasing bonds can be very risky because bond prices fluctuate in the second-hand market. If the bond owner wishes to sell the bond before the date of maturity, the price received for the bond may well be less than the price paid for the bond.

Bond prices are simply the present discounted value *(PV)* of the coupon payments and the maturity value. But as we described above, there is an inverse relationship between interest rates and present values. As interest rates rise, investors will pay *less* for the stream of coupon payments offered by a bond. As interest rates fall, investors will pay *more* for the stream of coupon payments offered by the bond.

From the vantage point of the purchaser, corporate bonds have an advantage over stock in that they have a prior claim on corporate profits. The corporation must pay the annual coupon to avoid bankruptcy. The lender knows with a high degree of certainty how much money will be received from the corporation until the date of maturity. A disadvantage of bonds is that, unlike the owner of the stock of the corporation, the bondholder cannot vote for the board of directors or share in unusually high profits.

The Issue of Stock

A second means of raising financial capital is for the corporation to sell additional shares of stock. Suppose ZYX corporation has 100,000 shares of stock that is already owned by stockholders. Each share of stock currently sells for $10 on the second-hand market for stocks. These second-hand markets for corporate stock are called *stock exchanges:* the two most prominent stock exchanges in the United States are the New York Stock Exchange (NYSE) and the American Stock Exchange (ASE), both located on Wall Street in New York City.

The corporation decides that it needs to raise $500,000 to build a new plant and arranges with an *investment bank* or an *underwriter* to sell 50,000 new shares of stock to investors. The company will prepare a *prospectus* (as required by the Securities and Exchange Commission) that describes to potential buyers of the stock the financial condition of the company and the proposed uses to which the raised funds will be put. The investment bank will charge an underwriting fee to sell the 50,000 shares.

The amount of money investors will be willing to pay for the 50,000 new shares depends upon their assessment of the impact of the proposed investment on ZYX corporation earnings. If investors expect the new plant to raise company earnings substantially, they will offer a higher price than if they expect the investment to have a small effect.

Experts believe that corporations will issue new stock only if they can avoid a decline in the price of the stock in the second-hand market. Let us suppose this is the case with ZYX corporation. When the investment bank is able to sell the 50,000 new shares at the $10-per-share price, ZYX corporation raises $500,000 through the stock issue.

The corporation now has 150,000 shares *outstanding* (owned by stockholders) rather than the previous 100,000. The owners of the new 50,000 shares are entitled to vote on corporate matters and to receive dividends. Unlike corporate bonds that legally obligate the corporation to pay fixed interest payments, there is no obligation on the part of the corporation to pay dividends. As noted earlier, the corporation cannot pay dividends before meeting its interest obligations; therefore, dividends are only paid if there are sufficient profits left over after paying interest. When corporations experience hard times, dividends are frequently cut or even omitted entirely.

Conceptually, it is easy to describe how the price of a share of stock is established:

> **The price of a share of stock is the perceived present value of the future earnings per share of the stock.**

Stock prices fluctuate dramatically because the future is unknown. No one knows for sure what the future earnings of any company might be. There will be disagreement among those who currently own the stock and those who are considering buying the stock. No one can predict how the economy as a whole will behave in the future; no one can predict for sure whether a particular company's fortunes will improve, deteriorate, or remain the same. When a company announces the development of a new product, the investment community may become convinced that this development will raise future earnings. This event will change investors' assessments of the present value of the company, and the stock price will rise.

The **price/earnings ratio** (*PE*) signals whether investors believe the profits of the company will rise or fall from current profit levels.

> The **price/earnings ratio** (*PE*) is the stock price divided by the earnings per share.

If the average company has a *PE* of 6, companies with a *PE* greater than 6 are expected to have profits rising at above-average rates. Companies with a *PE* less than 6 are expected to have profits rising at below-average rates (see Example 2).

> **A high *PE* indicates that investors believe that current profits understate the future profits of the corporation. A low *PE* indicates that investors believe that current profits overstate the future profits of the corporation.**

The price of stocks have an important effect on the allocation of capital resources. Consider what would happen if ZYX corporation's research-and-development team develops a promising anticancer drug and obtains Food and Drug Administration approval to market this drug. The investor community will realize (probably well before government approval is even granted) that ZYX corporation earnings will rise substantially, so the price of the stock will take off. In our earlier example, the price of ZYX stock was $10, and the company was able to raise $500,000 by selling 50,000 new shares of stock. If, on the other hand, the prospect of the new drug causes the price of the stock to rise to $50 (the new plant would be built to manufacture the new drug), the issue of 50,000 new shares would raise $2,500,000 instead of $500,000.

As stock prices rise, corporations find it easier to raise financial capital for expansion. Corpora-

Example 2   The Price/Earnings Ratio as a Barometer of Future Genentech Earnings

One of the most exciting scientific developments of the 20th century is genetic engineering—the ability through gene splicing to alter the genetic characteristics of lower and higher animal forms. Genentech Corporation, a scientific leader in the area of genetic engineering, is in the process of altering the genetic characteristics of bacteria to cause them to produce *interferon*. Interferon, which previously could be produced only at great expense from blood, is thought to be a promising anticancer drug that may one day have a large market. As of 1984, Genentech's earnings have been almost nonexistent. In 1982, it earned $0.05 per share, but its stock price averaged $24, for a *price/earnings (PE) ratio* of 480. In 1983, it earned $0.08 per share, and its average price was $37—

resulting in a *PE* ratio of 462; in 1984 its earnings per share were $0.11, and its average stock price was $35—for a *PE* ratio of 318.

When most other stocks have price/earnings ratios of 5 or below, why does Genentech have such an astronomical *PE* ratio? Stock-market investors are betting on the fact that commercial applications of genetic engineering will prove enormously profitable in the future. Thus, they are predicting increases in future earnings for companies like Genentech. For example, if in 1990, Genentech's earnings are $50 per share and rising, today's price of $35 per share would be quite a bargain. Stock-market investors who bought at that price could sell out at a substantial capital gain. ■

tions with falling stock prices cannot raise large sums of money for expansion. In this sense, the second-hand markets for corporate stocks serve as barometers that signal the direction of the allocation of financial capital. Dissatisfied stockholders can express their dissatisfaction by "voting with their feet." By selling their shares, they drive down the price of the stock. If dissatisfaction is widespread, the stock price can fall considerably, preventing the firm from raising much capital by selling new shares (see Example 3).

Taxation and Business Behavior

One important lesson gained from studying business enterprises is that taxes influence business behavior. The double taxation of corporate income influences whether a business will be set up as a partnership or as a corporation. If the advantages of the corporate form (limited liability, greater ability to raise capital) are not important, the business will likely be set up as a proprietorship or a partnership to avoid double taxation.

The double taxation of corporate income means that corporations must invest their financial capital in projects that offer higher rates of return than partnerships or proprietorships.

The double taxation of corporate income also affects the dividend policies of corporations. Individuals invest in corporations because stocks of-

fer two types of returns: a dividend and a **capital gain.**

A **capital gain** is the increase in the market value of any asset (stocks, bonds, houses, automobiles, art, etc.) above the price originally paid. The capital gain is *realized* when the asset is sold. According to current tax law, a capital gain is short-term if the asset was held less than 6 months and long-term if the asset was held longer than 6 months.

In the United States, realized capital gains are taxed at a much lower rate than other forms of income (wages and salaries, dividends, interest) if the asset is held for more than 6 months (a long-term gain). Currently, the tax on long-term capital gains is only 40 percent of the tax on other forms of income. For example, an investor in the 50 percent tax bracket in ordinary income would pay only $200 tax on a $1,000 capital gain. It is therefore argued that tax rules discourage the payment of dividends by corporations and encourage the plowing back of profits. Tax-reform proposals made by the U.S. Treasury in 1985 call for changing the preferential treatment of capital gains.

If corporate earnings are not distributed as dividends but are plowed back into the company, the earnings of the company should grow (if the

Example 3　The Initial Public Offering of Stock

Privately owned companies can "go public" by publicly selling stock shares to buyers. A privately owned company that has earnings of, say, $10 million in the current year, can offer to sell 50,000 shares to the public, retaining another 50,000 shares for the current owners for a total of 100,000 shares. If the public believes that the earnings of this company will rise in the future, there will be a high price/earnings ratio on the stock. If they expect stable or declining earnings, the price/earnings ratio will be low. If the market establishes a price/earnings ratio of 10, the stock price is $1,000 per share because the earnings per share equal $10 million ÷ 100,000 shares (or $100) times the P/E ratio of 10. The 100,000 shares will sell for $100 million ($1,000 per share times 100,000 shares), and the company will receive $50 million in new capital from the sale of one half (1,000) of the company's shares.

The stock prices and price/earnings ratios of companies that are going public are determined in the *initial public offering (IPO)* market. Large investment firms, called *underwriters,* offer shares of the company to the public at a price the underwriter believes will equate supply and demand.

During the offering period (the period during which the shares are initially offered for sale), the underwriter is prepared to buy shares of stock not purchased by the public at the offering price. After the initial offering, the stock price rises and falls according to supply-and-demand conditions in the markets for second-hand stocks.

The amount of funds that can be raised in the *IPO* market is affected by general stock-market conditions. If stock prices and *PE* ratios are generally high, the public tends to place higher values on stocks than if the stock market is low. Thus, it is easier to raise capital during a booming stock market. Stock prices reached new highs in 1983, and formerly private firms raised $12.4 billion in the IPO market. In the first part of 1984, there was a general retreat in stock prices, and the IPO market reacted in a predictable manner. In the first eight months of 1984, only $2.5 billion of new capital was raised in the IPO market.

The accompanying table lists the leading underwriters of initial public offerings in 1984 (based on IPOs of $5 million or more from January 1 to September 14). ■

	1984 Issues Managed	1984 Volume* (millions of dollars)	1983 Volume* (millions of dollars)
Merrill Lynch**	16	$247	$891
Shearson Lehman/American Express**	13	213	794
First Boston	4	189	99
Morgan Stanley	6	173	378
Drexel Burnham	17	162	226
Goldman, Sachs	7	109	174
Dean Witter Reynolds	10	83	198
Kidder, Peabody	8	62	224
Bear, Stearns	6	61	126
Paine Webber	7	60	139
Alex, Brown & Sons	7	59	374
E.F. Hutton	8	53	664
Hambrecht & Quist	8	51	317
Prudential-Bache Securities	4	46	653
L. F. Rothschild	5	44	545

*Volume is calculated using a method in which equal proportionate credit is given to each co-manager with a double proportionate share going to the lead manager.
**Data for 1983 were determined by consolidating Merrill Lynch volume and issues with those of A. G. Becker. Merrill purchased Becker's corporate finance division in 1983. Same method applied for Shearson Lehman/American Express. Shearson purchased Lehman Brothers Kuhn Loeb Inc. in May.

Source: *Securities Data Company,* Inc.

money is invested wisely), and eventually the market price of the stock should rise. Investors who have held the stock for more than one year could then sell the stock and take a capital gain on which they would pay a relatively small income tax. If the company had, instead, paid out corporate profits as dividends, there would be less investment, the value of the stock would rise more slowly, and the recipient of the dividend payment would have to pay a heavy tax on the dividend.

For these reasons, it is argued that the differential taxation of capital gains encourages reinvestment of corporate earnings and discourages the payment of dividends. Roughly 80 percent of the new funds of U.S. corporations come from reinvested earnings rather than from borrowing or issuing stocks and bonds.

THE FOUR MARKET MODELS

The classification of business enterprises into sole proprietorships, partnerships, and corporations is useful because it tells us who makes the decisions, how risks are shared, and how capital is raised. This classification does not tell us in what type of market the business enterprise is operating. How much competition does it face? How much control does it have over its prices? These are all crucial questions.

To a certain extent, business behavior is determined by the kind of market in which the firm is operating. Economists differentiate between four basic market models: **perfect competition, pure monopoly, monopolistic competition,** and **oligopoly.**

Perfect Competition

Perfect competition has the following features:
1. There is a large number of buyers and sellers in the market.
2. Each buyer and seller has perfect information about prices and product quality.
3. The product being sold is homogeneous; that is, it is not possible (or even worthwhile) to distinguish the product of one firm from that of other firms.

4. There are no barriers to entry into or exit from the market. New firms may enter the market; established firms may leave the market.
5. All firms are *price takers*. No single seller is large enough to exert any control over the product price. Instead, the seller must accept as given the price dictated by the market.

Price taking is the most important feature of perfect competition. The number of sellers is "large" if each individual firm is so small compared to the total market that no single firm can affect the market price by increasing or decreasing production. The firm can sell as much as it likes at the going market price.

In perfectly competitive markets, there are two levels of analysis: one can analyze the behavior of the individual firm as well as the behavior of the market itself. No single firm can affect the market, but all firms together do determine how the market behaves.

Pure Monopoly

Pure monopoly has the following characteristics:
1. The market consists of one producer, the pure monopolist. The industry and the firm are one; there is usually a large number of buyers.
2. The producer sells a product for which there are no close substitutes.
3. The producer is protected from the entry of competitors into the market by barriers to entry.
4. The producer is a *price searcher*. The producer can control the price and, therefore, must select the price that is best for the monopolist.

The first three characteristics explain why the pure monopolist is a price searcher. *Price searching* is the most significant feature of monopoly. The monopolist has competitors in the sense that there are other products that can substitute for the monopolist's product, but these products are not close substitutes. Potential competitors are kept out of the market by barriers to entry. Barriers may be technological (there is only room in the industry for one producer); there may be government restrictions on entry (an exclusive franchise granted by government); or crucial natural resources might be owned by one firm (as in the case of the nickel and diamond industries). As a consequence of these features, the monopolist is in a position to affect the price by increasing or decreasing production.

Monopolistic Competition

Monopolistic competition has the following characteristics:

1. There is a large number of firms in a market that contains many buyers.

2. These firms sell a differentiated product. The product of one firm will be different from the products of the other firms.

3. There is freedom of entry and exit. New firms can enter freely, and established firms can exit.

4. Firms exert a limited degree of control over their price but are still price searchers.

Monopolistic competition combines features of perfect competition and pure monopoly, as the name suggests. The competitive features are the large number of firms and the freedom of entry. The monopolistic features are product differentiation and price searching.

To understand monopolistic competition, one must understand why firms are price searchers but only to a very limited degree. Price searching follows from the fact that each firm produces a differentiated product. The firm can raise its price without losing all its customers because the product's special features develop some product loyalty, but this product loyalty will be weak because of the large number of close substitutes. In the language of elasticities, the monopolistically competitive firm faces a highly elastic demand curve for its product.

The relationship between the firm and market is more complicated in the case of monopolistic competition. Each firm produces a differentiated product; therefore, the market is really not the sum of all these differentiated producers. The definition of the market in the case of monopolistic competition is not obvious.

Oligopoly

Oligopoly has the following characteristics:

1. There are a few *mutually interdependent* sellers in a market that contains many buyers.

2. Producers may produce homogeneous or differentiated products.

3. There are significant barriers to entry into the market.

4. Producers are price searchers.

Mutual interdependence is the most important feature of oligopoly. Firms are mutually interdependent because each firm is aware that its actions affect the other firms in the market and vice versa. If one oligopolist raises price, the sales of the other oligopolists will be affected, and they will react to this price increase. These reactions make oligoply difficult to analyze. The presence of barriers to entry explains why there are only a few producers in the market and why there is mutual interdependence. The sources of barriers to entry are varied and can range from technological obstacles to enormous advertising expenses.

The features of the four basic market models will be discussed in great depth in the following chapters. This chapter considered business organization as the first step in the study of the supply side of product markets. The next chapter will examine the role of production costs in determining product supply.

Summary

1. Business firms allocate the land, labor, and capital resources they own or rent by managerial coordination. Business firms work both through market allocation in their dealings with other firms and consumers and through managerial allocation. An agency relationship exists when one party—the *agent*—acts on behalf of another party—the *principal*. Principal/agent relationships are useful in describing the behavior of business firms. Firms exist because economies of scale, risk, transactions costs, or a need for team production are present.

2. Most economists assume that the goal of business firms is the maximization of profits.

3. The three forms of business organization are the *sole proprietorship* (a business owned by one individual), the *partnership* (a business owned by two or more partners who share in making business decisions), and the *corporation* (a business enterprise owned by stockholders). Although there are more sole proprietorships in the United States than there are partnerships or corporations, corporations (due to their larger average size) account for the bulk of business sales and profits.

4. Corporations can raise capital by selling bonds or issuing more stock. Corporate bonds are IOUs that obligate the corporation to make fixed interest payments and to repay the principal at the date of maturity. The amount of money a corporation can raise will depend upon the price of its stock in the second-hand market for stocks. The stock market helps to allocate capital to various industries and firms.

5. Economists distinguish between four basic market models: *perfect competition* (a market with a large number of buyers and sellers), *pure monopoly* (a market with one seller), *monopolistic competition* (a market with a large number of sellers each of which is a price searcher), and *oligopoly* (a market with a few mutually interdependent sellers).

Key Terms

managerial coordination
principal
agent
economies of scale
profit maximization
natural-selection theory
sole proprietorship
partnership
corporation
common stock
preferred stock
convertible stock
bonds
present value *(PV)*

bankruptcy
price/earnings ratio *(PE)*
capital gain
perfect competition
pure monopoly
monopolistic competition
oligopoly

Questions and Problems

1. You are deciding whether to build a home yourself or whether to have an established building firm build the home. What are the transaction costs of arranging to have the home built without the use of the building company? Under what circumstances would these costs be low enough for you to decide to build the home yourself?

2. Risk bearing is one function served by business firms. What risk does the owner of a new restaurant bear?

3. The statistics on sole proprietorships reveal that they are on average smaller than partnerships and that partnerships are smaller on average than corporations. From what you know about the legal features of business organizations, explain why this is so.

4. In the real world, limited partnerships exist in which the liability of each partner for the debts of the company is limited. Explain why such partnerships may be more attractive than the traditional form of partnership.

5. Explain why corporations can issue bonds that mature in the next century while partnerships and proprietorships can borrow for only short periods of time.

6. Explain why a corporation would be reluctant to issue new shares of stock to raise capital when the price of the stock is at an all-time low.

7. One stock has a price/earnings ratio of 2; a second stock has a price/earnings ratio of 20. The average *PE* ratio is 10. What would be the investment community's best guess as to the course of future profits for each company?

8. You own 100 shares of ZYX corporation, and the management of ZYX corporation allows you to vote on whether stockholders will receive dividends on the stock or whether the management will plow earnings back into the company. How would your tax bracket affect the way you vote?

9. ZYX corporation offers to sell bonds maturing in 20 years at an interest rate of 15 percent. If you buy a $10,000 bond from ZYX, what would be the annual coupon payment? Would you be more likely to buy the bond if you expected interest rates to fall?

10. The 100 shares of ZYX corporation that you purchased two years ago for $10 per share are now selling for $20 per share. If you sell the stock, what is the profit called? How will this profit be taxed?

11. For the following transactions, explain which party is the principal and which is the agent and why:
   a. Smith hires a remodeling company to add a room to her house.
   b. A university buys a computer from IBM.
   c. An engineer signs a contract with Aramco to work for a year in Saudi Arabia.

12. The price of one share of an airline stock is $4. The airline has not made a profit for four years. If share prices reflect corporate profitability, why is the price not zero?

13. Professional football teams take detailed films of each football game so that they can observe the performance of each player on each play. Using the Alchian/Demsetz theory, explain why they are doing this.

14. Boeing Corporation has typically not manufactured its own jet engines. Instead, it buys them on subcontracts from other manufacturers. Using Coase's arguments about why firms exist, explain why Boeing would make this decision.

Suggested Readings

Alchian, Armen and Harold Demsetz. ''Production, Information Costs, and Economic Organization.'' *American Economic Review* 57, 5 (December 1972): 777–95.

Coase, Ronald H. ''The Nature of the Firm.'' *Economica* 4 (1937): 386–405.

Knight, Frank H. *Risk, Uncertainty, and Profit.* New York: Harper Torchbooks, 1957.

28

Costs and Productivity

Chapter Preview

The preceding chapter examined the basic forms of business organization. Once a business firm has chosen its basic organizational form—whether it be single proprietorship, partnership, or corporation—it must get down to the main task of a business firm: making a profit. To make *profit* means that the business firm must earn revenues in excess of costs. Business activities may be complicated (like the production of a huge jet airliner) or simple (like the little girl or boy setting up a lemonade stand to earn money for a new bicycle). To make correct business decisions, the firm must look at both revenues and costs. If either revenue or cost is misunderstood, the firm can make incorrect or poor decisions.

This chapter looks at the cost side of the profit equation; the next several chapters look at the revenue side. Here we ask: What are costs? What costs are important to business decisions? How is productivity related to costs? The answers to these questions form the basis for determining how markets work. ■

Example 1 Why Economic Decisions are Based on Marginal Costs

Economist Thomas Wyrick gives a common-sense example of why economic decisions are based upon the marginal (opportunity) cost of an action. Suppose you are in a supermarket, and the manager announces that in the next five minutes you can buy two bottles of your favorite soft drink for the price of one. You hurry over and buy two bottles for $1 (the normal price of one bottle). When you arrive back at your home, your neighbor, who has unexpected company, comes over and asks to buy from you one bottle. What price would you decide to charge? As far as your costs are concerned, you have purchased 2 bottles for $1, for an average price of $0.50. There are three options: 1) Assume the bottle you are selling your neighbor is the "free" bottle and charge nothing. 2) Charge the average price of $0.50. 3) Charge

$1. An economically rational person would settle on the $1 price. Why? Once you have parted with the bottle, it would cost you $1 to buy another. The two-for-one offer has expired, and you must now pay the regular price. The marginal cost of the action (parting with the bottle of soft drink) is $1. If you part with the bottle for the average cost ($0.50), your wealth would be reduced by $0.50 when you replace the bottle at a $1 price. The moral of this story is that people and businesses make economic decisions on the basis of opportunity costs, not dollar costs. ■

Source: Thomas Wyrick, "Marginal-Cost Policy Making and the Guy Next Door," *Wall Street Journal*, April 12, 1984.

BASIC CONCEPTS

Opportunity Costs

Suppose your rich aunt gives you a brand new sports car, which has a market value of $15,000. She tells you: "This car is yours. You may keep it or sell it. If you sell it, the $15,000 is yours. As long as you keep it, I'll pay for all gas, oil, maintenance, repairs, and even your insurance. The car is yours—free in every way." This is a nice gift. But is the car in fact free? The car would be free if it costs you nothing to *use*. What is the cost of *using* the car?

To an economist the cost of using the car under these conditions may actually be higher than the annual cost of a small car. Suppose that the $15,000 that the car is worth now could be put into a savings account earning 12 percent interest per year to bring in $1,800 per year in interest income. Suppose that using the car for one year will reduce its resale value from $15,000 to $11,000—a cost to you of $4,000. Hence, the total cost to you of using the car for one year is the $4,000 loss of resale value you (not your aunt) must suffer plus the $1,800 of lost interest income. The total yearly *cost* of using the car is

$5,800 (= $1,800 + $4,000).[1] Thus, a "free" car is far from free if the car is used! The lesson is that *costs are not necessarily what has been paid but what has been given up by taking one action rather than another* (see Example 1). **Opportunity cost** is the measure of what has been given up.

The **opportunity cost** of an action is the value of the best forgone alternative.

The concept of opportunity costs was embodied in the production-possibilities frontier studied in Chapter 2. When more of one good (such as tanks) is produced, a certain amount of some other good (such as wheat) must be given up. As the car example shows, an opportunity cost may be an **implicit cost** or an **explicit cost.**

An **explicit cost** (also called an *accounting cost*) is incurred when an actual payment is made.

---

1. This $5,800 can be derived in another way. Keep the car for one year and you can sell it for $11,000. Sell the car now and you receive $15,000 today; in one year the $15,000 will grow to $16,800 at an interest rate of 12 percent. The difference between $16,800 and $11,000 is $5,800, the annual cost of using the car for the first year.

An **implicit cost** is incurred when an alternative is sacrificed but no actual payment appears to be made.

Consider a business firm engaged in the production of some good. To produce the good requires that resources be used. To acquire these resources, prices or payments must be paid to the owners of the resources because the resources have alternative uses. The minimum payments that are just necessary to attract resources into the production of the good are the opportunity costs of production. Some of these payments may be explicit (as money changes hands), and some will be implicit. The manager of the firm must consider the implicit costs (the value of those resources if used elsewhere) of the resources owned by the firm. The hired resources (labor, land, equipment) have explicit costs that must be paid to acquire them.

For example, pharmacist Smith is the owner and operator of Smith's Drugstore. Smith's managerial and pharmaceutical talents might be hired out to a chain drugstore for $2,000 per month; Smith's capital investment in the drugstore may earn $500 per month invested elsewhere. This $2,500 (= $2,000 + $500) is an *implicit* cost of doing business. (Although this $2,500 is a true opportunity cost, no money changes hands.) The explicit (accounting) costs are Smith's rent payments on the building, inventory costs, business taxes, and wage payments to clerks and other pharmacists. These explicit monthly payments add up to $37,000 per month. Smith's total opportunity cost (per month) is the sum of explicit costs ($37,000) and implicit costs ($2,500), or $39,500.

Economic Profits

Economic profits are not the same as **accounting profits.** Economists do not measure profits the same way as accountants do, nor do they use the term *profits* in the way most people do.

Accounting profits equal company revenues minus (explicit) accounting costs.

Accounting profits can give a misleading picture of the firm's well-being. Economic profits

can be used to signal whether or not resources are being directed to their best use.

Economic profits are the excess of revenues over total opportunity costs.

For example, Smith's Drugstore has accounting profits of $3,000 per month (that is, sales = $40,000; accounting costs = $37,000) that must be reported to the Internal Revenue Service. Smith's economic profit, however, is only $500 because accounting costs ignore the implicit costs that must be paid to Smith for using Smith's entrepreneurial talents and funds. This implicit cost is $2,500—the sum of money necessary to persuade the entrepreneur/owner to commit entrepreneurial resources and financial capital to the business. In this case, if accounting profit were below $2,500, the entrepreneur would not enter the business because the entrepreneur would not be earning a normal profit. A **normal profit** is an economic profit of zero.

A **normal profit** is the return that the time and capital of the entrepreneur would earn in the best alternative employment and is earned when total revenues equal total opportunity costs. (Economic profit is earned when total revenues *exceed* total opportunity costs.)

The Average/Marginal Relationship

In economics, the relationship between *average* values or quantities and *marginal* values or quantities comes up again and again. For example, this chapter examines the relationship between average costs and marginal costs. Later chapters will discuss the relationship between average revenues and marginal revenues. There is a common arithmetical background to all average/marginal relationships.

Suppose that you are taking a course in chemistry and that there are eight (equally weighted) examinations. Your performance for the course is determined by your average score on all exams. Table 1 shows how the average score is computed, and Figure 1 graphs both marginal and average scores. On test number 1, you score 80 points; your average is 80. On test number 2, you score only 50; your *total* score is now 130 (= 80

Table 1   Average and Marginal Relationships: Test Scores

Test	Test Score = Marginal Score	Average Test Score	Explanation
0		0	
	80		
1		80	Average and marginal values are the same
	50		
2		65	When the marginal score is below the previous average, the new average falls
	100		
3		76.67	When the marginal score is above the previous average, the new average rises
	70		
4		75	When the marginal score is below the previous average, the new average falls
	60		
5		72	When the marginal score is below the previous average, the new average falls
	50		
6		68.22	When the marginal score is below the previous average, the new average falls
	80		
7		70	When the marginal score is above the previous average, the new average rises
	70		
8		70	When the marginal score equals the previous average, the new average is unchanged

+ 50) and your average falls to 65 (= 130/2). Your average is the total accumulated points scored divided by the number of exams taken.

The marginal score is the increase in the total accumulated points obtained by taking one more exam. Clearly, the marginal score is simply your score on the last examination taken. On the first exam your average and marginal scores are the same: 80. The second exam score is 50, which is below the previous average of 80. What will happen to the new average? *Whenever the marginal value is below the previous average value, the new average will fall.* In this case, the average falls from 80 to 65 because it is *pulled down* by the low marginal test score. The third exam score is 100, well above the 65 average to that point. What will happen to the new average? *When the marginal score is above the previous average test score, the new average will rise.* The average will be *pulled up* by the high marginal score.

Whenever the marginal value exceeds the previous average value, the new average value will rise. Whenever the marginal value is below the previous average value, the new average value will fall.

A second rule is illustrated by the final marginal test score. The average test score of the first seven exams is 70. The eighth exam score is 70. Because the marginal score, thus, *equals* the previous average score, the new average will remain the same because the marginal value will pull the average neither up nor down.

If the marginal value equals the previous average value, the new average will not be changed.

Baseball fans are also familiar with these average/marginal rules. If a batter enters a game with a batting average of 0.250 (25 hits every 100 times at bat) and goes four-for-four on that day, the average will rise because the marginal score is higher than the previous average score. If the player had gone one-for-four on that day, the average score would not have changed because the marginal equals the previous average. If the player had zero hits, the average would have fallen because the marginal was below the previous average.

COST CURVES IN THE SHORT RUN

The Short Run Versus the Long Run

A business firm expands the volume of its output by hiring or using additional resources. Every

Figure 1   Average and Marginal Relationships

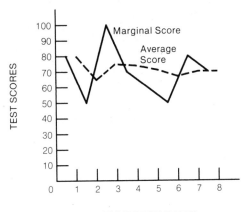

This figure graphs the data on hypothetical test scores given in Table 1. Whenever the marginal score is less than the previous average score, the average score declines. Whenever the marginal score is greater than the previous average score, the average score rises. If the marginal score equals the previous average score, the average score will not change.

good or service is produced by a combination of resources (land, labor, capital, raw materials, entrepreneurial or managerial talent). The package of resources used depends very much on three sets of factors: 1) the productivity of the resources; 2) the prices of the resources; and 3) the time available to the firm for altering output. The first two are important because the business firm will obviously try to keep costs as low as possible. The last is important because time is required to change the level of resource use. Some resources can be adjusted immediately. Other resources require considerable time to change.

A firm can work its existing labor force more intensively simply by asking each employee to work overtime. In this manner, more hours of work can be obtained quickly. The firm may also be able to acquire additional raw materials immediately. But the installation of a new piece of capital equipment or the construction of a new plant may require a significant amount of time. Economists distinguish between the **short run** and the **long run** when considering the time necessary to change input levels.

The **short run** is a period of time so short that the existing plant or equipment cannot be varied; it is fixed in supply. Additional output can be produced only by expanding the variable inputs of labor and raw materials.

The **long run** is a period of time long enough to vary all inputs.

The long run is not a specified amount of calendar time. The long run may be as short as a few months for a fast-food restaurant, a couple of years for a new automobile plant, or a decade or more for an electrical power plant. Generally speaking, engineering complexity determines whether the long run is a matter of weeks or years in actual calendar time.

Fixed and Variable Costs

In the short run, there is a difference between fixed and variable costs. In the short run, some factors (such as plant and equipment) are fixed in supply to the firm; even if the firm wanted to increase or reduce them, it would not be possible in the short run. The costs of these fixed factors are **fixed costs (FC)**. In the short run, greater output is obtained by using more of the *variable inputs* (such as labor and raw materials); the costs of these variable factors are **variable costs (VC)**.

Fixed costs (FC) are those costs that do not vary with output.

Variable costs (VC) are those costs that do vary with output.

In the long run, all costs are variable. Thus, in the long run, fixed costs are *zero*.

Fixed costs and variable costs have different effects on the behavior of the firm in the short run and in the long run. Rational firms should ignore fixed costs in the short run when making decisions because in the short run there is no way to change fixed costs. Fixed costs are not affected by any actions the firm can take in the short run. Only variable costs affect the firm's short-run decisions. If the firm's revenues exceed variable costs in the short run, the firm has something left over to pay part or all of fixed costs. The firm

Table 2   Cost Schedules in the Short Run for a Hypothetical Enterprise

Quantity of Output (units), Q (1)	Variable Cost (dollars), VC (2)	Fixed Cost (dollars), FC (3)	Total Cost (dollars), TC (4) = (2) + (3)	Marginal Cost (dollars), MC (5)	Average Variable Cost (dollars), AVC (6) = (2) ÷ (1)	Average Fixed Cost (dollars), AFC (7) = (3) ÷ (1)	Average Total Cost (dollars), ATC (8) = (6) + (7) = (4) ÷ (1)
0	0	4	4		0	∞	∞
				10			
1	10	4	14		10	4	14
				6			
2	16	4	20		8	2	10
				8			
3	24	4	28		8	1.33	9.33
				10			
4	34	4	38		8.5	1	9.5
				12			
5	46	4	50		9.2	0.8	10
				14			
6	60	4	64		10	0.67	10.67

This is the family of cost schedules for a hypothetical business enterprise operating in the short run with total fixed cost of $4 (column 3). *Fixed cost* does not vary with the level of output (column 1). *Variable cost* (column 2) rises with the level of output. *Total cost* (column 4) is the sum of total fixed cost and total variable cost. *Marginal cost* (column 5) is the increase in total variable cost due to increasing output by one unit. *Average variable* cost (column 6) is total variable cost divided by the number of units produced. *Average fixed cost* (column 7) is total fixed cost divided by the number of units produced. *Average total cost* (column 8) is the sum of average fixed cost and average variable cost.

The following equations show the relationships among the various measures:

$$TC = FC + VC \qquad MC = \Delta TC/\Delta Q = \Delta VC/\Delta Q \qquad ATC = AFC + AVC$$

that can pay fixed cost in addition to variable cost is paying its **total costs (TC)**.

Total costs (TC) are fixed costs plus variable costs:

$$TC = VC + FC.$$

How Costs Behave

Table 2 assembles cost and output information about a hypothetical firm that produces a single product. The costs shown include all opportunity costs (explicit and implicit). The firm is operating in the short run since fixed costs are not zero. For simplicity of illustration, the enterprise is assumed to have fixed costs of only $4 per day, as shown in column (3). This fixed cost is primarily the interest on the firm's capital lease payments and depreciation. When the firm produces 1 unit of output per day, its variable costs are $10. As more output is produced, variable costs must rise

because more inputs, such as labor and raw materials, must be hired or purchased. Column (2) shows the behavior of variable costs. Total costs are shown in column (4), which is simply the sum of columns (2) and (3) for each level of output.

Notice that as output increases, both total cost and variable cost increase by the same amount. In increasing output from 0 units to 1 unit, variable cost increases by $10 from $0 to $10; total cost also increases by $10 from $4 to $14. When 2 units of output are produced, variable cost rises by $6 to $16, and total cost also rises by $6 to $20. The increase in cost associated with producing one more unit of output is called **marginal cost (MC)**.

Marginal cost (MC) is the addition to total cost (or equivalently to variable cost) of producing one more unit of output:

$$MC = \frac{\Delta TC}{\Delta Q} = \frac{\Delta VC}{\Delta Q}.$$

The marginal cost of the first unit of output is $10, the *MC* of the second unit is $6, the *MC* of the third unit is $8, and so on up to the sixth unit of output, where *MC* = $14. Hence, Table 2 assumes that *MC* at first falls and then rises. Marginal cost eventually rises because as the firm increases its output, more variable inputs are being used relative to the fixed inputs. As will be explained later in this chapter, changing the ratio of variable to fixed inputs calls into action the *law of diminishing returns*. The law of diminishing returns explains why marginal cost tends to rise.

Column (6) divides variable costs *(VC)* by output *(Q)* to arrive at **average variable cost** *(AVC)*—that is, variable cost per unit produced. Column (7) divides fixed cost *(FC)* by output *(Q)* to arrive at **average fixed cost** *(AFC)*—that is, fixed cost per unit produced. Notice that average fixed cost declines throughout because the same fixed cost is being spread out over more and more units of output. Finally, column (8) adds average fixed cost and average variable cost to obtain **average total cost** *(ATC)*. Clearly, average total cost can also be obtained by dividing total cost *(TC)* by output *(Q)*.

Average variable cost *(AVC)* is variable cost divided by output:

$$AVC = VC \div Q.$$

Average fixed cost *(AFC)* is fixed cost divided by output:

$$AFC = FC \div Q.$$

Average total cost *(ATC)* is total cost divided by output, or the sum of average variable cost and average fixed cost:

$$ATC = TC \div Q = AVC + AFC.$$

Table 2 (and the graph of the curves in Figure 2) illustrates the relationship between marginal cost and average variable cost or between marginal cost and average total cost. Recall the nature of the average/marginal relationship, explained earlier. When *MC* is below *AVC* (or *ATC*), the margin is pulling down the average. Thus, in increasing output from 1 unit to 2 units, *AVC* falls

Figure 2   The Family of Cost Curves

(a) Total Cost Curves

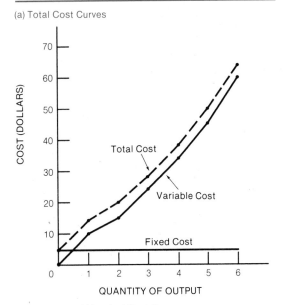

(b) Average and Marginal Cost Curves

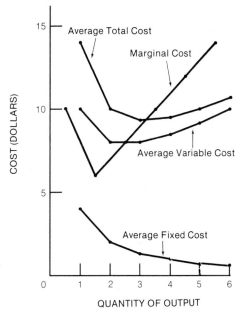

These cost curves are plotted from Table 2. In panel (a), variable cost changes with output; fixed cost does not vary with output. Total cost is the sum of variable cost and fixed cost. In panel (b), marginal cost is the change in total cost that results from producing one more unit of output. Average variable cost is variable cost divided by the number of units produced. Average fixed cost is fixed cost divided by the number of units produced and declines throughout. Average total cost is the sum of average variable cost and average fixed cost.

Figure 3   The Relationship Between Marginal and Average Costs

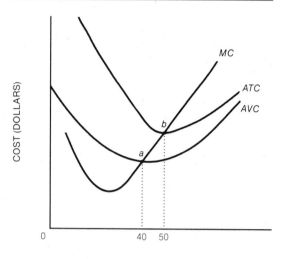

When output is less than 40 units, marginal cost *(MC)* is less than both average variable cost *(AVC)* and average total cost *(ATC)*, pulling both down. When output is between 40 and 50 units, *MC* is above *AVC* and below *ATC*, pulling *AVC* up and pulling *ATC* down. When output is greater than 50 units, *MC* pulls *ATC* up as well. The *ATC* and *AVC* curves get closer together as output increases.

from $10 to $8, and *ATC* falls from $14 to $10. The marginal cost of $6 is below *AVC* and *ATC* and pulls them both down. When output is 2 units, *MC* = *AVC*(at $8); therefore, *AVC* at 3 units of output remains constant at $8. When output is increased from 2 units to 3 units, however, *MC* is still less than *ATC*, so *ATC* falls from $10 to $9.33. When *MC* is above *AVC* or *ATC,* the margin pulls up the average. For example, when output is increased from 3 units to 4 units, both *ATC* and *AVC* rise because the *MC* of $10 exceeds both the $8 AVC and the $9.33 *ATC.*

Figure 2 graphs the cost curves corresponding to the costs given in Table 2. Panel (a) shows total, variable, and fixed costs. Panel (b) shows average total, average variable, average fixed, and marginal costs. Note: This book graphs marginal curves at the *midpoints* between the two values on the horizontal axis. For example, the marginal cost of producing the third unit of output (going from 2 to 3 units of output) is $8. We follow the convention of graphing the marginal cost, $8, halfway between 2 and 3 (at 2.5) on the horizontal axis. In tabular form, the marginal cost figure appears in the row between the output quantities 2 and 3.

Cost curves show the relationship between the level of output and the cost of producing that output. Output is on the horizontal axis, and cost is on the vertical axis. Cost curves show what happens to costs of production as the level of output changes.

Panel (b) of Figure 2 illustrates an important principle: the *MC* curve intersects the *AVC* and *ATC* curves at their minimum points because of the average/marginal rule. At the minimum point, the average value is neither rising nor falling; therefore, the marginal and average values must be equal.

A Graphical Summary

Figure 3 gives an independent summary of the cost curves of another firm. It summarizes the relationship between the marginal-cost curve, the average-variable-cost curve, and the average-total-cost curve. The minimum point on the *AVC* curve occurs at point *a* where output quantity is 40 units; the minimum point on the *ATC* curve occurs at point *b* where output quantity is 50 units. When output is less than 40 units, marginal cost is less than both *AVC* and *ATC*—therefore, both *AVC* and *ATC* are declining. When output equals 40 units, *MC* equals *AVC*, and *MC* is less than *ATC*. Therefore, *ATC* is declining, and *AVC* must be at its minimum. At output levels between 40 units and 50 units, *MC* is below *ATC* and above *AVC*, pulling *ATC* down and *AVC* up. At point *b*, *ATC* hits its minimum value when *MC* equals *ATC*. At output levels greater than 50 units, *MC* exceeds *ATC* and pulls *ATC* up. Notice that minimum *ATC* occurs after the minimum *AVC.*

Since *ATC* = *AVC* + *AFC,* the distance between the *AVC* and *ATC* curves represents *AFC.*

As a given fixed cost is spread over a larger and larger output, *AFC* gets smaller and smaller. Thus, the *AVC* and *ATC* curves get closer together as output rises.

> The marginal-cost curve will intersect the average-variable-cost curve and the average-total-cost curve at their respective minimum values. When marginal cost equals average variable cost, *AVC* will be at its lowest value. When marginal cost equals average total cost, *ATC* will be at its lowest value.

DIMINISHING RETURNS

The behavior of production costs reflects two sets of forces. First, the prices of the land, labor, and capital used in the enterprise are determined by conditions outside the firm (in the markets for those resources). Second, the technology the firm possesses is determined by the ability of the management team to absorb the engineering and technical knowledge relevant to the firm's business. Short-run cost curves can be expected to be *U*-shaped because of a feature common to all technologies: the law of diminishing returns.

Production Functions

To understand the law of diminishing returns, it is necessary to understand what a **production function** is.

> A **production function** summarizes the relationship between labor, capital, and land inputs and the maximum output these inputs can produce.

A production function is something like a recipe. It tells how much output can be produced from a given combination of inputs and tells by how much output will increase if one (or all) input(s) increase(s). A production function can be expressed in mathematical, graphical, or tabular form. The first three columns of Table 3 show a simple production function in tabular form; panel (a) of Figure 4 shows the same production func-

Figure 4   The Short-Run Production Function

(a) Total Product

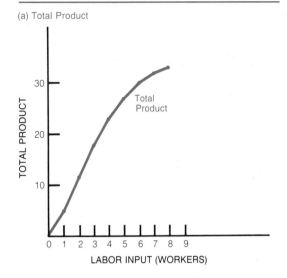

(b) Marginal Physical Product

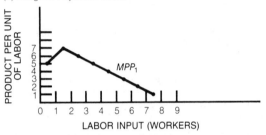

Panel (a) shows the short-run production function, based on columns (1) and (3) of Table 3. Panel (b) shows the marginal physical product curve (MPP_1), based on columns (1) and (4) of Table 3. The law of diminishing returns sets in after the second worker when *MPP* starts to decline.

tion in graphical form. The production function summarizes a production technology that uses two inputs, labor *(L)* and capital *(K)* to produce output *(Q)*.

The production function in Table 3 is a *short-run production function* because at least one factor of production (in this case, capital) is fixed in supply. In this example, capital is fixed at one unit, and labor is the variable input. To keep the example simple, these are the only two inputs.

Table 3   Production Function and the Law of Diminishing Returns

Labor Input (workers), L (1)	Capital Input (fixed at one unit), K (2)	Output (units), Q (3)	Marginal Physical Productivity of Labor (units), MPP_1 (4)	Fixed Cost (dollars), FC_1 (5)	Variable Cost (dollars), VC_1 (6)	Average Total Cost (dollars), ATC_1 $(7) = \dfrac{(5) + (6)}{(3)}$	Marginal Cost (dollars), MC_1 (8)
0	1	0		20	0	∞	
			5				2
1	1	5		20	10	6	
			7				1.43
2	1	12		20	20	3.33	
			6				1.67
3	1	18		20	30	2.78	
			5				2
4	1	23		20	40	2.61	
			4				2.50
5	1	27		20	50	2.59	
			3				3.33
6	1	30		20	60	2.67	
			2				5
7	1	32		20	70	2.81	
			1				10
8	1	33		20	80	3.03	

The *production function* is given in the first three columns. Because the capital input is fixed at one unit, the enterprise is operating in the short run. As the variable input—labor—increases, output increases. The fourth column, marginal physical productivity, shows the increase in output as labor increases by one unit. The *law of diminishing returns* states that as variable inputs are added to a fixed input, a point will be reached beyond which the *MPP* will decline.

Average total cost and *marginal cost* are calculated from the production function. In this example, each unit of labor costs $10 and each unit of capital costs $20. To obtain *ATC,* labor (variable) costs (column 6) and capital (fixed) costs (column 5) are added together and the sum is divided by the quantity of output. Marginal cost is calculated by dividing the increase in labor costs ($10) by the increase in output *(MPP).*

Marginal Physical Product

What will happen to output as labor, the variable input, increases while capital remains fixed depends on the **marginal physical product** *(MPP)* of labor.

> The **marginal physical product** *(MPP)* of a factor of production is the increase in output that results from increasing the input by one unit, holding all other inputs constant.

The *MPP* of labor, for example, is the increase in output brought about by increasing labor by one unit *(MPP = $\Delta Q/\Delta L$).*

In the 19th century English economist David Ricardo noted that agricultural land was essen-

tially fixed in supply. Even though other factors of production, such as labor and capital, could be increased in supply, Ricardo believed the ability of an agrarian economy to expand its output would also be limited. Ricardo felt that as more and more labor and capital inputs—the variable inputs—are combined with land—the fixed input—these variable inputs would yield smaller and smaller *additions* to output.

According to Ricardo, an economy with an expanding population, fixed agricultural land, and variable inputs that become less and less effective would soon reach a stationary state in which the growth of living standards (and of population) would cease. Ricardo's theory is known as the **law of diminishing returns.**

The **law of diminishing returns** states that as ever larger amounts of a variable input are combined with fixed inputs, eventually the marginal physical product of the variable input will decline.

If a variable input (such as labor) is added to a fixed input (such as capital), eventually the fixed input will become overcrowded with the variable input. For example, when workers continue to be added, each additional worker has less fixed capital with which to work, and the marginal physical product of labor begins to decline.

In column (4) of Table 3, or in panel (b) of Figure 4, the marginal physical product of labor rises, reaches a peak, and then begins to fall steadily in conformity with the law of diminishing returns. Clearly, *MPP* is largest (at 7 units) when 2 units of labor are used. *MPP* then declines as labor is increased beyond 2 units of labor. Why does the *MPP* of labor at first tend to rise? The basic reason is that one person working alone cannot effectively work with the available capital. Because two workers can specialize and save the time of passing from one job to another, the *MPP* of the second worker is higher than the first. The one unit of fixed capital could be a small broom factory with two specialized machines for cutting the handles and shaping the straw. When there is only one worker, the first worker must operate both machines, moving back and forth between jobs. With two workers, each could specialize. However, six workers would overcrowd the small plant, so the *MPP* of the sixth worker would be small. (See Example 2 on diminishing returns.)

Costs and Diminishing Returns

The law of diminishing returns and the level of fixed costs determine the shape of the family of short-run cost curves. The production function shows how much output can be produced from different combinations of inputs. The cost of producing output is the cost of the inputs. In our example (Table 3), the fixed factor is capital; the fixed cost is the fixed amount of money the business must pay for this capital. One unit of capital

Figure 5   Productivity and Costs

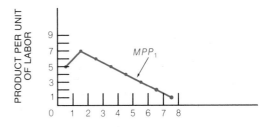

(a) Marginal Physical Product

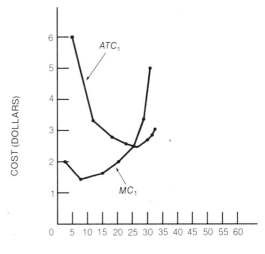

(b) Average and Marginal Costs

The curves shown here are plotted from the data in Table 3. In panel (b), the marginal-cost curve (*MC*₁) is a mirror image of *MPP*₁ in panel (a). As the marginal physical product of labor rises, the marginal cost of output falls, and vice versa.

costs \$20; therefore, *FC* = \$20. Labor is the sole variable factor; therefore, the variable cost *(VC)* will be the labor cost. With each unit of labor costing \$10, the variable cost can be calculated at each level of output. Average total cost is the sum of labor costs and fixed costs, divided by output. For example, the *ATC* of producing 23 units of output is \$2.61—which equals \$40 (the variable labor cost) plus \$20 (the fixed cost) divided by 23. (See Figure 5.)

Figure 6   The Effects of a Change in Plant Size

(a) Marginal Physical Product

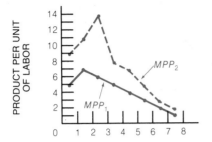

(b) Marginal Cost and Average Total Cost

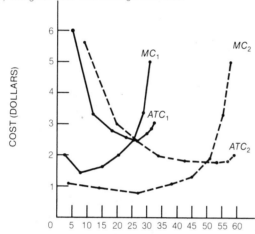

Panel (a) shows that the marginal physical product of labor shifts up from MPP_1 to MPP_2 when the stock of capital increases from one unit to two units (Table 4 contains the data for the production function when two units of capital are used; Table 3 describes the production function when one unit of capital is used). Panel (b) shows the associated shifts in the cost curves resulting from the increase in capital input. The average-total-cost curve shifts to the right from ATC_1 to ATC_2; the marginal-cost curve also shifts to the right from MC_1 to MC_2. The change in plant size represented by the increase in the capital input enables the firm to reach lower unit-cost levels.

Marginal cost is calculated by taking the *increase* in variable cost associated with one more unit of labor (which always equals $10 in this example) and dividing by the *increase* in output (which is the marginal physical product).[2] For example, the second unit of labor raises variable costs by $10 and raises output by 7 units (the *MPP*); the marginal cost is $10/7 units or $1.43. Figure 5 graphs the cost and productivity data of columns (4), (7), and (8) of Table 3.

> When *MPP* is increasing, *MC* is declining; when *MPP* is falling, *MC* is increasing.

When marginal physical product is rising, each additional worker produces a larger addition to output than the previous worker. When each worker is paid the same wage, the addition to cost *(MC)* will decline. When *MPP* is falling, each additional worker produces a smaller addition to output; therefore, the addition to cost *(MC)* will rise. Thus, according to the law of diminishing returns, *MC* will tend to rise in the short run as output is expanded.

> According to the law of diminishing returns, marginal physical product will fall as output expands in the short run. But marginal cost rises when marginal physical product falls. Therefore, according to the law of diminishing returns, marginal cost will rise as output expands in the short run.

LONG-RUN COSTS

The basic characteristic of the long run is that enterprises do not have any fixed costs; all costs are variable. Insofar as fixed costs arise because of fixed factors of production, enterprises have no fixed factors of production in the long run.

In the long run, the business enterprise is free to choose any combination of inputs to produce output. Once long-run decisions are executed (the company completes a new plant, the commercial farming enterprise signs a 10-year lease for addi-

---

2. The formula for calculating marginal cost from *MPP* is: $MC = W/MPP$, where *W* denotes the wage rate.

Table 4   Production Functions and the Average Cost/Marginal Cost Relationship

Labor Input (workers), L (1)	Capital Input (fixed at 2 units), K (2)	Output (units), Q (3)	Marginal Physical Productivity of Labor (units), MPP_2 (4)	Fixed Cost (dollars), FC_2 (5)	Variable Cost (dollars), VC_2 (6)	Average Total Cost (dollars), ATC_2 (7) = [(5) + (6)] ÷ (3)	Marginal Cost (dollars), MC_2 (8)
0	2	0		40	0	∞	
			9				1.11
1	2	9		40	10	5.56	
			11				0.91
2	2	20		40	20	3	
			14				0.71
3	2	34		40	30	2.06	
			8				1.25
4	2	42		40	40	1.91	
			7				1.43
5	2	49		40	50	1.84	
			5				2
6	2	54		40	60	1.85	
			3				3.33
7	2	57		40	70	1.93	
			2				5
8	2	59		40	80	2.03	

This table is constructed like Table 3 but shows what happens when the capital is fixed at 2 units instead of 1.

tional acreage), the enterprise again has fixed factors of production and fixed costs. In the long run, enterprises are free to select the cost-minimizing level of capital, labor, and land inputs. Long-run cost-minimizing decisions are based on the prices the firm must pay for land, labor, and capital.

Shifts in Cost Curves

Returning to the production function in Table 3, consider what happens when the enterprise is free to select any combination of labor and capital inputs, when capital is no longer fixed at one unit of input. Once the enterprise selects a new level of capital input, it is again in the short run, and its capital costs again become fixed costs. To keep the example simple, assume the enterprise can select either one or two units of capital in addition to its choice of labor inputs. The production function with capital fixed at one unit was given in Table 3; the production function with capital fixed at 2 units is given in Table 4. The marginal-physical-product, average-cost, and

marginal-cost schedules from both tables are now graphed in Figure 6.

A different family of short-run cost curves is associated with each of the two amounts of capital input. Because MPP is higher for each level of labor input when there are two units of capital, marginal cost will be lower at each level of output (marginal cost is the mirror image of marginal physical product). What happens to average total cost as capital increases? ATC_2 is the cost curve at 2 units of capital; ATC_1 is the cost curve at 1 unit of capital. The minimum point of the ATC_2 cost curve occurs at a higher level of output than the minimum point of the ATC_1 curve. In effect, the addition of extra capital causes the average-cost and marginal-cost curves to *shift to the right*.

> For every level of fixed input, there is a different short-run cost curve. As the fixed input expands, the short-run cost curve shifts right.

In the long run, enterprises have the option of choosing among the different short-run cost curves by selecting the level of capital input.

Example 2   Is the Law of Diminishing Returns Realistic?

An economic law should be able to predict results with great regularity to deserve to be called a "law." How true is it of modern economies that marginal physical productivity will eventually decline when variable inputs are added in ever-increasing quantities to a fixed input?

1. If the law applies to Iowa corn land, as more variable inputs (fertilizer, corn seed, tractors, farm workers) are applied to a given acre of fertile Iowa corn land, the extra cost of an additional bushel of corn must eventually rise. On average, an acre of Iowa corn land yields more bushels of corn than an acre of Texas corn land. Why is not all corn grown in Iowa? The law of diminishing returns supplies the answer. As more variable inputs are added to Iowa corn land, the *MPP* of these inputs falls. Eventually the *MPP* will fall to the point where it is less than the *MPP* of variable resources on Texas corn land. To grow all corn in Iowa would mean using resources with very low *MPP* relative to alternative uses making it more profitable to grow corn in another state where the *MPP* would be higher.

2. There was a large influx of small foreign cars into the United States after the price of gasoline rose dramatically from 1974 to 1981. The law of diminishing returns helps explain why Americans did not buy American small cars. Even if the American automobile manufacturer had been able to produce a small car of comparable quality to those made in Japan and Germany, existing production facilities for manufacturing small cars were limited. If American manufacturers had attempted to substantially increase their output of small cars, they would have faced a rapidly declining *MPP* of variable inputs (or rising marginal costs of production). Rising costs would have made it difficult, if not impossible, to compete with foreign imports if larger numbers of small cars were produced.

3. The law of diminishing returns is observed on a regular basis in many restaurants. During slack periods, one or two waiters or waitresses can handle all the business more efficiently if part of the dining area is closed off. The fixed inputs are the one or two waitresses; the variable input is the dining room space. During slack times the marginal physical productivity of dining room space is not only declining but is negative—therefore, it pays the restaurant to reduce the amount of space available!   ■

Once the capital input has been selected, they must operate on a new short-run cost curve. If they choose one unit of capital, they will operate on the first set of short-run cost curves in Figure 6. If they choose two units of capital, they will operate on the second set of short-run cost curves.

The Long-Run Cost Curve

There is a different *ATC* curve for each level of fixed input. If there are an infinite number of fixed input levels from which to choose, there would be an infinite number of associated *ATC* curves. Recall that in the long run all costs are variable; therefore, there is no distinction between long-run variable costs and long-run total costs—there is only **long-run average cost (*LRAC*).**

> **Long-run average cost (*LRAC*)** consists of the minimum average cost for each level of output when all factor inputs are variable (and when factor prices are fixed).

In the long run, the enterprise is free to select the most effective combination of factor inputs because none of the inputs is fixed. The long-run cost curve "envelopes" the short-run cost curves, forming a long-run curve that touches each short-run curve *(SRATC)* at only one point, as shown in Figure 7. In the short run, the fact that some factors of production are fixed causes the average-total-cost curve to be *U*-shaped. The law of diminishing returns need not apply to the long run because, in the long run, all inputs are variable.

Why the *LRAC* Curve Is *U*-Shaped

The long-run average-cost curve will also be *U*-shaped for several reasons. Figure 7 depicts the long-run average-cost curve as being *U*-shaped. Why would long-run average costs *(LRAC)* first decline as output expands and then later increase as output expands even further? The reason is that firms experience first economies of scale, then

Figure 7   The Long-Run Average-Cost Curve as the Envelope of the Short-Run Average-Total-Cost Curves

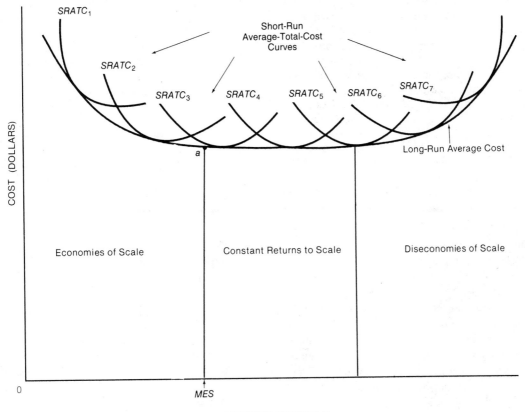

For each level of fixed input, there is a corresponding short-run average-total-cost curve. The long-run average-cost curve is the envelope of the short-run average-total-cost curves. The long-run average-cost curve is *U*-shaped. The declining portion shows economies of scale. The rising portion shows diseconomies of scale. The horizontal portion shows constant returns to scale. Point *a* shows the *LRAC* when the firm is producing at minimum efficient scale.

constant returns to scale, and finally diseconomies of scale as output expands.[3]

Economies of Scale.   The declining portion of the *LRAC* curve is due to economies of scale that arise out of the indivisibility of the inputs of

labor and physical capital goods or equipment. In a large firm, the division of labor will be much more specialized than in a small firm; as Adam Smith observed in his *Wealth of Nations*, workers will be able to specialize in various activities, will increase their productivity or dexterity through experience, and will save much time by "passing from one species of work to another." People are simply indivisible; it is difficult for one person to be one part mechanic, two parts supervisor, and three parts electrician and still remain as efficient

---

3. The following discussion of economies and diseconomies of scale is based on Frederic Scherer, *Industrial Market Structure and Economic Performance*, 3rd ed. (Boston: Houghton Mifflin, 1980), chap. 4.

Example 3   The Do-It-Yourself Car: Economies of Scale

Classic Motor Carriages, a company located in Florida, sells to do-it-yourself hobbyists a kit of automobile parts that can be assembled in your own garage. Not included is the automobile drive-train (which contains the engine and transmission), which the hobbyist can obtain already assembled. Even with the advantage of starting with an assembled drive train, Classic Motor Carriages estimates that it would take a person 200 hours to assemble the car. To get some idea of the advantages of specialization and large-scale production, consider General Motors' assembly plant in Tarrytown, New York. The plant employs 2,000 workers per 8-hour shift and turns out approxi-

mately one car per minute (about 500 cars per day). Dividing 500 cars by the 2,000 workers yields one car for every four workers—or, equivalently, one-fourth of a car per worker per day. Under conditions of specialization, large capital use, and mass production, the average worker produces one complete car every four days. The difference between 4 days (or 32 hours) per worker and 200 hours per worker illustrates in dramatic fashion the notion of economies of large-scale production. ∎

Sources: Roger W. Shmenner, *Production/Operations Management: Concepts and Situations* (Chicago: SRA, Inc., 1981), chap. 5, and the author.

as one who specializes in just one of these tasks. The classic example of worker specialization is the assembly line of an automobile plant. The same principles apply to machines. A small firm might have to use general-purpose machine tools whereas a large firm might be able to build special equipment or machines that will substantially lower costs when large quantities are produced. Small-scale versions of certain specialized machines simply cannot be made available.

Economies of scale can occur because of the greater productivity of specialization in any of a variety of areas, including technological equipment, marketing, research and development, and management. The optimal rate of utilization for some types of machinery may occur at high rates of output. Some workers may not be able to perfect specialized skills until a high rate of output allows them to concentrate on specific tasks. As the output of an enterprise increases with all inputs variable, average costs will decline because of the **economies of scale** associated with increased specialization of labor, management, plant, and equipment. (See Example 3.)

> **Economies of scale** are present when a given percentage change in inputs leads to larger percentage change in output.

Constant Returns to Scale.   Economies of scale will become exhausted at some point when expanding output no longer increases productiv-

ity. The evidence suggests that for a large range of outputs there will be **constant returns to scale,** where the average costs of production remain constant.

> **Constant returns to scale** are present when a given percent change in inputs results in the same percent change in output.

Diseconomies of Scale.   As the enterprise continues to expand its output, eventually all the economies of large-scale production will be exploited, and long-run average costs will begin to rise. The rise in long-run average costs as the capital stock of the enterprise expands is the result of **diseconomies of scale.**

> **Diseconomies of scale** are present when a given percentage change in inputs leads to a smaller percentage change in output.

Diseconomies of scale can be caused by a series of factors. As the firm continues to expand, management skills must be spread over a larger and larger firm. Managers must assume additional responsibility, and managerial talents may eventually be spread so thin that the efficiency of management declines. The problem of maintaining communications within a large firm grows, and red tape and cumbersome bureaucracy become commonplace. Large firms may find it difficult to correct their mistakes. Employees of large firms may lose their identity and feel that their contributions to the firm are not recognized. As the out-

Example 4   The Cost Curves of American Dairy Farms

The accompanying figure shows actual short-run cost curves of American dairy farms ranging from large-scale farms (more than $40,000 sales annually) to small-scale farms (less than $2,500 sales annually), with figures derived from the 1964 census of agriculture. The actual short-run cost curves show that the short-run average-total-cost curves shift downward and to the right as the scale of output increases. Economies of scale are experienced up to approximately 500,000 pounds of output, but the minimum point on the next average-total-cost curve (that of the largest class of dairy farm) yields virtually the same average total cost at 1.2 million pounds per year as at 500,000 pounds per year. Over the output range from 500,000 to 1.2 million pounds, returns to scale in dairy farming appear to be constant.

The long-run average-cost curve of dairy farming could be drawn as the envelope of the short-run average-cost curves and would show a pattern of economies of scale up to 500,000 pounds, after which the LRAC curve would become flat.

The ATC curves are numbered to correspond to firms whose annual sales are: 1) under $2,500, 2) $2,500–$4,999, 3) $5,000–$9,999, 4) $10,000–$19,000, 5) $20,000–$39,999, and 6) more than $40,000. ■

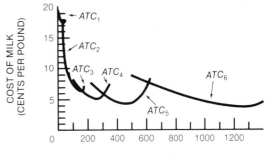

QUANTITY OF MILK
(THOUSANDS OF POUNDS PER YEAR)

Source: Leonard Weiss, *Case Studies of American Industry*, 2nd ed. (New York: John Wiley & Sons, 1971), p. 76.

---

put of an enterprise continues to increase average cost will eventually rise because of the diseconomies of scale associated with the growing problems of managerial coordination.

Minimum Efficient Scale

Cost and productivity schedules help explain a wide variety of real-world phenomena, such as why some companies are more profitable than others, why some industries are more concentrated than others, or why a particular company is doing well or poorly. Actual short-run and long-run cost curves for the dairy industry, for example, show the pattern of returns to scale in dairy farming (see Example 4).

Figure 7 shows a fairly typical long-run average-cost curve. Notice that the bottom portion is flat over a fairly large range. Empirical studies for a number of industries suggest that constant returns occur over a fairly sugnificant range of output. The output level associated with point *a* is called the **minimum efficient scale** *(MES)* of the firm.

The **minimum efficient scale** *(MES)* is the lowest level of output at which average costs are minimized.

In the real world, economies of scale differ substantially among industries. Some industries experience economies of scale up to output levels that are a high proportion of total industry sales. These industries tend to have a small number of firms. Economies of scale are an important explanation of the degree of concentration in different industries.

Empirical studies of economies of scale show that some industries (electricity, automobiles) have significant economies of scale.[4] Other industries, such as airlines, do not have any significant economies of scale. Table 5 reports the results of two studies of selected industries that show that

---

4. Some techniques for measuring economies of scale are discussed in William G. Shepherd, *The Economics of Industrial Organization* (Englewood Cliffs, N.J.: Prentice-Hall, 1979), chap. 12 and James V. Koch, *Industrial Organization and Prices*, 2nd ed. (Englewood Cliffs, N.J.: Prentice-Hall, 1980), chap. 6.

Table 5   Estimates of the Minimum Efficient Scale (MES) In U.S. Industries, 1967

Industry (1)	Minimum Efficient Scale (MES) (2)	MES as a Percentage of U.S. Demand (3)
Diesel engines	not available	21–30
Electronic computers	not available	15.0
Refrigerators	800,000 units per year	14.1
Cigarettes	36 billion cigarettes per year	6.6
Beer brewing	4.5 million barrels per year	3.4
Bicycles	not available	2.1
Petroleum refining	200,000 barrels per day	1.9
Paints	10 million U.S. gallons per year	1.4
Flour mills	not available	0.7
Bread baking	not available	0.3
Shoes (nonrubber)	1 million pairs per year	0.2

Sources: F. M. Scherer, Alan Beckenstein, Erich Kaufer and R. D. Murphy, *The Economics of Multiplant Operation* (Cambridge, Mass.: Harvard University Press, 1975), pp. 80–94. Leonard W. Weiss, "Optimal Plant Size and the Extent of Suboptimal Capacity," in eds. Robert T. Masson and P. D. Qualls, *Essays on Industrial Organization in Honor of Joe S. Bain* (Cambridge, Mass.: Ballinger, 1975), pp. 128–31; adapted in part from C. F. Pratten, *Economies of Scale in Manufacturing Industry* (Cambridge, England: Cambridge University Press, 1971).

the minimum efficient firm size is as high as 21–30 percent of sales in the case of diesel engines and as low as only 0.2 percent in the case of shoe sales.

This chapter examined how production costs behave in the short run and in long run. The next chapter will study how perfectly competitive firms use these costs to determine their output level.

Summary

1.   The opportunity cost of an action is the value of the best forgone alternative. Economic profit is defined as total revenue minus opportunity costs. When economic profits are zero, the firm is still earning a normal profit. The average of a series of values falls when the marginal value is below the previous average value; the average stays constant when the marginal value equals the previous average; the average rises when the marginal value exceeds the previous average.

2.   In the short run, the time period is so short that existing plant and equipment cannot be varied; in the long run, all inputs are variable. Variable costs are those costs that vary with output; fixed costs do not vary with output. In the long run, all costs are variable. Marginal cost is the increase in cost associated with increasing output by one unit. Average variable cost *(AVC)* is variable cost divided by output; average total cost *(ATC)* is total (fixed plus variable) cost divided by output. The average-variable-cost and average-total-cost curves tend to be *U*-shaped with the *MC* intersecting *AVC* and *ATC* at their minimum values.

3.   Marginal physical product is the increase in output due to increasing an input by one unit, holding all other inputs constant. The law of diminishing returns states that as one input is increased (holding other inputs constant), the marginal physical product of the variable input will eventually decline. If labor were the only variable input, marginal cost in the short run would be the wage rate divided by the marginal product of labor. The law of diminishing returns explains why marginal cost tends to rise as output expands.

4.   In the long run, there are different-sized plants. Associated with each sized plant is a particular short-run average-total-cost curve. The envelope of all such short-run average-total-cost curves is the *long-run average-cost curve*. The long-run average-cost curve gives the minimum unit cost of producing any given volume of output. Along the long-run average-cost curve the firm is choosing the least-cost combination of

inputs. Increasing returns to scale prevail when increasing all inputs by the same percentage increases output by a greater percentage; the long-run average-cost curve is declining. Constant returns to scale prevail when increasing all inputs by the same percentage increases output by that percentage; the long-run average-cost curve is constant or horizontal. Decreasing returns to scale prevail when increasing all inputs by the same percentage increases output by a smaller percentage; the long-run average-cost curve is rising. A firm's minimum efficient scale *(MES)* is the lowest level of output at which average costs are minimized.

Key Terms

opportunity cost
explicit cost
implicit cost
accounting profits
economic profits
normal profit
short run
long run
fixed costs *(FC)*
variable costs *(VC)*
total costs *(TC)*
marginal cost *(MC)*
average variable cost *(AVC)*
average fixed cost *(AFC)*
average total cost *(ATC)*
production function
marginal physical product *(MPP)*
law of diminishing returns
long-run average cost *(LRAC)*
economies of scale
constant returns to scale
diseconomies of scale
minimum efficient scale *(MES)*

Questions and Problems

1. Your bank advertises a no-service-charge checking account for customers who keep a minimum of $100 in their account. Is this truly a ''free'' checking account?

2. Explain the distinction between accounting profits and economic profits. Why are economic profits a better guide to resource-allocation decisions?

3. Contrast the *ATC* curve of a firm that has very large fixed costs relative to variable costs with the *ATC* curve of a firm that has very small fixed costs relative to variable costs.

4. Explain why fixed costs should not affect business decisions in the short run.

5. Answer the following questions using the production-function information in Table A and assuming that one unit of labor costs $5 and one unit of capital costs $10.

Table A

Labor (units)	Capital (units)	Output (units)
0	2	0
1	2	5
2	2	15
3	2	20
4	2	23
5	2	24

a. Derive the *MPP* schedule. Does it obey the law of diminishing returns?
b. Derive the short-run cost schedules.
c. Derive the *MPP* and short-run cost schedules if labor productivity doubles (with one labor unit, for example, being used to produce an output of 10 units instead of 5 units).
d. Explain why the short-run cost curves would shift if the amount of capital input changed.

6. If the previous average total cost is $25, and marginal cost is $15, what will happen to the new average total cost? To the new average variable cost? If *ATC* stays at $25 and *MC* increases to $25, what will happen to the next *ATC?*

7. Suppose $FC = \$25$, $VC = Q^2$, and $MC = 2Q$. Draw the *AFC, AVC, MC,* and *ATC* curves. Where does the minimum *ATC* occur?

8. What is the role of the law of diminishing returns in explaining the shape of the cost curves? Construct a numerical example.

9. If *MC* falls, what can be said about *ATC* or *AVC?*

10. What is the opportunity cost of a worker to a firm that mistakenly pays the worker $40 an hour instead of the worker's wage of $25 an hour?

11. Industry A with $10 million in sales is comprised of three equal-sized large firms. Industry B, also having $10 million in sales, is made up of 50 equal-sized firms. From this information, make rough sketches of the long-run average-cost curve of a typical firm in each industry. Also make predictions about *MES* at a given percentage of industry output in both cases.

12. The *MPP* of the third worker is 100 units of output per week. The *MPP* of the fifth worker is 50 units of output per week. Each worker is paid $25 per week, and labor is the only variable input. What is the marginal cost associated with the output of the third worker? What is the marginal cost associated with the output of the fifth worker?

13. Using Table B, plot all the short-run cost curves given in this chapter. Do the cost curves have the expected shapes? Explain your answer.

Table B

Output (units)	Fixed Costs (dollars)	Variable Costs (dollars)
1	10	5
2	10	8
3	10	12
4	10	20
5	10	40

14. A firm's accounting costs are $15,000 per month. In addition, the firm's implicit opportunity costs are $5,000. What are the firm's total opportunity costs? How much revenue must be earned for a normal profit to be earned? If revenue were $17,000, how much profit would the firm earn?

Suggested Readings

Kohler, Heinz. *Intermediate Microeconomics: Theory and Applications,* 2nd ed. Glenview, Ill.: Scott, Foresman, 1986.

Scherer, Frederick. *Industrial Market Structure and Economic Performance,* 3rd ed. Boston: Houghton Mifflin, 1980, chap. 4.

28A

The Least-Cost Method of Production

Appendix Preview

How should a firm go about choosing the right combination of resources? The correct answer is: the firm should choose the *least-cost method* of production. This appendix will show how firms determine the level of output that uses the least costly combination of resources.

Recall that a production function shows the maximum output that can be achieved by a given combination of inputs. Figure 1 shows a hypothetical firm that employs only two factors—capital and labor—to produce its output. The horizontal edge measures the labor input from 1 to 8 workers; the vertical edge measures the capital in-put from 1 to 8 machines. The amount of output that can be produced from any combination of labor and capital is shown in the cells corresponding to the intersection of a row of capital input and column of labor input. For example, 8 machines and 1 worker produce 50 units of output; 8 machines and 2 workers produce 71 units of output. Thus, the production function shown in Figure 1 gives the possible methods of producing the outputs shown at each intersection.

Figure 1 illustrates the concept of marginal physical product, the law of diminishing returns, and the principle of substitution. ∎

Figure 1   The Production Function

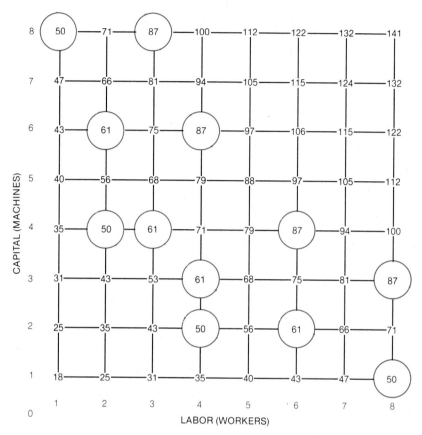

Capital inputs are measured vertically; labor inputs are measured horizontally. The number at the intersection of a row and column shows the output for that level of capital and labor input. For example: 4 machines and 2 workers produce 50 units of output. The law of diminishing returns can also be seen because when the input of machines is held constant at 4 units, additional units of labor bring about smaller additions to output; thus, along a given row output *increases* but at a *decreasing* rate.

THE PRODUCTION FUNCTION

Marginal Physical Product

Recall that the marginal physical product *(MPP)* of a factor is the extra output associated with increasing input of the factor by one unit, holding all other factors constant. Suppose that the amount of capital is held constant at 4 machines. With 1 worker, output is 35 units; with 2 workers, output is 50 units; and so on. Clearly the marginal product of labor is 35 for the first

worker and 15 for the second worker (since output rises from 35 to 50). The *MPP* of labor can be read in the figure by simply noting the difference between consecutive outputs along a given row. By similar reasoning, the marginal product of capital could be determined by varying the machine input, holding labor constant.

The Law of Diminishing Returns

According to the law of diminishing returns, the marginal physical product of a factor eventually declines as more of the factor is used while holding all other productive inputs constant. In Figure 1, when capital equals 4 machines, the *MPP* of the second worker is 15 and the *MPP* for the third worker is only 11.

The production function summarized in Figure 1 assumes constant returns to scale. When there are 3 units of capital and 3 units of labor, output is 53 units; when inputs double to 6 units of capital and 6 units of labor, output doubles to 106 units. When there are 3 units of capital and 3 units of labor, the fourth unit of labor has an *MPP* of 8 units as output rises from 53 to 61. When there are 4 units of capital and 4 units of labor, the fifth unit of labor also has an *MPP* of 8 units as output rises from 71 to 79. Thus, *the marginal physical product of labor remains the same as long as the ratio of capital to labor remains the same.* The source of the law of diminishing returns is the varying ratio of workers to machines.

The Principle of Substitution

Figure 1 also illustrates the principle of substitution. In Figure 1, 50 units of output can be produced by four different combinations of capital and labor. These combinations are listed in columns (2) and (3) of Table 1.

The production function alone cannot tell us how to produce the 50 units of output. From the information so far provided, there is no reason for choosing the combination of 8 units of capital/1 unit of labor over the combination of 1 unit of capital/8 units of labor to produce 50 units of output.

LEAST-COST PRODUCTION

The price of labor (P_L) and the price of capital (P_C) help us determine what combination of capital and labor the firm will use. Suppose $P_L =$ $50 per worker and $P_C =$ $25 per machine. Column (4) of Table 1 shows the costs of each combination of labor and capital that yields 50 units of output. For example: Combination *a* costs $250 because 8 machines cost $200 ($= 8 \times$ $25) and 1 worker costs $50. From Table 1 we can determine that the minimum cost combination is combination *b*—4 units of capital and 2 units of

Table 1   Factor Combinations for Producing 50 Units of Output

	Output (units), Q (1)	Capital (machines), C (2)	Labor (workers), L (3)	Total Cost (dollars), TC (4)
a	50	8	1	250
b	50	4	2	200
c	50	2	4	250
d	50	1	8	425

Note: The price of capital is $25 per machine; the price of labor is $50 per workers.

labor, the total cost *(TC)* of which is $200. The average total cost of production is $ATC = TC/Q =$ $200/50 = $4 per unit, which is the lowest possible cost per unit when total output is 50 units.

In moving from combination *a* to combination *b*, an extra unit of labor can be substituted for 4 machines without a loss of output. Labor costs $50; but 4 machines cost $100. Thus, the firm saves $100 in machine costs by substituting 1 worker for 4 machines and spends $50 on the added worker for a net gain of $50 (without a loss in output). Clearly, it pays the firm to select *b* over *a*.

The Equal-Output Curve

The above principles of least-cost production can be illustrated using graphs. Figure 2 plots combinations *a, b, c,* and *d* from Table 1 and connects these points by a smooth curve. The curve *abcd* shows all the combinations of capital and labor input that produce 50 units of output; hence, it can be called the **equal-output curve** for 50 units of output.

An **equal-output curve** shows the various combinations of two inputs (such as labor and capital) that produce the same output.

The equal-output curve is very similar to the indifference curves studied in the appendix to the chapter on demand and utility. Just as the indifference curves were convex to the origin, so an equal-output curve is convex to the origin. The

Figure 2   The Equal-Output Curve

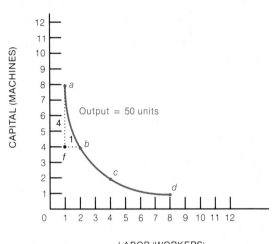

The equal-output curve shows all the combinations of labor (number of workers) and capital (number of machines) that produce the same 50 units of output. It is bowed toward the origin because the law of diminishing returns dictates that substituting capital for labor becomes more difficult as the ratio of workers to machines increases.

ratio of the line segment *af* to *fb* is the amount of capital that is substituted for the extra unit of labor. The slope of the curve between *a* and *b* demonstrates that the marginal physical product of labor is 4 times the marginal physical product of capital because the vertical distance *af* is 4 times the horizontal distance *fb*. The ratio of the marginal physical products measures the marginal rate of substitution, or the rate at which labor can be substituted for capital, and equals the slope (in absolute value) of an equal-output curve between two points or the absolute slope of the tangent to any point on the equal-output curve.

The Marginal Rate of Substitution of Capital for Labor

$$= \frac{\text{Marginal Physical Product of Labor}}{\text{Marginal Physical Product of Capital}}$$

$$= \text{the (absolute) slope of the equal-output curve}$$

The equal-output curve is bowed toward the origin because when workers are substituted for machines, the *MPP* of labor falls relative to the *MPP* of capital; to keep output constant one worker will not substitute for as many machines as the number of workers increases.

Equal-Cost Lines

Assuming that the price of labor (P_L) is \$50 per worker and the price of capital (P_C) is \$25 per machine, the total cost *(TC)* of production is:

$$TC = (P_L \times L) + (P_C \times C) = \$50L + \$25C$$

where L = the number of workers and C = the number of machines. In Figure 3, the line $TC = \$300$ consists of all the combinations of labor and capital that cost \$300. For example, if $C = 12$ and $L = 0$, $TC = \$300$; if $C = 0$ and $L = 6$, $TC = \$300$; the combination 6 machines and 3 workers also costs \$300. Thus, line TC is the **equal-cost line** for costs of \$300.

The **equal-cost line** shows all the combinations of labor and capital that have the same total costs.

Figure 3 gives three illustrative equal-cost lines, but there is one for every level of total costs. These equal-cost lines are parallel because each has the same slope. The absolute slope of any equal-cost line is simply P_L/P_C. In the present case, the (absolute) slope is 2 since the price of a unit of labor is twice that of a unit of capital. If a unit of labor costs twice as much as a unit of capital, 2 units of capital can be substituted for a unit of labor without increasing or decreasing total costs.

The (absolute) slope of the equal-cost line is the price of labor divided by the price of capital, which represents the rate at which firms can substitute labor for capital without affecting total costs.

Figure 3   Equal-Cost Curves

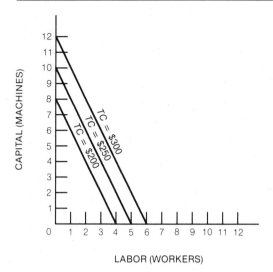

The equal-cost lines show all the combinations of labor and capital that cost the same amount. The line for *TC* = $300 shows all the combinations costing $300. The slope of each equal-cost line is measured by the ratio of the price of labor to the price of capital; in this case, labor is $50 per worker and capital is $25 per machine, so each equal-cost line has an absolute slope of 2.

Figure 4   The Least-Cost Rule

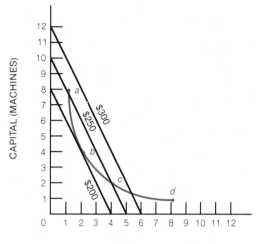

The least-cost method of producing 50 units of output can be found at the point where the equal-output curve, *abcd*, touches the lowest equal-cost line, *TC* = $200. At point *b*, the slope of the equal-output curve equals the slope of the equal-cost line. At point *b*, the two curves are tangent; here the ratio of the marginal physical product of labor to that of capital equals the ratio of the price of labor to the price of capital.

THE LEAST-COST RULE

Figure 4 shows how the firm minimizes the cost of producing a given volume of output (in this case, output is 50 units). When the equal-output curve for 50 units of output and the equal-cost lines for three representative cost levels are drawn on the same graph, one can determine the least-cost combination by observing where the equal-output line *abcd* intersects the *lowest* equal-cost line (at point *b*). The lowest equal-cost line that curve *abcd* can reach is *TC* = $200. All other combinations of labor and capital on *abcd* cost more than $200. Thus, point *b* is the least-cost production point. According to the **least-cost rule,** *b* is the best combination of labor and capital (4 machines and 2 workers) for producing 50 units of output.

In Figure 4, it is obvious that the slope of the equal-output curve is the same as the slope of the

equal-cost line since both are tangent (they touch without crossing) at that point. Thus,

$$\frac{MPP_L}{MPP_C} = \frac{P_L}{P_C}. \qquad (1)$$

Using a little algebra, the least-cost rule can be rewritten in a second equivalent way:

$$\frac{MPP_L}{P_L} = \frac{MPP_C}{P_C}. \qquad (2)$$

In other words, least-cost production requires that the extra output from the last dollar spent on labor must equal the extra output from the last dollar spent on capital. A third way of writing the least-cost rule [by taking the reciprocals of equation (2)] is

$$\frac{P_L}{MPP_L} = \frac{P_C}{MPP_C}. \qquad (3)$$

Table 2   Productivity and Costs

Capital (machines), C (1)	Labor (workers), L (2)	Marginal Physical Product of Labor (units), MPP_L (3)	Output (units), Q (4)	Marginal Cost (dollars), MC (5)	Fixed Cost (dollars), FC (6)	Variable Cost (dollars), VC (7)	Total Cost (dollars), TC (8)	Average Total Cost (dollars), ATC (9)
4	0		0		0	0	0	0
		35		1.43				
4	1		35		100	50	150	4.29
		15		3.33				
4	2		50		100	100	200	4.00
		11		4.54				
4	3		61		100	150	250	4.10
		10		5.00				
4	4		71		100	200	300	4.23
		8		6.25				
4	5		79		100	250	350	4.43

Note: The price of labor is $50 per worker; the price of capital is $25 per machine.

The **least-cost rule** is that the least-cost combination of two factors can be found at the point where a given equal-output curve is tangent to the lowest equal-cost line.

The price of labor divided by the *MPP* of labor is labor cost per unit of output, which is nothing but the marginal cost of output using labor (recall that marginal cost is the extra cost of producing one more unit of output). Similarly, the price of capital divided by the *MPP* of capital is the marginal cost of production using capital. According to the third equation, least-cost production (in the long run) requires using capital and labor in such a way that the marginal cost of production is the same whether output is increased using capital or using labor. If these two weren't equal, one would be substituted for the other.

When $P_L/MPP_L = P_C/MPP_C$, the long-run marginal cost of production is the common ratio.

The Link Between the Short Run and the Long Run

The long run is a period of time so long that both workers and machines can be varied. In the short run, the number of machines is fixed. If it takes time to find the right machine, install it, and train workers to use it properly, fixed costs would be the machine costs; variable costs would be the labor costs. In the short run, marginal cost would be the ratio P_L/MPP_L. As shown in Table 2, the number of machines is fixed at 4 in the short run, and the number of workers can be varied from 0 to 5. The first four columns of Table 2 can be derived from Figure 1. Column (5) of Table 2 is the short-run marginal cost. Columns (6) through (9) show the short-run costs of production. Column (9) illustrates the average total cost *(ATC)* of production. Note that *ATC* hits its minimum at an output of 50 units where *ATC* = $4.00.

Applying the Least-Cost Rule

What would the firm do if the price of capital rises from $25 per machine to $100 per machine, while the price of labor remains the same at $50 per worker? The firm, of course, would begin to substitute the now cheaper labor for the now more expensive machinery. The price of capital is now twice as great as the price of labor, so the slope of the new equal-cost lines is ½ instead of 2. Figure 5 shows what happens. The old *TC* line was *mn*—with the minimum-cost point *b*. The new minimum *TC* line is *m'n'*, which is tangent to point *c* on the equal-output curve. The total cost of production is now $400 (4 units of capital now costs $400 and 8 units of labor costs $400). Since

Figure 5   A Change in Factor Price

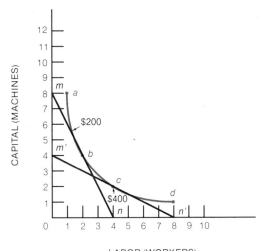

LABOR (WORKERS)

The equal-cost line *mn* shows the minimum cost of producing 50 units of output when capital is $25 per machine and labor is $50 per worker. (Line *mn* is the same as *TC* = $200.) If the price of capital rises to $100 per machine, the equal-cost line *m'n'* shows that the lowest cost of producing 50 units of output rises to $400 and the least-cost combination of capital and labor shifts from point *b* to point *c* as cheaper labor is substituted for machines.

50 units are still produced, the average cost of production is now $8 (= $400/50). Before capital quadrupled in price the average cost was $4. Quadrupling the price of capital causes the average cost of production to double. The optimal ratio of machines to workers is now 2 machines per 4 workers, or ½ machine per worker. The production process has now become less capital-intensive and more labor-intensive.

Summary

1. An equal-output curve shows all the combinations of two factors that will produce a given level of output.
2. An equal-cost line shows all the combinations of two factors that have the same total costs.
3. The least-cost combination of two factors can be found at the point where the equal-output curve intersects the lowest equal-cost line.

Key Terms

equal-output curve
equal-cost line
least-cost rule

Questions and Problems

1. Why is an equal-output curve convex to the origin? Why is it downward-sloping?

2. What should be the cost objective of the firm?

3. Show that raising the price of capital relative to capital will lead a firm to choose more labor-intensive techniques of production.

29

Perfect Competition

Chapter Preview

Adam Smith concluded that the "invisible hand" would lead people pursuing their own interests to serve the interest of society through the process of *competition*. Competition among the various actors on the economic stage channels the narrow and sometimes selfish interest of each person in a socially desirable direction. How this remarkable mechanism works is the subject of this chapter.

This chapter will describe how a firm facing perfect competition will make its profit-maximizing decisions in both the short run and the long run, how market prices are determined in both the short run and the long run, and how producers and consumers benefit from trading in a competitive market.

In a world of scarcity, available resources are not adequate to satisfy everyone's wants. Competition for scarce resources is a necessary and unavoidable characteristic of any economy. One may dislike competition, but there is no way to avoid it. Competition can take a variety of forms. A free-for-all system of catch-as-catch-can or steal-as-much-as-one-can is one possible scheme. In such a system, there are no property rights and each person can have whatever he or she can find. It does not take much imagination to see that such a system would not work well. Another arrangement—deplored by Adam Smith—is to grant certain people special privileges *(monopolies)* to use particular scarce resources. Another system is to allow people to buy and sell property rights in all sorts of things *freely* with property rights protected by the state. If property rights were not protected by law, no person would have an incentive to buy or produce property. Why produce something if somebody else can take it? ∎

THE MEANING OF COMPETITION FOR THE FIRM AND THE MARKET

Individuals endowed with property rights will compete for different things. Buyers will compete with other buyers; sellers will compete with other sellers. Economists distinguish between **perfect competition** and **imperfect competition.**

Perfect competition between buyers or sellers exists if no single buyer or seller has a perceptible influence on the market price of the good.

Imperfect competition exists if a single buyer or seller can influence the price. The less competition there is among sellers (or buyers), the more power each individual seller (or buyer) exercises over price.

Note: we will assume in this and in the following four chapters that buyers have no control over the prices they pay. This assumption holds generally for households but is less true for big businesses that buy from other businesses.

In the real world, almost every seller exercises some influence over price, but the more competition the seller faces the less control the individual sellers can exercise over the prices charged. In the limiting case, the seller has absolutely no control over price. Each individual seller faces so much competition from other sellers that the market price is taken as a given. When the price is given to the individual seller by the market, the seller is said to be a **price taker.**

A **price taker** is a seller that does not have the ability to control the price of the good it sells.

The five characteristics of perfect competition are: 1) the number of sellers and buyers is large; 2) the product is homogeneous; 3) each buyer and seller has perfect information about prices and product quality; 4) there is freedom of entry into and exit from the industry; 5) each seller is a price taker.

In perfect competition, all firms in the industry sell a homogeneous or identical product. No firm exercises an advantage over other firms in terms of quality, location, or other product features. If Firm A charges a higher price than Firm B for the identical product, no rational buyer will buy from A. In a perfectly competitive market, buyers have perfect information about the prices charged by different sellers. Every buyer knows that Firm B's price is lower than Firm A's price.

The difference between the perfectly competitive firm and the market (or the industry as a whole) is illustrated in Figure 1. Panel (b) shows the market demand curve, *D,* for the product. When the market price is $7, the quantity demanded in the market is 10,000 units. The individual firm, shown in panel (a), can sell all it wants (from a practical standpoint) at the going market price of $7. Whether the firm sells 3 units or 10 units, the price is still the $7 market price. (See Example 1.)

The demand curve facing the perfectly competitive firm is *horizontal* or *perfectly elastic* at the going market price.

The individual firm in a perfectly competitive market produces very small amounts relative to the market as a whole. An individual firm cannot change the market price by altering the quantity of the good it offers in the marketplace. Because the individual firm faces a perfectly elastic demand schedule, the firm is a price taker. If the firm tried to sell at a price higher than the market price, it would sell nothing.

PROFIT MAXIMIZATION IN THE SHORT RUN

In the short run, a perfectly competitive firm makes its output decisions by varying the quantity of its variable inputs (such as labor, raw material, energy) that are used with its fixed plant and equipment. The fixed plant and equipment is both a burden and a blessing. It is a blessing to established firms because in the short run fixed costs prevent new firms from entering the industry. Time is needed to build more plants, install more equipment, and find new locations. Fixed plant and equipment is also a burden. Even if the firm

Figure 1   Industry, or Market, Demand Versus Firm Demand

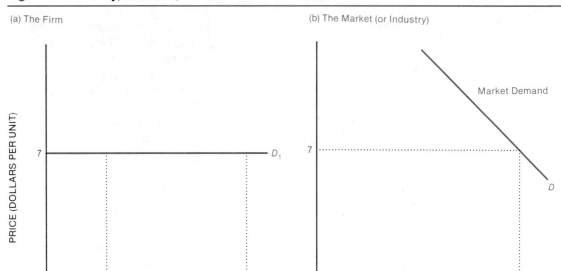

(a) The Firm

(b) The Market (or Industry)

The market demand curve, *D,* in panel (b) shows the total market demand for a homogeneous product being produced by many relatively small firms. The demand curve, D_1, in panel (a) shows how the demand is perceived by the individual firm. Because the individual firm is so small relative to the market, it cannot significantly influence the market price. The firm is, thus, a price taker and can sell all it wants at the going price.

shuts down temporarily, the firm in the short run is obliged to make certain contractual payments (taxes, rent payments, contractual obligations to some employees) and to forgo interest receipts that could be earned if the plant and equipment could be sold, even if the firm shuts down temporarily.

In the short run, the firm must make two decisions: 1) whether to temporarily shut down and produce nothing, and 2) how much to produce if it decides not to shut down. In the long run, the firm has the additional options of building more plants and acquiring more equipment or leaving the business permanently. Recall that the competitive firm does not decide the price. The firm is a *price taker;* the market sets the price.

The firm's supply curve shows how much it is prepared to sell at each price. The quantity supplied at each price is simply the firm's profit-maximizing output. The profit-maximizing rate of output depends on two factors: 1) the price in

relation to average variable cost and 2) marginal cost.

The Two Rules of Profit Maximization

The Shutdown Rule.   The firm is guided by the goal of profit maximization (or loss minimization). To maximize profit (or minimize losses), the firm will follow some simple rules.

Fixed costs should not affect decision making in the short run. In the short run, there is no way for the firm to alter fixed costs. The firm's fixed costs will continue whatever output decisions the firm makes in the short run. Even if the firm shuts down, these fixed costs must be paid. Only in the long run can fixed costs be avoided.

Thus, the first decision made by the perfectly competitive firm is: Should it shut down temporarily or should it produce some output? Surprisingly, it is not important whether or not the reve-

Example 1   Egg Farming and Price Taking

The world's largest egg farm (located in California) produces 730 million eggs per year. Total U.S. egg production averages about 70 billion eggs per year. Thus, the world's largest egg farm produces roughly 1 percent of U.S. egg output. If the largest firm in the egg market were to increase its output by, say, 10 percent, there would be no noticeable effect on the price. Even the largest firm is too small a share of the total to make a difference. The world's largest egg farm is, therefore, a *price taker*. It cannot influence the price of eggs by producing more or fewer eggs. If this is true of

the world's largest egg farm, it must be true of any individual egg farmer. Even though no single firm (even the world's largest egg farm) can influence price, the price can change (even if demand is stable). If something happens that affects all egg farms (such as the development of a new high-protein low-cost feed), the marginal costs of each egg farm (ranging from the smallest to the largest) are lowered, and the supply curve of each producer shifts to the right. The market supply curve cannot be affected by a single competitive firm, but is does shift when all supply curves shift.   ■

---

nues that the firm earns cover fixed costs. Instead, the decision to shut down will depend on the relationship between revenues and *variable costs,* as the **shutdown rule** explains.

> The **shutdown rule** is: If the firm's revenues at all output levels are less than variable costs, it minimizes its losses by shutting down. If there is at least one output level at which revenues exceed variable costs, the firm should not shut down.

For example, brick manufacturer Smith has fixed costs of $1,000 per week. She can sell $3,000 worth of bricks per week while incurring a variable cost *(VC)* of $2,900. Should the bricks be produced or should the plant be shut down? If no bricks are produced (the shutdown case), the fixed costs of $1,000 must be paid in any case, so the manufacturer will incur a loss of $1,000. By producing $3,000 worth of bricks, the manufacturer can *reduce* her losses to $900 because producing bricks results in an excess of $100 of revenues ($3,000) over variable costs ($2,900). The reasoning behind the shutdown rule is that any excess of revenues over variable costs can be applied to covering a portion of fixed costs. (See Example 2.)

The Profit-Maximization Rule.

Once the firm has decided not to shut down, what rule should the firm follow to maximize profits or minimize losses? The decision about *how much* to produce is based upon marginal analysis. If at any point producing another unit of output raises the

profit of the firm (or reduces its losses), more output should be produced. Adjustments in the level of output will continue to be made as long as each change adds more profit or reduces losses. As we learned in the preceding chapter, marginal cost *(MC)* is the increase in costs due to increasing output by one unit.

Once a firm decides not to shut down, the fundamental **profit-maximization rule** is that output should be produced up to the point where the extra cost of an additional unit of output (marginal cost) is just equal to the extra revenue derived from the additional unit of output, or the **marginal revenue** *(MR)*.

> **Marginal revenue** *(MR)* is the increase in total revenue *(TR)* that results from each one-unit increase in the amount of output:
>
> $$MR = \frac{\Delta TR}{\Delta Q}.$$

> The **profit-maximization rule** is that a firm will maximize profits by producing that level of output at which marginal revenue *(MR)* equals marginal cost *(MC)*. (This rule applies to all firms, be they perfectly competitive or imperfectly competitive.)

As long as an extra unit of output adds more to revenues than to costs, the profits of the firm are increasing (or its losses are being reduced). If the *MC* of an additional unit of output exceeds its *MR,* the profits of the firm would be reduced (or its losses increased) if output is expanded. To a

Example 2   Opportunity Costs, the Shutdown Rule, and U.S. Farming

The 1982 revenues and accounting costs of the U.S. farm industry are given in the accompanying table. These figures show that farm operators had $22.1 billion of net income after deducting fixed costs and variable accounting costs from revenue. With approximately 2.5 million farm operators, net income averaged $8,840 per farm operator. The U.S. median income of employed males was $14,748 in 1982. Thus, farm operators generally earned less than people working in nonfarm activities. Assuming the opportunity cost of operating a farm is the cost of passing up the opportunity to work in nonfarming jobs, we can conclude that farm economic profits (revenues minus total opportunity costs) were negative in 1982. In 1982, farmers could have earned more than the $22.1 billion of farm income if they had worked in nonfarm jobs earning the median income. Measured in terms of economic profit, farmers suffered a loss as a group. Why did most farmers stay in business? The shutdown rule provides the answer. The cost figures point out that the fixed costs of farming are quite high (almost one half of variable accounting costs). For farming as a whole, revenues ($162.2 billion) exceeded accounting variable costs ($97.2 billion). Assuming that the 2.5 million farm operators could have earned the median income for males, then the imputed value of their own labor would be $37 billion for an opportunity cost of $134 billion (= $97 billion + $37 billion). Revenues exceeded variable costs by $29 billion.

Category	Amount (billions of dollars)	
Total Revenue		$162.2
Total Costs		$140.1
Variable costs	$97.2	
Operating costs (fertilizers, seed, etc.)	$85.1	
Wages of hired labor	$12.1	
Fixed costs (rent, interest, property taxes)	$42.9	
Net income (total revenue minus total cost)		$ 22.1

This $29 billion could be applied to cover a portion of the $42.9 billion fixed cost, thereby holding down the economic loss. By shutting down, farmers would have lost their entire fixed cost. ∎

Source: Table is from the *Statistical Abstract of the United States,* 1984, p. 661.

---

competitive firm, the price *(P)* of the product measures the extra revenue of an additional unit of output, or the marginal revenue *(MR)* because the perfectly competitive firm can sell as much output as it wants at the prevailing market price, *P*. The increase in revenue brought about by increasing output by one unit, therefore, equals *P*.

Since *P* and *MR* are the same for a competitive firm, a profit-maximizing firm should produce that quantity of output at which *P = MC*.

Consider the hypothetical competitive firm described in Table 1. The firm must decide how much to produce. The firm's variable costs *(VC)* for different levels of output are shown in column (2). The firm's total costs *(TC)* are shown in column (3). Since the difference between *TC* and *VC* is $10 for all levels of output, the firm's fixed costs *(FC)* are $10.

Marginal costs for this competitive firm are shown in column (6) of Table 1. As in the previous chapter, the *MC* figures derived from the *TC* figures are positioned *between* the rows corresponding to consecutive output levels. Each *MC* figure that is in parentheses is simply the average of the preceding and following figures. For example, when output is 3 units, *MC* = $9 because reducing output by one unit lowers costs by $8 and raising output by one unit raises costs by $10—an average of $9.

Column (4) shows average variable costs *(AVC),* and column (5) shows average total costs *(ATC).* Notice that *AVC* reaches a minimum of $8 at output levels of both 2 units and 3 units. *ATC* reaches its minimum at an output of 4 units.

How much output the firm will produce de-

Table 1   Profit Maximization for a Perfectly Competitive Firm

Quantity, Q (1)	Variable Cost, VC (2)	Total Cost, TC (3)	Average Variable Cost, AVC (4)	Average Total Cost, ATC (5)	Marginal Cost, MC (6)	Profits when P = $7 (7)	Profits when P = $9 (8)	Profits when P = $13 (9)
0	$0	$10	—			− $10	− $10	− $10
					$10			
1	10	20	$10	$20	(8)	− 13	− 11	− 7
					6			
2	16	26	8	13	(7)	− 12	− 8	+ 0
					8			
3	24	34	8	11.33	(9)	− 13	− 7	+ 5
					10			
4	34	44	8.50	11	(11)	− 16	− 8	+ 8
					12			
5	46	56	9.20	11.20	(13)	− 21	− 11	+ 9
					14			
6	60	70	10	11.67		− 28	− 16	+ 8

Note: numbers in boxes show output levels where profits are maximized (or losses are minimized) at different prices.

pends upon the price. If price is less than $8 (minimum AVC), the firm will shut down (produce where output is 0) because for any level of output, revenues will not cover variable costs. Losses are, thus, minimized by shutting down. For example, if the price is $7, the firm's losses are held to the $10 fixed cost by simply shutting down. If output is any higher than 0 units, losses are larger than $10—as shown in column (7)—because price does not cover average variable costs. When price does not cover AVC, total revenue does not cover variable costs $(TR = P \times Q$ and $VC = AVC \times Q)$. Thus, losses would equal fixed costs plus that portion of variable costs not covered by total revenue.

If the price is $9, however, the firm will not want to shut down but will want to produce some level of output. How does it decide how much to produce once it decides not to shut down? If the firm were to produce 1 unit of output, its revenues would be $9/unit × 1 unit = $9 and its total costs would be $20—yielding losses of $11, as shown in column (8). The firm knows that the marginal cost of producing a second unit is only $6 compared to the marginal revenue from a second unit of $9. Thus, the firm can reduce its losses from $11 to only $8 by producing a second unit. Once it is producing 2 units of output, its total revenue is $9/unit × 2 units = $18 and its total costs are $26—yielding losses of $8, as

shown in column (8). The firm again compares marginal cost and marginal revenue to determine whether or not it should move to an output level of 3 units. The MC of moving from an output of 2 units to an output of 3 units is $8, but MR is $9. Thus, the firm can reduce its losses by $1 if 3 units are produced instead of 2 units. Should the firm produce a fourth unit of output? No. The MC of moving from 3 units of output to 4 units of output is $10 compared to the MR (= P) of only $9; the firm would increase its losses by $1 if it produced 4 units of output instead of 3 units. At a $9 price, losses are clearly minimized at an output of 3 units because that is the output level where P = MC.

If the price rises to $13, the firm will want to produce 5 units of output. Again, the firm decides whether or not to move from one output level to the next by comparing marginal cost and marginal revenue. When the firm gets to the point where it is producing 4 units of output, its total revenue is $13/unit × 4 units = $52 and its total costs are $44—yielding a profit of $8, as shown in column (9). To produce another unit of output would raise costs by only $12 but would increase revenues by $13. The firm can increase profit by $1 if it raises output from 4 units to 5 units. Can the firm do any better raising output again? No. If the sixth unit of output is produced, costs rise by $14, which is more than the price of $13. Hence, at a

$13 price, the firm maximizes profit at 5 units of output, where $P = MC$.[1]

The Two Rules and the Firm's Supply Schedule

Applying the shutdown rule and the profit-maximization rule[2] told us what quantities our hypothetical firm should produce at three specific prices (see Table 1). Recall that a supply curve shows quantities supplied at different prices by a seller or sellers. The three price/quantity combinations determined by using the two rules are three points on the firm's supply curve: 0 units/$7; 3 units/$9; 5 units/$13.

Graphical Analysis of the Profit-Maximizing Firm

The cost schedules in Table 1 have been plotted in Figure 2. The AVC and ATC curves are U-shaped, and the MC curve intersects each average curve at its minimum point. Average fixed cost (AFC) is the vertical distance between ATC and AVC.

Loss Minimization: Price Greater than AVC but Less than ATC.

Panel (a) shows the case where the market price equals $9. At this price, the firm will not shut down because price is greater than the lowest point on the AVC curve ($8). By staying in operation, the firm can cover its variable costs and pay for a portion of its fixed costs. To minimize losses, the firm will produce that output (3 units) at which P and MC are equal (point e).

---

1. In numerical examples involving discrete levels of output such as these, the $P = MC$ rule may not hold exactly. The reason is that going from (say) $Q = 1$ to $Q = 2$ is a discontinuous jump in output; the $MR = MC$ or $P = MC$ (for perfect competition) rule requires that the firm be able to choose not only whole numbers like $Q = 3$ but also fractional numbers like 2.5. One advantage of graphs over tables is that this problem does not arise; in graphs we can work with fractional numbers as easily as whole numbers. That the $P = MC$ rule does not hold exactly in the discrete case does not mean that it is not applied. The firm will expand output as long as P is greater than MC; it will contract output if P is less than MC. In other words, the firm will come as close as it can to observing the $P = MC$ rule.

2. In brief, the two rules are:

(1)   If $P < AVC$, set $Q = 0$ (shut down).

(2)   If $P > AVC$, adjust Q until $P (= MR) = MC$.

Figure 2   Profit Maximization for the Perfectly Competitive Firm

(a) Short-Run Loss Minimization

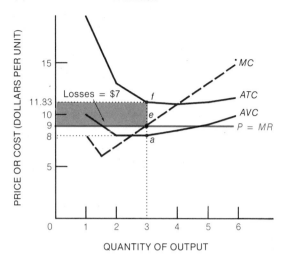

(b) Short-Run Profit Maximization

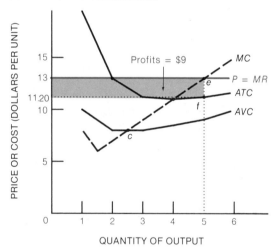

These cost curves are based on the data in Table 1. In panel (a), the market price of the good is $9; the firm's demand curve is, therefore, a horizontal line at $P = MR = \$9$. The firm produces 3 units of output since $MC = P$ ($9) at that point. Losses are minimized at this level of output. The black shaded area represents losses (loss per unit of $2.33 multiplied by total quantity of 3 units = $7.00, approximately). When the output level is 3 units, $AVC = \$8$. Since $P > AVC$ at that point, the firm has a margin of revenue over variable cost with which to defray some of the fixed costs; it should remain in production.

In panel (b), the market price is $13. The firm maximizes profits at an output level of 5 units (where $P = MC$). At $P = \$13$, price exceeds ATC ($11.20) by $1.80; the firm makes a profit of $1.80 times the quantity of output, or $9.

The firm's losses can be read directly from the graph. At an output quantity of 3 units, the average total cost *(ATC),* or cost per unit, equals $11.33, while price is $9. The *loss per unit of output* equals $2.33, or the vertical distance *ef.* The total loss, therefore, is the area of the black rectangle, or $2.33/unit × 3 units = $7 (approximately). That the firm is better off producing 3 units of output than shutting down is indicated by the vertical distance *ea* (which equals the price of $9 minus average variable cost of $8), where the market price exceeds *AVC* by $1. This $1 can be used to cover a portion of fixed costs.

Panel (a) shows one point on the firm's supply schedule. It reveals that at a market price of $9, the firm will supply 3 units of output.

Profit Maximization: Price Greater than *ATC.*
Panel (b) shows the case where the market price equals $13. Profits are maximized at the output level where $P = MC$, or at 5 units of output; the firm will, therefore, produce 5 units of output. At this output level, price ($13) exceeds *ATC* ($11.20) by $1.80, so the firm is making a profit per unit of output of $1.80 (the vertical distance *ef*). The total profit is the area of the color rectangle (= 5 units × $1.80/unit = $9). Notice that the maximum distance between the price line and the *ATC* curve occurs at 4 units of output, but 4 units is not the output level chosen by the firm because at 4 units, *MC* is less than *P.*

Perfectly competitive firms choose that level of output where $P = MC$—or, in graphical terms, where the $P (= MR)$ line intersects the *MC* curve—provided price is greater than the minimum level of *AVC.*

The competitive firm's supply curve (how much it is willing to sell at different prices) is that portion of the firm's *MC* curve above the *AVC* curve.

Economic Profit Versus Accounting Profit

Profit equals revenue minus costs. As noted in the preceding chapter, *economic profits* equal revenues minus opportunity costs, not just revenue minus accounting costs. *Opportunity costs* are the best alternatives sacrificed by the business firm when it engages in some particular production plan. *Included in these alternatives is the return that could be earned by the owner/entrepreneur if the owner's money capital, labor, and managerial time had been used elsewhere* (along with explicit payments for materials, labor, and interest). Economic losses are incurred when the return to the resources used in the business firm is less than the normal return those resources could earn in the next best alternative. When economic profits are zero, the business firm is earning a normal profit.

Industry Equilibrium in the Short Run

When one knows how the profit-maximizing (or loss-minimizing) competitive firm behaves in the short run, one can determine how a perfectly competitive industry, composed of many such firms, behaves in the short run. Recall that the short run is a period so short that old firms cannot build new plants and equipment; new firms cannot enter; old firms cannot leave. Thus, a short-run situation is one in which there are a fixed number of competitive firms of given plant sizes. Since each firm is behaving competitively, each firm's supply curve for the product is its own *MC* curve above its *AVC* curve.

How does the industry (all the firms together) behave in the short run? Figure 3 shows how the market price is determined. For simplicity, Figure 3 shows a market with only two firms and two consumers; in reality, competitive markets have a large number of firms and consumers, but the principles for constructing market supply and market demand curves are the same. Panels (d) and (e) show the supply curves S_1 and S_2 of Firms 1 and 2, respectively; these supply curves are really the firms' *MC* curves above minimum *AVC.* These two supply curves are summed horizontally to obtain the *market supply curve, S,* in panel (c). Panels (a) and (b) show the demand curves for Consumers 1 and 2, labeled D_1 and D_2, respectively. The two demand curves are summed horizontally to obtain the *market demand curve, D,* in panel (c). The market equilibrium price, *c,* clears the market and coordinates the decisions of the independent buyers and sellers.

Figure 3   Competitive Equilibrium in the Short Run

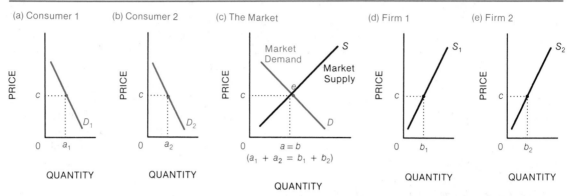

This figure depicts a competitive market with only two consumers and two producers (for simplicity). The demand curves D_1 and D_2 are the demand curves for the two consumers; the supply curves S_1 and S_2 are the supply curves for the two firms. Curve D in panel (c) is the market demand curve and is the horizontal sum of D_1 and D_2; curve S in panel (c) is the market supply curve and is the horizontal sum of S_1 and S_2. At the equilibrium price, market supply just matches market demand.

> **In the short run, the market supply curve is the horizontal summation of the supply curves of each firm, which in turn are their *MC* curves above minimum *AVC*.**

Figure 3 shows how price and output are determined in the short run in a perfectly competitive industry. Figure 4 shows in more detail how the firm's individual behavior is consistent with market behavior, and vice versa, when there are many firms.

Panel (b) of Figure 4 shows an industry consisting of 1,000 firms, and panel (a) shows a representative firm. The market supply and market demand curves in panel (b) determine the market equilibrium price of $15. This market price of $15 clears the market where a total of 20,000 units are traded. To the representative firm, the $15 price becomes the firm's horizontal demand curve. In response to this price, the firm produces 20 units of the output, where the *MC* curve intersects its demand curve. Since this representative firm is one of 1,000 firms in the industry, the industry as a whole will produce 20,000 units of output (20 × 1,000). Thus, the profit-maximizing behavior of the individual firm is consistent with the profit-maximizing behavior of all the firms in the market. The individual firm's supply curve,

the thick portion of the *MC* curve above *AVC*, is a small part of the market supply curve, *S*.

Panel (a) shows a representative firm that is *making an economic profit: ATC* at the profit-maximizing output level of 20 units is $12; therefore, the firm is making a per-unit profit of $3 (= $15 − $12) on each of the 20 units for a total of $60 economic profit. The representative firm could just as easily have made losses, since in the short run the firm will not shut down as long as it can pay part of its fixed costs.

The effect of economic profits on perfectly competitive industries is felt primarily in the long run when new firms can enter the industry and established firms can exit. As competitive firms respond to economic profits or losses, the industry short-run supply schedule shifts, and prices change.

PERFECT COMPETITION IN THE LONG RUN

The persistence of economic profits *(P > ATC)* or economic losses *(P < ATC)* is not a stable or equilibrium situation in the long run for a competitive industry. If losses continue to be sustained, in the long run some firms will choose to exit from the industry because the long run is a

Figure 4   Short-Run Equilibrium: The Firm and the Market

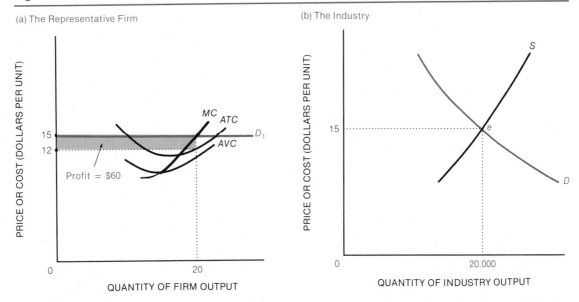

(a) The Representative Firm

(b) The Industry

Panel (a) shows the representative firm; panel (b) shows the market. There are 1,000 firms. Firm demand is D_1 when market demand and supply are in equilibrium at point e with a $15 price and an equilibrium market output of 20,000 units. The individual firm produces 20 units of output and makes a profit of $60 ($3 × 20 units) from the per-unit profit of $3 ($15 − $12 = P − ATC).

period of time long enough for firms to eliminate fixed-cost obligations by leaving the industry. If economic profits continue to be made, there will be an incentive in the long run for new firms to enter the industry to earn above-normal profits.

In the long run, the number of firms in a perfectly competitive industry is not fixed. If the typical firm is making economic profits, the number of firms will expand. If the typical firm is sustaining economic losses, the number of firms will contract. In other words, if $P > ATC$, the number of firms will increase. If $P < ATC$, the number of firms will contract.

Until the number of firms stops changing, the industry is not in long-run equilibrium. For a market to be in long-run equilibrium, there must be no incentive for new firms to enter or old firms to leave. In the long run, existing firms operate at a level of output at which average costs are minimized. Firms producing with inefficient plants

cannot compete with firms producing with efficient plants.

Long-run equilibrium occurs for the competitive industry when economic profits are zero and long-run average costs are minimized.

Figure 5 shows a perfectly competitive market in long-run equilibrium. In the long run, the firm operates at an efficient scale of operation. Thus, the ATC curve for the optimal plant will have a minimum average cost equal to the minimum average cost in the long-run average-cost curve. The long-run equilibrium for the representative firm occurs at q_0, where $P = ATC = LRAC$.

When $P = MC$ and $P = ATC = LRAC$ at the long-run equilibrium output, and when MC intersects ATC at its *minimum point*, the perfectly competitive firm is producing at the lowest average cost in the long run.

Figure 5   Long-Run Equilibrium: The Firm and the Market

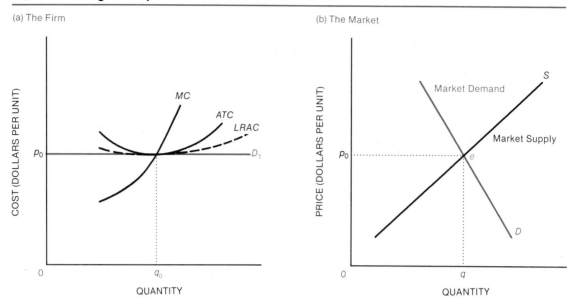

(a) The Firm

(b) The Market

These graphs illustrate the relationship between the firm and the market in long-run equilibrium. In long-run equilibrium, three conditions are satisfied: 1) quantity supplied equals quantity demanded, 2) price equals marginal cost, and 3) price equals average total cost equals long-run average cost. (The representative firm makes zero economic profit.) The representative firm in panel (a) produces where the D_1 curve intersects the MC curve $(P = MC)$, and the profits are zero because price just covers the minimum average total cost of production. The supply curve S in panel (b) is based on the number of firms in existence in long-run equilibrium.

This finding suggests that perfectly competitive firms will operate at maximum efficiency (produce at minimum $LRAC$) in the long run.

The Mechanism of Entry and Exit

A perfectly competitive industry adjusts toward a long-run equilibrium of zero economic profits through entry and exit. For the economy as a whole, entry and exit are opposite sides of the same coin. If it is profitable to enter one industry, resources must be exiting another industry. In other words, if revenue exceeds opportunity costs in some industries, revenue falls short of opportunity costs in other industries.

Entry.   The mechanism of free entry eliminates economic profits and insures that in the long run goods are produced at minimum average cost with an efficient-sized plant.

Consider the perfectly competitive industry consisting of 100 firms in panel (b) of Figure 6. Panel (a) shows the ATC and MC curves of a typical firm in this industry; we assume ATC is the short-run average-total-cost curve in an efficient scale of plant. Panel (b) shows the market supply curve derived by summing the supply curves of 100 such firms. When the market demand curve is D, the equilibrium price is \$10. At this price, the representative firm is making zero profits (a normal return). The demand curve facing the representative firm is D_1; each of the 100 firms produces 7 units of the product, making for a market output of 700 units. Equilibrium e_1 is both a short-run equilibrium and a long-run equilibrium.

Suppose that consumers increase their demand for the product, and the market-demand curve shifts from D to D'. The short-run equilibrium price rises to \$12, and the short-run equilibrium output of the industry rises to 800 units.[3] At this higher price, the firm's short-run equilibrium is

---

3. Remember in the short run, the number of firms is fixed. As market demand increases, there is a movement along the short-run supply schedule, S. In the long run, new firms can enter, at which point there is a rightward shift of the supply curve to S'.

Figure 6   Free Entry Drives Economic Profits to Zero and Unit Costs to a Minimum

(a) The Representative Firm

(b) The Market

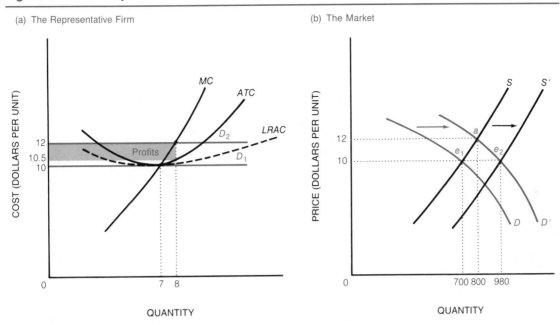

The initial long-run equilibrium is e_1, the intersection of D and S in panel (b). When demand shifts to D', the short-run equilibrium price rises to \$12 (point a), creating economic profits for the individual firm facing the new demand curve D_2 in panel (a). In the long run, new firms enter until the supply curve shifts to S'. The long-run equilibrium is established at point e_2, where price again equals \$10. Each firm returns to producing 7 units of output, but the number of firms rises from 100 (700 ÷ 7) to 140 (980 ÷ 7).

now at 8 units of output, where price and marginal cost are equal. The typical firm now makes economic profits. In the short run, which may be a few months or many years, the individual firm will enjoy above-normal returns.

In the long run, above-normal profits will attract more firms. *As these new firms enter the market, the supply curve shifts to the right,* because the market supply is the sum of individual supply curves. The entry of new firms will continue as long as economic profits are positive. But as the supply curve shifts to the right (to S'), the market price falls, putting a squeeze on profits. Eventually, in the new long-run equilibrium, economic profits must again be zero. The new long-run (and short-run) equilibrium is e_2, which is at the old equilibrium price of \$10. In the new long-run equilibrium, the individual firm again produces 7 units; but there are now 140 such firms producing 7 units each (or 980 total units for the market as a whole).

Efficient Scale.   Competition induces the perfectly competitive firm to produce at $P = MC$; free entry causes $P = ATC = LRAC$, thereby eliminating economic profits. Both forces together bring about *efficient* production, or production in which the good is being produced at the minimum cost to society. The firm in a competitive industry cannot be inefficient in the long run; the firm cannot select an inappropriate plant size. The plant size in Figure 6 must be the best possible size for producing 7 units, or the firm would not be around in the long run.

Exit.   The reverse of entry is exit. Like entry, the mechanism of exit also leads to a long-run equilibrium with the average firm producing at the minimum average cost and with price equal to marginal cost (see Figure 7).

In Figure 7, the original equilibrium is at e_1, which is both a short-run and a long-run equilibrium. There are 100 firms. Point e_1 is a short-run

Figure 7   The Exit of Firms Eliminates Losses and Drives Unit Costs to a Minimum

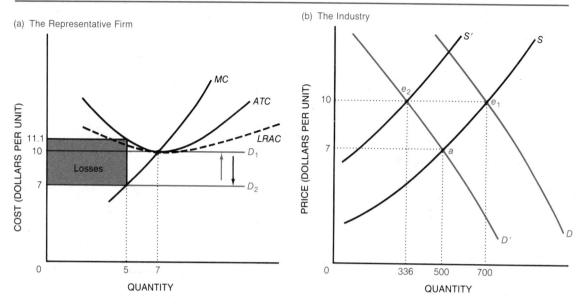

(a) The Representative Firm

(b) The Industry

The initial long-run equilibrium is e_1, the intersection of D and S in panel (b). Demand drops to D', causing the short-run equilibrium price to fall to $7 (point a). The representative firm makes losses as D_1 shifts downward to D_2. The exit of firms in the long run shifts the supply curve to S', which lifts price back to $10 and eliminates losses. Each firm returns to producing 7 units of output, but the number of firms falls from 100 (700 ÷ 7) to 48 (336 ÷ 7).

equilibrium point because, in panel (b), the market quantity supplied equals the market quantity demanded and because, in panel (a), $P = MC$ for the representative firm. The market is in long-run equilibrium because when price is $10 (demand curve is D_1), the representative firm makes zero profits.

When the demand curve shifts from D to D' in panel (b), the short-run equilibrium shifts from e_1 to a. The short-run price falls to $7, and the short-run quantity falls to 500 units, with the representative firm producing 5 units. Since $7 is less than ATC, the representative firm makes economic losses. In the long run, firms will begin to exit (the weaker ones first). The exit of firms shifts the industry supply curve to the left until economic losses are eliminated (at S'), and price is driven back up to the original $10. The new equilibrium is at e_2, where total output is 336 units and there are now only 48 firms who again produce an average of 7 units each.

The Long-Run Industry Supply Curve

In Figures 6 and 7, increases or decreases in de-

mand serve to raise or lower price in the short run. But in the long run, prices remain the same! In the case of Figure 6, the increase in demand is answered by an increase in supply that drives the price back down to the original level. Similarly, in Figure 7, the decrease in demand is answered by a decrease in supply that drives the price back up to the original level.

The long-run industry supply schedule shows the quantities that the industry is prepared to supply at different prices *after* the entry or exit of firms is completed.

Constant-Cost Industries.   The long-run industry supply curve corresponding to Figures 6 and 7 is perfectly elastic (horizontal) at the price of $10, which equals the minimum unit cost of production (minimum $LRAC$). The case of a perfectly elastic industry supply curve is illustrated in Figure 8, where S_L is the long-run industry supply curve. Shifts in demand, such as the shift from D to D', simply change the equilibrium quantity in the long run; there is no change in

Example 3   The Effects of Entry on VCR Prices

The theory of perfect competition suggests that positive economic profits in any given industry invite the entry of new firms, increasing supply and causing the price to drop to the point where a normal return is earned by the representative firm.

A recent example of these effects from the entry of new firms in an industry is provided by the video-cassette-recorder (VCR) industry. Sony introduced the VCR in 1975, with a price tag of $1,400—about $2,700 in 1984 dollars. The average VCR in 1984 cost about $500. Thus, the real price tumbled more than 80 percent. In 1975, there was one producer. In 1984, there were three dozen brands from which to choose. In addition to Sony, consumers can choose from among RCA, General Electric, Zenith, Panasonic, and many others. There could be as many as 70 brands be-

fore firms stop entering the industry as new firms from Korea and Taiwan continue to flood the market with VCRs. The price would then drop even further.

The difference in price between $2,700 and $500 is an understatement of the impact of entry because the quality of VCRs has improved almost yearly. Today's VCR is smaller, has a better sound, and even has a better picture than the first Sony.

This example vividly illustrates the impact of entry on price. Even if the product is moderately complicated, within a decade entry can wipe out economic profits. ■

Source: "Innovations Spur Boom in VCR Sales," *New York Times,* November 12, 1984.

---

prices or costs. When shifts in demand do not change prices or cost in the long run, the industry is a **constant-cost industry.**

What determines whether an industry will be a constant-cost industry? If the individual firms' cost curves remain the same when the industry expands (or contracts), the industry will be a constant-cost industry. Firms in constant-cost industries purchase labor, raw materials, land, and the like at the same prices whether the industry is expanding or contracting. The constant-cost industry's demand for resources is a relatively small part of the total demand, and the industry's factor inputs usually are not highly specialized.

> A **constant-cost industry** is relatively small and, hence, can expand or contract without significantly affecting the terms at which factors of production used in the industry are purchased. The long-run industry supply curve for a constant-cost industry is horizontal.

Increasing-Cost Industries.   As the number of firms in an **increasing-cost industry** expands, the prices of the factors of production used by that industry are bid up. Industries whose factor purchases make up a large percentage of the market and industries that use factors of produc-

Figure 8   The Long-Run Supply Curve for a Constant-Cost Industry

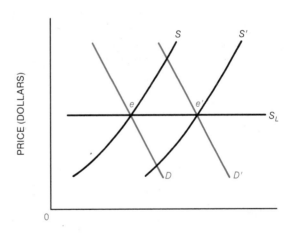

QUANTITY OF INDUSTRY OUTPUT

A constant-cost industry can buy all the inputs or productive factors it wants at constant prices; hence, the minimum average total cost of production is independent of industry size. When demand increases, as from D to D', in the long run the price stays the same and only quantity increases as supply increases by a corresponding amount from S to S'. Price must stay the same to keep economic profits at zero. Thus, the long-run supply curve, S_L, is perfectly elastic.

Figure 9   The Long-Run Supply Curve for an Increasing-Cost Industry

(a) The Firm

(b) The Market

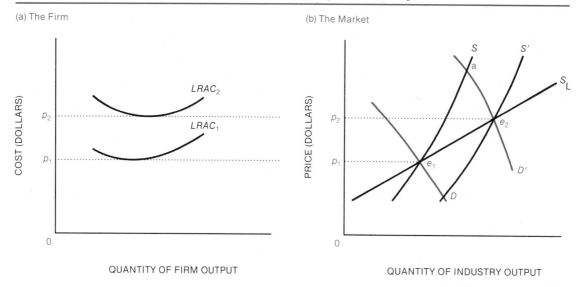

The expansion of an increasing-cost industry drives up some important factor prices facing individual firms; hence, the cost curves shift up as the size of the industry increases, as illustrated in panel (a). When demand shifts from D to D', the long-run equilibrium price increases from p_1 to p_2. The cost curve $LRAC_1$ in panel (a) corresponds to the equilibrium, e_1, in panel (b); the cost curve $LRAC_2$ corresponds to e_2. The long-run supply curve, S_L, is upward-sloping but is still more elastic than the short-run supply curves, such as S or S'.

tion specialized to that industry are usually increasing-cost industries. Thus, when the industry is expanding, the individual firms must pay higher prices for their resources—so their costs of production will rise. (See Example 4.)

> As the number of firms in an **increasing-cost industry** expands, the factor prices of resources used in the industry are bid up. As the number of firms in the industry contracts, the prices of these factors fall. Hence, the long-run industry supply curve for an increasing-cost industry is upward-sloping.

The long-run adjustment in an increasing-cost industry is illustrated in Figure 9. The equilibrium is initially at e_1, with the demand curve at D. The demand curve shifts to D', causing the price to rise in the short run to the level indicated at point a. The typical firm now earns economic profits. New firms enter, the industry expands, and the price of the good itself falls, squeezing profits toward zero, as in a constant-cost industry. But factor prices are also bid up as the number of firms increases and cause the $LRAC$ curve to shift up-

ward from $LRAC_1$ to $LRAC_2$. In the final equilibrium, indicated at e_2, profits have been squeezed to zero by the entry of new firms *and* rising costs. The long-run supply curve is shown as S_L.[4]

Differential Rents and the Representative Firm

Thus far we have assumed that perfectly competitive industries are composed of a large number of firms, all producing with *similar costs of production*. But is it not true that the production costs of competitive firms are quite different? One coal mine will offer rich veins just below the surface; another offers poor veins thousands of feet below the surface. One farm has rich fertile land; another farm has poor soil. Will these natural differences not lead to large differences in average

---

4. There is yet a third category of industry called the *decreasing-cost industry*. In decreasing-cost industries, prices paid for resources decline as the industry expands. Because decreasing-cost industries are rare and the causes of decreasing costs are complicated, we do not deal with them here.

costs among different competitive firms in the same industry? The answer is, surprisingly, no.

Consider the two different coal mines in Figure 10. The superior mine in panel (a) has lower average variable costs at each level of output than the inferior mine in panel (b) *when the cost of renting the mine from its owner is excluded.*[5] Because coal mining is a competitive industry, the coal produced from Mine A will sell for the same price as the coal from Mine B (the demand is shown as *D* in both cases).

The operator of Mine A will choose to produce q_A units of output and the operator of Mine B will produce q_B units. *If there were no rental payment,* the operator of Mine A would make an economic profit represented by the shaded area in (a); the operator of Mine B would make a much smaller economic profit—the shaded area in (b).

Because Mine A is a superior mine with lower production costs, however, coal operators would be willing to pay a higher *rent* for the privilege of operating *A.* In both cases, an economic profit (an above-normal return) is being earned if there were no rental payment; operators would, therefore, be willing to pay the owners of the mine property a *rent equal to the shaded area* for the privilege of using both mines. If the rent were greater than the shaded area, *ATC* would exceed price so that below-normal returns would be earned, and the operator would choose another occupation. If the rent were less than the shaded area above-normal returns would be earned, so other operators would be willing to pay a higher rent and would outbid the current operator.

The net result of paying rent for scarce resources is to equalize average costs among different competitive firms. A higher rent would be paid for Mine A than for Mine B, and this *differential rent* would equalize the average costs of production. The return from the more productive mine accrues to the owner of the scarce resource in the form of a rental payment, not to the mine operator in the form of an economic profit.

This general principle can be applied to other competitive industries in which firms are differ-

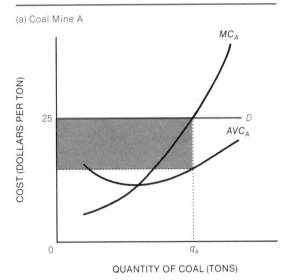

Figure 10   Differential Rents on Coal Mines of Varying Richness

Coal Mine A, depicted in panel (a), is easier to mine than Coal Mine B, depicted in panel (b). Thus AVC_A is lower than AVC_B, where the average variable cost curves exclude the costs of paying the rent on the mine itself. If the price of coal is $25 per ton, the shaded areas correspond to the rental that will be paid on the two coal mines. It will cost more to rent Mine A than to rent Mine B.

ent. A farmer who is located on particularly fertile land will earn more than neighboring farmers. A particular entrepreneur who is more ingenious than other entrepreneurs in the industry will earn a higher return. These returns are included in ac-

Example 4   Constant-Cost and Increasing-Cost Industries

Retail trade is a *constant-cost industry* because it usually accounts for a relatively small share of total employment in most labor markets; it employs personnel who do not have specialized skills; the capital used in retail trade (primarily buildings) is not specialized and represents a relatively small share of total capital. These conditions mean that the output of the retail-trade industry can be expanded or contracted without affecting the factor prices that retail-trade establishments must pay.

Another example of a constant-cost industry is banking. Like retail trade, banking employment accounts for only a small percentage of total employment; banking recruits employees who do not have highly specialized skills; the equipment used by the banking industry (principally structures) represents a very small portion of the total. The expansion of the banking industry would indeed affect the prices paid for equipment specific to the banking industry (such as automated-teller equipment), but this equipment would account for only a small portion of banking industry costs.

Examples of *increasing-cost industries* are not hard to find. Residential construction is an increasing-cost industry. The residential-construction industry accounts for a substantial portion of the total demand for gypsum, heating equipment, and plumbing fixtures. Moreover, the residential-construction industry is a major employer of labor with specific skills: carpenters, electricians, and plumbers. When the residential-construction industry expands, the prices of the inputs used in

home building—from lumber to carpenters—will be bid up. When the industry contracts, these prices fall, as illustrated by the collapse of lumber prices in 1981–82.

The petrochemicals industry—an industry that produces plastics, synthetic rubber, fertilizer, and synthetic fabrics—is another example of an increasing-cost industry. Petrochemical products are produced from crude petroleum and natural gas and are major users of petroleum and natural gas (about one quarter of these resources goes to the petrochemical industry). Therefore, expansion of petrochemicals will bid up the prices of petroleum products.

Coal mining is a third example of an increasing-cost industry. In coal-mining regions, coal mining is a major employer of labor (Pennsylvania, Kentucky, and West Virginia). As the coal industry expands, the wages of coal miners are bid up. In addition, coal mines differ in important respects. Some contain rich veins of coal that are close to the surface; others contain poor veins that are buried deep under the surface. The supply of mine sites that offer rich, easily accessible coal is limited. As the demand for coal increases, mining companies must turn to more and more of the inferior mines. As the cost of producing a ton of coal will be higher in inferior mines, increased demand will increase the average cost of coal production. As a result, the prices (called rents) paid for the superior mines will be bid up. ∎

---

counting profits, but they are not considered economic profits. Economists consider these returns *rents* to scarce factors of production.

The theory of differential rent reconciles the zero-economic-profit property of perfect competition with the fact that some people earn large incomes in perfectly competitive industries in the long run. The fact that some farmers and some coal-mine owners are very rich even though their industries are competitive is not inconsistent with zero long-run economic profits. If every firm were exactly alike in a competitive industry the entrepreneurs simply could not earn more than a normal return for their effort; they would probably have incomes that were very similar to the average in the community. But all firms are not ex-

actly alike. The fact that some firms have advantages over others simply means that the composition of opportunity costs differs from firm to firm. Part of these opportunity costs may simply be higher returns to superior resources. The superior resource (such as the rich vein of coal) means lower variable costs (such as mining the coal) and higher factor prices paid to the superior resource. (See Example 5.)

This "differential rent theory" owes its origin to David Ricardo, who, in his 1817 classic, *The Principles of Political Economy and Taxation,* called attention to the fact that fertile farmland paid higher rents than marginal farmland. The theory of differential rent applies to other factors of production in addition to farmland.

THE GAINS FROM VOLUNTARY EXCHANGE OR TRADE

The theory of perfect competition can be used to demonstrate how both producers and consumers can gain from voluntary exchange between many independent buyers and sellers.

Figure 11 shows a market that is in equilibrium when price is $9 and output is 400 units. Since the market supply curve begins at $5, the first unit can be coaxed out of some supplier by paying just $5; anything less than $5 would yield a zero output. To coax the 100th unit out of another supplier, a price of $6 has to be paid; to coax out the 400th unit would require a price of $9. Although the market price is $9, there would have been some production of this good if its price had been less than $9. Those firms that would have been willing to supply the good at lower prices are getting a surplus when the market price is $9. The supplier of the first unit is receiving a surplus of $4 (= $9 − $5); the supplier of the 100th unit is receiving a surplus of $3 (= $9 − $6). All the suppliers of this good taken together are getting a total surplus equal to the area of the triangle *ceb*. Alfred Marshall, the great 19th-century British economist, called this area above the supply curve and below the price the **producer surplus.**

> **Producer surplus** is the excess of what producers receive over the minimum value the producers would have been willing to receive.

In Figure 11, producer surplus is the area *ceb* when the market price is $9. The area *ceb* equals $800.

The concept of producer surplus is similar to the concept of **consumer surplus** discussed in an earlier chapter.

> **Consumer surplus** is simply the excess of the consumer benefits (the dollar value of total utility) from consuming a good over the dollar expenditure on the good.

In Figure 11, when the market price is $9, the consumer surplus is the area *aec*. This area equals $1600.

The benefits of trade or voluntary exchange are simply those benfits represented by the consumer surplus combined with those benefits represented by the producer surplus. The first unit has a worth

Figure 11   The Gains from Trade

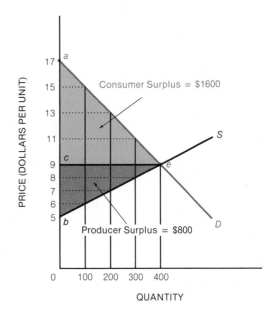

When the price is $9, producer surplus is the area *ceb,* and consumer surplus is the area *cea.* The first unit is worth $17 to buyers and costs $5; it yields a gain from trade of $12 to society. All 400 units are worth the area *aeb*—the consumer surplus + the producer surplus yielded by the market equilibrium price of $9. The total of consumer and producer surplus is $2,400 (area of triangle *aeb* = ½ × base × height = ½ × $12 × 400 = $2,400).

of $17 to some consumer since the demand curve intersects the vertical axis at $17. The first unit can be coaxed out of some producer for $5. Thus, the first unit is worth approximately $12 to society [($17 − $9) + ($9 − $5)]. This $12 is the gain from trade shared by the supplier who values the first unit at only $5 and the buyer who values the first unit at $17. Similarly, the 100th unit is worth $15 to some buyer and $6 to some supplier and, thus, yields a net gain of $9 [($15 − $9) + ($9 − $6)] when the seller sells to the buyer for the market price of $9. The 400th unit squeezes out all the gains from trade, and one price brings together many individual buyers and sellers.

Since the consumer surplus *aec* = $1600, and the producer surplus *ceb* = $800, society's net gain in the market illustrated in Figure 11 is $2400. The triangle area *aeb* can be interpreted as the potential loss to society if this market were to be eliminated.

Example 5   The World's Fastest Noodle Maker: Economic Rent as a Cost Equalizer

According to the Guinness Book of World Records, Mark Pi of the China Gate Restaurant in Toledo, Ohio, holds the world record as the world's fastest noodle maker (1,024 five-foot-long noodle strips in 60 seconds). The Chinese restaurant that employs the world's fastest noodle maker would appear to have a cost advantage compared to other restaurants that employ average noodle makers. The theory of perfect competition explains why this cost advantage will not be present. Assume that Pi's exceptional skill lowers the China Gate Restaurant's average variable cost by 10 percent. Because of the competitive nature of Chinese restaurants, all must charge about the same prices; therefore, it would appear that the restaurant that has the good fortune to have Pi would earn an economic profit. Other restaurant owners would come to recognize that the economic profits of the China Gate Restaurant were really due to Pi's unique skills. Competitors would bid among themselves for Pi's services. As the chapter points out, this bidding would stop only when Pi's earnings have risen sufficiently above those of other noodle makers so that his employer would no longer earn economic profits. At this point, the temporary economic profits would have been converted into a *rent* payment for Pi's unique talents. (It may be strange to talk about people receiving rents for unique talents, but this type of rent will be explained more fully in a later chapter). ■

Source: Ross McWhinter, ed. *Guinness Book of World Records,* (New York: Bantam, 1982), p. 485.

In the real world, the gains from trade are enormous. Through the mechanism of the market, people can specialize in the production of certain goods and trade them for resources that can, in turn, be traded for the wider variety of goods people demand. The benefits to people of specializing rather than trying to produce all that they demand are represented by the triangle area formed by the combination of the producer and consumer surpluses in each market (this triangle area is formed by the demand curve to the left of the equilibrium quantity, by the supply curve to the left of the equilibrium quantity, and by the vertical axis).

Competitive markets are the mechanism by which specialization can be coordinated. Competitive markets coordinate the specialization of different economic units and assure that goods will be provided at minimum average cost if the entry/exit mechanism is allowed to operate.

PERFECT COMPETITION IN PRACTICE

The theory of perfect competition describes how business firms behave in a perfectly competitive environment. These conditions of perfect competition are met in a number of markets: most agricultural markets—fibers, grains, dairy products, vegetables, oranges—are perfectly competitive. Stock markets and commodity markets are perfectly competitive as well. More important than these pure markets are industries that closely *approximate* the conditions of perfect competition. In such markets, the number of producers may not be large enough to make each firm a perfect price taker, but the amount of control over price may be negligible. Information on prices and product quality may not be perfect, but consumers may have a great deal of information at their disposal. The product may not be perfectly homogeneous, but the distinctions among products may be inconsequential. The number of firms actually in the industry may not be exceptionally large, but a large number of firms may be waiting in the wings to enter on short notice if economic profits are earned. An industry need not meet all the conditions of perfect competition for the theory of perfect competition to apply to buiness behavior.

The theory of perfect competition tells us, first, that economic profits will be squeezed out in the long run by the entry of new firms. Second, the theory tells us that when the markets are in equilibrium, price and marginal cost will be equal. Third, the theory tells us that short-run behavior will differ from long-run behavior. In the short run, firms will stay in business as long as the price covers average variable cost. In the long run, if the price fails to cover average costs (remember in the long run there are no fixed costs), firms will leave the industry. In the short run, demand increases will lead to price increases; in the long run, the price will ultimately depend upon the costs of the representative firm. Fourth, theory tells us that extraordinary earnings can persist in the long run in competitive markets, but these earnings will be rental returns to the owners of scarce factors, not economic profit.

Two of the most important characteristics of perfectly competitive industries are: 1) that perfectly competitive firms will operate at minimum average cost in the long run and 2) that perfectly competitive firms will produce that quantity of output at which price equals marginal cost in both the short run and the long run. These characteristics will be important to keep in mind when evaluating the other types of markets—monopoly, oligopoly, and monopolistic competition—that will be studied in the chapters that follow. The next chapter will examine the behavior of firms that are able to exercise some control over price. Monopolists exercise considerable control over their prices; monopolistically competitive firms have only limited control over their prices.

Summary

1.   A perfectly competitive market exists when there is a large number of sellers and buyers, when buyers and sellers have perfect information, when the product is homogeneous, and when there is freedom of entry and exit. These conditions insure that each seller will be a price taker. The price will be dictated to sellers by the market. No single seller can influence the market price. The theory of perfect competition explains the behavior of perfectly competitive firms and the behavior of perfectly competitive industries.

2.   In the short run, the number of firms in the industry is fixed, and the firm has fixed costs. In the long run, the number of firms can change through entry and exit, and fixed costs become variable costs. Profit-maximizing competitive enterprises make two decisions in the short run: whether to shut down (whether to produce anything) and (if they decide not to shut down) how much to produce. If the market price covers average variable cost, the competitive firm will not shut down. The competitive firm will produce that quantity of output at which price and marginal cost are equal. The firm's supply curve is its marginal cost curve above average variable cost. The industry supply schedule is the horizontal summation of all the supply schedules of individual firms in the industry. Where the quantity supplied equals the quantity demanded determines the market price. Each firm takes this market price as given.

3.   In the long run, firms enter competitive industries where economic profits are being made. They exit from industries where a below-normal profit is being earned. Economic profits must be zero for the competitive industry to be in equilibrium. In the long run, goods are produced at minimum average cost with price equal to marginal cost for the average competitive firm. Returns to scarce factors of production like land or managerial skills are called *economic rents* and are not included in economic profits.

4.   The gains from voluntary exchange or trade are the sum of consumer surplus and producer surplus.

5.   An industry need not meet all the conditions of perfect competition for the theory of perfect competition to be able to explain the behavior of firms in that industry.

Key Terms

perfect competition
imperfect competition
price taker
shutdown rule
marginal revenue *(MR)*
profit-maximization rule
constant-cost industry
increasing-cost industry
producer surplus
consumer surplus

Questions and Problems

1. Discuss why each firm may not be a price taker in an industry in which there is product differentiation among firms.

2. A firm is contemplating whether to produce its 10th unit of output and finds its marginal costs for the 10th unit are $50 and its marginal revenue for the 10th unit equals $30. What advice would you give this firm?

3. A firm has fixed costs of $100,000. It receives a price of $25 for each unit of output. Average variable costs are lowest (equal to $20) at 1,000 units of output. What advice would you give this firm? Would this advice be the same in the short run as in the long run?

4. Explain the relationships between accounting profits, normal profits, and economic profits. Will they always be different?

5. The representative firm in the widget industry, which is perfectly competitive, is making a large economic profit. What predictions can you make about what will happen in this industry in the long run?

6. "The theory of perfect competition claims that economic profits will disappear in the long run. This assumption is incorrect because I know a family that has a farm that earns more than $1 million per year." Evaluate this statement.

7. What is the difference between a constant-cost industry and constant returns to scale (where the *LRAC* curve is horizontal)?

8. Jones is an absolute genius at farming. He has an uncanny ability of knowing what to plant and when. As a result, Jones's farm consistently earns higher profits than other farms. From the economist's perspective, are these really higher profits or something else?

9. In Table 1, fixed costs are $10. If fixed costs were raised to $20, how would the supply schedule be affected in the short run? How will the supply schedule be affected in the long run?

10. Imagine a firm faces the cost schedule given in Table A.
  a. Calculate the firm's profit or loss for each

Table A

Quantity, Q	Variable Cost, VC	Fixed Cost, FC	Total Cost, TC
0	$ 0	$5	$ 5
1	6	5	11
2	14	5	19
3	24	5	29
4	36	5	41

level of output when the price = $5.99, $6.01, and $10.01, respectively.
  b. How many units of output will the profit-maximizing or loss-minimizing firm produce at those three prices?
  c. What is the firm's supply schedule?

11. You observe the (competitive) airline industry making economic losses. What do you expect to happen to ticket prices, to the quantity of airline passangers, and to the number of airline companies as time passes?

12. You observe a highly profitable new industry producing a product of advanced technology (such as computers). What do you expect to happen to the price of the product, to profits, to the industry's output, and to the number of firms as time passes?

13. Explain why in the long run the industry supply curve is perfectly horizontal in the case of a constant-cost industry.

14. What is the key difference between a constant-cost industry and an increasing-cost industry?

15. If dry cleaning is a constant-cost industry, what would you expect to happen to the price of dry cleaning in a particular town as the size of the town increased in both the short run and the long run?

Suggested Readings

Kirzner, Israel. *Competition and Entrepreneurship.* Chicago, Ill.: University of Chicago Press, 1973.

Mansfield, Edwin. *Microeconomics: Theory and Applications.* New York: W. W. Norton, 1979, chap. 8.

Weiss, Leonard. *Case Studies in American Industry.* New York: John Wiley, 1971, chap. 2.

30

Monopoly and Monopolistic Competition

Chapter Preview

Perfect competition exists when firms take the market price as given: each competitive firm is a price taker. A firm that has monopoly power has the ability to control (select) the prices of its products. Such a firm is called a *price searcher*. The greater the monopoly power, the greater the control over price. Most firms are price searchers. When the price searcher controls the entire market in which it operates, it is a *pure monopolist*. When the price searcher is a small firm that sells a product that is only slightly differentiated from its competitors', it is a *monopolistic competitor*. When the price searcher is an industrial giant competing with a few other industrial giants, it is an *oligopolist*. This chapter studies monopoly and monopolistic competition; oligopoly is discussed in the chapter after the next. This chapter explains how price-searching firms go about maximizing profits, the impact of entry barriers on profits, as well as the issues of product durability, price discrimination, and markup pricing.

Literally, *monopoly* means "single seller." A **pure monopoly** has the following characteristics.

A **pure monopoly** exists 1) when there is one seller in the market for some good or service that has no close substitutes, 2) when the seller has considerable control over price, and 3) when barriers to entry protect the seller from competition.

Like perfect competition, examples of monopoly in this pure form are rare, but the theory of pure monopoly does shed light on the behavior of firms that approximate the conditions of pure monopoly. Many firms possess at least a little bit of monopoly power. For example, a certain corner at a busy intersection may be the best spot in a town for a service station, and only one firm can occupy that spot. ■

CONDITIONS FOR MONOPOLY

Why Monopoly Is Not So Pure

''Pure'' monopoly is hard to find for several reasons. First, substitutes of some kind exist for almost all products. Trucking substitutes for railroad freight; national magazines and TV news substitute for local newspapers; stainless steel and copper substitute for aluminum; aluminum foil substitutes for cellophane; foreign imports substitute for domestically produced goods. A pure monopoly requires that there be no good substitutes, but where does one draw the line between good and poor substitutes?

Second, modern enterprises tend to be multiproduct firms. Pharmaceutical manufacturers produce different kinds of prescription drugs; steel companies produce rolled steel and specialty steels; automobile manufacturers produce cars, trucks, and tanks; the telephone company supplies data-transmission service as well as local telephone service. It is rare for a multiproduct firm to have a pure monopoly in *all* its product lines. A drug manufacturer may have a monopoly in one drug while competing with other drug manufacturers in its other product lines.

Third, a sole supplier in a particular market may not act like a pure monopolist if it fears that rival firms may enter the market. If the monopolist's economic profits become too high, rivals may find ways to overcome existing barriers to entry. (See Example 1.)

Barriers to Entry

The basic source of pure monopoly is the presence of *barriers to entry*. The main barriers are:

1. economies of scale,
2. patents,
3. exclusive ownership of raw materials,
4. public franchises, and
5. licensing.

Economies of Scale.   The average costs of one large firm may be much lower than the average costs of many smaller firms. When new firms cannot compete effectively with a larger firm, it is difficult for new firms to enter the market. Large established firms are protected by econom-

ies of scale that bar the entry of new firms. A *natural monopoly* occurs when economies of scale are so large that there is room for only one firm in the industry. Competition is either unworkable or highly inefficient. Examples of natural monopolies are the local public utilities that deliver telephone services, gas services, water services, and electricity.

Patents.   American *patent* laws allow an inventor the exclusive right to use the invention for a period of 17 years. During that period, the patent prohibits others from using the invention; the patent holder is protected from competition. The IBM Corporation's patents on tabulating equipment, Xerox's patents on copying equipment, the United Shoe Machinery Company's patents on shoemaking machinery, and Smith Kline's patent on the drug Tagamet are examples of this type of entry barrier. The Bell System achieved a monopoly in the 19th century when Alexander Graham Bell was granted a patent just hours before a rival inventor.

Exclusive Ownership of Raw Materials.

Established companies may be protected from the entry of new firms by their control of raw materials. The International Nickel Company of Canada owns virtually all the world's nickel reserves; 80 percent of the world's known diamond mines are under the control of the DeBeers Company of South Africa. American Metal Climax Corporation controls most of the world's supply of molybdenum.

Public Franchises.   State, local, and federal governments grant to individuals or organizations exclusive *franchises* to be the sole operator in a particular business. Competitors are legally prohibited from entering the market. The U.S. post office is a classic example of a public franchise. Along tollways, the state grants exclusive franchises to operate restaurants and service stations; duty-free shops in airports and at international borders are also franchise operations. Many public utilities operate under state or local franchises.

Licensing.   Entry into an industry or profession may be regulated by government agencies and by autonomous professional organizations. The American Medical Association licenses med-

Figure 1   Price Searching Versus Price Taking

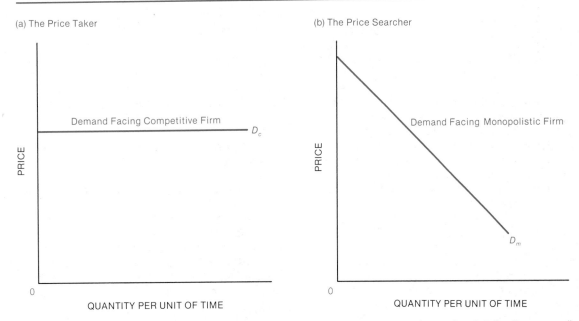

(a) The Price Taker

Demand Facing Competitive Firm D_c

PRICE

0   QUANTITY PER UNIT OF TIME

(b) The Price Searcher

Demand Facing Monopolistic Firm

PRICE

D_m

0   QUANTITY PER UNIT OF TIME

In panel (a), the demand curve D_c facing the competitive firm is perfectly horizontal, meaning that the firm can sell additional units without lowering its price. The price taker can sell all it wants at the going market price. In panel (b), the demand curve D_m facing the monopolistic firm is downward-sloping. This firm is a price searcher.

ical schools and allocates hospital staff privileges to physicians. The Federal Communications Commission licenses radio and television stations and controls entry into the broadcasting industry. Most companies license airlines and, thus, limit entry into the industry. Nuclear power plants must be licensed by the federal government.

PRICE-SEARCHING BEHAVIOR

The most fundamental difference between monopoly and perfect competition is that the competitive firm must accept whatever price the market dictates. The perfectly competitive firm is literally a *price taker*, while the monopolist is a **price searcher.** The monopolist has its own market demand curve. Thus, the monopolist has the problem of searching the demand curve for the profit-maximizing price. Such price-searching behavior is not restricted to just *pure* monopolies. Even the local grocery store has some control over price and must determine the right price.

The behavior of each price-searching firm is governed by certain general principles. First, *a*

price searcher faces a downward-sloping demand curve. Unlike the perfect competitor, the price searcher cannot sell all it wants at the going market price. For the firm to sell more, it must lower the price of the product. If it raises its price, it will sell less.

A **price searcher** is a firm with the ability to control to some degree the price of the good or service it sells.

Figure 1 illustrates the difference between price takers and price searchers. The price taker's demand curve is perfectly elastic because the price is dictated by the market and because more units can be sold without lowering the price. In contrast, the price-searching firm must lower its price on all units sold in order to sell more. To determine if the revenue gains from selling more output outweigh the revenue losses of lower prices, the firm must examine the **marginal revenue *(MR)*** and marginal cost of an additional unit of output.

Marginal revenue *(MR)* is the addition to total revenue brought about by a one-unit increase in quantity sold.

Example 1   Monopolies: From Tobacco and Diamonds to the Local Newspaper

Familiar examples of monopolies are the local telephone company and the local gas and electric companies. These monopolies are called *public utilities* and are typically regulated by state or local government. When public utilities are chartered by the relevant government body, they are given a legal monopoly over the market because competitors are legally prohibited from entering the market. Public utilities, however, are not very useful examples of monopoly because their rates and services are regulated by government.

There are numerous contemporary and historical examples of monopolistic firms that are not subject to government regulation. Until 1911, the American Tobacco Company and the Standard Oil Company controlled more than 90 percent of the output of their respective industries. Until 1945, the Aluminum Company of America controlled virtually the entire U.S. output of virgin aluminum ingots. In the 1950s, Pfizer monopolized the market

for the broad-spectrum antibiotic, tetracycline. Currently the Smith Kline Corporation is the sole supplier of the ulcer drug, Tagamet. The Boeing Corporation currently supplies 85 percent of the world's demand for commercial jet aircraft. The DeBeers Company of South Africa controls 80 percent of the world output of raw diamonds. On a smaller scale, there is typically one local newspaper and one movie theater in most small towns. Usually only one airline offers service between a small city and major airports.

As these varied examples show, the structure of the market (the number of suppliers or the percentage of the market) does not fully explain monopoly behavior. As the reader will see, there is a big difference between the behavior of Standard Oil (in 1911) or a Smith Kline in the 1970s on the one hand and the one airline offering service to a small city, the Boeing Corporation, or the local newspaper on the other.   ■

Like price takers, price searchers also want to maximize profits. All profit-maximizing firms attempt to produce that level of output at which marginal revenue *(MR)* and marginal costs *(MC)* are equal. The main difference between price takers and price searchers is that for the price taker, price equals marginal revenue, while for the price searcher, price does not equal marginal revenue.

Price in Relation to Marginal Revenue

The perfect competitor can always sell additional output at the going market price.

For perfect competitors, the market price is the extra revenue from selling one more unit *(MR):*

$$P = MR.$$

For price searchers, the price does not equal marginal revenue. To sell an additional unit of output, the price searcher must lower the price on the units previously sold at a higher price. Why?

The quantity of output produced before adding the marginal unit could be sold at a higher price than the quantity produced after adding the marginal unit. When a price searcher sells one more unit, the extra revenue generated equals the (new) price of the extra unit sold minus the loss in revenue from having to sell all but the marginal unit of output at a lower price. For the price searcher, price exceeds marginal revenue because of the necessity of lowering prices to sell additional output.

For a price searcher, price is greater than marginal revenue:

$$P > MR.$$

For example, suppose a price searcher faces a demand schedule in which 1 unit per week can be sold if price is $19; 2 units can be sold if the price is $17. The total revenue generated is the number of units multiplied by the price per unit for that quantity. When the number of units sold is 1, revenue is $19 (= $19 × 1); when the number of units sold is 2, revenue is $34 (= $17 × 2).

Example 2   Spoiling the Market: Daimler-Benz

For the price searcher, price exceeds marginal revenue. A price searcher who attempts to increase its sales may "spoil the market" by driving prices down. If by throwing a greater quantity of goods on the market, the price of a firm's product falls, the firm has lowered the price not only of the extra production, but also of the units sold previously at a higher price. Price searchers must weigh the advantages of increased production against the risk of spoiling the market.

Daimler-Benz, located in Sindelfingen, West Germany, provides a classic example of not spoiling the market. Each year, Daimler-Benz plans a very limited production of Mercedes-Benz automobiles despite waiting lists for thier cars. In other words, Daimler-Benz could easily sell more cars than it chooses to produce, but more production will "spoil the market" by driving down the price the market is prepared to pay. The result of this strategy is seen in the high premium that buyers pay for Mercedes-Benz cars over other luxury cars. ■

Marginal revenue is the extra reveneue raised by increasing output by one unit. Therefore, by comparing revenues at each output level, the change in revenue can be calculated. The marginal revenue of a change from 1 to 2 units is $34 − $19 = $15. Why is the price of the second unit ($17) greater than the marginal revenue for the second unit ($15)? To sell the second unit, the firm must lower price on both the first and second units from $19 to $17. The firm gains $17 in revenue on the sale of the second unit, but loses $2 on the sale of the first unit. Hence, the marginal revenue of the second unit is $17 − $2 = $15. In effect, selling one more unit "spoils the market" on the first unit because the price falls (see Example 2 for further discussion of spoiling a market).

There is another way to explain why price exceeds marginal revenue. The chapter on costs and productivity described the relationship between average and marginal values. Recall that when a new average value falls, the marginal value must go below the previous average. This relationship also exists between **average revenue (AR)** and marginal revenue (MR).

Average revenue (AR) equals total revenue (TR) divided by output.

In general, $TR = P \times Q$, and $TR = AR \times Q$. Hence, AR and P amount to the same thing when all units are sold at the same price. To say that the price searcher faces a downward-sloping demand schedule is to say that AR or P falls as output increases.

Whenever an average value is declining, the marginal value must be below the previous average value, pulling it down. In the case of the price searcher, AR is the average value; MR is its corresponding marginal value. If AR is declining, MR must be less than AR. Since $AR = P$, P must be greater than MR. Just as the demand schedule shows prices (or average revenue) for different quantitites, the **marginal-revenue schedule** shows the marginal revenues for different quantities.

The **marginal-revenue schedule** shows what happens to MR as the quantity of output changes.

Columns (1) and (2) of Table 1 show the demand schedule facing a price-searching firm. Column (3) shows the revenue produced at each level of output $(P \times Q)$, and column (4) gives the marginal-revenue schedule.

The marginal-revenue values are positioned vertically between the rows corresponding to different output levels in Table 1. Each number that appears in parentheses in column (4) is the average of the preceding and following marginal-revenue values. For example, the MR at an output level of 2 units is $13 because reducing output to 1 unit lowers revenue by $15 and increasing output to 3 units raises revenue by $11 ($13 is the average of $15 and $11).

The demand and marginal-revenue schedules of Table 1 are graphed as demand and marginal-revenue curves in Figure 2.[1] The firm's demand

1. The advantage of using an MR curve over a numerical schedule is that with a graph MR can be read at or between different levels of output.

Table 1   Monopoly Equilibrium

Output (units), Q (1)	Price or Average Revenue, P = AR (2)	Total Revenue, TR = P × Q (3) = (1) × (2)	Marginal Revenue, MR (4)	Total Cost, TC (5)	Marginal Cost, MC (6)	Profit = TR − TC (7) = (3) − (5)
0	$21	$ 0		$10		− $10
			$19		$10	
1	19	19	(17)	20	(8)	− 1
			15		6	
2	17	34	(13)	26	(7)	8
			11		8	
3	15	45	(9)	34	(9)	11
			7		10	
4	13	52	(5)	44	(11.5)	8
			3		13	
5	11	55	(1)	56	(14)	− 1
			− 1		15	
6	9	54	(−3)	70	(16)	− 16
			− 5		17	
7	7	49	(−7)	87	(18.5)	− 38
			− 9		20	
8	5	40	(−11)	107	(21)	− 67
			− 13		22	
9	3	27	(−14)	129	(23.5)	− 102
			− 15		25	
10	1	10		144		− 134

This table shows the demand and marginal-revenue schedules of a price searcher. The demand schedule is given in the first two columns. Because all customers are charged the same price, price and average revenue are the same. Revenue—in column (3)—equals P × Q. Marginal revenue is the increase in total revenue brought about by increasing output by one unit. The monopolist's profit is maximized by producing 3 units of output, where profit equals $11. If the monopolist had attempted to produce one more unit of output, total revenue would have increased by $7 and costs by $10, and profit would have fallen by $3. If the monopolist had produced one less unit, total revenue would have fallen by $11 and costs would have fallen by $8, reducing profit by $3. The firms expands output as long as MC does not exceed MR. Each MC and MR figure in parentheses is the average of the two figures above and below it.

curve, labeled *D*, shows that the firm is a price searcher (it must lower price to sell more quantity).

The position of the *MR* curve below the demand curve shows graphically that price is greater than marginal revenue for any quantity of output (except for the first unit sold). Whenever the demand curve is a straight line, the *MR* curve will always be horizontally halfway between the demand curve and the vertical axis because the slope of the *MR* curve is twice as steep as the slope of the demand curve. In Table 1, when price falls by $2, marginal revenue falls by $4.

Marginal Revenue and Elasticity

Panel (b) of Figure 2 shows the behavior of total revenue *(P × Q)* as output increases and graphs column (3) of Table 1. Revenue increases as output rises up to the quantity of 5.25 units, and thereafter revenue decreases as output rises. The relationship between *MR* and total revenue is simple; when *MR* is positive, the total-revenue curve is upward-sloping; when *MR* is negative, the total-revenue curve is downward-sloping; when *MR* = 0, the total-revenue curve reaches its highest point.

Whether *MR* is positive or negative depends on whether demand is elastic or inelastic at that point. Remember the total-revenue test of elasticity from the chapter on demand and elasticity: *If demand is inelastic ($E_d < 1$), total revenue falls as the price falls. If demand is elastic ($E_d > 1$), total revenue rises as the price falls.* When demand is elastic, a reduction in price raises total revenue and *MR* is positive. When demand is inelastic, a reduction in price lowers total revenue and *MR* is negative.

Figure 2 Demand, Marginal Revenue, and Elasticity

(a) Demand and Marginal Revenue

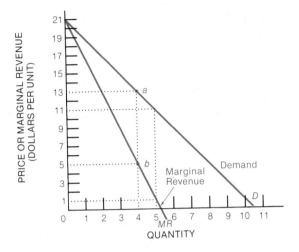

(b) Elasticity

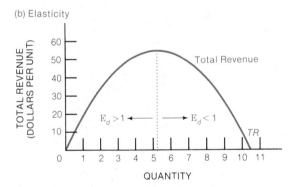

In panel (a), the demand and marginal-revenue schedules of Table 1 are plotted as *D* and *MR*. At an output level of 4 units, the price is $13 and the marginal revenue is $5. In other words, the value of *MR* for any given price is read vertically as that point on the *MR* curve directly below the point on the demand curve corresponding to that price. If the demand curve is a straight line, the marginal revenue curve will be located horizontally halfway between the demand curve and the vertical axis. In panel (b), the total-revenue schedule of Table 1 is plotted directly below the *MR* curve, showing the relationship between *MR* and total revenue. When *MR* is positive (above the horizontal axis), total revenue is rising; when *MR* is negative, total revenue is falling; when *MR* is zero, total revenue reaches its highest value. The price elasticity of demand (E_d) is greater than 1 when total revenue is rising and less than 1 when total revenue is falling. When demand is elastic, reductions in price raise total revenue; when demand is inelastic, reductions in price lower total revenue.

> When *MR* is positive, demand is elastic; when *MR* is negative, demand is inelastic.

This rule indicates that a price searcher will always operate at a level of output where demand is elastic (where $E_d > 1$). If the firm expands to the point where demand is inelastic, it is experiencing negative marginal revenue. Thus, by expanding its output, the monopoly is actually driving down its revenue.

The relationship between marginal revenue and elasticity is direct: for any given price, the higher is the elasticity of demand the higher is the marginal revenue. If demand is highly price elastic, a given percentage increase in output can be sold with a relatively small percentage reduction in price. Thus, the reduction in price on the previous units sold is relatively small, and marginal revenue is high (marginal revenue is close to price). The less elastic is the demand, for a given price, the smaller is the marginal revenue. If demand is highly price inelastic, a given percentage increase in output can be sold only with a relatively large percentage reduction in price. The reduction in price on previous units sold is relatively high, and marginal revenue is negative (marginal revenue is well below price).

All price-searching firms—be they monopolies, oligopolies, or monopolistic competitors—share three common characteristics:

1. For every price searcher facing a downward-sloping demand curve, $P = MR$ (except on the first unit sold) because the price must be lowered on previous units to sell additional units.
2. *MR* is positive when the demand is elastic; $MR = 0$ when the elasticity of demand is unity; *MR* is negative when the demand is inelastic.
3. The higher the elasticity of demand for a given price, the higher the marginal revenue. The more elastic is the demand, the closer is *MR* to price.

MONOPOLY PROFITS

How Monopolies Determine Output

The monopolist maximizes profit by choosing an output level where marginal cost (*MC*) equals marginal revenue (*MR*).

If the *MR* of an additional unit of output is $10 and the *MC* of the additional unit is $6, $4 is added to profit by producing the additional unit. Whenever *MR* exceeds *MC,* it pays the firm to expand output. The monopoly firm will increase output—and lower its price—as long as *MR* exceeds *MC.* The monoplistic firm lowers the price as output is increased in order to sell that larger output.

If the firm finds that *MR* is less than *MC,* it pays the firm to cut output and raise price. If *MC* = $15 and *MR* = $9, a cut in output by one full unit would lower costs by $15 and lower revenue by only $9. Profits would rise by $6 (or losses would fall by $6).

The monopolistic firm can raise profit by expanding output (or by lowering price) when *MR* > *MC*. The firm can raise profit by cutting output (or by raising price) when *MR* < *MC*. The monopolist—or the price searcher in general—maximizes profit by producing that quantity where *MR* = *MC*.

Table 1 gives cost schedules for a monopolistic firm in addition to the demand and revenue schedules already discussed. Like the marginal-revenue values in column (4), the marginal-cost values in column (6) are positioned vertically *between* the rows corresponding to different output levels. Again, each number in parentheses is the average of the preceding and following marginal-cost values. What level of output will the monopolist choose to produce? Column (7) shows that profit is largest (maximized) when 3 units of output are produced. The monopolist will, therefore, produce 3 units of output. The monopolist will expand output as long as *MR* exceeds *MC.* The first unit of output raises total revenue by $19 (*MR* = $19) and raises costs by only $10 (*MC* = $10), thus contributing $9 to paying the monopolist's $10 fixed cost—reducing a $10 loss at zero output to a $1 loss at 1 unit of output. The second unit of output raises revenue by $15 and adds $6 to costs. The second unit, therefore, changes a $1 loss to an $8 profit. The third unit adds $11 to revenue and $8 to cost, adding $3 to profit. If the fourth unit were produced, only $7 would be added to revenue while $10 would be added to

Figure 3 Monopoly Profit Maximization

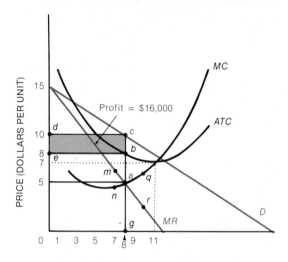

QUANTITY (THOUSANDS OF UNITS)

This monopolist has cost curves *ATC* and *MC* and faces demand curve *D*. Note that *MC* intersects *ATC* at its minimum point, where marginal cost and average total cost equal $7 and output is 11,000 units. The maximum profit occurs where *MR* = *MC*. The equilibrium price/quantity combination is found by drawing a vertical line from the demand curve through the point *(a)* where *MR* = *MC* down to the horizontal axis. The output level represented by the point where the vertical line hits the horizontal axis (8,000 units) is the optimal output level. The point where the vertical line hits the demand curve (at *c*) is the optimal price. Profit is represented by the rectangle *cbed*, or the difference between price and *ATC* multiplied by the number of units ($2 × 8,000 = $16,000).

---

cost, decreasing profit by $3. Note that at the output level where profit is maximized (3 units), *MR* = *MC* = $9.

Once the monopolist selects an output level of 3 units, the monopolist will charge the price of $15 dictated by the demand schedule. The monopolist can set either price or quantity. Once one is chosen, the other will be dictated by the market demand schedule. Monopolists maximize profits *either* by selecting the profit-maximizing output level and letting the market set its price *or* by selecting the profit-maxizing price and letting the demand curve determine the quantity of output (see Example 3).

Figure 3 shows another example of profit maximization in graphical form. The demand schedule is graphed as the demand curve, *D;* the marginal-revenue schedule is graphed as *MR.* When

Example 3   Setting the Price Versus Setting the Quantity

Most of the examples in this chapter show how a monopolist determines that quantity of output that gives it the most profit. Once the monopolist produces that ouput, the price is set in the market by the demand curve. The monopolist, alternatively, could just as well have determined the price that would cause buyers to demand the profit-maximizing quantity. Both procedures yield the same end result. Some monopolists maximize profit by determining output. The DeBeers Company of South Africa, a syndicate which controls 80 to 85 percent of the sales of raw diamonds, maximizes profits by determining what quantity of raw diamonds to offer on the world raw diamond market. DeBeers markets diamonds through an unusual marketing procedure called a *sight*. About three weeks before each sight, DeBeers sends notices to the 300 largest diamond purchasers, who are asked to send in requests in carats for the amount of diamonds they wish to buy. Two days before the sight (held in London, Luzerne, and Kimberley, South Africa), the buyers are informed how many carats they have been allocated—an amount often below the quantity requested. At the

sight, each buyer is handed a container of raw diamonds. In theory, the buyer can refuse the purchase if not satisfied with the quality, but the buyer would then run the risk of not being invited back for future sights. The market price of diamonds is regulated by the number of diamonds offered in each sight. The world's second largest raw-diamond producer, the Soviet Union, does not market through DeBeers, but it does sell at the prices that are maintained by DeBeers.

Other monopolists follow the strategy of setting price and then letting the demand curve determine the quantity. This strategy is used by AT&T in pricing its long-distance service. Although AT&T must compete with other long-distance phone services, it still accounts for 90 percent of all interstate long-distance calls. AT&T determines the interstate long-distance rates that will cause telephone users to demand the profit-maximizing quantity. In the AT&T case, it would be difficult if not impossible to maximize profits by regulating the amount of output (customer access to long distance). ∎

---

output is 7,000 units, marginal revenue exceeds marginal cost (point m is higher than point n), so profits rise if more than 7,000 units are produced. When output is 10,000 units, marginal revenue is less than marginal cost (point r is lower than point q), so profits rise if fewer than 10,000 units are produced.

To maximize profit, the monopolist selects that output at which marginal revenue and marginal cost are equal. The *MR* and *MC* curves intersect at point a. The output level, price, and profit per unit of output can be determined by drawing a vertical line through a. Where the vertical line crosses the horizontal axis (at g) is the monopolist's output level (8,000 units); where the vertical line intersects the demand curve (at c), is the price ($10); where the vertical line intersects the *ATC* curve (at b) shows the average total cost of producing 8,000 units ($8). The distance between c and b ($10 − $8) is economic profit per unit of output ($2). *Total* economic profit is therefore profit per unit times the number of units, or the color shaded area of the rectangle *cbed*. Algebra-

ically, total economic profit = $(P - ATC) \times Q$ = ($10 − $8) × 8,000 = $16,000.

Monopoly Profits in the Long Run

When there is competition, the distinction between the short run and the long run is crucial. In the short run, the number of firms in the industry is fixed; in the long run, new firms can enter the industry or old firms can exit in response to economic profits or losses. This long-run entry and exit insures that economic profits will be squeezed out of perfectly competitive industries. In the case of the monopolist, the long-run/short-run distinction is not as important because barriers to entry prevent new firms from entering the industry and squeezing out monopoly profits. There is no automatic tendency for monopoly profits to be eliminated by the *entry of new firms*.

Unlike competitive profits, monopoly profits can persist for long periods of time.

In the real world it is difficult to find pure monopolies because of actual or potential substitutes and because absolute barriers to entry are rarely present. Most real-world monopolies are not pure monopolies; they are *near monopolies*. Near monopolies are indeed subject to the profit squeeze in the very long run, particularly if monopoly profits are exceptionally high.

Exceptional monopoly profits have historically promoted the development of closer substitutes for the monopolist's product. The railroads' monopoly over freight transportation was eventually broken by the development of trucking and air freight; the Bell System's monopoly over long-distance telephone service is being broken by the advent of microwave transmission. (See Example 4 on coal-slurry pipines).

Although monopoly profits will not automatically be driven down to the normal return, there is a tendency for high monopoly profits to promote the development of substitutes in the very long run.

Being a monopoly does not guarantee automatic economic profits. Monopolies can incur losses just like competitive firms. The major distinction is that monopoly profits have a tendency to persist over time, while the above-normal profits of competitive firms are squeezed out by the entry of new firms.

Consider the monopolist pictured in Figure 4. The demand curve, *D,* passes between the average-total-cost *(ATC)* and the average-variable-cost *(AVC)* curves before it intersects *AVC.* In this example, the monopolist suffers a loss when producing the 2,000-unit output level where *MR = MC* because the price at 2,000 units of output is $10, which is less than the $13 *ATC.*

Like competitive firms, the monopolist must decide whether or not to shut down. The monopolist's short-run shutdown rule is the same as a competitive firm's: if price covers *AVC,* stay in business. When price is greater than *AVC,* the firm can cover all variable costs and can also recover a portion of fixed costs. If the price falls below average variable cost, the monopolist will shut down. In the long run, if the demand curve remains below the average-cost curve, the monopolist will leave the industry permanently (see the explanation of the shutdown rule in the preceding chapter).

Figure 4   Monopoly Losses

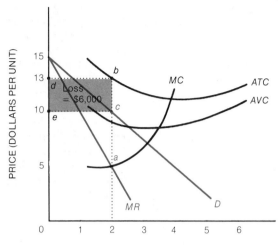

This monopolist minimizes losses (as long as price exceeds average variable cost) by producing 2,000 units of output (where *MC = MR*). The monopolist must charge a price of $10 at an average total cost of $13. The monopolist loses $3 per unit of output for a total loss of $6,000 (the rectangle *bced*).

In Figure 4, the shutdown rule says to stay in operation. When the monopolist produces 2,000 units of output (where *MC = MR*), the monopolist's price of $10 is greater than the *AVC* of $9 but is less than the *ATC* of $13. The monopolist, therefore, has a loss of $3 for each unit, for a total loss (the area of the shaded rectangle *bced*) of $6,000.

FACTS AND FALLACIES ABOUT MONOPOLY

Our analysis sheds light on some common facts and fallacies concerning monopoly.

Common fallacies are:

1. *Monopolists charge the highest possible price.* Monopolists must weigh the revenue gains from higher prices against the revenue loss of lower sales. They will select the price that clears the market for the output level at which *MR = MC.* In Figure 3, it is possible for the monopolist to charge a price above $10, but at these higher prices *MR > MC* and profits are being sacrificed.

Example 4   Coal-Slurry Pipelines: Monopoly and Long-Run Competition

The theory of monopoly suggests that a monopolist will be able to continue to earn monopoly profits as long as potential competitors are kept out by barriers to entry. This theory, therefore, predicts that monopolists will do their best to keep entry barriers high.

A case in point is the railroads' monopoly of coal transport. Although the railroads must compete with trucking and air frieght in providing transportation service, the railroads hold a virtual monopoly over coal transport. Coal is very bulky and heavy, and trucking cannot provide an economical alternative to rail transport. The hauling of coal is currently the most profitable line of business for the nation's railroads, particularly the railroads that haul coal from the western states.

Technology has now developed an alternative form of transport for coal: the *coal-slurry pipeline*. These pipelines carry a mixture of powdered coal and water from coal fields to coal-burning utilities and ports and compete directly with the railroads. Although major companies (Bechtel Corporation, Boeing, and Texas Eastern Transmission Company) have proposed to build such pipelines (currently there is only one in existence), it is not possible to build one without government approval.

Right-of-way privileges must be obtained, and only the government can grant such a privilege.

Lobbying by the railroads in Congress has blocked such legislation for 19 years. The latest lobbying victory by the railroads came in September 1983 when the House of Representatives soundly voted against coal-slurry legislation. The railroads argue that coal pipelines would deprive them of their most profitable business, thereby retarding the rehabilitation of the railroad industry. Coal-burning utilities favor such legislation as a means of obtaining coal more cheaply.

The coal-slurry example illustrates that: 1) Even monopolies must worry about competition from substitutes in the very long run. These substitutes are often provided by new technology. 2) Substitutes are attracted to compete with established monopolies by the existence of monopoly profits. If coal transport did not yield monopoly profits, the railroads would not be threatened by coal-slurry pipelines. 3) Firms often rely on the government to protect the barriers to entry into their industry. ∎

Source: "Coal-Slurry Pipeline Measure Is Rejected by House as Railroad Lobbying Succeeds," *The Wall Street Journal*, September 28, 1983.

---

2. *Monopolies always earn profits.* Some monopolies make above-normal profits; others earn normal profits; others suffer losses. Whether or not a monopolist makes profits depends on the demand curve and the cost curves. (For example, every patent issued by the U.S. patent office is a monopoly, but only a handful are used because price is less than average cost at all output levels for many patent holders.) The monopolists that do earn monopoly profits, however, are more likely to keep on earning these profits in the long run than competitive firms.

3. *Monopolists do not have to worry about demand.* Although the monopolist is the sole producer, the monopolist cannot ignore the law of demand. Once the monopolist has determined how much output to produce, the demand curve will determine the price at which that output will sell. If the monopolist attempts to set the price above the market-dictated price, some output will not be sold.

Facts about monopoly are:

1. *Monopolists do not produce where average costs are minimized.* In the long run, perfectly competitive firms will be forced to produce that quantity of output at which average costs are minimized. Monopolists, however, both in the long run and in the short run tend to produce a level of output less than necessary to minimize average costs. In Figure 3, *ATC* is minimized at an output of 11,000 units, but the monopolist produces only 8,000 units. In this sense, monopolists are less efficient than perfectly competitive firms.

2. *Monopolists charge a price higher than marginal cost.* The monopolist equates marginal revenue and marginal cost, and price is greater than marginal revenue. Thus, in the case of monopoly, $P > MC$.

3. *Monopolists produce where demand is elastic.* The profit-maximizing monopolist produces that quantity of output at which $MR = MC$. We have demonstrated that marginal revenue is only positive when demand is elastic. If the monopolist expanded into the inelastic portion of the demand schedule, total revenue would decline, and the firm's profits would fall. This characteristic of monopoly pricing can be used as a test for the existence of monopoly behavior. If the demand for a profit is inelastic at the current price, the seller is not behaving like a profit-maximizing monopoly.

4. *There is no supply curve for a monopolist.* The monopolist supplies a certain quantity of output given demand and cost conditions. The monopolist does not have a supply curve showing how much output will be supplied at different prices because *the monopolist sets prices*.

MONOPOLISTIC COMPETITION

All price-searching firms are not monopolists. In fact, few price searchers are monopolies. Price searchers can be anything from a pure monopoly to a firm that bears a close resemblance to a perfect competitor. The characteristic common to all price searchers is that they all face a downward-sloping demand schedule for their product. In order to sell more of their product, they must lower their price.

In the real world, there is usually some basis for distinguishing between the goods and services produced by different sellers. These distinctions may be based on the physical attributes of the product (hamburgers at one restaurant are different in some respects from hamburgers at other restaurants), on location (one gas station may be more conveniently located than another), on the type of service offered (one dry cleaner offers 2-hour service; another offers one-day service), and even on imagined differences (one type of aspirin is "better" than another). The point is that there are differences—real or imagined—among products. Sellers of these different products have some monopoly power over the customers who have a preference for their product. How much monopoly power they have depends upon the strength of this preference.

The theory of **monopolistic competition** was developed by the American economist Edward Chamberlin and the English economist Joan Robinson to deal with markets that produce heterogeneous products. A monopolistically competitive industry is one that blends the features of monopoly and competition.

> The four essential characteristics of **monopolistic competition** are: 1) the number of sellers is large enough so that each seller acts independently of the other; 2) the product is differentiated from seller to seller; 3) there is free entry into and exit from the industry; 4) sellers are price searchers.

When sellers are acting independently, each seller, when deciding upon its price and output, presumes that its decisions have no discernible effect on the rest of the market. The price-searching characteristic follows from the differentiation-of-products characteristic. Because products are different (by physical traits, location, type of service, or imagined differences), the seller has some control over price. The degree of control may be quite limited, but it is there. The seller who raises the price will not lose all customers (as would the perfect competitor) because some customers will have a strong enough preference to accept the higher price. The determinants of the strength of consumer preferences are a key topic in the study of monopolistic competition. The monopolistically competitive firm faces a downward-sloping demand curve. The firm's marginal-revenue curve lies below its demand curve, just as a monopolist's does.

Profit Maximization by the Monopolistically Competitive Firm

To maximize profits, firms produce that quantity of output at which *MR* equals *MC*. The monopolistic competitor is no exception to this rule. Like the monopolist, the monopolistic competitor faces a downward-sloping demand curve; marginal revenue will be less than average revenue (price). It, therefore, selects that *quantity* at which *MR* equals *MC* and charges the *price* that clears the market. Analytically, in the short run the theory of monopolistic competition is the same as the theory of the monopoly. The analysis of Table 1 and Figure 3 apply just as well to monopolistic competition as to monopoly in the short run.

Indeed, in the short run, the main difference between monopolistic competition and monopoly is the price elasticity facing the firm. Since a monopolistic competitor faces more competition from the substitute products of other firms in the industry, its price elasticity of demand will greatly exceed that of a typical monopolist.

In the long run, however, the two types of market organization are strikingly different. Barriers to entry protect the monopolist from the entry of competitors. If a monopoly earns substantial profits, the entry of new firms will not automatically squeeze out those profits. Monopolistic competition, however, shares with perfect competition the characteristic of *freedom of entry.* Free entry means that if a monopolistic competitor earns economic profits in the short run, new firms can (and will) enter the market; new firms can gain access to these economic profits, eventually driving them down to zero.

One example of a monopolistic competitor is a service station located on a busy intersection. It earns substantial economic profits in the short run. Like the monopolist, its price is above average total cost after equating *MR* and *MC.* If the station were a monopolist (say, a gas station with an exclusive franchise along a tollway), new firms could not gain access to these profits. This gas station would be protected from competition. The monopoly could keep on earning profits for a long period of time. Not so with the monopolistic competitor.

In the long run, new firms can enter the monopolistically competitive market. Attracted by high profits, another service station will be built on the opposite corner of the intersection—a close but not a perfect substitute. The two stations will differ in terms of access, number of gas pumps, friendliness of service, operating hours, and so on. The entry of the second firm will have two effects on the demand schedule of the first: 1) When customers are attracted away from the first station, the demand schedule for the first station's product will shift to the left. 2) Because buyers now have more substitutes for the product of the first station, the demand schedule will become more elastic. If both stations continue to make economic profits, even more gas stations will be built—two more at the same intersection and then another at the nearest intersection. Each new entrant will reduce the demand facing other stations and make their demand schedules more elastic.

Figure 5   The Long-Run Equilibrium of a Monopolistically Competitive Firm

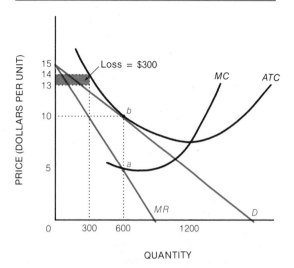

A firm engaged in monopolistic competition faces a downward-sloping demand curve, such as *D.* In the long run, because of free entry, economic profits will be driven down to zero. Thus, the long-run equilibrium must be a point such as *b* where *D* is just tangent to the *ATC* curve. For any price other than $10, profits are negative. Profits are at a maximum when price is $10 and output is 600 units. Since profits are at a maximum at 600 units of ouput, *MR* must equal *MC* at 600 units. Thus, the *MC* and *MR* curves must intersect directly below point *b.*

As in the case of perfect competition, this process ends when economic profits have been driven down to zero.

The long-run equilibrium of a typical monopolistically competitive firm is shown in Figure 5. In the long run, new firms will enter until economic profits are driven down to zero. Graphically, profits equal zero at a point to the left of the lowest point on the *ATC* curve, where the downward-sloping demand curve is tangent to the *ATC* curve. In Figure 5, point *b*—where output is 600 units and price is $10—is the point of zero profits and, therefore, the point of long-run equilibrium. In Figure 5, 600 units is the quantity that equates marginal cost and marginal revenue, and $10 is the price that corresponds to 600 units on the demand curve. Therefore, point *b* is the point of maximum profit. Notice that since the demand curve is tangent to *ATC* at point *b,* price is less than *ATC* to the left or to the right of point *b.*

Profit is zero at point *b* and negative elsewhere. For example, at an output of 300 units, price is $13 and *ATC* is $14, resulting in a $1 loss per unit. We have already shown that profits are maximized where marginal cost equals marginal revenue. Accordingly, the *MC* and *MR* curves intersect directly below the tangency of the demand curve and the *ATC* curve at point *b*.

The optimum, or minimum-unit-cost, level of output is clearly 1200 units in Figure 5 because at that output level, *MC* = *ATC*. In long-run equilibrium, each firm in a monopolistically competitive industry will produce an output that is smaller than the optimal capacity. This smaller than optimal output is produced because the demand curve is downward-sloping and tangent to the average-cost curve. Thus, there is *excess capacity,* making monopolistic competition less efficient than perfect competition. Many regard such excess capacity as the price we must pay for variety.

Product Differentiation and Advertising

The threat of the entry of new firms and the loss of economic profits are facts of life for monopolistic competitors. If they can erect artificial barriers to entry (by exclusive government franchises, licensing, zoning ordinances, and so on), they can delay the day when their economic profits are driven down to zero. Monopolistic competitors, by definition, produce goods and services that are different. If they can succeed in making their product more distinct from their competitors by engaging in **nonprice competition,** customer loyalty will be stronger. The stronger is this customer loyalty, the smaller will be the loss of customers as new firms enter and the less elastic will be the demand for their product.

> **Nonprice competition** is any action other than the lowering of prices that differentiates one product from the competition and delays the disappearance of economic profits.

Advertising to differentiate products is encountered frequently in monopolistically competitive markets. In fact, nonprice competition can earn considerable short-run profits for the firm and offers the potential of long-run profits if new entrants cannot copy the nonprice attribute. Profits on some brand-name products, like Bayer aspirin or Borden's condensed milk, have persisted for very long periods of time. In other cases, profits are transitory. If the gas-station owner differentiates the product by staying open all night or by offering a free car wash with fillups, then competitors can do the same. (See Example 5.)

Market Size and Efficiency

Monopolistic competition has two important characteristics in common with perfect competition: freedom of entry and a large number of firms. In both types of industries, economic profits are driven down to zero in the long run. The major difference between the two markets is that the product is homogeneous in the case of perfect competition and heterogeneous in the case of monopolistic competition. Monopolistic competition most closely approximates perfect competition *in large markets.*

An example of a large monopolistically competitive market would be service stations in a large metropolitan area. Service stations in a large market could be distinguished from service stations in a small market (such as a small town) by the kinds of service available: convenient location, self-service pumps, car repairs, automatic car wash, long hours of operation.

In a small town, it may be that the service station is the only place that can offer some of these services. In a large city, each service station faces far more competition not only for gasoline but for all the other services as well. There are firms that specialize in car repair, car washing, or automobile service. In the large market, there is a greater availability of close substitutes; the large number of service stations and specialist firms makes the demand curve for the product of any one service station quite elastic. In the small market, because each service station faces less competition from close substitutes, the demand curve for the product of any one service station is not quite as elastic.

In large markets, the distinction between monopolistic competition and perfect competition becomes less pronounced.

Figure 6   Monopolistic Competition and the Size of the Market

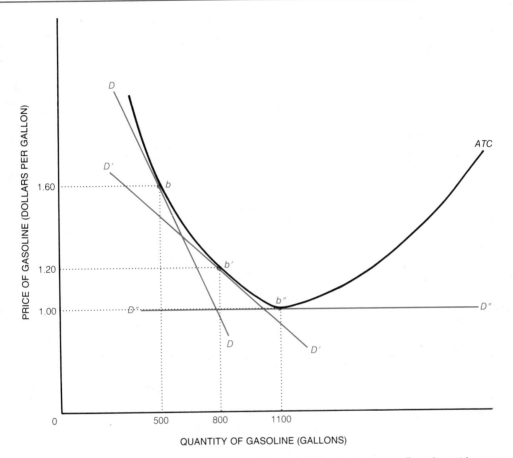

With a larger market for gasoline (more buyers), the demand curve is flatter because a smaller price cut is necessary to sell one more unit of the product. Thus, D' would correspond to the demand curve for a larger market than the market with demand curve D. Since in the long run profits are zero in monopolistic competition, a larger market brings with it a smaller price (b' as opposed to b) and a greater exploitation of economies of scale within the individual firm. The bigger the market the closer is the monopolistically competitive equilibrium to the perfectly competitive (long-run) equilibrium, illustrated by the horizontal demand curve D''.

In Figure 6, the small-town demand curve, D, is steeper (and less elastic) than the big-city demand curve, D'. The small-market long-run equilibrium occurs at b, where price is $1.60 per gallon and output is 500 gallons. The large-market long-run equilibrium occurs at b', where price is $1.20 and output is 800 gallons. If the large market continues to grow and the distinctions between the products of the different firms become negligible, eventually the demand curve would become perfectly elastic. The market would become perfectly competitive, producing in the long

run an output of 1100 gallons at a price of $1.00 per gallon.

APPLICATIONS

The theories of monopoly and monopolistic competition explain why price-searching firms behave the way they do. These theories explain a variety of behavior patterns encountered every day in the real world, including price discrimination, markup pricing, and discrepancies in product durability.

Example 5   Monopolistic Competition and Generic Gas

Gasoline stations are a good example of monopolistic competition. There are many of them; entry is easy; economic profits tend to disappear in the long run; there is product differentiation by brand, service, and location. Gas stations are either owned by the oil companies themselves or by "independents" who are franchised by an oil company to sell that company's gas. In a suit filed in 1971, the independent gas-station operators filed suit against the major oil companies claiming that they should be allowed to buy gas from the cheapest wholesale source of supply. Under a typical franchise agreement, the independent is required to buy gas only from the franchising oil company. In a settlement reached in September 1984, the independents acquired the right to buy gasoline from the source of their choice. The requirement imposed by the oil companies was that if the independent sells "debranded" gasoline (gasoline not purchased from the franchising company), this gas must come out of a separate pump marked as generic gas.

Experts in the field predict that debranding will lessen product loyalty. As debranding proceeds, it will be less clear to buyers exactly what brand they are buying when they buy generic gas. At the wholesale level, all gas is the same. Different additives are added at the retail level, and many consumers have developed a brand loyalty to the additive mixture of a particular oil company. Debranding should weaken this loyalty.

The weakening of brand loyalty will show itself as an increase in the price elasticity of the demand curve facing a particular gas station. Prior to debranding, a customer might prefer one station over another because of its location, its service, or its brand of gasoline. After debranding, one reason for customer preference will disappear. Gas-station demand curves, therefore, will become more horizontal, prices may fall, and the gas-station industry should more closely resemble perfect competition. ■

Source: "Brand Loyalty May Waver at Gasoline Stations," *New York Times*, September 25, 1984.

Price Discrimination

Thus far this chapter has assumed that the price searcher charges the same price to all buyers, but this is not always the case. Customers often pay different prices for the same product. Large users of electricity (factories, for example) pay lower rates than small users (households); movie prices are lower during the day than in the evening; doctors and lawyers often charge wealthy clients more than poor clients; airlines charge business travelers higher fares by requiring advance ticket purchases and minimum stays for discounts. All of these situations are examples of **price discrimination.**[2]

> **Price discrimination** exists when the same product or service is sold at different prices to different buyers.

Conditions for Price Discrimination.   In order for firms to engage in price discrimination,

1. the seller must exercise some control over the price; price discrimination is possible only for price searchers.
2. the seller must be able to distinguish easily among different types of customers.
3. it must be impossible for one buyer to resell the product to other buyers.

If the firm is not a price searcher, it cannot control its price. The seller who cannot distinguish between customers will not know which buyers should be charged the lower price. The electric company meters electricity usage and can readily distinguish high-volume from low-volume users; doctors and lawyers can fairly well identify wealthy clients on the basis of appearance, home address, and stated profession. By placing advance-purchase requirements and minimum-stay requirements on tickets, airlines can create conditions that many business travelers cannot meet. If one buyer can sell to another, low-price buyers can sell to high-price buyers, and no one will be willing to pay the high price. Midday movies can-

---

2. For detailed discussions of price discrimination in the real world, see F. M. Scherer, *Industrial Market Structure and Economic Performance*, 2nd ed. (Boston: Houghton Mifflin, 1980), chap. 11; James V. Koch, *Industrial Organization and Price*, 2nd ed. (Englewood Cliffs, N.J.: Prentice-Hall, 1980), chap. 12

Figure 7   Price Discrimination: Electricity

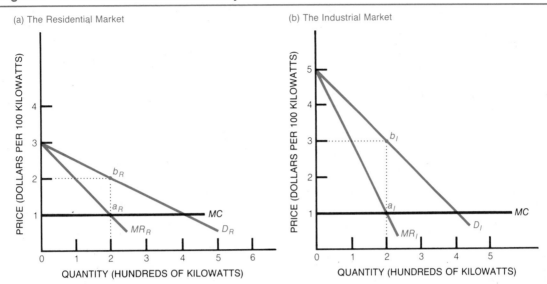

(a) The Residential Market

(b) The Industrial Market

The demand and marginal-revenue curves of residential customers are drawn as D_R and MR_R in panel (a). They are more elastic than the demand and marginal-revenue curves $(D_I$ and $MR_I)$ of industrial customers in panel (b). The marginal cost of providing electricity (MC) is the same for industrial and residential customers and is constant at $1 per kilowatt. The electric company will maximize profits in each market by equating MR and MC in each market. In the industrial market, $MR = MC$ at a price of $3; in the residential market $MR = MC$ at a price of $2.

not be resold to evening moviegoers; poor clients cannot resell legal and medical services to the wealthy; industrial users of electricity cannot sell their electricity to households. Airline tickets with a minimum-one-week-stay requirement cannot be sold to someone departing on a two-day business trip.

If the above conditions are met, the seller can divide the market in various noncompeting groups. A profit-maximizing seller will then charge prices according to the price elasticity of demand of each group. For example, if residential users of electricity have a more elastic demand for electricity than industrial users, it pays the electric company to charge a higher price to industrial users. The higher the price elasticity of demand, the lower the price charged.

To see how price discrimination raises profits, assume that the electric company charged the same price in both markets. Suppose that the demand of residential users had a price elasticity of 4 and that the demand of industrial users had a price elasticity of 2. The electric company's MR from selling another unit to residential customers would then exceed its MR from selling one less

unit to industrial customers. Accordingly, it would pay the firm to shift output from industrial users to residential users by raising the industrial price and lowering the residential price. The process of raising the price to the users with a low price elasticity of demand and lowering price to users with a high price elasticity of demand would continue until the marginal revenue the firm earns in each market is the same. Clearly, as long as MR differs between markets it pays to reduce the quantity sold with a low MR and raise the quantity sold with a high MR.

Panel (a) of Figure 7 shows the demand curve of residential users, D_R; panel (b) shows the demand curve of industrial users, D_I. The marginal-revenue curve in (a) is MR_R and in (b) is MR_I. The marginal cost (MC) of a unit of electrical service is assumed to be $1 per 100 kilowatt hours.

The electric company equates MR and MC in each market by charging $2 to residential users and $3 to industrial users. The $2 residential price corresponds to the output quantity that equates MC and residential MR; The $3 industrial price corresponds to the output quantity that equates MC and industrial MR. Thus, the monopolist charges different prices because more profit can be earned by exploiting the differences in demand elasticities.

Markup Pricing

If one were to ask price-searching business managers how they set prices, they would likely answer: "We just set the price *x* percent above our average cost." Such price searchers would be referring to the practice of **markup pricing.**

> **Markup pricing** is the setting of prices at a given percentage above average cost.

According to this chapter, the business managers should be setting prices so that *MR* = *MC* at the quantity demanded. Does the widespread use of markup pricing mean that business firms do not follow the *MR* = *MC* rule? Because the amount of the markup depends upon the elasticity of demand, markup pricing is consistent with the theory of the profit-maximizing price searcher.

Retailers—supermarkets, drugstores, department stores, and specialty shops—buy their goods at wholesale prices (from the producers) and sell them at higher retail prices. In retailing, the percentage markup is the difference between the retail and wholesale prices divided by the wholesale price. Retailers face a downward-sloping demand curve. They offer a service (retailing) that is differentiated by location, hours of service, product lines, friendliness of service, and so on.

The supermarket, for example, offers a wide variety of goods ranging from basic food staples like flour, sugar, potatoes, and meats, to specialty items like toys, lightbulbs, greeting cards, and delicatessen foods. Each good is purchased at a wholesale price, and its retail price will be a markup over the wholesale price. Which items have a high percentage markup and which have a low percentage markup?

As we know, a profit-maximizing firm sets prices to equate marginal revenue and marginal cost. Retailers can buy one more unit of the product at the wholesale price; therefore, neglecting handling costs, the wholesale price is the marginal cost of the retailer.

Figure 8 shows what the demand curves for flour and envelopes facing a particular supermarket will look like. The price elasticity of demand for food staples (flour, sugar, vegetable oils) will be quite high to each supermarket. (Remember, the elasticity of demand facing a particular supermarket that must compete with other supermarkets is not the same thing as the elasticity of market demand for specific items like flour or lightbulbs.) These staples are items that are frequently purchased and well advertised. Supermarkets compete among themselves for such sales; slight changes in prices bring about large changes in sales.

The price elasticity of demand for discretionary items (envelopes, school supplies, beauty aids) will be less elastic to each supermarket. These items are purchased with less frequency; they are likely to be picked up because the shopper is already in the store; the shopper tends to be less aware of the prices of these items at competitive stores. Therefore, the demand curve for flour (*D_F* in Figure 8) is more elastic than the demand curve for envelopes *(D_E)* facing each store.

Assume the *MC* of flour (the wholesale price) is \$0.25 and the *MC* of envelopes (also the wholesale price) is \$0.15. The profit-maximizing supermarket manager will set prices to equate *MR* and *MC*. As Figure 8 shows, *MR* = *MC* at a price of \$0.42 per pound for flour and a price of \$0.50 per box for envelopes. The percentage markups are 68 percent [(\$0.42 − \$0.25)/\$0.25] for flour and 233 percent [(\$0.50 − \$0.15)/\$0.15] for envelopes. Actual supermarket markups reveal that—as the theory predicts—the percentage markups of discretionary items tend to be higher than the percentage markups of staple items.[3]

> If the price elasticity of demand is relatively high, the percentage markup will be small. If the price elasticity of demand is relatively low, the percentage markup will be high. The percentage markup is negatively related to the elasticity of demand.

Product Durability

Where is the 10-year lightbulb? Do business firms suppress ways of increasing product durability in

---

3. "Emergence of Savvy Consumers Forces Painful Rethinking by Supermarkets," *Wall Street Journal,* September 29, 1980. For instance, the percentage markups on lightbulbs and school supplies are 55 and 47 percent, respectively, while the markups on flour and coffee are 16 and 10 percent, respectively.

Figure 8   The Theory of Markup Pricing: Flour and Envelopes

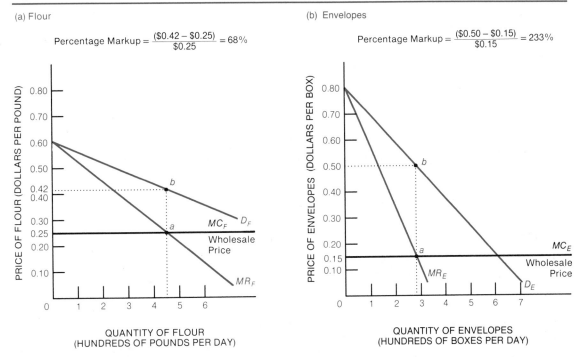

(a) Flour

$$\text{Percentage Markup} = \frac{(\$0.42 - \$0.25)}{\$0.25} = 68\%$$

(b) Envelopes

$$\text{Percentage Markup} = \frac{(\$0.50 - \$0.15)}{\$0.15} = 233\%$$

The demand for flour, D_F, facing the supermarket is elastic. The demand for envelopes, D_E, is less elastic. Because the supermarket maximizes profits by equating MR and MC for each product, there will be a higher percentage markup for envelopes than for flour. Percentage markups tend to be higher the less elastic is the demand for the product.

order to maintain long-run demand? This practice is sometimes referred to as *planned obsolescence*. How many of us have heard that there are tires that last twice as long, a lightbulb that lasts 10 years, more durable cars, motor oils that never have to be changed—but that these products have been suppressed so that consumers will have to buy the less durable goods more often?

Imagine that a firm has a complete monopoly in lightbulb production. Because it need not fear competition from other producers, there is no incentive to produce a more durable product simply to differentiate the firm's product from the competition's. Because people want lightbulbs because of the light they produce, the demand for lightbulbs is derived from the demand for light or, more specifically, from the demand for *lightbulb hours*.

Suppose that the monopolist discovers a costless method of doubling the life of a lightbulb; that is, the monopoly learns that it can continue

to produce a lightbulb for the same MC but the lightbulb will now last twice as many hours. Will the monopolist introduce the new lightbulbs? Clearly, this discovery would cut the cost of producing a *lightbulb hour* in half. Any monopolist would be happy to have lower costs of production. This monopolist could increase its profits just by doubling the price of the (improved) product and cutting the output in half. (See Figure 9.) Since the price of a *lightbulb hour* would remain the same if the price of a 2-hour bulb were twice the price of a 1-hour bulb, people could satisfy their demand by buying half as many lightbulbs each period as before. If the firm maintained the price of a lightbulb hour (by doubling the price of a lightbulb), the firm's profits would rise because revenue would stay the same while costs fell. As Figure 9 shows, however, the firm could do even better. Since the firm's marginal cost of producing *lightbulb hours* has fallen, it would pay the firm to reduce the price per lightbulb hour in or-

Figure 9   Lightbulb Durability and Monopoly Profits

(a) 1 Lightbulb = 1 Lightbulb Hour

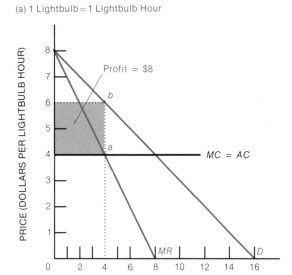

(b) 1 Lightbulb = 2 Lightbulb Hours

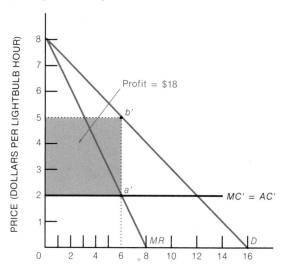

The demand curve *D* shows the demand for lightbulb hours (not lightbulbs). Panel (a) shows a situation where 1 lightbulb equals 1 lightbulb hour (each lightbulb burns only 1 hour). If the *MC* of lightbulbs is $4, monopoly profits are maximized where output is 4 bulbs, where *MC* equals $4, and where price equals $6. Monopoly profits are $8. A costless doubling of lightbulb durability (to make 1 lightbulb burn 2 lightbulb hours) is shown in panel (b). Marginal cost per lightbulb hour is now reduced to $2, but demand for lightbulb hours remains the same. The monopolist now maximizes profit at an output level of 6 lightbulb hours (= 3 bulbs). The monopoly price is now $5 per lightblub hour, and monopoly profit equals $18.

der to equate *MR* and *MC*. In Figure 9, the firm *increases* its profits by charging $5 per lightbulb hour ($10 per bulb) for its improved bulb.

The reason why business firms do not extend the durability of a good more than they do is that it costs firms to make goods more durable. To produce a space vehicle with virtually no chance of breaking down costs millions of dollars; the cost could be reduced dramatically if all the backup systems and safety checks were eliminated. Similarly, to produce more durable cars requires certain trade-offs; either the car must have a higher price (like the Mercedes-Benz or Rolls-Royce), or other characteristics like styling and handling performance must be sacrificed (as in the Toyota Corolla).

The theory of price searching explains that both monopolists and monopolistic competitors produce that quantity of output at which marginal revenue equals marginal costs. In the long run, monopolies can maintain monopoly profits, while

the profits of monopolistic competitors are squeezed out by the entry of new firms.

The chapter that follows will try to evaluate monopoly and monopolistic competition in relation to perfect competition. Characteristics that will be important in such a comparison include 1) the fact that monopolists are not pressured to produce at minimum average cost in the long run and 2) the fact that price searchers do not equate marginal cost and price.

Summary

1.   A pure monopoly exists when there is one seller producing a product that has no close substitutes. Barriers to entry keep out competitors. The monopolist is a price searcher and has considerable control over price. Pure monopoly is rare in the real world because of

substitutes and the absence of absolute barriers to entry, especially in the long run. Sources of monopoly are: economies of scale, patents, ownership of crucial raw materials, public franchises, and collusion.

2. Price searchers face downward-sloping demand curves; they must lower their price in order to sell more. As long as the price searcher charges all customers a uniform price, price and average revenue are the same. For price searchers, price will exceed marginal revenue. When marginal revenue is positive, demand is elastic; when marginal revenue is negative, demand is inelastic. Therefore, a profit-maximizing price searcher will never produce at an inelastic point on the demand curve.

3. Monopolists maximize profits by producing that output quantity at which marginal revenue and marginal cost are equal or by charging that price at which $MR = MC$. Once the monopolist has chosen the optimal output, the market will dictate the price, and vice versa. Monopolists do not always make profits. When monopolies are unprofitable, they follow the same shutdown rule as competitive firms.

4. Popular fallacies about monopolies are: a) monopolists charge the highest price possible; b) monopolists do not have to be concerned with market demand; c) monopolists always make a profit. Monopolists do not produce where price equals marginal cost. Monopolists do not produce in the long run where average costs are minimized. Monopolists produce where demand is elastic.

5. A monopolistically competitive industry has many sellers, sells a differentiated product, has freedom of entry and exit, and contains individual firms that are price searchers. Monopolistic competitors also produce where MR equals MC. In the long run, the entry of new firms will drive profits down to zero. When profits are zero and $MR = MC$, the firm's output must be less than the minimum efficient scale; that is, unit costs are not minimized as in perfect competition. By engaging in nonprice competition—through product differentiation and advertising—monopolistically competitive firms can delay the disappearance of economic profits. In large markets, monopolistic competition approximates perfect competition.

6. Price searchers can raise their profits through price discrimination. Buyers with inelastic demand will pay higher prices than those with elastic demand. The practice of markup pricing is consistent with the MR-equals-MC rule. The percentage markup will be negatively related to the elasticity of demand. Product durability will depend upon the cost of supplying durability.

Key Terms

pure monopoly
price searcher
marginal revenue *(MR)*
average revenue *(AR)*
marginal-revenue schedule
monopolistic competition
nonprice competition
price discrimination
markup pricing

Questions and Problems

1. Firm A can sell all it wants at a price of $5. Firm B lowers its price from $6 to $5 to sell more output. Explain why the marginal revenue of Firm A is not the same as the marginal revenue of Firm B even though they are both charging a $5 price.

2. "The shutdown rule applies only to firms operating in competitive markets. Monopolies don't use any shutdown rule." Evaluate this statement.

3. Explain why a price searcher can choose either its profit-maximizing output level or its profit-maximizing price. Why is it that when one choice is made, the firm has no choice about the other?

4. A monopolist produces 100 units of output, and the price elasticity of demand at this point on the demand curve is -0.5. What advice would you give the monopolist? From this information, what can you say about marginal revenue?

5. A price searcher produces output at a constant MC of $5 and has no fixed costs. The demand curve facing the price searcher is indicated in Table A.

a. Determine the price searcher's profit-maximizing output, price, and profit.

b. Show that by producing more or less output, the firm would decrease its profit.

c. Explain what happens to marginal revenue when output is raised from 15 to 20 units.

Table A

Price (dollars)	Quantity Demanded (units)
12	0
10	5
8	10
6	15
4	20

---

6. A food concession in a sports stadium makes an economic profit of $100,000 in the first year of operation. Explain what will happen to profits in subsequent years

a. if the concessionaire is granted an exclusive franchise to stadium concessions and

b. if potential competitors have the freedom to set up concession stands in the stadium. In the latter case, can the concessionaire do anything to protect long-run profits?

7. Prices of movie tickets and tickets to sports events and concerts are typically lower for children than for adults. Explain why using the theory of price discrimination.

8. Explain why the entry of new firms into a monopolistically competitive market makes the demand curves of established firms more elastic.

9. Assume a monopoly is making an economic profit. The monopoly is sold to the highest bidder. Would the new owner make an economic profit? Why or why not?

10. Suppose the price at which a monopolist can sell its product is $P = 10 - Q$, where Q is the number of units sold per period. The monopolist's $MC = ATC = \$4$.

a. Graph the demand curve.

b. Graph total revenue for output levels from 0 units to 10 units.

c. Graph the MR for each output level.

d. Which output level maximizes profit?

e. How much is maximum profit?

11. A monopolist is making an economic profit of $100,000 per year. What would happen under the following circumstances to the monopolist's price and output?

a. The government imposes a fixed tax of $90,000 a year on the monopolist.

b. The government imposes a fixed tax of $110,000 a year on the monopolist.

12. A monopolist sets output by maximizing revenue. What advice would you give the monopolist?

13. "The medical-care industry is not a monopoly because the price elasticity of demand for medical care is less than unity. Monopolists would charge higher prices." Evaluate this statement.

14. Explain why MR is less than price for a price searcher.

Suggested Readings

Chamberlin, Edward H. *The Theory of Monopolistic Competition,* 6th ed. Cambridge: Harvard University Press, 1980.

Kitch, Edmund W. *et al.* "The Regulation of Taxicabs in Chicago." *Journal of Law and Economics* (October 1971), pp. 285–350.

North, Douglass C. and Roger LeRoy Miller. *The Economics of Public Issues,* 5th ed. New York: Harper and Row, 1980, chap. 2.

Smith, Adam. *The Wealth of Nations,* ed. Edwin Cannan. New York: The Modern Library, 1939, chap. 7.

31

Monopoly and Competition Compared

Chapter Preview

Ever since Adam Smith argued that the invisible hand of competition would lead profit-maximizing producers and utility-maximizing consumers to an efficient allocation of society's resources, economists have been captivated by its charm. In addition to the praise offered by economists, the antitrust laws of the United States, beginning with the Sherman Act of 1890 (to be discussed in a later chapter), have made a competitive order the law of the land.

This chapter explains why perfect competition is more efficient than monopoly in the absence of external costs but also describes the advantages and disadvantages of monopoly.

When thinking about how competition influences the way the economy works as a whole, it is easy to commit the fallacy of composition. People might reason that because everyone in a competitive order is looking out for himself or herself, society's interests will suffer. The study of competition shows that social interests can be promoted when each person promotes his or her self-interest.

We cannot prove that competition leads to efficiency for the economy as a whole unless we can examine a situation in which all the conditions of perfect competition are met. Thus, we will begin by considering an economy with no monopoly elements and with perfect information about prices and product quality. In addition, in this economy there are no costs or benefits accruing to those not involved in the activity. Thus, buyers gather all the benefits of the goods they buy; sellers pay all the costs of producing the goods they sell. In other words, we are talking about markets made up of well-informed consumers who face many producers of shoes, shirts, housing, and so on—where property rights are well-defined and strictly enforced. How will this economy function? ■

THE CASE FOR COMPETITION: EFFICIENCY

The concept of *economic efficiency* is far from simple, but it basically means that nothing is being wasted. Consider the following examples of inefficiency:

1.   Ann and Betty live on a deserted island with only 50 apples and 100 bananas per week upon which to subsist. Ann will not eat bananas, and Betty will not eat apples. Each has 25 apples and 50 bananas, and they do not trade.
2.   Wheat is being grown on Iowa corn land, and corn is being grown on Kansas wheat land.
3.   The price of wheat is $10 per bushel in Chicago and $2 per bushel in Kansas City. The wheat is used in the finest Illinois bakeries and as animal fodder in Kansas.

In each of these three cases, a slight rearrangement in production or consumption can make everyone better off. Both Betty and Ann will be better off if Ann gives Betty her bananas and Betty gives Ann her apples; consumers and producers of wheat and corn would benefit if wheat were grown in Kansas and corn were grown in Iowa; because both farm products would be produced more cheaply. Consumers in Illinois and producers in Kansas would benefit if wheat were shipped to Illinois. Such rearrangements would change situations characterized by economic **inefficiency** into situations characterized by economic **efficiency**.[1]

> **Efficiency** is present when society's resources are so organized that it is impossible to make everyone better off by *any* reallocation of resources.

> **Inefficiency** is present when resources can be reallocated to make everyone better off or when at least one person could be made better off without hurting anyone else.

The above examples clearly show that inefficiency is present when profitable trading opportunities are not being exploited. Ann can trade her bananas to Betty in return for Betty's apples. Similarly, farmers will make more profits by devoting Kansas wheat land to wheat and Iowa corn land to corn. Traders can buy wheat in Kansas City and sell it for a handsome profit in Chicago. It was Adam Smith's insight that individuals, guided by their own self-interest, will eliminate any economic inefficiencies. The invisible hand operates when each person's quest for profit leads to economic efficiency for all.

Economic Efficiency

Market equilibrium in perfectly competitive markets brings about the right balance between consumer utility and costs of production. When this balance is achieved, economic efficiency is the result.

Consumers buy a variety of goods—milk, shirts, cars, housing, books, and so on. As the chapter on demand utility showed, well-informed and rational consumers carry out their purchases of any particular good until the ratio of its marginal utility *(MU)* to price is the same as that ratio for all other goods. Thus, individual consumers arrange consumption so that the prices of the goods they buy reflect the marginal utilities of those goods: low-priced goods have low *MU*s and high-priced goods have high *MU*s. Thus, the price of a good is a dollar measure of the good's marginal utility to the individual; indeed, we can say that the marginal benefit of the good to the consumer equals its price. Because the price is the same to all buyers and to all sellers in a perfectly competitive market, each consumer in a perfectly competitive market pays the same price.

> **The price of a good measures its marginal benefit to society because each utility-maximizing consumer equates the good's *MU/P* to that of all other goods.**

Now consider the other side of the market: the competitive firms that produce milk, cars, bread, shirts, and houses. Each producer will carry out production until price and marginal cost are equal. If price exceeds marginal cost, the competitive producer finds profit opportunities in expand-

---

1. This notion of efficiency was first developed by the Italian economist, Vilfredo Pareto. This concept of economic efficiency is named in his honor as *Pareto optimality*.

ing production until diminishing returns drive marginal cost up to the level of price. When price equals marginal cost, additional profit opportunities to each individual producer are exhausted.

> In perfect competition, every producer faces the same price and produces to the point where marginal cost equals price. Therefore, each producer has the same marginal cost of production. Thus, the marginal cost of bread for one producer, which equals the marginal cost for other producers, is the same as the marginal cost of bread to society.

The good is produced using a minimum of society's resources when each producer has the same marginal cost. If the good were produced by firms at different marginal costs, the same quantity could be produced at lower total cost by shifting production from high-marginal-cost producers to low-marginal-cost producers. Market equilibrium entails producing the good at minimum cost and up to the point where marginal benefit (price) is just balanced by marginal cost. The economy is efficient when society's extra cost of producing a good equals the marginal benefit of that good. When $P = MC$ and markets clear, opportunities to increase profits have been exhausted.

Social Efficiency

The difference between price and marginal cost is not only a profit opportunity for individual producers, it also signals a social opportunity. If $P > MC$, there is a social payoff to producing more of the good. Remember that marginal cost is the opportunity cost at the margin—what is being given up elsewhere. To say that price exceeds marginal cost is to say that the resources used in the production of this particular good have a higher marginal benefit to society than those resources have elsewhere since marginal costs are measured as opportunity costs.

In Figure 1, an output of 5,000 units is 3,000 units short of the equilibrium quantity. The marginal cost to society is $70 (at point a), and the marginal benefit to society is $120 (at point b). Moving from an output of 5,000 units to an output of 8,000 units benefits society by the shaded area abc. Point c is an efficient output level.

Figure 1 Perfect Competition and Social Efficiency

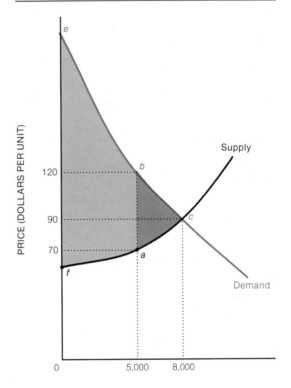

When output is restricted to 5,000 units, the marginal cost of the 5,001st unit of output is the price at point a, or $70; the marginal benefit is the price at point b, or $120. Moving to the equilibrium quantity of 8,000 units results in a net gain to society of area abc, because marginal benefits exceed marginal costs on the intervening 3,000 units. Social welfare is maximized when price is $90 and the total of consumer and producer surplus equals area ecf.

> If price does not equal marginal cost for all goods, there is inefficiency in the system, and all people can be made better off (or at least some better off and none worse off) by reallocating resources until price equals marginal cost.

THE LIMITATIONS OF COMPETITION

Even in a perfectly competitive world, the invisible hand may not lead to the best of all possible worlds for at least three reasons:

1. Perfect competition may lead to inequalities in the distribution of income that are not regarded by a democratic majority as equitable.

2. When the operation of a competitive firm results in costs to someone outside the firm, perfectly competitive markets may cause inefficient resource allocation.

3. Perfect competition may not be conducive to a high rate of technological progress.

Equity Versus Efficiency

As demonstrated above, perfect competition leads to economic efficiency. Efficiency means nothing is being wasted. In an efficient situation, to help one person, someone else must be hurt.

Efficiency can prevail even when the resulting distribution of income is widely believed to be unethical, unjust, or unfair. In a perfectly efficient economy, **economic equity** need not be present: some people may live in a state of grinding poverty, while those owning large quantities of scarce resources may live in luxury. Resources may be allocated efficiently under perfect competition, but there is no guarantee that resources will be divided equitably among the members of society. In order to make the poor better off in an efficient economy, however, the rich must be made worse off because there are no extra resources around that are being wasted.

> **Economic equity** is present when resources are distributed fairly according to widely accepted social-welfare criteria.

In our real world of poverty and scarcity, a society that purposely enacts policies that lead to inefficiencies (or wastefulness) might be just as negligent as the efficient society that ignores those people in real need. If society wishes to alter the distribution of resources among the members of society to achieve economic equity, it should seek to do so without reducing economic efficiency. The later chapter on public finance shows that this is easier said than done.

Externalities

A perfectly competitive allocation of resources will be economically inefficient if **externalities** are present.

> **Externalities** are present when an economic activity results in direct economic costs or benefits for third parties not immediately involved in the activity.

Externalities arise when a factory belches black smoke that raises the cost of laundry or medical care for those people living in the vicinity, when the chemical plant dumps wastes that affect fishing and agricultural production, when the pulp mill pollutes the air others must breathe, or when the airport pollutes an area with deafening noise.

In order to understand the effects of an externality, it is necessary to distinguish between **private costs** and **external costs** and between **private benefits** and **external benefits.**

> **Private costs** (or **benefits**) are the costs (or benefits) borne (or enjoyed) by the firm producing a good.

> **External costs** (or **benefits**) are the costs (or benefits) borne (or enjoyed) by someone other than the firm producing the good.

When externalities are present, then, the full cost to society of producing a good is determined by adding the private costs and external costs together; the full benefit to society is the sum of the private benefits and external benefits. The costs or benefits to society of producing a good are the **social costs** or **social benefits.**

> **Social costs** are private costs plus external costs.

> **Social benefits** are private benefits plus external benefits.

The main feature of an externality is that the *marginal private cost (MPC)* of production does not necessarily reflect the *marginal social cost (MSC)*. The marginal social cost of producing steel includes not only the marginal private costs of the steel mill but also the marginal external costs imposed on others (the extra laundry costs, medical-care costs, and so on). The steel plant does not take these external costs into account when making its economic decisions.

Externalities lead to economic inefficiency because the marginal social benefit of steel *as measured by its market price* will be less than its marginal social cost.

Figure 2 shows a competitive steel industry that imposes external costs on others. At equilibrium, 1 million tons are produced at a price of $100 per ton (point *a*). The *MSC* curve measures marginal social costs while the supply curve measures only marginal private costs *(MPC)*. With a marginal social cost of $160 per ton at the equilibrium output level, an output of 1 million tons is too much steel production from the standpoint of society. Marginal social costs ($160) do not equal marginal social benefits ($100) when 1 million tons are produced because externalities are present. Too much steel is produced when marginal social cost is greater than price. Efficiency requires that 0.8 million tons of steel be produced (point *e*), where both marginal social cost and price are equal to $120.

Economic activities can have external benefits as well as external costs. When one neighbor plants flowers, surrounding neighbors also benefit. The person who considers only personal pleasure to be the benefit from growing flowers will plant flowers only to the point where marginal costs and marginal benefits are equal. The marginal costs to the person of growing the flowers does not equal the marginal benefits enjoyed by society (the neighborhood) because other neighbors get some marginal benefits as well. Economic inefficiency is present because too few flowers get planted. Externalities do not create problems only under conditions of perfect competition. All systems of resource allocation—from monopoly to planned socialism—are plagued by externalities. Pollution is as much a problem in the Soviet Union as it is in the United States; externalities are not unique to competitive capitalism. The presence of externalities is simply a problem that the invisible hand of perfect competition does not automatically solve. Different economic systems may cope better or worse with the problem of externalities.

Technological Progress

There is no guarantee that competition will be efficient in a *dynamic* (changing) situation. Perfect competition has been shown to be efficient when resources and technology are *static* (unchanging). Is it possible that competition is poorly suited to creating and promoting technological change?

Figure 2   Externalities and Competition

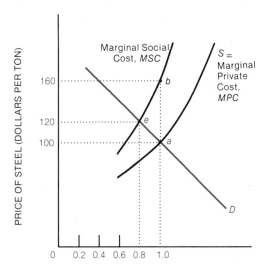

QUANTITY OF STEEL
(MILLIONS OF TONS PER PERIOD)

The supply and demand curves of this hypothetical steel industry intersect at the price/quantity combination of $100 per ton and 1 million tons of steel (point *a*). The supply curve, *S*, reflects only marginal *private* costs. The *MSC* curve shows marginal *social* costs. At the equilibrium point *a*, the marginal social cost of an extra ton of steel is $160, but the marginal social benefit is only $100, as measured by the height of the demand curve. Too much steel is produced from the society's point of view.

There is considerable controversy surrounding this question, which will be addressed in the next section.

THE CASE AGAINST MONOPOLY

Opponents of monopoly argue that monopoly is 1) inefficient and 2) unfair.

Sources of Inefficiency in Monopoly

Monopoly is inefficient for three reasons. First, monopoly leads to contrived scarcities. Second, the resources used to acquire monopoly power could have been used elsewhere in the economy. Third, monopoly does not force efficiency in production.

Contrived Scarcity. The basic argument against monopoly is that monopolies maximize profit by restricting output to the scale where price exceeds marginal cost. Remember that monopolies maximize profit where $MR = MC$, but $P > MR$. Therefore, price will exceed marginal cost at that output which maximizes monopoly profit.

> **Price measures marginal social benefit, and marginal cost measures marginal social cost (if externalities are not present); therefore, when $P > MC$ there is contrived scarcity in the economy.**

Contrived scarcity occurs when the economy would be better off—more efficient in the sense of giving more to everyone—if more of the monopolized good were produced. When $P > MC$, one more unit of output adds more to social welfare than to social costs, and it is possible to rearrange the allocation of resources (to produce more of the good and less of other goods) to make everyone better off.

To compare monopoly with perfect competition, consider a situation in which both are possible. Figure 3 depicts an industry where there are no economies of scale; average costs are the same for all levels of output. Therefore, average cost and marginal cost are the same: $AC = MC$. Either one large firm (a monopoly) or a large number of small firms (a perfectly competitive market) could satisfy consumer demand at the same average cost. Marginal cost ($= AC$) is a constant $4 per unit. The monopoly output level (300 units) is found where MR is also $4; the monopoly price is $7. Monopoly profits are represented by the color shaded area, which equals $900. Under perfect competition, on the other hand, free entry would squeeze out economic profits. The long-run competitive price would, therefore, be $4, and the competitive output would be 600 units (point c).

The cost of monopoly can be calculated from Figure 3. If this industry could be converted to perfect competition from monopoly, the equilibrium price/quantity combination would shift from point b to point c, and the price would fall from $7 to $4. The increase in consumer surplus resulting from the shift from monopoly to competition is the sum of the color shaded area (the mo-

Figure 3   Monopoly and Competition Compared

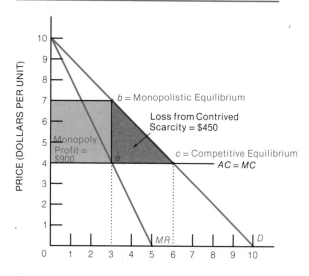

QUANTITY (HUNDREDS OF UNITS)

This industry has constant returns to scale where $AC = MC = \$4$ for all levels of output. If the industry were perfectly competitive, price would be $4 and output would be 600 units. If this industry were a single-firm monopoly, price would be $7 and output would be 300 units with a monopoly profit of $900($ = \$3 \times 300$). Monopoly profit is the color area. The monopolist creates profits by the contrived scarcity of 300 units (the monopolist produces 300 units less than the competitive industry). The loss from contrived scarcity is the grey area, which equals $450, or the deadweight loss to society. Moving from monopoly to competition creates consumer surplus of $1,350 ($900 + $450) while destroying only $900 worth of profits for the monopolist. More is gained by all parties taken together than is lost.

nopolist's profit of $900) and grey shaded area ($450). The gain in consumer surplus would, therefore, equal $1350. But the monopolist, who is also a member of society, loses monopoly profits of $900 in the process. The net gain to society of converting from monopoly to perfect competition (the consumers' gain minus the monopolist's loss) is simply the grey shaded triangle, which equals $450.[2] Notice that everyone involved

---

2. The deadweight loss can also be calculated another way. When $Q = 300$ and $P = \$7$, the margin between marginal social benefits and marginal social costs is $3 ($7 − $4). Hence, it pays society to expand output beyond the 300th unit. In effect, the 301st unit adds $3 to social welfare. The 601st unit adds nothing to social welfare since $P = MC$. From $Q = 300$ to $Q = 600$, the extra benefit per unit declines from $3 to $0. Thus, on the average, the 300 additional units from 300 (the monopolist's Q) to 600 (the Q under perfect competition) add $1.50 each (the average of $3 and $0), or $450.

could be made better off as a result of the move to perfect competition. Since consumers gain $1350 in consumer surplus, they could buy off the monopolist with a payment (say, $901) greater than the original monopoly profit—which would make the monopolist better off by $1 and the consumers better off by $449. The $450 loss from monopoly is a **deadweight loss** since nothing is received in exchange for the loss. The deadweight loss of monopoly is equivalent to throwing away valuable scarce resources.

A **deadweight loss** is a loss to society of consumer or producer surplus that is not offset by anyone else's gain.

How large are losses from contrived scarcities in the American economy? Economist Arnold Harberger has estimated the deadweight loss from all monopolies to be a very small fraction of total U.S output.[3] A number of other researchers roughly estimate these losses at about 1 percent of GNP. (See Example 1.)

Monopoly Rent Seeking.   Gordon Tullock and Anne Krueger have argued that the above-cited estimates of the deadweight losses from monopoly represent lower bounds to the true loss of society from monopoly.[4] In terms of Figure 3, if the industry were perfectly competitive, the price/quantity combination would be $4/600 units, or point *c,* and there would be no deadweight losses. If someone could turn this industry into a monopoly, that person could gain the potential monopoly profit of $900 (color area). People would be willing to spend real resources—or engage in **monopoly rent seeking**—to turn the industry into a monopoly and acquire the monopoly profit. The monopoly profit can be thought of as the rent received in return for expending the resources needed to turn a competitive industry into a monopoly or to maintain an existing monopoly.

Monopoly rent seeking is the activity of anyone trying to achieve or maintain a monopoly in order to gain the monopoly profits, or "rent."

A prime example of monopoly rent seeking would be lobbying costs. Monopolies can be achieved and maintained through government charters, franchises, and regulation. Example 4 in the preceding chapter mentioned the railroad lobby's opposition to coal-slurry pipelines. To maintain the railroads' monopoly over coal transport, real resources have to be spent on lobbying. Another prominent case is the lobbying in Congress by American automobile manufacturers for protection from foreign imports. Monopoly profits yield benefits to the monopolist, even though they harm the consumer through contrived scarcity.

If *all* monopoly profits are absorbed in monopoly rent seeking, consumers would lose the grey shaded area in Figure 3 (the loss of consumer surplus) and the monopolist would *not* gain the color shaded area (monopoly profit). Monopoly rent seeking, in this extreme case, has multiplied the deadweight loss of monopoly.

Monopoly rent seeking can lead to substantial social losses. To limit monopoly-rent-seeking behavior, it would be necessary to lessen substantially the possibility of "buying" monopoly through the manipulation of government. This is easier said than done.

X-**Inefficiency.**   The third loss from monopoly power is called *X*-**inefficiency,** a term coined by Harvard economist Harvey Leibenstein.[5] To understand *X*-inefficiency, recall that perfect competition forces enterprises to produce as cheaply as possible to stay in business. The competitive producer that fails to minimize costs will go bankrupt in the long run. What if the firm has a monopoly? While it is beneficial to the monopolist to minimize costs of production, it is not as costly to the monopolist who fails to do so as it is to the competitor. Unlike the competitive business, the monopolist will not be driven out of business if it fails to minimize costs. Hence, it is likely that "organizational slack" will develop in monopolistic industries.

3. Arnold Harberger, "Monopoly and Resource Allocation," *American Economic Review* 44 (May 1954): 77–87. We can mention only a few of the economists who have contributed to this estimate: David Schwartzman, Dean Worcester, Jr., David Kamerschen, and Michael Klass.
4. Anne Krueger, "The Political Economy of the Rent-Seeking Society," *American Economic Review* 64 (June 1974): 291–303; and Gordon Tullock, "The Welfare Cost of Tariffs, Monopolies, and Theft," *Western Economic Journal* 5 (June 1967): 224–32.

5. Harvey Leibenstein, "Allocative Efficiency vs. *X*-Inefficiency," *American Economic Review* 56 (June 1966): 392–415.

Example 1   The Case of Valium: Monopoly Versus Competition

This chapter explains why a monopoly produces less than a competitive industry and why consumers pay higher prices under monopoly. If an industry could be converted from monopoly to competition, consumers would be made better off by having more output at lower prices.

An examination of the prescription-drug industry reveals numerous instances in which the introduction of competition into a previously monopolistic market lowered prices. Prescription drugs developed by research-oriented drug companies are protected by patents for a 17-year period, giving the original manufacturer a monopoly over production and marketing for the duration of the patent. When the patent expires, other manufacturers are allowed to manufacture the drug in its generic (chemical equivalent) form. The original company usually continues to market the drug under its brand name but now in competition with other manufacturers.

One of the most prescribed prescription drugs in the United States is Hoffman-LaRoche's valium. Hoffman-LaRoche's patent on valium expired in the early 1980s, and the appearance of generic valium manufactured by rival firms is expected shortly after the federal government completes its certification procedures. Currently, some 40 million valium prescriptions are filled annually at an average price of about $10 for sales revenue to Hoffman-LaRoche of some $400 million. As generic brands appear on the market, experts predict that Hoffman-LaRoche will lower the price on its brand-name valium. The generic manufacturers will likely price generic valium at about one quarter of the brand-name price. To maintain sales despite generic competition, Hoffman-LaRoche has already changed the appearance of its valium (a heart-shaped hole is now placed in the center of each tablet) to further differentiate its valium from generic valium. On average, the price of valium should drop to about half of its original price as a consequence of these actions.

Lower prices mean an increase in consumer surplus. One estimate of the possible consumer-surplus gain is shown in the accompanying hypothetical figure. If the price dropped from $10 per prescription to $5 (from *d* to *c*), the quantity demanded would increase from 40 million to 50 million prescriptions, if the demand curve for valium looked like curve *b*. Consumer surplus would have risen by the area *acde* (the area of the rectangle

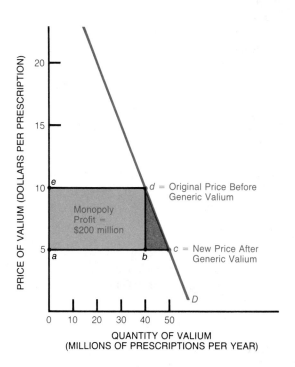

abde plus the area of the triangle *bcd*) or by $225 million (= $200 million + $25 million). Consumers would clearly be better off. How about producers? Before the change, the profits represented by the rectangle *abde* would have accrued to the monopolist. After the price change, the monopolist would lose this $200 million profit, but consumers would gain $225 million. Society as a whole would gain $25 million—the area of the triangle *bcd*. (This hypothetical figure probably overstates the monopolist's loss. Because of brand-name identification, the former monopolist's product will probably still command a higher price in the market place, thereby limiting the loss in profits below the above-estimated figure.) ■

Example 2   How Cable-TV Franchises Recapture Monopoly Profits

Cable-TV companies must obtain *franchises* from municipal governments because to provide their service they must lay cable under city streets and through people's back yards. Once a particular cable company has acquired a franchise, it has been granted a legal monopoly to be the sole cable TV operator in that municipality. Although cable TV franchises have yet to return substantial profits (due likely to the high capital costs of cable installation), it is expected that eventually cable TV operators will earn monopoly profits.

Some economists argue that the public should be allowed to capture some of the monopoly profits by either auctioning off the rights to the monopoly franchise to the highest bidder or by taxing the monopolist with high franchise fees. In both cases, all or a portion of the monopolist's future profits will be captured by the municipality that grants the monopoly.

Municipal governments appear to be following, at least partially, the recommendations of these economists. The Federal Communications Commission is currently investigating allegations that city and county governments have required cable companies to pay "improperly high" franchise fees. Federal rules permit a franchise fee of up to 3 percent of gross revenues. Federal rules further state that no fee may total more than 5 percent and that in order to charge between 3 and 5 percent, Federal Communication Commission approval must be obtained. A survey has found that 67 percent of the cable operators are being charged a franchise fee of between 3 and 5 percent without the proper waiver on file with the Federal Communications Commission.

If the granting of a legal monopoly creates monopoly profits, should city and county governments be allowed to capture a portion of these profits? Existing federal regulations appear to have responded to this normative question by restricting the local government's ability to capture these profits. ■

Sources: "Cable-Television Firms and Cities Haggle Over Franchises that Trail Expectations," *The Wall Street Journal,* December 28, 1983; National Cable Television Association.

X-inefficiency is the organizational slack that results from the lack of competition in monopolies. *X*-inefficiency results in costs that are higher than necessary.

How large are monopoly *X*-inefficiencies? Estimates of *X*-inefficiency as high as 2 percent of national output have been presented by industrial-organization experts, but accurate estimates are impossible to achieve. Although *X*-inefficiency is a very logical concept, it is very hard to quantify with any precision.[6]

Monopoly and Income Distribution

Is monopoly unfair because it creates too much wealth for monopolists? What is the effect of monopoly on the distribution of income?

In Figure 3, the transformation of the industry from monopoly to perfect competition would lower the price from $7 to $4; the consumer would pay $3 less for each unit purchased.

Income is redistributed from the monopolist to the consumer when the monopoly becomes competitive.

When an industry converts from being composed of competitors to being composed of a monopoly, income is redistributed from the consumer to the monopolist. Thus, the existence of monopoly profits affects the distribution of income among individuals. Are monopoly profits fair? This is an ethical question that economists are ill-equipped to answer, but many people regard the transfer of income from the consumer to the monopolist as unfair. (See Example 2.)

How large an impact has monopoly had on the American distribution of income? Again, it is difficult to get reliable estimates, but one study of the wealthiest 0.25 percent of U.S. households re-

---

6. Walter Primeaux conducted an interesting test of *X*-inefficiency: Primeaux found that in 49 cities, there is competition between at least two electric companies. Primeaux found that the costs of those companies that face competition is 11 percent below those of monopoly suppliers. *See* Primeaux, "An Assessment of *X*-Efficiency Gained Through Competition," *Review of Economics and Statistics* 59 (February 1977): 105–108.

veals that their share of wealth would fall from 18.5 percent to between 12 and 14 percent if all monopoly power were eliminated.[7]

Taxing Monopoly Profits

A normative objection to monopolies is that they can make above-normal, or economic, profits. Since the monopolist is protected from competition, its profits are secure from the inroads of competing firms.

Recall that monopoly is inefficient because too little is being produced. What can be done about monopoly profits without making the economy more inefficient? If monopoly profits can be taxed away without affecting in any way the output decision of the monopolist, there would be no loss of efficiency, and one objection to monopoly would be removed. Economists believe a **lump-sum tax** could accomplish these goals.

> A **lump-sum tax** is a tax that does not vary with any indicator of the firm's performance; that is, it does not vary with the firm's output, profit, or employment. It is like a fixed cost.

The effect of lump-sum taxation on monopoly output and profits is shown in Figure 4. Figure 4 shows a monopolist making substantial economic profits. Economic profits are $100,000 per year, since the profit-maximizing output is 20,000 units and the profit per unit is $5. How can the government tax away these profits without causing the monopolist to reduce output?

The tax collector could levy a $100,000 lump-sum tax on these profits. To the monopolist, such a tax would be like a fixed cost. The monopolist would continue to produce the same output and charge the same price as before the lump-sum tax. The lump-sum tax merely reduces the monopolist's economic profit (after tax) to zero. The ATC curve shifts up to include the tax, and the MC curve remains the same because a lump-sum tax cannot affect marginal costs.

A lump-sum tax does not influence marginal

7. William Comanor and Robert Smiley, "Monopoly and the Distribution of Wealth," *Quarterly Journal of Economics* 89 (May 1975): 177–94.

Figure 4   Taxing the Monopolist: Lump-Sum Taxation

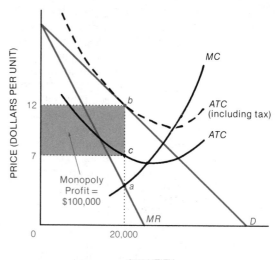

This monopolist maximizes profit by producing 20,000 units of output, which are sold at a price of $12 per unit. The average cost is $7; the monopolist earns a total profit of 20,000 units × $5, or $100,000. If the government levies a lump-sum tax of $100,000, the monopolist will continue to produce the same quantity and charge the same price because this tax is a fixed cost. The MC curve does not shift; only the ATC curve shifts when the tax is included.

costs or marginal revenue; hence, enterprise decision making is not influenced by a lump-sum tax. A lump-sum tax does not affect the productivity or efficiency of the economy as a whole. A lump-sum tax that exceeds economic (monopoly) profits would drive the monopolist out of business in the long run. The tax would drive resources into some other activity.

The main economic objection to monopoly is not that monopolists make high profits; it is always possible to tax away above-normal profits and redistribute the proceeds to the poor and to orphans. Even if all monopoly profits were taxed away and given to the most deserving members of society, monopoly would still be inefficient: if price is greater than marginal cost, society is not putting enough resources into the monopolized activity. Inefficiency is the main economic objection to monopoly.

Example 3   Is the Patent a Spur to Innovation?

The major rationale for patents—which give patent holders a legal monopoly for 17 years—is that patents are necessary to spur innovation. Why should a company or individual expend time and money on an invention that can be copied by a rival firm? Thus, patents are a price society must pay for innovation. Economists Edwin Mansfield, Mark Schwartz, and Samuel Wagner have studied the protection a patent actually provides from competition in the real world. They conclude that patents provide surprisingly little protection from competition. Basically, a patent protects the inventor by making it difficult to legally invent around a patented product. If an electronics firm, for example, has a patented production technology that gives it a cost advantage, rivals will find it difficult to develop a substitute technology that does the same thing but in a different enough way so as not to infringe on the patent.

In a survey of 48 product innovations, 31 of them patented, Mansfield and his associates find that patents have increased the cost of legally imitating the original invention by only 11 percent. They also find that 60 percent of the patented inventions were successfully imitated within four years—far less time than the 17-year life of the patent. They further find that patent protection was not essential for the development and introduction of at least 75 percent of the inventions they studied. Surprisingly, patents have played a relatively small role in the most innovative fields of the past 25 years—electronics and bioengineering. Bioengineering and electronics companies have relied more on secrecy than on patents to protect their inventions. The major exception to the rule that patents have not protected the inventor from competition is the prescription-drug industry, in which patents have effectively protected inventions for long periods of time (see Example 1).

The research of Mansfield and associates raises a very important question: If patents do not effectively discourage imitation, are patents really necessary to encourage innovation? Secrecy may be more productive. For example, companies like Coca Cola or McDonalds have made large profits for years by keeping their recipes secret. ∎

Source: "The Patent is Expiring as a Spur to Innovation," *Business Week,* May 11, 1981; Edwin Mansfield, Mark Schwartz, and Samuel Wagner, "Imitation Costs and Patents: An Empirical Study," *Economic Journal,* December 1981, pp. 907–918.

THE CASE FOR MONOPOLY: INNOVATION?

Some economists believe that monopoly is conducive to technological innovation that a competitive order would not generate. (See Example 3.) If such were the case, the disadvantages of monopoly noted above—inefficiency and unfair income distribution—might be offset by its dynamic advantages. Greater outward shifts in the production-possibilities frontier over time could compensate for monopoly's failure to operate on the frontier at any single point in time.

Economists have asked what type of market structure—perfect competition or monopoly—is better suited to creating significant new inventions. *Monopoly* and *big business* are not the same; as we have shown, monopolies can be relatively small. But more often than not, monopolies (or companies that possess considerable monopoly power) are giant concerns. Giant corporations like AT&T, DuPont, and IBM maintain enormous, privately financed laboratories and employ thousands of scientists. Indeed, Nobel Prizes for the discovery of the laser and the transistor were awarded to scientists employed by giant corporations.

The ability of large companies to finance research and product development has caused some prominent economists to argue that big businesses are more likely to come up with significant scientific inventions than competitive businesses. (See Example 4.)

The noted Austrian-born economist Joseph Schumpeter argues:

As soon as we go into the details and inquire into the individual items in which progress was most conspicuous (since 1899), the trail leads not to the

Example 4   Size and Innovation: The Bell Labs

One argument in favor of monopoly is that large companies protected from the challenges of competition can afford large research-and-development expenditures. It has been argued that modern research and development requires large labs and scientific facilities and that some projects require years and even decades before they can have commercial applications. Whether small, competitive firms or large, monopolistic firms are better settings for innovation is a controversial issue. This chapter points out that many major inventions have come from individuals or small companies. However, the Bell Labs (with current employment of 18,000 people) of AT&T is an example of how a large monopoly can successfully foster research and development. Bell Labs began operation in 1925 with the charge of conducting fundamental research and development. From the beginning, Bell Labs was given the authority to consider a broad range of physical problems whether or not their results were immediately ap-

plicable to the telephone business. Moreover, Bell Lab scientists were encouraged to work together in an interdisciplinary setting—engineers, physicists, psychologists, linguists, and so on all working together. As of 1984, Bell Lab scientists had won seven Nobel prizes for science. By far the most important discovery to come out of Bell Labs was the transistor—the discovery that sparked the computer revolution. When the Bell System was broken up into separate parts in 1984, Bell Labs remained with the parent company, AT&T. Bell Labs scientists fear that the company will not be willing to continue to underwrite such fundamental research (the payoffs from which are necessarily achieved in the short run) in the now more competitive telecommunications environment. ■

Source: Jeremy Bernstein, *Three Degrees Above Zero: Bell Labs in the Information Age*) New York: Scribner, 1984).

doors that work under conditions of comparatively free competition but precisely to the doors of the large concerns—which, as in the case of agricultural machinery, also account for much of the progress in the competitive sector—and a shocking suspicion dawns upon us that big business may have had more to do with creating (our high) standard of life than keeping it down.[8]

Why does Schumpeter refer to this conclusion as a "shocking suspicion"? Before Schumpeter's writings, economists maintained that monopolies were not especially innovative because they are not pressured by the forces of competition to innovate. Yet Schumpeter argues that monopolies are responsible for our important technological advances!

Schumpeter did not believe that innovation by monopoly would yield a permanent competitive advantage or that it would shield monopolists from long-run competition. Schumpeter believed in "creative destruction." Innovations that give a monopolist large economic profits spur economic

progress, but the monopoly position will be only transitory. Eventually, another large concern will come up with a superior innovation, the original monopoly will lose out, and a new monopoly will take its place, until in turn, it is replaced by a more innovative monopoly.

Schumpeter's theme of the innovational efficiency of monopoly has been taken up by other economists. John K. Galbraith argues in a slightly different way:[9]

A benign Providence has made modern industry of a few large firms an almost perfect instrument for inducing technological change. . . . There is no more pleasant fiction than that technological change is the product of the matchless ingenuity of the small man forced by competition to employ his wits better than his neighbor. Unhappily, it is a fiction. Technical development has long since become the preserve of the scientist and engineer. Most of the cheap and simple inventions have, to put it bluntly, been made.

What are we to make of the arguments for and

8. Joseph Schumpeter, *Capitalism, Socialism, and Democracy,* 2nd ed. (New York: Harper and Brothers, 1942), pp. 81–82.

9. John K. Galbraith, *American Capitalism,* rev. ed. (Boston: Houghton Mifflin, 1956), p. 86.

against the dynamic efficiency of monopoly? On the one hand, it is argued that competition forces business firms to be innovative. On the other hand, we hear that monopoly and big business are required to create significant technological breakthroughs. Which view is correct?

What has been the actual relationship between market structure and technological innovation?[10] While the evidence is not overwhelming, it is safe to say that the evidence does not support the extreme Galbraith-Schumpeter position, despite the plausibility of their arguments.

In a major study, John Jewkes, David Sawers, and Richard Stillerman compiled case histories of 61 important 20th-century inventions.[11] They found that less than one third were discovered in large industrial laboratories. A little more than one half were the product of academic investigators or of individuals working independently of any research organization. In another study, Willard F. Mueller found that of the 25 most significant inventions pioneered by DuPont, only 10 were developed in DuPont laboratories. The rest came from small independent researchers.[12]

F. M. Scherer summarizes the evidence and its bearing on public policy: "No single firm size is uniquely conducive to technological progress. There is room for firms of all sizes. What we want, therefore, may be a diversity of sizes, each with its own special advantages and disadvantages."[13]

Diversity can be important to technological innovation. A small firm might discover a new product or process, but a large firm may be required to put the invention on the shelf for the consumer to enjoy it. Basic ideas may come from small firms or even individuals, but a large laboratory may be required to develop the idea to the point where it can be put to practical use.

10. For a survey of this literature, see Morton Kamien and Nancy Schwartz, "Market Structure and Innovation: A Survey," *Journal of Economic Literature* 8, 1 (March 1975): 1–38.

11. John Jewkes, David Sawers, and Richard Stillerman, *The Sources of Invention* (New York: St. Martins Press, 1959), pp. 71–85.

12. Willard F. Mueller, "The Origins of the Basic Inventions Underlying DuPont's Major Product and Process Inventions," in *The Rate and Direction of Innovative Activity* (Princeton: Princeton University Press, 1962), pp. 323–46.

13. F. M. Scherer, *Industrial Market Structure and Economic Performance, 2nd ed.* (Boston: Houghton Mifflin, 1980), p. 418.

THE EXTENT OF MONOPOLY: EVIDENCE FROM PRICE CEILINGS

Earlier this chapter noted that the losses from monopoly have been estimated to be relatively small in the U.S. economy. An indirect method for appraising the extent of monopoly is to test the predictions of the two models.

Chapter 4 demonstrated how *price controls* in a competitive industry cause shortages. Without controls, the competitive industry is in equilibrium when price equals marginal cost for each firm. Only at the equilibrium price will the quantity demanded by buyers equal the quantity supplied by firms. When a price ceiling is set below the equilibrium price, the quantity demanded exceeds the quantity supplied, and a shortage arises.

In a competitive industry, price ceilings below the equilibrium price cause shortages.

But the argument that price controls cause shortages depends on the existence of competition. In the case of monopoly, price ceilings below equilibrium do not necessarily result in shortages.

Figure 5 shows why price ceilings do not cause shortages when monopoly prevails. The demand curve facing the monopoly is D. For simplicity, assume $MC = AC = \$4$. The monopoly price/quantity combination is \$7/300 units (point b). If the ceiling price is set at \$6, the monopoly will be able to sell 400 units. If the monopolist chooses to sell 400 units at a \$6 price, consumers are also prepared to buy 400 units, and there would be no shortage. Would the monopolist decide to sell 400 units at a \$6 ceiling price? Clearly the monopolist will want to sell all 400 units because profits (= \$800) would be larger than if any smaller quantity were sold at the price of \$6. For example, if the monopolist continued to produce 300 units at the \$6 ceiling price, profits would fall by \$200 (by the area of the rectangle $acdg$). There is no reason for the monopolist not to sell the quantity demanded by the market at the ceiling price. Thus, in a monopoly, an effective price ceiling established below the uncontrolled monopoly price but above marginal cost will not cause a shortage.

Figure 5   The Effect of Price Ceilings on Monopoly

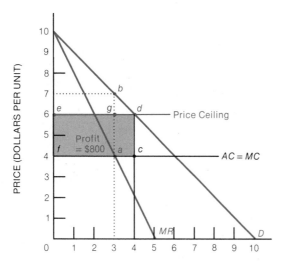

QUANTITY (HUNDREDS OF UNITS)

If there were no price ceilings, this monopolist would produce that output at which marginal revenue and marginal cost are equal—namely, an output level of 300 units—and would charge a price of $7 per unit. If a price ceiling is imposed below the monopoly price but above marginal cost, the monopolist will sell more. At a price of $6, the monopolist will sell 400 units because profits will be maximized (the area of the rectangle *edcf*) at that output. Price ceilings can increase output in the case of monopoly.

A price ceiling imposed on a monopoly below the monopoly price but above marginal cost will not cause a shortage.

Historical evidence does not support the assumption that business behavior is, overall, monopolistic: virtually every price control that has been instituted in history has been associated with shortages.

As far as the effects of price controls are concerned, history shows that the world behaves more like competition than like monopoly. Although the real world is often a blend of both monopoly and competition, the blend leans more toward the competitive side in this particular respect.

This chapter has compared the extremes of monopoly and competition under the assumption that both are feasible. The next chapter examines the many varieties of oligopoly behavior that combine elements of monopoly and perfect competition.

Summary

1. In an ideal world, perfect competition would exist in every industry. Consumers would be well informed, and externalities would be absent. Efficiency is present when society's resources are so organized that it is impossible to make at least one person better off by any reallocation of resources without harming someone else. Efficiency prevails when price and marginal cost are equal—which occurs under conditions of perfect competition.

2. Even though perfectly competitive economies are efficient, the resulting distribution of income may not be equitable from the viewpoint of society. Perfect competition is compatible with an unfair distribution of income. *Externalities* are unpriced costs and benefits of economic activities. When externalities exist, perfect competition is not efficient.

3. Monopoly can be inefficient because of contrived scarcity, monopoly rent seeking, or *X*-inefficiency. Monopoly may also result in an unfair distribution of income because of monopoly profits. Monopoly profits can be taxed away by lump-sum taxation without affecting output and prices.

4. Schumpeter and Galbraith argue that large business firms or large concentrations of monopoly power are conducive to technological progress. Modern research fails to support this view.

5. A price ceiling imposed on a monopoly below the monopoly price but above marginal cost will not cause a shortage. The fact that price controls have historically been associated with shortages suggests that world markets behave more like competition than monopoly.

Key Terms

efficiency
inefficiency
economic equity

externalities
private costs
external costs
private benefits
external benefits
social costs
social benefits
deadweight loss
monopoly rent seeking
X-inefficiency
lump-sum tax

Questions and Problems

1. Restate the reason why $P = MC$ is the condition for economic efficiency.

2. Give examples of positive external benefits and of negative external costs.

3. Why do economists say that monopolists contrive scarcity?

4. The *MC* of production in Industry A is $8 and is equal to average cost. The demand schedule is linear and is given in Table A. What is the deadweight loss of monopoly in this case due to contrived scarcity? What is the maximum loss due to monopoly rent seeking?

Table A

Price (dollars per unit)	Quantity (units)
20	0
15	500
10	1,000
5	1,500
0	2,000

5. Explain why a lump-sum tax on monopoly profits would not affect monopoly output and prices while a tax on each unit of output would.

6. Explain the resource-allocation problem that would exist in a competitive market economy if the following undertakings had externalities: a) the production of electricity by burning coal and b) the immunization of chidlren against communicable diseases. Draw a supply-and-demand diagram for each indicating both the market and the correct resource-allocation result.

7. What does the evidence indicate about the relationship between the size of business firms and technological progress? Is technological innovation a "monopoly" of large business enterprises?

8. What is the difference between monopoly rent seeking and the losses due to the monopolist producing where $MR = MC?$

9. Why is production at an output level where $MC = MR$ socially inefficient for monopolies but socially efficient under perfect competition?

Suggested Readings

Galbraith, John Kenneth. *Economics and the Public Purpose*. Boston: Houghton Mifflin, 1973, parts I–III.

Harberger, Arnold. "Monopoly and Resource Allocation." *American Economic Review* 44 (May 1954): 77–87.

Kamien, Morton, and Nancy Schwartz. "Market Structure and Innovation: A Survey." *Journal of Economic Literature* 8, 1 (March 1975): 1–38.

Mansfield, Edwin. *Microeconomics: Theory and Applications*. New York: W. W. Norton, 1979, chap. 10.

Schumpeter, Joseph. *Capitalism, Socialism, and Democracy*, 3rd ed. New York: Harper and Row, 1950.

Tullock, Gordon. "The Welfare Cost of Tariffs, Monopolies, and Theft." *Western Economic Journal* 5 (June 1967): 224–32.

32

Oligopoly

Chapter Preview

Oligopoly is an umbrella term that covers market forms between monopoly and monopolistic competition. This chapter explains why some oligopolies behave like monopolies while others act like competitive industries. Oligopoly behavior is rich and varied and presents many puzzles that require solution. This chapter will describe the characteristics of oligopoly, how oligopolies behave, and the pitfalls of collusive behavior.

An **oligopoly** is an industry characterized by:
1. the relatively small number of firms in the industry,
2. moderate to high barriers to entry,
3. price searching (oligopolists are able to exercise some control over price), and
4. recognized mutual interdependence.

When the number of firms in an industry is "relatively small," each firm is aware of the others on an individual basis (Ford is aware of General Motors, for example), and the industry is more likely to be characterized by **mutual interdependence.**

> **Mutual interdependence** is characteristic of an industry in which the actions of one firm will affect other firms in the industry and in which these interrelationships will be recognized.

Mutual interdependence is the most important feature of oligopoly because oligopolists may collude in some circumstances and vigorously compete in other circumstances. The purpose of oligopoly theory is to spell out the different circumstances that determine firm behavior. Some oligopolies produce a homogeneous product (like aluminum or steel), while others produce a differentiated product (like automobiles or breakfast cereals). Entry barriers are higher in some oligopolies but low in others. Variety is the name of the game. ∎

CHARACTERISTICS OF OLIGOPOLY

Barriers to Entry

An important characteristic of oligopoly is the relatively small number of firms in the industry. Barriers to entry explain the limited number of firms. A pioneering researcher in this area, Joe S. Bain, defines a **barrier to entry** in the following way:[1]

> A **barrier to entry** is any advantage that existing firms hold over firms that might seek to enter the market.

Economists recognize several different types of barriers to entry, including economies of scale, product differentiation, control over input supplies, government barriers to entry, large capital requirements, technological advantages, and sunk costs.

Economies of Scale.   Economies of scale provide established firms with cost advantages over potential entrants. The established firm that produces a large volume of output will operate farther out on the generally declining long-run average-cost curve. New firms normally must enter the market producing small volumes of output relative to established firms.

Figure 1 depicts a situation in which a new firm's costs are higher because it must—at the beginning—have a smaller plant size than established firms. Clearly new firms will operate at less than the minimum efficient plant size and will produce at higher average cost than established firms.

Examples of oligopolistic industries protected by economies-of-scale barriers are automobile and tractor manufacturing and electrical-power generation. Industries with low economies-of-scale barriers to entry are passenger airlines, canned goods, cigarettes, meat packing, and tire manufacturing.

Product Differentiation.   The more highly differentiated the product in the eyes of the con-

1. Joe S. Bain, *Barriers to New Competition* (Cambridge, Mass.: Harvard University Press, 1965).

Figure 1   The Cost Advantage of Established Firms Over New Firms

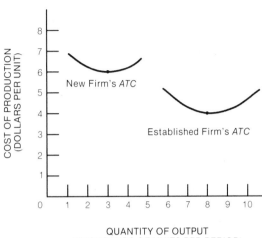

When there are economies of scale in an industry, established firms with large plants will have a lower average total cost than new firms that might operate with a smaller plant size.

sumer, the more difficult it is for new firms to enter an industry. If the buyer is convinced that a particular brand of medication is supoerior to competitive brands or that a particular brand of cigarettes tastes better than others, the manufacturer has succeeded in erecting a barrier to entry. (See Example 1.)

One major means of differentiating products is advertising. If advertising successfully differentiates the product, higher prices can be charged without causing the entry of competitors who drive the price back down. For this reason, some economists view advertising as anticompetitive. Others stress that advertising is procompetitive because it increases the amount of product information available to the consumer.

Control Over Input Supplies.   If established firms control crucial inputs and can deny new firms access to these inputs, a barrier to entry has been erected. An example of this type of entry barrier was provided by the American steel industry in the 1960s. The 9 largest steel producers and the 4 major iron-ore merchants accounted for

---

Example 1   Product Differentiation Through Advertising: Aspirin

---

A classic example of product differentiation through advertising is the case of Bayer and St. Joseph's aspirin. Bayer has typically spent large sums of money advertising its adult-strength aspirin, while St. Joseph has spent very little. Both companies, however, have spent equal sums on advertising their children's aspirin. The result: the Bayer adult aspirin sells at a price 60 percent above St. Joseph's, while the children's brands sell for the same price. ■

Source: This case study is based upon 1971 testimony before the Subcommittee on Monopoly, Select Committee on Small Business, and cited in James V. Koch, *Industrial Organization and Prices,* 2nd ed. (Englewood Cliffs, N.J.: Prentice-Hall, 1980), p. 324

---

more than 95 percent of ore reserves in the nation's richest iron-ore area. Moreover, only U.S. Steel Corporation had sufficient iron-ore reserves, and other companies had to rely on U.S. Steel for ore. The major U.S. steel producers also enjoyed a commanding lead over small companies in the ownership of foreign ore reserves in Venezuela, Liberia, and Labrador.[2]

Government Barriers to Entry.

If state, local, or national governments protect established firms with exclusive franchises, operating charters, and licensing arrangements that keep other firms out of the market, the entry of new firms is restricted not by economic factors, but by the force of the law.

There are numerous examples of governmental barriers to entry. Local governments grant exclusive franchises to operate concessions at municipal airports, and they often control entry into the taxicab business. The federal government for many years limited entry into the commercial airline and trucking industries, and protected the Bell System from the competition of independent long-distance companies. The Federal Communications Commission has controlled entry into radio and television broadcasting by administratively allocating broadcast frequencies.

Large Capital Requirements.

In many industries, the amount of capital required to operate a firm at its efficient size is enormous. In the steel industry, the average firm equipped with blast furnaces used about $141 million in capital assets (in

1985 dollars). The average cigarette manufacturer has capital assets of $118 million. Such capital requirements may serve to protect existing firms from the competition of new firms.

Technological Advantages.

Established firms may have a crucial technology that is denied to potential competitors. The exclusive right to use a technological innovation may be granted by the government in the form of a patent, or it may be achieved as a result of superior research and development by an established firm.

Examples of concentrated oligopolies that have exploited technological advantages or patents are the prescription-drug industry, shoe manufacturing, and telephone-equipment manufacturing.

Sunk Costs.

An important entry barrier is a barrier to exit. Suppose a firm knows that some of the fixed costs it incurs when it enters the industry are **sunk costs** that it can never recover.

> **Sunk costs** are those fixed costs that cannot be recovered even in the long run.

One example of sunk costs would be setup costs. When a firm enters a particular industry, it may have to pay for the training of its employees, for the hiring of attorneys to see if any trademark or copyright laws are being violated, and for the purchase of any licenses that may be required to sell the product. These costs often are not recoverable (although sometimes licenses can be resold on a competitive basis). The firm may also have to purchase specialized capital goods that have no use except in that particular industry. The salvage value of such machinery may be very small if it is difficult to sell to anyone outside the industry

---

2. Walter Adams, ed., *The Structure of American Industry,* 4th ed. (New York: Macmillan, 1971), pp. 77–78.

Example 2   Classification of Manufacturing Industries by Barriers to Entry

When manufacturing industries are grouped according to the amount of barriers to entry, it is clear that some manufacturing industries are protected by high barriers to entry; others have very little protection from the entry of new competition.

Barriers to entry explain the small number of firms characteristic of some oligopolies. ■

Source: Based on William Shepherd, *Market Power and Economic Welfare* (New York: Random House, 1970), p. 126.

High Barriers to Entry	Moderately High Barriers to Entry	Low Barriers to Entry
Distilled liquors	Cereals	Meat packing
Wood pulp	Flour mixes	Flour
Newspapers	Bread	Canned fruits and vegetables
General periodicals	Sugar	Woolen and cotton textiles
Drugs	Soft drinks	Clothing
Soaps	Cigarettes	Brick and tile
Explosives	Lumber	Small metal products
Glass and glass products	Paper	Wooden furniture
Automobiles	Periodicals	Corrugated containers
Aircraft and parts	Gypsum products	Printing
Photographic supplies	Metal cans	Footwear
Steel	Typewriters	Cement
Copper	Books	Foundries
Tractors	Gases	Airlines (Since 1978)
Computers	Organic chemicals	
Copying equipment	Inorganic chemicals	
Heavy electrical equipment	Synthetic rubber	
Electrical lamps	Toilet preparations	
Telephone equipment	Fertilizers	
Buses	Petroleum refining	
Locomotives	Tires and tubes	
Shipbuilding	Aluminum	
	Heavy industrial machinery	
	Large household appliances	

(for example, railroad tracks and certain kinds of telephone exchanges). The firm may have to advertise to let buyers know of its existence. Clearly, sunk costs will be a barrier to entry because the firm realizes that if it goes out of business its losses may be enormous.

Example 2 classifies 60 industries according to whether the barriers to entry into the industry are high, medium, or low. Industries with high barriers are likely to be populated by a tight group of oligopolistic producers. Industries with low entry barriers are likely to be populated by a relatively larger number of loosely knit producers.

Trends in Concentration

There is no magic formula for measuring the extent of oligopoly in the American economy. Some economists believe that oligopoly is the predominant form of industrial organization; others argue that oligopoly is not so important. A tool economists use to gauge the extent of oligopoly is the **concentration ratio** (see Table 1).

An *x*-firm **concentration ratio** is the percentage of industry sales (or output, or labor force, or assets) accounted for by the *x* largest firms.

The 4-firm sales concentration ratio, for example, is the percentage of industry sales accounted for by the four largest firms in the industry. Concentration ratios are an imperfect guide to the extent of oligopoly for four reasons. First, concentration ratios do not reflect competition from foreign producers or from substitute products at home. The 4-firm concentration ratio of

Table 1   Selected Concentration Ratios in Manufacturing, 1977

Industry	4-Firm Concentration Ratio (percent)	Number of Firms
Motor vehicles and car bodies	93	254
Cereal breakfast foods	89	32
Photographic equipment	72	702
Tires and inner tubes	70	121
Aircraft	59	151
Metal cans	59	153
Soaps and other detergents	59	544
Cookies and crackers	59	263
Radio and TV sets	51	546
Farm machinery	46	1,868
Blast furnaces and steel mills	45	395
Toilet preparations	40	644
Hardware	39	1,063
Gray iron foundries	34	865
Men's footwear	31	113
Petroleum refining	30	192
Women's footwear	29	243
Periodicals	22	2,860
Mobile homes	24	308
Paper mills	23	171
Pharmaceutical preparations	24	655
Canned fruits and vegetables	22	648
Tufted carpets	21	397
Men's and boys' suits	21	619
Radio and TV equipment	20	1,873
Corrugated and solid fiber boxes	19	863
Sawmills	17	6,966
Wood household furniture	14	2,795
Nuts and bolts	13	723
Valves and pipe fittings	13	741
Women's dresses	8	6,753
Ready mixed concrete	5	4,317

Source: U.S. Department of Commerce, "Concentration Ratios in Manufacturing," 1977 *Census of Manufacturers*, MC77-SR-2.

the U.S. automobile industry is more than 93 percent—a figure that fails to measure the competition of foreign imports. The 4-firm concentration ratio in metal cans (59 percent) does not show the competition from stainless steel, plastic, and so on.

Second, concentration ratios may not measure concentration in the relevant market. The 4-firm concentration ratio in the aircraft industry is 59 percent, but it is 97 percent in the commercial-transport type aircraft industry, where Boeing and McDonnell-Douglas dominate sales.

Third, many markets, such as newspapers, cement, and real estate, are local or regional. Concentration ratios for percentages of national sales are misleading in such markets. A local or re-

gional firm may dominate its relevant market, and this dominance would not necessarily be reflected by the national concentration ratio.

Fourth, concentration ratios do not measure *potential* competition. They do not indicate in which industries new firms can find ways and means to overcome existing barriers to entry if existing firms earn extraordinary profits.

Despite these difficulties, concentration ratios—carefully used—can be useful in measuring oligopoly. A leading authority on industrial organization, F. M. Scherer, argues that a 4-firm concentration ratio of 40 percent or more indicates that the industry can be considered an oligopoly and that a 4-firm ratio of 50 percent or more is fairly conclusive evidence of oligopoly. Using these criteria for industry classification, 50 percent of all American manufacturing industry could be characterized as oligopolistic in the late 1960s and early 1970s.[3]

There is a widespread false impression that the degree of concentration of the American economy has been increasing over time. In manufacturing, this is not the case, as column (1) of Table 2 shows. The share of manufacturing output accounted for by highly concentrated industries did not change markedly for more than 70 years. One reason for the impression of growing concentration is that the share of manufacturing output of the largest 100 companies has grown from 23 percent in 1947 to 34 percent in 1977, as shown in column (2) of Table 2. This increase is largely the result of company mergers across industries, however, not of increasing concentration within a particular industry.[4]

Economist William G. Shepherd made a bold attempt to measure trends in the level of concentration for the U.S. economy as a whole from 1939 to 1980.[5] Using published data on concentration ratios in manufacturing, data provided by antitrust cases, government reports, research monographs, and specific articles, Shepherd classifies each industry listed in Table 3 according to the degree of competition. Shepherd considered the extent of oligopoly in the economy could be found by combining the percentage shares in output of what he classified as ''dominant firms'' and ''tight oligopolies'' (see Table 3).

Shepherd's results are tentative and are likely to be hotly debated. After virtually no increase in competition between 1939 and 1958, Shepherd finds that the U.S. economy became markedly more competitive between 1958 and 1980. The average share of each sector of the economy that was ''effectively competitive'' rose from 56.4 percent in 1958 to 76.7 percent in 1980, with large increases in construction, manufacturing, trade, finance, insurance, real estate, and ser-

Table 2 Trends in Concentration in American Manufacturing: Two Measures

Year	Percentage of Output by Firms with 4-Firm Concentration Ratio of 50 percent or Above (1)	Percentage of Output of 100 Largest Firms (2)
1895–1904	33	n.a.
1947	24	23
1954	30	30
1958	30	32
1972	29	33
1977	—	34

Sources: G. Warren Nutter, *The Extent of Enterprise Monopoly in the United States, 1899–1939* (Chicago: University of Chicago Press, 1951), pp. 35–48, 112–150; F. M. Scherer, *Industrial Market Structure and Economic Performance* (Boston: Houghton Mifflin, 1980), pp. 68–69; *Concentration Ratios in Manufacturing, 1977 Census of Manufacturing,* MC77-SR-9.

vices. Between 1958 and 1980, the share of total output produced by monopoly fell only slightly, while the share produced by oligopoly (dominant firms plus tight oligopoly) fell dramatically from 40.6 percent to 20.8 percent of output. In his analysis of the causes of the trend toward more competition, Shepherd finds three dominant factors: increasing import competition, antitrust actions, and deregulation. (The last two factors will be discussed in a later chapter.)

Oligopoly Versus Monopoly

Some economists think the distinctions between oligopoly and monopoly are small. In the words of John Kenneth Galbraith, ''So long as there are only a few massive firms in an industry, each must act with a view of the welfare of all.''[6] While some oligopolies act like a **shared monopoly,** many do not.

> A **shared monopoly** is an oligopoly in which all the firms in the industry coordinate price and output by some means. In its extreme form, the industry behaves like one gigantic firm.

3. F. M. Scherer, *Industrial Market Structure and Economic Performance,* 2nd ed (Boston: Houghton Mifflin, 1980), p.67.

4. See Scherer, *Industrial Market Structure,* pp. 68–70; James V. Koch, *Industrial Organization and Prices,* 2nd ed. (Englewood Cliffs, N.J.: Prentice-Hall, 1980), p. 181.

5. William G. Shepherd, ''Causes of Increased Competition in the U.S. Economy, 1939–1980,'' *Review of Economics and Statistics,* November 1982, pp. 613–26.

6. John K. Galbraith, *American Capitalism,* rev. ed. (Cambridge: The Riverside Press, 1956).

Table 3   The Trends in Competition in the U.S. Economy, 1939–1980

Sectors of the Economy	Total Net Output of Each Sector, 1978 (billions of dollars)	The Share of Each Sector that Was Effectively Competitive (percent)		
		1939	1958	1980
Agriculture, forestry, and fisheries	54.7	91.6	85.0	86.4
Mining	24.5	87.1	92.2	95.8
Construction	87.6	27.9	55.9	80.2
Manufacturing	459.5	51.5	55.9	69.0
Transportation and public utilities	162.3	8.7	26.1	39.1
Wholesale and retail trade	261.8	57.8	60.5	93.4
Finance, insurance, and real estate	210.7	61.5	63.8	94.1
Services	245.3	53.9	54.3	77.9
Total	**1,512.4**	**52.4**	**56.4**	**76.7**

The Share of Each Category in Total Output	(billions of dollars)	Percentage Shares		
		1939	1958	1980
1. Pure monopoly	38.2	6.2	3.1	2.5
2. Dominant firm	42.2	5.0	5.0	2.8
3. Tight oligopoly	272.1	36.4	35.6	18.0
4. Others: effectively competitive	1,157.9	52.4	56.3	76.7
Total	**1,512.4**	**100.0**	**100.0**	**100.0**

Shepherd considered an industry to be 1) a pure monopoly if market share was near 100 percent, entry barriers were high, and there was evidence of monopoly pricing; 2) a dominant firm if market share was between 50 percent and 90 percent, there was no close rival, entry barriers were high, and rates of return were above the competitive rate; 3) a tight oligopoly if the 4-firm concentration ratio was above 60 percent, market shares were stable, and there was a tendency toward cooperation; 4) effectively competitive if the 4-firm concentration ratio was below 40 percent, entry barriers were low, market shares were unstable, and prices were flexible. The extent of oligopoly in the economy is the measure of the combined shares of dominant firms and tight oligopolies.

Source: William G. Shepherd, "Causes of Increased Competition in the U.S. Economy, 1939–1980," *Review of Economics and Statistics*, November 1982, pp. 613–26.

Galbraith's view that concentrated oligopoly and monopoly are virtually equivalent is disputed by most industrial-organization specialists.[7] If oligopoly were simply a complex monopoly, this chapter would be very short: it could just refer the reader back to the monopoly-theory chapter. The truth is that oligopoly encompasses a broad range of market behavior and performance. The task of oligopoly theory is to study the circumstances under which oligopoly might approximate either monopoly (on the one hand) or competition (on the other hand).

Some oligopolies behave much like shared monopolies; they agree on prices, and they agree on which firms get which contracts. Other oligopolies make pricing decisions according to tradition; one acts as a price leader, and others automatically follow. Still other oligopolies engage in competitive pricing wars, behaving much like a perfectly competitive or monopolistically competitive industry. One question oligopoly theory must answer is: why is there no single model of oligopoly behavior?

OLIGOPOLISTIC INTERDEPENDENCE

Oligopoly theory is more complicated than the theories of perfect competition, pure monopoly, or monopolistic competition because there is no one theory of oligopoly. For example, in either perfect competition or monopoly, the firm need

---

7. Oliver Williamson, *Markets and Hierarchies: Analysis and Antitrust Implications* (New York: The Free Press, 1975), p. 234.

only equate marginal cost and a well-defined marginal revenue.

There are so few firms in oligopoly that each firm's actions will influence the market as a whole and may also influence the behavior of rival firms. Oligopolistic firms are interdependent. In an oligopoly, Firm A's behavior depends on Firm B's behavior, and Firm B's behavior depends on Firm A's behavior.

In oligopoly there is a mutual interdependence of actions among firms.

The Oligopolist's Demand Curve

Because of the mutual interdependence of firms in an oligopoly, the demand curve for an oligopolist's product cannot be defined until the behavior of rival firms is specified. The behavior of rival firms can range from complete independence of other oligopolists to complete coordination.

Consider the Ford Motor Company. It produces cars and competes with a handful of other automobile manufacturers around the world. Suppose that at the current price of $6,000 Ford is selling 1 million units of its compact car, with the comparable compact cars of Toyota, Volkswagen, Datsun, Chrysler, and General Motors selling for comparable prices. Point *a* in Figure 2 describes the current situation confronting an oligopolist.

Point *a* lies on Ford's demand curve, since 1 million units are being sold at a price of $6,000. What happens to Ford's demand curve if Ford reduces its price to $5,000? Figure 2 shows two extreme scenarios. Point *b* represents Ford's quantity demanded if the rest of the industry (General Motors and foreign producers) behaves *in an exactly parallel fashion,* lowering prices by the same percentage as Ford. In this case, Ford increases its sales to 1.25 million cars because auto prices in general have fallen relative to the prices of substitutes for autos. Point *b* represents the shared-monopoly effect on Ford's quantity demanded.

Point *b'* represents Ford's quantity demanded when the rest of the industry behaves *completely independently* of Ford: when Ford lowers its price, the rest of the industry continues to charge

Figure 2   Why the Oligopolist's Demand Curve Is Indeterminant

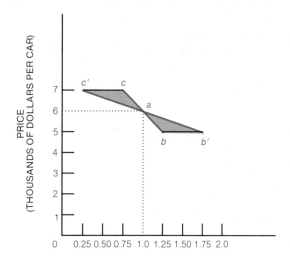

QUANTITY
(MILLIONS OF CARS PER YEAR)

At point *a,* Ford sells 1 million cars at a price of $6,000. If Ford lowers its price to $5,000, what happens to sales depends upon how Ford's competitors react. Point *b* results when Ford's rivals match Ford's price reduction. Point *b'* results if they do not follow Ford's price reduction. If Ford raises its price to $7,000, what happens to sales again depends upon the reactions of competitors. Point *c'* results if they keep their prices constant; point *c* results when they match Ford's increase.

the same prices as before. In this case, there will be a large increase in Ford's sales to 1.75 million. The price of Ford cars has fallen relative to those of its closest substitutes. In Figure 2, *b* and *b'* represent the extremes of the possible positions of the demand curve. The actual position could be anywhere between *b* and *b',* depending upon how competitors react.

If Ford raises its price to $7,000, the same range of outcomes is possible. Point *c* is a point on Ford's demand curve when there is complete coordination of pricing actions by all oligopolists. In this case, Ford sales fall to 0.75 million units. Point *c'* is a point on Ford's demand curve when there is complete independence of actions, with the other oligopolists holding the line on prices. Ford sales might then fall considerably to point *c',* where only 0.25 million units are sold. The range of possible outcomes is represented by the line $c'c$.

In Figure 2, the demand curve for Ford's compact cars can be anywhere in the shaded region of the two triangles. The slope of the demand curve can vary from the slope of the line cab to the slope of $c'ab'$.

The demand curve and, hence, marginal revenue cannot be determined in oligopoly until the actions of rival firms are known.

The Kinked-Demand Model

The behavior of an oligopoly can take many forms. One way to explain oligopoly behavior is the theory of the **kinked-demand curve,** developed by Paul Sweezy. The model serves as a useful introduction to oligopoly theory because it nicely illustrates one possible way oligopolistic firms might anticipate the behavior of their rivals, but the kinked-demand model applies only to certain situations.

Suppose Ford discovers its rivals tend to match Ford's price *cuts* but hold their prices when Ford raises its price. In this case, Ford's demand curve would be $c'ab$. The demand curve would have a "kink" in it at point a, the current price.

A **kinked-demand curve** results when other firms match a firm's price decreases but don't match the firm's price increases.

The assumptions of the kinked-demand curve appear to be plausible in certain industries. They describe an oligopoly firm that is not the industry's **price leader** because when the firm raises its prices, the other firms keep their prices constant. There is, therefore, some independence of action when the oligopolist raises its prices. If Oligopolist A raises its price, Oligopolists B, C, and D may take the opportunity to expand their markets by holding prices constant. On the other hand, if Oligopolist A lowers its prices, the remaining firms may fear the loss of customers and many cut their prices as well.

A **price leader** is a firm whose price changes are consistently imitated by rival firms.

The kinked-demand model appears to hold for some industries (and firms) but not others. In the cigarette industry, Liggett & Meyers (which accounts for 2 percent of cigarette sales) has found in the past that its price increases are not followed by other cigarette manufacturers but that its price decreases are followed. If Phillip Morris, which accounts for 31 percent of industry sales, raises its prices, however, other firms tend to follow suit. Thus, Phillip Morris (the manufacturer of Marlboros) may not face a kink. A company like GM (which has lower costs than its domestic rivals) may not face a kink, but Ford and Chrysler may.

If a firm is the price leader in its industry, it will not face a kink in its demand curve because rival firms follow both price increases and price reductions. If the firm is not the industry's price leader, it is likely to face a kink unless it is so small relative to the industry that its pricing actions are ignored.[8]

Figure 3 shows an oligopoly firm facing a kinked-demand curve. The current price being charged by this firm is $12. Since this firm's price increases are not followed by rivals but its price cuts are matched, then this firm's demand curve, D, is more elastic above the $12 price than below the $12 price. Thus, the firm's demand curve has a kink at the current price. Because of the kink, the MR curve drops sharply at the price of $12. In Figure 3, marginal revenue is $7 at a price just above $12 and only $2 at a price just below $12. Since the marginal-revenue curve has a vertical segment (*feg*) just below the demand kink, there is a *range* of MR values associated with the $12 price; the oligopolist is maximizing profits at the price of $12 if the MC curve intersects the MR curve anywhere in that range of values represented by the vertical segment *feg*. In this situation, MC intersects MR at point e.

Note: If the firm's costs changed a bit and the MC curve shifted up or down within the range f to g, MR would still equal MC at the current price! The firm would not change its output and

---

8. Scherer, *Industrial Market Structure*, p. 184.

Figure 3   An Oligopoly Firm Facing a Kinked-Demand Curve

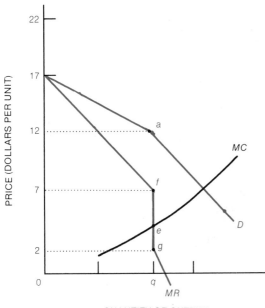

This firm's rivals will follow price reductions but will not follow price increases. Therefore, for prices below the current $12 price, the demand curve D is less elastic than above $12. The marginal-revenue curve, MR, drops sharply from f to g. MC can shift up or down (as long as it remains within this vertical portion of the MR curve) without changing the firm's price or output decisions. The kinked-demand schedule is one explanation for the inflexibility of oligopoly prices.

price. Moreover, there could even be slight changes in demand conditions without altering the profit-maximizing price.

> According to the kinked-demand theory, 1) prices will be more stable in a kinked-demand oligopoly than in perfect competition; 2) prices will be more stable in a kinked-demand oligopoly than in a pure monopoly because (as the monopoly chapter showed) monopoly prices change when costs change.

The kinked-demand model of oligopoly raises as many questions as it answers. The kinked-demand curve applies to a limited range of situations. It does not answer the most important

question of all; namely, why the kink is located where it is. (See Example 3.)

One reason for the appeal of the kinked-demand model is that it predicts that oligopoly prices will be more stable than in perfect competition or monopoly. A number of studies have found that oligopoly prices on the average tend to change less than other prices. There is still debate among authorities who have investigated this issue, but for those who believe oligopoly prices tend to be more stable, the kinked-demand curve is a logical explanation.[9]

COLLUSION AND OLIGOPOLY

The kinked-demand model of oligopoly assumes there is no overt coordination among firms. Each firm knows that price increases will not be followed but that price reductions will be, and firms make their pricing decisions on the basis of this industry behavior pattern.

Other models of oligopoly assume there is collusion (secret agreements or cooperation) on pricing and output decisions. Methods of coordination range from formal agreements on price and market shares made in secret (in those countries like the United States where they are normally against the law) or openly (in cases where such agreements are legal and even sanctioned by government) to tacit coordination without any formal agreement. The effectiveness of coordination will vary. In some cases, coordination will be rigidly enforced; in other cases, it will be loosely enforced and will tend to break down.

The three major methods of oligopoly coordi-

9. J. Fred Weston and Steven Lustgarten investigated price changes between 1954 and 1973 and found that, typically, the higher the concentration ratio the lower the annual percentage price change. This study is one of a long series that followed the 1935 studies of Gardner Means, who coined the term *administered prices* to characterize inflexible oligopoly prices. The major challenge to the administered-price notion was mounted by George Stigler and James Kindahl, who maintain that the list prices of oligopoly products like steel, automobiles, and aluminum conceal many hidden discounts that understate oligopoly price flexibility. *See:* J. Fred Weston and Steven H. Lustgarten, "Concentration and Wage-Price Changes," in eds. Harvey J. Goldschmid et al., *Industrial Concentration: The New Learning* (Boston: Little, Brown, 1974), p. 312; George Stigler and James K. Kindahl, *The Behavior of Industrial Prices* (New York: National Bureau of Economic Research, 1970).

Example 3   The Airline Industry and the Kinked-Demand Curve

One example of a kinked-demand oligopoly is the airline industry. Since 1978, airline prices have been almost completely freed of government controls, so the airlines can set their own prices. In the early years of deregulation, some smaller airlines such as Air Florida, Southwest Airlines, and Texas International could lower their fares without the larger national airlines following. Due to the recessions of 1980 and 1981, the volume of air traffic fell, and the larger airlines such as United, Eastern, TWA, and Pan American began to offer lower fares in 1981 and 1982. At this point, the demand curve became kinked. Other major airlines followed fare reductions for fear of losing market shares. Traditionally, nondiscount airlines such as Delta and American matched virtually all fair reductions. When the largest American airline—United—attempted in 1981 to raise its fares and the other airlines did not follow, United abandoned its experiment with higher fares. Kinked-demand behavior for price reductions is evident in the cases where airlines offer to match the fares of competing airlines, as most did in 1982, 1983, and 1984.

In September of 1984, the new Braniff (which operates out of its Dallas/Fort Worth hub) lowered fares to attract more customers. Braniff apparently was guessing that its major competitors (American and Delta) would regard its lower fares as a minor irritation and would not follow with price cuts of their own. However, American and Delta, after considerable deliberation, matched Braniff's lower fares. Only very small discount airlines that offer a limited number of flights in a busy market appear to be able "to beat the kink" (to lower fares without being matched). ■

---

nation are: 1) cartel agreements, 2) price leadership, and 3) conscious parallelism.

Cartel Agreements

The simplest way for an oligopoly to coordinate pricing and output policy is to enter a **cartel** agreement, binding on all parties, to set the prices or market shares of each producer. Presumably, such agreements would allow the oligopolistic firms to operate their industry as a shared monopoly—to earn monopoly profits for the industry as a whole.

> A **cartel** is an arrangement that allows the participating firms to operate the industry as a shared monopoly. In effect, the participating firms coordinate their output and pricing decisions to yield that industry price and output combination that would have prevailed had this industry been a pure monopoly with each firm as a branch of one giant firm.

Consider an oligopolistic industry that consists of three indentical firms (with the same costs and producing the same product). Assume that barriers to entry are so high that the three established firms need not worry about the attraction of new entrants should profits be high. The three identical firms agree to each share one third of the market and to charge the same monopoly price.

Joint Profit Maximization.   How each firm selects its profit-maximizing price is shown in Figure 4. The industry demand curve is D. Firm A's demand and marginal revenue curves (which are the same as those of firms B and C) are shown as D_A and MR_A. Since a cartel agreement is in force to share the market equally, Firm A's demand curve is D_A $(= \frac{1}{3} \times D)$. The monopoly price is determined by drawing the MR_A curve corresponding to D_A and locating its intersection with the MC curve. Firm A would maximize its profit by producing 100 units at a price of $50 per unit (point a). The other two firms also charge $50 and produce 100 units each. Industry output is 300 $(= 3 \times 100)$.

The Temptation to Cheat.   Notice now the position of Firm A. The two rival firms are selling 200 units at the price of $50. What would prevent Firm A from stealing some customers from the other firms by offering a slightly lower price? Firm A could charge, for instance, $49.50 and possibly obtain a great deal more business. In ef-

Figure 4   Collusive Oligopoly

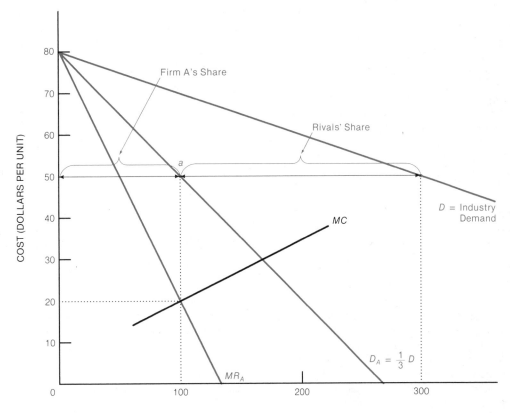

QUANTITY OF INDUSTRY OR FIRM OUTPUT

Curve *D* represents the industry demand curve. The industry consists of three oligopolistic firms who agree to share the market equally and charge the same price. D_A is the demand schedule of Firm A; it is one third of the industry demand schedule. MR_A is the marginal-revenue curve of Firm A. Firm A will maximize profits by producing that output at which *MC* equals *MR*, or 100 units at $50 per unit (point *a*).

Why would Firm A be tempted to cheat on the agreement? If A lowers price a little, Firm A gains sales from its two rivals. As long as A's lower price exceeds A's *MC*, Firm A's profits will increase. The cost of cheating is that if all three firms cheat, a competitive bidding war would break out, and they could end up earning virtually no economic profits.

fect, the cartel price approximately equals the marginal revenue to the firm if it can make secret sales at slightly less than the cartel price. As long as its secret sales remain small and don't drive down the cartel price, $49.50 is now essentially the cheating firm's marginal revenue. The marginal revenue of $49.50 clearly exceeds marginal cost ($20) to each firm. Hence, substantial gains accrue to the firm that breaks the cartel agreement. Cheating on the agreement has its long-run costs, of course, since it may lead the other two firms to break the agreement. Price warfare could erupt, and economic profit would be driven down.

Cartel theory has two great and contradictory themes: 1) Every cartel member can gain through the attainment of monopoly profits if every member adheres to the cartel agreement. 2) Each cartel member can gain by cheating on the agreement if the others do not cheat.

Most cartels come and go unless they have the legal backing of governments. They have a history of instability because of the extreme difficulty of enforcing the cartel agreement. Greed leads firms into cartels; greed also leads firms to

Example 4   The Instability of Cartels: OPEC

The most highly publicized cartel of the 1970s and 1980s is the Organization of Petroleum Exporting Countries, or OPEC. OPEC was founded in 1960 by the five major oil exporters: Iran, Iraq, Kuwait, Saudi Arabia, and Venezuela. Its founders hoped that OPEC would someday be able to set world oil prices and allocate production quotas among OPEC members. By the 1970s, most of the major oil-exporting countries had joined OPEC, and the major industrial countries were no longer producing enough oil at home to cover domestic demand.

By October of 1973, OPEC found itself in a shared monopoly position. The price of OPEC oil rose from $3.01 per barrel in 1973 to $34 per barrel in 1982. The oil revenues of the OPEC countries skyrocketed, and complaints were heard that OPEC was holding the world economy hostage.

The OPEC cartel has operated by establishing a uniform set of prices for its members to charge oil importers. Little OPEC effort had been devoted to regulating the production of OPEC members. In this regard, each OPEC country behaves like the oligopoly firm in Figure 4. OPEC's goal is to set world price equal to the profit-maximizing price.

The OPEC cartel brought considerable prosperity to its members, but its weaknesses are apparent. First, the substantial rise in oil prices has caused oil importers to search out substitutes for oil. The demand for imported oil has become more elastic in the long run. Second, the oil production of non-OPEC countries—such as Mexico—has increased. Third, the industrialized countries have suffered through three recessions since 1973. During these recessions the world demand for imported oil has stagnated. The recession of 1981 put a severe damper on the world demand for imported oil.

Under these conditions, it has become increasingly difficult to maintain a stable cartel. With demand shrinking and market shares being eaten up by noncartel producers who are not obliged to follow the cartel rules, there is a real temptation among OPEC members to cheat. By offering discounts below the cartel price, customers can be wooed away from higher-priced producers. As long as the marginal revenue obtained from additional sales is above the marginal cost, the cheaters have benefited. If discipline breaks down and all cartel members begin to cheat, then there will no longer be an effective cartel. In January of 1985, OPEC oil ministers found that they were unable to agree on a common pricing strategy. At this point, a real question arose as to whether or not OPEC was able to dictate the price of oil.   ■

---

break up cartels. Very few cartels are successful over the long run.

There are numerous examples of cartel agreements on pricing. The member nations of the Organization of Petroleum Exporting Countries (OPEC) meet regularly, with full coverage by the world's press, to set (or attempt to set) the price of crude oil. (See Example 4.) The International Air Transport Association (IATA) also meets openly with the blessing of the member country governments to set airfares for travel between countries.

With some minor exceptions, formal price-setting agreements violate U.S. law, but a number of price-conspiracy cases have come to light where oligopolistic producers have met together in secret to set prices and distribute sales.

The most widely publicized case was the electrical-products conspiracy case of 1961 involving top executives from General Electric, Westinghouse, Allis Chalmers, and other well-known companies. These executives met secretly to set prices and allocate contracts among companies participating in the agreement. While formal secret agreements continue to be uncovered (see Table 4), there are other less risky means of coordinating prices.

Informal agreements can also be used to coordinate pricing and output decisions. The most notable historical case of informal agreement was the so-called Gary Dinners of the early 20th century. Mr. Gary, president of U.S. Steel Corporation, would invite steel-company executives representing more than 90 percent of the output of

Table 4   Selected Price-Fixing Conspiracies, 1961–1970

Market	Geographical Scopes	4-Firm Concentration in the Market (percent)	Number of Conspirators (and their percentage share of sales)		Number of Firms in the Market
Wrought steel wheels	National	85	5	(100)	5
Bed springs	National	<61	10		20
Metal library shelving	National	60	7	(78)	9
Self-locking nuts	National	97	4	(97)	6
Refuse collection	Local		86		102
Women's swimsuits	National	<69	9		
Steel products (wholesale)	Regional	66	5	(72)	
Gasoline	Regional	>49	12		
Milk	Local	>90	11	(>80)	13
Concrete pipe	Regional	100	4	(100)	4
Drill jig bushings	National	56	9	(82)	13
Linen supplies	Local	49	31	(90)	
Plumbing fixtures	National	76	7	(98)	15
Class rings	Regional	<100	3	(90)	5
Tickets	Regional	<78	9	(<91)	10
Baked goods (wholesale)	Regional	46	7		8
Athletic equipment	Local	>90	6	(100)	6
Dairy products	Regional	>95	3	(95)	13
Vending machines	Local	93	6	(100)	6
Ready-mix concrete	Local	86	9	(100)	9
Carbon steel sheets	National	59	10		
Liquid asphalt	Regional	56	20	(95)	

Note: The omitted figures are not available.
Source: George A. Hay and Daniel Kelly, "An Empirical Survey of Price Fixing Conspiracies," *Journal of Law and Economics* 17 (April 1974): 29–38.

steel to dinner regularly to urge his guests to co-operate in holding prices where they were. Walter Adams describes the Gary dinners:

> He exhorted them like a Methodist preacher at a camp meeting to follow the price leadership of U.S. Steel. There was no need for any formal agreements. U.S. Steel simply assumed the lead incumbent on a firm its size; its rival followed, fully realizing the security and profitablity of cooperation.[10]

Gary Dinners and their like confirm Adam Smith's perception that "people of the same trade seldom meet together, even for merriment and diversion, but the conversation ends in a conspiracy against the public, or in some contrivance to raise prices."[11]

10. Adams, *The Structure of American Industry*, p. 71.
11. Adam Smith, *The Wealth of Nations*, ed. Edwin Cannan (New York: Modern Library, 1937).

Price Leadership

A more subtle method of collusion occurs when a recognized price leader emerges among a set of oligopolists. The price leader keeps a sharp eye on market demand and costs that are common to all firms. As noted, the price leader's price increases and decreases are followed by rival firms.

Examples of price leadership are plentiful: During the 1920s and 1930s, the "big three" cigarette manufacturers (R. J. Reynolds, American Tobacco, and Liggett & Meyers) set the classic pattern with R. J. Reynolds (Camels) serving as the price leader. In today's cigarette industry, Philip Morris has become the price leader by virtue of the market dominance of Marlboro cigarettes. The ready-to-eat breakfast-cereal industry, including Kelloggs, Post, and General Mills (the big three), has an interesting pattern of price leadership. Kelloggs leads for most product lines while General Mills and Post lead for their own best product lines. The same pattern exists for the steel industry.

Conscious Parallelism

The most subtle form of collusion is **conscious parallelism,** which uses a *focal point* as a means of price setting. A focal point is an obvious benchmark by which prices or output could be co-ordinated without an explicit agreement. Thomas Schelling gives the following general analogy of how focal points are discovered:

> You are to meet someone in New York City. You have not been instructed where to meet; you have no prior understanding with the person on where to meet; and you cannot communicate with each other. . . . You are told the date but not the hour of this meeting; the two of you must guess the place and exact minute of the day for the meeting.[12]

According to Schelling, given these instructions, most people familiar with New York City would choose the information booth at Grand Central Station at high noon.

How do focal points apply to the economic behavior of oligopolists? Oligopolist firms will be intimately acquainted with their own industries. Business practices followed in the industry are well known. The focal points may involve certain standardized business practices—such as common percentage markups, the use of round numbers, the charging of prices like $4.95, and policies like "splitting the difference" or charging high season rates. As long as each oligopolist understands these standard practices, it can anticipate how rival firms will behave in given situations.

> Through **conscious parallelism,** the actions of producers can be coordinated within certain ranges without formal or even informal agreements. All oligopolists use their understanding of the industry to make their own decisions and anticipate the behavior of other oligopolists.

The clearest example of conscious parallelism is the following experience of the U.S. Veterans Administration, recounted by F. M. Scherer.[13]

> On June 5, 1955, five different companies submitted sealed bids to fill an order for 5,640 100-capsule bottles of the antibiotic tetracyclin, each quoting an effective net price of $19.1884 per bottle. . . . But although one can never be certain, it is probable that there was no direct collusion connected with this transaction. . . . The curious price of $19.1884 per bottle was arrived at through the application of a series of round-number discounts to round-number base prices: $19.1884 is the standard trade discount of 2 per cent of $19.58, which (after rounding) is 20 percent off the wholesale price of $24.48, which in turn is 20 percent off the $30.60 charged to retail druggists, which is 40 percent off the prevailing retail list price of $51.00, which in turn reflected an earlier 15 percent cut from the original list price of $60.00 per 100 capsules.

What appears to be an incredible coincidence explainable only by a secret price agreement may in fact be simply the application of focal points by the firms involved. Focal points may also help explain why oligopoly prices are sometimes inflexible. Firms accustomed to making decisions based on focal points may be reluctant to make large moves that put them outside the customary range of focal points.

Obstacles to Collusion

Despite the considerable gains to oligopolists from cooperation, collusion may not work. The chances for effective and lasting collusion decrease when there are 1) many sellers, 2) low entry barriers, 3) product heterogeneity, 4) high rates of innovation, 5) high fixed costs, 6) infrequent orders, 7) opportunities for cheating, and 8) legal restrictions.

Many Sellers.   The more sellers or firms there are in the industry, the more difficult it is for the sellers to join in a conspiracy to raise prices. The communication network becomes much more complicated as the number of conspirators grows. When there are two sellers, there is only one communication link; when there are three sellers, there are three different information

---

12. Thomas Schelling, *The Strategy of Conflict* (Cambridge: Harvard University Press, 1960), p. 56.

13. Scherer, *Industrial Market Structure,* p. 191.

links. When there are 10 sellers, there are 45 ways information must flow! The number of information channels increases at a far greater rate than the rate at which the number of sellers increases. It becomes far more difficult to coordinate collusive actions as the number of colluders grows. (The formula for the number of information flows is $n(n - 1)/2$, where n is the number of sellers.)

Low Entry Barriers.   If it is easy for new firms to enter an industry, existing firms may not find it worthwhile to enter into cumbersome agreements to raise prices. Effective collusion would only bring in new firms.

High prices create profitable opportunities for new firms. For example, imagine an industry has constant returns to scale (no economies or diseconomies of scale) and only one firm. Suppose that the average cost of production—including a normal return—is $10. With complete free entry, the existing firm could not charge more than $10 in the long run. Any price above $10 would bring in new firms to capture above-normal returns. The entry of firms would eventually drive the price down to $10 where only a normal return is being earned.

Product Heterogeneity.   The more heterogeneous or differentiated the product is from firm to firm, the more difficult it will be for the industry to achieve coordination or collusion. Reaching an agreement creates both costs and benefits. It is costlier to reach an agreement if the product is not homogeneous. Since steel is homogeneous, an agreement on prices and market shares between U.S. Steel and Bethlehem Steel may be fairly easy to conclude. But an agreement between McDonnell Douglas and Boeing over the relative prices of DC-10s and Boeing 747s may be quite difficult because of the differences in and the complexity of the product. An agreement between the producers of high-quality goods and low-quality goods may break down because of differences of opinion over one good's quality relative to the other good's quality.

High Rates of Innovation.   If there is a high rate of innovation in an industry, collusive agreements will be more difficult to reach. In unstable, quickly changing situations, oligopolies have more difficulty finding the joint profit-maximizing solution. The costs of reaching an agreement are higher in relation to benefits when the industry is constantly turning out new products and developing new techniques.

High Fixed Costs.   The higher fixed costs are relative to total costs, the more likely it is that price wars or price breaks will occur in collusive agreements. Firms will ask themselves what they can gain by cheating on the pricing agreement. If fixed costs are high, variable costs are a low percentage of total costs. As long as the price covers average variable costs, there is something left over to pay fixed costs. By granting a secret price concession, a firm may gain a great deal in the short run if marginal costs are very low. Thus, the benefits to secret price reductions are increased by high fixed costs.

Infrequent Orders.   If orders for the product come in infrequently, the individual firms have an incentive to break a collusive agreement. The gains to a particular firm from price cheating will be greater when orders are large and infrequent than when orders are small and frequent because the cheating will be harder to detect and more profitable per unit.

Opportunities for Cheating.   If it is easy to cheat without being detected, firms will tend to break a collusive agreement. It is easier to cheat on price agreements when actual prices charged by one party cannot be known with certainty by the other parties to the agreement. For example, barbers often can agree upon and charge uniform prices within the same city because the prices of haircuts must be posted. It is easy for rival barbers to detect barbers who are undercutting the agreed-upon price. Thus, in many cities with a strong barbers' union the price of haircuts is uniform, and there are few price wars. On the other hand, when the terms of price negotiations are not revealed (as in the cases of long-term oil-delivery contracts or purchases of commercial aircraft by the airlines), it is easier to cheat on pricing agreements.

Legal Restrictions.   In the United States, the Sherman Antitrust Act (1890) holds that combinations in restraint of trade are illegal. Such a law can obviously reduce collusion by increasing the cost of forming agreements. (Legal restrictions will be discussed in more detail in a later chapter.)

GAME THEORY

If the obstacles to collusion are sufficiently strong, oligopoly behavior will be noncooperative. In these circumstances, each oligopolist must make guesses about what its rivals will do under alternative circumstances. If McDonald's advertises heavily on television, can Wendy's or Burger King be expected to follow suit? If Kelloggs introduces a new breakfast cereal, will General Mills and Post introduce yet another brand of cereal?

When oligopolists do not collude, they must act strategically. Oligopoly is like a game. As in sports, poker, chess, or war, each player must play in response to the strategies adopted by his or her opponent. In 1944, mathematician John von Neumann and economist Oskar Morgenstern together developed an approach for studying strategic interactions among individual agents. Appropriately enough, their approach is called *game theory*.[14]

Nash Equilibrium

If oligopolists must guess about what their rivals will do, how can they ever reach an equilibrium? What if they guess wrong? While they are likely to guess wrong in any initial situation, after some mutual but noncooperative adjustments their guesses might prove to be correct. In a competitive market, for example, price adjusts until suppliers and demanders are brought into balance. Might not firm strategies also adjust in a noncooperative world? An early 19th-century French economist, Augustin Cournot, and later a modern game theorist, John Nash, suggested a way to analyze this situation. An oligopolistic industry will reach a **Nash equilibrium** when each firm's guess about the strategy of other firms is correct and each firm is able to employ its best strategy for responding to the behavior in which it believes its rivals are engaged. In other words, a behavior pattern in an industry reaches a Nash equilibrium if no firm finds it advantageous to depart from its behavior pattern as long as the others continue to behave the way the firm believes they are behaving.

> A **Nash equilibrium** exists in an oligopolistic market if each firm's profit-maximizing behavior is based on a correct guess about the behavior of rivals.

One of the difficulties with cartels is that they cannot achieve a Nash equilibrium. If everybody else is playing by the rules of the cartel game, it pays each participant to break the rules. Similarly, focal-point pricing will not achieve a Nash equilibrium. If all sellers of a particular drug are submitting bids on the basis of costs plus 30 percent, it pays one seller to submit a bid of costs plus 29 percent!

There are many examples of oligopoly behavior that achieves a Nash equilibrium. The behavior described by the kinked-demand model can achieve a Nash equilibrium when each oligopolist holds price steady in the expectation that its rivals will match price cuts but not price increases. As long as rivals persist in this behavior, the oligopolist cannot gain by raising or lowering price itself.

Three important examples of behavior through which firms in an oligopolistic industry reach a Nash equilibrium are:

1. firms playing the *prisoners' dilemma game* and deciding to cooperate rather than act independently;
2. firms playing the advertising game and deciding to spend more on advertising when their rivals increase their advertising budgets;
3. a firm making a *credible threat* and deciding to make a costly commitment in order to prevent a potential competitor from entering the market.

The Prisoners' Dilemma Game

The famous ''prisoners' dilemma'' game developed by game theorists is a way to analyze a situation much like that often faced by oligopolistic

---

14. Oskar Morgenstern and John von Neumann, *Theory of Games and Economic Behavior* (Princeton: Princeton University Press, 1944).

producers. The setup for the game is that two bank robbers have been apprehended by the police; they are being interrogated in separate rooms. If both talk, both go to jail but with light sentences. If one talks and the other remains quiet, the one who talks gets off with a very light sentence while the silent bank robber gets a long jail sentence. If neither talks, both go free. Each prisoner is in a dilemma. Each knows that by keeping quiet both can get off free provided the other remains quiet; but keeping quiet is risky, since the other prisoner might talk. A situation in which both prisoners keep quiet is not a Nash equilibrium because either one could improve the position he or she would be in if the other confessed by also confessing. If both bank robbers take a conservative strategy of avoiding the worst possible outcome, they will both confess. Is this a Nash equilibrium? Yes. If one believes the other will confess, his or her best strategy is also to confess. If both actually confess, each one has guessed correctly about the other's behavior and is able to employ the best strategy for the situation in which the other confesses.

The prisoners' dilemma is much like an oligopolist's dilemma of deciding whether to collude or to act independently. In both cases, the consequence of one ''player's'' decision depends upon the decision of another ''player.'' Suppose Firm A and Firm B each sell a differentiated product. Suppose also that when the two products have equal prices, both firms enjoy exactly the same profit. If one charges a slightly lower price than the other, however, that firm will make large profits while the high-priced firm loses money.

Figure 5 shows the simplest possible set of outcomes. Each firm has the option of choosing a price of either $20 or $19. The prices Firm A might charge are shown down the left side of the figure; the prices Firm B might charge are shown along the top. The *profits* earned by each firm are the payoffs from any set of prices the *two firms together* might charge. Firm A's profit payoffs are shown in the lower-left corner of each box (in color); Firm B's profit payoffs are shown in the upper-right corner of each box (in black). As Figure 5 shows, when both charge $20, both earn $2,500; when both charge $19, both earn $1,500. When one charges $20 and the other charges $19, the lower-priced firm earns $3,000 while the higher-priced firm earns only $1,000.

Figure 5   Profit Payoffs to a Two-Firm Oligopoly

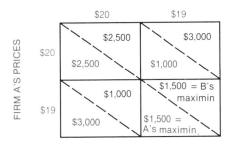

Each square (cell) shows the profits that each firm would earn when various combinations of prices are charged by the two firms. Firm A's profits are shown in color in the lower left-hand corner of each cell, and Firm B's profits are shown in black in the upper right-hand corner of each cell. For example, if A charges $19 and B charges $20, A would earn a profit of $3,000 and B would earn $1,000. What strategy will each pursue? There are two likely options. 1) If the two firms collude, they would both receive the maximum benefit of $2,500 if each charged $20. 2) Each firm might decide to use a *maximin* (maximize the minimum) strategy to find the best of the worst possible outcomes. If A charges $19, the worst that can happen to A is a profit of $1,500. If A were to charge $20, the worst possible outcome for A is a profit of $1,000. By charging a $19 price, A can insure that the worst outcome will not happen. B's best of the worst possible outcomes is the $1,500 gained by charging $19. The maximin solution is for both firms to choose a price of $19. The maximin strategy also yields a Nash equilibrium: each firm is worse off if it raises prices while the other firm sticks to its $19 price.

The two firms reach a Nash equilibrium when both firms charge $19. If each believes the other is charging $19, the best strategy for each one is also to charge $19. When both actually charge $19, each has guessed correctly and each is able to employ the best strategy for the situation in which the *other* charges $19.

The Nash solution of both firms charging $19 is also called the *maximin* (maximize the minimum) strategy. Firms following such a strategy choose the best of the worst possible outcomes. If Firm A charges $20, the worst that could happen to A is if B charged $19 because A's profits would then be $1,000. If A charged $19, the worst that could happen to A would be a $1,500 profit, which would result if B also charged $19. B's worst outcome for charging $19 is a profit of $1,500. B's worst outcome for charging $20 is a

Example 5   TIT-FOR-TAT and the Prisoners' Dilemma Game

Economist Robert Axelrod has studied how people play the prisoners' dilemma game. In particular, Axelrod is interested in learning how people play the game if it is repeated over and over again so that they can learn from experience. Axelrod invited 14 authorities on the prisoners' dilemma game to compete in a tournament. Each contestant was required to submit a strategy for the following game: For each of the 200 rounds of the game, each player's strategy should generate either a C (cooperate) or D (don't cooperate—defect). If both players produce a C, then each receives 3 points. If both produce a D, they each receive 1 point. If one offers a D while the other offers a C, the defecting player gets 5 points and the cooperating player zero points. The reward for successfully suckering your opponent is quite high. The winning program was the shortest program of all—called TIT-FOR-TAT by its author, Anatol Rapoport. Its strategy was very simple: Offer a C on the first move, and then do whatever your partner did on the previous move. As long as your opponent cooperates, you cooperate too. If your opponent defects, you punish by defecting on the next move. The TIT-FOR-TAT program amassed the highest number of points in the first tournament and beat out 62 entrants from six countries in Axelrod's second tournament. The simplest winning strategy achieved its victory by being cooperative. Game theorists are studying whether or not people naturally employ cooperative behavior in real-life business "games" that are played frequently. ∎

Source: William F. Allman, "Nice Guys Finish First," *Science 84,* October 1984, pp. 25–32.

profit of $1,000. In this case, both firms will charge $19 and earn a $1,500 profit, which for each is the best of the worst possible outcomes. If the conservative maximin strategy is followed, prices are rather stable, just as in the kinked-demand theory.

If A and B played this game repeatedly over a fairly long period of time, it is likely that A and B would somehow learn that they are both better off charging higher prices. They might learn to cooperate and choose the strategy that maximizes joint profits. In this case, both would charge $20 and earn profits of $2,500 each. (See Example 5 for a further discussion.)

The Advertising Game

If a firm's rival advertises, "my product is better than all others" it is difficult for the firm to fail to respond with its own advertising message. When the Wendy's hamburger chain, in their "Where's the Beef?" campaign, claimed their rivals produced hamburgers containing less beef, McDonald's and Burger King stepped up their own advertising campaigns.

Consider a hypothetical rivalry between two hamburger giants: Big Burger and Best Burger. Table 5 shows what the strategy of each hamburger company would be in response to the various amounts of daily national television commercials by its rival.

Big Burger strategists calculate that the company could maximize its profits by running 3 ads per day if Best Burger placed 0 ads per day, by running 6 ads if Best Burger placed 8 ads, and by running 9 ads if Best Burger placed 16 adds. The black curve in Figure 6 shows the graph of Big Burger's optimal strategy. On the other hand, Best Burger strategists calculate that the company could maximize its profits by running 4 ads per day if Big Burger placed 0 ads per day, by running 8 ads if Big Burger placed 6 ads, and by running 12 ads if Big Burger placed 12 ads per day. The color curve in Figure 6 shows a graph of Best Burger's optimal strategy. The Nash equilibrium occurs where Best Burger's strategy curve intersects Big Burger's strategy curve. Thus, when Big Burger is running 6 ads a day and Best Burger is running 8 ads per day, there is a Nash equilibrium. Big Burger maximizes its profit with 6 ads when Big Burger places 8 ads; Best Burger maximizes its profit with 8 ads when Big Burger places 6 ads. At this point, each company is employing its best strategy for dealing with a correct assessment of how many ads the other company will place.

Table 5   Advertising Strategies

Big Burger's Strategies (Ads per day)		Best Burger's Strategies (Ads per day)	
Big Burger Optimum	Best Burger Number	Best Burger Optimum	Big Burger Number
3	0	4	0
6	8	8	6
9	16	12	12

This table shows the profit-maximizing number of TV advertisements for each hypothetical hamburger chain in response to its rival. The Nash equilibrium occurs when Best Burger runs 8 ads per day and Big Burger runs 6 ads per day because at this point, each firm's profit-maximizing behavior is based on a correct guess about the other firm's behavior.

Figure 6   Nash Equilibrium: Advertising

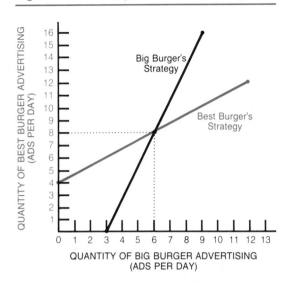

The black line shows Big Burger's best response to Best Burger's ads. The color line shows Best Burger's best response to Big Burger's ads. Where the two curves intersect is a Nash equilibrium, where each firm's guess about the other firm's strategy is confirmed. In other words, Big Burger wants 6 ads when Best Burger places 8 ads, and Best Burger wants 8 ads when Big Burger places 6 ads.

The advertising example is interesting because the firms advertise much more in the Nash equilibrium than they would if they reached an informal agreement to deliberately keep their advertising expenditures to a minimum.

The Credible Threat

One example of a Nash equilibrium involves an oligopolistic firm making a *credible threat* about starting a price war. The firm wants to prevent a rival from being able to compete by making a threat that causes the rival to think the costs of competing in the market exceed the benefits. Imagine an oligopolistic industry contains one actual monopolist and one *potential* entrant and that the monopolist is trying to prevent the rival from entering the business. The monopolist can take two actions: do nothing or let the rival know that the entry of a new firm will result in a *price war* (that is, the monopolist will cut prices below costs to drive out the new firm. The rival may not believe the monopolist's threat unless the monopolist makes some commitment that makes this threat credible. An empty threat may be ignored—any potential entrant may simply calculate that the monopolist would also lose from the price war and would eventually have to settle down into a more stable oligopoly situation. But the monopolist can make an irreversible commitment. For example, the monopolist might spend $10 million to secure the services of the best advertising agency before the potential rival enters the business. Or the monopolist might convert assets in order to accumulate large cash resources so that any would-be rival would be afraid to engage in a price war. The credible threat makes it easier for the potential entrant to make a correct assumption about the monopolist's behavior. A Nash equilibrium results when the monopolist maximizes profits by making a costly commitment a credible threat that succeeds in keeping out the potential entrant (on the correct assumption that the potential entrant would become an actual entrant in the absence of the costly commitment) and when the potential entrant minimizes losses by not entering the market (on the correct assumption that the monopolist would start a price war if a new firm did enter the market).

The behavior of a wide variety of noncooperative oligopolies can be explained using the concept of a Nash equilibrium. Indeed, the Nash-equilibrium concept can even be applied to many social behaviors. Game theorists are hard at work

Example 6   The Credible Threat and Breakfast-Cereal Advertising

Breakfast cereals provide the most notable example of a highly concentrated oligopoly based upon product differentiation. In 1950, there were 25 brands in distribution, and by 1980 there were more than 80 brands. The broad evidence suggests that the minimum efficient plant size of a cereal producer is 5 percent of the market; engineering economies of scale would not lead one to expect high concentration in the breakfast-cereal industry. Yet the four largest breakfast-food manufacturers—Kellogg, General Mills, General Foods, and Quaker Oats—control 90 percent of the ready-to-eat breakfast-cereal market. Each spends large sums on advertising its cereals: about $0.13 of each dollar of sales is spent on advertising.

These four large breakfast-cereal manufacturers have been able to earn profit rates that are well above average for manufacturing firms and have been able to increase their market share from 68 percent in 1940 to around 90 percent in the 1980s. The high concentration in breakfast cereals is not explained by economies of scale or by collusive agreements because there are too many manufacturers. Concentration in the breakfast-cereal industry has been created by successful product differentiation through advertising.

Product differentiation raises barriers to entry. If a new entrant introduces a new product, the big four could embark upon an advertising blitz in favor of their own products that would limit the sales of the newcomer. By offering a dazzling array of brands and package sizes, established firms make it difficult for new entrants to find an unexploited market niche. New firms must seek to enter without a product that can be readily differentiated from existing products. By standing ready to increase already large advertising budgets, the big four cereal manufacturers have a credible threat to deter entry. ∎

---

on new concepts of equilibrium that can explain even more complicated oligopolistic strategies—such as setting low prices today and high prices tomorrow—in an effort to shed more light on the behavior of noncollusive oligopolies. (See Example 6.)

CONTESTABLE MARKETS: COMPLETE FREEDOM OF ENTRY AND EXIT

Even if an industry is highly oligopolistic in terms of concentration ratios, economists William J. Baumol, John Panzer, and Robert Willig argue that potential entrants can constrain the industry to act competitively.[15] In short, a monopoly or oligopoly market can be contested by those who could compete under the right conditions. A **contestable market** is one where the potential for competition has the same effect on firm behavior as actual competition. The theory of contestable markets applies to an oligopolistic market or even to a natural monopoly in which new firms can enter and exit with complete ease.

> A **contestable market** is one in which 1) entry and exit by new firms is completely free, 2) the new firms can produce with the same costs as the incumbent firms, 3) firms can easily dispose of their fixed assets by selling them elsewhere (fixed costs are not sunk but are recoverable), and 4) customers buy from the firm (or firms) that first posts the lowest price.

Imagine a monopoly firm that has declining average total cost and that produces a product that can be duplicated by many other firms that have access to the same technology. If the firm charges a monopoly price, new firms can enter, can sell at a lower price, and can leave the monopolist holding the bag. Such hit-and-run entry can effectively prevent the monopoly from fully exploiting its position in the market or from earning any economic profits. The presence of such complete freedom of entry would force the "monopolist" to charge a price equal to its average total costs.

What about the situation where an industry re-

15. William J. Baumol, "Contestable Markets: An Uprising in the Theory of Industry Structure," *American Economic Review* 72 (March 1982): 1–15.

quires several firms for economic efficiency? Imagine all firms have free access to the same U-shaped cost curve and that the cost curve reaches a minimum ATC at $1 per unit and 1,000 units of output. To keep matters simple, assume that at a price of $1 exactly 4,000 units are demanded by the market. Efficiency demands that 4 firms each produce 1,000 units of the product at a cost of $1 per unit. If this market were contestable, how would it function? According to the definition of a contestable market, if all four firms charged a price higher than $1—say $1.20—they would face hit-and-run entry. Another firm (or firms) could enter and charge, say, $1.10, make a profit, and induce losses for the incumbent firms. Indeed, any price higher than $1 will invite hit-and-run entry. Thus, to prevent the entry of potential competitors, the 4 firms would produce 1,000 units each and charge exactly $1 per unit. Since the price equals the minimum ATC, the price also equals MC—as it would in a perfectly competitive market.

In a contestable market with two or more firms, the market works much like perfect competition. The solution is efficient in the sense of giving the product to consumers at the lowest possible cost. A contestable market does not require many actual firms, only many potential entrants, to achieve this efficient result. When entry is completely free and exit is absolutely costless, the number of potential firms is enormous.

One possible example of a contestable market is the market for airline service between two particular cities. If only one airline is serving the route between city A and city B, monopoly pricing might be impossible because other airlines could enter and exit swiftly if the airline attempted to charge a monopoly price. Many airlines would be able to assign planes to service the route between A and B on very little notice. If a new rival airline wished to exit, it could simply reassign its planes to other routes.

The theory of contestable markets is still being researched. Traditional industrial-organization economists still prefer to look at markets in terms of whether they are tight or loose oligopolies. If complete freedom of entry and exit determines the way firms in a given market behave, external rather than internal market conditions are more important. If the presence of sunk costs determines the behavior of the oligopolistic firms, then internal market conditions are more important.[16]

IMPLICATIONS OF OLIGOPOLY THEORY

The Diversity of Oligopoly

Oligopoly is too varied to draw general conclusions that apply to all forms of oligopoly. In less concentrated oligopolies, the number of firms is too large for formal or tacit collusion to occur, and it is difficult to prevent competitive behavior from erupting. According to Scherer, if firms supply a homogeneous product, it generally takes only 10 to 12 evenly matched suppliers for them to ignore each other's influence on price.[17]

When the oligopoly is loose due to low barriers to entry, the behavior of the oligopolistic firm should not differ very much from that of monopolistically competitive or even perfectly competitive firms. Large economic profits would not be expected.

Only in highly concentrated oligopolies with high entry barriers is coordinated action possible, but the temptations to cheat are substantial, and collusive agreements often fall apart. In its most successful form, however, a cartel arrangement yields a result that is really no different from monopoly.

Criticism of Oligopoly

The previous chapter described positive features of perfect competition—efficiency, production at minimum average cost, lower prices with higher output—and negative features of monopoly—production above minimum average cost, long-term monopoly profits, prices not equal to marginal costs, restricted output with higher prices.

As already noted, some oligopolies bear a strong resemblance to competitive markets while other oligopolies, especially in their collusive form, can bear a strong resemblance to monop-

---

16. For a critique of the contestable-market theory, see William G. Shepherd, " 'Contestability' vs. Competition," *American Economic Review* 74 (September 1984): 572–87. Other critics of the theory include Martin Weitzman, Marius Schwartz, and Robert Reynolds.

17. Scherer, *Industrial Market Structure*, p. 199.

oly. If the reader was convinced in the previous chapter that monopoly is bad and competition is good, then it is likely that same reader will conclude that less concentrated oligopolies are better than collusive oligopolies.

There has been substantial debate among industrial-organization researchers about whether or not oligopolies earn extraordinary profits. This question is difficult to study because of the difficulty of measuring economic profits (as opposed to accounting profits) and the problem of determining the degree of oligopoly, which is typically determined by measuring concentration ratios or the existence of entry barriers.

Joe S. Bain and H. Michael Mann showed that profit rates in the 1930s and 1950s tended to rise with barriers to entry and with concentration, although these results were more pronounced in the 1950s than in the 1930s.[18] More recent studies find that, particularly at high concentration ratios (70 percent and above), concentration is strongly and positively related to profits and that barriers to entry have an even stronger correlation with profits than concentration ratios. Other oligopolies (with concentration ratios below 70 percent) have profit rates that are more weakly associated with concentration or barriers to entry.[19]

The theory of contestable markets appears to imply that profit rates will be uncorrelated with internal market structure (concentration ratios, size of firm, etc.) when the market is contestable. Thus, a well-documented study showing concentration ratios are related to profits would indicate those markets were not contestable.

Defense of Oligopoly

Some economists defend oligopoly as an efficient form of economic market. Harold Demsetz sees the positive relationship between profit rates and concentration or barriers to entry as an indicator of efficiency rather than as an indicator of market power.[20]

Demsetz maintains that higher profits are the result of the superior cost performance of larger firms in the industry. If prices are set in a competitive manner so that each firm acts more or less like a price taker (exerting no monopoly power over prices), then economic profits will accrue only to those firms that have lower costs, not to all firms in the industry. There is evidence that oligopoly profits are earned only by the largest firms in oligopolistic industries, not by all firms. Demsetz, therefore, concludes that oligopoly profits are not the result of the exercise of excessive market power; rather, oligopoly profits are the result of the superior efficiency of large oligopolistic firms.

Figure 7 illustrates the Demsetz argument. It assumes that a homogeneous product is being produced and that perfect competition prevails. Each firm equates marginal costs to the price. Figure 7 shows that when these conditions prevail, economic profits are earned by the low-cost producer. The Demsetz thesis is relatively new and has not been subjected yet to appropriate empirical testing.[21]

John K. Galbraith agrees with Demsetz that large oligopolies are much more efficient than their smaller counterparts. In fact, Galbraith argues that there is a power imbalance between the competitive sector and the oligopoly/monopoly sector.

In Galbraith's view, the competitive sector is being gradually worn down by the technically superior technostructure of the oligopoly sector. Rather than the competitive sector efficiently utilizing resources and monopoly/oligopoly underutilizing resources, as theory teaches, Galbraith maintains that the reverse is true. The competitive

18. Joe S. Bain, *Barriers to New Competition*, pp. 192–200; H. Michael Mann, "Seller Concentration, Barriers to Entry, and Rates of Return in Thirty Industries," *Review of Economics and Statistics*, August 1966, pp. 296–307.
19. Leonard W. Weiss, "Quantitative Studies of Industrial Organization," in ed. Michael D. Intriligator, *Frontiers of Quantitative Economics* (Amsterdam: North Holland, 1971); Leonard Weiss, "Concentration-Profits Relationship and Antitrust," in eds. Goldschmid et al., *Industrial Concentration: The New Learning* (Boston: Little, Brown, 1974), pp. 184–233.
20. Harold Demsetz, "Industry Structure, Market Rivalry, and Public Policy," *Journal of Law and Economics* 16 (April 1973): 1–10.
21. Scherer argues that a proper test of the oligopoly-superiority hypothesis has yet to be undertaken. Such a test must take into account the interdependence between profitability, concentration, market shares, and differentiation. The superiority hypothesis would be easy to test if oligopolies produced a homogeneous good and no other. But in the real world oligopolies tend to produce many differentiated products that may be reflected in different costs. To assume that higher profits reflect the same price for the same good and, thus, lower unit cost remains to be demonstrated. *See* Scherer, *Industrial Market Structure*, pp. 290–91.

Figure 7   The Demsetz Thesis

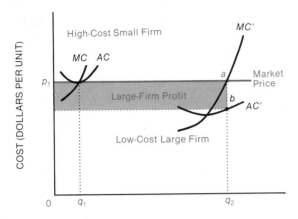

The large, efficient firm produces an output of q_2 units with a per-unit profit of ab. The small, inefficient firm produces an output of q_1 units with a zero economic profit. According to Demsetz, perfect competition can be consistent with the positive association between concentration rates and economic profits.

sector cannot advertise like the large corporations, which can manipulate the demand for their products.[22]

Joseph Schumpeter argues that the large corporation is ideally equipped to generate technological progress. This technological progress is the moving force behind economic progress; it establishes some firms as dominant in their industry but not forever. Through the process of ''creative destruction,'' Schumpeter believes that new ideas and new technologies replace the old and that the monopoly power created by technological innovation will prove to be transitory. The previous chapter raised serious questions about the validity of this argument.

This chapter completes our study of the four basic market models. The next chapter will examine how the costs of gathering information about buyers, sellers, resources, and products af-

fects market behavior and how markets provide information about present and future scarcity.

Summary

1.   An oligopoly is an industry characterized by the small number of firms, barriers to entry, and mutual interdependence. The number of firms is so small that the actions of one firm will have a significant effect on other firms in the industry. The presence of barriers to entry explains the small number of firms in an oligopoly. Types of barriers to entry are economies of scale, product differentiation, control over input supplies, government barriers to entry, large capital requirements, technological advantages, and sunk costs. Even though the concentration ratio is an imperfect guide to the measurement of oligopoly, it is used to measure the extent of oligopoly. The degree of concentration in an oligopoly varies; some oligopolies act more like a monopoly than a competitive industry, while others behave more competitively.

2.   Because of mutual interdependence, the oligopolist's demand curve cannot be defined until the reaction pattern of rival firms is specified. The demand curve can vary from the kinked-demand curve to the perfectly coordinated demand curve of a cartel arrangement. The kinked-demand curve is one explanation of the apparent inflexibility of oligopoly prices. It explains how costs and demand can change without a change in the price. The kinked-demand curve is based on the assumption that rivals will follow price decreases but will not follow price increases.

3.   There are several methods of oligopoly coordination that range from formal agreements (cartels) to informal arrangements, such as price leadership or conscious parallelism. Collusive agreements, if successful, allow the participating firms to earn monopoly profits. Because there are incentives to cheat on the cartel agreement, however, collusive agreements tend to be unstable. Collusion is difficult when there are many sellers, low barriers to entry, heterogeneous products, high rates of innovation, high fixed costs, infrequent transactions, easy price cheating, or laws against collusion.

22. John K. Galbraith, *The Affluent Society* (Boston: Houghton Mifflin, 1957); *American Capitalism* (Boston: Houghton Mifflin, 1956); *Economics and the Public Purpose* (Boston: Houghton Mifflin, 1973); *The New Industrial State* (Boston: Houghton Mifflin, 1967).

4. Game theory explains and analyzes the incentives to cheat on collusive agreements. A *Nash equilibrium* prevails in an oligopolistic market if each firm's profit-maximizing behavior is based on a correct guess about the behavior of rivals. Examples of behavior through which firms can achieve a Nash equilibrium are the playing of the prisoners' dilemma game, advertising, and the making of a credible threat.

5. A *contestable market* is a market in which the potential for competition has the same effect on firm behavior as actual competition.

6. Empirical studies show that at high levels of concentration, there is a positive relationship between economic profits and concentration, and between economic profits and barriers to entry. Some economists argue that the higher profits of concentrated oligopolies are the result of the superior technological and cost performance of large firms (Demsetz, Galbraith, and Schumpeter), but there is substantial disagreement among industrial-organization experts on this point.

Key Terms

oligopoly
mutual interdependence
barrier to entry
sunk costs
concentration ratio
shared monopoly
kinked-demand curve
price leader
cartel
conscious parallelism
Nash equilibrium
contestable market

Questions and Problems

1. According to Table 1, the 4-firm concentration ratio for motor vehicles is 89 percent. Is this an accurate measure of the extent of oligopoly? Explain.

2. What is the relationship between the small number of firms and mutual interdependence in oligopoly theory? Why was mutual interdependence not considered in the chapter on monopoly and monopolistic competition?

3. Firm ZYX is one of three equal-sized firms in the widget market. It currently charges $20 per widget and sells one million widgets per year. It is considering raising its price to $22 and needs some estimate of what will happen to its widget sales. Why would it be difficult to make such an estimate?

4. Firm ZYX and the two other widget manufacturers meet in secret and agree to charge a uniform price of $50 and share the market equally (each gets one third of sales). At the price of $50, each firm's marginal cost is $10. What are the rewards to cheating on the agreement if ZYX does not get caught? What happens if all three try to cheat?

5. The prisoners' dilemma game is also used to explain how oligopolists devise advertising strategy. Try to apply the prisoners' dilemma game to advertising in highly concentrated oligopolies.

6. Why is nonprice competition encountered frequently in oligopolistic industries?

7. In an oligopolistic industry comprised of 3 large firms and 10 small firms, the large firms earn an economic profit while the small firms earn normal profits. What do you know about the sources of economic profit in this industry?

8. How does oligopoly theory explain why there are so many different types of oligopoly behavior—collusion, nonprice competition, conscious parallelism, price leadership?

9. What is a *Nash equilibrium?*

10. Which of the following are examples of a Nash equilibrium?
    a. The prisoners' dilemma game.
    b. Cartel pricing.
    c. The credible threat.
    d. Pricing by focal points.

11. Can a contestable market register economic profits?

12. William G. Shepherd has written that the theory of contestable markets ''treats a specialized, extreme set of conditions, which are

probably found in no real markets which have significant internal market power.'' Evaluate this statement.

13. What is the difference between *sunk costs* and *fixed costs?* Why is the difference important?

14. What is the relationship between profit rates and concentration ratios? Why would market contestability be expected to affect this relationship?

Suggested Readings

Adams, Walter, ed. *The Structure of American Industry,* 4th ed. New York: Macmillan, 1971, pp. 77–78.

Bain, Joe S. *Barriers to New Competition.* Cambridge, Mass.: Harvard University Press, 1965.

Caves, Richard. *American Industry: Structure, Conduct, Performance.* Englewood Cliffs, N.J.: Prentice-Hall, 1981.

Galbraith, John K. *American Capitalism,* rev. ed. Cambridge: The Riverside Press, 1956.

Koch, James V. *Industrial Organization and Prices,* 2nd ed. Englewood Cliffs, N.J.: Prentice-Hall, 1980, p. 181.

Scherer, F. M. *Industrial Market Structure and Economic Performance,* 2nd ed. Boston: Houghton Mifflin, 1980, p. 67.

Williamson, Oliver. *Markets and Hierarchies: Analysis and Antitrust Implications.* New York: The Free Press, 1975, p. 234.

33

The Economics of Information

Chapter Preview

Perfect competition is an efficient way of organizing society's resources. If the economy is perfectly competitive, it will not be possible to raise the well-being of some without reducing the well-being of others. For this reason, perfect competition is viewed by economists as yielding an efficient allocation of resources.

Yet competition in its perfect form is rarely found in the real world for several reasons: Most products are not homogeneous; they differ according to quality, location, time, and imagined effects. Second, perfect freedom of entry and exit is hard to realize in the real world. Some barriers to entry—in the form of capital requirements, economies of scale, and so on—typically are present even in competitive industries. Third, the

condition of perfect information concerning prices and quality is met in the real world only in exceptional circumstances. Information is itself a scarce commodity; there are costs and benefits to acquiring information. This chapter focuses upon the role that information gathering plays in our economy.

This chapter will examine why information is a valuable commodity; the role of intermediaries (or "middlemen"), speculators, and hedgers; and the costs of gathering information about markets and products. Information costs are also the key to understanding why it pays to shop for the lowest price, why there are the problems of product quality and safety, and why contracts contain certain features. ■

TRANSACTION COSTS AND INFORMATION COSTS

It is costly to bring buyers and sellers together. All the costs associated with making exchange possible are called **transaction costs.** Some examples are the cost of travel, the cost of negotiation, the cost of property-rights enforcement, and the cost of acquiring information.

> **Transaction costs** are the costs associated with bringing buyers and sellers together.

In real-world markets—even those that are highly competitive—there is considerable uncertainty about the prices that prevail now, the prices that we must pay in the future, and even about product qualities. If information on current and future prices and product qualities were available instantaneously at no cost of time or money to individuals, such uncertainty would evaporate. But acquiring information typically does have its costs, and **information costs** have a substantial effect on real-world markets.

> **Information costs** are the costs of acquiring information on prices, product qualities, and product performance.

Information costs include the costs of telephoning, shopping, checking credentials, inspecting goods, monitoring the honesty of workers or customers, placing ads, and reading ads and consumer reports in order to acquire more economic information.

A major part of the cost of making a transaction between a buyer and a seller is the cost associated with searching for and acquiring economic information. The buyer and seller must first find each other and then agree on the price and other terms of the contract. Knowledge of the existence and location of a willing buyer is valuable information to the seller, just as knowledge of a willing seller is valuable information to the buyer. Without this information, economic transactions cannot take place.

Information is typically a scarce and valuable commodity. Information is costly because human beings have limited capacity to acquire, process, store, and retrieve facts and figures about prices, qualities, and location of products. Each person specializes in certain types of information. Chemical engineers may know a great deal about producing plastics but may know little about building houses. The produce clerks know a great deal about displaying lettuce or apples but little about how they are grown. Homemakers know a great deal about the prices of groceries in their town but little about the prices of industrial machinery. Industrial purchasing agents know more about machinery prices than about grocery prices. Information is costly to acquire because it is distributed over the population in bits and pieces. Example 5 in Chapter 3 explained why no one person knows how to make a pencil from start to finish. Some people—the industrial purchasing agent, the realtor, the stock-market broker—even make a profession of specializing in information, but their knowledge is limited to very specific areas.

Because information is costly, each individual accumulates information that is specific to that person's particular circumstances of time and place. This special information can be valuable. To quote the Noble Prize laureate, Friedrich A. von Hayek:[1]

> . . . a little reflection will show that there is beyond question a body of very important but unorganized knowledge which cannot possibly be called scientific in the sense of knowledge of general rules: the knowledge of particular circumstances of time and place. It is with respect to this that every individual has some advantage over all others in that he possesses unique information of which beneficial use might be made.

By allowing people to be paid for their scarce information, the price system economizes on information costs. The auto mechanic does not have to learn nuclear physics, and the physicist does not have to know how to repair a car.

THE ECONOMICS OF SEARCH

Centralized and Decentralized Markets

A market can be a highly **centralized market** or a **decentralized market.**

---

1. F. A. Hayek, "The Use of Knowledge in Society," *American Economic Review* 35 (1945):510–30.

A **centralized market** is one in which all buyers and sellers of a particular product make their transactions in one location.

A **decentralized market** is one in which buyers and sellers of a particular product make their transactions in a large number of different physical locations.

Stocks, bonds, and commodities (like wheat, gold, and soybeans) are traded in highly centralized markets. Other products, such as retail items, dry-cleaning services, real estate, and furniture are traded in decentralized markets.

Why are some markets centralized and others decentralized? Imagine what would happen if any one of our large cities (or even a medium-sized or small city) were to abolish all grocery stores and set up one central market for grocery products. Such a market, besides being hectic, would prove very inconvenient. The transaction cost of purchasing groceries would be much higher: consumers would need more time (and more gas) to drive to the centralized market, and they would need more time to purchase the desired goods once there (the centralized market could not specialize in particular products because it must service all customers). To avoid the cost and hassle, families would have to maintain much larger inventories of groceries in thier homes.

A decentralized market for staple groceries is cheaper for the consumer, even though the consumer may pay lower purchase prices in the centralized market. The higher transaction costs of a centralized grocery market more than outweigh any savings in shelf prices at the centralized market.

In decentralized markets, it is more difficult for customers to know the prices charged for the same items in different stores, and even if consumers are aware of price differences, the transaction costs of going always to the cheapest store may outweigh the advantages of the lower price. As a consequence, prices in decentralized markets will differ from location to location. A *perfectly competitive market* was described in an earlier chapter as one in which all buyers paid the same price for the same product. Decentralized markets are usually imperfect because different buyers ap-

pear to pay different prices for the same product. From an economic viewpoint, however, the same good in different locations is a different product. This imperfection saves the consumer enormous transaction costs.

Information Gathering and Price Dispersion

Shopping or search costs explain why products sold in decentralized markets sell for different prices, although they are homogeneous with respect to every characteristic except location. A 19-inch Zenith color TV set may sell for different prices in stores one block apart; the same brand of milk may sell for different prices in adjacent grocery stores; the same brand of automobile may sell at different prices in two dealerships located in the same part of town.

If information about the prices charged by different retail outlets were free (assuming that no location is more convenient than another), the same commodity would sell for the same price, as predicted by the theory of perfect competition. But information is not free; real resources must be devoted to gathering information. Therefore, in the real world, the prices of homogeneous products sold in decentralized markets will be dispersed.

In gathering costly information, people follow the same rule that governs most economic behavior:

People will continue to acquire economic information as long as the benefits of gathering information exceed the costs.

That individuals follow economic rules in gathering information may seem far fetched at first glance, but this notion is really quite reasonable. For example, when a person decides to buy a new car, the more information that person has on prices and on the technical qualities of various automobiles, the better the eventual choice is likely to be. But it is costly to gather such information. It is costly to drive all over town to the various dealers; it is costly to take time off from work or from leisure activities to compare prices;

Example 1   The Dispersion of Coffee and Tea Prices in Houston Supermarkets

The proposition that the price dispersion on identical items would be lower the higher is the total expenditure on the item was tested in 1981 by gathering prices on two homogeneous products at five Houston supermarkets. Prices of a one-pound can of Folgers coffee and of a box of 48 Lipton tea bags were gathered at five different stores on the same day, in the same neighborhood. According to standard statistical measures, the price of the Lipton tea varied twice as much as the price of Folgers coffee. The prices are plotted in the accompanying figure. (The ratio of the standard deviation to the mean was 0.031 for coffee and 0.061 for tea).

This result is exactly what the economic theory of search predicts. It costs as much to shop for coffee as for tea, but Americans spend much more for coffee than for tea. The benefits of searching out the lowest coffee prices are, therefore, much higher than the benefits of searching out the lowest tea prices. Hence, we expect more

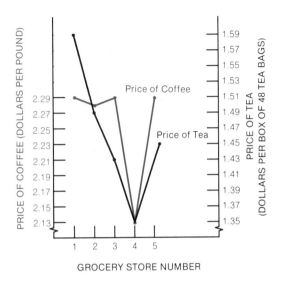

GROCERY STORE NUMBER

comparison shopping and far less price dispersion for coffee than for tea. ■

---

it may be expensive in terms of time and money to acquire and master technical information contained in the various consumer-guide reports on new automobiles. To gather all the available information about new cars would take an inordinate amount of time and money; therefore, the prospective buyer would have to draw the line somewhere. That line would be drawn approximately at the point where the person felt that the marginal benefit from acquiring more information is less than the marginal cost of acquiring more information.

The theory that consumers search until marginal benefits equal marginal costs can be used to predict the extent of price dispersion on different products. Clearly, anything that raises the marginal benefits of search relative to the marginal costs of search will increase the amount of searching (shopping, reading, consultation of experts). The greater the volume of resources devoted to searching, the closer will be the prices of homogeneous products. The marginal benefits of search should be higher the larger are the expenditures on a given item; therefore, the theory of search suggests that prices of items that are more expen-

sive (as a percent of total expenditures) will be less widely dispersed than those of less expensive items (see Example 1).

There is considerable evidence to support this proposition. George Stigler, in his investigation of automobile and washing-machine prices, found that prices were less widely dispersed for identical makes of automobiles than for identical brands of washing machines.[2]

An interesting paradox is that the more people search, the less the individual needs to search. If everyone devoted considerable resources to information searching, price dispersion—and the gains to further search—would be reduced because the sellers would be aware of the search behavior. (See Example 2.)

INFORMATION PROBLEMS

When information is costly, it can become difficult for one party in a contract to monitor the

---

2. George Stigler, *The Theory of Price* (New York: Macmillan, 1952), p. 4.

Example 2   Uncertainty and Search Costs in the New England Fishing Market

The New England fishing market is an example of how uncertainty, information, and search costs caused real-world markets to diverge from the uniform-price feature of perfect competition. On the surface, this market appears to have the characteristics of perfect competition: there are more than 1,800 fishing vessels; there is relative freedom of entry; there are more than 400 licensed dealers who buy directly from the fishing vessels. One would expect the New England fishing market to be perfectly competitive with everyone paying the same price for the same product.

On the contrary, on the same day the same type and quality of fish sells for radically different prices. Some sellers sell at high prices; others sell at low prices. Uncertainty and high information costs explain why there is such disparity in prices.

Fishing vessels catch fish in nets and deposit their catch in their holds, never certain of the exact quantities and qualities of fish they have caught. When they arrive in port, the costs of getting alternative prices on their catch are prohibitive. The fish must be "offloaded" (at the fishing vessel's expense), and the fish are likely to lose their freshness in the process. Vessel owners simply are not in a position to shop from one dealer to another for alternative bids. Moreover, there is no centralized market for freshly caught fish (no spot market); fish sellers have little information on the price of fish on that particular day and are at a distinct informational disadvantage to the buyers. The result: on the same day, fish of the same type and quality sell at different prices. Sellers do not know the spot price of fish. In fact, there is no single organized spot market. Sellers cannot shop around for the highest price because the costs of such shopping around would be prohibitive. The costs of acquiring price information in such a market are very high because the fish sellers would have to have agents monitoring all the transactions taking place at different dock locations on each day to know what prices are. When information costs are taken into account, however, the market is probably as efficient and competitive as possible. ■

Source: Based upon James Wilson, "Adaptation to Uncertainty and Small Numbers Exchange: The New England Fresh Fish Market," *Bell Journal of Economics* 11 (Autumn 1980): 491–504.

other party's performance, and it can be difficult to check the claims made by economic agents trying to secure favorable contracts.

The Moral-Hazard Problem

If someone buys an insurance policy that will cover any losses the person might incur if his or her car is in a collision, that person may drive less cautiously than if he or she did not have insurance. In other words, the person has an incentive to change his or her behavior as a result of the contract written with the insurance company. The insurance company cannot write into the contract that the person must drive defensively, because such behavior is simply impossible to monitor.

In a different context, if a seller gives an absolute guarantee that a certain product will never break down, such a guarantee might encourage some buyers to abuse the product—or at least to be less careful in using the product. The behavior of such buyers is affected by the contract. It is difficult to make the guarantee conditional on the buyer not abusing the product because it is too costly for the seller to obtain information on how and when a product is abused.

Both of these situations are examples of the **moral-hazard problem.**

The **moral-hazard problem** occurs when a buyer or seller alters his or her behavior after a contract is made to profit from the contract at the other party's expense and arises because it is too costly for the other party to obtain information about the first party's post-contractual behavior.

The moral-hazard problem exists when contracts dealing with future performance are abused by economic agents who cannot be fully monitored. Insurance companies attempt to solve the moral-hazard problem by requiring people to share in the costs of losses. The insured person who has a car accident must often pay the first $250 or $500 to repair the damage. The moral-hazard problem explains why insurance companies must investigate large claims, why product guarantees sometimes appear to protect the seller as much as the buyer, and why many types of insurance are not even available.

The Adverse-Selection Problem

While the moral-hazard problem deals with the postcontractual behavior of economic agents, the **adverse-selection problem** deals with the precontractual behavior of agents. When buyers and sellers have different information about the product, it is possible for the one with superior information to lure the other into writing a favorable contract.

> The **adverse-selection problem** occurs when a buyer or seller enters a disadvantageous contract on the basis of incomplete or inaccurate information because the cost of obtaining the relevant information is higher for this buyer or seller than for the other party to the transaction.

For example, if an insurance company does not know that Joe Nervous is an accident waiting to happen, it may sell him car insurance at the same rate that applies to other people in Joe's age group. Because Joe knows he is a terrible driver, he jumps at the chance to buy car insurance at the same rate that other drivers in his group pay. If the insurance company did not face high information costs finding out about Joe's driving habits, it could simply ask for a compensating higher insurance rate or refuse insurance.

The adverse-selection problem plagues the used-car market as well as the car-repair business. The seller of a used car may know the car has a history of problems. If the used-car buyer had the same information as the seller about the car, the buyer would either not buy the car or would pay a price that compensated the buyer for the car's defects. If the seller wants to protect its reputation, the buyer may rely on receiving complete information about the car. But when reputation is not a factor, used-car markets and car-repair markets work very sluggishly.

The adverse-selection problem is also encountered by those administering government programs. If a government undertakes a program that distributes aid to poor people, some people who are well off will pretend to be poor in order to obtain government benefits. Such opportunism limits the extent to which the program can really help the poor. If the government knew who was poor and who wasn't, there would be no adverse-selection problem.

When opportunistic agents are able to write favorable contracts because the characteristics of their "product" cannot be observed when the contract is first written, the adverse-selection problem has occurred. The adverse-selection problem occurs when a perfectly healthy 70-year-old can't buy health insurance at a rate befitting his or her health or when a teenager who can drive better than his parents has to pay more for car insurance.

Markets have developed responses to a variety of information problems. Every effort is made by buyers and sellers to devise contracts that will somehow reveal the true character of the parties involved. For example, insurance companies put in clauses so that they can either cancel a person's insurance or raise the rates as experience dictates. By changing the relative sizes of the basic insurance rate and the penalties, drivers will self-select themselves into good and bad risks! A low insurance rate with a high penalty for an accident will attract good drivers. A high insurance rate with a low penalty will attract bad drivers. The same principle applies to different categories of coverage. If you have *liability insurance,* the insurance company pays for the damage you cause to the other party. If you have *collision* insurance, the insurance company pays for part of the damage to your own car. Those who are good drivers might opt for liability insurance instead of collision insurance if they can.

Examples of quality-revealing contracts also appear in the labor market. A good worker might agree to a low wage today in exchange for a high wage tomorrow whereas a poor worker would want the high wage today knowing he or she might be fired tomorrow! Thus, firms have an incentive to offer long-term labor contracts with attractive long-term benefits in order to attract high-quality workers.

In cases involving the adverse-selection problem, the consumer must either rely on the reputation of the seller or turn to the intermediaries who can give buyers the assurance of quality.

THE ROLE OF "MIDDLEMEN," OR INTERMEDIARIES

"Middlemen," or **intermediaries,** specialize in information concerning
1.   exchange opportunities between buyers and sellers;
2.   the variety and qualities of different products;
3.   the channels of marketing distribution of produced goods.

> "Middlemen," or **intermediaries,** buy in order to sell again or simply bring together a buyer and a seller.

Real-estate brokers, grocery stores, department stores, used-car dealers, auctioneers, stock brokers, insurance agents, and travel agents are all intermediaries, or "middlemen." All these professions "mediate" or stand between ultimate buyers and sellers in return for a profit.

Suppose that an individual is willing to sell a multimillion dollar private airplane for no less than $20 million, and a potential buyer residing in some distant country is willing to pay at most $25 million for such an airplane. How will they locate one another? Someone with information about the existence of the potential buyer and seller could act as an intermediary and bring the two together. It would be possible for the seller to get $20 million, for the buyer to pay $25 million, and for the intermediary to charge as much as $5 million for the service of bringing the two together.

Transactions of this sort take place all the time, although most transactions are less spectacular. The buyers and sellers of residential homes are brought together by realtors who charge a fee for this service. Stock-market brokers bring together buyers and sellers of a particular stock. Auction houses bring together sellers of rare works of art with potential buyers, and charge a fee for this service. Are such "middlemen" cheating innocent buyers and sellers, or are they providing a service that is worth the price?

The role of intermediaries in providing information to buyers and sellers is often misunderstood. The export-import agent who brings the airplane buyer and seller together and pockets $5 million may be regarded as a near-criminal by people who think that this "go-between" is trading on the ignorance of others. When food prices rise, many consumers blame the intermediaries. Buyers and sellers of real estate often become upset with the high fees charged by realtors. Implicit in these complaints is the belief that the intermediaries are getting a reward for doing nothing or for doing very little.

The intermediary's share of the price varies substantially from good to good. In real estate, the broker receives typically a 5 to 10 percent fee for bringing together the buyer and seller. This fee depends upon competitive conditions in the market. In stock-market transactions the fee varies from about 0.5 percent to about 2 percent of the price of the stock. Supermarkets charge an intermediary fee of perhaps 10 percent to 55 percent of the wholesale price at which they buy.

The fee that intermediaries charge for their services depends, like other economic activities, on the amount of competition, on the degree of freedom of entry into the business, and on the opportunity costs of bringing goods to the market. If the business is competitive, the fee will reflect in the long run a normal profit, as in any other competitive market. For example, retail grocery stores are in a very competitive business; the typical supermarket earns an accounting profit of about 1 percent on its sales. The markups found in the supermarket are almost entirely used for paying rent, stock clerks, checkout clerks, produce specialists, and butchers. The grocery store, for example, must hire employees to prepare produce and meat for display in quantities convenient for inspection and purchase; the store must maintain inventories of products on which it must pay carrying charges. The grocery store must select a location convenient to its customers and must pay substantial rents for a good location. In return for the intermediary fee, consumers receive from the grocery store a convenient location, the convenience of inspecting goods before purchase, and the convenience of finding the quantity and quality of goods they want without packing, sorting, and searching for themselves. The net result of these expenses is that the rate of return on stockholders' equity is about 12% for the two largest retail grocery chains (Safeway and Kroger).

Buyers and sellers could in most situations avoid paying the "middleman's" fee. Homemakers could drive to farmers' markets and to whole-

Example 3   The Lemons Principle: Adverse Selection

Certifying quality helps prevent market breakdown due to adverse selection. In the case of used cars, the seller knows the value of the product, but the buyer must guess the quality. Most buyers would probably assume that the car is of average quality. If every used-car dealer operated on a disreputable basis, the only used car that would trade would be the *lemons*—those of lowest quality. If there were used cars in the market ranging from $1,000 to $6,000 in true value (a range known, say, to all potential buyers), but potential buyers could not tell the difference among them, would any rational consumer buy a used car priced at $5,000? No one would. At a price of $5,000, cars worth more than $5,000 would not be offered for sale; only those worth $5,000 or less would be put on the market—so that the average car offered for sale would be worth $3,000. Why pay $5,000 for a car that is more than likely worth much less than $5,000? At a price of $3,000, only cars worth $3,000 or less would be placed on the market (so the average car offered would be worth only $2,000). Why pay $3,000 for a car that is likely worth much less than $3,000? Indeed, any price above $1,000 would bring forth cars worth less than the price. What type of cars would, therefore, be traded in this fly-by-night market? Only those lemons that are worth exactly $1,000 since buyers paying more could only expect to be ripped off. In these circumstances, only when established dealers serve as certifiers of quality will nonlemons be placed on the market. ■

Source: Based upon George Akerlof, "The Market for 'Lemons': Quality, Uncertainty, and the Market Mechanism," *Quarterly Journal of Economics* 84 (August 1970): 488–500.

sale distributors of meats and dairy products. They could even drive to canning factories. The intermediary, by specializing in bringing together buyers and sellers, is able to provide the service at a lower cost than if the individuals involved performed the service themselves.

Another function of intermediaries like Sears, Safeway, J.C. Penney, used-car lots associated with new-car dealers, and so on is to certify the quality of goods. The consumer is confronted with a vast array of goods, some of which are so complicated that the buyer is at an enormous information disadvantage relative to the producer. In short, the consumer faces the adverse-selection problem. The number of producers is larger than the number of actual stores the consumer deals with. In such circumstances, the intermediary performs the function of certifying the quality of the good for the buyer. The customer is prepared to pay a price for this valuable service; thus, the intermediary is able to charge a higher markup over costs.

The real world consists of both disreputable dealers and those who serve, at least to some degree, as certifiers of quality. Certifiers of car quality enter the market in response to profit opportunities. "Middlemen" who are better informed about the quality of cars (because they can hire skilled mechanics) than the persons who buy cars will take advantage of profit opportunities. They will buy used cars (perhaps from their new-car customers), and they will then resell them on their used-car lots. They may even provide a guarantee (usually with a time limit) that the used car is not a "lemon." Customers will be willing to pay a fee (in the form of a price markup) for this certifier-of-quality service (see Example 3).

The same principle applies to the products sold by major grocery chains or major department stores. Customers know that the retailer serves as a certifier of quality, and, if the product happens to be defective, their money will be returned. Safeway or Sears wants its customers to come back for repeat business. Manufacturers also certify quality by identifying their products with brand names. If consumers could not distinguish the product of one manufacturer from that of all other manufacturers, there would be little incentive for the manufacturer to produce products of reasonable or uniform quality. Brand names like Sara-Lee, Levi's, Maytag, and Xerox serve as certifiers of product quality. (See Example 4.)

Example 4   Intermediary Fees in the Airline-Bonus-Coupon Market

Most of the nation's airlines offer frequent-flyer bonus programs according to which travelers who accumulate a certain number of miles on an airline are rewarded with coupons for discounts on additional travel. For example, a frequent flyer who travels 50,000 miles on Pan Am might receive two free first-class round-trip tickets to any Pan Am domestic destination. Traveling 50,000 miles on TWA could bring a free first-class round-trip ticket to any TWA international destination plus a second first-class ticket for the price of an economy ticket. A number of frequent-flyer programs allow the participant to transfer the bonus coupon to another person. This practice has created a market in frequent-flyer bonus coupons. If a passenger who has accumulated enough mileage for a bonus coupon did not want to use it (especially after flying 50,000 or 100,000 miles) but was willing to sell it, how would he or she find a willing buyer? A number of coupon-broker firms have emerged to bring together buyers and sellers of airline bonus coupons. They advertise in national newspapers; they buy the travel coupons from the frequent flyers and then resell them. The seller is happy to receive cash for an unwanted bonus; the buyer is happy to be able to buy tickets at a price well below the established price.

In an average transaction for airline coupons that would have sold for $3,500 as regular tickets, the coupon broker buys the coupon for $1,000 and resells at $2,200. Here, the intermediary pockets the $1,100 difference. The intermediary fee appears to be substantial even though this business is easy to enter. The different coupon brokers buy and sell at roughly the same prices, so it is unlikely that excessive economic profits are being earned. The substantial risks borne by the coupon-broker firms are the explanation for the high intermediary fees. The airlines would not honor the coupon if they were able to prove that the coupon had been sold; therefore, there can be no written contract on the obligations of the buyer and seller of the coupon. The coupon broker cannot sue either party if the terms of the agreement are broken. (Thus, the potential for a moral-hazard problem is great.) Once the frequent flyer has designated the buyer (located by the broker) as the coupon recipient, the coupon can be purchased only by the person whose name is on the coupon. If the buyer backs out of the agreement, the coupon broker cannot find another customer for the coupon. The $1,100 intermediary fee noted above is just high enough to compensate for risk without bringing in additional firms.   ∎

PRODUCT INFORMATION

Advertising

Insofar as advertising provides information to potential buyers, one might expect advertising to reduce market imperfections by reducing price dispersion. As we have already seen in an earlier chapter, however, when advertising helps to differentiate products, it can erect a barrier to entry that reinforces monopoly power. There are essentially two views of advertising. According to the procompetitive view of advertising, advertising provides information about prices and product qualities to buyers. As a result, advertising increases competition by making consumers aware of substitutes. Supporters of the anticompetitive view of advertising, however, believe that adver-

tising reduces competition by giving large, established firms a competitive advantage over smaller, less established firms. Advertising creates barriers to entry that limit competition and allow established firms to earn long-run profits.

Advertising can, in principle, either increase or reduce competition in an industry. Advertising's net effect on competition is, therefore, largely an empirical issue. If advertising's effect is largely anticompetitive, advertising would be likely to raise profit rates and industry concentration. If advertising is procompetitive, advertising would be likely to reduce industry concentration and even out profit rates among firms.

What do the facts indicate? Different researchers have reached contradictory conclusions. Moreover, advertising's impact is not uniform across industries; it appears to depend upon the particular industry.[3]

1. Advertising has different effects on different products. Studies show that advertising has a greater positive effect on the profitability of nondurable goods than on durable goods. Durable goods (TV sets, washing machines, automobiles) are usually more expensive products for which the marginal benefits to search are high. Nondurables (groceries, kitchen products, deodorant sprays, mouthwashes) are usually less expensive items for which the marginal benefits of search are small. Advertising appears to have a larger positive effect on profitability in the area of convenience goods, such as paper towels and aspirin.

2. Advertising has a procompetitive effect on retail trade. This result is quite consistent with our analysis of search costs and suggests that retail advertising conveys information on prices and product qualities to consumers and reduces the cost of search. Empirical studies show that the higher the advertising intensity, the lower the profit margins of retail and service industries. The opposite result is obtained for industries that manufacture consumer goods, where advertising creates barriers to entry and increases product differentiation.

3. There are significant economies of scale of advertising present in specific industries. In the beer industry and in the cigarette industry, the advertising of large firms has a substantially greater sales impact than that of small firms. In the cigarette industry, for example, the ratio of advertising expenditures to sales declines steeply up to sales of 20 to 30 billion cigarettes, a level of sales that may take years to attain.[4]

Advertising can lead to lower prices paid by consumers when its function is to provide infor-

mation on prices and quality. In this regard, consumers benefit from the advertising of retailers because advertising lowers search costs. But what of those cases where advertising reduces competition? Are consumers made worse off by advertising?

The higher price the consumer pays for advertised convenience products, such as over-the-counter drugs, children's clothes, or bleaches, may be a price willingly paid for the assurance of product quality. If, however, information were costless, and the consumer were perfectly informed about prices and product qualities, it is unlikely such price differentials would persist. (See Example 5.)

Product Quality, Durability, and Safety

Since information is costly to acquire, consumers will stop short of acquiring perfect information about the product's quality, durability, and safety. Advertising, insofar as it informs consumers about quality, durability, and safety, makes more information available to the consumer. Because people are uncertain about the quality, safety, and durability of the product being purchased, consumers avoid adverse-selection problems by relying on brand names to certify the quality of the product.

Some firms guarantee that the product will meet the customer's expectations and promise to refund the customer's money or allow the customer to exchange a defective product for another one when the product fails to meet the quality, safety, or durability standards the customer expects. For example, every product sold by Quaker Oats carries such a guarantee: buyers can get their money back by sending in the label with a brief explanation of what was wrong. Firms presumably do not want to be deluged with demands to reimburse buyers for defective products, so they seek to produce a product that meets consumer expectations.

But what about cases where severe damages are inflicted upon unsuspecting buyers, even by brand-name products? Teenagers have been killed in automobiles with poorly designed gas tanks

---

3. The literature on advertising has been developed by numerous economists including Lester Telser, Nicholas Kaldor, Richard Schmalensee, Phillip Nelson, William Comanor, Thomas Wilson, Michael Porter, Randall Brown, and many others. The available evidence is summarized in William Comanor and Thomas Wilson, ''The Effect of Advertising on Competition,'' *Journal of Economic Literature* 17 (June 1979): 453–76.

4. Randall Brown, ''Estimating Advantages to Large-Scale Advertising,'' *Review of Economics and Statistics* 60 (August 1978): 428–37.

Example 5   The Effect of Advertising on the Prices of Eyeglasses

Economist Lee Benham studied the effect of advertising on the prices of eyeglasses in a research report published in 1972. The advertising of eyeglasses is prohibited in some states and is allowed in others. Benham compared the prices of eyeglasses in states that allowed advertising with those where advertising is not allowed.

Benham found that the average price of eyeglasses in states that barred advertising was more than double the average price in states where advertising was allowed. This study shows how advertising can promote competition. Advertising, by providing information on prices and product quality, renders the demands for the products of individual suppliers more elastic and, thus, lowers the prices paid by consumers. The chapter on oligopoly described a case (breakfast cereals) where advertising increased product differentiation and raised prices. This example shows how advertising can play a procompetitive role. ■

Source: Lee Benham, "The Effect of Advertising on the Price of Eyeglasses," *The Journal of Law and Economics* 15 (October 1972): 337–52.

(that ignite on impact). Babies have been born deformed due to a drug taken by their mother during pregnancy; fingers have been severed by poorly designed lawnmowers. Who should be liable for such incidents? The two basic approaches to this question are *caveat emptor* (let the buyer beware) and *caveat venditor* (let the seller beware).

Caveat Emptor.   There is a big difference between professional buyers employed by large enterprises and the ordinary consumer. The large enterprise employs a purchasing agent who is a specialist in the goods purchased by the firm. Such agents know as much (or more) as the seller about the products they buy. Centuries ago, the average customer may have been in roughly the same position as this specialized purchasing agent. Goods were simple, and the buyer could assess their quality rather easily. The buyer was not at an information disadvantage relative to the seller. Thus, there was no adverse-selection problem.

Under these circumstances—where the buyer and seller possess the same information—the legal doctrine of *caveat emptor* (let the buyer beware) would be efficient and would work well.

Circumstances are different today. Products are exceedingly complex. When consumers select automobiles, television sets, home furnaces, or electrical wiring, they are at an enormous information disadvantage relative to the seller. For this reason, the legal doctrine of *caveat emptor* has been modified to protect the buyer from fraud, warranty violations, and negligence.

Fraud is an act of deceit or misrepresentation. Fraud occurs when the purchased product is never delivered or when a promised service is not supplied as contracted. A *warranty* is a guarantee of the integrity of a product and of the seller's responsibility for the repair or replacement of defective parts. Warranties may be expressed or implied. A good is supposed to do what it is designed to do (a washing machine is expected to wash clothes, a reclining chair is expected to recline). Whether the warranty is written or not, if the good does not perform its function, the seller has legally violated the warranty. *Negligence* occurs when the seller does not reveal to the buyer a hidden defect that later causes injury.[5]

The rule of *caveat emptor,* even in our modern world of complex products, does have some advantages. First, it provides the customer with an incentive to gain information about product quality, durability, and safety. If the user of the good is not liable for damages incurred while using the product, the consumer may not be as careful in choosing products.

Second, if the seller were liable for all damages caused by the use of a product, even by careless users, the cost of the product to the consumer could become excessive. If, for example, manufacturers of sulphuric acid were liable for all personal injuries associated with the use of the prod-

---

5. For this reason, in court cases involving personal injury due to manufacturing defects—such as a case against Ford Motors involving a fire-prone gas tank—it is very important for the claimant to establish that the company was aware of the defect.

uct, there would be little sulphuric acid supplied, and it would sell at a very high price. A moral-hazard problem could arise if sellers were liable for all loss or damage associated with the use of their products because this liability would encourage consumers to be less careful in the use of the products. It is more efficient for society as a whole to require the manufacturer to simply label the product as dangerous. If the user fails to heed this warning, the manufacturer is not liable for damages.

A third argument in favor of *caveat emptor* is that products are put to different uses by different consumers. It would be impossible for the manufacturer to anticipate all these uses, and it would be prohibitively expensive to design a product that would be safe in all uses. An automobile can be used either for transportation in a quiet suburb or for high-speed stock-car racing. The car manufacturer who is held liable for brake failure when the car is racing at 130 miles per hour would be forced to produce a car that would cost the average buyer much more and would have technical characteristics of little use to the majority of users. As Roland McKean observes:[6]

> The buyer is in a better position than anyone else to know the exact use to which he plans to put a product and what alternative qualities, or degrees of safety, in the product would mean to his costs and gains. The customer, if he is liable, has an extra incentive to acquire and make appropriate use of the information.

Caveat Venditor.   *Caveat emptor* does not work well when the cost of acquiring information is very high to the consumer. Manufacturers know more than anyone else about their products. When it is very costly for consumers to acquire information, producer responsibility *(caveat venditor)* may be a more efficient system of assigning liability.

Information costs can be kept down for consumers by organizations like Consumers Union, which basically hires itself out to check out products scientifically for its subscribers. Government

6. Roland McKean, ''Product Liability: Implications of Some Changing Property Rights,'' *Quarterly Journal of Economics* 84 (November 1970): 611–26.

can also reduce information costs by establishing minimum standards and carrying out inspections to insure that these standards are being observed. Municipal governments usually have health inspectors to inspect public dining places and public swimming pools. There are universal standards of weights and measures and inspections to insure that the butcher's scale is accurate. Without these governmental regulations and inspections, the costs of personal inspection and information gathering would be excessive. (See Example 6.)

SPECULATION

Although product information is important to consumers, information about changes in the market conditions for any number of goods and services is important to **speculators.** The homemaker who stocks up on peanut butter after hearing of a shortage of peanuts, the frozen-orange-juice distributor who buys oranges in response to a late frost in Florida, and the young couple that buys a house now because they fear home prices will rise beyond reach if they wait another year are all speculators. The professional speculator, however, is more maligned than any other economic agent.

> **Speculators** are those who buy or sell in the hope of profiting from market fluctuations.

Most people do not associate the term *speculator* with the family that stocks up on goods whose prices are expected to shoot up or the family that purchases a home as an inflation hedge. Most people associate the term *speculator* with the person who buys up agricultural land and holds it for future shopping-center development or the person who buys and sells foreign currencies or gold in the hopes of buying low and selling high. Such speculators buy or sell commodities in huge quantities hoping to profit from a frost, war scare, bumper crop, bad news, or good news.

The Role of the Speculator in the Economy

Speculators do, indeed, often profit from the misfortunes of others. They buy from the hard pressed farmer when prices are low, and they sell

Example 6   Producer Liability in the Case of Pistols

The doctrine of *caveat emptor* (let the buyer beware) is usually used in the case of products for which there is no substantial information imbalance between the buyer and the seller. If the product is so complex that the buyer cannot assess the performance characteristics of the products or the dangers of using the product, the seller may be held liable for deficient performance or injury. An unusual suit was filed in Texas in 1984 over an accidental pistol discharge that left a 15-year-old student paralyzed. Lawyers for the paralyzed youth sued the pistol's manufacturer and distributor on the grounds that pistols are, by their nature, unsafe and hazardous products and that manufacturers and sellers should be held liable for injuries or deaths resulting from pistols. The defense argued that the suit stretches the producer-liability law too far—that it is unfair to hold manufacturers liable for any subsequent use of their product. From the standpoint of economic theory, one of the major issues was whether the buyer was at an information disadvantage relative to the seller in being able to assess the potential hazards of owning a pistol. The suit proved to be very controversial because groups that oppose controls on handguns (such as the National Rifle Association) argued that if pistol manufacturers could be held liable for damages resulting from handguns, the costs of manufacturing handguns would soar, and economic (rather than legal) limits would be placed on the ownership of handguns. The outcome: the judge decided in favor of the pistol manufacturer and distributor. ■

---

later at much higher prices. Has the farm family been robbed by the speculator? Upon hearing of a frost in Florida, speculators buy oranges in large quantities, thereby driving up the prices of orange juice for the consumer. Speculators, at the first sign of international trouble, may buy gold and sell American dollars, thereby weakening the American dollar. The popular view of speculators is that they do only harm. This chapter will explain how speculators often perform a useful economic function.

The fundamental economic role of the speculator is to engage in **arbitrage** *through time*.

> **Arbitrage** is buying in a market where a commodity is cheap and reselling it in a market where the commodity is more expensive.

The arbitrator buys wheat at Chicago at $5 per bushel and resells it for $5.10 the next minute in Kansas City. Arbitrageurs, therefore, serve to keep the price of wheat in Chicago and Kansas City approximately equal.

Simple arbitrage of this type is not very risky since information about prices in Chicago and Kansas City can be obtained instantly from commodity brokers. Arbitrageurs must act quickly and have sharp pencils and keen minds if they are to prosper. Unlike the arbitrageur, who buys in one location and sells in another, the speculator buys goods *at one time* and resells *at another time*. Speculation is a risky business because tomorrow's prices cannot be known with certainty.

> **Arbitrage serves to equalize prices in different markets, because when price differences arise, arbitrageurs buy in the cheap market and resell in the expensive market.**

Profitable Speculation

The objective of the speculator is to make a profit by buying low and selling high. When the speculator is making a profit—and when there are enough speculators—prices will be driven up by speculation when they are low, and they will be driven down by speculation when they are high. When speculators buy at low prices, they add to the demand and drive prices up. When speculators sell when prices are high, they drive prices down by adding to the supply.

> **Profitable speculation (that is, speculation that succeeds in buying low and selling high) stabilizes prices and consumption over time by reducing fluctuation in prices and consumption over time.**

Figure 1   Profitable Speculation

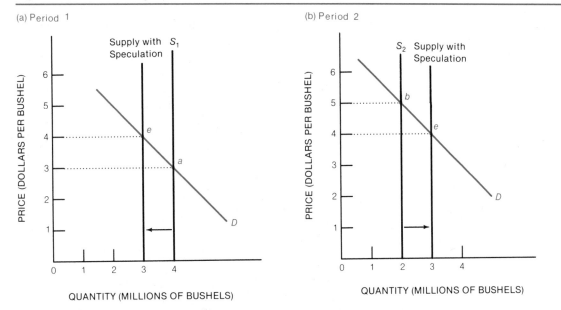

Period 1's wheat harvest is 4 million bushels, while period 2's wheat harvest is only 2 million bushels. If there were no speculation, the price would be $3 in period 1 and $5 in period 2. Perfect speculation will cause 1 million bushels of wheat to be purchased and stored by speculators in period 1, to be sold in period 2. As a result, the price is driven up to $4 in period 1 and driven down to $4 in period 2. Both price and consumption are stabilized by speculation in this case.

Profitable speculation is illustrated in Figure 1. Panel (a) shows that the supply of wheat in the first period (say, 1987) is S_1, or 4 million bushels. Panel (b) shows that the supply of wheat in the second period (say, 1988) is S_2, or 2 million bushels. If there were no speculation, the price of wheat would be $3 in period 1 and $5 in period 2 (we assume that demand does not change between the two periods). Thus, without speculation, prices and consumption would vary dramatically between the two periods.

Profitable speculation shifts supplies from periods when supplies are relatively abundant and prices potentially low to periods when supplies are relatively scarce and prices potentially high. In this sense, profitable speculation provides the valuable economic service of stabilizing prices and consumption over time.

If speculators correctly anticipate that next year's wheat crop will be small, they could make handsome profits by buying at $3 and selling next year at $5. But what happens as speculators begin to buy this year's wheat? When speculators buy wheat, they withdraw it from the market and place it in storage. As a result, the supply of wheat offered on the market is reduced. If speculation is profitable, the profits of the marginal speculator will be driven down to zero. When speculators buy 1 million bushels in the first period, the effective supply shifts (left) to 3 million bushels, and the price rises to $4. When speculators resell this wheat in the second period, the effective supply also shifts (right) to 3 million bushels in year 2. With profitable speculation, the price would remain stable at $4 in both periods, and the quantity of wheat sold on the market would remain stable at 3 million bushels—despite substantial differences in the wheat harvest in the two periods. In this example, we assume that storage costs are zero. Had storage costs been positive, the price of wheat in the second period would have been higher by the cost of storage.

Unprofitable Speculation

Speculation is risky. Speculators cannot always guess right. They may buy when they think prices are low only to find that they sink even lower. They may sell when they think prices are at their peak, only to watch the prices rise even further. In such cases, speculation destabilizes prices and consumption over time. When prices would otherwise be high, such speculators are buying and driving prices even higher; when pices would otherwise be low, such speculators are selling and driving prices even lower.

Unprofitable speculation is shown in Figure 2. The supply of corn is 5 million bushels in period 1 and will also be 5 million bushels in period 2. Because demand remains the same in the two periods, the equilibrium price of corn will be $4 in both periods without speculation. Now assume speculators incorrectly guess that the supply of corn will fall in period 2 due to an anticipated poor harvest. Speculators buy 2 million bushels, which they place in storage for later sale, driving up the price to $6 in period 1 (point *a*). The speculators then wait in vain for a decline in supply that never materializes. They must sell the 2 million bushels in period 2, and they drive the price down to $2 a bushel (point *b*).

Without speculation, the price and consumption of corn would have been the same in both periods (point *e*). With unprofitable speculation, consumption is 3 million bushels in period 1 and 7 million bushels in period 2. Period 1's price is $6 and period 2's price is $2. Unprofitable speculation is inefficient for the economy as a whole.[7]

Unprofitable speculation is destabilizing because it creates artificial scarcities in some periods and artificial abundance in other periods. In this sense, speculation can be costly to society.

---

7. Because the economy is worse off, both speculators and nonspeculators together (the consumers of corn) are made worse off, but consumers are made better off. The consumers of corn lose consumer surplus of $8 million in period 1 when the price rises from $4 to $6, but they gain it all back and more when consumer surplus rises $12 million above what it would have been had the price remained at $4. The gain to consumers is $4 million worth of consumer surplus. But speculators lose $8 million (the 2 million bushels bought at $6 and sold at $2). This loss exceeds the gain of consumers.

Ex Ante and *Ex Post* Efficiency

Speculators make guesses about future supplies and prices. Since the future is uncertain, speculators will often make wrong decisions. On balance, does society benefit from speculation?

After the event has occurred, it is easy to evaluate the prediction made by the speculator. But judging speculation on the basis of *ex post facto* (after the fact) performance is a poor way to determine whether speculation helps or hurts the economy on balance.

Most economists agree that the business of speculation is populated by a core of expert, professional speculators and a rotating periphery of nonexperts. Since decisions must be made about uncertain future events, it is better for *ex ante facto* (before the fact) decisions to be made by the best informed specialists (the professional speculators) than by poorly informed individuals.

The important question is whether the professional speculator employs *ex ante* decision rules that are efficient in the sense that they are most likely to yield the correct answer concerning future prices and quantities. A million *ex post* examples of unprofitable speculation do not prove that speculation should be abolished. Although it is difficult to prove empirically, it is probably true that the millions of *ex ante* decisions by professional speculators that turn out to be correct overwhelm the number that turn out to be incorrect.

Although no one can foresee the future, in some cases predicting future events is not as difficult as one might expect. For example, it is widely known that spring wheat is harvested in September and winter wheat is harvested in June or July. The amount of wheat harvested in other months is negligible. The seasonal pattern of wheat supply is, therefore, known to a rather sharp degree. What if no one were to speculate in this situation? In harvest months, farmers would harvest and sell their wheat; wheat prices would be driven down to very low levels. In the remaining months when very little wheat is harvested, wheat prices would be astronomical. Such a situation, it is obvious, would not be satisfactory. Because the pattern of wheat harvesting is well-known, speculators (who include, by the way, the farmers who put their grain into storage rather

Figure 2   Unprofitable Speculation

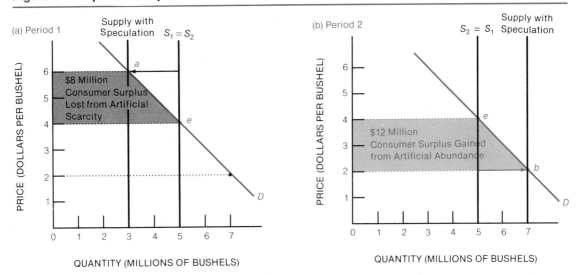

In this example, period 1 and period 2 have the same demand and supply conditions. Without speculation, the price would be $4 in both periods. Speculators guess incorrectly that the supply of corn in period 2 will be less. They buy 2 million bushels in period 1 and drive period 1's price up to $6. When they must resell the 2 million bushels in period 2, they drive the price down to $2. In the case of unprofitable speculation, price and consumption are seriously destabilized.

than sell it immediately) purchase grain at harvest time, put it into storage, and then sell it throughout the rest of the year. This activity assures that society will not lack for wheat during the remainder of the year and that consumers will not have to pay wildly fluctuating prices. Speculators will, of course, make some errors in the process; they may incorrectly predict the size of the upcoming harvest. However, these mistakes appear to be relatively minor when compared to what the world would be like in the total absence of speculation.

In some cases, speculators do trade on the ignorance of others and, thus, fail to perform a useful social function even in the case of profitable speculation. In our examples of speculation, we assumed that professional speculators would not have access to inside information that would give them an unfair advantage over all other speculators. In 1973, western agricultural experts grossly underestimated the size of the Russian wheat harvest, due in part to deliberate Soviet efforts to misrepresent their forthcoming harvest. The Soviets, having inside information that the world supply of wheat would be less than most specu-

lators thought, quietly purchased wheat through French-based companies to cover their deficit before the price of wheat began to shoot up.

THE FUTURES MARKET

The business of speculation is so highly specialized that markets have developed that separate the business of storage of the commodity being bought and sold from the business of speculation. The grain speculator does not have to worry about what the purchased grain looks like, where it is stored, and how much to take out of storage. These matters are handled by a **futures market.**

A **futures market** is one where a buyer and seller agree now on the price of a commodity to be delivered at some specified date in the future.

Many are familiar with futures markets only through sensational press reports, like those about the oil-rich Hunt family seeking to corner the silver market, about European and Asian speculators driving the price of gold to dizzying heights, or about the increase in coffee prices following a freeze in Brazil that is blamed on speculators. The type of market most people know best is one in which there is an actual outlay of cash (or the arrangement of credit) for the immediate delivery of a good. The market in which a good is purchased today for immediate delivery is called a **spot** (or **cash**) **market.**

> In a **spot (cash) market,** agreements between buyers and sellers are made now for payment and delivery of the product now.

Most of the goods consumers buy and sell are transacted in spot markets. In the grocery store, consumers pay now for goods that are delivered now. Stocks, foreign exchange, gold, and commodities like wheat, pork bellies, lumber, and copper are traded in organized exchanges. The organized markets in which commodities are traded are called *commodities markets*. In commodities markets, contracts can be made now for payment and delivery now.

Futures markets work quite differently from spot markets. *Futures contracts* are bought and sold in futures markets. In a futures contract, the terms (the price and the quantity) of a future transaction are set today. The buyer of a futures contract enters a contract today to purchase a specified quantity of a good (say, wheat) at a specified price at some specified date in the future. Both delivery and payment are to be made *in the future*. The seller is obliged to deliver the specified quantity of the good at the specified price at the specified future date. The seller of a futures contract need not even own the commodity at the time of the sale (but will in many instances).

> The *seller* of a futures contract is in a *short position* since something is being sold that is not owned.

> The *buyer* of a futures contract is in a *long position* since a claim on a good is being acquired.

When the seller agrees to sell and the buyer agrees to buy at a specified price at a specified date in the future, what guarantees that both parties live up to their ends of the bargain? The buyer and seller must each put up cash—called a *margin requirement*—equal to a small percentage of the value of the contract.[8]

The Mechanics of Futures Trading

Futures trading is different from the types of transactions with which most people are familiar. Futures trading is a topsy-turvy world: traders can sell something before they buy it; traders are buying and selling obligations to buy or sell in the future a commodity they will likely never even see. Most daily newspapers supply futures prices. For example, on October 4, 1984, the price of July 1985 wheat was $3.40 per bushel in Chicago. The futures price is the price agreed upon now for a commodity to be paid for and delivered on some future date. Any time between now and the future date, the seller or buyer can *close out* the futures contract by engaging in an offsetting transaction. The seller offsets the transaction by simply buying another futures contract with the same delivery date; a buyer closes out by selling another futures contract with the same delivery date. Two examples of futures trading, illustrating a long position and a short position, follow.

A Long Position.   George Bull thinks that wheat prices will rise in the future more than other buyers generally expect them to rise. George thinks that the July 1985 wheat price of $3.40 is too low; he expects the July 1985 price to be well above $3.40. On October 4, 1984, George buys 5,000 bushels of July 1985 wheat, paying the futures price of $3.40. George is now in a long position in wheat. George has had to put up $2,000 as a margin requirement with his commodity broker. Time passes, and the futures price of July 1985 wheat changes. If the futures price rises above $3.40, George gains. If the price of July 1985 wheat falls below $3.40 in the future, George loses.

---

8. The actual percentage *margin requirement* varies from commodity to commodity. Wheat usually has a 5 percent requirement. If you are wealthy and an established customer, it would have been possible to deposit some of your assets (stocks, bonds) with your commodity broker to guarantee the contract. The amount of cash put up is negligible; it basically screens out individuals who may run out on the contract if things go badly.

On December 1, 1984, the price of July wheat rises to $3.50. George has made a profit because he bought the wheat at $3.40 a bushel and can now sell it for $3.50 a bushel. If George closes out his long position by *selling* a contract for 5,000 bushels of July 1985 wheat, he will make a profit of $500 (or $0.10 × 5,000 bushels). His deposit with his commodity broker has increased from $2,000 to $2,500. Surprisingly, even if George does not close out his position by selling, his broker will automatically credit George's account for $500. If George continues his long position, he will have $2,500 on deposit with his broker (or can have the broker send him a check for $500). By continuing to hold a long position without closing out, George runs the risk that the price of July 1985 wheat will fall and that he will lose his $500 profit or more.

A Short Position.   Sue Bear has already paid the margin requirement for a futures contract for 5,000 bushels of July 1985 wheat and thinks, on the other hand that July 1985 wheat will be lower in price than people currently anticipate. She thinks that if she sells July 1985 wheat at $3.40 per bushel, the futures prices will fall, and she can make a profit. Sue Bear sells 5,000 bushel of July 1985 wheat on December 1, 1984 at the market futures price of $3.40 a bushel. Sue is now in a short position in wheat (she sold something she doesn't completely own). While this will probably not be the case, it is convenient to think of Sue as the one who sells to George. If the price of July 1985 wheat rises above $3.40, Sue loses; if the price falls below $3.40, Sue wins. As we already indicated, on December 1, 1984 the futures price of July 1985 wheat is $3.50. When Sue closes out her short position, she loses $0.10 per bushel, or $500. Sue, who has also deposited $2,000 as a margin requirement, now has only $1,500 on deposit with her commodity broker. Even if Sue had not closed out her short position, her broker would have automatically debited Sue's account for $500 when the futures price rose to $3.50 a bushel. If the price continues to rise and Sue keeps an open position, she will receive a *margin call* from her broker for more cash when her account balance is zero, or the broker will automatically close out her position. Sue has the choice of closing out her short

position or continuing to hold it in the hope that the price will fall and she can recoup her losses.

Hedging

The person who "hedges a bet" bets both sides in order to minimize the risks of heavy losses. Such a person might bet $5 it will rain tomorrow and $4 it won't rain. **Hedging** also takes place in futures markets.

> **Hedging** is the temporary substitution of a futures market transaction for an intended spot transaction.

Futures markets can provide an opportunity to traders of commodities in both spot and futures markets to reduce the risks of price fluctuations over time as well as to increase their profits. A futures market allows those involved in the distribution, processing, or storage of a good to concentrate on their specialized productive activities by taking advantage of the relationship between spot and futures prices.

Suppose, for example, that on July 1, the operator of a grain elevator buys 5,000 bushels of wheat from a farmer for $5 a bushel (the spot price on that date). The grain is put into storage for intended sale at some date in the future. What are the risks to the operator? If the price of wheat were to drop, the operator could incur substantial losses. Through the futures market, the elevator operator hedges by immediately selling a futures contract for 5,000 bushels of wheat to be delivered at a price of $5.15 in November. The elevator operator has sold November wheat for $5.15.

If the elevator operator holds his wheat until November, the wheat purchased for $5 can be delivered on the futures contract for $5.15. The elevator operator has locked in a profit of $0.15 per bushel to cover his carrying charges.

Now suppose the spot price of wheat drops, and one month later, the elevator operator sells this wheat for $4 on the spot market to General Mills. On this spot transaction, he has lost $5,000 ($1 per bushel on 5,000 bushels). But what about the November futures contract that he has previously sold? Because wheat prices are falling, the price of November wheat has dropped to $4.10. Having bought a November contract for 5,000 bushels, the elevator operator can earn $1.05 ×

5,000, or $5,250, by closing out the position. Remember the elevator operator had previously sold a November contract for $5,150. Through hedging, the elevator operator has not only limited the risks from falling grain prices but has made a profit. The elevator operator lost $5,000 from the spot market and gained $5,250 in the futures market and, in effect, earned $250—$0.05 per bushel—by holding wheat for one month.

Large grain users, such as General Mills, can also hedge against the risks of fluctuating wheat prices by using the futures market. General Mills knows in July that it will require 100,000 bushels of wheat in December. It does not know what the price of wheat will be in December, but it can purchase a December futures contract for 100,000 bushels of wheat at $5 per bushel and, thus, protect itself against the risk that wheat will be selling well above $5 in December.

Hedgers and speculators play highly complementary roles in the economy. Hedgers are interested primarily in storing commodities or in using these commodities in their business. Hedgers are interested in their particular business and in minimizing the risks of price fluctuations. The speculator, on the other hand, does not have to be concerned with the details of storing grain or making flour and grain products. The speculator specializes in information about supply and demand in the future. There is division of labor between the hedger and the speculator.

Information and Speculation

The futures market provides information concerning the future. This information is not always accurate; sometimes it predicts that prices will rise but instead they fall, and vice versa. Prices in futures markets reveal to the economy what speculators *anticipate* will happen to the prices of different commodities in the future. If the futures price of wheat is well above the current spot price, then speculators, who attempt to anticipate future developments of supply and demand, feel that wheat prices will rise. These futures prices represent the best information available to the economy on the course of prices in the future.

Economic decisions must be made today concerning actions that must be taken in the future.

Farmers must plant crops that will not be harvested for many months; mine operators must plan the expansion of mine capacity. If prices in the future were known with certainty, such planning would be grossly simplified, but the future is always uncertain. Clearly, having a futures market that establishes effective future prices today is of great benefit in an uncertain world. For those who need to know future prices, a futures market provides a summary indicator of market sentiment—a single price reflects much of what people know today about tomorrow.

Departures from perfect competition caused by information costs do not generally require government action, except to enforce contracts and to establish rules of liability. The next chapter examines departures from perfect competition that are caused by barriers to entry and oligopolistic collusion. In these cases, government has a more active role to play.

Summary

1.   Information is costly because of our limited ability to process, store, and retrieve facts and figures about the economy and because real resources are required to gather information. Individuals acquire information to the point where the marginal cost of acquiring more information equals the marginal benefit of more information.

2.   Search costs explain the observed dispersion of prices. When the benefits to further search are large, price dispersion will be limited.

3.   Two problems encountered by buyers and sellers because of the cost of information are the *moral-hazard problem* and the *adverse-selection problem*. The moral-hazard problem occurs when one party is able to alter his or her behavior after a contract is made in order to profit from the contract at the other party's expense and arises because it is too costly for the other party to obtain information about the first party's postcontractual behavior. The adverse-selection problem occurs when a buyer or seller enters a disadvantageous contract on the basis of incomplete or inaccurate information because the

cost of obtaining the relevant information is higher for this buyer or seller than it is for the other party to the transaction.

4. Intermediaries bring together buyers and sellers; they often buy in order to sell again and sometimes serve as certifiers of quality.

5. Advertising can have both procompetitive and anticompetitive effects. By providing information, advertising makes markets more competitive. Advertising can also erect barriers to entry and thereby create monopoly power. In a complex world where the seller has more information about product quality, durability, and safety, the doctrine of *caveat emptor* (let the buyer beware) has its limitations. But even in such a world, there are still some advantages to *caveat emptor*.

6. Speculators buy now in order to sell later for a profit. If speculators are profitable, they stabilize prices and consumption over time. If they are unprofitable, they destabilize prices and consumption over time. Speculators should be judged on the basis of *ex ante* rather than *ex post* efficiency.

7. In a futures market, contracts are made now for payment and delivery of commodities in the future. Futures markets provide information about the uncertain future and allow hedging by those who wish to reduce risks.

Key Terms

transaction costs
information costs
centralized market
decentralized market
moral-hazard problem
adverse-selection problem
"middlemen" or intermediaries
speculators
arbitrage
futures market
spot (cash) market
hedging

Questions and Problems

1. Investors can purchase shares of stock through a full-service broker (who provides information and investment advice) or through a discount broker. The commission charged by the full-service broker is much higher than that of the discount broker. They both provide the service of buying the shares of stock ordered by the buyer. Explain why most investors use the services of the higher-priced brokers.

2. The market for wheat is highly centralized. In fact, one can say there is a world market for wheat. Why is this market centralized while other markets, like the market for automobiles, are decentralized?

3. What are the transactions costs of selling a home? What effect do real-estate brokers have on these costs?

4. Explain why more is spent on the advertising of deodorants than on the advertising of farm machinery.

5. If search costs in a market are zero and the market is competitively organized, what predictions can you make about prices in this market?

6. Under what conditions does *caveat emptor* work well? Under what conditions would *caveat emptor* not work well?

7. The stock market is highly competitive with thousands of speculators trying to buy low and sell high. Using the concepts of information and search costs, explain why we all can't get rich with a little study and research by playing the stock market.

8. What is the *moral-hazard problem?* Give examples.

9. Chicago Cubs baseball player Ron Cey received an "extra" $500,000 in the 1984 season because of an attendance clause in his contract. Explain how this behavior is a result of the moral-hazard problem.

10. What is the adverse-selection problem? Give examples.

11.   Assume that on January 1 July wheat is selling for $4. How could a speculator profit from the expectation that July wheat will sell for $3.50? How could a speculator profit from the expectation that July wheat will sell for $4.50?

Suggested Readings

Akerlof, George. "The Market for 'Lemons': Quality, Uncertainty, and the Market Mechanism." *Quarterly Journal of Economics* 84 (August 1970): 488–500.

Hayek, F. A. "The Use of Knowledge in Society." *American Economic Review* 35 (1945): 510–30.

Heyne, Paul and Thomas Johnson. *Toward Understanding Microeconomics.* Chicago: SRA, 1976, chap. 8.

Kohler, Heinz. *Intermediate Microeconomics: Theory and Applications* 2nd ed, Glenview, Ill.: Scott, Foresman, 1986, chap. 10.

Stigler, George. "The Economics of Information." *Journal of Political Economy* (June 1961), pp. 213–25.

34

Antitrust Law and Regulation

Chapter Preview

Public distrust of big business is not a new phenomenon. It is deeply rooted in economic theory and in the public's perception of harm being done to them by monopoly power. Adam Smith's famous warning issued in 1776 about the dangers of monopoly has been reinforced by the formal theory of monopoly presented in earlier chapters. This chapter will explain why governments decide to control monopoly power and will describe how governments can use public ownership, regulation, and the legal system to limit monopoly power.

Opponents of "bigness" in business argue three points. First, a monopoly will restrict output below what would have been produced if the industry were competitive, forcing the consumer to pay a higher price for a smaller quantity of output. Monopoly, therefore, causes *deadweight losses* to society that can be accentuated if there is monopoly rent seeking. Second, if potential competition is weak, the monopolist has little incentive to innovate. Monopolists will not be motivated to introduce new products or to find new cost-saving technologies. Third, when monopoly profits increase the wealth of monopolists and of their heirs, an undesirable distribution of income can result.

The case for big business also rests upon three points. First, if the monopolist operates in an industry where there are substantial economies of scale, a larger producer will be able to produce at lower average costs than a number of smaller producers and can, therefore, charge a lower price. Second, the monopoly power of big business is overrated. Even if a monopolist does not have immediate competitors (a railroad may offer the only rail service between two cities), monopolists must still compete with companies both at home and abroad that offer substitute products (trucking firms will compete for the railroads' customers). Moreover, if monopoly profits become too large, potential competitors may be enticed into the market. Third, only large companies can afford the enormous research-and-development costs required to develop modern technology. Small competitive firms simply cannot finance the laboratories and research staffs that have become essential to modern research and development. ■

THE NATURAL MONOPOLY

Where there is a real choice of industrial organization, government policy can be used to alter industrial structure in the desired direction. For example, a large company may be broken up into several smaller companies if the government believes that the company has used its monopoly power in a harmful way. There is no real choice of industrial structure in the case of a **natural monopoly.**

> A **natural monopoly** exists when the technology of producing a certain product is such that it is cheaper for one firm to produce the product over the relevant range of output than for two or more firms to produce the product.

The case of the natural monopoly is shown in Figure 1. The natural monopoly occurs when a single firm can produce the industry level of output at a long-run average cost below that of any firm that tried to produce less than the industry level of output. Examples would be electric-power and natural-gas utilities and local telephone service. For such enterprises, long-run average costs typically fall as output is increased.

If the industry is a natural monopoly, industry output will be produced at much lower average cost by one firm than if the industry were made up of more than one producer. Imagine, for example, having three electric utilities operating in the same market with three systems of power lines and underground cables. In the case of the natural monopoly, economies of large-scale production are so prominent that there is little choice but to operate as a single-firm industry. (See Example 1.)

Since a certain amount of monopoly power is unavoidable, government must decide *whether or not* and *how* to control monopoly power.

THE GOVERNMENT'S INSTRUMENTS FOR CONTROL OF MONOPOLY POWER

If the government chooses to control monopoly power, what instruments does it have at its disposal? Basically, governments have three options:

Figure 1   The Natural Monopoly

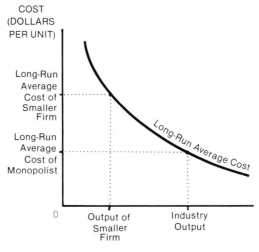

This figure shows the long-run average-cost curve of producing a certain product. As the curve shows, the long-run average costs of producing this product are lower at the output level corresponding to total-industry output than for any output level less than total-industry output. A single producer can, therefore, produce at much lower average cost than could any of the smaller producers who would *together* try to produce the industry quantity by each producing a portion of total-industry quantity.

government ownership, regulation, and antitrust legislation.[1]

Government Ownership

The government can purchase the monopoly from private owners and run the monopoly ''in the public interest.'' Public ownership of business in the United States is more common at the municipal and state level than at the federal level. Municipal services such as local transportation, wa-

---

1. A fourth method for controlling monopoly power—not used in the United States—is to utilize the state's power to tax and subsidize monopolies. This method was promoted by the English economist, A. C. Pigou, and later by American economist Arnold Harberger. The idea is to pay the monopolist a subsidy as an incentive to produce the level of output that would have been produced had this been a perfectly competitive industry. The state would then seek to tax away (by a lump-sum tax) the increase in profits resulting from the subsidy, and the consumer would be made better off by being offered more output at a lower price. In this way, the state would eliminate the deadweight loss of monopoly. See Arnold Harberger, ''Monopoly and Resource Allocation,'' *American Economic Review* 44 (May 1954): 77–87.

ter, sanitation, gas, and electricity are often owned and operated by state and local government. In 1983, more than 23 percent of all electrical energy was generated by government-owned enterprises.[2]

At the federal level, government enterprises are more limited. They include, among others, the Tennessee Valley Authority (a giant government-owned electrical utility), the U.S. Postal Service (now a semigovernmental organization), government home-mortgage programs (the Veterans Administration and Federal Housing Authority programs), various weapons-producing arsenals, and the Government Printing Office.

These activities may appear substantial, but they account for only 2 percent of American national output. The unusual feature of government policy in the United States has been the decision to leave monopolies in the hands of private owners and to control monopoly by other means.

Regulation

Regulation of monopoly prices and services is a second means of controlling monopoly. The enterprise remains in private hands, but its activities are regulated by government agencies.

In the United States, regulation at the state and local level is largely directed at monopolies—the electric, gas, water, and telephone companies. At the national level, federal regulatory commissions regulate a number of industries, ranging from long-distance telephone service to broadcasting to trucking. Federal and state regulatory agencies enforce environmental standards (the Environmental Protection Agency) and worker safety (the Occupational Safety and Health Administration, or OSHA) and license professionals. The Federal Aviation Agency (FAA) is responsible for airline safety, and the Food and Drug Administration (FDA) is responsible for the safety of foods and drugs sold in the United States. Much government regulation is also directed toward potentially competitive industries, as discussed later in the chapter.

The four major federal regulatory commissions are:

1. the Interstate Commerce Commission (established in 1887), which regulates railroads, interstate oil pipelines, and interstate motor and water carriers;
2. the Federal Power Commission (established in 1920), which has jurisdiction over power projects and the interstate transmission of electricity and natural gas;
3. the Federal Communications Commission (established in 1933), which regulates interstate telephone and telegraph and broadcasting;
4. the Securities and Exchange Commission (established in 1934), which regulates securities markets.

The Civil Aeronautics Board (established in 1938), supervised domestic and international aviation until its dissolution at the end of 1984.

Currently, a general movement is underway to deregulate the economy, and the responsibilities of many of these commissions are being reduced. The Civil Aeronautics Board, for example, was eliminated in 1984 after almost a half century of regulating commercial aviation.

Regulation is supposed to ensure the availability of service, to establish standards for the quality of service, and to guarantee the public "reasonable" prices.

Antitrust Law

A third approach to monopoly control is legislation to control market structure and business conduct. The most important antitrust acts are the Sherman Act of 1890, the Clayton and Federal Trade Commission Acts of 1913, the Wheeler-Lea Act of 1938, and the Celler-Kefauver Act of 1950. These acts prohibit general and specific business practices that increase or abuse market power. Antitrust legislation also outlaws particular market structures.

GOVERNMENT OWNERSHIP

Public ownership of monopolies is not as widespread in the United States as elsewhere, but it is one method for controlling monopoly power. Figure 2 shows a natural monopoly owned by government.

---

2. *Statistical Abstract of the United States*, 1984, p. 585.

Figure 2   The Dilemma of a Public Enterprise

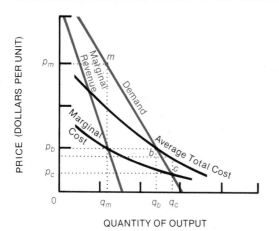

This figure depicts a monopoly that is owned by the public. It is not clear which rules the manager of this public enterprise should follow to operate this public enterprise "in the public interest." The manager could equate marginal cost and price (point c), but the enterprise would be operating at a loss. The manager could attempt to break even (point b)—by operating where price and average total cost are equal—but the manager would have little incentive to economize on costs as higher costs would translate into higher prices and higher revenues. Finally, the manager could attempt to maximize profits (point m), but consumers would receive a relatively small quantity of output and would pay relatively high prices while monopoly profits accrued to the state.

How does the government operate a public enterprise in the public interest? What instructions should be given to the manager of the public enterprise? Should it produce that quantity of output at which price and marginal cost are equal (point c in Figure 2)? Point c is efficient because the marginal cost (of society's resources) is equated with the marginal benefit (received by society) as reflected in the price. But, the $P = MC$ rule means that the enterprise will be run at a loss, and taxpayers must make up that loss. Taxpayers who do not use the service will subsidize those who do.

Alternatively, the public enterprise could be instructed to *break even*—to produce where price equals average total cost (at b in Figure 2). In our example, price is almost two times greater than marginal cost, and the efficiency rule $(P = MC)$ is broken. But the customer is offered a larger

quantity of output (q_b) at a lower price (p_b) than if this firm were an unregulated monopoly.

The third option would be to instruct the public enterprise to maximize profits, just like a private unregulated monopoly. This option would yield the outcome of point m (the enterprise would choose the quantity that equates marginal revenue and marginal cost). Again, the basic efficiency rule is broken: price is more than three times marginal cost in this example. The public is offered a relatively small quantity of output (q_m) for which it must pay a relatively high price (p_m). The only advantage such a government-owned monopoly has over a private monopoly is that the resulting monopoly profit will revert to the government, and the government can use these profits to pay for other government services.[3]

REGULATION OF MONOPOLIES

The American public has chosen overwhelmingly to regulate monopolies rather than to own them. Regulation is exercised by a variety of state, local, and federal agencies. Administrative regulation is carried out by officials of the executive branch of government and by semi-independent commissions that operate under general legislative authority.

Who Is Regulated?

Natural monopolies like the gas and electric companies and local telephone service are regulated at the state and local level. However, much state and local regulation is directed at basically competitive industries (taxicab licensing, concession franchises in sports stadiums, licensing of barbers and beauticians) for the purpose of limiting competition and creating more monopoly power. Federal commissions also regulate *potentially* competitive industries, such as transportation and broadcasting, and often limit competition in these industries. *Government regulation is not consistent.* Some government regulation is clearly de-

---

3. In the Federal Republic of Germany, the state owns the telephone company and operates it like a private unregulated monopoly. The monopoly profits from the telephone company are then used to support other government services (like the post office) that operate at a loss.

signed to combat monopoly power; other types of regulation discourage competition.

In recent years, there has been a movement toward federal *deregulation* of industries that are basically competitive, such as airlines, trucking, banking, and broadcasting. In fact, deregulation was emphasized during both the Carter and Reagan presidencies.

It is difficult to estimate exactly what proportion of the U.S. economy is regulated because most businesses are regulated in one way or another. On the one hand, regulated industries could include only those industries in which rates and prices are controlled by government agencies (transportation, communications, utilities, banking, and insurance). According to this criterion, as much as 10 percent of national output may be produced by regulated firms. If businesses that are government-supervised (such as the drug or meat-packing industries) are added, the regulated sector may be as high as one fifth of national output.[4]

Any single measure of the scope of the regulated sector is misleading because some businesses are more closely supervised than others (the prescription-drug industry is more strictly supervised by the Food and Drug Administration than the automobile industry is regulated by the Environmental Protection Agency).

Objectives of Regulation

There are three basic reasons to regulate business.[5] Businesses are regulated

1. to prevent monopoly profits from being earned without preventing the firm from operating at a normal profit.

---

4. The figures of 20 percent for 1939 and 21.5 percent for 1958 for the "government supervised" sector come from the studies of G. Warren Nutter, *The Extent of Enterprise Monopoly in the United States, 1899–1939* (Chicago: University of Chicago Press, 1951); G. Warren Nutter and Henry A. Einhorn, *Enterprise Monopoly in the United States, 1899–1958* (New York: Columbia University Press, 1969); and George Stigler, *Five Lectures on Economic Problems* (London: Longmans, Green and Company, 1949).

5. For a discussion of the objectives of regulation, see William J. Baumol, "Reasonable Rules for Rate Regulation: Plausible Policies in an Imperfect World," in ed. Paul MacAvoy, *The Crisis of the Regulatory Commissions* (New York: W. W. Norton, 1970), pp. 187–206; Robert E. Litan and William D. Nordhaus, *Reforming Federal Regulation* (New Haven: Yale University Press, 1983); and Lawrence J. White, *Reforming Regulation* (Englewood Cliffs, N.J.: Prentice-Hall, 1981).

2. to encourage the regulated business to operate efficiently and safely.

3. to prevent predatory competition that would result in less competition.

The basic instrument regulators use to achieve these objectives is rate regulation, or control of the prices (rates) that regulated enterprises are allowed to charge. Regulators in some cases control entry into the industry by issuing licenses and franchises. Regulators also establish rules or standards for the quality of goods or services. Although regulators do more than simply set rates, this chapter will concentrate on rate setting and its effects on the three basic objectives of regulation.

Principles of Rate Regulation

Figure 2 represents the demand and cost schedules of a typical privately owned natural monopoly. This monopoly is regulated by a regulatory commission, whose responsibility it is to protect the interests of users of the product. In practical terms, the regulatory commission must set "reasonable" rates for the service of the monopoly, establish standards for minimum quality of service, and guarantee to all customers access to the service without discrimination.

Regulatory commissions are bound by the safeguards of private property embodied in the Fifth and Fourteenth Amendments to the U.S. Constitution. Regulators must protect the property rights of the owners of the monopoly and are not permitted to set rates that do not cover operating costs plus a "fair" rate of return on invested capital. If regulators set rates that fail to cover operating costs and a fair rate of return, the monopoly can claim illegal seizure of private property and appeal to the courts for redress.

The Pricing Formula.   The usual regulatory pricing formula is:

Price of service = average operating cost + fair rate of return on invested capital

---

This pricing formula seems simple but raises as many questions as it answers. How are operating costs to be established? What constitutes a "fair"

Example 1   The Case of *U.S.* v. *IBM*

In 1969, the U.S. government filed an antitrust suit against IBM for alleged violations of the Sherman Antitrust Act. Thirteen years later in January of 1982, the Antitrust Division of the Justice Department dismissed the suit against IBM declaring the case "without merit." In the 13 years the case was tried, millions of dollars of IBM and federal-government funds were expended, a trial transcript of more than 100,000 pages was created, and thousands of documents were placed in the official record. *U.S.* v. *IBM* is one of the great monopoly cases of all time, rivaling the Standard Oil, the AT&T, and the Alcoa antitrust cases in importance. Critics of the government case point to it as an example of the inability of U.S. antitrust laws to deal with technologically advanced industries.

The government's case against IBM rested on a number of points. First, the government contended that IBM had a dominant share of the computer market and was, thus, a monopolist. Second, the government contended that IBM was earning monopoly profits. Government witnesses noted that IBM's profit rate was high (above profit rates of other industries), which the government took to be a sign of monopoly. Third, IBM was accused of unfair competitive practices (charging low prices and bundling its mainframe sales with maintenance and software contracts). Fourth, the government argued that there were significant barriers to entry (in the form of economies of scale) into the computer industry that gave IBM a competitive advantage.

IBM's defense consisted of the following arguments. First, IBM emphasized the competitive nature of the computer business since its birth in the 1950s. From the very beginning, the computer industry has been characterized by considerable entry and exit. A number of early entrants into the business fell by the wayside, and some of IBM's current rivals are recent entrants to the business. In fact, computers were first called *univacs* (after Univac Corporation). The intense competitive pressures of the computer market (operating under conditions of rapid technological change) actually resulted in dramatically falling prices and improved product quality instead of the restricted output and rising prices characteristic of monopoly. The fall in IBM's prices since 1964 is recorded in the accompanying table that describes five generations of IBM mainframes. Second, IBM pointed out the error of narrowly defining the computer industry. By the 1970s, IBM did not dominate the computer industry broadly defined—an industry crowded by new entrants as well as established producers. By the late 1970s, IBM continued to dominate only a portion of the computer market (accounting for 77 percent of the mainframe computer market). IBM also argued that government-cited statistics on IBM's market shares were based on the stock of existing com-

rate of return to invested capital? The formula does rule out marginal-cost pricing because marginal-cost pricing (point *c* in Figure 2) typically yields a loss and would not offer the regulated firm a fair rate of return. The fair-rate-of-return pricing formula is thought to lead to an inefficient use of resources. Increases in operating costs (whether justified or not) will be passed on to the consumer by the pricing formula in the form of higher prices; the regulated firm need not be overly concerned with minimizing its costs of production. Regulators typically do not have the information to detemine whether reported costs are padded or legitimate. Regulatory commissions do have the authority to examine accounting records for extravagant costs, exorbitant managerial salaries, or excessive advertising expenditures, but regulators are reluctant to substitute their judgments on what costs are reasonable for those of management.

The Rate Base.   The ability of regulated monopolies to pass cost increases on to consumers is one source of inefficiency. Rate regulation to provide a fair rate of return on invested capital creates a second type of inefficiency by encouraging the regulated monopoly to use too much capital.

Suppose regulators have determined that 12 percent is a fair rate of return. The regulated firm

System Name	Year Introduced	Maximum Memory Size (in megabytes)	Cost Per MIP[a] (in thousands)	Still Sold by I.B.M.	Price per Megabyte When Introduced (in thousands)
360	1964	1	$3,500	No	$1,600
370	1970	16	2,000	No	100
3030	1977	32	400	No	25
308x	1981	128	240	Yes	16
3090	1985	192	180	Yes	7

[a]MIP = millions of instructions per second.

puters, not on current sales of computers. Third, IBM argued that its high profits were the necessary rewards to successful innovation in a high-risk market. Computer firms that failed to innovate were forced to drop out of the market. Without a high rate of return for the successful innovators like IBM, no one would be willing to take the risks of operating in such a dynamic and risky market. Fourth, IBM argued that the computer industry is not characterized by significant economies of scale. In the modern computer industry, there are successful small companies and successful large companies. There appear to be few distinct cost advantages that accrue to large concerns like IBM. Fifth, IBM pointed out that it had abandoned its practice of bundling its maintenance and soft-ware contracts by the late 1960s—a practice the government criticized as anticompetitive. In sum, IBM's defenders argued that the only sin of IBM was that it acted as an aggressive competitor—delivering a quality product at a competitive price to the benefit of the consumer. These arguments convinced the Justice Department to dismiss the charges against IBM. ■

Source: "Additional Power from IBM," *New York Times,* February 13, 1985, p. 27; Franklyn Fisher, John J. Mc-Gowan, and Joen E. Greenwood, *Folded, Spindled, and Mutilated: Economic Analysis and U.S. v. IBM* (Cambridge: M.I.T. Press, 1983). The authors of this authoritative book on the IBM case were economists who assisted in IBM's defense. Table from International Data Corporation.

will be allowed to earn annual profits equal to 12 percent of invested capital. The value of invested capital is the regulated firm's *rate base.*

If the company has a rate base of $10 million worth of invested capital and the profit-rate ceiling is 12 percent, this company will be allowed to earn a maximum profit of $1.2 million per annum.

An unregulated company will add to its invested capital only if the present value of the resulting business profits exceeds the costs of acquiring the capital. The regulated monopoly, however, can increase its profits merely by expanding its rate base. By investing an additional $5 million, the rate base is expanded by $5 mil-lion (to $15 million), and the regulated company can now earn $1.8 million profit per annum. Accordingly, regulated firms have an incentive to acquire more capital than unregulated firms. According to economists, this incentive to acquire capital will lead to inefficiencies in the economic system because regulated firms will invest at the margin in projects with lower rates of return than those acceptable to unregulated firms. Therefore, regulators must decide whether certain additions to capital should be included in the rate base.[6]

6. The tendency of regulated monopolies to use too much capital was first analyzed by H. Averch and L. L. Johnson, "Behavior of the Firm Under Regulatory Constraint," *American Economic Review* 52 (December 1962).

Regulatory Lag

A fundamental problem of rate regulation is that it appears to eliminate rewards to efficiency and innovation *if regulators raise rates immediately when operating costs rise.* This rate adjustment is not necessarily very speedy, however. Regulated utilities must appeal to regulatory officials to raise rates, and the red tape and foot dragging associated with lengthy hearings can create substantial delays. If rate increases are delayed while operating costs are rising, the regulated firm will not be able to earn its fair rate of return.

Some authorities argue that **regulatory lag** does put some pressure on regulated monopolies to economize on costs and to innovate. If operating costs rise and if years are required for the approval of higher rates (called *rate relief* by regulated industries), company earnings fall. By the time rate relief is eventually granted, the new rates may already be outdated, and the incentive to hold down costs may still be present. Regulatory lag is especially harmful to utility profits during inflationary periods when costs are increasing rapidly while rate relief is slow in coming.

> **Regulatory lag** occurs when government regulators adjust rates some time after operating costs and the rate base have increased.

Regulatory lag reintroduces some of the incentives for regulated firms to use their resources efficiently, but it is only a partial (and very imperfect) solution to the fundamental problem: How can regulators encourage efficient operation when they are basically guaranteeing a fair rate of return?

The Effects of Regulation

To evaluate the rate regulation of natural monopolies, one must be able to compare the rates, services, and costs that would have existed in the absence of regulation to those that result with regulation. There is no ideal method of comparing actual regulated rates with hypothetical unregulated rates, but researchers have gone back in time to periods of U.S. history when there were both regulated and unregulated utilities to determine whether regulated rates were indeed lower.

The most authoritative study of this sort was conducted by George Stigler and Claire Friedland for the period 1912 to 1937 for electric utilities in states with and without regulatory commissions.[7] After 1937, virtually all electric utilities were regulated, so there would no longer be any basis for comparison. Stigler and Friedland found that, holding other factors constant, there was no difference between the rates charged by regulated and unregulated electric utilities. Thus, regulation made no difference in rates! Studies for more recent periods conclude that utilities "appear to be only moderately restrained by regulation."[8]

A surprising result of studies of the effects of regulation on utilities is that the overall effect has been so small. It is important to ask why regulation has not had more of an impact on prices. Several answers have been suggested.

First, regulators are outgunned by the regulated enterprises. The legal and professional staffs of regulatory agencies are small and underpaid and cannot compete with the large and well-paid staffs of the regulated firms. Moreover, only the regulated firms know the details of the operation of the company. The regulated firms are, therefore, in a position to circumvent orders from the regulatory commission. Monopoly profits in excess of the fair rate of return can be concealed by creative accounting (in determining how the rate base is to be valued, the proper amount of depreciation, and the allocation of joint costs) without the regulators' knowledge.[9]

Second, the monopoly power of regulated monopolies is exaggerated. If there are indeed effective substitutes (natural gas for electricity) or if users (primarily industrial and commercial customers) are prepared to move to another utility region if rates become excessive, then one would not expect rate regulation to make much difference.

7. George Stigler and Claire Friedland, "What Can Regulators Regulate? The Case of Electricity," reprinted in ed. Paul MacAvoy, *The Crisis of the Regulatory Commissions* (New York: W. W. Norton, 1970), pp. 39–52.

8. William G. Shepherd, "Causes of Increased Competition in the U.S. Economy, 1939–1980," *Review of Economics and Statistics,* November 1982, p. 617. This conclusion is based on studies by Alfred Kahn, Almarin Phillips, Stephen Breyer and Paul MacAvoy.

9. For a description of how regulated companies are able to evade regulatory decrees, see Richard Posner, "Natural Monopoly and its Regulation," in ed. Paul McAvoy, *The Crisis of the Regulatory Commissions* (New York: W. W. Norton, 1970), pp. 30–38.

Third, regulators tend to be captives of, or to have a certain loyalty to, the industry they regulate. Regulators often have more in common with the companies they regulate than with the public they are supposed to represent. Regulators are often recruited from the ranks of the regulated companies and often join the regulated companies upon leaving the regulatory agency.

REGULATION OF POTENTIALLY COMPETITIVE INDUSTRIES

Regulation in the United States is not limited to monopolies. There are numerous examples of the regulation of potentially competitive industries. Examples of industries that are (or have been) regulated and that have the potential for significant competition are radio and television broadcasting, trucking, passenger and freight airlines, railroads, and banking.

The Case For and Against Deregulation

The Case For Deregulation.
Over the years, most economists have favored deregulation of industries that are potentially competitive. They argue that deregulation would permit customers to get what they pay for, would eliminate the inefficiency of setting rates that do not reflect cost differences, and would eliminate stifling bureaucratic rules.

There are numerous examples of inefficient regulatory rules.[10] During the heyday of interstate trucking regulation, the rules of the Interstate Commerce Commission forced truckers to travel circuitous routes and to return with empty trucks from long hauls. The Civil Aeronautics Board required airlines to charge the same fare per passenger mile even if the plane were habitually full on one route and habitually half empty on another route. Throughout most of its history, the Interstate Commerce Commission sought to equalize the prices charged by motor carriers and railroads. Regulation often prevented enterprises from using

the most cost-efficient methods and from competing with one another on price. The consumer paid for this inefficiency in higher prices. The thrust of the deregulation argument is that where the potential for competition exists, it is better for professional managers to make decisions about fares and services than for government bureaucrats to make these decisions. The public will likely get better (and more diversified) service at lower cost. As Alfred Kahn, chairman of the Civil Aeronautics Board (CAB) when airline deregulation was initiated, put it: "I have more faith in greed than in regulation."[11]

Various economists have attempted to place a price tag on the costs of federal regulation. For the year 1977, the estimated price was between $14 billion and $36 billion, (between 0.7 percent and 1.8 percent of 1977 gross national product). The highest regulation costs were found in transportation.[12]

The Case Against Deregulation.
The case against deregulation rests on three arguments. The first is that substantial elements of the market may be denied an essential service as a result of deregulation. The regulated industry is required to provide access to the service to virtually all customers. If the industry is deregulated, firms will serve only the most lucrative markets. For example, small communities may find themselves without rail or air service after deregulation. The second argument is that if deregulation occurs, competition may be eliminated by the emergence of a dominant producer, who will then act like a monopolist. For example, it has been argued that deregulation of banking could lead to the domination of the industry by a few large banks. The third point is that regulation permits public control of the quality of the service. For example, if access to the airwaves were not regulated, people worry that public-interest programming would disappear.[13]

10. Case studies of the higher costs of regulated industries are presented in MacAvoy, *The Crisis of the Regulatory Commissions*, parts 3–5.

11. *The New York Times*, October 7, 1980.

12. Litan and Nordhaus, *Reforming Federal Regulation*, p. 23. These figures are based on studies by Murray Weidenbaum and R. DeFina, T. G. Moore, Ann Friedlander, Gerald Jautscher, G. W. Douglas, James C. Miller, and W. Comanor and B. Mitchell.

13. "Deregulation is Back on Track," *New York Times*, September 7, 1980; "FCC Battleground: Deregulation of TV," *New York Times*, October 20, 1980; "The U.S. Drive for Deregulation," *New York Times*, October 7, 1980.

Deregulation Legislation

In October 1978, President Jimmy Carter signed the Airline Deregulation Act, the first of the major deregulation acts of the 1970s and 1980s. The Airline Deregulation Act allowed the airlines, rather than the Civil Aeronautics Board, to set their own fares (within a broad range set by the CAB) and to select their own routes. Service to smaller communities was to continue for 10 years financed by government subsidy if necessary. The act also called for the phasing out of the CAB by 1984.

Other deregulation legislation soon followed. The Motor Carrier Act of 1980 curbed the ICC's control over interstate trucking. It allowed truckers greater freedom to set their own rates or to change their routes and permitted new firms to enter the business of interstate trucking. The Staggers Rail Act of October 1980 gave the railroads more flexibility in setting their own rates, banned the railroad industry's practice of collective rate setting, and allowed railroads to drop unprofitable routes. The year 1980 also saw the passage of the Depository Institutions Deregulation and Monetary Control Act, which will eventually eliminate interest-rate ceilings on bank savings deposits and allows savings and loans to offer checking accounts, car loans, and full-service credit cards. In 1982, the Thrift Institutions Restructuring Act enabled savings-and-loan institutions to operate on a more equal footing with commercial banks. The Bus Deregulatory Reform Act, also of 1982, allowed intercity bus lines to operate without applying for federal licenses in many circumstances. Since 1972, the FCC has been gradually deregulating the television-broadcast industry by increasing the number of channels, removing barriers to direct satellite broadcasting, licensing new low-power television stations, and removing restrictions on cable television. In 1981, the number of allowable VHF channels was increased, thus creating the possibility of a fourth major network.

Deregulation is a recent phenomenon; it is too early to determine whether the optimistic predictions of better service and lower prices will prove correct. It is also too early to tell whether deregulation will lead to an upsurge in productivity growth as industries are freed from bureaucratic controls. Airline deregulation was carried out during two costly recessions and a period of escalating fuel bills. The deregulation of trucking has been fought by unions and by major trucking companies, and, as a result, most truckers are still subject to federal regulation. As a consequence, it is very difficult at this point in time to evaluate the effects of deregulation.

A major fear of the opponents of deregulation is that deregulation will leave customers in small markets without a vital service—such as railroad trucking, or air service. The experience of the airlines shows that these fears have not been justified. Smaller commuter airlines have replaced the major carriers and now typically offer more frequent service than the major airlines before them. (See Example 2.)

ANTITRUST LAWS AND COURT RULINGS

The major alternative to direct regulation of monopolies is legislation to control market structure and market conduct. Rather than regulating monopolies directly by telling them what prices they can charge and what service they must offer, the government can set the legal rules of the game.

In the United States, federal legislation passed for the purpose of controlling market structure and conduct is called *antitrust law*. The cornerstone of antitrust legislation is the Sherman Antitrust Act of 1890. The Sherman Act was enacted as a reaction to the public outrage against the **trust** movement of the late 19th century in the railroad, steel, tobacco, and oil industries.

> A **trust** is a combination of firms that come together to act essentially as a monopolist. A trust sets common prices, agrees to restrict output, and punishes member firms who fail to live up to the agreement.

The Sherman Act of 1890

The Sherman Act contains two sections. Section 1 provides that

> every contract, combination in the form of a trust or otherwise, or conspiracy, in restraint of trade or commerce among the several States, or with foreign nations, is hereby declared to be illegal.

Example 2   Airline Deregulation After 1978

The Airline Deregulation Act of October 1978 ushered in a new era of competition in the airline business. The original opponents of airline deregulation warned that deregulation would mean higher fares, less service to small communities, lower airline profits, reduced airline employment, a general breakdown of the existing airline network, and the emergence of one or two dominant carriers.

It is still too early to judge the full effects of airline deregulation because it was carried out during unusual and trying times. Fuel prices soared in the late 1970s, the air-traffic-control system had to be restructured in the early 1980s, and economic downturns in 1980 and 1981 cut the demand for airline travel. How the airlines will perform under more normal conditions remains to be established. It is clear, however, that a number of the warnings of the opponents of deregulation have proven to be false.

First, the number of carriers has risen from 35 in 1978 to near 100 in 1984. Although one major airline (Braniff) and some small ones (Air 1, Capitol, and Air Florida) declared bankruptcy and ceased operation (a new Braniff, however, subsequently resumed operation), a large number of new airlines (Muse, People Express, and some commuter airlines) entered the market. There are few signs of growing monopoly power. In fact, the large trunk carriers are caught up in a competitive struggle with new entrants to keep existing markets. As a general rule, the midsize airlines have outperformed other airlines under deregulation.

Second, the rise in airline-ticket prices (particularly in large markets) has lagged behind the rise in the general price level. Most observers agree that airline travel remains a bargain and that increased competition is the explanation.

Third, small communities have not been deprived of airline service. A Civil Aeronautics Board study shows that airline service in the 239 small communities that had air service increased by 7 percent between 1978 and 1982.

Fourth, deregulation has not resulted in a decrease in passenger safety on the major carriers. The number of accidents (and fatalities) has remained relatively stable or has even declined since 1978 despite major disruptions in the air-traffic-control system. (However, some observers feel the increased markets served by small commuter airlines are not well monitored by federal safety regulators and point to many commuter airline groundings and crashes.)

Fifth, employment in the airline industry increased during the early years of deregulation and then returned to its 1978 level with the economic downturns of the early 1980s. The number of revenue miles flown after deregulation exceeded 1978 levels even during the economic downturns of the early 1980s.

Airline profits have been low since 1978. As a group, airline profits were negative in 1980, 1981, and 1982, rebounding to positive profits in 1983 and 1984. The losses of 1980–1982 have weakened a number of carriers, and one or two airlines may go out of business over the next few years. It is hard to sort out the effects of rising fuel prices and economic recession (which hurt airline profits) from the effects of deregulation. In a competitive environment, some carriers will prove more efficient and innovative than others. Well-managed airlines have earned consistent profits.

There have been losers from deregulation. Pilot and flight-attendant salaries have not kept pace with inflation (or, in some cases, have even been cut) as airlines cut their costs to remain competitive. Salaries in the airline industry had achieved a comfortable level prior to deregulation because ticket prices were well above competitive levels. The other losers are passengers in smaller cities who were previously charged the same price per mile as passengers flying between two major cities. In effect, the profits earned from the major-city market were used to subsidize the losses suffered on low-density flights. Because of competition, passengers flying between major hubs now pay a lower fare per mile than do those flying from a small city. ■

Section 2 provides that

> every person who shall monopolize, or attempt to monopolize, or combine or conspire with any other person or persons to monopolize any part of the trade or commerce among the several States, or with foreign nations, shall be guilty of a misdemeanor. . . .[14]

Section 1 prohibits a particular type of market *conduct* (conspiring to restrain trade), while section 2 outlaws a particular market *structure* (monopoly). The vague language of section 2 has led to varying court interpretations over the years. Section 2 prohibits *monopolization,* not *monopolies.* Although the act of creating a monopoly is clearly prohibited, the legality of existing monopolies is unclear.

The Clayton Act and the Federal Trade Commission Act, 1914

The Sherman Act contained a general prohibition of acts in restraint of trade but did not specify actual restrictive or monopolistic practices that were in violation of the law. Moreover, the Sherman Act did not establish any agency (other than the existing Department of Justice) to enforce the provisions of the Sherman Act.

The Clayton Act of 1914 declared illegal the following four specific monopolistic practices if their "effect was to substantially lessen competition or tend to create a monopoly":

1. price discrimination (charging different prices to different customers for the same product),
2. exclusive dealing and *tying contracts* (requiring a buyer to agree not to purchase goods from competitors),
3. acquisition of competing companies, and
4. *interlocking directorates* (in which the directors of one company sit on the board of directors of another company in the same industry).

The Clayton Act gave private parties the right

to sue for damages for injury to business or property as a result of violations of the antitrust laws along with other penalties.

The Federal Trade Commission Act established the Federal Trade Commission (FTC). The FTC's role was to secure compliance with the ban on "unfair methods of competition" stated in the FTC Act. It was empowered to prosecute unfair competition and also to issue cease-and-desist orders to violators.

Revisions of the Clayton Act

The Robinson-Patman Act of 1936 amended the anti–price-discrimination section of the Clayton Act. The Robinson-Patman Act modifies the Clayton Act's prohibition of price discrimination where the effect is "to substantially lessen competition" with a clause stating " . . . or to injure, destroy, or prevent competition with any person who either grants or knowingly receives the benefit of such discrimination, or with customers of either of them." The basic purpose of the Robinson-Patman Act—which was passed during Depression times when the rate of failure for small businesses was high—was to protect small businesses from the competition of the growing chain stores. The chain stores were receiving price discounts from their suppliers because of their large purchases and were then passing these discounts on to their customers. The Robinson-Patman Act sought to ensure equal competitive opportunities for small businesses. Because it protected small businesses from the lower prices of large competitors, many authorities regard the Robinson-Patman Act as anticompetitive. Its purpose seemed more to protect competitors than competition.

The Wheeler-Lea Act of 1938 extended the general ban on "unfair methods of competition" to include "unfair or deceptive" acts or practices. The FTC was empowered under this amendment to deal with false and deceptive advertising and the sale of harmful products.

The Celler-Kefauver Act of 1950 broadened the Clayton Act's ban on corporate mergers by limiting mergers that occurred through the acquisition of one company's assets by another company. This antimerger provision applied if the acquisition served to lessen competition

14. This discussion is based upon: A. D. Neale, *The Antitrust Laws of the United States of America* (Cambridge: The University Press, 1962), pp. 2–5; Eugene Singer, *Antitrust Economics* (Englewood Cliffs, N.J.: Prentice-Hall, 1968), chap. 2.; Marshall C. Howard, *Antitrust and Trade Regulation* (Englewood Cliffs, N.J.: Prentice-Hall, 1983).

substantially or to create a monopoly. The Hart-Scott-Rodino Antitrust Procedural Improvements Act of 1980 replaced the word *corporations* with the word *persons*. This change made the antimerger legislation applicable to large unincorporated business firms (such as large accounting partnerships). The act also requires that pending mergers be reported in advance to antitrust authorities.

Interpretation of the Sherman Act

American antitrust policy is decided in the courts as well as in Congress. The Sherman Antitrust Act, the mainstay of antitrust legislation, left unresolved a basic issue: Do antitrust laws prohibit only market *conduct* that leads to monopoly or is monopoly by the fact of its existence a violation of antitrust law?

The "Rule of Reason," 1911–1945.   In early court rulings, the courts interpreted the Sherman Act as outlawing specific market *practices* in restraint of trade (mergers, price fixing, price slashing to drive out competition), not the existence of monopoly in and of itself. This interpretation became known as the **rule of reason.**[15]

> The **rule of reason** stated that monopolies were in violation of the Sherman Act if they engaged in unfair or illegal business practices. Being a monopoly in and of itself was not considered a violation of the Sherman Act according to this rule.

The early landmark tests of the Sherman Act were the Standard Oil and American Tobacco Company cases, both tried in 1911. In both cases, the court ruled that these companies should be broken up into smaller companies (many of the major oil companies of today are spinoffs of Standard Oil). Both Standard Oil and American Tobacco accounted for more than 90 percent of output in their respective industries. The court's ruling, however, was not based upon this fact.

The court ruled that Standard Oil and American Tobacco violated the Sherman Act because they had both engaged in unreasonable restraints of trade, not because they were in fact monopolies.

The implication of the Standard Oil and American Tobacco rulings was that if a monopoly does not engage in unfair business practices, it is not in violation of the Sherman Act.

This rule of reason was upheld in the U.S. Steel Case of 1920. U.S. Steel at the time produced more than one half of the industry's output, but it had not treated its competitors unfairly or sought to control steel prices. U.S. Steel was in effect a "benevolent" monopolist. In the U.S. Steel case, the court upheld the rule of reason, stating that the law does not consider mere size or the existence of "unexerted power" to be an offense.

Questioning the Rule of Reason.   The rule of reason prevailed until the Aluminum Company of America (Alcoa) Case of 1945. The courts ruled that Alcoa was in violation of the Sherman Act because it controlled more than 90 percent of the aluminum ingot market in the United States. Alcoa was also accused of using unfair pricing (setting ingot prices too high relative to aluminum sheet prices). The courts (in a famous decision written by Judge Learned Hand) ruled that size alone was a violation of the Sherman Act.

The Alcoa decision appeared to overturn the rule of reason and to remove an important inconsistency. The rule of reason suggested that companies that engaged in practices that would ultimately lead to monopoly were in violation of the Sherman Act, while companies that were already monopolies, if they were well behaved, did not violate the Sherman Act. The Alcoa case appeared to reject the older "abuse theory" that required proof of the monopoly's predatory conduct. In its place a "structure test" was applied in which size was the determining factor. Actual monopolization—not the attempt to monopolize—was deemed Alcoa's offense.

Definition of Market.   The Alcoa decision raised a fundamental issue: if the existence of monopoly is itself a violation of the Sherman Act, how is the market to be defined?

---

15. This discussion of court rulings is based upon the previous references and upon Frederic Scherer, *Industrial Structure and Economic Performance,* 2nd ed. (Boston: Houghton Mifflin, 1980); Oliver Williamson, *Markets and Hierarchies: Analysis and Antitrust Implications* (New York: the Free Press, 1975); and Howard, *Antitrust and Trade Regulation.*

In the Alcoa case, the way in which the aluminum market was defined was crucial to the decision in the case. Alcoa controlled 90 percent of the virgin aluminum ingot market, but it had to compete in the scrap ingot market and to face competition from stainless steel, lead, nickel, tin, zinc, copper, and imported aluminum. In its 1945 Alcoa decision, the court ruled that because substitutes for aluminum should not be included in Alcoa's market, Alcoa was a monopoly.

The DuPont Cellophane Case of 1956 broadened the definition of markets. DuPont in 1956 produced almost 75 percent of the *cellophane* sold in the United States but accounted for less than 20 percent of the sales of all *flexible wrapping materials*. The Justice Department filed suit against DuPont for monopolization of the cellophane market. The Supreme Court ruled that DuPont was not in violation of the Sherman Act because the market should be defined to include products that are "reasonably interchangeable" with cellophane (such as aluminum foil, waxed paper, or vegetable parchment). The court found that DuPont controlled only 20 percent of the flexible-wrapping-materials market and ruled that this share was insufficient to establish monopoly power.

In 1975, the Justice Department won an antitrust judgment against Xerox Corporation. At the time of the 1975 decision, Xerox produced more than 90 percent of plain-paper copiers and a substantial 65 percent of all copying equipment. The courts ruled that Xerox monopolized the copying-equipment market and required Xerox to make some of its patents available to competitors to increase competition in the market.

In January of 1982, the government's 13-year-old suit against IBM was dismissed by the Justice Department. In 1969, when the Justice Department filed suit against IBM for monopolizing the "general-purpose computer and peripheral-equipment industry," IBM controlled about 70 percent of the mainframe-computer market but had less than 40 percent of the office-equipment market. The specific complaint against IBM was its combining of the price of hardware, software, and support services, thereby preventing competition in the software and support markets. Again, the issue was: what constituted IBM's market?

After more than a decade of litigation involving 66 million pages of documents, the Justice Department decided in 1982 to drop the case. In the intervening years, IBM's competition in the computer industry had increased substantially. In 1982, IBM dominated only the mainframe computer industry (with 70 percent of the U.S. market). In its other lines of business, IBM's shares were relatively small: 20 percent of the minicomputer market, 18 percent of the word-processor market, and less than 5 percent of the telecommunications and computer-services markets. On the basis of these changes, the Justice Department decided that IBM did not monopolize the computer industry as broadly defined. In general, court rulings of the 1950s and 1960s appeared to move away from the Alcoa ruling by using a more liberal interpretation of what constitutes the market.

In 1982, a compromise court decision was reached in which American Telephone and Telegraph agreed to divest itself of its local operating companies. AT&T agreed to give up its regional Bell affiliates (which remained subject to rate regulation) in return for being allowed to enter unregulated telecommunications and computer markets. (See Example 3.)

Reversing the Alcoa Decision.   Since the Alcoa case declared that size alone was a violation of the Sherman Act, business was concerned that the Alcoa decision would, in the words of Donald Baker, former head of the Justice Department's Antitrust Division, be used "to punish innovative success."[16] Even the Alcoa Decision warned against turning against the successful competitor who has been urged to compete.

Some companies gain monopoly positions not due to unfair business practices but due to superior innovation. Is a company that gains a dominant position through superior foresight, good planning, proper risk taking, and aggressive technological innovation violating the Sherman Act?[17]

---

16. The *Wall Street Journal*, November 10, 1980.

17. The Grinnel case of 1966 noted that if monopoly was the "consequence of a superior product, business acumen, or historic accident," the Sherman Act was not violated. *See* Williamson, *Markets and Hierarchies*, pp. 209–10.

Example 3   The Divestiture of AT&T

In what was termed the most important antitrust development since the dissolution of Standard Oil in 1911, American Telephone and Telegraph (AT&T) and the Justice Department settled a seven-year-old antitrust suit in January 1982. The Justice Department had charged AT&T with violating the Sherman Act through its monopoly over local telephone service. Potential competitors to AT&T's long-distance service had been denied—it was charged—equal access to AT&T's network to beat down the challenge to AT&T's monopoly of long-distance telephone service. If AT&T had been found guilty, injured parties could have sued to collect damages from AT&T. In the case of an adverse ruling, such damages could have cost AT&T some $14 billion.

The AT&T case was settled by an agreement between the Justice Department and AT&T in which AT&T did not have to admit wrongdoing. Thus, injured parties would have to prove wrongdoing by AT&T—an expensive and time-consuming task. The principal provisions of the agreement were: 1) AT&T agreed to divest itself of its 22 local operating companies, which accounted for $87 billion of AT&T's $136 billion assets; 2) AT&T kept its long-distance telephone service, its manufacturing arm (Western Electric) and its research arm (Bell Laboratories); 3) AT&T was allowed to enter into the unregulated business it chooses. Its long-distance rates are still to be regulated by the Federal Communications Commission as long as AT&T retains its virtual monopoly over long-distance service. The local telephone companies remain subject to regulation by state and local agencies.

Basically, the AT&T agreement allowed AT&T to give up its monopoly over local telephone service in exchange for less regulation. Prior to the settlement, AT&T was restricted by a 1956 consent decree that prevented it from entering into any unregulated business. Since its divestiture, the new AT&T has expanded into the new high-technology areas of data transmission, electronic message services, teleconferencing, electronic blackboards, voice-generated computers, personal computers, and computer programming. These computer-data-transmission activities have brought AT&T into direct competition with another industrial giant, IBM.

AT&T had to divest itself of its 22 local telephone companies within 18 months of the ruling, and the local companies were obliged to provide AT&T and its long-distance competitors with equal access to local exchanges.

In July of 1984, local companies began switching to equal-access long-distance service, whereby customers designate which long-distance service they wish to use (Sprint, MCI, AT&T). They then access long distance by dialing "1" irrespective of the system they select, and the local phone service does the rest. So far in head-to-head competition with lower-priced long-distance services, AT&T has kept about three quarters of its long-distance customers (if customers make no choice, their calls are automatically routed to AT&T).

How well AT&T will do in the long run in the competitive telecommunications industry remains to be seen. So far, its results have been impressive. ∎

An important test case of this issue was the Eastman Kodak case. In 1972, Berkey Photo Inc. filed an antitrust suit against Eastman Kodak charging that Eastman Kodak's method of introducing its pocket-sized instamatic camera and film gave Kodak an unfair advantage over Berkey and other film processors. After a lower court ruled in favor of Berkey, higher courts ruled in favor of Eastman Kodak, concluding that Kodak had earned certain advantages as a result of "reaping the competitive rewards attributable to efficient size."[18]

A second test case was the charge brought by the FTC staff against DuPont Company. In a 1978 complaint, the FTC staff accused DuPont of illegally using unfair competition to overwhelm

---

18. This case is summarized in "FTC Dismisses Charges Against DuPont in Major Statement of Its Antitrust Policy," *Wall Street Journal*, November 10, 1980.

smaller rivals in the titanium dioxide market. In its ruling, the FTC dismissed antitrust charges against DuPont:

> The essence of the competitive process is to induce firms to become more efficient and to pass the benefits of the efficiency along to consumers. That process would be ill served by using antitrust to block hard, aggressive competition that is solidly based on efficiencies and growth opportunities, even if monopoly is an inevitable result.[19]

These judgments seem inconsistent with the ruling in the Alcoa case, since the apparent intent of the Alcoa ruling was to declare monopoly *per se* illegal, irrespective of how that monopoly came about. The DuPont and Eastman Kodak rulings again required the courts to weigh how a monopoly came into being—through restrictive or unfair business practices or through better management and innovation.

Price Fixing

The U.S. courts have generally found price-fixing agreements to be illegal restraints of trade. Exceptions have been allowed, but formal arrangements for fixing prices have consistently been ruled as illegal restraints of trade.

The United States stands virtually alone among the industrialized countries in its law that *formal* price-fixing arrangements are illegal in and of themselves whether or not the resulting prices are reasonable. In this way, the thorny issue of distinguishing reasonable from unreasonable price fixing has been avoided.

Conscious parallelism has provided the most difficult enforcement problem. (*Conscious parallelism* refers to orchestrated pricing actions—such as price leadership or uniform pricing—taken by mutually interdependent companies that appear to be the result of tacit agreement among the companies.) Prior to 1948, the courts held that clear cases of conscious parallelism were illegal even if formal price conspiracy could not be shown. After 1948, it had to be shown that the pattern of pricing could not have occurred if the company had acted alone in its own self-interest. This interpretation has established the legality of price-lead-

---

19. *Wall Street Journal,* November 10, 1980.

ership arrangements and other forms of oligopoly pricing that result in parallel behavior without formal agreements. Some experts view this interpretation as a clear weakness in existing antitrust legislation. If no formal arrangement exists, violations are difficult to prove.

Nevertheless, the courts have continued to use strict standards for what constitutes a pricing conspiracy. Systematic exchanges of pricing information among competitors have been ruled illegal, and in the 1970s, antitrust agencies launched an attack on the signaling of price changes. *Signaling* in this instance means publicly talking about the need for price increases or informing the media about upcoming price increases.

Mergers

Antimerger Legislation.   The Clayton Act of 1914 and the Celler-Kefauver Act of 1950 prohibit the acquisition of one company by another if this action reduces competition. The courts (especially since 1950) have adopted a virtual prohibition of mergers between firms in the same industry if both have substantial market shares. An unlawful merger may be either a **horizontal merger** or a **vertical merger.**

> A **horizontal merger** is a merger of two firms in the same line of business (such as an insurance company merging with another insurance company or a shoe manufacturer merging with another shoe manufacturer).

Exceptions are allowed when one firm takes over another firm that is on the verge of bankruptcy. For example, Jones & Laughlin Steel and Youngstown Steel were allowed to merge in 1978 to form the third largest producer of basic steel. The reason such a merger was allowed is that it was considered better to keep the assets of the failing company in the business than to maintain competition.

> A **vertical merger** is a merger of two firms that are part of the same materials, production, or distribution network (such as a personal computer manufacturer merging with a retail computer-distribution chain or a machinery manufacturer merging with a machinery parts supplier).

Figure 3   Mergers in the United States, 1890–1984

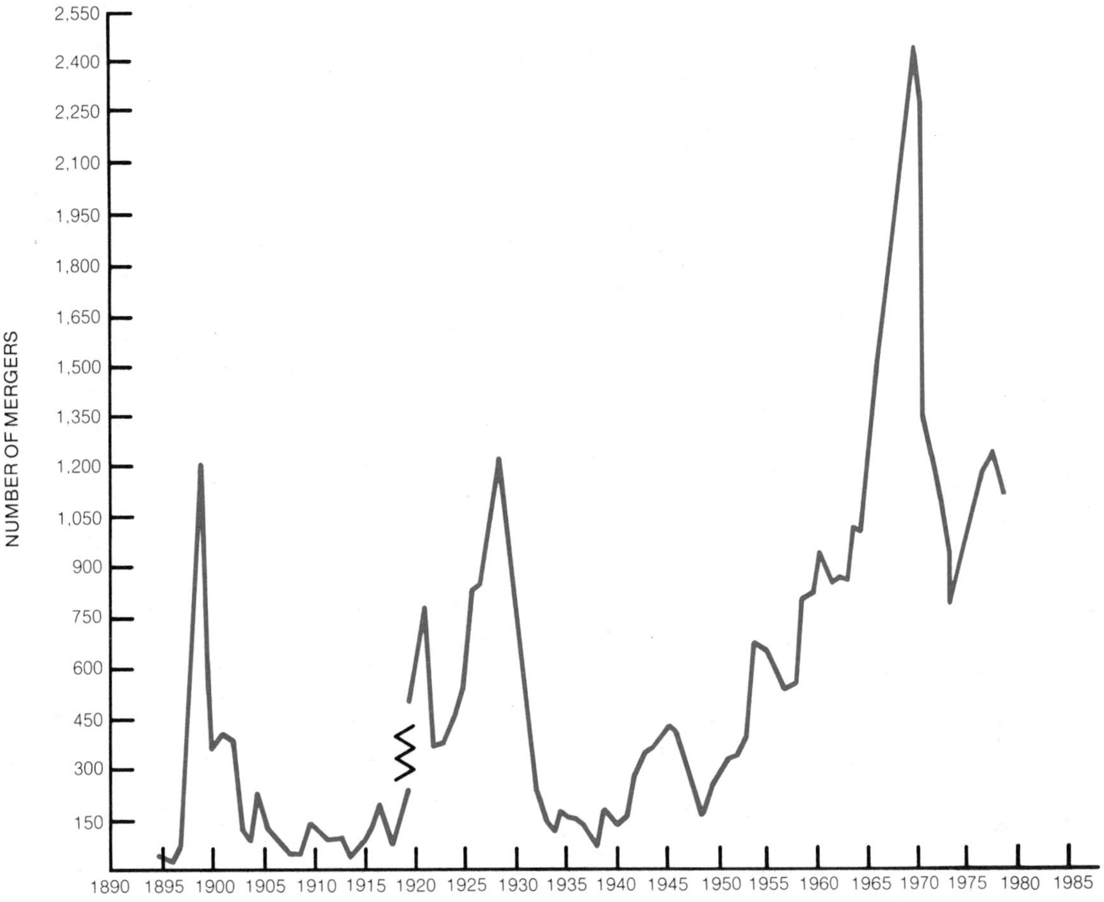

Source: The National Bureau of Economic Research and the Federal Trade Commission.

Vertical mergers are in violation of the Clayton Act if a buyer merges with a supplier and thereby is able to limit the access of other buyers to the supplier or if the vertical merger results in a transfer of significant market power. On these grounds, DuPont (a major supplier of automotive fabrics and finishes) was required to sell its 23 percent of General Motors stock in 1957 because DuPont's influence over GM gave it a competitive advantage versus other automotive suppliers. For similar reasons, Brown Shoe Company was not allowed in 1962 to acquire Kinney (a large shoe-retailing chain).

Conglomerate Mergers.   The major exception to the prohibition of mergers among large

companies is the **conglomerate merger.** Conglomerate mergers are less likely to be opposed by the Justice Department because they do not involve mergers of competing companies. Thus, U.S. Steel was permitted to acquire Marathon Oil, and DuPont was allowed to acquire Conoco because the merging companies operated in different markets.

A **conglomerate merger** occurs when one company takes over another company in a different line of business.

Conglomerate mergers have led to a substantial increase in the share of corporate assets controlled by the largest U.S. corporations over the past 30 years (see Figure 3). According to FTC statistics,

---

Example 4   The Herfindahl Index: Another Measure of Concentration

In the summer of 1982, the Justice Department issued new guidelines reflecting the Reagan administration's policy on mergers. Instead of using the traditional 4-firm concentration ratio (the total of the market shares of the industry's 4 largest firms) to determine whether a merger would restrain competition beyond acceptable limits, the Justice Department now uses the *Herfindahl index* (named for the late Orris Herfindahl), which is the total of the *squared values* of the market shares of all the firms in an industry. If an industry consists of firm 1 with a 60 percent market share and firm 2 with a 40 percent share, the Herfindahl index *(H)* is $(60)^2 + (40)^2 = 3,600 + 1,600 = 5,200$. The general formula is:

$$H = (S_1)^2 + (S_2)^2 + (S_3)^2 + \ldots + (S_n)^2,$$

where S_1 through S_n are the market shares (totaling 100 percent) of firms 1 through n.

Since the market shares are squared, large firms have a much larger impact on the index than small firms. For example, both the telephone-equipment and lightbulb industries have 4-firm concentration ratios of about 90 percent. AT&T's dominance of the telephone-equipment industry leads to a Herfindahl measure of 5,026, however, while the lightbulb industry has a Herfindahl measure of 2,036, because the dominant firms are more equal in size in the lightbulb industry.

Industrial organization experts generally agree that an industry with 10 equal-size firms would behave competitively. The Herfindahl index for an industry with 10 firms each of which has a 10 percent market share is 1,000 ($= 10^2 \times 10$). In the new Justice Department guidelines, a merger will probably not be challenged if the resulting Herfindahl index for the industry is less than 1,000. ■

Source: *Business Week,* May 17, 1982, p. 120; the *Wall Street Journal,* June 15, 1982. p. 3.

---

the 451 largest corporations controlled 50 percent of corporate assets in 1960; by 1976, they controlled 72 percent of the corporate assets.[20]

The pace of mergers in the United States has been highly uneven over the years (see Figure 3). In part, this pattern reflects the fact that antimerger legislation has changed over the years as has the rigor of enforcement of antimerger legislation.

The FTC and the Justice Department have led the battle against conglomerate takeovers. In the 1960s, they were able to win about one half of the cases brought against conglomerate mergers. Prior to 1973, the government was able to fight proposed mergers on the grounds that the merger *potentially* threatened competition. If a steel company wanted to acquire an aluminum company, this merger could be denied because the aluminum company might have the potential to compete eventually with the parent company—whether it currently did so or not. For instance, Proctor & Gamble was not allowed to acquire

Clorox in 1963 and 1967 because Proctor & Gamble was viewed as a potential entrant into the liquid bleach market.

Since 1973, the government lost all attempts to stop conglomerate takeovers. This trend can be traced to the fact that, since 1973, the government has had to prove that the proposed merger would actually (not potentially) reduce competition. Now the burden of proof is on the government to prove concretely that a conglomerate merger will indeed reduce competition. (See Example 4.)

Principal/Agent Theory, Contestable-Markets Theory, and Merger Policy. According to contestable-markets theory, discussed in an earlier chapter, the structure of a market (as determined by current concentration ratios) may be a poor measure of monopoly power. In a contestable market (which is characterized by complete freedom of entry), if a "monopoly" firm attempted to charge monopoly prices, competitive firms would immediately enter the market. New firms would undercut prices and take profits away from the established firm. Contestable-markets theory argues that horizontal merger decisions should be based on the speed and ease of entry of

---

20. These FTC statistics are from "Government May Abandon Fight to Stop Conglomerate Takeovers," *Wall Street Journal,* November 24, 1980.

Example 5   Mergers, Contestable Markets, and the Holdup Problem

The theory of contestable markets is used by the Civil Aeronautics Board (CAB) to evaluate airline mergers. In 1978, for example, Texas International (now Continental Airlines) sought to acquire National Airlines (which was ultimately acquired by Pan American). The Justice Department opposed the merger on the grounds that National and Texas International combined would dominate the New Orleans air-traffic market. The CAB, however, decided not to oppose the merger on the grounds that airline markets are contestable. In a contestable market, in which there is complete freedom of entry, new carriers would quickly enter and take profits from a carrier that was inefficient or was charging monopoly prices. The Civil Aeronautics Board, therefore, concluded that even though conventional measures of the structure of the market (like concentration ratios) pointed to monopoly power, the merged airline would still behave in a competitive and efficient manner.

The merger of General Motors and Fisher Body was a response to a holdup problem. In 1919, Fisher Body Corporation and General Motors entered into a 10-year contract in which GM agreed

to buy closed bodies exclusively from Fisher Body at a price equal to cost plus 18 percent. In return, Fisher Body agreed to make a highly specific investment in stamping machines and dies to turn out closed auto bodies that at the time were being used primarily by GM. The contract made it possible for Fisher Body to hold up GM. Fisher pushed up its prices by refusing to locate its plants near GM facilities and by holding down its capital costs (the interest on which could not be passed through to GM in the form of higher prices). Moreover, the demand for closed automobile bodies grew substantially during the 10-year contract period. Fisher's investment in closed bodies became less tied to purchases from GM, and Fisher's cheating potential rose. GM's holdup problem was resolved in 1926 when Fisher Body merged with General Motors. ■

Sources: Elizabeth E. Bailey, "Contestability and the Design of Regulatory Antitrust Policy," *American Economic Review,* May 1981, pp. 178–83; and Benjamin Klein, "Contract Costs and Administered Prices: An Economic Theory of Rigid Wages," *American Economic Review,* May 1984, pp. 332–38.

potential competitors, not on prevailing structural measures like concentration ratios.

When a manufacturer has a principal/agent relationship with a supplier and finds that the supplier's goals are not compatible with the manufacturer's goals (or when the supplier finds the manufacturer's goals are incompatible), a vertical merger may become a necessity. For example, a buyer firm (the principal) may be in a position to "hold up" a supplier firm (the agent) that has made specific investments in a product for which only that buyer would be a potential customer. Once the supplier has made the specific investment, the buyer could threaten the supplier with reductions in purchases to gain concessions. On the other hand, a supplier firm (the agent) may be able to hold up a buyer firm (the principal) who has become contractually dependent on the supplier. To induce a supplier firm to make specific investments, a buyer may have to sign exclusive purchase contracts, which give the seller leeway to manipulate the price or quality of the product. Because of different objectives, it may be impos-

sible to write quality, price, and delivery contracts that anticipate every potential holdup problem. According to conventional wisdom, a vertical merger of a large buying firm with a large supplier firm reduces competition and should not be allowed. Where a holdup problem exists, however, a vertical merger may be the best solution. (See Example 5.)

PROPOSALS FOR GOVERNMENT CONTROL OF MONOPOLY

As this chapter has outlined, U.S. government control of monopoly currently takes three forms: government ownership, government regulation, and antitrust law. None of these represents an ideal solution. A variety of proposals have been made to improve government control of monopoly, including: selling monopoly franchises, requiring consumer representation in management, and repealing antitrust laws.

Selling Monopoly Franchises

Some economists argue that natural monopolies will be better managed if they are not regulated.[21] Proponents of the deregulation of natural monopolies argue that an unregulated monopoly will be motivated to minimize costs, to limit prices to keep potential competitors out of the market, and to seek out innovation. Regulated monopolies, on the other hand, are inefficient; bureaucratic decisions are less efficient than private managerial decisions.

If natural monopolies are deregulated, the government could sell *monopoly franchises* (licenses to operate the monopoly) to the highest bidder, and the government could recapture most of the monopoly profits that the private monopoly would earn, thereby avoiding most of the negative income-distribution effects of monopoly. Competitive bidding would cause private investors to pay the present value of future monopoly profits. The monopoly would continue to produce an output less than the social optimum, however, and to charge a price higher than the optimal price.

Requiring Consumer Representation in Management

A second proposal is to place consumer representatives on the board of directors of natural monopolies or to grant consumers a voting interest in firms designated as public utilities. Important actions of the board of directors could be referred to the consumer by means of municipal elections.

If these measures were undertaken, it is argued, management would identify more closely with the interests of consumers and would refrain from abusing monopoly power.[22]

Repealing Antitrust Laws

A number of economists argue that the costs of antitrust laws outweigh the benefits to consumers. Antitrust battles cause corporations to spend billions of dollars on legal expenses, and litigation can stretch over decades. The IBM case, for example, lasted 13 years before its dismissal and cost the government more than $12 million and IBM even more.

The growth in international trade has more or less antiquated antitrust laws, which were passed in the early part of this century. Major U.S. corporations that account for substantial shares of U.S. production must now compete with foreign companies. Modern technology is able to develop substitutes for the products that monopolists sell, and the emergence of substitutes threatens all monopolies with potential competition if their monopoly profits are too high. Finally, monopolies may indeed be the result of superior innovation and better management (Eastman Kodak, DuPont, IBM, Boeing). To break these companies up may reduce rather than increase efficiency. Divestiture orders could signal other companies that aggressive innovation will be punished rather than rewarded.[23]

The vacillation of antitrust policy over the years stems in the first instance from changes in the composition of the Supreme Court itself. Yet the Supreme Court justices do not live in a vacuum; they are educated people responding in part to the changing views of the economics profession. In 1945 at the time of the Alcoa decision, the economics profession had a very severe standard of a good competitive order. They wanted an economy very close to perfect competition. Today, economists are coming to realize that it is not so much the world that is imperfect but the theory of perfect competition. Because information costs and transaction costs exist, perfect competition in its pure form is not possible. The consequent departure of real-world industries from the assumptions of perfect competition need not represent a case for antitrust action. Economists realize that the world is complex, and efficient arrangements may take on many forms.

This chapter completes our study of product markets. The five chapters in the next section will turn to the bottom half of the circular-flow dia-

21. This position is associated with Milton Friedman and George Stigler. See Milton Friedman, ''Monopoly and Social Responsibility of Business and Labor,'' in ed. Edwin Mansfield, *Monopoly Power and Economic Performance,* 3rd ed. (New York: W. W. Norton, 1974), pp. 57–68; George Stigler, ''Government of the Economy,'' in ed. Paul Samuelson, *Readings in Economics,* 7th ed. (New York: McGraw-Hill, 1973), pp. 73–77.

22. Edward Renshaw, ''Possible Alternatives to Direct Regulation'' in ed. Paul MacAvoy, *The Crisis of the Regulatory Commissions* (New York: W. W. Norton, 1970), pp. 209–211.

23. For one view of why antitrust laws should be abolished, *see* Lester Thurow, ''Let's Abolish the Antitrust Laws,'' *New York Times,* October 19, 1980.

gram: factor markets. The next chapter will give an introduction to factor markets and how they compare to product markets before subsequent chapters examine the markets for the different kinds of factors—labor, land, capital, entrepreneurship—individually.

Summary

1. The case *against* monopolies is that a) monopolies restrict output and charge higher prices, b) monopolies have less incentive to lower costs and develop new technologies, and c) monopoly profits make the distribution of income more unequal. The case *for* monopolies is that a) monopolies can take advantage of economies of scale, b) monopolies have less monopoly power than is commonly thought, and c) monopolies can afford to spend large sums on research and development.
2. The natural monopoly is an industry that must consist of one producer because economies of scale are experienced over the entire range of the industry's output.
3. The government uses three instruments to control monopoly: government ownership, regulation, and antitrust legislation.
4. Government ownership is not as widespread in the United States as in other countries. It is not clear how to operate government monopolies "in the public interest." Marginal-cost pricing will normally lead to losses. If the government monopoly is told to break even, there will be little incentive to reduce costs or to innovate. If the government monopoly is told to maximize profits, the consumer is no better off.
5. Regulation of natural monopolies aims at preventing monopoly profits while allowing the monopoly to operate profitably, encouraging efficient operation, and preventing predatory competition. Regulated monopolies are normally allowed to charge a price that covers operating costs plus a "fair" rate of return on invested capital. This pricing formula encourages inefficiency because higher costs can be passed on to the consumer and higher investment will automatically yield higher profits. Regulatory lag provides some incentive to minimize costs.
6. Regulation of potentially competitive industries has been criticized by economists as

leading to inefficiencies and to poor service. There is now a significant deregulation movement under way to free competitive industries from government supervision.
7. Antitrust legislation seeks to control market structure and market conduct by setting the legal rules of the game for business. The Sherman Act outlaws actions that restrain trade and outlaws the act of monopolization. The Clayton Act specifies the business practices that illegally restrain trade (price discrimination, mergers, tying contracts). The Federal Trade Commission Act established the Federal Trade Commission and banned unfair methods of competition. The Celler-Kefauver Act toughened the antimerger provisions of the Clayton Act. The "rule of reason" that only unreasonable restraint of trade violates the Sherman Act was applied by the courts until 1945. The rule of reason was apparently overturned in 1945 with the Alcoa decision when the courts ruled that size alone is a violation of the Sherman Act. In subsequent cases, the courts have ruled that monopolies created by superior technological achievement do not violate the Sherman Act.
8. Some of the alternative methods of controlling monopoly that have been proposed include a) deregulating natural monopolies and selling monopoly franchises to the highest bidder, b) placing consumer representatives on boards of directors, and c) repealing antitrust laws.

Key Terms

natural monopoly
regulatory lag
trust
rule of reason
horizontal merger
vertical merger
conglomerate merger

Questions and Problems

1. Explain why, in the case of a natural monopoly, there is not enough room in the industry for more than one producer.

2. Devise a set of rules that would, in your opinion, allow a government-owned natural monopoly to operate "in the public interest." Would these rules be different if the firm were not a natural monopoly?

3. You are the president of a regulated monopoly. You know that the regulators will allow you to set rates to cover operating costs plus a "fair" rate of return on invested capital. How would you behave? Would you behave differently if you were not regulated?

4. One explanation for why regulation of electric utilities has not made much of a difference in utility rates is that electric utilities face competition. How can a monopoly like an electric-power utility face competition and still be a monopoly?

5. You operate a regulated monopoly that sells in both a competitive and a monopolistic market. What steps would you take to improve your position in the competitive market?

6. Deregulation of the television-broadcasting industry has been opposed by the three major networks. How would deregulation affect their profits?

7. Explain the contradiction raised by the rule of reason.

8. Why would innovative and risk-taking firms such as Boeing and Eastman-Kodak oppose the Alcoa decision?

9. Evaluate the proposal to auction off monopoly franchises to the highest bidder. Why would this return most of the monopoly profits to the government?

10. "Several ill-informed people have suggested doing away with our antitrust laws. To do so would return us to the robber barons of the 19th century." Evaluate this statement.

11. Would regulatory lag tend to raise or lower economic efficiency? Why?

12. In which of the following cases would antitrust authorities be more likely to allow the merger?

    a. A merger of General Motors and Chrysler.

    b. A merger of Prudential Insurance with McDonald's Hamburgers.

    c. A merger of Hyatt Corporation and the bankrupt Braniff Airlines.

    d. A merger of U.S. Foods with Safeway Stores.

    e. A merger of U.S. Steel with Ford Motors.

    f. A merger of B. F. Goodrich with General Motors.

13. Economists who have studied the regulation of electric utilities have found that regulation hasn't had much of an effect on prices. How can this be when the regulators are able to set prices?

14. Explain why the definition of the market has become a crucial issue in antitrust law.

Suggested Readings

Baumol, William J. "Reasonable Rules for Rate Regulation: Plausible Policies in an Imperfect World." In *The Crisis of the Regulatory Commissions,* ed. Paul MacAvoy. New York: W. W. Norton, 1970, pp. 187–206.

Fisher, Franklyn, John J. McGowan, and Joen E. Greenwood. *Folded, Spindled, and Mutilated: Economic Analysis and* U.S. *v.* IBM. Cambridge: MIT Press, 1983.

Howard, Marshall C. *Antitrust and Trade Regulation: Selected Issues and Case Studies.* Englewood Cliffs, N.J.: Prentice-Hall, 1983.

Litan, Robert E. and William D. Nordhaus. *Reforming Federal Regulation.* New Haven: Yale University Press, 1983.

Mansfield, Edwin. *Monopoly Power and Economic Performance,* 3rd ed. New York: W. W. Norton, 1974, pp. 57–68.

Singer, Eugene. *Antitrust Economics.* Englewood Cliffs, N.J.: Prentice-Hall, 1968, chap. 2.

Swartz, Thomas R. and Frank J. Bonello, eds. *Taking Sides: Clashing Views on Controversial Economic Issues.* Guilford, Conn.: Duskin Publishing Group, 1982, pp. 58–73.

Weidenbaum, Murray L. *Business, Government and the Public,* 2nd ed. Englewood Cliffs, N.J.: Prentice-Hall, 1981.

White, Lawrence J. *Reforming Regulation: Processes and Problems.* Englewood Cliffs, N.J.: Prentice-Hall, 1981.

Williamson, Oliver. *Markets and Hierarchies: Analysis and Antitrust Implications.* New York: The Free Press, 1975.

Part **V**

Factor Markets

- Factor Markets
- Labor Markets
- Labor Unions
- Interest, Rent, and Profit
- Income Distribution and Poverty

35

Factor Markets

The individual firm operates in two distinct markets: the product (or output) market and the factor (or input) market. The preceding chapters focused on the firm's behavior as a seller in the product market. They studied how different degrees of competition in the market affect the firm's pricing and output decisions. Firms also act as buyers in the **factor market.**

> The **factor** (or input) **market** is the market in which firms purchase the land, labor, and capital inputs required to produce their output.

In terms of the circular-flow diagram (see Figure 1), the activities of firms in the product or output market (the upper half of the diagram) determine the solution to the *what* problem of economics. The activities of firms in the factor market (the lower half of the diagram) determine the solutions to the *how* and *for whom* problems.

This chapter examines the *how* and *for whom* problems by explaining how factor markets work.

The prices of labor, land, and capital are determined in factor markets, and these prices determine the incomes of the individuals and agents who own these productive factors.

This chapter identifies the main economic forces at work in the factor market. Rather than concentrating on one specific factor of production—like labor—this chapter will examine the general rules that govern the behavior of firms in factor markets. This chapter explains why the demand for the factors of production is a derived demand that depends upon the product market and how the prices the factor market assigns to the factors of production are the outcome of profit-maximizing decisions. Just as firms in the product market are motivated by profit maximization, the actions of firms in the factor market are also motivated by the desire to maximize profits. The rules for decisions made in both the product and factor markets actually boil down to a single general rule. ∎

Figure 1   The Circular Flow of Economic Activity

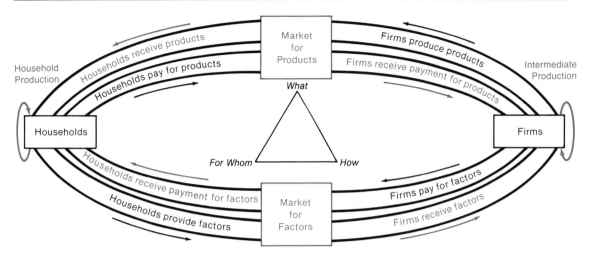

The circular-flow diagram shows that firms operate simultaneously in the product market and in the factor market. The upper half of the circular flow shows the flows of products and purchases between the business and household sectors. The bottom half shows the flows of factors from the households to business firms and the payment of factor income from business firms to households for the factors of production.

THE TWO FACES OF THE FIRM

The firm has two faces it displays to the outside world. One face is that of a *seller of the goods and services it produces* in product markets. As a seller, the firm can be either a price taker or a price searcher (as described in an earlier chapter). The other face is that of a *buyer of inputs* in factor markets. A firm can produce no output without factor inputs. In a factor market, the firm can again be either a price taker or a price searcher.

Price Searching and Price Taking in the Factor Market

The definitions of a **price taker** and **price searcher** in factor markets are analogous to the definitions of price takers and price searchers given in the chapters on product markets.

A **price taker** in a factor market is a buyer of an input whose purchases are not large enough to affect the price of the input. The price-taking firm must accept the market price as given.

A **price searcher** in a factor market is a buyer of inputs whose purchases are large enough to affect the price of the input.

Figure 2 shows the four possible market conditions the firm may face in its role as either a seller of products or a buyer of factor inputs and in its role as either a price taker or a price searcher:

1. The firm may be a price taker in both the product and factor markets—panels (a) and (b).
2. The firm may be a price searcher in both the product and factor markets—panels (c) and (d).
3. The firm may be a price taker in the product market and a price searcher in the factor market—panels (a) and (d).
4. The firm may be a price searcher in the product market and a price taker in the factor market—panels (b) and (c).

There is no necessary link between the amount of competition a firm faces on one side of the market and the amount it faces on the other side. A monopolist may purchase its land, labor, and capital inputs as a price taker. A perfectly competitive firm may be a price searcher in the factor market. Although there are numerous exceptions,

Figure 2   The Two Faces of the Firm: Product Market and Factor Market

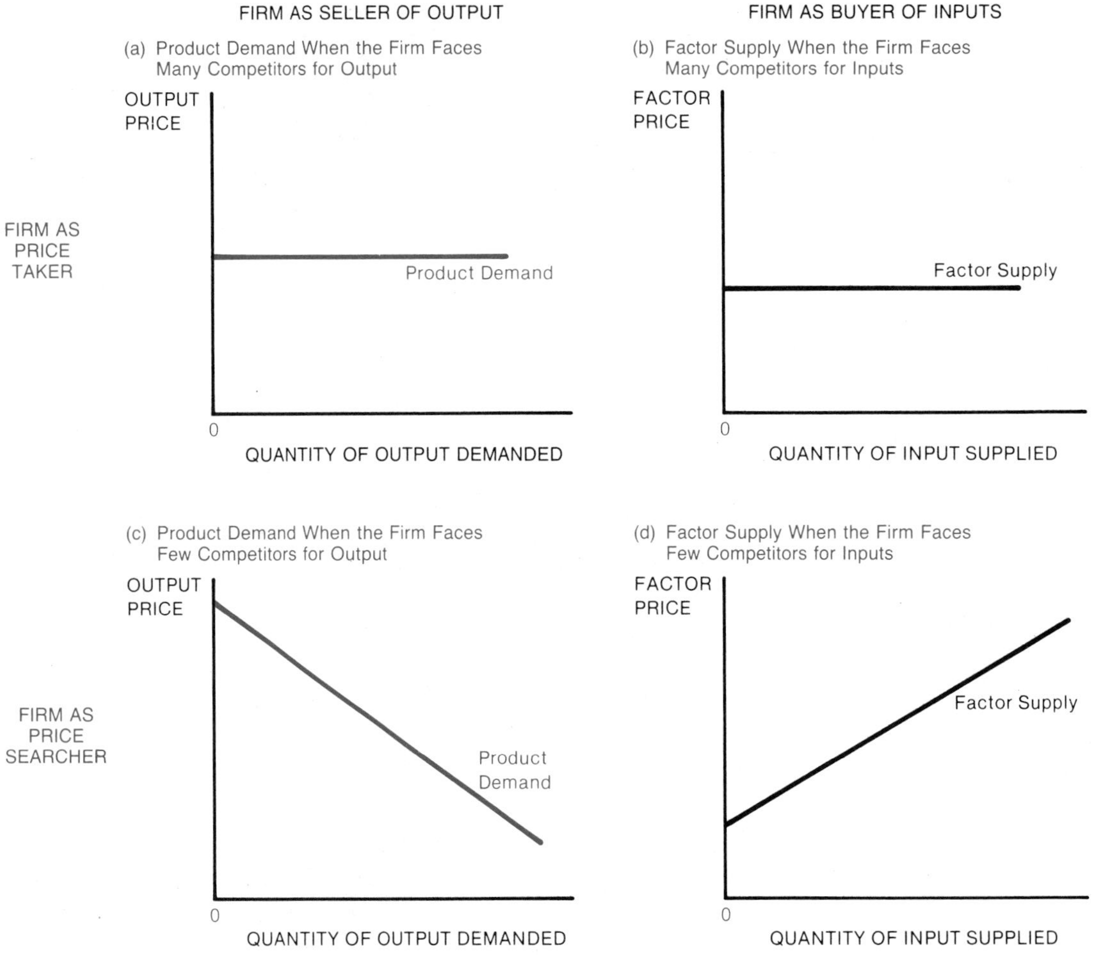

FIRM AS SELLER OF OUTPUT

FIRM AS BUYER OF INPUTS

(a) Product Demand When the Firm Faces
    Many Competitors for Output

(b) Factor Supply When the Firm Faces
    Many Competitors for Inputs

FIRM AS
PRICE
TAKER

OUTPUT
PRICE

FACTOR
PRICE

Product Demand

Factor Supply

0

0

QUANTITY OF OUTPUT DEMANDED

QUANTITY OF INPUT SUPPLIED

(c) Product Demand When the Firm Faces
    Few Competitors for Output

(d) Factor Supply When the Firm Faces
    Few Competitors for Inputs

FIRM AS
PRICE
SEARCHER

OUTPUT
PRICE

FACTOR
PRICE

Product
Demand

Factor Supply

0

0

QUANTITY OF OUTPUT DEMANDED

QUANTITY OF INPUT SUPPLIED

Panels (a) and (b) show a price-taking firm in the product and factor markets, respectively. Price taking on the product side means that the firm can sell all it wants at the existing market price (demand is perfectly elastic). Price taking in the factor market means that the firm can hire all the factors it wants at the prevailing factor price (factor supply is perfectly elastic).

Panels (c) and (d) show price searching in the product and factor markets, respectively. Price searching on the product side means that the firm faces a downward-sloping product demand curve—to sell more, it must lower its price. Price searching on the factor side means that the firm faces an upward-sloping factor supply curve. To hire more factor inputs, the firm must pay a higher factor price.

the most likely scenario is that the firm will face more competition on the input (factor) side than on the output (product) side. In selling its products, the firm faces competition from other firms that produce either the same product or a product that serves as a substitute for the goods it produces. As demonstrated in previous chapters, such competition may be limited. The picture is different in factor markets. Factors, unless highly specialized, can typically be used by different firms and by different industries. Essentially all firms compete with one another for skilled and unskilled labor; they all compete with one another for capital and for land.

Although some factors have use in only specific industries (for example, mountainous terrain is ill-suited to wheat farming but is well-suited to grape vineyards or vacation resorts), most factors can be used by a wide variety of industries. The firm, therefore, faces competition for inputs not only from those firms with which it competes in the product market but also from firms in entirely different industries. Oil companies, universities, law offices, and retailers all compete for skilled secretaries. Restaurants, motels, gas stations, retailers, and home builders all compete for land in major cities.

A firm will usually face more competition from other firms when hiring inputs than when selling outputs.

As with most generalizations, there are exceptions to the rule that firms face more competition on the input side than the output side. A textile mill located in a small, isolated town may face little competition from other employers in its hiring of local labor, while its sales on the output side may be in a perfectly (or near perfectly) competitive product market. Certain skilled people—professional athletes, for example—are so specialized that they are suited for employment in only one industry. The employer is, therefore, likely to be a price searcher in this factor market. Certain types of capital—such as oil-drilling rigs—are suited to only one use, unlike trucks, lathes, and computers. Firms purchasing such specialized equipment are more likely to be price searchers.

When the firm has the power to influence the price at which it purchases inputs, the firm has **monopsony** power.

A **monopsony** is a market in which buyers can affect the price of the product by altering the quantities they purchase. A *pure monopsony* is a market with only one buyer.

Like pure monopoly, pure monopsony is rare. Few firms are the sole buyer of a factor of production. Even if the isolated textile mill—which appears to have a monopsony over the local labor market as the sole major employer in town—offers wages that are too low, people may move to other cities, or outside firms might be attracted into the market by the prospect of cheap labor. This textile mill faces competition from factories located in other cities (in the case where people move) and also from new firms entering the local labor market.

Marginal Factor Cost

The concepts of marginal revenue and marginal cost play a decisive role in the theory of product markets described in the preceding chapters. Profit-maximizing firms produce that level of output at which marginal revenue and marginal costs are equal. If they follow the $MC = MR$ rule, they will maximize profits or minimize losses. In the theory of factor markets, there are concepts analogous to marginal cost and marginal benefit that are applicable to the input side of the firm. Inputs have costs and benefits to the firm, just as production has costs and benefits to the firm. In making its input decisions, the most important cost the firm must consider is the additional cost of hiring one more unit of an input, or **marginal factor cost (MFC)**.

Marginal factor cost (MFC) is the extra cost to the firm of using one more unit of a factor of production.

The marginal factor cost *(MFC)* of labor to the firm is, therefore, the extra cost of hiring one more unit of labor. The *MFC* of capital is the extra cost of using one more unit of capital.

The price of a factor of production is the wage (in the case of labor) or the rental (in the case of capital or land) that the firm must pay to hire or use the factor. Recall that, in the product market, price exceeds marginal revenue if the firm is a price searcher but that price equals marginal revenue when the firm is a price taker. Being a price taker means that the buyer is too small a part of the market to affect the factor's price.

In the factor market, if the firm is a price taker, marginal factor cost is simply the factor's market price. The firm can hire one more unit of the factor (or more than one unit) at the going market price. The firm's actions have no effect on the input's price.

If the firm is a price searcher in the factor market, the firm's marginal factor cost will exceed the market price of the factor. As a price searcher, the firm is a large enough portion of the

Example 1   The Many Faces of Coca Cola

Businesses operate in two markets: the product market and the factor market. A firm may be a perfectly competitive demander in the factor market and a monopolistic supplier in its product market, or it may be a monopsonist in the factor market and perfectly competitive in the product market. Coca Cola, for example, competes in its input markets as a perfect competitor for some factors and as a monopsonist for others. Coca Cola is the world's largest buyer of sugar. In fact, Coca Cola is such a large buyer that it can affect the price of sugar. If Coca Cola increases its buying of cane sugar, it drives up the price of cane sugar. If Coca Cola switches to corn-syrup sweeteners, it drives down the price of cane sugar. In other input markets, Coca Cola is a perfect competitor. In the labor market, Coca Cola is not an exceptionally large employer. By hiring more employees, Coca Cola does not bid up market wages. By buying more delivery trucks, Coca Cola does not affect truck prices. Thus, Coca Cola is both a monopsonist and a perfect competitor in its input markets. In its product market, Coca Cola is an oligopolist, competing with the other major soft-drink manufacturers such as Pepsi, Seven-Up, and Dr. Pepper. In its pricing and advertising decisions, it must take into account the reactions of its major rivals. ■

particular factor market so that it cannot buy more of the factor without driving up its market price. To use one more unit of the input per period, the firm must pay the same higher price for all units that it would need to pay for the last unit hired. In other words, the extra unit of the factor will cost the firm not only its market price but also the higher price paid on the previous units hired.

For example, Figure 3 shows that because Firm A is a price taker, it can rent as much farmland as it wants at the market price of $500 per acre. It currently rents 100 acres. Firm B is a price searcher that currently rents 1,000 acres at $500 per acre, but B would have to pay $500.10 to rent 1,001 acres. The marginal factor cost of Firm A is the market price of $500. The marginal factor cost of Firm B is the price of the 1,001st acre ($500.10) plus the $100 extra ($0.10 × 1,000) it must pay for the original 1,000 acres. Thus, the marginal factor cost of Firm B at an input level of 1,000 acres is $600.10.

In panel (a), Firm A is a price taker in the factor market (it can hire all of the input it wants at the market price). For this firm, the price of the input and the marginal factor cost are equal. In panel (b), Firm B is a price searcher in the factor market. To hire one more unit of more of the input, it must pay a higher price for that unit *and* raise the price it pays for all previous units. Its marginal factor cost is greater than the market price. Thus, B's *MFC* curve lies everywhere above the factor's supply curve.

For price searchers in factor markets, marginal factor cost is greater than the factor price.

As noted earlier, price taking is more likely in factor markets than is price searching (monopsony). The remainder of this chapter will deal with firms that are price takers in factor markets—firms in which marginal factor cost and factor price are the same. (A later chapter will examine the behavior of price-searching firms in the factor market.)

THE FIRM'S DEMAND FOR FACTORS OF PRODUCTION

The firm's demand for a factor input depends upon the input's physical productivity and upon the demand for the good the factor is being used to produce.

Marginal Physical Product

An earlier chapter analyzed the relationship between the **production function** and costs of production.

> The **production function** indicates the maximum amount of output that can be produced from different combinations of labor, capital, and land inputs.

Figure 3   Competition Versus Monopsony in the Market for Inputs

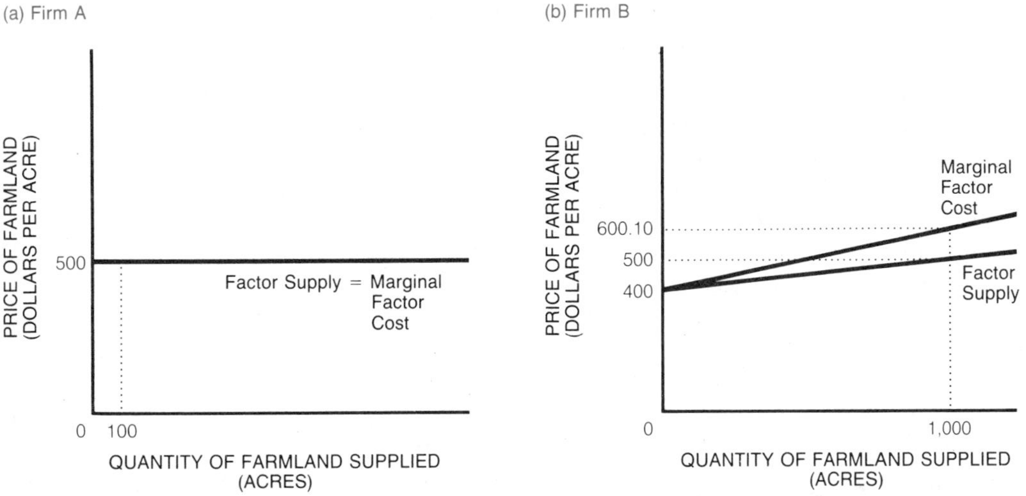

(a) Firm A

(b) Firm B

Panel (a) shows a price-taking firm that can hire all the inputs it wants at the going market price. The horizontal supply curve facing the firm is its marginal-factor-cost curve.

Panel (b) shows a price-searching firm on the factor side that must pay higher input prices to get larger quantities of the input. Since to use more input per period requires a higher price for all quantities of the input, the extra cost of hiring one more unit of the input is the price *plus the increase in the cost of using the old input quantity.* Thus, the *MFC* curve lies above the factor's supply curve.

A factor's **marginal physical product *(MPP)*** can be determined from the production function.

> The **marginal physical product *(MPP)*** of a factor of production is the increase in output per period that results from increasing the factor by one unit, holding all other inputs and the level of technology fixed.

Each factor's marginal contribution to output depends in part on how much of the factor is being used. A fundamental law of all production functions is the **law of diminishing returns.**

> The **law of diminishing returns** states that as ever larger quantities of a variable factor are combined with fixed amounts of the firm's other factors, the marginal physical product of the variable factor will eventually decline.

Derived Demand

Consumers buy products because they yield consumer satisfaction. The firm buys factors of production for a different reason. Inputs are purchased because they produce goods and services that create revenue for the firm. No matter how

productive the input is in producing output, that input will not be demanded unless it produces an output that commands a positive price in the marketplace. The garment industry buys sewing machines because they help to produce suits, shirts, and dresses that consumers will buy. Automobile workers are hired because they help produce automobiles that people will buy. Wheat land is rented because it yields wheat that people will consume. If the most productive tailor in the world made only three-armed shirts, the demand for the tailor's services would be zero because the demand for three-armed shirts is zero. The demand for workers, the demand for wheat land, and the demand for tailors are all examples of **derived demand.**

> The demand for a factor of production is a **derived demand** because it results (is derived) from the demand for the goods and services the factor of production helps produce.

The principle of derived demand is essential to understanding the workings of factor markets. If consumers reduce their demand for lettuce, the demand for workers employed in lettuce growing, the demand for farmland used for lettuce, and even the demand for water used in farm irrigation would also fall. When the demand for automobiles falls, there is unemployment in Detroit. When retail sales are permanently higher, rental rates paid on shopping-center land rise. When world demand for Boeing commercial aircraft is booming, employment in Seattle and Wichita (the cities where Boeing is located) rises. In short, the nature of the market for the good itself will be reflected in the derived demand for the factors used to produce it.

Joint Determination of Factor Demand

Another elementary but important fact about the demand for factors of production is that the production of a good requires the cooperation of different factors of production. Farmhands can produce no corn without corn land; corn land without farm labor is useless. Both corn land and farmhands require farm implements (ranging from hand tools to sophisticated farm machinery) to produce corn.

> **In general, the marginal physical product of any factor of production depends upon the quantity and quality of the cooperating factors of production.**

The marginal physical product of the farm worker will be less if the cooperating factor is one square yard of farmland than if it is one acre of land. The farm worker's *MPP* will be higher on one acre of fertile Iowa land than on one acre of rocky New England land. The *MPP* of the farm worker will be higher when working with modern heavy farm machinery than with hand implements. The interdependence of the marginal physical products of land, labor, and capital makes the problem of factor pricing in a market setting difficult to analyze.

Marginal Revenue Product

The demand for a factor of production—land, labor, or capital—is a derived demand. The dollar value of an extra worker, an extra unit of land, or an extra machine is that factor's **marginal revenue product** *(MRP)*—or the revenue from selling the marginal physical product *(MPP)* that the factor produces.

> The **marginal revenue product** *(MRP)* of any factor of production is the extra revenue generated by increasing the factor by one unit.

There are two ways of calculating a factor's marginal revenue product. Both approaches yield the same value.

Method 1.   The first method of calculating *MRP* is to simply change the quantity of the factor and observe the change in revenue. According to this direct method, *MRP* is the change in revenue divided by the change (increase or decrease) in the factor.

$$MRP = \frac{\Delta TR}{\Delta \text{Factor}}$$

Table 1 demonstrates this method. The different quantities of labor the firm employs are given in column (1), and the resulting output is given in column (2). Columns (1) and (2), therefore, represent the production function. Column (3) shows the market prices that clear the market for the various output levels produced. This firm is a price searcher in the product market because the price falls with higher output levels. The firm's total revenue (price times quantity of output) is given in column (4). Because marginal revenue product, in column (5), is the difference between the revenues generated at consecutive levels of labor input, it is recorded between the rows corresponding to the input levels. The revenue generated when one worker is employed is $95; the revenue when two workers are employed is $135. The *MRP* is, therefore, $135 − $95 = $40. In other words, the firm's total revenue would increase by $40 if the firm hired a second worker.

Method 2.   A factor's *MRP* can be calculated indirectly as well. The marginal physical product *(MPP)* is the increase in output associated with a one-unit increase in the factor but does not indicate the dollar value of this extra output. Marginal

Table 1 Marginal Revenue Product

Labor (workers), L (1)	Units of Output, Q (2)	Price P (3)	Total Revenue, TR (4) = (2) × (3)	Marginal Revenue Product, MRP (5) = (6) × (7) = Δ(4) ÷ Δ(1)	Marginal Revenue, MR (6) = Δ(4) ÷ Δ(2)	Units of Marginal Physical Product, MPP (7) = Δ(2)
0	0	$24	$ 0			
				$95	$19	5
1	5	19	95			
				40	10	4
2	9	15	135			
				9	3	3
3	12	12	144			

Columns (1) and (2) give the production function (the amount of output produced by 0, 1, 2, and 3 units of labor input). Columns (2) and (3) give the demand schedule facing the firm. Marginal revenue product (MRP) is calculated by taking the increase in total revenue associated with one-unit increases in the labor input. It can also be calculated by multiplying MR times MPP. Marginal revenue in column (6) is calculated by dividing the increase in revenue, in column (5), by the increase in output, which is the difference between rows in column (2). Marginal physical product in column (7) is the increase in output for every unit increase in the factor, or the difference between rows in column (2).

revenue (MR) indicates the increase in revenue associated with an increase in output of one unit.[1] Therefore:

$$MRP = MPP \times MR.$$

That this formula works for the price searcher is shown in Table 1. Because the firm increases its output from 5 to 9 units as a consequence of adding a second unit of labor, MPP equals 4. The 4 extra units of output add $40 to revenue, or $10 per extra unit ($40/4); therefore, the marginal revenue is $10. Using the formula, $MRP = MR \times MPP$, one can calculate that marginal revenue product equals $10 × 4, or $40. Thus, the indirect method of calculating MRP yields the same answer as the direct method. The MRP in column (5) is just the product of MR in column (6) and MPP in column (7).

To clarify why $MRP = MPP \times MR$, consider a corn farm that is a price taker in the output market. Because the firm must take the market price as given, price and marginal revenue are equal. On this farm, the marginal physical product of an

acre of land is 500 bushels, which means that an additional acre adds 500 bushels to the total output of the firm. The dollar value of the output produced by the additional acre of land is its marginal revenue product. As a price taker, the firm receives the prevailing market price of $4 per bushel. Therefore, the extra acre adds $4 × 500 bushels, or $2,000, to revenue; $2,000 is the MRP of an additional acre.

The marginal revenue product of a factor can be calculated directly by determining the increase in revenue at different input levels or indirectly by multiplying marginal physical product times marginal revenue.

PROFIT MAXIMIZATION

In the product market, the firm maximizes profit by producing that output at which marginal revenue and marginal cost are equal. The firm is also guided by profit maximization in the factor market. Profit-maximizing decisions in the product market are basically the same as profit-maximizing decisions in the factor market because deciding on the quantity of inputs determines the level of output.

1. For a price taker in the product market, $P \times MPP = MR \times MPP$. For a price searcher in the product market, $P \times MPP > MR \times MPP$. In intermediate textbooks, the product $P \times MPP$ is called the value of the marginal product.

Figure 4   Firm Equilibrium: The Hiring of Factor Inputs

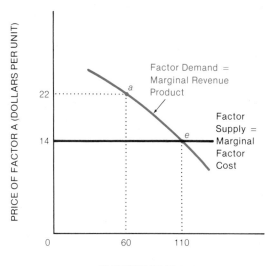

The firm's derived demand for Factor A is the marginal-revenue-product curve. The supply schedule of Factor A as seen by the firm is perfectly horizontal at the market price of $14. Equilibrium *(e)* will be reached at a price of $14 and a quantity of 110 units of Factor A. At this point, marginal revenue product equals marginal factor cost.

To understand how firms choose the profit-maximizing level of factor inputs, consider the case of a firm deciding how much unskilled labor to hire. *The firm will hire one more unit of unskilled labor if the extra revenue (the extra benefit) the firm derives from the sale of the output produced by the extra unit exceeds the marginal factor cost of the extra unit of unskilled labor.* Recall that if the firm is a price taker, marginal factor cost will be the market wage. As in any other economic activity, a firm will hire inputs to the point where marginal benefits equal marginal costs.

The *MRP* = *MFC* Rule

The firm will continue to hire inputs as long as their marginal revenue product *(MRP)* exceeds their marginal factor cost *(MFC)*. For a price taker in the factor market, the market prices of the inputs the firm uses (wage rates, rental rates,

interest rates) are the unchanging marginal factor costs of these inputs. The marginal benefit of an additional unit of factor input is its marginal revenue product. As long as the *MRP* exceeds the price of the input, it pays the firm to hire the factor. If the *MRP* of Factor A is $40 and its price is $30, it pays the firm to hire the factor. By hiring an additional unit of the factor, the firm increases its profit by $10 (= *MRP* − *MFC*).

Figure 4 shows the marginal-revenue-product curve of Factor A. The *MRP* curve is downward-sloping because the more of Factor A that is used, the lower will be its marginal physical product (because of the law of diminishing returns). Also, if the firm is a price searcher in the product market, higher levels of output mean a lower marginal revenue. Thus, as the quantity of Factor A increases, both *MPP* and *MR* tend to decline, so that *MRP* (which is *MR* × *MPP*) declines. The firm will hire Factor A until its price equals *MRP*.

> The *MRP* curve is the firm's demand curve for a factor because the firm hires that factor quantity at which the price of the factor equals the *MRP* of the factor.

The supply curve of Factor A to the firm is horizontal at the market price of $14. The factor price-taking firm can hire all it wants at $14. If the firm hired only 60 units of Factor A (point *a*), it would not maximize its profit: at 60 units, A's *MRP* equals $22 and A's *MFC* equals $14. The firm's incentive to hire additional factors continues as long as *MRP* exceeds $14. Thus, the firm will continue to hire to the point where *MRP* and *MFC* are equal, which occurs at 110 units of Factor A (point *e*). The firm will be in equilibrium (earning a maximum profit or minimizing its losses) when each factor is employed up to the point where marginal factor cost (which equals the price of the factor when the input market is competitive) equals the marginal revenue product of the factor.

> In equilibrium, $MRP_A = MFC_A$, $MRP_B = MFC_B$, and so on, where A and B are specific factors.

Table 2   Two Ways of Looking at Profit Maximization

Labor Hours, L (1)	Units of Marginal Physical Product, MPP (2)	Price Equals Marginal Revenue, P = MR (3)	Wage Equals Marginal Factor Cost, W = MFC (4)	Marginal Revenue Product, MRP (5) = (2) × (3)	Marginal Cost, MC (6) = (4) ÷ (2)
0 —					
	5	$10	$20	$50	$ 4
1 —					
	4	10	20	40	5
2 —					
	2	☐10☐	⊙20⊙	⊙20⊙	☐10☐
3 —					

This firm is a price taker on both sides of the market. Column (5) equals column (2) times column (3) because the additional revenue from one more unit of labor is simply the marginal product multiplied by the price (or marginal revenue). Column (6) equals column (4) divided by column (2) because marginal cost equals the wage per unit of marginal physical product.

The Two Sides of the Firm

In the product market, the rule of profit maximization is $MC = MR$. In the factor market, the rule is $MRP = MFC$ for each factor. These rules are logically the same. Recall that marginal cost is the mirror image of marginal physical product. That is:

$$MC = \frac{W}{MPP_L}, \qquad (1)$$

where MPP_L is the marginal physical product of labor and W is the wage rate.

The rule for profit maximization in the product market is:

$$MR = MC. \qquad (2)$$

Since MC equals W/MPP_L according to equation (1), equation (2) can be rewritten as:

$$W = MR \times MPP_L. \qquad (3)$$

Since the wage for a factor is equal to the marginal factor cost (when a firm is a price taker in the factor market), and since $MR \times MPP$ equals MRP, equation (3) can become:

$$MFC = MRP, \qquad (4)$$

which is the profit-maximizing rule in the factor market.

Table 2 provides a numerical example of how profit maximization in the product market is equivalent to profit maximization in the factor market. The firm is a price taker in both markets, so $W = MFC$ and $P = MR$. The product price is $10 and the wage rate is $20 per day. The marginal-physical-product schedule is given in columns (1) and (2) of Table 2. Column (3) shows MR (which equals P in this case), and column (4) shows MFC (which equals W in this case). Marginal revenue product is simply column (2) multiplied times column (3) and is shown in column (5). Marginal cost is the wage for an additional unit of labor divided by the change in output resulting from the additional unit, or $W \div MPP$, and is shown in column (6). When $P = MC$ (both $10), it is also true that $MRP = MFC$ (both $20). When one rule is satisfied, the other rule is also satisfied.

COST MINIMIZATION

The rules of profit maximization explain the behavior of firms in the factor market. These rules predict that firms will employ that level and combination of inputs that maximizes their profit. In the product market, firms produce that level of

Example 2   Marginal Revenue Product and Baseball Players

The proposition that factors of production will be paid their marginal revenue products is difficult to test empirically but is supported by the behavior of the market for star baseball players. Marginal-productivity theory teaches that firms will hire factors of production as long as the extra revenue (the *MRP*) of the factor is not lower than the wage. The *MRP* of an extra star player on a team that already has a large number of star players on its roster is likely to be lower than on a team with few star players. If the star player is the first star to be added to a roster, the *MRP* of that player would be very large, and the team's owners should be will-

ing to pay a high salary to that player. Teams with few star players are, therefore, likely to win the bidding war for star players. In 1975, a National Labor Relations Board ruling allowed certain players for the first time to sell their services to any team as free agents. Of the first 29 free agents signed, 20 were signed by teams that had poorer records than the teams they left. This pattern is exactly what the marginal-productivity theory predicts. ■

Source: Ronald G. Ehrenberg and Robert S. Smith, *Modern Labor Economics* (Glenview, Ill.: Scott, Foresman, 1982), pp. 55–56.

output (and charge the associated price) that maximizes their profit.

To maximize profit, it is necessary to minimize the cost of producing a given quantity of output. Thus far, we have explained how a firm selects the optimal level of *one* factor input. But firms produce output with cooperating factors. How will they know when they are combining *all* their inputs in a least-cost fashion? Suppose a firm has decided to produce 200 units of output and currently uses 15 labor hours and 25 machine hours to produce this output. The wage rate (the price of labor) is $5 per hour, and the rental rate on the machinery is $20 per hour. An extra hour of machine time costs four times as much as an extra hour of labor. The marginal physical product of capital is 30 units of output. The marginal physical product of labor is 10 units of output. An extra hour of machine time produces three times as much as an extra hour of labor. Is the firm using the optimal amount of labor and capital?

In this example, the firm is using too much capital and too little labor. If the firm were to substitute 3 hours of labor for one hour of capital, total output will not change, but costs will be reduced by $5. One hour of capital (at the margin) is three times as productive as one hour of labor. Adding 3 units of labor increases output by 30, and subtracting 1 machine hour decreases output by 30; there is no net change in output. However, cutting back on one machine hour saves $20, while hiring 3 more hours of labor costs $15. Output remains the same, but costs fall by $5.

What signals to the firm that a substitution of this sort will increase profits? The firm will look at marginal physical product *per dollar of cost*. In this example, because an extra hour of labor increases output by 10 units and increases costs by $5, an extra dollar spent on labor produces 2 units (10/$5) of output. Because an extra machine hour increases output by 30 units and increases costs by $20, an extra dollar spent on capital produces 1.5 units of output. In our example, a dollar spent on more labor is more effective than a dollar spent on more capital.

The marginal physical product *per dollar* of a factor is its *MPP* divided by its price. The price-taking firm takes both the wage rate for labor *(W)* and the rental rate on capital *(R)* as given. As the above example shows, if the marginal physical product per dollar of labor is greater than the marginal physical product per dollar of capital, the firm is not combining inputs in a least-cost fashion. It can produce the same output at lower cost by substituting labor for capital until:

$$\frac{MPP_L}{W} = \frac{MPP_K}{R},$$

where MPP_K is the marginal physical product of capital.

According to the least-cost rule, the firm is producing at minimum cost only if the marginal physical products per dollar of the various factors are equal.

Figure 5   Determination of the Market Price (Wage) of Truck Drivers in a Competitive Market

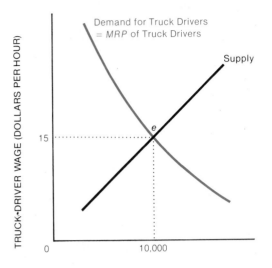

The market supply of truck drivers is upward-sloping, which indicates that individuals are prepared to work more hours as truck drivers at high wages than at low wages. The market demand curve is derived from the marginal-revenue-product curve of truck drivers across several industries. Equilibrium is achieved at point *e*, where the quantity supplied of truck drivers equals the quantity demanded. At the equilibrium wage of $15, there are 10,000 labor hours used in the various industries using truck drivers.

THE MARGINAL-PRODUCTIVITY THEORY OF INCOME DISTRIBUTION

Economists distinguish between the **functional distribution of income** and the **personal distribution of income.** Both are determined in the factor market.

The **functional distribution of income** is the distribution of income among the four broad classes of productive factors—land, labor, capital, and entrepreneurship.

The **personal distribution of income** is the distribution of income among households, or

how much income one family earns from the factors of production it owns relative to other families.

The profit-maximizing and least-cost rules resolve the *how* problem in economics. They show how firms go about combining inputs to produce output. These same rules also resolve the *for whom* problem.

Factors of production, unless they are highly specialized (such as 7-foot basketball players), are demanded by many firms and by many industries. For example, the market demand for truck drivers will come from a wide cross section of American industry: the steel industry, retailers, the moving industry, and the local florist will all have a derived demand for truck drivers. The demand for urban land will also come from a broad cross section of American industry: heavy industry requires land for its plant sites; motel chains require land for their motels; home builders require land to develop subdivisions. Similarly, the demand for capital goods will come from a cross section of American industry.

How the price (wage) of truck drivers is determined is shown in Figure 5. The wage rate of truck drivers reflects two forces: the derived demand for truck drivers as represented by their marginal revenue product and the supply of truck drivers. At equilibrium, the market wage will equate quantity supplied and quantity demanded, and the wage will equal the marginal revenue product. In other words, truck drivers will be paid their *MRP*. The same is true of the other factors of production. According to the **marginal-productivity theory of income distribution,** skilled labor and unskilled labor will be paid their respective *MRP*s. Capital goods will be paid their *MRP*s. Land will be paid its *MRP*.

According to the **marginal-productivity theory of income distribution,** the functional distribution of income between land, labor, and capital is determined by the relative marginal revenue products of the different factors of production. The price of each factor will equal the *MRP* of that factor.

Why some factors have high *MRP*s and others low *MRP*s will be discussed later in this chapter.

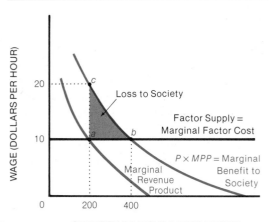

Figure 6   The Monopolist Hires Too Few Inputs

The firm is a monopolist in the product market and a price taker in the factor market. The value of the marginal product to society is $P \times MPP$ (the marginal benefit to society), and the marginal benefit to the monopolist is its marginal revenue product. If the wage rate is $10, the monopolist employs 200 labor hours because at that point marginal revenue product equals the wage. If the monopolist were forced to employ 400 labor hours, society would gain the area *abc*.

Marginal Productivity and Efficiency

The preceding chapters on product markets were interested in the relative efficiency of different market structures, particularly perfect competition and monopoly. It was argued that monopoly is inefficient because it creates contrived scarcity by failing to expand output to the point where price (the measure of the marginal benefit to society) and marginal cost (the measure of the extra cost to society) are equal.

If a firm has monopoly power in the product market, $P > MR$. Although the monopolistic firm will pay its inputs their marginal revenue products, which will equal $MR \times MPP$, the factor is actually worth $P \times MPP$ to society because each unit of output of MPP is valued at P. Because $MR \times MPP$ is less than $P \times MPP$, the monopolist is paying factors less than what they're worth to society.

Figure 6 illustrates a monopolist in the product market who is a price taker in the factor market. The curve $P \times MPP$ shows the marginal benefits

to society of an additional unit of the factor. The marginal-revenue-product curve shows the marginal benefit to the monopolist of hiring an additional unit to the factor. When the monopolist operates at point *a* rather than a point *b*, the monopolist stops hiring workers short of their marginal worth to society (or pays them less than they're worth to society, as represented by point *c*). The fact that the monopolist hires too little of the factor from the viewpoint of society is the other side of the coin to the conclusion that monopolists produce too little output from society's viewpoint.

If the firm is perfectly competitive in the product market, the marginal revenue product of a factor will be equal to the marginal benefit of the factor to society. Because price equals marginal revenue in a competitive firm, the firm will hire factors until the point where $P \times MPP$ equals the factor's price. Each factor adds a net marginal benefit to society equal to the factor's market price. This market price reflects its opportunity cost to society.

Marginal Productivity and Factor Incomes

The marginal-productivity theory of income distribution suggests that productive factors are usually paid their marginal revenue products. The marginal revenue product of one factor depends upon the quantity and quality of cooperating factors. Two textile workers, one in the United States and the other in India, may be equally skilled and diligent, but one works with a $50 sewing machine while the other works with a $100,000 advanced knitting machine. The New England farmer may be just as skilled as the Kansas farmer but may have a low MRP because of the low quality of the land. MRP also depends upon the supplies of factors. Residential land is quite limited in supply in Hawaii but abundantly supplied in Iowa. The equilibrium MRP of land is, therefore, higher in Hawaii. If women are limited to employment oportunities in only a few professions, they will *overcrowd* these professions and drive down the MRP and, thus, wages. Finally, MRP, as stated earlier, depends upon the demand for the product being produced. If product demand falls, so will the factor's MRP.

The marginal productivity theory of income distribution states that competitively determined factor price reflects the factor's marginal revenue product. *MRP* is the result of 1) the relative supplies of the different factors, 2) the quantity and quality of cooperating factors, and 3) the market demands for the goods the factors produce.

The Aggregate Production Function

The marginal-productivity theory of income distribution can be applied both widely and narrowly. In its narrow form, it can explain why one person earns more than another or why one plot of land rents for more than another. The aggregate economy is the summation of all the participants in the economy; therefore, it is possible to talk about average wages, average land-rental rates, and average interest rates. The economy churns out millions of goods and services using the different quantities and qualities of labor, capital, and land inputs at its disposal. The economy as a whole can be represented by an **aggregate production function.**

> The **aggregate production function** shows the relationship between the total output produced by the economy and the total labor, capital, and land inputs used by the economy.

The aggregate production function is a stark representation of the economy, but it is a useful tool for investigating the functional distribution of income among the broad factors of production—land, labor, and capital (see Figure 7).

To simplify the analysis, assume the economy produces only one product—corn—and that it is perfectly competitive in all markets. The demand curve for corn is then the marginal physical product of labor for the entire economy. If we assume that the price of a bushel of corn is $1, then the demand curve for corn measures both the marginal physical product and marginal revenue product for the entire economy and is also the demand curve for labor. The supply of labor is fixed at 50 million workers. The equilibrium wage rate is w_0, which brings about a quantity of labor demanded of 50 million (the quantity supplied).

The total output of the economy is the area under the demand curve in Figure 7 because the

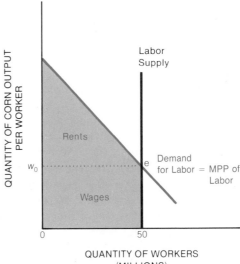

Figure 7 **The Aggregate Production Function and the Functional Distribution of Income**

This figure represents the aggregate production function of an entire economy. The economy produces a generalized physical output at a product price of $1. All markets are assumed to be perfectly competitive. Because the price of a unit of output is $1, the demand curve for labor is the marginal physical product of labor; it declines according to the law of diminishing returns. The vertical supply line represents the supply of labor, which is fixed at 50 million workers. The *MPP* curve will be the demand for labor, and the market wage will be set at w_0, where the quantity of labor supplied equals the quantity of labor demanded.

How much output has the economy produced and how much will go to labor? Each unit of labor adds to the economy's output. The area under the demand curve is the total output of the economy at that point. The 50 million workers will produce an output equal to the entire shaded area. Workers will receive their wage, w_0, times the number of workers. Their share of output is the shaded rectangle labeled *Wages*. The cooperating nonlabor factors (land and capital) will get what is left over, or the shaded triangle labeled *Rents*.

curve shows the additional corn produced by each worker.[2] Of this total output, labor will receive the area of the rectangle labeled *Wages* and the nonlabor factors, such as capital and land, will

---

2. The demand curve shows the *MPP* at each level of labor input. The *MPP*s for each successive unit of labor can be added together to yield total output. For 50 million workers, total output is the entire shaded area in Figure 7.

receive the area of the triangle labeled *Rents*. Each workers is paid the dollar value of the *MPP* of the 50 millionth unit rather than the dollar value of earlier units that have larger *MPP*s (as measured by the height of the demand curve).

The marginal-productivity theory states that the factors of production will be paid their marginal revenue products. If the world is sufficiently competitive, the theory suggests that the factors of production will be paid their marginal products.

Table 3 shows the actual distribution of earnings between labor and capital in the American business sector from 1948 to 1984. According to Table 3, the share of labor has remained fairly constant at around 65 percent of earnings (ranging from a low of 61 percent to a high of 66 percent), and the share of capital has ranged from 34 percent to 39 percent of total income.

Is the marginal-productivity theory consistent with these facts? Why should the labor share be roughly constant over this 36-year period? In fact, labor's share has been roughly constant since 1929. Between 1929 and 1984, the economy's capital stock more than doubled, while the number of hours worked increased only 20 percent.[3] Under these conditions why did not the share of capital increase?

The explanation can be found in the marginal-productivity theory of income distribution. Because the cooperating factor to labor—capital— has been increasing relative to labor, we would expect the marginal physical product of labor to rise relative to the marginal physical product of capital. This rise in the *MPP* of labor, according to marginal-productivity theory, would be reflected in an increase in the price of labor relative to the price of capital. Indeed, the price of labor (relative to capital) did indeed rise substantially over this period. The fact that the slower growth of labor was, therefore, offset by the increase in its relative price explains the constant shares of labor and capital.

This chapter gave an overview of how factor markets work, but each factor market—the labor

---

Table 3   Percentage Distribution of Earnings in the U.S. Private Business Sector, 1948–1984

Year	Labor	Capital
1948	62.2	37.8
1949	64.2	35.8
1950	61.3	38.7
1951	61.8	38.2
1952	64.8	35.2
1953	66.4	33.6
1954	66.1	33.9
1955	63.3	36.7
1956	63.9	36.1
1957	64.6	35.4
1958	64.6	35.4
1959	63.5	36.5
1960	63.6	36.4
1961	62.9	37.1
1962	62.2	37.8
1963	61.4	38.6
1964	61.6	38.4
1965	60.9	39.1
1966	61.8	38.2
1967	62.5	37.5
1968	62.9	37.1
1969	64.5	35.5
1970	65.8	34.2
1971	65.0	35.0
1972	65.6	34.4
1973	65.0	35.0
1974	66.4	33.6
1975	63.8	36.2
1976	63.9	36.1
1977	63.3	36.7
1978	64.3	35.7
1979	65.4	34.6
1980	65.5	34.5
1981	64.6	35.4
1982	65.9	34.1
1983	64.8	35.2
1984	63.3	36.7

Source: U.S. Department of Labor, Bureau of Labor Statistics, *Trends in Multifactor Productivity, 1948–81*, Bulletin 2178, September 1983, p. 20, 1982–1984 data estimated by authors.

---

market, the capital market, and the market for land—has its own special features. In the labor market, the supply of labor is determined by how individuals choose among market work, work in the home, and leisure. These are choices not faced by the owners of capital and land. Moreover, the labor market is affected by the organization of workers into unions and by the effect of

---

3. Edward Denison, *Accounting for Economic Growth in the United States, 1929–1969* (Washington, D.C.: The Brookings Institution, 1974), pp. 32, 54.

education and training on labor's marginal physical product. In the capital market, intertemporal choices are involved: buyers of capital can receive the benefits of capital over a long period of time; suppliers of capital must choose between consumption today and more consumption tomorrow. The market for land is characterized by the relative fixity of the supply of land.

The next three chapters will examine each factor market in detail, but these discussions will all be based upon the general theoretical framework established in this chapter.

Summary

1. Firms operate in two markets: the product (output) market and the factor (input) market. Firms sell their output in the product market, and they buy inputs to produce output in the factor market. The *what* problem is solved in the product market. The *how* and *for whom* problems are solved in the factor market. Marginal factor cost *(MFC)* is the extra cost of hiring one more unit of the factor of production. A price-searching firm in the factor market will have a marginal factor cost that is greater than price. A price taker in the input market will have a marginal factor cost equal to the price of the input.

2. The firm's demand for a factor of production will depend upon the demand for the product being produced and upon the factor's productivity. The marginal physical product *(MPP)* of a factor of production is the increase in output that results from increasing the factor by one unit, other things equal. The demand for a factor of production is a derived demand because it depends on the demand for the goods and services the factor helps produce. Production requires the cooperation of the factors of production. The marginal physical product of one factor will depend upon the quantity and quality of cooperating factors. Marginal revenue product *(MRP)* is the increase in revenue brought about by hiring one more unit of the factor of production.

3. Profit-maximizing firms will observe the following rule in factor markets: factors of production will be hired to the point where *MFC*

$= MRP$. The $MFC = MRP$ rule in the factor market is equivalent to the $MR = MC$ rule in the product market. If firms are perfectly competitive in the factor market, they will hire the various factors of production to the point where the *MRP* of each factor equals its price.

4. The least-cost rule for firms is to hire factors of production so that *MPP* per dollar of one factor equals the *MPP* per dollar of any other factor.

5. The marginal-productivity theory of income distribution explains the functional distribution of income (among the four classes of production factors) and the personal distribution of income (among households).

Key Terms

factor market
price taker
price searcher
monopsony
marginal factor cost *(MFC)*
production function
marginal physical product *(MPP)*
law of diminishing returns
derived demand
marginal revenue product *(MRP)*
functional distribution of income
personal distribution of income
marginal-productivity theory of income distribution
aggregate production function

Questions and Problems

1. The *MPP* of a 100th worker is 33 units of output. The marginal revenue of the firm for the corresponding level of output is $2, the price of the product is $3, and the wage rate is $99.
   a. Is the firm maximizing its profit?
   b. What would the wage rate have to be for 100 workers to maximize profit?

2. Explain how workers in Country X could earn $10 per hour while workers in the same industry in Country Y earn only $0.50 per hour.

Do the higher wages in Country X mean that workers in this country work harder than those in Country Y?

3. The last unit of land rented by a farmer costs $100 and increases output by 1,000 bushels. The last unit of capital costs $1,000 to rent and increases output by 20,000 bushels. Is this farmer minimizing costs? If not, what should he or she do?

4. In Soviet industry, capital has been growing about 10 times as fast as labor. What would you expect to happen to the marginal physical product of capital?

5. Evaluate the following statement: "Income distribution as explained by the marginal-productivity theory is entirely fair. After all, people are simply getting back what they personally have contributed to society."

6. A manufacturing plant in a small town accounts for 85 percent of employment in the town. The plant receives a large contract and decides to expand its work force by 40 percent. What will be the relationship between marginal factor cost and the wage rate in this case? Construct a graph to illustrate your answer.

7. One type of equipment—such as specialized oil-drilling equipment—can be used only in one particular industry. Another type—such as general-purpose lathes—can be used in a wide variety of industries. How would the amount of competition differ for these two types of equipment?

8. Complete Table A by filling in columns (4) and (5).

    a. Is the firm Table A describes a price searcher or a price taker in the product market?

    b. If the wage rate is $55, how many units of labor should the firm hire?

Table A

Labor (number of workers), L (1)	Units of Output, Q (2)	Price, P (3)	Units of Marginal Physical Product, MPP (4)	Marginal Revenue Product, MRP (5)
0	0	$8		
				$
1	10	8		
2	17	8		
3	23	8		
4	28	8		

9. Assume the MPP of a first worker is 20 units of output, the MPP of a second worker is 30 units, the MPP of a third worker is 20 units, and the MPP of a fourth worker is 15 units. If four workers are hired, how many units of output are produced?

Suggested Readings

Kohler, Heinz. *Intermediate Microeconomics: Theory and Applications,* 2nd ed. Glenview, Ill.: Scott, Foresman, 1986.

North, Douglass C. and Roger LeRoy Miller. *The Economics of Public Issues.* New York: Harper and Row, 1980, chap. 3.

Stigler, George, *The Theory of Price,* 3rd. ed. New York: Macmillan, 1966, chap. 14.

36

Labor Markets

This chapter will examine why some people earn more than others, why some jobs pay more than others, why wages and productivity are positively related, and why some people remain out of the labor force.

The preceding chapter showed that the profit-maximizing firm hires inputs up to the point where marginal factor cost *(MFC)* equals marginal revenue product *(MRP)*. This rule applies generally to the hiring of land, labor, and capital inputs. The labor market differs from other factor markets because of the human element. There are four special features of labor:

1. A person cannot be bought like an acre of land or a piece of equipment; slavery is against the law. Land and capital assets can be bought and sold, but the owner of labor can only rent out his or her labor services. A professional athlete may be under contract for a number of years; many workers in Japan appear to have lifetime labor contracts. But professional athletes and Japanese workers can be used only for the specific tasks designated in the contract; a slave, a piece of land, or a machine can be used for anything the owner wants.

2. Unlike the owner of land and capital, the owner of labor services can use his or her resources for useful alternatives to labor service. If land and machines are not put to productive use, they stand idle, and the owners do not normally benefit. When the owners of labor services do not engage in labor-market activity, they can spend time in work in the home or in leisure.

3. Land and capital do not care to which use they are put. The owners of labor services have preferences regarding the type of work they perform and the location of the work.

4. The existence of labor unions also differentiates labor from the other factors of production. Workers join together into labor unions in order to affect conditions in the labor market. *Labor unions* (to be discussed in the next chapter) are organizations that seek to affect the supply of and demand for the workers they represent and to establish rules and procedures concerning general employee/employer relationships.

This chapter will explain how supply, demand, and market equilibrium are determined in the labor market and will examine wage structure and alternative uses of time for the owners of labor services. ■

DEFINITIONS, FACTS, TRENDS

A market is an arrangement that allows buyers and sellers of a particular good or service to come together for the purpose of making transactions. The **labor market** is a market in this sense of the term. Its distinguishing feature is that labor services are being bought and sold rather than inanimate goods and services.

> A **labor market** is an arrangement whereby buyers and sellers of labor services come together to agree on working conditions such as compensation, fringe benefits, and hours of work. The agreement may be a formal contract or an informal, unwritten arrangement.

Labor markets differ in many ways. Labor markets may be national or local in scope. Examples of national and even international labor markets are the markets for some engineers, academics, airline pilots, and upper-level executives. Examples of local labor markets are the markets for sales clerks, teenage employees, unskilled workers, and sanitation workers.

Labor markets can also vary in their formality and structure. Some labor markets are highly informal. Job openings are announced by posting notices at the factory gate, by placing "help wanted" ads in the local newspaper, or by word of mouth. Other labor markets operate according to a well-defined set of rules. Government civil-service jobs are regulated by detailed legislation and rules. In unionized industries, rules governing hiring and firing are spelled out in considerable detail. Union rules may specify which employees are the first to be laid off, which tasks a worker can or cannot perform, or how overtime work is to be compensated.

The term *labor market*, therefore, encompasses a wide range of market behavior. If the buyer of a labor service must pay the wage rate dictated by the market regardless of how much labor is hired, the buyer is a price taker in the labor market. If the buyer of a labor service raises the wage rate by buying more and lowers it by buying less of a labor service, this buyer is a price searcher in the labor market and has monopsonistic power in the labor market. If the seller of a labor service must accept the market wage as given, the seller is a perfectly competitive seller of labor services. If the seller affects wage rates by selling more or less of the labor service, the seller has monopoly power in the labor market.

The discussion in this chapter deals only with perfectly competitive buyers of labor. As the preceding chapter argued, competition in the labor market (and other factor markets) is a relatively more common phenomenon than competition in the product market. (The next chapter on labor unions will deal explicitly with monopsony.)

To be useful, labor-market analysis must be able to explain observed trends and patterns in the labor market. Some of the empirical facts that economic analysis must account for in explaining labor market behavior are:

1. *Average hours worked per week have declined over the long run.* In 1914, workers in manufacturing worked an average of 49.4 hours per week (see Table 1). By 1982, this number had fallen to 38.9 hours per week.

2. *Real wages have risen over the long run.* After adjustment for inflation, the real hourly wage rate of American manufacturing workers increased more than 4 times between 1914 and 1982 (see Table 1). In other words, an hour of work in 1982 bought more than 4 times the quantity of goods and services as an hour of work in 1914.

3. *The labor-force participation rate of American women has risen dramatically over the last 50 years.* The *female labor-force participation rate* is the ratio of women 16 years or older in the labor force to the total number of women 16 years or older. Since 1930, the female labor-force participation rate has risen from 24.8 to 52.6 percent (Table 1).

4. *Some people earn more than others.* Coal miners earn about $12.50 per hour on average while textile workers earn $6.00 per hour. The president of a large corporation may earn $800,000 per year, a surgeon may earn $250,000 per year, a school teacher may earn $20,000 per year, and a roustabout on an offshore drilling rig may earn $45,000 per year.

The theory of labor-market behavior should be able to provide explanations for each of these facts.

Table 1   Facts About the Labor Market

Year	Average Hours Worked per Week in Manufacturing (1)	Index of Hourly Earnings in Manufacturing, 1900 = 100 (adjusted for inflation) (2)	Female Labor-Force Participation Rate (3)
1914	49.4	100	22.8 (1910)
1930	42.1	151	24.8
1940	38.1	214	27.4
1950	40.5	273	31.4
1960	39.7	348	34.8
1970	39.8	396	42.6
1975	39.4	408	45.9
1982	38.9	430	52.4
1983	40.1	434	52.7
1984	40.7	436	53.3

Sources: Hours and real wages are from Ronald Ehrenberg and Robert Smith, *Modern Labor Economics: Theory and Public Policy* (Glenview, Ill.: Scott, Foresman, 1982), Table 2.5. The female-participation-rate data are from *Historical Statistics of the United States: Colonial Times to the Present*, series D29–41, p. 133; and from *Statistical Abstract of the United States*, 1983, p. 407. Updated to 1984 from *Economic Report of the President*.

THE DEMAND FOR A SINGLE GRADE OF LABOR

The wage rate for a particular type of labor is determined in the labor market. The equilibrium wage rate/labor quantity combination is determined by the forces of demand for and supply of labor of that grade, just as product price/quantity combinations are determined by supply and demand.

The Firm's Demand for Labor

How does a firm decide how much labor of a single grade to hire at different wage rates? According to the preceding chapter, profit-maximizing firms hire factors up to the point where the marginal factor cost *(MFC)* equals the marginal revenue product *(MRP)* of the factor. The firm, therefore, will continue to hire labor as long as the marginal revenue product of the additional worker exceeds that worker's marginal factor cost. The firm in Figure 1 is perfectly competitive in the stenographer market (it must take the market wage rate as given), and its *MFC* is the market wage rate. This firm can hire all the labor it wants at the prevailing market wage rate. Its labor supply schedule is a horizontal line (perfectly elastic) at the market wage.

Columns (1) and (2) of Table 2 show the amounts of output that are associated with various amounts of labor input for this firm. Columns (3) and (4) give the marginal physical product and marginal revenue product for each level of input. Table 2 assumes that the firm's product will sell for $2 per page and that the capital input is fixed in the short run. Both columns (2) and (3) show that under these circumstances, the law of diminishing returns applies to the labor input. Figure 1 graphs the data from column (1) and (4) of Table 2.

This firm is a price taker in the product market as well as in the factor market; therefore, its *MRP* equals its product price, *P*, times labor's marginal physical product *(MPP)*. As the preceding chapter demonstrated, the firm will demand the quantity of labor at which $W = MRP$.

When the market wage is $28 per hour, the firm will demand that quantity of labor at which *MRP* is $28. Table 2 shows that the *MRP* of the second stenographer hour is $28; therefore, the firm will demand 2 stenographer hours. If the market wage falls to $16 per hour, the firm will no longer demand 2 stenographer hours because

Figure 1   The Firm's Demand for Stenographers

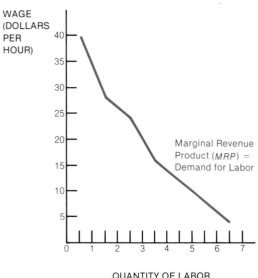

QUANTITY OF LABOR
(WORKER HOURS)

The labor demand curve shows the *MRP* of different quantities of labor hours. This firm is competitive in both the labor market and the product market. The firm uses 4 stenographer hours when the wage rate is $16 per hour (the *MRP* of the fourth hour is equal to the market wage of $16 per hour). If the market wage rate rises to $28 per hour, the $16 *MRP* of the fourth worker hour is well below the wage rate. The firm would not wish to employ 4 hours at a wage of $28 but would employ only 2 stenographer hours because the *MRP* of the second hour equals $28.

Table 2   The Demand for Stenographers

Labor Input (hours) (1)	Quantity of Output (pages transcribed) (2)	Marginal Physical Product, *MPP* (3)	Marginal Revenue Product, *MRP* = *P* × *MPP* (4)
0	0		
		20	$40
1	20		
		14	28
2	34		
		12	24
3	46		
		8	16
4	54		
		6	12
5	60		
		4	8
6	64		
		2	4
7	65		

The price of this firm's output is $2 per page. Its capital input is fixed in the short run.

$28 (the *MRP* of the second hour) is greater than $16 (the wage being paid), and the firm is paying for the last hour a wage that is less than the hour's contribution to the firm's revenue. The situation offers a profit opportunity to the firm; it would react by hiring more stenographer hours. As the firm increases employment, *MRP* will fall because of the law of diminishing returns. The firm will continue to increase labor until the last hours *MRP* just equals the market wage of $16. At a $16 wage, the firm would use 4 stenographer hours because the *MRP* of the fourth hour is $16. If the market wage had risen (instead of fallen), the firm would have reacted by hiring less labor. The quantity of labor demanded varies inversely with the wage rate, which can be seen by comparing columns (1) and (4) or by observing the

downward-sloping shape of the demand curve in Figure 1. More labor will be hired at lower wages than at higher wages, *ceteris paribus*.

The individual firm's demand curve for labor is its marginal-revenue-product curve.

The Market Demand for Labor

If there are 400 firms demanding stenographers, the market demand for stenographers is the summation of the demand of all 400 firms that purchase labor of that grade. The market demand curve shows how the total quantity of labor demanded varies as the wage changes.

The market demand curve for labor is a derived demand curve for labor that reflects the demands for the product that the particular grade of labor is used to produce.

A typical market demand curve for labor is given in Figure 2. This market demand curve for stenographers shows the quantities of a single grade of labor that are demanded by all 400 employers of that type of labor at different wage

Figure 2   The Market Demand for Stenographers

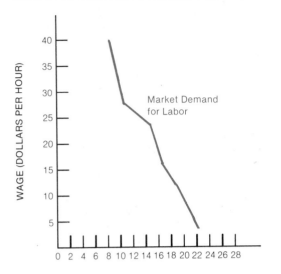

The market demand curve for stenographers indicates the number of stenographer hours that would be demanded by all firms that hire stenographers at different wage rates. Because the demand curves of each firm are negatively sloped, the market demand curve is also negatively sloped.

rates. Because the labor-demand curves of individual firms are negatively sloped, the market demand curve will be negatively sloped as well.[1]

Elasticity of Demand for Labor

The market demand also reflects the cooperation of labor with the other factors of production (land, capital, and other grades of labor). Just as the price elasticity of product demand curves reflects the responsiveness of quantity demanded to changes in product prices, so the price elasticity of labor-demand curves reflects the responsiveness of the quantity of labor demanded to changes in the wage rate.[2]

Three factors determine whether the market demand for labor of a single grade is elastic or inelastic: 1) the price elasticity of the product labor helps produce, 2) the substitutability of other factors, and 3) the ratio of labor costs to total costs.

The derived demand for labor will be more elastic the more price elastic is the demand for the product that labor produces. When labor costs rise, the cost of producing the product increases. Therefore, an increase in the wage rate is passed on in the form of a higher product price. When price elasticity is high, the quantity of the product demanded drops sharply with each price increase, and, hence, the quantity demanded of labor and other factors used in its production drops sharply. For example, the price elasticity of demand for meat cutters by one supermarket will be higher than the price elasticity of demand for all meat cutters, simply because the price elasticity of demand for supermarket A's beef will be higher than that for beef in general.

The derived demand for labor will be more elastic the easier it is to substitute other productive factors for labor. The more substitutes there are for anything, the greater the elasticity of demand. If machines are available that can do the work of people, the demand for workers will be more price elastic than if these machines were not available. The ease of substitution is also determined by technical factors.

The derived demand for labor will tend to be more elastic the greater is the ratio of labor costs to total costs. If costs for labor of a particular grade are a large fraction of total costs, a larger fraction of wage increases will be passed on to product buyers in the form of higher prices. The higher prices will cause a larger decline in the quantity demanded of output—and, hence, of labor—than if labor were a small fraction of costs.

Many real-world phenomena are explained by the elasticity of demand for labor. As the next

1. The market demand curve for labor is *not* the horizontal sum of all the individual demand curves for labor. The individual-firm demand curves for labor can hold product prices constant; but, as all the firms expand output, the fall in product prices affects the *MRP*s of the individual firms. It is still true that at any given wage rate, the market demand is the sum of all the individual-firm demands (in the quantity-demanded sense). In the demand-schedule sense, the market demand curve for labor will be steeper than the simple horizontal sum of the individual demand curves since the product price must fall to sell additional industry output.

2. The *elasticity of demand for labor* is defined as the percentage change in the quantity demanded of labor divided by the percentage change in the wage rate. If this ratio is greater than unity, demand is elastic. If it equals one, demand is unitary elastic. If it is less than one, demand is inelastic.

Example 1   Who Pays for the Employer Payroll Tax?

In 1985, employers and employees paid a social-security payroll tax of 7.05 percent of the first $38,500 in wages earned by an employee. Employees must pay the Social Security Administration an equivalent sum, which is deducted from their paychecks. By dividing the contribution equally between the employer and employee, it appears that employers foot a least one half of the bill for the social-security system. Is it true that the existing system splits the burden of financing social security equally between employer and employee?

A worker with a base wage of $10,758 per year is receiving only $10,000 (after deduction of the employee's share of the payroll tax), and the employer is paying $11,574 ($10,758 to the employee + $816 to the government). The total tax per employee, therefore, is $1,574 on wages of $10,000. Who bears the burden of this tax depends upon the price elasticities of demand and supply of labor.

The payroll tax causes a reduction in the demand for labor (a downward or leftward shift in the demand curve) because the firm wants fewer workers at the $11,436 wage than at the $10,000 wage. The demand curve shifts down by exactly the amount of the combined tax on the employer and employee, or by $1,574.

The accompanying figure shows that as the demand for labor falls as a result of a hypothetical $7 tax, the wage rate falls below what it would have been in the absence of the tax. The tax shifts the demand curve down by the vertical distance ae', and the wage drops from w_1 to w_2 (from $11 to $6 in this case). Employers now pay $13 rather than $11 as a result of the tax.

Who ultimately pays the tax? In order for the ultimate burden of the tax to be divided evenly between employer and employee the price elasticity of demand for labor would have to equal the price elasticity of supply. The accompanying figure presupposes that the price elasticity of demand is more than the price elasticity of supply, which means that employees are less price sensitive than employers and, hence, that they will pay more than their share.

Economists have sought to estimate what proportion of the employer's social-security contribution is passed on to employees in the form of lower

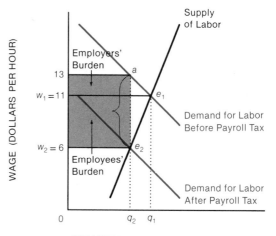

QUANTITY OF LABOR (WORKER HOURS)

wages. Although there is no unanimity, the most recent findings suggest that less than half (perhaps less than one third) of the increases in employer social-security taxes are passed on to the employee in the form of lower wages.   ∎

Source: Daniel Hamermesh, "New Estimates of the Incidence of the Payroll Tax," Southern Economic Journal 45 (February 1979): 1208–19; Ronald Ehrenberg, Robert Hutchens, and Robert Smith, Distribution of Unemployment Insurance Benefits and Costs, Technical Analysis Paper, no. 58, U.S. Department of Labor, October 1978.

chapter shows, the behavior of unions is affected by the elasticity of demand for the labor of union members. Why firms substitute capital for labor more readily in some industries than in others is also explained by the determinants of elasticity of demand for labor. The elasticity of demand for labor also explains who ultimately bears the burden of the social-security payroll tax (see Example 1).

Factors That Shift the Labor-Demand Curve

Factors other than wages can affect the demand curve for a particular grade of labor. The demand curve for labor will shift to the right (that is, demand will increase) if:

1. the demand for the final product produced using that grade of labor increases.

Example 2   Productivity and Wages in the United States, 1960–1984

The accompanying figure shows the pattern of compensation changes and productivity changes between 1960 and 1984. It illustrates the close positive relationship between wages and labor productivity. Economic theory provides an explanation for this relationship. Increases in labor productivity should cause the demand for labor to increase. As the demand for labor increases, the wage rate should rise, *ceteris paribus* (as long as the labor-supply curve is upward-sloping). Thus,

the positive relationship between labor productivity and wages is predicted by theory.

Notice that the correlation between wages and productivity is far from perfect. As the theory suggests, a number of factors affect the behavior of wages over time; productivity is only one of those factors. ■

Source: U.S. Bureau of the Census.

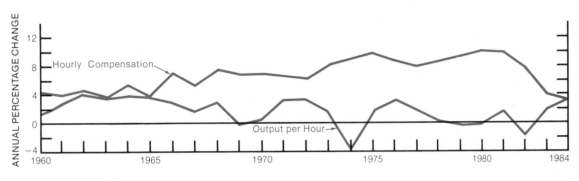

2. the price of a substitute factor of production increases.

3. the price of a complementary factor of production decreases.

4. the productivity (marginal physical product) of labor increases.

If the demand for the final product increases, there will be an increase in that product's price, *ceteris paribus*. This price increase will raise the marginal revenue product of labor, shifting the demand curve to the right.

Substitute factors are those that can be substituted for the type of labor in question in the process of production. Automated equipment may be sustituted for bank tellers; sophisticated word-processing equipment may be substituted for secretaries; skilled labor may be substituted for unskilled labor; the farmer may substitute chemical fertilizers for farm workers. If the prices of substitute factors increase, firms will increase their demand for labor.

Complementary factors are those that are used in combination with the factor in question. Mate-

rials, such as steel, aluminum, and plastics, are used in combination with labor to make automobiles, for example. If the prices of these materials rise, the demand for labor will fall.

When labor productivity increases, more output can be produced from the same amount of labor. When the marginal physical product of labor increases, *ceteris paribus*, the marginal revenue product of (and, therefore, the demand for) labor rises. The positive relationship between productivity and wages is explained by the fact that rising productivity increases the demand for labor, thereby raising wages. Competitive industries will pay a real wage *(W/P)* that equals the marginal physical product of labor because competitive firms hire to the point where $W = P \times MPP$. Accordingly, real wages should rise when the marginal physical product of labor rises. The phenomenon of increasing real wages noted in Table 1 is explained largely by rising labor productivity. Example 2 shows that there is a close (but not perfect) positive relationship between increases in average wages and increases in productivity. The main causes of labor-productivity improvements

Example 3   The Volunteer Army: Why Workers Are Paid Their Opportunity Costs

The U.S. all-volunteer army needs to attract 300,000 recruits yearly to keep the uniformed force at the targeted 2.1 million level. The armed services must recruit enough high-school graduates with average grades or above to fill high-technology positions. The armed services understand opportunity-cost principles. If a potential recruit can earn $600 per month in civilian employment (the opportunity cost of enlistment) but only $500 per month in pay and benefits in the armed services, that recruit is not being paid his or her opportunity costs and will not enlist.

Opportunity costs explain why the military had little difficulty meeting its quantity recruiting goals from the years 1981 to 1983. The military's success in meeting quality goals was even more remarkable. In 1980, 50 percent of the recruits had reading skills below the 9th-grade level. By 1983, 93 percent of the recruits were high-school graduates with average or above-average grades. Two factors explain these recruiting successes. First,

pay for new recruits increased from $447 per month at the beginning of 1980 to $574 in 1982. Recruits also receive free housing, food, and medical care along with travel and educational benefits. In addition to pay increases, the military offers an enlistment bonus of several thousand dollars. The second factor was the economic recessions of the early 1980s. The unemployment rate of young persons aged 18 to 19 rose from 14.6 percent in 1979 to 22.1 percent in 1982. Between 1979 and 1982, median weekly earnings of men 16–24 years old rose from $201 per week to $231 per week—a total increase of 15 percent and well below military pay increases for these years.

Military planners predict that the economic recovery of the mid-1980s will have an adverse effect on army recruiting. As the civilian economy improves, the opportunity costs of military careers increases. If military pay does not keep pace with improving conditions in the civilian economy, young people will opt for civilian jobs. ■

---

are increases in technological knowledge, increases in the volume of cooperating factors (particularly capital), and investment in human capital.

THE SUPPLY OF A SINGLE GRADE OF LABOR

Now that we've determined that the market demand curve for labor of a single grade is negatively sloped, what are the determinants of the supply of labor to buyers of a particular grade of labor?

The Labor-Supply Curve

If all other factors are held constant, the amount of a single grade of labor that will be supplied will depend on the wage rate offered by employers. Workers, in making their labor-supply choices, compare the wage they can earn in one occupation with their opportunity cost (the wage they could receive from employment in another occupation). The higher the wage offered for la-

bor of that grade, the greater will be the number of workers of that grade who offer their services.

Workers will typically be paid their opportunity cost. Employers must pay workers a wage that is at least equal to the opportunity cost of the next best alternative that the worker sacrifices in accepting that employment.

The employer who fails to pay workers their opportunity costs will have no workers because they would all take the next best alternative—which then becomes their best alternative. (See Example 3.)

Figure 3 is a representative market supply curve that shows the number of hours stenographers are willing to work at different wage rates. The supply curve is positively sloped because at higher wages stenographic employment becomes more attractive relative to employment in other occupations. Workers will, therefore, shift hours from other occupations for which they are qualified (receptionists, office managers, grocery-store clerks) into stenographic work. The market labor-

Figure 3   The Market Supply of Stenographers

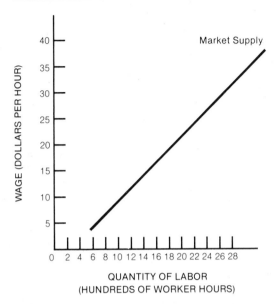

This market supply curve shows the number of hours stenographers are willing to work at different wage rates, all other things remaining the same. The labor supply curve is positively sloped because at higher wages, stenographic employment is more attractive relative to other types of employment.

supply curve is the summation of the individual labor-supply curves of stenographers.

Factors That Shift the Labor-Supply Curve

The labor-supply curve of Figure 3 is drawn holding all factors other than wages constant. There are two basic factors other than wages that affect the supply of labor to a particular occupation: 1) the wages that can be earned in other occupations and 2) the nonpecuniary aspects of the occupation. The wages paid in other occupations affect the supply of labor to a particular occupation. If receptionist wages increase, the supply of stenographers should fall, for example. The supply of labor responds to different types of work conditions. Other things remaining the same, people prefer to avoid heavy, unpleasant, or dangerous work or work in harsh climates. An increase in the unpleasantness or danger associated with a particular job (for example, an increase in the risk

Figure 4   Equilibrium in the Market for Stenographers

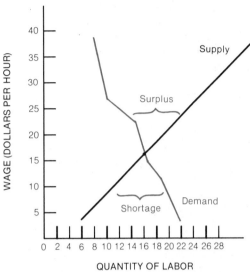

The market supply of stenographers (from Figure 3) and the market demand for stenographers (from Figure 2) are brought together in this figure. The equilibrium wage rate is $16 per hour. At the $16 wage, the quantity demanded (1,600 hours) equals the quantity supplied. At wage rates above $16, there is a surplus (quantity supplied exceeds quantity demanded); at wage rates below $16, there is a shortage of labor (quantity demanded exceeds quantity supplied).

of getting lung cancer in an asbestos factory) will cause a decrease in the supply of labor to that industry. Such an increase in the danger of the job would shift a supply curve leftward. The effect of unions on the supply of labor will be discussed in the next chapter on unions.

LABOR-MARKET EQUILIBRIUM

Wage rates are determined in a competitive labor market by the interaction of the forces of supply and demand. The market demand curve for labor of a single grade is negatively sloped; the market supply curve of labor of a single grade is positively sloped.

The market supply and demand curves for stenographers given in Figures 2 and 3 are brought together in Figure 4. The wage rate of $16 equates the quantity of stenographer hours sup-

Example 4   The Subminimum Wage

This chapter explains that wage rates for labor of a specific grade reach an equilibrium at which quantity demanded equals quantity supplied. Many economists argue that minimum-wage laws prevent specific labor markets from reaching equilibrium (the current minimum-wage law requires that employers pay $3.35 per hour). The result of minimum-wage laws is that very low-skilled and inexperienced workers (such as teenagers) are willing to work at the minimum wage but are unable to find jobs. In 1984, teenage unemployment reached 19.4 percent for all teens and 42.9 percent for black teens. As a response to this teenage unemployment, the Reagan administration has urged Congress to pass a "subminimum" wage of $2.50 per hour that would be in effect only during the summer months. By lowering the teenage minimum wage to $2.50, it is hoped that the disequilibrium between the number of teens wishing to work and the number of teenage jobs will be eliminated.

The subminimum wage is controversial. It is opposed by organized labor, which argues that the subminimum wage will cost adult jobs and raise employer profits. The subminimum-wage proposal is supported by the nation's black mayors who see it as a way to cut back on the social problems of summer teenage unemployment. The diversity of opinion surrounding this proposal is illustrated by the following two quotes:

> "It makes no sense to encourage employers to fire mothers and fathers in order to hire sons and daughters."
>
> —*Sen. Alan Cranston, D-Calif.*

> "If there were a subminimum-wage law, there would be an increase in total employment. For example, hotels might decide to keep their corridors cleaner by hiring kids; theaters might hire ushers once again; and we might have home delivery of packages again."
>
> —*Walter Williams, George Mason University*

■

Source of Quotes: *USA Today,* May 23, 1984.

---

plied with the quantity of stenographer hours demanded, or 1,600 hours. At any wage above $16, the number of hours stenographers wish to work exceeds the number demanded. At any wage below $16, the number of hours firms wish stenographers to work exceeds the number stenographers are willing to work.

> **The equilibrium wage rate in the labor market is that wage rate at which the quantity of labor demanded equals the quantity of labor supplied**

Labor Shortages and Surpluses

In a free labor market, wage rates adjust until they equal the equilibrium wage rate. If there is a **labor surplus,** some workers willing to work at the prevailing wage will be without jobs. Some will offer their sevices at lower wages and, thus, drive down the wage rate. If there is a **labor shortage,** some firms wishing to hire workers at the prevailing wage rate will go away empty-handed. Some will offer higher wages to attract employees and, thus, drive up wage rates.

A **labor surplus** occurs when the number of workers willing to work at the prevailing wage rate exceeds the number firms wish to employ at that wage rate.

A **labor shortage** occurs when the number of workers firms wish to hire at the prevailing wage rate exceeds the number willing to work at that wage rate.

In certain cases, wages are not permitted to adjust to equate quantity demanded with quantity supplied. Example 4 on the minimum wage explains what can happen in such a situation.

Shifts in Labor Supply and Demand

Unless something happens to prevent the labor market from seeking out the equilibrium wage, the market wage will be that wage which equates the quantity of labor demanded with the quantity of labor supplied. If any of the factors capable of shifting a demand or supply curve were to change, the equilibrium would be disrupted and a new wage rate would be established by the market.

Figure 5   Shifts in Labor Supply and Demand

(a) Labor Supply Decreases

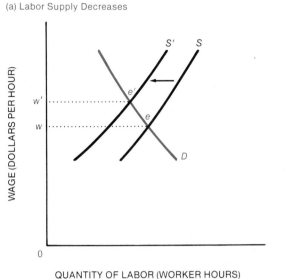

(b) Labor Demand Decreases

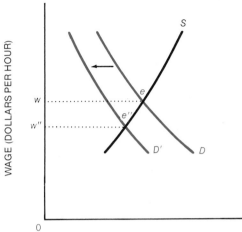

Panel (a) shows the effect of a decrease in the supply of labor. When there is a reduction in supply from S to S', there is a shortage of labor (firms want to use more worker hours than workers are willing to work) at the equilibrium wage, w. The competition among firms for labor will bid the wage up to w'. Panel (b) shows the effect of a decrease in demand. When the demand curve shifts from D to D', there is a surplus of labor (workers wish to work more hours than employers wish to use) at the original equilibrium wage. Competition among workers will drive the wage down to w".

Changes in conditions other than the wage rate can shift the supply or demand curve. The supply curve of labor may shift to the left because of higher wages in other occupations or increased health hazards on the job. As Figure 5 shows, if the supply of labor falls (shifts left) from S to S', there will be a shortage of labor at the wage, w, that initially equated quantity supplied and quantity demanded. Therefore, the wage will rise (to w'). If the demand for labor falls (shifts left), there will be a surplus of labor at the old wage, w, and the wage rate will fall to w". The possible causes of a demand reduction include a decline in labor productivity, a fall in the demand for the final product labor is used to produce, or a change in the prices of other inputs that cooperate with labor.

WAGE STRUCTURE

The preceding explanation of how the wage rate for labor of a single homogeneous grade is determined did not explain why some people earn more than others or why some occupations command a higher wage than others. These wage differences occur, very simply, because people are different and because jobs are different. Under competitive conditions, if all people were the same and if all jobs were the same, then everyone would earn the same wage.

Compensating Wage Differentials

Underground coal miners are paid more than workers in manufacturing industries in both capitalist and socialist countries. For example, miners in Canada earn 20 percent more than Canadian manufacturing workers. In Hungary and the Soviet Union, the percentages are even higher. In the United States in 1985, workers in coal mining were paid an average wage of $13.70 per hour–compared to the average wage of $8.32 per hour in nonagricultural industries.[3]

Why are coal miners paid more than other pro-

---

3. U.S. Department of Labor, *Employment and Earnings 29*, 3 (March 1982):80; Federal Reserve Bulletin, December 1984.

Figure 6   Wages in Coal Mining and Textiles

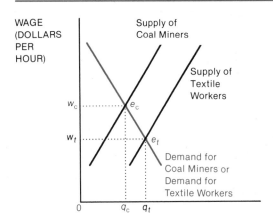

For simplicity, the demand curve for coal miners is assumed to be identical to the demand curve for textile workers. Wages are higher for coal miners because the quantity supplied of coal miners is less than the quantity supplied of textile workers at each wage rate.

duction workers? Coal mining does not require highly specialized skills or training; the skills that most manufacturing workers possess could readily be used in underground coal mining. The reason for the wage difference lies on the supply side of the labor market: jobs are different.

One of the factors capable of shifting the labor-supply curve is the general desirability of the job. People prefer to avoid dirty, monotonous, and dangerous jobs, other things equal. Coal mining is one of the most dangerous professions with a rate of 0.3 fatalities per million work hours. The fatality rate in minerals mining is 0.2 fatalities per million work hours (two thirds that of coal mining), and the hourly wage in minerals mining is 85 percent that of coal mining.[4]

Figure 6 shows the effect of differences in the danger of the occupation on relative wages. For simplicity, the demand curve for coal miners is assumed to be identical to the demand curve for textile workers. The labor-supply curves are quite different. The position of the coal miners' supply curve (higher than the textile workers' supply curve) reflects the fact that workers prefer, *ceteris*

paribus, less dangerous employment. To get an equivalent supply of coal miners, coal-mine employers must offer higher wages than textile employers.

This model can be used to explain a wide variety of **compensating wage differentials:** why welders on the Alaskan pipeline have to be paid so much (to compensate for the harsh climate and higher living costs) or why sanitation workers are usually better paid than clerical workers (to compensate for the unpleasantness and social stigma).

> **Compensating wage differentials** are the higher rewards (wages or fringe benefits) that must be paid workers to compensate them for undesirable job characteristics.

Numerous studies by economists have demonstrated that compensating wage differentials are indeed paid to offset undesirable job characteristics. Although individuals do differ a great deal (some enjoy heavy outdoor work and would detest office work; others enjoy work in the office but hate being outdoors), almost everyone wishes to avoid injury and disease. Eight separate studies by economists all show that wages are positively associated with the risk of being killed or seriously injured on the job. These studies show that workers receive, depending upon the job, between $20 and $300 more per year for every 1 in 10,000 increase in the death rate associated with a job.[5] As already noted, the occupational fatality rate in other mining occupations is two thirds that of coal mining, and coal miners earn an hourly wage 17 percent above minerals miners—even though both jobs require similar skills. Improvements in safety in coal mining would lead to a narrowing of this differential, according to economic theory.

Noncompeting Groups

The discussion of the labor market in this chapter has assumed to this point that all labor is the same (homogeneous). The difference in the wages earned by different workers was attributed to differences in job characteristics. In reality, both

4. *Statistical Abstract of the United States, 1981,* 102nd ed., p. 730.

5. Ronald Ehrenberg and Robert Smith, *Modern Labor Economics: Theory and Public Policy,* 2nd ed. (Glenview, Ill.: Scott, Foresman, 1985), chap. 8.

jobs *and* people are different. Because people are different, firms must take the trouble to distinguish high-productivity workers from low-productivity workers. Some individuals are qualified by mental and physical skills and training for a wide variety of occupations. Others are qualified for only a few occupations. Only a limited number of people have the peculiar abilites to become brain surgeons, trial lawyers, or theoretical physicists. Surgeons must have extremely sensitive and sure hands; trial lawyers must be articulate and be able to think quickly on their feet; and theoretical physicists must have an enormous analytical aptitude. The number of individuals qualified to be professional athletes is limited to those possessing the necessary physical attributes. On the other hand, the number of individuals who are qualified to be stock clerks, management trainees, factory workers, and so on is much greater.

Adam Smith pointed out that the natural differences among people are less than commonly supposed, while training is responsible for the significant differences among people. While the philosopher and electrician may not be genetically that different, background, education, and experience differentiate them to the point where it becomes difficult for electricians to compete with philosophers. Labor suppliers are divided into **noncompeting groups,** the existence of which has a substantial effect on the distribution of income.

> **Noncompeting groups** are groups of labor suppliers that are differentiated by natural ability and abilities acquired through education, training, and experience to the extent that one group does not compete with another for jobs.

If people were the same and had equal access to all occupations, the wage differences that would remain would be the consequence of different job conditions. The brain surgeon would earn as much as the garbage collector if the two jobs were equally desirable.[6] In the absence of differences in people, if brain surgery was regarded as a more pleasant job (or a higher-status job) than garbage collection, it is even conceivable that garbage collectors would receive higher wages.

Signaling and the Internal Labor Market

Because people are different, it is often costly for the potential employer to determine the marginal physical product of each worker. Employers typically do not know exactly how productive a potential employee will be in a particular position. The problem of gathering information on the marginal physical products of different workers is similar to the consumer's problem of gathering information on product quality and product prices discussed in an earlier chapter. Consumers solve the problem of costly information by buying brand names and by limiting searching time in the case of less expensive items. Employers have developed similar techniques to deal with the problem of distinguishing low-productivity workers from high-productivity workers.

Credentials or Screening. Employers must bear the costs of training employees, but they presumably want to minimize these costs by hiring the most able persons for the job. It is costly for firms to investigate intensively the backgrounds of potential employees or to administer comprehensive examinations designed to determine worker qualifications. When training costs (for example, the costs of teaching new employees how to operate sophisticated equipment) are substantial, firms will spend more on testing employees and investigating their backgrounds. A recent study by the Carnegie Foundation for the Advancement of Teaching, for example, found that corporations spent about $40 billion per year training employees. This expenditure approaches the total annual expenditures of U.S. colleges and universities. Companies like IBM who must expend large sums of money to train new employees do indeed devote considerable resources to **screening** potential employees.

> **Screening** is the process used by employers to raise the probability of selecting the most qualified workers on the basis of observable characteristics.

---

6. To become a brain surgeon may require years of study while the garbage collector may begin work immediately after schooling. Wage differences attributable to differences in the amount of training and education would still remain, but everyone would have the "opportunity" to become brain surgeons.

Employers can reduce screening costs by relying upon worker **signals.** Employers may know from experience, for example, that college graduates in math and business are on average more productive in certain occupations than high-school graduates or college graduates from other disciplines. Such employers, therefore, specify that a business or math degree is a requirement for the job. Employers may believe that, on the average, scholastic grades are an indicator of worker productivity. These employers may, therefore, specify that only students with a B average or better will be hired for particular positions.

> **Signals** are credentials or qualifications—such as formal schooling—that can be acquired by workers and that employers believe to be indicators of productivity

Workers try to send out signals to employers telling them that they are high-productivity workers. Because there are costs to the worker of acquiring the signal (such as a college education), however, the worker will weigh the costs and benefits he or she believes are associated with the signal before acquiring it. By requiring college degrees or minimum grade-point averages employers screen out job candidates who, on average, are not qualified for the job in question. The use of tested credentials allows them to reduce the costs of distinguishing qualified from unqualified job applicants. They know that these techniques will be correct only on average, however. They know that not every person who holds the desired credentials will actually be suited for the job, while some individuals who do not hold the right credentials may be ideally suited for the job.

Internal Labor Markets.   One way employers can resolve the problem of obtaining the best qualified persons with a minimum of hiring costs is to draw workers from an **internal labor market.**

> A firm establishes an **internal labor market** when it fills all jobs—from general laborers to top-level executives—except entry-level jobs by promoting or transferring workers already employed by the firm.

Entrance into the internal labor market is through general entry-level positions, such as management trainee, bookkeeper, or apprentice machinist. In internal labor markets, rules and established procedures determine who will be promoted and when, the role that the union organization will play, and the manner in which vacancies will be filled. Rather than screening potential employees on the basis of credentials, firms that rely on an internal labor market hire a large number of people without much testing, interviewing, or screening. A large department store will hire a large number of management trainees; a factory may hire a large number of general laborers. Once on the job, the management of the firm has the opportunity to observe job performance and to determine actual worker productivities. The major benefit of using the internal labor market to fill job vacancies is that the firm can learn a great deal about the person being considered for a job. The major cost of using the internal labor market is that the firm passes up the opportunity to hire more qualified persons from outside the firm by restricting its hiring and promotions to those already employed by the firm.

Monitoring Costs and the Principal/Agent Problem

The goal of the employer is to maximize the long-run profits of the firm. Employees often have personal objectives for their behavior that are different from the firm's objectives for employee behavior. The objective of one employee may be to maximize the amount of income earned on a particular job. Another employee may wish to minimize the amount of stress and exertion the job requires subject to earning a target level of income. Employees are different, and they behave differently. As long as the employer and employee have different objectives, a **principal/agent problem** exists.

> A **principal/agent problem** exists between the firm and any of its employees when the firm (as a principal) and the employee (as an agent) have different goals and objectives for the employee's behavior.

The employer cannot constantly monitor the performance of each employee because the information costs would be prohibitive. The size of the management staff would have to be increased dra-

Example 5   Stock Options and Attendance Bonuses in Incentive-Pay Contracts

A principal/agent problem exists when the goals of the agent differ from the goals of the principal. In modern corporations, the principals (the ownership of the corporation as represented by an elected board of directors) seeks to ensure that the hired managerial agents (the president, vice-presidents, department heads, and so on) pursue goals that are the same as those of the principal. The principal wishes its agents to maximize the long-run profits of the corporation. Long-run profits will raise the share values of the principal's stock. One common incentive mechanism is to grant managerial employees stock options. A *stock option* is the right to purchase shores of stock at a fixed price (say, the share price on the date the managerial employee was hired). Stock options, therefore, make the managerial employee interested in long-run profitability that will raise the share value of the corporation's stock. Higher share prices mean that the employee can make an instant profit on share purchases. The principal need not monitor the managerial employee as long as the employee's main objective is to maximize the share value of the stock.

Another incentive device used by the ownership of professional sports teams (the principal) is an attendance bonus for star players. The star baseball player receives a substantial bonus, for example, if annual attendance exceeds a specified target. The principal's profit depends upon attendance, and if the principal's star players are also interested in attendance, they will play to maximize the number of games won, which stimulates attendance. Less general incentive contracts (based, say, upon the number of strike-outs a pitcher accumulates) may cause perverse behavior that leads to lost games. The pitcher may maximize strike-outs but at the expense of an excessive number of base-on-balls.

Stock option and attendance contracts work best if granted to individuals whose performance can make a difference. Rank-and-file workers, if granted stock options, would conclude that their performance will not affect long-run corporation profits. Professional athletes of nonstar quality would realize that their performance does not affect attendance. Neither would be motivated to better performance. ■

---

matically in order to observe the performance of each worker. When workers are part of a team, it is even more difficult to monitor the productivity of any one member of the team. When it is easy to monitor performance (as in the case of salespersons), the principal/agent problem is less difficult to solve. Firms attempt to minimize the principal/agent problem in a number of ways. To prevent assembly-line workers from shirking, the firm may pay workers extra bonuses for exceeding production norms or goals. Professional athletes may be given performance-based incentive contracts. A baseball player may be given a bonus for every extra-base hit over 50 in a season; a football running back may be given a bonus for gaining more than 1,000 yards per season. A company may give its employees an annual bonus if the company exceeds a profit target. All these bonus and incentive schemes are designed to improve the work performance of the agent (the worker) without raising the monitoring costs of the principal (the employer).

It is not easy to design incentive-pay systems that eliminate the principal/agent problem. Assembly-line workers may achieve their bonuses by increasing the quantity of output but in the process may reduce the quality of their work. Employers may find that more output is coming off the assembly line but that more of it is of unacceptable quality. Professional baseball players may lose games for their employers by attempting to get extra-base hits when a sacrifice fly is required. When workers whose bonuses depend upon company profits feel they are too small a part of the company to affect company profitability, the incentive scheme has no effect on their performance. The more specific the incentive target, the more likely the employee is to achieve the target by sacrificing some other worthwhile outcome (such as sacrificing quality for quantity). The more general the incentive target—such as a bonus based on company profits—the less likely the employee is to believe that his or her actions affect the outcome. (See Example 5.)

LEISURE AND HOUSEHOLD PRODUCTION

Individuals do have options other than work in the labor force. These other options have an effect upon the total supply of labor to the economy. Individuals must choose among work in the labor force, **household production,** and **leisure.**

Household production is work in the home, including such activities as meal preparation, do-it-yourself repair, child rearing, and cleaning.

Leisure is time spent in any activity other than work in the labor force or work in the home.

What determines how an individual will allocate his or her time among these three activities? The theory of the allocation of time developed by Gary Becker, Jacob Mincer, Yoram Ben Porath, and others is designed to analyze this choice in the framework of rational economic decision making.

Labor/Leisure Choices

The opportunity cost of leisure is the income (or household production) that must be given up to enjoy leisure. The opportunity cost of leisure, therefore, rises when the price of market work rises. If real wages have risen over time, one would expect the quantity of market work that each person performs to have increased over time. As Table 1 shows, real wages have in fact risen, while average hours worked per week have declined dramatically.

The evidence in Table 1 suggests that the labor-supply curve representing the relationship between wages and hours worked per person is *backward-bending* (it has a section with a negative slope), as shown in Figure 7. When the wage rate rises, two things happen: First, leisure becomes more expensive to the individual. Second, the individual's income increases. When leisure becomes more expensive because its opportunity cost (earnings sacrificed) has increased, *leisure is discouraged;* when income rises, *leisure is encouraged.*

The chapter on demand and utility identified

Figure 7   The Backward-Bending Labor-Supply Curve

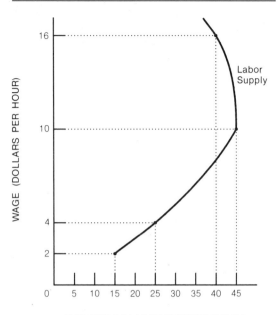

QUANTITY OF LABOR (WORKER HOURS)

The labor supply curve is upward-sloping until a wage of $10 per hour is reached. Below $10 the substitution effect of higher wages dominates the income effect of higher wages. At wage rates above $10, the quantity of labor supplied falls as the wage rate increases because the income effect dominates the substitution effect.

two effects of a price change on the consumption of goods: the *income effect* (the impact of the change in real income that results from a price change) and the *substitution effect* (the substitution of cheaper goods for more expensive goods that results from a price change).

The increase in wages (or the "price" of leisure) also results in income and substitution effects. The increase in the relative price of leisure (that occurs when wages rise) motivates individuals to substitute other things—in this case market work—for leisure, thereby discouraging leisure. On the other hand, the increase in wages increases income (an income effect), making more income available for leisure. Typically, as income rises, more consumption of a good occurs—if the good is a *normal good* (a good the demand for which increases as income rises). If the substitution effect of a wage increase discourages leisure, and the income effect of a wage increase encour-

Example 6   Animal Workers and the Backward-Bending Labor-Supply Curve

Economic theory teaches that as wages increase, workers can afford to "buy" more leisure. Eventually, their increased willingness to buy more leisure outweighs the opportunity cost of forgoing earnings, and higher wages can actually cause people to work less. The labor-supply curve bends backward after a high level of wages is reached. Indeed, American workers over the past century have opted to work fewer hours and to demand more leisure as real wages have risen.

Surprisingly, the backward-bending labor-supply curve characterizes the behavior of animal workers as well as human workers. Economists have conducted experiments with animal workers (in this case pigeons) in which they observe how the hours worked by animal workers change as the animal's wage rate changes. Pigeons were trained to work at key pecking and treadle running. In one such experiment, the wage rate of pigeons (the amount of mixed pigeon grains "paid out" per unit of work) was varied and the amount of pigeon work time was recorded for each wage rate. The results of this experiment, as graphed in the accompanying figure, show that pigeon workers first increase their hours worked as the wage rate rises, but eventually they cut back on hours worked as the wage rate rises. (Wages are ex-

pressed as an index. The "100" level denotes a wage rate of 1 grain of food per 100 pecks, but at the *higher* levels 1 grain of food was paid out for *fewer* pecks.) ■

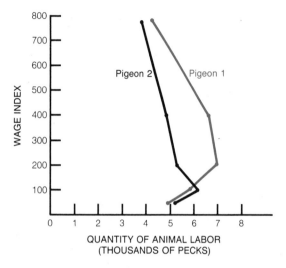

Source: Raymond Battalio, Leonard Green, and John Kagel, "Income-Leisure Trade-Offs of Animal Workers," *American Economic Review,* September 1981, pp. 621–32.

ages leisure, what then will be the overall effect on leisure of the wage increase? The overall effect depends upon which effect is stronger, the substitution effect or the income effect.

In Figure 7, when the wage is only $2 per hour and hours worked are only 15 hours per week, a dollar increase in wages adds up to only an additional $15 per week; the income effect is weak. When wages are $4 per hour and hours worked are 25 per week, a dollar increase in wages is like an extra $25 per week; the income effect is stronger. When wages are $10 per hour and 45 hours are worked per week, the income effect is even stronger. Figure 7 assumes that the income effect begins to dominate the substitution effect after wages reach $10 per hour. Further increases in wages cause hours worked per person to actually decline, as shown by the backward-bending section of the labor-supply curve.

The data presented in Table 1 suggest that in the long run the income effect is stronger than the substitution effect, which explains why average hours worked per week have been dropping despite rising real wages. The data are generally consistent with a backward-bending labor-supply curve. (See Example 6.)

Over the long run, mechanization has raised labor productivity, which translates into higher real wages. Higher real earnings enable people to opt for more leisure and fewer hours worked. The ultimate payoff of mechanization is that it has enabled people to have more leisure while still earning high incomes.

Wages and Household Production

One explanation for the dramatic rise in the labor-force participation rate of women reported in Table 1 is that the social roles of men and women have been changing. High divorce rates, a larger number of one-parent families, an increase in the number of part-time jobs, the growth of service and sales employment, and the enforcement of antidiscrimination legislation help explain rising female labor-force participation.

Economic theory provides another plausible explanation. According to economic theory, whether people work in the labor force or in household production depends in part upon the value of their household production relative to the wage they could earn in market employment. If work in the home (child rearing, cleaning, food preparation) is worth, say, $10 per hour, and the market wage a woman could earn in the labor market is $8 per hour, she would not enter the labor force. If, however, the market wages of women rise more rapidly than the value of household production, then one would expect women to enter the labor force. The rise in the real wages of women in recent decades is the explanation cited by some economists for the rise in the labor-force participation rates of women.

This chapter examined how labor markets work. The next chapter will take a look at the effect of labor unions on the labor market.

Summary

1. Labor markets operate like other factor markets, but labor is different because workers desire leisure and because workers have preferences concerning different jobs. Labor cannot be bought and sold like the other factors of production. A labor market brings buyers and sellers of labor services together. If the buyer of the labor service must accept the market wage as given, this buyer is perfectly competitive in the labor market. If the buyer affects wage rates, the buyer has some monopsonist power.

2. Individual firms hire labor to the point where $MFC = MRP$. The firm's MRP schedule is its labor demand schedule. The labor-demand curve will be negatively sloped both for firms and for the market. The labor-demand curve will shift if demand for the firm's final product changes, if the price of either substitute factors or complementary factors changes, or if the productivity of labor changes.

3. The labor-supply curve for a particular occupation will be positively sloped because workers must be paid their opportunity costs. The labor-supply curve will shift if job conditions or wages in other industries change.

4. The market wage rate is typically that wage at which the quantity demanded of labor of a single grade equals the quantity supplied. A shortage exists when the quantity demanded exceeds the quantity supplied at that wage. A surplus exists when the quantity supplied exceeds the quantity demanded at that wage. A new equilibrium wage/quantity combination will result when either the market supply or market demand curve shifts because of changes in productivity, product prices, the prices of other factors, or job conditions.

5. The theory of labor markets explains why workers in dangerous occupations are paid more. Noncompeting groups are workers with different abilities who do not compete for the same jobs. In the real world, it is costly for employers to determine the real productivities of potential employees. They therefore use signals, and internal labor markets to distinguish high-productivity workers. Employers use incentive-pay schemes to deal with the principal/agent problem.

6. When wage rates in general rise, the opportunity cost of leisure increases as does income. Whether the aggregate labor-supply curve will be backward-bending depends upon the relative strengths of the income and substitution effects. Whether people work in household production or in the market labor force depends upon the value of time in the home compared to their market wage.

Key Terms

labor market
labor surplus
labor shortage
compensating wage differentials
noncompeting groups
screening

signals
internal labor market
principal/agent problem
household production
leisure

Questions and Problems

1. Explain why labor's special features cause the labor market to work differently from the other factor markets.

2. Take a firm that fills all positions by promoting from within. What is this firm's strategy with regard to information and screening costs?

3. A price-taking firm in both its product and factor markets is currently employing 25 workers. The 25th worker's *MRP* is $300 per week and the worker's wage is $200 per week. Is this firm maximizing its profits? If not, what would you advise the company to do?

4. This chapter has shown that there is a close positive association between labor productivity and wages. Using the theory presented in this chapter, explain this relationship.

5. State law in New Jersey requires that employees in licensed gambling casinos be residents of New Jersey for a specified period of time. What effect does this legislation have upon the elasticity of demand for casino employees in New Jersey? What effect does this legislation have upon the incidence of the employee payroll tax?

6. During recessions and periods of falling wages, the number of volunteers for the all-volunteer army rises. Using the economic theory of this chapter, explain why this supply of labor rises.

7. Explain why a worker in India earns much less than a worker in West Germany.

8. "If all jobs were the same, everyone would earn the same wage." Evaluate this statement.

9. "If all people were the same, everyone would earn the same wage." Evaluate this statement.

10. You are a surgeon earning $200,000 per year. When the demand for your services increases, the charge for each operation increases by 25 percent. What effect will this increase have on the number of operations you perform?

11. Rank each of the following jobs according to the difficulty of devising an incentive-pay system for the job that is compatible with the overall objectives of the firm. Explain your ranking.

a. Janitorial work performed at night in an office building.
b. Assembly-line work in a washing-machine factory.
c. Traveling sales work.
d. The creation of hand-carved figures for a crafts company.
e. Professional basketball playing.

12. "If there were no monitoring costs, there would be no principal/agent problem between firms and employees." Evaluate this statement.

13. Referring to Table 2, explain what would happen to the wage of stenographers if the number of pages produced per hour were to double for each level of labor input. Explain what would happen if the price of the product fell to $1.

Suggested Readings

Addison, John T. and W. Stanley Siebert. *The Market for Labor: An Analytical Treatment.* Glenview, Ill.: Scott, Foresman, 1979.

Becker, Gary. *Human Capital,* 2nd ed. New York: National Bureau of Economic Research, 1975.

Doeringer, Peter and Michael Piore. *Internal Labor Markets and Manpower Analysis.* Lexington, Mass.: D.C. Heath, 1971.

Dunlop, John T. and Walter Galenson, eds. *Labor in the Twentieth Century.* New York: Academic Press, 1978.

Ehrenberg, Ronald G. and Robert S. Smith. *Modern Labor Economics: Theory and Public Policy,* 2nd ed. Glenview, Ill.: Scott, Foresman, 1985.

Reynolds, Lloyd E. *Labor Economics and Labor Relations,* 8th ed. Englewood Cliffs, N.J.: Prentice-Hall, 1982.

Welch, Finis. *Minimum Wages: Issues and Evidence.* Washington, D.C.: American Enterprise Institute, 1978.

37

Labor Unions

Chapter Preview

Labor unions are an integral part of modern capitalist economies. Some people view labor unions as a positive force for justice, equality, and even economic efficiency and believe unions protect workers from the monopsony power of employers. Others see labor unions as monopolistic and often corrupt organizations that benefit their own members while imposing costs on nonmembers and on society as a whole. Some economists argue that the economic role of labor unions is substantial, while others maintain that the power of unions to affect wages and employment has been exaggerated.

This chapter will examine the role of labor unions in the labor market and will discuss the history of the American labor movement and the effects of unions on wages, employment, and economic efficiency.

Workers in the same industry, with the same general occupation, or with some other characteristic in common may join together in a **labor union.**

> A **labor union** is a collective organization of workers and employees whose objective is to improve conditions of pay and work.

The labor union's primary objectives are to improve the pecuniary and nonpecuniary conditions of employment of its members. ■

Figure 1   Union and Employee Association Membership as Percent of Labor Force, 1870–1984

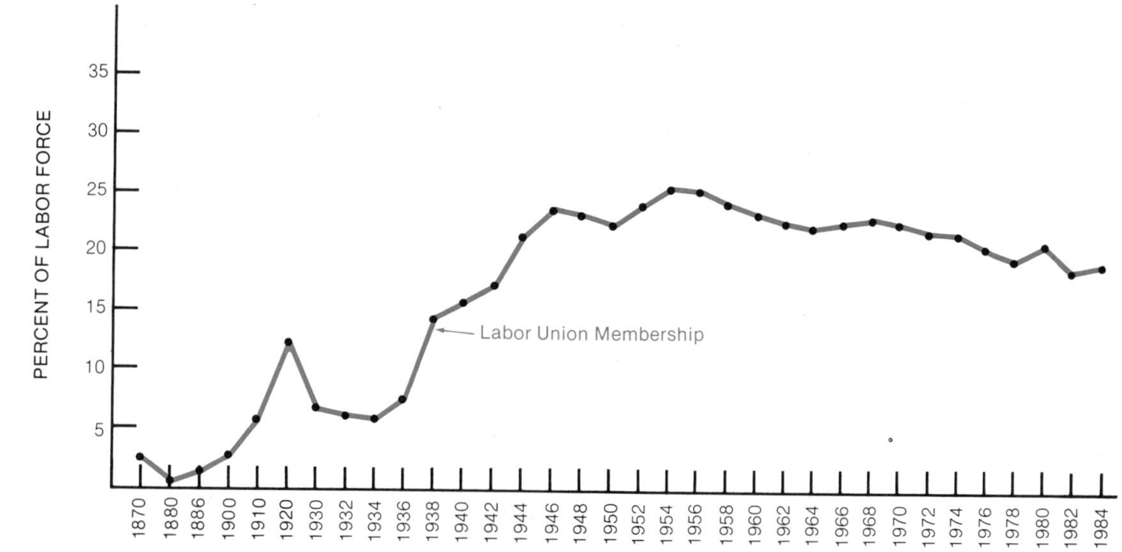

About one out of five members of the labor force in the United States belongs to unions. Union membership rose from 6.7 percent in the 1930s to a peak of 25 percent in the 1950s before declining to recent levels.

Source:*Statistical Abstract of the United States;* 1984, Table 726, 728; *Handbook of Labor Statistics* (U.S. Department of Labor, Bureau of Labor Statistics, December 1980), Table 165; *Historical Statistics of the United States, Colonial Times to 1970,* 1976, part I, series D. The 1983 figure is from Leo Troy and Neil Shefflin, *The Union Sourcebook;* the 1984 figure is from U.S. Department of Labor.

DEFINITIONS, FACTS, AND FIGURES

Labor unions are traditionally one of three types: 1) a **craft union,** 2) an **industrial union,** or 3) an **employee association.**

A **craft union** is a union that represents workers of a single occupation.

A craft union could be an electricians' union or a plumbers' union.

An **industrial union** is a union that represents employees of an industry or a firm regardless of their specific occupation.

Examples of industrial unions are the United Automobile Workers (a union that represents automobile workers of all types) and the United Mine Workers (a union that represents all types of workers engaged in mining).

Historically, employee associations, such as the National Education Association, the American Association of University Professors, the American Bar Association, the American Medical Association, and state employee associations, were primarily concerned with maintaining professional standards, but in recent years they have become increasingly involved in the primary union function of improving the pecuniary and nonpecuniary conditions of employment of their members.

An **employee association** is an organization that represents employees in a particular profession.

Unions perform a variety of functions. Their most visible function is to engage in *collective bargaining* with the employers of their members. Instead of each employee negotiating individually with the employer concerning wages, fringe benefits, and work conditions, the union represents all employees in negotiations or discussions with employers. Unions may bargain collectively about a number of issues, ranging from wage rates, vacation pay, and group health insurance to job-security provisions, lay-off rules, and safety conditions.

In the United States, there are fewer than 20 million union members; slightly less than one out of five members of the labor force belongs to unions (see Figure 1). In the 1930s, union members accounted for between 6 and 7 percent of the labor force. This percentage rose in the late 1930s and 1940s and peaked at 25 percent in the mid-1950s. Since then, the share of union members has fallen steadily to 18.8 percent in 1984.

Union membership as a percentage of employment has declined in recent years for several reasons. The percentage of women in the labor force has been rapidly increasing, and women have tended historically not to join unions. The share of white-collar workers in total employment has been rising as well; white-collar employees also tend not to join unions. Moreover, there has been a well-publicized shift in population from the northeastern and midwestern states to the southern and southwestern states, which are the states where union membership has been weakest. The rapid unionization of public employees after 1963 has kept the percentage of union members from falling even more. In 1964, only 7.7 percent of state- and local-government employees belonged to unions. By 1978, the proportion had risen to 17.4 percent. The rise in public-sector unionism, while significant, has not been sufficient to stem the fall in the share of union members in total employment.

Most American unions are affiliated with the AFL–CIO (American Federation of Labor–Congress of Industrial Organizations). Unions affiliated with the AFL–CIO account for 78 percent of union members. The Teamsters and the United Automobile Workers are the two largest industrial unions not affiliated with the AFL–CIO and constitute 16 percent of union members (see Table 1).

Table 1	Membership in Large Unions, 1980
Union	Membership (in thousands)
Teamsters	1,891
Automobile workers	1,371
Steelworkers	1,238
Electrical workers (IBEW)	1,041
Machinists	754
Carpenters	784
State, county workers (AFSCME)	1,098
Retail clerks (RCIA)	699
Laborers (LIUNA)	608
Service employees (SEIU)	650
Meat cutters	510
Clothing and textile workers	502
Communications workers	551
Teachers (AFT)	551
Hotel and restaurant workers	400
Engineers, operating	420
Ladies garment workers (ILGWU)	323
Musicians	299
Paper workers	275
Mine workers	245
Transportation workers	265
Government workers (AFGE)	255
Postal workers	251
Electrical workers (IUE)	233
Plumbers	352
Letter carriers	230
Railway, steamship clerks	180
Rubber	151
Retail workers, wholesale	190
Painters	164
Iron workers	184
Oil, chemical workers	154
Firefighters	178
Sheet-metal workers	161
Government workers (NAGE)	200
Transit union workers	161
Transport workers	130
Boilermakers	145
Bakery, confectionery workers	160
Bricklayers	135
Maintenance-of-way workers	102
Printing and graphic workers (IPGCU)	122
Woodworkers	112
Typographical workers	100
Graphic-arts workers	93
Federal government workers (NFFE)	(NA)

Source: *Statistical Abstract of the United States*, 1984, p. 440.

HISTORY AND LEGISLATION

The Growth of the AFL–CIO

As Figure 1 shows, unions were not a powerful force in American life until the late 1930s, although the first national conventions of labor unions met as early as 1869 to lobby for restric-tions on Chinese immigration. Union membership expanded rapidly after 1886 when the traditional craft unions banded together in the American Federation of Labor (AFL) under the leadership of Samuel Gompers, the "father of the American labor movement." Gompers made a lasting imprint on the American labor-union movement through his espousal of a nonpolitical, nonsocialist approach to unionism. Gompers believed that unions should be organized by craft and should not include unskilled workers.

Unskilled and semiskilled workers joined the Knights of Labor (organized in 1869), which experienced phenomenal growth in the early 1880s. Unlike the AFL, the Knights of Labor was committed as much or more to political goals as to wage increases. When violence in Chicago's Haymarket Square in 1887 stiffened employer resistance to the Knights of Labor and turned public opinion against organized labor, the Knights of Labor suffered a fatal collapse.

One reason for the difficulty in organizing the American labor force into unions is the unfavorable political climate that prevailed until the 1930s. Antitrust laws (the Sherman Antitrust Act of 1890) were applied against "monopolistic" labor unions; companies used private police forces, threats, and intimidation to prevent the formation of labor unions. It was not until 1932 that the government adopted a conscious policy favoring the free organization of unions. Prior to 1932, management was often able to obtain court orders that prohibited union activity, and employers were allowed to require new employees to sign "yellow dog" contracts in which the employee had to agree not to join a union as a condition of employment.[1]

Industrial unionism (which suffered a severe setback with the collapse of the Knights of Labor) made a comeback in the 1930s under the leadership of John L. Lewis. The failure of the AFL to organize unskilled and semiskilled workers in assembly-line production caused conflicts within the AFL organization. As a consequence, the Congress of Industrial Organizations (CIO) was formed in 1936 to organize workers on an industrial rather than a craft basis.

In 1955, the AFL and CIO merged to form the combined AFL–CIO, to which 78 percent of all union members now belong. At this point, no one can tell whether continuing efforts to bring major non-AFL–CIO unions—the Teamsters, the United Auto Workers—back into the AFL–CIO will succeed.

The Courts and Legislation

Until the passage of federal legislation in the 1930s, the courts ruled on union activities using common-law principles. Common law, however, presented the courts with difficult choices. On the one hand, it is a common-law principle that intentional harm to private property is illegal. Yet strikes, picketing, and boycotts are designed to place economic hardship on the private property of employers. On the other hand, the right of people to combine for mutual assistance was also accepted by common law. In the early 19th century, the courts typically held that union efforts to raise wages through strikes, picketing, and boycotts constituted criminal conspiracies. Under such rulings, union leaders were criminally prosecuted and sued for damages. The basic legality of trade unionism was not settled until 1842 when the Supreme Court of Massachusetts ruled that union legality depended upon union objectives. Unions *per se* were not illegal. Following the 1842 ruling, peaceful strikes for improved wages, hours, or working conditions were generally accepted as legal, while violent strikes or sympathy strikes to aid workers in other industries were not accepted by the courts.

In the 1880s, employers began using court *injunctions* to prevent strikes, pickets, and boycotts. The injunction was originally designed to prevent threatened damage to property under conditions when regular court processes would be too slow. Employers could go to sympathetic judges when threatened with strikes to obtain a restraining order which could close down a picket line or head off a strike within a matter of hours. The use of injunctions was eventually broadened to safeguarding businesses' "justifiable expectation of profit." The liberal use of injunctions in the late 19th and early 20th centuries made it very difficult for unions to strike a company without being restrained by an injunction. The company only needed to claim that the strike threatened damage to the employer's property. In the early 20th century, court rulings further weakened unions by

---

1. For a history of the American labor movement, see Lance E. Davis et al., *American Economic Growth* (New York: Harper and Row, 1972), pp. 219–27; Robert F. Flanagan, Robert S. Smith, and Ronald G. Ehrenberg, *Labor Economics and Labor Relations* (Glenview, Ill.: Scott, Foresman, 1984); Lloyd G. Reynolds, *Labor Economics and Labor Relations,* 8th ed. (Englewood Cliffs, N. J.: Prentice-Hall, 1982).

upholding the validity of "yellow dog" contracts. In effect, the courts ruled that employers could legally require a nonunion pledge as a legitimate condition for employment. A further problem for unions was the uncertainty about whether the restraint-of-trade provisions of the 1890 Sherman Act were meant to apply to union activities.

Two pro-union laws passed during the Great Depression paved the way for the growth of the organized labor movement in the 1930s and 1940s. The Norris-LaGuardia Act of 1932 declared that a worker "has full freedom of association, self-organization, and designation of representatives of his own choosing, to negotiate the terms and conditions of his employment. . ." and that workers should be "free from the interference, restraint, or coercion of employers" in the choice of union representatives. The Norris-LaGuardia Act restricted the use of court orders and injunctions to combat union organizing drives and strikes and prohibited "yellow dog" contracts. The National Labor Relations Act (The Wagner Act) of 1935 defined specific unfair labor practices. Employers were required to bargain in good faith with unions representing a majority of employees, and it became illegal to interfere with employees' rights to organize into unions. The National Labor Relations Board (NLRB) was established and given the authority to investigate unfair labor practices. The NLRB was also authorized to conduct elections to determine which union the employees wanted, if any, to represent them.

The Norris-LaGuardia Act of 1932 and the Wagner Act of 1935 encouraged union growth in the 1930s and 1940s. Table 1 makes it clear that until these laws were passed, labor unions were relatively insignificant in size. After World War II, unions lost some of their popular support. The Taft-Hartley and Landrum-Griffin Acts were the result of anti-union sentiment. The Taft-Hartley Act of 1947 gave states the right to pass *right-to-work laws* that prohibited the requirement that union membership be a condition for employment. *Closed-shop agreements* that required firms to hire only union members were outlawed for firms engaged in interstate commerce. Major strikes that could disrupt the economy could be delayed by an 80-day cooling-off period if ordered by the President.

The Landrum-Griffin Act of 1959 was designed to protect the rights of union members and to increase union democracy. It included provisions for periodic reporting of union finances and for regulating union elections.

UNION OBJECTIVES

What are the objectives of labor unions? Surprisingly, the answer to this question is not as obvious as it appears. Unions would like to obtain higher wages, better fringe benefits, and safer working conditions for their members. They would also like to prevent the unemployment of their members. Are the two objectives of higher wages and lower unemployment compatible—given the fact (demonstrated in the previous chapter) that the firm will hire more labor at low wages than at high wages, *ceteris paribus?*

Assume that two different unions—A and B—collectively bargain about wages with management. For simplicity, we assume that the average worker in each union is earning the same wage, w_c, and that employment is the same in both cases (at l_c). The derived demand curve for each union's labor force is shown in Figure 2. The demand in the case of Union A is inelastic: moving from point c to point a in panel (a) means a large percentage increase in the wage (to w_a) compared to the percentage reduction in the quantity of labor demanded (from l_c to l_a). The demand is elastic in the case of Union B: moving from c to b in panel (b) means a small percentage increase in the wage compared to the percentage reduction in quantity of labor demanded (from l_c to l_b).

The **wage/employment trade-off** confront any labor union that faces a downward-sloping demand curve: higher wages can be obtained only by sacrificing the number of jobs; lower unemployment can be obtained only by sacrificing higher wages.

The leadership of Union B is faced with a dilemma. If it pushes for wages higher than w_c, such as w_b, the number of jobs available to union members will decline from l_c to l_b. Jobs will be traded off for higher wages, and the rank and file of the union will likely be dissatisfied with the current union leadership. (See Example 1.) This

Figure 2   The Trade-Off Between Wages and Employment: The Competitive Case

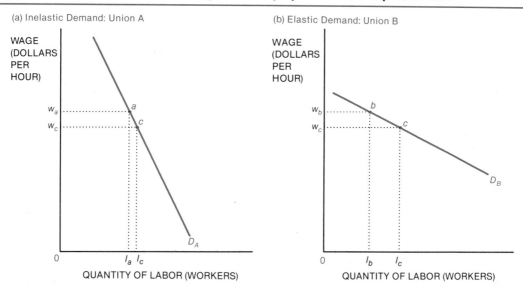

The demand curve for the members of Union A is relatively inelastic, while the demand curve for the members of Union B is relatively elastic. If both unions, in the collective-bargaining process, push for the same wage increases, more jobs will be lost by workers in Union B (where demand is elastic) than by workers in Union A.

wage/employment trade-off is less acute in the case of Union A because the same increase in wages causes the loss of fewer jobs (because of the difference in elasticity between A and B).

Union Behavior

The wage/employment trade-off explains a great deal of observed union behavior. First, it allows economists to predict which types of industries will be most easily unionized: one would expect unions to be formed first in those industries where the demand for labor is relatively inelastic. Indeed, history shows that the first occupations to be unionized were those crafts—carpenters, printers, glassblowers, and shoemakers—where the demand for labor was relatively inelastic.

The demand for labor is relatively inelastic in the case of skilled labor because the availability of close substitutes is limited. It is not easy to substitute unskilled for skilled labor or to substitute a skilled printer for a skilled glassblower. The occupations that were the last (and presumably most difficult to organize) were the unskilled occupations in which the demand for labor is

highly elastic, such as wholesale and retail trade.

Second, the model suggests that unions should seek to do two things: they should attempt not only to increase the demand for labor, but to reduce the elasticity of demand for labor. By increasing the demand for labor, labor unions can obtain both higher wages and higher employment. By reducing the elasticity of demand for labor, unions can raise wages with a smaller cost in lost employment.

Unions attempt to increase the demand for union labor and lower its elasticity of demand in a variety of ways. Unions lobby for tariffs and quotas on foreign-produced products to increase the demand for the products produced by union workers. Unions conduct advertising campaigns telling the public to "look for the union label" or to "buy American." Unions oppose relaxation of immigration laws and support the repatriation of illegal aliens. Unions have traditionally supported raising the minimum wage—an act that makes unskilled labor more expensive relative to the more skilled workers that tend to belong to unions.

Unions have lobbied for minimum staffing requirements, such as the rule that the new-genera-

Example 1   The Wage/Employment Trade-Off: A Union Strikes for Lower Wages!

One of the most unusual strikes in union history was called by the New Jersey Building and Construction Trades Council of the AFL–CIO in September of 1984 on behalf of unionized insulation installers. The strike, which lasted two days, was called to force employers to agree to pay union workers $1.60 an hour less than the employers had offered! Why would a union go on strike to gain lower wages? The union leadership interpreted management's offer as a subtle attempt to price union members out of the market. At the higher wage, firms would have the excuse to hire more nonunion labor and to cause a decline in union membership. In this case, the union members clearly understood the wage/employment trade-off. They were willing to accept lower wages for more jobs. ∎

Source: "Union Asks for Lower Wages to Save Jobs," *Christian Science Monitor*, September 24, 1984.

---

tion MD-80 aircraft be staffed by three cockpit personnel (two pilots and a flight engineer) rather than the two pilots that airline management wanted. Staffing requirements that call for the use of additional labor for jobs that have become redundant (such as fire stokers on diesel-powered locomotives) are called *featherbedding*. Unions may also bargain for rules that make it difficult or impossible to substitute other grades of labor for union labor. In construction, unions specify in detail which jobs can be performed only by electricians and by no one else, and there are sanctions against builders who hire nonunion employees.

Limitations of Labor Supply

Some unions seek to drive up the wage by limiting the supply of union labor. The union typically controls who will be allowed to work in a particular occupation by means of certification and qualification requirements. In craft unions, the number of union members can be limited by long apprenticeships, by rules limiting entry into the union, by difficult qualifying exams, and by state licensing. In the process of limiting labor supply, the union screens out unqualified workers but may also exclude some qualified people who are prepared to work in that occupation.

Figure 3 shows the effect of limiting labor supply on wages. The decrease in supply (from *S* to *S'*) moves the equilibrium wage/employment combination from *e* to *e'*; at *e'* wages are higher, but the number of jobs is fewer. When unions seek to control wages through limitations on the supply of union labor, it is especially important to prevent employers from substituting nonunion labor. For this reason, craft unions favor rigid certification requirements and rules prohibiting nonunion workers from performing certain tasks.

Strikes and Collective Bargaining

Industrial unions that represent all the workers in a particular industry have a more difficult time limiting the supply of labor. Such unions can indeed affect overall labor-supply conditions by favoring restrictions on immigration, mandatory retirement, shorter work weeks, and laws against teenage employment. But they, unlike plumbers, electricians, and physicians, find it difficult to control the number of union members. Industrial unions, therefore, use **collective bargaining** to raise the wages of union members.

> **Collective bargaining** is the process whereby the union bargains with management as the representative of all union employees.

Collective bargaining gives workers a stronger voice than they would have if each worker bargained separately with management.

The threat of **strike** is the union's most effective weapon in collective bargaining. The effect of the collective-bargaining process (with threat of strike) is represented in Figure 4. The supply curve, *S*, represents the supply of labor to the industry if each individual were to bargain separately with management. When the union threatens to strike, the union is, in effect, telling management that: at wages less than w_c, no labor will be supplied; at the wage of w_c, management

Figure 3   Craft Unions and Wages: Limiting Supply

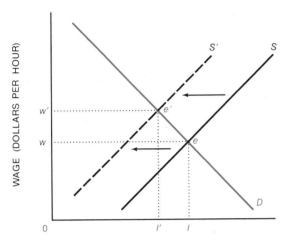

QUANTITY OF LABOR (WORKERS)

By limiting entry into the profession, a craft union shifts the labor-supply curve to the left (from S to S'), and the wage rate of union members is raised above what it would have been without the union.

Figure 4   Collective Bargaining with the Threat of Strike

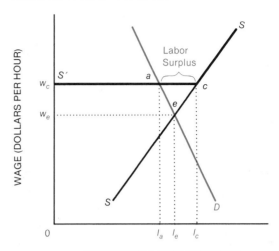

QUANTITY OF LABOR (WORKERS)

The supply curve, S, represents the labor supply if each worker were to bargain separately with the employer. The heavy black supply curve that is S' to the left of point c and S above c is the supply curve with collective bargaining because no union labor will be supplied at a wage below w_c. Point e is the equilibrium wage/employment combination without collective bargaining or the threat of a strike; point a is the equilibrium wage/employment combination with collective bargaining. The *benefit* to union members of collective bargaining is that a wage higher than the one that would have prevailed is achieved (w_c is higher than w_e). The *cost* is that the number of jobs available to union members is reduced. Some union members who are willing to work at w_c are without jobs in the industry (the number represented by the difference between l_c and l_a is the number left without jobs); however, l_c workers minus l_e workers is the number of workers attracted by the higher wages.

can hire as much labor as it wants up to l_c of labor; as wages increase above w_c, management can hire ever-increasing amounts of labor beyond l_c. Thus, the new labor-supply curve with the threat of a strike is indicated by the heavy line that connects w_c on the vertical axis with point c and then continues up the original supply curve above point c. Without the threat of strike, the supply curve would be the original curve S, and point e would be the equilibrium wage/employment combination. With the threat of a strike, the demand curve would meet the new supply curve at point a, and the firm would hire l_a workers at a wage of w_c.

> A **strike** occurs when all unionized employees cease to work until management agrees to specific union demands.

From the standpoint of union members, collective bargaining has its costs and benefits. The benefits are the higher wages that collective bargaining brings (w_c is higher than w_e). If the industry is entirely unionized, the costs are that some union members who are willing to work at

the negotiated wage will not be employed in this industry. Although l_c workers are willing to work at w_c, only l_a workers will be hired. The unemployment effects of collective bargaining are softened by numerous rules within the union (an internal labor market) governing which members will be laid off first. Typically, union members who have *seniority* (have been in the union the longest time) are laid off last.

Collective Bargaining with Monopsony

If employers have monopsony power over their labor market, the trade-off between higher wages

Table 2   The Monopsonist's Labor Cost

Labor (workers), L (1)	Wage (dollars per hours), W (2)	Labor Cost (dollars) (3) = (1) × (2)	Marginal Factor Cost (dollars), MFC (4)
1	5	5	
			9
2	7	14	
			13
3	9	27	
			21
4	12	48	

The monopsonist must pay a higher wage to employ more workers. The marginal factor cost of an extra worker is, therefore, greater than the wage. For example, the wage of the second worker is $7 per hour, but the marginal factor cost is $9 (or $7 plus the $2 difference between the wage necessary to hire one worker and the wage necessary to hire two workers).

and union employment does not hold. An employer has monopsony power if the employer accounts for a large enough portion of total hiring in the labor market to affect the market wage. The labor-supply curve to a monoposonistic firm is not horizontal at the prevailing market wage because the employer cannot hire all the labor it wants at the market wage. Instead, to hire more labor, the monopsonistic firm will have to offer higher wages to all its employees.

Consider a monopsonist faced with the labor supply schedule given in Table 2. As demonstrated in an earlier chapter, the wage rate is not the marginal factor cost *(MFC)* in the case of the monopsonist. To hire one more unit of labor, the monopsonist must pay a higher wage not only to the new worker but also to workers previously hired. To hire the second worker, the monopsonist must pay a higher wage ($7 rather than the previous $5) to the first worker. The *MFC* of the second worker is, therefore, the wage paid the second worker ($7) plus the increase in the wage of the first worker ($2) for a total of $9. The *MFC* for each additional worker is shown in the fourth column.

Figure 5   Monopsony and Collective Bargaining

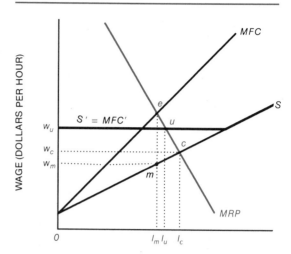

QUANTITY OF LABOR (WORKERS)

Because this industry is a monopsonist, *MFC* is greater than the wage at each quantity. The monopsonist will hire that quantity of labor at which *MFC* = *MRP* and pay the wage that corresponds to that labor quantity on the supply curve, or w_m. Without unions, *MFC* = *MRP* at point *e;* the monopsonist will hire l_m workers and pay the wage of w_m. If a union collectively bargains for a wage of w_u, the monopsonist's *MFC* curve shifts to *MFC'* because of the change in labor supply and becomes a horizontal line at w_u; *MFC* will now equal *MRP* at point *u*. In this case, collective bargaining actually increased both wages (from w_m to w_u) and union employment (from l_m to l_u).

The marginal factor cost of the monopsonist is greater than the wage rate paid by the monopsonist.

The relationship between *MFC* and wages is shown in Figure 5. The monopsonist will hire that quantity of labor at which *MFC* and *MRP* are equal (but will pay the wage corresponding to that quantity on the labor-supply curve). In the absence of collective bargaining, *MFC* = *MRP* at point *e,* so the monopsonist will hire l_m workers, but the wage required to induce l_m workers to work is only w_m; therefore, the monopsonist will operate at point *m* in the absence of collective bargaining, hiring l_m workers at a wage of w_m.

Since *MFC* exceeds the wage rate, the mon-

Example 2   A Case of Monopsony: The One-Horse Town that Died

An example of monopsony is the Anaconda Company, a copper smelter in Anaconda, Montana. For over 100 years, the Anaconda Company smelted copper from its Butte Copper Mine in Anaconda, Montana, which has 10,000 residents. In 1981, the Anaconda Company shut down its smelting plant, throwing some 1,000 residents out of a job. The only new industrial company in the town (a machine-parts foundry) had less than 12 workers on its payroll at the time of its closing. Local officials claimed that 70 percent of the town's earnings came from the now-closed copper smelter. The Anaconda Company smelter is a classic example of monopsony. Because it employed a large percentage of total employment, it could cause wages to drop by reducing its work force, and it would have to raise wages to hire more workers. The marginal factor of additional employment to this smelter would have been greater than the wage. ■

Source: *Business Week,* February 23, 1981, p. 28.

---

opsonist will hire less labor than would be the case if the industry were competitive in the labor market and each firm treated the wage rate as its *MFC*. In Figure 5, the competitive industry would operate at point *c,* where *S* (which equals the competitive firm's *MFC*) equals *MRP*.

If a union collectively bargains for a wage of w_u in Figure 5, the monopsonist's *MFC* curve becomes a horizontal line at w_u (*MFC'* in Figure 5). Collective bargaining makes the supply of union labor perfectly elastic (horizontal) at the union wage. By demanding w_u the union makes this wage the *MFC* of the monopsonist. In this case, *MFC* = *MFC* at point *u,* where the monopsonist hires l_u of labor. Collective bargaining has succeeded in raising both wages and union employment when the firm is a monopsonist.

There are no measures of the degree of monopsony in the labor markets of our economy. Earlier it was argued that monopsony in factor markets is less likely than monopoly in product markets. Although important cases of monopsony can be found (see Example 2), the observed behavior of labor unions—the obvious efforts of unions to soften the wage/employment trade-off—suggests that monopsony is not prevalent and that in most cases unions must trade off jobs for higher wages.

The wage/employment trade-off need not exist when the employer is a monopsonist.

THE EFFECT OF UNIONS ON WAGES

Unions can affect the wages of their members by limiting the supply of union labor, by increasing the demand for union labor through staffing requirements and programs to increase the demand for the product, and through collective bargaining. Considerable effort of labor economists has gone into estimating the extent to which unions have been able to raise the wages of their members relative to comparable nonunion workers.

Union Effect on Union Wages

Studies of the effect of unions on wages find that unions have indeed succeeded in raising the wages of their members above what they would have been without unions.[2] The effects of unions have varied among industries, over time, and by gender and race. Studies for the 1960s, for example, show unions raising the wages of laborers by the highest percentages but having little or no effect on managerial and professional wages. Table 3 shows that from 1967 to 1975, the wage

---

2. The pioneering study of the effects of unions on wage rates is by H. G. Lewis, *Unionism and Relative Wages in the United States* (Chicago: University of Chicago Press, 1963). A survey of this literature is provided by C. J. Paisley, "Labor Union Effects on Wage Gains: A Survey of Recent Literature," *Journal of Economic Literature* 18, 1 (March 1980): 1–31. *See also* Flanagan, Smith, and Ehrenberg *Labor Economics and Industrial Relations,* pp. 560–66.

Table 3   Estimated Union Wage Advantage Over Nonunion Workers, 1967, 1973, and 1975

	Percentage Union Wage Effect			Percentage Unionized		
	1967	1973	1975	1967	1973	1975
All workers	11.6	14.8	16.8	23	26	25
White males	9.6	15.5	16.3	31	33	31
Black males	21.5	22.5	22.5	32	37	37
White females	14.4	12.7	16.6	12	14	14
Black females	5.6	13.2	17.1	13	22	22

Source: Orley Ashenfelter, "Union Relative Wage Effects: New Evidence and a Survey of Their Implications for Wage Inflation," in *Econometric Contributions to Public Policy*, eds. R. Stone and W. Peterson (New York: St. Martin's, 1979), Tables 2.1 and 2.2

advantage of union members increased from around 12 percent to a near 17 percent advantage. The most substantial improvements were experienced by white male and black female union members, while white female union members scarcely increased their wage advantage relative to nonunion members. Black males appear to have benefited the most from union membership. In 1975, black male union members earned 22.5 percent higher wages than their nonunion counterparts.

Studies show that, historically, craft unions in construction and transportation have achieved the largest relative wage effects (20–25 percent). Industrial unions have had a smaller relative wage effect (10–15 percent). In competitive industries such as textiles and apparel, unions have had the smallest impact on relative wages.

Union Effect on Nonunion Wages

It is more difficult to establish the effect of unions on the general level of wages or on the wages of nonunion workers. Theory suggests that unions could either depress or increase the wage rates of nonunion workers.

According to economic theory, the labor market in any given industry consists of a union sector and a nonunion sector. For example, Figure 1 showed that one U.S. worker out of 5 is a union member. The economy's labor force is indeed made up of both unionized and nonunionized sectors. If unions in the unionized sector bargain for substantial increases in the union wage and trade off jobs for large wage increases, some union members who are willing to work at the union wage are unemployed, and they "spill over" into

the nonunion sector. The young union members with low seniority are the ones most likely laid off in the unionized sector. When they seek employment in the nonunionized sector, the labor supply curve in the nonunionized sector shifts to the right (increases), and wages in the nonunionized sector are bid down. This *spillover effect* is one reason why unions may depress the wages of nonunion workers.

A highly simplified view of the spillover effect is shown in Figure 6. Before Industry A is unionized, both industries pay $8 per hour; A uses 50 workers, and B uses 90 workers. When A is unionized, employment in A falls to 30 workers and employment in B rises to 110 workers. The wage rate in A rises to $12, and wages in B fall to $6 as a result of A's unionization. This example assumes perfect competition in the firm's product market, perfect information about jobs, and homogeneous labor. Here the 30 original members of Industry A benefit at the expense of the 20 workers who move to Industry B and must take lower wages.

On the other hand, unions could possibly raise wages in the nonunionized sector in two ways. First, employers of nonunion workers may fear that if they do not match union wage increases, pressure will build among their workers to form a union. Second, when a unionized worker is laid off, there is a possibility that that worker will not spill over into the nonunionized sector but will wait until he or she is recalled to a job in the union sector. The probability of such *wait unemployment* is greatest when there is a substantial wage differential between the nonunion and union job, when the likelihood of recall is high, and when the costs of unemployment are low (because

Figure 6   The Effect of Unions on Nonunion Wages: The Spillover Effect

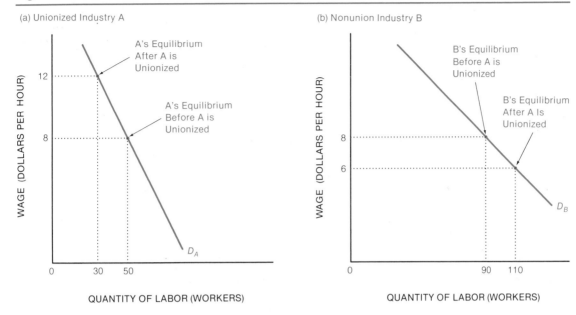

(a) Unionized Industry A

(b) Nonunion Industry B

Before industry A is unionized, wages are $8 per hour in both A and B; 50 workers are employed in A and 90 are employed in B. After A is unionized, workers in A earn a new wage of $12, and 20 workers lose their jobs and must be absorbed into industry B. A's unionization drives the wage down to $6 in the nonunionized industry by increasing the supply of workers to industry B. This example assumes that the employer is perfectly competitive, that workers have perfect information about jobs, and that labor is homogeneous.

of the availability of unemployment benefits or union unemployment funds). If unemployed union workers do not spill over into nonunionized jobs, the downward pressure on nonunion wages would be removed.

The empirical evidence on the question of union effects on nonunion wages is not extensive, but it does suggest that unions depress wages in nonunionized jobs. For example, the wages of nonunion workers are typically lower in cities where the percent of unionized workers is high.[3]

THE EFFECT OF UNIONS ON EFFICIENCY

The Traditional View

The traditional view of the effect of unions on economic efficiency is that unions have a negative

3. Lawrence Kahn, "The Effect of Unions on the Earnings of Nonunion Workers," *Industrial and Labor Relations Review* 31 (January 1978): 205–16.

effect on efficiency and productivity. The reasons for this view include the following:

1. Unions tend to bargain for staffing requirements *(featherbedding)* that prevent employers from using labor and capital in the most efficient manner. If union rules prevent carpenters from turning a screw on any electrical fixture, for example, the economy will operate below its potential.
2. Union strikes disrupt output and cause the economy to produce below its production potential. Strikes in major industries, like steel and rail transportation, can disrupt other sectors of the economy and cause losses of real output.
3. Unions drive a wedge between the wages of comparable workers in union and nonunion employment.

If workers of comparable quality are paid different wages because one belongs to a union and the other is in nonunion employment, the economy has again lost some potential output. In both the unionized and nonunionized sectors, workers will be employed to the point where their wage equals their *MRP*, but the *MRP*s of union workers will be higher than those of comparable nonunion workers. The economy could have increased its output by reallocating workers from the nonunionized sector (where *MRP* is lower) into the union sector (where *MRP* is higher). But the task of unions is to raise the wages of their members above what they would have been without the union. Whenever significant spillover effects occur, *MRP*s will be different.

Economists have attempted to estimate the loss of output due to the presence of unions. Economist Albert Rees, for example, has estimated this loss at approximately 0.8 percent of gross national product from the 1930s to the 1960s.[4] This loss has to be balanced against the perceived benefits that unions have brought workers.

Unions as a Voice Institution

Economists Albert Hirschman, Richard Freeman, and James Medoff maintain that unions actually improve productivity rather than reduce efficiency, as has been traditionally suggested.[5] In their view, unions improve productivity by acting as a collective voice for union members. Without unions, if workers are dissatisfied with their employer, their only recourse is to use the *exit mechanism,* or to revolt against bad employers and bad work conditions by quitting and seeking another job. In this way, bad employers are penalized, good employers are rewarded, and the efficiency of the social system is improved. However, the exit mechanism results in heavy job turnover, which costs the economy lost output as employees must learn new jobs and spend time in often lengthy job searches.

Unions offer an alternative to the exit mechanism by making it possible for workers to discuss with an employer conditions that must be changed. In other words, unions give workers a voice. As individuals, workers will not have an effective voice at the workplace for two reasons. First, there is a limited incentive for an individual worker to seek to improve important aspects of

Table 4   Effect of Unions on Quit Rates

Sample	Percentage by Which Quits Are Reduced by Unionism
All workers, 1968–1978	45
All workers, 1973–1975	86
Men 48–62 in 1969	107
Men 17–27 in 1969	11
Manufacturing workers	34–48

Source: Richard Freeman and James Medoff, "The Two Faces of Unionism," *The Public Interest 57* (Fall 1979): 79.

work conditions such as safety, grievance procedures, and work sharing. Few individuals want to run all the risks and devote the time to issues that affect other workers' welfare as much as their own. Each individual would prefer to let someone else do the protesting and wait for the benefits. Second, there are risks to individual workers in expressing their true feelings to their employers; employers may seek to get rid of activists. In order for unions to have an effective voice, activists must be protected by the union organization. This fact is recognized in the National Labor Relations Act, which protects collective (but not individual) actions at the workplace.

Unions can have a positive effect on productivity in three ways. First, when worker grievances are handled by the union, workers need not leave the firm in order to bring about an improvement in their work conditions. If fewer workers quit because the union gives them a voice for their protests or complaints, the firm can reduce its hiring and training costs, and the functioning of work groups is smoother. Workers with a voice are more willing to train in skills that are useful in only that industry. Second, senior workers (who are most important politically in the union organization) are more likely to provide informal training and assistance in enterprises where unions give them a voice. When the union provides a channel of communication between workers and management, the improved information flows between workers and managers can improve the efficiency of the enterprise. Third, a well-established seniority system tends to reduce friction between junior and senior workers.

4. Albert Rees, "The Effects of Unions on Resource Allocation," *Journal of Law and Economics* 6 (October 1963): 69–78.

5. Richard B. Freeman and James L. Medoff, *What Do Unions Do?* (New York: Basic Books, 1982).

Table 5	Effect of Unions on Productivity
Industry	Percentage Increase in Output per Worker Due to Unions
Manufacturing, 1972	20–25
Wooden furniture, 1972	15
Cement, 1953–76	6–8
Underground coal, 1965	25–30
Underground coal, 1975	–20– –25
Construction, 1972	29–38

Sources: Richard Freeman and James Medoff, "The Two Faces of Unionism," *The Public Interest 57* (Fall 1979): 80; Kim Clark, "The Impact of Unionization on Productivity: A Case Study, *Industrial and Labor Relations Review* (July 1980), pp. 451–69.

Evidence

What does the empirical evidence suggest about the effect of unions on productivity? First, there is strong evidence that the presence of unions causes a dramatic reduction in employee turnover (see Table 4). Although the quit rates of young workers (who happen to be the first laid off in unions) are only slightly reduced by unionization, all other workers' quit rates are reduced by the presence of unions from 34 to 107 percent.

The view of unions as a positive factor in labor productivity is fairly new to the economics literature and remains to be subjected to careful scrutiny and debate. The final word on whether unions raise or lower economic efficiency remains to be written.

The evidence that unions reduce quit rates does not necessarily prove that unions do improve labor productivity. The evidence cited by Freeman and Medoff and by Kim Clark (see Table 5) does suggest that unions have increased output per worker in those industries studied with the exception of underground bituminous coal mining. The negative effect of unions in underground bituminous coal mining may be due to deteriorating industrial relations in that industry in the late 1960s that prevented the United Mine Workers from being an effective union voice.

The productivity advantage of union workers (according to Freeman and Medoff) may be large enough to offset the wage advantage of union workers. If union workers are 20 percent more productive and earn 20 percent more than non-

union workers, average labor costs per unit of output are the same (see Example 3). Richard Ruback and Martin Zimmerman, however, cite evidence to dispute this point. They find that share prices of companies typically fall (by about 4 percent, on average) when that company becomes unionized—which means that the investment community views unions as reducing the long-run profitability of firms.[6]

This chapter continued the discussion of labor markets begun in the preceding chapter by examining how unions affect wages and economic efficiency. The next chapter will turn to the nonlabor factors of production: land, capital, and entrepreneurship.

Summary

1. A union is a collective organization of workers and employees whose objective is to improve the pecuniary and nonpecuniary conditions of its members. A craft union represents workers of a particular occupation. An industrial union represents workers of a particular industry. Currently less than 20 percent of the labor force belongs to unions—a decline from the high of 25 percent in the 1950s. The declining percentage is due to the rise of white-collar employment, the rising share of women in the work force, and the shift of industry to the south and southwest. The most substantial gains in union membership in recent years have been in public employment.

2. During the 19th century, the courts used common-law rulings and injunctions to limit union activity. The formation of unions was aided by prolabor legislation beginning with the Norris-LaGuardia Act of 1932, which facilitated union organizing drives. The National Labor Relations Act of 1935 made it illegal for employers to interfere with the rights of employees to organize. The Taft-Hartley Act of 1947 was a reaction against the pro-union legislation of the 1930s.

---

6. Richard S. Ruback and Martin B. Zimmerman, "Unionization and Profitability: Evidence from the Capital Market," *Journal of Political Economy*, December 1984, pp. 1134–57.

Example 3   Unions and Productivity: The Continental Airlines Bankruptcy Case

Recent Supreme Court rulings have altered bankruptcy laws to allow comparatively healthy companies to file for bankruptcy if the company projects that it will become insolvent. Under earlier rulings, a company actually had to be insolvent (unable to pay its bills) to file for bankruptcy. In 1984, Continental Airlines filed for bankruptcy because it argued that its existing high-wage union contracts would have caused it to become insolvent. By filing for bankruptcy, Continental Airlines sought to abrogate existing union contracts on the grounds that these contracts would eventually force it to cease operation. Continental maintained that it had to compete with smaller regional airlines operating at lower costs because they employed nonunionized pilots and flight attendants who were working for lower wages.

One of the issues in the court hearings on the Continental bankruptcy case was whether or not airline flight-attendant and pilot unions raised Continental's productivity sufficiently to compensate for their higher wages relative to nonunionized employees. If (as suggested by some economists) unions can raise productivity sufficiently to compensate for higher wages, Continental's argument would not be correct. The courts sided with Continental and allowed Continental to abrogate its existing union contracts. ■

---

3. Unions must weigh the advantages of higher wages against the disadvantages of less union employment. Unions respond to the trade-off between jobs and employment by increasing the demand for union labor and by promoting measures to reduce the elasticity of demand for union labor. In collective bargaining, the most potent weapon of the union is the threat of strike. In the case of labor monopsony, the trade-off between higher wages and employment may not be present. That unions do attempt to reduce this trade-off suggests that monopsony is not prevalent.

4. Unions are able to raise the wages of union members relative to comparable nonunion members. The amount wages are raised varies by industry and by union. Unions can have both a positive and a negative effect on nonunion wages. When unions raise wages in the union sector, the workers who are laid off spill over into the nonunion sector, and the increase in labor supply lowers nonunion wages. However, when unions raise wages in the union sector nonunion employers may raise wages because they fear the formation of a union if they do not raise wages. The empirical evidence suggests that the net effect of unions on nonunion wages is negative.

5. There are two views on the effect of unions on productivity. The traditional view maintains that unions adversely affect labor productivity.

The new view argues that unions serve as a voice institution that raises the labor productivity of union workers.

Key Terms

labor union
craft union
industrial union
employee association
wage/employment trade-off
collective bargaining
strike

Questions and Problems

1. Assume that the elasticity of demand for labor (the percentage change in quantity of labor demanded divided by the percentage change in the wage) is 1.5 in the widget industry and is 0.5 in the ratchet industry. Which industry would be easier to unionize? In which industry is the trade-off between employment and higher wages more costly?

2. If you were the president of a major industrial union, what would your attitude be toward free immigration into the United States? What would your attitude be toward the minimum-wage law? Explain.

3. Explain why the employment/wage trade-off does not exist for a monopsonistic industry.

4. Explain why both the automobile unions and the management of the automobile industry favor import restrictions on imported cars.

5. Assume that you belong to a union of bank tellers. What would your attitude be toward automated bank tellers? Explain.

6. Explain why the impact of higher union wages on nonunion wages might depend upon the extent of wait unemployment.

7. Which of the following policies would unions tend to favor? Explain your answer.
  a. Liberal immigrations laws.
  b. Free trade.
  c. Reductions of quotas on foreign goods.
  d. A higher minimum wage.

8. If unions do succeed in raising productivity, what effect would this productivity increase have on the costs of production of unionized companies versus nonunionized companies?

9. Explain why common-law principles made it difficult for judges in the 18th and 19th centuries to rule on the legality of strikes.

10. A firm currently employs 100 workers at a wage of $50 a week. In order to hire 5 more workers, the employer must raise the wage rate to $55.10. What is the marginal factor cost of hiring one more worker? What is the relationship between marginal factor cost and the wage rate? What kind of firm is this?

11. If unions lower quit rates, why would productivity be expected to increase?

12. A firm is currently paying labor $5 per hour. If this firm can double its labor force and still pay $5 per hour, what kind of a firm is this?

Suggested Readings

Barbash, Jack. "The Labor Movement After World War II." *Monthly Labor Review,* November 1976.

Bowen, William G. and Orley Ashenfelter, eds. *Labor and the National Economy,* rev. ed. New York: W. W. Norton, 1975.

Ehrenberg, Ronald G. and Robert S. Smith. *Modern Labor Economics: Theory and Public Policy,* 2nd ed. Glenview, Ill.: Scott, Foresman, 1985.

Freeman, Richard B. and James L. Medoff. "The Two Faces of Unionism." *Public Interest 57* (Fall 1979): 69–93.

Freeman, Richard B. and James L. Medoff. *What Do Unions Do?* New York: Basic Books, 1982.

Paisley, C. J. "Labor Unions and Wages: A Survey." *Journal of Economic Literature* 18 (March 1980): 1–31.

Reynolds, Lloyd G. *Labor Economics and Labor Relations,* 8th ed. Englewood Cliffs, N. J.: Prentice-Hall, 1982.

38

Interest, Rent, and Profit

Chapter Preview

Interest, rent, and profit accounted for approximately 27 percent of national income in the early 1980s; wages and salaries constituted the remaining 73 percent (see Table 1). The last two chapters described wages, or the payments to labor; this chapter will describe the income earned by the remaining factors of production: land, capital, and entrepreneurship. The owner of each of these three factors of production offers the use of the factor in return for payment.

The payment for the use of capital is *interest*. The supply of capital is the accumulation of savings by households and firms. The payment for the use of land and other natural resources is *rent*. The supply of land or natural resources is relatively fixed. The payment for the use of an entrepreneur's services is *profit*. The supply of entrepreneurship is heavily dependent on the detailed

social, educational, and economic characteristics of the society from which entrepreneurs are

Table 1 Shares of National Income by Type, 1984

Type of Income	Share (percent)
Compensation of employees	73.3
Proprietors' income	5.1
Rental income of persons	2.1
Corporate profits	9.9
Net interest	9.6

Source: *Federal Reserve Bulletin.*

drawn. This chapter will identify the principal forces determining interest, rent, and profit. ∎

INTEREST

Interest is the price paid for funds borrowed for investment in capital or for funds borrowed to purchase consumer durables. Capital goods are required for the indirect, or roundabout, production of consumer goods. Chapter 2 noted that roundabout production is typically more productive than direct production. For example, productivity is raised when a net is used instead of bare hands in catching fish. Productivity is raised when workers assemble cars on an assembly line with sophisticated equipment rather than by hand. Interest is determined in credit markets, where the desire to invest is balanced with the willingness to save.

> **Interest** is the price of credit and is determined in credit markets, where the amount businesses wish to invest is balanced with the amount people are prepared to save.

Capital goods such as trucks, conveyors, buildings, lathes, cranes, hammers, and computers enlist the mechanical, electrical, and chemical powers of nature to expand the production possibilities of society far beyond what otherwise could be accomplished by unaided human hands or minds. Interest is determined by the forces of supply of and demand for capital.

The Stock of Capital

Economists distinguish between *tangible capital* and *intangible capital*. Tangible capital differs from the other factors of production in that in its concrete form (from trucks and computers to fish nets and shovels) it has already been produced. Land that has been improved by irrigation, by the clearing of forests, or by the draining of swamps is also "produced" and as such is a capital good just like machines and factories.

Intangible capital takes two general forms: *research and development* (R&D) *capital* is accumulated investments in technology, productive knowledge, and know-how; *human capital* is accumulated investments in human beings—investments in training, education, and improved health that improve the productive capacities of human beings. The stock of intangible capital available to a society at one point in time can be measured

by the cost of the resources that have been devoted to R&D investment and to human-capital investment. Human-capital investments, which are an important determinant of the distribution of income, will be discussed in more detail in the next chapter. Human-capital theory suggests that the human capital embodied in trained labor is "produced" in the same economic sense as a truck or factory.

The inventory or stock of capital that exists in an economy at any moment of time depends on 1) the accumulated savings and investment decisions that have been made in the past and 2) the extent to which old capital goods have undergone **depreciation** through use or obsolescence.

> **Depreciation** is the wearing down of the economic value of capital goods as they are used in the production process.

Each year, households decide how much they are prepared to save; each year, firms decide how much they wish to invest in new capital goods. Each year, new capital goods are added to the stock of capital depending on how much consumers are saving and how much firms are investing. Over time, capital goods (broadly defined to include human capital and investments in land improvements) accumulate and depreciate. If the rate of accumulation exceeds the rate of depreciation, the stock of capital will grow.

> The current stock of capital is the result of past savings and investment decisions. The stock of capital grows if the rate of capital accumulation exceeds the rate of depreciation. The stock of capital declines if the rate of accumulation is less than the rate of depreciation.

Credit Markets

The production of capital goods is made possible in a modern society through **credit markets,** which are also called *capital markets*.

> **Credit markets** are markets for borrowing and lending funds.

Robinson Crusoe, living alone on a deserted island, had no need for credit markets. Crusoe would simply *save* (give up some present consumption) so he could *invest* (engage in roundabout production to increase his future consumption). When Crusoe took three days off from fishing to weave a net, he was both saving and investing. Simultaneous saving and investing is also characteristic of primitive agricultural societies. Farmers both save and invest by taking time off from current production to drain a swamp or build an earthen dam (that is, to produce capital goods). In a modern economy, however, financial assets—stocks, bonds, bank credit, and trade credit—are used to finance the accumulation of capital goods. In a modern economy, investors and savers are often separate. Credit markets make possible the separation of the act of saving from the act of investing.

Credit, or capital, markets are necessary because of specialization. A business firm that has the foresight to increase future production by investing today (building a larger plant, installing new equipment) usually needs to borrow funds in credit markets in order to be able to make the investment.

Households specialize in saving because they do not have the information to act on profitable investment opportunities. Business firms that specialize in production are able to seek out and take advantage of profitable investment opportunities. There is, therefore, a natural trade that can be set up between households and businesses. In credit markets, firms wishing to invest in capital goods borrow from households (and other businesses); similarly, savers (households and businesses) lend to investors.

The growth of the stock of tangible capital is paralleled by the growth of the financial assets of those individuals or firms who accumulate savings. These financial assets (stocks, bonds, and various IOUs) are specific types of claims on the net productivity of real capital. The owners of such capital receive *interest* (or dividend) *income* from investors as payment for the use of capital.

The Rate of Interest

As a convention, the **interest rate** is usually expressed as an annual percentage rate.

The **interest rate** measures the yearly cost of borrowing as a percent of the amount loaned.

If $1,000 is borrowed on January 1 and $1,100 (the $1,000 borrowed plus $100 interest) is repaid on December 31, the $100 interest represents a 10 percent rate of interest on an annual percentage basis. If the loan were for only six months, and $1,050 were repaid on June 30, the $50 interest still represents a 10 percent annual rate.

Referring to the rate of interest as the "price of money" is confusing and misleading because of the problem of interpreting the word *money*. Strictly speaking, in economics *money* is the medium of exchange used by an economy. Interest was defined earlier as the payment for funds borrowed to invest in capital. Since capital is financed through borrowing and lending, interest can also be considered the *price of credit*. The "price of credit" is a better definition than the "price of money" because the term *credit* assumes the passage of time between borrowing and repayment. The rate of interest represents the terms of trade between the present and future. A high interest rate means that future goods are cheap relative to present goods; a low interest rate means present goods are cheap relative to future goods. If ice cream is $1 a gallon both this year and next year, a 0 percent interest rate means that to give up 1 gallon of ice cream today (saving $1) will yield only 1 gallon next year; a 50 percent interest rate means that to give up 1 gallon of ice cream today will yield 1.5 gallons next year. At a 0 percent interest rate, the opportunity cost of 1 gallon of ice cream today is 1 gallon of ice cream next year. At a 50 percent interest rate, the opportunity cost of 1 gallon today is 1.5 gallons next year.

As a price of credit or borrowing, the interest rate indicates the terms of trade between things today and things tomorrow. The interest rate is the price that links the present and the future. Money, on the other hand, is the medium of exchange *for present transactions*.

Since the interest rate can be used to link the present and future, it can be used to convert future values into present values. The simplest case of present value is that of a perpetual income stream. As shown in the chapter on business organization, the present value *(PV)* of a *perpetual income stream* (a fixed amount of income to be received every year forever) is:

Example 1   Bond Prices and Interest Rates

The present value formula reveals that *there is an inverse relationship between present values and interest rates*. The higher the interest rate, the lower the present value, and vice versa.

The prices that savers are willing to pay for a financial asset that promises payments in the future—such as bonds—will equal the asset's present value. Thus, bonds that promise a specific sequence of dollar payments in the future will fall in price whenever interest rates rise. If the price of a long-term bond is $1,000 when the interest rate is 10 percent, the market price will fall if the interest rate rises to 15 percent because at an interest rate of 15 percent, a new bond pays 15 percent. To compete with the new bonds, the old bonds must be sold at a discount from their original price. The increase in the interest rate causes the present value of the future interest payments to fall. If the bond is sold after the interest rate rises, the owner will suffer a capital loss (the price at which the owner sells will be less than the price at which the owner bought). Thus, substantial capital losses can be incurred on bond holdings as interest rates rise. Conversely, if interest rates fall, the prices of bonds rise. Owners of such bonds can then sell them at a profit (that is, they can experience capital gains). ∎

$$PV = \frac{R}{i}, \qquad (1)$$

where R = the annual income stream, and i = the rate of interest expressed in decimal form. For example, the present value of $100 a year in perpetuity with an interest rate of 10 percent is $100/0.10 = $1,000.

Typically, financial assets do not yield perpetual income streams. Instead, financial assets typically make payments of specified amounts for a limited number of years. For example, the present value of an IOU that pays $100 per year for 3 years would be calculated using the following formula already given in the business-organization chapter for the present value of a future sum of money.

$$PV = \frac{R_n}{(1 + i)^n}, \qquad (2)$$

where R_n is the sum of money to be paid in the nth year and i is the interest rate in decimal form. At a 10 percent interest rate, the $100 to be received one year from now is worth $90.91 (= $100/1.10). In other words, if one deposited $90.91 in a savings account paying 10 percent interest, one would have accumulated $100 at the end of the first year. The $100 to be received 2 years from today is worth $82.65 (= $100/1.21) because if $82.65 were deposited in a 10 percent savings account for 2 years, one would have accumulated $100 after 2 years. Similarly, the $100 to be received 3 years from now is worth $75.19 (= $100/1.33). Thus, the *PV* of the IOU that pays $100 per year for 3 years would be calculated as:

$$\begin{aligned} PV &= \frac{R_1}{1 + i} + \frac{R_2}{(1 + i)^2} + \frac{R_3}{(1 + i)^3} \\ &= \frac{100}{1.10} + \frac{100}{1.21} + \frac{100}{1.33} \\ &= \$90.91 + \$82.65 + \$75.19 = \$248.75. \end{aligned}$$

Present values fall as the interest rate rises and rise as the interest rate falls. At a 15 percent interest rate, the present value of the above 3-year $100-a-year IOU would be $228.50. At a 5 percent interest rate, the present value of the 3-year $100-a-year IOU would be $272.36. (See Example 1.)

Interest-Rate Determination

The interest rate is determined by the interaction of the supply of and demand for loanable funds.

The Supply of Loanable Funds.   The rate of interest is determined in the market for **loanable funds.**

Figure 1   The Market for Loanable Funds

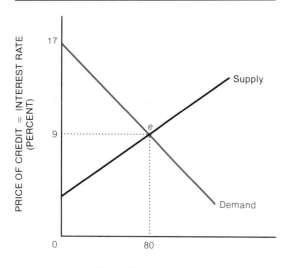

QUANTITY OF LOANABLE FUNDS
(BILLIONS OF DOLLARS)

The supply curve shows the quantity of loanable funds offered by lenders at different interest rates; lenders will offer more at high interest rates. The demand curve shows the quantity of loanable funds demanded by borrowers at different interest rates; less will be demanded at high interest rates. The market for loanable funds is in equilibrium at an interest rate of 9 percent, where the quantity demanded equals the quantity supplied.

Loanable funds are the amount of lending from all households, governments, and businesses, or the bank credit made available to borrowers in credit markets.

For credit markets as a whole, the supply of loanable funds during a given period comes primarily from the net savings of businesses and households during that period. The supply curve in Figure 1 shows the quantity of loanable funds savers are willing to save (and, thereby, make available to lenders) at each interest rate. This supply curve is positively sloped because a larger quantity of loanable funds will be saved (made available to lenders) at high interest rates than at low interest rates, *ceteris paribus*.

The Demand for Loanable Funds.   The demand for loanable funds is principally the demand for new investments in capital goods of businesses. Households also demand loanable funds for automobile loans, consumer credit, and

home mortgages, but this chapter will concentrate primarily on business investment.

What determines the demand for capital goods? New capital raises the output (and, therefore, the revenue) of the firm for a number of years because capital goods are in use for more than one year. For example, a machine will be used for 8 years on average, and a plant will be used for 35 years on average. Capital's *marginal revenue product* (the amount an extra unit of capital will contribute to a firm's revenues) must be estimated over each year of the capital's useful life in order to determine the **rate of return of a capital good.**

> The **rate of return of a capital good** is that rate which makes the present value of the stream of marginal revenue products for each year of the good's life equal to the cost of the capital good.

Business firms will increase the use of capital as long as marginal benefits exceed marginal cost.

> The cost of additional capital is usually the interest rate that firms must pay for credit. The marginal benefit of capital is its rate of return. The equilibrium amount of capital for the firm will be that amount at which the rate of interest and the rate of return on the last investment project are equal.

Example 2 shows how this rate of return could be calculated in the case of a typewriter.

The law of diminishing returns applies to capital just as it applies to labor. Additional capital investment projects will yield successively lower rates of return. In making their investment plans, businesses will consider a variety of investment projects. By adding on a new wing of their plant, they may achieve a high rate of return. By acquiring new equipment to replace older-generation equipment, they may achieve a substantial but lower rate of return. Successive projects bring lower and lower rates of return due to the law of diminishing returns.

The demand curve for loanable funds in Figure 1 is downward-sloping. The demand curve reflects the rate of return on capital investment projects because business firms will be willing to add to their capital stock as long as the rate of return

Example 2 Calculating Rates of Return for a Typewriter

A firm may purchase for $200 a typewriter that will be used for only two years. The firm estimates that the typewriter will have a marginal revenue product of $110 in the first year and $121 the second year. After the second year it will be retired from service and will have a $0 salvage value. The typewriter costs $200. What is its anticipated rate of return?

As noted in the chapter, the rate of return of a capital good is that rate of interest that makes the present value of the stream of *MRP*s for each year of the life of the capital good equal to the cost of the capital good, or in this case that value of *r* (denoting rate of interest or rate of return in decimal form) that solves the equation:

$$\$200 = \frac{\$110}{(1 + r)} + \frac{\$121}{(1 + r)^2}$$

Solving for *r* yields *r* = 0.10, or 10 percent. The firm will not undertake this investment project unless the rate of interest on the $200 necessary to buy the typewriter is less than 10 percent (the rate of return on the typewriter). ∎

---

of investment projects exceeds the rate of interest. In Figure 1, the demand curve shows the quantity of loanable funds investors are prepared to borrow at each interest rate.

> **The demand curve for loanable funds is negatively sloped because at high interest rates there are fewer investment projects that have a rate of return equal to or greater than the interest rate. At low interest rates, there are more investment projects with rates of return equal to or greater than the interest rate.**

The Equilibrium Interest Rate.

Like any other price, the equilibrium (market) rate of interest established by the credit market is that rate at which the quantity of loanable funds supplied equals the quantity demanded.

In Figure 1, when the interest rate is 9 percent, there are $80 billion worth of investment projects that yield a rate of return of 9 percent or above. Since the quantity supplied of loanable funds equals the quantity demanded of loanable funds at that point, the equilibrium rate of interest is 9 percent.

> **The equilibrium interest rate equates the quantity demanded and quantity supplied for loanable funds so that investment projects yielding rates of return less than the equilibrium rate are choked off. Only those investments yielding the market interest rate or above are financed.**

The Productivity of Capital.

The demand for loanable funds reflects the basic productivity of capital. Firms demand loanable funds for investment as long as rates of return are greater than or equal to the rate of interest. Anything that makes capital more productive will shift the demand curve to the right and cause the interest rate to rise. The supply curve of loanable funds reflects the basic thriftiness of the population. Anything that causes the population to be more thrifty (that is, to save more at each interest rate) will shift the supply curve to the right and cause the interest rate to fall.

If an important technological breakthrough raises the productivity of capital, the demand curve would shift to the right and would drive up the interest rate, *ceteris paribus*. If there were a change in tax laws to reward those families that save, the supply curve would shift right and lower the market rate of interest, *ceteris paribus*.

Real Versus Nominal Interest Rates

Inflation occurs when the money prices of goods, on the average, rise over time. How does inflation affect interest rates? Supply-and-demand analysis provides a clear answer. Anticipated inflation affects both the demand for and supply of loanable funds. Loans are repaid in dollars over the course of the loan. Inflation causes these dollars to become cheaper over time. Lenders will become less anxious to lend and the borrower more anxious to borrow if the rate of inflation is expected to increase. As a result, anticipated inflation

Figure 2   Anticipated Inflation and Interest Rates

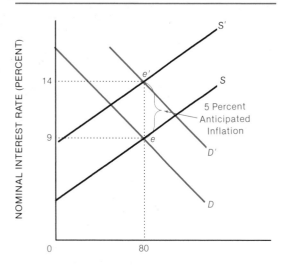

QUANTITY OF LOANABLE FUNDS
(BILLIONS OF DOLLARS)

When there is a 0 percent rate of inflation, the original equilibrium is at point e. When a 5 percent inflation rate is anticipated, borrowers will be willing to pay an interest rate 5 percent higher than before, and lenders must be paid an interest rate 5 percent higher because repayments are in cheaper dollars. Both S and D shift upward by 5 percent. The new equilibrium is e' at a 14 percent interest rate. The real interest rate is still 9 percent (equal to the nominal rate minus the anticipated rate of inflation).

causes the demand curve for loanable funds to shift to the right and the supply curve of loanable funds to shift to the left (see Figure 2).

In Figure 2, the initial equilibrium interest rate is 9 percent when there is 0 percent inflation. If borrowers and lenders anticipate a 5 percent rate of inflation, lenders will want to be compensated for the declining value of the dollars in which the loan is repaid, and borrowers will be willing to pay a higher interest rate because they can repay the loan in cheaper dollars.

What matters to borrowers and lenders is not so much the **nominal interest rate** but the **real interest rate.**

The **nominal interest rate** is the cost of borrowing expressed in terms of current dollars (unadjusted for inflation).

The **real interest rate** equals the nominal interest rate minus the anticipated rate of inflation.[1]

A 14 percent nominal rate of interest with a 5 percent rate of inflation yields the same real rate of interest as a 9 percent interest rate with 0 percent inflation. In Figure 2, the supply and demand curves for loanable funds at 14 percent nominal interest intersect at the same quantity of loanable funds (in constant dollars) as at 9 percent nominal interest, or $80 billion worth of loanable funds. (See Example 3 on real interest rates.)

The Structure of Interest Rates

Although the interest rate is the price of credit, this price is not the same for all borrowers. Some borrowers pay higher interest rates than others. Savings-and-loan associations may pay as little as 5¼ percent when they borrow from their depositors. Individuals who borrow from the savings and loan may be charged interest rates of 12 percent for automobile and home-mortgage loans. The U.S. treasury may pay 8 percent to purchasers of its six-month treasury bill and 10 percent on a three-year treasury bond, while a near-bankrupt company must pay 21 percent on a six-month bank loan. *Different interest rates are paid on different financial assets.* Interest rates differ because of differences in the conditions of *risk, liquidity,* and *maturity* associated with a loan.

Risk.   Borrowers with high credit ratings will pay lower interest rates than borrowers with low credit ratings. Lenders must be compensated for the extra risk associated with lending to borrowers with low credit ratings if they are to be competitive and earn a normal profit. If a certain type of borrower fails to repay bank loans 1 percent of

---

1. This formula holds approximately. Where r = the real interest rate, p = the inflation rate, and i = the nominal interest rate, the actual formula is:

$$r = i - p - rp$$

When r and p are small, rp is close to zero. If $r = 0.10$ and $p = 0.05$, then $rp = 0.005$.

Example 3   Nominal Versus Real Interest Rates

The chapter explains that the real rate of interest is the nominal rate of interest minus the anticipated rate of inflation. The nominal rate of interest is determined in credit markets; nominal interest rates are widely reported in the financial press and in government reports. Nominal interest rates (on high-grade corporate bonds) are reported in the accompanying figure for the period 1975 to 1984. To determine the real rate of interest, one must know the inflation rate that was anticipated at the time the decision was made to lend or borrow loanable funds. To answer this question, we would have to be able to look inside the minds of borrowers and lenders, something we cannot do. Therefore, we cannot know the real rate of interest for sure; we can only guess at its value. One way to look at inflationary psychology is to assume that people determine their expected rate of inflation by looking to the past. The current anticipated rate of inflation will be some average of past inflation rates. In the accompanying figure, it is assumed that the rate of inflation anticipated in each year is the (unweighted) average value of inflation over the previous three years. The real interest rate

shown in the figure is the difference between the nominal interest rate and the average inflation rate of the previous three years (the anticipated rate of inflation). There are a number of alternative ways

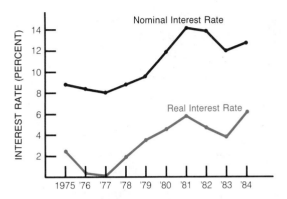

to calculate the anticipated rate of inflation; this is only one method. As the figure shows, the movement of the real interest rate calculated in this way closely parallels the movement of the nominal interest rate. ■

the time, banks will require such a borrower to pay an interest rate at least 1 percent above the interest rate charged borrowers with a 0 percent risk of default. The extra 1 percent is called a *risk premium*.

Liquidity.   A financial asset that can be turned into cash quickly or with a small penalty is said to be *liquid*. People are willing to hold savings accounts paying 5.5 percent interest when six-month certificates of deposits pay 12 percent simply because the former can be turned into cash (the medium of exchange) quickly and without penalty. The general rule is that interest rates will vary inversely with liquidity, *ceteris paribus*.

Maturity.   Interest rates will also vary with the term of maturity. A corporation borrowing $1,000 for one year may pay a lower rate of interest than if it borrows the same $1,000 for two

years because credit-market conditions during the second year are expected to differ from conditions in the first year. If the credit market expects the interest rate on one-year loans to be 10 percent during the first year and 14 percent during the second year of a two-year loan, the interest rate on a two-year loan will be 12 percent. If $1,000 were invested for one year at 10 percent, it would yield $1,100 in one year; if the $1,100 were then reinvested at 14 percent it would yield $1,254. On the other hand, if $1,000 were invested at 12 percent for two years, it would also yield $1,254. Thus, $1,000 invested at 10 percent for one year with the proceeds invested for one more year at 14 percent is the same thing as investing $1,000 for two years at 12 percent. Roughly speaking, the two-year interest rate (expressed on an annual basis) will be an average of the one-year interest rates the credit market anticipates over the two years.

Figure 3   Interest Ceilings and Credit Rationing

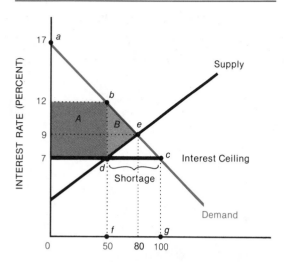

QUANTITY OF LOANABLE FUNDS
(BILLIONS OF DOLLARS)

The equilibrium interest rate at point *e* is 9 percent, where $80 billion worth of loanable funds are borrowed. When an interest ceiling of 7 percent is imposed, $100 billion worth of investment projects are demanded with returns ranging from 17 percent to 7 percent. At an interest rate of 7 percent, only $50 billion worth of these projects can be financed (point *d*). Therefore, some credit rationing must occur. There are $50 billion worth of investment projects that yield returns of from 17 percent to 12 percent (along segment *ab* of the demand curve). There are another $50 billion worth of projects that yield returns of from 12 percent to 7 percent (segment *bc* of the demand curve). If rationing is efficient, the best half of all the desirable projects—those with returns ranging from 17 percent to 12 percent along segment *ab*—would receive financing. If only these high-return projects are financed, society loses the welfare represented by triangle *B*. If only those projects that earn the lowest rates of return— those represented by segment *bc* of the demand curve, earning 12 to 7 percent rates of return—are financed, society loses Area *A + B,* which is the maximum loss from interest ceilings. Switching from the first $50 billion (along *ab*) to the second $50 billion (along *bc*) would lower total returns from 0*abf* to *fbcg.*

Interest-Rate Ceilings

Usury laws (that place ceilings on interest rates charged by lenders) are in effect in many states and countries. An interest-rate ceiling is said to be *effective* if the legislated rate is below the market interest rate that would have prevailed without the usury law.

Usury laws have considerable popular support because they claim to protect the poor from excessive interest rates charged by the rich. Insofar as the rich are the large lenders and the poor are the ones who must borrow, usury laws are thought to redistribute wealth from the rich to the poor. However, most economists agree that effective interest-rate ceilings may redistribute wealth differently.

Wealth Redistributions.   If the interest-rate ceiling lowers the interest rate, the quantity of loans demanded will rise and the quantity supplied will fall. Thus, the ceiling causes an excess demand for loans. The interest rate cannot rise sufficiently to ration the scarce supply of loanable funds.

Figure 3 shows how interest-rate ceilings create shortages of loanable funds. The interest-rate ceiling of 7 percent means there will be an excess of $50 billion in loanable funds demanded by borrowers over what lenders are willing to supply. The excess demand means that some potential borrowers will be unable to get the financing they desire at the interest-rate ceiling. Lenders will be made worse off by the ceiling (at least those lenders that abide by the law) because they are able to lend fewer funds at lower interest rates. The borrowers who actually obtain financing at lower rates are made better off because they will be earning high rates of return on their investment projects but need pay back their loans at the lower ceiling rate of interest. Those shut out of the loan market lose the returns they could have gained if they had had funds for investment. Ceilings, therefore, redistribute wealth from the unlucky (those who are unable to obtain financing at the ceiling rate) to the lucky (those who are able to get financing at the ceiling rate).

Interest-rate ceilings tend to redistribute loanable funds from those who can earn lower rates of return to those that can earn higher returns because the ones who can earn higher returns are better risks. Unfortunately, a larger fraction of poor people are bad credit risks, and they will be the ones who suffer the major burden of the ceiling. In many cases, the only alternative of poor people driven out of the legal loan markets is to find a loan shark charging much more than what the interest rate would be in the absence of ceilings. The loan shark is an entrepreneur for taking risks and must be compensated for breaking the law and dealing with people, who through self selection, reveal themselves to have inferior credit ratings.[2]

Economic Efficiency.

Credit rationing reduces economic efficiency because there is no guarantee that scarce loanable funds will go to finance those investment projects yielding the highest rates of return. Under credit rationing with a 7 percent interest ceiling, for example, a borrower with a 17 percent project may not receive credit while one with a 7 percent project does receive credit. In Figure 3, the loans could just as easily go to the borrowers with low-return investments (on segment bc of the demand curve) as to the borrowers with high-return investments (on segment ab), resulting in lower returns on investments. When this happens—as it can under credit rationing—society loses economic output. This loss of output is a deadweight loss to society. Figure 3 explains how to calculate society's loss of output due to credit rationing. It shows that credit rationing causes deadweight losses even if loans go to those projects with the highest rates of return because credit rationing causes a lower volume of loans.

When there is an excess demand for loanable funds that cannot be eliminated by higher interest rates, there is no guarantee that available loanable funds will be allocated to their highest and best use.

The highest and best use of scarce loanable funds (or resources in general) can be secured by a credit market that sets equilibrium interest rates. An interest-rate ceiling can result in credit rationing that reallocates scarce loanable funds from high-yielding investment projects to low-yielding investment projects.

---

2. It was probably through the usury laws that the early economists such as Adam Smith were alerted to the unfortunate effects of interfering with the market mechanism. Adam Smith realized that what legislators intended was often quite different than the actual impact of laws such as interest-rate ceilings.

RENT

The rent on land is a relatively small proportion—about 2 or 3 percent—of the total of all payments to factors of production in the United States. This figure includes payments based on the natural fertility of the land and its locational advantages but excludes the returns to investments erected on the land or capital improvements in the land (such as irrigation). The crucial feature of land and other natural resources is that they are relatively inelastic in supply. They are nature's bounty, and the quantity supplied is not affected by the price received as a factor payment.

Even though land rents account for such a small portion of factor payments, relative inelasticity of supply can characterize productive factors other than land and natural resources. Because other types of factor payments resemble land rents, the study of rents for land and natural resources is much more important than the small percentages of factor payments to land suggests.

"Rents" paid for apartments, cars, tools, or moving trucks should not be confused with the *economic rents* studied in this section. "Rental payments" for the temporary use of a particular piece of property owned by someone else can be returns to land, labor, or capital. Apartment rent is a payment both to land (for the land on which the apartment resides) and to capital (for the structure itself). Thus, the common term *rent* is simply a price or rental rate rather than a payment to a specific factor of production.

Pure Economic Rent

Figure 4 shows the determination of the competitive price for a fixed amount of land. The market demand curve is generated from the demand curves of all firms for the land; its height at any point equals the marginal revenue product of different amounts of land inputs. The supply curve is completely inelastic: more land is not forthcoming at higher prices. The competitive rent paid to land is that price which equates the fixed quantity supplied with the quantity demanded. As such, the equilibrium price rations the fixed supply of land among the various claimants for the land.

Figure 4   Pure Economic Rent

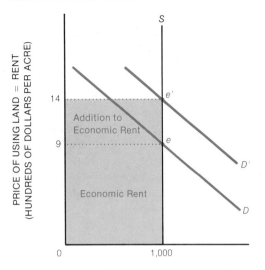

QUANTITY OF LAND (ACRES)

Because the supply of land is fixed at 1,000 acres, the supply curve, *S,* is perfectly inelastic. The equilibrium rent of $900 per acre at *e* gives rise to pure economic rents, since the land has no alternative uses. The entire rental payment is a surplus over opportunity costs. In this case, opportunity costs are zero. If the demand curve for land increases from *D* to *D',* due to an increase in the demand for the product the land is used to produce, the economic rent will rise from $900 to $1,400 per acre at *e'.* Changes in economic rents are demand-determined because supply is fixed.

The main economic role of **pure economic rent** is to assure that the factors of production that are fixed in supply are used in the highest and best use.

A **pure economic rent** is the price paid to a productive factor that is completely inelastic in supply. Land is the classic example of such a factor.

Figure 4 illustrates the concept of pure economic rent. If the price of land were $0, the same quantity of land would be supplied as if the price were $900 or $1,400 per acre, as shown by the vertical supply curve. The quantity demanded, however, at a zero price would likely be very large. Even if the land were prime agricultural land, at a zero price, instead of being used to produce food, the land might be used as a garbage dump or as a dumpyard for old cars. A higher price of land will cut off the various demands for

the land that have a low *MRP*. If the price is too high, the land will not be fully used, and there will be an excess supply. If the price is too low, the land may not be put to its best use. Just as interest-rate ceilings may allow investments with relatively low rates of return to be financed, so land rents that are below equilibrium can allow land to be put to uses that yield relatively low *MRP*s. Efficiency requires that the price be set where the quantity supplied equals the quantity demanded of land.

> The pure economic rent that is paid to a productive factor does not serve the incentive function of increasing the quantity supplied of the scarce factor because the supply is perfectly inelastic. Pure economic rent in a competitive market serves as a guide to efficient resource use by rationing the available supply to the most efficient use.

When something is perfectly inelastic in supply, price incentives cannot lead to an increase in its supply. The price of a good or factor that is perfectly inelastic in supply must, therefore, be demand-determined. If the demand curve in Figure 4 shifts from *D* to *D'* due to technological advances in the use of the land or increases in the final demands for goods that the land is used to produce, competitive economic rents will be bid up.

From the standpoint of an individual firm using agricultural land, economic rent is most certainly a cost of production. In order to bid the land away from other uses, the individual firm must pay the competitive price. From the standpoint of the economy as a whole, however, rent is not a true opportunity cost to society. The amount of available land and other resources that are fixed in supply is a free gift of nature. In the case of pure rent, the payment to the factor of production exceeds the payment required to keep the resource available to the economy by the entire amount of the rental payment. The land is fixed in supply; the economy has use of the land whether it pays something or nothing. But the individual firm does not have use of the land unless it is willing to bid the land away from alternative users. For the economy as a whole, the opportunity cost of land that is fixed in supply is zero. For the indi-

Example 4   Land Taxes and Efficiency

A tax on the natural fertility or locational advantages of a piece of land will have no impact on the supply of the land. The same amount of land is offered for rent on the market even if the economic rent received by the owner is lowered. Therefore, the market-clearing price will not change if a tax (to be paid by the owner) is levied. This feature of land makes it an attractive target of taxation because it means that a tax on land will not harm economic efficiency. The tax does not affect the quantity of land supplied, unlike a tax on labor and capital that would reduce the quantity supplied.

Suppose the government institutes a 50 percent tax on land rents and that prior to the tax, land was renting for $1,000 per acre. What effect will the tax have on land rents? Who will "pay" the tax? From the perspective of businesses renting the land, the tax does not affect the *MRP* of the land, so the demand curve for the land will remain the same. In order for the land owner to pass the tax on to the user, the supply of land would have to be reduced, thereby raising the rental price to the user. In the case of land, the individual landowner gains no advantage from withdrawing the land from use, since rental income would fall to zero. Thus, the rental price would remain as it was before the tax, and the landowner would "pay" the entire tax. Land would continue to rent for $1,000 per acre, but the landowner would receive only $500 after paying the tax to the government. Economic efficiency has not been impaired because the quantity of land in use has remained the same.

The distribution of the burden of a 50 percent tax on land rents is illustrated in Figure 5. Since the tax does not affect the marginal revenue product of the land (as measured by the height of the demand curve before the tax), the rent the market is willing to pay per acre for any given total quantity of land will remain the same. The tax collector, however, will take 50 percent of the rental price. A 50 percent tax shifts the demand curve facing

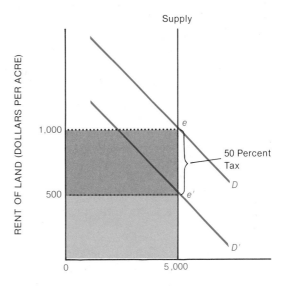

landowners from *D* to *D'* because the tax collector takes half the rental price land users are willing to pay. The net price received by landowners falls from $1,000 per acre to $500 per acre. The landowners bear the entire burden of the tax. The equilibrium rental price that renters must pay remains at $1,000 per acre. ∎

vidual user of that land, the equilibrium economic rent is a real cost of production that must be paid in order to prevent the land from being used in an alternative way. (See Example 4.)

Quasi Rents

Naturally productive land and land located in prime urban and manufacturing areas is inelastic in supply in the long run. No matter what is done, no matter what economic rents are paid, such land cannot be increased in supply. Payments to such land are *pure economic rents*. Because the opportunity cost to society of this land is zero in both the long and short runs, the entire factor payment is a payment of economic rent. Many factors that are fixed in supply in the short run, however, are more elastic in supply in the long run.

There are many examples of factors that are fixed in supply in the short run. In a booming sunbelt city, the amount of space in office buildings is fixed in supply in the short run; when the

Example 5   Economic Rents and Classical Musicians

Symphony orchestras complain that their financial difficulties are caused by the soaring fees that the top concert artists earn. In 1981, the top fees per performance earned by musicians were: Luciano Pavarotti (tenor) and Vladimir Horowitz (pianist)—$40,000; Rudolf Serkin (pianist) and Joan Sutherland (soprano)—$25,000; M. Rostropovich (cellist), Leonard Bernstein (conductor), and George Solti (conductor)—$15,000.

How much economic rent these performers earn as musicians would depend upon their next best alternative earnings as nonmusicians. Some may have good options outside of music. Leonard Bernstein, for example, could perhaps be a politician or TV announcer, earning, say, $5,000 per appearance. Bernstein's economic rent would, therefore, be $10,000 per performance ($15,000–$5,000). Others of these musicians may have limited earning potential outside of music. Their economic rent would be even more substantial.

Why are extraordinary economic rents paid? From the viewpoint of the symphony orchestra, music society, or opera company, these fees must be paid because others are paying these fees. Opera companies, for example, bid among themselves for top stars. Although the Metropolitan Opera of New York attempted to maintain a top fee of $6,000, the company found that other companies were paying $10,000 and even more. If the Met is to attract top performers, it simply must pay the going rate.

The supply of musical superstars is inelastic because the superstars offer something other performers cannot match, an ingredient that sells out every concert. Other musicians may have equal skill, but they do not have the charisma and attraction of the superstar. ■

Source: "Soaring Fees for Star Musicians Are Disrupting the Concert World," *New York Times,* November 30, 1981.

---

demand for office space increases, office rental rates rise dramatically. The demand curve shifts up (or right) along a vertical supply curve. In the long run, however, developers will respond to soaring office rents by constructing new office buildings, but it may take two to five years to plan and complete significant additions to the stock of office buildings. In the long run, as these office buildings are completed, the supply curve becomes more elastic and office rents are reduced.

The supply of professional tennis players is essentially fixed in the short run, for it takes years of training and practice to develop players of professional caliber. If the demand for professional tennis players increases due to an increase in the popularity of the sport, the earnings of the fixed number of tennis professionals will increase. In the short run, they will be able to earn extraordinary salaries. In the long run, however, new professional-caliber players who are attracted by high prize earnings will enter the profession; the supply becomes more elastic, and the extraordinary earnings of tennis professionals will be bid down. (See Example 5.)

As these examples show, the owners of resources that are fixed in supply in the short run will receive economic rents. But such a payment is not a pure economic rent but a **quasi rent** because it cannot be maintained in the long run.

A **quasi rent** is a payment over and above the short-run opportunity cost necessary to induce the owners of the resources to offer their resources for sale or rent in the short run.

In the long run, quasi rents will disappear as the supply curve becomes more elastic. In the long run, the supply curve will become more and more elastic until quasi rents have been dissipated. At this point, the factor of production will be paid its opportunity cost.

Economic Rent and Other Factors of Production

Pure economic rents represent an extreme case of factor payment. At the other extreme is a payment to a factor that just equals its opportunity cost. A factor of production that is perfectly elastic in supply earns no economic rents because the factor is paid its *opportunity cost* (its earnings in its next best alternative use). For example, a small farmer must compete with other farmers and potential users of the land. If the farmer does not pay what the land could earn in its next best use, the land will be used elsewhere.

In between factors of production that are perfectly elastic in supply and those that are perfectly inelastic are numerous cases where factors of production earn some surplus return over their opportunity costs, or **economic rent.**

> **Economic rent** is the excess of the payment to the factor over its opportunity cost.

The major distinction between *economic rent* and *pure economic rent* is that a factor that earns pure economic rent has an opportunity cost of zero. A factor that earns economic rent has an opportunity cost that is positive but smaller than the payment to the factor.

The amount of economic rent earned by a factor depends upon the perspective from which the factor is viewed. The corn land rented by an Iowa farmer does not earn economic rent—because the *individual* farmer is paying the land's opportunity cost—but Iowa corn land *in general* does earn economic rent. In other words, *rents accrue to factor owners, not factor users.* The economic rent of John Smith as an engineer differs from the economic rent of John Smith as an engineer *for General Motors.* Smith can earn $30,000 per year working for GM, $29,000 working for Ford, and $20,000 working in his best nonengineering job. Smith's economic rent as a GM engineer is $1,000 (the excess of his earnings over his opportunity cost); his economic rent as an engineer is $10,000 (the excess of his earnings as an engineer over his next best nonengineering alternative).

The prices paid to an attractive movie star, a late-night talk-show host, the winningest pitcher in major league baseball, Iowa farm land, and offices in New York City surprisingly have much in common: a large fraction of the factor's income is economic rent. These factors receive payments in excess of their opportunity cost (their earnings in alternative uses). The factor payment serves the function of assuring that the factor is employed efficiently in its highest and best use. Boxing great Mohammed Ali's million-dollar contracts served the important economic function of assuring that his assets were efficiently utilized; the utility of sports fans would have been reduced if he were employed as a waiter at a local restaurant. Paying one of the world's most talented tenors $40,000 per performance assures that he devotes himself to opera and not to working as a plumber.

Although people often resent individuals with inherited talents, rare skills, or good looks who earn substantial salaries, it should be recognized that oil-drilling rigs, Hawaii real estate, Iowa corn land, and high-speed computers are earning similar rewards; namely, payments in excess of their opportunity costs. Although land rents account for only a small portion of total factor earnings, economic rents are paid to a wide variety of economic factors. Actors, professional athletes, musicians, surgeons, professors, and television repair persons can earn economic rents.

PROFITS

People are often suspicious of the ethics of those individuals and companies who earn high profits. In the Middle Ages, high profits were seen as a sure sign that a pact had been made with the devil, who would soon get another lost soul for Hades' fire.

Profits that are headlined on the business pages are *accounting profits* that often have little to do with *economic profit.* From an economist's point of view, **accounting profits** can be misleading because they do not take into account the firm's *opportunity costs,* which include actual payments to factors of production as well as the costs of the next best alternative that the firm has sacrificed. Economists prefer to evaluate a firm's profitability on the basis of **normal profits** and **economic profits.**

> **Accounting profits** are simply enterprise revenues minus explicit enterprise costs.

> **Normal profits** are the profits required to keep resources in that particular business. Normal profits are earned when revenues equal opportunity costs.

Economic profits are the excess of revenues over total opportunity costs (which include both actual payments and sacrificed alternatives). Economic profits are profits in excess of normal profits.

In practice, it is very difficult to calculate a firm's economic profits because it is difficult to know all implicit opportunity costs. The practical difficulty of calculating economic profits does not detract from the important role of economic profits in economic theory. As earlier chapters explained, economic profits regulate entry into and exit from an industry.

Sources of Economic Profits

There are three basic sources of economic profits. The first source is the existence of barriers to entry in an industry or business. Such economic profits, called *monopoly profits,* are the basis of popular misgivings about profits. The second source of profits is the dynamic and ever-changing nature of the economic system. Such profits arise from the uncertain or risky nature of economic activity. The third source of economic profits is innovation. The individual (or group of individuals) who engage in risk taking and innovation are called *entrepreneurs*. For this reason, economic profits that are not the result of monopoly restrictions are often considered the reward to entrepreneurship.

Entry Restrictions.   As we have shown, monopolies can earn a profit rate in excess of normal profits. Moreover, unlike competitive profits, which are transitory in nature, monopoly profits can persist over a long period of time. In other words, under conditions of monopoly, businesses can earn revenues that exceed the opportunity costs of the factors they employ. In this sense, monopoly profits are like economic rents; for this reason, economists often refer to monopoly profits as *monopoly rents*. Monopoly profits can also be earned in a potentially competitive industry where entry is restricted by government licensing or franchising. If monopoly profits cannot be competed away by the entry of new firms, existing firms can enjoy monopoly rents. The source of these monopoly rents is the restriction on supply caused by entry restrictions.

Examples of monopoly profits due to entry restrictions are not hard to find. Cable-television franchises are granted by municipal authorities and by local governments. Once the franchise is granted, the cable-television company is protected by law from the entry of competitors. In many cities, taxicab drivers must be licensed, and entry into the business is controlled by the high cost of the license. Monopoly profits in the prescription-drug industry are protected by patents. Economies of scale also limit the entry of competitors into power generation, telecommunication services, and parcel deliveries.

Monopoly profits are often difficult to detect because they will be *capitalized* (converted to their present value) when the firm is sold to a new owner. For example, in New York City, when taxicab drivers sell their licenses (called *medallions*) to others, the market price that the license brings will be the present value of the cab's monopoly profits. The cab driver who purchases the license is earning no economic profit because the economic profit has gone to the original owner of the license (see Example 6 for a more detailed discussion).

Risk Taking.   If there were no entry restrictions, if people could predict the future perfectly, and if there were no costs for obtaining information about current market opportunities, there would be no economic profit. All businesses would earn normal profits. If an opportunity arose to earn economic profits, it would be anticipated and the free entry of new firms would serve to keep profits down to a normal return.

Unfortunately, no one can predict the future. Industry is unprepared for wars, changes in fashions and preferences, weather, and new inventions. Even with free entry, at any given time, some industries will earn economic profits, and others will suffer negative economic profits. Unanticipated shifts in demand or costs cause economic profits to rise and fall. The majority of people wish to limit their exposure to the ups and downs of the economy; they want a steady income. Therefore, there must be rewards to those who are willing to risk the ups and downs of economic fortunes. Just as those who lend money to poor credit risks require risk premiums, so those who desire economic profits must be willing to reward risk bearing. In his book, *Risk, Uncer-*

Example 6   Monopoly Profits and Medallion Cabs in New York City

A New York City cab *medallion* (taxi license) entitles the seller to earn economic profits. The New York City Taxi and Limousine Commission has frozen the number of medallions at 11,787 for 40 years. The fixed number of licenses controls entry and creates monopoly profits. The medallion license entitles the licensed taxi to respond both to radio calls and to hails. The 1984 price of a medallion was around $80,000. What determines this price? A medallion buyer is willing to pay $80,000 for a medallion because a licensed taxi can earn economic profits. The $80,000 price reflects the fact that (with 1984 interest rates at around 13 percent) the medallion is expected to bring in economic profits of $10,400 per year. If the $80,000

were put in a savings account yielding 13 percent annual interest, it would yield a perpetual income stream of $10,400 per year. If the taxi license yielded less than this amount, the 1984 buyer would not be willing to pay $80,000 for it. The purchaser of the medallion does not earn economic profits because the normal operating costs plus the interest costs of purchasing the medallion should yield only a normal rate of profit. The monopoly profit accrues to the seller of the license who has received the monopoly profit in a lump-sum payment. It is difficult to detect economic profits when they must be traced back to the seller monopolist. ■

---

tainty, and Profit (1921), economist Frank Knight emphasized that uncertainty and risk taking are the ultimate source of profit. Knight noted that there will be a large element of luck in the fortunes of different enterprises. Economic profits cannot be assured in an uncertain world; the outcome of the profit game will be to a large extent random.

Uncertainty turns the quest for profits into something resembling a game of chance in which there will be winners and losers even in the long run. Entrepreneurs are the ones who bear this risk. The winners will earn economic profits; the losers will make losses. Like games of chance, there will be some big winners and some big losers. Most business firms will earn either more or less than the average return to risk bearing. Some firms will have extreme good luck and experience large returns; others will experience large misfortunes. All is not fair in love, war, and . . . business. As in a game of chance, profits will average out to a normal return over all firms but there will be a wide range of profit outcomes with a few big winners, a few big losers, and a larger number of intermediate winners and losers.

Innovation.   Blind luck cannot explain all economic profits. The economy is in a constant state of flux. New technologies are developing; consumer tastes are changing; new markets are being discovered. Resource availabilities are

changing. To be an innovator requires ability, foresight, luck, and the willingness to bear risk.

Austrian-born economist Joseph Schumpeter (1883–1950) maintained that profits were primarily the return to the entrepreneur and innovator, but that these entrepreneurial profits were temporary. Economic progress requires a succession of new innovations to replace the old. A successful entrepreneur will earn substantial economic profits only temporarily until another entrepreneur with a newer and better idea comes along to take customers and profits away.

Business history is replete with success stories of business geniuses—Henry Ford and the Model-T, Edwin Land and the Polaroid camera, Richard Sears and Alvah Roebuck and mass retailing, and Louis Marx and his children's toy empire. It is difficult to believe that ability and entrepreneurial genius did not lead to the success of each of these companies. More was involved than a game of chance with an uncertain outcome. Yet even ability does not guarantee success. Many able people are trying to become the next Henry Ford or the next Sears or Roebuck, but few succeed.

Empirical Evidence

According to economic theory, profits arise from monopoly restrictions and barriers, uncertainty and risk, and entrepreneurial innovation. Does the factual record support these propositions? It is

Figure 5   Compensation of Employees and Corporate Profits, 1960–1984

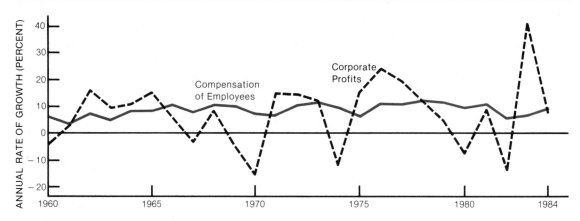

This graph shows that corporate profits are characterized by greater variability than wage income over time—suggesting that it is more risky to be dependent on profits than it is to be dependent on wage income.

Source: *Economic Report of the President;* 1984 (Washington, D.C.: U.S. Government Printing Office, 1984), pp. 244, 315; *Federal Reserve Bulletin.*

very difficult for economists to test the relationship between economic profit and these three factors. It is virtually impossible to measure economic profit. Although it is easier to measure accounting profit—a measure that includes elements of normal returns to land, labor, and capital—accounting profit is less valuable as an economic measure. Empirical studies typically assume that rates of return based on accounting profits are indicative of rates of return based on economic profits.

Barriers to Entry and Profits.   The empirical literature supports the theory that economic profits are strongly associated with monopoly barriers to entry. For example, prescription drugs protected by patents sell at 60 to 100 times average costs, and price-fixing conspiracies have been shown to create extraordinary profits. Other examples of the correlation between barriers to entry and profit rates can be found in the chapter on oligopoly.

Risk and Profits.   The problem in determining the relationship between risk and profit rates is that it is very difficult to measure the amount of risk a firm or an industry faces. In empirical studies, risk is typically measured by the variabil-

ity of profits. If there are considerable ups and downs in profits over time or among firms in a particular industry, substantial risk is said to be present.

Figure 5 plots annual growth in wage income (employee compensation) and corporate profits over time. The most striking differences between the two series is the much greater variability of profits. Unlike earnings from labor, which tend to rise smoothly from year to year, profits rise and fall—sometimes with very substantial declines from one year to the next. If risks are indeed measured by ups and downs, it is definitely more risky to be dependent upon profits than on wages, at least as far as the aggregate economy is concerned. The annual ups and downs of aggregate profits may not be an accurate guide to risk, however, because more serious risk stems from longer-run dangers from new technology and new competition that can cause a permanent decline in the profits earned by individual firms.

Economists that have studied the relationship between the rate of profit and risk (as measured by the variability of profits) find (although there is some dispute on this matter) that profit rates are indeed higher in risky industries. Firms and industries that are subject to greater risk earn *risk premiums*. Entrepreneurs and stockholders are compensated in the form of higher average profits for being called upon to bear more risk than others.[3]

Innovation and Profits. The association between entrepreneurial activity and profit rates is difficult to establish empirically because it is difficult to find measurements of trends in entrepreneurial activity to associate with the ups and downs of profits. Although statistical tests remain to be conducted, economic history shows that great fortunes (the fortunes of the Rockefeller, Carnegie, Mellon, and Ford families) have been amassed by great entrepreneurs. Although good fortune may have played a role in the accumulation of these fortunes, a more likely interpretation is that the fortunes were the consequence of entrepreneurial innovation.

The last three chapters surveyed how the economy determines wages, rents, interest, and profit—the payments to the productive factors of labor, land, capital, and entrepreneurship. The next chapter will turn from the functional distribution of income to the personal distribution of income and will address questions like: How equally or unequally is income distributed among persons? What has happened to the personal distribution of income? How does America's income distribution compare to that of other countries? What can be done about poverty?

Summary

1. Interest, rent, and profits account for some 26 percent of factor payments in the United States.

2. Interest is payment for the use of capital. The supply of capital is the result of past saving and investment decisions. Interest rates are determined in credit markets, which make possible the specialization of savings and investment decisions. The structure of interest rates depends upon risk, liquidity, and maturity. Interest rates are determined in the market for loanable funds by the demand and supply of loanable funds. The real rate of interest is the nominal interest rate minus the anticipated rate of inflation.

3. Rent is payment for the use of land or natural resources. Pure economic rent is the payment to a factor of production that is completely inelastic in supply and is demand-determined. A quasi rent is payment to a factor of production above short-run opportunity costs. In the long run, quasi rents tend to disappear. Economic rent is the excess of the payment to a factor over its opportunity cost.

4. Economic profits are the excess of revenues over total opportunity costs. The sources of economic profits are: restrictions to entry into an industry, uncertainty, and entrepreneurship. Empirical evidence supports the relationship between profits and entry barriers, between profits and risk taking, and between profits and innovation.

Key Terms

interest
depreciation
credit markets
interest rate
loanable funds
rate of return of a capital good
nominal interest rate
real interest rate
pure economic rent
quasi rent
economic rent
accounting profits
normal profits
economic profits

---

3. Empirical studies of the relationship between risk and profitability have been conducted by I. N. Fisher and G. R. Hall, "Risk and Corporate Rates of Return," *Quarterly Journal of Economics* 83 (February 1969): 79–92 and P. Cootner and D. Holland, "Rate of Return and Business Risk," *Bell Journal of Economics* 1 (Fall 1970): 211–16. Both studies found a positive association between risk and corporate profit rates. A different interpretation of these findings has been suggested by Richard Caves and Basil Yamey, "Risk and Corporate Returns: Comment," *Quarterly Journal of Economics* 85 (August 1971): 513–17 and by W. G. Shepherd, *The Treatment of Market Power* (New York: Columbia University Press, 1975), who argue that these higher rates of return are the result of oligopoly structure rather than greater risk.

Questions and Problems

1. Why is it misleading to call interest the price of money?

2. This chapter emphasized that the credit market is another example of specialization in economics. Explain how this specialization works and its effect on economic efficiency.

3. If you borrow $10,000 from the bank and repay the bank $12,000 in one year, what is the annual rate of interest?

4. A business earns $1,000 per year in economic profits and is expected to earn these annual profits in perpetuity. The current market interest rate is 10 percent. What is the present value of this business? How is the present value related to the rate of interest?

5. A machine that costs $1,000 will last two years, after which it must be scrapped with no salvage value. If the machine is purchased it will raise profits by $0 the first year and $1800 the second. What is the rate of return on this investment? Would the firm invest if the interest rate were 20 percent?

6. A company has four investment projects that yield returns of 20 percent, 15 percent, 10 percent, and 5 percent. Explain how the company will decide which of these projects to carry out.

7. The interest rate is currently 10 percent, and the inflation rate is 5 percent. If people anticipate that the inflation rate will rise to 10 percent, what effect could this expectation have on interest rates?

8. Distinguish between *pure economic rents* and *quasi rents*.

9. "Pure economic rents play no useful role in the economy because the supply of the factor in question is fixed. The factor will be supplied no matter what rent is paid." Evaluate this statement.

10. Why should the profit rate be higher in businesses that are risky? How do we measure risk?

11. What is the logic of taxing economic rents as opposed to taxing other kinds of factor incomes?

12. Identify the source of economic profits earned:
    a. by steel companies after the government imposed restrictions on competitive steel imports from foreign countries.
    b. in the coal industry after the Organization of Petroleum Exporting Countries quadrupled the price of oil in 1974.
    c. by a firm that developed a sure-fire method of increasing gas mileage.

Suggested Readings

Heyne, Paul and Thomas Johnson. *Toward Understanding Microeconomics*. Chicago: SRA, 1976, chaps. 2, 13.

Knight, Frank. *Risk, Uncertainty, and Profit*. New York: Harper Torchbooks, 1957.

Schumpeter, Joseph. *Theory of Economic Development*. Cambridge, Mass.: Harvard University Press, 1949.

39

Income Distribution and Poverty

Chapter Preview

This chapter will consider why some people are poor and others are rich. The distribution of personal income among households and among private individuals is determined first in factor markets. One's factor income equals the sum of the earnings of one's factors of production—one's land, labor, capital, and entrepreneurship. These earnings will be high if one owns relatively large quantities of factors that command relatively high prices in factor markets. The one who owns only one factor of production—say, unskilled labor—that commands a very low price in the labor market will have a low factor income. Government can change the distribution of income received from the ownership of the factors of production through differential taxes, through the unequal distribution of government services, and through transfer payments. The government's role in determining the distribution of income is an important topic in this chapter. Previous chapters have already described how factor markets operate—how wage rates, interest payments, and rents are determined; this knowledge is necessary to understand income distribution. ∎

Figure 1   The Lorenz Curve

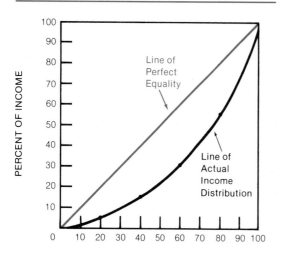

PERCENT OF HOUSEHOLDS

The Lorenz curve measures the cumulative percentage of households (ranked from lowest to highest incomes) on the horizontal axis and the cumulative percentage of income earned by these households on the vertical axis. If all households earned the same income (perfect equality), the Lorenz curve would be a 45-degree line. The 45-degree line is called the *line of perfect equality*. The bowed Lorenz curve shows an unequal distribution of income. The more the Lorenz curve for a society is bowed away from the line of perfect equality, the greater is the inequality in the distribution of income in that society.

MEASUREMENT OF INCOME INEQUALITY

The Lorenz Curve

The most common measure of the degree of inequality in the distribution of income is the **Lorenz curve.**

The **Lorenz curve** shows the percentage of all income earned by households at successive income levels. The cumulative share of households (ranked from lowest to highest incomes) is plotted on the horizontal axis of the Lorenz curve, and the cumulative share of income earned by the cumulative percent of households is plotted on the vertical axis.

Typically Lorenz curves are plotted in *quintiles*, or fifths. A household in the top fifth of the

Table 1   A Hypothetical Lorenz Curve

Quintile (1)	Share of Income (percent) (2)	Cumulative Share of Income (percent) (3)
Lowest fifth	5	5
Second fifth	10	15
Third fifth	15	30
Fourth fifth	25	55
Highest fifth	45	100

income distribution earns more than at least 80 percent of all households. A household in the bottom fifth earns less than at least 80 percent of all households. A hypothetical Lorenz curve is drawn in Figure 1 and plots the cumulative percentage of households against their cumulative share of income, given in column (3) of Table 1. For example, the cumulative share of income for the first four quintiles is 55 percent. That is, the bottom 80 percent of households accounts for 55 percent of all income. The bottom 20 percent of households earns only 5 percent of all income, and the top 20 percent earns 45 percent of all income.

A 45-degree line can be drawn to show absolute equality in the distribution of income: if income were equal, the bottom 20 percent of households would receive 20 percent of all income; the bottom 40 percent of households would receive 40 percent of all income; and so on. When the Lorenz curve deviates from the 45-degree line, which is called the *line of perfect equality,* the income distribution departs from perfect equality.[1] The more bowed the Lorenz curve is from

---

1. Another measure of the inequality of income distribution is the Gini Coefficient. The *Gini coefficient* is a numerical measure of inequality. The Gini coefficient is defined as the area between the 45-degree line and the Lorenz curve divided by the total area under the 45-degree line. If there is perfect equality, the Lorenz curve and the 45-degree line coincide, and the Gini coefficient is zero. If there is perfect inequality (one household gets all the income), then the difference between the Lorenz curve and the 45-degree line equals the entire area under the 45-degree line, and the Gini coefficient equals 1. In between these two extremes, the Gini coefficient can measure whether one income distribution is more or less unequal than another.

Table 2   The U.S. Distribution of Income (before taxes)

Quintile of Households	1929		1982	
	Share of Income (percent)	Cumulative Share of Income (percent)	Share of Income (percent)	Cumulative Share of Income (percent)
Lowest fifth	3.9	3.9	4.7	4.7
Second fifth	8.6	12.5	11.2	15.9
Third fifth	13.8	26.3	17.1	33.0
Fourth fifth	19.3	45.6	24.3	57.3
Highest fifth	54.4	100.0	42.7	100.0
Top 5 percent	30.0		15.7	

Source: *Historical Statistics of the United States, Part 1*, p. 300; *Statistical Abstract of the United States*, 1984, p. 465; *Federal Reserve Bulletin*, September 1984.

the line of perfect equality, the more unequal is the distribution of income.

Facts and Figures

Table 2 gives some facts about the American distribution of income before taxes in 1929 and 1982. The corresponding Lorenz curves are drawn in Figure 2. Over the past 60 years, there has been a noticeable leveling in the American distribution of income—a distinct trend toward more equality. Households in the top fifth accounted for 54.4 percent of all income in 1929 but for only 42.7 percent in 1982. The top 5 percent accounted for 30 percent of all income in 1929 but for only 15.7 percent in 1982. The share of the lowest 40 percent of households rose from 12.5 percent in 1929 to 15.9 percent in 1982. The *middle class* (households in the third and fourth quintiles) increased its relative standing most over the past half century: its share of income rose from 33.1 percent to 41.4 percent.

Despite the long-term trend toward a more equal distribution of income before taxes, there is still considerable inequality in the distribution of income. The top 5 percent of U.S. households accounts for 15.7 percent of all income, while the bottom 20 percent accounts for only 4.7 percent of all income. Since the top 20 percent earns 42.7 percent of all income, households in the top 20 percent earn on average about 9 times as much as those in the bottom 20 percent.

Why do some individuals and households earn a great deal more than others? Why is it that actual distribution of income departs so much from the line of perfect equality?

Figure 2   Lorenz Curves of the U.S. Distribution of Income, 1929 and 1982

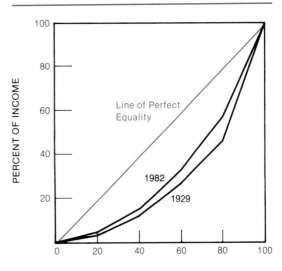

Over the past 53 years, there has been a distinct trend toward more equality in the U.S. distribution of income.

Source: Table 2.

SOURCES OF INEQUALITY

To determine what can be done (or should be done) about the distribution of income, it is important to understand the causes of inequality, including differences in ability, in chance and luck, in discrimination, in occupation, in human-capital investment choices, and in inheritance.

Differences in Ability

People have different mental and physical abilities that they are born with or that they acquire during their childhood years. Because of differences in ability, individuals are limited in their choice of occupation. Not everyone has the ability (mental skills and manual dexterity) to become a surgeon; few have the physical endowments to become professional athletes or high-paid fashion models. On the other hand, many possess the necessary skills to perform unskilled labor, to do typing, or to serve as bank tellers or store clerks. Because people are different, the labor market segregates them into noncompeting groups, as mentioned in the chapter on labor markets. The limited numbers of individuals with high IQs compete among themselves for jobs as physicians, lawyers, and engineers. The limited numbers of individuals with superb athletic ability compete among themselves for jobs as professional athletes. Those individuals with extroverted personalities and communication skills compete among themselves for jobs as sales representatives, public-relations agents, politicians, and union organizers. Because people are segregated into noncompeting groups, substantial wage differentials may emerge that can persist over a long period of time. Workers from a noncompeting group will not be able to enter the higher-wage market because such persons are excluded by ability, strength, or just outright discrimination from working in the higher-paying profession. The six-figure earnings of the surgeon will not cause people to switch from ditchdigging to surgery. The requirement of being able to lift 100 pounds will keep many people from seeking employment on offshore-drilling rigs even though high wage rates are being paid.

According to some studies, ability probably has only a relatively small independent effect on differential earnings because employers use for-

mal schooling as a screening device. Michael Spence and Nobel Laureate Kenneth Arrow maintain that the amount of formal schooling an individual has signals to employers that that individual is likely to possess sought-after traits. Lack of schooling credentials also serves to filter out for prospective employers individuals who are likely to be less productive. As long as schooling simply serves to screen employees for potential employers, the effect of ability should be modest. Employers will accept college graduates for positions with good career prospects and will not spend that much effort trying to distinguish among college graduates on the basis of ability.

The screening approach deviates from traditional human-capital theory, which argues that individuals with more schooling and training earn more because they are more productive. Screening theory suggests that schooling simply serves as a filter to admit some to high-paying jobs while excluding others who lack schooling credentials.[2]

Discrimination

Discrimination according to age, sex, skin color, or national origin can also contribute to income inequality. If individuals are denied equal access to education and training, they will be unable through no fault of their own to accumulate the same amounts of human capital as those who are not subject to discrimination. If individuals are denied access to jobs in craft unions or industrial unions for reasons of race, color, or creed, then these individuals will be the ones who spill over into the nonunionized sector, creating a favorable wage differential for unionized workers. If individuals are restricted by employers in their choice of occupation even though they may possess the necessary qualifications, they they will be forced into noncompeting groups, unable to compete for the higher-paying positions for which they may be qualified. (See Example 1.)

The effect of discrimination on the distribution of income is an important empirical issue. Is a substantial portion of observed inequality by race and sex the consequence of discrimination? For

---

2. Signaling theory is treated in Michael Spence, "Job Market Signaling," *Quarterly Journal of Economics* 87, 3 (August 1973): 355–74; Kenneth Arrow, "Higher Education as a Filter," *Journal of Public Economics* 2, 3 (July 1973): 193–216.

Example 1   The "Comparable Worth" Trap

Many economists warn against using the concept of "comparable worth" as an argument for eliminating the approximately 60 percent male/female wage differential. The Supreme Court and Federal Courts in rulings since 1981 have ruled that employees (be they male or female) have a right to equal pay for "comparable" work. This is a significant extension of the established principle of equal pay for equal work (according to which two people performing identical work under identical conditions should receive equal pay). In recent years, suits have been filed by persons who claim that they have been unlawfully discriminated against because they were paid less than others who performed comparable work. One example would be female prison guards in female institutions who received lower pay than male prison guards working in male institutions. In rulings in Oregon and Washington, the courts ordered employers to hire independent consultants to evaluate different jobs to determine whether or not jobs were of comparable worth. Pay scales were ordered to be adjusted according to an independent evaluation so that those performing comparable jobs would receive the same pay. In obeying court orders, the state of Washington established a committee to assign points to each job on the basis of knowledge and skills, mental demands, accountability, and work conditions. Registered nurses won the highest evaluation (573 points), computer-systems analysts were assigned 426 points. A clerical supervisor won a higher rating than a chemist; an electrician was assigned lower points than a beginning secretary; truck drivers were rated lower than retail clerks. In all these examples, the market had assigned different relative wages than the comparable-worth point system.

Economists warn of the consequences of pay according to "expert" rating systems as opposed to pay negotiated through the market. The market sets a wage rate to equate quantity supplied and quantity demanded. If employers are indeed required to pay registered nurses more than computer-systems analysts (the current market pay differential is about 56 percent), employers would find that they cannot keep computer-systems analysts (who would go to another employer or state), but would be deluged by registered nurses wishing to work at that pay scale. The firm that is required to pay truck drivers less than beginning secretaries would have too many applicants from secretarial workers but no truck drivers on the payroll. A surprising feature of the comparable-worth doctrine is that it, in the long run, could widen the male/female wage differential it is designed to close. By raising wages in the low-paid traditionally female professions, it would limit the incentive of women to enter into higher-paying male professions. Instead of encouraging women to become computer-systems analysts, it would encourage them to continue to study nursing and school teaching. ■

Sources: June O'Neill, "The 'Comparable Worth' Trap," *Wall Street Journal*, January 20, 1984; Robert Higgs, "The Economic Consequences of Comparable Worth," *The Collegiate Forum*, Spring 1984.

---

the postwar period as a whole, the median income of nonwhite households was slightly less than 60 percent that of white households. The postwar trend in the ratio of black to white incomes has been upward, beginning at 51 percent in 1947 and rising to an average of about 60 percent in the mid-1970s. The severe economic downturn of the late 1970s and early 1980s caused a slight reversal of the upward movement. In 1982, the ratio of median black to white income was 55 percent.

There are also substantial differences in the average incomes of males and females. Women who work full time have had an average income equal to slightly more than 60 percent of the incomes of their male counterparts since the late 1950s. Although the ratio of black to white earnings has increased since 1947, the female/male income differences remained pretty much the same up until 1980. The relative position of average female earnings actually worsened during the mid-1950s during a period when other (black/white, North/South) earnings differentials were improving. However, between 1980 and 1983, women's pay jumped from 60 percent to 64 percent of men's. It is too early to tell whether or not this is the start of an upward trend. Figure 3 shows income differences by race and sex for the years 1965, 1975, and 1982.

Figure 3   Income Differentials by Sex and Race

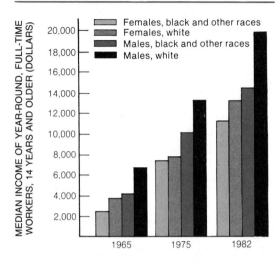

MEDIAN INCOME OF YEAR-ROUND, FULL-TIME WORKERS, 14 YEARS AND OLDER (DOLLARS)

Legend:
- Females, black and other races
- Females, white
- Males, black and other races
- Males, white

Years: 1965, 1975, 1982

This figure illustrates that substantial differences in the income of blacks and whites and in the incomes of males and females are still present in the United States.

Source: U.S. Bureau of the Census; *Handbook of Labor Statistics, 1983.*

The fact that whites earn, on average, more than nonwhites or that males earn, on average, more than females does not prove by itself that discrimination is present. Discrimination occurs when the entry of qualified individuals to jobs and occupations is blocked or when workers of equal skills and qualifications performing the same tasks are treated differently on the grounds of race, sex, or creed. Average differences in earnings may also be the consequence of differences in natural ability, human capital, drive, and ambition, not of labor-market discrimination. How much is due to discrimination?

Studies of the effects of discrimination on black/white earnings differences conclude that about one half of observed differences in earnings can be attributed to schooling differences. Thus, a major cause of earnings differences is the disparity between the quantity and quality of schooling received by the different races. The percent of persons 25-29 who completed at least 4 years of higher education was 25 percent for whites and 11.5 percent for blacks and hispanics. The most effective means, therefore, of reducing non-

white/white earnings differentials is to provide equal access to quality education irrespective of race. Notably, the male/female differential in college completion rates is much smaller (25 percent to 21 percent); therefore, the male/female income differential is less well explained by differences in years of schooling. A recent study finds that if years of education and years of job experience are taken into consideration, women's wages would average about 80 percent of men's.[3]

Once in the job market, individuals may be subject to labor-market discrimination. Certain unions or professional organizations may not accept blacks, hispanics, or women. Discrimination may be more subtle in the form of certain jobs being set aside for specific races or for women. Moreover, women may receive less on-the-job training on the grounds that they will be less permanently attached to the labor force than men. It is difficult to gauge the full effects of labor-market discrimination.

Labor-market discrimination according to sex and race does not normally assume the form of discriminating between two workers (of different race or sex) performing the same job. In fact, there are federal laws guaranteeing equal pay for equal work (see Example 2). More often discrimination occurs when nonwhites and women are channeled into occupations regarded as "suitable" for nonwhite or female employment. This channeling may be the result of the employee's own preferences (a woman may want to be a school teacher and nothing else) or employer discrimination (an employer may be unwilling to hire women for assembly-line work). The employer may be using simple screening rules (such as not hiring women for manual labor) to hold down screening costs. As long as simple screening rules are used, workers will continue to be denied access to certain jobs and professions. As a consequence, these "suitable" professions—say, nursing and school teaching for women or bus driving for black males—become *crowded,* and the relative earnings of these professions are driven down. If there were fewer formal and informal restrictions on the occupational choices of women and blacks, then public-school teaching,

3. James Smith and Michael Ward, *Women's Wages and Work in the Twentieth Century,* (New York: Rand Corporation, 1984).

Example 2   Occupational Distributions of Women and Blacks, 1982

The accompanying table supplies statistics on the occupational distribution of women and blacks for selected occupations in 1982. Although women accounted for 43.5 percent of the total labor force, women were disproportionately concentrated in sales, clerical work, services, and private household work—professions that rank low in relative earnings. Blacks accounted for 9.2 percent of the labor force, but they were concentrated in occupations like bus driving, manual labor, and private household work—also occupations noted for low relative earnings. In the industrial professions, women and blacks tended to be packers, dry-cleaning attendants, and textile operatives, rather than higher-paying workers like artisans, butchers, and precision-machine operators. The table also shows that women and blacks account for a very small percentage of dentists and craft workers. ■

Source: *Statistical Abstract of the United States; 1984,* pp. 419–20.

Occupation	Percent Female	Percent Black
Total employment	43.5	9.2
Professional and technical workers	45.1	6.4
Dentists	3.3	2.5
Physicians	14.8	2.3
Pharmacists	23.8	3.6
Registered nurses	95.6	8.2
Public-school teachers	70.7	9.0
Managers and administrators	28.0	3.9
Sales clerks, retail	70.0	5.1
Clerical workers	80.7	9.4
Secretaries	99.2	.5.9
Telephone operators	91.9	16.3
Craft workers	7.0	6.7
Operatives	40.7	13.5
Dressmakers	95.4	14.6
Laundry operatives	66.5	21.3
Butchers and meat cutters	6.6	7.7
Packers and wrappers	60.8	17.5
Precision-machine operators	12.4	7.3
Transport-equipment operatives	8.9	13.1
Bus drivers	46.6	19.5
Taxicab drivers and chauffeurs	9.9	19.1
Laborers	11.7	15.1
Service workers	59.0	15.7
Private-household workers	96.9	47.2

bus driving, and nursing would be less crowded and relative earnings in these professions would be less depressed.

Occupational Differences

Other things being the same, most people prefer to work in occupations that are not dangerous, that offer pleasant surroundings, and that do not involve heavy and dirty work. The supply of labor to attractive occupations and jobs will be greater than the supply of labor to dangerous, dirty, and unattractive jobs, *ceteris paribus*. Even though the coal miner and the garbage collector earn more than many others with the same physical and mental skills, labor does not move automatically into these higher-paying jobs to wipe out the wage differential. Compensating wage differentials exist because people require a reward for working in unpleasant jobs.

The existence of compensating wage differences means that some inequality is in fact a matter of conscious choice. The low-paid high-school dropout who switches from a job as a grocery clerk to a job on a drilling rig in the Alaskan permafrost or to a job as a garbage collector can improve his or her relative income position. (See Example 3.) The fact that an individual chooses to forgo compensating wage differences means that his or her utility or satisfaction is greater at the lower level of earnings. The nonpecuniary advantages of one type of occupation may outweigh the compensating wage differences offered by another occupation.

Some people may value leisure more than others. One person may work a 60-hour week, while another (who earns the same hourly wage) works a 30-hour week. The first person will have weekly earnings twice those of the second, but the second will have twice as much leisure. This

Example 3   Compensating Wage Differentials: Arctic Drillers

What high-school graduate would not want to earn $90,000 per year? An arctic driller works on an offshore drilling rig in arctic temperatures of 40 degrees below zero. On some days, the temperature falls to 90 degrees below zero. Drillers work 14 consecutive 12-hour days before taking 7 days off. Dropping a wrench down the drilling hole is grounds for immediate dismissal. Drillers live in a camp of connected trailers; they have no living expenses and the food is good. The job is dangerous. A wrong move with one lever will result in injuries. Frostbite is common. Drinking, gambling, drugs, and fighting are not allowed. Drillers with a few years' experience were paid more than $90,000 per year in the late 1970s. The one who helped the cook was paid $40,000. ■

extra leisure is worth something to the recipient that is not reflected in his or her money income.

Inequality through individual choice applies as well to occupational choices under conditions of uncertain income prospects. Different occupations involve different degrees of risk. The small-business owner has more uncertain income prospects than the tenured university professor. The wheat farmer, whose crops may be destroyed by blights and droughts, has a more uncertain income than the union employee with seniority. The real-estate speculator stands to make a fortune if lucky but will go bankrupt if unlucky.

Society is comprised of individuals with differing attitudes towards risk. *Risk seekers* are more willing to incur risks than others, while *risk avoiders* are reluctant to take on risks.[4] If society consists largely of risk avoiders and has only a small number of risk seekers, the distribution of income would be unequal for this reason alone. Some of those willing to incur risks will strike it rich and rise to the top income level. Other risk seekers will be less fortunate and will be at the bottom of the totem pole. The vast majority—the risk avoiders—will be in the middle, earning steadier incomes.

Human-Capital Investment Choices

Human-capital theory suggests that some inequality can be the consequence of choice, not chance. This theory, pioneered by Theodore W. Schultz, Gary Becker, and Jacob Mincer, is based on the premise that individuals are faced with the choice of different lifetime-earnings streams.[5] Individuals will make rational personal optimizing decisions based upon the costs and benefits of the different earnings streams.

Just as businesses invest in plant and equipment to increase the firm's productive capacity, so human beings invest in themselves to raise their own productivity and, hence, their future earning capacity. They (and their parents) can invest in extra schooling and technical education. They can pay the costs of migrating to areas where job opportunities are better. They can invest in medical care to improve their health.

These activities are regarded as investment because any activity that raises productive capacity can be classified as investment. Building a new plant, acquiring a new assembly line, installing an irrigation system are all forms of investment in tangible capital. All of these activities are designed to raise the productive capacity of the firm undertaking the investment. The same holds true for individuals: by acquiring more training and education, individuals can increase their own productivity.

If human-capital investment translates into higher lifetime productivity and, therefore, higher lifetime earnings, why does not everyone demand the same amounts of human-capital investment? Although human investment yields benefits, it also has its costs. To acquire a college degree requires paying not only for tuition and books but

4. The theory of individual choice of inequality was formulated by Milton Friedman in the article "Choice, Chance, and the Personal Distribution of Income," *Journal of Political Economy* 61, 4 (August 1953): 277–90.

5. The pioneering articles in human-capital theory are: Gary Becker, "Investment in Human Capital: A Theoretical Analysis," *Journal of Political Economy* 70, 5 (October 1962): 9–49; Theodore W. Schultz, "Capital Formation by Education," *Journal of Political Economy* 68, 6 (December 1960): 571–83.

also for the loss of current earnings due to prolonging formal education. To move to another city to seek a better job means the payment of moving costs, the loss of income between jobs, and the personal costs of leaving family and friends behind. Each form of human-capital investment has its costs and benefits. Confronted with these costs and benefits, individuals (and their parents) are assumed to make rational investment decisions; that is, they will acquire more human capital as long as the marginal benefits exceed the marginal costs. Insofar as the benefits from human-capital investment will be spread out over a number of years in the form of higher earnings in the future, the appropriate measure of benefits is the present value of the increase in future earnings.

The human-capital theorists view inequalities in the distribution of income as partly the result of conscious and rational decision making. Individuals must select between more money now (going to work after high school, for example) and more money later (going to college and not earning money now). This decision will depend upon the anticipated rate of return to additional human-capital investment, and this rate of return will depend upon the interest rate used to capitalize future earnings and the anticipated increase in future earnings. Individuals who place a high value on having money *now* (a high implicit interest rate) are less likely to acquire human capital.[6]

Human capital may be affected by social policy. Over the years (especially in the 1960s), various government programs have been put in place to increase the human capital of the poor and the young. These government programs (such as the Job Corps, Manpower Training and Development, and Neighborhood Youth Programs) all

aimed at training disadvantaged persons at government expense to learn marketable skills.

Chance and Luck

Another source of income inequality is chance (random occurrences) and luck. Accidents and poor health can unexpectedly destroy one's earning capacity. Choosing to train for a profession (such as teaching English or modern languages) in which there is an unexpected decline in demand can lead to low earnings. Likewise, having the good fortune to train for a profession (such as petroleum engineering in the late 1970s) in which there is an unexpected increase in demand can have a significant positive and unplanned effect on one's lifetime earnings. Luck determines whether individuals earn the economic rents discussed in the preceding chapter. Having the good fortune to be in the right place at the right time can have a marked impact on relative income. Having the bad fortune to be in the wrong profession or industry during downswings in the business cycle can also harm earnings. Involuntary unemployment not only reduces current earnings but also cuts down on the amount of work experience and training an individual accumulates. This loss will affect earnings even after the individual is employed again.

Typically, chance and luck have a short-term effect on a family's place in the income distribution. Spells of unemployment usually pass; the entrepreneur who has good luck in one period has bad luck in the next period. The other factors (ability, human capital, and occupational differences) tend to have longer-run effects.

Inheritance

Thus far, this chapter has offered several explanations for inequalities in the distribution of *labor income*. But income from other factors of production—land, capital, and entrepreneurship—is also unequally distributed. In fact, income from the ownership of land, mineral, and capital property is distributed more unequally than income from labor. Most nonlabor income derives from the ownership of **wealth** (stocks, bonds, real estate).

> Personal **wealth** (or net worth) is the value of one's total assets minus one's liabilities.

---

6. To show how human-capital investment decisions are made, assume an investment in an 8-year medical-degree training program costs $100,000. Once the training is complete, it promises to raise annual earnings $15,000 each year above what they would have been without additional training. In making this decision, the present value of the extra income ($15,000 in the ninth year, $15,000 in the tenth year, and so on until retirement from practice) must be calculated by converting each year's earnings to a present value. If the sum of the present values for each year's earnings exceeds the $100,000 cost, this human-capital investment is profitable.

Alternatively, one could calculate the rate of return that equates the cost and the present value. If this rate of return exceeds the rate of interest at which the $100,000 could be borrowed, then investment is a profitable one.

Example 4   The Sources of the Net Wealth of American Households, 1982

The Federal Reserve Board periodically estimates the net worth (the value of assets minus liabilities) of all American households. The net worth of the nation's households is divided into *tangible assets* (such as houses, land, and consumer durables) and *financial assets* (such as corporate stock, life-insurance and pension funds, and deposits at financial institutions). In 1982, the net worth of the entire nation was $11.2 trillion, while total income was $3,073 billion. On average, there were approximately $3.61 of net wealth for every dollar of income earned in 1982. The distribution of American net wealth is given in the accompanying figure. (Nonprofit organizations and private trusts were counted as households in this estimate.) ■

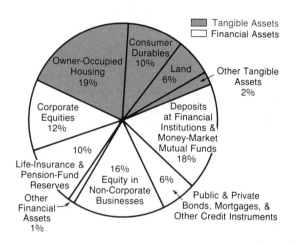

Source: *The Washington Post*, November 28, 1983, p. 19. Data in diagram from The *Federal Reserve Bulletin*, September 1983.

The sources of household wealth in the United States are illustrated in Example 4. The distribution of income from wealth can be inferred from the distribution of wealth (see Table 3). In 1983, the top 2 percent of wealth holders in the United States accounted for 30 percent of all financial assets (they accounted for 20 percent of property assets and one third of all business assets). The top 10 percent accounted for more than 50 percent of all assets. On the income side, the top 5 percent of households accounted for 15.7 percent of all income; thus, wealth is distributed more unequally than income. Like the distribution of income, the distribution of wealth has become more equal over the years. In 1929, the top 1 percent had 36.3 percent of all wealth.

One important cause of the unequal distribution of wealth is *inheritance*, or the process by which one generation passes wealth on to the next after death. Originally this wealth may have been created by luck, by refraining from consumption (saving), or by superior entrepreneurship. Wealth continues to be passed from one generation to the next because of several factors. First, the children of the wealthy, in addition to inheriting property, typically receive better education and training and

develop important social contacts. Second, the children of the wealthy tend to marry others who are likely to inherit wealth. Third, the wealthy may pass on a genetic inheritance to their heirs—such as inherited entrepreneurial ability or intelligence.

Empirical studies of the effects of inheritance on the overall distribution of income fail to uncover a significant role for inherited wealth in the United States. The share of income from wealth has been declining, and even for high-income families (those earning $50,000 and above in 1979), income from wealth accounted for only 10.7 percent of total income. One study finds that inherited wealth accounts for only 2 percent of the overall index of inequality in the United States.[7]

Although inherited wealth may not have a large direct effect on the distribution of income, it can have a substantial indirect effect that is difficult to measure. Inherited wealth may carry with it larger endowments of human capital in the form of better education, social contacts, and travel ex-

7. Alan S. Blinder, *Toward an Economic Theory of Income Distribution* (Cambridge, Mass.: MIT Press, 1974).

Table 3 Selected Characteristics of Asset Owners and Assets by Type of Asset, 1983

Type of Asset	Percent of All Families Owning Asset	Percent Held by Selected Families, Ranked by Income	
		Top 10 Percent	Top 2 Percent
Total financial assets			
Liquid assets...	88	51	30
Checking account....................................	79	41	23
Savings account.....................................	62	26	8
Money-market account	14	40	15
Certificates of deposit	20	33	15
IRA or Keogh account..............................	17	48	17
Savings bonds.......................................	21	26	12
Other financial assets			
Stocks...	19	72	50
Bonds...	3	70	39
Nontaxable holdings[a]................................	3	86	71
Trust..	4	46	34
Other assets			
Property	19	50	20
Business...	14	78	33

[a]Municipal bonds and shares in certain mutual funds.

Source: *Federal Reserve Bulletin*, September 1984, p. 689.

periences, as mentioned earlier. These advantages are called "fortunes" by Nobel-Prize-winning English economist James Meade. Those who are fortunate enough to inherit these fortunes (wealth, education opportunities, abilities) have the opportunity to earn not only substantial income from wealth but also substantial labor income from their fortunate human-capital situation.

Studies of the Causes of Inequality

Considerable empirical work has been devoted to estimating the contribution of each of the inequality-creating factors—human-capital investments, luck, ability, inheritance, discrimination, occupational differences—to observed inequality. As is often the case, there is no universal agreement on the relative importance of each factor. Most researchers, however, agree that human-capital investments account for a substantial portion of observed inequality. For example, a prominent researcher in this field, Jacob Mincer, has found that human capital accounts for one half of the total inequality. Other researchers may disagree

on the exact percentage, but there is agreement that differences in human capital explain much of the observed income differences among households.

Economists are not in unanimous agreement about whether investment in schooling and training leads to higher earnings or whether individuals with more ability or more fortunate family backgrounds simply happen to be those with more schooling and training. In other words, what is the effect of human-capital investment on inequality if ability and family background are held constant? Estimates vary widely: some researchers find that ability or family environment have only a small independent effect (Zvi Grilliches and William Mason, James Morgan and Martin David) while others (Samuel Bowles) find that family environment has a substantial independent effect on inequality.

The unequal distribution of education is clearly not the sole source of income inequality. If the unequal distribution of education were the sole cause of income inequality, we would expect educational achievements (say, as measured by

Table 4   U.S. Lorenz Curves, Before and After Income and Payroll Taxes, 1972

Quintile	Before Taxes		After Taxes	
	Share of Income (percent)	Cumulative Share (percent)	Share of Income (percent)	Cumulative Share (percent)
Lowest fifth	5.4	5.4	6.3	6.3
Second fifth	11.9	17.3	13.3	19.5
Third fifth	17.5	34.8	18.3	37.8
Fourth fifth	23.9	58.7	24.1	61.9
Highest fifth	41.4	100.0	38.0	100.0

Source: Edgar K. Browning, "The Trend Toward Equality in the Distribution of Net Income," *Southern Economic Journal* 43, 1 (July 1976): 914.

completed years of schooling) to be as unequally distributed as income. The research of Lester Thurow shows that education is distributed much more equally among the adult population than income.[8] A relatively small proportion of American adult males have completed less than 5 years of schooling; the largest proportion has completed between 11 and 13 years; almost 20 percent have attended or completed college.

Ability (as measured by IQ scores) is also much more equally distributed among the adult population than income. Adults with either high or low IQ scores are relatively rare with most adults falling in between the high and low scores. In the distribution of income, most families are concentrated in the lower income groups. There is a less even spread.

Comparisons of the income, education, and IQ distributions of the American adult population show that, while education is an important source of inequality, it is not the only source. Most experts agree that natural ability—which tends to be distributed fairly equally—is not a major source of income inequality.

HOW UNEQUAL IS U.S. INCOME DISTRIBUTION?

The Effect of Taxes

In the United States, the distribution of money income among households is not changed substan-

8. Lester C. Thurow, *Poverty and Discrimination* (Washington, D.C.: Brookings Institution, 1969), p. 68.

tially by the system of income taxes. Figure 4, which is based on Table 4, shows the effect of income and payroll taxes on the U.S. distribution of income in 1972. The Lorenz curve before income and payroll taxes is shown as curve *B*, and curve *A* shows the Lorenz curve after taxes. Income and payroll taxes do equalize the distribution of income slightly; the share of the lowest 20 percent rises from 5.4 percent to 6.3 percent, and the share of the top 20 percent falls from 41.4 to 38.0 percent. These changes are relatively minor, however. The next chapter discusses proposals for reforming the American tax system and the potential effects of those reforms on the income distribution.

International Comparisons

Figure 5 compares the Lorenz curves of Brazil, the United States, Sweden, and Taiwan. Brazil is an example of a country with a highly unequal distribution of income. Sweden and Taiwan are at the other extreme—their inequality in the distribution of income is considered to be relatively mild. The data show that Sweden, with a reputation for equality, is at about the same position as Taiwan but with more inequality at the lower end of the income distribution and less inequality at the upper end. The pattern of distribution in the United States is clearly closer to Sweden than to Brazil. In general, the poorer the nation, the more unequal its income distribution. Thus, it is to be expected that the U.S. income distribution is more equal than Brazil's. One important reason why income-distribution differences are strong among high-income countries is that in some

Figure 4 The Effect of Income Taxes and Payroll Taxes on the U.S. Distribution of Income, 1972

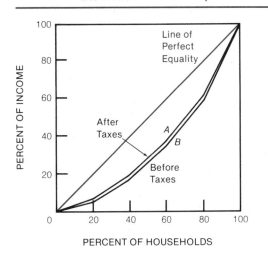

Income and payroll taxes have only a minor equalizing effect on the U.S. distribution of income, as shown by the difference between curve *B* (the distribution before taxes) and curve *A* (the distribution after taxes).

Source: Based on Edgar K. Browning, "The Trend Toward Equality in the Distribution of Income," *Southern Economic Journal* 43, 1 (July 1976): 914.

Figure 5 The Distribution of Income in Four Countries

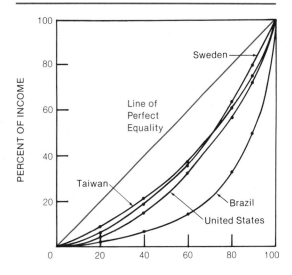

While Brazil has a highly unequal distribution of income, inequality in Sweden and Taiwan is relatively mild. The U.S. income distribution falls between these two extremes.

Source: The World Bank.

countries, like Sweden, the state does much to equalize the income distribution after taxes.

Life-Cycle Effects

Income varies systematically during each person's lifetime. Incomes tend to be low at the beginning of one's career (say, age 20–24); earnings then rise until the person's mid-fifties and then drop off at retirement age. These trends in lifetime earnings are plotted in Figure 6. The appropriate measure of inequality, therefore, is the distribution of the *lifetime incomes* of households.

Because incomes vary over the life cycle, the degree of actual inequality will be overstated by the standard Lorenz curves already cited. Households at different stages in their earnings cycle are grouped together. Households with wage earners in their twenties or sixties will typically have lower incomes than those with wage earners in their thirties, forties, or fifties, even though their lifetime earnings may actually be identical.

Economist Morton Paglin has estimated that the U.S. lifetime Lorenz curve (the distribution of income adjusted for differences in age) shows about 50 percent less inequality than the ordinary Lorenz curve. Other authors find that the correction for age should not reduce measured inequality by nearly as much as Paglin has estimated, but there is agreement that if age is held constant, the amount of inequality is reduced.[9]

9. Morton Paglin, in "The Measurement and Trend of Inequality: A Basic Revision," *American Economic Review* 65, 4 (September 1975); 598–609, reports that there is a significant trend towards a more equal distribution of income between 1947 and 1972 if the effects of age on the distribution of income are removed. Paglin's findings have been disputed by several authors, in particular by Sheldon Danziger, Robert Haveman, and Eugene Smolensky, in "The Measurement and Trend of Inequality: Comment," *American Economic Review* 67, 3 (June 1977): 502–13. For a survey of this literature, see Alan Blinder, "The Level and Distribution of Economic Well-Being," in ed. Martin Feldstein, *The American Economy in Transition* (Chicago: The University of Chicago Press, 1980), pp. 450–53.

Figure 6   Age and Earnings of U.S. Males, 1984

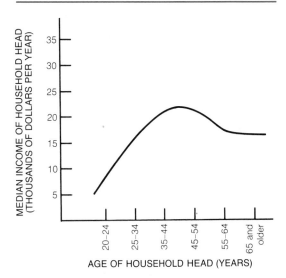

Incomes tend to be low at the beginning of one's career, tend to rise until one's fifties, and tend to tail off at retirement age.

Source: *Statistical Abstract of the United States,* 1984, p. 469.

Figure 7   The Distribution of Income Before and After Taxes and Benefits

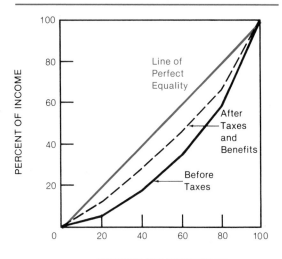

The distribution of U.S. income becomes much more equal when all sources of income and in-kind benefits are included as income.

Source: Based on Edgar K. Browning, "The Trend Toward Equality in the Distribution of Net Income," *Southern Economic Journal* 43, 1 (July 1976): 914.

The Unequal Distribution of Public Services

Household income consists of money income and **in-kind income.**

> **In-kind income** consists primarily of benefits—such as free public education, school lunch programs, public housing, or food stamps—for which the recipient is not required to pay.

As already shown in Table 4, transfers of income through the income-tax system (taxing the more fortunate to finance money payments to the less fortunate) do not materially alter the distribution of income. What happens to the distribution of income when in-kind services are included? Figure 7 shows the 1972 Lorenz curve based on one researcher's effort to calculate the distribution of income after taxes, including receipts of public services like public education, government medical services, and other categories of income not captured in the official money-income statistics. This calculation is by no means exact and requires numerous assumptions and qualifications, but it does show that the distribution of income becomes much more equal when all sources of income and in-kind benefits are included as income because the poor receive a larger share of public services than the rich. One reason why such calculations are inexact is that it is difficult to place an appropriate price tag on in-kind benefits. The recipient of a public service that costs $20 to produce (say, public health or public education) may value that service at less than $20 or may even place a zero value on the service. Calculations of the effect of the in-kind benefit are typically based upon the cost of supplying the service because it is difficult to know

Example 5   The Rising Number of U.S. Millionaires

The number of millionaires in the United States has risen substantially since 1976. In both 1972 and 1976, there were about 180,000 individuals with a net worth of $1 million or more. By 1981, this number had risen to between 350,000 and 500,000. The rise in stock-market prices since 1981 has undoubtedly raised the number of U.S. millionaires to at least the half million mark. Moreover, the number of "wealthy" individuals in the U.S. (people with gross assets of $300,000 or more) reached 4.5 million in 1981—some 2 percent of the U.S. population. On the other side of the coin, it should be noted that because of rising prices, $1 million in 1985 was roughly equivalent in value to $620,000 in 1976: $1 million doesn't go as far as it once did. ■

Source: "More Millionaires in U.S. Now, but then a Million is Worth Less," *Christian Science Monitor,* August 26, 1983.

---

the value that the recipient places on the service.[10]

WHAT IS A JUST DISTRIBUTION OF INCOME?

Philosophers have debated the distribution of income for centuries. Is it fair to have extremes of wealth and poverty? What is a just distribution of income? Are unequal rewards required in order to bring out extra effort and talents? The issue of *distributive justice* is largely an ethical issue. Economists are in a better position to describe the economic consequences of different distributions of income than to judge whether one distribution of income is better than another. Over the years, different philosophies of distributive justice have been formulated. Some argue for more equal distributions of income than others.

Natural Law and the Leaky Bucket

According to the natural-law philosophers of the 17th century, each individual has the right to the fruits of his or her labors. In terms of modern economic theory, this philosophy translates into the marginal-productivity theory of income distribution. According to this theory, the owners of the factors of production will receive a price that equals the marginal revenue product *(MRP)* of the factor. Under this system, those who are more productive (those who have high *MRP*s because of special skills or hard effort) will receive more than those with low *MRP*s.

Critics can point out with some justification that marginal-productivity theory will lead to inequities. Some individuals will inherit factors with high *MRP*s; some will be fortunate enough to be born to rich or brilliant parents; those who are lucky will receive high rewards.

The major advantage of distribution according to marginal productivities is that the owners of factors of production are encouraged to raise the marginal productivity of their factors. Individuals are encouraged to invest in human capital; owners of capital are encouraged to save to acquire more capital; entrepreneurs are encouraged to assume risks. If factors of production were not paid in accordance with marginal productivity, there would be a tendency to reduce effort, to acquire less human and tangible capital, and to take fewer risks. The end result would be that the economy would earn less income in total.

For this reason, most economists agree that there is a trade-off between more equality and more income. If income is redistributed from those who possess high-priced factors of produc-

---

10. Alternate calculations showing a smaller effect of in-kind services have been prepared by Timothy Smeeding, "On the Distribution of Net Income: Comment," *Southern Economic Journal* 46, 1 (January 1979): 932–44.

tion to those less fortunate (by means of a high tax on the fortunate, for example), the efficiency of the economy would decline, and less income would be available for society as a whole. Economist Arthur Okun describes the equity/efficiency trade-off using the analogy of a leaky bucket.[11] Redistributing income from the fortunate to the unfortunate is like transfering water from one barrel to another with a leaky bucket. In the process of making the transfer, water (income) is lost forever. If the leak is a slow one, then the costs to society of the redistribution are small. If the leak is large, then the losses of total income will be substantial. Society must decide whether the costs of greater equality are worth the price.

The Utilitarian Case for Equality

Natural-law philosophy and the marginal-productivity theory of income distribution support an unequal distribution of income. Inequality allows individuals to reap the fruits of their efforts and raises economic efficiency. At the other end of the spectrum is the argument that equal income distribution will maximize the utility of society.

The law of diminishing marginal utility supplies the basic rationale for the *utilitarian theory* of income distribution. If people are basically alike (if they have the same tastes, obtain the same satisfaction from the same amount of income, and so on), then the total utility of society will be greatest when income is distributed equally because everyone is subject to the law of diminishing marginal utility. If Jones were rich and Smith were poor, Jones would be getting much less utility from his last dollar than Smith. If income were shifted from Jones to Smith, Smith's utility would increase more than Jones's would be reduced. Therefore, the reduction in inequality would increase the total utility of society. If indeed everyone is alike, then the total utility of society would be greatest when income is distributed perfectly equally among individuals.

The obvious criticism of this case for equality is that people are indeed different. Some care little for money and worldly goods; others care a

great deal. Therefore, it is not at all certain that the rich person gets less marginal utility from his or her last dollar than does the poor person. Modern economists agree that because one cannot make interpersonal utility comparisons of this sort, one cannot argue scientifically that the total utility of society is greatest when income is equally distributed.

Rawlsian Equality

A different argument for equality has been proposed by Harvard philosopher John Rawls.[12] Rawls maintains that inequality and injustice result from the fact that people already know too much about their endowments of resources and abilities when entering into bargaining concerning their economic, social, and political rewards. Economic, social, and political contracts determine the distribution of income and privileges. Those who already know that they are better endowed with economic resources, social contacts, or political influence would not agree to arrangements (such as highly redistributive taxes) that give away these advantages. The rational self-interest of the privileged will not allow a social consensus for a more equal distribution to emerge. According to Rawls, if everyone were operating behind a "veil of ignorance" (if people did not know in advance whether they would be rich or poor), rational, self-interested individuals would act as risk avoiders. They would agree that everyone should have equal liberty and equal educational and political opportunities. Moreover, they would agree that any inequalities must be to the greatest expected benefit of the least advantaged. For example, if there were three possible outcomes, A, B, and C—where A meant the bottom 20 percent got 1 percent of all income, B meant the bottom 20 percent got 10 percent of all income, and C meant that the bottom 20 percent got 15 percent of all income—people would opt for C if operating in ignorance of their advantages.

Not knowing how they would fare (not knowing their advantages and disadvantages in ad-

11. Arthur Okun, *Equality and Efficiency; The Big Trade-Off* (Washington, D.C.: The Brookings Institution, 1975).

12. John Rawls, *A Theory of Justice* (Cambridge: Harvard University Press, 1971); and "Some Reasons for the Maximin Criterion," *American Economic Review* 64, 2 (May 1974): 141–46.

vance), individuals would opt to take the least risky position. If they were unlucky enough to end up in the bottom 20 percent, they would be better off in situation C than in A or B. In Rawls's system, there would be a strong tendency towards an equal distribution of income because risk aversion would require individuals to be concerned about the welfare of the poor because people couldn't be sure that they wouldn't end up being poor themselves.

The policy implication of the Rawls model is that government should step in to equalize the distribution of income. The government should push society toward that income distribution that would prevail if people did not know in advance who would be privileged and who would be without privilege.

Critics of Rawls's notion of distributive justice argue that there is no guarantee that individuals placed in Rawls's original position would indeed reach a consensus for an equal income distribution. Even in the original position, there would be some risk seekers who would dissent, believing that they could benefit at the expense of another. Moreover, Rawls's critics note that he ignores the problem of the efficiency/inequality trade-off. If the trade-off is substantial, a scheme that concentrates on protecting the least-advantaged could lead to a considerable loss of efficiency.

POVERTY

The causes of poverty are the same as the causes of inequality in the distribution of income. The poor are poor because of their limited endowments of ability and skills, their limited amount of human capital, bad luck, discrimination, and (some might even argue) conscious choice. The poor are poor because their capacity to earn a ''sufficient'' income is for some reason impaired.

Defining poverty is not an easy task, because establishing poverty levels of income requires important judgments on the part of the analyst. There will always be disagreement over what constitutes a poverty income. Some analysts define poverty in terms of the amount of income necessary to provide a family of a certain size with the minimum essentials of food, clothing, shelter,

and education. This approach provides an **absolute poverty standard.**

> An **absolute poverty standard** establishes a specific income level for a given-sized household below which the household is judged to be living in a state of poverty.

But is an absolute measure of poverty appropriate? Poverty can, after all, be relative. One's sense of poverty depends upon the incomes of others in the community. If one's income is 10 percent of everyone else's, one may feel poor even if one's income is above that required to purchase the minimum essentials. What Americans consider poor, however, would not necessarily be considered poor by some other countries. The American poor would be considered wealthy in the poorest Asian or African nation. The American poor measure themselves against other Americans, however, not against the poor in other countries. A second approach to poverty, therefore, is to measure it in relative terms. A **relative poverty standard** might classify a household as poor if the household's income is, say, 25 percent of an average household's income.

> A **relative poverty standard** defines the poor in terms of the income of others.

The choice of a poverty definition will determine to a great extent the number of poor and the rate at which poverty is perceived as being eliminated. If the absolute standard is selected, rising real living standards will push more and more families above the poverty line. According to a relative standard, poverty can be eliminated only by equalizing the distribution of income. If the rich and the poor both experience equal percentage increases in income, the poor will not have improved their relative position. As economist Alan Blinder writes about relative poverty standards: ''Under this definition, the War on Poverty would be unwinnable by definition, and the Bible would be literally correct: ye have the poor always with you.''[13] The discussion of trends in poverty that follows uses the official absolute poverty standards of the U.S. government. We

---

13. Blinder, ''The Level and Distribution of Economic Well-Being,'' p. 456.

Table 5　Persons Living in Households with Money Incomes Below Poverty Levels, 1959 to 1983

Year	Number of Persons Below Poverty Level (millions)	Percentage of Population	Poverty Income for Household of 4 (dollars)
1959	39.5	22.4	2,973
1960	39.9	22.2	3,022
1965	33.2	17.3	3,223
1966	28.5	14.7	3,317
1968	25.4	12.8	3,553
1970	25.4	12.6	3,968
1972	24.5	11.9	4,275
1974	24.3	11.6	5,038
1976	25.0	11.8	5,815
1978	24.5	11.4	6,662
1979	25.3	11.6	7,412
1980	29.3	13.0	8,414
1981	31.8	14.0	9,287
1982	34.4	15.0	9,862
1983	35.3	15.2	10,158

Source: *Statistical Abstract of the United States*, 1984, p. 471; *Economic Report of the President 1985*, p. 264.

have already discussed trends in relative poverty in the discussion of trends in income distribution.

Trends in Poverty

Table 5 lists the official statistics on the number of persons below poverty levels in the United States for the period 1959 to 1982. According to the absolute poverty standards of the U.S. government, the number of persons in households below the poverty level declined from 39.5 million to 35.3 million between 1959 and 1983. As a percent of the U.S. population, the figure has declined from 22.4 percent to 15.2 percent. Progress has been uneven, however. Large percentage declines were experienced in the 1960s; the number of people below the poverty level remained roughly the same through the 1970s, rising with the severe recessions of the early 1980s.

The overall improvement in poverty rates is not unexpected in a world of rising living standards. Rising real output pulls up the poor along with the rich. As the figures for the 1980s show, the incidence of poverty remains quite sensitive to general economic downturns.

The figures in Table 5 refer only to reported money income. Money-income figures do not include in-kind services received by the poor but do include government cash transfers, such as welfare payments and unemployment insurance. Yet government antipoverty programs emphasize in-kind benefits more than cash transfers. The government currently spends $3 in noncash benefits for every $2 in cash payments.

What effects do government cash and noncash antipoverty programs have on the number of persons living below the poverty line? Table 6 reports the number of persons living below poverty levels in 1976 before and after government antipoverty programs. (These figures differ from those in the previous table because they consider households to be unrelated individuals as well as those living in families.) These figures show that the percentage of Americans living below the poverty line would be much higher in the absence of government cash-transfer programs. Cash payments reduce the number of persons below the poverty line by roughly 50 percent. When in-kind transfers are included along with cash payments, government programs reduce the number living below poverty by more than two thirds. Without cash payments, 27 percent of the American population and almost 44 percent of the nonwhite U.S. population would be below the poverty line. The inclusion of government in-kind services further reduces the incidence of poverty. If both cash

Table 6   The Percentage of Persons Below Poverty Before and After Government Antipoverty Programs, 1976

Classification	All Households (percent)	White Households (percent)	Nonwhite Households (percent)
Income before taxes and cash payments	27.0	24.7	43.8
Income after cash payments	13.5	11.4	28.9
Income after cash and in-kind payments	8.1	7.1	15.9

Source: Congress of the United States, Congressional Budget Office, Background Paper No. 17, *Poverty Status of Families Under Alternate Definitions of Income,* June 1977.

payments and in-kind benefits are included in income, the percentage of those living below poverty levels falls to 7.1 percent of the white population and 15.9 percent of the nonwhite population.

The percentage of elderly persons living below poverty is reduced more than that of other groups by in-kind benefits. Their poverty incidence falls from 15 percent to 4.5 percent. This reduction results almost entirely from government Medicare and Medicaid programs that help pay the medical bills of the elderly.[14]

Who Are the Poor?

Table 7 provides a statistical profile of poor families. The poor tend to be disproportionately black and of Hispanic origin. They tend to live in large families; the family head tends to have little education, to be young, and to be female. Over 40 percent of the American poor are children under the age of 18. The poor tend to concentrate in central cities and in rural areas. Contrary to popular myth, a majority of the poor are working poor; not all the poor receive cash assistance. In 1982, in 77 percent of male-headed poor white families and in 60 percent of male-headed black families, the household head worked; more than one third of the female household heads of poor families worked (see Table 8). In 1979, only 64 percent of the poor received some form of cash assistance from government antipoverty programs.

14. U.S. Bureau of the Census, *Alternative Methods for Valuing Selected In-Kind Benefits and Measuring Their Effect on Poverty* (Washington, D.C.: U.S. Government Printing Office, 1982).

The figures cited above suggest that the majority of the poor are poor because of their limited earning capacity. Employment *per se* does not pull them and their families out of poverty. Only

Table 7   Characteristics of Poverty

Category	Percentage of Persons in Category Below Poverty Levels, 1982
Race	
White	12.0
Black	35.6
Spanish origin	29.9
Size of family	
2 persons	10.0
4 persons	10.8
5 persons	16.1
7 or more persons	32.5
Education of family head	
Less than 8 years	28.0
8 years	16.2
1–3 years high school	20.0
4 years high school	10.2
1 or more years college	4.8
Sex of family head	
Male	8.0
Female	14.8
Age of family head	
15–24 years	18.7
25–44 years	9.8
45–54 years	6.8
55–64 years	6.0
65 or more years	9.1
Location	
Central cities	16.7
Suburbs	7.5
Outside metropolitan areas	14.5

Source: *Statistical Abstract of the United States,* 1984, pp. 470–78.

in poor families headed by females do a majority of household heads not hold jobs.

The official poverty income standard does not provide for an attractive standard of living. The 1982 poverty income standard of $9,862 for a family of four allowed for $2.25 per person per day in food expenditures. A Gallup poll of the same year asked Americans what poverty income would be required to make ends meet and yielded a figure of $15,392—more than 50 percent larger than the official poverty standard.[15]

SOLUTIONS TO THE POVERTY PROBLEM

Income Maintenance

One solution to poverty is to raise the incomes of the poor. The two mechanisms used to accomplish this effect—voluntary charitable contributions and government cash-assistance programs—require a transfer of income from those above the poverty line to those below it. A later chapter on externalities explains why private charity alone will not eliminate poverty. The redistribution of income, however, can affect the efficiency of society's resource utilization. First, the redistribution from the rich to the poor may discourage work effort on the part of the rich and, thus, reduce the size of the income pie available for redistribution. Second, if the assistance to the poor discourages *their* work effort, the size of the income pie will be further reduced.

The Current Welfare System.

In the United States, the current welfare-assistance program follows the basic principle that public assistance should be granted primarily on the basis of demonstrated need. For this purpose, government programs have been established—such as Aid to Families with Dependent Children (AFDC), Food Stamps, public housing, and Medicaid—whereby the amount of public assistance is typically based upon family income. Under such programs, welfare authorities first determine what resources the family has (totaling the earnings of the family

---

Table 8   Labor Force Participation of Poverty Population, 1982

	Percent Whose Household Head Worked During 1982	
	Poor	Nonpoor
Male-headed families with children		
White	77	94
Black	60	89
Female-headed families with children		
White	42	89
Black	36	86
Aged persons		
Males	9	26
Females	5	12

Source: U.S. Bureau of the Census.

---

head, contributions from relatives, and so on). Public assistance is then granted on the basis of the need perceived by the welfare authority. The higher the resources of the family (its income from all sources and its savings), the less public assistance it is supposed to receive. The welfare family is, therefore, discouraged by this system from increasing its earnings because additional earnings—if detected by welfare authorities—will cause a reduction in public assistance. If the trade-off is a $1 loss of public assistance for every $1 of extra income, the incentive to earn extra income will be negligible.

The *disincentive effects* of current public-assistance programs have been noted by economists and politicians alike, and proposals have been made to build better incentives into the existing system. In particular, it has been proposed to Congress that welfare recipients be permitted to keep a specified percentage of extra earnings without a reduction in existing public-assistance benefits.

A second drawback of the current public-assistance system is that the documentation of needs and resources is very costly in terms of society's resources, requiring an army of welfare workers to staff the program. Dollars that could have been devoted to public assistance are diverted into the bureaucratic costs of operating the system. (See Example 6.)

---

15. Bradley R. Schiller, *The Economics of Poverty and Discrimination*, 4th ed. (Englewood Cliffs, N.J.: Prentice-Hall, 1984), pp. 18–19.

Table 9   A Hypothetical Negative Income Tax (with a guaranteed income of $6,000 and a negative tax rate of 50 percent)

Earnings (dollars)	Amount of Negative Income Tax Received (dollars)	Total Disposable Income = Earned Income + Tax Receipt (dollars)
0	6,000	6,000
3,000	4,500	7,500
6,000	3,000	9,000
9,000	1,500	10,500
12,000	0	12,000

Figure 8   The Workings of the Negative Income Tax

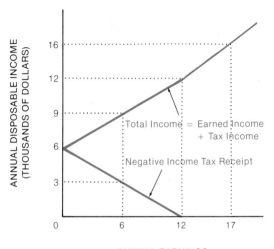

ANNUAL EARNINGS
(THOUSANDS OF DOLLARS)

This figure illustrates the workings of a hypothetical negative income tax. Here, the negative tax rate is set at 50 percent and a floor income is set at $6,000, below which no family income would be allowed to fall. A family with $0 income would receive $6,000 in benefits. Any family that earned more than $0 would have their $6,000 benefits reduced by $0.50 for every dollar earned. For example, a family earning $3,000 would receive $6,000 − (0.50 × $3,000) or $4,500 in addition to the $3,000 they earned. Up to an income of $12,000, families would still receive some benefits in addition to their income (benefits equal to $6,000 minus $0.50 times the amount of income earned). At an income of $12,000, however, families would receive no benefits in addition to their income because the $6,000 would be reduced by 0.50 × $12,000, or by $6,000 ($6,000 − $6,000 = $0). Beyond an income of $12,000, families would pay taxes. For example, a family earning $17,000 would pay taxes on the $5,000 difference between $17,000 and $12,000. If the tax rate were 20 percent, the family earning $17,000 would pay $1,000 in taxes (0.20 × $5,000) and would have a disposable income of $16,000.

The Negative Income Tax. Economists have proposed that the current system be replaced by a **negative income tax (NIT)**.

> A **negative income tax (NIT)** would supplement incomes that are less than a certain amount by giving recipients who earn less than the *break-even income* an amount equal to a minimum acceptable income and subtracting a given percentage of a dollar for each dollar the family earns on its own.

A negative income tax would work as outlined in Table 9 (and in Figure 8). First, the government would set a floor below which family incomes would not be allowed to fall. For purposes of illustration, Table 9 sets this floor at $6,000 for a family of four. Second, the government would set a negative tax rate. In our example, this negative tax rate is 50 percent.

Families of four who earn less than the $6,000 floor would be guaranteed an income of $6,000. If the family earned zero income, it would receive a negative-income-tax payment of $6,000. But what about the family that earns between $0 and $6,000? If a family that earned $3,000 were to receive a negative income tax of $3,000 to bring it up to the $6,000 floor, it would be no better off than the family that has zero income, in which case there would be little incentive to earn income. This is where the 50 percent tax rate comes in. If a 50 percent negative tax rate were in effect, benefits would be reduced by $0.50 for every extra collar earned. In this case, the family earns $3,000, and its benefits are reduced by one half

of the $3,000 earnings from $6,000 to $4,500. The total income of the family will, therefore, be $3,000 plus $4,500, or $7,500. By earning the $3,000, the family has been made better off compared to not working. The benefits of a family that earned double the guaranteed income— $12,000—would decrease at the rate of $0.50 for each extra dollar earned, or by $6,000, so the $6,000 benefits would be reduced by $6,000. The family earning $12,000, therefore, will receive no negative-income-tax payment from the govern-

Example 6   How the Poor Evaluate Government Services

The inclusion of government noncash poverty programs reduces income inequality and lowers significantly the percentage of American families living in poverty. Recent government studies have attempted to evaluate government poverty assistance programs using two approaches. The first is the *market-value approach,* which values the goods and services received by the poor according to their prices if they had been bought on the market. The second *cash-equivalent approach* measures the recipient's own valuation of the goods and services received. For example, a free medical-clinic program, which may be priced at $15 per visit in the market, may be valued by the recipient at only $5 per visit.

The results of a 1982 government study reveal how the poor value various government-assistance programs. They value government housing and food programs about the same as their market prices, but they value government medical-assistance programs well below their market prices. This result is true both for all poor people and, surprisingly, for the elderly poor (the major users of government medical programs). According to the market-price evaluation, the inclusion of government medical programs reduces the percentage of elderly poor from 12.9 percent to 5.2 percent. According to their own evaluation, the elderly poor feel that government medical programs reduce their poverty rate to only 9.3 percent.

This example illustrates why it is so hard to measure the incidence of poverty. People are receiving goods and services that may be valued below the cost of supplying them. ∎

Source: U.S. Bureau of the Census, *Alternative Methods for Valuing Selected In-Kind Transfer Benefits and Measuring Their Effect on Poverty,* Technical Paper 50, 1982.

---

ment. Its income will consist of its earnings of $12,000 plus a $0 negative-income-tax payment. In this example, the $12,000 income is called the *break-even income.* At $12,000 and above, the family's total income will equal its own earnings minus the income tax for that level.

Figure 8 shows what happens to disposable income as earned incomes increase from $0 to $17,000.

The negative-income-tax scheme offers two advantages over the existing system. First, it preserves work incentives up to the break-even income level by allowing low-income families to keep a prescribed portion of earnings. Second, it promises to do away with the costly bureaucracy of the existing welfare system. Administration of the negative income tax would be carried out by the same authority—the Internal Revenue Service—that administers the current personal-income-tax system.

The basic disadvantage is that work incentives will depend on the negative tax rate. A 50 percent negative tax rate means that families will be able to keep only one half of their own earnings below the break-even point. Incentive effects can be raised by lowering the tax rate—say, to 25 per-

cent, but this lowering of the rate raises the break-even income level to $24,000—well above any conceivable poverty level. To insure strong incentives requires low tax rates and negative-income-tax payments to those who are obviously not poor. Empirical studies show that 50 percent is about the highest tax rate an NIT program could impose without significant disincentives.

The idea of a negative income tax has widespread support among economists. Two U.S. Presidents—Presidents Nixon and Carter—proposed NIT programs, but to date a negative-income-tax program has not been adopted.

Long-Run Solutions

Income-maintenance programs—be they of the negative-income-tax or assistance-according-to-demonstrated-need variety—offer only a short-run solution to the poverty problem. The long-run solution of poverty requires an attack on the fundamental sources of poverty—limited human capital and discrimination—that are responsive to government action. Income-maintenance programs may assist the children of the poor by providing the money resources to maintain health and by funding the acquisition of training and education. Income-maintenance programs may perpetuate the poverty problem if they discourage work effort. To provide a long-run solution to the problem of poverty, government policy should aim at eliminating job-market discrimination and discrimination in the delivery of education to individuals according to color and sex. Moreover, government policy should encourage the children of the poor to invest in human-capital resources. The problem is how to devise a policy that does not defeat itself by reverse discrimination or by making the trade-off between equity and efficiency too costly. The intended effects of legislation can often differ dramatically from the actual effects. In the 1960s and 1970s, the government embarked on a series of training programs (called the "Great Society" programs in the 1960s) aimed at providing education and training for the children of the poor. Many of these programs have been abandoned in recent years because of their cost-ineffectiveness, but they represented an important social effort to eliminate the root sources of poverty.

This chapter examined the causes of inequality in the distribution of income and directed attention to the role of government in the redistribution of income to the poor. The next four chapters will focus on the role of government in the economy and the relationship between political and economic systems.

Summary

1.   The distribution of income among households is determined first in factor markets. Household income is the sum of the payments to the factors of production that the household owns. The government may change this distribution of income through taxes and the distribution of public services. The Lorenz curve measures the degree of inequality in the distribution of income. It shows the cumulative percent of all income earned by households at successive income levels. If the Lorenz curve is a straight 45-degree line, income is distributed perfectly equally. The more the Lorenz curve bows away from the 45-degree line, the more unequal is the distribution of income. The U.S. distribution of income has become more equal since 1929.

2.   The sources of inequality are: different abilities, discrimination, occupational differences, different amounts of human-capital investment, chance and luck, and property inheritance. Differences in schooling may affect earnings because employers use educational credentials to screen and select job candidates for high-paying careers. Although earnings differentials between whites and nonwhites have been reduced in recent years, earnings differentials between males and females have not been reduced by as much.

3.   The distribution of income appears to be more equal when one makes adjustments for taxes, in-kind services, and life-cycle effects.

4.   There are different views on what constitutes distributive justice. Marginal-utility theory calls for a distribution of income according to the marginal productivity of the resources owned by households. The utilitarian school believes an equal distribution of income maximizes total utility. John Rawls calls for a distribution of income that maximizes the utility of the least-fortunate members of society.

5.   Poverty can be measured either in absolute or relative terms. The absolute measure is based on an estimate of the minimum income necessary to allow a household to buy the minimum essentials. The relative standard measures poverty in terms of the household's location in the income distribution. According to government absolute measures of poverty, the number of those living below the poverty line has declined substantially since the 1950s. There has been little progress in the 1970s toward further reductions in the number of Americans living below the poverty line as measured by money income. If in-kind payments are included in income, slightly more than 7 percent of Americans are living below the poverty line. Poor Americans tend to be nonwhite, poorly educated, members of households headed by females, and either very young or very old.

6.   Income-maintenance programs are a short-run solution to the problem of poverty. The long-run solution is to raise the income-earning capacity of the children of the poor.

Key Terms

Lorenz curve
wealth
in-kind income
absolute poverty standard
relative poverty standard
negative income tax (NIT)

Questions and Problems

1. Draw a Lorenz curve for absolute equality. Draw a Lorenz curve for absolute inequality. Explain in words what the absolute-inequality Lorenz curve means.

2. "If all people were the same, the Lorenz curve would be a 45-degree line." Evaluate this statement.

3. "The fact that a woman earns on average two thirds of what a man earns proves beyond a shadow of a doubt that there is sex discrimination." Evaluate this statement.

4. There are two views of the causes of poverty. One school says that the poor are poor through no fault of their own. The other says that the poor are poor through choice. Give arguments for each position.

5. How does screening theory explain the apparently poor correlation between ability and inequality?

6. Contrast the utilitarian view of distributive justice with the Rawlsian view.

7. Explain why measured Lorenz curves that use disposable income before and after taxes may not give an accurate picture of the distribution of real income.

8. Would the work incentives be greater with a 25 percent negative-income-tax rate or a 50 percent NIT rate? Rework Table 9 and Figure 8 in the text to illustrate your answer.

9. Assume a society consists of 8 risk avoiders and 2 risk seekers. Contrast that society with one that consists of 5 risk seekers and 5 risk avoiders. Which society would have a more equal distribution of income?

10. In society A, 50 percent of the adult population is between 18 and 25 or over 65. In society B, 25 percent of the adult population is between 18 and 25 or over 65. Using Lorenz curves, which society would appear to be more unequal in its distribution of income because of life-cycle effects?

11. Joe wants goods today; Bill is more willing to wait until tomorrow for goods. Which one would be more likely to invest in human capital?

12. The official U.S. poverty income standard is adjusted upward each year to account for the general increase in prices. If a family's income just keeps up with the poverty income over the years, what is happening to its relative poverty position?

Suggested Readings

Blinder, Alan S. *Toward an Economic Theory of Income Distribution*. Cambridge, Mass.: MIT Press, 1974.

Blinder, Alan S. "The Level and Distribution of Economic Well-Being." In Martin Feldstein, ed. *The American Economy in Transition*. Chicago: The University of Chicago Press, 1980, pp. 450–53.

Friedman, Milton. "Choice, Chance, and the Personal Distribution of Income." *Journal of Political Economy* 61, 4 (August 1953): 277–90.

Kohler, Heinz. *Scarcity and Freedom*. Lexington, Mass.: D.C. Heath, 1977, pp. 339–80.

Lloyd, Cynthia B., ed. *Sex, Discrimination, and the Division of Labor*. New York: Columbia University Press, 1975.

Okun, Arthur. *Equality and Efficiency: The Big Trade-Off*. Washington, D.C.: The Brookings Institution, 1975.

Paglin, Morton. "The Measurement and Trend of Inequality: A Basic Revision." *American Economic Review* 65,4 (September 1975): 598–609.

Rawls, John. *A Theory of Justice*. Cambridge: Harvard University Press, 1971.

Rawls, John. "Some Reasons for the Maximin Criterion." *American Economic Review* 64, 2 (May 1974): 141–46.

Schiller, Bradley. *The Economics of Poverty and Discrimination*. Englewood Cliffs, N.J.: Prentice-Hall, 1973, chap. 10.

Microeconomic Issues

40

Public Finance

Chapter Preview

The distinguishing feature of economic behavior in the private sector is private ownership of the factors of production. Preceding chapters have described how private firms and private owners of the factors of production behave in different market environments. The private sector, however, does not account for all economic activity. A significant amount of economic activity is carried out by the *public sector,* or local, state, and federal governments. Public-sector economics is the study of the resource-allocation activities of government. One branch of public-sector economics is **public finance.**

Public finance is the study of government revenues and expenditures at all levels of government—local, state, and federal.

This chapter will study government expenditure and taxation and will examine the effects of government spending and taxation on private economic activity.

In 1984 the government purchased 21 percent of all goods and services produced by the economy. In an economy that produced some $3.7 trillion worth of goods and services, government purchases added up to $744 billion. The two types of government expenditures are **exhaustive expenditures** and **transfer payments.**

Exhaustive expenditures in 1983 accounted for 60 percent of total government spending. The remaining government expenditures are government transfer payments.

Exhaustive expenditures are government purchases of goods and services that divert real economic resources from the private sector, making them no longer available for private use.
Transfer payments transfer income from one individual or organization to another.

Government transfer payments do not change the amount of economic resources that the government consumes. For example, the social-security program transfers income from currently employed workers to retired or disabled workers and their families. The federal government transfers funds to state and local governments. Transfer payments affect the distribution of income among families but do not change the amount of goods and services exhausted (consumed) by government. Transfer payments may affect economic activity by changing the distribution of income and economic incentives. ■

Table 1   Exhaustive Expenditures and Transfer Payments of Government in 1983

Government	Purchase of Goods and Services, Including Interest Payments (billions of dollars)	Transfer Payments (billions of dollars)	Total Expenditures for Goods and Services and Transfers (billions of dollars)	Total Expenditure as Percent of GNP
Federal government	275	455*	730	22.1
State and local governments	415	17	432	13.1
Total government	690	472	1,162	35.2

*Federal transfers exclude grants to state and local governments.

Source: *Economic Report of the President,* February 1984, pp. 309–311, p. 220.

THE SCOPE OF GOVERNMENT ECONOMIC ACTIVITY

As Table 1 reports, total government expenditures accounted in 1983 for 35.2 percent of gross national product (GNP). The ratio of total government expenditures to gross national product is a common measure of the economic scope of government.

The average citizen's impression of the scope of government is formed by the share of personal income that he or she must pay to the government in personal tax payments—such as income taxes, inheritance taxes, or social security contributions. In 1984, government collected $435 billion in personal income taxes, which amounted to 15 percent of total personal income earned in that year. In addition to personal tax collections, governments collected $304 billion from sales and excise taxes and $306 billion in Social Security taxes and insurance. Together, all these taxes add up to about 33 percent of personal income.

Trends in Government

Government revenues and expenditures have been increasing at a rapid pace. Figure 1 shows the enormous acceleration of total government expenditures and transfer payments since 1929. Dollar figures exaggerate the growth of government because of the general rise in prosperity and prices (Recall the discussion in Appendix 1A of inflation and growth distortion.) We would expect government revenues and expenditures to rise along with the general economy. The more relevant yardstick of the changing role of government is the ratio of total government spending to total economic activity, or GNP (see Figure 2). In 1890, government expenditures accounted for 6.5 percent of GNP, but by 1984, this ratio had risen to 34 percent.

The economic role of government, especially of the federal government, has increased dramatically over the past half century for at least five reasons:

1. The United States, as one of the world's two major military superpowers, has had to devote an increasing share of its economic resources to national defense. On the eve of the Second World War, national defense expenditures accounted for 1.3 percent of GNP. At the peak of the Vietnam conflict, national defense accounted for almost 9 percent of GNP, falling to 5 percent of GNP in 1980 but rising to 6 percent by 1984.
2. Since 1929, government, especially the federal government, has increasingly taken responsibility for the health, education and income security of the American population. Prior to the Great Depression of the 1930s, it was primarily the responsibility of the individual to provide for family health, income security, and retirement needs. Educational needs were provided for by the local community, and private charitable organizations cared for the needy. Since the 1930s, this attitude has steadily eroded. In 1929, prior to the establishment of the Social Security Program, government social-welfare programs cost $3.9 million, a minute fraction of 1 percent of GNP. Today, government expenditures for health, edu-

Figure 1   Total Government Expenditures, 1929–1983

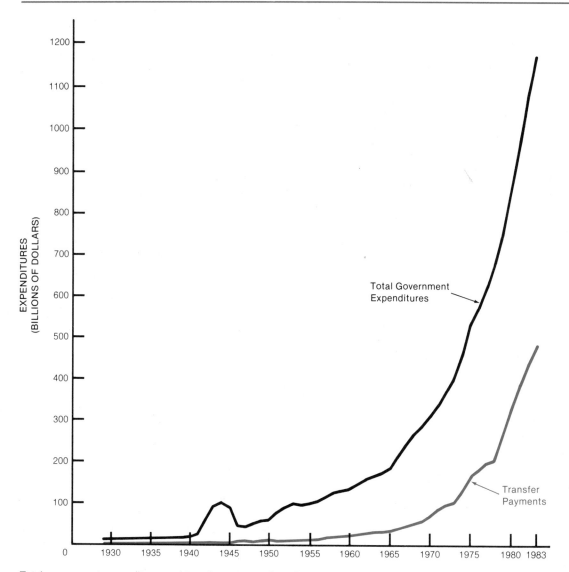

Total government expenditures and transfer payments have increased at an accelerating rate since 1929.

Source: *Economic Report of the President*, 1984, pp. 221, 308.

cation, and welfare account for almost 10 percent of GNP. Responsibility for health, education and welfare has been transferred from the family and private charitable organizations to government.

3.   The more modern and complex an economy becomes, the more government services it requires. Urban societies require more government services—sanitation, traffic control, water sup-

plies—than rural societies. Congested areas require more police protection than low-density communities. Modern industrial societies require a more complex legal system.

4.   Another explanation for the relative growth of government lies in the relative costs of supplying government services. Unlike manufacturing or agriculture, which have experienced substantial

Figure 2   Total Government Spending as a Percent of GNP, 1890–1983

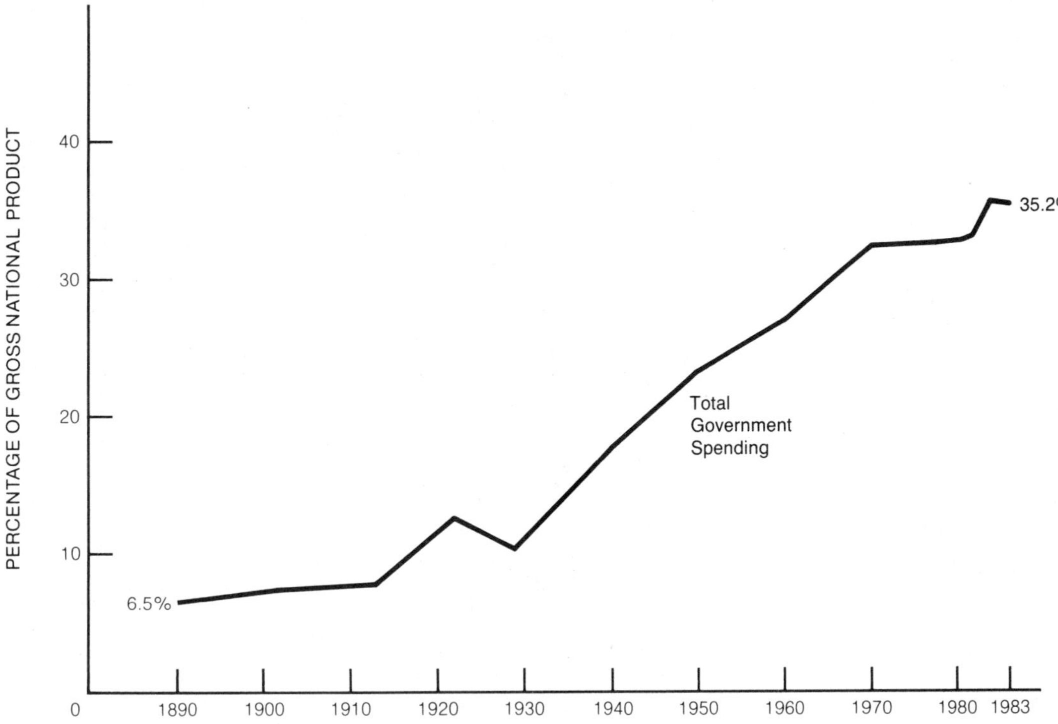

The ratio of total government expenditures to total economic activity (or GNP) is a better measure of the changing role of government than measures of government spending alone.

Source: *Economic Report of the President,* 1984, pp. 220, 308.

increases in productivity, efficiency gains in the government sector have been slow. It is easier to increase productivity in the private sector than it is in the public sector where *services*—such as school teaching, police protection, judicial services, and general record keeping—rather than *goods* are being provided. Because of slow productivity growth, price increases have been more rapid in the public sector than in the private sector. Since 1950, there has been a sixfold increase in the prices paid by government to purchase goods and services compared to a fourfold increase in consumer prices.

5. Because of the power of special-interest groups and lobbyists, democratic societies have been gradually increasing their support of government spending (see the chapter after next for further discussion).

Shares of Federal, State, and Local Governments

Government economic activities are distributed among federal, state, and local governments. Each society must determine at what level of government a given public service should be provided. Should roads be built by federal or local government? Should the municipalities, the states, or the federal government supply public education? There has been intense debate over issues like these since the founding of this country. Some citizens fear that the federal government is too removed from the people and from local conditions and sentiments and that it has acquired too much economic power. They view the states and localities as having too little power in relation to the federal government. Others consider the fed-

Figure 3   State and Local Expenditures Versus Federal Expenditures, 1930–1983

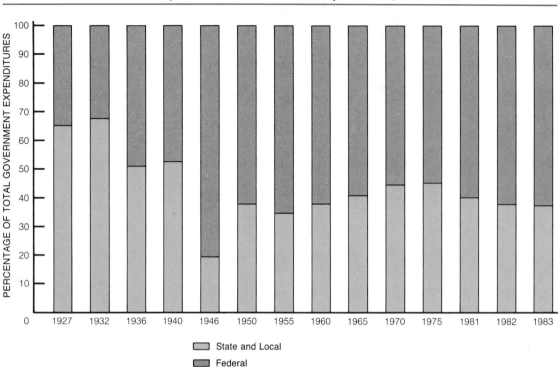

This graph shows that the dominance of federal over state and local spending is a fairly recent phenomenon. Note: Federal expenditures do not include grants in aid to state and local governments.

Source: *Economic Report of the President*, 1984, p. 308; *Historical Statistics of the United States*, vol. 2, pp. 1124–29.

eral government to be the most efficient and rational supplier of government services and the best enforcer of national standards and legislation.

In 1983, the federal government accounted for 63 percent of all government expenditures, while state and local government accounted for 37 percent. Figure 3 shows that the dominance by federal government is a fairly new phenomenon. In 1932, state and local government accounted for slightly less than 70 percent of government expenditures, while the federal government accounted for only 30 percent. As late as 1940, state and local government still accounted for about one half of all government revenues and expenditures. World War II dramatically altered the balance between federal and state/local spending. By the war's end in 1946, the federal government accounted for more than 80 percent of government spending. From 1955 to the mid-1970s,

state and local government grew in importance—from 34 percent to more than 45 percent of total government. Since the mid-1970s, the federal share has again been on the rise.

Government Surpluses and Government Deficits

Governments collect revenue (through taxes and sales of services) and make expenditures (on purchases of goods and services and transfer payments). In this regard, the government operates just like a household or business firm. If its revenues (its income) exceed its outlays, it is saving, or running a **government surplus.** If, on the other hand, its outlays exceed its revenues, it is dissaving, or running a **government deficit.** The relationship between government revenue and outlays is shown by the government budget.

Table 2   Facts and Figures on Government Budgets and Debt, 1983

	Receipts (billions of dollars)	Expenditures (billions of dollars)	Surplus of Deficit (billions of dollars)	Total Debt (billions of dollars)	Total Debt as Percent of GNP
Total government	1,040	1,172	−132	1,661	49%
Federal government	643	826	−183	1,382	42%
State and local governments	483	432	51	229*	7%

*Estimated.

Source: *Statistical Abstract of the United States,* 1984.

A **government surplus** is an excess of government revenues over government outlays.

A **government deficit** is an excess of government outlays over government revenues.

A government unit (be it a state, local, or federal government) that runs a deficit must engage in **deficit financing.**

Deficit financing is the borrowing of funds in credit markets to cover a government deficit.

If a government unit has to borrow funds over a number of years to finance its deficits, it will accumulate a **government debt.**

The **government debt** is the cumulated sum of outstanding IOUs that the government unit owes its creditors.

A government debt can be reduced by running a surplus. If the government debt were $100 billion and the government unit ran a $10 billion surplus, the government debt would be reduced by approximately $10 billion.

Table 2 provides some facts and figures on government budgets, surpluses, deficits, and debt in the United States for the year 1983. In 1983, the receipts of all government units (state, local, and federal governments) were $1,040 billion, while outlays were a higher $1,172 billion. This means that the total-government deficit was −$132 billion. Dividing these figures between the federal government and state and local governments, Table 2 shows that the federal govern-

ment ran a $183 billion deficit while state and local governments ran a $51 billion surplus. The combined deficit of −$132 is the federal deficit (−$183 billion) reduced by the amount of the state and local surplus ($51 billion). In 1983, the federal debt was $1,382 billion. Since 1950, the federal government has run surpluses in only 5 years. In 1950, the federal debt was $257 billion—18.5 percent of the 1983 figure. The federal debt has grown considerably over the years and is indeed large in absolute terms. It should be noted, however, that the federal debt was shrunk in relative terms. In 1950, for example, the federal debt was almost 90 percent of total economic output. In 1983, it was 42 percent of total output.

Macroeconomics deals with the economic consequences of government deficits and the national debt. In this chapter, we will provide only some basic background information.

An International Perspective

Government has become a $744 billion business and employs 15 out of every 100 workers in the economy. Is the economic role of government in the United States relatively larger than in other countries? As noted earlier, a convenient measure of government size is government tax revenues as a percentage of GNP. According to this measure, Figure 4 shows that government in the United States does not stand out as extraordinarily large or small. In fact, relative to the other industrialized countries, the economic role of U.S. government appears to be moderate, despite the generally heavier U.S. defense burden. The overall

Figure 4   The Comparative Tax Burden in Selected Industrial Countries, 1980

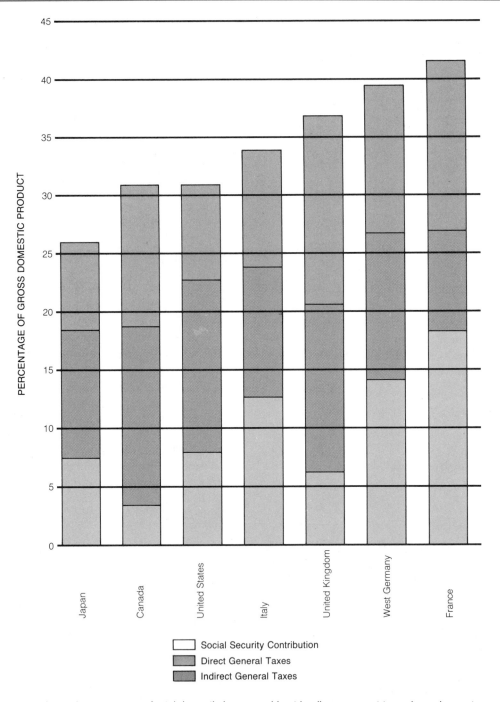

PERCENTAGE OF GROSS DOMESTIC PRODUCT

☐ Social Security Contribution
▨ Direct General Taxes
▨ Indirect General Taxes

This diagram shows the percentage of total domestic income paid out in all government taxes in each country.

Source: *Handbook of Economic Statistics, 1984;* p. 11.

U.S. tax burden is lower than in the industrialized Western European countries.

The government's share of economic activity generally rises with economic development. Low-income countries like Turkey, Portugal, and Spain have small shares of government, while the more advanced economies like Sweden, Denmark, the United Kingdom, Belgium, and Austria have large shares of government. For its level of economic development, the United States has a relatively low amount of government economic activity that is comparable to lower-income countries like Chile, Italy, Ireland, and Brazil.

COST/BENEFIT ANALYSIS OF GOVERNMENT ACTIVITY

The single rule that guides the private sector's economic decision making has been repeated over and over again in this book: *Any economic activity should be carried out as long as its marginal benefit exceeds or equals its marginal cost.* The profit-maximizing firm expands its production to the point where marginal costs and marginal revenues are equal. The business firm carries out investment projects as long as the rate of return exceeds the interest rate.

Private decision making usually follows the logic of cost/benefit analysis. In principle, cost/benefit analysis could play the same role in public decision making as it does in private decision making.

Cost/benefit analysis in the public sector requires the assessment of the costs and benefits of public-expenditure programs. Economic efficiency requires that a public-expenditure project be carried out as long as its marginal social benefit equals or exceeds its marginal social cost.

The public-sector cost/benefit rule is similar to the private-sector profit-maximization rule. Instead of comparing a firm's marginal benefits and marginal costs, the marginal benefit *to society* is compared to *society's* marginal cost. A government project that yields $10 million in benefits while costing $5 million is worth undertaking ac-

cording to this rule. A project that yields $50 million in benefits while costing $200 million should not be undertaken.

The optimal amount of government spending is that amount at which the marginal social costs and marginal social benefits of the last public expenditure program are equal.

Government cost/benefit analysis is often difficult to apply. The major problem is how to assess the social costs and benefits of different government expenditure programs. If a dam is to be built that will benefit down-river communities with better flood control and cheaper electricity but will displace long-time residents or threaten an endangered species of fish with extinction, what cost/benefit price tags should be placed on the project? The private firm can readily assess its private costs and benefits, but in society at large there will often be substantial differences of opinion on costs and benefits.

Cost/benefit analysis also ignores questions of income distribution or equity. The benefits of a government program may go to one group, and the costs may be imposed on another group. Unless the people who pay the costs are somehow compensated—which seldom occurs—the government program entails some redistribution of income.

Despite its problems, there has been an increasing trend towards the use of cost/benefit analysis in government. Many major government programs—such as dams, new highways, environmental-protection programs, and labor-training programs—are being assessed in terms of costs and benefits.

A Substitute for the Market Test

In the private sector, the market provides safeguards to prevent costs from exceeding benefits. If private firms produce a product whose benefit to society (as reflected in its market price) is less than its cost, the firm will incur losses. In the long run, it will either go out of business or switch to producing products that yield a benefit equal to or greater than cost. This process is called the **market test.**

Example 1   Voting with One's Feet in Houston, Texas

One argument for relatively more government spending at the state and local level than at the federal level is that people can vote for government services with their feet. If a family does not like the public services provided by one community, they can vote with their feet by moving to another community. At the national level, however, if voters do not like the government services provided, moving to a foreign country is a less practical option.

The Houston metropolitan area provides a typical example of this phenomenon. Within the Houston city limits are two independent city governments, and on the perimeter of the city limits are a large number of independent governments and independent school districts. One community (located in the middle of Houston) offers outstanding police and fire protection and numerous public parks, but its residents have to pay higher taxes for these services (along with higher prices for their homes). People who place a high value on police and fire protection can vote for these services with their feet by buying homes in this community. Other communities that lie outside the Houston Independent School District devote more resources per resident to public education. Residents of these communities pay for higher-quality public education by higher school-district taxes. Families with school-age children can vote for these services by buying homes in communities that offer the best schools. Families that do not have school-age children will be unlikely to move into these communities because they do not benefit from these special educational services. ■

The **market test** is the process that ensures that goods and services in the private sector yield a benefit equal to or greater than their cost.

Public goods are not subject to this market test. There is no guarantee that public expenditures will yield benefits equal to or greater than cost. One can argue that voters in a democratic society can always vote the politicians out of office or fire public officials who make unwise expenditures. However, if these decisions are made at high levels—say, in Washington—it is difficult for voters who cast their ballots every two or four years to voice by means of the ballot box their disagreement with specific government expenditures. Moreover, voters may lack sufficient information on complex government programs.

Publicly produced goods cannot satisfy everyone. In private markets, consumers buy what they want, for the most part. But as voters, people have to take the good with the bad. For example, a voter may support his or her congressional representative's position on defense spending but may oppose the representative's position on social security. These and other matters are discussed in the chapter on public choice.

Should a Program Be Local or National?

At lower levels of government, however, the ballot box can often provide the market test on public expenditures. In municipal elections, voters are often asked to vote on specific expenditure projects (whether or not to issue bonds to build a new school, whether to raise police officers' salaries). At the local level, households can vote for public services "with their feet." Different communities offer different mixes of public expenditures. One community offers good schools but high property taxes. Another community offers low taxes but poor schools. Young couples with school-age children may choose to settle in the community with good schools; older couples or couples without children may settle in the community with low taxes and poor schools. In this manner, communities will provide the mix of public services that its residents desire. (See Example 1.)

The case for decentralization of public expenditures to the level of local government is persuasive but leaves important questions unresolved. By giving more responsibilities to the states and localities, government-spending decisions will be made by those in closest touch with local needs. Criticisms of increased state and local responsibility focus on the supposedly lesser competence and training of state and local bureaucrats and on the greater corruption at the local level.

Certain government programs can only be national in scope. The nation must have a uniform legal system. National defense can be provided only for the nation as a whole. Many government-expenditure projects transcend state and local boundaries, such as the interstate highway system or a dam that affects several states. A whole range of public expenditures must be carried out above the local or even state level. Where the boundary is to be drawn between the various levels of government is a question that cannot be resolved by simple economic analysis.

PRINCIPLES OF TAXATION

To finance its expenditures, government—whether local, state, or federal—must have revenues. Taxation is the major source of general government revenue in the United States (see Table 3). Sales of and charges for government products and services account for only a minor portion of government revenues. As Table 3 reports, 60.4 percent of government revenue was derived in 1981 from taxes (income, sales, and property taxes), and 20.9 percent was derived from social-insurance contributions (primarily Social Security and unemployment insurance). The remaining 18.6 percent of government revenue was obtained through charges for products and services sold to buyers (postal services, tuition in state-run schools, public hospitals, government-run utilities, licenses, state liquor-store sales, and so on).

The composition of state and local taxes has shifted dramatically since the 1960s, when property taxes accounted for almost 50 percent of state and local revenue. By the 1980s, the share of property taxes dropped to less than 30 percent of state and local revenue. One reason for the falling share of property taxes was the revolt against property taxes that hit many large states in the 1970s and forced them to seek other revenue sources.

Table 3   Sources of Local, State, and Federal General Government Revenue, 1981

Source of Revenue		Percent of Total
Taxes		6.04
Individual income	30.9	
Corporate income	7.0	
Sales taxes	12.5	
Property and other taxes	10.0	
Social Security, employee retirement, unemployment insurance		20.9
Charges for goods and services		15.9
Utilities and liquor stores		2.8
Total		**100.0**

Source: *Statistical Abstract of the United States*, 1984, 273.

Distributing the Burden

Taxes have been with us since recorded history began, as has the debate over what constitutes a fair tax system. If people believe that taxes are unfairly levied, they will seek to evade taxes and will otherwise engage in taxpayer revolts. In some countries, tax evasion is an accepted social practice (see Example 2). In other countries, tax evasion is regarded as immoral. Public reaction depends upon whether the tax system is perceived as fair.

Over time, two principles of fairness have emerged. The first is the principle that the tax burden should be distributed according to benefits received. The second and opposing principle is that the tax burden should be distributed according to the ability to pay.

The Benefit Principle. The *benefit principle* of taxation states that those who benefit from the public expenditure that a tax finances should pay the tax. According to this principle, the persons who benefit from a new state highway, from a new airport, or from a flood-control project—all financed from tax revenues—should be the ones to pay. If community members are not willing to pay for a public project—for example, if citizens vote against a flood-control project in their community—they are indicating that they do not consider the project's benefits to outweigh its

Example 2   Tax Evasion in Other Countries

Almost all countries—even the Soviet Union—have underground economies that generate earnings that are not taxed. The magnitude of underground untaxed earnings appears to depend upon tax rates. Swedish workers pay tax rates twice those of comparable American workers. As a consequence, many Swedish workers enter the underground economy of bartered labor, work for cash only, and use other arrangements to avoid records of income earned. Despite efforts by Swedish authorities to discourage such activities, otherwise law-abiding Swedes are simply unwilling to pay the high tax rates required by Sweden's welfare state. Unreported income in Sweden is estimated to equal 13 percent of total income.

In Italy—a country with a cherished historical tradition of tax evasion—the underground economy is so large that economic planners must include it in their economic plans. It is estimated that one third of Italian workers are secretly employed, and income from underground labor is estimated at around 10.5 percent of GNP. Small firms are able to remain competitive in overseas markets by using hidden labor. Italian authorities fear that a crackdown on hidden labor would put too many people out of work and seriously damage the economy. Most Italian companies keep two books—one that records actual transactions and another prepared for tax authorities.

In Thailand, it is estimated that only 10 percent of the work force files tax returns. Virtually all products are exchanged under the table. Auto sellers offer cars at 10 to 30 percent off if the buyer pays cash and forgets about the deal. No one can even estimate the percentage of tax revenues lost to tax evasion.

Tax evasion is also practiced in the United States. Many taxpayers are tried and convicted for tax evasion, but the remarkable feature of the U.S. tax system is the relatively small magnitude of illegal tax evasion relative to other countries where tax evasion is a national pasttime. According to a Department of Commerce Study published in the June 1984 issue of *Survey of Current Business,* only $47.6 billion of income was underreported in 1977 (less then 3 percent of the total) for the purpose of avoiding legal tax obligations. This 3 percent figure is quite small by international standards. ∎

Sources: "Cheating on Taxes—A Worldwide Pursuit," U.S. News and World Report, October 22, 1979. Bruno S. Frey and Werner Pommerehne, "The Hidden Economy: State and Prospects for Measurement," *Review of Income and Wealth,* March 1984, pp. 1–24.

---

costs. If all taxes were levied on the principle that the beneficiaries bear the full burden of the tax (and if the beneficiaries were given the opportunity to vote on each public expenditure), benefits of projects undertaken would exceed costs. One example of a benefit tax is a tax on gasoline that is used to finance highway construction. In many communities, special taxes are assessed for specific road repairs, streetlighting, and sidewalks.

One disadvantage of the benefit principle is that it is often difficult to identify the beneficiaries of different government expenditures. While it is obvious that automobile drivers benefit from public highways and that residents of New York City benefit from public expenditures on the New York subway system, it is often difficult to determine who benefits and by what amount in the case of other public expenditures. Who benefits from national defense? Who benefits from police protection and from the legal system? Do the poor benefit more than the rich? Or is it the other way around? Who benefits most from the conduct of foreign policy? In order to apply the benefit principle, one must first know who is the beneficiary.

The Ability-to-Pay Principle.   The second approach to fairness in the tax system is the *ability-to-pay principle*. This principle maintains that those better able to pay should bear the greater burden of taxes whether or not they benefit more from the resulting government expenditure. According to the principle, the rich may benefit less from public education and from publicly financed hospitals because they use private hospitals and send their children to private schools, but because they are better able to pay than the poor, they should bear a heavier burden.

A tax system that adopts the ability-to-pay principle must have both **vertical equity** and **horizontal equity.**

Vertical equity exists when those with a greater ability to pay bear a heavier tax burden.

Horizontal equity exists when those with equal abilities to pay pay the same amount of tax.

If vertical equity is lacking, then taxes are not being paid on an ability-to-pay basis. If horizontal equity is not present, then the ability-to-pay principle is being violated because taxpayers with equal abilities to pay are being treated differently.

Like the benefit principle, the ability-to-pay principle leaves important questions unresolved. How is ability to pay to be measured? If one uses income as an indicator, how does one adjust for differences in family size, catastrophic medical expenses, and families that are sending three children to college at once? If one uses money income as the measure, how does one account for nonpecuniary income arising from differences in leisure and work conditions? If one defines ability to pay in terms of family wealth rather than income, should the tax be levied on the basis of the value of stock, bonds, and real estate that a family owns? What about the elderly couple that owns a $1 million home but has very little income?

Types of Taxes

A key feature of any tax system is whether taxes are used to redistribute income. An important ingredient of the redistributive impact of a tax system is the fraction of income taxpayers who earn different amounts of income must pay. A tax can be either a **proportional tax,** a **progressive tax,** or a **regressive tax.**

A **proportional tax** is one where each taxpaying unit pays the same percentage of its income as taxes.

A **progressive tax** is one where the higher is the income, the larger is the percentage of income paid as taxes.

A **regressive tax** is one where the higher is the income, the smaller is the percentage of income paid as taxes.

An example of a progressive tax is the federal income tax. In 1984, a married couple with $10,000 in taxable income paid $823 in taxes; a married couple with a $20,000 income paid $2,466; a married couple earning $40,000 paid taxes of $7,866. Taxes were about 8.2 percent of income for those with a $10,000 taxable income but 19.7 percent for those with a taxable income of $40,000.

An example of a regressive tax would be the sales tax because the wealthy spend a smaller portion of their income than poor people. For example, suppose the family with $40,000 of taxable income spends $20,000 and saves the rest, while the family with $10,000 taxable income spends the full $10,000. Each pays a 5 percent sales tax; the wealthy ($40,000) family pays sales taxes of $1,000, or 1/40th of its income, while the poor ($10,000) family pays sales taxes of $500, or 1/20th of its income. Although the poor family spends fewer dollars on sales tax, it spends a larger percentage of its income.

The people who believe that high-income families should pay a larger percentage of their income in taxes favor a progressive tax system. The supporters of a proportional tax system don't think the wealthy—who pay more taxes anyway when rates are constant—should pay a larger percentage of their income as taxes than the less affluent. What type of tax system is "best" is largely on issue of normative economics.

THE U.S. TAX SYSTEM

Society must decide for itself who should bear the burden of taxes. Society must resolve whether taxes are to be levied according to the ability-to-pay principle or the benefit principle and whether the tax system should be proportional, progressive, or regressive. Once these decisions are made, tax authorities must devise a tax system that fulfills these goals. At first glance, it seems simple. If society wants the rich to pay 40 percent of their income and the poor to pay 10 percent, then income-tax rates need only be set at 40 percent and 10 percent for these two groups. Right? Or, if society decides that cigarette manufacturers and big oil companies should pay a heavy share of taxes, then it must simply levy a tax on each carton of cigarettes and on each barrel of oil. Right?

The Incidence of Taxation

In reality, the individual or company that is being taxed is not necessarily the one who ends up actually bearing the full burden of the tax. In many cases, the **incidence of a tax** can be shifted to someone else.

The **incidence of a tax** is the actual distribution of the burden of tax payment.

For example, when a $1 tax is placed on each carton of cigarettes, cigarette manufacturers may reduce the supply of cigarettes to the market. When the price of cigarettes rises, the manufacturer has shifted the tax forward so that the consumer is paying at least part of the tax in the form of a higher price. If the price rises by $0.80 as a consequence of the $1 tax, then 80 percent of the tax has been shifted to the consumer, in which case most of the tax burden is borne not by the manufacturer but by the final consumer.

A tax is shifted to the consumer when the consumer of the product being taxed pays a portion of the tax by paying a higher price for the product.

Taxes can be shifted to suppliers of factors as well. If employers respond to the Social Security payroll tax by reducing their demand for labor, the wage rate falls and the tax has been shifted from the employer to the supplier of labor: the employee. If a $50 monthly payroll tax for each employee causes wages to fall by $25, then the employer has shifted 50 percent of the tax to employees.

Virtually any tax—an income tax, a sales tax, a wealth tax, an inheritance tax, or a tariff on foreign goods—can be shifted. Some taxes can be shifted almost entirely to others; other taxes must be completely paid by the individual or organization that nominally pays the tax. An increase in income-tax rates may persuade physicians to reduce their patient load. If physicians generally reduce their supply of labor, physicians' fees (prices) rise. Who has paid the tax? Surprisingly,

the patient pays a portion of the tax in the form of higher doctors' bills. If the government places a tax on imported cars, who pays? If automobile prices rise, purchasers of cars pay in the form of higher automobile prices.

To determine whether a tax system is progressive, regressive, or proportional, one must first determine the incidence of taxation. If the rich are taxed at highly progressive rates yet shift their taxes to the poor, then progressive taxation is only an illusion.

Federal Taxes

More than 90 percent of federal tax receipts are from taxes that are related to income. In 1984, individual income taxes accounted for 43.7 percent of federal revenues, Social Security contributions accounted for 37.3 percent, and corporation income taxes accounted for another 10.9 percent.

The Federal Individual Income Tax. The major source of federal tax revenues is the individual income tax. Individual income-tax liabilities are determined by applying a tax schedule to taxable income.

In the United States (for income earned in 1984), taxes were 0 percent (no taxes) on taxable income below $3,400 for a married couple filing a joint return. Graduated income-tax rates varied from 11 percent of taxable income to 50 percent. For example, a married couple with a taxable income of $20,000 paid in 1984 a tax of $2,466, or 12 percent of taxable income. On a $60,000 taxable income, a married couple paid $15,168, or 25 percent of their taxable income.

The Economic Recovery Act, passed by Congress in 1981, made substantial changes in the federal income tax. The Economic Recovery Act was implemented between October 1981 and July 1983 and reduced individual income-tax rates from the 1980 range of 14 percent to 70 percent to the new range of 11 percent to 50 percent. The overall rate reduction was approximately 25 percent. The law also reduced the maximum tax on "unearned" income (income from interest, dividends, and profits) from 70 percent to 50 percent, so that all forms of income would be subject to the same maximum rate. In addition, the Economic Recovery Act called for the **indexing** of tax rates.

> **Indexing** is the tying of tax rates to the rate of inflation. Tax rates are lowered as prices generally increase.

The Economic Recovery Act indexed tax rates to inflation because inflation typically pushes up both prices and wages (earnings). When individuals whose nominal incomes have been raised by inflation are pushed into higher tax brackets, their real income after taxes may be reduced. For example, suppose a couple pays 10 percent of their $20,000 income in taxes, leaving them $18,000 after taxes. If there were a 5 percent inflation, and their income also rose by 5 percent (to $21,000), they would have to pay 12 percent of their income in taxes ($2,520) because income taxes are progressive (higher incomes are taxed at higher rates, or percentages). After taxes, they now have $18,480. Because of the 5 percent rise in prices, their income after taxes can buy only $17,600 worth of goods and services in the prices of the previous year—less than their after-tax income could buy a year earlier. Indexing of tax rates to inflation prevents this erosion of purchasing power. As people's incomes are pushed up by inflation, tax rates are automatically lowered.[1]

The effect of highly progressive tax rates is softened by the numerous deductions and exemptions from taxable income allowed by law. These deductions and exemptions are often called *tax loopholes* and have aroused the fury of tax reformers over the years. Items excluded from taxable income reduce individual tax liabilities in three ways: 1) by deducting some forms of income from taxable income, 2) by deducting certain expenditures from taxable income, and 3) by deducting personal exemptions from taxable income.

Some forms of income are not included in reported income. The first $400 of dividends are exempted. Interest paid on bonds of local and state government (so-called *tax-exempt bonds*) is also excluded from income. Interest earned on *all-

saver certificates under the 1981 tax law is not included in taxable income. Most transfer payments are not counted as a part of income, although in 1984 some Social Security recipients had to pay taxes on their Social Security income. Certain contributions to retirement programs (Individual Retirement Accounts and Keogh Accounts) are not counted in taxable income.

The most important exclusion from taxable income is 60 percent of a **realized capital gain.**

> A **realized capital gain** is income gained when property is sold at a higher price than its purchase price. According to current tax laws, the capital gain is long-term if the asset is held longer than six months.

If someone sells stocks, bonds, or real property that has been owned for at least one year for a profit, only 40 percent of this profit must be included as income. The preferential treatment of capital gains means that the highest tax rate on capital-gains income (as of 1984) is 20 percent (40 percent of the capital gain times 50 percent, the maximum tax rate).

The government allows taxpayers to deduct certain expenditures (taxes paid to state and local government, medical expenditures, interest payments, charitable contributions, fire and theft losses, and child-care costs for working mothers) from taxable income. These deductions are called *itemized deductions*. There are two rationales for itemized deductions. The first is that adjustments should be made for special and unusual circumstances that affect one's ability to pay taxes. The family that has had catastrophic medical expenses or the family that has lost its home to fire has a reduced ability to pay income taxes. Other deductions are designed to encourage certain expenditures: the itemized interest deduction encourages home ownership; deductions for charitable contributions encourage voluntary giving to worthy charities; deductions of taxes paid to local and state governments protect taxpayers against excessively high tax rates from the combination of all government taxes and give state and local governments the opportunity to gather revenues.[2]

---

1. Tax rates in 1984 were lowered to meet the indexing requirements of the 1981 tax bill. In 1983, a family with a taxable income of $20,000 paid $2,611 in taxes. In 1984, a family with a $20,000 taxable income paid $2,466. For a family with a constant taxable income, the tax bill dropped by the inflation rate (slightly more than 5 percent).

2. Not all taxpayers itemized deductions. Individuals who do not have large itemized deductions are permitted to deduct a *standard deduction*, which currently is set at 10 percent of adjusted gross income (or at a maximum, or *zero-bracket amount*, of $3,710 for a married couple).

Table 4   The Relationship Between Personal Income and Taxable Income, 1981

Income Category	Amount (billions of dollars)	Percent of Personal Income
Personal income	2,427	100.0
minus		
Exclusions	−655	−27.0
equals		
Adjusted gross income	1,772	73.0
minus		
Deductions and personal exemptions	−388	−16.0
equals		
Taxable income	1,384	57.0

Source: *U.S. Internal Revenue Service, Statistics of Income, Individual Tax Returns.*

Table 5   Effective and Marginal Tax Rates for a Married Couple with Two Dependents, 1983

Income Level (dollars)	Effective Tax Rate (percent)	Marginal Tax Rate (percent)
10,000	3.0	13.0
20,000	9.2	19.0
25,000	11.3	23.0
35,000	15.2	30.0
50,000	19.7	35.0
75,000	25.4	44.0

The effective tax rate is the ratio of the tax payment to income before exclusions and deductions. The marginal tax rate is the ratio of the increase in tax payments to the increase in income.

Source: *Statistical Abstract of the United States,* 1984, p. 329.

Personal exemptions can also be deducted from taxable income. Each family member is allowed a personal exemption of $1,090 and extra exemptions are allowed for those over 65 and for the blind. A family of four with one family member over 65 would have 5 personal exemptions and would subtract $5,450 from its income (5 times $1,090). The major function of personal exemptions is to differentiate among families of different sizes and circumstances that have the same income. The percentage of income paid out in taxes depends on the amount of one's **taxable income.**

> **Taxable income** is the income that remains after all deductions and exemptions are subtracted.

The tax schedule (listing the tax rates for each income level) is applied to taxable income, not to actual income. If substantial subtractions are made, the difference between income and taxable income can be great. Deductions from taxable income cause an erosion of the tax base. Figures for 1981 (see Table 4) show the effect of each type of exclusion on the tax base. After all exemptions and deductions, taxable income was only 57 percent of personal income. Deductions erode the tax base by slightly less than one half.

The **effective tax rate** measures the ratio of tax liability to adjusted gross income. *Adjusted*

gross income is essentially personal income minus personal business expenses, contributions to retirement programs, and moving expenses.

> The **effective tax rate** is the percent of adjusted gross income that is actually paid in taxes. Effective tax rates show the effect of deductions and exclusions on tax rates.

The effective tax rate is reduced by each deduction made from taxable income. Effective tax rates for different earnings levels are given in Table 5. Effective tax rates for a four-person family range from 3.0 percent for an income of $10,000 to 25.4 percent for an income of $75,000.

The **marginal tax rate** shows what happens to tax rates as income increases.

> The **marginal tax rate** is the ratio of the *increase* in tax payments to the *increase* in income. The marginal tax rate shows how much extra taxes must be paid per dollar of extra earnings.

Marginal tax rates play an important role in economic decision making. Marginal tax rates are also shown in Table 5. Individuals who earn $10,000 have a marginal tax rate of 13 percent. In other words, if someone earning $10,000 earns an extra $100, his or her tax will rise by $13. Individuals who earn $75,000 have a marginal tax rate of 44 percent; if such an individual earns an extra $100, his or her tax would rise by $44. As the table shows, the marginal tax rate is higher than the average tax rate (the effective tax rate)—a result that is consistent with the marginal/average rule. In a progressive tax system, the average rate rises with income. In order for an average to rise, the marginal value must be higher than the average value.

Social Security and Payroll Taxes.

Since it was founded in 1935, the Social Security Program has been financed by a payroll tax, half of which is paid by the employer and half of which is paid by the employee. Unlike the individual income tax, where deductions exempt low-income families from paying the tax, Social Security payroll taxes are paid starting with the first dollar of earnings. In 1984, the payroll tax was 14 percent of the first $37,800 of earnings with the employer paying one half of the tax. For example, a worker earning $15,000 per year paid $1,050 in payroll taxes (and the employer paid the same sum). Because the tax is imposed only on the first $37,800 of income earned in a year, an employee earning $500,000 would pay the same tax as one earning $37,800. For this reason, the Social Security payroll tax is a regressive tax. In 1984, for example, an employee earning $10,000 typically paid a payroll tax of 7 percent of income and a personal income tax of 3 percent (from Table 5), while an employee earning $50,000 paid a payroll tax of 5.3 percent of income and an income tax of 19.7 percent of income. As income rises, the share of the payroll tax falls while the share of the income tax rises. Not all workers belong to the Social Security system. Federal employees and some state-government employees have their own retirement programs, as do railroad workers.

Social Security payroll taxes finance the Social Security retirement, health, and disability programs. The Medicare program that subsidizes medical care for the elderly is part of the Social Security system. Retirement benefits depend upon average monthly earnings during the years the worker paid into the program. According to existing benefit schedules, a poor worker retiring at age 65 receives retirement benefits greater than what earnings were while working, while the retired worker who had higher earnings receives about one half of previous earnings. The fact that poor workers can draw monthly benefits in excess of their monthly contributions is felt to soften the regressive nature of contributions to the system. In 1980, Social Security old-age pensions replaced 66 percent of the earnings retired couples had earned immediately before retirement.

Corporation Income Taxes.

Corporations are subject to a federal tax on their profits. Corporation income-tax rates in 1984 started at 15 percent for corporations with earnings of $25,000 per year, rose to 18 percent for the next $25,000, and then rose to a maximum of 46 percent on earnings in excess of $100,000. Like the individual income tax, the corporation income tax has provisions that erode the tax base. The major loopholes are the *investment tax credit* (which enables corporations to deduct up to 10 percent of the value of new capital equipment directly from their tax liabilities), fast depreciation write-offs, and special treatment for the minerals industry. Existing tax laws permit corporations with losses to, in effect, transfer these losses to profitable corporations so that they can reduce their tax liabilities. Economists have estimated that the average effective tax rate for corporations was little more than 35 percent in the 1960s and early 1970s. The effective tax rate varies considerably by industry.[3] In 1983, the average effective tax rate for large corporations was 15 percent of corporate income with capital-intensive corporations paying little or no taxes. (See Table 6.)

Corporate profits that are distributed to stockholders as dividends are taxed twice. The profits are taxed once as corporate income and taxed again as "unearned" income when stockholders receive their dividends (see the chapter on business organization for a more detailed discussion of the effects of double taxation). Many public-finance specialists have argued against the double taxation of corporate dividends, and some propose that there be one tax on income because the double taxation of dividends discourages the paying out of dividends. In effect, changes in tax codes have reduced substantially the relative share of the corporate income tax in federal tax revenues. In the mid-1950s, corporate taxes ac-

---

3. George Break and Joseph Pechman, *Federal Tax Reform: The Impossible Dream?* (Washington, D.C.: Brookings Institution, 1975), p. 91.

counted for one quarter of federal tax revenues. By 1983, this share had dropped to 6 percent. Liberalization of rules governing corporate taxes has pushed the U.S. tax system in the direction of one federal tax on income as the share of corporate taxes has declined.

Excise, Customs, and Gift Taxes.

A small proportion of federal tax receipts (about 7.5 percent) is gathered from **excise taxes, customs duties,** and **gift taxes.**

> **Excise taxes** are per-unit taxes on the production or sale of specific goods or services.

> **Customs duties** are taxes on the transfer of certain goods from one country into another.

> **Gift taxes** are taxes on the transfer of property from one owner to another.

Federal excise taxes are levied on a wide range of goods and services including alcohol, cigarettes, gasoline, tires, firearms, telephones, airline tickets, and trucks.

State and Local Taxes

State and local governments must also finance their expenditures, but taxpayers are more heavily burdened by the federal income tax. Moreover, state and local governments must be careful not to tax their constituents markedly more than neighbor governments for fear of losing population and industry. One reason for allowing taxpayers to deduct tax payments to state and local governments from taxable income on their federal tax returns is to give state and local governments the opportunity to raise revenues without exhausting the taxpaying capacity of their citizens. It has even been proposed (but never implemented) that the federal government give a tax credit (of, say, 50 percent) on taxes paid for state income taxes. Under such circumstances, for every $100 in state taxes, one's federal income tax would be reduced by $50.

Unlike the federal government that relies heavily on income taxes for its revenues, state and local governments obtained in 1981 only 12.0 percent of their revenue from individual and

Table 6   How Corporate Tax Rates Vary by Industry

Industry	Effective 1983 U.S. Tax Rate (percent)
Aerospace	14.0
Airlines	Loss
Beverages	18.7
Broadcasting	18.5
Chemicals	(1.0)
Computers, office equipment	26.3
Construction	0.7
Electronics, appliances	7.4
Financial institutions	6.4
Food processors	25.9
Glass, concrete	17.5
Instruments	32.8
Insurance	9.9
Investment companies	9.3
Metal manufacturing	Loss
Metal products	15.1
Mining	Loss
Motor vehicles	3.5
Paper, wood products	(0.5)
Petroleum	21.3
Pharmaceuticals	27.2
Railroads	3.3
Retailing	20.0
Rubber	19.6
Soaps, cosmetics	35.6
Telecommunications	4.8
Tobacco	33.8
Trucking	34.5
Utilities (electric, gas)	7.1
Wholesalers	34.8

Rates in parentheses are negative tax rates, indicating that the industry received a refund. No tax rate is computed for industries that recorded a loss in a year.

Source: *Joint Committee on Taxation,* cited in *New York Times,* December 1, 1984, p. 21.

corporate income taxes. Property and sales taxes yielded 31.8 percent of revenue. Payroll taxes for employee retirement and unemployment compensation contributed another 10.5 percent. In the 1960s and 1970s, taxpayers in many states revolted against high property taxes and passed laws reducing property-tax rates. As a consequence, property taxes fell from 32 percent of state and local-government revenue in 1960 to 18 percent in 1982. The major single source of state and local revenue in 1981 was revenue from the federal government for public welfare, highways, education, and unemployment compensa-

Example 3   The Efficiency Costs of the Tax System

Any tax that is not neutral can influence people to change their behavior and can, therefore, reduce economic efficiency. Taxpaying units respond to marginal tax rates in determining their economic behavior. Economic efficiency requires that the economy operate on its production-possibilities frontier. If a society produces less output under a given tax system than it would have produced under a neutral tax system, then the tax system has cost the economy some of its efficiency.

No one knows for sure how much output is lost by the current tax system. In a 1979 study for the Brookings Institution, economist Jerry Hausman found that the U.S. tax system causes people to work less. According to the Hausman study, if there were no taxes at all, men would work 8 percent more. The top 20 percent of male earners would increase their hours of work by 13 percent. Women would be even more strongly affected. Another form of inefficiency is introduced by the more favorable tax treatment of capital investment. Currently, businesses that invest in capital equipment receive a number of tax advantages that are not available when they hire human capital (highly skilled people). The favorable tax treatment of

capital equipment causes firms to devote more resources at the margin to capital equipment even though the hiring of highly skilled people would have added more to the output of the firm. Once the tax advantages are calculated, firms find themselves better off devoting additional resources to capital. Because the interest paid by state and municipal governments is tax exempt, state and local governments can finance investment projects at lower rates of interest than can private industry. This means that state and local governments can invest in projects that yield a rate of return below those offered by private investments. Economic efficiency, however, requires that rates of return be equal at the margin. If the last investment project of local government yields 8 percent, while the last investment project of private industry yields 12 percent, output would be increased by reshuffling resources to private investment. Another source of inefficiency is the compliance cost of a tax system (see Example 4). If people have to devote time to record keeping and tax preparation that they could have used in alternate productive pursuits, the economy has suffered further efficiency losses. ■

---

tion, which accounted for 17.8 percent of state and local revenues.

The federal government is a major financier of state and local programs. The manner in which federal assistance is handled has been a controversial issue over the years. Those disturbed by the growing importance of Washington maintain that the federal government should provide money to state and local governments with no strings attached. The argument is that the federal government has preempted state and local governments by imposing heavy federal taxes, leaving the taxpayer with limited capacity to pay state and local taxes. This no-strings approach is called *revenue sharing*. It is argued that revenue sharing would allow state and local governments to make their own decisions on how to spend money. State and local governments, the advocates of revenue sharing maintain, are better judges of where the money is really needed. In 1983, only 4.8 percent

of state- and local-government revenues were from revenue sharing. Federal funds are granted primarily as grants-in-aid for specific programs. In other words, federal money is granted for a specific purpose, and the states are obligated to spend the money as instructed by the federal government.

Is the U.S. Tax System Progressive?

The U.S. tax system consists of different taxes at the local, state, and federal level. The federal tax system relies primarily on individual income taxes, corporation income taxes, and payroll taxes. State and local governments use sales and property taxes to raise their revenues. The federal individual income tax is progressive: effective tax rates are higher the higher is the income of the taxpayer. Social Security payroll taxes are regressive: families with low wages pay a higher per-

Figure 5   Two Views of the Tax Burden

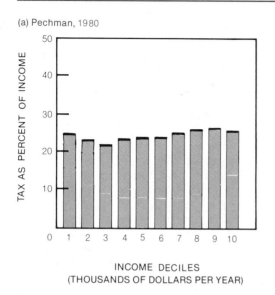

(a) Pechman, 1980

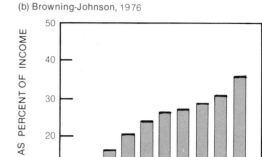

(b) Browning-Johnson, 1976

INCOME DECILES
(THOUSANDS OF DOLLARS PER YEAR)

INCOME DECILES
(THOUSANDS OF DOLLARS PER YEAR)

Browning and Johnson's findings indicate that the U.S tax system is more progressive than Pechman's findings suggest.

Sources: Joseph Pechman, *Who Paid the Taxes, 1966–85* (Washington, D.C.: Brookings Institution, 1985). Edgar K. Browning and William R. Johnson, *The Distribution of the Tax Burden* (Washington, D.C.: American Enterprise Institute, 1979).

centage of their income. Sales taxes are generally considered regressive because the poor spend a larger percentage of their income on the items taxed than do the rich.

When all these taxes are combined, is the overall U.S tax system regressive, proportional, or progressive? Is the progressivity of the federal individual income tax strong enough to outweigh the regressivity of payroll taxes and sales taxes? To answer this question, economists must first determine the incidence of taxation.

It is very difficult to estimate the incidence of taxation. Economists who have worked on this question disagree substantially on the distribution of the burden of taxes among different income groups.

In a major study of taxes conducted in 1974, Joseph Pechman and Benjamin Okner concluded that the U.S. tax system was basically proportional. According to their study, only the very poor (those in the bottom 5 percent of the income distribution) and the very rich (those in the top 5 percent) paid a higher proportion of their income in taxes. But for other families, the percentage of

income paid in taxes was basically uniform. The Pechman and Okner results are shown in panel (a) of Figure 5.

In a 1985 study, Pechman concludes that the U.S. tax system remains basically proportional (except at the very top and bottom) and that recent tax changes have raised the effective tax rates of the poor while lowering the effective rates of the rich because of the declining importance of property and corporate-income taxes and the rising importance of payroll taxes over the past decade.[4]

A 1979 study by Edgar Browning and William Johnson disputes the conclusions of Pechman and Okner.[5] Browning and Johnson found that the overall tax system was, as of 1972, highly progressive, as shown in panel (b) of Figure 5. Fam-

4. Joseph Pechman and Benjamin Okner, *Who Bears the Tax Burden?* (Washington, D.C.: Brookings Institution, 1974); Joseph A. Pechman, *Who Paid the Taxes, 1966–85* (Washington, D.C.: Brookings Institution, 1985).

5. Edgar K. Browning and William R. Johnson, *The Distribution of the Tax Burden* (Washington, D.C.: American Enterprise Institute, 1979).

ilies in the bottom 10 percent of the income distribution paid 10.7 percent of their income as taxes, while families in the top 10 percent paid 46.4 percent of their income.

Why is it that these two studies come to such different conclusions? The basic point of disagreement is the incidence of sales taxes. Browning and Johnson argue that the transfer payments received by the poor (Social Security, welfare, and so on) are raised almost automatically when prices rise because transfer payments are typically adjusted for inflation. If a sales tax causes prices to rise, the price increase will not be passed on to the poor because the poor's incomes will rise along with the price. Therefore, sales taxes are not regressive as had been thought but are actually progressive because they are shifted primarily to the rich.

The difference of opinon over the burden of the tax system is an explosive issue. If the tax burden is indeed heavier on the poor than on the rich, tax reformers could argue that the rich should be taxed more heavily. On the other hand, if the current tax system is as progressive as Browning and Johnson found, then society may be content with the existing system.

TAXES AND EFFICIENCY

Taxes can motivate individuals and firms to change their economic behavior. Tax laws that give favorable treatment to capital gains and that tax dividends doubly encourage corporations not to pay dividends. Increases in effective income-tax rates may cause high-income earners to reduce their supply of effort. High property taxes in areas with good schools will affect relocation decisions. Tax breaks on the restoration costs of historic buildings cause historic buildings to be preserved. Sales taxes may reduce supply and cause prices to rise. A **neutral tax** is hard to find.

A **neutral tax** is a tax that does not cause any change in private production, consumption, or investment decisions.

The goal of any economy is to obtain a maximum output from its limited resources. Economies would like to operate on their production-possibilities frontiers. If taxes cause output to be less than what could have been produced without the tax, then the tax has reduced the efficiency of the economy.

Some public-finance specialists favor a neutral tax system that leaves private economic actions unchanged. Others argue that a neutral tax system is impractical and that the tax system should be used to actively promote economic goals. If a government wishes to discourage alcohol consumption, for example, it should place a heavy tax on alcoholic beverages; if a government wishes to encourage home ownership, it should provide income-tax breaks to homeowners. If a government wishes to encourage marriages, it should place a heavier tax burden on singles.

Public-finance specialists agree that it is very difficult, if not impossible, to devise a neutral tax system. Any tax that individuals could reduce as a consequence of their actions is not neutral. If a tax is neutral, individuals cannot alter their tax liabilites by taking actions to reduce it. A $1,000 tax on each adult male between the ages of 20 and 55 would be a neutral tax because there is nothing the taxpayer can do to avoid or reduce the tax (outside of a sex-change operation). But such a tax would violate both the benefit principle and the ability-to-pay principle and would not be widely accepted.

Taxes will continue to affect economic decision making. The challenge to politicians and tax authorities is to devise a tax system that minimizes the efficiency losses of nonneutral taxes while moving society in the direction of desirable social goals. If income taxes must be progressive, what tax system minimizes the loss of work effort? If government desires to encourage private home ownership, how can this objective be achieved in the least disruptive manner and with as little abuse as possible? (See Example 3.)

Taxes and Work Effort

Labor-supply decisions are often affected by the tax system. Individuals, in deciding whether to work overtime, in deciding whether both husband and wife should work, or in deciding whether to play golf one or two days a week, examine their marginal tax rate. As defined above, the marginal tax rate is the ratio of the increase in taxes to the increase in taxable income.

The distinction between average and marginal tax rates is important. Suppose Ann Smith is a physician who earns $150,000 annually and who pays an effective tax rate of 40 percent. Smith pays $60,000 a year in taxes and her average tax rate is 40 percent. If working a few more hours per week would increase her taxable income by $50,000 (from $150,000 to $200,000), her taxes would rise to $90,000. The $50,000 increase in taxable income would cause taxes to rise by $30,000. Her marginal tax rate, then, is the ratio of the increase in taxes ($30,000) to the increase in earnings ($50,000), or 60 percent.

Marginal tax rates are important because taxpayers tend to base their economic decisions on marginal tax rates rather than on average tax rates. For example, faced with a marginal tax rate of 60 percent, Smith may decide it is not worth the extra effort to earn an additional $50,000 of taxable income if she can only keep $20,000 of it. If she decides not to work the extra hours, economic efficiency has been reduced because the economy is producing fewer goods and services than it would have without the tax.

Some tax reformers favor a lowering of marginal tax rates to encourage greater work effort. The theory is that a lowering of marginal tax rates would give individuals a greater incentive to work extra hours, for homemakers to enter the work force, and for greater entrepreneurial risks to be taken. The proponents of lower marginal tax rates argue that the output of goods and services would increase without a change in the underlying resource base; that is, lower marginal tax rates would improve economic efficiency.

Workability

In addition to being fair, a good tax system must be *simple* and *certain* and must have reasonable *compliance and collection costs*. A tax is *simple* if taxpayers can determine their tax liability without substantial costs. The tax system should not force people to bear large accounting and legal costs. A tax is *certain* if taxpayers are able to ascertain the tax consequences of their actions when they make their economic decisions. The rules of the game must be known by all, and changes in the rules of the game should not affect actions

that have already been taken. The tax system should not have high collection costs. A tax is inefficient if it costs almost as much to collect as the tax brings in. (See Example 4.)

PROPOSALS FOR FEDERAL TAX REFORM

Our system of federal taxation has evolved over the years through a series of tax reforms, legislative amendments, and court interpretations. The present tax system is a maze of regulations that supports the legion of professional accountants and tax specialists that are needed to advise the taxpaying public.

Can our existing system of tax collection be made significantly more efficient or equitable through tax reform? Public-finance specialists have recommended over the years a number of reforms of the existing system.[6] Currently, a number of significant changes in U.S. tax laws are being considered by Congress.

Taxing Consumption, Not Income

Personal taxes are normally levied on personal income. The more one earns, the higher one's income-tax payments. Numerous distinguished economists and social thinkers—John Stuart Mill, Irving Fisher, Alfred Marshall, Thomas Hobbes, and Nicholas Kaldor—have supported the taxing of consumption rather than income for two reasons. First, supporters of this reform believe people should be taxed according to what they take out of production (consumption) rather than according to what they put in (saving). Society benefits from saving by gaining a larger stock of capital. Second, reformers argue that expenditures are a more accurate measure of a household's permanent spending power or ability to pay taxes than is income. Taxpayers could reduce consumption-tax payments by spending less (and saving more).

---

6. For a collection of studies by public-finance experts on tax reform, *see* Michael J. Boskin, ed., *Federal Tax Reform: Myths and Realities* (San Francisco: Institute for Contemporary Studies, 1978).

Example 4   The Compliance Costs of the U.S. Income-Tax System

In a study made of the 1982 tax year, two economists, Joel Slemrod and Nikki Sorum, found that the average cost of compliance for each of the nation's 97 million taxpaying households is $275 per year. This figure breaks down as follows: It takes the average American taxpayer about 22 hours to prepare federal and state income taxes and maintain the necessary records. This time, if devoted to work, would have earned the taxpayer an additional $231 on average. Moreover, the average taxpayer spends $44 per year on professional tax assistance. For those with incomes of more than $50,000, the average cost of tax compliance was $1,400 or greater. These figures show that wealthy taxpayers—the ones who benefit most from tax loopholes and special provisions—may lose a portion of their advantages in the form of much higher compliance costs. These estimates do not include the costs to federal and state governments of collecting taxes nor do they include the expenses to businesses of deducting taxes from employee wages. ■

Source: "A Household's Cost of Figuring Income Taxes Adds Up to a Pretty Penny," *Christian Science Monitor*, September 13, 1984.

Consumption taxes are typically collected as sales taxes. The *value added tax* (or VAT) that is used in Europe is a prime example of a consumption tax. As already noted, sales taxes tend to be regressive, but must a consumption tax be regressive? Public-finance specialists argue that consumption taxes, like income taxes, can be made progressive if society so desires. For example, taxpayers could report their income minus savings (which would equal their consumption), and then government could tax income minus savings using progressive tax rates.

Eliminating Corporate Income Taxes

As explained in an earlier chapter, corporations are useful devices for raising capital in a world of costly information and uncertainty. Many economists argue that taxing corporate income reduces the social gains obtained from this institutional innovation. The double taxation of corporate income through the double taxation of dividends dams up billions of dollars of investment funds inside corporate treasuries and, thus, encourages investment of retained earnings by the corporation itself. Eliminating the tax on corporate dividends would free these funds up for their best employment. The elimination of the corporate income tax would be opposed by many as a pro-business reform, but economists Martin Feldstein and Daniel Frisch have estimated the *social* loss due to the corporation income tax at $4 billion to $6 billion per year at 1976 income levels—or between 0.2 percent and 0.3 percent of total income.[7] As noted earlier, the corporate income tax is declining in importance. The gradual disappearance of the corporate income tax means that the tax income gained from it is being replaced by tax income from personal income taxes and sales taxes.

Taxing Only Real Capital Gains

The current tax system—although it does give favorable treatment to realized capital gains—does not adjust for the effects of inflation on capital gains. Stock purchased 10 years ago may have doubled in value, but if prices have doubled as well, the investor is no better off in terms of purchasing power. Presumably, inflation would reduce the incentive to invest and to take risks. If only *real* capital gains were taxed—that is, if capital gains were taxed only after adjustment for inflation—investors would have an added incentive to take risks. The U.S. Treasury's tax reform proposal (discussed below) calls for taxing only real capital gains.

---

7. Martin Feldstein and Daniel Frisch, "Corporate Tax Intergartion: The Estimated Effects on Capital Accumulation and Tax Distribution of Two Integration Proposals," *Discussion Paper 541* (Cambridge, Mass.: Harvard University Institute of Economic Research, 1980).

Levying a Flat Tax

Critics of the current federal income-tax system claim that the confusing and complex mass of deductions, exemptions, and special provisions render the existing system too complicated and too often unfair. The wealthy, by investing in tax shelters and taking advantage of tax loopholes, can end up paying lower taxes than middle-income families. The costs of record keeping, tax preparation, and expert advice also place a burden on the American taxpayer.

The "Fair and Simple Tax Act of 1984" proposed by Senator Robert Kasten and Representative Jack Kemp would tax all taxable income at the same 25 percent rate. The Kemp-Kasten bill is called a *flat tax* because it taxes all taxable income (from low to high incomes) at the same rate. The Kemp-Kasten tax would allow few if any deductions and exemptions from taxable income. In this way, they argue, the tax would be fair because it is the upper-income taxpayers that benefit most from existing exemptions and deductions. Moreover, they argue that the flat tax would be so simple that tax preparation and compliance costs would be substantially reduced. Taxpayers would be saved the substantial costs of tax preparation that they currently incur under the existing system.

An alternate to the Kemp-Kasten flat tax is the "Fair Tax Act of 1983" proposed by Senator Bill Bradley and Representative Richard Gephardt. The Bradley-Gephardt bill calls for a simple, progressive tax with three rates—14 percent, 26 percent, and 30 percent—that vary with income. The maximum tax rate would be lowered, if this bill were enacted, from its current 50 percent to 30 percent.

Lowering Tax Rates While Raising the Tax Base

In May of 1985, the Reagan administration announced its proposals for modifying U.S. personal and corporate income-tax laws. The most important features of the Reagan-sponsored proposal are listed in Table 7. The basic idea behind the Reagan proposal was to lower both personal and corporate income-tax rates while, at the same time, increasing the amount of taxable income to avoid serious losses of federal revenues. The Reagan proposal calls for simplifying the existing 14 rates ranging from 11 percent to 50 percent down to 3 rates: 15 percent, 25 percent, and 35 percent. The highest tax rate on taxable income would become 35 percent instead of the present 50 percent. Corporate tax rates would be cut from the maximum rate of 46 percent to 33 percent.

In return for lowering tax rates, a large number of deductions and exemptions from taxable income would be cut by the Reagan proposal. For personal income taxes, deductions for state and local taxes would be dropped, deductions for non-mortagage interest would be limited as would deductions for charitable contributions. Capital gains would be taxed like other forms of income, but only real capital gains (after adjustment for inflation) would be taxed. Moreover, fringe benefits (such as company-paid insurance plans) would be counted in taxable income. For corporate income taxes, a number of important deductions would be dropped. The investment tax credit and accelerated depreciation provisions would be dropped.

According to Treasury estimates, 56 percent of taxpayers would pay less under the new scheme; 22 percent would pay more; the rest would see their tax bill unchanged. The taxpayers who would be hurt would be those with large capital gains, large itemized deductions, and substantial fringe benefits. Taxpayers living in states and localities with high state and local taxes would also be hurt. The losers among corporations would be capital-intensive corporations who benefit most from investment tax credits and accelerated depreciation.

In general, if enacted, the Reagan proposal would raise taxes owed by corporations (by an estimated 25 percent) and would lower the taxes owed by individuals (by an estimated 8.5 percent). The Reagan tax proposal would, therefore, reverse the trend toward a smaller share of corporate taxes.

The three specific tax-reform proposals just discussed all call for lower personal income-tax rates and for the elimination of many exemptions and exclusions from taxable income. Any attempts to make significant changes in the existing tax codes, however, call forth heated debate and discussion. Most people and businesses would greet lower tax rates. Lower marginal tax rates

Table 7   Comparing the 1984 Treasury Proposal With Current Law

	1986 Under Current Law	Reagan Plan for 1986
Individual Tax Rates	14 rate brackets from 11% to 50%	Three rate brackets: 15%, 25% and 35%
Exemptions		
Self, spouse	1,090	$2,000
Dependents	$1,090	$2,000
Zero-Bracket Amounts		
Single returns	$2,510	$2,900
Joint returns	$3,710	$4,000
Heads of households	$2,510	$3,600
Indexing for Inflation		
Rate brackets, exemptions and zero-bracket amounts	Yes	Yes
Personal Deductions		
Mortgage interest	Deductible	Deductible for principal residences
Other personal interest	Deductible	Deduction limited to $5,000 over investment income
Medical expenses	Deductible above 5% of adjusted gross income	Deductible above 5% of A.G.I. (adjusted gross income)
Charitable contributions	Deductible	Deductible but only on itemized returns
State and local income taxes	Deductible	Not deductible
Two-earner deduction	Yes	No
Retirement		
Individual Retirement accounts	$2,000 Tax-deferred contribution permitted each year	$2,500 tax-deferred contribution permitted each year
Spousal I.R.A.	$250	$2,000
Corporate pensions	Tax deferred	Tax deferred up to $8,000/year
Social Security	Generally not taxed	Generally not taxed
Fringe Benefits		
Health insurance	Excluded from taxable income	Taxed up to $10/mo. (single), $25/mo. (family)
Group life and legal insurance	Excluded from taxable income	Taxed
Capital and Business Taxes		
Corporate tax rates	Graduated up to 46%	33% top rate, graduated rates up to $75,000
Dividend relief	$100/$200 exclusion	Exclusion repealed, 50% dividend-paid deduction
Depreciation	Accelerated Cost Recovery System, which provided for fast write-offs	Somewhat accelerated but less generous than current law
Investment Tax Credit	6% to 10%	Repealed
Capital gains	60% excluded from taxation	50% excluded for 17.5% top rate, but fewer items covered
Interest income/expense	Fully taxable/deductible	Indexed to inflation, partially excludable/nondeductible
Municipal Bonds		
Public purpose	Tax-exempt	Tax-exempt
Private purpose	Tax-exempt	Taxed

Source: Treasury Department, Office of Tax Analysis; *New York Times,* November 28, 1984; *Wall Street Journal,* May 30, 1985.

would spur greater economic effort. But if tax rates are lowered, many deductions and exemptions from taxable income must be removed to prevent significant losses of federal revenues. Yet each deduction and exemption is favored by their beneficiaries, and many of them were created to promote social goals (the interest deduction was designed to promote home ownership, for example; state and local tax deductions were designed to allow state and local governments to tax their citizens). The price of lowering corporate tax rates appears to be either the virtual disappearance of corporate taxes (as many economists have proposed) or the dropping of measures (such as investment tax credits and accelerated depreciation) designed to promote capital formation. If the corporate tax is allowed to wither away, revenue shortfalls must be made up by creating government revenues through other means. If the Reagan proposal is adopted, presumably there would be less capital formation as many of the extra tax advantages for investment would disappear. Because corporate taxes would be more evenly applied across different industries, however, investments would be allocated to their most productive uses rather than to those projects with the best tax treatment.

This chapter examined how government collects revenues and spends income and the effects of taxes and government expenditures on private economic activity. The next chapter will explore the reasons why government activity may be necessary to correct certain failures in the private economy.

Summary

1. Public finance is the study of the effects of government taxes and spending on private economic activity. Government expenditures are either exhaustive expenditures or transfer payments. Exhaustive expenditures divert resources to the public sector. Transfer payments affect the distribution of income in the private sector. Government spending rose from 10 percent of GNP in the late 1920s to 35 percent in the 1980s. Expenditures shifted away from local government to state and federal government. The relative size of government in the U.S. does not appear to be exceptionally large by international standards.

2. Cost/benefit analysis applied to government spending suggests that government spending should be carried to the point where marginal social benefits and marginal social costs are equal. Cost/benefit analysis could serve as a substitute for the market test that private goods must pass. Local programs stand a greater chance of passing the cost/benefit test.

3. There are two competing principles of fairness in taxation. One is that taxes should be levied according to benefits received. The other is that taxes should be allocated on the basis of ability to pay. If the ability-to-pay principle is used, the tax system should have both vertical and horizontal equity. *Progressive* tax rates rise with income; *regressive* tax rates fall with income; *proportional* tax rates do not change with income.

4. Federal taxes rely most heavily on individual income taxes, payroll taxes, and corporation-profits taxes. State and local governments use primarily sales and property taxes. Although tax rates on taxable income are highly progressive, effective tax rates are lower because of the exclusions and deductions (loopholes) allowed by law that erode the tax base by almost 50 percent. There is no agreement on how progressive the U.S. tax system is. Two major studies of this question are in sharp disagreement.

5. A neutral tax system is one that does not influence production, consumption, and investment decisions. In reality, neutral taxes are almost impossible to devise. Taxes do affect economic efficiency. The challenge is how to devise a tax system that moves the economy in a socially desired direction without severe losses of efficiency. Taxpayers are presumed to base their economic behavior on marginal tax rates. A tax system should be simple and certain and should not involve large collection costs.

6. Proposals for federal income-tax reform call for taxing expenditures not income, integrating the personal and corporate income tax, taxing only real capital gains, and levying flat taxes. Proposals placed before Congress in 1985 called for lowering tax rates while raising the tax base.

Key Terms

public finance
exhaustive expenditures
transfer payments
government surplus
government deficit
deficit financing
government debt
market test

vertical equity
horizontal equity
proportional tax
progressive tax
regressive tax
incidence of a tax
indexing
realized capital gain
taxable income
effective tax rate
marginal tax rate
excise taxes
customs duties
gift taxes
neutral tax

Questions and Problems

1. Explain how the market test for private spending balances costs and benefits and how cost/benefit analysis may substiute for the market test in the case of public spending.

2. Explain how "voting with one's feet" may make local-government spending more efficient than national-government spending.

3. Explain the different principles of fairness in taxation. Why can't the benefit principle simply be applied to all taxes?

4. What is meant by vertical and horizontal equity in a tax system?

5. Mr. Jones has a taxable income of $25,000. He pays a tax of $5,000. Ms. Smith has a taxable income of $50,000. How much tax would Smith have to pay for the tax system to be a) proportional? b) progressive? c) regressive?

6. "A tax on shoe sales that requires the dealer to pay a $2 tax on every pair of shoes sold should not be of concern to consumers because the dealer has to pay the tax." Evaluate this statement.

7. Define the following terms: a) *effective tax rate* and b) *erosion of the tax base*.

8. Explain double taxation of corporations.

9. Why is there a trade-off between equity and efficiency in any tax system?

10. When Jones's taxable income increases by $1,000, Jones's income tax increases by $200. What is Jones's marginal tax rate?

11. Explain why a consumption tax would likely result in a higher national saving rate than an income tax.

12. Proponents of the flat taxes maintain that flat taxes are more fair than the existing tax system. How can they make this argument when both high-income and low-income taxpayers would pay the same tax rate under a flat tax?

13. The State of Michigan hires an assistant professor to teach at one of its state universities. The State of Michigan pays and unemployed automobile worker $500 unemployment compensation out of state funds. Which transaction is an exhaustive expenditure? How will the two transactions differ in their effect on resource allocation?

14. Which of the following taxes satisfies the benefit principle? Which satisfies the ability-to-pay principle?
   a. A gasoline tax.
   b. A progressive income tax.
   c. A general sales tax.
   d. A special levy on a community to build a dam.

Suggested Readings

Boskin, Michael J., ed. *Federal Tax Reform: Myths and Realities*. San Francisco: Institute for Contemporary Studies, 1978.

Break, George and Joseph Pechman, *Federal Tax Reform: The Impossible Dream?* Washington, D.C.: Brookings Institution, 1975, p. 91.

Browning, Edgar K. and William R. Johnson. *The Distribution of the Tax Burden*. Washington, D.C.: American Enterprise Institute, 1979.

Musgrave, Richard A. and Peggy B. Musgrave. *Public Finance Theory and Practice,* 3rd ed. New York: McGraw-Hill, 1980.

Pechman, Joseph and Benjamin Okner. *Who Bears the Tax Burden?* Washington, D.C.: Brookings Institution, 1974.

Pechman, Joseph A. *Who Paid the Taxes, 1966–85.*Washington, D.C.: Brookings Institution, 1985.

41

Market Failure, the Environment, and Energy

Chapter Preview

This chapter will discuss the reasons for government intervention in the economy. Government intervention is usually justified as an attempt to deal with one of five problems that the market fails to solve sufficiently on its own: 1) monopoly power, 2) macroeconomic instability, 3) poverty, 4) externalities, and 5) the provision of public goods. Previous chapters examined government action in relation to monopoly, macroeconomic instability, and poverty. This chapter, first, restates the economics of externalities (previewed in an earlier chapter) and shows the circumstances under which government action on externalities is necessary. Second, it examines why government involvement is necessary in the provision of public goods. Third, the chapter discusses the problem of environmental pollution along with possible cures. Finally, in describing the economics of nonrenewable resources, the chapter raises the question of whether government intervention is necessary to protect the interests of future generations who have to live with the energy resources left by the present generation. ■

INTERNALIZING EXTERNALITIES

Externalities are a classic example of **market failure.**

> **Market failure** occurs when the price system fails to produce the quantity of a good that would be socially optimal.

Externalities are present whenever the actions of one agent have direct economic effects on neighboring agents.

> **Externalities** exist when a producer or consumer does not bear the full marginal cost or enjoy the full marginal benefit of an economic action.

For example, a factory imposes external cleaning or health-care costs on the community by polluting its air or water. The unique feature of these costs is that they are not paid by the factory, but by economic agents external to the factory. The factory does not have to pay the cleaning and health-care costs it imposes on the community; they do not show up anywhere in the factory's accounting.

On the other hand, the consumer who pays for an education is not the only one who benefits from that education. Society benefits when individuals receive education because education provides a common culture and language and encourages scientific progress.

When external costs or external benefits are present, economists measure social efficiency by comparing **social costs** and **social benefits.**

> **Social costs** = private costs + external costs.

> **Social benefits** = private benefits + external benefits.

As noted in an earlier chapter, whenever externalities are present, perfect competition does not lead to economic efficiency.

> **Social efficiency requires that marginal social benefits and marginal social costs be equal, but private participants equate only marginal private benefits with marginal private costs.**

Figure 1   Perfect Competition with External Costs

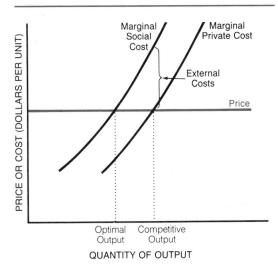

When external costs are present, competitive firms produce too much output. They produce at the output level where marginal private costs equal price, not where marginal social costs equal price.

When external costs are present, the competitive firm produces too much output because the firm produces that level of output at which marginal private costs and marginal private benefits are equal; it ignores the external costs of its actions. At the profit-maximizing level of output, marginal social costs exceed marginal social benefits. Society as a whole would be better off if the factory reduced its output to the point where marginal social costs and marginal social benefits are equal. These propositions are illustrated in Figure 1, which shows the optimal level of output for a competitive firm when external costs are present.

When externalities are present, market transactions between two parties will have harmful or beneficial effects on third parties. The effects are external to the price system and are not the outcome of mutual agreement between all the interested parties.

Examples of the harmful effects of externalities are not hard to find. Pollution of the air and water by industry and by the private car impose substantial external costs on the community. Ocean fishing grounds tend to be depleted because of the failure of one commercial fishing business to consider the external costs it imposes on others by overfishing. Modern skyscrapers built with reflective glass impose external costs on neighboring buildings by raising their air-conditioning costs. Any family that allows its house and lawn to deteriorate reduces the pleasure neighbors get from their own house and lawn. The buffalo almost became extinct because of the overkilling on the part of individual buffalo hunters who failed to consider the external costs imposed on others by overkilling.

Economists agree that externalities cause departures from the social optimum, and they are generally agreed about the manner in which to solve the externality problem: the individual consumer or producer must include the internal costs or benefits in its calculations of private gain. The solution is to *internalize,* or put a private price tag on, externalities. This price must be paid by the one imposing the cost or received by the one imposing the benefit.

Internalization of an externality is the process of putting private price tags on external costs or benefits.

If an economic agent pays for the costs imposed on others or receives a price for the benefits that others experience, it will take into account such costs and benefits in private cost/benefit calculations. A simple example of internalization would be the merger of two factories located on a river. Prior to the merger, the downstream factory has to pay water-purification costs incurred because the upstream factory is polluting the water. After the merger, the external costs imposed on the downstream factory become internal costs to the merged firms. Pollution costs will now be considered in private cost/benefit calculations. An externality can be internalized in three ways: 1) by redefining property rights, 2) by making voluntary agreements, or 3) by taxing or subsidizing the externality generator.

Redefinition of Property Rights

Property rights specify who owns a resource and who has the right to use that resource. Many externalities are a result of poorly defined property rights. Do firms or the community own the property rights to the air people breathe? Who owns the property rights to fish in the seas? If the property rights for a resource are held by the community, but each person has free access to the resource, the resource will likely be exploited and abused. Fishing businesses will overfish ocean waters; factories will overpollute the air.

If private property rights for the resource could be established, the externality would likely disappear. If hunting land is privately owned, the private owner can charge hunters fees to hunt game on that land. The rational private owner would set fees high enough to prevent game from being depleted. The same principle could be applied more broadly. For example, if one person in the community were somehow given ownership of the community's air, that person would have the legal right to charge the polluting factory for its use of the air. Every month, the polluting factory would get a bill from the owner of the community's air. If one country held the property rights to the ocean's fishing grounds, it could charge fishing businesses from all countries for their use of the ocean. (See Example 1.)

As these examples show, it is often not easy to eliminate externalities by changing property rights. Redefining property rights will not work when it is very costly to define or enforce property rights—as is the case for whales, which tend to be overkilled. How does one determine who owns the whales and how does one protect the owner's property rights? The case of pollution is another example of poorly defined property rights. The ownership rights to clean air are too poorly defined to allow those with property rights to clean air to sue polluters. In all these cases, the amount of information required to enforce property rights is excessive. The external costs each agent imposes must be known to redefine the rights. Exactly, how much pollution has each car emitted? How many whales are there and how many has each whaler killed? What is the real marginal cost to society of each whale?

Voluntary Agreements

Voluntary agreements between those that create the externality and third parties are a second means of internalizing externalities. The above

Example 1   Smoking on Airplanes: A Question of Property Rights

Smoking in public places is a classic example of external costs. The smoker imposes external costs on nearby people, some of whom are bothered by the smoke. Smoking in airplanes is a controversial issue because smokers and nonsmokers must be confined in a limited space often for a number of hours, during which smokers impose external costs on nonsmokers. The Civil Aeronautics Board—responding to petitions from nonsmoking air passengers—seriously considered in 1984 the banning of all smoking on commercial flights. Although the CAB came close to deciding in favor of such a ban, it ultimately decided against this action. In effect, a ban on smoking would mean that the property rights to the air in the airplane are assigned to nonsmokers. Economic theory suggests some interesting alternatives to the outright ban if property rights to the air were assigned to nonsmokers. On each flight, smokers could attempt to strike a deal with nonsmokers, offering a monetary incentive to allow them to smoke. Presumably, if the offer were sufficiently attractive, nonsmokers would voluntarily agree to let the smokers light up—but at a significant cost to the smokers. Economic theory also suggests that this solution would not be workable because so many parties are involved. The flight would likely be over before the parties could reach a mutually agreeable settlement. ■

example of a merger of two factories on a river illustrates a voluntary agreement. The number of individuals involved in a voluntary agreement must be small in order to keep bargaining costs down and to prevent other parties from "riding free." With well-defined property rights, voluntary agreements negotiated through the legal system can internalize external costs.

The proposition that voluntary agreements can handle some externality problems is called *the Coase theorem*, after Ronald H. Coase. Coase argues that external costs and benefits can be internalized by negotiations among affected parties. Coase gives the example of a rancher whose cattle occasionally stray onto a neighboring farm and damage the neighbor's crops. If the rancher were legally liable for the damage to the farmer, then private bargaining would result in a deal between the rancher and the farmer in which the farmer would be paid for the increased cost of growing crops imposed by the straying cattle. These extra costs would induce the rancher to reduce the size of the herd (or build better fences) and the potential externality would disappear. (See Example 2.)

Likewise, efficiency would still result even if the rancher's cattle had the legal right to stray onto the farmer's land. The farmer in this case would make a deal in which the rancher would agree to reduce the size of the herd or build a fence in return for a cash payment from the farmer. Again, when a price tag is placed on the externality, it disappears. In either case, the same amounts of crops and cattle would be produced. The social effect is the same, but the income-distribution effects are quite different. In the first case, the rancher transfers income to the farmer. In the second case, the farmer transfers income to the rancher. The distribution of income depends on who has the property rights.

There is some evidence that economists have underestimated the ability of negotiated voluntary agreements to solve externality problems. Nobel laureate James Meade used honey and apples as a classic example of externalities. The production of honey is stimulated by apple blossoms; the pollination of apple blossoms is facilitated by bees. Owners of apple orchards provide a benefit to bee keepers that does not directly enter into their private cost/benefit calculations. Bee keepers provide a benefit to apple growers that does not enter their private cost/benefit calculations.

Steven S. Cheung discovered in his research that not even this seemingly clear-cut example is perfect.[1] Cheung investigated the nectar and pollination business and found that externalities are bought and sold in the marketplace. Bee keepers and apple growers have worked out a compensation system that covers external benefits. Apple

---

1. Steven S. Cheung, "The Fable of the Bees: An Economic Investigation," *Journal of Law and Economics,* April 1973.

Example 2   Cattle Grazing: Externalities and Property Rights

Cattle grazing is an example of how externalities can be internalized by changing property rights. Before the establishment of private-property rights for grazing land, cattle owners allowed the common grazing property to be overgrazed. No one owned grazing land (or could enforce property rights by keeping other cattle off their property); individual cattle owners did not have to consider the costs they imposed on other cattle owners or farmers by allowing their cattle to wander and graze at will.

The barbed-wire fence gave cattle owners the technological and legal ability to enforce private-property rights. By keeping their fences repaired (and keeping others out with their six-shooters), owners of grazing land were able to restrict the use of their grazing land to their own cattle. If overgrazing occurred, the owners would bear the private costs of overgrazing. The barbed-wire fence internalized the externality. The individual owner of cattle now had the incentive to prevent grazing land from being ruined by overgrazing. ■

growers actually pay bee keepers for the pollination activities of their bees. Cheung found, in the state of Washington, that the beekeeper's fee for pollination is smaller the greater is the expected yield of honey because apple-tree pollination improves honey production. By reducing the pollination fee, the bee keeper is, in effect, paying the apple grower for the external benefit of the apple blossoms.

This example illustrates the Coase theorem that if small numbers are involved and bargaining costs are small the market will internalize the externality.

Government Taxes and Subsidies

The third way for an externality to be internalized is for the government to impose corrective taxes or subsidies. When private activities impose external costs, the volume of transactions will exceed what is efficient because private agents ignore the costs imposed on others (refer again to Figure 1). If an appropriate tax is placed on the externality-generating action, the economic agent must take into account the costs imposed on others and will, accordingly, reduce the amount of activity to the efficient level where marginal social costs equal marginal social benefits. When market transactions are accompanied by external benefits, the volume of transactions will fall short of the efficient level. In this case, a government subsidy will encourage private firms to increase the activity to the efficient level.

This third approach to internalization is appropriate when private bargaining costs are too high and voluntary agreements cannot be reached. When the government steps in with corrective taxes or subsidies, the government takes on the bargaining costs of the private parties. If the externality affects many people, it is cheaper to use collective or government action to internalize the externality. If external costs are imposed on thousands of individuals, voluntary agreement among the affected parties is unlikely.

Externalities do not automatically require government action, however. Making collective decisions is costly in and of itself, and society must weigh the costs and benefits of government action. For example, a small externality is involved in the choice of what color shirt or tie to wear; outrageous dress may offend some people. Yet society cannot afford to use collective action to deal with all trivial external costs or benefits. On the other hand, the emission by factories of highly toxic fumes that create acid rain and kill forests impose substantial social costs that require government action.

Both government action to correct externalities and externalities themselves can impose costs on individuals. Both the market mechanism and government action have advantages and disadvantages. There are, therefore, few hard and fast rules on whether the government or the market should solve the problem. It is necessary to weigh the advantages and disadvantages in each particular instance.

Some examples of externalities that probably require some government action would be automobile pollution, factory pollution that contaminates the air for miles in every direction, the abuse of scenic beauty, and the killing of whales and fish. In these cases, the costs of negotiating and enforcing private contracts exceed the potential gains. Some examples of potential externalities that may not require government action would be honey and apple production or localized pollution. In the case of localized pollution (air or noise), people who feel the external costs are too high can move (can vote with their feet). The worker who lives near a foul-smelling paper mill may receive a compensating wage differential for being willing to work in the community; residents who choose to buy homes near an airport have lower home costs. Whenever people have the choice of avoiding the external costs by moving or whenever people receive compensating wage differentials or lower living costs because of the presence of external costs, government action may not be necessary.

PUBLIC GOODS

Public goods are another example of market failure because competitive markets will fail to supply or will undersupply them. Public goods and services that are provided by the government—like public schools, public parks, public roads and bridges, national defense, police protection, or public health services—are generally made available to the public at no explicit charge and are financed by taxes (although in some instances, governments charge for government services, as in the case of postage or admission fees to public parks). People must decide whether or not government should provide **public goods.**

> **Public goods** are goods or services characterized by 1) nonrival consumption and 2) nonexclusion.

Nonrival Consumption

If a dam is built that protects a particular geographic area from flooding, everyone who lives in the protected area benefits. Moreover, the fact that one person's house is protected by the dam does not reduce any other house's protection. A television program is another "good" that is characterized by **nonrival consumption.** One person can listen to a program without reducing the amount of the program any other listener enjoys. All listeners are nonrival consumers.

> A good is characterized by **nonrival consumption** if its consumption by one person does not reduce its consumption by others, given the level of production.

The classic example of nonrival consumption is national defense. If the government builds an antimissile system that substantially reduces the likelihood of nuclear attack by a foreign nation, everyone in the protected geographical area enjoys the benefits. The protection of one person's life and property does not reduce the protection enjoyed by others.

Nonrival consumption does not mean that everyone benefits to the same degree. A pacifist may not like the national-defense effort—nor would an enemy spy. A family with a large estate may benefit more from flood control than one living in a wooden shack.

Most goods and services that are exchanged in markets are characterized by **rival consumption.**

> A good is characterized by **rival consumption** when the consumption of the good by one person lowers the consumption available to others, given the level of production.

Food and drink, cars, houses, shoes, dresses, and medical services are rival in consumption. A hamburger eaten by one person cannot be eaten by someone else; a house occupied by one family cannot be occupied by another. Some goods can be either rival or nonrival depending on the circumstances. Uncrowded movies or sporting events are nonrival. One person can enjoy an uncrowded movie without reducing another person's consumption, but consumption of a crowded movie or sporting event is rival, because each additional spectator displaces another possible spectator. (See Example 3 for another example.) The problem of rationing the available supply of most rival goods is solved by charging prices; those

Example 3   Rivalry and Nonrivalry: Cars, Fire Stations, and Libraries

Nonrival consumption depends very much on the physical contiguity of the consumers. If Jones and Smith are neighbors, they could conceivably use the same car for work or shopping as long as they do not have to shop or work at the same time in different places. In this particular case, Smith and Jones are nonrival consumers of the car. In the case of a shared car, it would be unusual for Smith and Jones to avoid rivalry. A library is an example of nonrival consumption of a common good. Strictly speaking, when one person checks out a book, that book is not available to others. But the probability of two people wanting the same book at the same time is small. The probability is higher for recent best sellers, which are loaned out for shorter periods. For most other books, from the viewpoint of probable use, a library offers nonrival consumption to a large collection of diverse people. The same is true of a fire station. While fire fighters cannot put out two fires at once, it is unlikely that fires will occur at the same time.   ■

who consume the rival good place a higher value on it than those who do not consume the good.

Nonexclusion

The second characteristic of public goods is **nonexclusion,** or the extreme cost required to exclude people from using the good (once it has been produced). National defense and flood control are classic examples. It is virtually impossible to exclude any person in the protected area from enjoying the benefits of the good; **exclusion costs** are prohibitive.

> A good is characterized by **nonexclusion** if the exclusion costs are so high that it is not possible (or practical) to exclude some people from using the good.

> **Exclusion costs** are the costs of defining and enforcing private property rights to some good, or the cost of preventing those who do not have property rights to the good from enjoying the good.

Nonrivalry should not be confused with nonexclusion. An uncrowded movie theater is nonrival in consumption, but nonpayers can be prevented from viewing a movie.

Identifying a public good can be difficult. Nobel laureate Paul Samuelson used the lighthouse as an example of a public good, since any one ship's use of the light does not detract from any other ship's use (nonrivalry) and since it is diffi-cult for the lighthouse to exclude nonpaying ships from using the light (nonexclusion). Economist Ronald H. Coase, however, found that in England lighthouses were for many years privately owned and operated.[2] From 1700 to 1834 the number of privately operated lighthouses increased, so the business was obviously profitable. Instead of being unable to provide this public good, the private market in lighthouses appeared to be thriving. Lighthouse owners were paid by the ship owners at the docks according to the tonnage of the ship. The economists did not realize that usually only one ship is near the lighthouse at a time; the light could be turned off at dusk if the ship did not fly the flag of a fee-paying vessel. Thus, exclusion costs were not high.

Most private goods are rival in consumption and have low exclusion costs so that nonpayers can be excluded from consuming them. Some goods, however, are rival in consumption and also have high exclusion costs. An example is crowded city roads during rush hour; to exclude some users would require building expensive toll gates. One person's use of the congested road can reduce another person's enjoyment of the road, but it is too costly to exclude nonpayers under normal circumstances (see Example 4 for a notable exception). Goods with high exclusion costs, be they rival or nonrival, are normally provided through the government.

---

2. Ronald H. Coase, "The Lighthouse in Economics," *Journal of Law and Economics*, October 1976.

Example 4   Charitable Giving as a Public Good

Public goods provide a rationale for government action. An earlier chapter noted that government is also active in the area of income redistribution. Why is income redistribution not handled by the market through private charity and voluntary giving? Surprisingly, voluntary charitable giving is subject to many of the same problems as public goods.

Most of us feel better off when the position of poor people improves. Because human beings are affected by motives of altruism, one person's welfare is affected by the well-being of others. The welfare of those with strong altruistic feelings towards the poor will be improved by a redistribution of income in favor of the poor. Again, however, voluntary contributions cannot be relied upon because of the free-rider problem.

Imagine that 50 million upper-income (nonpoor) people want to help 1 million poor people. If each of the 50 million nonpoor were willing to give $100, then $5,000 could be transferred to each poor person, and the poverty problem would be reduced. Everyone would be better off. The nonpoor would have assisted the poor in a substantial way, satisfying their altruistic motives, and the poor would each be $5,000 richer. Why is it unlikely for a voluntary program of income redistribution of this magnitude to come about? Each person realizes that giving $100 has no impact whatsoever on the poverty problem, as $100 spread over 1 million people amounts to one cent per hundred people; the individual has no incentive to contribute. Only if the individual knows that all 50 million are going to contribute (that there will be no free riders) will there be any noticeable effect on poverty. In this situation, the free riders will not contribute because they will believe it is likely that virtually everyone else will be a free rider. Government is left with the responsibility for income redistribution.

Another reason for government involvement in income redistribution is that it is impossible to take out private insurance policies against being poor. Consumers can buy fire insurance, life insurance, health insurance, or car insurance, but they cannot buy "poverty" insurance. The absence of poverty insurance is a market failure. One can think of being poor as an unfortunate event, just like a fire or accident. Private insurance companies do not offer policies against being poor because of the *moral-hazard problem* and the *adverse-selection problem* discussed in the chapter on the economics of information.

The person who takes out poverty insurance has less of an incentive to avoid being poor. In the insurance business, *moral hazard* is the problem insurance companies face when those who have bought insurance alter their behavior to increase the probability of collecting insurance. For example, property owners who have fire insurance may become careless or even set fires. Similarly, a person with poverty insurance may become lazy or careless about working to earn income.

Those who feel their chances of being poor are low probably would not buy poverty insurance. Hence, those who buy will be mainly those people that are most likely to be poor. *Adverse selection* is a problem that occurs when those who buy insurance are more likely to collect it than the average population. Because only those likely to be poor will buy, poverty insurance rates will be quite high, and the business of poverty insurance will be privately unprofitable.

Yet all sorts of random events such as bad health, technological progress, accidents, and changes in tastes can cause poverty. Since private insurance is impractical, government redistribution programs can act as an insurance program for the nonpoor. ∎

Nonrival Goods with High Exclusion Costs. The private provision of public goods is dependent upon the voluntary contributions of beneficiaries. Since those who benefit cannot be excluded from its use whether or not they are paying for it, people need not pay. A person who attempts to enjoy the benefits of the good without paying is a **free rider.**

A **free rider** is anyone who enjoys the benefits of a good or service without paying the cost.

When some of the beneficiaries are free riders, the private revenues voluntarily contributed to pay for a public good will be less than the social benefits the good generates—in which case, the good

Figure 2   Classifying Selected Goods as Private Goods or Public Goods

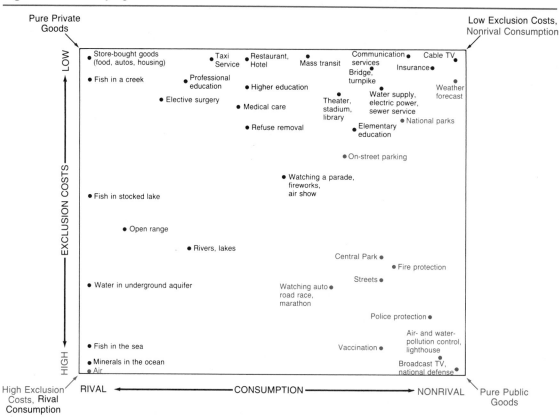

Pure private goods, in the upper-left corner, are characterized by low exclusion costs (free riders can be excluded easily) and by rival consumption. Pure public goods, in the lower-right corner, are characterized by high exclusion costs (free riding can't be prevented) and by nonrival consumption (one person's consumption of the good does not detract from another's consumption of the same good). Goods in the other two corners meet only one of the two characteristics of a public good. In the lower-left corner, goods are characterized by high exclusion costs but rival consumption. In the upper-right corner, goods are characterized by nonrival consumption but low exclusion costs.

Source: E. S. Savas, *Privatizing the Public Sector* (Chatham, N. J.: Chatham House Publishers, Inc., 1982), p. 34.

will not be produced or will be underproduced by the private market. Public television is a case in point. Noncontributors cannot be prevented from viewing public-television programming. Typically, public-television stations need government subsidies to maintain their operations.

The free-rider problem confounds the production of public goods. Suppose a dam costing $2,000 will protect a community of 10 people from flooding and that the flood protection of the dam is worth $400 to each person. The total value

of the dam is $4,000; it is worth building because it costs only $2,000. Building the dam by charging $200 to each person would clearly benefit everyone.

Voluntary agreement among the 10 people may be difficult. Any one might realize that if the other 9 build the dam without his or her contribution, he or she could still enjoy the benefits. Such free riders attempt to enjoy the benefits of the dam without paying their share of the costs. In this example, will the dam be built? If 6 people behave as free riders, the dam will not be built by voluntary agreement; the non-free-riders can raise only $1,600. If only 4 people behave as free riders the dam will be built.

Voluntary agreements will work if the amount of free riding is not excessive. Voluntary cooperation is more likely the smaller is the group, the more often collective decisions are made, and the greater is the individual gain from adopting cooperative behavior.

Examples of cooperative behavior abound. Dams are built by municipalities; public grounds in subdivisions are landscaped; most people obey the law; volunteers work to improve the community. But if the group is large, if collective decisions are made infrequently, and if the individual gains to cooperation are small, free riding will be more prevalent.

Nonrival Goods with Low Exclusion Costs.

For many nonrival goods, however, exclusion costs are not excessive. Pay television is an example of a nonrival good with low exclusion costs. Will private markets provide enough pay TV? What do we mean by "enough" in this case? In a world of diverse tastes, any price charged for pay TV will exclude some people from the market. If it costs society nothing to add one more user (because of nonrivalry), it seems wasteful to exclude that user.

Viewers can consume ordinary TV and radio as much as they like (once they have a receiver); the private market ingeniously finances private TV and radio by advertising. An alternative procedure for radio and TV production would be to ban advertising, set up a public TV monopoly, and let everyone pay the costs in taxes.

The problem of publicly providing nonrival goods with low exclusion costs is that the cost of producing the good must somehow be paid. Is it fair for people who hate baseball games to be forced to pay for entertaining those who love baseball games? Charging a toll on an uncrowded bridge leads to economic inefficiency because some users are excluded even though they do not keep others from using the bridge. Without the toll, however, nonusers would be forced to pay for the bridge in taxes.

Why is it that toll bridges are publicly owned while movies and sporting events are privately produced? The justification for public ownership of bridges is that a private owner would have a monopoly position and could charge monopoly prices. Figure 2 ranks selected goods along a continuum from private goods (characterized by low exclusion costs and rival consumption) to public goods (characterized by high exclusion costs and rival consumption).

The Information Problem

The problems of externalities and public goods are ultimately problems of information. If everyone had perfect information, bargaining and transaction costs would be minimal or zero. With perfect information, free riders could be identified and property rights could be defined as finely as one wished (even to the point of assigning property rights to each fish in the ocean or assigning property rights to the air). With property rights assigned, exact price tags could be placed on external costs or benefits. The agent incurring the externality would pay the price tag either as a result of voluntary agreement or government action. In a world of perfect information, competitive markets would internalize all potential external costs and benefits and would produce optimal amounts of goods and services.

In a world of imperfect information, many difficulties arise in applying the theory of externalities or public goods. There are usually several policy options that can be followed; it is easy to make mistakes in identifying the externality or public good. There are enormous controversies over the external costs of nuclear power or depletion of the ozone layer, for example. It is difficult to measure external costs and benefits for the purpose of establishing appropriate taxes or subsidies; externalities may be more apparent than real. In short, the information costs that are implicit in any externality also make it difficult to apply government solutions to the market failure.

Example 5   Electronic Road Pricing in Hong Kong

The severe traffic congestion in Hong Kong has motivated officials there to charge motorists for the privilege of driving on the Crown Colony's most congested roads. By law, each of Hong Kong's 350,000 private cars must be fitted with a tamper-proof electronic number plate. Buried under the road surface at congested intersections are electronic devices that broadcast the car's number to a central computer, which adds a fee to the car owner's account. By avoiding congested streets, the car owner can reduce his or her monthly bill. It is even possible to charge different fees for different streets—the greater is the congestion, the higher can be the price. The idea behind this pilot program is that by charging for the use of congested roads, drivers will cut back on the use of more congested roads, thereby alleviating Hong Kong's congestion problem.

The Hong Kong experiment shows how innovative methods can be used to control the free-rider problem without incurring excessive monitoring costs. If electronic road pricing works, it will be possible to tax road users with only small outlays for gathering road-use information. ■

Source: "Hong Kong to Test Electronic Road Pricing to Ease Traffic Chaos," *Houston Post*, April 13, 1983, p. 16A.

ENVIRONMENTAL ECONOMICS

The problem of pollution is a classic externality problem when the private agent that discharges waste into the air, into water, or even into outer space does not bear the full costs to society.[3]

Waste-Disposal Costs

Modern production and consumption patterns impose significant **waste-disposal costs** on society. When firms produce goods and services, wastes in the form of air pollutants, toxic chemicals, solid wastes, and noise are created. Wastes are also created by modern consumption; we as consumers produce wastes (automobile exhausts, noise, solid wastes). Wastes must be disposed of either in the ground, in water, or in the air. (Someday, they may be disposed of in outer space).

> **Waste-disposal costs** are the sum of: 1) pollution-prevention costs, 2) the private and public costs of avoiding pollution damage once pollution has occurred, and 3) the welfare loss society suffers when pollution is not prevented or pollution damage is not corrected.

---

3. The following discussion is based largely on Joseph Seneca and Michael Taussig, *Environmental Economics,* 3rd ed. (Englewood Cliffs, N.J.: Prentice-Hall, 1984).

Waste-disposal costs are real opportunity costs. If public or private resources are devoted to pollution prevention (scrubbers on smokestacks, for example), these resources are not available for other uses. If individuals purchase unpolluted water to prevent health damages from drinking polluted water, they also incur opportunity costs. If the health of individuals in the community deteriorates because of pollution from toxic-waste dumps, there are costs to the individual and community be they explicit cash outlays or less visible opportunity costs.

Insofar as modern societies produce vast quantities of wastes that must be disposed of, decisions must be made about how much of society's resources should be devoted to pollution abatement. Cost/benefit analysis provides, at least in principle, a practical guideline. Figure 3 shows the marginal social costs and marginal social benefits of different quantities of pollution abatement—in this case, the number of gallons of water purified through filtration procedures). For simplicity, we let the marginal social cost of each successive unit of abatement be constant. Marginal social benefits decline with more abatement because society will likely value the first units of abatement more highly than subsequent units. The optimal level of abatement occurs when the marginal social cost of an extra unit of abatement equals the marginal social benefit. If additional abatement is undertaken beyond this optimal

Figure 3   Optimal Pollution Abatement

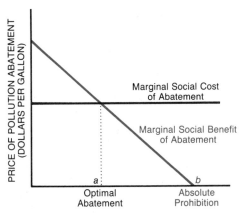

Marginal Social Cost
of Abatement

Marginal Social Benefit
of Abatement

a

b

Optimal
Abatement

Absolute
Prohibition

PRICE OF POLLUTION ABATEMENT
(DOLLARS PER GALLON)

QUANTITY OF POLLUTION ABATEMENT
(GALLONS OF WATER PURIFIED BY FILTRATION)

This figure shows how the optimal amount of pollution abatement would be determined. The marginal-social-benefit curve is downward-sloping (people place a higher value on the first units of abatement). The marginal social cost of pollution abatement is assumed constant. The optimal amount of abatement is quantity *a* (where marginal social costs equal marginal social benefits). Point *b*, the total prohibition of population, is not optimal because the marginal social benefit (zero) is less than the marginal social cost.

level, the extra benefits society enjoys fall short of the extra opportunity costs to society. Figure 3 also shows why society should not aim for the total elimination of pollution. To totally eliminate pollution, society would have to devote scarce resources to pollution abatement until the marginal social benefits are driven down to zero. The last dollar spent on pollution abatement yields zero benefits but has a positive marginal cost to society.

Figure 3 provides a theoretical standard for evaluating pollution-abatement programs. The application of cost/benefit analysis has, however, enormous practical problems. First, it is very difficult to know the exact costs and benefits of various pollution-abatement activities. Some costs and benefits are incurred only over time. It is difficult to measure the full costs even at one point in time because of the large number of people and things that are affected to varying degrees. Second, waste-disposal problems involve complicated physical, biological, and chemical interactions with the total environment. A particular

abatement procedure that increases water purity may work by shifting discharges to the atmosphere. Third, there are fundamental income-distribution effects associated with pollution abatement. Someone in society must pay if waste-disposal costs are to be reduced. Who should receive the benefits and who should bear the costs of pollution abatement? Should private firms pay? Should only affected individuals pay? Should the general public pay?

Solutions to Environmental Problems

Suppose a community is located on a river downstream from a factory that is dumping toxic wastes into the river. Because the environmental problem of waste disposal is a problem of externalities, the methods of approaching this problem are the same methods discussed in the earlier section of externalities: the problem can be resolved through the redefinition of property rights, through voluntary agreements, or through government programs.

Redefining Property Rights.   If there were an enforceable system of property rights to the air or water, an optimal level of pollution abatement could be reached, at least in principle. Suppose that the community has property rights to the river. Because it would have the legal right to use this property (and to allow others to use the property) as the community sees fit, the community could prohibit the dumping of wastes in the river. If the firm failed to obey this prohibition, the community could sue for damages in a court of law. If the community did not have property rights to the river, this option would not be open.

Private Agreements.   If the community had property rights to the river, it could also charge the firm for its clean-up costs. The firm and the community could agree on a mutually acceptable compensation, which would be included in the firm's private costs. Even if property rights to the river were not established, the community could pay the firm to find another means of disposing of its wastes. The social outcome would be the same under both sets of property rights, but the resulting income distribution would be different. In the

Example 6   The Problem of Acid Rain

Acid rain is the fog, snow, mist, or rain that carries a mixture of sulfur-dioxide (SO_2) gases and nitrous-oxide (NO_x) emissions. Acid rain is thought to destroy forests and poison lakes and rivers. Acid rain has received considerable publicity in the United States, Canada, and Europe. West Germany, Switzerland, and Austria are particularly concerned about the already extensive damage to their forest lands.

Acid rain is an externality problem that is not easily solved by private agreements. First, acid rain appears to damage common-property resources like lakes, rivers, and forests. Second, scientists are still unclear as to the actual chemical causes of acid rain. Some argue that the major culprit is industrial emissions of sulfur dioxide. Other scientists point the finger at nitrous oxide and hydrocarbons from automobile exhausts that combine to produce ozones. Third, it is very difficult to isolate the sources of these emissions even if scientists could agree on the exact sources of acid rain. Canada claims that acid rain originates in the United States; the Midwest claims that the pollution comes from 31 Eastern states; the Eastern states accuse the industrial midwestern states (who burn sulfur-rich coal) of being the problem. The sources of nitrous-oxide emissions are even harder to identify. Even if acid rain affected resources with clearly defined property rights, the property owners would have difficulty in deciding exactly whom to sue.

It is clear that the costs of reducing acid rain will be substantial. As long as scientists cannot determine who is creating the acid rain, it will be impossible to devise a payment scheme that follows the principle that the polluter must pay. One proposal (that was rejected by Congress) called for the acid-rain cleanup to be financed by a nationwide tax on electricity even though it is unclear to what extent electricity generation has contributed to acid rain. Given the scientific uncertainty about the causes and effects of acid rain, it is virtually impossible to conduct a cost/benefit analysis of acid-rain abatement. In order to assess different programs, one needs to know the benefits that will result (How many lakes and rivers will come back to life? How many forests will stop dying?) before one can determine the optimal amount of acid-rain abatement.

Acid rain is such a complex phenomenon that the private perpetrators of the external costs cannot be identified. There is too little scientific knowledge about the marginal benefits to be achieved from acid-rain abatement. In the absence of such vital information, it is very difficult to conduct a rational environmental policy. ■

Source: "Cleaning Up the Clouds," *Christian Science Monitor,* September 7, 1984.

---

first case, the polluting firm would transfer income to the community. In the second case, the community would transfer income to the polluting firm.

In most cases, the redefinition property rights or the making of private agreements does not yield optimal pollution levels. How does one assign property rights to a river, a lake, the air, or to outer space? The legal costs of suing another party for violating a property right can be quite high. Even with assigned property rights, it is difficult to enforce private contracts when there may be a number of polluters or when the costs of monitoring each firm are excessive. The causes of modern pollution are many and maybe spread over a wide geographic area. Modern pollutants cross numerous political boundaries. Many parties suffer to varying degrees from pollution problems, and these parties are difficult to organize. Once a community enters an agreement to pay a firm to stop polluting, other firms may issue credible (and costless) threats that they will begin pollution activities. Such agreements leave the community open to the threat of extortion. The arrangement of private agreements among parties is very difficult in a world of thousands of polluting firms imposing external costs on millions of people. As noted above, in such cases, the government may have to step in and impose corrective action (See Example 6.)

Government Action: The Environmental Protection Agency.   Because redefining property rights and making private agreements are unlikely to solve the waste-disposal problem, government action is typically used as a remedy.

In the United States, a number of state, local, and federal agencies are involved in pollution control. The most important such federal agency is the Environmental Protection Agency (EPA), which since 1970 has been charged with regulating pollution activities, acting through the states and through its own authority. The EPA derives its legislative authority through a number of Congressional Acts (the Clean Air Act, the Water Pollution Control Act, the National Environmental Policy Act, the Toxic Substances Control Act, and many other environmental acts).

In enforcing federal environmental laws, the EPA has chosen in most cases to follow a regulatory approach. The EPA specifies what each individual waste discharger must do with respect to air, water, and noise pollution. The EPA sets ceilings on the amounts of pollutants that can be discharged and requires that the discharger meet these ceilings by a specified date using the best practical (or best available) pollution-control technology. The EPA issues permits to each pollution source, and the permit specifies how much of each pollutant can be discharged and a time schedule for pollution reduction.

Aside from difficult enforcement issues, the most basic problem that the EPA faces in its pollution-reduction programs is deciding how much pollution is to be allowed. Environmental laws are not always specific in their charges. Elementary cost/benefit analysis shows that the absolute prohibition of pollution discharges is not a reasonable social goal. This policy would cause all pollution-abatement activities to be carried out to levels where marginal social costs of pollution abatement far outweigh marginal social benefits. The resource costs to society of this action would be prohibitive.

It is difficult to devise direct controls that are calibrated to lead to optimal abatement policies. The EPA sets discharge limits without reference to the marginal costs and benefits of its actions. Yet there is a growing realization that environmental policies (which are already costly) require a balancing of costs and benefits. For this reason, the EPA has experimented with economic-incentive-based environmental policies.

In an ideal incentive-based policy, the government would impose fees—called *effluent charges*—for the discharge of pollutants that equal the marginal external cost of the pollutant. Such effluent charges would cause the polluting firm to consider the external costs of pollution in its private economic calculations. Obviously, it is difficult to establish optimal effluent charges because of the difficulty of estimating the marginal external costs of each pollution-discharge activity. Because of the difficulty of setting and enforcing appropriate effluent charges, the EPA has experimented with a number of "market solutions." In one program, the EPA allows firms or groups of firms to determine their own pollution-abatement programs (which they presumably do at the least cost to themselves) subject to a total emissions limit assigned to the plant or region. If several firms are involved, they are allowed (in certain cases) to trade pollution rights among themselves and even to buy and sell rights to pollute. Another EPA program permits new pollution sources to operate if they are able to obtain an offset (a reduction in pollution discharges) from existing firms.

The basic notion behind these incentive schemes is that the costs of pollution abatement will be reduced if dischargers are allowed to make their own decisions. Firms that can reduce discharges cheaply will sell pollution rights to firms that can only reduce emissions expensively. Even if the end result is not an optimal balance of costs and benefits, at least the costs of pollution control will be reduced under such programs.

THE ALLOCATION OF EXHAUSTIBLE RESOURCES

Externalities and public goods are likely to lead to market failure, and government action is seen as one way to deal with externalities. Some argue that the problem of allocating exhaustible resources is another example of potential market failure. In their view, private resource allocation could lead to the too-rapid depletion of an **exhaustible resource**. Is government action also required to prevent the exhaustion of the globe's nonrenewable resources?

An **exhaustible** (or nonrenewable) **resource** is any resource of which there is a finite stock in the long run because the stock is fixed by nature.

A firm that produces a **renewable resource**—such as timber or livestock—does not behave differently in substance from the competitive and monopolistic firms described in various chapters. Additional quantities of the renewable resource can be produced if the firm is willing to bear the additional cost. For example, there is not a fixed supply of timber that will be exhausted at some point in the future. By incurring the marginal costs of planting saplings, fertilizing them, and protecting them from disease, timber producers can increase or renew stocks of trees.

A **renewable resource** is any resource of which the stock is not fixed in the long run.

The firm that produces renewable resources follows the standard profit-maximizing rule: in each period it produces that quantity of output at which the marginal revenue from the last unit of output equals its marginal cost. If the firm follows this simple rule, its profits will be maximized over the years. Unless externalities or monopolies are present, there will be social efficiency.

Consider a firm that supplies an exhaustible resource—the stock of which is fixed by nature. The firm cannot increase its stock of the exhaustible resource. Instead, the firm must decide how to allocate its fixed stock of the nonrenewable resource over time. The firm that extracts natural gas from a fixed reservoir must decide how much to supply to the market this year, next year, 5 years from now, and 20 years from now.

The nonrenewable-resource firm faces an opportunity cost not present for renewable-resource firms. In the case of renewable resources, the decision to supply x units this year does not mean that these x units cannot be supplied again (another tree can be planted). In the case of nonrenewable resources, every unit supplied this year will be one unit not available for subsequent years. Equivalently, units supplied next year will not be available this year.

Because supplies of nonrenewable resources must be traded off between current and future consumption, suppliers of nonrenewable resources must make an *intertemporal* (across time) comparison of the costs and benefits of supplying the resource today versus supplying it tomorrow.

Suppose a crude-oil firm can extract crude oil from a reservoir containing 1,000 barrels at a zero marginal extraction cost (the oil simply rises by itself to the surface). For simplicity, suppose also that the firm must sell its entire stock of 1,000 barrels within a two-year period. The market rate of interest is 10 percent.

How will this firm allocate its stock of crude oil between the two years? If the price of crude oil today is $20 per barrel, and the price expected next year is $21.50, the firm should sell all 1,000 barrels this year. By selling now, the firm gets $20 per barrel that can be invested at 10 percent interest; in one year, the firm will have $22 per barrel ($20 × 1.1). Each barrel the firm sells next year will yield only $21.50; so the firm is better off selling now. If next year's price were to be greater than $22, the firm's best course of action would be to wait to sell all 1,000 barrels next year. *If the price rises at the same rate as the interest rate (in this case, by 10 percent per annum), the firm would be indifferent as to whether it sold its stock of the nonrenewable resource this year or next year.*

Turning from the exhaustible-resource firm to the market, suppose a perfectly competitive market consists of a large number of price-taking firms (see Figure 4). The stock of the exhaustible resource owned by all the firms together is fixed (at 30 units), and firms must sell their entire stock within a two-year period (either in period 0 or period 1).

In Figure 4, the horizontal axis is 30 units long because only 30 units of the resource are available; what is supplied in period 0 will not be available for period 1. The period 0 demand curve is a standard demand curve read from left to right, but the period 1 demand curve is unusual because it must be read backwards; it should be read from right to left. Both demand curves indicate what quantities will be demanded in each period at various prices. Because only 30 units are available, once period 0's supply is set, whatever remains of the 30 units is what is available for period 1.

If 20 units were sold in period 0 and 10 units were sold in period 1, Figure 4 indicates that the period 0 price would be $6 per unit (point *a*) and the period 1 price would be $11 per unit (point *b*). Would the individual firms be content with this outcome? No. Each unit sold in period 0 and invested at 10 percent interest would be worth only $6.60 in period 1, whereas each unit sold in period 1 yields $11. Clearly, firms would want to

Figure 4   Market Equilibrium for an Exhaustible Resource in Two Periods

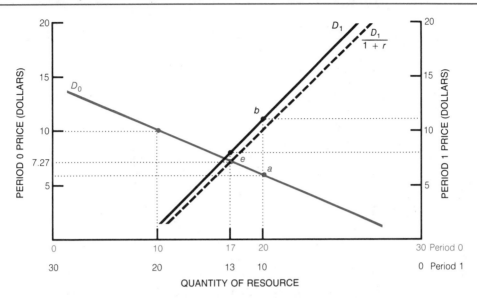

This figure represents a competitive market composed of a large number of perfectly competitive firms. The firms in the market together have a fixed supply of 30 units of the nonrenewable resource, and these 30 units must be used either in period 0 or period 1. The market demand curves are D_0 for period 0 and D_1 for period 1. (Period 1 quantity increases from right to left rather than from left to right.) Firms will contrast the price received in period 0 with the present discounted value of the price received in period 1. $D_1 \div 1.1$ is the present discounted value of the period 1 demand curve when the interest rate is 10 percent. When the available supply is allocated between periods 0 and 1, the prices in the two periods are established. As long as the period 0 price is less than the present value of the period 1 price (as it is when the period 1 quantity is 20 and the period 1 quantity is 10), firms will reallocate supplies from period 0 to period 1. Equilibrium will be reached when quantity is 17 in period 0 and 13 in period 1 and when price is $8 in period 1 and $7.27 in period 0. The ratio of the price in period 1 to the price in period 0 will be 1 plus the interest rate, or 1.1, in equilibrium.

supply less than 20 units in period 0 and more than 10 units in period 1.

An equilibrium would be attained when the period 0 price equals the present discounted value of the period 1 price, or when the period 0 price equals the period 1 price divided by 1.1. At this point, there would no longer be an incentive for firms to switch supplies from one preriod to the other. The dashed demand curve in Figure 4 shows the period 1 prices divided by 1.1 and represents the present discounted values of the period 1 prices. The quantity where the dashed curve intersects the period 0 demand curve (at point *e*) is the equilibrium quantity. The quantity corresponding to point *e* is 17 units in period 0 and 13 units in period 1. In Figure 4, the period 0 price for 17 units is $7.27, and the period 1 price for 13 units is $8. The present discounted value of $8 is $7.27 at a 10 percent rate of interest. At these prices, firms no longer have an incentive to shift supplies from one period to the other.

When marginal extraction costs are zero and the market is perfectly competitive, the price of an exhaustible resource will rise at the same rate as the interest rate.[4]

If period 1's demand increases between periods 0 and 1, D_1 would shift up, as would its discounted present value. The new equilibrium would be reached at higher prices in both periods, but with period 0's supply reduced. In equilibrium, the present value of period 1's price would still equal period 0's price. The anticipation of an increase in demand in some future period will tend to redistribute supplies of exhaustible resources from the present to the future.

---

4. Another important condition underlies this conclusion—namely, that technology is held constant. The importance of this assumption will be discussed later in the chapter.

Figure 5   Real U.S. Crude Oil Prices, 1880–1984

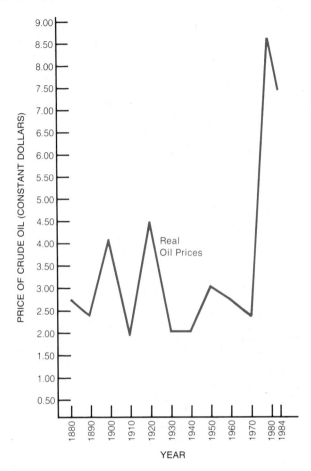

Since 1880, overall *real* U.S. crude oil prices neither increased nor decreased significantly until the late 1970s. Since the early 1980s, the real price has been falling.

Sources: U.S. Bureau of Mines, U.S. Bureau of Labor Statistics.

The Technology of Resource Extraction

Figure 4 delivers a reassuring message: competitive markets deal automatically with the rising scarcity of exhaustible resources. The annual growth rate of the prices of exhaustible resources should tend to equal the market rate of interest in the long run. In other words, the natural rise in the prices of nonrenewable resources should discourage their consumption. Moreover, if increasing scarcity is expected, supplies of the nonrenewable resource will be shifted to the future.

Figure 5 shows the long-run trend in the real price of a barrel of oil since 1880. The prices in Figure 5 are the ratio of the oil price to consumer prices in general. As the reader can readily see, there was no trend in the real price of oil until the late 1970s, at which time the real price rose. In the 1980s, the real price of oil has been falling. Since 1800 there has been a distinct downward trend in the real price of such exhaustible resources as copper, aluminum, and pig iron. Why have the real prices of exhaustible resources not risen steadily as the theory predicts? The answer is that falling extraction costs and technological

Example 7   When Will We Run Out of Nonrenewable Resources?

Will we run out of nonrenewable resources by the year 2000 as some doomsday experts claim? By using exhaustible resources now, are we condemning future generations to poverty and starvation? The prospect of running out of crucial nonrenewable resources appears especially alarming if one divides known reserves of specific exhaustible resources—such as oil or copper—by current annual consumption of the resource (or worse still by projections of the growth of consumption). Such exercises indicate that supplies of oil, copper, zinc, and about everything else will run out in our children's lifetime.

Before accepting such alarmist conclusions, let us consider the notion of reserves. Typically, engineers and geologists use the term *reserves* to refer to the quantity of the resource that can be economically produced with prevailing prices and technology. When prices rise and technology improves, reserves tend to increase. For example, known world reserves of oil were 75 billion barrels in 1950. By 1979, world reserves had risen to 679 billion barrels—a 905 percent increase. This enormous increase in reserves was caused by the discovery of new deposits and technological improvements that allow higher recovery rates in established fields.

The American Petroleum Institute estimates that the original oil in place in all oil fields in the United States is about 450 billion barrels. Of this amount, 115 billion barrels have been produced, and there are 30 billion barrels of known reserves. Experts currently expect only 32 percent recovery of oil already discovered. American oil reserves would be doubled if the recovery rate were to rise from 32 to 40 percent.

The rapid increase in known world reserves is characteristic of most nonrenewable resources. Manganese reserves have increased 27 percent, zinc 61 percent, lead 115 percent, copper 179 percent, bauxite 279 percent, chromite 675 percent, iron 1,221 percent, and phosphates 4,430 percent from 1950 to 1970.

The accompanying table shows the number of years known reserves of exhaustible resources will last at prevailing consumption rates. Known reserves will last from 9 years (gold) to 481 years (phosphorus). Using the U.S. Geological Survey's estimates of ultimate recovery resources, we find that the various resources will last from 102 years (gold) to 68,066 years (aluminum). Using the amount of the resource estimated to be in the earth's crust, we find that rsources are virtually inexhaustible—lasting millions of years.

When a particular resource threatens to become scarce in supply, its relative price would be expected to rise. Rising relative prices would discourage consumption; therefore, it is not apprpriate to assume that current consumption rates would continue into the future if the resource were threatened with depletion. ∎

Sources: William Nordhaus, "Resources as a Constraint on Growth," *American Economic Review* 64, 2 (May 1974): 23; *Handbook of Economic Statistics,* 1980; James Griffin and Henry Steele, *Energy Economics and Policy* (New York: Academic, 1980), pp. 311–12; Julian Simon, *The Ultimate Resource* (Princeton: Princeton University Press, 1981), p. 34.

	Years of Potential Consumption if Known Reserves Are Divided by Annual Consumption	Years of Potential Consumption if Ultimate Recoverable Resources Are Divided by Annual Consumption	Years of Potential Consumption if Amount Estimated in Earth's Crust Is Divided by Annual Consumption (millions)
Copper	45	340	242
Iron	117	2,657	1,815
Phosphorus	481	1,601	870
Molybdenum	65	630	422
Lead	10	162	85
Zinc	21	618	409
Sulphur	30	6,897	N.A.
Uranium	50	8,455	1,855
Aluminum	23	68,066	38,500
Gold	9	102	57

advances can cause prices to behave differently from the theory outlined above (which does not take into account marginal extraction costs and technological change).

Marginal Extraction Costs.

As shown in Figure 4, when marginal extraction costs are zero, firms will allocate supplies between the two periods so that the period 0 price equals the present value of the period 1 price. When positive marginal extraction costs are introduced, this equilibrium condition changes. Firms will allocate supplies so that the period 0 price (after deduction of marginal extraction costs) equals the present value of the price in period 1 (after deduction of marginal extraction costs). If marginal extraction costs are falling (say, they are positive in period 0 and zero in period 1), the price rises by less than the rate of interest.[5]

> If marginal costs are rising over time, the price of an exhaustible resource can rise more rapidly than the interest rate. If marginal costs are falling over time, the price can rise more slowly than the interest rate.

Technological Advances.

If technological advances occur that allow exhaustible-resource producers to increase their recovery rates, prices would not be expected to rise at the rate of interest. In fact, if technological advances are large, exhaustible-resource prices can fall.

Consider a resource firm that develops a new technology that will allow it to recover more of the exhaustible resource in period 1 than in period 0. Suppose an oil company with existing technology can recover one out of every two barrels un-

---

5. In this specific case, the equilibrium condition is

$$P_0 - MC_0 = \frac{P_1}{1 + r},$$

where P_0 is the period 0 price, P_1 is the period 1 price, MC_0 is the period 0 marginal extraction cost, and r is the interest rate. This equation is equivalent to

$$\frac{P_1}{P_0 - MC_0} = 1 + r.$$

In this case, P_1/P_0 is less than $1 + r$. Price rises by less than the interest rate.

derground and has a total of 200 barrels underground. A new technology that will be available in period 1 allows it to recover 1.5 barrels from every two barrels underground. For every barrel sold in period 0, the firm passes up the opportunity to sell 1.5 barrels (with the new technology) in period 1. As a result, more supplies will be shifted to period 1, thereby lowering the period 1 price and raising the period 0 price.

> Technological advances that are scheduled to take place in the future cause supplies of exhaustible resources to be shifted to the future, thereby raising current prices and lowering future prices.

Backstop Resources.

If a **backstop resource** exists, the pattern of pricing of the nonrenewable resource over time is affected.

> A **backstop resource** is a close substitute for an exhaustible resource that is available in virtually unlimited supply but at a higher cost.

Examples of backstop resources are solar energy as a backstop for conventional energy and shale oil and tar sands as backstops for conventional crude oil.

What effect does the availability of a backstop fuel—such as shale oil—have on the allocation of crude oil and oil prices over time? Suppose that shale oil is available in virtually unlimited supply at a price of $40 per barrel. The backstop fuel sets a price limit of $40 per barrel on conventional crude oil because consumers would switch to shale oil if the crude oil price went above $40. Until the $40 backstop price is reached, the price should increase by the rate of interest. Once the backstop price is reached, however, the price will then remain constant.

The advantage of the backstop resource is that it allows greater consumption of the nonrenewable resource in the present at lower prices than would be possible without the backstop resource. With the backstop resource, supplies of the nonrenewable resource need cover demands only up to the backstop price. As a result, more of the resource can be consumed now and in the near future with the knowledge that the distant future will be taken care of by the alternate resource.

The Working of the Price System

As demonstrated in this chapter, natural market forces should cause nonrenewable resources to be allocated efficiently over time. Suppliers of non-renewable resources must consider the opportunity costs of selling resources today and thereby raising their scarcity tomorrow. Unless rapid technological progress increases the supply of recoverable nonrenewable resources, their prices will tend to rise at the rate of interest. Suppliers must always weigh the returns from exploiting the resource now against waiting for the resource to become more scarce (and, thus, to sell for a higher price) tomorrow.

The major threat to the rational use of nonrenewable resources is interference in the pricing of resources. If prices are controlled—for example, if price ceilings are placed on oil or natural gas—then resource firms will have to make resource-allocation decisions on the basis of prices that do not correctly reflect scarcities today and tomorrow. In other words, price controls could result in too little being allocated to present consumption and too much being allocated to future consumption.

This chapter discussed some of the possible arguments for government action. Externalities, particularly the environmental problem of waste disposal, and public goods represent legitimate cases of market failure. The next chapter will explore the question: If government action is needed, how does government work in a world of limited information, majority rule, and self-interest?

Summary

1. Market failure occurs when the price system fails to produce the quantity of a good that would be socially optimal. Two examples of market failure are the presence of externalities and the provision of public goods. Externalities occur when marginal social costs (or benefits) do not equal marginal private costs (or benefits). Social efficiency requires that marginal social benefits and marginal social costs be equal, but private market participants equate marginal private benefits with marginal private costs. Externalities can be internalized by redefining property rights, by making voluntary agreements, or by taxing or subsidizing the externality generator.

2. Pure public goods have two characteristics: a) the consumption of the good is nonrival among all users; b) no one can in practice be prevented from using the good (nonexclusion).

3. Waste-disposal costs are the sum of pollution-prevention costs, the costs of avoiding pollution damages, and the welfare loss society suffers when pollution is not prevented or remedied. Pollution problems cannot easily be solved by redefining property rights or by voluntary agreement; government action is typically required. In the United States, the Environmental Protection Agency is charged with environmental protection. The EPA sets pollution standards but in recent years has been experimenting with market solutions.

4. Firms that produce nonrenewable resources must determine how to allocate the available fixed supply over time. When marginal extraction costs are zero, when the industry is perfectly competitive, and when there is no technological progress, they will allocate the resource so that the present discounted values of the prices in each period are the same. Prices will rise at the rate of interest. If increasing scarcity is anticipated in the future, supplies of the nonrenewable resource will be reallocated from the present to the future. The prices of nonrenewable resources in general have not risen in real terms because of declining marginal extraction costs and rapid technological progress. Natural market forces should cause the efficient allocation of nonrenewable resources over time.

Key Terms

market failure
externalities
social costs
social benefits
public goods
nonrival consumption
rival consumption
nonexclusion

exclusion costs
free rider
waste-disposal costs
exhaustible resource
renewable resource
backstop resource

Questions and Problems

1. Factory A produces 1,000 tons of sulfuric acid. It costs A $10,000 to produce 1,000 tons. As a consequence of producing 1,000 tons of sulfuric acid, people in the community must increase their medical payments by $5,000; they lose $4,000 in wages by being sick; their dry-cleaning bills increase by $1,000. What are the private and social costs of the 1,000 tons of sulfuric acid?

2. Explain how the external costs calculated in the previous example might be internalized. Will this internalization be handled differently when there are three people who are hurt by the factory from when 300,000 people are hurt? In which case is government action more likely?

3. Most everybody thinks we need national defense. Why is it, therefore, difficult to get people to pay voluntarily their share of national defense? Why is there no problem in getting people to pay for shoes?

4. Explain why two people are nonrival consumers of a big-city expressway if they are driving at 3:00 A.M. but are rival consumers when driving at 5:00 P.M.

5. An oil producer has 100 barrels of oil that must be sold within a two-year period. The interest rate is 20 percent and the price of crude oil expected next year is $35 per barrel. At which prices would the oil producer sell all the oil this year? At which prices would the oil producer sell all the oil next year? If the oil producer expects an improvement in technology to increase the recovery rate by 10 percent next year, how will this affect the decision?

6. If new cost-efficient technologies were developed that reduced the marginal costs of pollution abatement, what would happen to the optimal level of pollution abatement?

7. Does the pollution-trading concept used in recent years by the EPA solve the problem of choosing the optimal level of pollution?

8. Explain why economists do not favor the total elimination of pollution. Why would it not be efficient to totally eliminate pollution from our environment?

Suggested Readings

Cheung, Steven S. "The Fable of the Bees: An Economic Investigation." *Journal of Law and Economics,* April 1973.

Coase, Ronald H. "The Lighthouse in Economics." *Journal of Law and Economics,* October 1976.

Coase, Ronald H. "The Problem of Social Costs." *Journal of Law and Economics,* October 1960.

Griffin, James A. and Henry B. Steele. *Energy Economics and Policy.* New York: Academic, 1980.

Heyne, Paul and Thomas Johnson. *Toward Understanding Microeconomics.* Chicago: SRA, 1976, chap. 14.

Krutilla, John V. and Anthony C. Fisher. *The Economics of Natural Environments.* Baltimore: Johns Hopkins, 1975.

Ruff, Larry E. "The Economic Common Sense of Pollution." *The Public Interest* 18 (Spring 1970): 69–85.

Simon, Julian. *The Ultimate Resource.* Princeton: Princeton University Press, 1981, p. 19, appendices A2–A5.

42

Public Choice

Chapter Preview

The two preceding chapters explored how governments raise revenues to finance their expenditures and why governments might be needed to allocate resources in the case of market failures. This chapter will examine how a government allocates its resources—or makes its expenditures—in a way that reflects the preferences of the different individuals that compose the society. This question is especially important in a democratic republic where individual choices do matter.

Research in the area of *public-choice theory* has contributed to a greater understanding of the circumstances that determine government successes and failures. This chapter is devoted to the economics of public choice.

A market failure creates a potential role for government action. Public choices must often be made. The attitude that was popular for many years was that if the market failed to function efficiently, the government should step in to fill the gap and that even imperfect government action was better than doing nothing. It is entirely pos-

sible, however, for government action to make a bad situation even worse. Public-choice economists consider how public decisions can be made that will contribute to economic efficiency.

In an ideal world, government would work so well that everyone would be unanimous in their approval of government action and public choices. The criterion of a perfect government is similar to that of a perfectly working price system. The price system is considered efficient (perfect) when it is impossible to make anyone better off without hurting someone else. An efficient economic system is making as large a pie as possible; in an efficient system, to give one person a larger piece is to give someone else a smaller piece. An *inefficient* economic system is one in which the pie could be made larger. In a sense, unanimity is at the base of an evaluation of a good price system. When two people engage in an exchange, they are both made better off: they are unanimous in agreeing to the deal. ■

UNANIMITY: THE IDEAL WORLD

The turn-of-the-century Swedish economist, Knut Wicksell, has suggested that the analog to the private market in questions of public choice is **unanimity.**

> **Unanimity** is the result of a vote in which all voters agree on or consent to a particular government action or decision.

Under certain circumstances, government action can reflect the voluntary and unanimous actions of each individual. Consider a hypothetical community that has no information costs or bargaining costs. Everyone knows everything about everyone else. In such a community, unanimous collective decisions are no longer difficult. Consider the adoption of a flood-control project. In the real world flood control is a pure public good because it is nonrival in consumption and no one can be excluded from its benefits. The market will fail to provide it; the community must, therefore, decide how much flood control to produce. In our imaginary community, each person's demand schedule for flood control is known to everyone else.

Suppose the community consists of individuals A, B, and C. Figure 1 shows their three demand schedules. The demand curve D_A shows person A's marginal valuation of flood control at different amounts of flood control. (Assume that the quantity of flood control is measured in terms of the height of a dam. A higher dam provides a larger "quantity" of flood control.) For example, the 100th foot of a dam is worth $1 to person A. If the community provides a 100-foot dam, the same amount of flood control is available to A as is available to B or C. According to the three demand schedules, A's marginal valuation of the 100th foot of a dam is $1, B's valuation is $5, and C's valuation is $6. The community's total marginal valuation of the 100th foot of a dam is, thus, $12. The total demand curve is the vertical summation of each of the individual demand curves.

The ideal quantity of flood control in Figure 1 is a 100-foot dam because the marginal social cost *(MSC)* of this quantity of flood control is $12, which we assume to be constant for simplic-ity. The optimal quantity of flood control is a 100-foot dam because at that amount of flood control, marginal social benefits equal marginal social costs.

> The demand curve for a nonrival (public) good differs from the demand curve for a rival (private) good. The market demand curve for a nonrival good is the vertical summation of each individual's demand curve. (Recall for contrast that the market demand curve for a rival good is the horizontal summation of all the individual demand curves.)

In our hypothetical community, optimality (unanimity) can easily be attained. The ideal government knows the demand schedules of all concerned and simply taxes people according to each person's marginal valuation. Thus, A pays a price of $1 per unit of flood control; B and C pay the higher prices of $5 and $6 per unit of flood control. The prices paid by each individual exactly match the benefits they receive. If such taxes were imposed on each person, each would vote for a 100-foot dam's worth of flood control. All members of the community would vote unanimously for a 100-foot dam.

This voluntary-exchange view of collective action assumes governments have more information than they actually have. If the individual demand schedules for a public good are not known, some voting process other than unanimity would have to be used.

The costs of discovering the government expenditure and tax program that would bring about unanimous approval of all members of the population are prohibitive; hence, it is necessary to accept some principle of collective action short of unanimity. When the community departs from the unanimity principle, how efficient is public choice?

MAJORITY RULE

The most popular method of making political decisions is **majority rule.** In the three-person community considered above, any proposal for flood control would require only 2 yes votes to be carried out.

Figure 1   Unanimity: Ideal Benefit Taxes

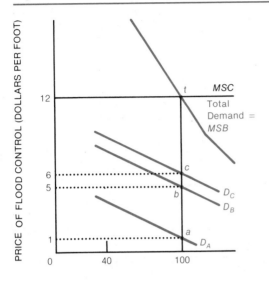

QUANTITY OF FLOOD CONTROL
(HEIGHT OF DAM IN FEET)

This graph represents an ideal three-person community where the demand curves of A, B, and C for a nonrival good, flood control, are known to all. The total demand for flood control is the vertical sum of the three individual demand curves because, with a nonrival good, providing one person with flood control provides all with flood control. The marginal social cost (MSC) of flood control is $12; the height of the demand curve measures the marginal social benefit (MSB) of flood control. The optimal amount of flood control is a 100-foot dam because MSC equals MSB at 100 units. With the individual demand curves known to all, benefit taxes of $1, $5, and $6 (per unit of flood control) imposed on A, B, and C would lead them to unanimously choose 100 units of flood control.

Figure 2   Majority Rule

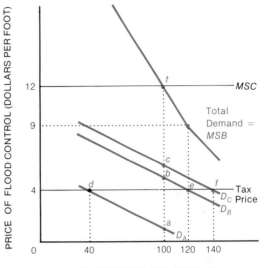

QUANTITY OF FLOOD CONTROL
(HEIGHT OF DAM IN FEET)

This figure represents the same three-person community portrayed in Figure 1, except that now majority rule reigns and the individual demand curves are not known to all. For simplicity, suppose that the $12 per unit cost of flood control is shared equally by all so that the tax price is $4 per unit of flood control per person. At this price A will want 40 units, B will want 120 units, and C will want 140 units of flood control. Voter B is the median voter; under majority rule the median voter determines the outcome. Thus, 120 units of flood control will be provided. This quantity is inefficient because the marginal social benefit of the 120th unit is only $9 (compared to the marginal social costs of $12).

Majority rule is a system of voting in which a government action or decision is approved if more than 50 percent of the voters approve.

For simplicity, assume that the $12 marginal cost per unit of flood control is divided equally among the three persons. The "tax price" of flood control would then be $4 per person per unit of flood control. The total tax liability of each individual would depend on the number of units the community chooses to produce.

Figure 2 illustrates the majority-voting process. With a tax price of $4 per person, A prefers a 40-foot dam, B prefers a 120-foot dam, and C prefers a 140-foot dam. If any dam lower than 40

feet is proposed, which is the dam height desired by the person who desires flood control the least, all three members would favor flood control. But B and C would realize that such a proposal is very costly to them. At a tax price of $4, B and C want a 120-foot and a 140-foot dam, respectively. To them a 40-foot dam is far to small for the price. If a 100-foot dam (the optimal height) is proposed, A (who wants only a 40-foot dam) would vote against the proposal, but B and C would favor it over a 40-foot dam. However, B and C would still realize that a 100-foot dam is not enough flood control for the price. The **median voter,** B, wants a 120-foot dam.

Voters B and C will press for higher and

Table 1   Building Access Roads for Farmers B and C: Benefits Exceed Costs

Beneficiaries	Net Benefit (+) or Cost (−) of Access Road for B	Net Benefit (+) or Cost (−) of Access Road for C
A	− $2	− $2
B	+ $5	− $2
C	− $2	+ $5
Society	+ $1	+ $1

In this example, access roads cost $6; these costs are shared equally by each farmer ($2 each). But each access road is worth $7 to the affected farmer. Building both roads is socially efficient in this case because total benefits ($14) exceed costs ($12). Under simple majority rule without logrolling, neither road is built because the *number* of voters benefiting does not exceed the number of voters who do not benefit. But if Farmers B and C link their votes (if both vote for both roads), then both roads can be built and society benefits.

higher levels of flood control until this median voter is satisfied. If a 120-foot dam is proposed, A will vote against it, but both B and C will vote for it. If a dam higher than 120 feet is proposed, A and B will vote against it. Thus, the median voter (B) gets his or her wish: a 120-foot dam. Using the principle of majority rule, the spending proposal of providing a 120-foot dam costing a total of $1440 (= $12 × 120 feet) will defeat all other proposals. Each voter will be assessed $480 to pay for flood control.

> The **median voter** on a public-expenditure program wants more expenditure than half the remaining voters and less expenditure than the other half of the remaining voters.

> Under majority rule, the median voter determines the outcome. The median voter's preferences count most because precisely half of the remaining voters prefer less of the public good and half prefer more.

Three important conclusions follow from the decisive role of the median voter in simple, direct voting under majority rule:

1. *Social choices need not respond to individual wants.* Many people are dissatisfied with how the government reacts to the individual because the votes of those in the minority (or 49 percent of the voters on some issues) do not count. The most disgruntled members of our society are those whose preferences are almost always in the minority.

2. *Majority-voting rules may not reflect the rel-*

ative intensity of preferences. Since the median voter determines the outcome, a change in the intensity of anyone else's preferences has no impact. Shifting the demand curve of A downward and C upward in Figure 2 would have no impact on the outcome. The intensity of A's preferences and C's preferences are irrelevant. Only the median voter's preference intensities count. This system is in sharp contrast to the market for private goods where dollar votes for goods duly register the intensity of each person's preferences.

3. *Majority voting need not be efficient.* In Figure 2, majority rule led to a 120-foot dam, which is higher than the 100-foot dam an efficient economy would provide. Although the intensity of preferences of nonmedian voters is irrelevant, as we just saw, the intensity of preferences of nonmedian voters affects marginal social benefits. In Figure 2, too much of the public good is produced. Whether too much or too little is produced depends on the distribution of demands around the median voter. (See Example 1.)

VOTING PROBLEMS

In our example of majority rule the policy that was adopted was supported by the majority of voters. When more than one issue is involved, **logrolling,** or "pork-barrel politics," can result in the approval of policies that are actually opposed by a majority. Majority voting may also paradoxically lead to inconsistent outcomes.

> **Logrolling** is the trading of votes to secure a favorable outcome on decisions of more intense interest to each voter.

Table 2   Building Access Roads for Farmers B and C: Costs Exceed Benefits

Beneficiaries	Net Benefit (+) or Cost (−) of Access Road for B	Net Benefit (+) or Cost (−) of Access Road for C
A	−$2	−$2
B	+$3	−$2
C	−$2	+$3
Society	−$1	−$1

In this case, access roads still cost $6 each and cost is still shared equally by all three farmers. But each access road is worth only $5 to the affected farmer. Building the roads is socially inefficient in this case. Under simple majority rule without logrolling neither road is built, but when Farmers B and C link their votes both roads are built even though the benefits to the two farmers do not exceed the costs to society.

Logrolling

One characteristic of majority rule is that intensities of preferences do not matter. The vote of a person who is passionately against some measure and the vote of one who is only marginally in favor of the measure are given equal weight in deciding the final outcome. On a single issue, the difference in preference intensity has no effect on the outcome. But the political process involves not just one decision but a stream of decisions that are both complex and simple. The person who is only mildly in favor of one proposal might trade his or her vote with a person strongly against the proposal in exchange for a similar trade when their positions are reversed.

Consider three farmers, A, B, and C. Suppose B and C could each use a separate access road to the main highway. Farmer B would gain $7 from one access road and Farmer C would gain $7 from the other access road, and each access road would cost the community $6. The $6 cost would be equally shared by all three farmers ($2 each). Table 1 describes the net benefits (+) or costs (−) to each farmer from building these access roads at the public expense.

Since the $6 cost would be shared equally, building each road has a $2 cost per farmer. Roads built for B or C do not benefit A at all. But a road built for B gives B a net benefit of $5, as the gains from the road are worth $7 and B's share of the cost is only $2. If a road is built for C, B is in the same position as A, but C gains a net benefit of $5.

According to majority rule, if an access road for B is proposed, farmers A and C will vote against it; similarly, an access road for C will be defeated by A and B. Majority rule without logrolling causes the defeat of such special-interest legislation.

But farmers B and C will each perceive that they can gain by voting for the other farmer's access road. If farmers B and C link their votes, both roads will be built, and farmer A will have to shell out $4 in taxes. Farmers B and C each gain $3 (= $7 − $4), which is their net gain from building both roads.

Whether logrolling increases or decreases economic efficiency depends on the circumstances. In this example, building both roads has a net social benefit of $2. Each road costs $6; each road brings benefits of $7. Thus, from a purely social point of view, it is worthwhile to build the two roads. Hence, logrolling in this case is a good thing because without logrolling the roads would not have been built.

But logrolling can also result in inefficiencies. If each road brings in net benefits of only $5 each to farmers B and C instead of $7 each, farmers B and C, if they link their votes, must each pay out $4 ($2 for each access road) and A must contribute $4 ($2 per road). Since the benefit to B and C ($5 each) exceeds their cost ($4 each), it is still worthwhile to them to logroll. But now the net social benefit is − $2 rather than + $2. The new net benefits and costs in this case are shown in Table 2.

The example described in Table 2 demonstrates that majority rule with logrolling can result in policies that lower the size of the total economic pie. Indeed, for this reason some political scientists have recommended political reforms

Table 3	Policy Rankings		
Policy	Voter A	Voter B	Voter C
a	1st choice	3rd choice	2nd choice
b	2nd choice	1st choice	3rd choice
c	3rd choice	2nd choice	1st choice

Table 4	Possible Contests and Outcomes
Contest	Winning Policy
a vs. b	a
b vs. c	b
a vs. c	c

that eliminate logrolling opportunities.[1] (See Example 2.)

The Paradox of Voting

Even in simple majority-rule voting situations without logrolling, a definite outcome may not emerge. The real world is filled with examples of many policy inconsistencies. Governments pass minimum-wage laws that create unemployment and then create job-training programs to put people to work. The government raises the cost of food to the poor through farm price supports and then hands out food stamps to the poor. Governments subsidize college students (who tend to be from affluent families) and then enact policies that benefit middle-income or poor families.

This inconsistency can be explained using an example. Suppose three voters (A, B, and C) must vote on three policies (policy a, policy b, and policy c). Policy a redistributes income to voter A, policy b redistributes income to voter B, and policy c redistributes income to voter C. Table 3 describes how voters A, B, and C rank these various policies. Naturally, the first choice of each voter is the policy that benefits him or her. But each voter also has preferences for the other policies as well. Voter A, for instance, might like voter B more than voter C. Hence, policy b is A's second choice and policy c is A's third choice. Table 3 shows that voter B prefers policy c to policy a, and that voter C prefers policy a to policy b.

Notice that in Table 3 every policy is one person's first choice, another's second choice, and a third person's third choice. The table is, there-

fore, perfectly symmetrical in this respect. Only two issues are voted on at a time. In a contest between policies a and b, voter C determines the outcome because A and B vote for their own policies. Since voter C prefers a to b, policy a wins.

Table 4 shows the three possible contests and outcomes. In each of the three possible contests, a different policy wins. No one policy wins more than one contest. If someone witnessed only the first two contests and saw that a was preferred to b and that b was preferred to c, logic would suggest to that person that a should be preferred to c. However, the third row of Table 4 shows that in fact c is preferred to a. Majority rule has resulted in an inconsistent outcome. This inconsistency is the **paradox of voting.** If one reverses the second and third choices of just one of the voters, the paradox disappears, however.

> The **paradox of voting** is that majority rule can yield inconsistent social choices. Even if each voter is perfectly rational, the majority of voters can choose a over b, b over c, and then choose c over a.

THE POLITICAL MARKET

The political market consists of voters, politicians, political parties, special-interest groups, and government bureaucracy. How does each of these groups affect the public choices made by democratic governments?

Voters

It is common after an election for journalists and television announcers to bemoan the difficulty of motivating people to vote. The decline in voter

---

1. Dennis C. Mueller, *Public Choice* (Cambridge: Cambridge University Press, 1979), pp. 49–51.

Example 1   The Median-Voter Rule and School-District Budgets

The median-voter hypothesis is that the preferences of the median voter will dominate in single-issue elections. Like most propositions in economics, this proposition can be subjected to hypothesis testing. A number of economists have looked at public-school finance referenda to determine if the level of public-school expenditure per pupil typically corresponds to the level desired by the median voter. Public-school finance referenda tend to be single-issue votes and should conform to the median-voter hypothesis. Insofar as the median voter cannot be identified directly, the median voter is defined in such studies as the voter who embodies the median socioeconomic characteristics of the community. In other words, the median voter is the voter with median income, median education, owning the median-priced home, and so on.

Studies of finance referenda in Michigan school districts (by Randall Holcombe), in New York State school districts (by Vincent Munley), and in Long Island School districts (by Robert Inman) find that the actual level of spending per pupil is very close to that preferred by the median voter. Thus, they find empirical support for the median-voter hypothesis.

Surprisingly, a study for Oregon school districts fails to support the median-voter hypothesis.

Economists Radu Filmon, Thomas Romer, and Howard Rosenthal find that the level of spending tends to exceed that desired by median voters in Oregon school districts. What is the explanation for these different results? In voting on school-funding referenda, voters must consider the alternative to supporting the spending package proposed by the school board. If the alternative is to revert to a very low level of spending (as apparently is the case in Oregon), school boards can propose levels of spending higher than desired by the median voter, yet the median voter will approve because of the undesirable alternative. In other school districts (such as in Michigan and New York state), if the spending package proposed by the school board fails to pass, the school budget reverts to the status-quo budget. In this case, the median voter feels freer to vote against school spending programs that are higher than the median voter wishes. ∎

Sources: Radu Filimon, Thomas Romer, and Howard Rosenthal, "Asymmetric Information and Agenda Control," *Journal of Public Economics* 17 (February 1982); Randall Holcombe, "An Empirical Test of the Median Voter Model," *Economic Inquiry* 18 (April 1980); Robert Inman, "Testing Political Economy's *as if* Proposition: Is the Median Voter Really Decisive?" *Public Choice* 33 (1978).

turnout between the U.S. elections in 1960 and 1972 and the continued decline in the 1980 election indicated to some far too much apathy on the part of voters—although this decline in voter participation was not evident in the 1984 election.

What motivates a voter to vote? Objectively, there is a marginal cost (in time and effort) of going to vote. The probability of any single person's vote deciding an election is close to zero. According to one study,[2] most people vote out of a sense of obligation and duty, but an important determinant of voter turnout is the cost of going

to the polls and the closeness of the election. If people expect a close election, the chances of voting are larger.

The evidence suggests that people do make a cost/benefit calculation when they decide whether or not to vote. The benefit voters enjoy is the knowledge that they have performed their duty as a citizen; this benefit increases the closer the election is supposed to be.

Do people make informed decisions when they do go the polls? Anthony Downs calls the lack of information on the part of the voting public **rational ignorance.**[3]

2. O. Ashenfelter and S. Kelly, Jr., "Determinants of Participation in Presidential Elections," *Journal of Law and Economics* 18 (December 1975): 695–733.

3. Anthony Downs, *An Economic Theory of Democracy* (New York: Harper & Row, 1957).

Example 2   Dairy Subsidies: Rational Ignorance and Logrolling

In 1983, the U.S. government paid $2.7 billion to the dairy-farming industry in the form of purchases of dairy products that were produced but not purchased on private markets. The reason quantity supplied did not equal quantity demanded in private markets is that the U.S. government agreed to support the price of dairy products at $13.10 for the equivalent of 100 pounds of milk. As a result of government buying under this price-support program, the U.S. government stockpiled dairy products equal to 16 billion pounds of milk. In November of 1983, a new dairy-support bill was signed by President Reagan that retained dairy price supports (lowering the supported price by about 4 percent) and put into effect a program for paying dairy farmers to reduce the amount of dairy products they produce. Under the new law, the dairy farmer could reduce milkings between 5 and 30 percent below the previous year's marketings and receive $10 for every 100 pounds not produced.

The dairy subsidy program is a classic example of special-interest legislation. Why did Congress pass this dairy-subsidy program? Why did the President sign it into law? First, the benefits to specific dairy farmers (particularly, the very large dairy farms that receive the bulk of the benefits) are very large. Big dairy operators (the 6 percent who own one third of the dairy cows) stand to be the big winners. The losers are the consumers of milk who must pay for the program by paying higher milk prices. Farm experts estimate that the production cutback program would raise retail milk prices by 4 percent if dairy farmers cut back production 10 percent. But in 1984, the average American family spent approximately $210 per year on milk, so a 4 percent price increase may cost the average household $8 per year of $0.02 per day. This figure understates the entire cost of the program to the milk consumer. To obtain this figure, one must know what the price of milk would be without the entire dairy-support program. The costs of the dairy-subsidy program are also widely diffused among American taxpayers who must pay the direct subsidy. The dairy-subsidy program costs the average taxpayer an extra $18 per year on his or her federal income taxes.

The dairy-support program is a complicated program. To understand its implications, one must be able to estimate its effects on retail prices and to determine by how much it raises tax bills. The average taxpayer may be better off paying the $18 (being rationally ignorant) than going through the trouble of gaining this complex information. Moreover, even if the individual voter gathered the information to convince himself or herself that the program should be abolished, the best that voter could do would be to write letters of protest to his or her senator or congressional representative. If the senator or representative voted for the dairy bill anyway, the individual voter still may not want to vote against that official in the next election because that official's other votes may have been to the liking of the voter.

The passage of the dairy-subsidy package also illustrates the importance of vote trading in a multi-issue political world. The large dairy cooperatives (the largest of which received a subsidy payment of $339 million in 1983) were generous givers to the major political parties. The dairy bill was supported by key politicians from tobacco-producing states because it was combined with a tobacco-support bill. Moreover, the senator from the major milk-producing state lobbied colleagues heavily claiming that the defeat of the bill would cost him reelection and threaten the Republican Senate majority. These logrolling and vote-trading efforts ensured the passage of the dairy-support bill even though it was opposed by consumer coalitions, the American Farm Bureau, and the National Cattlemen's Association. ∎

Source: "Dairy Industry Making Money Two Ways: Milking and Not Milking," *Houston Chronicle,* February 12, 1984.

Rational ignorance is a decision not to acquire information because the marginal cost of acquiring the information exceeds the marginal benefit of having the information.

An earlier chapter on information costs explained that people gather information about choices as long as the extra benefits of information gathering exceed the extra cost. The cost of acquiring information about public choices is greater than the cost for private choices because public programs are more complicated than most private goods, and the link between the act of voting and the benefits received is very uncertain.

Hence, most people will know much more about private choices than about public choices. This ignorance is rational because it is a response to the costs of information.

Special-Interest Groups

The major implication of rational ignorance is that voters will know much more about legislation that affects them than about legislation that affects someone else. Thus, **special-interest groups** will emerge.

> **Special-interest groups** are minority groups with intense, narrowly defined preferences about specific government policies.

Dairy farmers will be very well-informed about milk-price supports; many consumers may not know they exist. The benefits to dairy farmers from higher milk-price supports are enormous; the costs to the typical voter of these supports are comparatively small. To the individual voter, the cost of finding out about the milk-price-support program exceeds the increase in the price caused by the program. Thus, the dairy farmers will have intense preferences for milk-price supports, and the rest of the public will be nearly indifferent. This is just the type of situation where logrolling and vote trading among politicians can result in special-interest legislation that is economically inefficient.

Politicians and Political Parties

President John F. Kennedy was fond of quoting the typical mother who wanted her offspring to grow up to be President, but who did not want a politician in the family. For reasons imbedded deeply in human psychology, people expect politicians to behave on a higher or more altruistic level than the average person. When they act just like anyone else does, people are disappointed in their low moral character.

The successful politician is a political entrepreneur. Politicians, through voting and logrolling, determine government policies. Like a business entrepreneur who stays in business by offering consumers what they want, the political entrepreneur can only stay in business by offering a platform of positions that will attract enough votes at election time. The politician earns his or her living by getting reelected. The rewards of reelection are many: popularity, power, prestige, and increased income opportunities. The public-choice economist assumes that politicians are more interested in votes than in serving the public interest. Even if they are completely unselfish, politicians cannot serve society unless they are reelected.

Remembering that voters are rationally ignorant about the complex of policies a particular politician supports, a vote-maximizing politician can put together a package of policies in support of special-interest legislation that benefits a minority but hurts the majority. Each member of each minority will benefit enormously while each member of the majority will be hurt only a trivial amount. By preparing a package of such policies, the politician can attract enough support from a coalition of minority groups to actually win. The politician who opposes all the special-interest legislation might be looking for a job after the next election.

> The central problem of public choice in our society is that the benefits of government policies are highly concentrated while the costs are highly diffused.

Restricting Japanese car imports makes the American automobile manufacturer and worker better off in an obvious way. The costs of import restrictions, however, are distributed over the entire population in such a subtle fashion that the public cannot distinguish between the increase in the price caused by the policy and, say, inflation. The French economist, Frederick Bastiat, referred to this as *what is seen* and *what is unseen*. What is seen is the fact that farmers are better off with price supports; what is unseen is that the price of dairy products is a few cents higher to everyone. The consumer does not know how much of the price paid for a TV set is due to the U.S. tariff on imported TV sets. American TV manufacturers and assembly workers, however, are very aware of the protection.

All government policies do not make the public worse off. The same political process that provides valuable pure public goods may result in inefficient levels of public goods (which may be unavoidable) and costly special-interest policies.

Bureaucrats

Aside from assorted lobbyists and pressure groups, the final actor on the political stage is the much-maligned **bureaucrat.**

> A **bureaucrat** is a nonelected government official responsible for carrying out a specific, narrowly defined task.

Basically, a bureaucracy is needed to run the government programs enacted by politicians. The bureaucrats tend to be the experts (social scientists, lawyers, accountants) who execute the programs.

Many observers have pointed out that bureaucracies tend to produce budgets that are too large. In market firms, profits provide the incentive to minimize costs. If the firm's resources are not allocated efficiently, profits will fall or the firm will go out of business. In bureaucracies, there are few incentives to minimize costs—instead bureaucrats may maximize "personal profits" in the form of plush offices or European trips. If bureaucrats succeed in running their offices or agencies more efficiently, the ultimate beneficiaries (the taxpayers) will be unaware of this fact because of rational ignorance. Large budgets cannot be monitored because of rational ignorance on the part of the elected politicians that approve the budgets. Legislators, who must be concerned with thousands of different programs, get the bulk of their information from the very bureaucracies they are trying to oversee. The bureaucrat has an enormous information advantage over the typical legislator. Since the bureaucrat is interested in expanding the budget and since the legislator is not too interested in cutting out the program completely (due to the importance of special interests), the budget will tend to be larger than necessary.

Competition Among Local Communities

Although voting at the ballot box is one form of voting, economist Charles Tiebout points out that voters can "vote with their feet." Tiebout hypothesized that households are not frozen in particular localities but, instead, can shop around to seek out the bundle of public goods and taxes that most closely approximates their demands for local public goods, such as parks, police protection, roads, zoos, and schools.[4] Consumers have some discretion over their consumption of public services. The competitive aspects of the provision of public services by different cities or states may stimulate local officials to try to minimize costs and to respond to consumer tastes.

PROPOSALS FOR GOVERNMENT REFORM

Economic analysis suggests that some government resource-allocation activities may be carried too far while others are not carried far enough. Many people support the view that government is too large. Opponents of large government criticize the combination of special interests, logrolling, and rational ignorance on the part of both the public and our representatives. Public spending in support of particular groups or industries—such as agriculture or the steel industry—is criticized as not being in the public interest.

Anthony Downs has pointed out that rational ignorance is also responsible for government being too small. According to Downs, the voter will usually underestimate the *benefits* (not just the costs) of fully justifiable government expenditures because they are remote and uncertain. In Down's view, a fully informed voter would vote for larger budgets, but voters are not so informed because of private information costs. John Kenneth Galbraith has also argued that private advertising makes people more aware of private needs than public needs.

Many public-choice economists believe that government has grown too large. James Buchanan argues that constitutional limits must be imposed on democratic governments in order to constrain their inherent tendencies to overexpand:

> Modern America confronts a crisis of major proportions in the last decades of the twentieth century. In the seven decades from 1900 to 1970, total government spending in real terms increased forty times over, attaining a share of one-third in national prod-

---

4. Wallace E. Oates, "On Local Finance and the Tiebout Model," *American Economic Review* 71 (May 1981): 93–98.

uct. These basic facts are familiar . . . The point of emphasis is that this growth has occurred, almost exclusively, within the predictable workings of orderly democratic procedures.[5]

Modern public-choice theory suggests that, regardless of the size of government, there are substantial government failures involved in the way public choices are made. The preferences of everyone, from the lowest worker to the captain of industry, should be duly registered when public choices are made. Currently, however, the median voter dominates; logrolling and vote trading allow the passage of special-interest legislation; voters are rationally ignorant about the costs and benefits of government programs. Public-choice economists have proposed a variety of reforms to make government more responsive to individual preferences, including the following:[6]

1. A three-fourths majority should be required for some types of legislation (particularly obvious special-interest legislation, such as tariffs, price supports, minimum-wage laws, and loans to bankrupt-prone firms).
2. Decisions on major proposals should be made by direct majority voting by the general public.
3. All expenditure programs should be linked to a visible tax increase.
4. Members of Congress should be determined by a process of random selection from the general public.

These reforms attempt to address the problems of rational ignorance, logrolling, and the overrepresentation of special interests.

This chapter examined how government works. The self-interest of politicians and bureaucrats combined with limited information can often result in poor public policies. This chapter looked at only one political-economic system: democratic capitalism; the next chapter will look at another type of economic system.

5. James M. Buchanan, *The Limits of Liberty* (Chicago: The University of Chicago Press, 1975), p. 162. Chapter 9 of Buchanan's book contains compelling reasons why governments can get too large.
6. The proposals are given in E. Browning and J. Browning, *Public Finance and the Price System* (New York: Macmillan Publishing Co., 1979).

Summary

1. The government must make resource-allocation decisions because the market fails to efficiently allocate public goods. In an ideal world, all government actions would have the unanimous support of all citizens. Unanimous collective decisions, however, require perfect information and zero bargaining costs. Governments would price public goods according to each individual's marginal valuation of the good, and each individual would vote for the proposal.
2. Unanimity is virtually impossible in the real world. The most popular alternative in democratic societies is majority rule. Under majority rule, the median voter decides on public goods. Social choices, therefore, do not reflect the relative intensities of preferences of different voters. Majority rule does not guarantee that the socially optimal amount of the public good will be produced.
3. Majority rule makes possible logrolling and pork-barrel politics in situations involving more than one decision. By forming vote-trading coalitions, beneficiaries of public goods can create majorities that would not have been possible otherwise. Majority voting can also lead to the paradox of voting.
4. The political market consists of voters, politicians, political parties, special-interest groups, and the government bureaucracy. Voters use personal cost/benefit analysis in their voting decisions; they vote when the perceived costs are low and the perceived benefits are high. Voting decisions are characterized by *rational ignorance*. The costs to most voters of acquiring information on complex public issues are high, and the benefits are low. For special-interest groups, however, the benefits are high relative to the costs of acquiring information. Politicians must adopt policies that will improve their chances of reelection. The fact that voters are rationally ignorant and do not see the effects of many government policies encourages special-interest legislation.
5. Economic analysis indicates that government undertakes many programs for which the marginal social benefits do not exceed the marginal social costs or that government fails to

undertake many programs for which the marginal social benefits exceed the marginal social costs. Public-choice economists have offered suggestions on how to improve public choices. These suggestions attempt to solve the problems of rational ignorance, logrolling, and overrepresentation of special interests.

Key Terms

unanimity
majority rule
median voter
logrolling
paradox of voting
rational ignorance
special-interest groups
bureaucrat

Questions and Problems

1. What factors limit unanimity on political decisions?

2. Some politicians have been observed to switch their positions in the course of political contests (for example, between the primary and the general election). Is this fact consistent with the theory of the role of the median voter in majority-rule elections? Why or why not?

3. If people are rational, how can public choice result in government actions with benefits that are less than the costs?

4. Explain why government bureaucrats would be less interested in cost minimization than would managers of private firms.

5. Do you think government will be more or less efficient than competitive enterprise? Will it be more or less efficient than private monopoly? Explain.

6. Do you think lobbying promotes or reduces the general welfare? Explain.

7. How would you reform the political process to make majority rule work better?

8. "The more localized are public goods, the more likely it is that unanimity can be achieved in public choices." Evaluate this statement.

9. There has been much discussion of a balanced-budget amendment in the popular press during the Reagan administration. How would you justify such an amendment in terms of the concepts used in this chapter?

10. How can majority rule be inefficient? Does inefficiency mean majority rule should be avoided?

11. Must logrolling result in economic inefficiency? Explain.

12. Bob prefers apples over bananas and bananas over oranges. Maria prefers oranges to apples and apples to bananas. Sam prefers bananas to apples and apples to oranges. If majority rule is used to choose among these goods, is there a voting paradox in this case?

13. In a world with zero information costs would there be economic inefficiency in the provision of government services?

Suggested Readings

Browning, E. and J. Browning. *Public Finance and the Price System.* New York: Macmillan, 1979.

Buchanan, James M. and Gordon Tullock. *The Calculus of Consent.* Ann Arbor: University of Michigan Press, 1962.

Buchanan, James M. *The Limits of Liberty.* Chicago: The University of Chicago Press, 1975, p. 162.

Downs, Anthony. *An Economic Theory of Democracy.* New York: Harper and Row, 1957.

Mueller, Dennis C. *Public Choice.* Cambridge: Cambridge University Press, 1979, pp. 49–51.

43

The Soviet Economy

Chapter Preview

This book has described the workings of the American economy, but no two economies are exactly alike. In many ways, the study of the American economy is a useful introduction to economics because the American economy uses primarily the market forces of supply and demand to solve the economic problem of *what, how,* and *for whom*. Although the economic role of government appears to be large to most of us, in proportion to the huge size of the American economy, it is still smaller than in most other countries. Although the government does redistribute income through taxes and the allocation of government services, the redistributive role of American government is still less than in other industrialized countries.

The American economy comes about as close as possible in our modern world to being a textbook example of a capitalist market economy. Some economies, however, rely more on government planners than on markets to allocate resources. In some economies, there is virtually no private ownership of land or capital. In other economies, substantial differences between the rich and poor are eliminated by government action. In some countries, consumers have a great say in determining what will be produced; in others, government officals assume this responsibility. Each country solves the economic problem using its own particular type of **economic system.**

> An **economic system** is the set of ownership, resource-allocation, incentive, and decision-making arrangements that a society uses to solve the economic problem.

This chapter examines the functioning and evaluates the performance of the Soviet economic system as the major alternative to the capitalist economic system that prevails in the United States. ■

ECONOMIC SYSTEMS

Economies differ according to a number of attributes. An economic system cannot be defined or categorized on the basis of one characteristic alone. Typically, economic systems are differentiated according to:

1. the form of resource ownership,
2. the form of resource allocation,
3. the type of incentives, and
4. the level of decision making.

Form of Resource Ownership

Who owns the factors of production is an important identifying trait of an economic system. The factors of production may be owned primarily by society (or by a government that is supposed to represent society), by private individuals, or by a combination of the two. The owner has the right typically to determine how the resource is used and to receive the income the resource generates.

Form of Resource Allocation

Goods and the factors of production can be allocated by the forces of supply and demand, or they can be allocated by government planners. How resources are allocated will determine how a society solves the *what* and *how* problems. In some economic systems, individual firms decide what and how to produce, and in others government officials give orders to enterprises.

Type of Incentives

Most economic systems use one of two basic mechanisms for motivating the participants in the economic system to carry out their economic tasks. The first mechanism is to provide *economic incentives* to motivate people. The other alternative is to provide *moral incentives* (medals, adulation in the press) or even *threats* to induce individuals to work and produce.

Level of Decision Making

Different economic systems make economic decisions at different levels. The individual partici-

pants in the economic system (households and individual firms) may make their own decisions (a decentralized arrangement), or their decisions may be made for them at higher levels (a centralized arrangement). When resource allocation decisions are made by government officials, they may be made at the local, regional, or national level.

CAPITALISM VERSUS SOCIALISM

Using the four characteristics of an economic system, **capitalism** and socialism can be defined more exactly.

> **Capitalism** is an economic system characterized by private ownership of the factors of production, market allocation of resources, the use of economic incentives, and decentralized decision making.

Socialism exists in two variants: **planned socialism** and **market socialism.**

> **Planned socialism** is an economic system characterized by state ownership of the factors of production (other than labor), the use of moral as well as economic incentives, resource allocation by economic plan, and centralized decision making.

> **Market socialism** is an economic system characterized by state ownership of the factors of production, the use of primarily economic incentives, market allocation of resources, and decentralized decision making.

No real-world economy fits exactly into one of these three abstract molds. In all economies, there is a mixture of private and public ownership, administrative and market allocation, economic and moral incentives, and centralized and decentralized decision making. However, in most economies, the major traits of one particular economic system will dominate. The American economy is a capitalist economy because private ownership, market resource allocation, economic incentives, and decentralized decision making dominate. The Soviet economy is a planned socialist economy because public ownership, resource allocation by plan, and centralized decision making dominate in that economy.

Examples of market socialism—economies where resources are publicly owned, yet where allocation occurs by way of the market—are harder to find in the contemporary world. Yugoslavia is a notable current example of market socialism, and Hungary is experimenting with different forms of market socialism. In recent years, China has begun experimenting with combinations of socialism and capitalism.

This book has already provided a thorough introduction to one economic system—capitalism—in its presentation of the American economic system. The functioning of the major alternative to the capitalist system—planned socialism—is best illustrated by an analysis of the Soviet economy. Of course, one cannot directly generalize from the Soviet and American economies to the abstract economic systems they represent. The Soviet and American economies differ in more than just their type of economic system. After all, the Soviet economy, despite its impressive military power, is still a much more backward economy than the United States. When the Soviet Union began its industrialization drive in the 1930s, it was one of the poorest countries of Western Europe and remains so today despite considerable economic growth. Nevertheless, the Soviet Union is a country much like the United States in the richness of its resources and in its position as an economic and political power in its sphere of influence.

THE HERITAGE OF MARX

The revolutionary writings of Karl Marx (1818–1883) and Marx's collaborator and financial backer, Friedrich Engels (1820–1895) provide the theoretical framework for the Soviet economy, just as the writings of Adam Smith provide the theoretical framework for capitalism. Marx's message was clear: capitalism is subject to internal contradictions that will lead to its inevitable collapse. A socialist workers' revolution will overthrow capitalism, and a new and superior economic system—socialism—will replace the old capitalist order. Marx's analysis of capitalism explains why capitalism is a doomed economic system.

Labor Theory of Value

The downfall of capitalism is preordained by its tendency towards ever-worsening economic crises, unemployment, and declining profits. According to Marx's **labor theory of value,** the value (price) of every commodity is ultimately determined by the amount of labor used to produce it.

> Marx's **labor theory of value** states that the value of a commodity *(C)* equals the sum of direct labor costs *(v)*, indirect labor costs *(c)*, and surplus value *(s)*.

$$C = c + v + s$$

In the above equation, fixed capital expenditures *(c)* are outlays for plant, equipment, inventories, and materials. The *v* stands for wage costs, called "variable capital" by Marx. The *s* denotes *surplus value,* Marx's term for profits.

Surplus Value.   Surplus value is the root cause of the class conflict, according to Marx. The feature that distinguishes labor from other factors of production is that capitalists can compel workers to produce **surplus value.**

> **Surplus value** is the value of any labor over and above the amount of labor service the worker would have to provide to meet subsistence needs.

Employers do not have to pay workers the full value of their production—only enough to allow workers to subsist. A worker may have to work 8 hours to produce enough output for subsistence needs; yet, the employer can force the worker to create a surplus by working 12 hours—4 hours more than required for subsistence.[1]

Fixed capital, though essential to production, cannot create surplus value; only labor can create surplus value. Workers are exploited because their surplus value produces profits for the capitalist class. Exploitation is the basic source of class conflict. Surplus value plays a central role

---

1. Marx was unclear about how *subsistence* should be defined—whether it was physical subsistence or some socially accepted norm of existence. Scholars and ideologists after Marx have long debated this particular point.

in Marxian theory, which assumes that the capitalist's desire to maximize profits is the driving force behind capitalism.

Unemployment.

Workers are prevented from receiving a share of the surplus value because of unemployment. Marx believed that wages would hover at subsistence because capitalism naturally produces a large amount of unemployment. The major cause of unemployment in Marx's view is the replacement of workers by machines. Massive unemployment keeps wages from rising above subsistence: if an employed worker is unwilling to work at the subsistence wage, a number of unemployed workers would be more than happy to take his or her place.

Marx believed that in the long run capitalist profits will eventually decline. According to Marx's "law" of declining profit rates, as an economy becomes more capital-intensive and less labor-intensive, the profit rate falls. Marx believed that competition compels capitalists to become more capital-intensive because capitalists are forced by competition to introduce cost-saving innovations. When one capitalist firm introduces a labor-saving technology and attracts its competitors' customers through lower prices, its profits increase temporarily. These extra profits, however, are short-lived as competitors eventually introduce the same cost-saving techniques and as new firms enter the market. Excess industry profits are eliminated, and capital has been substituted for labor.

> According to Marx, the inherent tendency for capitalists to substitute capital for labor, even though labor is the sole source of surplus value, will have disastrous long-run consequences for capitalism.

As the profit rate falls, the internal contradictions of capitalism become apparent. In an effort to halt the decline in profits, capitalists will try to increase the exploitation of their workers by raising surplus value, and the class conflict intensifies. The declining rate of profit will cause mass business failures, and bankrupt small capitalists will join the ranks of the unemployed.

Marx predicted that the economy will then begin to suffer overproduction and disproportions. Workers will be kept at subsistence incomes, capitalists will not be willing to increase their spending on luxury goods. Moreover, the ranks of the capitalists will thin as monopolists drive smaller capitalists out of business. Yet all the while, the productive capacity of the economy will be growing. Aggregate demand will fall chronically short of aggregate supply and recessions and depressions will become commonplace.

At this point, the stage is set for the qualitative change from capitalism to socialism. The workers, unable to bear their economic misery any longer, will unite against the weakened capitalist class and a violent world revolution will install a new socialist order. Capital will then become the property of the working class, who will take control of government.

The New Socialist State

Marx and Engels had surprisingly little to say about what happens after the socialist revolution installs the first socialist state. Marx felt that the new socialist society would go through two phases, later called *socialism* and *communism* by V. I. Lenin. During the first transitional phase, elements of the old capitalist order would remain; the powers of the new socialist state—called the *dictatorship of the proletariat* by Marx—would have to be directed against these capitalist forces. During this transitional phase, a strong state would be required to direct the class struggle against capitalist elements and to build up society's productive capacity. Scarcity would still be present, and the old capitalist system of rewarding labor would be continued. Marx's formula for distribution during this first phase was "to each according to his contribution."

Eventually, a stage of abundance would be reached. At this point, full communism would be established, the state would wither away, and there would be enough to go around for everyone. There would no longer be any class struggle because there would be only one class, the class of workers. Work would cease to be a chore, and distribution could now proceed according to the formula: "from each according to his ability, to each according to his needs."

THE SOVIET ECONOMY

In 1917, the Soviet Communist party (then called the Bolshevik party) under the leadership of V. I. Lenin took control of Russia. The Bolshevik revolution overthrew the moderate but ineffective government that took over after the revolutionary ouster of the Russian monarchy. The Russian revolution had little in common with the socialist revolution predicted by Marx—it occurred in one of the most backward and agrarian European countries and was more a consequence of exhaustion from the First World War than of class struggle between capitalists and workers. Once in command, Lenin and his successor, Josef Stalin, faced the task of building the world's first planned socialist economy.

It is not possible to understand how the Soviet economy works without understanding the ideology and political system of the Soviet Union. For deep-rooted ideological reasons and because of perceived negative experiences with the market in the 1920s, the leadership of the Soviet Union has been and remains deeply distrustful of market resource allocation. The leadership of the Soviet Communist party believes it is the responsibility of the party (and the state) to decide what is to be produced, how it is to be produced, and for whom. The purpose of the 1917 revolution in Russia was to place the Communist party in charge of resource allocation.

Soviet leaders believe that the Communist party knows what is best for society at large and that the market leads only to anarchy. Therefore, they believe it is essential for the party, not the market, to resolve the economic problem.

The Communist party begins the process of solving the economic problem by setting economic priorities. These priorities are handed down to government and industry officials by government planners in the form of general instructions, or "control indicators." These instructions set general goals for major industries, announce major changes in economic policy, set targets for Soviet agriculture, and detail the defense budget.

In the Soviet Union, the main planning body is *Gosplan* (the State Planning Agency), and Gosplan is directly responsible to the highest officials of the Communist party. The industrial ministries and large trusts participate in the planning process by assisting in the preparation of detailed plans for the enterprises that they control. Enterprises are associated together in combines or *trusts* that carry out some planning and control responsibilities. Together, Gosplan, the industrial ministries, and the trusts make up the planning apparatus of the Soviet Union.

Soviet planners translate the priorities of the Communist party into actual directives and orders for each enterprise in the Soviet Union. Because there are currently several hundred thousand such enterprises in an economy that produces a gross national product (GNP) of more than $2.0 trillion, this task is not easy.

Balancing Supplies and Demands

In the 1930s, there was a lively debate among economists about the feasibility of a planned socialist economic system. The sceptics in this "socialist controversy"—Friedrich von Hayek and Ludwig von Mises—argued that a modern economy, comprised of thousands of enterprises, millions of consumers, and producing millions of distinct products, could not conceivably be planned in a satisfactory manner. The job of balancing supplies and demands would simply be too large even in a world of high-speed computers. But the Soviet economy—despite the dire predictions of Hayek and Mises—has survived as a centrally planned economy for more than 60 years. How have Soviet planners managed to plan an increasingly complex economy?

The planning method developed by the Soviets in the 1930s (and still used in virtually the same form today) is called **material-balance planning.**

> **Material-balance planning** is a system of resource allocation in which centralized planning is restricted to controlling the output levels of only the most important industrial commodities that the economy produces and in which the production of other less important commodities is controlled at lower levels in the planning hierarchy.

Commodities such as electricity, steel, concrete, coal, oil, motor vehicles, cotton textiles, industrial chemicals, and machine tools determine the direction of the economy and are, therefore, planned and allocated from Moscow. Other less important commodities—such as services, garments, and toys—are planned, but they are managed at lower planning levels. The highest planning authorities determine in detail which economic units receive supplies of basic industrial commodities. Other less important commodities are planned by the ministries or by regional or even local authorities. Some commodities are not planned at all; in rare cases some commodities are even allocated by the market. The notion of dealing centrally with only the most important industrial commodities derives from practical necessity and from the theory that the Communist party could control the whole economy by controlling its most important industrial commodities.

For each of the several thousand commodities that are planned at the center, Gosplan (and the responsible ministry) must determine a **material balance.** For example, Gosplan knows from its preliminary production targets that 500 million tons of coal are to be produced in the coming year. It also knows that there are existing contracts to export 50 million tons of coal. A domestic supply of 450 million tons then remains. On the demand side of the market, Gosplan knows (largely on the basis of past experience) the coal requirements of each industry that are necessary to meet their anticipated production targets and also the coal requirements of the housing sector. Thus, Gosplan can estimate the anticipated demand for coal during the coming year.

> A **material balance** is achieved when anticipated demands and supplies of a critical good are equated by administrative means.

Gosplan and the ministries must draw up a material balance for each critical commodity—for steel, for cement, for sulfuric acid, for trucks, and so on. Once Gosplan has listed all the anticipated supplies and demands, it must make sure that there is an overall balance. Gosplan may find, for example, that the anticipated demand for coal exceeds the anticipated supply of coal. In addition to balances of materials, Gosplan draws up labor balances, machinery balances, and financial and money balances. The total cash in the hands of the population should balance the value of consumer goods placed on the market.

In capitalist economies, imbalances between supply and demand are corrected by spontaneous changes in relative prices. If there is an excess demand for coal and an excess supply of steel, coal prices will rise and steel prices will fall. In this way, capitalist economies can equate supplies and demands. Soviet material-balance planning corrects imbalances by making administrative changes in planned supplies and demand. If there is an excess demand for coal, planners can either raise production targets for coal or reduce the planned allocations of coal. In the Soviet Union, there is rarely an excess supply of any critical commodity. The problem planners typically must correct is excess demand. Responding to excess demands by raising production targets could disrupt other balances. Gosplan, therefore, has typically corrected imbalances by reducing planned allocations (by reducing demand) and not by increasing supply.

Setting Priorities.   Gosplan does not reduce material allocations in a haphazard manner. It will not, for example, say that every firm must take a 10 percent cut in coal allocations if it is necessary to reduce the demand for coal by 10 percent. Instead, Gosplan will follow a strict **priority principle.**

> The **priority principle** is that the industries most important to the Communist party will be the last to take cuts in supplies. Historically, light industry, which produces goods for the consumer, has been the low-priority industry. Therefore, when cuts have had to be made, they are absorbed by light industry and, ultimately, by the consumer.

There are two reasons for the strict observance of the priority principle over the years. The first is that the Soviet leadership has consistently favored heavy industry over light industry because heavy industry provides military hardware and because heavy industry is supposed to provide the basis for the future communist society. The second reason is that it is better to avoid plan shortfalls in heavy industry than in light industry. If steel, oil, or coal targets are not met, these shortfalls will disrupt the entire plan. If the plan for men's suits or children's shoes is not met, the overall impact on the plan will be limited.

Executing the Plan.

After intense negotiation and tough bargaining among all interested parties—the Communist party, Gosplan, the ministries, the trusts, regional authorities, and enterprise managers—Gosplan prepares an operational economic plan for the U.S.S.R. economy. This national economic plan is then submitted to the Soviet government for final approval, after which the economic plan becomes the law of the land. It is then the responsibility of every Soviet citizen and every Soviet enterprise to fulfill the tasks set out in the national plan.

Each enterprise receives a detailed enterprise plan—a thick document—that tells it what commodities it must produce, how many employees to have on the payroll, what materials it is to receive, what new machinery to install, what bank credits to draw on, and so on down to the finest details of enterprise operation. The enterprise director is responsible for fulfilling this enterprise plan. Enterprise plans are broken down into weekly, monthly, quarterly, and annual segments.

Surprisingly, the national economic plan is only the first phase in the resource-allocation process. Plan targets are never fulfilled in their entirety. In the course of plan fulfillment, it may become evident that some targets cannot be achieved or that not all promised supplies can be delivered. Again, administrative decisions about what parts of the plan will be fulfilled and what targets must be set aside are made according to the priority principle. There is no formal process for making such decisions. What is evident from Soviet economic history is that a strict priority principle has been observed, whereby low-priority branches bear the burden when resources are juggled. When the plan is announced with great fanfare, ambitious increases in consumer goods are typically called for, but when the plan is completed, the shortfalls are concentrated in the consumer-goods area.[2]

Soviet Managers

Official accounts of Soviet planning portray the Soviet manager as an unimportant actor in the resource-allocation process. After all, the economic plan provides the manager with a detailed set of instructions concerning what is to be produced, how it is to be produced, and who is to receive the material supplies. It would appear that all the Soviet manager has to do is to follow these instructions. Nothing could be further from the truth. Because the Soviet manager is given so many instructions—many of which are contradictory—he or she has considerable discretionary authority in the conduct of the enterprise's business. The fact that the enterprise manager is the one who decides what plan directives to follow and which directives to ignore makes the enterprise manager an important participant in the resource-allocation process.

Soviet managers—just like American managers—want to be successful, and to be successful, they too must please their bosses. The manager's boss is his or her immediate superior (perhaps a regional minister or, if it is a large firm, it may even be the national minister). The immediate superior is then responsible to his or her superior, and so on up the hierarchy. Eventually, everyone is responsible to the Communist party.

Over the years, Soviet managers have learned that success is measured by one's ability to fulfill those plan targets that one's superiors regard as most important. The relative importance of different plan targets has changed over the years—one year cost-reduction targets are important; the next year the labor-productivity plan is more important—but what remains constant is that one's success as a manager is judged primarily on the basis of one's ability to fulfill output targets. All other targets are secondary in comparison to the output target. Therefore, it is not surprising that Soviet managers have devoted most of their attention to making sure that they meet output targets.

The Principal/Agent Problem

A principal/agent problem arises when a principal and its agent have different goals and the cost of monitoring the agent is high. In the Soviet planned economy, there are a number of complex principal/agent relationships. The industrial ministries are agents for the state and for the party, as represented by Gosplan. The enterprises are agents for their industrial ministries. Enterprises of national importance are often directly agents of

---

2. It is difficult to pin down the record of plan fulfillment. During the course of a plan, plan targets are continuously revised so that at the end of the plan, party officials can announce the plan's success.

Gosplan. Gosplan wants the industrial ministries to meet their output targets, producing high-quality products at minimum cost and delivering them to designated receiving units. Gosplan also wants the ministries to introduce new technologies despite the risks associated with new technologies. The ministers, for their part, want to keep the state and party content with their performance. They know that Gosplan cannot monitor them fully (not knowing local conditions) and that Gosplan will, therefore, have to judge performance on the basis of readily observable indicators—like quantities of products produced. For Gosplan to monitor all the dimensions of performance (like product quality, cost-saving innovations, product mix) would be too costly. The ministry maximizes its well-being by taking the least risky path: ministries seek to meet quantity output targets and sacrifice other goals desired by the state if they stand in the way. In pursuing this strategy, the ministries know that Gosplan (the principal) cannot monitor them well enough to penalize them for their failure to meet other targets.

A similar principal/agent problem exists between the ministry (as the principal) and the enterprises (as the agent). The ministry would like its enterprises to achieve all the targets set out in the enterprise plan (output, inputs, new technology, productivity improvements, new products, and the like.) Yet the costs of monitoring the multiple dimensions of enterprise-plan fulfillment are too high. The ministry, therefore, evaluates enterprise performance on the basis of easily observable indicators—output quantities.

The use of output targets as the criterion for judging managerial success has led to paradoxical economic behavior on the part of the Soviet manager. Soviet managers are led by their own incentive system to engage in activities that reduce output and waste economic resources. From the viewpoint of the Soviet manager, an ideal plan is one that gives the manager more resources than are necessary to produce an output well below the enterprise's capacity. Under these circumstances, the manager knows that the plan targets can be met with little risk of failure. The worst thing that can happen is that the manager gets a plan that supplies few resources and requires the production of an output beyond the capacity of the enterprise. It is in managers' best interests to provide false or misleading information to their superiors—to overstate their input requirements and to understate their output capacities. During the Stalin years, managers who failed to meet output targets were branded as capitalist saboteurs and sent to Siberia or summarily executed. Although contemporary penalties for such failures are by no means so drastic, the search for managerial success continues.

When the manager receives the ideal plan of ample resources and small output requirements, one might expect that the manager would like to impress his or her superiors by overfulfilling the targets. On the contrary, however, the manager who reports an impressive degree of overfulfillment would risk receiving a much more ambitious set of targets next year. Soviet managers fear the *ratchet effect,* whereby planners respond to plan overfulfillment by "ratcheting up" plan targets for the next year. Soviet managers, therefore, avoid impressive plan overfulfillment, preferring to overfulfill the output plan by a modest margin.

The difficulty of exactly defining the desired mix of output encourages the Soviet manager to engage in other kinds of opportunistic behavior. If the manager is told to produce 10 million rubles worth of children's shoes, the easiest thing to do is to produce all shoes of the same size and color and flood the market with goods the consumer does not want. If the manager is told to produce a specific mix of sizes and colors, he or she may skimp on materials and produce defective shoes, technically fulfilling the output targets.

The manager will hesitate to innovate because the risks of trying new things will be large, and the perceived benefits will be small. New production technologies may disrupt existing supply channels; construction delays may endanger fulfillment of the all-important output plan. Planners might not recognize that a better product is being produced or that output is being produced more efficiently.

MARKET ALLOCATION IN THE SOVIET UNION

Although most industrial commodities and investment goods are allocated by the administrative orders of planners and party officials, market resource allocation does play a reasonably important role in the Soviet economy. The major areas of market resource allocation are in the buying and selling of consumer goods, labor, and underground commodities.

Consumer Goods

The amounts and qualities of consumer goods produced in the Soviet Union are planned by government and party officials, although enterprise managers do have some leeway to determine what will be produced. In the whole process of determining what to produce, the consumer has remarkably little say. Soviet consumers must spend their income on those goods that the state and enterprise managers have decided to produce. Once produced, consumer goods are, with important exceptions, allocated to consumers much as they are allocated in capitalist countries. Soviet consumers make up their own minds as to what they want to buy with their earned income, and the state generally attempts to set prices to equate supplies and demands.

In terms of supply and demand curves, consumer goods are allocated as in Figure 1. The supply of good X is completely inelastic; the demand curve is no different from the demand curves drawn in earlier chapters. If the state, which sets virtually all prices in the Soviet Union, fails to set the price at equilibrium, there will be either a shortage or a surplus. Surpluses are not unknown, especially for shoddy or defective merchandise that accumulates unsold in Soviet stores. Shortages are more common, but Soviet pricing authorities have learned that if shortages are too widespread consumers will find that they cannot use their earnings to buy what they want and will lose interest in higher earnings. This loss of incentives can harm the economy; therefore, in general, the Soviets have attempted at least in recent years to keep prices of consumer goods near equilibrium levels.

The rule of pricing consumer goods to equate supply and demand is broken in many instances. Housing, automobiles, high-quality merchandise imported from the West, and other prestige items are typically sold at prices too low to equate supply and demand. Housing rents are maintained at ridiculously low levels both for purposes of income distribution (Socialists believe no one in a Socialist society should be denied housing for reasons of income) and for reasons of social control.

Figure 1   Retail Pricing in the Soviet Union

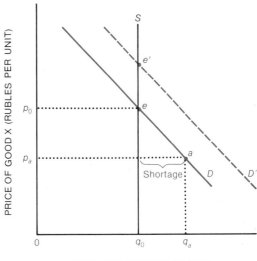

In the Soviet Union, the supply of consumer goods is basically determined by planners without reference to price. Thus, the supply curve is virtually vertical (perfectly inelastic). The demand curve, however, obeys the law of demand and is downward-sloping. For many products, Soviet authorities attempt to set retail prices at the equilibrium price (at p_0). Other products, however, are priced below equilibrium (at p_a, for example) for reasons of income distribution and social control. An important feature of the Soviet system is that increases in demand (an increase from D to D') do not lead to increases in quantity supplied.

If prized apartments are allocated not by price but by political authorities or plant managers, then authorities have another tool for controlling and motivating the population. The same can be said of private automobiles, access to French or West German goods, and seaside resorts. Government officials allocate such goods as rewards for good workers and the party faithful.

Labor

With some exceptions, Soviet citizens can select their own occupations and places of employment. One exception is that college graduates are assigned their first job and must remain in these jobs for a prescribed period of time. Authorities also limit the number of people who are allowed to move to major urban centers like Moscow and

Leningrad. Otherwise, the Soviet labor force makes its own decisions about where to work.[3]

Planning authorities determine the demand for labor in different occupations and in different industries. To insure that these demands will be met, industrial wages are set to equate supply and demand. As a result, occupations in undesirable locations or dangerous, unpleasant, or dirty jobs are paid more than others. In fact, Soviet wage differentials appear to be much like those in the United States or other capitalist countries. Workers in the Far North who work under extreme weather conditions earn wages 2 to 3 times those in central U.S.S.R. The Soviet economy most resembles a capitalist economy in the area of labor allocation. The Soviets have learned that incentives will be low if occupational choice is not relatively free. People cannot be ordered around from one job or occupation to another like steel and cement. A relatively free labor market is the price that must be paid to maintain worker incentives.

The Second Economy

Karl Marx had hoped that the creation of a socialist state would create a "new socialist man"—a new type of individual who would place the interests of society above personal self-interest. As we have shown, however, the Soviet labor market operates much like a capitalist market. Recent research shows that a substantial unplanned sector of the Soviet economy—called the "second economy"—may be as important in the Soviet Union as it is to Western capitalist economies. In capitalist economies, the underground economy supplies goods and services and serves as a device for evading taxes. In the U.S.S.R., the underground economy specializes in supplying goods and services planners are incapable of or unwilling to supply.

There is no way to measure the relative size of the Soviet second economy. Newspapers report spectacular court proceedings in the Soviet Union that unearth self-made Soviet millionaire entrepreneurs. Emigrants from the Soviet Union also report a wide range of second-economy activities: physicians have large earnings from private practices (which are not allowed by law); materials from state enterprises are diverted into the production of high-quality consumer goods; important positions in the Communist party are sold by party officials. Scarce supplies are made available to industrial firms by under-the-table deals between enterprises. In fact, in the Soviet Union, a recognized profession is that of the *expeditor*— the individual who arranges for industrial materials outside of normal supply channels.

The activities mentioned above are illegal activities, but there is one form of legal private economic activity that is openly tolerated by Soviet officials: the collective-farm market. Farmers in socialist agriculture are allowed to keep small plots of land for their own cultivation or for sale if they decide. The products from these private plots are sold in collective-farm markets at prices determined by the forces of supply and demand. Collective-farm markets can vary from a large organized outdoor market in a large city to a peasant woman selling apples on a street corner. The output of private agriculture—which comes from land that is only 1 percent of total cultivated acreage—accounts for a large proportion of the Soviet consumption of meat, dairy, and vegetable products. The role of these farm markets is so important in feeding the Soviet population that party authorities have no choice but to accept it.

SOVIET ECONOMIC PERFORMANCE

The preceding section described briefly how the Soviet economy solves the *what, how,* and *for whom* problems. This description of the Soviet economy suggests that there are certain weak points. Material-balance planning is a clumsy and cumbersome process that aims more at finding balances of supplies and demands than at finding the best way to combine inputs. Managers are

---

3. This was not always the case. During the early years of the Soviet regime (1918–1921), labor was treated pretty much like military conscripts (this was, after all, the time of the Russian civil war), and the state told people where they were to work and whether or not they could quit their jobs. The same was true during the Second World War, when there were severe penalties for tardiness or changing jobs without permission. But with these exceptions, Soviet citizens have been relatively free in their choice of occupations.

more interested in meeting output targets than in combining resources in the most efficient manner. Managers are not motivated by the incentive system to take risks.

Market economies also have their own weaknesses. When firms possess monopoly power, output is restricted below the social optimum. When externalities are present, only private costs and benefits will be considered. Capitalism may lead to an income distribution that many people may regard as unfair.

Assessing how well one existing economy performs relative to another is a tricky business. It is even more difficult to determine how well a theoretical economic system should perform relative to another. One conceptual problem confounds such comparisons: by whose standards should one judge economic performance? By the standards of the Soviet Communist party, Soviet economic performance may be regarded as satisfactory. By standards that place more emphasis on living standards, Soviet performance is less satisfactory. Value judgments must be made to draw conclusions concerning economic performance, and there is no scientific way to prove that one person's (or one group's) judgments are better than any other's.

The various criteria that are typically used to evaluate economic performance include: economic growth, economic efficiency, economic stability, military power, and income distribution. Once the performance of the Soviet economy in each area has been evaluated, it is then up to the individual reader to decide just how well or how poorly the Soviet economy has performed.

Economic Growth

From the viewpoint of the Soviet leadership, rapid economic growth has always been an important goal for several reasons. Rapid economic growth lays the economic foundation for communism; it allows the Soviet Union to catch up and overtake its capitalist enemies; economic growth, particularly the growth of heavy industry, makes possible a strong military. Moreover, the Soviet leadership has consistently claimed that the superiority of the Soviet economic system would be demonstrated by its ability to grow more rapidly than the declining and decadent capitalist West.

Table 1   Annual Rates of Economic Growth: U.S.S.R., United States, and Major Capitalist Economies

Country	Growth Rate (percent)
U.S.S.R.	
1885–1913	3.3
1928–1940	5.4
1950–1981	4.8
1928–1981	5.0
United States	
1834–1929	4.0
1929–1981	3.0
United Kingdom (1855–1980)	2.2
France (1831–1980)	2.5
Belgium (1900–1980)	2.3
Netherlands (1860–1980)	2.6
Germany (1850–1980)	2.9
Denmark (1865–1980)	3.1
Japan (1874–1980)	4.6
Canada (1870–1980)	3.6

Source: Paul Gregory and Robert Stuart, *Soviet Economic Structure and Performance*, rev. ed. (New York: Harper and Row, 1981), p. 335, 337.

Table 1 supplies data on the long-term economic growth of the U.S.S.R. and of the major capitalist countries. These data show that the Soviet economy has indeed grown rapidly since the initiation of its industrialization drive in 1928, more rapidly in the long run than any major capitalist country with the exception of Japan. The data also show that the Soviet growth rate has been declining over the past two decades; Soviet economic growth is now no more rapid than the average growth of capitalist countries—in fact, since 1980 it is well below the Western average. Soviet ambitions to overtake the U.S. economy must, therefore, be put aside unless a means can be found to revive the ailing Soviet growth rate.

The most rapid Soviet growth took place in the early 1950s, after the death of Stalin, when the new leadership loosened the more restrictive features of the Stalin dictatorship. This upsurge in growth, however, did not lead to growth that was more rapid than the fast-growing capitalist countries like West Germany and Japan.

The declining growth rate troubles the Soviet leadership. It forced them to experiment in the mid-1960s with modest economic reforms—reforms that gave slightly more authority to managers and gave consumers more of a voice in the choice of consumer goods. These modest reforms failed to produce the desired result and have largely been abandoned. It has also forced them to expand their trade with the West.

Economic Efficiency and Productivity

There is no direct statistical measure of how efficiently an economy utilizes its available resources—of how close it is to its production-possibilities frontier—but there is a great deal of indirect evidence of economic inefficiency in the Soviet economy. The perverse behavior of Soviet managers in response to output targets, the extent to which economic activities are forced into the second economy, and the cumbersome material-balancing system have already been described. Moreover, the practice of pricing many goods below equilibrium has caused an unproductive use of time because of the vast amount of time spent in lines.[4]

Soviet productivity growth (the growth of output per unit of input) is average or below average when compared to the Western world. The Soviet Union was a technologically backward country in 1917, and an objective of the Soviet leadership has been to catch up with Western technology. But Soviet productivity growth has not exceeded productivity growth in the capitalist West. The technology gap, thus, remains quite large.

Earlier, it was noted that long-term Soviet growth has been rapid but that productivity growth was at best average. This combination of facts suggests that Soviet economic growth is explained primarily by the growth of labor and capital inputs. Output per unit of inputs has not increased at a significant rate.

---

4. Even official Soviet sources admit to low output per unit of input. Soviet industrial workers produce about one half as much as their American counterparts. American estimates show that the Soviet economy produces about 60 percent as much output from one unit of input (whether labor, capital, or land) as does the American economy. Comparisons of Soviet productivity with that of Western Europe also show Soviet productivity to be well below that of most European countries but about equal to that of Italy. By themselves, such figures do not demonstrate that the Soviet economic system is less efficient than its capitalist counterpart. Many factors other than the economic system determine efficiency.

Military Power

The Soviet leadership came to power in a militarily weak country surrounded by capitalist foes, and the leadership had strong pretensions of initiating a world communist revolution to convert the world from capitalism to Marxist ideals. For these reasons, the goal of military power—to maintain and expand communist power—has always been important to the Soviet leadership.

In this area of economic performance, there can be little doubt of Soviet successes. Although the overall size of Soviet gross domestic product (GDP) is roughly 60 percent that of the United States, Soviet military power exceeds or rivals that of the United States, as illustrated by comparisons of defense capital stock (such as personnel, tanks, bombers, or missiles).

The costs of achieving military parity with or superiority to the United States have been high. The best Soviet material and human resources have been devoted to defense and have been diverted from the production of industrial capital or consumer goods. The U.S. intelligence community estimates that some 14–16 percent of Soviet GDP is devoted to defense, whereas in the United States the percentage is 4–5 percent. Obviously, such large military outlays hinder the attainment of other goals—such as reviving the declining Soviet growth rate or raising Soviet living standards.

Economic Stability

The Soviet press and Soviet economics textbooks emphasize the great economic instability of capitalism. *Pravda* (the official newspaper of the Communist party) gleefully announces the latest American or British figures on unemployment and inflation. The sad lot of the capitalist worker is emphasized: there is an ever-present threat of losing one's job. In contrast to the anarchy of the market, Soviet officials emphasize the greater economic stability of their economic system. Unemployment, they declare, was liquidated in 1929. Everyone is guaranteed a job; no one is denied suitable housing because of low income. All workers are protected from cradle to grave by free health services and by state pensions. Education is free. Moreover, Soviet consumers are protected from the ravages of inflation by the state's control of consumer prices. In fact, official Soviet price indexes show that prices are lower in the Soviet Union today than they were in 1950—a remarkable claim in a world of double-digit inflation.

Considerable Western research has been devoted to testing these Soviet claims, and this research shows that there is indeed unemployment and inflation in the U.S.S.R. Inflation takes several forms: first, it takes the form of *repressed inflation* when people must stand in line longer (for goods that run out before the line does) rather than pay a higher price. Although repressed inflation is less prevalent than it was in earlier years, it is still an important factor. Second, inflation can take the form of price increases that are hidden from view by the official statistics. The official figures are fudged in a number of ways to understate inflation. Third, the inflation can spill over into the second economy, where the rate of inflation cannot be readily measured. Nevertheless, most Western studies show that both inflation and unemployment are much less severe than in most capitalist countries. The unemployment rate may be around 1.5 percent, while the inflation rate may be between 2 and 3 percent.

This result is not unexpected. Soviet industrial wages have been allowed to increase at rates equal to the rate of growth of labor productivity. Workers are guaranteed jobs whether they are redundant or not. Yet the Soviets have had to pay a price for this economic stability. Soviet workers know they cannot be fired unless they engage in extreme misconduct, and even then Soviet managers have little to gain by letting bad workers go. The price of stability in official price indexes has been greater hidden inflation and the direction of economic activity into the second economy where prices are not controlled. In general, one can say that greater economic stability has been purchased at the price of lower economic efficiency.

Income Distribution

During the Soviet industrialization drive of the 1930s, income distribution for Soviet workers was more unequal than for their American counterparts. The gap between the pay of skilled and unskilled workers was immense. The cause of these differentials was probably more economic than ideological. The Soviet economy was plagued by a shortage of skilled and educated workers. Many technicians had fled abroad, and the children of the working class did not possess the needed educational credentials. The large wage differentials were required to equate the supply to the extraordinary demand for skilled workers.

By the mid-1950s, the Soviet educational establishment had succeeded in graduating an impressive number of technically skilled and educated workers and employees. In recognition of this fact, substantial reforms in the system of industrial wages were begun in 1956 and completed in the mid-1960s. As a consequence of these reforms, wage differentials between skilled and unskilled workers were reduced, so that today wage differentials are smaller than in most capitalist countries.

The overall distribution of income in the Soviet Union is hard to estimate because Soviet statistical authorities do not readily publish information on the earnings of the ruling elite. Moreover, Soviet citizens' claims on economic resources are not determined entirely by income because members of the elite often receive more highly priced goods free of charge—such as chauffeur-driven cars, free vacations, or travel to the West—and those would not show up in income statistics.

Even with these reservations, it is safe to say that the distribution of income in the U.S.S.R. is much more equal than it is in the United States. Surprisingly, the same conclusion cannot be drawn strongly from comparisons of the U.S.S.R. income distribution with capitalist countries like Sweden and the United Kingdom in which the state plays a large redistributive role (Table 2). The main reason for the more equal Soviet distribution compared to U.S. distribution is the absence of income from land and capital in the Soviet Union.

This chapter has examined how planned economies solve the economic problem, using the Soviet Union as an example of a planned economy. It looked at the heritage of Marx and at actual resource-allocation practices in the Soviet planned economy in making its comparisons.

Table 2   An International Comparison of Income Shares of Selected Percentile Groups, Distributions of Households by per Capita Household Income, and GDP per Capita

Distribution, Country and Year	GDP per Capita (U.S. = 100)	Percentage Income Share of			
		Lowest 10%	Lowest 20%	Highest 20%	Highest 10%
Nonfarm households (pretext)					
USSR, 1967	38	4.4	10.4	33.8	19.9
Urban households (post-tax)					
USSR, 1972–1974	48	3.4	8.7	38.5	24.1
All households (pretax)					
Australia, 1966–1967	56	3.5	8.3	41.0	25.6
Norway, 1970	64	3.5	8.2	39.0	23.5
U.K., 1973	66	3.5	8.3	39.9	23.9
France, 1970	68	2.0	5.8	47.2	31.8
Canada, 1969	74	2.2	6.2	43.6	27.8
U.S., 1972	99	1.8	5.5	44.4	28.6
All households (post-tax)					
Sweden, 1972	80	3.5	9.3	35.2	20.5

Source: Abram Bergson, "Income Inequality under Soviet Socialism," *Journal of Economic Literature* 22 (September 1984).

Summary

1. No two economic systems are alike. Economic systems are multidimensional. They differ in their ownership of resources, their allocation of resources, their production incentives, and their decision making.

2. Capitalism is an economic system with private resource ownership, economic incentives, market allocation, and decentralized decision making. Planned socialism is an economic system with state resource ownership, the use of moral as well as economic incentives, plan rather than market allocation, and centralized decision making.

3. Karl Marx viewed capitalism as an unstable economic system, destined to be replaced by socialism through a violent socialist revolution. Marx believed that labor alone creates surplus value but that replacing labor with capital causes the profit rate to fall. When profits fall, the capitalist class increases worker exploitation, economic crises become more severe, and the capitalist system breaks down. The breakdown of capitalism is inevitable because the capitalist system is based upon class conflict between the working class and the capitalists.

4. The Soviet Union is the best example of planned socialism. In the Soviet economy, the Communist party decides what is to be produced and the planning agencies construct an economic plan that implements these instructions. Quantities supplied and demanded are equated by administrative orders, not by the price system. Each participant in the economy is obligated to fulfill the plan. Each enterprise receives a detailed plan that gives it detailed instructions on what, how, and for whom to produce. Soviet managers are given a large number of often conflicting targets. They decide which targets to fulfill on the basis of the priority principle.

5. There are important elements of market allocation in the Soviet Union. Consumer goods, once produced, are allocated primarily through the market, although there are significant exceptions. Labor is allocated primarily through the market, and the "second (underground) economy" operates strictly through the market.

6. Soviet economic performance must be judged in terms of economic growth, economic efficiency, income distribution, economic stability, and military power. After a period of rapid economic growth, economic growth has been declining in recent decades. Soviet productivity growth has failed to reduce the technology gap the Soviets inherited. The Soviet distribution of income is more equal than the U.S. income distribution, but is close to that of the capitalist welfare states. Soviet achievements have been greatest in the military sphere.

Key Terms

economic system
capitalism
planned socialism
market socialism
labor theory of value
surplus value
material-balance planning
material balance
priority principle

Questions and Problems

1. Explain how capitalism differs from socialism in terms of the four characteristics of an economic system.

2. Compare the ways in which the Soviet economy and a capitalist economy deal with a shortage of a particular industrial commodity.

3. What are the causes of an underground economy in the Soviet Union?

4. Why is Soviet long-term growth rapid by international standards while Soviet productivity has grown at only an average rate?

5. Explain why the Soviet Union is subject to the principal/agent problem. Would one expect the problem to be more severe in a planned economy?

6. Unlike industrial materials, labor and consumer goods tend to be allocated through markets in the Soviet Union. Speculate on the reason for the market allocation of labor and consumer goods.

7. Contrast Marx's labor theory of value with the supply/demand theory of value found in the early chapters of this book. On what points do they agree? On what points do they disagree?

8. In Marx's theory, explain why the tendency to substitute capital for labor will lead to a long-run decline in the profit rate.

Suggested Readings

Bornstein, Morris, ed. *Comparative Economic Systems: Models and Cases,* 5th ed. Homewood, Ill.: Richard D. Irwin, 1985.

Gregory, Paul R. and Robert C. Stuart. *Comparative Economic Systems,* 2nd ed. Boston: Houghton Mifflin, 1985.

Gregory, Paul R. and Robert C. Stuart. *Soviet Economic Structure and Performance,* 3rd ed. New York: Harper and Row, 1986.

Grossman, Gregory. *Economic Systems.* Englewood Cliffs, N.J.: Prentice-Hall, 1967.

Nove, Alec. *The Soviet Economic System.* London: Allen and Unwin, 1977.

Glossary

absolute advantage the ability to produce a unit of a good using fewer resources than any other producer (**22**).

absolute poverty standard establishes a specific income level for a given-sized household below which the household is judged to be living in a state of poverty (**39**).

accelerator principle that investment depends upon the growth of output; implies that investment will be unstable. Investment will fall simply because output grows at a slower rate. For investment to just remain stable, output growth must be constant (**10**).

accounting profits revenues minus explicit (accounting) costs (**28, 38**).

activist policy policy that selects money- and fiscal-policy actions on the basis of perceived economic conditions and that changes as economic conditions change (**17**).

adaptive expectations expectations that people form from past experience and modify only gradually as experience unfolds (**14**).

adverse-selection problem occurs when a buyer or seller enters a disadvantageous contract on the basis of imcomplete or inaccurate information because the cost of obtaining the relevant information is higher for this buyer or seller than for the other party to the transaction (**33**).

adverse supply shock occurs when the short-run aggregate-supply curve shifts to the left, causing the price level to rise and output to fall (**11**).

agent a party that acts for, on behalf of, or as a representative of a *principal* (**27**).

aggregate demand *(AD)* a schedule of the amounts of goods and services agents in the economy (households, business firms, and government) are prepared to buy at different price levels (**5**); the equilibrium aggregate expenditure levels (where desired expenditures and actual income are equal) at different price levels, holding the nominal money supply, tax rates, and real government expenditures constant (**10**).

aggregate expenditures *(AE)* a schedule of the desired amounts of total spending ($C + I + G$) at different income levels (**9**).

aggregate production function the relationship between the total output produced by the economy and the total labor, capital, and land inputs used by the economy (**35**).

aggregate supply *(AS)* a schedule of the quantities of real output the economy is prepared to supply at different price levels (**5**). (See also **short-run aggregate supply** and **long-run aggregate supply**.)

allocation the apportionment of scarce resources to specific productive uses or to particular persons or groups (**2**).

arbitrage buying in a market where a commodity is cheap and reselling it in a market where the commodity is more expensive (**33**).

auction market a market in which the market price is renegotiated on a regular basis (**19**).

automatic stabilizers government spending or taxation actions that take place without any deliberate government control and that tend to dampen the business cycle (**13**).

autonomous changes changes in tax rates or government spending that are independent of changes in income **(13)**.

autonomous expenditures   expenditures determined independently of income changes **(10)**.

average fixed cost *(AFC)*   fixed cost divided by output **(28)**.

average revenue *(AR)*   total revenue divided by output **(30)**.

average tax rate   one's tax payment divided by taxable income **(13)**.

average total cost *(ATC)*   total cost divided by output, or the sum of average variable cost and average fixed cost **(28)**.

average variable cost *(AVC)*   variable cost divided by output **(28)**.

"bads"   (see **economic "bads"**).

backstop resource   a close substitute for an exhaustible resource that is available in virtually unlimited supply but at a higher cost **(41)**.

balanced-budget multiplier   the ratio of changes in income to equal changes in government spending and taxes; always equals 1 because equal increases (or decreases) in government spending and taxes will cause income to increase (or decrease) by the amount of the change in government spending **(10)**.

balance of payments   a summary record of a country's economic transactions with foreign residents over a specified period **(24)**.

balance sheet   a summary of the current financial position of a firm that compares the firm's assets and liabilities **(8)**.

banks   (see **commercial banks**).

bank money   money that is on deposit in checking accounts **(7)**.

bankruptcy   the state of a corporation that cannot pay its bills or its interest obligations **(27)**.

barrier to entry   any advantage that existing firms hold over firms that might seek to enter the market **(32)**.

beneficial supply shock   occurs when the short-run aggregate-supply curve shifts to the right, causing the price level to fall and output to rise **(11)**.

benefit   (see **external benefit, private benefit, social benefits**).

bonds   IOUs of a corporation that bind the corporation to pay a fixed sum of money (the *principal*) at maturity and also to pay a fixed sum of money annually until the maturity date (the *interest* or *coupon payment*) **(27)**.

budget line   all the combinations of goods the consumer is able to buy given a certain income and set

prices. The budget line shows all the choices of consumer goods available to the consumer **(26A)**.

bureaucrat   a nonelected government official responsible for carrying out a specific, narrowly defined task **(42)**.

business cycle   the pattern of upward and downward movements in the general level of real business activity **(5)**.

capital   the equipment, plants, buildings, and inventories that are available to society **(2, 8)**. (See also **human capital**.)

capital deepening   an increase in the ratio of capital to workers in an economy **(20)**.

capital gain   the increase in the market value of any asset above the price originally paid. The capital gain is realized when the asset is sold **(27)**. (See also **realized capital gain**.)

capitalism   an economic system characterized by private ownership of the factors of production, market allocation of resources, the use of economic incentives, and decentralized decision making **(3, 43)**.

capital/output ratio *(K/Y)*   the value of capital *(K)* needed to produce a given level of output divided by the value of that output *(Y)*, or K/Y **(10)**.

cartel   an arrangement that allows the participating firms to operate the industry as a shared monopoly **(32)**.

cash leakage   occurs when a check is converted into cash instead of being deposited in a checking account **(8)**.

centralized market   a market in which all buyers and sellers of a particular product make their transactions in one location **(33)**.

ceteris paribus **fallacy**   the false attribution of the effects of changes in one set of variables to changes in another set of variables **(1)**.

check   a directive to the check writer's bank to pay lawful money to the bearer of the check **(7)**.

circular-flow diagram   summarizes the flows of goods and services from producers to households and the flows of the factors of production from households to business firms **(3)**.

classical quantity theory of money   that the price level is strictly proportional to the money supply **(7)**.

collective bargaining   the process whereby a union bargains with management as the representative of all union employees **(37)**.

commercial banks   banks that have been chartered either by a state agency or by the U.S. Treasury's Comptroller of the Currency to make loans and receive deposits **(8)**.

commodity money money whose value as a commodity is as great as its value as money **(7)**.

common stock confers voting privileges but no prior claim on dividends. Common stock dividends are paid only if they are declared by the board of directors in any given year **(27)**.

comparative advantage (see **law of comparative advantage**).

compensating wage differentials the higher rewards (wages or fringe benefits) that must be paid workers to compensate them for undesirable job characteristics **(36)**.

competing ends the different purposes for which resources can be used **(2)**.

competition (see **perfect competition, imperfect competition, monopolistic competition**).

complements any two goods such that the demand for one rises when the price of the other falls (or such that the demand for one falls when the price of the other rises) **(4)**.

concentration ratio the percentage of industry sales (or output or labor force or assets, as the case may be) accounted for by the x largest firms **(32)**.

conglomerate merger occurs when one company takes over another company in a different line of business **(34)**.

conscious parallelism occurs when the actions of producers can be coordinated within certain ranges without formal or even informal agreements. Oligopolists use their understanding of the industry to make their own decisions and anticipate the behavior of other oligopolists **(32)**.

constant-cost industry a relatively small industry that can expand or contract without significantly affecting the terms at which factors of production used in the industry are purchased. The long-run industry supply curve for such an industry is horizontal **(29)**.

constant-money-growth rule that the money supply should increase at a fixed percentage each year **(12)**.

constant returns to scale present when a given percent change in inputs results in the same percent change in output **(28)**.

consumer equilibrium occurs when the consumer has spent all income and the marginal utilities per dollar spent are equal on each good purchased $(MU_A/P_A = MU_B/P_B)$. At this point, the consumer is not inclined to change purchases unless some other factor (such as prices, income, or consumer preferences) changes **(26)**.

consumer surplus the excess of total consumer benefit that a good provides over what the consumers actually have to pay **(26, 29)**.

consumption/income schedule shows the amount of desired consumption at different levels of national income or output **(9)**.

contestable market a market in which 1) entry and exit by new firms is completely free, 2) the new firms can produce with the same costs as the incumbent firms, 3) firms can easily dispose of their fixed assets by selling them elsewhere (fixed costs are not sunk but are recoverable), and 4) customers buy from the firm (or firms) that first posts the lowest price **(32)**.

contractionary fiscal policy lowers aggregate demand by lowering autonomous government spending or by autonomously raising taxes **(13)**.

convertible stock a hybrid between a stock and a bond. The owner of convertible stock receives fixed interest payments but has the privilege of converting it to common stock at a fixed rate of exchange **(27)**.

corporation a form of business enterprise that is owned by a number of stockholders. The corporation has the legal status of a fictional individual and is authorized by law to act as a single person. The stockholders elect a board of directors that appoints the management of the corporation, usually headed by a president. Management is charged with the actual operation of the corporation **(27)**.

cost (see **explicit cost, implicit cost, external cost, opportunity cost, private cost, social costs**).

cost-push inflation (see **supply-side inflation**).

countercyclical monetary policy policy that increases aggregate demand when output is falling too much (or when its rate of growth is declining) and reduces aggregate demand when output is rising too rapidly **(12)**.

countervailing duty a duty imposed on foreign imports which are subsidized by their home governments **(23)**.

coupon payment the fixed interest-payment obligation due to the owner of a bond at stated, regular intervals **(18)**.

craft union a union that represents workers of a single occupation **(37)**.

credit markets markets for borrowing and lending funds **(38)**.

credit rationing occurs when interest rates are not allowed to rise to the rate at which the demand for loans equals the supply of loans. In this situation, the demand for investment funds at the prevailing interest rate exceeds the supply. Credit rationing limits investment by making investment funds unavailable to some firms that are prepared to invest at prevailing interest rates **(12)**.

cross-price elasticity of demand (E_{xy}) the percentage change in demand of one product divided by the percentage change in the price of a related product **(25)**.

crowding out (see **direct crowding out, indirect crowding out**).

crude birth rate the number of births per 1,000 population **(21)**.

crude death rate the number of deaths per 1,000 population **(21)**.

currency basket a bundle of currencies of different countries against which the dollar can be measured. The dollar on the average depreciates if this currency basket becomes more expensive and appreciates if this currency basket becomes less expensive **(24)**.

current-account balance equals exports of goods and services minus imports of goods and services minus net unilateral transfers abroad **(24)**.

customs duties taxes on the transfer of certain goods from one country into another **(40)**.

cyclical unemployment unemployment associated with general downturns in the economy **(5, 15)**.

deadweight loss a loss to society of consumer surplus or producer surplus that is not offset by anyone else's gain **(31)**.

debt (see **government debt**).

decentralized market a market in which buyers and sellers of a particular product make their transactions in a variety of different physical locations **(33)**.

decreasing costs are present when each unit costs less to produce the greater is the number of units produced **(62)**.

deficit (see **government deficit**).

deficit financing the borrowing of funds in credit markets to cover a government deficit **(40)**.

deflationary gap exists if equilibrium output falls short of the natural level of output **(11)**.

demand a schedule (which can be depicted by a curve) of the amounts of a good or service consumers are prepared to buy at different prices during a specified time period **(4)**. (See also **law of demand.**)

demand deposit a deposit of funds that can be withdrawn ("demanded") from a depository institution at any time without restrictions. The funds are usually withdrawn by writing a check **(7)**.

demand-side inflation occurs when the amount of money purchasers of goods and services want to spend increases more rapidly than the supply of such goods and services, resulting in the bidding up of prices **(5, 14)**.

demand shock an unanticipated shift in aggregate demand due to an unanticipated change in monetary or fiscal policy or a sudden change in private consumption or investment behavior **(19)**.

demographic transition the process by which countries change from rapid population growth to slow population growth as they modernize **(21)**.

dependent variable the variable that changes as a result of a change in the value of another variable **(1A)**.

deposit (see **demand deposit, time deposit**).

deposit multiplier the ratio of the change in total deposits to the change in reserves **(8)**.

depreciation the value of the existing capital stock that has been consumed or used up in the process of producing output; includes not only the physical wear and tear on capital goods but also the loss of value due to the obsolescence of old capital **(6)**; the wearing down of the economic value of capital goods as they are used in the production process **(38)**.

depression a very severe downturn in economic activity that lasts for several years. Real output declines during this period by a significant amount, and the unemployment rate rises to very high levels **(5)**.

derived demand factor demand that results from the demand for the goods and services the factor of production helps produce **(35)**.

dialectical materialism the view that class conflict will necessarily force societies to evolve from lower-order to higher-order economic systems **(43)**.

direct crowding out occurs when increased government spending substitutes for private spending by providing similar goods or services **(10)**.

discouraged worker an unemployed worker who becomes convinced that no job is or will be available in his or her field and stops looking for work—at which point that worker is no longer classified as unemployed **(5, 15)**.

discretionary fiscal policy a government spending or taxation action that has been deliberately taken to achieve a specified macroeconomic goal **(13)**.

diseconomies of scale are present when a given percentage change in inputs leads to a smaller percentage change in output **(28)**.

disinflation a decline in the rate of inflation **(16)**.

dissaving occurs when the economy's total saving is negative—when consumption spending exceeds disposable income—at which point the economy is either increasing its indebtedness or financing consumption by drawing down its savings **(9)**.

dumping occurs when a country sells a good in another country at a price less than the price charged in the home country **(23)**.

economic "bads" goods or services that do not contribute to society's economic well-being **(6)**.

economic equity the fair distribution of resources according to widely accepted social-welfare criteria **(31)**.

economic growth an increase from one period to the next in *real GNP per capita* (which is real GNP divided by the country's population); an increase from one period to the next in *real GNP* **(20)**.

economic profits the excess of revenues over total *opportunity costs* (which include both actual payments and sacrificed alternatives); profits in excess of normal profits **(28, 38)**.

economic rent the excess of the payment to the factor over its opportunity cost **(38)**.

economics the study of how scarce resources are allocated among competing ends **(2)**; the study of how people choose to use their limited resources (land, labor, and capital goods) to produce, exchange, and consume goods and services **(1)**.

economic system the set of organizational arrangements and institutions that are established to solve the economic problem **(2)**; the set of ownership, resource-allocation, and decision-making arrangements that society establishes to solve the economic problem **(43)**.

economies of scale are present in the production process when large output volumes can be produced at a lower cost per unit than small otuput volumes **(27)**; are present when a given percentage change in inputs leads to larger percentage changes in output **(28)**.

effectiveness lag the time it takes for a change in the money supply to affect the economy **(12)**.

effective tax rate the percent of adjusted gross income that is actually paid in taxes; shows the effect of deductions and exclusions on tax rates **(40)**.

efficiency is present when society's resources are so organized that it is impossible to make someone better off by any reallocation of resources without hurting someone else **(31)**; results when no resources are unemployed and no resources are misallocated **(2)**.

elasticity of demand (see **cross-price elasticity of demand, income elasticity of demand, perfectly elastic demand, perfectly inelastic demand, price elasticity of demand**).

elasticity of supply (see **perfectly elastic supply, perfectly inelastic supply, price elasticity of supply**).

employee association an organization that represents employees in a particular profession **(37)**.

entitlement program requires the federal government to pay benefits to any person or unit of government that meets the eligibility requirements stated in the entitlement legislation **(13)**.

entrepreneur one who organizes, manages, and assumes the risks for an enterprise **(2)**.

equal-cost line shows all the combinations of labor and capital that have the same total costs **(28A)**.

equal-output curve shows the various combinations of two inputs (such as labor and capital) that produce the same output **(28A)**.

equilibrium (see **consumer equilibrium, Keynesian equilibrium, long-run macroeconomic equilibrium, Nash equilibrium, short-run macroeconomic equilibrium**).

equilibrium (or **market-clearing**) **price** the price at which the quantity demanded by consumers equals the quantity supplied by producers **(3, 4)**.

equity (see **economic equity, horizontal equity, vertical equity**).

excess monetary growth occurs when the money supply grows more rapidly than money demand **(7)**.

excess reserves reserves in excess of required reserves **(8)**.

exchange rate (see **floating exchange rate, fixed exchange rate**).

excise taxes per-unit taxes on the production or sale of specific goods or services **(40)**.

exclusion costs the costs of defining and enforcing private property rights to some good, or the cost of preventing those who do not have property rights to the good from enjoying the good **(41)**.

exhaustible resource any resource of which there is a finite stock in the long run because the stock is fixed by nature **(41)**.

exhaustive expenditures government purchases of goods and services that divert real economic resources from the private sector, making them no longer available for private use **(40)**.

expansionary fiscal policy increases aggregate demand by raising autonomous government spending or by autonomously lowering taxes **(13)**.

expectations (see **adaptive expectations, rational expectations**).

expenditure multiplier the ratio of the change in output to the change in autonomous expenditures. The two expenditure multipliers are the *investment multiplier* and the *government-expenditure multiplier* **(10)**.

explicit cost (or *accounting cost*) a cost incurred when an actual payment is made **(28)**. (See also **implicit cost.**)

export promotion occurs when a country encourages exports by subsidizing the production of goods for export **(21)**.

extensive growth economic growth that results from the expansion of factor inputs **(20)**.

external benefits the benefits enjoyed by someone other than the firm producing the good **(31)**.

external costs   the costs borne by someone other than the firm producing the good (**31**).

externalities   exist when a producer or consumer does not bear the full marginal cost or enjoy the full marginal benefit of an economic action (**31, 41**).

factor market   the market in which firms purchase the land, labor, and capital inputs required to produce their output (**35**).

factors of production   the resources used to produce goods and services: land, labor, capital, and entrepreneurship (**2**).

fallacy   (see **false-cause fallacy, fallacy of composition**, *ceteris paribus* **fallacy, mercantilist fallacy**).

fallacy of composition   the false belief that what is true for each part taken separately is also true for the whole, or that what is true for the whole is true for each part considered separately (**1**).

false-cause fallacy   the false belief that, because two events occur together, one event has caused the other (**1**).

feedback rule   establishes a feedback relationship between activist policy and the state of the economy (**17**).

fiat money   money whose value or cost as a commodity is less than its value as money (**7**).

final goods   goods that are not used up in the production of any other goods in the current period (**6**).

financial intermediaries   borrow funds from one group of economic agents (people or firms with savings) and lend to other agents (**8**).

fine tuning   the frequent use of discretionary monetary and fiscal policy to counteract even small movements in business activity (**17**).

fiscal drag   the tendency for nonindexed progressive taxes to act as an automatic destabilizer (**13**).

fiscal policy   the deliberate control of federal government spending and taxes for the purpose of achieving macroeconomic goals (**11, 13**). (See also **contractionary fiscal policy, discretionary fiscal policy, expansionary fiscal policy**.)

fiscal surprise   occurs if government spending or taxation turns out different from what people expected (**19**).

fixed cost *(FC)*   the cost that does not vary with the level of output (**28**).

fixed exchange rate   an exchange rate that is set by government decree or intervention within a small range of variation and to which supply and demand must conform (**24**).

fixed investment   the addition of new plants, equipment, commercial buildings, and residential structures (**6**).

floating exchange rate   an exchange rate that is freely determined by the interaction of supply and demand (**24**).

flow variable   a variable that can be meaningfully measured only over a period of time (**6**).

foreign exchange   the national currency of another country that is needed to carry out international transactions. Normally, foreign exchange consists of bank deposits denominated in the foreign currency, but may sometimes consist of foreign paper money when foreign travel is involved (**24**).

free good   a good of which the amount available is greater than the amount people want at a zero price (**2**).

free rider   anyone who enjoys the benefits of a good or service without paying the cost (**41**).

free trade   international trade unimpeded by artificial barriers, such as tariffs or import quotas (**23**).

frictional unemployment   the unemployment associated with the normal changing of jobs in a dynamic economy (**5, 15**).

full-employment surplus (deficit)   what the government budget surplus (or deficit) would be if the economy is operating at the natural, or full-employment, rate of output (**13**).

functional distribution of income   the distribution of income among the four broad classes of productive factors: land, labor, capital, and entrepreneurship (**35**).

futures market   a market in which buyer and seller agree now on the price of a commodity to be delivered at some specified date in the future (**33**).

gift taxes   taxes on the transfer of property from one owner to another (**40**).

GNP   (see **gross national product, real GNP, nominal GNP**).

GNP gap   the difference between current GNP and *potential GNP* (the output the economy would conceivably have produced at full employment); a measure of the social costs of unemployed resources (**17**).

government debt   the cumulated sum of outstanding IOUs that a government unit owes its creditors (**13, 40**).

government deficit   an excess of government outlays over government revenues (**13, 40**).

government-expenditure multiplier $(\Delta Y/\Delta G)$ the ratio of the change in output to the change in government spending (**10**).

government surplus   an excess of government revenues over government outlays (**13, 40**).

Gresham's Law that bad money drives out good. When depreciated, mutilated, or debased currency is circulated along with money of high value, the good money will disappear from circulation; only the bad money will remain in circulation (**7**).

gross national income (GNI) the sum of all factor incomes (**6**).

gross national product (GNP) the market value of all final goods and services produced by an economy in one year's time (**6**).

gross wealth the value of one's assets (**6**).

growth (see **economic growth, extensive growth, intensive growth**).

growth distortion the measurement of changes in a variable over time that does not reflect the concurrent change in other relevant variables with which the variable should be compared, such as population size (**1A**).

hedging the temporary substitution of a futures market transaction for an intended spot transaction (**33**).

horizontal equity exists when those with equal abilities to pay pay the same amount of tax (**40**).

horizontal merger a merger of two firms in the same line of business (**34**).

household production work in the home, including such activities as meal preparation, do-it-yourself repair, child rearing, and cleaning (**36**).

human capital the accumulation of past investments in schooling, training, and health care that raises the productive capacity of people (**2**).

human-resource policy the use of government training programs, unemployment services, and unemployment insurance programs to lower the natural rate of unemployment over the long run (**17**).

hyperinflation a very rapid and often accelerating rate of inflation (**5**).

hypothesis a tentative assumption made in order to test its logical or empirical consequences (**1**).

immediate run a period of time so short that the quantity supplied cannot be changed at all. In the immediate run—sometimes called the *momentary period* or *market period*—supply curves are perfectly inelastic (**25**). (See also **long run, short run**.)

imperfect competition exists if a single buyer or seller can influence the price. The less competition there is among sellers (or buyers), the more power each individual seller (or buyer) exercises over price (**29**).

implicit cost cost incurred when an alternative is sacrificed but no actual payment appears to be made (**28**). (See also **explicit cost**.)

import quota a quantitative limitation on the amount of a specific product that can be imported during a given period (**23**).

import substitution occurs when a country substitutes domestic production for imports by subsidizing domestic production through tariffs, quotas, and other devices (**21**).

incidence of a tax the actual distribution of the burden of tax payment (**40**).

income (see **functional distribution of income, personal distribution of income, personal disposable income, personal income, national income**).

income effect occurs when a fall in the price of a good makes more income available for purchasing all goods and services, including the one whose price has fallen (**26**); the change in the quantity demanded of a good that is attributable to the welfare change that accompanies the price change (**26A**). (See also **substitution effect**.)

income elasticity of demand (E_i) the percentage change in the demand for a product divided by the percentage change in income, holding all prices fixed (**25**).

incomes policy a set of rules, guidelines, or laws devised by government to influence wage and price increases (**14**).

increasing-cost industry an industry in which, as the number of firms expands, the factor prices of resources are bid up; an industry in which, as the number of firms contracts, the prices of these factors fall; the long-run industry supply curve for such an industry is upward-sloping (**29**).

increasing costs are present when each unit has a greater opportunity cost the greater is the number of units produced (**22**). (See also **constant returns to scale, decreasing returns to scale, economies of scale**.)

independent variable the variable that causes the change in the value of the dependent variable (**1A**).

index (see **price index**).

indexing the tying of a variable's rate of increase to the actual inflation rate (**16, 40**).

indifference curve shows all the alternative combinations of two goods that yield the same total satisfaction and among which the consumer is indifferent (**26A**).

indirect crowding out occurs when increased government spending raises interest rates and causes autonomous spending elsewhere in the economy to decrease (**10**).

industrial union a union that represents employees of an industry or a firm regardless of their specific occupation (**37**).

inefficiency   is present when resources can be reallocated to make someone better off without making someone else worse off (**31**).

inferior good   a good the demand for which will fall as income rises, *ceteris paribus* (**4**).

inflation   a general increase in prices (**5**). (See also **supply-side inflation, demand-pull side inflation.**)

inflationary gap   exists if equilibrium output exceeds the natural level of output (**11**).

inflation distortion   the measurement of the dollar value of a variable over time without adjustment for the change in the inflation rate over that period (**1A**).

information costs   the costs of acquiring information on prices, product qualities, and product performance (**33**).

in-kind income   consists primarily of benefits, such as free public education, school lunch programs, public housing, or food stamps, for which the recipient is not required to pay (**39**).

input market   (see **factor market**).

intensive growth   growth that results from increases in output per unit of factor input (**20**).

interest   the price of credit, usually a percentage of the amount of money borrowed (**3**); the price of credit that is determined in credit markets, where the amount businesses with to invest is balanced with the amount people are prepared to save (**38**).

interest rate   measures the yearly cost of borrowing as a percent of the amount loaned (**38**). (See also **nominal interest rate, prime interest rate, real interest rate.**)

interest-rate effect   occurs when rising interest rates discourage investment expenditures and, thus, reduce aggregate spending as rising prices increase the demand for credit (or when falling interest rates have the opposite effect) (**10**).

interest-rate target   a rate of interest that the Fed seeks to achieve through monetary policy (**12**).

interest-sensitive industries   industries, like automobile manufacturing, construction, farming, and retailing, whose sales and/or profits fall when interest rates rise (**18**).

intermediaries   buy in order to sell again or simply bring together buyers and sellers (**33**). (See also **financial intermediaries**.)

intermediate goods   goods that are completely used up in the production of another good; the value of intermediate goods is reflected in the price of the final goods (**3, 6**).

internal labor market   the filling of all but entry-level jobs by promoting or transferring workers already employed by the firm (**36**).

inventory investment   the increase (or decrease) in the value of the stocks of inventories that businesses have on hand (**6**).

investment   additions to the stock of capital (**2**). (See also **fixed investment, inventory investment.**)

investment multiplier ($\Delta Y/\Delta I$)   the ratio of the change in output to the change in investment (**10**).

IS **curve**   shows all the combinations of interest rates and real income that are consistent with goods-market equilibrium (in which desired investment equals desired saving) (**10A**).

Keynesian equilibrium   occurs when the economy produces an output that equals desired aggregate expenditures (**9**).

kinked-demand curve   an oligopolistic firm's demand curve when other firms match the firm's price decreases but do not match the firm's price increases (**32**).

labor   the physical and mental talents that human beings contribute to the production process (**2**).

labor force   the number employed plus the number unemployed (**5, 15**).

labor market   an arrangement (either a formal contract or an informal agreement) whereby buyers and sellers of labor services come together to agree on working conditions (such as compensation, fringe benefits, and hours of work) (**36**). (See also **internal labor market.**)

labor shortage   occurs when the number of workers firms wish to hire at the prevailing wage rate exceeds the number willing to work at that wage rate (**36**).

labor surplus   occurs when the number of workers willing to work at the prevailing wage rate exceeds the number firms wish to employ at that wage rate (**36**).

labor theory of value   Marx's view that the value of a commodity equals the sum of direct labor costs, indirect labor costs, and surplus value (**43**).

labor union   a collective organization of workers whose objective is to improve conditions of pay and work (**37**).

lag   (see **effectiveness lag, recognition lag, regulatory lag**).

land   any part of nature's bounty—including minerals, forests, land, water resources, or oxygen (**2**).

law of comparative advantage   people or countries specialize in those activities in which they have the greatest advantage compared to other people or countries. Equivalently, people or countries specialize in those activities in which they have the least disadvantage compared to other people or countries (**3, 22**).

law of demand   there is a negative (or inverse) relationship between the price of a good and quantity demanded, holding other factors constant (**4**).

law of diminishing marginal rate of substitution   as more of one good is consumed, the amount of the other good that the consumer is willing to sacrifice for one more unit of the first good declines (**26A**).

law of diminishing marginal utility   as more of a good or service is consumed during a given time period, its marginal utility declines, holding the consumption of everything else constant (**26**).

law of diminishing returns   as ever larger quantities of a variable input are combined with fixed amounts of other inputs, the marginal physical product of the variable input will eventually decline (**2, 28, 35**).

law of increasing costs   as more of a particular commodity is produced, its opportunity cost per unit will eventually increase (**2**).

layoff   a suspension of employment without pay and without prejudice that lasts (or is expected to last) seven days or more; the laid-off worker is expected to return to the job if economic conditions improve (**15**).

leading indicators   measures of specific economic activities that tend to rise or fall prior to the general rise or fall in business activity (**5**).

least-cost rule   the least-cost combination of two factors can be found at the point where a given equal-output curve is tangent to the lowest equal-cost line (**28A**).

leisure   time spent in any activity other than work in the labor force or work in the home (**36**).

less developed countries (LDCs)   countries that have yet to reach a reasonably high level of economic development (**21**).

liabilities   anything one owes to other economic agents (**8**).

liquidity   the ease with which an asset can be converted into a medium of exchange without risk of loss (**7**).

liquidity-preference theory   the opportunity cost of holding money—a completely liquid asset—is the interest sacrificed (**12**).

LM curve   shows all the combinations of interest rates and real income that bring about equality between the demand for money and supply of money (**10A**).

loanable funds   the amount of lending from all households, governments, and businesses, or the bank credit made available to borrowers in credit markets (**38**).

logrolling   the trading of votes to secure a favorable outcome on decisions of more interest to each voter (**42**).

long run   a period of time long enough for new firms to enter the market, for old firms to disappear, and for existing plants to be expanded (**25**); a period of time long enough to vary all inputs (**28**). (See also **immediate run, short run**.)

long-run aggregate supply (*LRAS*)   a schedule of the output quantities supplied by business at different price levels, assuming that all wages and prices are flexible and that all expectations are fulfilled (**11**).

long-run average cost (*LRAC*)   the minimum average cost for each level of output when all factor inputs are variable and when factor prices are fixed (**28**).

long-run macroeconomic equilibrium   the equilibrium of price level and aggregate output that occurs when aggregate quantity demanded equals long-run aggregate quantity supplied (**11**).

long-run Phillips curve   a vertical line that shows that in the long run, the unemployment rate is independent of the inflation rate and that unemployment will not decline with more inflation in the long run (**16**).

Lorenz curve   shows the percentage of all income earned by households at successive income levels. The cumulative share of households (ranked from lowest to highest incomes) is plotted on the horizontal axis, and the cumulative share of income earned by the cumulative percent of households is plotted on the vertical axis (**39**).

Lucas demand curve   shows the quantity of real GNP demanded at each level of price surprise (**19A**).

Lucas supply curve   shows the quantity of real GNP supplied for every level of price surprise (**19A**).

lump-sum tax   a tax that does not vary with any indicator of the firm's performance; that is, it does not vary with the firm's output, profit, or employment (**31**).

luxuries   those products that have an income elasticity of demand greater than 1 (**25**).

M1   the sum of currency (and coins), demand deposits at commercial banks held by the nonbanking public, travelers' checks, and other checkable deposits like NOW (negotiable orders of withdrawal) accounts and ATS (automatic transfer services) accounts (**7**).

M2   M1 plus savings and small time deposits plus money-market mutual-fund shares plus other highly liquid assets (**7**).

macroeconomics   the study of the economy in the large; examines the economy as a whole rather than with individual markets and individual consumers and producers (**1**).

majority rule   a system of voting in which a government action or decision is approved of more than 50 percent of the voters approve **(42)**.

managerial coordination the disposition of the firm's resources according to the directives of the firm's manager **(27)**.

marginal analysis a strategy for decision making that examines the consequences of making relatively small changes from the current state of affairs **(1)**.

marginal cost *(MC)* the addition to total cost (or equivalently to variable cost) of producing one more unit of output **(28)**.

marginal factor cost *(MFC)* the extra cost to the firm of using one more unit of a factor of production **(35)**.

marginal output/capital ratio *(MOCR)* the change in output divided by the change in capital **(21)**.

marginal physical product *(MPP)* the increase in output that results from increasing a factor of production by one unit, holding all other inputs constant **(28, 35)**.

marginal-productivity theory of income distribution the functional distribution of income between land, labor, and capital is determined by the relative marginal revenue products of the different factors of production. The price of each factor will equal the *MRP* of that factor **(35)**.

marginal propensity to consume *(MPC)* the change in desired consumption brought about by a change in income of $1 **(9)**.

marginal propensity to save *(MPS)* the change in desired saving brought about by a change in income of $1 **(9)**.

marginal rate of substitution *(MRS)* how much of one good a person is just willing to give up to acquire one unit of another good **(26A)**.

marginal revenue *(MR)* the increase in total revenue that results from each one-unit increase in the amount of output **(29,30)**.

marginal revenue product *(MRP)* the extra revenue generated by increasing a factor of production by one unit **(35)**.

marginal-revenue schedule the relationship between marginal revenue and the quantity of output **(30)**.

marginal tax rate the ratio of the increase in taxes to the increase in taxable income **(13, 40)**.

marginal utility *(MU)* the increase in utility that a consumer experiences when consumption of a good or service (and that good or service alone) is increased by one unit **(26)**. (See also **law of diminishing marginal utility.**)

market an established arrangement by which buyers and sellers come together to exchange particular goods or services **(2, 4)**. (See also **auction market,** **centralized market, contestable market, credit markets, decentralized market, factor market, product market, futures market, labor market, spot market.**)

market demand curve the demand curve of all consumers of a particular product **(4)**; shows the total quantities demanded by all consumers in the market at each price and is the horizontal summation of all individual demand curves in that market **(26)**.

market failure occurs when the price system fails to produce the quantity of the good that would be socially optimal **(41)**.

market socialism an economic system characterized by state ownership of the factors of production, the use of primarily economic incentives, market allocation of resources, and decentralized decision making **(43)**.

market test the process that ensures that goods and services in the private sector yield a benefit equal to or greater than their cost **(40)**.

markup pricing the setting of prices at a given percentage above average cost **(30)**.

material balance the balance achieved when the anticipated demands and supplies of a key commodity are equated by administrative means **(43)**.

material-balance planning a system of resource allocation in which centralized planning is restricted to controlling the output levels of only the most important industrial commodities that the economy produces and in which the output of other less important commodities is controlled at lower levels in the planning hierarchy **(43)**.

median voter the voter on a public-expenditure program who wants more expenditure than half the remaining voters and less expenditure than the other half of the remaining voters **(42)**.

mercantilist fallacy that exporting is better than importing **(24)**.

merchandise-trade balance exports of merchandise minus imports of merchandise **(24)**.

merger (see **conglomerate merger, horizontal merger, vertical merger**).

microeconomics the study of the economic decision making of firms and individuals in a market setting; the study of the economy in the small **(1)**.

midpoints formula the coefficient of the price elasticity of demand equals the percentage change in quantity demanded divided by the percent change in price, where the percent change in quantity demanded is the change in quantity demanded divided by the average of the two quantities and where the percent change in price is the change in price divided by the average of the two prices **(25)**.

minimum efficient scale *(MES)* the lowest level of output at which average costs are minimized **(28)**.

monetarism the doctrine that monetary policy should follow a constant-money-growth rule **(12)**.

monetary-aggregate target a particular money supply or growth rate of the money supply that the Fed seeks to achieve through monetary policy **(12)**.

monetary base the sum of reserves on deposit at the Fed, all vault cash, and the currency in circulation, or the sum of the money supply and reserves at the Fed **(8)**.

monetary policy the deliberate control of the money supply and, in some cases, credit conditions for the purpose of achieving macroeconomic goals **(12)**. (See also **countercyclical monetary policy. procyclical monetary policy.**)

monetization of debt the creation of demand-deposit liabilities in the process of making bank loans **(8)**.

money anything that is widely accepted in exchange for goods and services **(3)**; the medium of exchange used by an economy; the commodity ordinarily used in transactions that transfer ownership of goods and services from one person to another **(7)**. (See also **bank money, commodity money, fiat money, M1, M2.**)

money illusion exists when economic decision makers mistakenly believe that a proportionate change in all money prices and money wages means that relative prices have changed as well **(11)**.

money multiplier the increase in the money supply for every dollar increase in the monetary base **(8)**; the ratio of the money supply to the monetary base **(12)**.

money price a price expressed in monetary units (such as dollars, francs, etc.) **(3)**.

money supply the sum of all commodity moneys, fiat moneys, and bank moneys that are held by the nonbanking public in a given country as of a given date **(7)**.

money surprise occurs if the actual money supply is different from that generally expected **(19)**.

monopolistic competition a type of market structure in which 1) the number of sellers is large enough so that each seller acts independently of the others. 2) the product is differentiated from seller to seller, 3) there is free entry into and exit from the industry, and 4) sellers are price searchers **(27, 30)**.

monopoly (see **pure monopoly, shared monopoly**).

monopoly rent seeking the activity of trying to achieve or maintain a monopoly in order to gain the monopoly profits, or ''rent'' **(31)**.

monopsony a market in which buyers can affect the price of the product by altering the quantities they purchase. A *pure monopsony* is a market with only one buyer **(35)**.

moral-hazard problem occurs when a buyer or seller alters his or her behavior after a contract is made to profit from the contract at the other party's expense and arises because it is too costly for the other party to obtain information about the first party's postcontractual behavior **(33)**.

motive (see **precautionary motive, speculative motive, transactions motive**).

multiple-deposit expansion occurs when an increase in reserves causes an expansion of the money supply that is greater than the reserve increase **(8)**.

multiplier (see **balanced-budget multiplier, deposit multiplier, expenditure multiplier, government-expenditure multiplier, investment multiplier, money multiplier, simple multiplier, tax multiplier**).

mutual interdependence characteristic of an industry in which the actions of one firm will affect other firms in the industry and in which these interrelationships will be recognized **(32)**.

Nash equilibrium exists in an oligopolistic market if each firm's profit-maximizing behavior is based on a correct guess about the behavior of rivals **(32)**.

national debt (see **government debt**).

national income net national product minus indirect business taxes; the sum of all factor payments made to the factors of production in the economy **(6)**.

national-income accounting the science of measuring the aggregate output and income of an economy **(6)**.

natural level of real GNP (y_n) the output produced when the economy is operating at the natural rate of unemployment **(11)**.

natural monopoly exists when the technology of producing a certain product is such that it is cheaper for one firm to produce the product over the relevant range of output than for two or more firms to produce the product **(34)**.

natural-rate hypothesis that prices must be higher than expected for output to exceed the natural output level and that prices must be lower than expected for output to fall below the natural output level **(11)**.

natural rate of unemployment (u_n) that rate at which there is an approximate balance between the number of unfilled jobs or vacancies and the number of qualified job seekers **(5)**; the rate of unemployment that can be sustained without accelerating or decelerating inflation **(11)**.

natural-selection theory if business firms do not maximize profits, they will be unable to compete with other firms and will be driven out of the market **(27)**.

necessities   those products that have an income elasticity of demand less than 1 **(25)**.

negative income tax (NIT)   would supplement incomes that are less than a certain amount by giving recipients who earn less than the *break-even income* an amount equal to a minimum acceptable income and subtracting a given percentage of a dollar for each dollar the family earns on its own **(39)**.

negative (inverse) relationship   exists between two variables if an increase in the value of one variable is associated with a reduction in the value of the other variable **(1A)**.

net national product (NNP)   GNP minus depreciation **(6)**.

net output   (see **value added**).

net wealth   the value of one's assets minus the value of one's liabilities **(6)**.

neutral tax   a tax that does not cause any change in private production, consumption, or investment decisions **(40)**.

nominal GNP (or *GNP in current dollars)*   the value of final goods and services for a given year in that year's prevailing market prices; GNP in current dollars **(6)**.

nominal interest rate   the rate of interest expressed in terms of current dollars, unadjusted for inflation **(5, 18, 38)**.

nonactivist policy   policy that is independent of prevailing economic conditions and that is held steady when economic conditions change **(17)**.

noncompeting groups   groups of labor suppliers that are differentiated by natural ability and abilities acquired through education, training, and experience to the extent that one group does not compete with another for jobs **(36)**.

nonexclusion   characteristic of a good for which the exclusion costs are so high that it is not possible (or practical) to exclude people from using the good **(41)**.

nonmarketed goods   goods and services exchanged through barter arrangements or acquired through do-it-yourself activities that take the place of goods and services that would otherwise have been purchased in organized markets **(6)**.

nonprice competition   any action other than the lowering of prices that differentiates one product from the competition and delays the disappearance of economic profits **(30)**.

nonprohibitive tariff   a tariff that does not wipe out all imports of the product **(23)**.

nonrival consumption   characteristic of a good the consumption of which by one person does not reduce its consumption by others, given the level of production **(41)**.

normal good   a good the demand for which increases as income rises, *ceteris paribus* **(4)**.

normal profits   the return that the time and capital of the entrepreneur would earn in the best alternative employment and that is earned when total revenues equal total opportunity costs **(28)**; the profits that are required to keep resources in that particular business **(38)**.

normative economics   the study of *what ought to be* in the economy **(1)**.

Okun's law   for every 1 percent increase in the unemployment rate there is a 2.5 percent drop in real GNP **(15)**.

oligopoly   a type of market in which 1) there are only a few mutually interdependent sellers but many buyers, 2) homogeneous or differentiated products may be produced, 3) there are significant barriers to entry, and 4) sellers are price searchers able to exercise some control over price **(27, 32)**.

open-market operations   purchases and sales of federal government securities by the Fed (as directed by the Federal Open Market Committee) **(8)**.

opportunity cost   the loss of the next best alternative **(2)**; the value of the best forgone alternative **(28)**.

paradox of voting   that majority rule can yield inconsistent social choices: even if each voter is perfectly rational, the majority of voters can choose *a over b, b over c*, and then choose *c over a* **(42)**.

partnership   a business enterprise that is owned by two or more people who make all the business decisions, share the profits of the business, and bear the financial responsibility for any losses **(27)**.

perfect competition   a type of market structure in which 1) there is a large enough number of buyers and sellers that no single buyer or seller has a perceptible influence on the market price, 2) each seller and buyer has perfect information about prices and product quality, 3) the product being sold is homogeneous, 4) there are no barriers to entry into or exit from the market, and 5) all firms are price takers **(4, 29)**.

perfectly elastic demand   demonstrated by a horizontal demand curve, where quantity demanded is most responsive to price **(25)**.

perfectly elastic supply   demonstrated by a horizontal supply curve, where quantity supplied is most responsive to price **(25)**.

perfectly inelastic demand   demonstrated by a vertical demand curve, where quantity demanded is least responsive to price **(25)**.

perfectly inelastic supply demonstrated by a vertical supply curve, where quantity supplied is least responsive to price **(25)**.

perfectly competitive market (see **perfect competition**).

permanent income an average of the income that an individual anticipates earning over the long run **(13)**.

personal disposable income personal income minus income-tax pyments **(6)**.

personal distribution of income the distribution of income among households, or how much income one household earns from the factors of production it owns relative to other households **(35)**.

personal income national income 1) *minus* retained corporate profits, corporate income taxes, and social-insurance contributions 2) *plus* transfer payments and consumer interest payments and net government interest payments **(6)**.

personal saving personal disposable income minus personal-consumption expenditures **(6)**.

Phillips curve shows the relationship between unemployment and inflation and seems to reveal that a reduction in the rate of unemployment requires an increase in the rate of wage (or price) inflation **(16)**. (See also **long-run Phillips curve, short-run Phillips curve.**)

planned socialism an economic system characterized by state ownership of the factors of production (other than labor), the use of moral as well as economic incentives, resource allocation by economic plan, and centralized decision making **(43)**.

policy (see **activist policy, fiscal policy, human-resource policy, incomes policy, nonactivist policy, monetary policy**).

policy instruments controllable variables that affect output, employment, and prices **(17)**.

positive economics the study of *what is* in the economy **(1)**.

positive (or **direct**) **relationship** exists between two variables if an increase in the value of one variable is associated with an increase in the value of the other variable **(1A)**.

poverty (see **absolute poverty standard, relative poverty standard**).

precautionary motive the desire to hold money in order to protect oneself against unforeseen emergencies **(7)**.

preferences people's evaluations of goods and services independent of budget and price considerations **(26)**.

preferred stock confers a prior claim on dividends but no voting privileges (dividends must be paid before paying common stock dividends but after meeting interest obligations) **(27)**.

present value *(PV)* the most anyone would pay today in order to receive money in the future; the most anyone is willing to pay today for an asset in order to be able to receive a stream of returns from that asset in the future **(27)**.

price (see **money price, relative price**).

price discrimination exists when the same product or service is sold at different prices to different buyers **(30)**.

price/earnings ratio *(PE)* the stock price divided by the earnings per share of stock **(27)**.

price elasticity of demand (E_d) a measure of the responsiveness of quantity demanded to a change in price; the percentage change in the quantity demanded divided by the percentage change in price **(25)**.

price elasticity of supply (E_s) a measure of the responsiveness of quantity supplied to a change in price; the percentage change in the quantity supplied divided by the percentage change in price **(25)**.

price index shows the current year's cost of a particular market basket as a percentage of the cost of the same market basket in some base year **(5)**.

price leader a firm whose price changes are consistently imitated by rival firms **(32)**.

price-level surprise occurs when the actual price level, P, is not equal to the expected price level, P_e **(19)**.

price risk the chance that the price of a bond will fall in secondhand markets: if the bond had to be sold before its maturity date (when the principal is due), it would have to be sold at a loss if interest rates rise **(18)**.

price searcher *in a factor market:* a buyer of inputs whose purchases are large enough to affect the price of the input **(35)**; *in a product market:* a seller with the ability to control the price of the goods it sells **(30)**.

price system coordinates economic decisions by allowing people with property rights to resources to trade freely, buying and selling at whatever relative prices emerge in the marketplace **(3)**.

price taker *in a factor market:* a buyer of an input whose purchases are not large enough to affect the price of the input **(35)**; *in a product market:* a seller that does not have the ability to control the price of the goods it sells **(29)**.

prime interest rate the base, or reference, rate on which banks decide to price their loans; the base cost of commercial bank credit **(18)**.

principal   a party that has controlling authority and that engages an agent to act subject to the principal's control and instruction **(27)**.

principal/agent problem   exists when the principal (such as a firm) and the agent (such as an employee) have different goals and objectives for the employee's behavior **(36)**.

principle of substitution   practically no good is irreplaceable in meeting demand because users are able to substitute one product for another to satisfy demand **(3)**.

priority principle   industries most important to the communist party will be the last to take cuts in supplies **(43)**.

private benefits   the benefits enjoyed by the firm producing a good **(31)**.

private costs   the costs borne by the firm producing a good **(31)**.

procyclical monetary policy   policy that decreases aggregate demand when output is falling and increases aggregate demand when output is rising **(12)**.

producer surplus   the excess of what producers receive over the minimum value the producers would have been willing to receive **(29)**.

production function   indicates the maximum amount of output that can be produced from different combinations of labor, capital, and land inputs **(28, 35)**.

production-possibilities frontier *(PPF)*   shows the combinations of goods that can be produced when the factors of production are utilized to their full potential; reveals the economic choices open to society **(2)**.

profit maximization   the search by firms for the product quality, the output, and the price that give the firm the highest possible profits **(27)**.

profit-maximization rule   a firm will maximize profits by producing that level of output at which marginal revenue equals marginal cost **(29)**.

profits   (see **accounting profits, economic profits, normal profits**).

progressive tax   a tax where the higher is the income, the larger is the percentage of income paid as taxes **(40)**.

prohibitive tariff   a tariff that is high enough to cut off all imports of the product **(23)**.

property rights   the right of an owner to use and exchange property **(3)**.

proportional tax   a tax where each taxpaying unit pays the same percentage of its income as taxes **(40)**.

public finance   the study of government revenues and expenditures at all levels of government **(40)**.

public goods   goods or services characterized by 1) nonrival consumption and 2) nonexclusion **(41)**.

purchasing-power parity *(PPP)*   exists between two currencies when changes in the exchange rate reflect only relative changes in the price levels of the two countries **(24)**.

pure economic rent   the price paid to a productive factor (such as land) that is completely inelastic in supply **(38)**.

pure monopoly   a type of market structure in which 1) there is only one seller, 2) the seller's product has no close substitutes, 3) the seller is protected from the entry of competitors by barriers to entry, and 4) the seller is a price searcher that can control the price **(27, 30)**.

quantity demanded   the amount of a good or service consumers are prepared to buy at a given price during a specified time period **(4)**.

quantity supplied   the amount of a good or service offered for sale at a given price **(4)**.

quantity theory of money   (see **classical quantity theory of money**).

quasi rent   a payment over and above the short-run opportunity cost necessary to induce the owners of the resources to offer their resources for sale or rent in the short run **(38)**.

rate of natural increase   the crude birth rate minus the crude death rate **(21)**.

rate of return of a capital good   that rate of interest which makes the present value of the stream of marginal revenue products for each year of the good's life equal to the cost of the capital good **(38)**.

ratification of supply-side inflation   results if the government increases the money supply to prevent supply-side shock from raising unemployment **(14)**.

rational expectations   expectations that people form about macroeconomic variables, such as the inflation rate and the unemployment rate, using their public knowledge about current and future monetary and fiscal policy, business and consumer spending plans, and how the economy works **(19)**; expectations that people form by using all available information and by relying not only on past experience but also on their predictions about the effects of present and future policy actions **(14)**.

rational ignorance   a decision not to acquire information because the marginal cost of acquiring the information exceeds the marginal benefit of having the information **(42)**.

real-balance effect   occurs when desired real consumption at each income level changes as price-level changes alter the purchasing power of assets, including money balances (**10**).

real GNP (or *GNP in constant dollars*) measures the volume of real goods and services by removing the effects of rising prices on nominal GNP (**6**).

real interest rate the nominal interest rate minus the anticipated rate of inflation (**5, 18, 38**).

realized capital gain income gained when property is sold at a higher price than its purchase price (**40**).

recession a decline in real output that lasts for six months or more (**5**).

recognition lag the time it takes the Fed to actually change the supply of money in response to a change in economic conditions (**12**).

regressive tax a tax where the higher is the income, the smaller is the percentage of income paid as taxes (**40**).

regulatory lag occurs when government regulators adjust rates some time after operating costs and the rate base have increased (**34**).

relatively uncontrollable outlays government expenditures whose outlay level is determined by existing statutes, by contracts, or by other obligations (**13**).

relative poverty standard defines the poor in terms of the income of others (**39**).

relative price a price expressed in terms of other commodities (**3**).

renewable resource any resource of which the stock is not fixed in the long run (**41**).

rent (see **economic rent, pure economic rent, quasi rent**).

required-reserve ratio the amount of reserves a bank is required to hold for each dollar of deposits (**8**).

reserve requirements rules that state the amount of reserves a bank must keep on hand to back bank deposits (**8**).

reserves the funds that the bank uses to satisfy the cash demands of its customers (**8**). (See also **excess reserves**.)

resource (see **backstop resource, exhaustible resource, renewable resource**).

return (see **rate of return**).

rival consumption the characteristic of a good the consumption of which by one person lowers the consumption available to others, given the level of production (**41**).

roundabout production the production of goods that do not immediately meet consumption needs; the production of intermediate goods (**3**).

rule of reason monopolies are in violation of the Sherman Act if they engage in unfair or illegal business practices, not because they are a monopoly (**34**).

saving the amount of national income (total factor income) that is not spent on consumption or direct taxes (**6**). (See also **personal saving**.)

saving/income schedule shows the desired amount of saving at different levels of national income or output (**9**).

Say's Law desired aggregate expenditures can never depart from actual aggregate expenditures; whatever output is produced will be demanded (**9**).

scarce good a good of which the amount available is less than the amount people would want if it were given away free of charge (**2**).

scatter diagram a number of separate points, each of which plots the value of the independent variable (measured along the horizontal axis) against a value of the dependent variable (measured along the vertical axis) for a specific time interval (**1A**).

scientific method the process of formulating theories, collecting data, testing theories, and revising theories (**1**).

screening the process used by employers to raise the probability of selecting the most qualified workers on the basis of observable worker characteristics (**36**).

shared monopoly an oligopoly in which all the firms in the industry coordinate price and output by some means; in its extreme form, the industry behaves like one gigantic firm (**32**).

shortage results if at the current price the quantity demanded exceeds the quantity supplied; the price is too low to equate the quantity demanded with the quantity supplied (**4**).

short run a period of time long enough for existing firms to produce more goods but not long enough for existing firms to expand their capacity or for new firms to enter the market. Output can be varied only by varying the variable inputs (of labor and raw materials) and only within the limits of existing plant capacity (**25, 28**).

short-run aggregate supply (*SRAS*) a schedule of the quantities of real output business is prepared to supply at different price level, holding other factors (particularly the expected price level) constant (**11**).

short-run macroeconomic equilibrium occurs at that price level where short-run aggregate quantity supplied equals aggregate quantity demanded (**11**).

short-run Phillips curve shows a negative relationship between inflation and unemployment (like the original Phillips curve) (**16**).

shutdown rule if the firm's revenues at all output levels are less than variable costs, it minimizes its losses by shutting down; if there is at least one output level at which revenues exceed variable costs, the firm should not shut down (**29**).

signal credentials or qualifications—such as formal schooling—that are acquired by workers and that employers believe to be indicators of productivity **(36)**.

simple multiplier shows the impact on income of a change in autonomous spending or taxes when the price level and interest rates are not affected by such changes **(10)**.

slope the ratio of the change in y to the run in x **(1A)**.

social benefits private benefits plus external benefits **(31, 41)**.

social costs private costs plus external costs **(31, 41)**.

socialism a society characterized by collective ownership of property and government allocation of resources **(3)**. (See also **market socialism, planned socialism**.)

social overhead capital capital goods (such as roads, canals, schools, and hospitals) that benefit society more than they benefit specific individuals **(21)**.

sole proprietorship a form of business that is owned by one individual who makes all the business decisions, receives the profits, and bears the financial responsibility for losses **(27)**.

special drawing right (SDR) an international money that can be used among monetary authorities **(24)**.

special-interest groups minority groups with intense, narrowly defined preferences about specific government policies **(42)**.

speculative motive the desire to hold money in order to take advantage of opportunities to profit from market fluctuations **(7)**.

speculators those who buy or sell in the hope of profiting from market fluctuations **(33)**.

spot (cash) market a market in which agreements between buyers and sellers are made now for payment and delivery of the product now **(33)**.

stabilizers (see **automatic stabilizers**).

stagflation the combination of high unemployment and high inflation **(5, 16)**.

stock (see **common stock, convertible stock, preferred stock**).

stock variable a variable that can be meaningfully measured at a given moment in time **(6)**.

strike occurs when all unionized employees cease to work until management agrees to specific union demands **(37)**.

structural unemployment the unemployment that results from the long-run decline of certain industries becaue of rising costs, changes in consumer preferences, or technological advances that make the industry's product obsolete **(5, 15)**.

substitutes any two goods such that the demand for one rises when the price for the other rises (or such that the demand for one falls when the price of the other falls) **(4)**.

substitution (see **principle of substitution**).

substitution effect occurs when the fall in the price of a good motivates consumers to substitute that good for other relatively more expensive goods **(26)**; the change in the quantity demanded of a good that occurs when the good's price changes and the consumer substitutes to keep utility or welfare constant **(26A)**.

sunk costs those fixed costs that cannot be recovered even in the long run **(32)**.

supply a schedule (which can be depicted by a curve) of the amounts of a good or service offered for sale at different prices during a specified time period **(4)**.

supply shock an event that unexpectedly causes the short-run aggregate-supply curve to shift **(14, 19)**. (See also **adverse supply shock, beneficial supply shock.**)

supply-side inflation occurs when increases in prices of inputs caused by autonomous reductions in their supply generally cause firms to reduce their offerings of goods and services to the market at prevailing prices, resulting in the bidding up of their prices **(5, 14)**.

surplus results if at the current price the quantity supplied exceeds the quantity demanded; the price is too high to equate the quantity demanded with quantity supplied **(4, 13)**. (See also **consumer surplus, producer surplus, government surplus.**)

surplus value the value of any labor over and above the amount of labor service the worker would have to provide to meet subsistence needs **(43)**.

surprise (see **fiscal surprise, money surprise, policy surprise, price-level surprise**).

T-accounts a summary of bank assets and liabilities **(8)**.

tangent a straight line that touches the curve at only one point **(1A)**.

target (see **interest-rate target, monetary-aggregate target**).

tariff a tax levied on imports or exports **(23)**. (See also **nonprohibitive tariff, prohibitive tariff**).

tax (see **customs duty, excise tax, gift tax, neutral tax, progressive tax, proportional tax, regressive tax**).

taxable income the income that remains after all deductions and exemptions are subtracted from gross income (40).

tax multiplier $(\Delta Y/\Delta T)$ the change in output divided by the change in the tax (10).

tax rate   (see **average tax rate, effective tax rate, marginal tax rate**).

terms of trade   the rate at which two products can be exchanged for each other between countries (22).

theory   isolates those factors that may be crucial determinants of the phenomenon being explained (1).

time deposit   a deposit of funds upon which a depository institution can legally require 30 days' notice of withdrawal and on which the financial institution pays the depositor interest (7).

total cost *(TC)*   the total of the variable and fixed costs of producing each level of output (28).

total revenue *(TR)*   the price of the commodity multiplied by the quantity sold (25).

total-revenue test   1) if price and total revenue move in different directions, demand is elastic; 2) if price and total revenue move in the same direction, demand is inelastic; 3) if total revenue does not change when price changes, demand is unitary elastic (25).

transaction costs   the costs associated with bringing buyers and sellers together (33). (See also **information costs**.)

transactions motive   the desire to hold money in order to carry out normal transactions (7).

transfer payments   payments to recipients who have not supplied current goods or services in exchange for these payments (6); transfers of income from one individual or organization to another (40).

trust   a combination of firms that come together to act essentially as a monopolist; the firms set common prices, agree to restrict output, and punish member firms who fail to live up to the agreement (34).

unanamity   the result of a vote in which all voters agree on or consent to a particular government action or decision (42).

underground worker   a worker whose income is unreported or not fully reported to the government (15).

unemployment   (see **cyclical unemployment, frictional unemployment, structural unemployment, natural rate of unemployment**).

unemployment rate   the number of unemployed divided by the number in the labor force (15).

unintended investment   the difference between desired saving and desired investment at each income level (9).

union   (see **craft union, industrial union, labor union**).

utility   the satisfaction that a person enjoys from consuming goods and services (26). (See also **marginal utility**.)

value added   the value of a firm's (or an industry's) output minus the value of its purchases from other firms (or industries); also called **net output** (6).

variable cost *(VC)*   the cost that varies with the level of output (28).

velocity of circulation   the number of times the average dollar is spent on final goods and services in one year's time (7).

vertical equity   exists when those with a greater ability to pay bear a heavier tax burden (40).

vertical merger   a merger of two firms that are part of the same materials, production, or distribution network (34).

voluntary export quota   the result of a bargain between a home government and a foreign government to limit the foreign country's exports over a specified period of time (23).

wage/employment trade-off   the situation confronted by any labor union that faces a downward-sloping demand curve: higher wages can be obtained only by sacrificing the number of jobs; lower unemployment can be obtained only by sacrificing higher wages (37).

wage/price spiral   the phenomenon of higher prices pushing wages higher and then higher wages pushing prices higher, or vice versa. This spiral occurs when workers anticipate inflation and demand and get higher wages and when the monetary authorities ratify the supply-side inflation. This process repeats itself (14).

waste-disposal costs   the sum of: 1) pollution-prevention costs, 2) the private and public costs of avoiding pollution damage once pollution has occurred, and 3) the welfare loss society suffers when pollution is not prevented or pollution damage is not corrected (41).

wealth   the value of one's total assets minus the value of one's liabilities (39). (See also **gross wealth, net wealth**.)

X-inefficiency   the organizational slack that results from the lack of competition in monopolies; results in costs that are higher than necessary (31).

Name Index

Subject Index

HB 171
.5   Ruffin, Roy
.R82   Principles of economics
1985

HB 171   212675
.5   Ruffin, Roy
.R82   Principles of
1985   economics

DEMCO

Table III Price Indexes and Interest Rates

Year	GNP Deflator (1972 = 100)	Consumer Price Index (1967 = 100)	Interest Rate on 3-Month Treasury Bills	Prime Rate Charged by Banks
1929	32.76	51.3	—	5½-6
1933	25.13	38.8	0.515	1½-4
1939	28.43	41.6	0.023	1.50
1940	29.06	42.0	0.014	1.50
1941	31.23	44.1	0.103	1.50
1942	34.32	48.8	0.326	1.50
1943	36.14	51.8	0.373	1.50
1944	37.01	52.7	0.375	1.50
1945	37.91	53.9	0.375	1.50
1946	43.88	58.5	0.375	1.50
1947	49.55	66.9	0.594	1½-1¾
1948	52.98	72.1	1.040	1¾-2
1949	52.49	71.4	1.102	2.00
1950	53.56	72.1	1.218	2.07
1951	57.09	77.8	1.552	2.56
1952	57.92	79.5	1.766	3.00
1953	58.82	80.1	1.931	3.17
1954	59.55	80.5	0.953	3.05
1955	60.84	80.2	1.753	3.16
1956	62.79	81.4	2.658	3.77
1957	64.93	84.3	3.267	4.20
1958	66.04	86.6	1.839	3.83
1959	67.60	87.3	3.405	4.48
1960	68.70	88.7	2.928	4.82
1961	69.33	89.6	2.378	4.50
1962	70.61	90.6	2.778	4.50
1963	71.67	91.7	3.157	4.50
1964	72.77	92.9	3.549	4.50
1965	74.36	94.5	3.954	4.54
1966	76.76	97.2	4.881	5.63
1967	79.06	100.0	4.321	5.61
1968	82.54	104.2	5.339	6.30
1969	86.79	109.8	6.677	7.96
1970	91.45	116.3	6.458	7.91
1971	96.01	121.3	4.348	5.72
1972	100.00	125.3	4.071	5.25
1973	105.69	133.1	7.041	8.03
1974	114.92	147.7	7.886	10.81
1975	125.56	161.2	5.838	7.86
1976	132.11	170.5	4.989	6.84
1977	139.83	181.5	5.265	6.83
1978	150.05	195.4	7.221	9.06
1979	163.40	217.4	10.041	12.67
1980	178.42	246.8	11.506	15.27
1981	195.60	272.4	14.029	18.87
1982	207.38	289.1	10.686	14.86
1983	215.34	298.4	8.63	10.79
1984	223.38	311.1	9.58	12.04

Source: *Economic Report of the President, 1985, pp. 236, 294, 310.*

Table IV Money Supply (M1 in billions of dollars)

Year	M1
1929	26.64
1933	19.91
1939	34.15
1940	39.65
1941	46.52
1942	55.36
1943	72.24
1944	85.34
1945	99.23
1946	106.46
1947	111.79
1948	112.31
1949	111.16
1950	114.14
1951	119.23
1952	125.22
1953	128.34
1954	130.27
1955	134.44
1956	136.02
1957	136.75
1958	138.35
1959	143.27
1960	141.59
1961	143.93
1962	147.00
1963	151.28
1964	157.22
1965	163.79
1966	171.05
1967	177.77
1968	190.41
1969	201.77
1970	209.98
1971	223.9
1972	241.7
1973	259.4
1974	272.2
1975	284.9
1976	301.5
1977	323.9
1978	350.3
1979	377.4
1980	401.4
1981	429.6
1982	458.0
1983	509.1
1984	542.5

Sources: *Historical Statistics of the United States from Colonial Times to the Present;* Series X, 410–419; Federal Reserve Bulletin, various issues.